W9-BPJ-133

# SAFe®
## REFERENCE GUIDE

SCALED AGILE FRAMEWORK® FOR LEAN
SOFTWARE AND SYSTEMS ENGINEERING

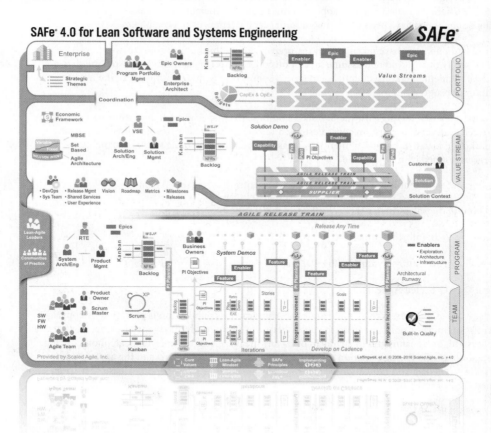

# Dean Leffingwell

with Alex Yakyma, Richard Knaster,
Drew Jemilo, and Inbar Oren

For information about buying this title in bulk quantities, or for special sales opportunities (which may include electronic versions; custom cover designs; and content particular to your business, training goals, marketing focus, or branding interests), please contact our corporate sales department at corpsales@pearsoned.com or (800) 382-3419.

For government sales inquiries, please contact governmentsales@pearsoned.com.

For questions about sales outside the U.S., please contact intlcs@pearson.com.

Visit us on the Web: informit.com/aw

Library of Congress Control Number: 2016943742

Copyright © 2017 Scaled Agile, Inc.

ISBN-13: 978-0-13-451054-5

ISBN-10: 0-13-451054-2

Text printed in the United States on recycled paper at RR Donnelley in Willard, Ohio.

2  16

# Contents

# Preface

On behalf of the entire Scaled Agile, Inc., team and the SAFe contributors, it is my personal pleasure to introduce the *SAFe 4.0 Reference Guide*.

SAFe is an online, freely revealed knowledge base of proven success patterns for implementing Lean-Agile software and systems development at enterprise scale. It provides comprehensive guidance for work at the enterprise Portfolio, Value Stream, Program, and Team levels.

## Why SAFe?

The world's economy, and the health and welfare of society as a whole, is increasingly dependent on software and systems. In support of this need, systems builders are creating increasingly complex software and cyber-physical systems of unprecedented scope and complexity with requirements for utility and robustness exceeding those that have come before them.

The methods that systems builders use to create these systems must keep pace with this larger mandate. However, the assumptive, one-pass, stage-gated, waterfall methods of the past are not scaling to the new challenge. New development methods are needed. Agile shows the greatest promise, but it was developed for small teams and, by itself, does not scale to the needs of larger enterprises and the systems they create. What's needed is a new way of working, one that applies the power of Agile but leverages the more extensive knowledge pools of systems thinking and Lean product development. The Scaled Agile Framework (SAFe) is one such approach.

SAFe is provided by Scaled Agile, Inc., where our core belief is simple: Better systems and software make the world a better place. Our mission is to assist those who build these systems through development and publication of the SAFe framework, as well as accompanying certification, training, and courseware. As case studies on the Scaled Agile Framework website (www.scaledagileframework.com) show, many enterprises—large and small—are getting outstanding business benefits from applying SAFe.

These typically include:

- 20 – 50% increase in productivity
- 50%+ increases in quality
- 30 – 75% faster time to market
- Measurable increases in employee engagement and job satisfaction

As you can imagine, with results like those, SAFe is spreading rapidly around the world. The majority of Fortune 100 U.S. companies have certified SAFe practitioners and consultants already on site, as do an increasing percentage of the Global 1000 enterprises. SAI also has an extensive network of more than 80 global partners providing consulting and implementation services in almost every region of the world. And while every business situation is unique, we have found that the straightforward Implementation 1-2-3 strategy always delivers results.

Our commitment is to continuously evolve SAFe to provide value to the industry—better systems, better business outcomes, better daily lives for the people who build the world's most important new systems—but only you, the adopters and practitioners, can tell us whether or not we have accomplished that. As we are fond of saying, "without you, SAFe is just a website."

## Why a *Reference* Guide?

The SAFe website is quite comprehensive, containing hundreds of pages of guidance for the various roles, responsibilities, activities, and artifacts that constitute SAFe, along with the foundational elements of values, Lean-Agile mindset, principles, and practices. This Reference Guide is intended to provide a hard-copy or e-copy companion to help you understand and apply SAFe, with the goal of helping you accomplish your mission of building better systems.

## More on SAFe

For more on SAFe, please browse the site, read the blog, watch the "updates" field, and follow us on Twitter (@ScaledAgile), where we will notify you of new developments. Also, click on the site's "Presentations & Downloads" tab to find free posters for the Big Picture, the House of Lean, and SAFe Lean-Agile Principles. You'll also find SAFe videos and recorded webinars, free presentations, and more. Finally, be sure to check out our corporate site www.ScaledAgile.com. Even better, attend a Training and Certification course (www.scaledagile.com/which-course); perhaps I will see you there. Stay SAFe!

—*Dean Leffingwell and the Scaled Agile Team*

# Acknowledgments

## Scaled Agile Framework Contributors

**Alex Yakyma, SAFe Fellow and Principal Consultant**

Alex is a SAFe methodologist, trainer, and principal consultant who has been involved with the development and field implementations of the Scaled Agile Framework since its inception. Alex's broad prior experience as an engineer, development manager, and program manager in highly distributed multicultural environments provides the experience needed to assist enterprises with improving their system development capabilities at the Program, multi-program, and Portfolio levels. Alex has published a number of articles and white papers on Agile and Lean and is the author of *Pacific Express*, a novella about launching an Agile Release Train.

**Drew Jemilo, SAFe Fellow and Principal Consultant**

Drew is a principal contributor to the Scaled Agile Framework, a consultant, and an instructor. Drew met Dean Leffingwell in early 2009 when he was developing a scaled Agile methodology for a management consulting company to bridge their strategic business framework with Agile. Since then, they have worked together with global clients to synchronize distributed teams using Agile Release Trains in the United States, Europe, and India.

**Richard Knaster, SAFe Fellow and Principal Consultant**

Richard has more than 25 years' experience in software development in roles ranging from developer to executive and has been involved in Agile for more than a decade. Prior to joining Scaled Agile, Inc., Richard worked at IBM, where his career spanned from product line management (PPM domain) and professional services to chief methodologist, Agile and Lean. Richard is a certified IBM Thought Leader and an Open Group Distinguished IT Specialist. He is also a certified SPC, PSM, Agile Certified Practitioner, PMP, and a contributor to the Disciplined Agile Delivery framework and PMI Portfolio/Program Management standards.

**Inbar Oren, SAFe Fellow and Principal Consultant**

Inbar has more than 20 years' experience in the high-tech market. For more than a decade, he has been helping development organizations—in both software and integrated systems—improve results by adopting Lean-Agile best practices. Previous clients include Cisco, Woolworth, Amdocs, Intel, and NCR. Inbar's current focus is on working with leaders at the Program, Value Stream, and Portfolio levels to help them bring the most out of their organizations and build new processes and culture.

## SAFe Community Contributors

We are also indebted to those SAFe Program Consultant Trainers (SPCTs) and SAFe Program Consultants (SPCs) who are doing the hard work of applying the framework in various enterprises every day. Many have contributed indirectly in discussions, certification workshops, LinkedIn forums, and more. More specifically, the following individuals have directly provided content that is included either here or in Guidance articles on the Scaled Agile Framework website (www.scaledagileframework.com).

- **Harry Koehnemann, SPCT** – Special contributor to SAFe for Lean Systems Engineering and 4.0 systems engineering content
- **Ken France, SPCT** – Guidance article: "Mixing Agile and Waterfall Development in the Scaled Agile Framework"
- **Scott Prugh, SPC** – Guidance article: "Continuous Delivery"
- **Eric Willeke, SPCT** – Guidance articles: "Role of PI Objectives," "A Lean Perspective on SAFe Portfolio WIP Limit"
- **Jennifer Fawcett, SAFe Fellow and Principal Consultant** – Product Manager and Product Owner contribution and focus
- **Colin O'Neill, SPCT** – SAFe 1.0 – 2.5 contributor
- **Gareth Evans, SPCT** – Guidance article: "Lean Software Development in SAFe"
- **Gillian Clark, SPCT** – Guidance article: "Lean Software Development in SAFe"
- **Maarit Laanti, SPC** – "Lean-Agile Budgeting" guidance and white paper
- **Steven Mather, SPC** – SAFe 2.0 glossary draft
- **Al Shalloway, SPCT** – Concept development and community support

## Additional Acknowledgments

**The Contributors to Agile Software Requirements**
The initial concepts behind the framework were first documented in the 2007 text *Scaling Software Agility: Best Practices for Large Enterprises*, by Dean Leffingwell. But the framework itself was first documented in Dean's 2011 book *Agile Software Requirements: Lean Requirements for Teams, Programs, and the Enterprise* (ASR), so it's appropriate to repeat and update the book acknowledgments here.

Thanks to the ASR reviewers, Gabor Gunyho, Robert Bogetti, Sarah Edrie, and Brad Jackson. Don Reinertsen provided permission to use elements of his book, *The Principles of Product Development Flow*. Thanks to my Finnish collaborators: Juha-Markus Aalto, Maarit Laanti, Santeri Kangas, Gabor Gunyho, and Kuan Eeik Tan. Alistair Cockburn, Don Widrig, Mauricio Zamora, Pete Behrens, Jennifer Fawcett, and Alexander Yakyma contributed directly to book content. Even that list is not exhaustive; many others—Mike Cottmeyer, Ryan Shriver, Drew Jemilo, Chad Holdorf, Keith Black, John Bartholomew, Chris Chapman, Mike Cohn, Ryan Martens, Matthew Balchin, and Richard Lawrence—contributed words, thoughts, or encouragement.

## A Special Acknowledgment to the Agile Thought Leaders

Of course, SAFe stands on the shoulders of many who came before us, particularly the Agile thought leaders who created the industry movement. It starts with the signers of the Agile Manifesto and continues with those outspoken thought leaders who have helped move the industry toward the new paradigm. The following have contributed most directly to our understanding of Agile development: Kent Beck, Alistair Cockburn, Ron Jeffries, Mike Cohn, David Anderson, Jeff Sutherland, Martin Fowler, Craig Larman, Ken Schwaber, Scott Ambler, and Mary and Tom Poppendieck. Still others are acknowledged in the Bibliography.

## A Special Acknowledgment to the Lean Leaders

In extending Agile to the enterprise and developing the broader Lean-Agile paradigm, we are fortunate to stand on the shoulders of Lean thought leaders as well, including Don Reinertsen, Jeffrey Liker, Taichi Ohno, Eli Goldratt, Dr. Alan Ward, Jim Sutton, Michael Kennedy, Dantar Oosterwal, Steve Womack, and Daniel Jones. Still others are acknowledged in the Bibliography.

## And to W. Edwards Deming

Finally, where would we be without the seminal works of W. Edwards Deming, to whom we perhaps owe the deepest gratitude of all? He was a visionary and systems thinker, whose tireless quest for the underlying truths and unwavering belief in people and continuous improvement led to a set of transformational theories and teachings that changed the way we think about quality, management, and leadership.

# Introduction to the Scaled Agile Framework (SAFe)

The Scaled Agile Framework (SAFe) is a freely revealed knowledge base of proven, integrated patterns for enterprise-scale Lean-Agile development. It is scalable and modular, allowing each organization to apply it in a way that provides better business outcomes and happier, more engaged employees.

SAFe synchronizes alignment, collaboration, and delivery for large numbers of Agile Teams. It supports both software solutions and complex cyber-physical systems that require thousands of people to create and maintain. SAFe was developed in the field, based on helping Customers solve their most challenging scaling problems. SAFe leverages three primary bodies of knowledge: Agile development, Lean product development and flow, and systems thinking.

## Overview

The SAFe website (www.scaledagileframework.com) provides comprehensive guidance for scaling development work across all levels of an enterprise. SAFe's interactive "Big Picture" (Figure 1) provides a visual overview of the framework. Each icon on the website is selectable, navigating the user to an article that provides extensive guidance on the topic area, along with links to related articles and further information.

The Big Picture has two views. The default "3-level view" (below left) is well suited for solutions that require a modest number of Agile Teams. The "4-level view" (below right) supports those building large solutions that typically require hundreds or more practitioners to construct and maintain.

*Figure 1. Big Picture: 3-level and 4-level SAFe*

SAFe provides three, and optionally four, organization levels, as well as a foundation, as follows:

- **Team Level** – SAFe is based on Agile Teams, each of which is responsible for defining, building, and testing stories from their backlog. Teams employ Scrum or Kanban methods, augmented by quality practices, to deliver value in a series of synchronized, fixed-length iterations.

- **Program Level** – SAFe teams are organized into a virtual program structure called the "Agile Release Train" (ART). Each ART is a long-lived, self-organizing team of 5 to 12 Agile Teams—along with other stakeholders—that plan, commit, execute, inspect and adapt, and deliver solutions together.

- **Value Stream Level** – The optional value stream level supports the development of large and complex solutions. These solutions require multiple, synchronized ARTs, as well as stronger focus on solution intent and solution context. Suppliers and additional stakeholders contribute as well.

- **Portfolio Level** – The portfolio level organizes and funds a set of value streams. The portfolio provides solution development funding via Lean-Agile budgeting and provides necessary governance and value stream coordination.

- **Foundation Layer** – The foundation layer holds various additional elements that support development. Elements include guidance for Lean-Agile Leaders, communities of practice, core values, the Lean-Agile mindset, the nine Lean-Agile principles that guide SAFe, and an overview of implementation strategy.

## Foundation Layer

The foundation layer of SAFe (the shadow backdrop on the big picture) contains the aspects of SAFe that are critical, necessary, and supportive of value delivery, but are not specific practices. This layer contains the following:

- **Lean Agile Leaders** – The ultimate responsibility for the success of the enterprise, and thereby any significant change to the way of working, lies with management. To this end, SAFe describes a new style of leadership, one that is exhibited by SAFe's *Lean-Agile Leaders*.

- **Communities of Practice** – The Lean approach to aligning around Value Streams typically causes the Lean enterprise to pivot from a functional organization to a more flexible and adaptive line-of-business approach. In response, SAFe also supports communities of practice, informal groups of team members and other experts who share practical, functional knowledge in one or more relevant domains.

- **Core Values** – There are four primary *core values* that help make SAFe effective: Alignment, Built-in Quality, Transparency, and Program Execution.

- **Lean-Agile Mindset** – SAFe Lean-Agile Leaders are lifelong learners and teachers who understand and embrace Lean and Agile principles and practices, and teach them to others. To achieve that effectively, leaders must first be trained in, and then become trainers of, these leaner ways of thinking and operating. This mindset is exhibited in part by the House of Lean and the Agile Manifesto.

- **Lean-Agile Principles** – SAFe's practices are grounded on nine fundamental principles that have evolved from Agile principles and methods, Lean product development, systems thinking, and observation of successful enterprises. These are:

    #1 – Take an economic view

    #2 – Apply systems thinking

    #3 – Assume variability; preserve options

    #4 – Build incrementally with fast, integrated learning cycles

    #5 – Base milestones on objective evaluation of working systems

    #6 – Visualize and limit WIP, reduce batch sizes, and manage queue lengths

    #7 – Apply cadence, synchronize with cross-domain planning

    #8 – Unlock the intrinsic motivation of knowledge workers

    #9 – Decentralize decision-making

- **Implementing 1-2-3** – Based on the learnings from hundreds of SAFe implementations, a basic "Implementing SAFe 1-2-3" pattern for successfully adopting SAFe has emerged. The pattern is, first, *train implementers and Lean-Agile change agents (SPCs)*. In turn, these external or internal consultants can then *train all executives, managers, and leaders*. After this, SPCs can *train teams and launch Agile Release Trains*.

## Team Level

The team level provides an organization, artifact, role, and process model for the activities of Agile Teams, as illustrated in Figure 2.

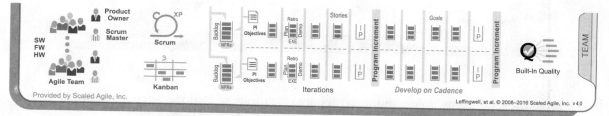

*Figure 2. SAFe team level*

All SAFe teams are part of one Agile Release Train (ART)—the central construct of the program level. Each Agile Team is responsible for defining, building, and testing stories from their team backlog in a series of fixed-length iterations, using common iteration cadence and synchronization to align with other teams, so that the entire system is iterating.

Teams use Scrum or Team Kanban, along with the Built-in Quality practices, to deliver working software every two weeks. The system demo creates a routine "pull event," which pulls the effort of the different teams together, bringing forward the hard work of integration and testing that phase-gated models often leave until too late in the life cycle.

Each team has five to nine members and includes all the roles necessary to build a quality increment of value in each iteration. Roles include the Scrum Master, Product Owner, dedicated individual contributors, and any specialty resources the team needs to deliver value.

A summary of this level is provided in the "Introduction to the Team Level" overview article.

## Program Level

The heart of SAFe is the program level, illustrated in Figure 3, which revolves around the organization called the "Agile Release Train," and which incorporates the team level by reference.

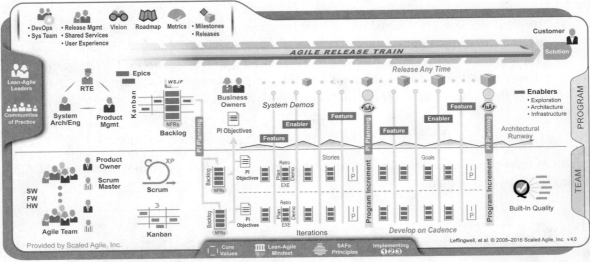

*Figure 3. Program level*

SAFe program level teams, roles, and activities are organized around the ART metaphor, a team of Agile Teams that delivers a continuous flow of incremental releases of value.

ARTs are virtual organizations formed to span functional boundaries, eliminate unnecessary handoffs and steps, and accelerate the delivery of value via implementation of SAFe Lean-Agile principles and practices.

While it is called the "program level," ARTs are generally very long-lived and therefore have a more persistent self-organization, structure, and mission than a traditional "program," which more classically has a start and an end date, as well as temporarily assigned resources. It is the long-lived, knowledge acquiring, flow-based, and self-organizing nature of the ART that powers the SAFe portfolio.

Value in SAFe is delivered by Agile Release Trains, each of which realizes a portion of a value stream (or, in some cases, the entire value stream). They deliver value incrementally in program increments (PIs) of 8 to 12 weeks in duration; each PI is a multiple-iteration timebox during which a significant, valuable increment of the system is developed. Each ART is composed of 5 to 12 Agile Teams (50 – 125+ people) and includes the roles and infrastructure necessary to deliver fully tested, working, system-level solutions. Many release trains are virtual, spanning organizational and geographic boundaries; others follow a line of business or product line management reporting structure.

A summary of this level is provided in the "Introduction to the Program Level" overview article.

## The Spanning Palette

There are a number of additional icons indicated on this level; they are located at the conjunction of the value stream and program level on the Big Picture. This is called the "spanning palette" and is illustrated in Figure 4.

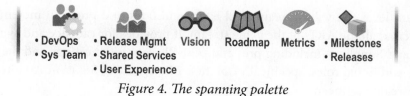

• DevOps     • Release Mgmt     Vision     Roadmap     Metrics     • Milestones
• Sys Team     • Shared Services                             • Releases
              • User Experience

*Figure 4. The spanning palette*

Each of these artifacts and roles contributes to the ART and program level, as described in the "Vision," "Roadmap," "Metrics," "Milestones," "Releases," "DevOps," "System Team," "Release Management," "Shared Services," and "User Experience" articles. However, these elements also "span" the levels because many of them are also useful at the other levels.

## Value Stream Level

The value stream level is optional in SAFe. Enterprises that build systems that are largely independent, or that can be built with a few hundred practitioners, may not need these constructs, and in that case the portfolio can operate with the 3-level view. Even then, however, those are far from trivial systems, and the constructs at the value stream level can be used in 3-level SAFe as needed.

The value stream level helps enterprises that face the largest systems challenges: those building large-scale, multidisciplinary software and cyber-physical systems. Building such solutions in a Lean-Agile manner requires additional constructs, artifacts, and coordination. The constructs of the value stream level are illustrated in Figure 5.

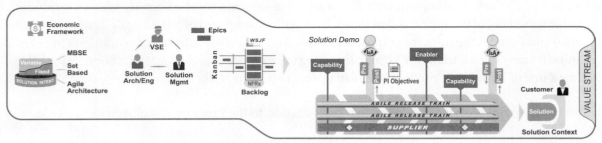

*Figure 5. Value stream level*

This level contains an economic framework, intended to provide financial boundaries for value stream and ART decision-making; solution intent as a repository for intended and actual solution behavior; solution context, which describes the way the solution fits in the deployment environment; and capabilities, describing the larger behaviors of the solution.

Like the program level, the value stream level is organized around program increments, which are synchronized across all the ARTs in the value stream. It provides for cadence and synchronization of multiple ARTs and Suppliers, including pre- and post-PI planning meetings and the solution demo. It also provides additional roles, specifically Solution Management, Solution Architect/Engineering, and the Value Stream Engineer.

A summary of this level may be found in the "Introduction to the Value Stream Level" overview article.

## Portfolio Level

The SAFe portfolio is the highest level of concern in SAFe. As illustrated in Figure 6, each SAFe portfolio has the value streams, people, and processes necessary to provide funding and governance for the products, services, and solutions required to fulfill the overall business strategy.

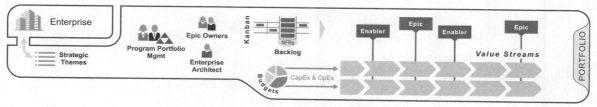

*Figure 6. SAFe portfolio level*

It provides the basic constructs for organizing the Lean-Agile Enterprise around the flow of value via one or more value streams, each of which develops the systems and solutions necessary to meet the strategic intent. The portfolio level encapsulates these elements and also provides the basic budgeting and other governance mechanisms that are necessary to ensure that the investment in the value streams provides the returns necessary for the enterprise to meet its strategic objectives.

The portfolio has a bidirectional connection to the business. One direction provides the strategic themes that guide the portfolio to the larger, and changing, business objectives. The other direction indicates a constant flow of portfolio context back to the enterprise.

The primary elements of the portfolio are value streams (one or more), each of which provides funding for the people and other resources necessary to build the solutions that deliver the value. Each value stream is a long-lived series of system definition, development, and deployment steps used to build and deploy systems that provide a continuous flow of value to the business or Customer. Program Portfolio Management represents the stakeholders who are accountable to deliver the business results.

A summary of this level may be found in the "Introduction to the Portfolio Level" overview article.

# Part 1
# The SAFe Foundation

scaledagileframework.com

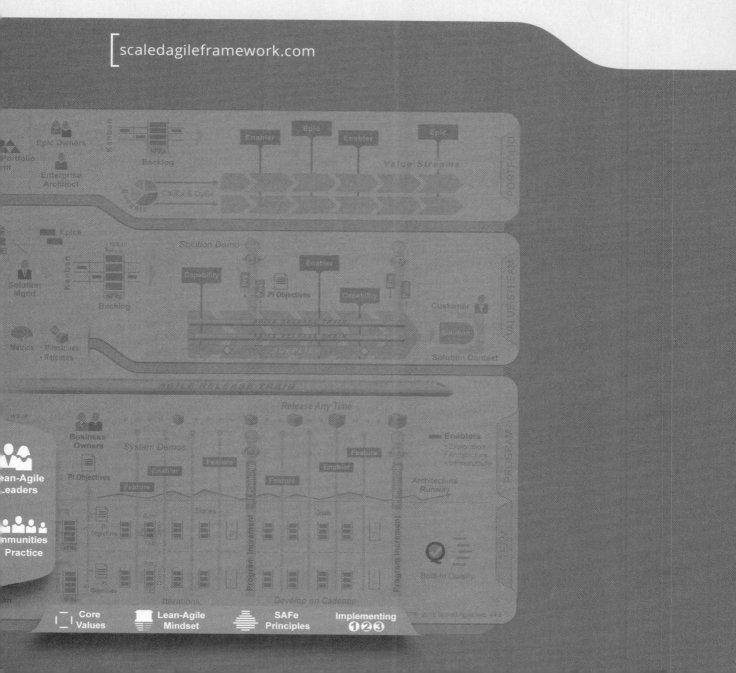

# Lean-Agile Leaders

*A leader is one who knows the way, goes the way, and shows the way.*
  —*John C. Maxwell*

## Abstract

The philosophy of SAFe is simple: As the enabler for the teams, the ultimate responsibility for adoption, success, and ongoing improvement of Lean-Agile development lies with the Enterprise's existing managers, leaders, and executives. Only they can change and continuously improve the systems in which everyone operates. To achieve this, leaders must be trained, and become trainers, in these leaner ways of thinking and operating. Many need to offer a new style of leadership, one that truly teaches, empowers, and engages individuals and teams to reach their highest potential.

While some of these management roles and titles do not appear specifically on the Big Picture, they serve a critical function nonetheless by providing the personnel, resources, management, direction, and support necessary to help the enterprise achieve its mission. This article describes the principles of these *Lean-Agile Leaders*.

## Details

SAFe *Lean-Agile Leaders* are lifelong learners and teachers who help teams build better systems through understanding and exhibiting the Lean-Agile Mindset, SAFe Principles, and systems thinking. Such leaders exhibit the behaviors below.

### #1 – Lead the Change

The work of steering an organization toward Lean and Agile behaviors, habits, and results cannot be delegated. Rather, Lean-Agile Leaders exhibit urgency for change, communicate the need for the change, build a plan for successful change, understand and manage the change process, and address problems as they come up. They have knowledge of organizational change management and take a systems view with respect to implementing the transformation.

## #2 – Know the Way; Emphasize Lifelong Learning

Create an environment that promotes learning. Encourage team members to build relationships with Customers and Suppliers and expose them to other world views. Strive to learn and understand new developments in Lean, Agile, and contemporary management practices. Create and foster formal and informal groups for learning and improvement. Read voraciously from the recommended reading list and on other topics. Share selected readings with others and sponsor book club events for the most relevant texts.

Allow people to solve their own problems. Help them identify a given problem, understand the root causes, and build solutions that will be embraced by the organization. Support individuals and teams when they make mistakes, otherwise learning is not possible.

## #3 – Develop People

Employ a Lean leadership style, one that focuses on developing skills and career paths for team members rather than on being a technical expert or coordinator of tasks. Create a team jointly responsible for success. Learn how to solve problems together in a way that develops people's capabilities and increases their engagement and commitment. Respect people and culture.

## #4 – Inspire and Align with Mission; Minimize Constraints

Provide mission and vision, with minimum specific work requirements. Eliminate demotivating policies and procedures. Build Agile Teams and trains organized around value. Understand the power of self-organizing, self-managing teams. Create a safe environment for learning, growth, and mutual influence. Build an Economic Framework for each Value Stream and teach it to everyone.

## #5 – Decentralize Decision-Making

(See "SAFe Principle #9" for further discussion.)

Establish a decison-making framework. Empower others by setting the mission, developing people, and teaching them to problem-solve. Take responsibility for making and communicating strategic decisions—those that are infrequent, long lasting, and have significant economies of scale. Decentralize all other decisions.

## #6 – Unlock the Intrinsic Motivation of Knowledge Workers

(See "SAFe Principle #8" for further discussion.)

Understand the role that compensation plays in motivating knowledge workers. Create an environment of mutual influence. Eliminate any and all management by objectives (MBOs) that cause internal competition. Revamp personnel evaluations to support Lean-Agile principles and values. Provide purpose and autonomy; help workers achieve mastery of new and increasing skills.

# Role of the Development Manager

As an instantiation of the principles of Lean and Agile development, SAFe emphasizes the values of nearly autonomous, self-organizing, cross-functional teams and Agile Release Trains. This supports a leaner management infrastructure, with more empowered individuals and teams and faster, local decision-making. Traditional, day-to-day employee instruction and activity direction is no longer required.

However, all employees still need someone to assist them with career development; set and manage expectations and compensation; and provide the active coaching they need to advance their technical, functional, individual, and team skills and career goals. They also have a right to serve as an integral member of a high-performing team.

In addition, self-organizing ARTs do not fund themselves or define their own mission. That remains a management responsibility, as it is an element of implementation of strategy.

Much of this responsibility traditionally falls to the traditional role of the *development manager*, and the adoption of Lean-Agile development does not abrogate their responsibilities. However, in SAFe these responsibilities fall to those who can adapt, thrive, and grow in this new environment.

## Responsibilities

The development manager (or engineering manager for system development) is a manager who exhibits the principles and practices of Lean-Agile leadership as described above. Further, the manager has personal responsibility for the coaching and career development of direct reports, takes responsibility for eliminating impediments, and actively evolves the systems in which all knowledge workers operate. They have final accountability for effective value delivery as well. A summary of responsibilities is highlighted below.

### Personnel and Team Development

- Attract, recruit, and retain capable individuals

- Build high-performing teams; establish mission and purpose for individuals and teams

- Perform career counseling and personal development

- Listen and support teams in problem identification, root cause analysis, and decision-making

- Participate in defining and administering compensation, benefits, and promotions

- Eliminate impediments and evolve systems and practices in support of Lean-Agile development

- Take subtle control in assignment of individuals to teams; address issues that teams cannot unblock; make personnel changes where necessary

- Evaluate performance, including team input; provide input, guidance, and corrective actions
- Serve as Agile coach and advisor to Agile Teams
- Remain close enough to the team to add value and to be a competent manager; stay far enough away to let them problem-solve on their own

**Program Execution**
- Help in building Agile Milestones and Roadmaps, as well as the building plans that enable them
- Help develop, implement, and communicate the economic framework
- Participate in Inspect and Adapt workshops
- Protect teams from distractions and unrelated or unnecessary work
- Assist the Release Train and Value Stream Engineers with PI Planning readiness and Pre- and Post-PI Planning activities
- Participate in PI planning, System Demo, and Solution Demo
- Build partnerships with Suppliers, subcontractors, consultants, partners, and internal and external stakeholders
- Provide other resources as necessary for teams and ARTs to successfully execute their Vision and roadmap

**Alignment**
- Work with Release Train and Value Stream Engineers and system stakeholders to help ensure alignment and effective execution of Strategic Themes
- Work with the System Architect/Engineer, Product Managers, and Product Owners to establish clear content authority
- Continuously assist in aligning teams to the system mission and vision
- Help ensure the engagement of Business Owners, Shared Services, and other stakeholders

**Transparency**
- Create an environment where the *facts are always friendly*
- Provide freedom and safety so individuals and teams are free to innovate, experiment, and even fail on occasion
- Communicate openly and honestly with all stakeholders
- Keep backlogs and information radiators fully visible to all
- Value productivity, quality, transparency, and openness over internal politics

**Built-in Quality**

- Understand, teach, or sponsor technical skills development in support of high-quality code, components, systems, and Solutions

- Foster Communities of Practice

- Understand, support, and apply Agile Architecture

---

## LEARN MORE

[1] Manifesto for Agile Software Development. http://agilemanifesto.org/.

[2] Reinertsen, Donald. *The Principles of Product Development Flow: Second Generation Lean Product Development.* Celeritas Publishing, 2009.

[3] Rother, Mike. *Toyota Kata: Managing People for Improvement, Adaptiveness, and Superior Results.* McGraw-Hill, 2009.

[4] Liker, Jeffrey and Gary L. Convis. *The Toyota Way to Lean Leadership: Achieving and Sustaining Excellence Through Leadership Development.* McGraw-Hill, 2011.

# Communities of Practice

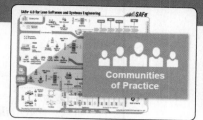

*It's said that a wise person learns from his mistakes. A wiser one learns from others' mistakes. But the wisest person of all learns from others' successes.*

—*Zen proverb adapted by John C. Maxwell*

## Abstract

A *Community of Practice* (CoP) is an informal group of team members and other experts, acting within the context of a program or enterprise, that has a mission of sharing practical knowledge in one or more relevant domains. CoPs are not new, nor are they mandated by Agile development. However, the Lean approach to aligning around Value Streams optimizes for delivery of value, which is a good thing. Over time, this typically causes the Lean Enterprise to pivot from a vertical, *functional* organization to a more flexible, *horizontal line-of-business* organization that can deliver value more rapidly. Further, within value streams, SAFe promotes long-lived Agile Release Trains (ARTs), which are built of people allocated to them for an extended period. What happens when practitioners of a discipline (whether or not their organization has become horizontal), who are from different programs but often have the same reporting structure, meet regularly, are led by managers and experts from their domain, and advance their specialist skills? Enter the SAFe CoP (*Guild*, in Spotify terminology [1]).

## Details

Lean-Agile promotes cross-functional teams and programs that facilitate value delivery in the Enterprise. Similarly, Lean thinking emphasizes organizing people with different skills around a Value Stream. However, developers need to talk with other developers within or outside of the team context, testers need to talk with other testers, Product Owners need to communicate with their peers from other Agile Teams, and so on. This is critical for leveraging the multiple experiences and different types of practical knowledge available from different people at scale. That is what drives craftsmanship and persistent knowledge acquisition and facilitates the adoption of new methods and techniques.

Such inter-team communication is often supported by *Communities of Practice* (CoP)—informal working groups designed specifically for efficient knowledge-sharing and exploration across teams and groups of professionals, as shown in Figure 1.

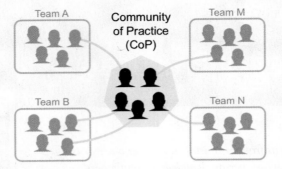

*Figure 1. Community of practice: Members normally work in their
Agile Teams but also regularly share best practices*

## Organizing a Community of Practice

A Lean enterprise has the ability to identify the relevant domains where communities of practice would be beneficial and then to foster and support such communities once they are in place.

CoPs can be ad hoc and need driven. They may or may not be permanent; they may form and disband based on current need and context. For example, an automated testing CoP could be composed of test engineers and developers who are interested in advancing these skills. An architecture and design CoP would foster the adoption of practices such as emergent design, intentional system architecture, Continuous Integration, and refactoring. It could also support the effort put into building and maintaining the Architectural Runway, foster designing for testability and deployability, deprecate old platforms, and more. Still others may be formed around Agile coaching, continuous integration, continuous delivery, coding standards, and other new practices and processes. Similarly, Scrum Masters from different Agile Teams may form a CoP to exchange facilitation best practices and experiences in building highly productive Agile Teams.

## Operating a Community of Practice

A CoP is defined by the knowledge specialization of its members. Each typically has a specific learning objective, Roadmap, and backlog. Membership is fluid and changes as members take on different roles, as new needs arise, or as individual members gain the knowledge they need. CoPs may be fostered or initiated spontaneously. They are largely self-organizing, although a leader or Scrum Master equivalent (the *Guild Coordinator* in Spotify terminology) may organize the initiative and help maintain its momentum. CoPs meet regularly for knowledge-exchange sessions and maintain and evolve internal community websites and wikis to institutionalize their knowledge. The CoP exists only for so long as the members believe they have something to learn or contribute.

However, CoPs are created for the purpose of learning and exchanging experiences, not for coordinating dependencies or current tasks.

For instance, the Scrum Master CoP would foster learning new facilitation techniques, while actual coordination and dependency management for current work in process would happen among the same people during the Scrum of Scrums.

The Innovation and Planning Iteration presents a great time for CoPs to hold learning sessions, formal or informal, as well as other activities such as coding dojos, coaching clinics, and the like.

It is the role of Lean-Agile Leaders to encourage and support people's desire to improve as this both helps the enterprise and builds the intrinsic motivation of knowledge workers, as is evident in SAFe Principle #9–*Decentralize decision-making*.

---

**LEARN MORE**

[1] Scaling Agility @ Spotify with Tribes, Squads, Chapters, and Guilds. https://dl.dropboxusercontent.com/u/1018963/Articles/SpotifyScaling.pdf.

# SAFe Core Values

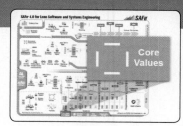

*Find people who share your values, and you'll conquer the world together.*
—*John Ratzenberger*

## Abstract

*Core Values* are the fundamental beliefs of a person or organization. The core values are the guiding principles that dictate behavior and action. Core values can help people to know what is right from wrong; where to put their focus and help companies to determine if they are on the right path and fulfilling their business goals; and they create an unwavering and unchanging guide.

A Lean-Agile Mindset, Lean-Agile Leaders, SAFe Principles, and the extensive benefits that Lean-Agile development provides all play important roles in defining what makes SAFe safe. But in synthesis, there are four *Core Values* that SAFe honors, supports, and helps deliver: *Alignment, Built-in Quality, Transparency,* and *Program Execution.* If an Enterprise does those four things well, a lot of goodness will surely follow.

## Details

SAFe is broad and deep and is based on both Lean and Agile principles. That's what it's built on, but what does SAFe itself stand for? SAFe upholds four *Core Values: Alignment, Built-in Quality, Transparency,* and *Program Execution.*

These are illustrated in Figure 1, and each is discussed in the paragraphs that follow.

Built-in Quality

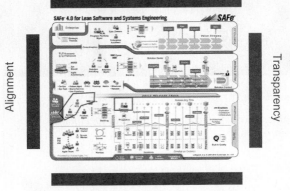

*Figure 1. SAFe core values: alignment,*
*built-in quality, transparency, program execution*

## Alignment

Like cars out of alignment, misaligned companies can develop serious problems. They are hard to steer and they don't respond well to changes in direction [1]. Even if it's clear where everyone thinks they're headed, the vehicle is unlikely to get them there.

*Alignment scales.* It is a necessary condition to be able to address the business reality of fast-paced change, turbulent competitive forces, and geographically distributed teams. While empowered Agile Teams are good (even great), the responsibility for strategy and alignment cannot rest with the accumulated opinions of the teams, no matter how good they are. Rather, alignment must be based on the Enterprise business objectives. Here are some of the ways in which SAFe supports alignment:

- It starts at the strategy level of the portfolio, is reflected in Strategic Themes and the Portfolio Backlog, and then moves down through the Vision, Roadmap, and Program Backlogs to the Team Backlogs. All is visible. All is debated. All is resolved. All is known.

- It is supported by clear lines of content authority, starting at the portfolio and then resting primarily with the Product and Solution Management roles, and extending to the Product Owner role

- PI Objectives and Iteration Goals are used to communicate expectations and commitments

- Cadence and synchronization are applied to ensure that things stay in alignment, or that they drift only within reasonable economic and time boundaries

- Program architecture, User Experience guidance, and governance help ensure that the Solution is technologically sound, robust, and scalable

- Lean prioritization keeps the stakeholders engaged in continuous, agreed-to, rolling-wave prioritization, based on the then-current context and changing fact patterns

Alignment, however, does not imply or encourage command and control. Instead, it provides a foundation for the enterprise where business objectives and outcomes are the continued focus. It also encourages decentralized technical and economic decision-making, thereby enabling those who implement value to make better local decisions.

## Built-in Quality

Built-in Quality ensures that every increment of the solution reflects quality standards. Quality is not "added later." Built-in quality is a prerequisite of Lean and flow; without it, the organization will likely operate with large batches of unverified, unvalidated work. Excessive rework and slower velocities are the likely outcome. There can be no ambiguity about the importance of built-in quality in large-scale systems. It is mandatory.

### Software

In complex solutions, *software* functionality often represents a fast-changing and increasingly high-investment area. In addition, given the high levels of complexity and the manual nature of much of the work, it is often the source of many solution defects. The relatively lower cost of change encourages rapid adaptation, which is good. But if attention is not paid, the software design may quickly erode, negatively affecting quality and velocity.

Put simply, *you can't scale crappy code.* The Agile Manifesto certainly focused on quality: "Continuous attention to technical excellence and good design enhances agility" [2]. To address software quality in the face of rapid change, software practitioners have developed and evolved a number of effective practices, many of which are largely inspired by eXtreme Programming. These include:

- Test-First: Test-Driven Development (TDD), Acceptance Test-Driven Development (ATDD), and Behavior-Driven Development (BDD)

- Continuous Integration

- Refactoring

- Pair work

- Collective ownership

**Hardware**

But coding aside, no one can scale crappy components or systems, either. Hardware elements—electronics, electrical, fluidics, optics, mechanical, packaging, thermal, and many more—are a lot less "soft." Errors here can introduce a much higher cost of change and rework. Tips to avoid this include:

- Frequent design cycles and integration [3]
- Collaborative design practices
- Model-Based Systems Engineering
- Set-Based Design
- Investment in development and test infrastructure

**System Integration**

Eventually, different components and subsystems—software, firmware, hardware, and everything else—must collaborate to provide effective solution-level behaviors. Practices that support solution-level quality include:

- Frequent system and solution-level integration
- Solution-level testing of functional and Nonfunctional Requirements
- System and Solution Demos

## Transparency

Solution development is hard. Things go wrong or do not work out as planned. Without transparency, facts are obscure and hard to come by. This results in decisions based on speculative assumptions and lack of data. No one can fix a secret.

For that *trust* is needed, because without trust no one can build high-performing teams and programs, or build (or rebuild) the confidence needed to make and meet reasonable commitments. Trust exists when one party can confidently rely on another to act with integrity, particularly in times of difficulty. And without trust, working environments are a lot less fun and motivating.

Building trust takes time. Transparency is the enabler for trust. SAFe helps an enterprise achieve transparency:

- Executives, Portfolio Managers, and other stakeholders are able to see into the Portfolio Kanbans and program backlogs, and they have a clear understanding of the PI goals for each train
- Programs have visibility into the team's backlogs, as well other program backlogs
- Teams and programs commit to short-term, clear, and visible commitments. They routinely meet them.

- Programs Inspect and Adapt with all relevant stakeholders; lessons learned are incorporated.

- Teams and programs have visibility into business and architecture Epic Kanban systems. They can see what might be headed their way.

- Status reporting is based on objective measures of working systems

- Everyone can understand the velocity and WIP of the teams and programs; strategy and the ability to execute are aligned

## Program Execution

Of course, none of the rest of SAFe matters if teams can't execute and continuously deliver value. Therefore, SAFe places an intense focus on working systems and resultant business outcomes. This isn't only for the obvious reasons. History shows us that while many enterprises start the transformation with Agile Teams, they often become frustrated as even those teams struggle to deliver larger amounts of solution value reliably and efficiently.

That is the purpose of the Agile Release Train, and that is why SAFe focuses implementation initially at the Program Level. In turn, the ability of Value Streams to deliver value depends on the ability of the ARTs.

But with *alignment, transparency,* and *built-in quality* on the team's side, they have a little "wind at their back." That enables a focus on *execution.* And if they struggle—and they will, because complex solution development is *hard*—they have the cornerstone of the inspect and adapt workshops. In that way, they close the loop and execute better and better during each Program Increment.

But program execution can't just be a team-based, bottom-up thing. Successful Lean-Agile execution at scale requires not just the teams but the active support of their Lean-Agile Leaders, who couple their internal leadership with an orientation toward system and Customer outcomes. That creates a persistent and meaningful context for the teams and their stakeholders.

That's the way the successful teams and programs are doing it, and that's why they are getting the many benefits—employee engagement, productivity, quality, and time to market—that Lean-Agile enterprises so enjoy.

---

**LEARN MORE**

[1] Labovitz, George H. and Victor Rosansky. *The Power of Alignment: How Great Companies Stay Centered and Accomplish Extraordinary Things.* Wiley, 1997.

[2] AgileManifesto.org.

[3] Oosterwal, Dantar P. *The Lean Machine: How Harley-Davidson Drove Top-Line Growth and Profitability with Revolutionary Lean Product Development.* Amacom, 2010.

---

# Lean-Agile Mindset

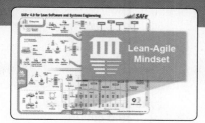

*It all starts with a Lean-Agile Mindset.*
  —SAFe Authors

## Abstract

SAFe is based on a number of newer paradigms in modern systems and software engineering, including Lean and systems thinking, product development flow, and Agile development. As reflected at the Team Level, Agile provides the tools needed to empower and engage teams to achieve unprecedented levels of productivity, quality, and engagement. But a broader and deeper *Lean-Agile Mindset* is needed to support Lean and Agile development at scale across the entire Enterprise.

**Thinking Lean**
Much of the thinking in Lean is represented in the SAFe "House of Lean" icon. It is organized around six key constructs. The "roof" represents the goal of delivering Value, the "pillars" support that goal via Respect for People and Culture, Flow, Innovation, and Relentless Improvement. Lean-Agile Leadership provides the foundation on which everything else stands.

**Embracing Agility**
In addition, SAFe is built entirely on the skills, aptitude, and capabilities of Agile Teams and their leaders. And while there is no one definition of what an Agile method is, the *Agile Manifesto* provides a unified value system that has helped inaugurate Agile methods into mainstream development.

Together, these create the *Lean-Agile Mindset*, part of a new management approach and an enhanced culture, one that provides the leadership needed to drive a successful transformation, and one that helps both individuals and businesses achieve their goals.

## Details

### The SAFe House of Lean

While initially derived from Lean manufacturing [1], the principles and practices of Lean thinking as applied to software, product, and systems development are now deep and extensive.

---

For example, Ward [2], Reinertsen [3], Poppendieck [4], Leffingwell [5], and others have described aspects of Lean thinking that put many of the core principles and practices into a product development context. In combination of these factors, we present the *SAFe House of Lean*, as illustrated in Figure 1, which is inspired by "houses" of Lean from Toyota and others.

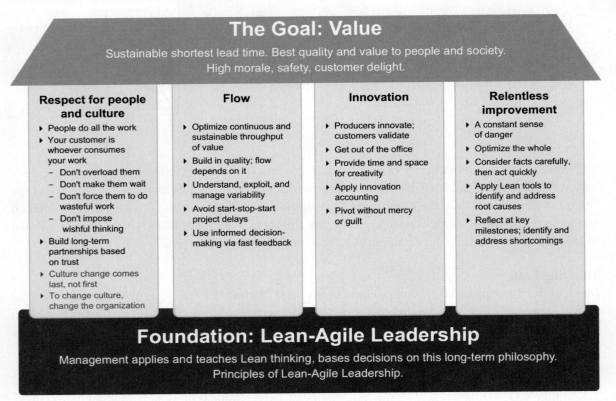

*Figure 1. The SAFe House of Lean*

## The Goal – Value

The goal of Lean is inarguable: to deliver the *maximum Customer value in the sustainably shortest lead time*, while providing the highest possible quality to Customers and society as a whole. High morale, safety, and Customer delight are further tangible targets and benefits.

## Pillar 1 – Respect for People and Culture

SAFe is a systematic framework for implementing Lean-Agile development at scale, but it does not instantiate itself, nor does it perform any real work. *People do all the work*. Respect for people and culture is a fundamental value of the SAFe House of Lean. People are empowered to evolve their own practices and improvements.

Management challenges people to change and may even indicate what to improve, but the teams and individuals learn problem-solving and reflection skills, and they make the appropriate improvements.

Culture is the driving force behind this behavior. To evolve a truly Lean organization, the culture will need to change. In order for that to happen, the organization and its leaders must change first. And culture and people are not solely an internal construct. The culture of the organization extends to long-term relationships with Suppliers, partners, Customers, and the broader community that supports the Enterprise.

Where there is urgency for positive change, improvements in culture can be achieved gradually by, first, understanding SAFe values and principles; second, implementing SAFe practices; and third, delivering positive results. Changes to culture will follow naturally.

## Pillar 2 – Flow

The key to successful execution in SAFe is establishing a continuous flow of work that supports incremental value delivery, based on continuous feedback and adjustment. Establishing continuous flow is critical to fast value delivery; effective quality practices; continuous improvement; and effective, evidence-based governance. The principles of flow, reflected in this pillar of the House of Lean, constitute an important subset of the SAFe Lean-Agile Principles and are instantiated in various practices throughout. These include understanding the full Value Stream, visualizing and limiting WIP, reducing batch sizes and managing queue lengths, and prioritizing work based on the cost of delay. Lean also has a primary focus on Built-in Quality, fast feedback, and the identification and constant reduction of delays and non-value-added activities.

These constructs provide a pivotal change to a better understanding of the system development process and provide new thinking, tools, and techniques that leaders and teams can use to move from phase-gated processes to more continuous value delivery.

## Pillar 3 – Innovation

Flow builds a solid foundation for the delivery of value, but without innovation, both product and process will stagnate. Innovation is a critical part of the SAFe House of Lean. In support of innovation, Lean-Agile Leaders:

- "Get out of the office" and into the actual workplace where value is produced and products are created and used (*gemba*). As Taiichi Ohno put it, "No useful improvement was ever invented at a desk."

- Provide time and space for people to be creative. Time for innovation must be purposeful. Innovations can rarely occur in the presence of 100% utilization and continuous firefighting. SAFe's Innovation and Planning Iteration is one such opportunity.

- Apply innovation accounting [6]. Establish non-financial, non-vanity Metrics that provide fast feedback on the important elements of the new innovation.

- Validate the innovation with Customers, then *pivot without mercy or guilt* when the hypothesis needs to change

## Pillar 4 – Relentless Improvement

The fourth pillar is relentless improvement. With this pillar, the organization is guided to become a learning organization through continuous reflection and relentless improvement. A constant sense of competitive danger drives the learning organization to aggressively pursue improvement opportunities. Leaders and teams do the following systematically:

- Optimize the whole, not the parts, of both the organization and the development process

- Consider facts carefully, then act quickly

- Apply Lean tools and techniques to determine the root cause of inefficiencies and apply effective countermeasures quickly

- Reflect at key Milestones to openly identify and address the shortcomings of the process at all levels

## Foundation – Leadership

The foundation of Lean is leadership, which is the ultimate enabling force for team success. Here, SAFe's philosophy is simple: *The ultimate responsibility for adoption and success of the Lean-Agile paradigm lies with the enterprise's existing managers, leaders, and executives.* "Such a responsibility cannot be delegated" (Deming [7]) to Lean/Agile champions, Lean/Agile working groups, development teams, a PMO, process teams, outside consultants, or any other party. To achieve success, leaders must be trained in these new and innovative ways of thinking and exhibit the principles and behaviors of Lean-Agile leadership.

Lean thinking deviates from common experience with Agile, which was often introduced as a team-based process that tended to exclude management. That does not scale. Here is a key differentiator between traditional Agile and one of the key drivers for SAFe:

In traditional Agile, the expectation has been that management simply *supports* the teams and helps eliminate impediments as they arise. In Lean-Agile development, the expectation is that management *leads* the teams, embraces the values of Lean, is competent in the basic practices, proactively eliminates impediments, and takes an active role in driving organizational change and facilitating relentless improvement.

## The Agile Manifesto

In the 1990s, in response to the many challenges of waterfall development methods, a number of lighter-weight and more iterative development methods arose. In 2001, many of the leaders of these methods came together in Snowbird, Utah. While there were differences of opinion on the specific merits of one method over another, the attendees agreed that their common values and beliefs dwarfed the differences in approach. The result was a *Manifesto for Agile Software Development* [8], which was a turning point that helped unify the approach and started to bring the benefits of these innovative methods to the industry at large. The Manifesto consists of a value statement, as exhibited in Figure 2, and a set of principles, as exhibited in Figure 3.

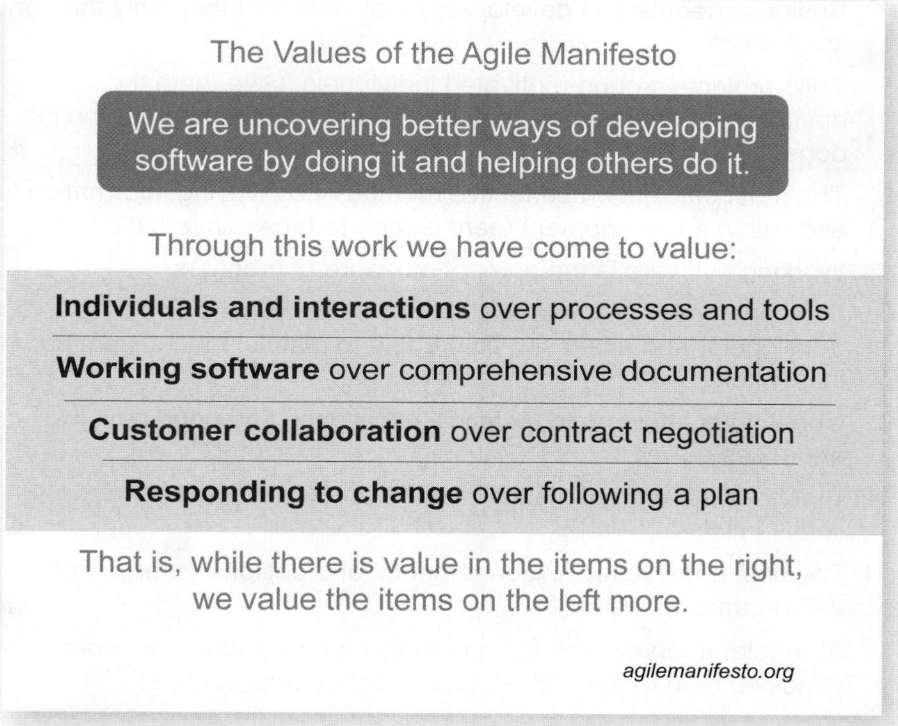

The Values of the Agile Manifesto

We are uncovering better ways of developing software by doing it and helping others do it.

Through this work we have come to value:

**Individuals and interactions** over processes and tools

**Working software** over comprehensive documentation

**Customer collaboration** over contract negotiation

**Responding to change** over following a plan

That is, while there is value in the items on the right, we value the items on the left more.

*agilemanifesto.org*

*Figure 2. Values of the Agile Manifesto*

## The Principles of the Agile Manifesto

1. Our highest priority is to satisfy the customer through early and continuous delivery of valuable software.

2. Welcome changing requirements, even late in development. Agile processes harness change for the customer's competitive advantage.

3. Deliver working software frequently, from a couple of weeks to a couple of months, with a preference for the shorter timescale.

4. Business people and developers must work together daily throughout the project.

5. Build projects around motivated individuals. Give them the environment and support they need, and trust them to get the job done.

6. The most efficient and effective method of conveying information to and within a development team is face-to-face conversation.

7. Working software is the primary measure of progress.

8. Agile processes promote sustainable development. The sponsors, developers, and users should be able to maintain a constant pace indefinitely.

9. Continuous attention to technical excellence and good design enhances agility.

10. Simplicity—the art of maximizing the amount of work not done—is essential.

11. The best architectures, requirements, and designs emerge from self-organizing teams.

12. At regular intervals, the team reflects on how to become more effective, then tunes and adjusts its behavior accordingly.

*agilemanifesto.org*

*Figure 3. Principles of the Agile Manifesto*

Along with the various Agile methods, the Manifesto provides the Agile foundation for effective, empowered, self-organizing teams. SAFe extends this foundation to the level of teams of teams and applies Lean thinking to understand and relentlessly improve the systems that support the teams in their critical work.

## LEARN MORE

[1] Womack, James P., Daniel T. Jones, and Daniel Roos. *The Machine That Changed the World: The Story of Lean Production—Toyota's Secret Weapon in the Global Car Wars That Is Revolutionizing World Industry*. Free Press, 2007.

[2] Ward, Allen and Durward Sobeck. *Lean Product and Process Development*. Lean Enterprise Institute, 2014.

[3] Reinertsen, Donald G. *The Principles of Product Development Flow: Second Generation Lean Product Development*. Celeritas, 2009.

[4] Poppendieck, Mary and Tom Poppendieck. *Implementing Lean Software Development: From Concept to Cash*. Addison-Wesley, 2006.

[5] Leffingwell, Dean. *Agile Software Requirements: Lean Requirements Practices for Teams, Programs, and the Enterprise*. Addison-Wesley, 2011.

[6] Ries, Eric. *The Lean Startup: How Today's Entrepreneurs Use Continuous Innovation to Create Radically Successful Businesses*. Crown Business, 2011.

[7] Deming, W. Edwards. *Out of the Crisis*. MIT Center for Advanced Educational Services, 1982.

[8] Manifesto for Agile Software Development. http://agilemanifesto.org/.

# SAFe Principles

*The impression that "our problems are different" is a common disease that afflicts management the world over. They are different, to be sure, but the principles that will help to improve the quality of product and service are universal in nature.*

—W. Edwards Deming

SAFe is based on a number of immutable, underlying Lean and Agile principles. These are the fundamental tenets, the basic truths and economic underpinnings that drive the roles and practices that make SAFe effective. The nine principles are:

### #1-Take an economic view

### #2-Apply systems thinking

### #3-Assume variability; preserve options

### #4-Build incrementally with fast, integrated learning cycles

### #5-Base milestones on objective evaluation of working systems

### #6-Visualize and limit WIP, reduce batch sizes, and manage queue lengths

### #7-Apply cadence, synchronize with cross-domain planning

### #8-Unlock the intrinsic motivation of knowledge workers

### #9-Decentralize decision-making

## Why the Focus on Principles?

Building enterprise-class software and cyber-physical systems is one of the most complex challenges the industry faces today. Millions of lines of software, complex hardware and software interactions, multiple concurrent platforms, demanding and unforgiving nonfunctional requirements—these are just a few of the challenges systems builders face.

Of course, the enterprises that build these systems are increasingly complex, too. They are bigger and more distributed than ever. Mergers and acquisitions, distributed multinational (and multilingual) development, offshoring, and the rapid growth that success requires are all part of the solution—but also part of the problem as well.

Fortunately, we have an amazing and growing body of knowledge to help us address this challenge. These include Agile principles and methods, Lean and Systems thinking, product development flow, Lean process and product development, and more. Many thought leaders have gone down this path before us and left a trail to follow in the hundreds of books and references we can draw on.

SAFe's goal is to synthesize some of this body of knowledge and the lessons learned from hundreds of deployments into a single framework—a system of integrated, proven practices that has been demonstrated to bring substantial improvements in employee engagement, time to market, solution quality, and team productivity. However, given the complexity of the industry challenges already discussed, there is truly no off-the-shelf solution to the unique challenges every enterprise faces. This means that some tailoring and customization may be required, as not every SAFe-recommended practice will apply equally well in every circumstance. Therefore, we always endeavor to make certain that SAFe practices are grounded in fundamental, and reasonably immutable, principles. In that way, we can be confident that they apply well in the general case. And when and if they don't, the underlying principles can guide those doing the implementation to make sure that they are moving on a continuous path to the "shortest sustainable lead time, with best quality and value to people and society." There is value in that too.

The nine SAFe Principles are discussed in greater detail in the next chapter.

# Implementing 1-2-3

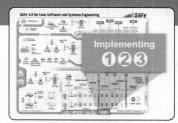

*It is not enough that management commit themselves to quality and productivity, they must know what it is they must do. Such a responsibility cannot be delegated.*

—W. Edwards Deming

## Abstract

Implementing the changes necessary to become a Lean-Agile technology enterprise is a substantial change for most organizations. Embracing a Lean-Agile Mindset, understanding and applying the Lean-Agile principles, and effectively implementing the SAFe practices all come *before* the business benefits. And, of course, the culture must evolve, too.

While SAFe is a freely revealed body of knowledge, available to all, it does not implement itself, nor does it prescribe the organizational change management process that is typically required for successful implementation. We leave that to the enterprise, because only they know their specific context, and they—typically assisted by their partners—must own the transformation.

But many enterprises have gone down this path already (see the "Case Studies" articles online at www.scaledagileframework.com), and the lessons learned are now becoming more widely accessible. Based on the learnings from hundreds of SAFe implementations, Scaled Agile, Inc., the owner of SAFe, has developed a basic *Implementing SAFe 1-2-3* pattern for successful SAFe adoption. It provides a simple roadmap that helps gets everyone aligned to a common implementation strategy.

This article describes an overview of this successful pattern for SAFe implementation, along with pointers to the growing community of service providers who are ready and willing to help your enterprise make this critical transformation.

## Details

Figure 1 on the next page provides a high-level summary of the *Implementing SAFe 1-2-3* approach. Each of the numbered items in this strategy is described in the paragraphs that follow.

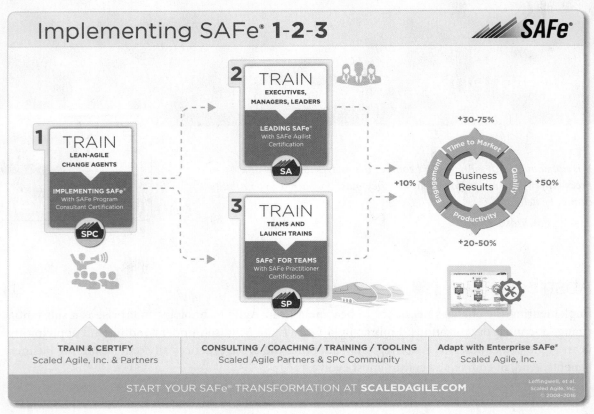

*Figure 1. Implementing SAFe 1-2-3*

## 1. Train Implementers and Lean-Agile Change Agents

Given the scope, challenge, and impact of rollouts, successful adoption of SAFe requires most enterprises to use a combination of internal and external change agents, leaders, mentors, and coaches. These people need to be skilled in teaching and delivering SAFe. To achieve this, Scaled Agile, Inc. provides an *Implementing SAFe 4.0 with SPC Certification* program. After taking this class, attendees will be able to:

- Lead an enterprise Agile transformation with SAFe

- Implement SAFe

- Launch Agile Release Trains and proctor and continuously improve the trains via Inspect and Adapt workshops

Those who take and pass the optional SPC Certification exam (included) will be licensed to:

- Train managers and executives in Leading SAFe and act as a SAFe Agilist (SA) certifying agent

- Train practitioners in SAFe 4.0 for Teams and act as a SAFe Practitioner (SP) certifying agent

The Implementing SAFe 4.0 with SAFe Program Consultant (SPC4) Certification course is delivered by certified SPC Trainers (SPCT) in open enrollment or on-site settings worldwide. Service providers who specialize in SAFe and Scaled Agile Partners can be found online at www.scaledagile.com. There are many independent SPCs as well; these can be found at the Scaled Agile SPC membership site at www.scaledagileacademy.com.

## 2. Train all Executives, Managers, and Leaders

It is critical that executives, managers, and leaders understand what is required to lead a Lean-Agile transformation, including how and why SAFe works. To help achieve this, Scaled Agile, Inc., provides a two-day course, *Leading SAFe 4.0, Leading the Lean-Agile Enterprise with the Scaled Agile Framework*. After attending, participants will be able to:

- Adopt a Lean-Agile mindset

- Apply Lean and Agile principles; base daily decisions on this long-term philosophy; understand, exhibit, and teach these principles

- Understand the practices, roles, activities, and artifacts of the Scaled Agile Framework

- Unlock the intrinsic motivation of knowledge workers

- Learn the practices and tools of relentless improvement and teach employees problem-solving and corrective-action skills

- Become hands-on in the new process adoption, eliminate impediments, and facilitate organizational change management

- Take responsibility for Lean-Agile implementation success

The audience for this class is executives, managers, and change agents responsible for leading a Lean-Agile change initiative, whereby they gain the knowledge necessary to lead the SAFe adoption.

A certification exam is optional for this course. Those who pass the optional exam will be certified as SAFe Agilist (SA), and will receive one year's membership to that community and its benefits.

The *Leading SAFe 4.0* course is delivered by certified SPC consultant/trainers in open enrollment or on-site settings worldwide. Service providers include Scaled Agile, Inc.; Scaled Agile Partners; and independent SPCs.

## 3. Train Teams and Launch Agile Release Trains

The primary value delivery mechanism in the enterprise is the Agile Release Train, but starting these trains is not a trivial task. One proven starting mechanism is an Agile Release Train Quickstart.

Suitable after some significant up-front preparation, the QuickStart is a one-week training and immersion program that:

- Organizes 50 – 100 team members into Agile Teams, training them simultaneously in the principles of Lean, Agile, and SAFe

- Aligns the teams on the train to a common mission and spends two days in face-to-face support of planning the next Program Increment

- Introduces prospective Product Owners and Scrum Masters to the skills and activities unique to their roles in the new Agile enterprise

- Builds context and a cadence-based, rolling-wave planning and delivery model that continuously incorporates business objective setting and program commitments, effective and reliable program execution, and adaptive feedback

SPCs can provide these services and download and use the SAFe ART Launch Pack (member login required) to prepare for a successful launch. It contains the tools to prepare the organization, programs, teams, and individuals for success and continuous improvement. You may also want to consider licensing the ART Training and Launch Pack Bundle. This bundle provides both the courseware and tools needed to quickly and effectively launch Agile Release Trains.

## Supporting Consulting Activities

Once the enterprise has a critical mass of in-house Lean-Agile Leaders, and a few Agile Release Trains rolling, a variety of consulting activities may be applicable and beneficial. These could include *coaching the train, training specialist roles,* and *continuous improvement.*

**Coaching the Train**

By sharing their knowledge and experience, coaches can help teams and individuals improve their newfound skills by:

- Providing program consulting and team coaching to build the organization's Lean-Agile capabilities

- Facilitating Agile Release Train readiness, including Program Backlog refinement and more

- Facilitating inspect and adapt workshops

- Facilitating Portfolio planning workshops

- Implementing relevant Metrics and governance

- Mentoring executives, managers, and other program stakeholders in SAFe adoption

- Shadowing and mentoring Release Train Engineers

Many of the these activities are supported by various Scaled Agile workshop kits, which are available to SPCs in good standing.

**Training Specialist Roles**

It is important to train specialists—including prospective Product Owners and Scrum Masters—in the principles and practices unique to their roles. Training courses for this purpose include:

- *SAFe 4.0 Scrum Master Orientation* – Half- to 1-day orientation to the role of a SAFe Scrum Master

- *SAFe 4.0 Product Manager / Product Owner with PMPO certification* – This 2-day certification course is for Product Managers, Business Owners, and Product Owners who will learn how to manage and prioritize backlogs, participate in SAFe events, define and support epics, capabilities, features, and user stories, and manage stakeholders at the various levels of the enterprise.

- *SAFe 4.0 Advanced Scrum Master with ASM Certification* – This 2-day advanced, certification course prepares current Scrum Masters for their leadership role in facilitating Agile team, program, and enterprise success. It enhances the Scrum paradigm with an introduction to scalable engineering and DevOps practices; the application of Kanban to facilitate flow; supporting interactions with architects, product management, and other critical stakeholders; and tips and techniques for building high-performing Agile teams.

Note: The courseware offerings are always advancing, so be sure and check ScaledAgile.com for the latest updates.

**Continuous Improvement**

Once the transformation is under way, there are a variety of opportunities for sustaining and enhancing improvements in speed and quality that can be best facilitated by the extensive community of skilled professionals. These activities can include Agile Release Train health checks; Portfolio, Value Stream, Agile Release Train, and Team agility self-assessments; and facilitated Inspect and Adapt sessions. For help, we again refer you to your in-house SPCs, Scaled Agile Partners, and other independent SPCs.

## Guidance and Governance with Enterprise SAFe

For those who would benefit from being able to modify a custom version of the Scaled Agile Framework website, all SAFe content is available for enterprise licensing. Organizations that are scaling Lean-Agile best practices leverage Enterprise SAFe so they can have access to the most up-to-date content for their teams and the thought leaders at Scaled Agile, Inc.

Enterprise SAFe allows organizations to align around common process objectives while providing the ability to adapt SAFe to their unique needs and culture. Enterprise SAFe allows organizations to create a custom version of the Scaled Agile Framework website while maintaining automated updates as the methodology advances.

**Fully Adaptable to Your Organization's Context**

Provisioned by Scaled Agile, Inc., and built on WordPress, Enterprise SAFe supports adaptation that enables organizations to revise the graphical representation of the SAFe Big Picture as well as the entire SAFe content offering. Content is controlled locally by the enterprise via a set of tools that support accepting or rejecting framework updates from Scaled Agile, Inc., as well as adding custom content, such as articles, icons, labels, and graphics.

Enterprise SAFe features include:

- A WordPress publishing platform that allows you to start capturing the specifics of your custom SAFe implementation in a matter of minutes

- A customizable Big Picture in Adobe Illustrator that allows you to capture key modifications to the framework at the front end of the website

- A PowerPoint version of all SAFe artwork that allows you to change the graphics that are integral to the story

- Provisions to modify or extend SAFe with your custom process content

- Local control of custom content via a set of tools that allow reviewing differences between local pages and content updates, and accepting or rejecting updates

- Administration utility for easy management of large numbers of user accounts

Enterprise SAFe is provisioned by Scaled Agile, Inc., via a private and secure cloud-based website.

# Part 2
# The SAFe Principles

scaledagileframework.com/**safe-lean-agile-principles**

#1-Take an economic view

#2-Apply systems thinking

#3-Assume variability; preserve options

#4-Build incrementally with fast, integrated learning cycles

#5-Base milestones on objective evaluation of working systems

#6-Visualize and limit WIP, reduce batch sizes, and manage queue lengths

#7-Apply cadence, synchronize with cross-domain planning

#8-Unlock the intrinsic motivation of knowledge workers

#9-Decentralize decision-making

SAFe
Principles

# #1 – Take an economic view

*While you may ignore economics, it won't ignore you.*
*—Donald Reinertsen, Principles of Product Development Flow*

## Abstract

Achieving the lean systems builder's goal—sustainably shortest lead time, with best quality and value to people and society—requires a fundamental understanding of the economics of the systems builder's mission. Without such an understanding, even a technically competent system may cost too much to develop, take too long to deliver, or have manufacturing or operating costs that cannot support economically efficient value.

To this end, systems builders—as represented by the entire chain of leadership, management and knowledge workers—must all understand the economic impact of the choices they are making. Traditionally, the economic constraints on the systems builder's activities is known to only a few—those decision makers and authorities who have the understanding of the business, marketplace, and Customer economics. However, centralizing such knowledge means that workers' everyday decisions are either a) made without such an understanding, or b) escalated to those who have it. The first choice directly sub-optimizes economic outcomes. The second increases delays in value delivery, which has the same ultimate effect.

## Details

SAFe highlights the important role that economics play in successful Solution development. Therefore, SAFe's first Lean-Agile Principle is to *take an economic view*. It is Principle #1 for a reason: If the solution doesn't meet the Customer's or systems builder's economic goals, then the long-term viability of the solution is suspect. Solutions fail for many reasons, and failed economics is a primary one. This article describes the two primary aspects of achieving optimum economic outcomes via Lean-Agile methods; these are *deliver early and deliver often*, and *understand the economic trade-off parameters for each program and value stream*. Each is described in the sections that follow. In addition, SAFe instantiates many of these principles directly in the various practices; that is the subject of the Economic Framework article.

## Deliver Early and Often

Enterprises arrive at the larger decision to embrace Lean-Agile development either because their existing processes are not producing the results they need, or because they anticipate that those processes will not do so in the future. In choosing a Lean-Agile path, they are choosing a model that is based on incremental development, and early and continuous value delivery, as Figure 1 illustrates.

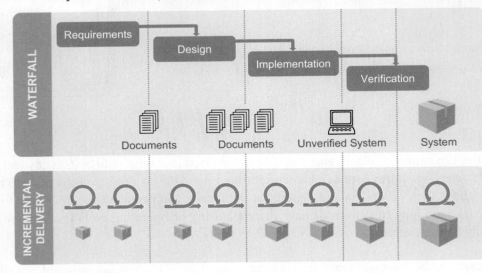

*Figure 1. Moving to early and continuous delivery*

That decision alone produces a  significant, and perhaps the primary, economic benefit, as is illustrated in Figure 2.

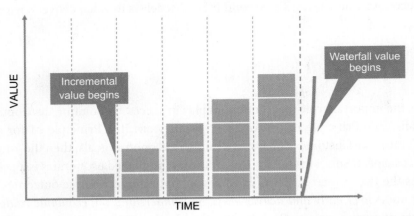

*Figure 2. Incremental development and delivery produces value far earlier*

This figure illustrates how value is delivered to the Customer much earlier in the process. Moreover, this value integrates over time—the longer the Customer has it, the more value they receive.

With the waterfall model, value can't even begin until the end of the planned development cycle. This difference is a material economic benefit of SAFe. Moreover, Figure 2 does not even account for the benefits of far faster feedback to the solution builder, as well as the lower probability that the waterfall end delivery will actually occur on time and, even then, have fitness for use. And, there is a third and final factor with the prime imperative, as is shown in Figure 3.

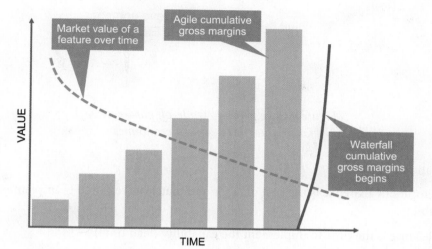

*Figure 3. Value is higher early on, producing higher margins over a longer period of time*

Figure 3 illustrates a key differentiator, so long as the quality is high enough: *Things that are delivered early to market are typically more valuable.* After all, if it's early enough, it isn't available from anyone else, and therefore it's worth a premium to the economic buyer. Over time, features become commoditized and cost, not value differentiation, rules the day. This means that even a Minimum Viable Product (MVP) can be worth more to an early buyer than a more fully featured product delivered later. The net effect is that cumulative gross margins for the solution builder are higher. This is the basic premise of Lean-Agile development, one that is firmly entrenched in the Lean-Agile Mindset, and one that drives solution builders to always strive for the shortest sustainable lead time.

## Understand Economic Trade-off Parameters

The prime imperative discussed above drives solution builders to this more effective economic model of delivering value more quickly. However, there is far more work to be done when executing a program, and the economic decisions made throughout the life of the solution will ultimately determine the outcome. Therefore it's necessary to take a deeper look at various additional economic trade-offs. Reinertsen [1] describes five primary parameters that can be used to consider the economic perspective on a particular investment, as Figure 4 on the next page illustrates.

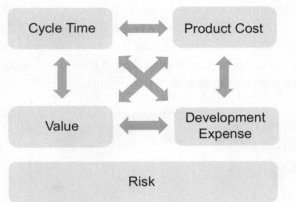

*Figure 4. Five primary trade-off parameters
for product development economics*

In this illustration:

- **Development Expense** is the cost of labor and materials required to implement a Capability

- **Cycle Time** is the time to implement the capability (lead time)

- **Product Cost** is the manufacturing (cost of goods sold), and/or deployment and operational costs

- **Value** is the economic worth of the capability to the business and Customer

- **Risk** is the uncertainty of the technical or business viability of the solution

Understanding these trade-offs helps optimize life cycle profits—the key to unlocking optimum economic value in development. But it requires a deeper project understanding. Here are two examples:

1. A team building a home automation system estimates that they can reduce the *Cost* of electronics parts by $100 by moving more functionality to software, but it would delay the release *Lead Time* by three months. Should they do so? Clearly the answer depends. It depends on the anticipated volume of the product to be sold compared to the cost of delay of not having the new release to market for three extra months. Some further analysis is required before that decision can be made.

2. A large software system with substantial technical debt has become extremely difficult to maintain. The *Development Expense* is largely fixed. Focusing on the technical debt now will clearly reduce the near-term *Value* delivery, but it will also reduce *Lead Time* for future features. Should they do it? Again, the answer depends; somewhat more quantitative thinking will need to be applied.

In addition to the trade-off parameters, Reinertsen describes a number of key principles that help teams make solid decisions based on economics. These include:

- *The Principle of Quantified Cost of Delay* – If you only quantify one thing, quantify the cost of delay

- *The Principle of Continuous Economic Trade-offs* – Economic choices must be made continuously

- *The Principle of Optimum Decision Timing* – Each decision has its optimum economic timing

- *The Sunk Cost Principle* – Do not consider money already spent

- *The First Decision Rule Principle* – Use decision rules to decentralize economic control

This last principle is particularly relevant to SAFe, and the corollary Principle #9 – *Decentralize decision-making*, and is described further in the "Economic Framework" article.

---

**LEARN MORE**

[1] Reinertsen, Donald. *The Principles of Product Development Flow: Second Generation Lean Product Development*. Celeritas Publishing, 2009.

# #2 – Apply systems thinking

*A system must be managed. It will not manage itself. Left to themselves, components become selfish, competitive, independent profit centers, and thus destroy the system. The secret is cooperation between components toward the aim of the organization.*

—W. Edwards Deming

Deming, one of the world's foremost systems thinkers, constantly focused on the larger view of problems and challenges faced by people building and deploying systems of all types—manufacturing systems, social systems, management systems, even government systems. One central conclusion was the understating that the problems faced in the workplace were driven by a series of complex interactions that occurred within the systems the workers used to do their work. Taking the larger systems view is key to unlocking the mysteries of the system, and to improving the development process and the quality of the products and services that are the aim of the system.

## The Solution Is a System

SAFe's purpose is to help systems builders achieve the shortest sustainable lead time, along with best quality and value to people and society. As such, the focus is primarily on the subject system—that big, cool, new thing. Here, the understanding that systems must be managed leads to a number of critical insights:

- Systems builders must clearly understand the boundaries of the system, what it is, and how it interacts with the environment and systems around it, as well as how its components interact to achieve the larger aim of the system in serving the needs of the Customer

- Optimizing a component does not optimize the system; instead, the system must be optimized as a whole. Systems builders must ensure that the components do not become selfish and hog the resources they need—computing power, memory, electrical power, whatever—and that other elements need as well.

- For the system to behave well as a system, intended system behavior, and some intentionality of architecture and nonfunctional system behaviors, must be understood in advance of implementation

- The value of a system passes through its interconnections; those interfaces—and the dependencies they create—are critical elements of providing ultimate value

- A system can evolve no faster than its slowest integration point; the faster the full system can be integrated and evaluated, the faster the actual knowledge of the system grows

## The Enterprise Building the System Is a System, Too

Applying systems thinking brings us to an important corollary, as well: The enterprise building the system is a system, too. The people, management, and functional and administrative departments of the enterprise constitute the system that builds the system.

The same system thinking caveats apply here as well, or else the components of the development and production system will become selfish and interfere with value delivery and economic benefit. This leads to another set of critical system thinking insights:

- Value crosses organizational boundaries. Accelerating value requires the elimination of functional silos, or the creation of virtual organizations that can be used to better deliver value.

- Building complex systems is a social endeavor. Systems builders must create an environment where people can collaborate on the best way to build the best system.

- Suppliers and Customers are integral to the value stream. They must be treated as partners, based on a long-term foundation of trust.

- Leaders must take a long-term view. Decisions made today impact future outcomes. Investing in enabling capabilities such as infrastructure, practices, tools, and training provide the foundation for future value delivery and advances in quality and productivity.

## Only Management Can Change the System

Deming arrived at other conclusions as well [1]: "Everyone is already doing their best; the problems are with the system" and "only management can change the system."

This prepares us for the final set of insights: Systems thinking requires a new approach to management as well, an approach where managers are problem-solvers, take the long systems view, and are proactive removers of impediments. These Lean-thinking manager-teachers:

- Exhibit and teach Lean, Agile, and Systems Thinking values, principles, and practices

- Eliminate functional silos and barriers to flow

- Build effective, long-term Supplier and Customer relationships

- Constantly engage in problem-solving and elimination of impediments

- Apply and teach root cause analysis and corrective action techniques

- Empower knowledge workers by unlocking their intrinsic motivation (Principle #8) and decentralizing decision-making (Principle #9)

- Partner with the teams to reflect at key milestones, and identify and address shortcomings

Understanding these systems thinking aspects helps leaders and workers truly understand why they are doing what they are doing, and the impact on those around them. In turn, this leads to a smarter enterprise, one than can better navigate the organization and solution development complexities and thereby improve economic outcomes.

---

**LEARN MORE**

[1] Deming, W. Edwards. *The New Economics*. MIT Press, 1994.

# #3 – Assume variability; preserve options

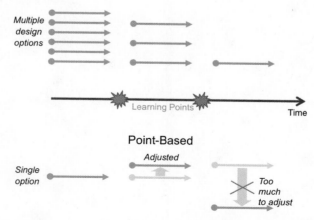

*Generate alternative system-level designs and subsystem concepts. Rather than try to pick an early winner, aggressively eliminate alternatives. The designs that survive are your most robust alternatives.*

—Allen C. Ward, Lean Product and Process Development

Systems builders tend to have a natural inclination to try to reduce variability. It just seems that the more you think you know and have already decided, the further along you are. But this is often not the case. While it is true that variability can lead to bad outcomes, the opposite case can also be true. Variability is not inherently bad or good. Rather, it is the economics associated with the timing and type of variability that determines the outcomes. A focus on eliminating variability too soon perpetuates a risk-avoidance culture wherein people can't make mistakes and gain experience by learning what works and what doesn't.

Other than a general understanding of system intent, Lean systems builders recognize that very little is actually known at the beginning of the project. If it was, they would have already built it. However, traditional design practices tend to drive developers to quickly converge on a single option—a point in the potential solution space—and then modify that design until it eventually meets the system intent. This can be an effective approach, unless of course one picks the wrong starting point; then subsequent iterations to refine that solution can be very time consuming and lead to a suboptimal design [1].

And the bigger and more technically innovative the system is, the higher the odds are that your starting point was not the optimal one. A better approach, referred to as set-based design or set-based concurrent engineering [2], is illustrated here.

In this approach, the systems builders initially cast a wide net by considering multiple design choices at the start. Thereafter, they continuously evaluate economic and technical trade-offs—typically as exhibited by objective evidence presented at integration learning points. They then eliminate the weaker options over time and finally converge on a final design, based on the knowledge that has been gained to that point.

This process leaves design options open as long as possible, converges as and when necessary, and produces more optimal technical and economic outcomes.

---

## LEARN MORE

[1] Iansiti, Marco. "Shooting the Rapids: Managing Product Development in Turbulent Environments." *California Management Review* 38 (1995): 37–58.

[2] Ward, Allan C. and Durward Sobek. *Lean Product and Process Development*. Lean Enterprise Institute Inc., 2014.

# #4 – Build incrementally with fast, integrated learning cycles

*The epiphany of integration points is that they control product development and are the leverage points to improve the system. When timing of integration points slip, the project is in trouble.*

—Dantar P. Oosterwal

## Building Systems Incrementally

In traditional, stage-gated development, investment cost begins immediately and accumulates until a solution is delivered. Often, there is little to no actual value delivered until all of the committed features are available, or the program runs out of time or money. During development, it is difficult to get any meaningful feedback because the process isn't designed for it, and the system isn't designed or implemented in such a way that incremental capabilities can be evaluated by the Customer. The risk remains in the program until the deadline, and even into deployment and initial use. This process is error prone and problematic and typically results in loss of trust between the systems builder and the Customer. In an attempt to adjust for this, Customers and systems builders try even harder to define the requirements and select "the best" design up front. They also typically implement even more rigorous stage gates. Each of these solutions actually compounds the underlying problem. This is a systems-level problem in the development process, and it must be addressed systemically.

## Integration Points Create Knowledge from Uncertainty

Lean systems builders approach the problem differently. Instead of picking a single requirement and design choice early—assuming that it is both feasible and will provide fitness for purpose—systems builders work within a range of requirements and design options (Principle #3) and build the solution incrementally in a series of short timeboxes. Each timebox results in an increment of a working system that can be evaluated by the systems builder and the Customer. Subsequent timeboxes build upon the previous increments and the solution evolves until it is released. The knowledge gained from integration points is not solely for the purpose of establishing technical viability. Many integration points can serve as minimum viable solutions or prototypes for testing the market, establishing usability, and gaining objective Customer feedback. Where necessary, these fast feedback points allow the systems builder to "pivot" to an alternate course of action, one that should better serve the needs of the intended Customers.

## Integration Points Occur by Intent

Cadence-based *integration points* become the primary focus of the systems builder, via a development process and a solution architecture that is designed in part for that specific purpose. Each integration point creates a "pull event" that *pulls* the various solution elements into an integrated whole, even though it addresses only a portion of the system intent. Integration points *pull* the stakeholders together as well, a routine synchronization that helps ensure that the evolving solution addresses the real and current business needs, as opposed to the assumptions that were established at the beginning. Each integration point delivers its own value by *converting uncertainty into knowledge* of the technical viability of the current design choice, and knowledge of the potential viability of the solution, all based on objective measures (Principle #5).

## Faster Learning Through Faster Cycles

Integration points are an instantiation of Shewhart's basic Plan-Do-Check-Adjust cycle [3] and thereby serve as the primary mechanism for controlling the variability of solution development.

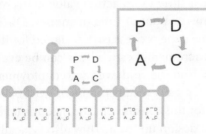

The more frequent the points, the faster the learning. In complex systems development, local integration points are used to ensure that each element or capability for the system is meeting its responsibilities in contributing to the overall solution intent. These local points must be further integrated at the next higher system level. The larger the system, the more such integration levels exist. Systems builders understand that the *top-level, least-frequent integration point* provides for the only true measure of system progress, and they endeavor throughout to achieve those points as frequently as possible. All stakeholders understand that *when timing of integration points slip, the project is in trouble.* But even then, this timely knowledge helps facilitate the necessary adjustments to scope, technical approach, cost, or delivery timing needed to get the project tracking to revised expectations.

### LEARN MORE

[1] Oosterwal, Dantar P. *The Lean Machine: How Harley-Davidson Drove Top-Line Growth and Profitability with Revolutionary Lean Product Development.* Amacom, 2010.

[2] Ward, Allan C. and Durward Sobek. *Lean Product and Process Development.* Lean Enterprise Institute Inc., 2014.

[3] Deming, W. Edwards. *Out of the Crisis.* MIT Press, 2000.

# #5 – Base milestones on objective evaluation of working systems

*There was in fact no correlation between exiting phase gates on time and project success … the data suggested the inverse might be true.*

—Dantar P. Oosterwal, *The Lean Machine*

## The Problem with Phase-Gate Milestones

The development of today's large systems requires substantial investment—an investment that can reach millions, tens of millions, and even hundreds of millions of dollars. Together, systems builders and Customers have a fiduciary responsibility to ensure that the investment in new solutions will deliver the necessary economic benefit. Otherwise, there is no reason to make the investment.

Clearly, stakeholders must collaborate in such a way as to help ensure the prospective economic benefit *throughout* the development process and not just "wishful thinking" that all will be well at the end. To address this challenge, the industry has evolved to phase-gated (waterfall) development processes, whereby progress is measured—and control is exercised—via a series of specific milestones. These milestones are not arbitrary; they follow the apparently logical and sequential process of discovery, requirements, design, implementation, test, and delivery. Of course it hasn't worked out all that well for many, as Figure1 shows.

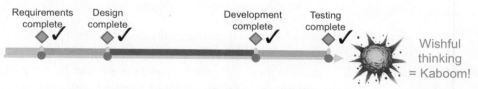

*Figure 1. The problem with phase-gate Milestones*

The root causes of this problem is the failure to recognize *four critical errors* within the basic assumption that phase gates reveal real progress and thereby mitigate risk:

1.  Centralizing requirements and design decisions in siloed functions that may not be integrally involved in the solution building

2.  Forcing too-early design decisions and "false positive feasibility" [1]: An early choice is made to the best-known option at that time; development proceeds under the assumption that everything is on track, only later to discover that the path chosen is not actually feasible (Principle #3)

3. Assuming a "point" solution exists and can be built right the first time. This ignores the variability inherent in the process, and provides no legitimate outlet for it. Variability will find a way to express itself.

4. Taking up-front decisions creates large batches of requirements, code and tests, long queues. This leads to large-batch handoffs and delayed feedback. (Principle #6)

## Base Milestones on Objective Evidence

Clearly, the phase gate model does not mitigate risk as intended, and a different approach is needed. Principle #4 – *Build incrementally with fast, integrated learning cycles* provides elements of a solution to this dilemma.

Throughout development, the system is built in increments, each of which is an integration point that demonstrates some evidence as to the viability of the current in-process solution. Unlike in the case of phase-gate development, every milestone involves a portion of each step—requirements, design, development, testing—together producing an increment of value (see Figure 2). Further, this is done routinely, on a cadence (Principle #7), which provides the discipline needed to assure periodic availability and evaluation, as well as predetermined time boundaries that can be used to collapse the field of less desirable options.

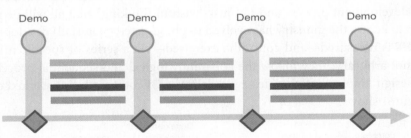

*Figure 2. Milestones based on objective evaluation of working systems*

What is actually measured at these critical integration points is subject to the nature and type of the system being built. But the system can be measured and assessed, and evaluated by the relevant stakeholders *frequently, and throughout the solution development life cycle*. This provides the financial, technical, and fitness-for-purpose governance needed to ensure that the continuing investment will produce a commensurate return.

---

**LEARN MORE**

[1] Oosterwal, Dantar P. *The Lean Machine: How Harley-Davidson Drove Top-Line Growth and Profitability with Revolutionary Lean Product Development*. Amacom, 2010.

# #6 – Visualize and limit WIP, reduce batch sizes, and manage queue lengths

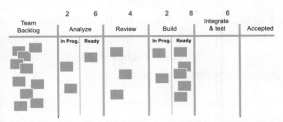

*Operating a product development process near full utilization is an economic disaster.*
  —*Donald Reinertsen*

To achieve the sustainably shortest lead time, Lean systems builders strive to achieve a state of continuous flow, whereby new system capabilities move quickly from concept to cash. Achieving continuous flow requires the elimination of the traditional start-stop-start project initiation and development process, along with the incumbent stage gates that hinder flow (Principle #5).

The three primary keys to implementing flow are to *visualize and limit work in process, reduce the batch sizes* of work items, and to *manage queue lengths*.

## Visualize and Limit WIP

Overloading teams and programs with more work than they can accomplish is a common and pernicious problem. Having too much work in process (WIP) in the system causes multiplexing and frequent context switching. It overloads the people doing the work, reduces focus on any task at hand, reduces productivity and throughput, and increases wait times for new functionality.

The first step is to make the current WIP visible to all stakeholders. This visualization illustrates the total amount of work at each step and also serves as an initial process diagnostic, showing the current bottlenecks. In some cases, simply visualizing the current work is a wake-up call that causes developers to start to address the systemic problems of too much work, and too little flow. The next step is to start balancing the amount of work in process against the available development capacity. When any step reaches its WIP limit, no new work is taken on.

However, limiting WIP requires knowledge, discipline, and commitment. It may even seem counter-intuitive to those who believe that the more work you put into the system, the more you get out. While that is true up to a point, after that point the system becomes turbulent and flow *decreases*. There is no substitute for effective management of WIP.

## Reduce Batch Size

Another way to reduce WIP and improve flow is to decrease the batch sizes of the work— those requirements, designs, code, tests, and other work items that move through the system. Simply, small batches go through the system faster, and with less variability, which fosters faster learning. The faster speed is obvious; the variability increases because of the accumulated variability of the items in the batch.

The economically optimal batch size is dependent upon both the holding cost (the cost for delaying feedback and value) and the transaction cost (the cost of implementing and testing the batch). The figure illustrates the "u-curve optimization" for batch size [1].

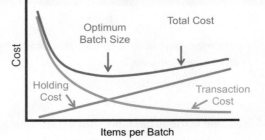

In order to improve the economics of handling smaller batches—and thereby increasing throughput— a primary focus must be placed on reducing the transaction costs associated with any batch. This typically involves increasing the attention and investment on infrastructure and automation, including things such as the continuous integration and build environment, DevOps automation, and system test setup times. This is integral to systems thinking (Principle #2), and a critical element in long-view optimization.

## Manage Queue Lengths

The last element in achieving flow is managing—and generally reducing—queue lengths. Little's Law— the seminal law of queuing theory—tells us that the wait time for service from a system is the ratio of the length of the queue divided by the average processing rate (this might seem complicated, but even the line at Starbucks teaches you that). Therefore, assuming any average processing rate, the longer the queue, the longer the wait.

For Solution development, this means that the longer the queue of work awaiting implementation by the team, the longer the wait time, *no matter how efficient* the team is in processing the work. If you need faster service, you must either reduce the length of the queue or increase the processing rate. While increasing the processing rate is a consistent and common goal, the fastest way to reduce wait times is to reduce the length of the queue. This is accomplished by keeping backlogs short and largely uncommitted. Visualizing the work helps this process immensely.

Reducing queue lengths decreases delays, reduces waste, and increases predictability of outcomes. The trifecta of *visualizing and limiting WIP*, *reducing batch size*, and *managing queues* is an extremely powerful way to increase throughput. Doing so can cause fast and measurable improvements in Customer satisfaction and employee engagement, to the overall economic benefit of systems builders and their Customers.

---

**LEARN MORE**

[1] Reinertsen, Donald G. *The Principles of Product Development Flow: Second Generation Lean Product Development*. Celeritas, 2009.

---

# #7 – Apply cadence, synchronize with cross-domain planning

*Cadence and synchronization limit the accumulation of variance.*
  —Donald Reinertsen, *Principles of Product Development Flow*

Solution development is an inherently uncertain process. If it weren't, then the solutions would already exist and there would be no room for the next generation of innovations. This inherent uncertainty conflicts with the business need to manage investment, track progress, and have sufficient certainty of future outcomes to be able to plan and commit to a reasonable course of action. Solution development lives at the intersection; it is its own conundrum—the conflict of uncertainty of outcomes and the needed certainty of the business. Perhaps that is why it's so fun.

The Lean systems builder operates in the safety zone where sufficient uncertainty provides the freedom for innovation, while sufficient certainty allows the business to operate. The primary means to achieve this is to maintain *true knowledge of the current state*. *Cadence, synchronization* and, *cross-domain planning* help provide this.

## Cadence

Cadence provides a rhythmic pattern, the dependable heartbeat of the process. Cadence *makes routine that which can be routine*, so the intellectual capacity of the systems builders can be devoted to managing the variable parameters. Cadence transforms unpredictable events into predictable ones, and has many additional benefits:

- Makes waiting times predictable; if the work you are waiting on isn't in this timebox, it can likely be in the next

- Facilitates planning and provides for more efficient use of resources

- Provides a forcing function and lowers the transaction costs of key events, including planning, integration, demonstrations, feedback, and retrospectives

## Synchronization

Synchronization causes multiple perspectives to be understood, resolved, and integrated at the same time.

Synchronization is used to:

- Pull the disparate assets of a system together to assess solution-level viability
- Align the development teams and business to a common mission
- Integrate the Customers into the development process

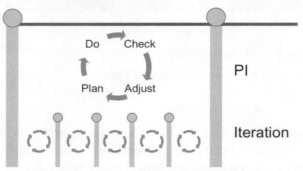

*SAFe cadence and synchronization harmonics*

Taken together, cadence and synchronization—and, most importantly, the associated activities—help the systems builder operate reliably within the uncertainty safety zone.

## Synchronize with Cross-Domain Planning

Of all the events that occur, one is the most critical: periodically, all stakeholders gather for cross-domain planning and synchronization. This event (the *Release (PI) Planning event* in SAFe) serves as the fulcrum around which all other events operate. It also serves as the plenary exhibition of *true knowledge of the current state*. The event serves three primary purposes:

1. **Assessment of the current state of the solution** – Objective knowledge of the current state is determined by an integrated, solution-level demonstration and assessment, which typically occurs immediately prior to the planning event

2. **Realign all stakeholders to a common technical and business vision** – Based on the current state, business and technology leaders reset the mission, with minimum possible constraints (Principles #8, 9). This aligns all stakeholders to a common vision, both near- and longer-term.

3. **Plan and commit to the next program increment** – Based on new knowledge, the teams plan for what can be accomplished in the upcoming timebox. The distribution of planning and control empowers teams to create *the best possible plans to achieve the best possible solution* within the given constraints.

The development of large-scale systems is fundamentally a social activity, and this planning event provides a continuous opportunity to build and improve the social network.

There is no cure for the inherent uncertainty of solution development. If there were, it would surely be worse than the disease. However, applying *cadence and synchronization*, and *periodic cross-domain planning*, provides Lean systems builders with the tools they need to operate in the safety zone.

## LEARN MORE

[1] Reinertsen, Donald. *The Principles of Product Development Flow: Second Generation Lean Product Development*. Celeritas Publishing, 2009.

[2] Kennedy, Michael. *Product Development for the Lean Enterprise*. Oaklea Press, 2003.

# #8 – Unlock the intrinsic motivation of knowledge workers

*It appears that the performance of the task provides its own intrinsic reward . . . this drive . . . may be as basic as the others . . .*

—Daniel Pink, *Drive*

Lean-Agile Leaders operate within a relatively new, fundamental truth—the "management" of knowledge workers is an oxymoron. As Drucker [2] points out, "knowledge workers are individuals who know more about the work that they perform than their bosses." In that context, how can any manager seriously attempt to manage, or even coordinate, the technical activities of those who are infinitely more capable of defining the activities necessary to accomplish their mission than they are?

Indeed they *cannot*. Instead, what they can do is to *unlock the intrinsic motivation of knowledge workers*. Some guidelines are provided in the paragraphs below.

## Leverage the Systems View

Before delving further into additional motivational constructs, we note that a significant understanding emerges. This is the understanding that the Lean-Agile principles of SAFe are themselves a system too. And the elements of this system collaborate to create a new and empowering paradigm. One wherein the knowledge worker is able to communicate across functional boundaries; make decisions based upon an understanding of the economics; achieve fast feedback as to the efficacy of their solution; participate in continuous, incremental learning and mastery; and more generally participate in a more productive and fulfilling solution development process. That is one of the most powerful motivations of all.

## Understand the Role of Compensation

*Many organizations still operate from assumptions about human potential and individual performance that are outdated … rooted more in folklore than in science. They continue to pursue practices such as short-term incentive plans and pay-for-performance schemes in the face of mounting evidence that such measures usually don't work and often do harm. [1]*

Pink [1], Drucker [2], and others have pointed out the fundamental paradox with respect to the motivational factor of compensation for knowledge workers:

- If you don't pay enough, people won't be motivated. Under-compensation is a major de-motivator.

- But after a point, money is no longer a motivator. That is the point of intellectual freedom and self-actualization. Here, the knowledge worker's mind is free to focus on the work, and not the money.

- After this point, adding incentive compensation elements is again, a *de-motivator*. It can serve as an insult to the intellectual integrity, or cause the worker to focus on the money, rather than the work.

Lean-Agile Leaders understand that ideation, innovation, and deep workplace engagement of knowledge workers can't be motivated by money—nor the reverse: threats, intimidation, or fear. Such incentive-based compensation, as often embodied by individual MBOs (management by objectives), causes internal competition and the potential destruction of the cooperation necessary to achieve the larger aim. The Enterprise is the loser in that competition.

## Provide Autonomy with Purpose, Mission, and Minimum Possible Constraints

*Drive* [1] also "drives" home the fact that knowledge workers have a need for *autonomy*—the ability to self-direct and to manage their own lives. Providing for autonomy, while harnessing it to the larger aim of the enterprise, is an important leadership responsibility.

Managers and workers also know that the motivation of self-direction must be within the context of the larger objective. To this end, leaders must provide some larger *purpose*—some connection between the aim of the enterprise and the workers' daily work activities.

When building systems, knowledge workers participate as part of a team. Being part of a high-performing team is yet another critical motivational dimension. Leaders can inspire teams to do their best by providing [4]:

- The mission: a general goal and strategic direction—a strong vision

- Little, minimal, or even no specific work or project plans

- Challenging requirements, along with the minimum possible constraints as to how teams meet these requirements

## Create an Environment of Mutual Influence

"To effectively lead, the workers must be heard and respected" [2] in the context of an environment of mutual influence [4]. Leaders create such an environment by giving tough feedback supportively, by a willingness to become more vulnerable, and by encouraging others to:

- Disagree where appropriate

- Advocate for the positions they believe in

- Make their needs clear and push to achieve them

- Enter into joint problem solving with management and peers
- Negotiate, compromise, agree, and commit

Contemporary systems builders live in a new age, an age where the workers are smarter and have more local context than management can ever have. Unlocking this raw potential is a significant factor in improving the lives of those doing the work, as well as providing for better outcomes for Customers and the enterprise as a whole.

## LEARN MORE

[1] Pink, Daniel. *Drive: The Surprising Truth About What Motivates Us.* Riverhead Books, 2011.

[2] Drucker, Peter F. *The Essential Drucker*. Harper-Collins, 2001.

[3] Bradford, David L. and Allen Cohen. *Managing for Excellence: The Leadership Guide to Developing High Performance in Contemporary Organizations*. John Wiley and Sons, 1997.

[4] Takeuchi, Hirotaka and Ikujiro Nonaka. "The New, New Product Development Game." *Harvard Business Review*. January 1986.

# #9 – Decentralize decision-making

*Knowledge workers themselves are best placed to make decisions about how to perform their work.*

—Peter F. Drucker

As we noted in the House of Lean, the goal is simple: *to deliver value in the sustainably shortest lead time.* Achieving this goal requires fast, decentralized decision-making. Any decision that must be escalated to higher levels of authority introduces a delay and can decrease the fidelity of the decision, due to the lack of local context, plus changes in fact patterns that occur during the wait time. Decentralized decision-making reduces delays, improves product development flow, and enables faster feedback and more innovative solutions.

However, this is not to say that all decisions are decentralized. Some decisions are strategic, critical, and far reaching enough to be centralized; these should be made by management. Since both types of decisions occur, the creation of an established and known *decision-making framework* is a critical step in ensuring the flow of value to the Customer.

## Centralize Strategic Decisions

Empowering knowledge workers to make decisions does not eliminate management's responsibility for strategy or ultimate outcomes. Managers are in their position for a reason; they have the deep market knowledge, longer-range technical perspectives, fiduciary responsibilities, and understanding of the financial landscape necessary to steer the enterprise to the right business outcomes. Managers are, and should be, empowered to make these high-level decisions.

These *centralized* decisions are those that are *infrequent, long lasting, and have significant economies of scale.*

## Decentralize Everything Else

The vast majority of decisions however, do not reach this threshold of strategic importance. These decisions *happen frequently, are often time-critical, and do not have significant economies of scale.*

These decisions should be *decentralized* to those who have better local context, detailed knowledge of the technical complexities, and who spend their time on the front lines of delivering value every day.

## Establish a Decision-Making Framework

Empowering others to make decisions does not abrogate leadership's responsibility for good decisions. To that end, the enterprise should establish a decision-making framework within which decisions at the various levels can be made. Based in part on the economic framework (Principle #1), the decision-making framework establishes the logic and economic reasoning behind a decision and empowers the various roles that individuals and teams have in making and implementing the decisions.

An effective decision-making framework provides many benefits to the enterprise. These include faster time to market and higher-quality products and services. It also *helps unlock the intrinsic motivation of knowledge workers* (Principle #8), thereby bringing higher levels of employee engagement and personal job satisfaction. A significant improvement in both the enterprise's performance and culture is a likely result.

---

**LEARN MORE**

[1] Drucker, Peter F. *The Essential Drucker*. Harper Collins, 2001.

[2] Reinertsen, Donald G. *The Principles of Product Development Flow: Second Generation Lean Product Development*. Celeritas Publishing, 2009.

# Part 3
# The Team Level

[ scaledagileframework.com/**team-level**

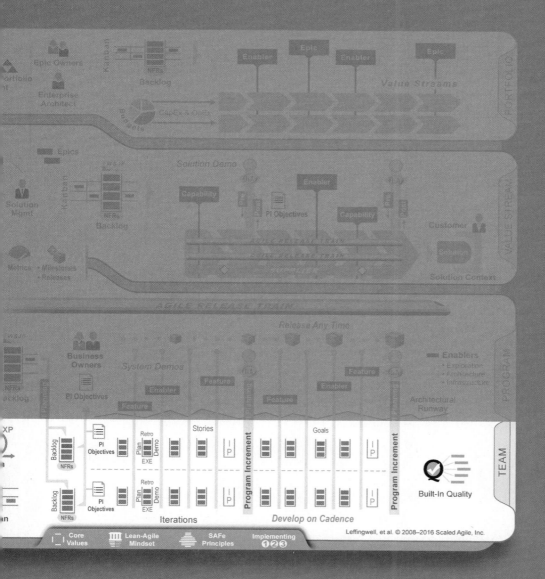

Leffingwell, et al. © 2008–2016 Scaled Agile, Inc.

# Introduction to the Team Level

*We, the work, and the knowledge are all one.*
   —Authors

## Abstract

While depicted somewhat separately, the SAFe *Team Level* is part of the Program Level. All SAFe teams are part of one Agile Release Train (ART)—the central construct of the program level. The team level provides an organization, artifact, role, and process model for the activities of Agile Teams. Each Agile Team is responsible for defining, building, and testing stories from their Team Backlog in a series of fixed-length Iterations, using common iteration cadence and synchronization to align with other teams, so that the entire system is iterating. Teams use ScrumXP or Team Kanban to routinely deliver high-quality systems and produce a System Demo every two weeks. This ensures that all the different teams on the ART create an integrated and tested system that stakeholders can evaluate and respond to with fast feedback. The system demo creates a routine "pull event," which pulls the effort of the different teams to a specific point, bringing forward the hard work of integration and testing that phase-gated models often leave until too late in the life cycle.

## Details

The *Team Level* describes how Agile Teams power the Agile Release Train (ART). They apply SAFe ScrumXP or Team Kanban, along with the Built-in Quality practices that help ensure a quality end product. Each team has five to nine team members (ScrumXP) and includes all the roles necessary to build a quality increment of value in each Iteration. ScrumXP roles include the Scrum Master, Product Owner, dedicated individual contributors, and any specialty resources the team needs to deliver value. Team Kanban roles are less rigorously defined, though many SAFe Kanban teams implement the ScrumXP roles as well. Each team is supported by the program personnel, including the Release Train Engineer, Product Management, System Architects/Engineering, System Team, Shared Services, DevOps, and anyone else required. Thereby, the team is fully capable of defining, developing, testing, and delivering working and tested systems every iteration (at least).

### Program Increments and Iterations

Teams share common iteration start/stop dates and durations—both the iteration boundary and the Program Increment (PI) boundary—so as to synchronize and integrate with other teams on the ART.

Each PI begins with the teams participating in PI Planning, where they build Team PI Objectives—which are aggregated to Program PI Objectives—that help guide the teams during the iterations.

Teams plan and execute two-week timeboxed iterations in accordance with agreed-to Iteration Goals. Each iteration provides a valuable increment of new functionality, accomplished via a constantly repeating pattern: *Plan* the iteration, *commit* to some functionality, execute the iteration by *building* and *testing* Stories, *demo* the new functionality, hold a *retrospective*, and *repeat for the next iteration*. At the end of each iteration, teams also support the System Demo, which is the critical integration point for the ART. In larger Value Streams with multiple ARTs, teams also support the Solution Demo, where the entire Solution from multiple ARTs comes together to be integrated and tested in its entirety.

The Innovation and Planning (IP) Iterations provide the teams with an opportunity for exploration and innovation, dedicated time for planning, retrospecting, and learning through informal and formal channels. And in the case where the Release is at the PI boundary, teams perform final system verification, validation, and documentation. In order to provide a buffer, teams don't plan stories for the IP iteration, so each PI is planned at less than 100% utilization. This increases flow, throughput, and delivery reliability.

The PI timebox is used to aggregate larger, system-wide functionality into valuable and evaluable program increments. The functionality can be released at the PI boundary, or that can happen more frequently. Programs should Develop on Cadence and Release Any Time.

## Number of Iterations per PI

SAFe divides the development timeline into a set of iterations within a PI. The Big Picture illustrates how a PI is initiated by a PI planning session and is then followed by four execution iterations, concluding with one innovation and planning iteration. *This pattern is suggestive but arbitrary, and there is no fixed rule for how many iterations are in a PI.* Experience has shown that a PI duration of between 8 and 12 weeks works best, with a bias toward the shortest duration.

## Stories and the Team Backlog

The teams use stories to deliver value, and the Product Owner has content authority over their creation and acceptance. Stories carry the Customer's requirements through the value stream into implementation. The Team Backlog consists of user and Enabler stories, most of which are identified during PI planning, when Product Management presents the Vision, Roadmap, and Program Backlog. Identifying, prioritizing, scheduling, elaborating, implementing, testing, and accepting stories are the primary requirements-management processes at work on the team level.

**LEARN MORE**

[1] Leffingwell, Dean. *Agile Software Requirements: Lean Requirements Practices for Teams, Programs, and the Enterprise.* Addison-Wesley, 2011.

# Agile Teams

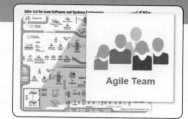

*Nothing beats an Agile Team.*
  —*SAFe mantra*

## Abstract

The Agile movement, as captured in part by the Agile Manifesto (2001), represented a major turning point in the way software and systems development are performed. SAFe builds on this change by empowering *Agile Teams* as the building blocks for creating and delivering value.

Without effective Agile Teams, composed of empowered and motivated individuals, organizations cannot scale Agile to achieve the larger business benefits of Enterprise Lean-Agile development. The primary responsibility of Lean-Agile Leaders becomes to create and mentor these Agile Teams.

The SAFe Agile Team is a cross-functional group of individuals who have the ability and authority to *define*, *build*, and *test* Solution value—all in a short Iteration timebox. The team includes the individuals necessary to successfully deliver this value, supported by Program Level or Value Stream Level specialists where applicable. This follows the SAFe Principle #9 – *Decentralized decision-making* by bringing the authority for local requirements and designs to the teams responsible for doing the actual work.

In SAFe, Agile Teams are not stand-alone units. Instead, they are an integral part of the Agile Release Train (ART), where they collectively have responsibility for delivering larger value. All teams are on a train; no train exists without its teams. Teams operate in the context of the train, adhering to its Vision, collaborating with other teams, and participating in key ART ceremonies. The teams and the train are inseparable; the whole is greater than the sum of its parts.

## Details

An *Agile Team* consists of a small group of dedicated individuals (5 – 9 in Scrum), who together have the skills necessary to *define* (elaborate and design their component/Feature), *build* (implement their component/feature), and *test* (run the test cases and validate the component/feature) increments of value in a short timebox.

Within the context of the Agile Release Train (ART), teams are empowered, self-organizing, and self-managing and are accountable for delivery of results that meet the Customer's needs and expectations. These teams develop software, hardware, firmware, or some combination, but most generally the team represents a collaboration of the disciplines necessary to deliver features.

By moving work to the teams and trains, instead of bringing people to the work, Enterprises help create teams, and teams of teams, that are long lived and dedicated to relentlessly improving their ability to deliver Solutions. In this way, SAFe is different from the traditional approach in which managers direct individuals to activities. SAFe teams—not their managers—determine what and how to build their features and components. Lean-Agile Leaders provide the Vision, leadership, and autonomy necessary to foster and promote high-performing teams. Tasking individual team members with work items is no longer required. This brings the chain of decentralized decision-making all the way to the level of the individual contributor.

## Roles and Responsibilities

SAFe facilitates withdrawal from the functional, silo-based, and stage-gated development model, in which user value is delivered at the end of a long life cycle with input from separate functional departments. Agile Teams perform or participate in all of these functions and do so in a way that delivers value in every Iteration:

- The *team* is responsible for managing their work
- The *team* estimates the size and complexity of the work
- The *team* determines the technical design in their area of concern, within the architectural guidelines
- The *team* commits to the work they can accomplish in an iteration or Program Increment (PI) timebox
- The *team* is responsible for value and builds to continuously improve the quality of their deliverables
- The *team* is continuously committed to finding ways to improve

## Intense Collaboration

Teams can meet their responsibilities only via constant communication and collaboration and fast, effective, and empowered decision-making. If at all possible, teams are collocated to facilitate hourly, daily, and weekly communication. Standard team meetings depend on the framework of choice but may include a daily stand-up, Iteration Planning and Team Demo, and a retrospective at the end of each iteration. Each team member is fully dedicated to a single team and works intensely during a responsible workweek. Team members continuously and actively engage with other teams to manage dependencies and resolve impediments.

Relationships within the team are fundamentally based on trust, and trust is facilitated by a common mission, common Iteration Goals, and team PI Objectives. Collaboration is continuously improved using regular feedback loops that are built into the learning cycle of the teams. Each tangible delivery of value encourages trust, reduces uncertainty and risk, and builds confidence. Agile Teams are motivated by a shared vision and their commitment to deliver value to the Customer.

## Teams Have a Choice of Agile Methods

SAFe teams use Agile practices of choice, based primarily on Scrum and Team Kanban. Most SAFe teams apply Scrum as the basic project management and delivery framework. The Scrum Product Owner participates in and supports decentralized decision-making, which is critical to team empowerment. The Scrum Master facilitates the team toward their delivery objectives and helps build a high-performing and self-managing team.

But Scrum is not exclusive. Teams apply User Experience (UX)-inspired engineering and Built-in Quality practices to drive disciplined development and quality. These practices—including collective ownership, pair work, coding standards, Test-First, and Continuous Integration—help keep things Lean by embedding quality and operating efficiency directly in the development process. Agile Architecture helps complete the picture for quality solution development.

However, as SAFe is a flow-based system, most teams also apply Kanban to visualize their work, establish WIP limits, and use Cumulative Flow Diagrams to illustrate bottlenecks and key opportunities for improving throughput. Some teams—especially maintenance teams, DevOps, and System Teams—often apply Kanban as their base practice, as the planning and commitment elements of Scrum may not apply as efficiently for workloads that are activity and demand-based, and where priorities change more frequently.

## Agile Teams Are on the Train

SAFe Agile Teams do not operate independently; they power the ART and collaborate on building ever more valuable increments of working solutions. Whether the teams apply Scrum, Kanban, or a blend of both, all teams operate within a common framework that governs and guides the train. They *plan together, integrate and demo together*, and *learn together*, as is illustrated in Figure 1.

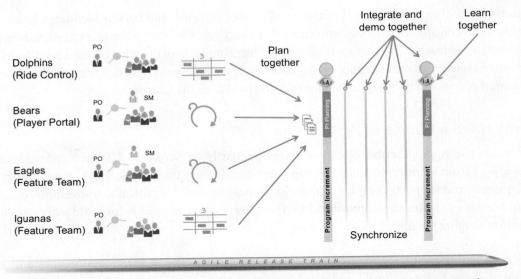

*Figure 1. Agile Teams plan together, integrate and demo together, and learn together*

## Plan Together

All teams—and wherever possible, all team members—attend PI Planning, where they plan and commit to a set of PI objectives together. They work with a common vision and Roadmap, and they collaborate on ways to achieve the objectives. Clear content authority roles facilitate the planning and execution process. The Product Owner is part of a larger Product Management content authority team (Kanban teams sometimes have a different name for this role). The team's individual Team Backlogs are driven in large part by the Program Backlog.

In addition, as part of the ART, and in accordance with the Economic Framework, all Agile Teams participate in a common approach to estimating work. This provides a meaningful way to help decision authorities guide the course of action based on economics. The means to accomplish this vary based on the method chosen, but the result is the same, as is further described in the "Scrum" and "Team Kanban" articles.

## Integrate and Demo Together

Delivering complex systems of high quality requires intense inter-team cooperation and collaboration. In support of this, teams work on a common ART cadence and publish and communicate iteration goals at the beginning of each iteration. They also update other teams during the ART sync and actively manage dependencies by interacting with team members from other teams.

Of course the goal is not to simply have the teams "sprint" toward the goal; rather, the objective is to have the system "sprinting" forward in quality, evaluable increments. In support of this, teams apply built-in quality and engage in continuous integration throughout the iteration—both inside the team and across the train—while working together toward an aggregate System Demo that occurs at the end of each iteration.

**Learn Together**

All SAFe teammates engage in *relentless improvement* (see Pillar 4 in the "Lean-Agile Mindset" article). In addition to Team Level retrospectives and ad hoc process enhancements, teams participate in the larger Inspect and Adapt meetings, where they identify and prioritize improvement Stories that are incorporated into the following PI planning sessions. In this way, the "loop is closed" as the teams and the ART progress forward one iteration, and one PI, at a time. And, of course, learning is not relegated exclusively to retrospectives; learning happens continuously in the context of Communities of Practice that have been formed to help individuals and teams advance their functional and cross-functional skills.

---

## LEARN MORE

[1] Leffingwell, Dean. *Scaling Software Agility: Best Practices for Large Enterprises*. Addison-Wesley, 2007.

[2] Lencioni, Patrick. *The Five Dysfunctions of a Team: A Leadership Fable*. Jossey-Bass, 2002.

[3] Cohn, Mike. *Succeeding with Agile: Software Development Using Scrum*. Addison-Wesley, 2009.

[4] Manifesto for Agile Software Development. http://agilemanifesto.org/.

# Product Owner

*Business people and developers must work together daily throughout the project.*

—Agile Manifesto

## Abstract

The *Product Owner* (PO) is the member of the team responsible for defining Stories and prioritizing the Team Backlog so as to streamline the execution of program priorities, while maintaining conceptual and technical integrity of the Features or components the team is responsible for. The PO has a significant role in quality and is the only team member empowered to accept stories as done. For most Enterprises converting to Agile, this is a new and *critical* role, which typically translates into a full-time job, requiring one PO to support each Agile Team (or, at most, two teams).

The role has significant relationships and responsibilities outside the local team, including working with Product Management (who are responsible for the Program Backlog) to prepare for the PI Planning meeting.

## Details

The *Product Owner* (PO) is the member of the Agile Team who serves as the Customer proxy and is responsible for working with Product Management and other stakeholders—including other Product Owners—to define and prioritize Stories in the Team Backlog so that the Solution effectively addresses program priorities (Features/Enablers) while maintaining technical integrity. Ideally, the Product Owner is collocated with the rest of the team, where they typically share management, incentives, and culture. But the Product Owner also attends most relevant Product Management meetings about planning and backlog/Vision refinement.

### Responsibilities

The SAFe Product Owner fulfills the primary responsibilities outlined in the following.

### Preparation and Participation in PI Planning

- As a member of the extended Product Management team, the Product Owner is heavily involved in Program Backlog refinement and preparation for PI Planning and also has a significant role in the planning event itself. Prior to the event, the Product Owner updates the team backlog and typically participates in reviewing and contributing to the vision, Roadmap, and content presentations.

- During the event, the Product Owner is involved with story definition, providing clarifications necessary to assist the team with their story estimates and story sequencing, and drafting the team's specific objectives for the upcoming Program Increment (PI).

### Iteration Execution

- **Backlog Refinement** – With input from System Architect/Engineering and other stakeholders, the Product Owner has the primary responsibility for building, pruning, and maintaining the team backlog. The backlog consists mostly of user stories but also includes defects and enablers. Backlog items are prioritized based on user value, time, and other team dependencies that are determined in the PI planning meeting and refined during the PI.

- **Iteration Planning** – The Product Owner reviews and re-prioritizes the backlog as part of the preparatory work for Iteration planning (see "Plan the Iteration" in the "ScrumXP" article), including coordination of content dependencies with other Product Owners. During the iteration planning meeting, the Product Owner is the main source for story detail and priorities and has the responsibility of accepting the final iteration plan.

- **Just-in-Time Story Elaboration** – Most backlog items are elaborated into user stories for implementation. This may happen *prior* to the iteration, *during iteration planning*, or *during the iteration itself*. While any team member can write stories and acceptance criteria, the Product Owner has the primary responsibility for keeping the process flowing. It is usually good to have approximately two iterations' worth of ready stories in the team backlog at all times. More would create a queue, while less might inhibit flow.

- **Supporting ATDD** – POs participate in development of story acceptance criteria, draft them when feasible, and provide examples in support of ATDD (Acceptance Test-Driven Development) specification by example. See the "Test-First" article.

- **Accepting Stories** – The PO is the only team member who can accept stories as done. This includes validation that the story meets acceptance criteria and has the appropriate, persistent acceptance tests, and that it otherwise meets its Definition of Done. In so doing, the PO also fulfills a quality assurance function, focusing primarily on fitness for use.

- **Understand Enabler Work** – While Product Owners are not expected to drive technological decisions, they are expected to understand the scope of the upcoming enabler work and to work with System and Solution Architect/Engineering to assist with decision-making and sequencing of the key technological infrastructures that will host the new business functionality. This can often best be accomplished by establishing a capacity allocation, as described in the "Program and Value Stream Backlog" article.

- **Participate in Team Demo and Retrospective** – As an integral member of the team and the one responsible for requirements, the PO has an important role in the Team Demo, reviewing and accepting stories; and in the Iteration Retrospective (see "Retrospect and Improve" in the "ScrumXP" article), where the teams gather to improve their processes. POs are also active participants in the ART's Inspect and Adapt workshop.

## Program Execution

- Iterations and teams both serve a larger purpose: frequent, reliable, and continuous release of value-added solutions. During the course of each PI, the Product Owner coordinates content dependencies with other Product Owners. This is often accomplished in part by attendance at weekly PO sync meetings. See the "Program Increment" article for more information.

- The Product Owner also has an instrumental role in producing the System Demo for program and Value Stream stakeholders.

## Inspect and Adapt

- Teams address their larger impediments in the PI inspect and adapt workshop. There, the Product Owner works across teams to define and implement improvement stories that will increase the velocity and quality of the program.

- The PI system demo occurs as part of the inspect and adapt workshop. The Product Owner has an instrumental role in producing the PI system demo for program stakeholders.

- POs also participate in the preparation of the PI system demo to make sure that they will be able to show the most critical aspects of the solution to the stakeholders.

## Content Authority

At scale, a single person cannot handle product and market strategy while also being dedicated to an Agile Team. Since Product Management and the Product Owner share the "content authority" for the program, it is important to have a clear delineation of roles and responsibilities, as is illustrated in Figure 1.

| Product Manager | Product Owner | Team |
|---|---|---|
| • Market/Customer facing. Identifies market needs. Collocated with marketing/business. | • Solution, technology, and team facing. Collocated with team(s). | • Customer/stakeholder facing. |
| • Owns vision and roadmaps, program backlog, pricing, licensing, ROI. | • Contributes to vision and program backlog. Owns team backlog and implementation. | • Owns story estimates and implementation of value. |
| • Drives PI objectives and release content via prioritized features and enablers. | • Defines iterations and stories. Accepts iteration increments. | • Contributes to intentional architecture. Owns emergent design. |
| • Establishes feature acceptance criteria. | • Drives iteration goals and iteration content via prioritized stories. | • Contributes to backlog refinement and creation of stories. |
| | • Establishes story acceptance criteria, accepts stories into the baseline. | • Integrates with other teams. |

*Figure 1. Release content governance*

## Fan-out Model of Product Manager, Product Owner, and Agile Teams

Successful development is, in part, a game of numbers in the Enterprise. Without the right number of people in the right roles, bottlenecks will severely limit velocity. Therefore, the number of Product Managers, Product Owners, and Agile Teams must be roughly in balance in order to properly steer the Agile Release Train (ART), or the whole system will spend much of its time *waiting* for definition, clarification, and acceptance. The Framework recommends a fan-out, as illustrated in Figure 2.

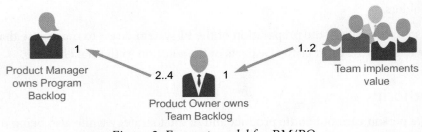

*Figure 2. Fan-out model for PM/PO*

Each Product Manager can usually support up to four Product Owners, each of whom can be responsible for the backlog for one or two Agile Teams.

## LEARN MORE

[1] Leffingwell, Dean. *Agile Software Requirements: Lean Requirements Practices for Teams, Programs, and the Enterprise.* Addison-Wesley, 2011, chapter 11.

[2] Larman, Craig, and Bas Vodde. *Practices for Scaling Lean & Agile Development: Large, Multisite, and Offshore Product Development with Large-Scale Scrum.* Addison-Wesley, 2010, chapter 3.

# Scrum Master

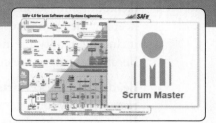

*Good leaders must first become good servants.*
  —*Robert K. Greenleaf*

## Abstract

Most SAFe teams apply ScrumXP, a lightweight team framework for effective Agile project management and product delivery flow. The *Scrum Master* role is assumed by a team member who has a primary responsibility to help the self-organizing, self-managing team achieve its goals. Scrum Masters do this by teaching and coaching and SAFe, implementing and supporting SAFe Principles and practices, identifying and eliminating impediments and facilitating flow.

SAFe teams can tune their process from a continuum of methods, picking the best practices from Scrum, Kanban, XP, and more. While this role is based largely on standard Scrum, most teams—even those teams that are primarily transaction or flow based (applying Kanban primarily)—effectively apply the Scrum Master role to help the team meet its goals and coordinate activities with other teams.

## Details

The *Scrum Master* role is a special role for an Agile Team member who spends much of her time helping other team members communicate, coordinate, and cooperate; generally, this person assists the team in meeting their delivery goals. The Scrum Master is a team-based management proxy and servant leader who helps teams self-organize, self-manage, and deliver via effective Agile practices. The Scrum Master supports and enforces the rules of the Scrum process and other rules that the team has agreed upon. The Scrum Master also helps the team coordinate with other teams on the Agile Release Train and communicates status to management as needed.

### Responsibilities on the Team

The effective SAFe Scrum Master is a team-based servant leader who:

- **Exhibits Lean-Agile leadership** – Exhibits the behaviors of a Lean-Agile Leader with a Lean-Agile mindset. Helps the team embrace SAFe Core Values, adopt and apply SAFe Principles, and implement SAFe practices.

- **Supports the rules** – The rules of Scrum are lightweight, but they are rules nonetheless, and the Scrum Master is responsible for reinforcing them. These include the rules of Scrum, WIP limits, and any other process rules the team has agreed to.

- **Facilitates the team's progress toward the goal** – The Scrum Master is trained as a team facilitator and is constantly engaged in challenging the old norms of development, while keeping the team focused on the goals of the Iteration. Helps the team achieve in areas including quality, predictability, flow, and velocity. Helps the team focus on daily and Iteration Goals in the context of current PI Objectives.

- **Leads the team's efforts in relentless improvement** – Helps the team improve and take responsibility for their actions. Facilitates the team retrospective. Teaches problem-solving and helps the team become better problem-solvers for themselves.

- **Facilitates meetings** – Facilitates all team meetings, including the daily stand-up, Iteration Planning, Team Demo, and Iteration Retrospective.

- **Supports the Product Owner** – The Product Owner has a special responsibility on the team. The Scrum Master supports the Product Owner in his efforts and facilitates a healthy intra-team dynamic with respect to priorities and scope.

- **Eliminates impediments** – Many blocking issues will be beyond the team's authority or will require support from other teams. The Scrum Master actively addresses these issues so that the team can remain focused on achieving the objectives of the iteration.

- **Promotes SAFe quality practices** – SAFe provides guidance to assist the teams in constantly improving the quality of their deliverables and meeting the Definition of Done; the Scrum Master helps foster the culture of technical discipline and craftsmanship that is the hallmark of effective Agile Teams. Fosters and supports relevant Communities of Practice.

- **Builds a high-performing team** – Focuses on ever-improving team dynamics and performance. Helps the team manage intrapersonal conflicts, challenges, and opportunities for growth. Escalates people problems to management where necessary, but only after internal processes have failed to achieve the objective. Helps individuals and teams through personnel changes.

- **Protects and communicates** – Communicates with management and outside stakeholders. Helps protect the team from uncontrolled injection of work.

## Responsibilities on the Train

The Scrum Master helps coordinate inter-team cooperation and helps the team operate as an effective "team on the train."

- **Coordinates with other teams** – The Scrum Master is typically the representative in the Scrum of Scrums meeting, and he passes information from that meeting back to the team. (See the "Program Increment" article for more details.) Often coordinates with the System Team, User Experience, DevOps, Shared Services, and Release Management. It is important to note, however, that the responsibility for inter-team coordination cannot be delegated entirely to the Scrum Master; every team member shares responsibility in that regard.

- **Facilitates preparation and readiness for ART ceremonies** – Assists the team in preparation for ART activities, including PI Planning, System Demos, and the Inspect and Adapt workshop.

- **Supports estimating** – Guides the team in establishing normalized estimating and helps the team and the ART estimate larger Features and Capabilities.

## Sourcing the Role

The Scrum Master can be a part-time or full-time role, depending on the size of the team, the context, and other responsibilities. However, at Enterprise scale, it can be a challenge to "sell" the need for a full-time Scrum Master for each Agile Team. After all, if the enterprise is organizing 100 new Agile Teams, it probably isn't economically or politically practical to take 100 full-time development team members and assign them to these new duties that don't include development or testing. Nor is it economically viable to hire a full- or half-time consultant for each team to help them learn and master the new methods. That could kill the transformation before it even gets started, and before the teams have had a chance to prove the value of the role.

Therefore SAFe takes a pragmatic approach and assumes, in general, that the Scrum Master is a part-time role assumed by an Agile Team member, project manager, team leader, or other individual. During initial SAFe adoption, however, the role may be more intensive; at this stage the organization may find it beneficial to bring external consultants on board to coach the teams while they become experienced in Scrum and SAFe. These outside consultant Scrum Master-coaches will often coach multiple teams in the organization.

---

**LEARN MORE**

[1] www.scrumalliance.org.

[2] Leffingwell, Dean. *Agile Software Requirements: Lean Requirements Practices for Teams, Programs, and the Enterprise.* Addison-Wesley, 2011.

# ScrumXP

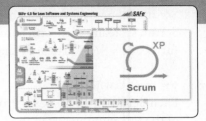

*. . . a holistic or "rugby" approach—where a team tries to go the distance as a unit, passing the ball back and forth—may better serve today's competitive requirements.*

—Nonaka and Takeuchi, *The New, New Product Development Game*

## Abstract

Most SAFe teams use Scrum as their primary, team-based project management framework. Scrum is a lightweight yet disciplined and productive process for cross-functional, self-organized teams to operate within the context of SAFe. Scrum prescribes three roles: Scrum Master, Product Owner, and development team members [3]. The Scrum Master is a servant leader who helps the team adhere to the rules of Scrum and works within and outside the team to remove impediments. The Product Owner (PO) is responsible for defining what gets built. He or she is the owner of the team's backlog (*Product Backlog* in basic Scrum, *Team Backlog* in SAFe). When extended by Lean quality practices and engineering techniques inspired by eXtreme Programing (XP), the SAFe *ScrumXP* team provides the basic Agile building block for SAFe.

But, of course, SAFe ScrumXP teams do not work in isolation. Each team is part of the larger Agile Release Train (ART), where they cooperate in building the larger system, which is the subject of the endeavor. To this end, to ensure that the entire system iterates and evolves incrementally over time, all Agile Teams *plan together, integrate and demo together*, and *learn together*.

## Details

The *ScrumXP* Agile Team is a self-organizing, self-managing, and cross-functional group of five to nine people, collocated wherever possible. The size and structure of the team are optimized for communication, interaction, and the ability to deliver value. Self-organization implies that there is no team leader or manager role that tasks the team members, estimates their work, commits the team to specific objectives, or determines how exactly they will advance the Solution. The team is presented with the intent of the Iteration and is solely responsible for determining how much of that scope they can actually commit to, and how they are going to build that increment of value.

The team is cross-functional, so it has all the roles and skills needed to deliver an increment. The self-organization and cross-functional nature of the team, along with constant communication, constructive conflict, and dynamic interaction, can create a productive team and a more enjoyable work environment for the team members.

Scrum defines two specific roles, the Product Owner and Scrum Master, who are members of the SAFe ScrumXP team, each with a unique and specific set of responsibilities. Each of these roles is elaborated further in a SAFe article by that name. A summary of the responsibilities for each is provided below.

### Product Owner (PO)

Each ScrumXP team has a Product Owner who is responsible for the Team Backlog. The interaction of the PO with the rest of the team is a significant, daily, and highly focused effort. Therefore, the most effective model is to have a dedicated PO for each team, or to share a PO across no more than two teams. That allows the PO to effectively support the team during Iteration Execution by answering questions, providing more detail on the functionality under development, and reviewing and accepting the completed stories into the baseline.

### Scrum Master (SM)

The Scrum Master is the facilitator and Agile coach for the team. Primary responsibilities include ensuring that the process is being followed, educating the team in Scrum, XP, and SAFe practices, and providing the environment for continuous improvement. The Scrum Master is also typically charged with leading the removal of impediments. The Scrum Master may be a full- or part-time role for a team member. Alternately, some dedicated Scrum Masters may support two to three Scrum teams.

## The Scrum Process

The Scrum process itself is a lightweight project management framework that fosters quick, iterative advancement of the solution Capabilities and facilitates continuous improvement in support of higher productivity and quality and better outcomes. The process is centered around the iteration (note: Scrum uses the term *sprint*; SAFe uses the more general term *iteration*)—a short timebox, two weeks in the case of SAFe—during which the team defines, builds, tests, and reviews results. The Scrum process is further described in the sections below.

### Planning the Iteration

The iteration starts with Iteration Planning—a timeboxed event (four hours or less) during which the Product Owner presents the stories for the iteration. The team then reviews the stories, defines the acceptance criteria, splits larger stories into smaller ones where necessary, estimates them in story points, and, finally, commits to what they can build, based on their known velocity (story points per iteration). Many teams further divide stories into tasks, estimating the tasks in hours to better refine their understanding of the work ahead. Finally, the team commits to a set of goals for the iteration.

Even before the iteration starts, the Scrum team is preparing content for the new iteration by *refining* the team backlog items to make sure they understand the work to be delivered during the upcoming iteration.

## Visualizing Work

During execution, the team builds and tests stories, with a goal of delivering a story or two every few days. This serialization limits work in process and helps avoid "waterfalling" the iteration. Teams use big visual information radiators" (BVIRs) to understand and track progress during iteration execution. The team's *story board* visualizes the stories and their progress throughout the iteration. In so doing, they often use development steps as the columns and move stories left to right over time, as Figure 1 demonstrates.

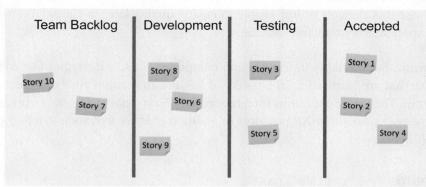

*Figure 1. An example of a team's story board*

Some teams also apply work in process limits to some steps to create a "pull" process within the iteration, and to continuously balance the work to increase throughput. Indeed, many teams integrate the best practices of Scrum and Kanban to facilitate the flow of work through the iterations. In this case, the simple story board above evolves into a more structured Kanban board. See the "Team Kanban" article for more on the use of Kanban by ScrumXP teams.

## Coordinating with Daily Stand-up Meetings

Each day, the team has a formal ceremony—the *Daily Stand-up Meeting* (DSU)—to understand where they are, escalate problems, and get help from other team members. During this meeting each team member describes what they did yesterday, what they are going to work on today, and any "blocks" they are encountering. As this is a *daily* coordination meeting, it has to be kept short and to the point by the Scrum Master. The DSU should take no more than 15 minutes and is done standing up in front of the story board.

Team communication does not end there, however, as team members interact continuously throughout the iteration. The facilitation of such communication is the main reason why ScrumXP prefers that the team be collocated whenever possible.

**Demonstrating Value and Improving the Process**

At the end of each iteration, the team conducts a Team Demo and an Iteration Retrospective. During the demo, the team demonstrates each story accomplished during the iteration, the summation of which is the team's increment of value for that iteration. This is not a formal status report; rather, it is a review of the tangible outcomes of the iteration. Thereafter, the team conducts a brief retrospective, a time to reflect on the iteration, the process, things that are working well, and current obstacles. Then the team comes up with improvement stories for the next iteration.

## Building Quality In

As a tenet of SAFe says, "You can't scale crappy code." Therefore, one of the Core Values of SAFe is "Built-in Quality." Built-in quality begins at the code and component levels by those who create the solution, otherwise it is difficult or impossible to ensure quality later as the solution integrates and scales from component to system and solution.

To make sure teams build quality in to code and components, SAFe describes five engineering and quality practices that are inspired by the tenets of XP and that augment the project management practices of Scrum. They are Continuous Integration, Test-First, refactoring, pair work, and collective ownership. Some teams use other XP practices in addition to these five, such as a pair programming and metaphor [2].

## ScrumXP Teams Are "on the Train"

While the teams are cross-functional, it isn't always realistic for a team of seven or eight to deliver end-user value when a large system includes different technology platforms and a spectrum of disciplines including hardware, software, and systems engineering. Many more teams are typically required. To address this, SAFe Agile Teams teams operate within an Agile Release Train (ART), which provides mission alignment and a collaborative environment whereby teams can cooperate with other teams to build the larger solution capabilities. As part of the ART, ScrumXP teams *plan together, integrate and demo together*, and *learn together*, as illustrated in Figure 2.

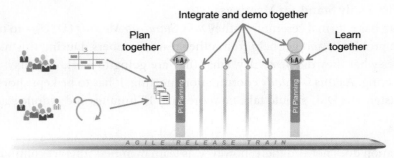

*Figure 2. SAFe Agile Teams plan together,*
*integrate and demo together, and learn together*

Each team's participation in this "shared responsibility program" is further defined in the "Agile Teams" article.

## Leadership of ScrumXP Teams

Managers are typically not part of the cross-functional team. However, the initial organization of such teams around Features, components, and subsystems and the design and structure of the ART is typically a management responsibility, based on input from the teams. Thereafter, the ongoing management of such teams typically undergoes a qualitative shift, from *manager as expert*, directing the team to specific technical achievements, to manager as a Lean-Agile Leader and *enabler and developer of people*.

---

**LEARN MORE**

[1] Kniberg, Henrik. *Scrum and XP from the Trenches.* lulu.com, 2015.

[2] Beck, Kent and Cynthia Andres. *Extreme Programming Explained: Embrace Change,* 2nd edition. Addison-Wesley, 2004.

[3] Sutherland, Jeff and Ken Schwaber. http://www.scrumguides.org.

# Team Kanban

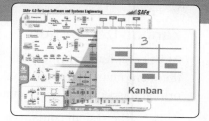

*The only way you can create excess inventory is by having excess manpower.*
—Eli Goldratt

*Or perhaps overspecialization?*
—SAFe Authors

## Abstract

Kanban systems are used, albeit for somewhat different purposes, at the Portfolio, Value Stream, Program, and Team Levels of SAFe. This article describes *Team Kanban*, a method that helps teams facilitate the flow of value by visualizing work flow, establishing work-in-process limits, measuring throughput, and continuously improving their process.

SAFe teams have a choice of Agile methods. Most use Scrum, a lightweight, effective, and ubiquitous method for managing work. Teams that develop new code also apply XP practices to bring focus to software engineering and code quality. Some teams, however, particularly System Teams, DevOps, and maintenance teams, choose to apply Kanban as their primary method. In these contexts, the response mandate, the rapid-fire nature of the work, fast-changing priorities, and the lower value of planning what exactly will be done in the next Iteration all lead them to this choice. This article will describe a Kanban system well suited to SAFe Agile Teams. However, these teams are "on the train," and certain rules of the train must be applied.

## Details

Generally, Kanban is described as a *pull system*; teams "pull" work when they have known capacity for it, rather than scope being "pushed" on them. This article describes *Team Kanban*, a method that helps teams facilitate the flow of value by visualizing work flow, establishing work-in-process limits, measuring throughput, and continuously improving their process.

A Kanban system is built up of work flow states. Most states have work-in-process (WIP) limits, whereby a work item can be pulled into a state only when the number of items at that state is lower than the WIP limit. A few states, typically beginning and end states, are not WIP limited.

WIP limits are defined and adjusted by the team itself, allowing for the quick adaptation to variations in flow that is characteristic of complex systems development. In SAFe, Team Kanban is applied in concert with the cadence and synchronization requirements of the Agile Release Train (ART). This provides for alignment; dependency management; and fast, integration-based learning cycles, which provide the objective evidence needed to advance the larger Solution.

## Kanban Description

At its core, Kanban (meaning "visual signal") is a method for visualizing and managing work. While there are many interpretations of how to apply Kanban in development, most would agree that the primary aspects of a development Kanban system include the following:

- The system contains a series of defined states that work moves through

- All work is visualized, and the progress of individual items is tracked

- Teams agree on specific WIP limits for each state and change them when necessary to improve flow

- Teams adopt specific policies covering how work is managed

- Flow is *measured*. Work items are tracked from the time they enter the system to the time they leave, providing continuous indicators of the amount of work in process and the current lead time (how long, on average, it takes an item to get through the system).

- Prioritization is done by assigning a class of service, which, in turn, is based on cost of delay

## Visualizing Flow and Limiting WIP

To get started, teams typically build an approximation of their current process flow and define some initial WIP limits. Figure 1 shows an example of one team's initial Kanban board, which captures their current work flow steps of *analyze – review – build – integrate – test*.

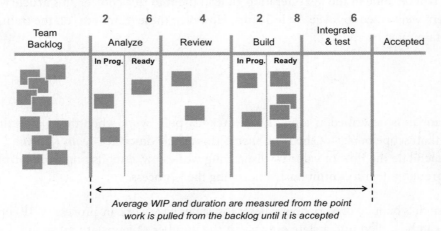

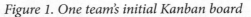

*Average WIP and duration are measured from the point work is pulled from the backlog until it is accepted*

*Figure 1. One team's initial Kanban board*

In Figure 1, the team has also decided to create two *buffers* ("Ready") to better manage variability of flow. One is in front of the "Review" step, which might require external subject matter experts (Product Management or others), whose availability may be limited and uneven. The other buffer is in front of "Integrate and Test," which, in their case, requires the use of shared test fixtures and resources. Since integration and testing is performed by the same people on the same infrastructure, the two steps are treated as a single state. Also, to justify the transaction cost, the team allows reasonably higher WIP limits for the "Review" and "Integrate and Test" steps.

A team's Kanban board evolution is iterative. After defining the initial process steps and WIP limits and executing for a while, the team's bottlenecks should surface. If not, the team refines the states or further reduces the WIP until it becomes obvious which state is "starving" or is too full, helping the team adjust toward more optimum flow. As the assumptions are validated, WIP limits are adjusted and steps may be merged, split, or redefined.

## Measuring Flow

In order to understand and improve their flow and process, Kanban teams use objective measures, including average *lead time*, *WIP*, and *throughput*. One common way is to use a Cumulative Flow Diagram (CFD), as illustrated in Figure 2.

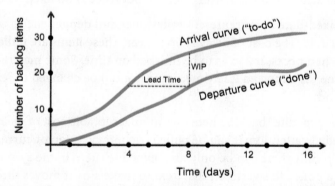

*Figure 2. Cumulative Flow Diagram (CFD) shows how lead time and WIP evolve over time*

Each backlog item is date stamped, both when it enters the work flow (pulled from the Team Backlog to begin implementation) and when it is completed. The arrival curve shows the rate at which backlog items are pulled into work. The departure curve shows when they have been accepted. The x-axis shows the average *lead time*—how long it takes, on average, for an item to get through the system. The y-axis shows the *WIP*—the average number of items in the system at any point in time. *Throughput*—the number of stories completed per a period of time—represents another critical metric. Since Kanban teams in SAFe operate on an Iteration cadence, they measure throughput in Stories per iteration.

The Cumulative Flow Diagram provides the data for the team to be able to calculate their current iteration throughput.

To do this, the team divides the average WIP by the average lead time, to arrive at the average number of stories processed per day. They then multiply by 14 (which is the iteration duration in days). This provides the iteration average throughput in number of stories per iteration, which helps with planning. (This will also be important in calculating "derived velocity," as described later in this article.)

The Cumulative Flow Diagram also provides a critical visualization of significant variation in flow, which may be a result of systemic internal impediments the team is not aware of or external forces that impede the flow. The CFD is an excellent example of an objective measure that facilitates relentless improvement for Kanban teams.

## Improving Flow with Classes of Service

In addition, teams need to be able to manage dependencies as well as ensure alignment with Milestones. Kanban uses the mechanism of *classes of service* to help teams optimize the execution of their backlog items. Classes of service provide a way of differentiating backlog items based on their cost of delay. Each class of service has a specific execution policy that the team agrees to follow. For example:

1. **Standard** – Most backlog items should fall in the *normal case*—new development, which is not specifically date dependent. The cost of delay is linear for standard items, in that value cannot be achieved until delivery occurs, but there is no fixed date requirement.

2. **Fixed date** – Fixed-date items represent milestones and dependencies with a predetermined date. The cost of delay is nonlinear. These items are pulled into development when necessary so as to be finished on time. Some may require additional analysis to refine the expected lead time; some need to be changed to "expedite" if the team falls behind.

3. **Expedite** – An "expedite" backlog item has an unacceptable cost of delay and therefore requires immediate attention; it can be pulled even in violation of current WIP constraints. Typically there can be only one "expedite" item in the system at a time, and teams may set a policy to swarm on that item to make sure it moves through the system expeditiously.

If teams find that many items require expediting, then the system may be overloaded. Either demand exceeds capacity, or the input process could be undisciplined. In any case, the process needs to be adjusted.

As illustrated in Figure 3, classes of service are typically visualized as "swim lanes."

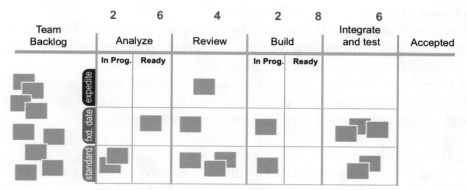

*Figure 3. Classes of service on the Kanban board*

In addition, the teams may reserve specific colors for different types of backlog items (see the "PI Planning" article), such as "new functionality," "research spike," "modeling," etc., which adds additional understanding to the work being performed.

Close attention to the structure of flow provides Kanban teams with improvement opportunities that otherwise would pass unnoticed. For example, changes in the Cumulative Flow Diagram may suggest increasing average WIP (which will cause an increase in lead time). While this can just be a symptom of a deeper problem, the team now has a way of spotting it. Regular reflection and adaptation of the process is a necessary measure to realize the benefit of high visibility of flow.

## The SAFe Kanban Team Is on the Train

SAFe Kanban teams operate in a broader context of building a solution that requires multiple Agile Teams and may even span multiple Agile Release Trains (ARTs). In order to accomplish this, the team needs to adhere to specific SAFe rules in addition to the regular Kanban guidelines. These rules are that the teams *plan together, integrate and demo together*, and *learn together*, as is described in more detail in the "Agile Teams" article. Planning together is one element that warrants further discussion, and is described below.

## Estimating Work

Generally, Kanban teams don't invest as much time in estimating or tasking as Scrum teams do. Rather, they take a look at the needed work, split the bigger items where necessary, and drive the resulting stories to completion, mostly without much concern for their size. However, SAFe teams have to able to estimate the demand against the capacity for PI Planning, and they also participate in economic estimation of larger backlog items. Also, in order to be able to forecast, there must be an understanding of the teams' velocity in a manner consistent with that of the other teams on the train, and of the total ART velocity.

### Establish a Common Starting Point for Estimation

Initially, a new Kanban team has no knowledge of its throughput, as that is a trailing measure based on history. To get started, SAFe Kanban teams must have a means to estimate work, often beginning with the first PI planning session. In a manner consistent with Scrum teams, estimation of initial capacity begins with normalized estimating (as described in the "Iteration Planning" article). Kanban teams then add their estimated stories into iterations, just as the Scrum teams do. Their starting capacity is their assumed velocity, at least for the first Program Increment (PI).

### Calculating Derived Velocity

After this starting point, Kanban teams can use their Cumulative Flow Diagrams to calculate their actual throughput in stories per iteration (or they can simply count and average them!). Kanban teams then calculate their "derived velocity" by multiplying the throughput by an average story size (typically 3 – 5 points). In this way, both SAFe Scrum and Kanban teams can participate in the larger Economic Framework, which, in turn, provides the primary economic context for the portfolio.

### Estimating Larger Work Items

At the Portfolio and Value Stream Levels, it is often necessary to estimate larger work items (Epics and Capabilities) to determine the potential economic viability of these initiatives. In addition, development of ARTs and Value Stream Roadmaps requires both a knowledge of estimating (how big is the item) and ART velocity (how much capacity does the ART have to do it). In order to do this, Kanban teams break larger initiatives into stories for estimating, just as the Scrum teams do. This provides the finer-grained resolution needed to estimate larger items. Stories are then estimated in normalized story points. This provides the ability for the Enterprise to aggregate estimates from various teams—and types of teams—without excessive debate.

---

**LEARN MORE**

[1] Anderson, David. *Kanban: Successful Evolutionary Change for Your Technology Business*. Blue Hole Press, 2010.

[2] Kniberg, Henrik. *Lean from the Trenches: Managing Large-Scale Projects with Kanban*. Pragmatic Programmers, 2012.

# Team Backlog

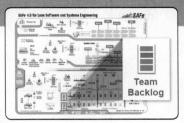

*Definition of BACKLOG:*

1. *A large log at the back of a hearth fire*
2. *An accumulation of tasks unperformed or materials not processed*

*Burn the first slowly and the second quickly.*

## Abstract

The *Team Backlog* represents the collection of all the things a team needs to do to advance their portion of the system. It can contain User or Enabler Stories, most of which are stories that originate from the Program Backlog, while some others are local to the team's specific context. The team backlog is owned by the Product Owner, although backlog "ownership" does not mean that the PO is the only one to populate it but rather that the PO prioritizes the work for execution.

Since both enabler and user stories are part of the backlog, it is important to apply capacity allocation to help ensure that investments are balanced across conflicting needs. This is based on the capacity allocation of the Agile Release Train as a whole and on the needs of the team.

## Details

While "backlog" seems to be a simple notion, there are a number of subtleties that create the power behind this simple construct.

- It truly contains *all* things. If a thing is in there, it *might* get done. If it isn't there, there is no chance that it will get done.

- It's a list of "want to do" items, not a commitment. Items can be estimated (preferable) or not, but neither case implies a specific time commitment as to when any of them will be done.

- It has a single owner—the team's Product Owner. This protects the team from the problem of multiple stakeholders, each with potentially divergent views of what's important.

- All team members can enter Stories that they think are important into the backlog

- It contains user stories, Enabler Stories, and "improvement stories," which are those stories that capture the results of the team's Iteration Retrospective

The *Team Backlog* is a simple and unifying construct, and one that conveniently hides some of the complexity of Agile at scale. Figure 1 illustrates a view of the team backlog, with its three primary input sources.

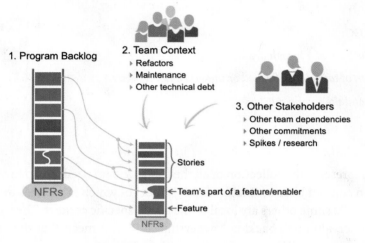

*Figure 1. Exploded view of a team backlog*

The Program Backlog consists of upcoming Features that are planned to be delivered by an Agile Release Train (ART). During PI Planning, the features that are planned for the Program Increment (PI) are broken into stories and tentatively allocated to individual upcoming Iterations in the team backlog. In addition, some future work is planned for upcoming periods; in this case the team backlog can also contain future features that have yet to be broken into stories. At other times a feature requires multiple teams for delivery, in which case a placeholder for that team's part of the work, and its size estimate, is maintained in the team backlog.

The team has its own context as well. In addition to the stories needed to fulfill features, the team typically has a backlog of local stories representing new functionality, refactors, defects, research spikes, and other technical debt. These latter must also be identified, written as enabler stories, estimated, and sequenced.

Teams on the release train are not islands, and their backlogs will reflect certain stories that are in support of other teams' and stakeholders' objectives. These can include research and estimating spikes for features, Capabilities and even Epics, stories to reflect team dependencies, and other external commitments.

## Optimizing Value Delivery and System Health with Capacity Allocation

Just like the ART itself, every team faces the problem of how to balance the backlog of internally facing work—maintenance, refactors, and technical debt—with the new user stories that deliver more immediate value. "All new functionality all the time" may work for a bit and even provide immediate gratification in the market, but this will be short lived as delivery velocity will be eventually slowed by a crushing load of technical debt. In order to avoid velocity reduction and to defer the need for wholesale replacement of the system due to technological obsolescence, teams invest continuously in evolving the technical underpinnings of the solution, as well as keeping existing Customers happy with bug fixes and enhancements.

This complicates the challenge of sequencing work, as the Product Owner is constantly trying to compare the value of three unlike things: 1) defects; 2) refactors, redesigns, and technology upgrades; and 3) new user stories. And there is no upper limit to the demand for any of these things! Much as in the program backlog, *capacity allocation* is used by the teams to make a policy decision as to how much of their total effort can be applied to each type of activity for a given period, as Figure 2 illustrates.

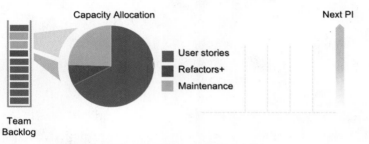

*Figure 2. Team backlog capacity allocation*

Once that decision is made, the teams still need to select the highest-priority backlog items from each "slice" to implement in each iteration. For stories that are committed to the program, sequencing is probably already predetermined by PI planning commitments. But for local stories, the Product Owner can sequence those using value/size, or even apply full WSJF where beneficial. In addition, in order to balance long-term product health and value delivery, the percentage allocation to each type can be changed over time (for example, for each PI).

## Backlog Refinement

We noted above that the backlog contains some stories that are in an advanced state of maturity, essentially ready for implementation without too much risk or surprise. Since the whole team is involved, most teams take a flow-based approach to this process as well, typically by having at least one team workshop per iteration (or even one per week) whose sole focus is to look at upcoming stories (and features, as appropriate), discuss and estimate, and establish an initial understanding of acceptance criteria.

There is no standard term for this meeting, but *backlog refinement* describes this meeting in SAFe, though it is recognized that the backlog refinement function is continuous and cannot be relegated to a single-meeting timebox. Teams applying Acceptance Test-Driven Development will typically invest even more up-front time in developing specific acceptance tests, sometimes in special sessions often called *specification workshops*. In addition, as multiple teams are doing backlog refinement, new issues, dependencies, and stories are likely to result. In this way the process of backlog refinement helps surface underlying problems with the current plan, which will come under discussion in ART sync meetings.

---

**LEARN MORE**

[1] Leffingwell, Dean. *Agile Software Requirements: Lean Requirements Practices for Teams, Programs, and the Enterprise.* Addison-Wesley, 2011.

# Iterations

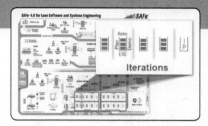

*None of my inventions came by accident. I see a worthwhile need to be met and I make trial after trial until it comes.*

—*Thomas Edison*

## Abstract

The *Iteration* is the basic building block of Agile development. Each iteration is a fixed timebox wherein the teams build an incremental element of business or product functionality. SAFe's two-week iterations provide the basic development cadence for Agile Teams building Features and components. During this short period, the team executes the Stories in their iteration backlog, integrates the output with that of the other teams, and prepares and participates in a System Demo. Each iteration is followed by another, providing the basic tempo of continuous value development and delivery.

The iteration cadence is the first cadence in SAFe, but SAFe also provides a nested harmonic of short iterations grouped into a longer Program Increment (PI) timebox. This timebox provides the outer cadence for all the teams on an Agile Release Train (ART) to be able to plan together, integrate and demo together, and learn together.

## Details

Since fast learning is the key goal of SAFe's learning cycles, Agile Teams execute a full Plan-Do-Check-Adjust cycle as quickly as possible, as illustrated in Figure 1.

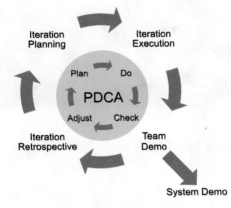

*Figure 1. PDCA in iterations*

Each PDCA cycle is an *Iteration*, which serves as the regular, predictable development cadence to produce an increment of value, as well as to refine previous increments. Each team plans, builds, tests, integrates, and demonstrates their work in the context of a full system increment every two weeks. These short iterations help the team, Product Owners, Product Managers, and other stakeholders test the technical and business hypotheses on a working system. Each iteration also anchors an integration point, a "pull event" that pulls together various system aspects—functionality, quality, alignment, and fitness for use—across all the teams' individual contributions.

## Plan the Iteration

The Iteration Planning meeting is the "Plan" step of the PDCA cycle. It aligns all team members to the common goals of the team, as described by the Team PI Objectives, and to the outcome that will be demoed at the Team and System Demos.

While the specifics of the planning function will differ based on whether the team works in ScrumXP or Kanban, the team reviews the Team Backlog and comes up with a set of Iteration Goals, detailing— from a system perspective—what will be ready for integration and demo by the end of the iteration.

## Execute the Iteration

Iteration Execution is the process of how the work takes place. During the iteration, the team completes the "Do" part of the PDCAj5

jcycle by building and testing the new functionality. Teams deliver Stories in an incremental fashion, demoing ready stories to the Product Owner as soon as they are done; they arrive at the demo ready to show their progress.

During execution there is also a smaller PDCA cycle, as represented, in part, by the daily stand-up. Every day, team members meet to evaluate their progress toward the iteration goals and update each

---

other on their progress. This meeting represents a full, daily PDCA cycle, which allows the team to plan, check, and adjust their iteration plan every day.

## Team Demo

The team demo is the "check" step in the PDCA cycle. In the demo, the teams show a tested increment of value to the Product Owner and receive feedback on what has been produced. The outcome of this meeting will help shape the team backlog for the next iteration. Some stories will be accepted and others refined by the learning gained during the iteration.

Following the team demo, team members participate in an integrated system demo. This is the first required, formal integration point among teams on the Agile Release Train (ART), and it serves as a pull event to ensure early integration and validation at the Program Level. Within the iteration, teams integrate and evaluate as continuously as their system context allows.

## Improve the Process

The Iteration Retrospective serves as the "check" step for the overall iteration. Here, the team evaluates its process and any improvement stories it had from the previous iteration, identifies problems and their root causes as well as bright spots, and comes up with improvement stories that enter the team backlog for the next iteration. This frequent retrospective is one of the key ways to ensure that relentless improvement (one of the pillars of SAFe's Lean-Agile Mindset) is happening at the Team Level. Iteration retrospectives also drive program level changes to process, either immediately or at the Inspect and Adapt workshop.

Before the next planning begins, the backlog is refined to include the decisions from the demo and retrospective. The Product Owner refactors and reprioritizes new and old backlog items as needed.

**LEARN MORE**

[1] Cockburn, Alistair. "Using Both Incremental and Iterative Development." *STSC CrossTalk* 21 (2008): 27 – 30.

[2] Maurya, Ash. *Running Lean: Iterate from Plan A to a Plan That Works*. O'Reilly Media, 2012.

# Iteration Planning

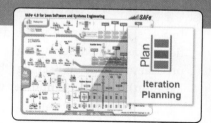

*Stay committed to your decisions, but stay flexible in your approach.*
—Tom Robbins

## Abstract

Team-based *Iteration Planning* is one of the key mechanisms for decentralizing control and empowering fast, local decision-making. In Scrum, teams plan by selecting Stories from the product backlog and committing a set of them for execution in the upcoming Iteration. This basic process is fundamental to SAFe as well, but the context is broader, as SAFe teams are part of an Agile Release Train (ART). As such, the team's backlog has already been seeded and partially preplanned during the PI Planning meeting. In addition, the teams have feedback, not only from their prior iterations but from the System Demo and other teams as well. That, and the natural course of events and changing fact patterns, provides the broader context for iteration planning. However, the iteration planning process is largely the same as in traditional Scrum, as each Agile Team plans the upcoming iteration in a timeboxed meeting. The output of this iteration planning meeting is:

1. The iteration backlog, consisting of the stories committed to the iteration, with acceptance criteria where appropriate

2. A statement of Iteration Goals, typically a sentence or two stating the business objectives of the iteration

3. A commitment by the team to the work needed to achieve the goals

## Details

The purpose of *Iteration Planning* is to organize the work and define a realistic scope for the Iteration. Each Agile Team agrees on a set of Stories for the upcoming iteration (the iteration backlog) and summarizes those stories into a set of Iteration Goals. The iteration backlog and goals are based on the team's capacity and allow for consideration of each story's complexity, size, and dependencies on other stories and other teams.

At the end of planning, the teams commit to the goal of the iteration and adjust stories as necessary to achieve the larger purpose. In return, management does not interfere or adjust the scope of the iteration, allowing the team to stay focused on the goals.

## Inputs to Iteration Planning

In SAFe, iteration planning is a refinement of the level of detail and an adjustment of the initial iteration plans created during Agile Release Train PI Planning. Teams approach iteration planning with a pre-elaborated Team Backlog (they have usually held a backlog refinement meeting during the previous iteration). There are a number of inputs to the planning meeting:

- The Team and Program PI Objectives, created at PI planning

- The team's PI plan backlog, which consists of stories that were identified during PI planning

- Additional stories that arise based on local context, including items such as defects, refactors, and new stories that have come about since the planning session

- Feedback from the prior iteration, including any stories that were not successfully completed (did not meet the Definition of Done; see "A Scaled Definition of Done" in the "Release" article) in that iteration

- Feedback from the System Demo

## Planning the Iteration

Prior to the meeting, the Product Owner will have prepared some preliminary iteration goals, based on the team's progress in the Program Increment (PI). Typically, the Product Owner starts the meeting by reviewing the proposed iteration goals and the higher-priority stories in the team backlog. During the meeting, the Agile Team discusses implementation options, technical issues, Nonfunctional Requirements (NFRs), and dependencies, then plans the iteration. The Product Owner defines the *what*; the team defines *how* and *how much*.

Throughout the meeting, the team elaborates the acceptance criteria and estimates the effort to complete each story. Based on their velocity, the team then selects the candidate stories. Many teams break each story down into tasks and estimate them in hours to confirm that they have the capacity and skills to complete them. Once confirmed, the team commits to the work and records the iteration backlog in a visible place, such as a story board or tooling. This meeting is timeboxed to a maximum of four hours.

### Establish Velocity
First, the team quantifies their capacity to perform work in the upcoming iteration. Each team member determines their availability, acknowledging time off and other potential duties. This activity also takes into account other standing commitments (see the "capacity allocation" section in the "Team Backlog" article)—such as maintenance—that are distinct from new story development.

### Iteration Goals

Once team member capacity has been established, the team turns their attention to understanding and agreeing on one or more iteration goals that are based on the team and program PI objectives from the PI planning session. The closer this iteration is to the PI planning session, the more likely the program objectives will remain unchanged.

### Story Analysis and Estimating

With the proposed iteration goals acting as a reference point, the team backlog is reviewed. Each story is discussed, covering relative difficulty, size, complexity, technical challenges, and acceptance criteria. Finally, the team agrees to a size estimate for the story. There are typically other types of stories on the team backlog as well, including Enablers that could constitute infrastructure work, refactoring, research spikes, architectural improvements, and defects. These are also prioritized and estimated.

### Tasks

Many teams then break each story into tasks. As the tasks are identified, team members discuss each one: who would be the best person(s) to accomplish it, approximately how long it will take (typically in hours), and any dependencies it may have on other tasks or stories. Once all this is understood, a team member takes responsibility for a specific task or tasks. As team members commit to tasks, they reduce their individual iteration capacity until it reaches zero. Often, toward the end of the session, some team members will find themselves overcommitted, while others will have some of their capacity still available. This situation leads to further discussion among team members to more evenly distribute the work.

### Commitment

When the team's collective capacity has been reached in terms of committed stories, no more stories are pulled from the team backlog. At this point, the Product Owner and team agree on the final list of stories that will be achieved, and they revisit and restate the iteration goals. The entire team then commits to the iteration goals, and the scope of the work remains fixed for the duration of the iteration.

## Attendees

Attendees of the iteration planning meeting include:

- The Product Owner
- The Scrum Master, who acts as facilitator for this meeting
- All other team members
- Any other stakeholders, including representatives from other Agile Teams or the ART, and subject matter experts

## Agenda

A sample iteration planning meeting agenda follows:

- The team determines the velocity available for the iteration
- The Product Owner presents the iteration goals; the team discusses and agrees on the goals
- The team discusses each story in ranked (sequenced or prioritized) order. For each story, the team:
    - Sizes/resizes each story in story points and splits them if necessary
    - Elaborates acceptance criteria through conversation
    - Based on size and value/time/risk, the PO may re-rank stories
    - Optional: In ranked order, the team breaks stories into tasks, estimated in hours, and takes responsibility
    - Planning stops once the team runs out of points
- The team and PO negotiate and finalize the selected stories
- Everyone commits to the iteration goals

## Guidelines

Below are some tips for holding a successful iteration planning meeting:

- Timebox the meeting to 4 hours or less
- This meeting is held by and for the team
- A team should never commit to work in excess of its adjusted capacity or historical velocity

## Relative Estimating, Velocity, and Normalizing Story Point Estimating

Agile Teams use relative estimating [2, 3] to estimate the size of a story in story points. With relative estimating, the size (effort) for each story is estimated relative to the size of other stories. The team's velocity for an iteration is equal to the sum of the size of all the stories completed in the iteration. Knowing a team's velocity assists with planning and is a key factor in limiting WIP, as teams simply don't take on more stories than their prior velocity would allow. Velocity is also used to estimate how long it takes to deliver larger Features or Epics, which are likewise estimated in story points.

### Normalizing Story Point Estimating

In standard Scrum, each team's story point estimating—and the resultant velocity—is a local and independent matter. The fact that a small team might estimate in such a way that they have a velocity of 50, while a larger team estimates so as to have a velocity of 12, is of no concern to anyone.

In SAFe, however, story point velocity must be normalized to a point, so that estimates for features or epics that require the support of many teams are based on rational economics. After all, there is no way to determine the return on potential investment if you don't know what the investment is.

In order to do this, SAFe teams start down a path where a story point for one team means about the same as a story point for another. In this way, with adjustments for economics of location (the U.S., Europe, India, China, etc.), work can be estimated and prioritized based on economics by converting story points to cost. This is particularly helpful in initial PI planning, as many teams will be new to Agile and will need a way to estimate the scope of work in their first PI. One starting algorithm is as follows:

- For every individual contributor on the team, excluding the Product Owner, give the team eight points (adjust for part-timers)

- Subtract one point for every team member vacation day and holiday

- Find a small story that would take about a half-day to develop and a half-day to test and validate. Call it a 1.

- Estimate every other story relative to that one

Example: Assuming a 6-person team composed of 3 developers, 2 testers, and 1 PO, with no vacations, etc., then the estimated initial velocity = 5 * 8 points = 40 points per iteration. (Note: The team may need to adjust a bit lower if one of the developers and testers is also the Scrum Master.)

In this way, all teams estimate the size of work in a common fashion, so management can thereby fairly quickly estimate the cost for a story point for teams in a specific region. They then have a meaningful way to establish the aggregate cost estimate for an upcoming feature or epic.

*Note: There is no need to recalibrate team estimating or velocities after that point. It is just a common starting point.*

While teams will tend to increase their velocity over time—and that is a good thing—in fact, the number tends to remain fairly stable, and a team's velocity is far more affected by changing team size, makeup, and technical context than by productivity changes. And, if necessary, financial planners can adjust the cost per story point a bit. This is a minor concern compared to the wildly differing velocities that teams of comparable size may have in the non-normalized case.

## LEARN MORE

[1] Leffingwell, Dean. *Agile Software Requirements: Lean Requirements Practices for Teams, Programs, and the Enterprise.* Addison-Wesley, 2011, chapter 9.

[2] Leffingwell, Dean. *Scaling Software Agility: Best Practices for Large Enterprises.* Addison-Wesley, 2007, chapter 10.

[3] Cohn, Mike. *Agile Estimating and Planning.* Robert C. Martin Series. Prentice Hall, 2005.

# Iteration Execution

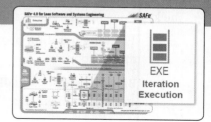

*Vision without execution is hallucination.*

—Thomas Edison

## Abstract

Each Agile Team has a single focus: the development of an increment of an effective, high-quality, working, tested system—all done within a short timebox. This is the fundamental challenge of every Lean-Agile Team, Program, Value Stream, Portfolio, and Enterprise. No matter the preparation, no matter the planning, without effective *Iteration Execution*, scaling is nearly impossible and Solution quality is compromised. The negative business effects will be felt by all.

This article provides guidance on how effective Agile Teams manage their work throughout the iteration timebox, both as individual teams and as members of the Agile Release Train.

During the iteration, the team collaborates intensely to define, build, and test the Stories committed during Iteration Planning. They demonstrate them *all* at the Team Demo. They track the iteration's progress and improve the flow of value using story and Kanban boards and daily stand-up meetings. They deliver stories throughout the iteration and avoid "waterfalling" the timebox. They reflect on their practices and challenges and make small improvements every increment. They work effectively with other teams on the train. They apply Built-in Quality to build big systems right. It's a big job, but effective Agile Teams are up to the task.

## Details

Empowering Agile Teams to focus on rapid value delivery fuels the team with energy, motivation, purpose, and a better sense of mission than that available with traditional management and development models. The centerpiece of all that goodness is the effective execution of each Iteration. Teams employ a variety of practices to achieve this result, but the focus is always the same: delivering the Stories they committed to during Iteration Planning in order to meet the Iteration Goals.

But even with effective, local *Iteration Execution*, teams are part of a larger purpose, which is optimizing *program execution*, one of the four Core Values of SAFe.

To achieve this, teams operate in the context of the Agile Release Train (ART), which coordinates teams toward agreed-to Team and Program PI Objectives. All teams use the same iteration cadence and duration to allow their work to be synchronized for integration, evaluation, and demonstration by the team during the Team Demo and the System Demo.

The key elements of a successful iteration execution include:

- **Tracking iteration progress** – Using story and Kanban boards to track the progress of the iteration

- **Building stories serially and incrementally** – Avoiding mini-waterfall and building stories incrementally

- **Constant communication** – Constant communication and synchronization via daily team stand-up meetings

- **Improving flow** – Optimizing flow by managing WIP, building quality in, and continuously accepting stories

- **Program execution** – Working together as an ART to achieve program PI objectives

## Tracking Iteration Progress

Tracking iteration progress requires visibility into the status of the stories, defects, and other activities that the team is working on during the iteration. Most teams use a big visible information radiator (BVIR) on a wall in the team room for this purpose. Kanban teams use their Kanban board, and ScrumXP teams would use a story board, perhaps like the one in Figure 1.

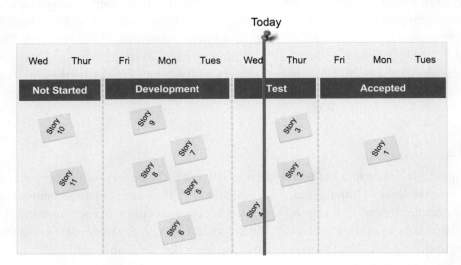

*Figure 1. Tracking progress with a team story board*

With this simple story board, the team just moves the red ribbon to the current day. This provides an easy-to-understand visual assessment of where the team is in the iteration. (Note how it is clear that the iteration in Figure 1 is at risk.) With that information, the team can discuss what is needed to successfully complete the iteration. If a remote participant or key stakeholder needs status information, the team can share it on a webcam, send it via e-mail, or post it in a wiki. At scale, of course, virtually all Agile Teams use contemporary Agile project management tools to capture stories and status, defects, test cases, estimates, actuals, assignments, burn-down, etc., but this is usually *in addition* to the BVIR.

## Constant Communication

An open environment and collocation are keys to team collaboration. Otherwise, delays due to questions and assumptions will quickly cause delays in value delivery. Where, in the worst case, teams are distributed, they can establish an open communication environment by leaving webcams, instant messaging, and other collaboration tools in an "always on" state.

### The Daily Stand-up (DSU)

Each day, the team meets at the same time and place to coordinate their work by answering the following questions:

- What stories did I work on yesterday (and their status)?
- What stories will I be able to complete today?
- What is getting in my way (am I blocked)?

The DSU is key to team synchronization and self-organization. It is most effective when it is held in front of the BVIR that highlights the stories that are the objective of the iteration. The DSU is strictly timeboxed to 15 minutes and is not a problem-solving meeting. It is a primary mechanism for identifying issues, dependencies, and conversations, many of which need to happen afterward. The Scrum Master writes topics that need further discussion on the "Meet After" board. During the Meet After, only the involved parties stay to discuss. Ineffective DSUs are symptoms of deeper problems that require a systematic approach that often falls to the Scrum Master to facilitate.

Note: While the DSU is a Scrum construct, many Kanban Teams also hold a DSU in front of their Kanban board to coordinate and inspect the board for bottlenecks or WIP problems.

## Improving Flow

### Managing WIP

WIP limits provide a strategy for preventing bottlenecks in development and helping improve flow. They also increase focus and information-sharing, and they foster collective ownership. All SAFe teams should have a solid understanding of their WIP and flow.

Kanban teams explicitly apply WIP limits; ScrumXP teams also use WIP limits. They can be explicit or implicit—for example, implicit when the team plans their own work and takes on only the amount of stories that their velocity predicts they can achieve. This forces the input rate (negotiated iteration goals and stories) to match capacity (the team's velocity). The iteration timebox also limits WIP by preventing uncontrolled expansion of work.

ScumXP teams may also use explicit WIP limits on their story board. For example, in Figure 1 above, what would a developer do if there were no WIP limits and he or she finished story 5 above? They would probably start another story. If a WIP limit of 3 is imposed on the "In Process" and "Test" stages, the developer would need to help test stories instead, and throughput would increase. To understand more about WIP limits, refer to SAFe Principle #6.

### Building Quality In

Agile Release Trains execute and deliver new functionality with the fastest sustainable lead time. In order to do so, they must create high-quality systems that promote a predictable development velocity. SAFe prescribes a set of five quality and engineering practices that materially contribute to the Built-in Quality of even the largest Solutions: Test-First, Continuous Integration, refactoring, pair work, and collective ownership. Ensuring that quality is built in from the beginning makes delivering value quicker, easier, and less costly.

### Continuously Accepting Stories

Accepting stories continuously improves flow. (Refer again to Figure 1 for symptoms of a non-flowing iteration; they are six days in, and only one story has been accepted.) Teams demo stories as soon as they are ready, not waiting for the team demo. Stories that are not accepted are reworked by the team. This way, problems can be addressed quickly and efficiently, the teams don't build new stories on top of nonworking stories, and they avoid the context switching that occurs otherwise.

### Test Automation

Where possible, the criteria for acceptable system behavior, as specified by the Product Owner and the rest of the Agile Team members, are converted to story acceptance tests that can be run repeatedly to ensure fitness for use and continued system conformance as the system evolves. Automation also provides the ability to quickly regression-test the system, enhancing continuous system-wide integration, refactoring, and maintenance. These tests are often created in a business-readable, domain-specific language, thereby creating the "automatically executable specification and test" of the system.

## Building Stories Serially and Incrementally

### Avoiding the Intra-Iteration "Waterfall"

Teams should avoid the tendency to "waterfall" the iteration and instead ensure that they are completing multiple define-build-test cycles in the course of the iteration, as Figure 2 illustrates.

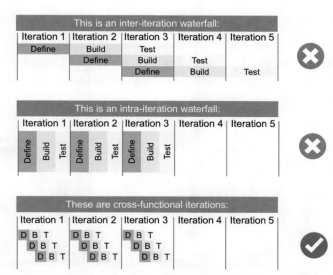

Figure 2. *Avoid the mini-waterfall with cross-functional iterations*

**Building Stories Incrementally**

Figure 3 illustrates how implementing stories in thin, vertical slices is the foundation for true incremental development, integration, and testing.

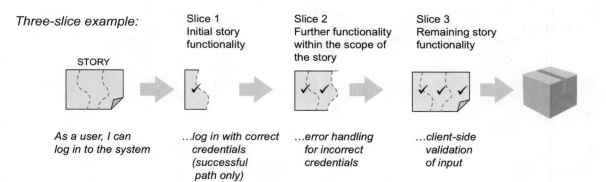

Figure 3. *Implementing stories in vertical slices is the key to incremental development*

This enables a short feedback cycle and allows the teams to operate with a smaller increment of the working system for continuous integration and testing. It enables Agile Team members to refine their understanding of the functionality, and it facilitates pairing and integration of working systems more frequently. The dependencies within and across teams and even trains can be managed more effectively, as the dependent teams can consume the new functionality sooner. This helps reduce uncertainty, validates architectural and design decisions, and promotes early learning and knowledge sharing.

## Focusing on Program Execution

While successful iterations are important, the ultimate goal of all teams is the execution of successful Program Increments. To help ensure that teams don't focus solely on local optimizations, SAFe teams *plan together*, *integrate and demo together*, and *learn together*, as Figure 4 shows.

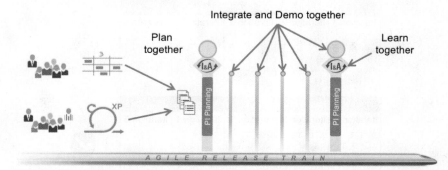

*Figure 4. Teams plan together, integrate and demo together, and learn together*

The practices used by teams to work together and achieve successful program increments are further detailed in the "Agile Teams" article.

---

**LEARN MORE**

[1] Leffingwell, Dean. *Agile Software Requirements: Lean Requirements Practices for Teams, Programs, and the Enterprise.* Addison-Wesley, 2011.

# Team Demo

*Working software is the primary measure of progress.*
  —Agile Manifesto

*Seeing is believing.*
  —Anonymous

## Abstract

Until people can see and touch the results of a Story or a Feature, it's just an abstract concept, so the demonstration of working, tested systems to Customers (or their proxies) is a concrete, seminal moment. To this end, depending on the scope of the Solution, there are *three* demos prescribed in SAFe: the Solution Demo, the System Demo, and the *Team Demo*. The system demo provides an aggregated view of all of the new system that has been delivered by all the teams on the Agile Release Train (ART), while the solution demo is the primary measure of progress for the Value Stream.

This article describes the team demo. This is the traditional Scrum-prescribed ceremony whereby the team reviews the increment that results from the Iteration; some Kanban teams apply them as well. Planning and presenting an effective team demo requires some work on the part of the teams, but without it they will not have the *fast feedback* they need to *build the right thing*.

## Details

The importance of the *Team Demos* cannot be overstated—they provide the only way that immediate, contextual feedback can be gathered from sponsors and Customers. As such, each demo serves three important functions:

- It brings closure to the Iteration timebox, to which many individuals have contributed to provide new value to the business

- It gives teams an opportunity to show the contributions they have made to the business, and to take some satisfaction and pride in their work and progress

- It allows Customers and stakeholders to see working Features and provide feedback

## Purpose

The purpose of the team demo is to measure the team's progress by showing working Stories to the Product Owner and other stakeholders and to get their feedback. This demo is a one- to two-hour demonstration of new functionality. The preparation for the demo begins during Iteration Planning, where teams start thinking about how they will demonstrate the stories they are committing to. Teams should be able to demonstrate every story, spike, refactor, and new Nonfunctional Requirement (NFR). This "beginning with the end in mind" facilitates iteration planning and alignment and fosters a more thorough understanding of the needed functionality.

## Process

The demo starts with a quick review of the Iteration Goals and then proceeds with a walk-through of all the committed stories. Each completed story is demonstrated in a working, tested system. Spikes are demonstrated via presentation of findings. After all completed stories are demonstrated, the team reflects on which stories were *not* completed, if any, and why the team was unable to finish them. This discussion usually results in discovery of impediments or risks, false assumptions, changing priorities, estimating inaccuracies, or overcommitment. These findings may result in further discussion in the Iteration Retrospective about how the next iterations can be better planned and executed. Figure 1 illustrates a team demo in action.

*Figure 1. Showing a working, tested system at the team demo*

In addition to showing how well the team did within this latest iteration, the team also reflects on how well it is progressing toward its PI Objectives.

## Attendees

Attendees at the team demo include:

- The Agile Teams, including Product Owner and Scrum Master

- Other ART stakeholders or Shared Services who were involved in the iteration

- Business Owners, executive sponsors, Customers, and members of other teams—perhaps. While they *may* attend, their interests and level of detail are usually better aligned with the System Demo. Otherwise, the team demos may be at too fine a level of detail, and "demo fatigue" may result.

## Agenda

A sample team demo agenda is as follows:

- Review the business context of the iteration and the iteration goals

- Demonstrate each story, spike, refactor, and applicable NFR; gather feedback

- Discuss any stories that were not completed and understand why (the answers may inform planning for the next iteration)

- Identify new current risks and impediments that may have emerged from the iteration or the demo

## Guidelines

Below are some tips for a successful team demo:

- Limit individual story demo preparation by team members to about one to two hours

- Timebox the meeting to one to two hours

- Minimize PowerPoint slides

- Demonstrate only working, tested systems of completed stories (reference the "Definition of Done" section of the "Release" article)

- If a major stakeholder cannot attend, the Product Owner should follow up to report progress and get feedback

---

**LEARN MORE**

[1] Leffingwell, Dean. *Agile Software Requirements: Lean Requirements Practices for Teams, Programs, and the Enterprise.* Addison-Wesley, 2011, chapter 9.

[2] Leffingwell, Dean. *Scaling Software Agility: Best Practices for Large Enterprises.* Addison-Wesley, 2007, chapter 15.

# Iteration Retrospective

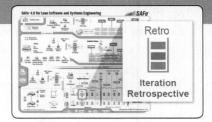

*At regular intervals, the team reflects on how to become more effective, then tunes and adjusts its behavior accordingly.*

—Agile Manifesto

## Abstract

At the end of each iteration, Agile Teams that apply Scrum (and many teams who use Kanban) gather for an *Iteration Retrospective*, where the team members discuss their practices and identify ways to improve. Timeboxed to an hour or less, each retrospective endeavors to uncover *what's working well*, *what isn't*, and *what the team can do better* next time.

Each retrospective has both *quantitative* and *qualitative* aspects. The quantitative review gathers and reviews any metrics the team is using to measure its performance. The qualitative part discusses the various team practices and the specific challenges that presented themselves in the course of the last iteration or two. When issues have been identified, root cause analysis is performed, potential corrective actions are discussed, and *improvement stories* are entered into the Team Backlog.

## Details

The *Iteration Retrospective* is used by Agile Teams to reflect on the Iteration just completed and to derive new ideas to improve the process. This helps instill the concept of relentless improvement—one of the pillars of the SAFe Lean-Agile Mindset—in the individuals and the team, and it helps ensure that every iteration makes some small improvements in the team's process.

The whole team participates in the retrospective, with the Scrum Master facilitating and applying the tools and processes for data collection and problem-solving. The team conducts the retrospective in two parts: quantitative and qualitative.

### Quantitative Review

The team assesses whether they met the Iteration Goals. This is a binary measure: yes or no. They also collect any other metrics they have agreed to analyze. This must include velocity—both the portion that is available for new development and the portion devoted to maintenance.

Agile Teams collect and apply other Iteration Metrics for visibility and to help with process improvement. This data also serves as context for the qualitative section that follows.

## Qualitative Review

First the team reviews the improvement Stories they had identified in the prior retrospective, then analyzes the current process, with a focus on finding one or two things they can do better in the next iteration. Since many improvement stories are significant in scope, the team should divide them into smaller improvement stories, so that they can focus on what they can improve in an iteration.

There are several popular techniques for eliciting subjective feedback on the success of the iteration (also see [1]):

- Individual – Individually write Post-its and then find patterns as a group

- Appreciation – Note whether someone has helped you or helped the team

- Conceptual – Choose one word to describe the iteration

- Rating – Rate the iteration on a scale of 1 to 5, and then brainstorm how to make the next one a 5

- Simple – Use three columns and open discussion

The latter is a common method, whereby the Scrum Master simply puts up three sheets of paper, labeled *What Went Well*, *What Didn't*, and *Do Better Next Time*, and then facilitates an open brainstorming session. It can be conducted fairly easily, making all accomplishments and challenges visible, as illustrated in Figure 1.

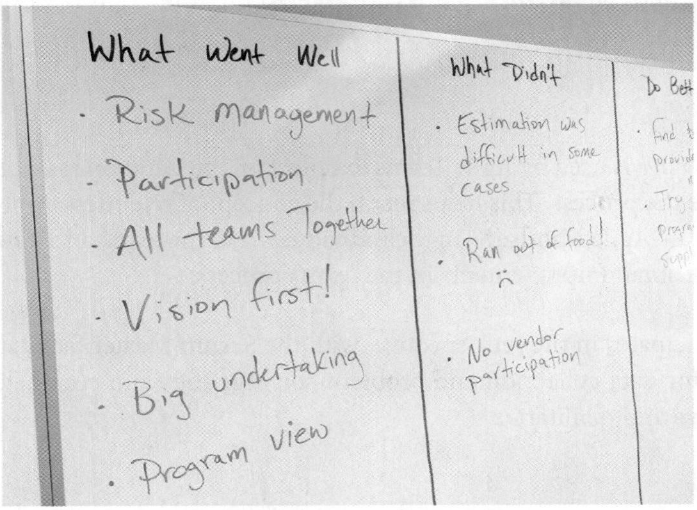

*Figure 1. One team's retrospective results*

## Agenda

A sample iteration retrospective agenda follows:

**Part 1: Quantitative**
Did the team meet the iteration goals (yes/no)? Collect and review the agreed-to iteration metrics.

**Part 2: Qualitative**
Review the improvement stories from the previous iteration. Were they all accomplished? If not, what do we want to do about them?

For this iteration, analyze:

- What went well?
- What didn't go so well?
- What we can do better next time?

## Guidelines

Below are some tips for holding a successful iteration retro:

- Keep the meeting timeboxed to an hour or less. Remember, it will come up every two weeks and the goal is small, continuous improvement steps.
- Pick only *one or two* things that can be done better next time and add them as improvement stories, targeted for the next iteration
- Make sure everyone speaks
- The Scrum Master should spend time preparing the retrospective, as it is a primary vehicle for improvement
- Focus on items the team can address, not on how others can improve
- Make sure improvement stories from the previous iteration are reviewed at the beginning of the quantitative review to show progress
- This is a private meeting for the team and should be limited to team members only

---

**LEARN MORE**

[1] Derby, Esther and Diana Larson. *Agile Retrospectives: Making Good Teams Great.* Pragmatic Bookshelf, 2006.

[2] Leffingwell, Dean. *Scaling Software Agility: Best Practices for Large Enterprises.* Addison-Wesley, 2007, Chapter 15, "Regular Reflection and Adaptation."

# Stories

*Stories act as a "pidgin language," where both sides (users and developers) can agree enough to work together effectively.*

—Bill Wake, co-inventor of eXtreme Programming

## Abstract

*Stories* are the primary artifact used to define system behavior in Agile development. Stories are not requirements; they are short, simple descriptions of a small piece of desired functionality, usually told from the user's perspective and written in the user's language. Each is intended to support implementation of a small, vertical slice of system functionality, supporting highly incremental development. In Agile development, stories largely replace the traditional requirements specifications, or they're used later to compile any mandated, traditional requirements documentation.

Stories provide just enough information for the intent to be understood by both business and technical people. They are a "promise for a conversation," intended to serve as a focal point for a more thorough discussion of the intended behavior and impact. Details are deferred until the story is ready to be implemented. Through acceptance criteria, stories get more specific as they are implemented, helping to ensure system quality. Acceptance criteria can be captured and automated in acceptance tests. These tests confirm that the functionality has been implemented properly, both when the story is written and later, as the Solution evolves. This is a critical element of SAFe Built-in-Quality practices.

*Enabler stories* are another type of story. They do not describe system functionality; rather, they are used by the teams to bring visibility to the work items needed in support of exploration, architecture, and infrastructure.

## Details

SAFe describes a four-tier hierarchy of artifacts that describe functional system behavior: Epic > Capability > Feature > *Story*. These, along with Nonfunctional Requirements (NFRs), are the Agile requirements (system behavioral) artifacts that are used to define system and Solution Intent, model system behavior, and build up the Architectural Runway.

Epics, capabilities, features, and Enablers are used to describe the larger intended behavior, but the detailed implementation work is described via *stories*, which constitute the Team Backlog. Most stories arise from business and enabler features in the Program Backlog, but others emerge from the team's local context.

Each story is a small, independent behavior that can be implemented incrementally and that provides some value to the user or the Solution; it is a vertical slice of functionality to help ensure that every Iteration delivers new value. To accomplish this, stories are split (see below) as necessary so they can be completed in a single iteration.

Initially, stories are typically written on an index card or sticky note. The physical nature of the card creates a tangible relationship between the team, the story, and the user and helps engage the entire team in story writing. They have a kinesthetic element as well; they help visualize work and can be readily placed on a wall or table, rearranged in sequence, passed around, and even handed off when necessary. They help teams better understand scope ("Wow, look at all these stories I'm about to sign up for") and progress ("Look at all the stories we accomplished in this iteration").

While anyone can write stories, approving stories into the team backlog and accepting them into the system baseline is the responsibility of the Product Owner. Of course, stickies don't scale well across the Enterprise, so stories often move quickly into Agile project management tooling. There are two types of stories in SAFe, user stories and enabler stories, as described below.

## Sources of Stories

In SAFe, stories are generally driven by splitting business features and enabler features, as Figure 1 illustrates.

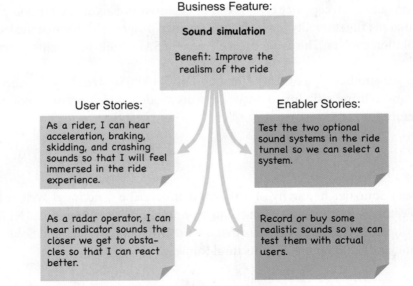

*Figure 1. Example of a business feature split into stories*

## User Stories

User stories are the primary means of expressing needed functionality. They largely replace the traditional requirements specification. (In some cases, however, they serve to understand and develop functionality that is later recorded in such a document in support of compliance, traceability, or other needs.)

User stories are *value centric* in that they focus on the user, not the system, as the subject of interest. In support of this, the recommended form of expression is the "user voice form," as follows:

**As a** <user role> **I can** <activity> **so that** <business value>

By using this format, the teams are constantly guided to understand *who* is using the system, *what* specifically they are doing with it, and *why* they are doing it. Applying the user voice routinely tends to increase the team's domain competence; they come to better understand the real business needs of their user. Figure 2 provides an example:

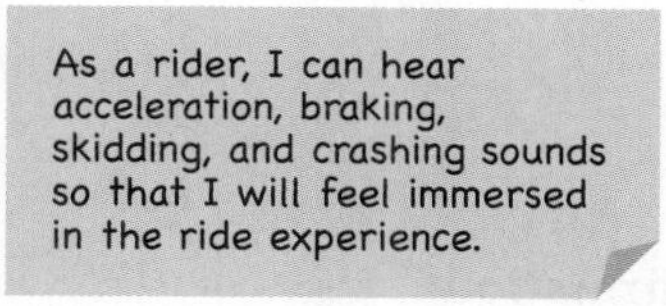

> As a rider, I can hear
> acceleration, braking,
> skidding, and crashing sounds
> so that I will feel immersed
> in the ride experience.

*Figure 2. Example user story in user voice form*

While the user story voice is the common case, not every system interacts with an end user. Sometimes the "user" is a *device* (example: printer) or other *system* (example: transaction server). In this case, the story can take on the form illustrated in Figure 3.

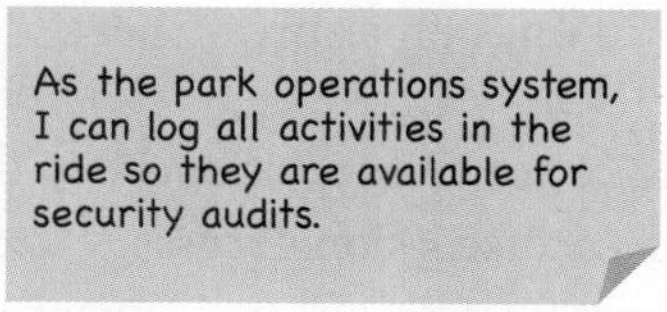

> As the park operations system,
> I can log all activities in the
> ride so they are available for
> security audits.

*Figure 3. Example of a user story with a system as a user*

## Enabler Stories

Teams also need to develop technical functionality that is needed to implement a number of different user stories, or support other components of the system. In this case, the story may not directly touch any end user. These are *enabler stories*, and they can support *exploration, architecture,* or *infrastructure,* just like all other enablers. In these cases, the story can be expressed in technical rather than user-centric language, as Figure 4 illustrates.

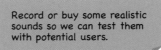

*Figure 4. Example enabler story*

Enabler stories may include any of the following:

- Refactoring and spikes (as traditionally defined in XP)

- Building or improving development/deployment infrastructure

- Running jobs that require human interaction (example: *Index 1 million web pages* )

- Creating required product or component configurations for different purposes

- Performing special types of system qualities verification (vulnerability testing, etc.)

And, of course, enabler stories are demonstrated just like user stories, typically via showing the artifacts produced or via UI, stub, or mock.

## Writing Good Stories

### The 3Cs: Card, Conversation, Confirmation

Ron Jeffries, one of the inventors of XP, is credited with describing the "3Cs" of a story:

**Card** represents the capture of the *statement of intent* of the user story on an index card, sticky note, or tool. The use of index cards provides a physical relationship between the team and the story. The card size physically limits the length of the story and, thereby, too-early specificity of system behavior. Cards also help the team "feel" upcoming scope, as there is something materially different about holding 10 cards in one's hand versus looking at 10 lines on a spreadsheet.

**Conversation** represents a "promise for a conversation" between the team, Customer/user, the Product Owner, and other stakeholders. This is the discussion necessary to determine the more detailed behavior required to implement the intent. The conversation may spawn additional specificity in the form of attachments to the user story (mock-up, prototype, spreadsheet, algorithm, timing diagram, etc). The conversation spans all steps in the story life cycle:

- Backlog refinement

- Planning

- Implementation

- Demonstration

Conversations provide shared context that cannot be achieved via formal documentation. It drives away requirements ambiguity via concrete examples of functionality. The conversation helps uncover gaps in scenarios and nonfunctional requirements. Some teams also use the confirmation section of the story card to write down what they will demo for the story.

**Confirmation** of the *acceptance criteria* provides the precision necessary to ensure that the story is implemented correctly and covers the relevant functional and nonfunctional requirements. Figure 5 provides an example.

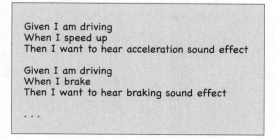

```
Given I am driving
When I speed up
Then I want to hear acceleration sound effect

Given I am driving
When I brake
Then I want to hear braking sound effect

. . .
```

*Figure 5. Story acceptance criteria*

Agile Teams automate acceptance tests wherever possible, often in a business-readable, domain-specific language, thereby creating the "automatically executable specification and test" of the code. Automation also provides the ability to quickly regression-test the system, which enhances Continuous Integration, refactoring, and maintenance.

**Invest in Good Stories**

People often use the mnemonic INVEST, developed by Bill Wake, to provide a reminder of the things that make a good story:

- **I** – Independent (of all other stories)

- **N** – Negotiable (a flexible statement of intent, not a contract)

- **V** – Valuable (providing a valuable vertical slice to the Customer)

- **E** – Estimable (small and negotiable)

- **S** – Small (fits within an iteration)

- **T** – Testable (understood enough to know how to test it)

Refer to [1] and [2] for more information.

## Estimating Stories

SAFe ScrumXP Agile Teams use story points and estimating poker [2 and 3] to estimate their work. A story point is a *singular* number that represents a combination of things:

- Volume – How much is there?

- Complexity – How hard is it?

- Knowledge – What's known?

- Uncertainty – What's not known?

Story points are relative; they are *not* connected to any specific unit of measure. The size (effort) of each story is estimated relative to the smallest story, which is arbitrarily assigned a size of 1. SAFe applies the modified Fibonacci sequence (1, 2, 3, 5, 8, 13, 20, 40, 100) to reflect the inherent uncertainty in estimating, especially large numbers (e.g. 20, 40, 100, etc.) [2].

### Estimating Poker

Agile Teams often use "estimating poker," which combines expert opinion, analogy, and disaggregation for quick but reliable estimates (note that there are a number of other methods used as well). The rules of estimating poker are:

- Participants include all team members

- Each estimator is given a deck of cards with 1, 2, 3, 5, 8, 13, 20, 40, 100, ∞, and ?

- The Product Owner participates but does not estimate

- The Scrum Master participates but does not estimate; an exception is if he or she is doing actual development work

- For each backlog item to be estimated, the Product Owner reads the description of the story

- Questions are asked and answered

- Each estimator privately selects an estimating card representing his or her estimate

- All cards are simultaneously turned over so that all participants can see each estimate

- High and low estimators explain their estimates

- After discussion, each estimator re-estimates by selecting a card

- The estimates will likely converge; if not, repeat the process

Some amount of preliminary design discussion is appropriate. However, spending too much time on design discussions is often wasted effort. The real value of estimation poker is to come to a common agreement on the scope of a story. And it's also fun!

**Velocity**

The team's *velocity* for an iteration is equal to the sum of the points for all the stories completed (that have met their Definition of Done) in the iteration. Knowing velocity assists with planning and is a key factor in limiting WIP, as teams don't take on more stories than their prior velocity would allow. Velocity is also used to estimate how long it takes to deliver larger epics, features, capabilities, and enablers, which are also estimated in story points.

**Common Starting Baseline for Estimation**

In standard Scrum, each team's story point estimating—and the resultant velocity—is a local and independent concern; the fact that a small team might estimate in such a way that they have a velocity of 50 while a larger team has a velocity of 12 is of no concern to anyone.

In SAFe, however, story point velocity must have a common starting baseline, so that estimates for features or epics that require the support of many teams are based on rational economics. In order to achieve this, SAFe teams start down a path on which a story point for one team is roughly the same as a story point for another, so that, with adjustments for economics of location (U.S., Europe, India, China, etc.), work can be estimated and prioritized based on converting story points to cost. After all, there is no way to determine the return on potential investment if there is no comparable "currency."

The method for getting to a common starting baseline for *stories* and *velocity* is as follows:

- For every developer-tester on the team, give the team eight points (adjust for part-timers)

- Subtract one point for every team member vacation day and holiday

- Find a small story that would take about a half-day to code and a half-day to test and validate. Call it a one (1).

- Estimate every other story relative to that one (1)

Example: Assuming a six (6)-person team composed of three (3) developers, two (2) testers, and one PO, with no vacations or holidays, the estimated initial velocity = 5 * 8 points = 40 points/iteration. (Note: Adjusting a bit lower may be necessary if one of the developers and testers is also the Scrum Master.)

In this way, story points are somewhat comparable to an ideal developer day, and all teams estimate size of work in a common fashion, so management can thereby fairly quickly estimate the cost for a story point for teams in a specific region. Then they have a meaningful way to figure out the cost estimate for an upcoming feature or epic.

*Note: There is no need to recalibrate team estimation or velocity after that point. It is just a common starting baseline.*

While teams will tend to increase their velocity over time—and that is a good thing—in fact the number tends to remain fairly stable. A team's velocity is far more affected by changing team size and technical context than by productivity changes. And if necessary, financial planners can adjust the cost per story point a bit. Experience shows that this is a minor concern, compared to the wildly differing velocities that teams of comparable size may have if they don't set a common starting baseline. That simply doesn't work at enterprise scale, because decisions can't be based on economics that way.

## Splitting Stories

Smaller stories allow for faster, more reliable implementation, since small things go through a system faster, reducing variability and managing risk. Splitting bigger stories into smaller ones is thus a mandatory survival skill for every Agile Team, and it is both the art and the science of incremental development. Ten ways to split stories are highlighted in [1]. A summary of these techniques is included below.

1. Work flow steps
2. Business rule variations
3. Major effort
4. Simple/complex
5. Variations in data
6. Data entry methods
7. Deferred system qualities
8. Operations (example: Create Read Update Delete, or CRUD)
9. Use-case scenarios
10. Break-out spike

Figure 6 illustrates an example of #9, splitting by use-case scenarios.

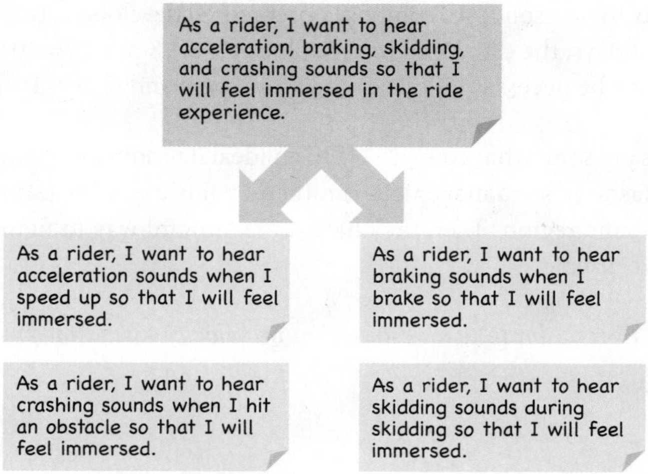

*Figure 6. An example of splitting a large story into smaller stories*

## Stories in the SAFe Requirements Model

As described in the SAFe Requirements Model, the framework applies an extensive set of artifacts and relationships to manage the definition and testing of complex systems in a Lean and Agile fashion. Figure 7 illustrates the role of stories in this larger picture.

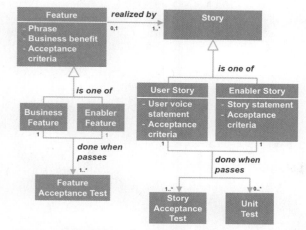

*Figure 7. Stories in the SAFe Requirements Model*

Figure 7 illustrates how stories are often, but not always, spawned by new features, and how each has an associated story acceptance test. Further, in XP and SAFe ScrumXP, each story should have a unit test associated with it. The unit test serves primarily to ensure that implementation of the story is correct. In addition, as unit tests are readily able to be automated, this is a critical starting point for test automation, as described in the "Test-First" article.

Note: Figure 7 uses UML notation to represent the relationships between the objects: zero to many (0,1), one to many (1..*), one to one (1) and so on.

---

**LEARN MORE**

[1] Leffingwell, Dean. *Agile Software Requirements: Lean Requirements Practices for Teams, Programs, and the Enterprise.* Addison-Wesley, 2011, chapter 6.

[2] Cohn, Mike. *User Stories Applied: For Agile Software Development.* Addison-Wesley, 2004.

# Iteration Goals

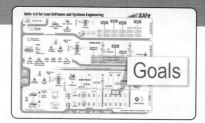

*Clarity adorns profound thoughts.*

   —Luc de Clapiers

## Abstract

*Iteration Goals* are a high-level summary of the business and technical goals that the Agile Team and Product Owner agree to accomplish in an Iteration. Iteration goals are integral to the effective coordination of an Agile Release Train (ART) as a self-organizing, self-managing team of teams. They help align the individual team members and the Product Owner to a common mission for the iteration, align the individual teams to the Program PI Objectives, and provide context for understanding and addressing cross-team dependencies. Finally, they provide a simple communication protocol between the teams, management, and Business Owners, so that all are working toward a common purpose and management is continuously apprised of the work in process.

Whether the teams apply Scrum or Kanban, iteration goals provide program stakeholders, management, and Agile Teams with a common language with which to maintain alignment, manage dependencies, and make any necessary adjustments during the execution of the Program Increment (PI).

## Details

As described in the "Iteration Planning" article, the planning process produces three outputs:

1. The Iteration backlog, consisting of the Stories committed to the iteration
2. A statement of *Iteration Goals*, as shown in Figure 1
3. A commitment by the Agile Team to the work needed to achieve the goals

**Iteration Goals:**

1. Finalize and push last name search and first name morphology

2. Index 80% of remaining data

3. Other stories:
   - Establish search replication validation protocol
   - Refactor artifact dictionary schema

*Figure 1. One team's iteration goals*

Iteration goals often reflect the following:

- Features, feature slices, or feature aspects, such as research, necessary infrastructure, etc.

- Business or technical Milestones

- Architectural, technical, or infrastructure effort

- Routine jobs

- Other commitments, such as maintenance, documentation, etc.

Iteration goals are achieved via completion of backlog items, but it may not be necessary to complete every story to meet the goals of the iteration. In other words, the goals for the iteration trump any particular story. On occasion, it may even be necessary to add unanticipated stories to achieve the goals of the iteration.

## Why Iteration Goals?

Iteration goals are mandatory in Scrum and SAFe (Scrum calls them the *sprint goals*). Agile Teams do their work via stories that are necessarily small enough to be completed in a single iteration. The ability to split user value into small, vertical, testable stories is essential to agility, but it can be difficult to *see the forest for the trees*. In the context of the Agile Release Train (ART), iteration goals help in understanding and maintaining a larger view of what the team intends to accomplish in each iteration, and what it intends to demo in the upcoming System Demo. They are fundamental to *transparency*, *alignment*, and *program execution*, three of the four Core Values of SAFe. Simply, committing to complete a set of stories in an iteration is insufficient; the team must be constantly looking at the business value of each iteration and be able to communicate that value in business terms to the Business Owners, management, and other stakeholders.

Iteration goals provide value in three aspects, which constitute a comprehensive approach to helping the teams and ART stay in alignment and continually commit to a common purpose and mission, as described in the following.

### Align Team Members to a Common Purpose

The execution of an iteration is a fast and furious process, and two weeks go by very quickly. Iteration goals help the team and Product Owner come to initial agreement on the business value they intend to deliver, align to Team and Program PI Objectives, and help ground the team to their agreed-to purpose, as Figure 2 illustrates.

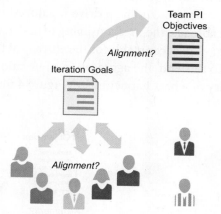

*Figure 2. Iteration goals help align the team*

### Align Program Teams to Common PI Objectives and Manage Dependencies

SAFe teams are not islands of agility. Rather, they are integral parts of a larger Program Level context and purpose. As such, each team must communicate the intent of upcoming iterations to the other teams and to the Release Train Engineer (RTE) so that they can ensure that they remain in alignment to the program PI objectives. In addition, individual team iteration goals provide the necessary context for dependency discovery and resolution, as Figure 3 illustrates.

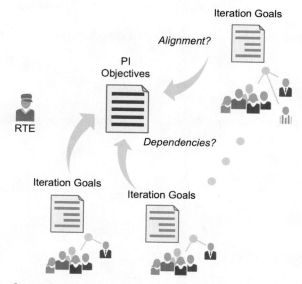

*Figure 3. Iteration goals align teams to PI objectives and to each other, and help identify dependencies*

## Provide Continuous Management Information

Scaling to the program level while remaining Lean and Agile is dependent on building self-managing, self-organizing Agile Teams. These teams should require very little management interdiction or daily supervision. In that way, managers can manage *up* and *across*, rather than *down*. This creates an empowered, leaner organization in which management can handle more responsibility and use their organization skills to eliminate impediments and help drive organizational improvements. However, management cannot and should not abrogate their responsibility to understand what the teams are doing and why they are doing it, for they are still accountable for the efficacy of the development organization and the value delivery outcomes. To this end, the aggregation of iteration goals for a train provides a simple, textual, fortnightly summary of what's happening, as Figure 4 illustrates.

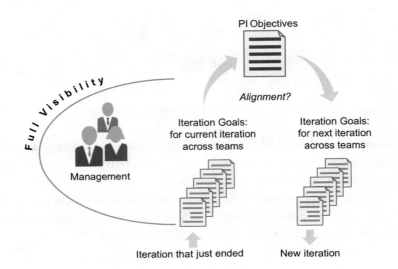

*Figure 4. Iteration goals provide visibility and communication with management*

## LEARN MORE

[1] Leffingwell, Dean. *Agile Software Requirements: Lean Requirements Practices for Teams, Programs, and the Enterprise*. Addison-Wesley, 2011.

# Built-In Quality

*Build incrementally with fast, integrated learning cycles*
  —*SAFe Principle #4*

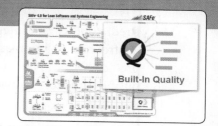

## Abstract

*Built-In Quality* is one of the four Core Values of SAFe. The Enterprise's ability to deliver new functionality with the *fastest sustainable lead time* and to be able to react to rapidly changing business environments is dependent on Solution quality. But built-in quality is not unique to SAFe. Rather, it is a core principle of the Lean-Agile Mindset, where it helps avoid the cost of delays associated with recall, rework, and defect fixing. The Agile Manifesto is focused on quality as well: "Continuous attention to technical excellence and good design enhances agility" [1]. There can be no ambiguity about the value of built-in quality in large-scale systems. It is mandatory. To this end, this article describes quality practices for software, firmware, and hardware.

The software practices—many of which are inspired and described by eXtreme Programming (XP)—help Agile software teams ensure that the solutions they build are high quality and can readily adapt to change. The collaborative nature of these practices, along with a focus on frequent validation, create an emergent culture in which engineering and craftsmanship are key business enablers.

With respect to firmware and hardware, the goal is the same, but the physics and economics—and therefore the practices—are somewhat different. They include a more intense focus on modeling and simulation, as well as more exploratory early Iterations, more design verification, and more frequent system-level integration.

## Details

When Enterprises need to respond to change, software and systems built on good technical foundations are easier to change and adapt. For large systems this is even more critical, as the cumulative effect of even minor defects and wrong assumptions can create unacceptable consequences.

Achieving high-quality systems is serious work that requires ongoing training and commitment, but the investment is warranted by many business benefits:

- **Higher Customer satisfaction** – Low defect-density products and services provide higher levels of Customer satisfaction, higher safety, better return on investment, and higher confidence for the business

- **Predictability and integrity of the development organization** – Without reliable control over Solution quality, it is impossible to plan new business functionality predictably, or to understand development velocity. This creates a lack of trust in the business, reduces individual pride of craftsmanship, and lowers morale.

- **Scalability** – When the components clearly express design intent, exhibit simplicity, and have supporting integration and test infrastructure, adding more teams and functionality will result in more business value delivered. Otherwise, adding more developers and testers slows the Enterprise down and creates unacceptably high variability in quality and Release commitments.

- **Velocity, agility, and system performance** – Higher quality fosters better maintainability and enhances the ability to add new business functionality more quickly. It also enhances the team's ability to maintain and enhance critical Nonfunctional Requirements, including performance, scalability, security, and reliability.

- **Ability to innovate** – Innovation occurs at the confluence of smart, motivated people and the environment in which they operate. High quality creates a fertile technical environment where new ideas can be easily prototyped, tested, and demoed.

The sections below summarize recommended practices for achieving *Built-in Quality* of software, firmware, and hardware.

## Software

SAFe is built on a decades-long evolution of better engineering practices, driven in large part by the success of innovative Lean and Agile methods. When it comes to software engineering, XP practices have led the way [2]. In addition to the key role that Agile Architecture plays in assuring system-level quality, SAFe describes additional critical Lean-Agile software engineering practices that help teams achieve the highest-level quality. The sections below provide a summary of these practices, two of which—Continuous Integration and Test-First are covered in more depth separately in this book.

### Continuous Integration

*Continuous Integration* (CI) is the software practice of merging the code from each developer's work space into a single main branch of code, multiple times per day. In that way, all developers on a program are constantly working with the latest version of the code, and errors and assumptions made among developers and among teams are discovered immediately. This helps avoid the risk of deferred system-level integration issues and their impact on system quality and program predictability.

Continuous integration requires specialty infrastructure and tools, including build servers and automated test frameworks. But even more important is the cultural mandate that *individuals and teams give themselves credit only for fully integrated and tested software.*

In SAFe, teams perform local integration at least daily, but equally important is the responsibility to integrate the full *system* and run regression tests as necessary, to ensure that the *system* is evolving in the intended manner. Initially that may not be feasible every day, so a reasonable initial goal may be to achieve full system-level integration at least one or two times per Iteration. This provides the baseline needed for a successful biweekly System Demo.

The "Continuous Integration" companion article offers more about this topic, particularly with respect to system- and Solution-level CI.

### Test-First

*Test-First* is a philosophy that encourages teams to reason deeply about system behavior prior to implementing the code. This increases the productivity of coding and improves its fitness for use. It also creates a more comprehensive test strategy, whereby the understanding of system requirements is converted into a series of tests, typically prior to developing the code itself.

Test-first methods can be further divided into *Test-Driven Development (TDD)* and *Acceptance Test-Driven Development (ATDD)*. Both are supported by test automation, which is required in support of continuous integration, team velocity, and development effectiveness.

In *Test-Driven Development*, developers write an automated unit test first, run the test to observe the failure, and then write the minimum code necessary to pass the test. Primarily applicable at the code method or unit (technical) level, this ensures that a test actually exists and tends to prevent gold plating and feature creep of writing code that is more complex than necessary to meet the stated test case. This also helps requirements persist as automated tests and remain up to date.

*Acceptance Test-Driven Development* is an advanced discipline in which the criteria for acceptable system behavior, as specified by the Product Owner, is converted to an automated acceptance test that can be run repeatedly to ensure continued conformance as the system evolves. ATDD helps keep the team focused on necessary system-level behavior that is observable to Customers, and it gives the teams clear success criteria.

The companion "Test-First" article offers more on this topic.

## Refactoring

*Refactoring* "is a disciplined technique for restructuring an existing body of code, altering its internal structure without changing its external behavior" [3]. As Agile eschews "Big Up-Front Design" (BUFD) and "welcomes changing requirements, even late in development" [1], this implies that the current code base is amenable to change as new business functionality is required. In order to maintain this resiliency, teams continuously refactor code in a series of small steps to provide a solid foundation for future development. Neglecting refactoring in favor of "always new functionality" will quickly create a system that is rigid and unmaintainable, and ultimately it drives increasingly poor economic outcomes.

Refactoring is a key enabler of emergent design and is a necessary and integral part of Agile. More guidance on refactoring is presented in the companion "Refactoring" article.

## Pair Work

As opposed to *Pair Work*, pair programming—a mandatory practice in XP—involves two programmers working at a single workstation. One person codes while the observer reviews, inspects, and adds value to the coding process. These roles are switched throughout a paired session. Before a line of code is written, the pair discusses what needs to be done and gains a shared understanding of the requirements, design, and how to test the functionality. The observer inspects the work, makes suggestions about how to improve the code, and points out potential errors. Peer review is done in real time and is integral.

Pair programming is integral to XP, but it is also controversial—some people believe that pairing increases costs because two people are working on the same lines of code. And there can be interpersonal and cultural challenges as well.

For many, pair programming is too extreme. However, in practice, there are a number of different styles of pairing work done by Agile Teams. Each has value on its own, and many can be used in combination. Some teams follow pair programming standards for all code development, as prescribed by XP. Others pair developers and testers on a Story; each reviews the other's work as the story moves to completion. Still others prefer more spontaneous pairing, with developers pairing for critical code segments, refactoring of legacy code, development of interface definition, and system-level integration challenges. Pair work is also a great foundation for refactoring, CI, test automation, and collective ownership.

## Collective Ownership

*Collective Ownership* "encourages everyone to contribute new ideas to all segments of the project. Any developer can change any line of code to add functionality, fix bugs, improve designs, or refactor. No one person becomes a bottleneck for changes" [4]. Collective ownership is particularly critical in SAFe, as big systems have big code bases, and it's less likely that the original developer is still on the team or program. Even when that person is on the team, waiting for one individual to make a change is a hand-off, and a certain delay.

Implementing collective ownership at scale requires following proven, agreed-to coding standards across the program; embracing simplicity in design; revealing intent in code constructs; and building interfaces that are resilient to changing system behaviors.

## Firmware and Hardware

But coding aside, no one can scale low-quality components or systems, either. Hardware elements—electronics, electrical, fluidics, optics, mechanical, packaging, thermal, and many more—are a lot less "soft"; they are more difficult and expensive to change. As illustrated in Figure 1 [5], errors and unproven assumptions in firmware and hardware can introduce a much higher cost of change and rework over time.

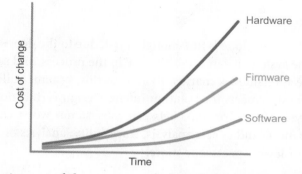

*Figure 1. Relative cost of change over time for software, firmware, and hardware*

As described in the sections below, this higher cost of later change drives Lean developers of cyber-physical systems to a number of practices that ensure built-in quality during solution development.

**Exploratory Early Iterations**

As highlighted in reference [6], even when building a Harley-Davidson—where it takes a fairly complete team to road test a new motorcycle—more frequent design cycles are the systems builders' tool to accelerate knowledge and reduce the risk and cost of errors discovered later. In this respect, SAFe treats firmware and hardware in the same way it does software; the cadence of iterations and Program Increments, and the expectations, are largely the same. However, the early iterations are particularly critical because the cost of change has not yet reached the higher levels. Lean systems builders apply "softer" tool systems to iterate more quickly, including:

- Agile Architecture
- Model-Based Systems Engineering
- Set-Based Design

### Frequent System-Level Integration and Testing

*Continuous* integration is a worthy and achievable goal for many software solutions. However, it is difficult to apply or even envision in cyber-physical systems, as many physical components—molds, mechanisms, fabricated parts, and more—evolve more slowly and cannot be integrated and evaluated every day. But that cannot be an excuse for late and problematic integration.

After all, eventually all the different components and subsystems—software, firmware, hardware, and everything else—must collaborate to provide effective solution-level behaviors. And the sooner, the better. To this end, Lean systems builders try for *early and frequent integration and testing* of subsystems and systems. This typically requires an increased investment in development, staging, and test infrastructure.

### Design Verification

However, integration and testing alone is not enough. First, due to the dependencies of availability of various components of the system, it can occur too late in the process; and second, it cannot possibly evaluate all possible usage and failure scenarios. To address this, systems builders perform design verification to ensure that a design meets the Solution Intent. Design verification can include steps such as specification and analysis of requirements between subsystems; worst-case analysis of tolerances and performance; failure mode and effects analysis; traceability; analysis of thermal, environmental, and other deployed system-level aspects; and more.

While many of these practices are important in the software domain as well, the cost of change is lower there, so not as much needs to be known in advance of commitment to a design option. With respect to firmware and hardware, however, more up-front design considerations and specifications work is warranted.

---

### LEARN MORE

[1] Manifesto for Agile Software Development. www.AgileManifesto.org.

[2] Beck, Kent, and Cynthia Andres. *Extreme Programming Explained: Embrace Change*. Addison-Wesley, 2004.

[3] Fowler, Martin. Refactoring.com.

[4] http://www.extremeprogramming.org/rules/collective.html.

[5] Rubin, Ken. http://www.innolution.com/blog/agile-in-a-hardware-firmware-environment-draw-the-cost-of-change-curve.

[6] Oosterwal, Dantar P. *The Lean Machine: How Harley-Davidson Drove Top-Line Growth and Profitability with Revolutionary Lean Product Development*. Amacom, 2010.

# Part 4
# The Program Level

[ scaledagileframework.com/**program-level**

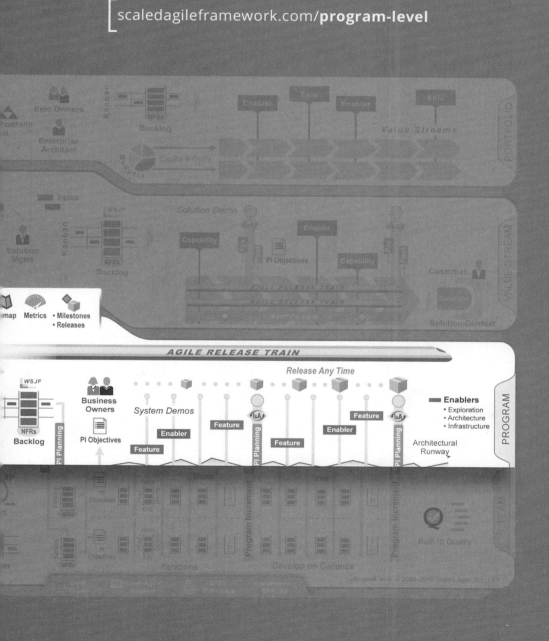

# Introduction to the Program Level

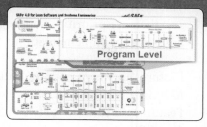

*A system must be managed. It will not manage itself. Left to themselves, components become selfish, competitive, independent profit centers, and thus destroy the system. . . . The secret is cooperation between components toward the aim of the organization.*

   —W. Edwards Deming

## Abstract

The *Program Level* is where development teams and other resources are applied to some important, ongoing development mission. SAFe program level teams, roles, and activities are organized around the Agile Release Train (ART) metaphor, a team of Agile Teams that delivers a continuous flow of incremental releases of value. Agile Release Trains are virtual organizations formed to span functional boundaries, eliminate unnecessary handoffs and steps, and accelerate the delivery of value via implementation of SAFe Lean-Agile principles and practices.

While it is called the program level, ARTs are generally very long-lived and therefore have a more persistent self-organization, structure, and mission than a traditional "program," which more classically has a start and an end date, as well as temporarily assigned resources. It is the long-lived, flow-based, and self-organizing nature of the ART that powers the SAFe portfolio.

## Details

Value in SAFe is delivered by long-lived Agile Release Trains, each of which realizes a portion of a Value Stream (or, in some cases, the entire value stream). They deliver value incrementally in Program Increments (PIs) of 8 to 12 weeks; each PI is a multiple-Iteration timebox during which a significant, valuable increment of the system is developed. Each ART is composed of 5 to 12 Agile Teams (50 – 125+ people) and includes the roles and infrastructure necessary to deliver fully tested, working, system-level software. Many release trains are virtual, spanning organizational and geographic boundaries; others follow a line of business or product line management reporting structure.

## Managing the Flow of Value

A primary responsibility of the *Program Level* is the discovery, definition, and development of Features and Enablers that are required by the business to realize the Vision and Roadmap. To manage this flow of work, and to make sure it is visible to all stakeholders, SAFe provides a Program Kanban system. This system is used to ensure that features are reasoned and analyzed prior to reaching the PI boundary, then are prioritized appropriately, and that acceptance criteria have been established to guide a high-fidelity implementation.

Features are maintained and prioritized in the Program Backlog. Upon implementation, they are sized to fit in a program increment such that each PI delivers new functionality with conceptual integrity. Features, in turn, lie between Stories, which are handled by a single team within an iteration, and Capabilities, which are Value Stream Level services that can span ARTs.

## Key Roles

Agile Release Trains are self-managing and self-organizing teams of Agile Teams that plan, commit, and execute together. However, a train does not create or steer itself. It needs guidance and direction so that the teams are aligned to a common mission, operate under architectural and User Experience guidance, and are assisted in delivery by a Release Train Engineer (RTE), the chief Scrum Master for the train. Figure 1 illustrates this "troika" of key roles.

*Figure 1. Program management, content management, and architecture troika*

These three primary functions help ensure successful execution of the vision and roadmap initiatives at the program level:

- **Program Execution** – The Release Train Engineer is a servant leader and the chief Scrum Master for the train. The RTE facilitates optimizing the flow of value through the program using various mechanisms, such as the Program Kanban, Inspect & Adapt workshop, PI Planning, and more.

- **Content Management** – Product Management is the internal voice of the Customer and works with Customers and Product Owners to understand and communicate their needs, define system features, and participate in validation. They are responsible for the program backlog.

- **Technology** – The System Architect/Engineer is an individual or small cross-discipline team that truly applies systems thinking. They define the overall architecture for the system, help define Nonfunctional Requirements, determine the major elements and subsystems, and help define the interfaces and collaborations among them.

In larger value streams, these roles also participate in Pre- and Post-PI Planning for the Solution.

## The Spanning Palette

There are number of additional icons indicated on this level; they are located at the conjunction of the value stream and program level on the Big Picture. This is called the "spanning palette" and is illustrated in Figure 2.

*Figure 2. Spanning palette*

Each of these artifacts and roles contributes to the ART and program level, as are defined in the "Vision," "Roadmap," "Metrics," "Milestones," "Releases," "DevOps," "System Team," "Release Management," "Shared Services," and "User Experience" articles. They span the levels, because many of these artifacts are also useful at the value stream level. Clicking on the right-hand "Collapse" button on the Big Picture results in hiding the value stream level, causing the palette to appear between the portfolio and program levels and indicating that it can be useful to have some or all of these elements play a role at the portfolio level, when applicable. This is an essential part of the configurability and modularity of the framework. When it comes to these items, the SAFe Enterprise can apply all that are needed, and no more, at any of the three levels.

## Connection to the Value Stream and Portfolio

Programs have a bidirectional connection to the value stream and/or portfolio. The program vision and roadmap provide a view of the solutions and capabilities to be developed, reflecting Customer and stakeholder needs and the approaches that are proposed to address those needs.

However, in a multi-ART value stream, the development of the program vision and roadmap are not created in isolation. They are done in concert with one another and must be synchronized with the solution, typically at PI boundaries. Program Portfolio Management and Product and Solution Management for each train collaborate on the development of the respective roadmaps and visions.

## Mixing Traditional Programs with ARTs

In enterprises transitioning to SAFe, and in cases where Supplier development practices are outside the control of the enterprise, traditional (waterfall) programs may still exist. Therefore SAFe Program Portfolio Management provides a governance model that can be applied to governing ARTs along with traditional, stage-gated programs. Guidance articles for this mixed mode of operation are provided in the "Guidance" section at www.scaledagileframework.com. (See the "Mixing Agile and Waterfall Development" article.)

---

**LEARN MORE**

[1] Leffingwell, Dean. *Agile Software Requirements: Lean Requirements Practices for Teams, Programs, and the Enterprise.* Addison-Wesley, 2011.

# Agile Release Train

*Principle of Alignment: There is more value created with overall alignment than local excellence.*

*—Donald Reinertsen*

## Abstract

The *Agile Release Train* (ART) is the primary value delivery construct in SAFe. Each ART is a long-lived, self-organizing team of Agile Teams, a virtual organization (5 – 12 teams) that plans, commits, and executes together. ARTs are organized around the Enterprise's significant Value Streams and live solely to realize the promise of that value by building Solutions that deliver benefit to the end user.

The ART aligns teams to a common mission via a single Vision, Roadmap, and Program Backlog. Program Increments (PIs) provide a development timebox (default 10 weeks) that uses cadence and synchronization to facilitate planning, limit WIP, provide for aggregation of newsworthy value, and ensure consistent retrospectives. PI timeboxes also provide a quantum unit of thinking for Portfolio Level consideration and roadmapping. Each train has the dedicated people and resources necessary to continuously define, build, and test valuable and evaluable capabilities in every Iteration. Trains provide architectural, engineering, and User Experience guidance to help teams build systems that support current and upcoming user and business needs.

## Details

SAFe Program Level teams, roles, and activities are organized around an *Agile Release Train*, a team of Agile Teams that delivers a continuous flow of incremental releases of value in a Value Stream.

Development of the Solution occurs on a standard cadence, but train teams can release at any time, as described in the "Develop on Cadence, Release Any Time" article. With respect to development cadence, the Big Picture illustrates a PI Planning session followed by four *development* Iterations and concludes with one Innovation and Planning (IP) Iteration. SAFe calls this timebox a Program Increment.

This PI cadence, as illustrated on the Big Picture, is suggestive but arbitrary, and there is no fixed rule for how many iterations are in a PI, nor for how much time should be reserved for IP iterations.

Many Enterprises choose to release software on the PI boundary, but releasing can also be independent of this cadence; it is left to the judgment of each train and/or value stream. Moreover, for larger systems, releasing is not an all-or-nothing event, and different parts of the solution (subsystems, services, etc.) can be released at different times, as described in the "Release" article.

Empowering individual teams to focus on rapid value delivery unlocks the raw energy, intrinsic motivation, and innovation that can be constrained by command-and-control models. However, that alone is not enough, as the teams will naturally tend toward *local optimization*. Teams will do what they can to deliver requirements to their Customer constituency, but it is hard for them to take a global view. But since the highest benefit comes from *global optimization*, the ART *helps* teams align to a common direction and achieve far more *force* to address global targets of opportunity.

## Key Concepts

The "Agile Release Train" metaphor is used to communicate several key concepts:

- The train departs the station and arrives at the next destination on a reliable schedule, which provides for fixed cadence, standard ART velocity, and predictable planning (and in many cases, cadence-based releases)

- All "cargo," including prototypes, models, software, hardware, documentation, etc., goes on the train

- Most people needed on the train are dedicated full-time, no matter what their functional reporting structure might be. If you want to participate, you need to be on the train.

The ART aligns the teams and helps manage risk and variability by providing cadence and synchronization. It is based on a set of common operating principles:

- Agile Teams power the train and are cross-functional, self-organizing entities that can *define*, *build*, and *test* a Feature or component

- Teams embrace and follow the principles of the Agile Manifesto and the values and principles of SAFe. Teams use SAFe, ScrumXP, and XP Agile practices.

- Teams apply frequent, face-to-face, rolling wave planning

- PI and iteration dates are fixed. Quality is fixed. *Scope* is variable.

- Teams determine the scope via decentralized planning

- Teams apply common iteration lengths and standardized estimating to support ART-level estimating, planning, and integration

- Continuous integration is implemented across all teams on the train

- Every iteration, the System Demo shows integrated, ART-level, working solutions to key stakeholders

- Innovation and planning iterations provide a guard band for estimating and dedicated time for PI planning, innovation (e.g., hackathons, etc.), continuing education, and infrastructure work
- Certain infrastructure components, such as models, prototypes, and other Enablers, should typically track ahead of development

In addition, in large value streams multiple ARTs cooperate to build larger value in the form of solution Capabilities. In such cases, some ART stakeholders participate in value stream ceremonies including the Solution Demo and Pre- and Post-PI Planning.

## Agile Release Train Roles

In addition to the Agile Teams, there are a number of additional key roles:

- The Release Train Engineer is a servant leader and operates as a full-time "Chief Scrum Master" for the train
- Product Management (PM) has content authority for the Program Backlog and works with Product Owners (POs) to actively manage scope and quality. At scale, a single person cannot handle both product and market strategy while also being dedicated to an Agile Team. Therefore, the "PM/PO" team steers the train together.
- Business Owners are key stakeholders, and they are "on the train."
- User Experience designers and System Architects and Engineering are responsible for defining the Architectural Runway that supports new feature development, as well as providing guidance for common solution behaviors, shared components, and separation of concerns
- The System Team helps with infrastructure, assists with integration, performs ART-level testing, is capable of evaluating conformance to Nonfunctional Requirements (NFRs), and assists with the train's system demo
- DevOps is integral to the train to ensure a faster flow of value to the end user. This role provides mechanisms for tighter integration of development and deployment operations.
- Shared Services assist the train with specialty functions that cannot be dedicated to the train

## Organizing Agile Release Trains

The organization of an Agile Release Train determines who will be planning and working together, as well as what products, services, features, or components the train will deliver. Organizing Agile Release Trains is part of the "art" of SAFe, and there are many factors to consider.

## Effective Train Size

One primary consideration is size. Effective Agile Release Trains typically consist of 50 – 125 people. The upper limit is based on Dunbar's number, which suggests a limit on the number of people with whom one can form effective, stable social relationships. Larger trains occur as well, but they face larger challenges, including:

- Logistics for Program Level events become more complex

- Longer or tighter timeboxes are needed for PI planning, the system demo, and the Inspect & Adapt workshop

- There are more dependencies to manage

- The program backlog becomes larger, and the queue size for a program increment increases WIP (work in process)

- Gaining and maintaining alignment to the mission becomes more difficult

So again, 50 – 125 is the most typical range of people on an ART.

The lower limit is based mostly on empirical observation of SAFe implementations in larger enterprises. However, trains with fewer than 50 people can still be very effective (the authors are part of such a train) and provide many advantages over legacy Agile practices for coordinating Agile Teams. However, smaller trains typically make adjustments to SAFe to better suit their context.

## ART Organization Depends on Value Stream Size

Given the size constraints, there are three outcomes for organizing ARTs, as illustrated in Figure 1 below.

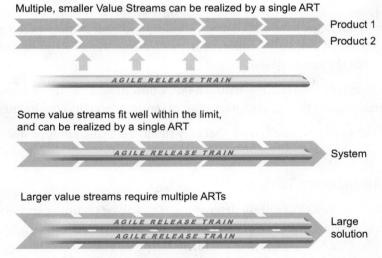

*Figure 1. Organizing ARTs based on value stream size*

1. Multiple value streams can be realized by a single ART: This is usually the exceptional case; it tends to occur in smaller enterprises, or in enterprises that build a large number of products with a modest number of people

2. The value stream can be realized by a single ART: This is a common case and the easiest to manage, as the ART and the value stream are one and the same

3. The value stream is large and requires multiple ARTs: This is also quite a common case for those building systems, but additional work is required, as described below

## Splitting Large Value Streams

In the larger enterprise, it is very common to have large value streams that need to be split into multiple ARTs. Splitting value streams is part technical, part art, and part social and organizational science. Below are some common patterns for splitting large value streams into ARTs:

- By solution capabilities or feature areas (see below)

- By subsystems (applications, components, platforms, etc.; see below)

- By Customer or market segment

- By subsets of value: enabling flows or value stream segments

- Other considerations may play a role:

  - Trains should be focused on a single, primary product or solution objective

  - Teams with features and components that have a high degree of interdependencies should plan and work together

  - Locale is a major consideration—wherever possible, train teams should be collocated, or at least geographic distribution should be as limited as is feasible, as that simplifies planning logistics and cooperation among the teams

  - Source of funding

The design of trains requires careful consideration of the trade-offs. In general, the design of trains usually involves a combination of the various patterns above. For example: Larger value streams with multiple ARTs typically require both capabilities *and* subsystems. The following section discusses the trade-offs of organizing trains with these two common patterns.

### Organizing Trains around Capabilities and Subsystems

Two of the major organizational patterns for ARTs are organizing around capabilities or organizing around subsystems, as illustrated in Figure 2 below. For example: A train can be organized around "Customer Enrollment" end-to-end functionality (*capability*), or, alternatively, it can be organized around mobile applications (*subsystem*).

- *Capability ARTs* are optimized for value flow and delivery speed. They are generally preferred; however, they require additional technical governance to keep architecture from decaying and, ultimately, decreasing velocity.

- *Subsystem ARTs* are optimized for architectural robustness, critical components, or components that are used by many other elements. However, they may require significant content coordination to manage dependencies, as well as prioritization of different trains to maintain a reasonable velocity.

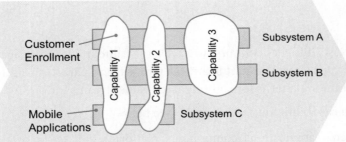

*Figure 2. ARTs can be organized by capabilities and/or subsystems*

## Organizing Teams on the Train

Once the ART boundary is established, it will be clear which Agile Teams will be involved in actually building the value. The next step, then, is for the teams to organize for the larger purpose of maximizing velocity by minimizing dependencies and handoffs, while sustaining architectural and engineering robustness and system qualities. Teams can be organized around:

- Features – A *feature team* is an Agile Team that is organized around user-centered functionality. Each team is generally capable of delivering end-to-end user value. Feature teams operate primarily with user stories, refactors, and spikes. However, technical stories may also occasionally occur in their backlog.

- Components – A *component team* is an Agile Team whose primary area of concern is restricted to a specific component or set of components. Accordingly, the team backlog typically consists of technical stories (as opposed to user stories), refactors, and enabler stories (e.g., spikes).

- Other – Platform, architectural layer, programming language, middleware, UI, DB, business logic, spoken language, technology, location, etc.

Most ARTs have a mix of feature teams and component teams:

- Whenever possible, lean toward *feature teams*, as they provide higher velocity and have fewer dependencies. They also facilitate the development of T-shaped skills, so that all team members can better flex to the work at hand.

- Use *component teams* when there are high reuse opportunities, high technical specialization, and critical NFRs. But component teams should work to the principle that each component is a potentially replaceable part of the system, with well-defined interfaces. This supports modularity, separation of concerns, and ease of reuse.

ARTs should generally avoid organizing around "other" (see above), as this creates tight coupling and generally impedes flow.

## LEARN MORE

[1] Leffingwell, Dean. *Agile Software Requirements: Lean Requirements Practices for Teams, Programs, and the Enterprise.* Addison-Wesley, 2011.

[2] Reinertsen, Donald. *Principles of Product Development Flow: Second Generation Lean Product Development.* Celeritas Publishing, 2009.

[3] Gladwell, Malcolm. *The Tipping Point: How Little Things Can Make a Big Difference.* Little, Brown and Company, 2000.

# Release Train Engineer and Value Stream Engineer

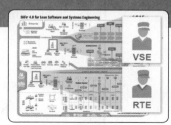

*It is a misuse of our power to take responsibility for solving problems that belong to others.*

—Peter Block

## Abstract

While Agile Release Trains (ARTs) are largely self-organizing and self-managing teams of teams, they don't necessarily drive or steer themselves. The responsibility for steering falls to the *Release Train Engineer* (RTE). The RTE is the one who facilitates Program Level processes and execution, escalates impediments, manages risk, and helps drive program level continuous improvement.

At the Value Stream Level, the *Value Stream Engineer* (VSE) plays a similar role, facilitating and guiding the work of all ARTs and Suppliers. RTEs and VSEs typically have a background as program or development managers and operate most effectively as servant leaders. They have a solid understanding of scaling Lean and Agile, and they understand the unique opportunities and challenges associated with facilitating and continuously aligning a large development program.

## Details

The *Release Train Engineer* and the *Value Stream Engineer* facilitate Agile Release Train and Value Stream processes and execution, respectively. They escalate impediments, manage risk, help ensure value delivery, and help drive continuous improvement. Many also participate in the Lean-Agile transformation, coaching leaders, teams, and Scrum Masters in the new processes and mindsets. They help adapt SAFe to the organization, standardizing and documenting practices.

### Responsibilities

RTEs and VSEs typically fulfill the following responsibilities:

- Manage and optimize the flow of value through the program using various tools, such as the Program and Value Stream Kanbans and information radiators
- Establish and communicate the annual calendars for Iterations and Program Increments (PI)

- Facilitate PI Planning readiness via fostering the preparation of Vision and backlogs, and via Pre- and Post-PI Planning meetings

- Facilitate PI planning

- Aggregate Team PI Objectives into Program PI Objectives (the RTE) and publish them for visibility and transparency

- Aggregate program PI objectives into Value Stream PI Objectives (the VSE) and publish them for visibility and transparency

- Assist with execution and Feature/Capability completion tracking (see the "Metrics" article)

- Facilitate periodic synchronization meetings, including the ART sync at the Program Level and the VS sync at the Value Stream Level

- Assist with economic decision-making by facilitating feature and capability estimation by teams and the roll-up to the value stream level and Portfolio Level

- Escalate and track impediments

- Encourage the collaboration between teams and System and Solution Architects, Engineering, and User Experience

- Work with Product Management, Product Owners, and other value stream stakeholders to help ensure strategy and execution alignment

- Help manage risks and dependencies

- Report status to Program Portfolio Management and Release Management and support related activities

- Understand and operate within the ART Budget

- Provide input on resourcing to address critical bottlenecks

- Attend System Demos and Solution Demos

- Drive continuous improvement via Inspect and Adapt workshops; assess the agility level of the program/value stream and help improve

- Encourage Team Level, program level, and value stream level Continuous Integration and Communities of Practice around SAFe, Agile, and Lean and around engineering and quality practices

- Coach leaders, teams, and Scrum Masters in Lean-Agile practices and mindsets

## Reporting Structure

SAFe doesn't prescribe a reporting structure, but the RTE and VSE typically report to the development organization or an Agile PMO, which, in SAFe, is considered a part of Program Portfolio Management. For enterprises with existing PMO organizations, a program manager often plays this role. While they typically have the organizational skills to perform the RTE duties, they may need to transition from traditional legacy mindsets to Lean/Agile Mindsets.

## RTEs and VSEs Are Servant Leaders

A mindset change is often required for new RTEs and VSEs in the transition from directing and managing activities to acting as a *servant leader*. Servant leadership is a leadership philosophy that implies a comprehensive view of the quality of people, work, and community spirit [1]. In the context of the RTE and VSE, the focus is on providing the support needed by the teams/ARTs to be self-organizing and self-managing. Characteristic servant leader actions include:

- Listen and support teams in problem identification and decision-making
- Create an environment of mutual influence
- Understand and empathize with others
- Encourage and support the personal development of each individual and the development of teams
- Persuade rather than use authority
- Think beyond day-to-day activities; apply systems thinking
- Support the teams' commitments
- Be open and appreciate openness in others

As Robert Greenleaf, the father of servant leadership, said, "Good leaders must first become good servants." Just as there are Lean-Agile transformational patterns for the Program Portfolio Management function, there are also transformational patterns for a traditional manager moving to a servant leader. The "from" and "to" states are:

- From *coordinating* team activities and contributions to *coaching* the teams to collaborate
- From *deadlines* to *objectives*
- From *driving* toward specific outcomes to *being invested* in the program's overall performance
- From *knowing* the answer to *asking* the teams for the answer
- From *directing* to *letting* the teams self-organize and hit their stride
- From *fixing* problems to *helping* others fix them

## LEARN MORE

[1] See Servant Leadership at http://en.wikipedia.org/wiki/Servant_leadership.

[2] Leffingwell, Dean. *Agile Software Requirements: Lean Requirements Practices for Teams, Programs, and the Enterprise.* Addison-Wesley, 2011.

[3] Trompenaars, Fons and Ed Voerman. *Servant-Leadership Across Cultures: Harnessing the Strengths of the World's Most Powerful Management Philosophy.* McGraw-Hill, 2009.

# System and Solution Architect/Engineering

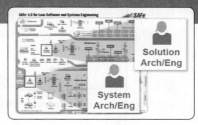

*Engineering is a great profession. There is the satisfaction of watching a figment of the imagination emerge through the aid of science to a plan on paper. Then it moves to realization in stone or metal or energy. Then it brings homes to men or women. Then it elevates the standard of living and adds to the comforts of life. This is the engineer's high privilege.*

—Herbert Hoover (1874 – 1964)

## Abstract

The SAFe System and Solution "Arch/Eng" icon represents the individuals and teams who have the technical responsibility for the overall architectural and engineering design of the system and solution, respectively.

*Architect/Engineering* are cross-discipline teams that truly "take a system view" on solution development. They participate in the definition of the higher-level functional and Nonfunctional Requirements, analyze technical trade-offs, determine the major components and subsystems, and define the interfaces and collaborations between them. They understand the Solution Context and work with the teams, Customers, and Suppliers to help ensure fitness for use in the Customer's environment.

In cooperation with Solution and Product Management, Architect/Engineering play a critical role in helping align teams in a common technical direction toward accomplishment of the mission, Vision, and Roadmap.

And, of course, they are Lean-Agile Leaders who understand the complexities of large-scale solution development, and they apply Lean and Agile practices to address them.

## Details

*Architect/Engineering* align the Value Stream and Agile Release Trains to a common technological and architectural vision of the Solution under development. They participate in defining the system and subsystems, validate technology assumptions, and evaluate alternatives. They support solution development through providing, communicating, and evolving the larger technological and architectural view of the solution.

Arch/Eng teams occur at both the Program and Value Stream Levels. System Arch/Eng operates mainly in the context of the Agile Release Train, where they work with Agile Teams and provide technical enablement with respect to subsystems and capability areas under the purview of the ART. Solution Arch/Eng teams provide technical leadership for evolving architectural capabilities of the entire solution.

Both involve tight collaboration with business stakeholders, teams, Customers, Suppliers, and third-party stakeholders in defining the technology infrastructure, decomposition into components and subsystems, and the definition of interfaces between subsystems and between the solution and Solution Context.

While providing a general view on solution architecture, they enable those who implement value by empowering them to make local decisions in order to provide a faster flow of value and better economics.

## Responsibilities

Architects and Systems Engineering teams are Lean-Agile Leaders who typically have the following responsibilities:

- Participate in planning, definition, and high-level design of the solution and explore solution alternatives

- Define subsystems and their interfaces; allocate responsibilities to subsystems; understand solution deployment, and communicate requirements for interactions with solution context

- Work with Customers, stakeholders, and Suppliers to establish high-level Solution Intent; help establish the solution intent information models and documentation requirements

- Establish critical Nonfunctional Requirements at the solution level; participate in the definition of others

- Operate within the Economic Framework to validate the economic impact of design decisions

- Work with portfolio stakeholders, particularly the Enterprise Architect, to develop, analyze, split, and realize the implementation of Enabler Epics

- Participate in PI Planning and Pre- and Post-PI Planning, System and Solution Demos, and Inspect and Adapt events

- Define, explore, and support the implementation of value stream and program enablers to evolve solution intent; work directly with Agile Teams to implement, explore, or support them

- Plan and develop the Architectural Runway in support of upcoming business Features/ Capabilities

- Work with Product and Solution Management to determine capacity allocation for enablement work

- Support technology/engineering aspects of Program and Value Stream Kanbans
- Supervise and foster Built-in Quality

## The Origin of the Roles in SAFe

### Role of the System Architect

The role of an *Architect* is common in software development and has been included in SAFe as one of the critical roles at the program and portfolio levels. Also, the role of an Architect often extends beyond just the software domain to include responsibilities that enable value delivery in a technologically diverse and heterogeneous, multi-domain solution environment, so SAFe takes a fairly expansive view of that role.

### Role of Systems Engineering

Enterprises building cyber-physical systems, however, also rely on *Systems Engineering*—a group of people who perform the systems engineering aspects of solution development. These teams typically encompass multiple disciplines, including hardware, electrical and electronic, mechanical, hydraulic, and optical and other aspects of a complex solution, as well as the software elements. INCOSE [1] defines Systems Engineering as:

> "... an interdisciplinary approach and means to enable the realization of successful systems. It focuses on defining customer needs and required functionality early in the development cycle, documenting requirements, then proceeding with design synthesis and system validation while considering the complete problem, including operations, performance, test, manufacturing, cost and schedule, training and support, and disposal. Systems Engineering integrates all the disciplines and specialty groups into a team effort, forming a structured development process that proceeds from concept to production to operation. Systems Engineering considers both the business and the technical needs of all customers with the goal of providing a quality product that meets the user needs."

## A Leaner Approach

Clearly, it is impossible to reason about how to build complex solutions without including the roles of software Architecture and Systems Engineering. However, a significant note of caution is warranted. The dominant, traditional methods for both strongly gravitate toward phase-gate, point-solution, Big Up-Front Design approaches. This is understandable because a) these are big systems and somebody has to know how one is supposed to go about building them, and b) the stage-gate waterfall model was the best model available at that time.

However, as described extensively in the SAFe Lean-Agile Principles, this approach is not supportive of product development flow, and it doesn't produce the best economic outcomes. SAFe views software Architecture and Systems Engineering as *enabling* functions for continuous product development flow. In the Lean-Agile Mindset, these functions focus on frequent cross-discipline collaboration, building systems incrementally through fast, feedback-driven learning cycles, understanding and leveraging the inherent variability of the product development process, and decentralizing control.

## Decentralized Decision-Making

Design decisions vary significantly in terms of their impact, urgency, and frequency of occurrence. This suggests a balanced combination of centralized and decentralized decision-making (Principle #9 of SAFe). The basic rule of decentralized decision-making is to centralize only those decisions that are not urgent and long lasting and that have significant economies of scale. Decentralize everything else.

With respect to system design, this means that:

- Certain larger-scale architectural decisions should be centralized. These include definition of primary system intent, subsystems and interfaces, allocation of functions to subsystems, selection of common platforms, definition of solution-level nonfunctional requirements, elimination of redundancy, and more.

- However, the rest, and thereby *most*, of the design decisions are delegated to Agile Teams. The balance is achieved by applying practices of emergent design in conjunction with intentional architecture (see the "Agile Architecture" article).

This is supported by frequent collaboration, whether in the form of informal and continuous face-to-face discussions or, more regularly, in PI planning, system and solution demos, inspect and adapt workshops, and specification workshops.

In any case, Arch/Eng exhibits the traits of Lean-Agile Leaders. They:

1. Collaborate with, enable, and empower engineers and subject matter experts with decision-making

2. Educate team members in design-related disciplines; lead technical Communities of Practice

3. Demonstrate Lean and Agile principles, as applied to system design, by example

## An Empirical Approach

In addition, success of any solution development program depends on the organization's ability to embrace the learnings from empirical evidence. This paradigm can challenge traditional mindsets that support detailed, committed early design based on reasoned but unverified hypotheses and implementation strategies. In that case, when the evidence belies the design, those responsible for design may see it as a personal affront and exhibit a tendency to defend the design, not the evidence.

The Lean-Agile Arch/Eng mindset relies on the firm belief that if there is a problem with the design, the problem is with the *design*, and not with the people who created it. No one could have anticipated the new learnings; it's *research* and development, after all. Everyone learns together.

This belief is further fostered by:

- Fact-based governance, where the facts are produced by frequent integration and objective evidence

- Set-based engineering, where a *spectrum* of possible solutions to a problem is considered, instead of a single idea picked early

- Learning Milestones that are planned and executed with the specific purpose of validating the technical *and* business hypotheses

- A bias toward economic decision-making, where trade-offs between architectural capabilities of the system and economic outcomes are made continuously and in collaboration with business stakeholders

---

**LEARN MORE**

[1] International Council on Systems Engineering. "What Is Systems Engineering?" http://www.incose.org/AboutSE/WhatIsSE.

[2] Leffingwell, Dean. *Agile Software Requirements: Lean Requirements Practices for Teams, Programs, and the Enterprise.* Addison-Wesley, 2011.

# Product and Solution Management

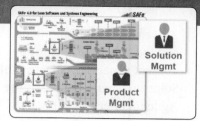

*Decentralize decision-making*

   *—SAFe Principle #9*

## Abstract

Lean-Agile Enterprises focus on delivering the right Solutions to Customers with the highest quality and shortest lead times. In a dynamic environment, this requires people with clear *content authority* to take responsibility for continuously defining, prioritizing, and validating requirements. These people work closely with development in short, integrated learning cycles, bringing the voice of the Customer to the developers and the voice of development to the Customer.

In accordance with *Decentralized Decision-Making*, SAFe prescribes a content authority chain that extends through three levels. *Solution Management* is responsible for guiding the solutions that constitute the Value Stream. *Product Management* is responsible for Program Vision and Backlog. Finally, *Product Owners* make fast, local content decisions on behalf of the Agile Team.

This article describes the important roles that Product Managers and Solutions Managers play in SAFe. While the roles are similar in most respects, they operate at different levels of the solution and manage different concerns.

## Details

*Solution Management* and *Product Management* are the main *content authorities* in SAFe, guiding the Value Stream and Program Levels respectively, where they have primary responsibility for Value Stream and Program Backlogs. They create the Vision; they work with Customers to understand their needs, define requirements, and guide work through the Value Stream and Program Kanbans. They prioritize work using WSJF, schedule it for Release via the Roadmap, validate the Customer response, and provide fast feedback.

### A Lean-Agile Approach to Content Management

What SAFe describes as *content* has traditionally been represented by marketing requirements documents, product requirements documents, and system and software specifications. In waterfall development, these specifications were typically done up front, with an expectation that all the requirements could be established in advance of Solution development. However, it didn't work out all that well that way, and the move to a Lean-Agile paradigm is driven in large part by that result. We now understand that assumptions about system requirements, design, and architecture all need to be validated through actual development, testing, and experimentation [1], and that teams must be open to emerging knowledge that can be quickly fed back into the solution.

As we see in Solution Intent, some of the requirements of the solution are likely to be well understood and fixed from the beginning, while others are variable and can only be understood during the development process. Managing this dynamic new paradigm is the primary responsibility of Product and Solution Management. In the Lean Enterprise, these responsibilities must be fulfilled in a far more Agile manner, as is illustrated in Table 1.

| Responsibility | Traditional | Agile |
|---|---|---|
| Understand Customer need | Up-front and discontinuous | Constant interaction; Customer is part of the value stream |
| Document requirements | Fully elaborated in documents; handed off | High-level vision; constant product and solution backlog refinement and informal face-to-face communication with Agile Teams |
| Schedule | Created in hard-committed roadmaps and milestones at the beginning | Continuous near-term roadmapping |
| Prioritize requirements | Not at all, or perhaps one-time only, often in requirements document form | Reprioritized at every PI boundary via WSJF; constant scope triage |
| Validate requirements | Not applicable; QA responsibility | Primary role, involved with Iteration and PI System Demos; acceptance criteria included; fitness for purpose understood |
| Manage delivery schedule | Typically one time, fixed well in advance | Released frequently, whenever there is enough value |
| Manage change | Change avoided—weekly change control meetings | Change embraced; adjusted at PI and iteration boundaries |

*Table 1. Changes in Product and Solution Management behavior in a Lean-Agile enterprise*

# Responsibilities of Product Management

The following section describes the primary responsibilities of the Product Manager in the context of a single Agile Release Train. For larger (multiple-ART) value streams, additional responsibilities are necessary. Those are described in later sections.

- **Understand Customer needs and validate solutions** – Product Management is the internal voice of the Customer for the ART and works with Customers (as well as Product Owners) to constantly understand and communicate their needs and participate in validation of the proposed solutions.

- **Understand and support portfolio work** – Every Agile Release Train lives in the context of a portfolio, so Product Management has a responsibility to understand the Budget parameters for the upcoming fiscal period, understand how Strategic Themes influence the strategic direction, and work with Epic Owners to develop the business case for Epics that affect their ART.

- **Develop and communicate the program vision and roadmap** – Product Management continuously develops and communicates the vision to the development teams and defines the features of the system. In collaboration with System and Solution Architect/ Engineering, they also define and maintain the Nonfunctional Requirements (NFRs), to help ensure that the solution meets relevant standards and other system quality requirements. They are responsible for the roadmap, which illustrates, at a high level, how features are intended to be implemented over time.

- **Manage and prioritize the flow of work** – Product Management manages the flow of work though the program Kanban and into the program backlog. Product Management is responsible for making sure that there are enough *ready* features in the backlog at all times. To be ready, they develop feature *acceptance criteria* that can be used to establish that the feature meets its Definition of Done. And since judicious selection and sequencing of features is the key economic driver for each ART, the backlog is reprioritized with WSJF prior to each PI Planning session.

- **Participate in PI planning** – During each PI planning session, Product Management presents the vision, which highlights the proposed features of the solution, along with any relevant upcoming Milestones. They also typically participate as Business Owners for the train, with the responsibility of approving PI Objectives and establishing business value.

- **Define releases and Program Increments** – Owning the *what* means that Product Management is largely responsible for release definition as well, including new features, architecture, and allocations for technical debt. This is accomplished though a series of program increments and releases, whose definition and business objectives are also determined by Product Management.

Product Management works with Release Management, where applicable, to decide when enough value has been accrued to warrant a release to the Customer.

- **Work with System Architect/Engineering to understand Enabler work** – While Product Management is not expected to drive technological decisions, they are expected to understand the scope of the upcoming enabler work and to work with System and Solution Architect/Engineering to assist with decision-making and sequencing of the key technological infrastructures that will host the new business functionality. This can often best be accomplished by establishing a capacity allocation, as described in the "Program Backlog" article.

- **Participate in demos and Inspect and Adapt** – Product Management is an active participant in biweekly System Demos, including the aggregate one at the end of the PI. They are also involved in assessment of Metrics, including evaluation of business value achieved versus plan, and are active participants in the inspect and adapt workshop.

- **Build an effective Product Manager/Product Owner team** – Though the Product Owner and Product Management roles may report to different organizations, forming an effective extended Product Management/Product Owner team is the key to efficient and effective development. Such a team also contributes materially to the job satisfaction that comes with being part of a high-performing team, one that routinely delivers on its quality and vision commitments.

## Product Management's Participation in Large Value Streams

The above section highlights the role of the PM in the context of the ART. For teams building value stream solutions that require multiple ARTs, Product Management has additional responsibilities:

- **Collaborate with Solution Management** – At the value stream level, Solution Management plays a similar role, but with a focus on the solution. But building an effective solution is no more effective than the collaboration between the two roles. This collaboration involves participation in value stream backlog refinement and prioritization, as well as splitting Capabilities into features, and NFRs, as the case may be.

- **Participate in Pre- and Post-PI Planning** – Product Management also participates in the Pre-PI Planning meeting, working with the value stream stakeholders to define the inputs, milestones, and high-level objectives for the upcoming PI planning session. In the Post-PI Planning session, Product Management helps synthesize findings into an agreed-to set of value stream PI objectives.

- **Participate in the Solution Demo** – Product Management participates in the solution demo, often demonstrating the capabilities that their ART has contributed and reviewing the contributions of the other ARTs, always with a systems view, and always with an eye toward fitness of purpose

- **Collaborate with Release Management** – In larger-scale systems, Release Management also plays a significant role. Product Management works with the key stakeholders on progress, budget, release strategy, and releasability of their elements of the solution.

## Responsibilities of Solution Management

Solution Management plays much the same role that Product Management plays, but at the value stream level. There, Solution Management is part of the critical troika—Solution Management, Value Stream Engineer, and Solution Architect/Engineering—that shares much of the responsibility for solution success. Solution Management is responsible for the solution intent, which captures and documents fixed and variable solution level behaviors. They also work with Release Management where applicable.

Responsibilities include working with portfolio stakeholders, Customers, and ARTs to understand needs and build and prioritize the solution backlog. They have similar vision, roadmap, value stream Kanban, and solution demo activities as well.

Solution Management plays a crucial role in pre- and post-PI planning, as well as value stream inspect and adapt workshops. They also work with Suppliers, making sure the requirements for Supplier-delivered capabilities are understood and assisting with the conceptual integration of these concerns.

---

**LEARN MORE**

[1] Ries, Eric. *The Lean Startup: How Today's Entrepreneurs Use Continuous Innovation to Create Radically Successful Businesses.* Crown Business, 2011.

[2] Leffingwell, Dean. *Agile Software Requirements: Lean Requirements Practices for Teams, Programs, and the Enterprise.* Addison-Wesley, 2011, chapter 14.

# WSJF (Weighted Shortest Job First)

*If you only quantify one thing, quantify the cost of delay.*
—Donald Reinertsen

## Abstract

SAFe is intended for application in situations in which Agile Release Trains (ARTs) are engaged in ongoing, continuous development—a *flow* of work—that makes up the Enterprise's incremental development effort. As such, it avoids the overhead and delays of the start-stop-start nature of traditional projects and programs, whereby various project authorizations and phase gates are used to control the program and its economics.

While this continuous flow model helps eliminate delays and keeps the system lean, we do have to ensure that the system's priorities are constantly updated so that the value provides the best economic outcomes for the business. In flow, it is item *sequencing* (rather than theoretical individual item ROI) that drives the best economic result. To that end, *WSJF* illustrates how the ART, the Solution, and the Portfolio Backlogs are reprioritized using the *Weighted Shortest Job First* via calculating the *cost of delay* and *job size* (proxy for duration). Using this algorithm at PI boundaries continuously updates the job's priorities based on current business context, value, time, development facts, risk, and effort considerations. It also conveniently and automatically *ignores sunk costs*, which is a key principle of Lean economics.

## Details

Reinertsen [2] describes a comprehensive model called *Weighted Shortest Job First* (WSJF) for prioritizing jobs based on the economics of product development flow. WSJF is calculated as the cost of *delay divided by job duration*. Jobs that can deliver the most value (or cost of delay) and are of the shortest duration are selected first for implementation. When applied in SAFe, the model supports a number of additional key principles of product development flow, including:

- Take an economic view
- Ignore sunk costs
- If you only quantify one thing, quantify the cost of delay
- Economic choices must be made continuously
- Use decision rules to decentralize economic control

The impact of properly applying WSJF can be seen in Figure 1. (See [2 or 3] for full discussion.) The areas shaded in blue illustrate the total cost of delay in each case. Doing the *weighted shortest job first* delivers the best economics.

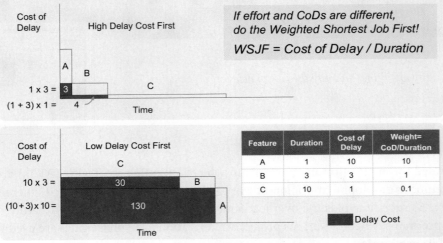

From *The Principles of Product Development Flow*, by Donald G. Reinertsen, Celeritas Publishing, © 2009 Donald G. Reinertsen

*Figure 1. The economic effect of doing the Weighted Shortest Job First (WSJF); cost of delay for work*

## Calculating the Cost of Delay

In SAFe, our "jobs" are the Epics and the Features and Capabilities we develop, so we need to establish both the cost of delay and the duration for each job. There are three primary elements that contribute to the cost of delay:

**User-Business Value** – Do our users prefer this over that? What is the revenue impact on our business? Is there a potential penalty or other negative impact if we delay?

**Time Criticality** – How does the user/business value decay over time? Is there a fixed deadline? Will they wait for us or move to another solution? Are there Milestones in the critical path impacted by this?

**Risk Reduction-Opportunity Enablement Value** – What else does this do for our business? Does it reduce the risk of this or a future delivery? Is there value in the information we will receive? Will this feature open up new business opportunities?

Moreover, since we are in continuous flow and should have a large enough backlog to choose from, we needn't worry about the absolute numbers. We can just compare backlog items relative to each other using the modified Fibonacci numbers we use in estimating poker.

Then the relative cost of delay for a job is:

$$Cost\ of\ Delay = User\text{-}Business\ Value + Time\ Criticality + RR\text{-}OE$$

## Duration

Next we need to understand job duration. That can be pretty difficult to figure, especially since early on we perhaps don't yet know who is going to do the work or what capacity allocation they might be able to give it. So we probably don't really know. Fortunately, we have a ready proxy: job *size*. In systems with fixed resources, job size is a good proxy for duration. (If I'm the only one mowing my lawn, and the front yard is three times bigger than the back yard, the front lawn is going to take three times longer to mow.) And we know how to estimate item size in story points already (see the "Features" article). Taking job size, we have a reasonably straightforward calculation for comparing jobs via WSJF, as Figure 2 illustrates:

$$WSJF = \frac{User\text{-}Business\ Value + Time\ Criticality + Risk\ Reduction\text{-}Opportunity\ Enablement\ Value}{Job\ size}$$

*Figure 2. A formula for calculating WSJF*

Then, for example, we can create a simple table to compare jobs (three jobs in this case), as shown in Figure 3:

| Feature | User-Business Value | Time Criticality | RR-OE Value | Job Size | WSJF |
|---------|---------------------|------------------|-------------|----------|------|
|         |                     |                  |             |          |      |
|         |                     |                  |             |          |      |
|         |                     |                  |             |          |      |

- Rate each parameter of each feature against the other features.
- Scale: 1, 2, 3, 5, 8,13, 20.
- Do one column at a time, start by picking the smallest item and giving it a "1". There must be at least one "1" in each column!
- The highest priority is the highest WSJF.

*Figure 3. A sample spreadsheet for calculating WSJF*

To use the table, the team rates each job relative to other jobs on each of the three parameters. (Note: With relative estimating, you look at one *column* at a time, set the smallest item to a one, and then set the others relative to that item.) Then divide by the size of the job (which can be either a relative estimate or an absolute number based on the estimates contained in the backlog) and calculate a number that ranks the job's priority.

*The job with the highest WSJF is the next most important item to do.*

One outcome of this model is that really big, important jobs have to be divided into smaller, pretty important jobs in order to make the cut against easier ways of making money (i.e., small, low-risk jobs that your Customers are willing to pay for now). But that's just Agile at work. Since the implementation is incremental, whenever a continuing job doesn't rank well against its peers, then you have likely satisfied that particular requirement sufficiently that you can move on to the next job.

As we have described, another advantage of the model is that it is *not* necessary to determine the absolute value of any of these numbers. Rather, you only need to rate the parameters of each job against the other jobs from the same backlog.

Finally, as the backlog estimates should include only the job size remaining, then frequent reprioritization means that the system will *automatically ignore sunk costs.*

## A Note on Job Size as a Proxy for Duration

However, we do have to be careful about the proxy we chose for duration. If availability of resources means that a larger job may be delivered more quickly than some other item with about equal value, then we probably know enough about the job to use *duration* to have a more accurate result. (If I can get three people to mow my front lawn while I mow the back, then these items have about the same duration, but not the same cost.) But this is rarely necessary in the flow of value, in part because if there is some small error in selection, that next important job will make its way up soon enough.

---

**LEARN MORE**

[1] Leffingwell, Dean. *Agile Software Requirements: Lean Requirements Practices for Teams, Programs, and the Enterprise.* Addison-Wesley, 2011.

[2] Reinertsen, Donald. *Principles of Product Development Flow: Second Generation Lean Product Development.* Celeritas Publishing, 2009.

# Program and Value Stream Kanban

*It is said that improvement is eternal and infinite. It should be the duty of those working with Kanban to keep improving it with creativity and resourcefulness without allowing it to become fixed at any stage.*

—*Taiichi Ohno*

## Abstract

SAFe supports the goal of continuous value delivery by implementing Kanban systems at all levels: Portfolio, Value Stream, Program, and Team. At the program and value stream levels, Features and Capabilities follow a common work flow pattern of exploration, refinement, prioritization, and implementing. The "pull" nature of the Kanban system allows programs to establish capacity management based on WIP limits and helps prevent the system from operating with large handoffs. Such continuous flow fosters collaboration and effective decision-making. Large initiatives, such as program and value stream Epics, are managed in a special section of the program and value stream Kanbans, resulting in features and capabilities intended to advance the Solution.

*Program and Value Stream Kanban* systems are aligned with the Program Increment (PI) cadence, allowing stakeholders and teams to elaborate, plan, and implement value in a routine, reliable manner, ensuring that none of the steps in the Kanban is overloaded or starving and that the solution is being reliably built in increments.

Together with the Portfolio Kanban, program and value stream Kanban systems constitute a SAFe enterprise content governance model that instantiates an economic decision-making framework and decentralization of control, vital to a fast, sustainable flow of value.

## Details

To facilitate the flow of value, Solution builders apply a Kanban system at the Program and Value Stream levels. These Kanban systems help teams:

- Increase visibility into new work, and into the flow of work
- Ensure continuous refinement of new value definition and acceptance criteria

- Foster role collaboration about the new work across disciplines, functions, and levels

- Instantiate economic decision-making

- Establish connections among the Portfolio, value stream, and program levels

The *Value Stream and Program Kanbans* are connected to the Portfolio Kanban; together these three Kanbans constitute a content governance system that accounts for most of the significant decisions about what gets built. In a fully expanded case, portfolio Epics that have acquired sufficient readiness and have been approved for implementation get split into Value Stream epics and Capabilities that get loaded into the value stream Kanban. Capabilities and value stream epics, as they progress through the value stream Kanban, get split into Features and program epics and loaded into the program Kanban. Figure 1 illustrates such a case.

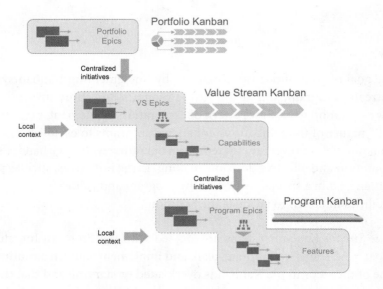

*Figure 1. Enterprise flow of value through Kanban systems*

The optimum economic benefits and efficacy of the solutions in the portfolio are achieved by integrating centralized decision-making (vertical arrows) with the local context (horizontal arrows), which are those features and capabilities that arise directly from the value stream, ART, or Customer context. The connected Kanbans instantiate much of the economic decision-making framework and provide the foundation for a continuous feedback mechanism on decisions made.

The following sections explore program and value stream Kanbans in more detail.

## Program Kanban

A program Kanban system facilitates the flow of features and program epics. While all Kanban systems are purpose-built, a typical structure is illustrated in Figure 2.

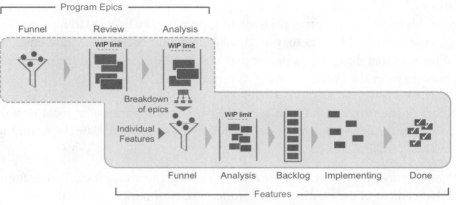

*Figure 2. Program Kanban*

The program Kanban consists of two main structural elements, the program epic section and the feature section, as described below.

**Program Epic Section**
The purpose of the program epic section of the program Kanban is to analyze and approve program epics and split them into features that will be further explored and implemented in the "downstream" feature section of the program Kanban (see Figure 2). This section is not always present in the program Kanban, depending on how frequently program epics occur in the local context of the program.

This part of the program Kanban system requires involvement of a higher level of stakeholders—typically at the value stream or portfolio level—to explore and approve program epics. The flow generally resembles the equivalent set of steps in the portfolio Kanban:

- All big initiatives are welcome in the *Program Epic Funnel*. There is no WIP limit at this step.

- The *Program Epic Review* step allows the assigned analysts to perform initial exploration of epics and rank them roughly, using WSJF, to determine which epics should move to the next step for deeper exploration.

- *Program Epic Analysis* provides the ability to explore the epic in more depth; refine size and WSJF compared to other epics in this step; consider solution alternatives; identify possible paths of the incremental implementation strategy; and determine the costs involved, technology and architectural enablement, infrastructure, etc. This information is captured in a lightweight business case. Based on that, stakeholders with sufficient content and budget authority consider approval of the epics. Approved epics are split into features and transitioned to a feature Kanban.

Similar to portfolio epics, program epics may require Epic Owners who will help with the definition, exploration, and implementation of an epic.

## Feature Section

The purpose of this section of the program Kanban system is to facilitate readiness, prioritization, and implementation of features. Features may originate locally (either from program epics or introduced as individual features that don't have a parent program epic) or come from the upstream Kanban. In either case, features enter the Feature Funnel.

The feature part of the program Kanban stays fully under the purview of local content authority: Product Management and System Architects. The following steps instantiate the feature section of the Agile Release Train (ART) Kanban:

- All new features are welcome in the *Feature Funnel*. These may include new functionality or enhancement of the existing system functions. New backlog items that enhance system qualities or produce architectural or infrastructure enablement also originate here.

- Features that align with the Vision and support strategic themes are moved to *Feature Refinement* for further exploration. This step requires refinement of the key attributes of a feature: business benefit, acceptance criteria, and WSJF. General sizing of features also occurs at this step, as features are estimated in normalized Story points. The purpose of such estimation is to support economic estimating and forecasting of value delivery over a longer period of time based on scope. Some features under analysis may require prototyping or other forms of exploration that involve Agile Teams. Typically such exploration work is included in the PI plan. The WIP limit at the analysis step is expressed based on overall availability of Product Management, other subject matter experts involved, and the capacity of teams dedicated to exploration activities.

- Highest-priority features that were sufficiently elaborated and approved by Product Management move to the next step—*Program Backlog*—where they are prioritized with WSJF relative to the rest of the backlog.

- At every PI boundary, the ART pulls the top features from the program backlog and moves them into the *Implementing* step. The transition is performed as a result of the PI Planning process, where selected features get broken down into stories and subsequently implemented by teams during the PI.

The program Kanban is managed by Product Management, who has content authority over business features, and System Architects, who support Enablers. They periodically involve external stakeholders with fiduciary responsibility and decision-making capacity to approve larger initiatives.

## Value Stream Kanban

The value stream Kanban generally repeats the structure and flow of the program Kanban system, so it won't be described further here. However, it operates with capabilities and value stream epics, respectively. The value stream Kanban is managed by the Solution Management team and supported by Solution Architects. Involvement of portfolio stakeholders is necessary to approve value stream epics.

## Supporting Ceremonies

Both program and value stream level Kanban systems require certain ceremonies that support the flow of value. Some of these serve a broader purpose, while others are specific to the Kanban system itself. Since value stream and program levels operate on a synchronous PI cadence, it is critical to align Kanban system activities to that cadence. Below are suggested ceremonies in the context of program and value stream Kanban systems. The Release Train Engineer and Value Stream Engineer typically facilitate these ceremonies at their respective levels.

### Epic Specification Workshop
Structured similarly to the specification workshop at the portfolio level, the epic specification workshop involves analysts and stakeholders who have authority over program and value stream epics. During the workshop, some epics can be pulled from funnel to review, others from review to analysis. For still others, a "go" / "no-go" decision will be made, followed by resultant features and capabilities being transitioned to the "downstream" part of the Kanban.

### Program/Value Stream Backlog Refinement
The goal of this workshop, which typically involves content and technical authority at the relevant level, is to build the backlog of features or capabilities, respectively. Sizing and elaboration of business benefits and acceptance criteria are performed at this time. Rough WSJF prioritization sequences the features and capabilities that can be pulled into the backlog.

### PI Planning
In the general case, PI Planning begins with a Pre-PI Planning session at the value stream level, where capabilities from the value stream Kanban are split into features and fed into the program Kanban systems for each train in the value stream. The input to this session is the set of top capabilities from the Value Stream Backlog. The session involves both Solution and Product Management. Each Product Manager will bring the resultant features to their program Kanban system and place them in the "feature funnel" step, if more elaboration is needed. The features will move through the Kanban system, and those that get through refinement will be pulled by the trains into their two-day PI planning session. The aggregated results of these sessions will be brought back up to the value stream level (Post-PI Planning) for better understanding of which capabilities made it into the implementation.

### Solution/System Demo
The goal of a flow system is to drive backlog items to completion. The Solution Demo and System Demo allow stakeholders to assess the amount of completed work and value delivered.

# Program and Value Stream Backlogs

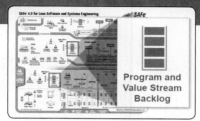

*The emphasis should be on why we do a job.*
  —W. Edwards Deming

## Abstract

The *Program and Value Stream Backlogs* are the definitive repositories for all the upcoming work anticipated to advance the Solution. The backlogs consist of upcoming Features (Program Backlog) and Capabilities (Value Stream Backlog) that are intended to address user needs and deliver business benefits, as well as Enablers that advance learning and build the Architectural Runway.

The items in the backlog arise from various stakeholders—Customers, Business Owners, Product Management, Product Owners, Architects, and more—but the management of the backlog is the responsibility of Product Management (Program Backlog) and Solution Management (Value Stream Backlog). Effectively identifying, refining, prioritizing, and sequencing the backlog items (using WSJF) is the key to the economic success of the solution.

Since the backlog contains both new business functionality and the enablement work necessary to extend the architectural runway, capacity allocation can be applied to help ensure near- and long-term velocity and quality.

## Details

The *Program and Value Stream Backlogs* are the repositories for all the upcoming work that affects the behavior of the Solution. Product and Solution Management develop, maintain, and prioritize the program and value stream backlogs, respectively. The backlogs are a short-term holding area for Features and Capabilities that have gone through the Program and Value Stream Kanbans and have been approved for implementation. Backlog items should be estimated in story points, as Figure 1 illustrates.

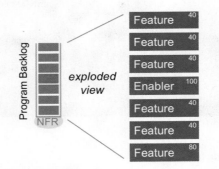

*Figure 1. Exploded view of program backlog, with story point size estimates*

## Refining the Backlog

The Value Streams (VSs) and Agile Release Trains (ARTs) run a steady 8 – 10 week Program Increment cadence of planning > execution > demo > inspect and adapt. This steady rhythm is the heartbeat that drives backlog readiness as well. Appearing at a Pre-PI Planning or a PI Planning without a well-elaborated backlog adds unacceptable risk to the upcoming PI. To this end, the time between PI planning events is a busy time for Product and Solution Management, as they are constantly in the process of refining the backlogs in preparation for the next PI planning. Making this process visible, and achieving "backlog readiness" for the upcoming PI, are the primary purposes of the ART and solution Kanbans. Backlog refinement typically includes:

- Reviewing and updating backlog item definition and developing acceptance criteria

- Working with the teams to establish technical feasibility and scope estimates

- Analyzing ways to split backlog items into smaller chunks of incremental value

- Determining the Enablers spawned by new features and capabilities, and establishing their capacity allocation

## Prioritizing the Backlogs

Prioritizing the backlogs is a key economic driver for the solution. To this end, product and solution management use the Weighted Shortest Job First prioritization method for job sequencing. To recap, WSJF ultimately translates to a simple formula:

$$WSJF = \frac{\textit{User-Business Value} + \textit{Time Criticality} + \textit{Risk Reduction-Opportunity Enablement Value}}{\textit{Job size}}$$

Applying the formula requires that the numerator items be ranked only on a relative basis to each other. The denominator, job size, can be either a relative measure or an estimate in story points. Note: The actual denominator of WSJF is job duration, though we use job size as a proxy.

This is because duration depends on who does the work and what capacity allocation they can give the new work; that can be almost impossible to determine in advance of allocating the work. Since large jobs typically take longer to do, job size is a reasonable first approximation.

With respect to job size, the denominator should represent only the *remaining work* for any items already under way. Then, if the remaining work for the item is too large to justify further investment relative to other jobs, the item can be called "good enough," and the teams can move on to other priorities. This implicitly implements Reinertsen's [2] key economic *Principle E17: The sunk cost principle: Do not consider money already spent*.

## Preparing for PI Planning

The week or two prior to PI planning is a very busy time. Product and Solution Management do final backlog preparation, update the vision briefings, and work with Product Owners to further socialize the backlog prior to the event. System and Solution Architects/Engineering update enabler definitions and models and often develop use cases that illustrate how the features and capabilities work together to deliver the end user value.

## Optimizing Value and Solution Integrity with Capacity Allocation

One of the challenges every ART and value stream faces is how to balance the backlog of business features and capabilities with the need to continuously invest in the Architectural Runway, provide time for exploration of requirements and design for future PIs, and create prototypes and models to enhance visibility into the problem areas. In order to avoid velocity reduction and to defer the need for wholesale replacement of components due to technological obsolescence, ARTs must invest continuously in implementing the enablers of the solution. This complicates the challenge of prioritizing work since different people can pull the teams in different directions, as Figure 2 shows.

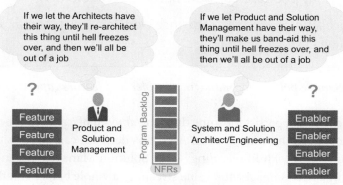

*Figure 2. Business vs. enabler backlog items dilemma*

To address this problem, teams apply *capacity allocation*, whereby they make a decision about how much of the total effort can be applied for each type of activity for an upcoming PI. Further, they establish an agreement to determine how the work is performed for each activity type. Examples of the results are given in Figure 3 and Table 1.

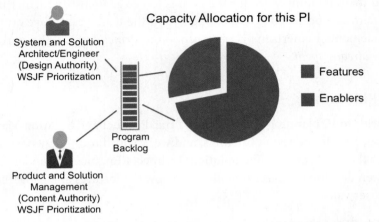

*Figure 3. Capacity allocation for architecture in an ART backlog for a single PI*

1.  At each PI boundary, we agree on the percentage of resources to be devoted to new features or capabilities vs. enablers

2.  We agree that System and Solution Architects and Engineering have authority to prioritize enabler work

3.  We agree that Product and Solution Management have authority to prioritize business backlog items

4.  We agree to jointly prioritize our work based on economics

5.  We agree to collaborate so as to sequence work in a way that maximizes Customer value

*Table 1: Sample policies for managing enabler and feature capacity allocation*

While the agreed-to *policies* can persist for some time, the *amount* of capacity allocated should vary over time based on the context. In the context of an ART, this decision can be revisited as part of backlog refinement in preparation for each PI planning, while Solution Management and Solution Architect/Engineering make similar decisions for the value stream as a whole before solution PI planning.

## On Backlogs, Queues, Little's Law, and Wait Times

It's important to take a brief aside and discuss the relationship between backlog, wait times, and flow. The principle *Manage queue length* discusses the relationship in detail; refer to SAFe Principle #6 for more complete understanding. However, it's important to summarize that discussion here, because the program and value stream backlogs are *the* backlogs that can have the biggest impact on delivery time and throughput. Here's a summary:

1. Little's Law illustrates that the average wait time for an item in a queue is equal to the average length of the queue divided by the average processing rate for an item in a queue. The longer the queue, the higher the wait time, *and* the higher the variability. (Think of the line at Starbucks: If the ten people ahead of you each order a tall coffee, you are going to be out of there in minutes; if they all order an extra-hot vanilla latte and a heated bagel, you might be late for your meeting, and it is not under your control.)

2. Long queues are all bad, causing decreased motivation, poor quality, longer cycle times, higher variability (think Starbucks), and increased risk [2].

3. Your program and value stream backlogs are not queues, as items can leapfrog others for faster delivery, and you can always choose not to service everything in the backlog. (Note that neither of these work at Starbucks.)

4. *However*, if all the items in your backlog are committed to stakeholders, *then your backlog behaves like a queue*, and the longer it is, the longer your stakeholders are going to have to wait for service. And if they have to wait too long, they will find another coffee shop, as your shop just can't meet their rapidly changing market needs.

Therefore, in order for a development program to be fast and responsive, *teams must actively manage the backlogs and keep them short*. Teams also must limit commitment to longer-term work, because some other item may come along that's more important than a prior commitment. If a team has too many fixed and committed requirements in the backlog, they cannot respond quickly, no matter how efficient they are. Teams *can be both reliable and fast only if they actively manage the backlog and keep it short*.

---

**LEARN MORE**

[1] Leffingwell, Dean. *Agile Software Requirements: Lean Requirements Practices for Teams, Programs, and the Enterprise*. Addison-Wesley, 2011.

[2] Reinertsen, Donald. *Principles of Product Development Flow: Second Generation Lean Product Development*. Celeritas Publishing, 2009.

# Nonfunctional Requirements

*I've been accused of being a shell designer—you start with a machine and enclose it. But in many cases, the shell is essential. A locomotive without a shell would be nonfunctional.*

—Raymond Loewy

## Abstract

*Nonfunctional Requirements* (NFRs, or system qualities) describe system attributes such as security, reliability, maintainability, scalability, and usability (often referred to as the "ilities"). They can also be constraints or restrictions on the design of the system (in which they may be referred to as *design constraints*). These requirements are just as critical as the functional Epics, Capabilities, Features, and user stories, as they ensure the usability and efficacy of the entire system; failing to meet any one can result in systems that do not meet internal business, user, or market needs or that do not meet mandatory requirements imposed by regulatory or standards agencies.

Nonfunctional requirements are persistent qualities and constraints and, unlike functional requirements, are typically revisited as part of the Definition of Done for each Iteration, Program Increment, or Release. NFRs exist at all four SAFe levels: Team, Program, Value Stream, and Portfolio.

Definition and implementation of NFRs is of critical concern for the systems builder. Over-specify them and the Solution may be too costly to be viable; under-specify them and the solution will not be adequate for its intended use. An adaptive and incremental approach to exploring, defining, and implementing NFRs is a key skill of the successful Lean-Agile systems builder.

## Details

Traditionally, one way to think about all the types of requirements that affect a Solution's overall fitness for use has been the acronym "FURPS," which is a traditional requirements categorization for *Functionality, Usability, Reliability, Performance,* and *Supportability* [5]. *Functional* requirements are largely expressed in user stories and in Features and Capabilities. This is where most of the work occurs: Teams build systems that deliver functional value to the user, and a majority of the time and effort in solution development is devoted to that functionality.

"FURPS" is the placeholder for *Nonfunctional Requirements*. Though they may be a bit more subtle, NFRs are as just as important to system success as are functional requirements. NFRs can be considered *constraints* on new development, in that each eliminates some degree of design freedom on the part of those building the system. For example: "We need to implement SAML-based single sign-on for all products in the suite" (SSO is a *functional* requirement; basing the technology on SAML is a constraint). NFRs can cover a wide range of business-critical issues that are not well addressed by functional requirements. As a reminder to system designers, a fairly comprehensive list of such potential requirements is described in [1].

## NFRs Occur at All Levels

Nonfunctional requirements are associated with backlogs at all four levels of SAFe, as Figure 1 illustrates.

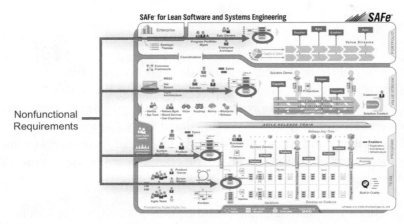

*Figure 1. NFRs occur at all four levels*

Because NFRs are significant attributes of the solution that the Agile Release Train and Value Streams create, the most obvious representation of NFRs are at the Program and Value Stream Levels. System and Solution Architect and Engineering are often responsible for defining and refining these NFRs.

All teams must be aware of these special attributes of the system they are creating. This helps foster Built-in Quality practices by accelerating NFR testing, rather than postponing it. Teams include the relevant NFRs into their Definition of Done, use them as constraints on local design and implementation decisions, and take responsibility for some level of NFR testing on their own. Otherwise, the solution may not satisfy key NFRs, and the cost of correction can be very high when it occurs late in the process.

In addition, Team Level NFRs can also be important, as they create constraints and performance requirements on the features and subsystems they create.

The Portfolio Level may require certain NFRs as well. This is often the case for inherently cross-system qualities, like the single sign-on example. Other examples include restrictions on open source usage, common security requirements, regulatory standards, and more.

If a specific portfolio level NFR is not yet achieved, it may require architectural Enablers to implement it. In other cases, portfolio level NFRs may naturally appear on business and enabler Epic success criteria.

## NFRs as Backlog Constraints

In SAFe, NFRs are modeled as "backlog constraints," as is illustrated in Figure 2.

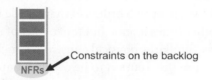

*Figure 2. A backlog with NFR constraints*

More technically, the SAFe Requirements Model specifies that NFRs may constrain *zero*, *some*, or *many* backlog items. Further, in order to know that the system is compliant with the constraint, most NFRs require one or more system qualities tests, as is illustrated in Figure 3.

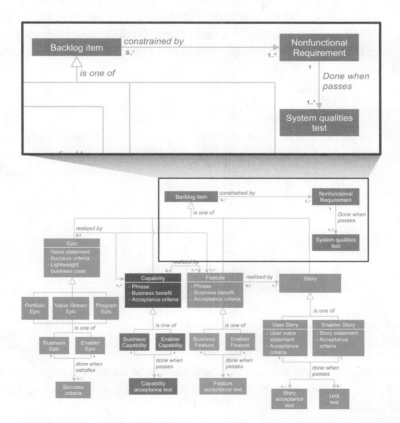

*Figure 3. Association between backlog items, nonfunctional requirements, and system qualities tests*

Many NFRs begin their lives as enablers that need to be addressed. Thereafter, they constrain the system and all new backlog items going forward.

## The Systemic and Economic Impact of NFRs on Solution Development

Nonfunctional requirements can have major impact on solution development and testing. NFRs are tricky to specify, and it's easy to go overboard. For example, a statement like "99.9999% availability" may increase development effort by one or two orders of magnitude more than "99.999% availability." Sometimes that's necessary and other times it's not, but the impact of the NFR must be well understood by those writing the specifications. Similarly, physical constraints such as weight, volume, or voltage, if not given enough thought, may cause the solution to be overly complicated and too costly.

The Economic Framework of the solution should hold criteria to evaluate the extent to which NFRs should be taken as a trade-off with costs and other considerations. Suppliers are likewise impacted by NFRs, and declaring them incorrectly or without the full trade-off ramifications of the economic framework might lead to unnecessarily complex and costly systems and components.

It is also important to reevaluate NFRs regularly. Unlike other requirements, NFRs are persistent constraints on the backlog, rather than backlog items themselves, and so they may not always come up during PI Planning. But nonfunctional requirements do change during development, and systems builders must be well aware.

## NFRs and Solution Intent

Solution Intent is the single source of truth about the solution, and as such it includes NFRs as well as functional requirements. It also includes links between NFRs, requirements they impact, and tests used to verify them. NFRs play a key role in understanding the economics of fixed versus variable solution intent.

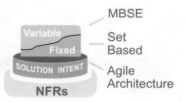

*Figure 4. Solution intent*

Early on, some of the functionality is not clear and will need to be tested and negotiated with Customers during development. The same goes for NFRs—some are fixed and well known up front, while others will evolve with the solution.

By imposing constraints, NFRs may impact a wide scope of system functionality. Therefore they are an important factor in Agile analysis:

- Analyzing business epics, capabilities, and features

- Planning and building the Architectural Runway

- Refactoring to better reflect increasing solution domain knowledge

- Imposing DevOps constraints by manufacturing, deployment, support, installation, maintainability, etc.

The tools used to help develop solution intent provide some mechanisms to help establish an economic approach to defining and implementing NFRs.

- **Agile Architecture** – A solid intentional architecture supports development of NFRs and helps maintain flexibility as they change

- **Model-Based Systems Engineering** – Models can be used to simulate the effect of NFRs and can link to the tests that validate them

- **Set-Based Design** – SBD provides different frames for achieving NFRs and can guide a range of edge-case testing in support of design decisions

## Specifying NFRs

Defining NFRs is assisted by consideration of the following criteria:

- **Bounded** – Some NFRs are irrelevant (or even impairing) when they lack bounded context. For example, performance considerations can be extremely important for the main application but irrelevant (or too expensive) for administration and support applications.

- **Independent** – NFRs should be independent of each other so that they can be evaluated and tested without consideration of or impact from other system qualities

- **Negotiable** – Understanding the NFR business drivers and bounded context mandates negotiability

- **Testable** – NFRs must be stated with objective, measurable, and testable criteria, because *if you can't test it, you can't ship it*

## Implementation Approaches

Many NFRs prescribe that some additional work be done—either now or in the future—to satisfy them. Sometimes the NFR must be implemented all at once; at other times the teams can take a more incremental approach. The trade-offs described in the economic framework should impact the implementation approach. Implementation should be built in a way that will allow several learning cycles to ascertain the right level of NFR.

1. **All at once** – Some NFRs appear as new, immediate concerns and just have to be done now. For example, a new regulatory rule for derivative trading, if not immediately accommodated, could take the company completely out of the market or cause a regulatory violation.

2. **Incremental story-by-story path** – At other times the teams have options. For example, the need for "substantially improved performance" can be dealt with over time, one story at a time, as Figure 5 illustrates.

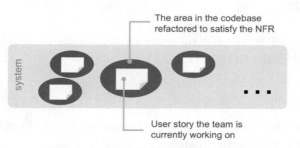

*Figure 5. Introducing an NFR to the solution incrementally*

NFR implementation is also impacted by the way ARTs have been organized. ARTs built around architectural layers will find it very hard to implement and test an NFR in its entirety. ARTs organized around capabilities will find it easier to implement, test, and maintain systemic NFRs.

## Testing Nonfunctional Requirements

Of course, in order to know that a system meets NFRs, it must be tested against them. Testing NFRs is most easily viewed from the perspective of the *four Agile testing quadrants*, as reflected in Figure 6 [2, 3].

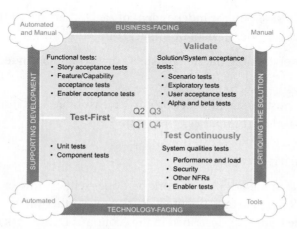

*Figure 6. Agile testing quadrants (adapted from [2, 3])*

Quadrant 4, *System Qualities Tests*, is the home of most NFR tests. Due to their scope and criticality, NFR testing often requires collaboration between the System Team and the Agile Teams. Wherever possible, teams should automate so that these tests can be run continuously, or at least on demand, to help prevent the growth of unexpected technical debt.

Over time, however, the accumulated growth of regression tests, even when automated, may consume too much resource and processing time. Worse, it can mean that NFR testing may be practical only on occasion, or only with specialty resources or personnel. In order to ensure practicality and continuous use, teams often need to create reduced test suites and test data, as is illustrated in Figure 7.

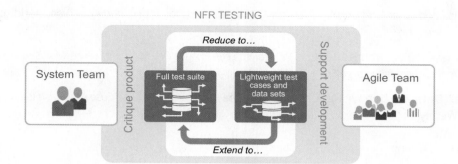

*Figure 7. Collaboration of the System Team and Agile Teams
to create a more practical NFR testing strategy*

Though "partial testing" sounds less than ideal, it can actually be beneficial in *increasing* system quality:

- When teams are able to apply reduced test suites locally, they may spot inconsistencies in the test data or testing approach

- Teams may create new and unique tests, some of which may be adopted by the System Team to help build the larger set

- Testing infrastructure and configurations will likely be continuously improved

- Teams gain a practical understanding of the impact of NFRs, which helps improve estimating of business and architectural features

Even so, in some cases the environment where the NFRs can be tested may not be available on a daily basis (example: field testing of vehicle guidance software). In these cases, the following approaches [4] can be used:

- Using virtualized hardware

- Creating simulators

- Creating similar environments

In all cases, efficiently testing nonfunctional requirements requires some thought and creativity. A lack of NFR testing, on the other hand, may increase the risk of substantive technical debt or, worse, system failure.

---

**LEARN MORE**

[1] https://en.wikipedia.org/wiki/Non-functional_requirement

[2] Leffingwell, Dean. *Agile Software Requirements: Lean Requirements Practices for Teams, Programs, and the Enterprise*. Addison-Wesley, 2011.

[3] Crispin, Lisa and Janet Gregory. *Agile Testing: A Practical Guide for Testers and Agile Teams*. Addison-Wesley, 2009.

[4] Larman, Craig and Bas Vodde. *Practices for Scaling Lean & Agile Development: Large, Multisite, and Offshore Product Development with Large-Scale Scrum*. Addison-Wesley, 2010.

[5] Leffingwell, Dean and Don Widrig. *Managing Software Requirements: A Use Case Approach* (second edition). Addison-Wesley, 2003.

# Program Increment

*Many people don't focus enough on execution. If you make a commitment to get something done, you need to follow through on that commitment.*
—Kenneth Chenault

*Doing is a quantum leap from imagining.*
—Barbara Sher

## Abstract

The *Program Increment* (PI) is the largest plan-do-check-adjust (PDCA) learning cycle in SAFe. A PI is to the Agile Release Train (or Value Stream) as an Iteration is to the Agile Team: a cadence-based interval for building and validating a full system increment, demonstrating value and getting fast feedback. Each PI is a development timebox that uses cadence and synchronization to facilitate planning, limit WIP, provide for aggregation of newsworthy value for feedback, and ensure consistent program-level retrospectives. Due to its scope, the PI also provides a strategic quantum of thinking for Portfolio Level consideration and Roadmapping.

The PI aggregates multiple teams—and multiple iterations of their work—into an amount of value and a timebox that the Enterprise can focus attention on. And while continuous integration and system/solution validation is always the goal, the PI timebox can also provide a forcing function for full system integration and validation that can significantly reduce the risk of deferred integration and, even worse, deferred or slow internal or external Customer feedback.

The PI cycle is distinct from the Release cycle. In some situations, the PI and release cadence are the same, which can be a major convenience. Other programs may need to release less or more frequently than the PI cadence. Still others will have multiple, independent release cycles for the various components of the solution.

## Details

SAFe divides the development timeline into a set of Iterations within a *Program Increment* (PI). The Big Picture illustrates how a PI is initiated by a PI Planning session and is then followed by four execution iterations, concluding with one Innovation and Planning Iteration.

*This pattern is suggestive but arbitrary, and there is no fixed rule for how many iterations are in a PI. Experience has shown that a PI duration of between 8 and 12 weeks works best, with a bias toward the shortest duration.*

The PI is the outer-loop cadence of the PDCA cycle; it aggregates a strategic unit of time and value into a meaningful point to objectively measure the Solution under development. And as "integration points control product development" [1], the PI is the routine point at which the meaningful emergent behavior of the full system or solution can be evaluated.

Both the Value Stream and its Agile Release Trains (ARTs) use the same PI cadence, as Figure 1 illustrates.

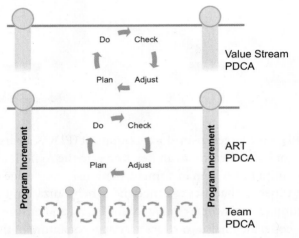

*Figure 1. Value streams and ARTs follow the same PI cadence*

The PI follows a classic PDCA learning cycle. PI planning is the "plan" step of the cycle, and the "do" step is the PI execution, the "check" is the demo, and the Inspect and Adapt workshop represents the "adjust." This applies to both the value stream and the ARTs, as can be seen in the "Coordination" article.

## Develop on Cadence, Release Any Time

Continuous end-to-end sequencing of PIs is the metronome of the Agile Release Train. ART assets grow continuously and incrementally. Releasing solutions, however, is a separate concern, which is covered in the "Release" and "Develop on Cadence, Release Any Time" companion articles. With these principles, programs and/or value streams are free to establish the best product development rhythm, continuously building incremental functionality. The business is free to deploy releases as and when the business or market requires.

## Executing the Program Increment

When it comes to execution, a sequence of program events creates a closed-loop system to "keep the train on the tracks," as illustrated in Figure 2.

Each program event is described in the sections below.

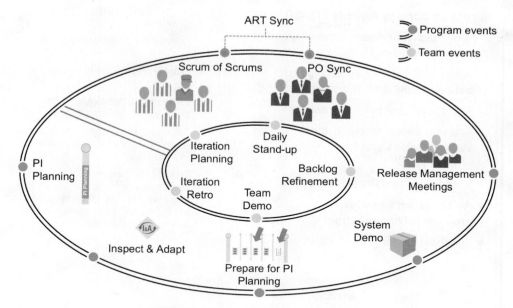

*Figure 2. Program execution events*

## PI Planning

Each PI begins with a PI planning session. Given the fixed cadence and routine nature of these critical events, dates can be fixed and scheduled well (often up to a year) in advance. This lowers facility, travel, overhead, and other transaction costs.

During PI planning, the teams estimate what will be delivered and when, and highlight their interdependencies. PI planning also creates the baseline for the integration and demo pull events by defining what will be built and demonstrated. One outcome of the PI planning is a set of program PI Objectives, detailing what the ART will have ready for integration and demo at the end of the PI.

## Scrum of Scrums

The Release Train Engineer (RTE) typically facilitates a weekly (or more frequently, as conditions require) Scrum of Scrums (SoS) meeting to continuously coordinate dependencies of the Agile Release Train and to provide visibility into progress and impediments. The RTE, Scrum Masters, and others (where appropriate) meet to update their progress toward Milestones, program PI objectives, and internal dependencies among the teams. The meeting is timeboxed to less than 30 minutes and is followed by a "meet-after" to solve problems identified. A suggested agenda for the SoS meeting is described in Figure 3.

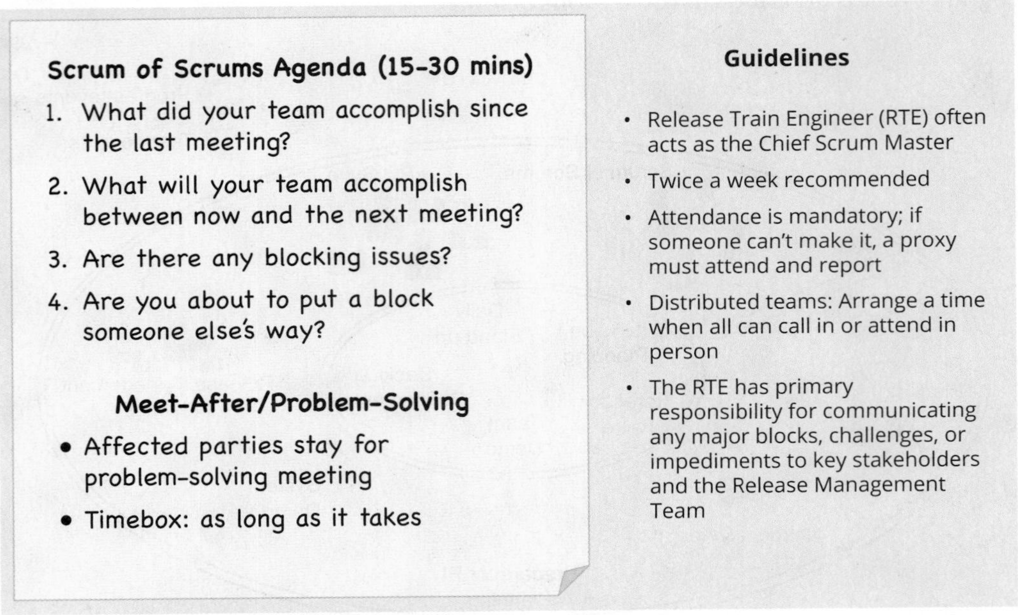

**Scrum of Scrums Agenda (15–30 mins)**

1. What did your team accomplish since the last meeting?
2. What will your team accomplish between now and the next meeting?
3. Are there any blocking issues?
4. Are you about to put a block someone else's way?

**Meet-After/Problem-Solving**

- Affected parties stay for problem-solving meeting
- Timebox: as long as it takes

**Guidelines**

- Release Train Engineer (RTE) often acts as the Chief Scrum Master
- Twice a week recommended
- Attendance is mandatory; if someone can't make it, a proxy must attend and report
- Distributed teams: Arrange a time when all can call in or attend in person
- The RTE has primary responsibility for communicating any major blocks, challenges, or impediments to key stakeholders and the Release Management Team

*Figure 3. Sample Scrum of Scrums agenda*

**PO Sync**

In a manner similar to the SoS, a PO Sync meeting is often held for Product Owners and Product Managers. This meeting typically occurs weekly, or more frequently as conditions require. The PO Sync is also timeboxed (30 to 60 minutes) and is followed by a "meet-after" to solve problems identified during the meeting.

This meeting may be facilitated by the RTE or Product Manager. The purpose of the meeting is to get visibility into how well the ART is progressing toward meeting the program PI objectives, to discuss problems or opportunities with Feature development, and to assess any scope adjustments. The meeting may also be used to prepare for the next PI (see below) and may include Program Backlog refinement, WSJF prioritization prior to the next PI planning meeting, and more.

Note: As illustrated in Figure 2, sometimes the Scrum of Scrums and PO Sync are combined into one meeting, often referred to as an *ART sync*.

**Release Management Meetings**

Release Management meetings provide governance for any upcoming Releases and also provide regular communication to management. These may occur weekly or as needed by the program context. The Release Management team has the authority to approve any scope, timing, or resource adjustments necessary to help ensure the release.

## System Demo

The hallmark of each PI is a biweekly System Demo. The demo is used to get feedback from the stakeholders about the efficacy and usability of the system under development. This demo also helps ensure that integration between teams on the same ART occurs on a regular basis and no less than every iteration.

## Prepare for the Next PI Planning Event

While we note this function as an event in Figure 3, in reality, preparing for the upcoming PI is a *continuous* process, with three primary focus areas:

1. Management alignment and organizational readiness for planning

2. Backlog readiness

3. The actual logistics for the event—facility readiness

Since any one of these can interfere with the potential outcome—an actual, specific, and committed PI plan—careful consideration of all three factors is warranted.

## Inspect and Adapt

The PI is "done" when the PI timebox expires. Each PI is followed by a final system demo, a newsworthy event that illustrates *all* the features that have been accomplished during the PI. This is usually done as part of the inspect and adapt (I&A) workshop, which is a regular time to reflect, problem-solve, and take on improvement actions needed to increase the velocity, quality, and reliability of the next PI. The result of the workshop is a set of *improvement stories* that can be added to the backlog for the upcoming PI planning. In this way, every ART improves every PI.

## PI Execution in Multi-ART Value Streams

In larger, multi-ART value streams, there are additional events and activities necessary to bring a similar focus to the progress of the solution.

## Pre- and Post-PI Planning for the Value Stream

The Pre- and Post-PI Planning meetings allow Agile Release Trains and Suppliers in large value streams to build an aligned plan for the next program increment. The pre- and post-PI planning meetings serve as a wrapper for the PI planning meetings at the Program Level, which is where the actual, detailed planning takes place, as can be seen in the IP iteration calendar (see the "Innovation and Planning Iteration" article).

## Value Stream Increment and Solution Demo

During the PI timebox, the ARTs build multiple increments of value, which accumulate into solution Capabilities. The new capabilities must be designed, developed, tested, and validated holistically, along with the existing capabilities of the system. The Solution Demo is the apex of the PI learning cycle.

This is a high-profile event where value stream stakeholders, Customers (or their internal proxies), and senior management view the progress that the solution has made during the past program increment.

At this event, the value stream demonstrates its accomplishments in the past PI. Senior managers and stakeholders review the progress in the broader solution context. It may also inform decisions about continuation, adjustment, or even cancellation of initiatives, as well as changes to the Budgets for the various value streams.

---

**LEARN MORE**

[1] Oosterwal, Dantar P. *The Lean Machine: How Harley-Davidson Drove Top-Line Growth and Profitability with Revolutionary Lean Product Development*. Amacom, 2010.

# PI Planning

Future product development tasks can't be predetermined. Distribute planning and control to those who can understand and react to the end results.

—Michael Kennedy, *Product Development for the Lean Enterprise*

There is no magic in SAFe . . . except maybe for PI Planning.
—Authors

## Abstract

A principle of the Agile Manifesto states, "The most efficient and effective method of conveying information to and within a development team is face-to-face conversation." SAFe takes this to the next level via *PI Planning*, the seminal, cadence-based synchronization point of the Agile Release Train (ART). PI planning is a routine, face-to-face event with a standardized agenda that includes presentation of business context and Vision, followed by team planning breakouts wherein the teams create the plans for the upcoming Program Increment (PI). Facilitated by the Release Train Engineer (RTE), attendees include all members of the ART whenever possible. It takes place over one and a half to two days and occurs within the IP Iteration, which means that it doesn't affect the timebox, scheduling, or capacity of other iterations in the PI. The result is a commitment to an agreed-to set of Program PI objectives for the next PI. In geographically distributed ARTs, the event may occur at multiple locations simultaneously, with constant communication between the locations.

In multi-ART Value Streams, Pre-PI Planning meetings are held to set the context and input objectives for the ART PI planning sessions. Post-PI Planning sessions are used to integrate the results of the ARTs that contribute to the Value Stream.

## Details

*PI Planning* is the seminal, cadence-based event that serves as the heartbeat of the Agile Release Train. It is integral and essential to SAFe (if you are not doing it, you are not doing SAFe). At scale, this can be quite a significant event, as Figure 1 implies.

*Figure 1. Large-scale, face-to-face PI planning. Remote teams in India and Slovakia are planning simultaneously with these teams in the U.S.*

PI planning delivers innumerable business benefits; its activities include:

- Establishing high-bandwidth communication across all team members and stakeholders
- Building the social network the ART depends upon
- Aligning development to business via business context, Vision, and Team and Program PI Objectives
- Identifying dependencies and fostering cross-team and cross-ART coordination
- Providing the opportunity for "just the right amount" of Architecture and User Experience guidance
- Matching demand to capacity, eliminating excess WIP
- Accelerating decision-making

Inputs to the event include the Roadmap and vision, the top 10 Features from the Program Backlog, and other business context. Attendees include all the team members and program stakeholders, including the Business Owners. PI planning has three primary outputs:

1. A set of "SMART" team PI objectives for each individual team, created by the team, with business value assigned by the Business Owners, and a synthesized and summarized set of program PI objectives

2. A "program board," which highlights the new features, anticipated delivery dates, and any other relevant Milestones, aggregated from the team objectives

3. A vote of confidence/commitment from the entire program to these objectives

In addition, in large Value Streams, multiple ARTS typically plan contemporaneously. Such events are typically bracketed by Pre- and Post-PI Planning events, which provide alignment and coordination of the ARTs to a common Solution purpose. These events are discussed briefly later in this article.

## Preparation

PI planning is a major event that requires preparation, coordination, and communication. Event attendees, including Product Management, Agile Teams, System and Solution Architect/Engineering, the System Team, and other stakeholders must be notified and well prepared.

Preparation for a successful event is required in three major areas:

- Organizational readiness – Strategic alignment and teams and trains setup

- Content readiness – Management and development preparedness

- Facility readiness – The actual space and logistics for the event

Below are descriptive highlights from the *Release Planning Readiness Checklist* in [1], Appendix C. See Chapter 15 of [1] for additional details.

## Organizational Readiness

Prior to planning, it's important to insure that programs have reasonable strategy alignment among participants, stakeholders, and Business Owners; teams are aligned to the value stream; and critical roles are assigned. To address this, preparedness questions include:

- Planning scope and context – Is the scope (product, system, technology domain) of the planning process understood? Do we know which teams need to plan together?

- Business alignment – Is there reasonable agreement on priorities among the Business Owners?

- Agile Teams – Do we have Agile Teams? Does each have dedicated developer and test resources and an identified Scrum Master and Product Owner?

## Content Readiness

It is equally important to ensure that there is clear vision and context and that the right stakeholders can participate. Therefore the PI planning must include:

- The executive briefing – A briefing that defines the current business context

- Product vision briefing(s) – Briefings prepared by Product Management, including the *top 10 Features* in the program backlog

- The architecture vision briefing – Briefing prepared by the CTO, Enterprise Architect, and/or System Architect to communicate new Enablers, features, and Nonfunctional Requirements

## Facility Readiness

Securing the physical space and technical infrastructure necessary to support the large number of attendees isn't trivial either, especially if there are remote participants. Considerations include:

- Facility – This must be roomy enough for all attendees, with breakout rooms if necessary

- Facilities/tech support – These people need to be identified in advance and reachable during setup, testing, and the event

- Communication channels – For distributed planning meetings, primary and secondary audio, video, and presentation channels must be available

## Event Agenda

The meeting generally follows a standard agenda, such as that in Figure 2. Descriptions of each agenda item follow.

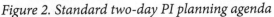

*Figure 2. Standard two-day PI planning agenda*

### Day 1

- **Business Context** – A senior executive/line-of-business owner describes the current state of the business and presents a perspective on how well current solutions are addressing current Customer needs.

- **ART/Solution Vision** – Product Management presents the current vision—typically represented by the next top 10 upcoming features—and highlights any changes from the previous PI planning meeting, as well as any upcoming Milestones.

- **Architecture Vision and Development Practices** – System Architect/Engineering presents the architecture vision. In addition, a senior development manager may present Agile-supportive changes to development practices, such as test automation and Continuous Integration, that are being advanced in the upcoming PI.

- **Planning Context** – The Release Train Engineer presents the planning process and expected outcomes of the meeting.

- **Team Breakouts #1** – In the breakout, teams estimate their capacity (velocity) for each Iteration and identify the backlog items they will likely need to realize the features. Each team creates their draft plans, visible to all, iteration by iteration.

During this process they identify risks and dependencies and draft their initial team PI objectives. The team also adds the features to the program board.

- **Draft Plan Review** – During the tightly timeboxed draft plan review, teams present key planning outputs, including draft objectives, potential risks, and dependencies. Business Owners, Product Management, and other teams and stakeholders review and provide input.

- **Management Review and Problem-Solving** – It is likely that the draft plans present challenges such as scope, resource constraints, and dependencies. During this review and problem-solving meeting, management negotiates scope and resolves these challenges by agreeing to various planning adjustments. The RTE facilitates and keeps key stakeholders together for as long as necessary to make the decisions needed to reach achievable objectives. In multi-ART value streams, a similar meeting may be held after the first day of planning to solve cross-ART issues that have come up, or, alternatively, the RTEs of the affected trains talk with each other to raise issues that are then resolved in the train management problem-solving meeting.

**Day 2**

- **Planning Adjustments** – The next day, the meeting begins with managers describing any changes to planning scope and resources.

- **Team Breakouts #2** – Teams continue planning based on their plan from the previous day, with the appropriate adjustments. They finalize their objectives for the PI, to which the Business Owners assign business value.

- **Final Plan Review** – During the final plan review, all teams present their plans to the group. At the end of each team's time slot, the team states their risks and impediments, but there is no attempt to resolve them in this short time slot. If the plan is acceptable to the Customers, the team brings their program PI objective sheet and program risk sheet to the front of the room so that all can see the aggregate objectives unfold in real time.

- **Program Risks** – During planning, teams have identified critical program-level risks and impediments that could affect their ability to meet their objectives. These are addressed in a broader management context in front of the whole group. One by one, risks are categorized into one of the following groups and addressed in a clear, honest, and visible manner:

    **Resolved** – The teams agree that the issue is no longer a concern

    **Owned** – The item cannot be resolved in the meeting, but someone takes ownership

    **Accepted** – Some risks are just facts or potential occurrences that simply must be understood and accepted

    **Mitigated** – Teams can identify a plan to mitigate the impact of an item

- **Confidence Vote** – Once program risks have been addressed, teams vote on their confidence in meeting their program PI objectives. Each team conducts a "fist of five" vote. If the average is three or four fingers, then management should accept the commitment. If the average is fewer than three fingers, then planning adjustments are made and plans are reworked. Any person voting two fingers or fewer should be given an opportunity to voice their concern. This might add to the list of risks, require some replanning, or simply be informative.

- **Plan Rework if Necessary** – If necessary, teams rework their plans until a high confidence level can be reached. This is one occasion where alignment and commitment are valued more highly than adhering to a timebox.

- **Planning Retrospective and Moving Forward** – Finally, the RTE leads a brief meeting retrospective to capture what went well, what didn't, and what can be done better next time. Following this, next steps are discussed, including capturing objectives and stories in the Agile project management tools, scheduling upcoming key activities and events … and cleaning up the room!

## Outputs of a Successful Event

A successful event delivers three primary artifacts:

1. A set of "SMART" objectives for each team, created by the team, with business value set by the Business Owners. This may include stretch objectives, which are goals built into the plan but not committed to by the team. Stretch objectives provide the flexible capacity and scope management options needed to increase reliability and quality of ART execution (reliably delivering on cadence requires capacity margin). Figure 3 shows a sample of one team's PI objectives.

| Objectives for PI 4 | BV |
|---|---|
| - Proof of concept with mock sounds | 10 |
| - Help with Radar POC | 4 |
| - Decide buy/make engine noises | 3 |
| ======== STRETCH OBJECTIVES ========== | === |
| - Proof of concept with real sounds | 7 |

*Figure 3. A team's objective sheet with business value and one stretch objective*

2. A "program board," which highlights the new feature delivery dates, dependencies among teams and with other ARTs, and relevant milestones, as illustrated in Figure 4.

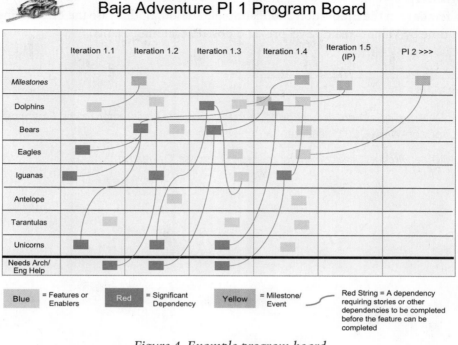

*Figure 4. Example program board*

3.   A vote of confidence/commitment from the entire ART to these objectives.

## Post-Event Activities

Teams leave the event with a pre-populated backlog for the upcoming PI. This serves as fresh input into the normal Iteration Planning processes that follow.

After the meeting, the RTE synthesizes the team PI objectives into program PI objectives (see the "PI Objectives" article for more information) and uses this to communicate expectations to stakeholders and to track progress toward the goal. This usually happens after and not during the PI planning meeting. The program board may or may not be maintained after that time. Given the PI plan, the roadmap is typically updated by product management.

Finally, and most important, the program proceeds to execute the PI, tracking progress and adjusting as necessary to changes that occur as new knowledge emerges.

## PI Planning in Multi-ART Value Streams

The above description focuses on the planning activities of a single ART. However, in larger value streams, multiple ARTs conduct such planning sessions and cross-ART coordination is also required.

Based on logistics, geography, and scope, these may be done contemporaneously, or they may be staggered over a few days in the Innovation and Planning Iteration. In this case the PI planning events are bracketed in time by Value Stream Level pre- and post-PI planning events.

---

### LEARN MORE

[1] Leffingwell, Dean. *Agile Software Requirements: Lean Requirements Practices for Teams, Programs, and the Enterprise*. Addison-Wesley, 2011, chapter 16.

[2] Kennedy, Michael. *Product Development for the Lean Enterprise*. Oaklea Press, 2003.

# Business Owners

*It is hard to imagine a more stupid or more dangerous way of making decisions than by putting those decisions in the hands of people who pay no price for being wrong.*

—*Thomas Sowell*

## Abstract

*Business Owners* are a role in SAFe played by a critical group of three to five (3 – 5) stakeholders who have shared fiduciary, governance, efficacy, and ROI responsibility for the value delivered by a specific Agile Release Train. For each train, the role is fulfilled by the people best suited to these responsibilities. Ultimately, Business Owners can be identified by answering the following question: "What key leaders can steer this train in the right direction; participate in planning; help eliminate impediments; speak on behalf of development, the business, and the Customer; and, ultimately, approve—and where necessary defend—a set of PI plans, while knowing full well that they will never satisfy everyone?"

The answer to that question will identify the Business Owners for a train; they play a key and active role in helping the train deliver value. Among other duties, they have a specific responsibility during PI Planning, where they participate in mission-setting, planning, drafting plan reviews, and management review and problem-solving. They assign business value to PI Objectives and, finally, approve the PI plan. But they don't disappear after planning. Active and continuous involvement by the Business Owners is a determining factor in the success of each train.

## Details

### Summary Role Description

Self-managing, self-organizing Agile Teams and Agile Release Trains are essential to the success of SAFe. This represents a significant change in management mindset. No longer do responsible managers directly manage development by assigning tasks and activities. Instead, they provide leadership via mission and vision, help the teams with coaching and skills development, but largely decentralize execution authority to the members of the ART. However, a transformation to a Lean-Agile way of working does not relieve management of their ultimate responsibilities. They remain accountable for the growth of the organization and its people, operational excellence, and business outcomes.

In order to navigate to this place, SAFe defines the role of *Business Owners*, the role key managers play in guiding the ART to the appropriate outcomes. The specific roles and activities for Business Owners in SAFe enable them to fulfill their obligations to the enterprise while also empowering the teams to do their best work. Business Owners are Lean-Agile Leaders who share ultimate responsibility for the value delivered by a specific Agile Release Train. They are responsible for understanding the Strategic Themes that influence the train. They have knowledge of the current enterprise and Value Stream context, and they are involved in driving or reviewing the program Vision and Roadmap.

## Responsibilities

Effective execution of the authority vested in Business Owners requires active, ongoing participation and fulfillment of their responsibilities. As execution centers around incremental development via Program Increments (PIs), the following sections describe the responsibilities primarily from that perspective.

**Prior to PI Planning**

The time prior to PI Planning is a busy time for Business Owners, as they will:

- Participate in Pre-PI Planning as applicable

- Understand and help ensure that business objectives are understood and agreed to by key stakeholders of the train, including the Release Train Engineer (RTE), Product Management, and System Architects

- Prepare to communicate the business context, including Milestones and significant external dependencies, such as those of Suppliers

**During PI Planning**

The importance of their role during PI planning cannot be overstated. Business Owners:

- Deliver relevant elements of the business context in the defined PI planning agenda timebox

- Are ready and available to participate in certain key ceremonies, including presentation of vision, draft plan review, assigning final business value to PI Objectives, and approving final plans

- Play a primary role in the draft plan review, understanding the bigger picture and how these plans, taken together, do or do not fulfill the current business objectives. Watch for significant external commitments and dependencies.

- Actively circulate during planning, communicate business priorities to the teams, and maintain agreement and alignment among the stakeholders as to the key objectives of the train

- Participate in the management review and problem-solving meeting. Review and adjust scope, compromise as necessary.

## Assigning Business Value

The assignment of business value during planning provides an important face-to-face dialogue between the team and their most important stakeholders, the Business Owners. It is an opportunity to develop a personal relationship between the Agile Teams and the Business Owners, to gain an understanding upon which a mutual commitment can be based, and to better understand the real business objectives and their relative value. An example is provided in Figure 1.

| PI Objectives | Business Value |
|---|---|
| Structured locations and validation of locations | 7 |
| Build and demonstrate a proof of concept for context images | 8 |
| Implement negative triangulation by tags, companies, and people | 8 |
| Speed up indexing by 50% | 10 |
| Index 1.2 billion more web pages | 10 |
| Extract and build URL abstracts | 10 |
| ========== Stretch Objectives ========== | |
| Fuzzy search by full name | 7 |
| Improve tag quality to 80% relevance | 4 |

*Figure 1. An example of a team's PI objectives ranked by business value*

During the assignment of business value, the user-facing Features will typically be ranked highest by the Business Owners. But mature Business Owners know that architectural and other concerns will also increase the velocity of the team in producing future business value, so placing business value on Enablers helps drive ultimate velocity and shows support for the team's legitimate technical challenges. In addition, because the road after PI planning takes its inevitable twists and turns, having objectives ranked by business value gives the teams guidance in making trade-offs and minor scope adjustments in a manner that allows them to deliver the maximum possible business benefit. Finally, these numbers also serve later in determining the PI Predictability Measure, a key indicator of program performance and reliability.

## At Inspect and Adapt

The Inspect and Adapt workshop is the larger, cadence-based opportunity whereby the ART comes together to reflect and to address the larger, systemic impediments that they are facing—many of which cannot be addressed without the active involvement of Business Owners.

During the workshop, Business Owners help assess actual business value achieved vs. plan, and they participate in the problem-solving that follows.

**During PI Execution**
The Business Owners' job is not complete when PI planning is done; they have an ongoing role in helping to assume the success of the PI. They:

- Participate in Release Management, with focus on scope management, quality, deployment options, Release, and market considerations

- Actively participate in ongoing agreements to maintain business and development alignment as priorities and scope are inevitably changed

- Attend the System Demo to view progress and provide feedback

- Attend occasional and Agile Team Iteration Planning and Iteration Retrospective meetings, as appropriate

**Other Responsibilities**
Business Owners may have additional duties beyond those described above, including:

- Participate and provide feedback from the Solution Demo relevant to the Capabilities and subsystems being built by the ART

- Actively address impediments, especially those that escalate beyond the authority of the key stakeholders on the train

- Participate in Post-PI Planning and assist the trains in adjusting the ART's PI plans as needed

- Participate, in some cases, in Program Portfolio Management, Product Management, and even Release Management and System Architecture

It cannot be emphasized enough: *Active participation of Business Owners is a critical success factor for the train.*

# PI Objectives

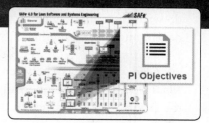

*Making and meeting small commitments builds trust. Ba must be energized with its own intentions . . .*

— Nonaka and Takeuchi, *The Knowledge-Creating Company*

## Abstract

*PI Objectives* are a summarized description of the specific business and technical goals that an Agile Team, ART, or Value Stream intends to achieve in the upcoming Program Increment. Their main purpose is to validate understanding of business and technical intent, focus alignment on outcomes rather than process or tactical concerns, and summarize data into meaningful information that enhances alignment and provides visibility for all.

PI objectives are formulated during PI Planning and, where applicable, Post-PI Planning. During PI planning, each team reviews the Vision and any other input objectives, defines initial Stories, and plans them into Iterations until their capacity is full. Teams then reflect on the iteration plans and synthesize and summarize the specific technical and business objectives for their team for that PI. The aggregation of each team's objectives becomes the *Program PI Objectives*, which are approved by the Business Owners. If Value Stream Level PI planning is needed, then the programs' PI objectives are synthesized and aggregated and become the *Value Stream PI Objectives*.

In this way, all stakeholders know what to expect from each team, each ART, and the value stream as a whole; all WIP is visible. Each team executes against a current, known, aligned, and definitive set of feasible, agreed-upon objectives based on plans that are created by, *not for*, the teams.

At the end of the PI, each team, each ART, and the value stream assess their results against their objectives and use this input to continuously improve performance. (For more on this important topic, see the "Role of PI Objectives" Guidance article online at www.scaledagileframework.com/the-role-of-pi-objectives.)

## Details

SAFe is commitment based, in that it relies on a rolling series of short-term commitments from the Agile Teams, Agile Release Trains (ARTs), and Value Streams to assist with meaningful business planning and outcomes.

This is a key element of trust that must exist between development and the business stakeholders. However, this shouldn't be confused with committing to a set of fixed, long-term, waterfall-like deliverables (as explained in the "Solution Intent" article). But in order for the business to do any meaningful planning, it depends on Solution builders for some amount of reliable, predictable forecasting. Too little, and it's "those ARTs can't commit to anything useful." Too much, and it's "those ARTs never do what they say they will." Neither is optimum, as both increase the distrust between business and development. That significantly hinders ultimate business success, not to mention the joy of work.

We need something in between, and that is a primary purpose of the *Team, Program,* and *Value Stream PI Objectives*. In addition to alignment, the process of feasible objective-setting is integral to reducing the excess work in process in the system.

SAFe PI objectives and plans are built bottom up, by Agile Teams who estimate and plan their own part of the solution. The team creates team PI objectives at the PI Planning meeting, indicating what they will have ready by the end of the Program Increment. The objectives created by the team are aggregated up to the Program Level and then aggregated again to the Value Stream Level, as can be seen in Figure 1.

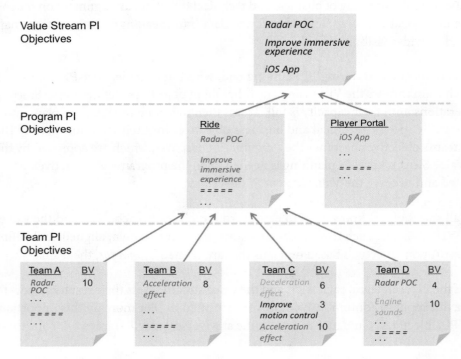

*Figure 1. From team to program to value stream PI objectives*

## Building the Team PI Objectives

During PI planning, teams set team PI objectives, which provide many benefits:

- Provide a common language for communication between business and technology
- Align teams to each other and to a common mission
- Create the near-term vision around which teams can rally and develop as a team
- Provide an important Metric, the Program Predictability Measure, that the team and Agile Release Train can use to improve performance
- Communicate with management and highlight each team's contribution to business value
- Expose dependencies between teams that must be addressed for system success

Setting team PI objectives is not a trivial thing, as it requires solid estimating and planning, a well-understood velocity, analysis of upcoming Features, defining Stories for the Team Backlog, and, finally, synthesis into simple business terms that can be understood by everyone. The net result, however, is straightforward and readily represented, as the example in Figure 2 illustrates.

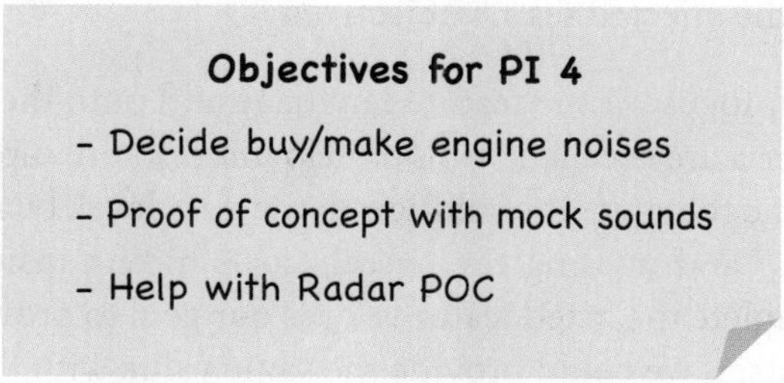

**Objectives for PI 4**

- Decide buy/make engine noises
- Proof of concept with mock sounds
- Help with Radar POC

*Figure 2. An example set of a Baja Ride team's initial PI objectives*

During PI planning, the teams look at the Program Vision and new features and plan the stories they need to deliver. In so doing, they also identify their specific *team PI objectives*.

## Differentiate Between Features and Objectives

The team's PI objectives often relate directly to intended features; indeed, many are the same. However, the mapping is not always straightforward, since some features require the collaboration of multiple teams, as Figure 3 illustrates.

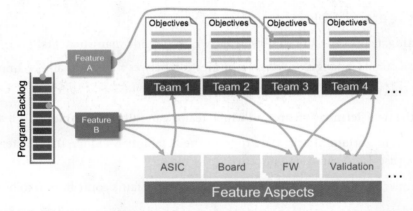

*Figure 3. From features to objectives; some features will appear on more than one team's objectives*

Note that some features (such as Feature A) can be delivered by individual teams; others (Feature B) require collaboration. In addition to features and inputs to features, other team objectives will appear as well. These can include technical objectives (for example, the proof of concept in Figure 2) that enable future features, enhancements to development infrastructure, Milestones, and more. All the results of this process are captured in the affected team's objectives.

PI objectives help teams shift focus off the feature language and onto the desired business outcomes. Features and acceptance criteria are excellent tools to help understand, capture, and collaborate around the work that needs to be done to iterate the solution to the next level, but it's all too easy to get caught up in "finishing the features" and missing the overall goals hiding inside them. The core question becomes, "Is our goal to complete the listed features, or is our goal to provide the outcomes desired by those features? In other words, if we could provide the same value with half the amount of work, and without building all of the features, would this be acceptable?"

Better understanding of the intent offered by direct conversations with the Business Owners often results in the teams providing new perspectives to System Architects/Engineering and Product Management and quickly finding ways to apply their expertise more effectively.

## Use Stretch Objectives

*Stretch* objectives provide a way to help ensure that the delivery timebox will be met (synchronizing to a delivery cadence requires capacity margins [2]). Teams *commit to deliver their non-stretch objectives*. In addition, teams also agree to do their best to deliver the stretch objectives, and they *are included* in the capacity for the PI. Realistically, however, those may or may not be achieved in the timebox, due to timing or other uncertainties. As these objectives might not be finished in the PI, stakeholders plan accordingly. Stretch objectives provide a number of benefits:

- **Improved economics** – Without them, if the team must commit to a 100% scope in a fixed timebox, they are forced to trade off quality or build other buffers into the system. Buffers convert *uncertain* "might-have-been" scope to *certain* but "less-than-what-might-have-been" scope, resulting in less overall throughput.

- **Increased reliability** – Stretch objectives provide an estimating error allowance, thereby increasing confidence in delivery of the main priorities. In turn, delivering commitments (stretch objectives are not committed objectives) is the most important factor in *building trust* between the teams and the stakeholders.

- **Adaptability to change** – In order to reliably deliver on a cadence, stretch objectives provide the capacity needed to meet commitments yet alter priorities if necessary when fact patterns change

Typically, the total allowance for stretch objectives is 10% to 15% of the total capacity. And one must constantly keep in mind that stretch objectives *are* used to identify what *can* be variable within the scope of a plan; stretch objectives *are not* the way for stakeholders to load the teams with more than they can possibly do.

## Write SMART Objectives

Team PI objectives serve as a brief summary of a team's plan for the PI. However, the fact that the objectives are at the higher level of abstraction means that they may tend toward fuzzy and non-verifiable "chunks of intent." To address this, teams use SMART objectives. Each objective is written in such a way that it is:

- **Specific** – States the intended outcome as simply, concisely, and explicitly as possible. (Hint: Try starting with an action verb.)

- **Measurable** – It should be clear what a team needs to do to achieve the objective. The measures may be descriptive, yes/no, quantitative, or provide a range.

- **Achievable** – Achieving the objective should be within the team's control and influence

- **Realistic** – Recognize factors that cannot be controlled. (Hint: Avoid making "happy path" assumptions.)

- **Time-bound** – The time period for achievement must be within the PI, and therefore all objectives must be scoped appropriately

## Communicate Business Value with Objectives

As objectives are finalized during PI planning, Business Owners assign business value to each of the teams' individual objectives in face-to-face conversation with the teams. The value of this particular conversation, from business-to-team and team-to-business, cannot be overstated, as it communicates the strategy and context behind these weighting decisions. Each objective is ranked by the Business Owners on a scale of 1 to 10. Business value should not be confused with any other measures, such as the associated effort, total story points associated with an objective, etc. Business value is assigned, not calculated, and serves as an input to execution considerations. Many of the team's objectives provide direct and *immediate* value to the solution.

Others, such as Enablers, advances in infrastructure, development environments, and quality initiatives, enable the faster creation of *future* business value. All of these factors must be weighed in the final balance.

## Finalize the Team PI Objectives

When objectives have been made "smarter," stretch objectives have been identified, and business value has been established, then the objectives in Figure 2 might evolve to look like those in Figure 4.

| Objectives for PI 4 | BV |
|---|---|
| - Proof of concept with mock sounds | 10 |
| - Help with Radar POC | 4 |
| - Decide buy/make engine noises | 3 |
| ====== Stretch Objectives ====== | |
| - Proof of concept with real sounds | 7 |

*Figure 4. Objective sheet with business value and stretch objectives*

## Commit to PI Objectives

Near the end of PI planning, once objectives have been agreed to, some scope margin has been provided by stretch objectives, and risks have been addressed, the teams hold a vote of confidence on their ability to meet the objectives. While, strictly speaking, a vote of confidence is not the same as a commitment, they are treated as about the same thing. Therefore, this commitment has to be a reasonable thing to ask for. In addition to the Agile prima facie case that a commitment has to *come from* the teams, not be *given for* the teams, a team's SAFe commitment has two parts:

1. Teams agree to do everything in their power to meet the committed objectives

2. If, during the course of the PI, facts dictate that some objectives are simply not achievable, then the teams agree to escalate *immediately* so that corrective action can be taken

In this way, all stakeholders know that either: a) the program results will be achieved as planned, or b) they will be provided sufficient notice so as to be able to mitigate and take corrective action, thereby minimizing business disruption. That's about as good as it gets, because this is, after all, *research* and development.

## Creating Program and Value Stream Objectives

The result of the PI planning process will be some number of approved objectives sheets, one per team. Teams vote on the confidence level for the objectives as a set, and if confidence is high enough, the aggregate set of objectives becomes the committed ART plan. (If not, planning continues until it is.)

This is all the input the Release Train Engineer needs, and he or she uses that team data to roll up the team objectives into the program PI objectives in a format suitable for management communication.

These objectives should be SMART, much like the team PI objectives, and have stretch objectives. Also, like the team PI objectives, these might be business Capabilities the ART is working on, enablers, or other business or technical goals.

During the Post-PI Planning meeting, after all the ARTs have planned, objectives are further rolled up to the value stream level by the Value Stream Engineer, and the value stream PI objectives are synthesized and summarized. This is the top level of PI objectives in SAFe, and they communicate to stakeholders what the value stream as a whole will deliver in the upcoming PI. Figure 1 (above) illustrates this aggregation from team to program to value stream PI objectives.

It is important to note that only team PI objectives have business value attached to them. This value is not rolled up to the other levels. When calculating the predictability measure for programs and value streams, the metric itself is rolled up to ascertain predictability at a higher level.

## Shed Excess WIP with Realistic Objectives

During review of the team PI objectives, it will typically become obvious that not everything that was envisioned by the various business stakeholders will likely be achieved in the PI timebox. Therefore, in order to gain agreement, some of the current in-flight development work (WIP) will need to be reevaluated. This happens throughout the PI planning process but is crystallized in the final agreement among *all* the stakeholders to the program PI objectives. Those lower-priority work items get moved back into the Program Backlog (a lower-cost holding pattern, also called "not doing this now"). Decreasing excess WIP reduces overhead and thrashing, and it increases productivity and velocity. The net result is a *feasible* set of objectives that are agreed to by all business stakeholders and team members, as well as increased efficiency and a higher probability of delivery success. And that's something that most everyone should be able to commit to.

Planning at the value stream level can work similarly: The planning of the ARTs will impact each other, pushing some work back into the Value Stream Backlog for reevaluation in a later PI.

---

**LEARN MORE**

[1] Leffingwell, Dean. *Agile Software Requirements: Lean Requirements Practices for Teams, Programs, and the Enterprise*. Addison-Wesley, 2011.

[2] Reinertsen, Donald. *The Principles of Product Development Flow: Second Generation Lean Product Development*. Celeritas Publishing, 2009.

# System Demo

*Working software is the primary measure of progress.*

  — Agile Manifesto

*Nothing works until it's tested . . . .*

  — A SAFe assumption

## Abstract

The primary measure of Agile Release Train (ART) progress in SAFe is the *System Demo*, a fortnightly demonstration of the subject system being built by the ART. The importance of the system demo cannot be overstated. It is the means for gathering immediate, ART-level feedback from the people doing the work, as well as from sponsors, stakeholders, and Customers. The demonstration of the fully integrated work from all the teams during the prior Iteration is the only true measure of value, velocity, and progress.

Planning for and presenting an effective system demo requires some work on the part of the teams, but it is the only way to get the *fast feedback* needed to build the right Solution.

## Details

The purpose of the *System Demo* is to test and evaluate the *full system* that the Agile Release Train is working on and to get feedback from the primary stakeholders—including Business Owners, executive sponsors, other Agile Teams, development management, Customers, and Customer proxies—on the efficacy and usability of the Solution under development. This feedback is critical, as *only they can* provide the feedback (see Figure 1) that the train needs to stay on course or take corrective action.

*Figure 1. The system demo*

The *System Demo* occurs at the end of every Iteration. It provides an integrated, aggregate view of the new Features that have been delivered by *all* the teams on the train in the most recent iteration. It provides the ART with a fact-based measure of current, system-level progress within the Program Increment (PI) and is the only *true* measure of ART velocity. Achieving this means that the teams must implement the scalable engineering practices necessary to support integration and synchronization across the ART.

At the end of each PI, a special system demo is held. It is a somewhat more structured and formal affair, as it demonstrates the accumulation of *all* the features that have been developed over the course of the PI. This demo is usually held as part of the Inspect and Adapt workshop, which feeds into the retrospective and various measures of PI progress, including the Predictability Measure.

Note: For purposes of clarity, the system demo is the integrated demo of the work of all teams on the train. It is in addition to—and does not replace—each team's local Team Demo, which also occurs at the end of every iteration. In multi-ART Value Streams, the system demo feeds into the aggregate Solution Demo.

## Timing of the System Demo

The system demo happens as near as possible to the end of the iteration—ideally, the next day. However, there are a number of complications that can make that impractical. These include:

- The result of the full integration effort is typically only available at the end of the iteration (of course the goal is to strive for Continuous Integration across the full stack, but that isn't always feasible)

- In addition, each new increment may require extensions to the demo environment, new interfaces, third-party components, simulation tools, etc. Of course, the System Team and the Agile Teams can plan for that, but some late-breaking items are inevitable.

However, the system demo *must occur no later than within the time bounds of the following iteration.* Otherwise, the feedback to the teams will be delayed so as to potentially put the program increment at risk. The ART must make all the necessary investments to make the system demo happen in a timely manner.

## Balancing Integration Effort and Feedback

The goal of the system demo is to learn from the most recent development experience and adjust the course of action. However, when the concerns for an ART span software, hardware, mechanical systems, supplier-provided components, etc., integrating all assets every two weeks may consume too much capacity and create an unacceptable transaction cost. Simply, continuous integration may not be economical or practical in such environments.

However, *no or deferred integration* is far worse; it significantly inhibits learning and creates a false sense of security and velocity. Therefore, if full integration is not practical, it is critical to find the right balance, and to also continuously improve integration and testing automation to lower the cost of future integrations. Figure 2 shows a U-curve cost optimization for integration efforts.

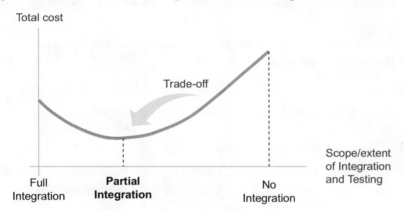

*Figure 2. Integration U-curve cost optimization*

When full integration at every iteration is too costly, the teams should consider:

- Integrating a subset of Capabilities, components, or subsystems
- Integrating to illustrate a particular feature, capability, or Nonfunctional Requirement (NFR)
- Integrating with the support of prototypes and mock-ups
- Integrating every other iteration

It is also important to remember that frequent integration represents a natural challenge for groups that are in the process of transitioning to Lean and Agile methods. That is normal and should not be an excuse to reduce the scope or extent of integration. Most of the challenges should disappear with the increasing maturity of the train, but only if the teams start immediately.

## Process and Agenda

Having a set agenda and fixed timebox helps lower the transition costs of the system demo. A sample system demo meeting script follows:

- Briefly review the business context and the PI Objectives (~5 – 10 mins.)
- Briefly describe each new feature that will be demonstrated (~5 mins.)
- Demonstrate each new feature in an end-to-end use case (~20 – 30 mins. total)
- Open the forum for questions and comments
- Identify current risks and impediments
- Wrap up by summarizing progress, feedback, and action items

## Attendees

Attendees typically include:

- Product Managers and Product Owners, who are usually responsible for running the demo
- One or more members of the System Team, who are often responsible for staging the demo on the QA or demo environment
- Business Owners, executive sponsors, Customers, and Customer proxies
- System Architect/Engineering, DevOps, and other development participants

Below are some tips for a successful system demo:

- Timebox the demo to *one hour*. This is critical to keep the *continuous, biweekly involvement* of key stakeholders. It also illustrates team professionalism and solution readiness.
- Share demo responsibilities among the team leads and Product Owners who have new features to demonstrate
- Minimize PowerPoint slides; demonstrate only working, tested solutions
- Discuss the impact of the current solution on NFRs

---

### LEARN MORE

[1] Leffingwell, Dean. *Agile Software Requirements: Lean Requirements Practices for Teams, Programs, and the Enterprise.* Addison-Wesley, 2011, chapter 9.

[2] Leffingwell, Dean. *Scaling Software Agility: Best Practices for Large Enterprises.* Addison-Wesley, 2007, chapter 15.

# Features and Capabilities

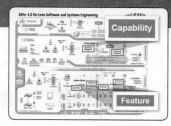

*There's innovation in Linux. There are some really good technical features that I'm proud of. There are capabilities in Linux that aren't in other operating systems.*

— *Linus Torvalds*

## Abstract

SAFe describes a hierarchy of artifacts that describe functional system behavior: Epics > Capabilities > Features > Stories. This article describes *Features and Capabilities*, which are used to describe system and Solution behavior.

The terms *features* and *capabilities* are not unique to SAFe. They are largely industry-standard terms, used by Product and Solution Managers, chief engineers, marketing, and sales personnel to describe products and solutions to Customers. A *feature* is a service provided by the system that addresses one or more user needs. A *capability* describes the higher-level behaviors of a solution at the Value Stream Level.

Features and capabilities are developed and managed through the Program and Value Stream Kanbans, respectively, where they progress to facilitate readiness, prioritization, and approval, and await implementation. This process assumes reasoned economic analysis, technical impact, and strategies for incremental implementation.

To avoid redundancy, most of this article is devoted to describing the definition, articulation, and implementation of features, as they provide the description of system behavior for each ART. Capabilities are simply a level of abstraction above features, applied to the solution in the optional value stream level, where they exhibit largely the same attributes.

## Details

*Features and Capabilities* are central to the SAFe Requirements Model (www.scaledagileframework.com/safe-requirements-model). They are critical to definition, planning, and implementation of value and represent the most basic mechanism of advancing the Solution in SAFe. Figure 1 provides the larger context for these artifacts.

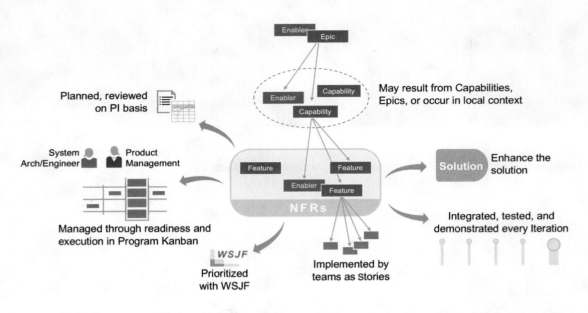

*Figure 1. Feature in context of SAFe*

As Figure 1 shows, features are the required, primary, functional system definition element. Each feature reflects a service provided by the system that fulfills some stakeholder need. Features are maintained in the Program Backlog and sized to fit in Program Increments, so that each PI delivers value. Features originate from the local context of the Agile Release Train, or they may arise as a result of splitting Epics or capabilities.

Features (and, similarly, capabilities) are managed in the Kanban systems. They are subject to Product Management and System Architect/Engineering authority and prioritized using Weighted Shortest Job First, or WSJF. They realize value in the context of certain Nonfunctional Requirements. Features are planned and reviewed at PI boundaries; implemented as Stories; and are integrated, tested, and demonstrated as the functionality becomes available.

Capabilities are similar to features; however, they describe higher-level solution behaviors and often take multiple ARTs to implement. Capabilities are sized to fit within PIs to ensure that each PI delivers incremental and measurable value. (Epics are used to describe initiatives that require multiple PIs to implement.) Capabilities may originate in the local context of the solution or occur as a result of splitting portfolio epics that may cut across more than one Value Stream. Another potential source of capabilities is the Solution Context, where some aspect of the environment may require new solution functionality.

## Describing Features

Features are described using a *features and benefits matrix (FAB)*.

- **Feature** – A short phrase giving a name and some implied context
- **Benefit** – A short description of the benefit to the user and the business; there may be multiple benefits per feature

Since features can span multiple user roles, SAFe generally recommends against using the user story voice to express them. Furthermore, the business is not usually familiar with user stories and it may cause confusion if the same format is used for both stories and features.

An example features and benefits matrix is illustrated in Figure 2.

| Feature | Benefit |
|---------|---------|
| In-service software update | Significantly reduced planned downtime |
| Hardware VPN acceleration | High-performance encryption for secure WAN |
| Traffic congestion management | Improved overall quality of service across different protocols |
| Route optimization | Improved quality of service due to faster and more reliable connectivity |

*Figure 2. Network router features and benefits matrix example*

## Creating and Managing Features

In collaboration with Product Owners and other key stakeholders, features are created by Product Managers in the local context of an ART. Others arise as a result of decomposition of epics. Enabler features pave the Architectural Runway, support exploration, or may provide the infrastructure needed to develop, test, and integrate the initiative. Enabler features are generally created by Architects or Engineers and maintained in the program backlog alongside business features.

Just like business features, enabler features may originate from epics or emerge locally at the ART level in support of the needs of the Agile Teams, ARTs, or value streams. Enablers that make it through the Kanban systems will be subject to capacity allocation in the program backlog to ensure that enough emphasis is placed on both, furthering the solution and extending the architectural runway. Capacity allocation can be applied for enabler work as a whole or it can be used to differentiate between the various types of enablers.

## Prioritizing Features

SAFe applies WSJF for continuous prioritization of features in the program backlog. Since selecting the right work items in the right sequence delivers the primary economic benefit to the ART—and thereby the solution—it's hard to overestimate the importance of this critical process.

## Estimating Features

Features estimation facilitates forecasting value delivery, applying WSJF prioritization, and sizing larger initiatives such as epics. Feature estimation usually occurs in the "refinement" state of Program Kanban and relies on normalized estimation techniques, equivalent to the approach used by Agile Teams for estimating stories (see the "Stories" article for more detail on estimating with normalized story points). Feature estimation at this point, however, does not require full breakdown into stories or involve all the teams that possibly will be involved in feature development. Instead, select subject matter experts may be involved in basic exploration and sizing.

## Accepting Features

Features also have acceptance criteria that are used to determine whether the implementation is correct and delivers the business benefits. Figure 3 provides an example of a feature with acceptance criteria:

**Feature:**

In-service software update

**Acceptance Criteria:**

- Nonstop routing availability
- Automatic and manual update support
- Rollback capability
- Support through existing admin tools
- All enabled services are running after the update

*Figure 3. Feature acceptance criteria example*

Elaboration of acceptance criteria not only mitigates implementation risks but also provides early validation of whether or not feature scope entails desirable value to the business. In addition, acceptance criteria are typically the source of various stories, as well as functional tests, that are developed and automated to support refactoring and regression testing.

Product Management is responsible for accepting the features. They use acceptance criteria to determine whether the functionality has been properly implemented and nonfunctional requirements met.

## Value Stream Capabilities

Most of this article is devoted to describing the definition, articulation, and implementation of features, as they are the most prevalent description of system behavior. Since capabilities are aggregations of features at the solution level, they exhibit the same characteristics and practices.

For example, capabilities:

- Are described using a similar matrix as the feature and benefits matrix and have associated acceptance criteria

- Originate in the local value stream context or are derived from epics

- Are sized to fit in a PI

- Are reasoned about and approved using the Value Stream Kanban. Approved capabilities are maintained in the value stream backlog.

- Have associated enablers to describe and bring visibility to all the technical work necessary to support efficient development and delivery of business capabilities

- Are accepted by Solution Managers, who use the acceptance criteria to determine whether the functionality has been properly implemented

## Splitting Features and Capabilities

Capabilities must be split into features to be implemented. Features, in turn, are split into stories consumable by teams within an Iteration timebox. The list below provides 10 patterns for "splitting work," as described in Leffingwell [1, Chapter 6]. They can be applied to all the above-mentioned cases.

1. Work flow steps
2. Business rule variations
3. Major effort
4. Simple/complex
5. Variations in data
6. Data methods
7. Deferring system qualities
8. Operations
9. Use-case scenarios
10. Breaking out a spike

An example of splitting a capability into features is illustrated in Figure 4.

**Capability:**
Hardware acceleration

**Feature:**
Encryption hardware
acceleration

**Feature:**
Quality of service
hardware acceleration

**Feature:**
Access control lists
hardware acceleration

*Figure 4. A capability split into features*

## LEARN MORE

[1] Leffingwell, Dean. *Agile Software Requirements: Lean Requirements Practices for Teams, Programs, and the Enterprise.* Addison-Wesley, 2011.

# Enablers

*Luck is what happens when preparation meets opportunity.*
— *Seneca*

## Abstract

*Enablers* are technical initiatives meant to enable and support the development of business initiatives. Enablers (reflected in red on the Big Picture) exist on all four levels of SAFe: *Enabler Epics* at the Portfolio Level, *Enabler Capabilities* at the Value Stream Level, *Enabler Features* at the Program Level, and *Enabler Stories* at the Team Level. Enablers can be used for any activities that are necessary to support upcoming business features, but generally they fall into one of three categories:

- Exploration – Exploration enablers are used to build understanding of what is needed by the Customer, to understand prospective Solutions, and to evaluate alternatives

- Architecture – Architectural enablers are used to build the Architectural Runway in order to enable smoother and faster development

- Infrastructure – Infrastructure enablers are used to build and enhance the development and testing (and occasionally deployment) environments, thereby facilitating faster development and higher-quality testing

## Details

*Enablers* are work items that capture and bring visibility to all the work necessary to support efficient development and delivery of future business Features. They are used primarily for exploration, system and Solution architectural evolution, and to enhance development and testing environments (see later sections of this article). Since they reflect real work, and sometimes plenty of it, they cannot be invisible. They are treated like all other value-added development activities and are thereby subject to estimating, visibility and tracking, WIP limits, feedback, and, finally, presentation of results.

## Types of Enablers

Enablers exist at all levels of the framework (and are indicated on the Big Picture by red shading). They inherit the attributes of the type of work they are associated with, as follows:

- **Enabler epics** are a type of Epic, and as such are written using the value statement format defined for epics. They tend to cut across Value Streams and Program Increments (PIs). They must include a lightweight business case to support their implementation and are identified and tracked through the Portfolio Kanban system.

- **Enabler capabilities and features** occur at the Value Stream and Program Levels, where they capture work of that type. As these enablers are a type of Feature or Capability, they share the same attributes, including a statement of benefits and acceptance criteria, and they must be structured so as to fit within a single PI.

- **Enabler stories,** as a type of Story, must fit in Iterations. However, while they may not require user voice format, they have acceptance criteria to clarify the requirements and support testing.

Enablers are written, prioritized, and follow the same rules as their respective epics, capabilities, features, and stories. For example: Features and enabler features are written using a features and benefits matrix, have acceptance criteria, use story points for estimation and WSJF for prioritization, etc.

## Creating and Managing Enablers

Most enablers are created when business initiatives, making their way through the different Kanban systems, require exploration enablers to validate the need or solution; architectural enablers to pave the runway; or infrastructure enablers to be ready to develop, test, and integrate the initiatives.

Enablers are often created by architects or by systems engineering at the various levels, whether by Enterprise Architects at the Portfolio Level or by Solution and System Architects/Engineering at the value stream and program levels. The architects who create the enablers steer them through the Kanban systems, providing both the guidance needed to analyze them and the information needed to estimate and implement them.

Some enablers will emerge locally from the needs of the Agile Teams, Agile Release Trains (ARTs), or value streams to improve the existing solution. Enablers that make it through the Kanban systems will be subject to capacity allocation in the Program and Value Stream Backlogs to ensure that enough emphasis is placed on both, furthering the solution and extending the Architectural Runway. Capacity allocation can be applied for enabler work as a whole or it can differentiate between the various types of enablers.

## Using Enablers

### Exploration

Applying *Enablers* for exploration provides a way for development teams to flesh out the details of requirements and design. The nature of Solution Intent is that many requirements begin as variables, since at the beginning of development little is known about exactly what the Customer needs or how to implement it. Often the Customers themselves don't understand exactly what they want, and only through iterative product development and demos do they gain an understanding of what they actually need.

On the solution side, there are many technical possibilities for how to implement a business need. These alternatives need to be analyzed and sometimes evaluated through modeling, prototyping, or even concurrent development of multiple solution options (set-based engineering).

### Architecture

The architectural runway is one of the means by which SAFe implements the concepts of Agile Architecture. The runway provides the basis for developing business initiatives more quickly, on appropriate technical foundations. But the runway is constantly consumed by business epics, features and capabilities, and stories, and so it must be constantly maintained. Enablers are backlog items used to extend the runway.

Some of these architectural enablers fix existing problems with the solution—for example, the need to enhance performance. These enablers start out in the backlog, but after implementation, they may become Nonfunctional Requirements (NFRs). In fact, many NFRs come into existence as a result of architectural enablers. They tend to build over time, as can be seen in Figure 1.

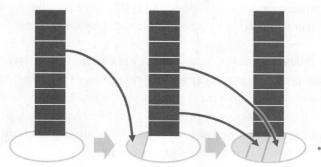

*Figure 1. Many nonfunctional requirements appear over time as a result of enablers*

### Infrastructure

Agile development is built on frequent integration. Agile Teams integrate their work with other teams on the ART at the System Demos in every iteration. The trains integrate every PI for the Solution Demo. Many Enterprises even implement Continuous Integration to ensure that the solution is always running and to reduce the risk at the integration points.

To support these frequent or continuous integration and testing constructs, there is a need to develop infrastructure at the Team Level, program level, and value stream level. New infrastructure is also sometimes needed to increase the rate of Release to the Customer. Agile Teams, working with the System Team, are responsible for building and maintaining this infrastructure. Infrastructure enablers are used as backlog items to advance this work and continuously enhance it, both to support new scenarios and to enhance the agility of the enterprise.

## Implement Architectural Enablers Incrementally

Architectural enabler work can be big. It is important to remember that it needs to be broken down into small enabler stories that can fit in iterations. This can be difficult, as architectural and infrastructure changes can potentially stop the existing system from working until the new architecture/infrastructure is in place. When planning enabler work, make sure to organize it such that the system can run for most of the time on the old architecture or infrastructure. That way teams can continue to work, integrate, demo, and even release while the enabler work is happening.

As described in the "System and Solution Architect/Engineering" article and [1], there are three options:

- Case A – The enabler is big, but there is an incremental approach to implementation. The system always runs

- Case B – The enabler is big, but it can't be implemented entirely incrementally. The system will need to take an occasional break

- Case C – The enabler is really big, and it can't be implemented incrementally. The system runs when needed; do no harm

Examples of incremental patterns are also described in [2] (Chapter 2), whereby the legacy subsystems are gradually "strangled" over time, using proven patterns such as asset capture or event interception.

Enablers drive better economics by creating the technology platforms that deliver business functionality. But innovative product development cannot occur without risk-taking. Therefore, initial technology-related decisions cannot always be correct. Hence the Agile enterprise must be prepared to reverse course on occasion. The Ignore Sunk Costs principle of product development flow ([3], principle E17) provides essential guidance: Do not consider money already spent. Incremental implementation helps, as corrective action can be taken before the investment grows too large.

## Plan Cross–ART and Cross–Value Stream Enablers

Enabler epics and enabler capabilities can cut across multiple value streams or ARTs respectively. During the analysis phase of the Kanban system, one of the important decisions to make is whether to implement the enabler in all VSs/ARTs at the same time or to do so incrementally.

This is a trade-off between the risk reduction of implementing one solution or system at a time vs. the cost of delay caused by not having the full enabler, as Figure 2 illustrates.

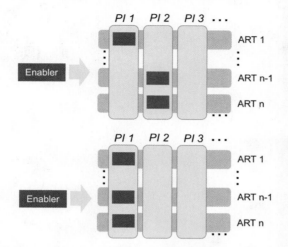

**Scenario A:** If the level of uncertainty, impact on existing systems, and overall risk is high, then incremental implementation is the wise choice.

**Scenario B:** If the cost of delay is unacceptably high, then the enabler can be implemented concurrently in all ARTs/VSs (example: new regulatory requirement).

*Figure 2. Two scenarios for implementing large enablers spanning multiple ARTs or VSs*

## LEARN MORE

[1] Leffingwell, Dean. *Agile Software Requirements: Lean Requirements Practices for Teams, Programs, and the Enterprise.* Addison-Wesley, 2011.

[2] Fowler, Martin. Strangler Application. http://martinfowler.com/bliki/StranglerApplication.html.

[3] Reinertsen, Donald. *The Principles of Product Development Flow: Second Generation Lean Product Development.* Celeritas Publishing, 2009.

# Innovation and Planning Iteration

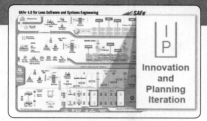

*Inertia is the residue of past innovation efforts. Left unmanaged, it consumes the resources required to fund next-generation innovation.*

— *Geoffrey Moore*

*100% utilization drives unpredictability.*

— *Donald Reinertsen*

## Abstract

Lean, Agile, and SAFe all provide a dedicated focus on continuous delivery of Customer value. Every Program Increment (PI) ends with a System Demo and an Inspect and Adapt workshop that create a focus and integration point for the entire Agile Release Train (ART) and Value Stream. It's a critical point in development, one that shows the progress of the Solution to all stakeholders and supports the need for continuous value delivery. To that end, during the PI, teams are busy working on the Features that they took on in PI Planning. Every Iteration counts, and the teams are mostly "heads down," focused on near-term delivery. PI after PI, the solution marches to market. The focus on delivery is unrelenting.

Of course, a focus on one thing, delivery, can lead to a lack of focus on another, in this case innovation. Given this constant urgency, there is a risk that if time is not put aside for innovation, the "tyranny of the urgent iteration" will trump the need to constantly innovate. To address this, SAFe provides for *Innovation and Planning Iterations*. These serve a variety of purposes, including a dedicated time for planning, retrospecting, and exploration and innovation. They serve a number of other purposes as well; all are described in the details below.

## Details

### Understand the IP Iteration Activities

*Innovation and Planning Iterations* provide a regular, cadence-based opportunity every PI for teams to work on activities that are difficult to fit into a continuous, incremental value delivery paradigm.

These can include:

- Time for innovation and exploration
- A dedicated time for the PI System Demo, Inspect and Adapt workshop, PI Planning events, and backlog refinement
- Final integration of the Solution
- Work on technical infrastructure, tooling, and other systemic impediments
- Enablement of continuing education

In addition, IP Iterations fulfill another critical role by providing an estimating buffer for meeting PI Objectives and enhancing release predictability. Agile Release Trains typically report that their overall efficiency, velocity, sustainability of pace, and job satisfaction are all enhanced by regular opportunities to "recharge their batteries and sharpen their tools."

## Allow Time for Innovation

One of the pillars of SAFe's Lean-Agile Mindset is innovation, but finding time for free association and innovation in the midst of delivery deadlines can be difficult. To this end, many enterprises use IP iterations for research and design activities and hackathons. The rules for a hackathon can be simple:

1. Team members can work on whatever they want with whomever they want, so long as the work reflects the mission of the company
2. They demo their work to others at the end of the hackathon

Hackathon learnings routinely make their way into Program Backlogs and thereby help drive innovation. They're fun, too!

## Dedicate Time to PI Events

The PI system demo, inspect and adapt workshop, and PI planning are critical events that take time to execute. Placing them in a dedicated IP iteration means that all other Iterations can have normal lengths and velocities and are not truncated by the time dedicated to these critical functions. Even more important, the events can be locked systematically into the program schedule, so that their occurrence is thereby better guaranteed.

In addition, it's likely that some just-in-time, last-responsible-moment Program and Value Stream Backlog refinement and Feature and Capability elaboration during this period can significantly increase the productivity of the upcoming planning session.

## Integrate the Complete Solution

The IP iteration contains the system demo and provides time for final testing of the solution, including final performance and other Nonfunctional Requirements (NFR) testing, standards and security validations, user acceptance testing, final documentation, and any other readiness activities that are not feasible or economical to perform at every iteration.

When a complex solution includes hardware and other tangible components that are more difficult to continuously integrate end to end, full integration at the Program Level as well as the Value Stream Level may be feasible only during the IP iteration. In these cases, it's just common sense to plan for that.

That being said, this should not be the only attempt to integrate the assets into the system. SAFe organizations rely on frequent integration, which—even when not fully end to end—addresses specific aspects of the solution and validates the assumptions early enough to be able to respond to significant problems and risks within the PI. These integrations are demoed at the system demo at the end of every iteration. The IP iteration is a placeholder for full, final solution integration that *must happen at least once per PI*. The System Team(s) typically assists the Agile Teams with this integration effort.

## Advance Development Infrastructure

Lean delivery puts additional pressure on the development infrastructure. New continuous integration environments must be erected, new test automation frameworks must be installed and maintained, project management tooling is adopted, intra- and inter-team communications systems may need to be upgraded or enhanced, and the list goes on. While many of these items can and should be addressed in the course of each iteration (they are often improvement stories from the team's Iteration Retrospective or Enablers), it can be more efficient to perform an upgrade or migration at a time when there isn't a critical demo just a few days away. We all understand that we have to sharpen our tools from time to time. Agile Teams are no different; indeed, they have an even higher dependency on their working environments than do regular teams, and so they need to spend time building this environment.

## Enable Continuous Learning

Lean engineers and leaders are lifelong learners. Changes in technology, as well as changes to method and practice, are routine; opportunities for continuing education, however, are far less common. In addition, the initial move to Lean-Agile requires many new techniques, including feature/Story writing, building in quality, automated testing, collective ownership, Lean-Agile architecture, Continuous Integration, pair work, Product Owner and Scrum Master skill mastery, and team building. Providing time for continuing education gives teams and leaders the time they need to learn and master these new techniques. This time can also be used to foster and support Communities of Practice devoted to these and other topics. The net results benefit both the individual and the Enterprise: employee mastery and job satisfaction increase, velocity goes up, and time to market goes down.

## Leverage the Built-in Estimation Buffer

Lean flow teaches us that operating at 100% utilization drives unpredictable results. Put simply, if everyone is planned to full capacity, there is no one available to flex when problems inevitably occur. The result is unpredictability and delays in value delivery.

To address this, the IP iteration is treated as a "guard band" or estimating buffer. During PI planning, no features or stories are planned for development in this iteration. This buffer gives the teams extra time to respond to unforeseen events, delays in dependencies, and other issues, thereby increasing their ability to meet Team and Program PI Objectives. This substantially increases the predictability of the program's outcomes, an attribute that is extremely important to the business. However, *routinely using that time for completing the work is a failure pattern*. Doing so defeats the primary purpose of the IP iteration, and innovation will likely suffer. Teams must take care that the estimating guard does not simply become a crutch.

## A Sample IP Iteration Calendar

Taking all the above into account, many teams' IP iterations take on a somewhat standard schedule and format. An example is illustrated in Figure 1.

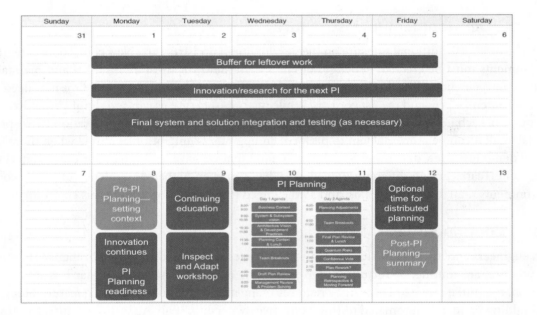

*Figure 1. Example calendar for an IP iteration*

---

**LEARN MORE**

[1] Reinertsen, Donald G. *The Principles of Product Development Flow: Second Generation Lean Product Development.* Celeritas Publishing, 2009.

[2] Leffingwell, Dean. *Agile Software Requirements: Lean Requirements Practices for Teams, Programs, and the Enterprise.* Addison-Wesley, 2011, chapter 17.

# Inspect and Adapt

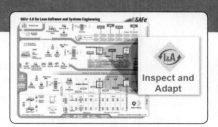

*Kaizen is about changing the way things are. If you assume that things are all right the way they are, you can't do kaizen. So change something!*

　—Taiichi Ohno

## Abstract

The philosophy of continuous improvement is integral to Agile ("… at regular intervals, the team reflects on how to become more effective …" Agile Manifesto), Lean Thinking (kaizen), and SAFe. SAFe emphasizes the criticality of this philosophy by embodying relentless improvement as one of the four pillars of SAFe's House of Lean. Opportunities for *relentless improvement* occur continuously throughout development. However, applying cadence and synchronization to this philosophy helps ensure that there is dedicated time to spend reasoning about "what we could do better." The two primary, programmatic opportunities are the team retrospective and this, the *Inspect and Adapt* workshop.

The inspect and adapt (I&A) workshop is a significant event held at the end of each Program Increment. I&A is a regular time to reflect, collect data, problem-solve, and take action on improvement actions needed to increase the velocity, quality, and reliability of the next PI. All program stakeholders participate in this workshop. The result of the workshop is a set of *improvement stories* that can be added to the backlog for the upcoming PI Planning. In this way, every ART improves every PI. For large Solutions, a similar I&A workshop also typically occurs at the Value Stream Level.

## Details

The main mechanism in SAFe for achieving *relentless improvement*, one of the pillars of SAFe's Lean-Agile Mindset, is the *Inspect and Adapt* (I&A) workshop. The I&A workshop is held at the end of each Program Increment, to reflect on the execution and results of the previous PI and build improvement backlog items for the next PI. It can be held at both the Program Level and the Value Stream Level. This article focuses primarily on the program event, as those who build the system are those best suited to change the process by which they do so.

Participants in the program I&A workshop should be, wherever possible, *all* the people involved in building the system. These include the Agile Teams, Release Train Engineer (RTE), System and Solution Architect/Engineering, Product Management, Business Owners, and others on the train.

---

Value Stream stakeholders may also attend this workshop. The I&A workshop consists of three parts:

1. PI System Demo
2. Quantitative measurement
3. Retrospective and problem-solving workshop

## PI System Demo

A system demo is the first part of the workshop. This particular system demo is a little different from the biweekly ones that precede it, in that it is intended to show *all* the accumulated Features that have accrued over the course of the PI. Also, typically the audience is broader, as, for example, additional Customer representatives may choose to attend this demo. Therefore the demo tends to be a little more formal in nature, and some additional preparation and staging is usually required. But like any other system demo, this one should be timeboxed to an hour or less, with the level of abstraction high enough to keep the important stakeholders engaged and providing feedback.

## Quantitative Measurement

In the second part of the workshop, teams review any quantitative Metrics they have agreed to collect, then discuss the data and trends. In preparation for this, the RTE and the Value Stream Engineer are often responsible for gathering the information, analyzing it to showcase interesting statistics and findings, and facilitating the presentation of the measurements.

One primary measurement is the *Program Predictability Measure*. During the PI system demo, the Business Owners, Customers, Agile Teams, and other key stakeholders collaboratively rate the actual business value achieved for each team's PI Objectives, as shown in Figure 1. Reliable trains should generally operate in the 80% – 100% range; this allows the business and its outside stakeholders to plan effectively. (Note: Stretch objectives don't count in the commitment but do count in the actual score, as can also be seen in Figure 1.)

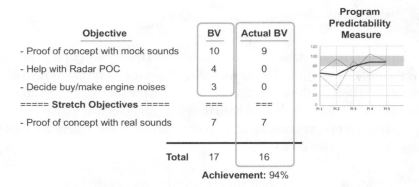

*Figure 1. Team PI performance report*

# Retrospective and Problem-Solving Workshop

## Retrospective

The teams then run a brief (30 minutes or less) retrospective, the goal of which is to identify whatever issues they would like to address. There is no one way to do this; a number of Agile retrospective formats can be used [3]. The objective of the selected format is to identify a *small number of significant problems* that the teams can potentially address.

Based on attendance at the retrospective, and the nature of the problems identified, the facilitator helps the group decide which ones they want to tackle. They then have a choice of resolving Team Level problems or, more typically, selecting a Program Level problem and joining others who wish to work on the same issue. This self-selection helps provide cross-functional and differing views of the problem, and it seeds the problem-solving team with those who are most likely to be impacted and those who are best motivated to address the issue.

Key ART stakeholders—including Business Owners, Customers, and management—join the teams in this retro. Often they, and they alone, can unblock the impediments that exist outside the team's control.

## Problem-Solving Workshop

For the larger, systematic program-level problems, a structured, root cause analysis-based, problem-solving workshop format can be applied. Root cause analysis is a set of problem-solving tools used to identify the root causes of a problem, rather than simply addressing the symptoms. The session is typically facilitated by the RTE, or other facilitator, in a timebox of two hours or less.

The steps in the workshop are depicted in Figure 2 below. Each is described in the following sections.

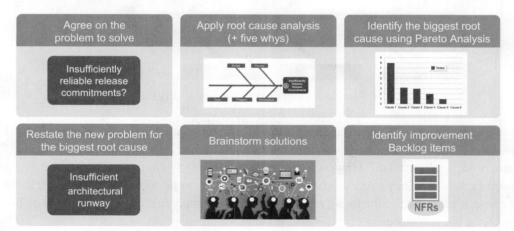

*Figure 2. Problem-solving workshop format*

## Agree on the Problem(s) to Solve

American inventor Charles Kettering is credited with the statement that "a problem well stated is a problem half solved." At this point, the teams have self-selected the problem they want to work on.

But do they really agree on what the problem is, or is it more likely that they have differing perspectives? To this end, the teams should spend a few minutes stating the problem, thinking about the *what, where, when*, and *impact* as succinctly as they can. Figure 3 illustrates a Baja Ride systems engineering example.

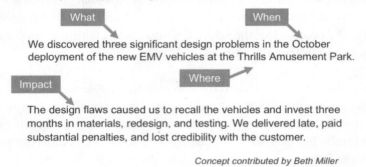

*Concept contributed by Beth Miller*

*Figure 3. Example problem statement*

## Perform Root Cause Analysis

We recommend the use of traditional and effective problem-solving tools, including *Fishbone Diagrams* and the *Five Whys*. Also known as an Ishikawa Diagram, the fishbone diagram is a visual tool used to explore the causes of specific events or sources of variation in a process. As can be seen in Figure 4, the name of the problem statement is written to the right at the end of the "backbone."

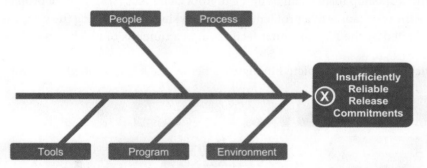

*Figure 4. Fishbone diagram with major sources identified*

Causes are identified and then grouped into major categories as bones off the main bone. For our problem-solving workshop, we preload the main bones with the categories "People," "Process," "Tools," "Program," and "Environment." However, these may be adapted as appropriate. Team members then brainstorm factors that they think contribute to the problem to be solved. Once a cause is identified, its root cause is identified with the *5 Whys* technique. By simply asking *Why*, as many as five times, each *cause of a cause* is easier to discover and is added to the diagram.

## Identify the Biggest Root Cause

Pareto Analysis, also known as "the 80/20 rule," is a statistical decision-making technique used to narrow down the number of actions that produce the most significant overall effect.

It uses the principle that *20% of the root causes can cause 80% of the problem.* It is particularly useful when many possible courses of action are competing for attention, which is almost always the case with complex, systemic problems.

Once all the possible causes of causes have been identified, team members then cumulatively vote on the item they think is the biggest factor causing the end problem. They can do this by placing stars (five stars are allocated to each group member, which can be spread among one or more items as they see fit) on the causes they think are most problematic. The team then creates a Pareto chart, such as the example in Figure 5, which illustrates their collective consensus on the largest root causes.

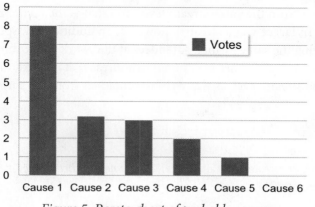

*Figure 5. Pareto chart of probable causes*

### Restate the New Problem
The next step is to pick the largest cause from the list and restate it clearly as a problem. This should only take a minute or so, as the teams are very close the root cause now.

### Brainstorm Solutions
At this point, the root cause will start to imply some potential solutions. The working group brainstorms as many possible corrective actions as they can think of in a 15 – 30 minute session. The rules of brainstorming apply here:

- Generate as many ideas as possible
- Do not allow criticism or debate
- Let the imagination soar
- Mutate and combine ideas

### Create Improvement Backlog Items
The team then cumulatively votes on up to *three* most likely solutions. These will serve as *improvement stories and features* to be fed directly into the PI Planning session that follows. During that session, the RTE helps ensure that the relevant improvement Stories are loaded onto the Iteration plans, thus ensuring that action will be taken and resources allocated, as with any other backlog item.

This closes the loop on the retrospective and ensures that people and resources are dedicated as necessary to improving the current state.

In this way, problem-solving is routine and systematic at both the program and VS levels, and *team members, program stakeholders, and value stream stakeholders can be assured that the value stream is solidly on its journey of relentless improvement.*

## Inspect and Adapt at the Value Stream Level

The above describes a rigorous approach to problem-solving in the context of the program. It often includes key stakeholders from the value stream level, and that is the recommended path to facilitate Solution development. In larger value streams, however, an additional inspect and adapt workshop may be required, following the same format. Attendees at that workshop cannot include all stakeholders, so stakeholders are selected that are best suited to address that context. This includes the primary stakeholders of the value stream level, as well as representatives from the various ARTs and Suppliers.

### LEARN MORE

[1] Leffingwell, Dean. *Agile Software Requirements: Lean Requirements Practices for Teams, Programs, and the Enterprise*. Addison-Wesley, 2011.

[2] Leffingwell, Dean. *Scaling Software Agility: Best Practices for Large Enterprises*. Addison-Wesley, 2007.

[3] Derby, Esther and Diana Larsen. *Agile Retrospectives: Making Good Teams Great*. Pragmatic Bookshelf, 2009.

# Develop on Cadence, Release Any Time

*Control flow under uncertainty.*

  *—Donald Reinertsen*

*Deliver software frequently, from a couple of weeks to a couple of months, with a preference to the shorter time scale.*

  *—Agile Manifesto*

## Abstract

**Develop on Cadence** – In a flow-based system, basing routine development activities on a fast, synchronous cadence—a regular, predictive rhythm of important events—is the best strategy for managing the inherent variability in systems development. Building complex, large-scale systems is, after all, *research* and development. This is a *fundamental* premise of SAFe, and its effects can be seen directly on the Big Picture with the fast cadence of synchronized, short Iterations, then the further integration of those iterations into larger Program Increments.

**Release Any Time** – However, SAFe provides a separation of concerns that gives development teams the cadence and synchronization tools they need to manage the complexity and rapid change in their environment, while allowing for either synchronous or asynchronous Releases to the market. This is another fundamental premise behind SAFe, and it is also expressed directly in the Big Picture by those little iconic, asynchronous *boxes of working software*.

## Details: Develop on Cadence

Cadence and synchronization are the key constructs we use to build our Solution assets. *Cadence* is the use of a regular, predictive development rhythm. *Synchronization* causes multiple dependent events to happen at the same time. Together, cadence and synchronization allow us to *make routine that which can be routine*, including PI Planning, System and Solution Demos, and system integration, as well as less frequent items such as adjusting resources and realigning work to teams. These principles (thanks to Donald Reinertsen, *Principles of Product Development Flow* [1]) are so critical to understanding *why* SAFe works the way it does that we describe some of Reinertsen's basic principles—along with how SAFe applies them—in Tables 1 and 2.

| Principles of Flow: Cadence | SAFe Practices |
|---|---|
| **F5: Use a regular cadence to limit the accumulation of variance** | Planning at regular Program Increment (PI) intervals limits variances to a single PI timebox, thereby increasing Agile Release Train and Value Stream predictability. |
| **F6: Provide sufficient capacity margin to enable cadence** | In order to reliably meet PI objectives, the Innovation and Planning Iteration is unplanned and provides schedule margin. Uncommitted, but planned, stretch goals provide capacity margin. Together they provide the schedule and scope margin needed to reliably meet PI goals. |
| **F7: Use cadence to make waiting times predictable** | If a Feature doesn't make it into a PI (or Release) and it remains high priority, its delivery can be anticipated to be on schedule in the next PI (or scheduled, frequent release), thereby avoiding the temptation to load excess WIP into the current increment. |
| **F8: Use a regular cadence to enable small batch sizes** | Short Iterations help control the number of Stories in the iteration batch. Feature batch sizes are controlled by short PIs and frequent releases, providing high system predictability and throughput. |
| **F9: Schedule frequent meetings using a predictable cadence** | PI planning, iteration planning, backlog refinement, Inspect and Adapt, architecture discussions, etc., all benefit from frequent meetings. Each meeting needs to process only a small batch of new information. Cadence helps lower the transaction costs of meetings and other significant events. |

*Table 1: Cadence principles applied in SAFe*

| Principles of Flow: Synchronization | SAFe Practices |
|---|---|
| **F10: Exploit economies of scale by synchronizing work from multiple projects** | Individual Agile Teams are aligned to common iteration lengths. Work is synchronized by system and solution demos. Portfolio business and Enabler Epics drive common infrastructure and Customer utility. |
| **F11: Capacity margin enables synchronization of deliverables** | Teams plan with stretch objectives; these are sacrificed as necessary when plans meet reality. |
| **F12: Use synchronized events to facilitate cross-functional trade-offs** | Value stream and program PI events synchronize Customer feedback, resource and Budget adjustments, mission alignment, inspect and adapt improvements, and program review and governance. They also drive collaboration and team-building. |
| **F13: To reduce queues, synchronize the batch size and timing of adjacent processes** | Teams are aligned to common timeboxes and similar batch sizes. The System Team at the Program and Value Stream Levels supports integration on a regular cadence. Backlogs are kept short and uncommitted to support rapid delivery of new ideas. |
| **F14: Apply nested cadence harmonic multiples to synchronize work** | Teams integrate and evaluate (at least) on iteration boundaries; programs and value streams integrate and evaluate on PI boundaries. |

*Table 2: Synchronization principles applied in SAFe*

Taken together, cadence and synchronization are critical concepts that help us manage the inherent variability in our work. This creates a more reliable, dependable software development and delivery process, one that our key business stakeholders can come to rely on.

# Details: Release Any Time

As we have seen, *developing on cadence* is indeed well and good, but when it comes to actually Releasing value, a different set of rules may apply. Given a reliable stream of Program Increments, the next and even larger consideration is to understand when and how to actually release all that accumulating value to the end user.

The Big Picture illustrates releases at various times during the flow of each Agile Release Train (ART). But that's just a picture, and every Enterprise, and every Program and Value Stream, has to have a strategy for releasing software that suits its development and business context. In the next section, we will discuss considerations with respect to release frequency.

## Toward Continuous Delivery

For many, the prospect of Continuous Delivery (www.scaledagileframework.com/continuous-delivery/) may represent a desired end state. After all, none of us panic when an automatic update becomes available for our phone; we assume it will deliver value and hit that *update now* button without much thought or concern. And surely there is as much or more software in that phone than there is in some of our enterprise systems. However, the enterprise world often marches to a different drummer. Perhaps, for reasons of security and availability, or for financial (banking, trading) or personal (medical equipment, man-rated systems) criticality, the Customer's operational environment may not be suited to continuous updates of significant new value. Perhaps our enterprise's development and release capabilities have not advanced to the point where that is a largely risk-free approach for our Customers. Perhaps, for *whatever* reason, it just doesn't make economic sense.

In addition, systems that support continuous delivery *must be designed for continuous delivery*. Even then, releasing is *not* a homogeneous thing. Even this simple website has multiple release paradigms. If, for example, we updated the Big Picture every week, those supporting SAFe with tooling and courseware would not think that was a good approach. At the same time, if we didn't have the ability to roll out new content (through the blog, Guidance, and updates to articles), we'd be inhibited in our goal of continuous value delivery. We couldn't be as Agile. You have to design for these things.

## Separating Development Concerns from Release Concerns

We therefore recognize that *developing* and *releasing* systems may be unlike events. For maximum flexibility and agility, SAFe provides a separation of concerns to decouple them. Each program value stream defines the development *cadence* for its Agile Release Train when it picks its Iteration pattern. With this conceptual model, there are three separate cases for releasing.

1. **Releasing on the Program Increment Cadence** – The simplest case is when an enterprise can release on the program increment boundaries. It's simplest because PI planning, releasing, and Inspect and Adapt are coordinated by the same cadence and calendar dates. In addition, Innovation and Planning Iterations can be timed, designed, and coordinated to support the more extensive release activities, which can include final verification and validation, UAT, release documentation, etc. Plus, all release dates can be known well in advance! (Fix the date, float the scope.) If an organization wants the efficiency and convenience of this model, and since the overall PI pattern is arbitrary, many enterprises find their way to this simple construct. (See Figure 1 in the "Roadmap" article for an example.)

2. **Releasing Less Frequently** – In many cases, however, releasing on a fast PI cadence may not be possible or even desirable. For example, in some enterprise settings, deployed systems constitute critical infrastructure for a Customer's operating environment. Even if the Customers would like to have the new software, service level and license agreements may be prohibitive, and there is the overhead and disruption of installation. In other cases, the time lines of enterprises that are building systems that contain both software and hardware, such as a mobile phone or geophysical mapping satellite, are driven by long-lead hardware items—displays, chip sets, and the like. The new hardware must be available first, so releasing early and incrementally is not an option. In these cases, releasing on PI cadence may not be an option, and the planning and releasing activities may be completely decoupled.

3. **Releasing More Frequently** – For enterprises building complex solutions (e.g., systems of systems), either of the above two cases are probably overly simplistic. While the larger system may lend itself to either of the models above, various components of the system may have to be released more frequently. The periodic planning function still provides the cadence, synchronization, and alignment the enterprise needs to manage variability and limit deviations from expectations, but forcing the release of all assets to the same cadence is unnecessary and constrains the system too much.

## Release Any Time

Let's be practical. Big systems are not homogeneous. They may contain different types of components and subsystems, each of which requires its own release model. So elements of each of these three models above may all be present at the same time, in which case it's probably easiest to consider the most general model: *Release whatever you want, whenever it makes sense within the governance and business model*, as the example in Figure 1 illustrates.

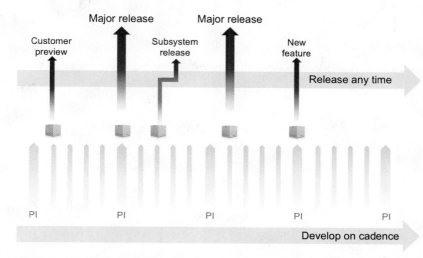

*Figure 1. Fully decoupling development concerns from release concerns*

In all cases, enterprises that apply SAFe can rest easy in the knowledge that development and releasing are not the same thing, and they can release any quality asset at any time required to meet business conditions.

---

**LEARN MORE**

[1] Reinertsen, Donald. *Principles of Product Development Flow: Second Generation Lean Product Development*. Celeritas Publishing, 2009.

[2] Leffingwell, Dean. *Scaling Software Agility: Best Practices for Large Enterprises*. Addison-Wesley, 2007, chapter 16.

[3] Leffingwell, Dean. *Agile Software Requirements: Lean Requirements Practices for Teams, Programs, and the Enterprise*. Addison-Wesley, 2011.

# Architectural Runway

*The best architectures, requirements, and designs emerge from self-organizing teams.*

—Agile Manifesto

*While we must acknowledge emergence in design and system development, a little planning can avoid much waste.*

—James Coplien and Gertrud Bjørnvig, Lean Architecture: for Agile Software Development

## Abstract

The *Architectural Runway* provides one of the means by which SAFe implements the concepts of Agile Architecture. An architectural runway exists when the Enterprise's platforms have sufficient existing technological infrastructure to support the implementation of the highest-priority Features in a near-term Program Increment without excessive, delay-inducing redesign. This runway provides the necessary technical basis for developing business initiatives and implementing new Features and/or Capabilities.

The runway is constantly consumed by Business Epics, capabilities, features, and Stories. They use the runway to accomplish their needed functionality. In order to support upcoming functionality, the enterprise must continually invest in extending the runway by implementing Enablers. Some of these enablers fix existing problems with the Solution—for example, the need to enhance performance—while others might implement foundational capabilities that will be used by future capabilities.

## Details

Agile development eschews waterfall thinking and Big Up-Front Design (BUFD) and replaces it with a simple belief that "the best architectures, requirements, and designs emerge from self-organizing teams" (Agile Manifesto [3]). Out of this comes the practice of *Emergent Design*—the Agile Architecture evolutionary process of discovering and extending the design only as necessary to implement and validate the next increment of functionality.

This new practice works extremely well, up to a point. As Agile practices mature and are adopted by larger teams and teams of teams, there comes a point at which *emergent design* is an insufficient response to the complexity of large-scale system development. The following problems start to occur:

- Excessive redesign and delays; flow bottlenecks
- Different architecture constructs in support of the same capabilities, increasing maintenance costs
- Reduced collaboration and synchronization among teams
- Low velocity
- Systems that are difficult to integrate and validate
- Deterioration of system qualities (Nonfunctional Requirements, or NFRs)
- Low reuse of components; implementation redundancies

The net result of all of the above can be poor solution performance, bad economics, and slower time to market.

## Intentional Architecture Supports the Bigger Picture

It simply isn't possible for all teams to anticipate changes that may occur well outside of their environment, nor for individual teams to fully understand the entire system and thereby avoid producing redundant and/or conflicting designs and implementations. Simply put, no one team in a larger Enterprise can see the bigger picture, nor reasonably anticipate some of the changes that are headed their way, many of which arise outside their local control.

For this reason, teams need some *intentional architecture*—a set of purposeful, planned architectural initiatives that enhance solution design, performance, and usability and provide guidance for cross-team design and implementation synchronization. These Enablers create the *Architectural Runway* needed to allow teams to deliver business value faster and more reliably.

Together, *intentional architecture* and *emergent design* enable programs to create and maintain large-scale Solutions. Emergent design enables fast, local control so that teams react appropriately to changing requirements without excessive attempts to future-proof the system. Intentional architecture provides the guidance needed to ensure that the system as a whole has conceptual integrity and efficacy. Achieving the right balance of emergent design and intentional architecture drives effective evolution of large-scale systems.

## Enable Flow and Agility with Architecture

Enablers are used to extend the architectural runway. Enablers are often defined by architects or by systems engineering at the various levels, whether by Enterprise Architects at the Portfolio Level or by System and Solution Architects/Engineering at the Value Stream and Program Levels.

The architects who define the enablers help steer through the various Kanban systems, providing both the guidance needed to analyze them and the information needed to estimate and implement them. This enablement ensures that the affected elements—subsystems, components, functions, protocols, internal system functions, etc.—have the architecture necessary to support the near-term Features and Capabilities on the Roadmap.

However, implementation of enabler Epics and capabilities and features is complicated by the fact that the "big up-front branch-and-merge" waterfall approach no longer applies. Instead, the enterprise commits to implementing architecture incrementally. Doing so means that enabler epics must be split into enabler features and/or capabilities, which are ultimately implemented by individual Agile Release Trains (ARTs). Each enabler feature must be completed within a Program Increment (PI) such that the *system always runs*, at least at the PI boundaries. In some cases, this means that new architectural initiatives are implemented piecemeal and may not even be exposed to the users in the PI in which they are implemented. In this way, the architectural runway can be implemented and tested behind the scenes, allowing shipment throughout, and then exposed to users when a sufficient capability exists to support the implementation of new business epics and the program-level features that instantiated them.

SAFe uses the PI cadence and synchronization of both planning and asset integration as a primary tool to manage the inherent variability of R&D. In this way, ARTs have constant availability of new product for potential shipments; the enterprise is then free to decide whether or not to ship that asset, based on mostly external factors. This means that having solid, high-quality, deployable system-level solutions at (and at least at) PI boundaries is critical. In turn, that means that some amount of architectural runway must exist going *into* the PI Planning session. Otherwise, there is a substantial risk that architectural rework—followed by the build-out of new features that depend on that rework—adds unacceptable risk to the program.

To mitigate the risk, programs must take care to ensure that the necessary architectural underpinnings for the most innovative new features are *already* in the system when planning for the PI. That is accomplished by *building* some runway, *using* the runway, and *extending* it, as we'll see in the following sections.

## Building the Architectural Runway

In the cases where new platforms are particularly innovative, or in the case of entirely new (greenfield) development, it is common that the System or Solution Architect/Engineer plays a role in the initial definition and build-out of the runway. There, usually the new infrastructure is initially put in place with just one or two Agile Teams—sometimes with the architect/engineer serving as Product Owner—over the course of a few Iterations, as illustrated in Figure 1.

*Figure 1. Initiating the architectural runway*

The rules for doing so are both simple and Agile:

1. These teams iterate like every other Agile Team on the program

2. Credit goes to working solutions, not models and designs

3. Time is of the essence. It should take no more than a few iterations to implement and prove the new architecture.

Very quickly thereafter, the program is expanded to add some feature teams, who test the new architecture with the initial, consumable features, as illustrated in Figure 2.

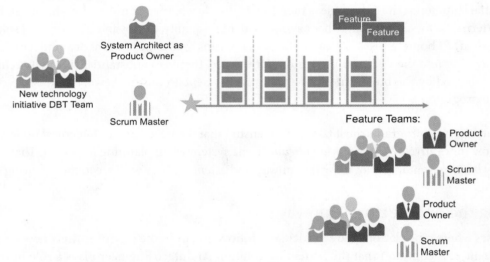

*Figure 2. Implementing some new features on the new runway*

In the meantime, the teams build up additional architectural runway, as illustrated in Figure 3.

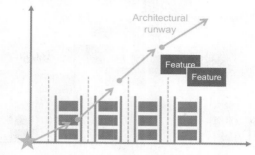

*Figure 3. Progress in building the architectural runway*

To support a stable velocity, the architectural runway needs to be continuously maintained and extended. Capacity allocations are used to ensure continuous investments in enablers, those activities that are intended to extend the runway. Product/Solution Management and Architects/Engineers, in collaboration with the affected teams, define many of these architectural initiatives, but implementation is the responsibility of the Agile Release Trains. While providing the enablement for near-term delivery success, the architectural runway should not over-constrain the development with long-range technical commitments. "Just the right amount" of architectural runway is required. Too much, and the architecture over-constrains the teams and is too disconnected from the current context; too little and the teams will have trouble reliably making and meeting near-term commitments.

## Using It: The Fragile and Temporal Nature of System Architecture

All is good up to this point. A new architecture is in place and valuable features have already been deployed on it. This initial success can be temporary, however, as a number of natural forces will tend to cause the architecture to be consumed over time:

1. Agile Teams are fast. They have an unparalleled focus and ability to deliver new features, thus consuming whatever runway exists.

2. Product Owners and Product/Solution Management are impatient. They've invested some time on internal system capabilities, and they will quickly move backlog priorities to the features that users are willing to pay for.

3. Architecture itself is fragile and needs to be continuously evolved. Technologies change in short time frames. Stuff obsolesces.

4. Customer needs change quickly, too

Unless the Agile Teams are really on their game, the result will be as depicted in Figure 4.

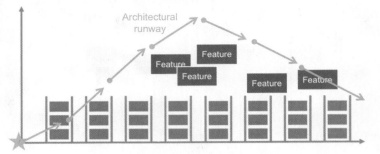

*Figure 4. Using up the architectural runway*

## Extending It

How can teams avoid ending up right back where they started? Simply, investing in architecture cannot be a one-time or sporadic event. This is a flow-based system, after all. Instead, teams commit to continuous elaboration, analysis, and implementation of enabler epics and capabilities and features, using the various Kanban systems. In addition, Architects/Engineers and Agile Teams have newfound skills that provide for splitting enabler epics and features into small slices that can be implemented during the course of each iteration and PI, thereby continuously delivering value to the Customer. (See the "System and Solution Architect/Engineering" article and ASR [2], Chapters 20 and 21, for incremental implementation strategies.)

## Note: The Source of the Metaphor

The term *Architectural Runway* started as an analogy with respect to observing PI-level burn-down charts. It is often the case that when there isn't enough architecture already extant in code when teams start a PI, then any features dependent on new architecture are high risk, and programs can't always "land those PIs" (bring the burn-down to 0 at the end of the PI). In that case, they fail to meet the PI objectives. There has to be some "runway" to land the thing.

In the SAFe Big Picture, the red architectural runway line is drawn the way it is, going up and down over time, because the team builds some, then uses some, builds some more, uses that too . . . there has to be just about the right amount at any point. Plus, to extend the metaphor a bit, the bigger the aircraft (system) and the faster the flying (velocity), the more runway that's needed to land the PI safely. Runway is explained further in the "Agile Architecture" article.

---

**LEARN MORE**

[1] Leffingwell, Dean. *Scaling Software Agility: Best Practices for Large Enterprises.* Addison-Wesley, 2007, chapter 16.

[2] Leffingwell, Dean. *Agile Software Requirements: Lean Requirements Practices for Teams, Programs, and the Enterprise.* Addison-Wesley, 2011.

[3] Manifesto for Agile Software Development. http://www.agilemanifesto.org.

---

# Part 5
# The Spanning Palette

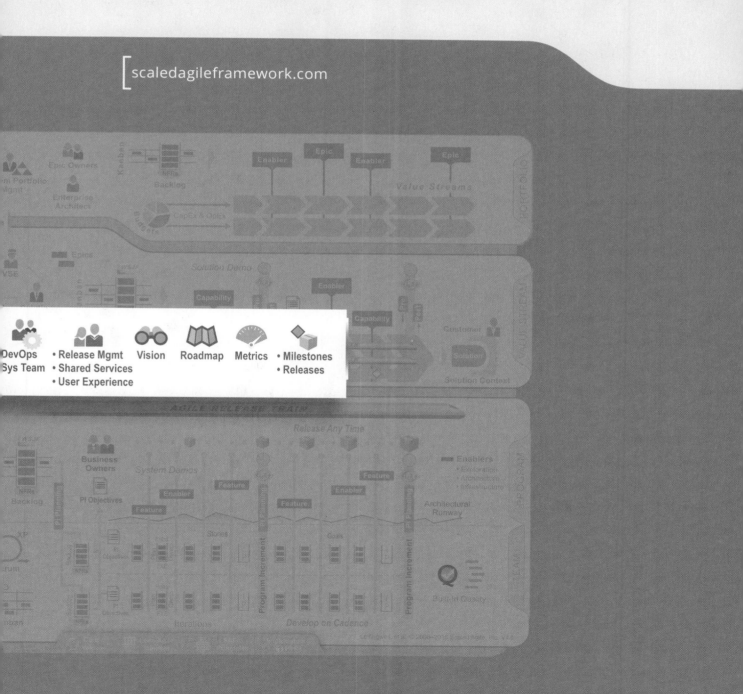

# DevOps

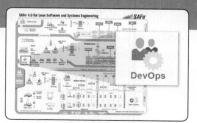

*In order for you to keep up with customer demand, you need to create a deployment pipeline. You need to get everything in version control. You need to automate the entire environment creation process. You need a deployment pipeline where you can create test and production environments, and then deploy code into them, entirely on demand.*

—Erik to Grasshopper, *The Phoenix Project* [2]

## Abstract

Real, tangible development *value* occurs *only* when the end users are successfully operating the Solution in their environment. This demands that the complex routine of *deploying to operations*, or *moving to production*, receives early and meaningful attention during development.

To ensure a faster flow of value to the end user, this article suggests mechanisms for tighter integration of development and deployment operations, typically referred to as *DevOps*. This is accomplished, in part, by integrating personnel from the operations/production team with the Agile Teams in the Agile Release Train (ART). There are also specific suggestions for continuously maintaining *deployment readiness* throughout the capability and feature development timeline. In turn, this gives the Enterprise the ability to deploy to production more frequently, and thereby lead its industry with the *sustainably shortest lead time*.

## Details

### Deployment Operations Is Integral to the Value Stream

The goal of software and systems engineering is to deliver usable and reliable Solutions to the end users. Lean and Agile both emphasize the ability to do so more frequently and reliably. "Leaning" the development process helps development shops gradually establish faster development flow by systematically reducing development cycle time and introducing "built-in quality" approaches. However, in most cases, development teams still deliver solutions to deployment or production in large batches. There, the actual deployment and release of the new solution is likely to be manual, error prone, and unpredictable, which adversely affects release date commitments and delivered quality.

In contrast, many shops have very effective Lean manufacturing facilities that are out of sync with the development side of the Value Stream.

To enable organizations to effectively deliver value to the business, a leaner approach must be applied, which incorporates smaller batch sizes and includes deployment readiness from Capability definition all the way through to the point where users actually benefit. Thereby we can move closer to continuous delivery, which is an end goal for many Enterprises. While this article is mainly focused on *DevOps* practices in the setting of internal and external IT software development, DevOps is more than just a set of practices and can be applied to the larger context of both software and systems development. More important, DevOps is also about changing the mindsets of people to break down silos; obtain fast, useful feedback; and improve the flow of work and collaboration to bring about the best economic outcomes and develop products that delight Customers.

## Deployment Operations Must Be "on the Train"

In SAFe, value streams cover all steps of software value *creation and delivery*. The Agile Release Train, a self-organized team of Agile Teams, is designed to enable effective flow of value in a particular value stream via a steady stream of Releases. Some value streams can be realized by a single ART, while some require many ARTs to deliver the solution. In order to establish an effective deployment pipeline and process, it is crucial that the *deployment operations* or *production* team members are active on the train and fully engaged in the process. In multi-ART value streams, DevOps is part of the trains, as well as part of the solution team at the Value Stream Level.

DevOps typically includes system administrators, database administrators, operational engineers, and network and storage engineers. However, DevOps principles, values, and practices can also be extended to manufacturing experts and others—those who are traditionally responsible for deploying or manufacturing the solution and keeping it running. They must operate in the shared, real-time development *and* delivery context of the Agile Release Train. The Internet of Things (IoT) is also set to be the next wave of disruption to the market to those building and connecting things. This will also require new thinking as to how to deal with the integration of widely distributed software, hardware and systems, IT operations, and quality practices needed for rapid deployment. Being part of the Agile Release Train means actively participating in ART events—interacting with teams, System and Solution Architect-Engineering, and Business Owners. It also includes developing and maintaining a backlog of DevOps activities aligned with Program PI Objectives. This implies some level of participation of the deployment operations team in the activities of PI Planning, backlog refinement, Scrum of Scrums, System Demo, Solution Demo, and Inspect and Adapt. It is also important that the pipeline of deployable work is *visualized*, so that development teams and operations/production can work collaboratively to ensure the flow of value from the time the capabilities are conceived until they get actually deployed and used.

## Six Recommended Practices for Building Your Deployment Pipeline

In order to establish an effective deployment pipeline—a continuous flow of new value from development to and through deployment—six specific practices are provided in the following sections. These are based on an understanding of a necessary, broader, and more automated environment, as Figure 1 illustrates.

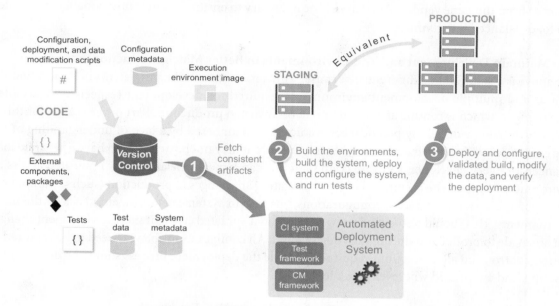

*Figure 1. Deployment pipeline environment*

We can see from Figure 1 that there are three main processes that must be supported:

1. Automatically fetching all necessary artifacts from version control, including code, scripts, tests, metadata, and the like

2. Automatically integrating, deploying, and validating the code in a staging environment and automating it as far as possible

3. Deploying the validated build from staging to production and validating the new system

### #1 – Build and Maintain a Production-Equivalent Staging Environment

Figure 1 illustrates a critical asset: a staging environment. The need for this environment is driven by the fact that most development environments are typically quite different from production. There, for example, the application server is behind a firewall, which is preceded by a load balancer; the much larger-scale production database is clustered; media content lives on separate servers; and more. During the handoff from development to production, Murphy's Law will take effect: The deployment will fail and debugging and resolution will take an unpredictable amount of time.

Instead, the company should build a staging environment that has the same or similar hardware and supporting systems as production. There, the program teams can continuously validate their software in preparation for deployment. While achieving true production equivalency may not become economically viable—it doesn't makes sense to replicate the hundreds or thousands of servers required—there are a variety of ways to achieve largely functional equivalence without such investment. For example, it may be sufficient to have only 2 instances of the application server instead of 20, and a cheaper load balancer from the same vendor—all that may be necessary to ensure that new functionality is validated in a load-balanced environment.

### #2 – Maintain Development and Test Environments to Better Match Production

The above is a solution to a different root cause, which itself can also be mitigated, and that is that the various and multiple development environments required for development (especially distributed development, which is routine at scale) do not closely match production. Part of the reason for this is cost, which may be driven by practical economics (unencumbered by a lack of understanding of the true cost of delay of deployment). So, for example, while it may not be practical to have a separate load balancer for every developer, software configurations can typically be affordably replicated across all environments. This can be accomplished by propagating all changes in production (such as component or supporting systems upgrades, configurations, changes in system metadata, etc.) back to the other environments. This should also include new development-initiated configuration/environment changes that are made to production during each deployment. All configuration changes need to be captured in version control, and all new actions required to enable the deployment process should be documented in scripts and automated wherever possible.

### #3 – Deploy to Staging Every Iteration; Deploy to Production Frequently

**3a – Deploy to Staging Every Iteration** – It is not possible to objectively understand the true state of any increment unless it is truly deployment ready. To better ensure this, one suggestion is a simple rule: *Do all fortnightly system demos from the staging environment, including the final system and solution demos.* In that way, *deployability* becomes part of Definition of Done for every user story, resulting in potentially deployable software every Iteration.

**3b – Deploy to Production Frequently** – And while continuous *deployment readiness* is critical to establishing a reliable delivery process, the real benefits in shortening lead time come from *actually deploying to production more frequently.* This also helps eliminate long-lived production support branches and the consequential extra effort required to merge and synchronize changes across all the instances. However, while Figure 1 shows a fully automated deployment model, we must also consider release governance before we allow an "automatic push" to production. This is typically under the authority of Release Management, whose considerations include:

- Conceptual integrity of the feature set, such that it meets a holistic set of user needs (see the "Releases" article)
- Evaluation of any quality, regulatory, security, or other such requirements

- Potential impacts to Customers, channels, production, and any external market timing considerations

**#4 – Put Everything Under Version Control**

In order to be able to reliably deploy to production, all deployable artifacts, metadata, and other supporting configuration items must be maintained under version control. This includes the new code, all required data (dictionaries, scripts, look-ups, mappings, etc.), all libraries and external assemblies, configuration files or databases, application or database servers—everything that may realistically be updated or modified. This approach also applies to the test data, which has to be manageable enough for the teams to update every time they introduce a new test scenario or update an existing one. Keeping the test data under version control provides quick and reliable feedback on the latest build by allowing for repeatedly running the tests in a deterministic test environment.

**#5 – Start Creating the Ability to Automatically Build Environments**

Many deployment problems arise from the error-prone, manually intensive routines that are required to build the actual run-time environments. These include preparing the operating environment, applications, and data; configuring the artifacts; and initiating the required jobs in the system and its supporting systems. In order to establish a reliable deployment process, the environment setup process itself needs to be fully automated. This automation can be substantially facilitated by virtualization, using Infrastructure as a Service (IaaS) and applying special frameworks for automating the configuration management jobs.

**#6 – Start Automating the Actual Deployment Process**

Last, it should be obvious that the actual deployment process itself also requires automation. This includes all the steps in the flow, including building the code, creating the test environments, executing the automated tests, and deploying and validating verified code and associated systems and utilities in the target (development, staging, and production) environment. This final, critical automation step is achievable only via an incremental process, one that requires the organization's full commitment and support, as well as creativity and pragmatism as the teams prioritize target areas for automation.

## Deployability and Solution Architecture

A Lean, *systems approach* to continuous deployment readiness requires understanding that the code itself, as well as configurations, integration scripts, automated tests, deployment scripts, metadata, and supporting systems, are equally important pieces of the entire solution. Faster achievement of user and business goals can be achieved only when the whole solution context is considered. As with the other Nonfunctional Requirements (NFRs), designing for deployability requires intentional design effort via collaboration of System Architects, Agile Teams, and deployment operations toward the goal of a fast and flawless delivery process, requiring minimal manual effort.

In addition, in order to support the adoption of more effective deployment techniques, the organization may need to undertake certain enterprise-level architectural initiatives (common technology stacks, tools, data preparation and normalization, third-party interfaces and data exchange, logging and reporting tools, etc.) that gradually enhance architecture, infrastructure, and other nonfunctional considerations in support of deployment readiness. Everything that jeopardizes or complicates the process of getting valuable software out the door must eventually be improved.

## LEARN MORE

[1] Humble, Jez and David Farley. *Continuous Delivery: Reliable Software Releases through Build, Test, and Deployment Automation*. Addison-Wesley, 2010.

[2] Kim, Gene, et al. *The Phoenix Project: A Novel About IT, DevOps, and Helping Your Business Win*. IT Revolution Press, 2013.

[3] Prugh, Scott. *Continuous Delivery*. http://www.scaledagileframework.com/continuous-delivery by Prugh, on the same topic, from DevOps Enterprise Summit, 2014.

# System Team

*The whole is greater than the sum of its parts.*
*—Aristotle*

## Abstract

In SAFe, Agile Teams are not stand-alone units. Instead, they are an integral part of the Agile Release Train (ART), where they collectively have responsibility for delivering larger value. Teams operate in the context of the train, adhering to its vision, collaborating with other teams, and participating in key ART ceremonies. The teams and the train are inseparable; the whole is greater than the sum of its parts. During the transition to Agile, it is typically the case that additional infrastructure work is required to be able to integrate assets frequently (hourly, daily, weekly), rather than once only at the end of a development cycle. To accomplish this, one or more specialized *System Teams* are often formed. They assist with system and solution integration, and they help demonstrate the evolving Solution as it unfolds.

## Details

### Summary Role Description

A *System Team* is a special Agile Team on the Agile Release Train or Value Stream that is typically chartered to provide assistance in building and using the Agile development environment infrastructure—including Continuous Integration—as well as integrating assets from Agile Teams, performing end-to-end Solution testing. They may participate in demonstrating solutions in the System Demo at the end of each Iteration, and at the Solution Demo at the end of each Program Increment, or more frequently as the case may be. This supports the teams and other stakeholders by providing quick feedback with respect to the efficacy and integrity of the evolving end-to-end solution. System Teams may also have a special role in assisting with each Release and with Coordination of larger value streams.

However, these efforts should be shared between the System Team and Agile Teams; otherwise, the System Team will become a bottleneck, and the Agile Teams cannot be fully capable of or accountable for real value delivery.

## The System Team in Larger Value Streams

System Teams are particularly invaluable in large, multi-ART value streams. Depending on the scope and complexity of the value stream, we have observed three organizational patterns in this larger case:

1. There is a System Team per ART, and that team can effectively coordinate the solution integration and validation without additional help

2. There is a System Team only at the Value Stream Level, and that team can fulfill these responsibilities for the ART

3. There are System Teams both at the value stream level and within the release trains

The decision regarding which pattern to use is highly dependent on the specific context of the value stream. However, generic factors may include Agile Team orientation (feature or component), ART structure within the value stream (built around capabilities or subsystems), solution architecture, branching and integration policies across the trains, system testability, and development infrastructure.

## Responsibilities

The System Team's primary responsibilities are indicated below.

### Building Development Infrastructure

Good infrastructure supports high ART velocity. Thus, the System Team may:

- Create and maintain infrastructure, including continuous integration, automated builds, and automated build verification testing

- Create platforms and environments for solution demonstration, QA, user testing, etc.

- Create products, utilities, and scripts to automate deployment

- Facilitate the technical aspects of collaboration with third parties, such as data or service providers, hosting facilities, etc.

### System Integration

Complex solutions also require that the System Team do the following:

- Participate in PI Planning and the Pre- and Post-PI Planning meetings at the value stream level, and in backlog refinement to define integration and test Capabilities and Features

- Determine and help maintain decisions and policies for appropriate branching models

- Run solution-level integration scripts or integrate manually where automation is not possible or has not yet been applied

- Assist component teams in defining inter-component interfaces

- Attend other teams' stand-ups in support of daily activities

**End-to-End and Solution Performance Testing**

The System Team may also perform a number of automated testing responsibilities:

- Create new automated test scenarios

- Extend test scenarios to larger data sets

- Organize test cases designed by individual teams into ordered suites

- Perform manual testing and run automated tests for new features and Stories

- Prioritize time-consuming tests, refactor, and run reduced test suites where applicable

- Assist teams in creating reduced test suites that they themselves can run

- Test solution performance against NFRs and assist System and Solution Engineering in identifying system shortfalls and bottlenecks

**System and Solution Demos**

At the appropriate time during every iteration, the teams need to demonstrate the current, *whole-system* solution to stakeholders in the system demos. Likewise, the value stream must integrate and show progress at the solution demo. The System Team typically helps stage these demos and helps ensure that demo environments are adequate to the challenge of reliably demonstrating new solution functionality.

**Release**

It is often the case that the System Team has unique skills and purview with respect to the evolving solution. The team may include senior QA personnel; perhaps the System Architect/Engineer serves as a member of this team. They have seen the solution across multiple iterations; they generally understand what it is, what it does, and how well it meets all the intended requirements. With this perspective, the System Team is likely to be directly involved in supporting the release, working closely with DevOps and doing whatever is necessary to help the train prepare, package, and release a solution into the target environment.

## Balancing Solution Integration and Testing Effort

However, the System Team can never be the entire solution to the integration challenge. Agile Teams must also have a clear vision of the bigger picture of what they are creating. Otherwise, even local excellence on the part of Agile Teams will not result in good economic outcomes. Effective solution development only occurs when these practices are appropriately shared. For example, if only the System Team is testing NFRs and individual teams don't perform even lightweight performance testing, then the entire ART velocity will be slowed by the rework necessary to pass these critical quality tests.

In a similar fashion, if Agile Teams are not continuously integrating at least the immediate components they interface with, the integration effort by the System Team will be a long and painful process.

Maximizing ART velocity requires *a sense of balance between Agile Teams and System Teams*, as Figure 1 illustrates.

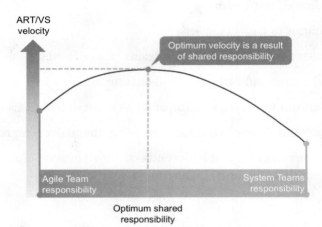

*Figure 1. The optimum balance in terms of integration effort between Agile Teams and the System Team. With maturity and automation, the optimum point moves to the left.*

## LEARN MORE

[1] Leffingwell, Dean. *Agile Software Requirements: Lean Requirements Practices for Teams, Programs, and the Enterprise.* Addison-Wesley, 2011, chapter 4.

# Release Management

*Success in management requires learning as fast as the world is changing.*
   —Warren Bennis

## Abstract

*Release Management* typically assists with planning, managing, and governing releases of the Solution and has the authority and responsibility to help guide the Value Stream toward the business goals. They help coordinate and facilitate the activities necessary to help internal and external stakeholders receive and deploy the new solution, and they help ensure that the most critical governance elements of quality—particularly internal and external security, regulatory, and other compliance-related aspects of the solution—have been appropriately addressed prior to deployment.

## Details

As the governing authority for the Release, *Release Management* typically consists of Solution Management, along with senior representation from those functions that are not full-time participants of the Value Stream, including marketing, quality, development, Program Portfolio Management, operations, deployment, and distribution. This function has the authority, knowledge, and capacity to foster and approve frequent releases of quality Solutions to Customers. In many cases, the Release Management team includes representatives from the Agile Release Trains that contribute to the solution.

Release Management meets regularly to evaluate content, progress, and quality. As SAFe espouses fixed quality/fixed-cost-schedule/flexible Features or Capabilities, Release Management will typically be actively involved in scope management, even late in a Program Increment. In addition, Release Management is concerned with other elements of the whole solution, including internationalization, packing and deployment, training requirements, internal and external communications, and ensuring conformance to the most critical quality standards (including external and regulatory requirements).

### Responsibilities

Planning a release is the easy part; the hard part is coordinating the implementation of all the capabilities and features over the multiple Iterations within a release, especially as new issues, roadblocks, dependencies, overlaps, over-scopes, and gaps in Vision and Backlogs are uncovered—all while the external environment is evolving.

This is the challenge for the self-managing, self-organizing ARTs; the scope of each release must be continually managed, revalidated, and communicated. But some of these changes and impediments may be outside the authority of the train, so they are typically assisted in this challenge by Release Management, who share the responsibility for coordinating releases and communicating to significant stakeholders.

Primary responsibilities include:

- Ensuring that the organization's release governance is understood

- Communicating release status to external stakeholders

- Ensuring that an appropriate deployment/distribution plan is in place

- Coordinating with marketing and with Product and Solution Management on internal and external communications

- Validating that the solution meets relevant quality and governance criteria

- Participating in Inspect and Adapt to improve the release process, value stream productivity, and solution quality

- Providing final authorization for the release

- Acting as a liaison with Program Portfolio Management, as appropriate

Note: Releasing is generally detached from development cadence in SAFe. "Planning a release" assumes the effort during PI Planning, directed toward a specific release or releases within the current PI boundaries, or close to them. In SAFe, solutions are developed on cadence but released any time, in support of business demand.

## Membership
The Release Management function typically comprises individuals from the following areas:

- Release Train Engineers and Value Stream Engineers

- Line-of-business owners, Solution and Product Managers

- Senior representatives from sales and marketing

- Development managers who have responsibility for the teams and technology

- Internal IT, production, and deployment personnel

- Senior and solution-level QA personnel who are responsible for the final assessment of solution-level quality, performance, and suitability for use

- System and Solution Architects, CTOs, and others who oversee architectural integrity

**Regular Coordination**

In many enterprises, Release Management meets weekly to address the following questions:

- Is the vision still understood, and are the trains and teams aligned to that purpose?

- Does everyone understand what they are building, and is it aligned with the understanding of the purpose of the value stream and current Strategic Themes?

- Are the scheduled releases still largely tracking?

- What impediments must be addressed to facilitate progress?

The weekly meeting provides senior management with regular visibility into the release status. This team also has the authority to approve any scope, timing, or resource adjustments necessary to help ensure the release. In this manner, Release Management represents the final authority on release governance issues.

---

**LEARN MORE**

[1] Leffingwell, Dean. *Agile Software Requirements: Lean Requirements Practices for Teams, Programs, and the Enterprise.* Addison-Wesley, 2011, chapter 4.

# Shared Services

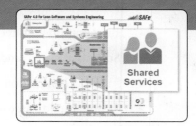

*My idea of heaven is a great big baked potato and someone to share it with.*
   —Oprah Winfrey

## Abstract

*Shared Services* represent specialty roles that are necessary for success of an Agile Release Train (ART) or Value Stream but that cannot be dedicated full time. These resources may include security specialists, information architects, DBAs, technical writers, quality assurance, IT operations personnel, and more. As the resources are specialized, often single-sourced, and typically quite busy, each ART and value stream must plan to engage the resources they need, when they need them.

## Details

Agile Release Trains and, by extension, Value Streams are characterized by the dedicated focus that can be accomplished when all necessary skills and abilities needed to deliver value are fully dedicated to the ART. However, in many cases it's simply impractical to dedicate some specialty functions to a single ART. There may be insufficient capacity of skills of that type, or, alternately, the need from the ART varies over time such that full-time dedication is not economically sensible. To address this, *Shared Services* support development by quickly bringing specialty expertise to bear on areas of the system or Solution that require unique knowledge and skills.

In some cases, the efforts must proactively track ahead of the Agile Teams (examples: security, information architecture), such that they contribute directly to the Architectural Runway that supports new Capability or Feature development. In other cases, the resources can trail core development a bit (examples: IT/deployment support, Customer training, localizations), and simply being quickly supportive and reactive is sufficient.

In either case, without timely support and synchronization, the programs will struggle to meet their objectives. Therefore, while the Shared Services may not be *on the release train* per se, they must travel synchronously with it, as the train has to carry some of their cargo, too.

## Summary Role Description

Potential members of the Shared Services group include those with specialty skills in areas such as:

- Data modeling, data engineering, and database support
- Enterprise Architecture
- Information architecture
- ScrumXP, Agile, and Built-in Quality coaches
- Internationalization and localization
- System quality assurance (QA) and exploratory testing
- Documentation
- End-user training
- IT and deployment operations
- Information security
- Desktop services
- Infrastructure and tools management
- Application/web portal management
- Configuration management

## Responsibilities

In order to be effective, Shared Services personnel should be trained in SAFe and participate in PI Planning as well as Pre- and Post-PI Planning. There they drive requirements where necessary and take ownership of their portion of dependent backlog items that emerge. Thereafter, they collaborate to fulfill dependencies that occur during Program Increment (PI) execution. They may also participate in System Demos, Solution Demos, and Inspect and Adapt workshops when appropriate, as many improvement backlog items may reflect challenges with specialty technology or with availability and dependencies.

Occasionally, members of the Shared Services group may choose to operate as a single team. When so doing, they iterate on the same cadence as the ARTs and perform Iteration planning and demo and retro activities, just as the Agile development teams do.

### Maintain Specialized Training

Because technical shared resources are highly specialized (as opposed to the *generalized specialists* of an Agile Team), their skills must be continuously refined to keep up with advancements in their respective fields.

**Periodically Embed in Agile Teams**

In order to better help an Agile Team that requires either sustained or transitional special expertise, Shared Services personnel may also be embedded with development teams for short periods of time. There they have the benefit of experiencing daily life on an Agile Team. This helps develop an appreciation for the Agile Team dynamic, as well as an understanding of the speed of development and the quality of the product being produced. It also accelerates the larger dynamic of teams of teams that, only acting together, can deliver Enterprise value.

**LEARN MORE**

[1] Leffingwell, Dean. *Agile Software Requirements: Lean Requirements Practices for Teams, Programs, and the Enterprise.* Addison-Wesley, 2011.

# User Experience (UX)

*Simple things should be simple, complex things should be possible.*

   —Alan Kay

## Abstract

*User Experience (UX)* represents a user's perceptions of a system's aspects, including ease of use, utility, and efficiency of the man-machine interface. User Experience design focuses on building systems that reflect a deep understanding of end users, what they need, and what they value, and it reflects an understanding of their abilities and limitations.

A common Agile challenge is how to incorporate the User Experience into a rapid Iteration cycle, including implementation of visual design, navigation, and user interface (UI) elements. When teams attempt to resolve complex (and seemingly subjective) user interactions while simultaneously trying to develop and test incremental deliverables, they often end up "churning" through many iterations. This can be a source of frustration with the Agile process. UX/UI implementation is further complicated by the necessity of User Experience testing. Since it may not always be practical to run User Experience tests and gain feedback within the same iteration that implements new functionality, the result can be delayed feedback that affects future iterations, reduces velocity, and introduces delays in delivery.

Fortunately, Agile Teams have found a number of practices for addressing this important design element. Keys include having the User Experience design track a bit ahead as part of the Architectural Runway for a system, centralizing design guidance but not implementation, and leveraging iterations and working code to drive out uncertainty and risk through fast user feedback.

## Details

### Summary Role Description

In SAFe, Agile Teams have responsibility for implementing the Solution, including the user interface (UI) elements. However, in order to provide a consistent *User Experience (UX)* across the components and systems of the larger solution, one or more User Experience designers is typically dedicated to the Agile Release Train (ART).

In general, they need to track a bit ahead and be ready with design guidelines, prototypes, wireframes, style sheets, and other artifacts as part of the Architectural Runway necessary to provide some common guidance for the new Program Increment functionality.

## Responsibilities

User Experience designers typically have the following responsibilities:

- Work with stakeholders to understand the specific business targets behind the user-system interaction

- Provide Agile Teams with the next increment of UI design, User Experience guidelines, and design elements in a just-in-time (but timely enough) fashion

- Continually validate User Experience via User Experience testing

- Work with System and Solution Architect/Engineering and teams to build and maintain the technical foundation for real-time User Experience validation, feedback, tracking statistics, etc.

- Share User Experience guidelines across the Program; educate developers on the best practices of maintaining good UI design

- Assist test engineers and the System Team in User Experience testing and testing automation

- Lead UI design and User Experience/UI Community of Practice workshops

- Attend Iteration Planning, backlog refinement meetings, System Demos, and Solution Demos whenever critical UI-related work is involved

## User Experience Design in Agile

Given the elimination of Big Up-Front Design (BUFD), the flow of User Experience design is somewhat different in Agile and typically includes the following characteristics:

- Includes fast, low-fidelity prototyping to develop runway for future implementation

- Is extremely incremental

- Relies on fast and frequent feedback via rapid code implementation

- Is highly collaborative between the users and the teams

- Uses Enabler Story spikes for User Experience research activities

- Includes UI criteria in the Definition of Done (see "Scaled Definition of Done" in the "Releases" article) and user story acceptance criteria

## User Experience in Relation to Design and Testing

In order to enable an effective User Experience design process and fast and reliable UI implementation, the following design criteria are important:

- Clear separation of UI and application logic

- Effective UI development conventions

- Effective organization of UI assets and ease of reuse, extension, and style modification

- Support for collection of usage statistics, UI error logging, and feedback mechanisms

Many of the User Experience guidelines and requirements are directly testable. Some can be automated more simply than other functional tests. (For example: A simple test script could check for "use horizontal menus on all screens" and thereby prevent developers from accidentally diverging from this criteria.)

## User Experience Designers on the Agile Release Train

Many system elements interact with the user in some fashion, so proper User Experience design is as important as are the other aspects of good software and system engineering, especially in larger systems and systems of systems. The User Experience design of devices (including aesthetics, shape, size, and weight) can be equally important factors. This impacts the way in which User Experience designers collaborate with the rest of the program. The following organizational models are common.

### Centralized User Experience Guidance and Implementation

Although it might appear attractive from the perspective of empowerment and velocity of the Agile Team, fully distributing User Experience development to the team can be problematic, in that the entropy of multiple team-based UI design approaches is not likely to serve the user well. Therefore, some organizations create a central User Experience design team that iterates a bit ahead of the development teams, as in Figure 1.

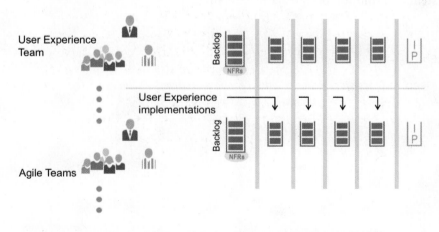

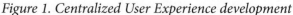

*Figure 1. Centralized User Experience development*

They run a common cadence and Iteration model, but their backlog will contain User Experience enabler story spikes, testing, prototyping, and *implementation* activities that are used to define a common User Experience.

### Distributed, Governed User Experience Development

However, it's likely that the central team will become a bottleneck for the development teams. Worse, the problem becomes larger at scale, because there are more dependencies that must be addressed. To mitigate this problem, a hybrid model can often be more effectively applied, as shown in Figure 2.

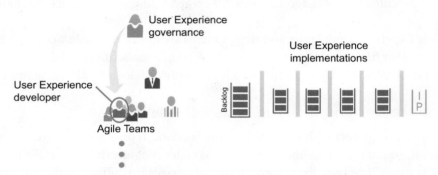

*Figure 2. Distributed, governed User Experience development*

In the "distributed but governed" model, there is a small, centralized User Experience design team (or individual) who provides the basic design approach and preliminary mock-ups (or prototypes) for each UI, but the teams do the actual implementation. In this case, the User Experience implementation skills are distributed among the teams, but the centralized design authority provides wireframes, style sheets, brand control guidance, mock-ups, physical hardware prototypes, usability guidelines, and other artifacts that can help provide conceptual integrity of the User Experience across the entire solution. The User Experience design team also typically attends Team Demos and system demos to see how the overall system and solution design are progressing.

---

### LEARN MORE

[1] Leffingwell, Dean. *Agile Software Requirements: Lean Requirements Practices for Teams, Programs, and the Enterprise.* Addison-Wesley, 2011, chapter 7.

# Vision

*People at work are thirsting for context, yearning to know that what they do contributes to a larger whole.*

 —Daniel Pink

## Abstract

The *Vision* describes a future view of the Solution to be developed, reflecting Customer and stakeholder needs, as well as Features and Capabilities that are proposed to address those needs. It also describes markets, Customer segments, and user needs to be served. It provides the larger, contextual overview and purpose of the solution under development. It sets the boundaries against which new features, Nonfunctional Requirements, and other content decisions are based.

The vision is both aspirational and tactical in nature. It may be driven largely by a specific set of contractual obligations, or it may respond to the systems builders' view of the opportunities the marketplace provides.

The vision icon lives on the "spanning palette" in SAFe. This reflects the fact that while the focus typically is on the solution at the Program and Value Stream Levels, the Portfolio Vision is also clearly relevant, and certainly Agile Teams can have longer-term views of the aspects of the systems that they are responsible for.

## Details

Few question the benefits of Lean-Agile's focus on near-term deliverables. Deferring decisions until the last responsible moment, limiting work in process—forgoing detailed, too-early requirements specifications, future proof architectures, detailed longer-term plans—and instead focusing on immediate value delivery are hallmarks of Lean-Agile development. There is no substitute for that kind of focus and bias for action: "Let's build it and then we'll know."

However, in the context of larger Solutions, every individual contributor makes decisions each day on what to do now and, in so doing, also on what will be easy—or not so easy—to do in the future.

In this way, they ultimately determine both the effectiveness of the current solution and the economics of developing future solutions. To this end, there is no substitute for keeping all team members continuously apprised of the solution *Vision*, for that is *why* they do *what* they do. Continuously developing, maintaining, and communicating the vision—both longer term and nearer term—is critical to creating a shared understanding of the program's goals and objectives, especially as those ideas evolve due to ever-shifting market needs and business drivers.

In SAFe the vision appears on the spanning palette, indicating that it is applied at different places depending on context. The solution vision can be either at the Program Level in 3-level SAFe or on the Value Stream Level in 4-level SAFe, indicating to Agile Release Trains and Agile Teams why they are building the solution. The Portfolio should also have a vision, reflecting how the Value Streams will cooperate to achieve the larger Enterprise objectives. And of course the teams can apply the vision constructs as well, helping to ensure their focus on the nearer- and longer-term views.

## Portfolio Vision

The portfolio vision sets a longer-term context for near-term decisions in a way that is both practical—local decisions are made in the light of a long-term context—and inspirational: "This is something really worth doing." Lean-Agile leaders largely have the responsibility for setting the strategic direction of the company and establishing the mission for the teams who will implement that strategy. *Switch* [1] calls this longer-term view a "Destination Postcard," as Figure 1 illustrates.

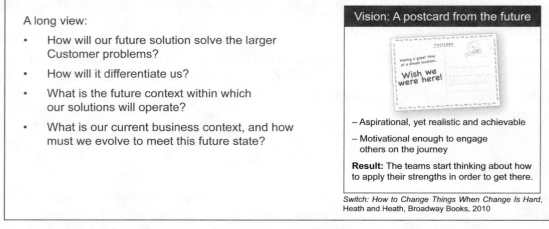

*Figure 1. The portfolio vision is an enterprise-level "postcard from the future"*

A portfolio vision exhibits the following characteristics:

- **Aspirational, yet realistic and achievable** – The vision has to be compelling and somewhat futuristic, yet realistic enough to be achievable over some meaningful time frame

- **Motivational enough to engage others on the journey** – The vision must align with the Strategic Themes, as well as to the individual team's purpose

This longer-term vision—and the business context that drives it—is typically delivered to the teams during the periodic PI Planning event. It may be delivered by the Business Owners, or possibly by the C-level executive who can best communicate the vision as well as inspire others to help achieve it. Given this vision, the teams will start thinking about how they will apply their unique strengths. True engagement begins with a destination in mind, one that helps the teams fulfill their purpose.

### Solution Vision

Given that longer-term view, Product and Solution Management have the responsibility for converting the portfolio vision to a solution vision indicating the reason and direction behind the chosen solution. In order to do so, specific questions must be asked and answered:

- What will this new solution do?
- What problem will it solve?
- What Features and benefits will it provide?
- For whom will it provide them?
- What performance (Nonfunctional Requirements) will it deliver?

### Inputs to the Solution Vision

In SAFe, this responsibility lies primarily with Product and Solution Management (depending on whether this is a 3- or 4-level instance of SAFe). They work directly with the Business Owners and other stakeholders to synthesize all the inputs and integrate them into a holistic and cohesive vision. There is no shortage of inputs, as Figure 2 illustrates.

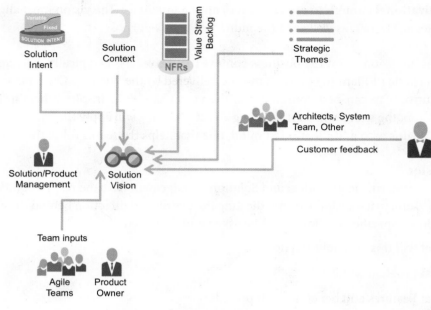

*Figure 2. Solution vision input sources*

These inputs include:

- Customers provide fast and intimate feedback

- Solution Intent contains some of the vision and is the destination for new elements

- Solution Context indicates the how the solution interacts with the Customer context

- Value Stream Capabilities Backlog contributes direction and guidance to the vision

- Continuous evolution of the Architectural Runway supports current and near-term Features

- Strategic Themes provide direction

- Finally, and not to forget the obvious, the foremost experts in the domain are typically the Agile Teams themselves. Primarily through the Product Owner, teams continuously communicate emerging requirements and opportunities back into the program vision.

### Capturing Vision in Solution Intent

Given the SAFe practice of cadence-based, face-to-face PI planning, vision documentation (various forms of which can be found in References 2, 3, and 4) is augmented, and sometimes replaced, by rolling-wave vision briefings. These provide routine, periodic presentations of the short- and longer-term vision to the teams. During PI planning, value stream level stakeholders, such as Solution Management, describe the current overall value stream vision, while Product Management provides the specific ART context and vision.

The relevant elements of the vision, along with details of the current and specific behaviors of the system, are captured in solution intent.

## Program Vision

In 4-level SAFe, in addition to the solution vision, each ART will likely have its own vision, detailing the direction of the specific capabilities or subsystems that it produces. This vision should be tightly coupled to the solution vision it supports.

## Roadmap View

Having a sense of direction is critical to planning and engagement. But unless there is some realistic plan for how teams intend to fulfill the vision, people won't actually know what they have to do. That purpose is filled by the Roadmap. Figure 3 provides an example.

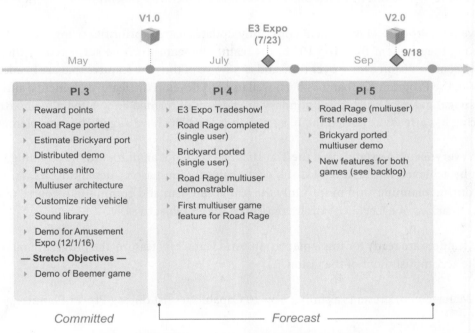

*Figure 3. The roadmap is part of the vision*

**PI Planning Vision—the Top 10 Features**

The roadmap is indeed helpful. But for action and execution, the immediate steps must be clear. To that purpose, Product and Solution Management have the responsibility to lay out the next steps. In the SAFe context, this translates to a series of steady steps forward, one PI at a time, and one feature at a time, as Figure 4 illustrates.

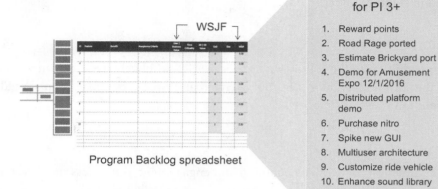

*Figure 4. Vision is achieved one PI at a time, via the "Top 10 features for the next PI"*

To achieve this, Product Management constantly updates feature priorities using WSJF. Then, during PI planning, they present the "Top 10" to the team. The team won't be surprised by the new list, as they have seen the vision evolve over time and are aware of the new features that are headed their way. In addition, the Program Kanban has been well used to develop the features, benefits, and acceptance criteria, so features that reach this boundary are fairly well formed and vetted already. Architecture/ Engineering has already reviewed them, and various Enablers have already been implemented.

However, everyone understands that the Top 10 is an input, not an output to the planning process, and what can be achieved in the next PI is subject to capacity limitations, dependencies, knowledge that emerges during planning, and more. Only the teams can plan and commit to a course of action, one that is summarized at every Program Increment in the PI Objectives.

But these features are ready for implementation. And feature by feature, the program marches forward toward the accomplishment of the vision.

Solution Management presents a similar Top 10 Capabilities list during Pre-PI Planning.

## LEARN MORE

[1] Heath, Chip and Dan Heath. *Switch: How to Change Things When Change Is Hard*. Broadway Books, 2010.

[2] Leffingwell, Dean. *Agile Software Requirements: Lean Requirements Practices for Teams, Programs, and the Enterprise*. Addison-Wesley, 2011.

[3] Leffingwell, Dean. *Scaling Software Agility: Best Practices for Large Enterprises*. Addison-Wesley, 2007.

[4] Leffingwell, Dean and Don Widrig. *Managing Software Requirements*. Addison-Wesley, 2001.

# Roadmap

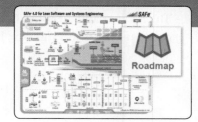

*Prediction is very difficult, especially if it is about the future.*
 —Neils Bohr

## Abstract

The *Roadmap* communicates Value Stream and Agile Release Train (ART) deliverables over a near-term timeline. Typically representing about six months of Program Increment (PI) Milestones, a roadmap includes committed confidence and visibility into the deliverables of the next PI, and a forecast with medium confidence for the next PI or two. The roadmap is developed and updated by Solution and Product Management as the Vision and delivery strategy evolve.

Of course, predicting the future is a hazardous business, and a Lean-Agile Enterprise must be able to respond to changing fact patterns and business conditions, so flexibility is warranted, even in the near term. The real world, however, occasionally demands even more, so it may be necessary for enterprises to predict even longer term, as some initiatives take years to develop, and some degree of commitment must be made to Customers, Suppliers, and partners. To this end, SAFe provides some guidance for forecasting over the longer term, based on the physics of Agile development and the predictability of program execution.

The desired horizon must be balanced carefully: too short, and the enterprise runs the risk of not obtaining the right level of alignment or ability to communicate future Capabilities and Features; too long, and the enterprise is attempting to predict the future. Even worse, the time for any new request to travel through a long, committed queue will cause unresponsiveness to changing Customer needs.

## Details

*Responding to change over following a plan* is one of the four values of the Agile Manifesto. In order to live up to that value, it should be obvious that it's actually quite important to have a plan, as otherwise everything is a change, and the backlog is the "tail of the dog that is constantly wagged" by changes that should have been readily anticipated. In turn, this causes thrashing, excess rework, and excess WIP. It is demotivating to all. Planning is good.

The *Roadmap* provides just such a plan. In the context of a roadmap, the teams know what their current commitments are and what the plan of intent is. The ability to routinely execute on those planned tasks provides a sense of personal satisfaction, as well as the extra mental and physical capacity necessary to respond to the real changes, those that could not have been anticipated.

The SAFe roadmap consists of a series of planned Program Increments (PIs) with various Milestones called out, as is indicated by Figure 1.

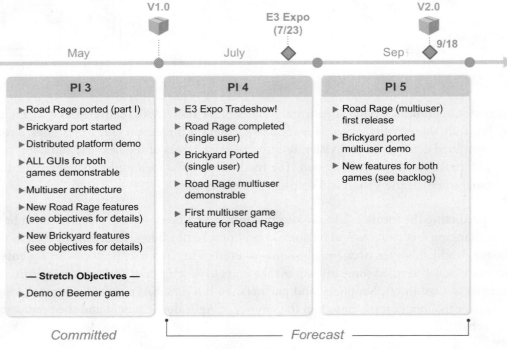

*Figure 1. An example PI Roadmap for a gaming company*

Each element on the roadmap is a milestone, either a learning milestone that has been defined by the teams or a date milestone that may be driven by external events.

## Building the PI Roadmap

The Figure 1 roadmap covers three PIs, or approximately 30 weeks. In many Enterprises, this is about the sweet spot—there's enough detail to be able to run the business, and yet a short enough time frame to keep long-term commitments from interfering with the ability to flex to changing business priorities. This roadmap consists of a "committed PI" and two "forecasted PIs," as described in the following sections.

### The Committed PI

During PI Planning, teams commit to meeting the program PI Objectives for the upcoming PI. Therefore the near-term plan is a high-confidence plan; the enterprise should be able to confidently plan for the impact of the upcoming new functionality. For Agile Release Trains (ARTs) that are new to SAFe and have yet to reach high confidence levels with their PI plans, the System Demo and Inspect and Adapt workshop will help increase confidence in each upcoming PI. In any case, reaching a predictable delivery of the upcoming PI is an important capability for every ART.

### Forecast PIs

Forecasting the next two PIs is a little more interesting. Value Streams and ARTs typically plan only one PI at a time. For most, it's simply imprudent to plan in detail much further (except perhaps for some Architectural Runway), because the business or technical context changes so quickly.

However, the Value Stream and Program Backlogs contain Capabilities and Features (which constitute future milestones) that have been working their way through the Kanban systems. They've been reasoned, socialized with the teams, have acceptance criteria in process, and have preliminary estimates for size in Story points. Given knowledge of the ART velocities, the PI Predictability Measure, relative priorities, and the history of how much work is devoted to maintenance and other business-as-usual activities, ARTs can generally lay the future features into the roadmap without too much difficulty. The result is that most trains have roadmaps with a reasonable degree of confidence over about a three-PI period.

## Long-Term Forecasting

The above discussion highlights how enterprises can have a reasonable, near-term plan of intent for all the ARTs in the portfolio. However, for many enterprises, especially those building large, complex systems, complete with Suppliers, long hardware lead times, major subsystems, critical delivery dates, external Customer commitments, etc., that amount of roadmap will be inadequate. Simply, building a satellite, a crop combine, or a new car takes a lot longer than the PI roadmap, and the enterprise must plan realistically for the longer-term future.

In addition, even when external events do not necessarily drive the requirement for long-term forecasting, enterprises need to be able to plan investment in future periods. They need to understand the potential recourse and development bottlenecks in support of the longer-term business demands, and the waxing and waning of investment in particular value streams.

So the conclusion is inevitable: It is most likely necessary to extend the forecast well beyond the PI planning horizon, even though the future work is largely unplanned.

## Estimating Longer-Term Initiatives

Fortunately, Agile work physics give us a means to forecast longer-term work. Of course, in order to forecast the work, estimation is required. In order to estimate, teams can use Agile story point physics, based on normalized estimating, and estimate larger initiatives at the Epic level, as Figure 2 illustrates.

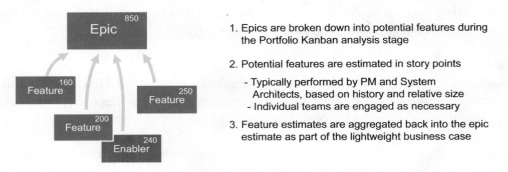

*Figure 2. Epics are estimated in story points rolled up from feature estimates*

Given these estimates, a knowledge of ART velocities, and some sense of the capacity allocation that can be provided to the new initiative, the business can then play out a "what-if" analysis, as Figure 3 illustrates.

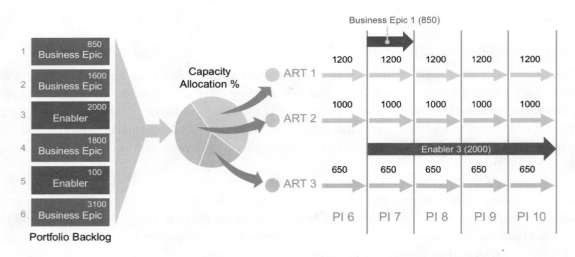

*Figure 3. Epic estimates, capacity allocations, and
ART velocities are used for longer-term forecasting*

Therefore, the enterprise has a way to build a roadmap that goes as far into the future as they need. However, every enterprise must be very careful about such forecasts, and while many see long-term predictability as the goal, Lean-Agile Leaders know that *every long-term commitment decreases the agility of the enterprise.*

Even in a case in which requirements can be fairly well established in advance, the unpredictability and variability of innovation, the tendency to estimate only the known activities, the difficulty in predicting future capacity, unforeseen events, and other factors all conspire to create a bias for underestimating reality. The net effect is that while fixed, long-term plans and commitments may feel good, and may even be required in some circumstances, they absolutely limit the ability of the enterprise to pivot to a new, and potentially more economically beneficial, outcome. You can't have it both ways.

As a result, the Lean-Agile enterprise strives to establish the right amount of visibility, alignment, and commitment, while enabling the right amount of flexibility. The correct balance can be obtained via a willingness to convert long-term *commitment* to *forecasts* and to continually reevaluate priorities and business value, as needs dictate, at each PI boundary.

## Avoid the Queue from Hell

Lean-Agile Leaders understand queuing theory and are well aware of the impact that long queues have on delivery time. Simply, the longer the committed queue, the longer the wait for any new initiative. Period. For example, in Figure 1 above, the second PI on the roadmap does not appear to be fully loaded. The math then tells us that the wait time for a new, unplanned feature is from 10 to 20 weeks; it can't be in the current PI, but it can be in the next.

The roadmap in Figure 4 below tells a different story.

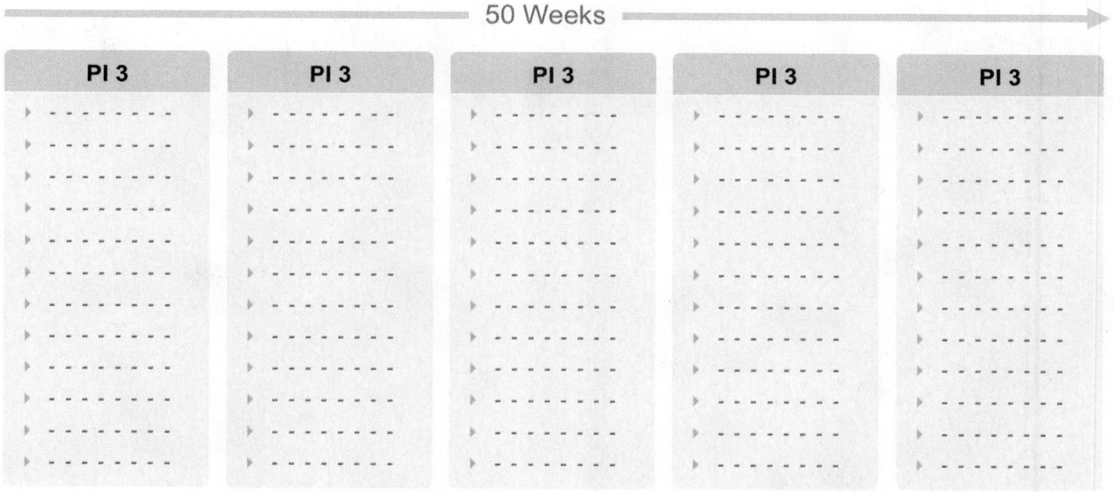

*Figure 4. A fully committed roadmap is the queue from hell*

If, for example, all the items on this roadmap are fully committed and the teams are running at nearly full capacity, then the wait time for a new capability is in excess of 60 weeks!

No matter how Agile the enterprise thinks it is, it is deluding itself. Little's Law will trump management's dreams, every time.

**LEARN MORE**

[1] Leffingwell, Dean. *Agile Software Requirements: Lean Requirements Practices for Teams, Programs, and the Enterprise*. Addison-Wesley, 2011.

# Metrics

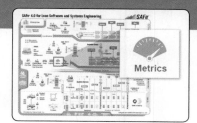

*The most important things cannot be measured. The issues that are most important, long term, cannot be measured in advance.*
　—W. Edwards Deming

*Working software is the primary measure of progress.*
　—Agile Manifesto

## Abstract

People adjust their behavior based on the metrics used to measure their systems and evaluate their performance, so they will naturally flex their efforts to improve the measures the Enterprise puts in place. But it's true that most measures are simply proxies for some real, and often intangible, results, so they need to be handled with care.

With its work physics, timeboxes, and fast feedback, Agile is inherently more measurable than prior documentation-oriented, indirect, waterfall-based measures of progress. Of course, the best measure by far comes directly from *working software and solutions*. It's best for teams, Agile Release Trains, managers, Program Management, and portfolio managers to pivot most of their measuring attention to this critical fact. All other metrics—even the extensive set of Agile metrics outlined below—are subordinate to that objective and the overriding goal of keeping the focus on rapid delivery of quality, working Solutions.

But measures are important in the Enterprise context. To that end, SAFe provides guidance for *Metrics* on each level of the Framework.

### Portfolio Metrics

**Lean Portfolio Metrics**
The *Lean Portfolio Metrics* set provided here is an example of a comprehensive but Lean set of metrics that can be used to assess internal and external progress for an entire Portfolio.

In the spirit of "the simplest set of measures that can possibly work," Figure 1 provides the leanest set that a few Lean-Agile Enterprises are using effectively to evaluate the overall performance of their transformations.

| Benefit | Expected Result | Metric Used |
|---|---|---|
| Employee engagement | Improved employee satisfaction; lower turnover | Employee survey; HR statistics |
| Customer satisfaction | Improved Net Promoter Score | Net Promoter Score survey |
| Productivity | Reduced average feature cycle time | Feature cycle time |
| Agility | Continuous improvement in team and program measures | Team, Program, and Portfolio self-assessments; Release Predictability Measure |
| Time to market | More frequent releases | Number of releases per year |
| Quality | Reduced defect counts and support call volume | Defect data and support call volume |
| Partner health | Improving ecosystem relationships | Partner and vendor surveys |

*Figure 1. Lean Portfolio Metrics*

## Portfolio Kanban Board

The primary motivation of the *Portfolio Kanban Board* is to ensure that Epics and Enablers are reasoned and analyzed prior to reaching a Program Increment boundary, are prioritized appropriately, and have established acceptance criteria to guide a high-fidelity implementation. Furthermore, the epics and enablers can be tracked to understand which ones are being worked on and which have been completed, as illustrated in Figure 2.

The Review and Analysis states are WIP limited (the numbers shown in the parentheses in Figure 2) and reflect the limit set by the PPM Team. Refer to the "Portfolio Kanban" article for information about each of the Kanban states.

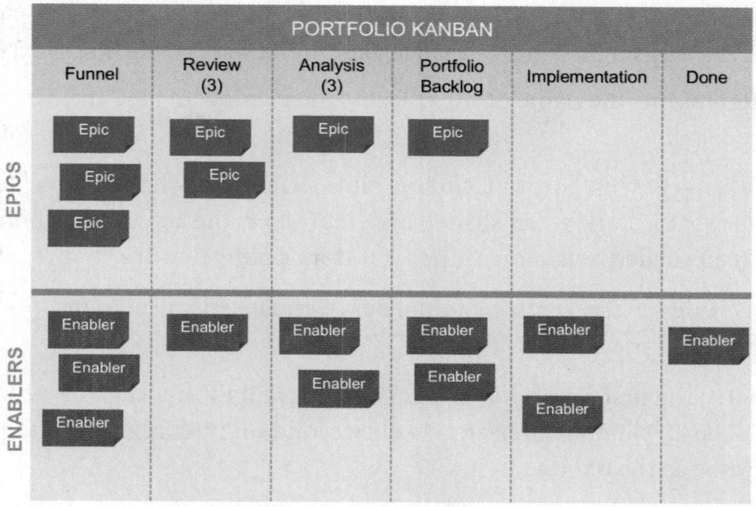

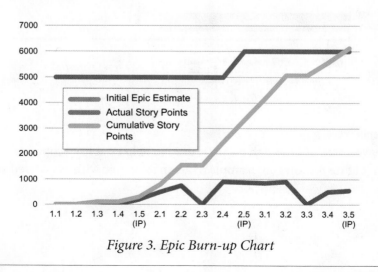

Figure 2. Portfolio Kanban Board

**Epic Burn-up Chart**

The *Epic Burn-up Chart* tracks progress toward an epic's completion. There are three measures:

1. **Initial epic estimate line** (blue) – Estimated Story points from the lightweight business case

2. **Work completed line** (red) – Actual story points rolled up from the epic's child Features and stories

3. **Cumulative work completed line** (green) – Cumulative story points completed and rolled up from the epic's child features and stories

These are illustrated in Figure 3.

Figure 3. Epic Burn-up Chart

## Epic Progress Measure

The *Epic Progress Measure* provides an at-a-glance view of the status of all epics in a Program portfolio.

1. **Epic X** – Represents the name of the epic; business epics are blue (below) and enabler epics are red

2. **Bar length** – Represents the total *current* estimated story points for an epic's child features/stories; the dark green shaded area represents the actual story points completed; the light green shaded area depicts the total story points that are "in progress"

3. **Vertical red line** – Represents the initial epic estimate, in story points, from the lightweight business case

4. **0000 / 0000** – The first number represents the current estimated story points, rolled up from the epic's child features/stories; the second number represents the initial epic estimate (same as the red line)

These measures are depicted in Figure 4.

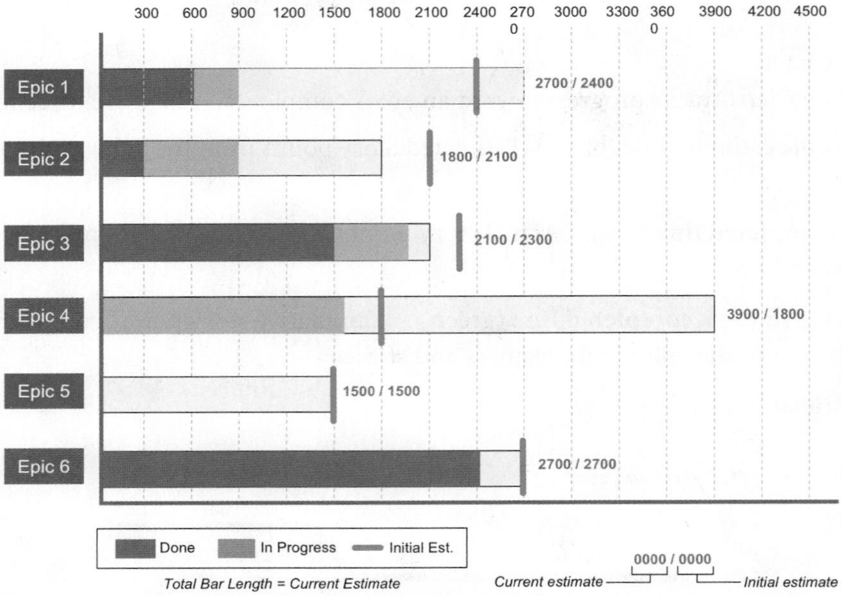

*Figure 4. Epic Progress Measure*

## Epic Success Criteria

Each epic should have *Success Criteria* that can be used to help establish scope and drive more detailed feature elaboration. Figure 5 shows an example of an enabler epic with associated success criteria.

1. API is secured and authentication methods are compatible with our partners' protocols

2. API documentation is released to the partners in the form of JavaDocs

3. All the domain logic in all systems, except our admin applications, should be exposed as Java APIs

*Figure 5. An example of success criteria for an enabler epic*

### Enterprise Balanced Scorecard

The *Enterprise Balance Scorecard* provides four perspectives to measure performance for each portfolio—although the popularity of this approach has been declining over time in favor of Lean Portfolio Metrics (see Figure 1). Nonetheless, these measures are:

1. Efficiency

2. Value Delivery

3. Quality

4. Agility

These measures are then mapped into an executive dashboard, as illustrated in Figures 6 and 7.

| **Efficiency** | **Value Delivery** |
|---|---|
| Sample Measures:<br>• Contribution margin<br>• Organizational stability<br>• Team velocity vs. capacity | Sample Measures:<br>• Number of releases<br>• Value feature points delivered<br>• Release date percentage<br>• Architectural refactors |
| **Quality** | **Agility** |
| Sample Measures:<br>• Defects<br>• Support calls<br>• Support satisfaction<br>• Product satisfaction<br>• Escalation rate percentage | Sample Measures:<br>• Product Ownership<br>• Release planning and tracking<br>• IP planning and tracking<br>• Teamwork<br>• Testing and dev practices |

*Figure 6. A Balanced Scorecard approach,
dividing measures into four areas of interest*

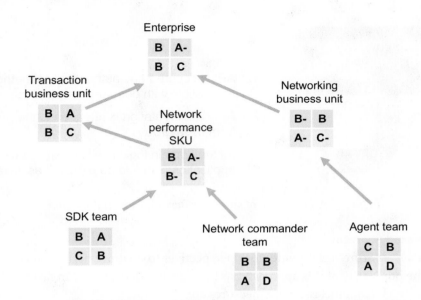

*Figure 7. Converting the above metrics to an alphabetical rating and aggregating
them can provide a look at the bigger picture for the enterprise*

For more on this approach, see [2], Chapter 22.

**Program Portfolio Management Self-Assessment**
The Program Portfolio Management (PPM) team continuously assesses and improves their processes. Often this is done using a structured, periodic *Self-Assessment*. When the PPM team completes the self-assessment form, it will automatically produce a radar chart like that shown in Figure 8, which highlights relative strengths and weaknesses.

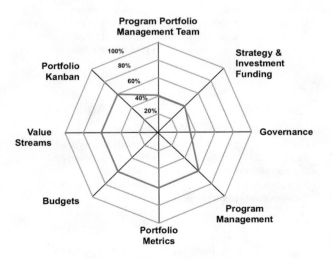

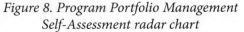

*Figure 8. Program Portfolio Management
Self-Assessment radar chart*

## Value Stream Metrics

### Value Stream Kanban Board

The primary motivation of the *Value Stream Kanban Board* is to ensure that Capabilities and Enablers are reasoned and analyzed prior to reaching a PI boundary and are prioritized appropriately, and that acceptance criteria have been established to guide a high-fidelity implementation. Furthermore, the features can be tracked to understand which ones are being worked on and which have been completed, as illustrated in Figure 9.

The Review and Analysis states are WIP limited, as shown by the numbers in the parentheses. Refer to the "Program and Value Stream Kanban" article for information about each of the Kanban states.

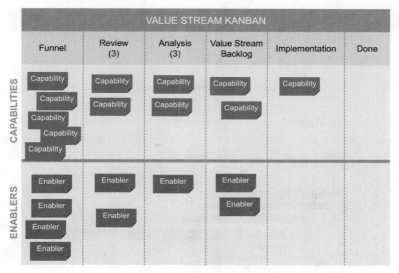

*Figure 9. Value Stream Kanban Board*

### Value Stream Predictability Measure

To assess the overall predictability of the Value Stream, individual predictability measures for an Agile Release Train (ART) can be aggregated to create an overall *Value Stream Predictability Measure*, as illustrated in Figure 10.

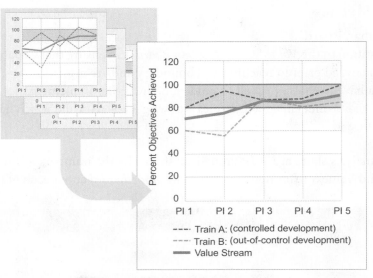

*Figure 10. Value Stream Predictability Measure*

## Value Stream Performance Metrics

To assess the overall performance of the value stream, individual performance measures for an ART can be aggregated to create an overall set of *Value Stream Performance Metrics*, as illustrated in Figure 11.

| Functionality | PI 1 | PI 2 | PI 3 |
|---|---|---|---|
| Program velocity | | | |
| Predictability measure | | | |
| # Features planned | | | |
| # Features accepted | | | |
| # Enabler features planned | | | |
| # Enabler features accepted | | | |
| # Stories planned | | | |
| # Stories accepted | | | |
| Quality | | | |
| Unit test coverage % | | | |
| Defects | | | |
| Total tests | | | |
| % automated | | | |
| # NFR tests | | | |

*Figure 11. Value Stream Performance Metrics*

## Program Metrics

### Feature Progress Report

The *Feature Progress Report* tracks the status of features and enablers during PI execution. It indicates which features are on track or behind at any point in time. The chart has two bars:

1. **Plan** – Represents the total number of stories planned for a feature.

2. **Actual** – Represents the number of stories completed for a feature. The bar is shaded red or green, depending on whether the feature is on track or not.

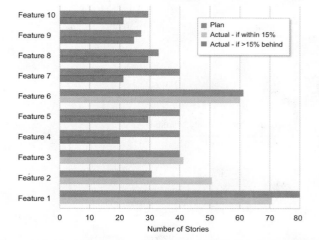

Facilitates decisions about what changes might be necessary to successfully deliver the PI

*Figure 12. Feature Progress Report, highlighting the status of each feature compared to the PI plan*

### Program Kanban Board

The primary motivation of the *Program Kanban Board* is to ensure that features are reasoned and analyzed prior to reaching a PI boundary and are prioritized appropriately, and that acceptance criteria have been established to guide a high-fidelity implementation. Furthermore, the features can be tracked to understand which ones are being worked on and which have been completed, as illustrated in Figure 13. The Review and Analysis states are WIP limited, as shown by the numbers in the parentheses. Refer to the "Program and Value Stream Kanban" article for information about each of the Kanban states.

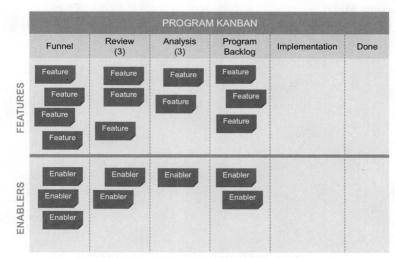

*Figure 13. Program Kanban Board*

## Program Predictability Measure

To assess the overall predictability of the release train, the "Team PI Performance Report" is aggregated, for all teams on the train, to calculate the *Program Predictability Measure*, as illustrated in Figure 14. The Team PI Performance report compares actual business value achieved to planned business value (see Figure 22).

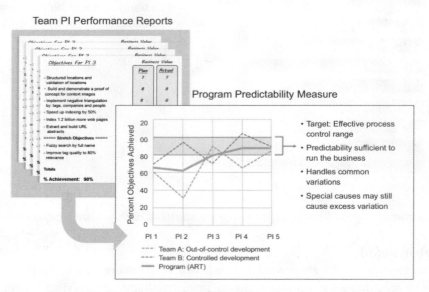

*Figure 14. Program Predictability Measure, showing two of the teams on the train and program (cumulative)*

For more on this approach, see [1], Chapter 15.

## Program Performance Metrics

The end of each PI is a natural and significant measuring point. Figure 15 is an example set of *Performance Metrics* for a program.

| FUNCTIONALITY | P1 | P2 | P3 |
|---|---|---|---|
| Program velocity | | | |
| Predictability measure | | | |
| # Features planned | | | |
| # Features accepted | | | |
| # Enabler features planned | | | |
| # Enabler features accepted | | | |
| # Stories planned | | | |
| # Stories accepted | | | |
| QUALITY | | | |
| Unit test coverage % | | | |
| Defects | | | |
| Total tests | | | |
| % automated | | | |
| # NFR tests | | | |

*Figure 15. One train's chart of Performance Metrics*

### PI Burn-down Chart

The *PI Burn-down Chart* shows the progress being made toward the program increment timebox. Use it to track the work planned for a PI against the work that has been accepted.

1. The *horizontal axis* of the PI burn-down chart shows the iterations within the PI
2. The *vertical axis* shows the amount of work (story points) remaining at the start of each iteration

Figure 16 exemplifies a train's burn-down measure. Although the PI burn-down shows the progress being made toward the program increment timebox, it does not reveal which features may or may not be delivered during the PI. The Feature Progress Report provides that information (refer to Figure 12).

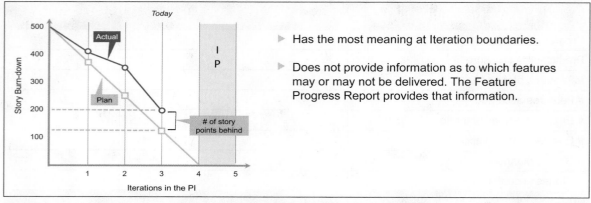

Figure 16. One train's PI Burn-down Chart

## Cumulative Flow Diagram

A *Cumulative Flow Diagram* (CFD) is made up of a series of lines or areas representing the amount of work in different stages of progression. For example, in software development, typical steps for development of a feature are:

- Funnel
- Analysis
- Backlog
- Execution
- Review
- Done

In the cumulative flow diagram in Figure 17, the number of features in each stage of development is plotted for each day in the chart.

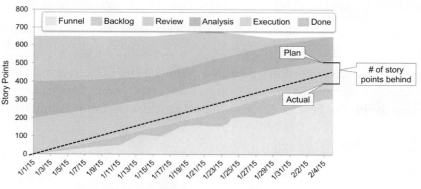

Figure 17. Sample PI Cumulative Flow Diagram

## Agile Release Train Self-Assessment

As program execution is a core value of SAFe, the Agile Release Train (ART) continuously works to improve its performance. A *Self-Assessment* can be used for this purpose at PI boundaries or any time the team wants to pause and assess their organization and practices.

Trending this data over time is a key performance indicator for the program. Figure 18 gives an example of the results of a self-assessment radar chart.

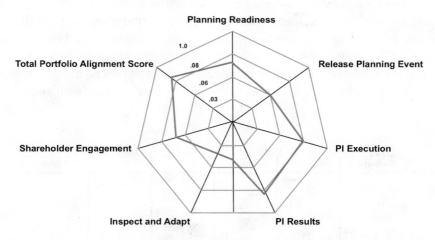

*Figure 18. ART Self-Assessment radar chart*

## Team Metrics

### Iteration Metrics

The end of each iteration is the time for each Agile Team to collect whatever *Iteration Metrics* they have agreed upon. This occurs in the quantitative part of the team retrospective. One such team's metrics set is illustrated in Figure 19.

| FUNCTIONALITY | ITERATION 1 | ITERATION P2 | ITERATION P3 |
|---|---|---|---|
| Velocity planned | | | |
| Velocity actual | | | |
| # Stories planned | | | |
| # Stories accepted | | | |
| % Stories accepted | | | |
| QUALITY | | | |
| Unit test coverage % | | | |
| # Defects | | | |
| # New test cases | | | |
| # New test cases automated | | | |
| Total tests | | | |
| Total % tests automated | | | |
| # Refactors | | | |

*Figure 19. One team's chart of Iteration Metrics*

## Team Kanban Board

A team's Kanban process evolution is iterative. After defining the initial process steps (e.g., *define – analyze – review – build – integrate – test*, etc.) and WIP limits, then executing for a while, the team's bottlenecks should surface. If not, the team refines the states or further reduces the WIP until it becomes obvious which state is "starving" or is too full, helping the team adjust toward more optimum flow.

As the assumptions are validated, WIP limits are adjusted and steps may be merged, split, or redefined. Figure 20 shows a Team Kanban Board that has surfaced bottlenecks, along with its current WIP limits (top row).

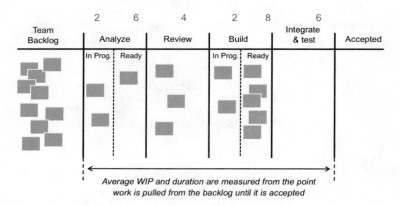

*Figure 20. One team's initial Kanban Board*

## Team PI Performance Report

During the PI System Demo, the Business Owners, Customers, Agile Teams, and other key stakeholders collaboratively rate the actual business value achieved for each team's PI objectives, as shown in Figure 21.

Reliable trains should generally operate in the 80% – 100% range; this allows the business and its outside stakeholders to plan effectively. Below are some important notes about how the report works:

1. The Planned total (BV) does not include stretch objectives to help the reliability of the train

2. The Actual total (Actual BV) includes stretch objectives

3. The *Achievement %* is calculated by dividing the Actual BV total / Planned BV total

4. A team can achieve greater than 100% (as a result of stretch objectives achieved)

5. The effort required for stretch objectives is included in the Iteration plan's load (i.e., it is not extra work the team does on weekends)

6. Individual team totals are rolled up into the Program Predictability Measure (see Figure 14)

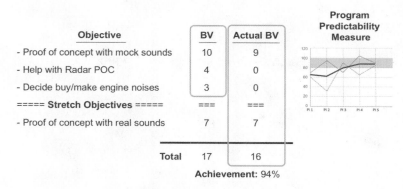

| Objective | BV | Actual BV |
|---|---|---|
| - Proof of concept with mock sounds | 10 | 9 |
| - Help with Radar POC | 4 | 0 |
| - Decide buy/make engine noises | 3 | 0 |
| ===== Stretch Objectives ===== | === | === |
| - Proof of concept with real sounds | 7 | 7 |
| Total | 17 | 16 |

Achievement: 94%

*Figure 21. Team PI Performance Report*

## SAFe Team Self-Assessment

Agile Teams continuously assess and improve their processes. Often this is via a structured, periodic *Self-Assessment*. This gives the team time to reflect on and discuss the key practices that help yield results. One such assessment is a simple SAFe Team practices assessment. When the team completes the assessment, it will automatically produce a radar chart such as that shown in Figure 22, which highlights relative strengths and weaknesses.

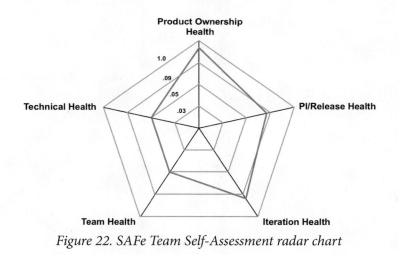

*Figure 22. SAFe Team Self-Assessment radar chart*

---

### LEARN MORE

[1] Leffingwell, Dean. *Agile Software Requirements: Lean Requirements Practices for Teams, Programs, and the Enterprise*. Addison-Wesley, 2011.

[2] Leffingwell, Dean. *Scaling Software Agility: Best Practices for Large Enterprises*. Addison-Wesley, 2007.

# Milestones

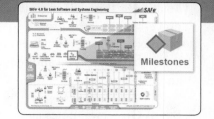

*There was in fact no correlation between exiting phase gates on time and project success ... the data suggested the inverse might be true.*

　—Dantar Oosterwal, *The Lean Machine*

*Base milestones on objective evaluation of working systems.*

　—SAFe Lean-Agile Principle #5

## Abstract

*Milestones* mark specific progress points on the development timeline, and they can be invaluable in measuring and monitoring the progress and risk of a program. Traditionally, many project milestones are based on phase-gate activities. In SAFe, however, progress is indicated differently in that it is supported by a fixed cadence of Iterations and Program Increments, allowing teams to acquire a sense of rhythm and help manage outcome variability. Most SAFe milestones, therefore, differ from milestones in traditional project and program management: *They are based on working systems and thereby support the ability to objectively evaluate the technical or business hypothesis.*

Not everything, however, occurs on cadence. The complexities of modern software and systems engineering involve multiple factors that rely on external events, third parties, fixed-date constraints, etc., that may offer irregular timeline patterns, distinct from the development cadence. In addition, *learning milestones* help validate business opportunities and business hypotheses, and they help measure emerging business performance of the Capabilities delivered to the market.

When handled properly, milestones can bring a required focus to the work, provide for some governance, and enable better business outcomes.

## Details

The development of today's large systems requires substantial investment—an investment that can reach millions, tens of millions, and even hundreds of millions of dollars. Together, systems builders and Customers have a fiduciary responsibility to ensure that the investment in new Solutions will deliver the necessary economic benefit. Otherwise, there is no reason to make the investment.

Clearly, stakeholders must collaborate in such a way as to help ensure the prospective economic benefit *throughout* the development process and not just rely on wishful thinking that all will be well at the end.

## The Problem with Phase-Gate Milestones

To address this challenge, the industry has historically followed phase-gated (waterfall) development processes, whereby progress is measured—and control is exercised—via a series of specific progress *Milestones*. These milestones are not arbitrary, but they are generally document based, and they follow the apparently logical and sequential process of discovery, requirements, design, implementation, test, and delivery.

But as Oosterwal notes above, they don't really work. The cause of this problem is the failure to recognize some *critical errors* with the basic assumption that phase gates reveal real progress and thereby mitigate risk. For example:

- Using documents as a proxy for solution progress; not only do these create a false sense of security for solution progress, they also drive various measures and metrics, such as work breakdown structures, earned value measures, and others, that may actually impede flow and real value delivery

- Centralizing requirements and design decisions in siloed functions that may not be integrally involved in building the solution

- Forcing too-early design decisions and "false-positive feasibility" [1]

- Assuming that a "point" solution exists, early in the cone of uncertainty, and that it can be built right the first time

The net effect of all the above is that phase-gate milestones have not always helped mitigate risks; instead, a point solution is picked far too early in the cone of uncertainty. Problems follow inevitably, as Figure 1 illustrates.

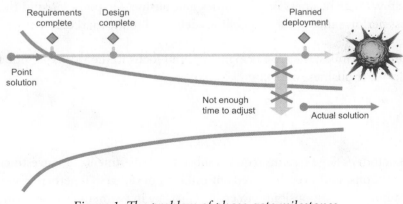

*Figure 1. The problem of phase-gate milestones*

With this backdrop, it becomes clear that a different approach is needed, as is described below.

## PI Milestones: Objective Evidence of Working Systems

SAFe provides a number of means to address the problems. In particular, Principle #4 – *Build incrementally with fast, integrated learning cycles*, especially when used in conjunction with Set-Based Design, provides elements of the solution.

With this approach, the system is built in increments, each of which is an integration and knowledge point that demonstrates evidence of the viability of the current in-process solution. Further, this is done routinely, on the Program Increment (PI) *cadence*, which provides the discipline needed to ensure periodic availability and evaluation, as well as predetermined time boundaries that can be used to collapse the field of less desirable options. Each PI thereby creates an objective measure of progress, as Figure 2 illustrates.

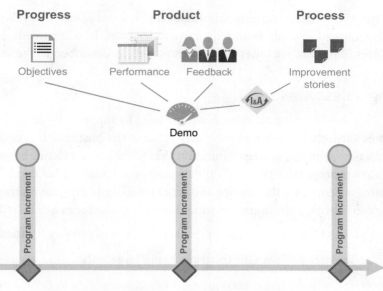

*Figure 2. PI milestones provide objective evidence*

This is true at both the Program (system integration and validation) and Value Stream (solution integration and validation) levels. Of course, what is actually measured at these critical integration points is subject to the nature and type of the system being built. But the system can be measured, assessed, and evaluated frequently by the relevant stakeholders throughout development. Most important, changes can be made while there is still time to make them, as Figure 3 illustrates.

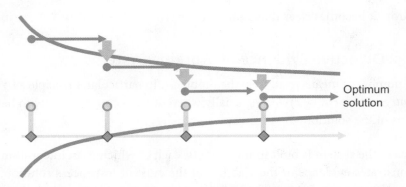

*Figure 3. PI milestones guide system developers to the optimum solution*

This provides the financial, technical, and fitness-for-purpose governance needed to ensure that the continuing investment will produce a commensurate return.

In SAFe, these are the most critical learning milestones that control solution development—so critical that they are simply assumed as credible and objective milestones. In other words, every PI is a learning milestone of a sort. But there are other milestones as well, as described in the sections that follow.

## Other Learning Milestones

In addition to the PI, other learning milestones can be used to support the central goal of building a solution that satisfies Customer needs and generates value to the business. It is critical that the value proposition behind a new solution, or a large initiative that advances an existing solution, is treated as a *hypothesis* that requires conceptualization and validation against actual market conditions. Translating a hypothesis into business demand is the science and art of Lean-Agile product management. It involves a great deal of intermediate organizational learning. Learning milestones can help. For example:

- Do the new product Capabilities have a market that is ready to pay for them?
- Do they solve the user problem for the users being targeted?
- Are the necessary non-financial accounting measures available to demonstrate real progress? [2]
- What revenue can the organization expect?
- Is there a viable business model to support the new product or capability?

These, and many other business concerns, formulate the basic hypothesis for any large initiative. Learning milestones provide the necessary means to understand the feasibility of the solution and frame the right set of capabilities. Testing a concept of a new capability with a focus group, building and releasing a minimum viable product (MVP), or validating User Experience assumptions for the new functionality are examples of learning milestones.

Such milestones do not necessarily occur on PI boundaries and may require significant effort, not only on behalf of the product development organization but also on the part of other business functions in the Enterprise, such as sales, marketing, operations, finance, etc.

Every learning milestone assumes that there is a certain degree of uncertainty that needs to be translated into knowledge and, ultimately, into business benefits for the organization. This requires set-based thinking and the ability to pivot, if necessary, to a different concept of the solution.

Since the outcome of any learning milestone impacts the understanding of intent, milestones are planned incrementally, as Figure 4 suggests.

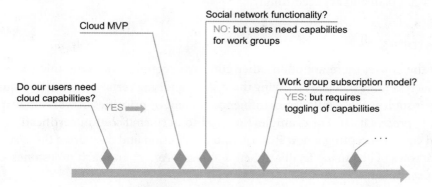

*Figure 4. Learning milestones help evaluate progress toward the goal*

Other elements, including the solution Vision, Solution Intent, and the Economic Framework, also evolve with the learning.

But learning doesn't stop even when new product capabilities hit the market and start to generate business benefits. Every new capability, and every significant nonfunctional aspect of the system, deserves facts to replace assumptions about anticipated value. In a Lean enterprise environment, learning is an integral part of development, even for mature products. Meaningful learning milestones can help.

## Fixed-Date Milestones

Every Lean-Agile enterprise wants to operate with minimum constraints. In part, that's where agility comes from. The real world, however, has different concerns, and fixed-date milestones are common in both traditional and Lean-Agile development. For example, fixed dates may arise from:

- Events such as trade shows, Customer demos, user group meetings, preplanned product announcements, etc.
- Release dates that are controlled by other internal or external business concerns
- Contractually binding dates for delivery of value, intermediate milestones, payment, demonstrations, etc.

- Scheduling larger-scale integration issues including hardware, software, Supplier integration, and anything else where a fixed date provides an appropriate forcing function to bring together assets and validate

There are many more examples. In Lean terms, fixed dates have a nonlinear cost of delay. That is, required system Features become a much higher priority as the date comes closer, as failure to meet the milestones has negative economic consequences. This is directly incorporated into Program and Value Stream Backlog prioritization via WSJF; the "time criticality" parameter gets higher as the fixed date gets closer, thereby increasing WSJF priorities for elements dependent on that date. In any case, any fixed-date milestones should be reflected on the relevant program or value stream Roadmap, so all stakeholders can plan and act accordingly.

## Other Milestones

In addition to the above, there are often other concerns required for economic success of product development, such as filing patents, certifying the system, auditing certain regulatory requirements, and so on. In many instances these milestones influence content or priorities of work; they may even alter the development *process* itself. For example, the need to perform solution certification may increase the transaction cost of accepting a new Release into production and may drive the systems builder to seek alternative ways of acquiring feedback before release. Again, any such milestones should appear on the relevant roadmap.

## Planning and Executing Milestones

An understanding of what types of milestones are required to support value creation may originate from different sources. It may be communicated to portfolios from the enterprise level, or identified during the analysis step in the Portfolio or Value Stream and Program Kanban systems, or even during the planning and roadmapping process for value streams and Agile Release Trains. Eventually, teams will have to create a specific plan of action during the PI planning process, build specific Stories in support of a milestone, reflect the milestone in their roadmaps and PI Objectives, understand and address dependencies with other teams and trains, and negotiate scope and time trade-offs with program stakeholders.

Thereafter, execution of milestones happens incrementally. Progress is demonstrated every PI.

## Measuring Success

Successful execution of milestones requires criteria for what "success" means, so there can be value in associating specific measures and Metrics with milestones. For example, a milestone of "capturing X% market share" may require understanding of revenue or usage indicators. A learning milestone of "a search engine being able to reliably identify persons' names on a web page" could be supported by a limited percentage of false positives across the pages in the "gold collection" of web data. In any case, thoughtful measures make for more meaningful milestones.

### LEARN MORE

[1] Oosterwal, Dantar P. *The Lean Machine: How Harley-Davidson Drove Top-Line Growth and Profitability with Revolutionary Lean Product Development.* Amacom, 2010.

[2] Ries, Eric. *The Lean Startup: How Today's Entrepreneurs Use Continuous Innovation to Create Radically Successful Businesses.* Crown Business, 2011.

# Releases

*Deliver software frequently, from a couple of weeks to a couple of months, with a preference to the shorter time scale.*

   —Agile Manifesto

*There are really three parts to the creative process. First there is inspiration, then there is the execution, and finally there is the release.*

   —Eddie Van Halen

## Abstract

The goal of Lean development is frequent delivery of valuable, working, and fully tested increments of the Solution. This is accomplished via a stream of *Releases* of value, each of which has been validated and approved for final efficacy of use, accompanied by the documentation necessary to ensure successful application. Accomplishing this requires leaner software and engineering practices, as well as a more continuous process of verification and validation. In addition, there are typically some final, pre-shipment validation, documentation, and support activities necessary for successful release into production, or directly into the Customer's world.

## Details

### Releasing Value More Frequently

Every *Release* delivers more value to the Customer. Also, some ideas, assumptions, and aspects of the Solution cannot be fully validated until and unless they are released into the Customer's environment. In those cases, truly meaningful feedback about efficacy, deployability, and usability can only be partially assessed in the development environment. For that reason, *releasing more frequently* is one of the goals of the Lean-Agile Enterprise.

For many, releasing is a homogeneous thing. A widget may be released to manufacturing or into the Customer's environment in a single event. However, complex solutions are, by definition, more complex, and in these cases different elements of the system may be released at different times.

Optimizing for overall value delivery means that each element might need to have its own delivery rhythm.

Take, for example, the Baja Ride. Software updates to the player portal can perhaps be delivered every two weeks, every day, or even on demand, and the Customer and users can thereby receive the benefit of fast, incremental delivery. Perhaps the vehicle control system can receive occasional over-the-air software updates, but it could easily require some necessary off-line, end user validation before deployment, so some batching and testing is required. Releasing that subsystem might be on a cadence or it might be ad hoc, based on context, problems, and opportunities, to improve reliability or some aspect of the ride experience. Finally, a newer motion base, with update firmware and hardware, might warrant being released and installed on the vehicle only annually. Figure 1 illustrates this example.

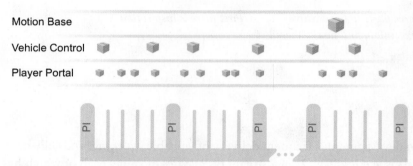

*Figure 1. Different elements of the solution may have different delivery rhythms*

## Develop on Cadence, Release Any Time

Given these opportunities and constraints, releasing does not have to be aligned with the development cadence. Develop on Cadence, Release Any Time (see the "Develop on Cadence, Release Any Time" article) supports the goals of synchronization, alignment, management of variability, and predictability of development velocity. Delivery can happen whenever the business needs it. That being said, however, many enterprises find it convenient to align delivery of some or all aspects of the solution to a Program Increment (PI) boundary. In these cases the development rhythm and delivery rhythm can be the same, and there can be many associated conveniences.

## Building the Release

Building large-scale systems that are ready for release and fit for use is a process most easily considered in stages, as Figure 2 illustrates.

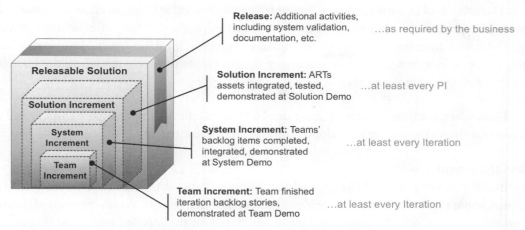

*Figure 2. Building a releasable solution*

### Team Increment

The first, and hopefully continuous, step in this process is each Agile Team on the Agile Release Train (ART) focusing on ensuring that they produce a working increment for the Stories and components they are responsible for. They do this by:

- Completing user stories from their Team Backlog, ensuring that each meets its story (local) Definition of Done

- Applying Continuous Integration practices with test automation whenever feasible to monitor and ensure progress

### System Increment

Every two weeks, teams build a *system increment*, an integrated stack of new functionality, which is the sum of all the team backlog items completed by all release train teams, during the current and all previous Iterations. Each system increment is the subject of the System Demo. In this way, one story at a time, new Features are added to the system incrementally, typically a few per program increment.

For those features that are completed within the increment, feature acceptance criteria must be met. Some features, however, can be still in progress, so the current increment may include some, but not all, of their functionality. To make sure that all the functionality is consistent, the train performs verification and validation of key scenarios and nonfunctional aspects, usually with the help of the System Team.

Each system increment is a result of the work of multiple teams and, as such, needs to be integrated, as indicated above. However, in some cases full integration of all program assets may represent a high transaction cost (assembly, configuration, testing, etc.), especially when the solution Capabilities involve hardware components. In such cases it is important to find the right balance of effort and frequency.

While the Definition of Done for a system increment can be relaxed at times, to allow for faster feedback without full integration, this should not be an excuse to abandon the practice of frequent integration and testing. The system increment is the *primary measure of progress* for ARTs (each a learning Milestone), and not having increments at a certain frequency simply means not knowing where the team is with respect to the system development.

At the PI boundary, each Agile Release Train does a final system demo during the Inspect and Adapt workshop that shows the features developed throughout the entire PI.

## Solution Increment

In a multi-ART Value Stream, ARTs typically build only a part of the solution, whether it's a set of subsystems, some solution capabilities, or a mix thereof. For that reason, *the real progress of the solution development effort* can only be objectively evaluated based on the *solution increment* that comprises all the capabilities, collaboratively delivered by ARTs, integrated, verified, and validated, with both the functional and Nonfunctional Requirements (NFRs) satisfied. This solution increment is the subject of the all-important Solution Demo, which brings all the increments together into a working system.

The full system integration process will likely require assistance by Program and Value Stream Level System Teams. Indeed, that is the major reason why they exist. SAFe suggests that this activity is less frequent than the others described in this article, with an emphasis on the PI boundary. On large systems, especially those with mixed hardware and software components, the transaction costs may be fairly high, thus the implication of a lower frequency.

Sometimes much of this work is performed during the Innovation and Planning (IP) Iteration, where the availability of personnel, Supplier subsystems and components, special skills and equipment, and other resources can be applied to that significant task. But that is not always the case. If the enterprise wants to acquire a better understanding of progress within the PI, it may choose to produce solution increments at a more frequent rate. In this case, the solution-level integration effort may be dispersed across multiple iterations within the PI, as opposed to all being encapsulated in the IP iteration. In that case, the system demo is a validation of the progress up to that point.

## Release

In this manner, solution development proceeds—one story, feature, capability, and nonfunctional requirement at a time, until the ultimate goal of the release. However, before all that new functionality can be actually released to Customers, some final activities, including *solution verification and validation*, *documentation*, and *supporting activities,* are typically necessary.

The release process may also involve the transition of the solution assets to another business unit, or even to a different organization that is responsible for actual delivery to the Customer. For example, the system, in the form of designs, can be released to manufacturing engineering, where the actual fabrication instructions are finalized.

In other cases, the solution can be released as is, but the delivery process requires considerable effort and is a major project of its own (in order to be useful, a satellite needs to be sent into its orbit). In either case, there are usually significant risks associated with the release process that may prevent the whole program from succeeding (examples: a new motion base is too costly to manufacture, or the satellite launch imposes too much vibration on the satellite).

The best way to prevent release issues is by:
  a) Designing the solution and the process with "release-ability" in mind
  b) Validating those assumptions as early and frequently as possible

In order to solve (a), the Economic Framework, the Value Stream Kanban, and the rest of the decision-making tools have to reflect the key release concerns. The system itself also needs to satisfy the nonfunctional requirements, which reflect, in part, release constraints. The PI Planning and *Pre- and Post-*PI Planning meetings are great occasions to involve people who can speak to the release aspects of the solution, and to assist the trains and teams in better understanding what building releasable increments entails.

To satisfy (b), a frequent validation/feedback model is required. In some cases, more frequent external releases are extremely helpful. In other instances, when releasing frequently is not possible, is too expensive, or is otherwise constrained, this type of validation needs to happen at the solution increment level at least every PI, though it may require special procedures and infrastructure to verify release-ability by emulating some or all of its aspects. The IP iteration can provide a helpful timebox for this.

## A Scaled Definition of Done

Taken together, the continuous buildup of system functionality, along with continuous verification and validation of the elements of the solution, as well as the final solution itself, can be reflected in a scaled Definition of Done. See the example illustrated in Table 1.

| Team Increment | System Increment | Solution Increment | Release |
|---|---|---|---|
| • Stories satisfy acceptance criteria | • Stories completed by all teams in the ART and integrated | • Capabilities completed by all trains and meet acceptance criteria | • All capabilities done and meet acceptance criteria |
| • Acceptance tests passed (automated where practical) | • Completed features meet acceptance criteria | • Deployed/installed in the staging environment | • End-to-end integration and solution V&V done |
| • Unit and component tests coded, passed, and included in the BVT | • NFRs met | • NFRs met | • Regression testing done |
| • Cumulative unit tests passed | • No must-fix defects | • System end-to-end integration, verification, and validation done | • NFRs met |
| • Assets are under version control | • Verification and validation of key scenarios | • No must-fix defects | • No must-fix defects |
| • Engineering standards followed | • Included in build definition and deployment process | • Included in build definition and deployment/transition process | • Release documentation complete |
| • NFRs met | • Increment demonstrated, feedback achieved | • Documentation updated | • All standards met |
| • No must-fix defects | • Accepted by Product Management | • Solution demonstrated, feedback achieved | • Approved by Solution and Release Management |
| • Stories accepted by Product Owner | | • Accepted by Solution Management | |

*Table 1. Example SAFe scalable Definition of Done*

## LEARN MORE

[1] Leffingwell, Dean. *Agile Software Requirements: Lean Requirements Practices for Teams, Programs, and the Enterprise.* Addison-Wesley, 2011.

# Part 6
# The Value Stream Level

[ scaledagileframework.com/**value-stream-level**

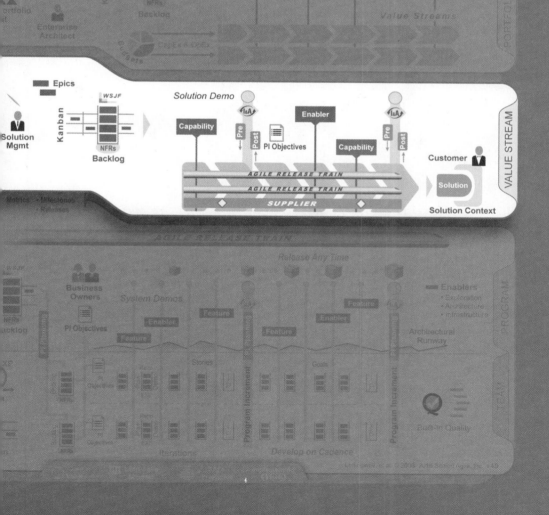

# Introduction to the Value Stream Level

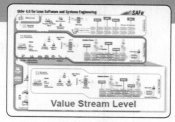

*Projects and practices fail when they optimize one part of the value stream at the expense of others or when the parts just don't fit—luxury customers with low-cost and low-quality suppliers, for example.*

—Alan C. Ward

## Abstract

The *Value Stream Level* is intended for builders of large and complex solutions, that typically require multiple ARTs as well as the contribution of Suppliers. The level provides a number of constructs that are new in SAFe 4.0. It was designed in large part based on the input of Enterprises that face the largest systems challenges, building multidisciplinary and cyber-physical systems that contain software, hardware, electrical and electronics, optics, mechanics, fluidics, and more. Building these systems often takes hundreds, even thousands, of practitioners, as well as internal and external Suppliers. These systems are mission crucial. Failure of the Solution, or even a subsystem, has unacceptable economic and societal consequences.

This is serious business, and yet traditional, stage-gated approaches do not always scale well to the challenge. A leaner and more Agile approach is required to deliver the right economics, as well as solution efficacy and safety. SAFe addresses this in general, but now with a particular focus on the largest systems at the value stream level, intended to help those defining, building, and deploying these, the world's most important systems.

## Details

The *Value Stream Level* is optional in SAFe. Enterprises that build systems that are largely independent, or that can be built with a few hundred practitioners, may not need the constructs of this level, in which case they can operate from the "collapsed view," which is called 3-level SAFe. Even then, however, those are far from trivial systems, and the constructs at the value stream level can be used in 3-level SAFe. It's a framework, after all.

But the primary purpose of this level is to describe Lean-Agile approaches to systems development that scale to the challenge of defining, building, and deploying large, mission-critical Solutions.

Building such solutions in a Lean-Agile manner requires additional constructs, artifacts, and coordination. Therefore, this level contains an Economic Framework to provide financial boundaries for Value Stream decision-making; Solution Intent as a repository for intended and actual solution behavior; Solution Context, which describes the way the solution fits in the deployment environment; and Capabilities, describing the larger behaviors of the solution.

Similarly to the Program Level, the value stream level is organized around Program Increments, which are synchronized across all the Agile Release Trains in the value stream. It provides for cadence and synchronization of multiple ARTs and Suppliers, including Pre- and Post-PI Planning meetings and the Solution Demo.

It also provides additional roles, specifically Solution Management, Solution Architect/Engineering, and the Value Stream Engineer.

## Key Roles

Much like the "troika" of the program level, the value stream level has its own troika of three critical roles necessary to coordinate and advance the value stream, as Figure 1 shows.

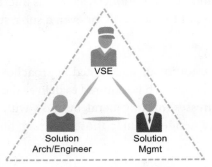

*Figure 1. Value Stream Engineer, Solution Architect/Engineering, and Solution Management troika*

**Execution and improvement** – The Value Stream Engineer is the servant leader of the value stream. He is responsible for seeing that the value stream is running smoothly and that bottlenecks are identified and resolved across the entire value stream. He facilitates the value stream level meetings and monitors the Value Stream Kanban and the value stream health via its Metrics.

**Content management** – Solution Management represents Customers' needs as well as the strategic themes of the portfolio Vision. They work with the ARTs' Product Management to define capabilities and decompose them into Features. They are responsible for the Value Stream Backlog and its prioritization via WSJF, as well as for the creation of an economic framework to govern the decision-making process for ARTs and Agile Teams.

**Technical excellence** – Solution Architect/Engineering is a team in charge of defining the overarching architecture that connects the solution across ARTs. They also work with the System Architect/Engineering team to help guide the architecture developed by the trains.

## Defining the Solution

Solution behavior and decisions are managed in solution intent, which serves both as a single source of truth and as a container for requirements in their transition from variable to fixed. In addition to vision and Roadmap, which also occur at this level via the spanning palette, the development of solution intent in an adaptive manner is supported by three additional practices:

1. **Model-Based Systems Engineering (MBSE)** – Describes how emergent requirements and design can be developed, documented, and maintained in more flexible and more accessible models

2. **Set-Based Design** – Practices that support preservation of options and the move from variable to fixed requirements over time, while deferring decisions to the last responsible moment

3. **Agile Architecture** – Supporting the balancing act between emergent design, which is built just in time by the Agile Teams, and intentional architecture, which is created collaboratively with the senior technical leaders and the teams

## Building the Solution

The main construct of the value stream level is the solution, which is the subject of the value stream. While the solution also appears at the program level in 3-level SAFe, additional practices and details are described at this level.

Solutions behave as described in solution intent, but they also live in the larger part of a solution context, which characterizes the environment in which a deployed solution operates. Solutions are built to satisfy needs of Customers and are built up of capabilities and Enablers, which are needed to realize the value stream vision and roadmap.

Capabilities are managed through the value stream Kanban system, which is used to verify that capabilities are evaluated and analyzed before they reach the value stream backlog, where they are queued for implementation. It also serves as a focusing mechanism and limits WIP to ensure that all the ARTs are synchronized and have the capacity to deliver capabilities together. Larger initiatives are managed as solution Epics and are broken down into capabilities during analysis.

Large solutions, in many cases, require Suppliers who develop components, subsystems, or capabilities for the value stream. These Suppliers participate in value stream level meetings.

## Coordinating ARTs

Another function of the value stream level is to handle the coordination of multiple ARTs that deliver a solution together. To support this, all ARTs in the value stream are synchronized around a single PI cadence, with synchronized Iterations to facilitate collaboration across ARTs and even Suppliers.

At the start of each PI, planning takes place for all ARTs at the same time. The planning is done by the ARTs themselves in PI Planning meetings, but in order to align and create a single plan across all trains, as well as manage dependencies between the trains, Pre- and Post-PI Planning meetings are also held, which results in aggregated Value Stream PI Objectives that can be communicated to stakeholders.

At the end of each PI (usually a bit into the next PI), a solution demo is held. This is an important event where the value stream shows Customers and stakeholders from the portfolio and from other value streams an integrated solution across all ARTs and Suppliers. After this demo, an Inspect and Adapt workshop is held to improve the process of the entire value stream.

## Using Constructs of the Value Stream Level in 3-Level SAFe

As described, some of the constructs of the value stream level are primarily relevant for large value streams that have to be realized by multiple ARTs, but some may well be relevant to ARTs in a 3-level SAFe environment. These constructs include solution intent and related practices, which are particularly necessary in building high-assurance systems. The solution context, the economic framework, and guidance for working with Suppliers may also be relevant. While they do not "descend" to the program level in a 3-level SAFe "collapsed view" (the way Customer and solution do), they are still relevant, and many programs can and should use them as needed.

# Value Stream Coordination

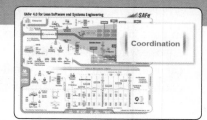

*Two captains sink the ship.*

  *– Turkish Proverb*

## Abstract

Value Streams are the most fundamental construct in SAFe. They provide a focus that helps the Lean-Agile Enterprise better understand the flow of value, from concept to delivery. As an enterprise better understands the various flows, they can focus their attention on organizing around them and further optimizing them by reducing waste, unnecessary steps, and delays. In this way the sustainably shortest lead time can be achieved and continuously reduced.

Therefore, it is sensible that value streams are organized to be largely independent. However, the fact is that *coordination of dependencies* among value streams is typically necessary. Even more important, effective *Value Stream Coordination* can create a differentiated and unmatchable Solution offering. To this end, managers and executives understand the challenge and opportunity that their value streams provide; they make them as independent as possible where appropriate, and simultaneously interconnect and coordinate them to the larger enterprise purpose.

When this is done well, the enterprise provides decentralization and autonomy of the value streams themselves—resulting in fast, independent, and unhindered value delivery. And this value is substantially enhanced by the effective exploitation of *opportunities that exist only in the interconnections.*

## Details

The SAFe Portfolio Level is where Value Streams are represented, funded, and guided to the larger purpose. It provides the general mechanisms for reasoning about the flows of value through the Enterprise. The primary constructs are the value streams themselves; Business and Enabler Epics, which serve as containers for the business initiatives that are crosscutting in nature; and the Program Portfolio Management function, which allocates Budgets to each value stream.

Often the value streams are largely independent. For example, a hardware or software concern may sell a number of products and services, largely decoupled in technology from each other. More likely, however, they have dependencies between them, and while we typically think of dependencies in a negative sense, Systems Thinking informs us that value flows through these dependencies.

Even more important, it is often the case that this additional value is *unique and differentiated*. Indeed, in part via those dependencies, an enterprise can offer a set of Solutions that cannot be matched by anyone who does not provide an equivalent set, as well as the mastery surfacing the unique and emerging capabilities that only coordinated value streams can provide. Achieving this requires a deeper look at coordinating value streams within a portfolio, as illustrated in Figure 1.

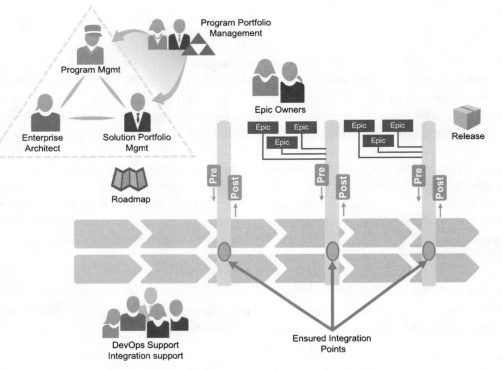

*Figure 1. Cross-value stream coordination details*

The primary aspects of *Value Stream Coordination* are described in the sections below.

## Cadence and Synchronization

To start, Figure 1 describes how the principles of *cadence and synchronization* apply equally well to the portfolio level as to the value streams and programs. The merits are the same, making routine things routine—thereby lowering the transaction costs associated with change—and synchronizing the various aspects of multi-value stream solution development.

Common cadence also provides the opportunity and mandate that the portfolio level solution (via business epics) moves forward in time with ensured planning and *integration points*, each of which provides the opportunity for objective evaluation of the solution set under development. These points are the only true measure of portfolio velocity. The more frequent the points, the faster the learning and the shorter the time to market.

## Injection of New Portfolio Level Work

Figure 1 illustrates another key point: The portfolio cadence determines the rate and timing by which new portfolio level work can be injected into the system. During the course of each Program Increment, the value streams and Agile Release Trains are necessarily "heads down," focusing on achieving the committed Objectives for that PI. Clearly, if new work is injected into the system in the interim, it causes substantive interruptions, task switching, realignment, and movement of people and other resources to the newly revised objectives. Since teams obviously can't meet their prior commitments *and* mix in new and unplanned work, this portfolio cadence provides the metronome for introducing new portfolio work and helps the programs achieve the predictability that the enterprise depends on.

This portfolio cadence also provides regular mechanisms for Epic Owners and others managing epics through the Portfolio Kanban system. Any epic that is not ready at the boundary must wait for future service, even though resources may otherwise have been available. This  timeboxing that the cadence provides also tends to limit work in process for the new, and substantial, work that is going to be injected into the system.

## Program Management, Content Management, and Enterprise Architecture

In support of the need to coordinate at this highest SAFe level, Figure 2 illustrates a set of three primary roles, each of which parallels comparable roles at the Program and Value Stream Levels.

*Figure 2. Program Management, content management, and architecture troika*

This "troika" provides three primary functions necessary to help ensure successful execution of portfolio initiatives:

1. **Program Management** – The PPM function has the highest-level governance function within the framework, so it is logical that a program manager, or someone with skill and experience in helping teams-of-teams-of-teams, reliably executes the strategic intent. This role directly parallels the Value Stream Engineer and Release Train Engineer roles that appear at the value stream and program levels, respectively.

2. **Solution Portfolio Management** – Someone must also steer the integrated portfolio solution set to the larger content intent. These responsibilities are ascribed to a solution portfolio manager role. This role also directly parallels the Solution Management and Product Management roles, which occur at the value stream and program levels.

3. **Enterprise Architect** – The Enterprise Architect may also play a role similar to those at the value stream and program levels, in this case helping to ensure common technical underpinnings, defining cross-value stream use cases, and helping to avoid unnecessary duplication of assets and effort.

In support of cadence and synchronization and decentralized planning, these roles—along with other portfolio stakeholders—may also participate in Pre- and Post-PI Planning.

## Portfolio Roadmap

Clearly, at this level of the portfolio, a plan of intent must be evident. As Figure 1 illustrates, a portfolio Roadmap is a useful artifact that highlights how new content, primarily in the form of epics, contributes to the plan of intent. In addition, this higher-level roadmap provides the opportunity to integrate various aspects of the lower-level roadmaps, and their associated Milestones, into a more comprehensive view, one suitable to communicate the larger picture to the enterprise stakeholders.

## Deployment and Release

Depending on the nature of the value streams and dependencies, deployment of integrated value may depend on effective DevOps capabilities at this portfolio level as well. While the DevOps function is primarily illustrated at the program and value stream levels, in many cases those capabilities may be all that is needed. In other cases, however, additional portfolio considerations require special treatment, and there may be dedicated or Shared Services and Systems Teams that help integrate the solution into a portfolio level Release.

# Economic Framework

*Take an economic view.*

*—SAFe Principle #1*

## Abstract

SAFe's first Lean-Agile Principle, *take an economic view,* highlights the key role that economics play in successful Solution development. The "Principle #1 – *Take an economic view*" article describes the primary aspects of taking an economic view, delivering early and often, and understanding the other economic trade-off parameters. Principle #9 – *Decentralize decision-making* is another SAFe principle.

These principles come together in this article, which describes the *Economic Framework*, a set of decision rules for a Value Stream or Program that aligns everyone to the mission and the financial constraints, including budget considerations driven from the program portfolio, as well as the trade-off parameters that effect a particular Solution. In such a context, portfolio fiduciaries can delegate decision authority to others, knowing that those decisions will be made in accordance with agreed-to economic parameters.

## Details

The primary purpose of the *Economic Framework* is to support effective, fast, decision-making within the bounds of the larger economic picture. In turn, that requires three things:

1. An understanding of the rules for decision-making

2. The current local context

3. Relevant authority

To this end, many of the needed economic decisions are embedded in various SAFe practices. Figure 1 on the next page summarizes where these decision rules and authorities occur.

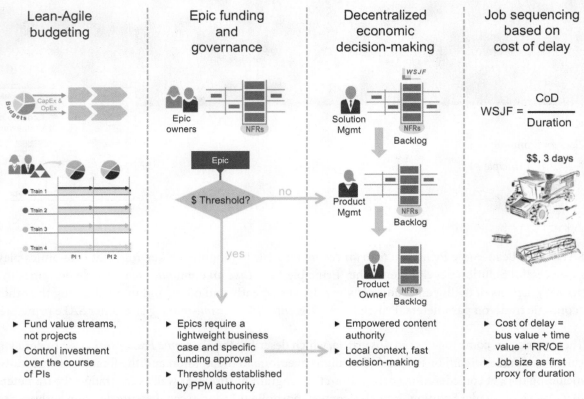

| Lean-Agile budgeting | Epic funding and governance | Decentralized economic decision-making | Job sequencing based on cost of delay |
|---|---|---|---|

$$WSJF = \frac{CoD}{Duration}$$

- ▸ Fund value streams, not projects
- ▸ Control investment over the course of PIs

- ▸ Epics require a lightweight business case and specific funding approval
- ▸ Thresholds established by PPM authority

- ▸ Empowered content authority
- ▸ Local context, fast decision-making

- ▸ Cost of delay = bus value + time value + RR/OE
- ▸ Job size as first proxy for duration

*Figure 1. SAFe constructs for economic decision-making*

Each of these areas is described in the sections that follow.

## Lean-Agile Budgeting

The first decision is a big one, as the Lean-Agile enterprise moves from project-based, cost-center accounting to a more streamlined budget process, whereby the funding is allocated to long-lived Value Streams. Thereafter, the cost for each Program Increment is largely fixed, and scope is varied as necessary. Each value stream budget can then be adjusted over time at PI boundaries, based on the relative value that each value stream provides to the portfolio. This process is described further in the "Budgets" article.

## Epic Funding and Governance

Allocating funds to the value streams (and thereby to the Agile Release Trains) is all well and good, but what happens when there are substantial, crosscutting concerns such as portfolio Epics, or significant local investment concerns as represented by value stream or program epics? The empowerment of funding requires the concomitant responsibility to communicate any investments that are beyond routine. This is the primary purpose of the Portfolio Kanban System and the related portfolio, value stream, and program epics. Each requires a lightweight business case and an explicit approval process.

## Decentralized Economic Decision-Making

With these budget elements in place, the enterprise then empowers people (particularly Product and Solution Management) with the relevant context, knowledge, and authority necessary to make content decisions at each level of the framework. Of course they don't act alone, as they work with their larger stakeholder community to determine the best course of action. But in the end, the decision is theirs, as that is their primary responsibility and authority.

## Job Sequencing Based on Cost of Delay

Every significant program has a host of new backlog Features and Capabilities just waiting to be implemented in order to increase the efficacy of the solution. But SAFe is a flow-based system, and flow-based system economics are optimized by job-sequencing rather than by theoretical job ROI, or, worse, first-come, first-served job selection. Picking the right next job is where the greatest economic benefit lies. This is enabled by the Program and Value Stream Kanban systems and the Program and Value Stream Backlog staging areas. Jobs are pulled into implementation based on WSJF, whereas estimate of job size is typically used as a proxy for duration.

## Practices Provide the Form; People Make the Decisions

This article describes the built-in SAFe constructs for economic decision-making. Together they provide the foundation for effective decision-making based on the economics of the portfolio and value stream. SAFe also defines the roles and responsibilities of those who live in the decision-making chain. However, the decisions don't make themselves. Lean-Agile Leaders continually apply these constructs and educate others in their use, so that economically responsible decision-making happens throughout the development organization, thereby bringing the full economic benefits of Lean-Agile development to the enterprise.

---

**LEARN MORE**

[1] Reinertsen, Donald G. *The Principles of Product Development Flow: Second Generation Lean Product Development*. Celeritas Publishing, 2009.

# Solution Intent

*Assume variability; preserve options.*

   —SAFe Principle #3

## Abstract

Building large-scale software and cyber-physical systems is one of the most complex and challenging endeavors in industry today. Systems builders must continuously align on "what, exactly, is this thing we are building?" as well as on "how are we going to build it?" They need sufficient and timely knowledge and decisions with respect to both questions. Further, these two questions are related. If systems builders don't know *how* to build it in an economically or technically feasible manner, then the *what* may need to be revisited in the context of the *how*. For example: current technology, capability, and capacity of the teams; and Customer context aligned with the required time frame and Economic Framework.

SAFe calls this critical knowledge pool the *Solution Intent* and uses it as the basic understanding of the current and evolving requirements, design, and intent—that larger purpose—of the Solution being constructed. Systems builders also recognize that some of the system understanding is *fixed*, with non-negotiable requirements for what the solution *must* do or already does; and some is *variable*, subject to further discussion and exploration as facts surface. Understanding and navigating these differences, and allowing variability to proceed even late into the timeline, is key to unlocking agility in large-scale solution development.

This article addresses one other critical item as well: Until now, many builders of critical, large-scale solutions have shied away from Agile methods because of the apparently lightweight treatment of system design and documentation. Scaling Lean-Agile development to the needs of those building the world's most critical systems will be addressed in this article as well.

## Details

When building systems that have an unacceptably high cost of failure, one significant barrier to Agile adoption is the need for a more rigorous definition and validation of system behavior. While many practitioners resonate with the Agile Manifesto [1] value statement of *working software **over** comprehensive documentation*, those can become conflicting priorities for enterprises that need *both*.

Engineering of complex and highly reliable Solutions requires and creates large amounts of technical information. Much of this information reflects the intended behavior of the solution—Features and Capabilities, Stories, Nonfunctional Requirements, system architecture, domain-level models and designs (e.g., electrical and mechanical), interfaces, Customer specifications, tests and test results, traceability, etc. Other relevant information records some of the key decisions and findings about the system. This may include information from trade studies, results of experiments, the rationale for design choices, and other items. In many cases, this information must become part of the official record, whether out of necessity or regulation.

## Introducing Solution Intent

*Solution Intent* is a critical knowledge repository to store, manage, and communicate *what* systems builders are building and *how* they are going to build it. It serves many purposes:

- Provides a single source of truth as to the intended and actual behavior of the solution
- Records and communicates requirements, design, and system architecture decisions
- Facilitates further exploration and analysis activities
- Aligns the Customer, the systems builders, and Suppliers to a common purpose
- Supports compliance and contractual obligations

Figure 1 illustrates the compound nature of solution intent:

- **Current and future state** – Builders of complex systems must constantly know two things: what, exactly, the current system does now, and what changes are intended for a *future* state
- **Specifications, designs, and tests** – Knowledge of both the current and future states can be captured in any form suitable to the solution builder, but it includes the three primary elements: specifications (documented definition of system behavior), design, and tests

When building systems for which behavior must be ensured, including life-critical systems, mission-critical systems, and other systems governed by regulatory standards for documents, *traceability* is a means to help ensure that the system behaves as intended. Traceability connects the elements of solution intent to each other, and to the components of the systems that realize the full system behavior. (Note: For more on building high-assurance systems with Lean-Agile development, refer to the Guidance white paper "*Agile Development in High-Assurance and Regulated Environments.*") Figure 1 illustrates this concept.

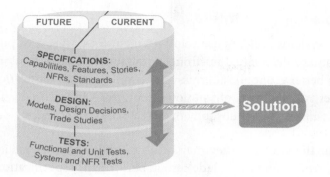

*Figure 1. Anatomy of solution intent*

The specific elements of solution intent can be realized in many forms, from documents, spreadsheets, and whiteboard sessions to formal requirements and modeling tools, as described in the "Model-Based Systems Engineering" article. But as solution intent is a means to the end of building the solution, methods for capturing solution intent should be sufficient but not create unnecessary overhead and waste (see the sufficiency discussion below).

## The Dynamic Nature of Solution Intent

Traditionally, the proxy for solution intent has existed largely as a fixed set of requirements, defined up front and often imposed on the solution builder by the Customer, or defined by the systems builder. Indeed, the very word "requirements" often implies waterfall thinking, biased by the assumption that requirements all need to be identified up front.

SAFe Principle #3 – *Assume variability; preserve options* describes the evidence that defining requirements and designs too tightly up front leads to *less successful* outcomes.

A different approach is needed, one that supports understanding the knowns and allows the unknowns to emerge over the course of development. Therefore, solution intent is not a one-time statement, frozen in time; it must support and evolve throughout the entire development process, as illustrated in Figure 2.

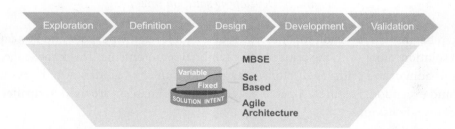

*Figure 2. Solution intent evolves with and supports all the steps in solution development*

## Fixed and Variable Solution Intent

As mentioned earlier, systems builders use solution intent for a variety of purposes. However, none of these mandate creating fully defined up-front "point-solution" specifications. Such early decisions restrict exploration of better economic alternatives and often lead to waste and rework [2]. In support of this, SAFe describes two elements of solution intent, *fixed* and *variable*, that support the general adaptive requirements and design philosophy that create the best economic benefit.

*Fixed* intent represents the knowns. They may be nonnegotiable, or they may have emerged during the course of development. Examples include certain performance specifications (e.g., "the pacemaker waveform must be as follows"), or the need to adhere to compliance standards ("comply with all PCI compliance credit card requirements"), or core capabilities that define the solution ("the Baja Adventure Ride holds four adult riders").

*Variable* intent represents the elements for which systems builders are free to explore the economic trade-offs of requirements and design alternatives that could meet the need. Once established, these new understandings will eventually become fixed requirements (e.g., "The ride vehicle has a maximum passenger load of 400 KG"). Even then, optionality should be preserved for as long as possible (e.g., "The current design supports 350 KG; let's discuss that with the Customer").

## Developing Solution Intent

SAFe's Lean-Agile approach to developing system knowledge differs from the traditional waterfall approach. Figure 3 illustrates the artifacts and processes used to develop solution intent via a more emergent approach.

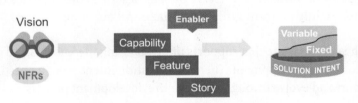

*Figure 3. Developing solution intent*

Solution intent begins with a Vision that describes, at a high level, the purpose and key capabilities of the intended solution, along with the critical nonfunctional requirements. This knowledge, along with an emerging Roadmap and critical Milestones, can provide sufficient guidance to the teams for initial PI Planning and execution. Features, capabilities, Stories, and Enablers are used to further define and realize the solution behavior.

In more complex and/or regulated environments, substantially more investment in solution intent documentation is required. Compliance needs may mandate the creation of standards-based or other technical specifications. Some even require recording the results of exploration and decisions.

Others mandate traceability to support analysis, efficacy, and demonstration of solution compliance to approved requirements. In these cases, some elements of solution intent will be formally documented. In the spirit of Lean, this documentation is a *compiled* result, rather than an up-front mandate.

## Collaborating on Solutions Intent

Product and Solution Management, typically working with a Solution Architect and Systems Engineering team and the Customer, is often responsible for the highest-level, system-wide decisions, such as system decomposition, interfaces, and allocations of requirements to various subsystems and capabilities. Solution engineering also establishes the solution intent's organizational structure and may define where various types of information are managed to support analysis and compliance needs.

Although solution intent is depicted at the Value Stream Level, ARTs build the capabilities and subsystems and make significant contributions to solution intent. Figure 4 shows how the collaboration between the Customer, Product and Solution Management, and ARTs contribute to solution intent; this assigns further behaviors to the ART components by influencing the Program and Value Stream Backlogs.

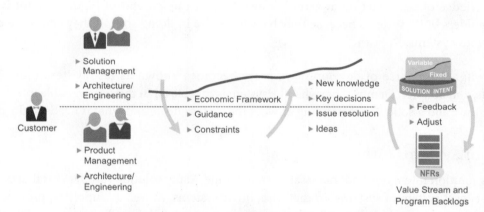

*Figure 4. The collaboration that develops solution intent*

Solution Management and Solution Architect/Engineering often delegate some solution intent requirements directly to the ARTs that build the capabilities and subsystems of the solution. ARTs also provide feedback on solution-level decisions and raise issues and ideas to solution engineering. And finally, the Customer's Solution Context has a material impact on solution intent.

## Moving from Variable to Fixed Solution Intent

Building and deploying a solution often requires systems builders to eventually know exactly what the system does and validate that it does exactly that and nothing else. In other words, at the time of final construction, requirements must all be fixed. Moving from variable to fixed is a process of exploring options and keeping optionality present, as long as possible, within the Economic Framework.

This is supported by Set-Based Design practices and the use of enablers, all intended to resolve uncertainty and mitigate risk. At the same time, teams build the system based on their current understanding; as more is known, they implement new features, as Figure 5 illustrates.

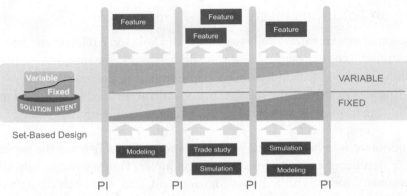

*Figure 5. Moving from variable to fixed solution intent*

Fixed knowledge doesn't start off at zero, because even at the left end of Figure 5, a lot is known. Systems builders build systems because they have expertise in doing so, and they can reuse elements from previous systems.

Then, through the course of development, more becomes known as fast as Iterations, Program Increments, and Solution Demos show what the system is capable of. In this way, variable intent becomes fixed over time and a solid understanding of what the system does, and what it needs to do, emerges.

## System of Systems Intent

A system's solution intent does not necessarily stand alone. Many solutions are *systems* that participate in a higher-level system of systems. In that case, other systems, as well as Suppliers, provide systems builders with unique knowledge and solution elements that accelerate development. Suppliers, for example, will often have separate and independent requirements, designs, and other specifications for their subsystem or capability.

From their perspective, that is their solution intent. The ultimate (top-level) solution intent must therefore include the relevant Supplier knowledge and information necessary to communicate decisions, facilitate exploration, align builders, and support compliance. The result is a "daisy chain" of requirements and design decisions that move up and down the system hierarchy, as illustrated in Figure 6.

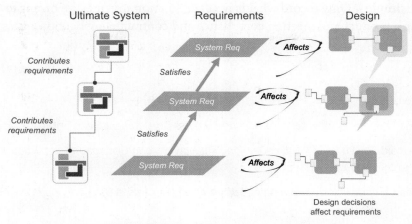

*Figure 6. Solution intent hierarchy*

## Minimal but Sufficient Documentation

Solution intent is a means to an end—a means to guide systems builders, communicate decisions, and demonstrate compliance. Planning the solution intent's content, organization, and documentation strategies should begin with those ends in mind. But more is not necessarily better. The Lean-Agile community recommends *keeping it light* with respect to documenting requirements, design, and architecture [5]. Best practices include:

- **Favor models over documents** – An environment of continuous change challenges a document-centric approach to organizing and managing solution intent. When applied properly, models can provide a more easily maintained way to manage solution intent, as is further discussed in the "Model-Based Systems Engineering" article.

- **Solution intent is a collaboration** – There is no monopoly on innovation, and solution intent is not the exclusive domain of the Product and Solution Managers, Architects, and Engineers. Many team members participate in the creation, feedback, and refinement of solution intent information.

- **Keep options open** – Defer decisions to local concerns. Make them as late as possible. An adaptive approach to requirements and design keeps promising options open as long as that is economically feasible. Set-Based Design practices help avoid committing too early to design and requirements.

- **Document items in only one place** – Record any requirements and design decisions in only one place, a single source of truth that serves as the repository of record for all.

- **Keep it high level** – Communicate at as high a level of abstraction as possible. Don't over-specify. Provide a range of acceptable behaviors. Describe solution behavior with intent, not specificity. Decentralize requirements and design decision-making authority.

- **Keep it simple** – Only record what is needed. Solution intent is the means to the end of building a product and meeting compliance and contractual obligations. Less is more.

---

## LEARN MORE

[1] Agilemanifesto.org.

[2] Ward, Allen and Durward Sobek. *Lean Product and Process Development*. Lean Enterprise Institute, 2014.

[3] Reinertsen, Donald. *Principles of Product Development Flow: Second Generation Lean Product Development*. Celeritas Publishing, 2009.

[4] Leffingwell, Dean and Don Widrig. *Managing Software Requirements: A Use Case Approach*. Addison-Wesley, 2003.

[5] Ambler, Scott. "Agile Architecture: Strategies for Scaling Agile Development." Agile Modeling, 2012. http://agilemodeling.com/essays/agileArchitecture.htm.

# Model-Based Systems Engineering

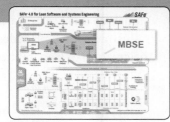

*All models are wrong, but some are useful.*
—George E. P. Box

## Abstract

Since humans began engineering systems and structures, they have used models to abstract, learn, and communicate. *Model-Based Systems Engineering (MBSE)* is the application of modeling of requirements, design, analysis, and verification activities as a cost-effective way to learn about system characteristics prior to construction. Models provide early feedback on system decisions and communicate intended aspects of the system to all involved, including Customers, stakeholders, developers, testers, etc.

While, as Dr. Box asserts, models are never a perfect representation of the real world, they provide knowledge and feedback earlier and more cheaply than could possibly be achieved through implementation. In practice, engineers use models to gain knowledge (e.g., performance, thermal, fluid), to serve as a guide for system implementation (e.g., SysML, UML) or, in some cases, to directly build the actual implementation (e.g., electrical CAD, mechanical CAD).

Models facilitate early learning by testing and validating system characteristics, properties, and behaviors early, enabling early feedback on requirements and design decisions.

## Details

Engineering disciplines have used modeling for years to discover and specify structure and behavior, explore alternatives, and communicate decisions early in the life cycle. Lean practices support fast learning through a continuous flow of small work to gain fast feedback on decisions. *Model-Based Systems Engineering (MBSE)* is a discipline and a Lean tool that allows engineers to quickly and incrementally learn about the system under development before the cost of change gets too high.

## Support Learning Cycles with Models

MBSE supports fast learning cycles and helps mitigate risks early in the product life cycle. Models facilitate early learning by testing and validating system characteristics, properties, and behaviors early, enabling early feedback on design decisions.

Models come in many forms—dynamic, solid, graphs, equations, simulation, and prototypes. As Figure 1 illustrates, each provides a different perspective into one or more system characteristics that enable the creation of Capabilities and Features.

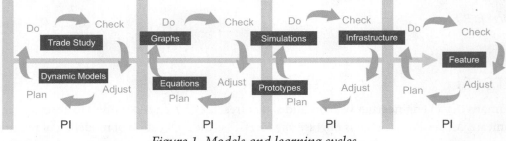

*Figure 1. Models and learning cycles*

Models may predict performance (response time, reliability) or physical properties (heat, radiation, strength), or they may explore designs for user experience or response to an external stimulus.

## Use Traceability for Impact Analysis and Compliance

Relationships among models can help further predict system utility and support analysis and compliance activities. Systems may have models from many disciplines—electrical, mechanical, software—as well as system-level requirements and design models. Traceability is achieved by relating system elements within and across models. It provides many benefits:

- Simplifies and automates most regulatory and contractual compliance needs

- Reduces time and effort for impact analysis needed to support new work and provides information for Inspect and Adapt activities

- Facilitates cross-discipline collaboration by allowing traceability from a model in one discipline to a model in another

- Encourages general knowledge discovery by making information, and related cross-discipline information, more accessible to teams

A Lean, continuous change environment amplifies the need for related models. While manual solutions to managing coverage and compliance may work adequately in a stage-gate process, they will be quickly overwhelmed by an Agile environment that encourages frequent and continuous change.

Figure 2 shows a high-level model link structure in which requirements are linked to tests in a test model and to system-level elements in a system model.

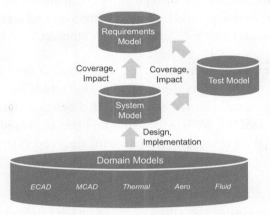

*Figure 2. Linking cross-domain models*

Domain models then link to the system model. Engineers can quickly and reliably understand the impact of a requirements change on the system and the domains, or the impact of a change at the domain level on other parts of the system and requirements. In addition, the existence or absence of links shows coverage and compliance gaps (e.g., requirements not tested).

Instead of manually creating and maintaining this traceability information, compliance documents can be generated from model information and the links between them. When the system requirements or designs change, traceability information shows the impact of a change, any gaps in test/requirements coverage, and any linked information that is now suspect and should be revisited.

## Record Models in Solution Intent

Technical knowledge and decisions are recorded in Solution Intent for communication with and reference by team members across the entire Solution development. In practice, engineers represent technical information in many forms, from documents to spreadsheets to modeling tools. While documents and spreadsheets are easy for an author to create, they do not encourage the knowledge transfer or the continuous collaboration required for Lean systems engineering. For that, what's needed is MBSE.

Solution intent will contain many different kinds of models, with many options for organizing and linking information. System and Solution Architects and Engineers are typically responsible for tasks from specifying the model information and organization to ensuring its quality. Agile Teams populate the model(s) with their respective knowledge and information.

With many contributors, large systems may assign a model owner role (often a member of Systems Engineering), who is responsible for model content and structural integrity.

## Generate Documentation for Compliance

While SAFe emphasizes models for early discovery and system documentation, many product and engineering domains require documents for regulatory compliance (FAA, FDA, etc.) or contractual obligations (CDRLs in government contracting). In addition, not all stakeholders will be well versed in models or their notations, and they will continue to communicate with documents.

Wherever possible, documents should be generated from information in system models. (Engineers should not duplicate their efforts by creating compliance documents—a Lean example of waste.) Further, documents can be generated for stakeholders with different system perspectives. Architectural framework standards (e.g., DoDAF, MODAF) define multiple stakeholder viewpoints and different views for communicating system information. Generating documents from models is the best way to ensure consistency across all stakeholder views.

While all products and programs will likely require formal documents, System Engineers are encouraged to work with Customers and/or regulatory agencies on the minimum set sufficient to meet their obligations. The source of most, if not all of, the information resides in engineering repositories that can and should be used for inspections and formal reviews where possible.

## Build Model Quality In

As stated previously, models can suffer a quality challenge due to the diversity and number of those who contribute information. Without proper oversight, continuous changes made by many people can cause quality to suffer. The model owner is responsible for working with the teams to define quality practices—model standards and model testing—and to help ensure that they are followed.

The quality practices discussed below facilitate early learning cycles. As SAFe notes, "You can't scale crappy code," and the same is true for system designs represented in models. Quality practices allow engineers to confidently and frequently make model changes and contribute to the system intent.

## Model Standards

Model standards help control quality and guide teams on how best to model. They can include:

- What information should be captured
- Modeling notations (e.g., SysML) and parts of those notations (e.g., Use Case) to use or exclude
- Where modeling information should be placed for solution and subsystem elements
- Meta-information that should be stored with different types of model elements

- Links within the model or with other cross-discipline models
- Common types and common dimensions used across the system
- Modeling tool properties and configuration (likely part of the engineering environment)
- Collaboration practices with any underlying version control system(s) (if relevant)

If documents are being generated from the models, the document templates should be defined early, as they influence many of these decisions. Systems designers need to know where to store the model elements and any metadata or links required on the model elements that may be used for queries, document generation, or compliance.

As a best practice, create an exemplar, high-level, full-system model early on. The example is ideally a skeleton model across the solution (one that defines all subsystems), and one element can illustrate how to model the structure and behavior of a single subsystem. Run any document generation tests against this configuration early to ensure completeness so the teams do not have to rework (waste) the model with missed information.

## Create Testable and Executable Models

SAFe's Test-First practices help teams build quality into their products early and facilitate the continuous, small changes we find in Agile software development. Test-first creates a rich suite of test cases that allow developers to more reliably make changes without causing an error in another part of the system.

Lean practices encourage testable, executable models where appropriate to reduce waste associated with downstream errors. Models should be testable against whatever assessment criteria exist for the domain or discipline. Mechanical models have tests for physical and environmental issues, electrical models for logic, software models for anomalies, and executable system models for system behavior. Most modeling tools provide the ability to check models or to create scripts that can iterate across the models and look for anomalies.

**Testing Requirements Models** – Textual requirements are used in almost every system and, under the current practice, are typically reviewed manually. The community has long sought executable specifications, where requirements are specified in a form that can be executed for testing. Success, however, has been limited to certain specific domains where the problem is well defined. Agile practices advocate a variant of executable specifications called Acceptance Test-Driven Development (ATDD). Some exploratory work has emerged to support ATDD in systems development. While a promising solution for requirements testing, ATDD has not yet been used at a large scale. Make requirements and tests one and the same where possible, and automate to the extent possible.

**Testing Analysis and Design Models** – Designs represented in models can be tested both statically and dynamically. Modeling tools typically have static model analyzers or "checkers" that examine the model looking for anomalies.

Model owners may add their own rules—model organization, modeling conventions and standards, required meta-information (e.g., SysML tags, stereotypes), etc. Where analyzers do not exist, scripts can iterate over the models looking for violations in the static model.

**Dynamic Testing –** The models from engineering disciplines have their own solutions for assessing quality and should be leveraged as part of testing practice.

**Testing Traceability –** Models must comply with the linking structure to ensure proper queries, document generation, and compliance.

**Document Generation –** While possibly redundant with the traceability scripts above, document generation may have scripts to ensure that the model is structured properly and all data exists to support all document templates. With large models, it is often easier to debug a script than a document template.

# Set-Based Design

## Abstract

Systems development can be described as a process of continuously reducing uncertainty to knowledge. No matter how well a system is initially defined and designed, real Customer needs and technological choices are both uncertain, and therefore the understanding of how a system needs to be implemented will have to adapt over time to reflect reality.

Point-Based Design—the process of committing to a specific, detailed requirements and system design early in the process—deprives the system developer of the potential benefit of later, more empirical data, which becomes available only as system development proceeds. The discovery that the chosen design doesn't work occurs far too late in the process, making it impossible to recover with any grace.

*Set-Based Design* is a practice that maintains multiple requirements and design options for a longer period in the development cycle. Later, as the deadline approaches, it uses empirical data to collapse focus to the final design option. With such an approach, systems builders can assume variability and preserve options late into the game, providing for maximum flexibility of approach rather than binding early to a final option.

## Details

*Point-Based Design* commits to a set of requirements and a single design strategy early in the process. It often leads to late discoveries that require substantive rework as the deadline approaches, necessitating shortcuts, quality compromises, and, worse, missed program commitments and deadlines. This is one of the primary problems with system development when it follows a traditional, linear (waterfall) requirements > design > implementation > test approach, and it is one of the main reasons for the continual cost and schedule overruns of such processes.

*Set-Based Design (SBD)* maintains multiple design options through a longer period in the development cycle. Set-Based Design is an important practice for economic efficiency in Lean product development and is described further in [1] and [2]. Figure 1 shows the conceptual difference between Set- and Point-Based Design approaches.

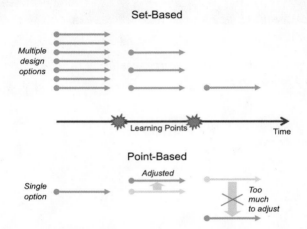

*Figure 1. Point-Based Design commits to a design up front. Set-Based Design maintains multiple alternatives for a longer period.*

## Set-Based Design and Fixed-Schedule Programs

Set-Based Design is particularly effective in programs that require a high degree of fixed schedule commitments. After all, since the schedule is unmovable, it makes sense to keep multiple design options present, even if some of the more reliable design options do not necessarily provide the degree of innovation or enhanced performance that the systems developers would otherwise prefer. But when the deadline is sacrosanct, teams must do what they can within the schedule.

## Achieving Economic Efficiency with Set-Based Design

Of course, maintaining more than one design option also comes at a cost—the cost of developing and maintaining the options, even if they are mostly model or paper based. (Note: Reinertsen [3] points out that maintaining multiple design options is one form of U-curve optimization, and sometimes the optimum number on the curve is one!) But in the case of a high degree of innovation or variability, and in the case of immovable deadlines ("This crop combine must leave the factory in January"), a Set-Based Design may be the best choice. In this case, design efficiency depends on a number of factors:

- **Flexibility** – Preserving a broad set of design options for as long as possible
- **Cost** – Minimizing the cost of multiple options through modeling, simulation, and prototyping
- **Speed** – Facilitating learning through early and frequent validation of design alternatives

In order to achieve this efficiency, some recommended practices are described below.

### Specifying Interfaces and Requirements, Not Design

Complex systems are built out of subsystems and component elements, which collaborate to produce system results. While elements may have different levels of coupling, design flexibility can be increased by specifying the performance requirements and interfaces rather than how an element achieves its result. This abstraction to a higher level of concern provides a broader spectrum of design options, as different designs of an element may each potentially satisfy the predefined interfaces.

For example, perhaps a team is developing a new CNC lathe, one with substantially higher performance requirements than an existing model. Specifications for increased operating speeds will have specific implications on certain components. Designers might have a choice of analog servo control motors or stepping motors. Stepping motors would decrease manufacturing cost but might not be able to meet the performance requirements. Maintaining both options for some period during the design process could help with the right economic trade-offs.

In addition, specifying interfaces supports building incrementally with fast, integrated learning cycles. In the lathe example, having agreed upon certain interfaces, the team can test the prototype lathe on the fixture with each type of component, without changing other elements of the design.

### Modeling, Simulation, and Prototyping

The process of modeling, simulating, and prototyping allows for empirical system validation early, and it provides early learning points that will help eliminate some design alternatives and validate others. Model-Based Systems Engineering is a disciplined, comprehensive, and rigorous approach to modeling. These techniques should be applied to the aspects of the system where the highest risk is likely to occur, thereby significantly reducing the cost of maintaining design alternatives for a longer period of time.

### Frequent Integration Points

During development periods where new designs are in flight, uncertainty abounds and true knowledge is scarce. The only way to resolve the uncertainty is to test the design via early and frequent integration of the system components. In SAFe, these integration points are driven in part by System Demos, which occur on a fixed two-week cadence, and by Solution Demos, which typically occur on the longer Program Increment (PI) cadence. In fact, without this frequent integration, SBD practices may create a false sense of security and thereby even increase risk, as perhaps none of the design alternatives will really meet the necessary performance requirements. Frequent integration supports this empirical learning with new knowledge that is used to reduce options as the system evolves, as Figure 2 illustrates.

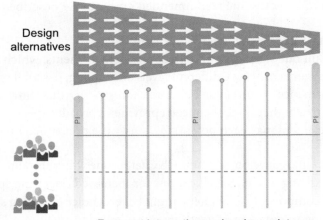

*Figure 2. Frequent integration provides critical learning points that narrow design alternatives*

Frequent system integration is even more critical when system development initiatives involve Suppliers. Even when interfaces are carefully defined, if there is infrequent integration then unexpected findings will occur too late, often leaving no time or resources to respond to the impending deadline.

## Adaptive Planning

Explicit and regular planning provides the opportunity for evaluating different design alternatives and directly supports set-based thinking. PI Planning defines the overall intent for the PI and fosters alignment on the constraints and requirements that will govern the design alternatives under consideration. Iteration Planning plays a more tactical role, allowing teams to adjust during PI execution as they learn more from frequently integrating and reviewing increments of value.

## Economic Trade-offs in Set-Based Design

Different design options have different economic implications, so understanding Set-Based Design requires an understanding of the macroeconomic goals and benefits of the system. One way to look at this is to place the alternatives on a spectrum, where a certain "weight" can be associated with each option.

Some of the economically significant indicators may include cost of development, cost of manufacturing, performance and reliability, cost of support, development time, and technical risks. These indicators help illustrate which design options provide the greater benefit. In the earlier lathe example, for instance, the trade-off between the accuracy of various types and brands of motors and the cost of manufacture can make a big difference, as Figure 3 demonstrates.

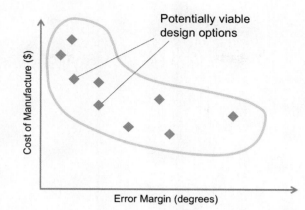

*Figure 3. A trade-off curve between an economic indicator (Cost) and a performance requirement (Error Margin) provides guidance for choosing among Set-Based Designs*

In summary, up-front commitment to a specific, detailed design can rarely survive contact with empirical evidence. With a proper understanding of the economic trade-offs, Set-Based Design provides an adaptive approach with a wider systems perspective and provides for better economic choices and more adaptability to existing constraints.

---

**LEARN MORE**

[1] Ward, Allen, and Durward Sobek. *Lean Process and Product Development*. Second edition. Lean Enterprise Institute, Inc., 2014.

[2] Oosterwal, Dantar. *The Lean Machine*. Amacom, 2010.

[3] Reinertsen, Donald. *Principles of Product Development Flow: Second Generation Lean Product Development*. Celeritas Publishing, 2009.

# Agile Architecture

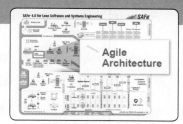

*While we must acknowledge emergence in design and system development, a little planning can avoid much waste.*

—James O. Coplien, *Lean Architecture*

## Abstract

*Agile Architecture* is a set of values and practices that support the active evolution of the design and architecture of a system, *concurrent with* the implementation of new business functionality. With this approach, the architecture of a system, even a large system, evolves over time while simultaneously supporting the needs of current users. This avoids Big Up-Front Design and starting and stopping of stage-gated methods. The *system always runs*, and it thereby supports a more continuous flow of value.

Agile architecture enables incremental value delivery by balancing between two end points—emergent design and intentional architecture. *Emergent design* provides the technical basis for a fully evolutionary, incremental implementation approach, and it helps the design respond to immediate user needs. The design *emerges* as the system is built and deployed. At the same time, however, organizations must respond to new business challenges with larger-scale architectural initiatives that require some intentionality and planning. *Intentional architecture* provides guidance and technical governance to Agile programs and teams for certain overarching technical constructs. These provide for commonality of approach, elimination of redundancy, and higher robustness of the full system. Together, these activities create the *Architectural Runway* needed to enable teams to deliver business value faster and more reliably.

SAFe's principles of Agile architecture, described in this article, illustrate how collaboration, emergent design, intentional architecture, design simplicity, designing for testability, prototyping, domain modeling, and decentralized innovation all support this important underpinning to Lean-Agile development.

## Details

By balancing emergent design and intentionality, *Agile Architecture* is a Lean-Agile approach to addressing the complexity of building Enterprise Solutions. It avoids Big Up-Front Design, starting and stopping, and the big-branch-and-merge problems associated with traditional development.

It's an approach that supports the needs of current users while simultaneously evolving the system to meet near-future needs. Used together, emergent design and intentionality continuously build and extend the Architectural Runway that provides the technical foundation for future development of business value.

Agile architecture spans all levels of SAFe. The following *Principles of Agile Architecture* provide the basic principles for the SAFe approach:

1. Design emerges. Architecture is a collaboration.

2. The bigger the system, the longer the runway

3. Build the simplest architecture that can possibly work

4. When in doubt, code or model it out

5. They build it, they test it

6. There is no monopoly on innovation

7. Implement architectural flow

## #1 – Design Emerges. Architecture Is a Collaboration.

Traditional, stage-gated development methodologies often use Big Up-Front Design (BUFD) to create a roadmap and architectural infrastructure intended to fully address the needs of the future system. The belief is that a one-time effort could capture requirements and architectural plans sufficiently to support the system for years to come.

However, this approach comes with many challenges. One is the delay in starting implementation. A second arises when the planned architecture—a large set of speculative, forward-looking constructs—meets the real world. Soon enough, the designs become brittle and hard to change, and eventually a big-branch-and-merge to a new set of speculative assumptions is the routine course of action. SAFe addresses this by combining emergent design and intentional architecture, driven by collaboration.

**Emergent Design**
Principle 11 of the Agile Manifesto [2] is the primary driver behind the concept of emergent design: The *best architectures, requirements, and designs emerge from self-organizing teams*. This implies that:

- The design is grown incrementally by those who are closest to it

- The design evolves hand-in-hand with business functionality. It is constantly tested and enabled by Refactoring, Test-First, and Continuous Integration.

- Teams rapidly evolve the design in accordance with the currently known requirements; the design is extended only as necessary to implement and validate the next increment of functionality

This new practice of emergent design is effective at the Team Level. However, emergent design alone is insufficient when developing large systems.

- It can cause excessive redesign for things that could have been anticipated. In turn, that drives bad economics and slows time to market.

- Teams are not always able to synchronize with each other, thus creating assumption entropy and architectural divergence

- Teams may not even be aware of some of the larger, upcoming business needs; factors outside their purview drive the need for future architecture

- Common architectural underpinnings enhance usability, extensibility, performance, and maintainability of the larger system of systems

- New, crosscutting user patterns affect future fitness of purpose

- Mergers and acquisitions drive integrations and the need for commonality of infrastructure

### Intentional Architecture

Therefore, there comes a point at which emergent design is an insufficient response to the complexity of large-scale system development. Simply, it is not possible for teams to anticipate changes that may well occur outside their environment, nor for individual teams to fully understand the entire system and thereby avoid producing redundant and/or conflicting code and designs.

For this some *intentional architecture* is needed—a set of purposeful, planned architectural initiatives to enhance solution design, performance, and usability and to provide guidance for inter-team design and implementation synchronization.

### Architecture Is a Collaboration

Clearly, it's best to have both: fast, local control of emergent design and a global view of intentional architecture. The combination provides the guidance needed to ensure that the system as a whole has conceptual integrity and efficacy. Achieving the right balance of emergent design and intentional architecture drives effective evolution of the system, as Figure 1 illustrates.

Figure 1 shows that these are not independent constructs. Intentional architecture constrains the emergent design, but at a high enough level of abstraction to allow the teams to effectively adapt the "intentional" part to their specific context. At the same time, emergent design influences and corrects intentional architecture and also feeds new ideas for future, centralized, intentional effort.

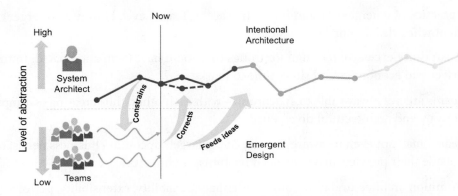

*Figure 1. Intentional architecture, emergent design, and collaboration support system evolution*

Such a deep reciprocity between emergent design and intentional architecture can occur only as a result of *collaboration* between Agile Teams, System and Solution Architecture, Enterprise Architects, and Product and Solution Management. The Agile Release Train creates a team-of-teams environment that fosters this particular collaboration.

## #2 – The Bigger the System, the Longer the Runway

An architectural runway exists when the enterprise's platforms have sufficient technological infrastructure to support the implementation of the highest-priority Features and Capabilities in the backlog without excessive, delay-inducing redesign. In order to achieve some degree of runway, the enterprise must continually invest in extending existing platforms, as well as building and deploying the new platforms needed for evolving business requirements. In the Lean-Agile enterprise, implementation of architectural initiatives is complicated by the fact that the "big-bang-up-front branch-and-merge" waterfall approach is abandoned. Instead, the enterprise commits to implementing architectural initiatives incrementally in the main code base. Doing so means that architectural initiatives must be split into Enabler Features, which build the runway needed to host the new business features, as Figure 2 illustrates.

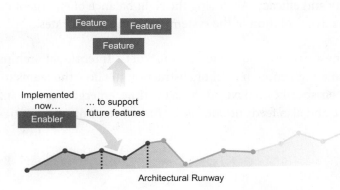

*Figure 2. The architectural runway continuously evolves to support future functionality*

Each enabler feature must be completed within a Program Increment such that the system always runs, at least at the PI boundaries. In some cases, this means that new architectural initiatives are implemented piecemeal and may not even be exposed to the users in the PI in which they are implemented. In this way, the architectural runway can be implemented and tested behind the scenes, allowing shipment throughout, and then exposed to users when a sufficient feature capability exists in the next PI or so.

The concept of runway illustrates how intentional architecture and emergent design effectively complement each other at scale: intentional, high-level ideas in support of future functionality are adapted and instantiated by Agile Teams; they are empowered to figure out the optimal emergent design.

## #3 – Build the Simplest Architecture That Can Possibly Work

*We welcome changing requirements even late in development* (Agile Manifesto [2]). Yes, we do, but surely enabling change is facilitated by systems that have understandable designs. As Kent Beck notes, "If simplicity is good, we'll always leave the system with the simplest design that supports its current functionality" [3]. Indeed, at scale, design simplicity is not a luxury but a survival mechanism. There are many considerations that help accomplish this. Here are a few:

- Use a simple, common language to describe the system
- Keep the solution model as close to the problem domain as possible
- Refactor continuously
- Ensure that object/component interfaces clearly express their intent
- Follow good old design principles [4, 5]

Certain approaches to designing the system, such as Domain-Driven Design [6], usage of design patterns [4], and applying metaphor [3], simplify both the design and the communication between the teams. This "social" aspect of design simplicity is critical as it enables collective code ownership, which in turn fosters feature—rather than component—orientation [7]. The dominant theme in evolving maintainable and extensible solutions is to consider the system as a set of collaborating entities. This prevents typical design flaws such as concentrating too much logic at the database layer, or creating a thick UI, or ending up with large and unmanageable classes. Simplicity requires design skill and knowledge. Communities of Practice help develop and spread these best practices.

## #4 – When in Doubt, Code or Model It Out

Coming to agreement on good design decisions can be difficult. There are legitimate differences of opinion about which course of action is best. Often there is no one right answer. And while Agile Teams and programs don't mind refactoring, they surely want to avoid *unnecessary* refactoring. In order to decide, Agile Teams can typically just *code it out*, using Technical or Functional Spikes and even rapid prototyping.

Iterations are short and spikes are small; the result is fast feedback with objective evidence, which can then be subject to A/B testing by the teams, designers, and architects—or even the users.

In cases where design changes are of such scope that coding, spikes, and prototyping are insufficient, it is useful to *model* the problem to gain an understanding of the potential impact prior to implementation. As illustrated in Figure 3, Domain Modeling (the subject of a Guidance article) and use-case modeling are two lightweight Agile modeling constructs that are particularly valuable.

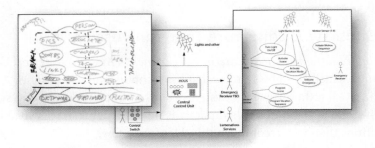

*Figure 3. A domain model and a use-case model, supported by a system context diagram*

### Record Models in Solution Intent

Of course, the models aren't useful if no one can find them. Therefore, models, technical knowledge, and even various design decisions are recorded in the Solution Intent, which provides a central point of communication. In practice, however, systems builders represent technical information in many forms, from documents to spreadsheets to the models described above. While documents and spreadsheets are easy for an author to create, they do not necessarily encourage the knowledge transfer or the continuous collaboration required for Lean systems engineering.

A better approach is Model-Based System Engineering (MBSE), which is the topic of another article.

With MBSE, solution intent will contain many different kinds of models, with many options for organizing and linking information. System and Solution Architects and Engineers are typically responsible for tasks ranging from specifying the model information and organization to ensuring its quality. Agile Teams populate the model(s) with their respective knowledge and information.

## #5 – They Build It, They Test It

The responsibility for knowing whether a design actually works rests with those who collaborate on the architecture. Testing system architecture involves testing the system's ability to meet its larger-scale functional and Nonfunctional operational, performance, and reliability requirements. To do this, teams must also build the testing infrastructure—automate wherever possible—that enables ongoing system-level testing.

And as the architecture evolves, the testing approaches, testing frameworks, and test suites must evolve with it. Therefore System Architects, Agile Teams, and the System Team actively collaborate in order to continuously Design for Testability.

## #6 – There Is No Monopoly on Innovation

Optimization of architecture is a collaborative effort of Agile Teams, architects, engineers, and stakeholders. This can help foster a *culture of innovation* whereby innovation can come from anyone and anywhere.

Though such ideas come from anyone, capturing and propagating them requires some centralization via communication and recording in system intent. One of the responsibilities of the Enterprise Architect is to foster an environment where innovative ideas and technology improvements that emerge at the team level do not pass unnoticed but can be synthesized into the building blocks of the architectural runway. And as Agile can foster the "tyranny of the urgent iteration," programmatic time for innovation should also be built into occasional Innovation and Planning Iterations.

## #7 – Implement Architectural Flow

Enterprise-scale architectural initiatives require coordination across Agile Release Trains and Value Streams. Effective flow of these architectural initiatives is made visible via the Portfolio Kanban. There, program and value stream enabler features and capabilities follow a common work flow pattern of exploration, refinement, analysis, prioritization, and implementation. In addition, the "pull" nature of the Kanban system allows programs to establish capacity management based on WIP limits. This helps avoid overloading the system. Together with the portfolio Kanban, the Program and Value Stream Kanban systems provide a SAFe enterprise content governance model. This instantiates portions of the Economic Framework and helps Decentralize Decision-Making, both of which are vital to a fast, sustainable flow of value.

---

**LEARN MORE**

[1] Leffingwell, Dean. *Agile Software Requirements: Lean Requirements Practices for Teams, Programs, and the Enterprise*. Addison-Wesley, 2011.

[2] Manifesto for Agile Software Development. http://agilemanifesto.org/.

[3] Beck, Kent. *Extreme Programming Explained: Embrace Change*. Addison-Wesley, 2000.

[4] Bain, Scott. *Emergent Design: The Evolutionary Nature of Professional Software Development*. Addison-Wesley, 2008.

[5] Shalloway, Alan, et al. *Essential Skills for the Agile Developer: A Guide to Better Programming and Design*. Addison-Wesley, 2011.

---

[6] Evans, Eric. *Domain-Driven Design: Tackling Complexity in the Heart of Software*. Addison-Wesley, 2003.

[7] Larman, Craig and Bas Vodde. *Practices for Scaling Lean & Agile Development: Large, Multisite, and Offshore Product Development with Large-Scale Scrum*. Addison-Wesley, 2010.

[8] Coplien, James and Gertrud Bjørnvig. *Lean Architecture for Agile Software Development*. Wiley and Sons, 2010.

# Solution Demo

*The objective of the pull event was simple. It was designed to focus the development organization on a tangible event to force completion of a learning cycle with the objective to physically demonstrate it.*

　—Dantar P. Oosterwal

## Abstract

The *Solution Demo* is the apex event of the Program Increment cycle for a Value Stream. This is the event where the results of all the development efforts from multiple Agile Release Trains—along with the contributions from Suppliers and other value stream participants—are made visible to the Customers and other stakeholders. This is the most critical time for a fully integrated, Solution-level demonstration; a time for objective evaluation and stakeholder and Customer feedback. And it is a time to celebrate the accomplishments of the last PI.

It also represents one of the most significant learning points in the history of the value stream; results here will determine the future course of action for a major element of the Enterprise Portfolio.

## Details

The *Solution Demo* is a major event in the life cycle of a Value Stream Solution. This cadence-based event is the time high-profile stakeholders come together to view, via objective evidence, the progress that the solution has made during the past Program Increment. During the event, development teams demonstrate the new Capabilities of the solution, its compliance with Nonfunctional Requirements, and its overall fitness for purpose. Key stakeholders, typically including Solution Management, Architects/ Engineering, and, whenever possible, Customers, participate in the event and provide direct feedback and observations.

The importance of this event cannot be overstated. It is a high-profile event, and the harbinger of near-future value stream and Portfolio investment decisions. It is the only true measure of progress, and the primary mitigator of investment risk for the value stream.

## Solution Demo as a "Pull" Event

As can be inferred from the quote at the top of this article, the solution demo is a purposeful, mandatory, and high-profile "pull" event. It pulls various aspects of the solution together and helps ensure that the Agile Release Trains and Suppliers are creating an integrated and tested solution that is fit for its intended purpose. Thereby, it accelerates the integration, testing, and evaluation of the solution under development—something that is otherwise all too easy to defer until too late in the solution life cycle.

In the portfolio context, Enterprises sometimes create even larger pull events during which several solutions come together for a "road show" of their accomplishments (see [1] for an example). There, senior managers, stakeholders, and portfolio fiduciaries review the progress in the broader portfolio context and make decisions about the continuation or cancellation of initiatives or changes to the budgetary investment in the value streams.

## Overview

### Preparation

Such a critical event requires preparation. This preparation often begins at Pre- and Post-PI Planning, where the results of the most recent System Demos are available. Those results inform those who are staging the demo as to what specific capabilities and other aspects of the solution can be demonstrated. In addition, even though the solution demo may not have a large group of attendees (scope considerations usually prevent most development team members from attending), logistics do matter. Those who do attend are important to the value stream, and some attention to logistics, timing, presentation format, and professionalism enhance the experience. They may even influence the outcome.

### Attendees

Attendees for a solution demo typically include:

- Solution Management
- Value Stream Engineer
- Architects/Engineering
- Customers
- ART representatives, typically Product Management, the System Team, Product Owners, and representatives of the development teams themselves (to experience the Customer feedback firsthand)
- Program Portfolio Management representatives
- Value Stream Level stakeholders, executive sponsors, and senior management
- DevOps

**Event Agenda**

A typical event agenda includes the following actions:

- Review the value stream PI Objectives that were agreed to at the beginning of the PI (10 minutes)

- Demonstrate each objective and capability in an end-to-end use case (30 – 60 minutes total)

- Identify business value completed per objective

- Open the forum for questions and comments

- Wrap up by summarizing progress, feedback, and action items

In the case where multiple solutions are demoed together, the day can be even more interesting. One common format is like a science fair, where each solution has an area to demo progress and allow stakeholders to ask questions and provide feedback. Each solution has a one-hour timebox to demo its accomplishments to a set of specific stakeholders as per the agenda above, but all solutions are constantly available for demo. Members from other solutions and other stakeholders can go to each solution to get a less formal demo and provide informal feedback.

**Guidelines**

Of course there is no one right way to conduct a successful solution demo, but here are a few tips to keep in mind:

- Timebox the demo to *one to two hours*. This is critical to keep the involvement of key stakeholders. It also illustrates professionalism and solution readiness.

- Share demo responsibilities among lead engineers and team members who have new capabilities to demonstrate

- Minimize PowerPoint slides; demonstrate only working, tested capabilities

- Discuss the impact of the current PI on the solution NFRs and Solution Intent

- Demonstrate in the solution context (see below)

**Demonstrate the Solution in Its Solution Context**

The latter bullet is particularly critical, as different solutions may have different degrees of coupling with their Solution Context. In some cases, a solution is largely independent of its environment, and an isolated solution demo may be adequate. However, when the solution is tightly dependent on the solution context (a system of systems, for example), then the isolated approach is inadequate and may even be misleading. In this case, the solution should be demonstrated in an environment that is fully representative of the solution context. When that is not routinely practical, development should plan for some cadence of integration with the larger solution context. However, in that case the real learning only occurs at the lowest integration rate.

## Strategy, Investment, and Timing of Solution Demos

Big systems can be hard to integrate. In order to be able to routinely demonstrate a solution increment, teams must typically invest in integration, testing, and supporting infrastructure. Even then, the extent of integration and testing may be less than 100% and may need to vary across multiple early integration points. To assist, teams can leverage virtualization, environment emulation, mocks, stubs, reduced test suites, etc. In addition, some effort for integration and demonstration, and time to invest in the supporting environment, may need to be explicitly allocated during PI Planning.

As for timing, the solution demo may lag for some time after the last system demos in the PI. However, this creates a delayed feedback loop that increases risk and decreases value stream velocity. Here are some tips for minimizing the lag:

- Plan to demonstrate just a subset of the PI scope. This may require some configuration management enablement to support the partial demonstration.

- Leave room in the Innovation and Planning Iteration for this high-level integration

- ARTs that broaden their areas of responsibility for integration and testing can create more overlap with the subsystems/capability areas of other trains. Thereby, even the individual system demos offer a better approximation of the fully integrated solution demo.

Finally, the solution itself may be designed to better support integration and testing, thereby significantly lowering the demo transaction cost. Standard interfaces and strictly defined APIs and containers for software are among the elements that help teams spot problems and inconsistencies early on, making end-to-end integration and testing of subsystems easier.

---

**LEARN MORE**

[1] Oosterwal, Dantar P. *The Lean Machine: How Harley-Davidson Drove Top-Line Growth and Profitability with Revolutionary Lean Product Development*. Amacom, 2010.

# Pre- and Post-PI Planning

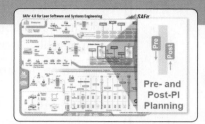

*Apply cadence, synchronize with cross-domain planning.*
—SAFe Principle #7

## Abstract

PI Planning (see the "PI Planning" article) is the critical, cadence-based synchronization point for every Agile Release Train (ART). For multi-ART Value Streams, there are two additional activities, *Pre- and Post-PI Planning*, which are the subject of this article. These additional activities support and coordinate the various ARTs involved in the value stream. Planning at this higher level helps bring alignment to the building of the Solution as a whole and provides direction and visibility into where the solution is going in the next Program Increment (PI).

While the timing and agenda for these meetings may vary based on Solution Context, they typically occur just prior to, and just after, the ART planning sessions. The pre-PI planning meeting is used to set context for the upcoming ART PI planning sessions. Immediately thereafter, value stream stakeholders participate in the ART planning sessions as well. The final meeting of the set is the post-PI planning session, wherein the results of ART planning are integrated into value stream objectives for the upcoming PI, as well as the solution Roadmap.

## Details

### Understand the Pre- and Post-PI Planning Meetings

The *Pre- and Post-PI Planning* meetings allow Agile Release Trains and Suppliers in large Value Streams to build an aligned plan for the next Program Increment (PI). The Pre- and Post-PI Planning meetings serve as a wrapper for the PI Planning meetings at the Program Level, which is where the actual, detailed planning takes place, as can be seen in the Innovation and Planning (IP) Iteration calendar. The pre-PI planning event is used to coordinate input objectives, key Milestones, and Solution Context and business context for the ART planning sessions. The Post-PI Planning event is used to integrate the results of planning into the Vision and Roadmap for the value stream. At the end of the post-PI planning meeting, there should be an agreement on a set of value stream PI Objectives to be implemented by the end of the PI and demoed at the next Solution Demo.

As with PI planning, the Pre- and Post-PI Planning meetings deliver innumerable business benefits:

- Provide for high-bandwidth communication through face-to-face alignment
- Align ARTs to value streams via the ART and value stream PI objectives
- Identify dependencies and foster cross-ART coordination
- Provide the opportunity for "just the right amount" of Solution-level architectural (and, where applicable, User Experience) guidance
- Match solution demand to ART capacities

Another benefit of the process is value stream-wide team building, which helps create the social fabric necessary to achieve high performance. In addition, as planning is based on known velocities, the post-PI planning meeting is a critical step in continuously assessing WIP and in shedding excess WIP whenever necessary.

Inputs to Pre- and Post-PI Planning include the value stream roadmap, vision, Solution Intent, and the top Capabilities from the Value Stream Backlog. Attendees include Customers; value stream stakeholders such as the Value Stream Engineer, Solution Management, Solution Architect/Engineering, solution System Team, and Release Management; and representatives from all the ARTs and Suppliers, usually Product Management, System Architect/Engineering, Release Train Engineers, and engineering managers. Outputs include three primary artifacts:

1. A set of aggregated "SMART" objectives for the value stream
2. A value stream planning board, which highlights the objectives, anticipated delivery dates, and any other relevant milestones for the solution
3. A vote of confidence/commitment to these objectives

This repetitive, "rolling-wave planning" process guides the solution through the inevitable technical obstacles and twists and turns of the business and technology environment.

## Gain Context in the Solution Demo

The solution demo is to the value stream what the System Demo is to the ART, in this case a regular opportunity to evaluate the fully integrated solution. Usually hosted by Solution Engineering, value stream stakeholders (who include Solution Management and the Value Stream Engineer) will typically attend. The learnings from that meeting inform these stakeholders of the current objective assessment of solution progress, performance, and potential fitness for use. While the timing of the solution demo will vary based on value stream and solution context, it provides critical context for the Pre- and Post-PI Planning meetings.

## Prepare for Pre- and Post-PI Planning

The Pre- and Post-PI Planning meetings bring together stakeholders from all parts of the value stream. They require content readiness preparation, coordination, and communication. The actual agendas and timelines listed below are a suggested way to run these meetings, but various value streams adapt these to their own capabilities and locations.

Regardless of how the actual timing and physical logistics are arranged, the various parts of these meetings must happen for a real alignment to be achieved across the trains and Suppliers. It is important to ensure that there is clear vision and context and that the right stakeholders can participate, including:

- The executive briefing – Defines current business, solution, and Customer context
- Value stream vision briefing(s) – Briefings prepared by Solution Management, including the top capabilities in the value stream backlog
- Clear definitions of the upcoming milestones

## Set Planning Context in Pre-PI Planning

The pre-PI planning meeting is used to build the context that allows the ARTs and Suppliers to create their plans. Individual sessions are described below, and a suggested overall agenda is shown in Figure 1.

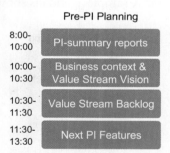

*Figure 1. Example pre-PI planning meeting agenda*

**PI Summary Reports** – Each ART and Supplier presents a brief report of accomplishments of the previous PI. This does not replace the solution demo, but it does provide the context of what has been achieved for the planning process.

**Business and Solution Context** – A senior executive presents a briefing about the current state of the value stream and program portfolio. Solution Management presents the current value stream vision and highlights changes from the previous PI. They will also present the roadmap for the upcoming three PIs, as well as milestones that fall during that period to ensure that they are known and addressed.

**Value Stream Backlog** – Solution Management will review the top capabilities for the upcoming PI. Solution Architect/Engineering will discuss upcoming Enabler Capabilities and Epics.

**Next PI Features** – Each ART's Product Management will present the Program Backlog that they prepared for the upcoming PI and discuss dependencies with other trains

## Value Stream Stakeholders Participate in ART PI Planning

The practical logistics of large value stream planning will be a limiting factor in participation by the value stream stakeholders. However, it is important that key ART stakeholders, particularly including Solution Management, Value Stream Engineer (VSE), and Solution Arch/Eng, participate in as many and as much of the ART PI planning sessions as is feasible. In many cases, ART planning sessions are largely concurrent, and these value stream stakeholders participate by circulating among the ART PI planning sessions during that time. Suppliers and Customers play a critical role as well, and they should be represented in ART PI planning.

## Summarize Results in Post-PI Planning

The post-PI planning meeting occurs after the ARTs have run their respective planning sessions, and it is used to synchronize the ARTs and create the overall solution plan and roadmap. Participants include value stream and key ART stakeholders. A sample agenda is shown in Figure 2; discussion follows.

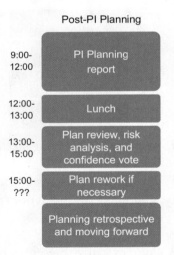

*Figure 2. Example post-PI planning meeting agenda*

**PI Planning Report** – Each ART's Product Management present the plans devised by their individual PI planning meetings, explaining the PI objectives and when each is anticipated to be available. RTEs fill out their ART's row of the value stream board and discuss dependencies with other ARTs or with Suppliers.

**Plan Review, Risk Analysis, and Confidence Vote** – All the participants review the complete plan. During PI planning, ARTs have identified critical risks and impediments that could affect their ability to meet their objectives. Relevant risks are addressed in a broader, value stream context in front of the full group. One by one, risks are categorized into one of the following groups and addressed in a clear, honest, and visible manner:

- Resolved – The group agrees that the issue is no longer a concern

- Owned – The item cannot be resolved in the meeting, so someone takes ownership

- Accepted – Some risks are facts or potential occurrences that simply must be understood and accepted

- Mitigated – The group can identify a plan to mitigate the impact of an item

Once all risks have been addressed, the group votes on its confidence in meeting the value stream PI objectives. The team conducts a "fist of five vote." If the average is three or four fingers, then management should accept the commitment. If the average is fewer than three fingers, then planning adjustments are made and plans are reworked. Any person voting two fingers or fewer should be given time to voice his or her concern, which might add to the list of risks.

**Plan Rework if Necessary** – If necessary, the group reworks its plans as long as it takes for commitment to be reached. This could cascade into follow-up meetings in the ARTs, as teams will need to be involved in any change to the plans.

**Planning Retrospective and Moving Forward** – Finally, the Value Stream Engineer leads a brief meeting retrospective to capture what went well, what didn't, and what could be done better next time. Following this, next steps are discussed, including capturing objectives, use of project management tooling, and finalizing the schedule of upcoming key activities and events.

## Create the Right Outcomes

A successful event delivers three primary artifacts:

1. A set of "SMART" objectives for the value stream, with business value set by Solution Management, Solution Architect/Engineering, and Customers. This may include stretch objectives, which are goals built into the plan but not committed to by the solution. Stretch objectives provide the flexible capacity and scope management options needed to increase reliability and quality of PI execution.

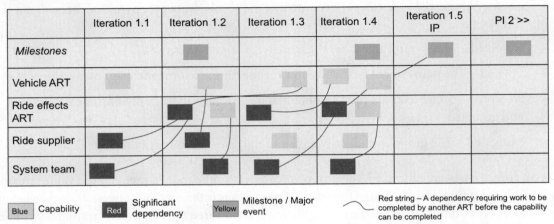

## Baja Ride – Value Stream board – PI 1

| | Iteration 1.1 | Iteration 1.2 | Iteration 1.3 | Iteration 1.4 | Iteration 1.5 IP | PI 2 >> |
|---|---|---|---|---|---|---|
| *Milestones* | | ▉ | | ▉ | ▉ | ▉ |
| Vehicle ART | ▉ | ▉ | ▉ | ▉ | | |
| Ride effects ART | | ▉ ▉ | ▉ | ▉ ▉ | | |
| Ride supplier | ▉ | ▉ | ▉ | | | |
| System team | ▉ | ▉ | ▉ | ▉ | | |

| ▉ Blue | Capability | ▉ Red | Significant dependency | ▉ Yellow | Milestone / Major event | | Red string – A dependency requiring work to be completed by another ART before the capability can be completed |
|---|---|---|---|---|---|---|---|

*Figure 3. Example value stream board*

2. A value stream planning board, which highlights the objectives, anticipated delivery dates, and any other relevant milestones, aggregated from the program boards, as illustrated by Figure 3.

3. A vote of confidence/commitment from the entire group to these objectives.

Thereafter, the value stream roadmap is updated based on the objectives for the planned PI.

# Supplier

*A long-term relationship between purchaser and supplier is necessary for best economy.*

—W. Edwards Deming [1]

## Abstract

Lean-Agile organizations deliver value to their Customers in the shortest possible lead time and with the highest possible quality. Wherever applicable, they engage *Suppliers* to develop and deliver components and subsystems that help them achieve their mission. Suppliers possess unique and distinctively competent skills and Solutions and are experts in their technology; they can provide a high leverage point for fast and economical delivery. Suppliers therefore participate in most Value Streams, and value delivery is very much dependent on their performance.

This article discusses how Suppliers are integrated into the value stream. How this is accomplished is somewhat dependent on the Supplier's own development and delivery methods, but, in any case, the Lean-Agile Enterprise treats Suppliers as long-term business partners and involves them deeply in the value stream. Further, these enterprises actively work with Suppliers to help them adopt Lean-Agile Mindsets and practices. That increases the economic benefit to both parties.

## Details

*Suppliers* play a key role in SAFe. Due to their unique Capabilities and Solutions, they represent significant economic value opportunities. To achieve the overarching goal of delivering value to Customers in the sustainably shortest lead time, Suppliers can have a large impact on lead time and value delivery of the Enterprise's Value Streams.

Suppliers can be external to the enterprise, or they can be other value streams within the organization. But enterprises are well aware that Suppliers have their own mission and their own solutions to deliver to other clients as well, not to mention their own Economic Framework. In order for both organizations to achieve optimal results, close collaboration and *trust* are required.

Historically, however, industries have suffered from the classic approach of dealing with Suppliers by delegating their selection and contracting to purchasing. The focus there is usually more on pricing than on whether or not the Supplier's solutions and services are an optimal fit for the buyer's purpose and culture, both now and in the future. Moreover, it can even be customary to routinely switch Suppliers in search of the lowest price possible, and to resource Suppliers across the globe in the lowest cost venue. Then, after a business secures a Supplier, they are usually held at arm's length and notified of information only on a need-to-know basis. They are often assigned specifications, timelines, and even pricing with little discussion.

The Lean-Agile enterprise takes an entirely different view, one that builds a far more collaborative, long-term, and trusted relationship with Suppliers. These Suppliers become an extension of the culture and ethos of the enterprise; they are treated like true partners. Their capabilities, policies, and economics are surfaced and understood.

However, reaching this state can be a challenge when the Supplier's basic mindset, philosophy, and development approach are materially different from that of the buyer. Generally there are two cases to be considered: one in which the Supplier has embraced and adopted Lean-Agile development, and the other in which they have not. Most typically, the larger enterprise has to address both, but the goal is the same—a more cooperative, long-term, adaptive, and transparent partnership.

## Working with Lean-Agile Suppliers

Involving Lean-Agile Suppliers as contributors to a portfolio value stream is the easier case. The working models and expectations are largely the same, and many current Lean-Agile practices can be simply assumed and extended:

- The Supplier is treated like an Agile Release Train and works in the same cadence as the other ARTs

- The Supplier participates in the PI Planning and Pre- and Post-PI Planning meetings, where they present what they plan to deliver in the next Program Increment, along with an indication of what will be delivered in each Iteration

- The Supplier demos their subsystem or components in the System Demo, participates in the Solution Demo, and continually integrates their work with the rest of the value stream, providing feedback to other trains

- The Supplier participates in Inspect and Adapt, both to improve the value stream as a whole and to help improve their own Lean-Agile practices

In addition to their role as Suppliers and their contribution to the enterprise's value stream, to the Supplier the enterprise is their Customer. That means that they will and should expect routine involvement of their Customer (the enterprise buyer) in their development value stream.

## Working with Suppliers Using Traditional Methodologies

It's a little trickier to work with Suppliers who employ traditional, phase-gated methods for development. It simply isn't reasonable or practical for a Lean-Agile enterprise to assume a Supplier will instantly transform to a Lean-Agile paradigm. After all, some Suppliers are much larger than their Customers, and change is not so easy in the larger enterprise. (However, such an expectation may exist for the longer term.)

Due to differences in working models (for example, larger batch size and non-incremental development), the enterprise may need to adjust its expectations:

- Some initial up-front design time will be needed in the early PIs to allow Suppliers to build their plans and to establish Milestones that they can demo or deliver. The Supplier may expect more formal requirements and specifications.

- The Supplier will likely not deliver incrementally

- Changes to requirements and design need to be understood earlier, and the response time can be expected to be longer

However, some expectations and behaviors can and should be imposed on these Suppliers:

- In the pre-PI planning meeting, Suppliers should indicate the upcoming milestones and their progress toward them

- In the solution demo, the Supplier should present the accomplishment during the PI timebox, even if these are documents and not working systems. They should also provide feedback on the demos of the other trains.

- Involvement in the inspect and adapt workshop is crucial, as many of these Suppliers will have longer learning cycles. They should use this opportunity to raise problems encountered in their working process.

In addition, Suppliers may have limited flexibility in adjusting their plans, and, as a result, other trains will need to be flexible to accommodate the Supplier's needs.

Note: Refer to the Guidance articles "Mixing Agile and Waterfall Development" and "Technical Strategies for Agile and Waterfall Interoperability at Scale" (on www.scaledagileframework.com) for more information on working with Suppliers using traditional methods.

## Applying Systems Thinking and Decentralizing Decision-Making

Since the goal is to improve the value stream as a whole, it's important to Apply Systems Thinking in all levels of decision-making about how and how much to involve Suppliers. The cadence of integration with the Supplier, for example, is impacted by their method of work, but also by the transaction cost of the integration.

Likewise, how far decisions can be decentralized to Suppliers is dependent on Solution Context. For example, if the Supplier is creating a subsystem that interfaces with the solution through well-established standards, it's easier to let them take more control. But if it's a proprietary interface that impacts several other Suppliers and thereby has economies of scale, more negotiation is required. Also, in a highly changing environment, constant collaboration and integration are more important than in environments that are more static.

In addition, setting very specific design requirements might be important in certain contexts but might drive poor outcomes in situations in which capabilities and Nonfunctional Requirements cross several trains. There, an over-specification could cause the Supplier to overinvest in an NFR.

It is important for each value stream to incorporate such thinking into their economic framework and govern their relationship with Suppliers accordingly.

## Collaborating with Suppliers

Collaboration with Suppliers occurs over all levels of SAFe. It starts by sharing strategic themes: "Honda tells the Suppliers what kinds of products it intends to introduce and what types of markets it plans to cultivate in the coming years" [4]. In order for Suppliers to be aligned with the enterprise, it is important that solution developers share with them what they are going to build.

It is also important to make sure they understand the economic framework that the value stream is working under. And it is equally important for the purchaser to understand the economic framework of the Supplier so that win-win relationships can be built: "Toyota uses the term *genchi genbutsu* or *gemba* (actual location and actual parts or materials) to describe the practice of sending executives to see and understand for themselves how Suppliers work" [4].

Collaboration continues by building the requirements together with the Suppliers. Solution Management works with Suppliers continuously and collaboratively to write capabilities and then decompose them into Features. Solution Architects/Engineering work with their Supplier counterparts to design the solution: "At the Toyota Technical Center, the 'design-in' room houses Suppliers who work in the same room on the same project" [4].

The same collaboration should cascade down. Agile Teams develop the actual solution, so it is important to have open communication channels between the Supplier's engineers and the systems builder's engineers to collaborate on the best design, given the constraints of the architecture and the economic framework. As Toyota's Supplier guidelines state, "Automobile manufacturing at Toyota is a joint endeavor with Suppliers and Toyota. To succeed in that endeavor, we and our Suppliers need to work together as a single company. We must maintain close communication, exchanging ideas frankly and coming to terms with each other on all matters of importance" [2].

In order to enable early integration and improve quality, Suppliers and ARTs need to share interfaces, tests, and simulators. All such interfaces should be documented in Solution Intent so that the information is available to everyone.

## Selecting Suppliers

As solutions get more complex, there is a general market shift away from Suppliers that create parts and components and toward Suppliers that create higher-value, integrated systems. Even in industries where Suppliers provide work for hire, there is a shift from hiring individuals to sourcing whole Agile Teams, and even to sourcing entire ARTs.

This makes selecting the *right* Suppliers even more critical. It's a long-term, high-value proposition. To make the right choice, multiple participants from engineering and purchasing will need to be involved in Supplier selection. Since the Lean-Agile organization will generally seek to have fewer Suppliers (but long-term relationships with each), these perspectives can better consider the long-term cultural and method fit of the two organizations.

## Helping Suppliers Improve

It is easier and more productive to work with Lean-Agile Suppliers; they can better fit within the cadence of the enterprise and can better adapt their plans as needed. In addition, trying to improve the value stream without improving supply chains is sub-optimal. To solve these problems, Lean-Agile enterprises work with their Suppliers to improve the Suppliers' processes and results, to the benefit of both companies. "While other automakers devote one day to a week to developing Suppliers, Honda commits 13 weeks to its development program. . . . Honda's Best Practices program has increased suppliers' productivity by about 50 percent, improved quality by 30 percent, and reduced costs by 7 percent. That isn't entirely altruistic; suppliers have to share 50 percent of the cost savings with Honda" [4].

Inviting Suppliers to join inspect and adapt workshops and other relentless improvement activities, as well as sending engineers who are proficient in Lean and Agile to help Suppliers improve their processes, can have a major impact on lead times and costs.

## Agile Contracts

In order to facilitate effective working relationships with Suppliers, it is important to build an environment of trust between the parties. Such trust is hard to build when the contracts governing the relationship assume something entirely different.

Traditional contracts often lead to a suboptimal result. Deming notes, "There is a bear trap in the purchase of goods and services on the basis of price tag that people don't talk about. To run the game of cost-plus in industry, a Supplier offers a bid so low that he is almost sure to get the business.

"He gets it. The Customer discovers that an engineering change is vital. The supplier is very obliging, but 'regrets,' he discovers, that this change will double the cost of the items" [1].

While this is still somewhat common in today's market, it does not optimize the economic benefit for either party. In its place, Lean-Agile buyers and Suppliers collaborate and embrace change, to the benefit of both parties. These relationships are built on trust. Increasingly, these relationships can be built via Agile Contracts, which provide a better way of working. This isn't new, as Toyota notes: "Contracts governing the relationships are ambiguous, consisting of general statements and nonbinding targets" [3].

---

### LEARN MORE

[1] Deming, W. Edwards. *Out of the Crisis*. MIT Center for Advanced Educational Services. 1982.

[2] http://www.toyota-global.com/sustainability/society/partners/supplier_csr_en.pdf.

[3] Aoki, Katsuki and Thomas Taro Lennerfors. "New, Improved Keiretsu." *Harvard Business Review*. September 2013.

[4] Liker, Jeffrey and Thomas Y. Choi. "Building Deep Supplier Relationships." *Harvard Business Review*. December 2004.

# Customer

*There is only one boss. The customer. And he can fire everybody in the company from the chairman on down, simply by spending his money somewhere else.*

—Sam Walton, Walmart founder

*Get closer than ever to your customer.*

—Steve Jobs

## Abstract

*Customers* are the ultimate economic buyer of every solution. In a globally competitive world, Customers—whether or internal or external—are increasingly demanding. They have choices. They want more value and they want it quickly. They expect solutions to work well and to solve their current needs. They also expect their solution providers to continuously improve the quality of their products and services.

Moreover, *engaged* Customers are integral to Lean-Agile Solution development. They are part of the Value Stream. They are inseparable from the process. They work frequently and closely with Solution and Product Management, and other key stakeholders, to shape the Solution Intent, Vision, and the Economic Framework in which development occurs. They have a strong influence in defining and prioritizing the solution's development and are active participants in solution planning, demos, and process improvement.

## Details

*Customers* are an integral part of Lean-Agile development and play a critical role in SAFe. They are part of the Value Stream. Their support for Lean and Agile principles and their active and continuous participation in the Solution definition, planning, demonstrations, and evolution are essential to successful execution.

In some cases, the Customer is internal (example: an IT shop delivering a supply chain application to the business). In others, the Customer is external and is the buyer of a custom-built offering by the systems builder (example: government purchasing a commercial or defense system). In still others, the Customer is a more remote third party, one of a larger class of economic buyers. There, the systems builder must understand the aggregate and synthesize requirements of the general case, craft solutions that fill the broader market needs, and provide an adequate internal proxy for much of development (example: an independent software vendor selling a suite of products).

## Summary of Responsibilities

No matter the type, Customers must be engaged continuously throughout Agile solution development. They participate either in person or by proxy to fulfill the following general responsibilities:

- Participate as Business Owner in PI Planning

- Attend Solution and possibly System Demo; help evaluate the solution increment

- Participate in Inspect and Adapt workshops; assist in removing some systemic impediments

- Interact with analysts and subject matter experts during specification workshops

- Collaboratively manage scope, time, and other constraints with Product and Solution Management

- Help define the Roadmap, Milestones, and Releases

- Communicate the economic logic behind the solution and help validate assumptions in the Economic Framework

- Review technical and financial status of the solution

- Participate in beta testing, UAT, other forms of solution validation

## The Customer Is Part of the Value Stream

The Lean-Agile Mindset spans beyond the development organization to encompass the entire value stream, which includes the Customer. The type of the value stream determines the context for interaction:

1. In the case of internal IT, the internal Customer is part of the operational value stream, as Figure 1 illustrates.

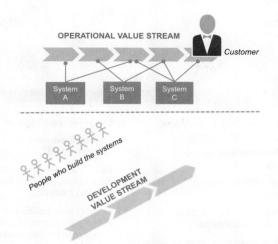

*Figure 1. The internal Customer*

An example would be a marketing director who has responsibility for a partner enrollment work flow (the operational value stream). The partner is the ultimate end user of the work flow and is the Customer, but to the development team, the marketing director and those who operate the value stream are the Customer.

2.  In the case of those who build solutions for an external end user, the Customer is the direct economic buyer of the solution, as Figure 2 illustrates.

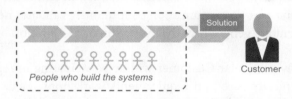

*Figure 2. External Customers are direct economic buyers*

In this case, the development value stream and the operational value stream are the same. The solution can be a final product that is sold or deployed directly, or it may need to be embedded into a broader Solution Context, such as a system of systems, to make it operational.

## Customer Engagement Drives Agile Success

Lean-Agile development is dependent on a high degree of Customer engagement, much higher than our former stage-gated models assumed. However, the means of engagement are different, based on whether the solution builder is building a *general solution*—one that can be used by or sold to a significant number of Customers—or whether the solution is a *custom built solution*—one that is built specifically for an individual Customer to their specifications. Figure 3 illustrates the relative level of indirect or direct Customer engagement in each case.

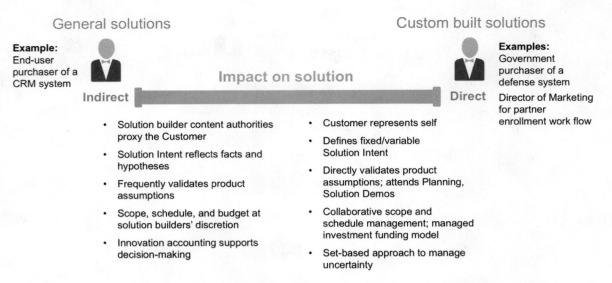

Figure 3. *Customer engagement models in general and custom-built solutions*

## General Solutions

On the left side, solution builders build systems that must address the needs of a larger audience. No one Customer can be assumed to be an adequate proxy for the market as a whole. In this case, Product and Solution Management serves as the indirect Customer proxy, and they have the authority over solution content. It is their responsibility to facilitate external interaction and make sure that the voice of the Customer will be heard, and that the organization continuously validates new ideas. Scope, schedule, and budget for development are generally at the discretion of the solution builder.

Since it is unlikely that any particular Customer will be participating in regular planning and demo sessions, interaction is typically based on requirements workshops, focus groups, usability testing, innovation accounting, limited beta releases, etc. By applying user behavior analysis, measures, and business intelligence to validate the various hypotheses, the solution evolves based on this feedback. During PI planning, a group of internal and external stakeholders acts as the Business Owners, the ultimate internal Customer proxy within a specific value stream.

## Custom-Built Solutions

On the right side of Figure 3, the Customer is typically "in charge." Such Customers define the solution and represent themselves. Product and Solution Management interact with the Customer and provide daily development support. However, even though the Customer is in charge, it is critical to establish a collaborative approach to scope and prioritization, both to foster incremental learning and to exhibit a willingness to adjust the course of action as facts dictate.

Active participation in PI planning, the Solution Demo, and selected specification workshops is required. This will often reveal inconsistencies in requirements and design assumptions, with potential contractual ramifications. This process should drive the Customer and solution builder toward a more collaborative and incremental approach.

Demonstrating results of the Program Increment to the Customer—in the form of a fully integrated solution increment—establishes a high degree of trust ("these teams can really deliver") and also provides Customers with the opportunity to empirically validate the current course of action. Forecasting ability, based on the measured predictability and velocity of the Agile Release Trains, is significantly improved.

Transition toward an Agile contract model will also help reduce the win-lose aspects of traditional relationships between systems builder and Customer. One such model is the SAFe managed investment model, whereby the Customer commits the funding for a PI or two, then adjusts funding based on objective evidence and incremental deliveries. This requires a fair bit of trust going in, but thereafter trust is built incrementally, based on a continuous flow of value received.

## LEARN MORE

[1] Ward, Allen and Durward Sobek. *Lean Product and Process Development.* Lean Enterprise Institute, 2014.

# Solution

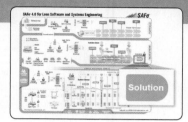

*Click. Boom. Amazing!*
   —*Steve Jobs*

## Abstract

All the words, pages, links, roles, activities, and artifacts in SAFe live for only one purpose: to help teams continuously deliver *Solutions* that provide value to the Customer. That, in turn, enables them to achieve their goals, which is the ultimate purpose of the endeavor.

However, even when teams and trains apply SAFe guidance and operate effectively within their areas of concern, value is not ensured. Customers do not buy Capabilities, Features, or components. Rather, they buy *solutions* that provide desirable business outcomes. For that reason, a solution is one of the central concepts in SAFe, and one that requires *taking a systems view* on value delivery.

## Details

Developing an effective *Solution*—one that is fit for its intended purpose—is the larger purpose of SAFe. As described in the "Value Streams" article, a solution is either a final product delivered to the ultimate economic buyer or, alternately, a set of systems that enables an operational value stream within the organization. In either case the work is largely the same: to determine the end user's needs and to reliably, efficiently, and continuously produce a flow of value to that end user. That is the process of solution development and the subject of all the roles, activities, and artifacts in SAFe.

### Overview of Solution Development in SAFe

Solution development is the entire subject of the Value Stream Level in SAFe, and that is the primary perspective of this article. Solution development involves a number of core practices and objects of SAFe, as Figure 1 illustrates.

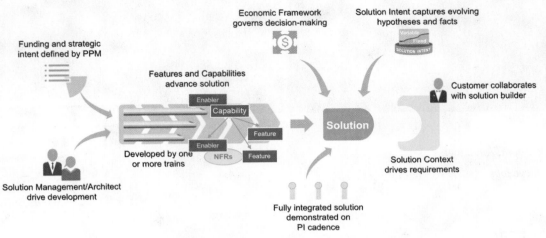

*Figure 1. Overview of solution development*

Every solution is delivered by a value stream, which is realized by the people on one or more Agile Release Trains. ARTs operate synchronously and build the solution in increments, which are fully integrated and evaluable via the Solution Demo, which occurs at every Program Increment at least. Solution Intent captures the goal of the solution and allows for exploring and defining fixed and variable requirements and designs, which are in part derived from the Solution Context. The Customer interacts with the solution builder to clarify the intent, validate assumptions, and review progress. Solution Management and Architects help drive development, make scope and priority decisions, and manage the flow of Features and Capabilities and Nonfunctional Requirements.

Governance is provided in part by the Economic Framework, which encompasses relevant economic decision rules that govern the logic around the solution. Value Stream budgeting and strategic themes provide additional boundaries and inputs.

Developing an economically viable solution requires a holistic approach to definition, planning, implementation, and review of the solution, as is further described below.

## Effective Solution Development Requires Systems Thinking

Principle #2 – *Apply systems thinking* guides the organization to adopt a systems view and to apply scalable and emergent practices around value definition, architecture, development practices, and process improvement. Many elements of the framework facilitate this, as described in the sections below.

### Solution Capabilities, Enablers, and NFRs

Capabilities are the end-to-end solution services that support the achievement of user goals. Capabilities are implemented via vertical, end-to-end slices of value, which enable incremental solution development. Enablers provide for exploration of new capabilities, contribute to solution infrastructure and architecture, and enhance NFRs. This drives early value delivery and architectural robustness.

### Solution Intent

Solution intent drives and captures a holistic view of the solution and includes different aspects that govern value definition, including structural, behavioral, functional, and other views. Model-Based Systems Engineering provides an effective way of reasoning about the solution and also serves as an efficient communication tool for sharing this knowledge. SAFe's fixed-variable solution intent paradigm enables value streams to enhance solution intent based on the objective knowledge that emerges over the course of many learning cycles.

### Customer and Solution Context

Taking a systems view helps ensure that the solution builder understands the solution context, the broader ecosystem in which the solution operates. Solution context provides the additional pieces that determine operational requirements and constraints.

And of course, Customers are part of the value stream. They participate in defining solution intent and solution context, and they help validate assumptions and fitness for use.

### Solution Integration, Testing, and Demo

Solution development is effective only when stakeholders and teams frequently evaluate integrated increments of the entire solution. While Solution Demonstration occurs on a fixed PI cadence, Continuous Integration and testing happen more frequently—whenever applicable, in fact. In order to progress on this objective, solution builders continuously enhance their integration and testing practices, configuration management, automation, and virtualization.

### Building an Economically Viable Solution

Building a complex solution requires informed, effective decision-making. The trade-offs of the Economic Framework help guide solution development. In addition, a continuous exploration process that includes learning Milestones, Customer feedback loops, and Set-Based Design informs and streamlines the learning process by validating good options and eliminating less viable ones.

## Managing Multiple Solutions in the Portfolio

Each SAFe Portfolio contains multiple value streams. Many are largely independent, while others may have a number of crosscutting concerns and dependencies, as is illustrated in Figure 2.

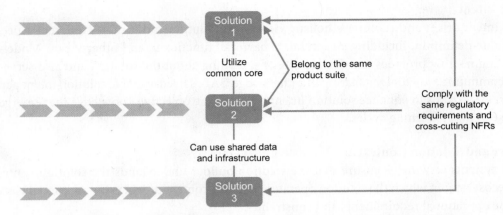

*Figure 2. An example of crosscutting solution concerns in a portfolio*

Sometimes these crosscutting concerns provide enhanced capabilities that provide strategy differentiation. At other times, they are just dependencies that must be addressed as part of the solution offering. When this is the case, Coordination across value streams is required.

# Solution Context

*Context is the key—from that comes the understanding of everything.*

—Kenneth Noland

## Abstract

The *Solution Context* identifies critical aspects of the target Solution environment and its impact on usage, installation, operating, support, and even marketing, packaging, and selling. Understanding solution context is critical to value delivery; it impacts development priorities, Capabilities, Features, and Nonfunctional Requirements, and it sets the focus for DevOps and other solution-level functions.

The solution context is often driven by factors that are outside of the control of the organization that develops the solution. The level of coupling between the solution and its context generally represents an architectural and business challenge of finding the fine balance between flexibility and interaction with the environment—an interaction that often crosses internal, Supplier, and Customer organizational boundaries.

## Details

Rarely do systems builders build systems for themselves; they build them for other people. This means that systems builders do not typically control, nor deeply understand, the context for deployment and use. Rather, a system is shipped, deployed, installed, and maintained in an environment that is unlike that in which it was developed. Even in the case of internal IT systems, newly developed systems are typically hosted by the IT maintenance and operations teams. There, for many reasons, the production environment is not the same as the development environment. In both cases, the *Solution Context* is integral to the solution efficacy. This adds risk to the process; an understanding of that context is required.

Understanding and aligning the Value Stream's Solution and Solution Intent with the solution context requires continuous interaction with the Customer stakeholders. They understand the Vision and have the requisite decision-making authority with respect to solution context. As Figure 1 illustrates, collaboration is required; its level depends heavily on the level of coupling between the solution and its environment.

*Figure 1. Solution intent and solution context inform each other*

To ensure this alignment, the Customer should participate in the Pre- and Post-PI Planning meetings and Solution Demos as frequently as possible. And the Customer should regularly integrate the solution in their context. This regular cadence of interaction and integration allows for building solution increments based on correct assumptions and provides validation of the result within the Customer's environment. Both sides play a role in adapting the context to achieve the best economic result (see the "Economic Framework" article).

## Solution Context Drives the Solution Intent

The Customer's context drives requirements and constrains design and implementation decisions that are described in the solution intent. Many of these contextual requirements are nonnegotiable and may render the solution unusable if not included. These requirements fall under the "fixed" category of the solution intent. Many aspects of the solution context surface as Non-Functional Requirements (NFRs) and need to be included as part of the Definition of Done for a solution Increment.

The solution context may also stipulate specific content that the solution intent must address. In a hierarchical system of systems, the system intents may also be hierarchically dependent (see the "System of Systems Intent" section in the "Solution Intent" article). The system context defines how the systems builder's system intent must be organized, packaged, and integrated for use by the Customer to meet any compliance, certification, and other objectives.

## Fixed vs. Evolving Solution Contexts

Some solution contexts are established Customer environments that the solution must simply "fit into" ("This is the way our system works; you have to fit in right here"). In that case, all solution context requirements are imposed on the solution via solution intent.

However, in many cases new solutions may require evolution of the Customer's deployment environment. In that case, the systems builders play an active role in tracking those changes, as both the system and deployment environment have to evolve to a common state. In this latter case, fixed vs. variable thinking and the preservation of options via multiple potentially viable solution contexts (see the "Moving from Variable to Fixed Solution Intent" section in "Solution Intent" article) are tools to manage risk. Simply, a more variable and evolving solution context requires more continuous collaboration.

## Types of Solution Contexts

Systems builders use the solution context to understand how their system will be packaged and deployed in its ultimate operating environment. Examples of solution contexts might include environments such as:

- System of systems (e.g., avionics system as part of the aircraft), product suite (word processor as part of an office suite)

- IT deployment environments (e.g., cloud environment where the solution is deployed)

There are other contexts as well, and combinations are also possible.

### Solution Context for a System of Systems

The solution Supplier-to-Customer relationship in large system-of-systems contexts is a unique and cascading thing, as Figure 2 shows.

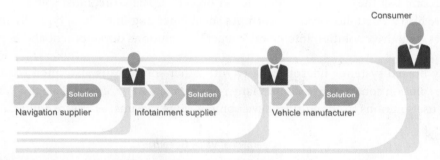

*Figure 2. Solution contexts wrap in a system of systems*

Each organization in the supply chain delivers its solution to the Customer's context, which specifies how the solution is packaged, deployed, and integrated. That Customer, in turn, provides a solution in context to their Customer, and so on. In Figure 2, for example, a vehicle navigation system Supplier operates first, in the infotainment Supplier's contexts, then in the vehicle manufacturer's context, and finally in the consumer's context. All of these contexts have the ability to impact viability of the solution, so the systems builder must be aware of the full end-to-end value chain.

### Solution Context for IT Deployment Environments

When developing software solutions for internal use, the Customer may be internal, but delivering solutions into the production environment still requires context. Deployment must consider specific interfaces, deployed OSs, firewalls, APIs to other applications, hosted or cloud infrastructure, etc., as Figure 3 shows.

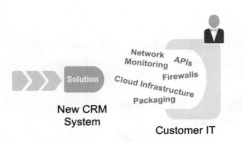

*Figure 3. Solution context for internal IT deployment*

In this example, the new CRM system should reflect the required interfaces, as well as how the application is packaged, released, hosted, and managed in the end environment.

**Solution Context Includes Portfolio-Level Concerns**

There is one final consideration. Generally, the products and services of an Enterprise must work together to accomplish the systems builder's larger objective. Therefore, most solutions do not stand alone; they are also a Portfolio Level concern. As such, emerging initiatives, typically in the form of portfolio Epics, also drive solution intent and impact the solution's development and deployment.

For internally hosted systems, interoperability with other solutions is also often required, further extending the solution context. For example, larger *Operational Value Streams* (see the "Value Streams" article) often use solutions from multiple development value streams, as Figure 4 illustrates.

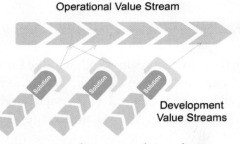

*Figure 4. Solutions work together to support the full operational value stream*

Each of those subject solutions must collaborate and integrate with the others, to provide the operational value stream with a seamless, end-to-end solution.

## Continuous Collaboration Ensures Deployability

Ensuring that a solution will operate correctly in its context requires continuous feedback. Solution builders need feedback that their solution will work properly in the deployed environment (see the "DevOps" article).

Cadence-based development frequently integrates the entire system-of-systems value stream to demonstrate progress toward the top-level context's Milestone and Release commitments. Continuous collaboration helps ensure that the solution can be deployed in the ultimate Customer's context:

- The Customer raises and discusses context issues during PI planning and solution demos
- Solution Management and the Customer continually ensure that the Vision, solution intent, Roadmap, and Value Stream Backlog align with the solution context
- Issues discovered in the Customer's context run through the Value Stream Kanban system for impact and resolution
- Systems builders and the Customer share relevant context knowledge, environment, and infrastructure, such as interface mock-ups, test and integration environments, test and deployment scripts, etc.
- Solution Architect/Engineering ensures technical alignment with solution context— interfaces, constraints, etc.

Consequently, there are many collaboration points between the systems builder and the various roles within the Customer organization. A number of SAFe roles carry that responsibility along with their Customer counterparts, as shown in Figure 5.

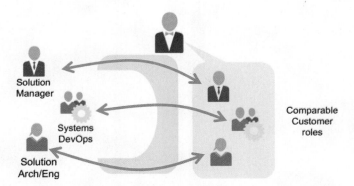

*Figure 5. Systems builder role collaboration with Customer roles*

Thereby, effective Customer/systems builder collaboration helps ensure that the system meets the Customers' needs, in *their* context.

# Part 7
# The Portfolio Level

[ scaledagileframework.com/**portfolio-level**

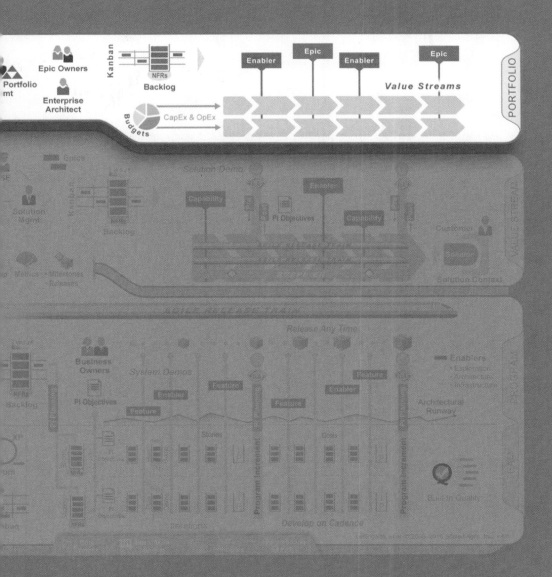

# Introduction to the Portfolio Level

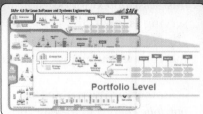

*To succeed in the long term, focus on the middle term.*
    —Geoffrey Moore

## Abstract

The SAFe *Portfolio* is the highest level of concern in SAFe. It provides the basic constructs for organizing the Lean-Agile Enterprise around the flow of value via one or more Value Streams, each of which develops the systems and Solutions necessary to meet the strategic intent. The portfolio level encapsulates these elements and also provides the basic budgeting and other governance mechanisms that are necessary to ensure that the investment in the value streams provides the returns necessary for the enterprise to meet its strategic objectives.

The portfolio has a bidirectional connection to the business. One direction provides the strategic themes that guide the portfolio to the larger, and changing, business objectives. The other direction indicates a constant flow of portfolio context back to the enterprise. This apprises the enterprise of the current state of the solution set, as well as key performance indicators and other business factors affecting the portfolio. Program Portfolio Management represents the stakeholders who are accountable to deliver the business results. Other significant roles, activities, and artifacts complete the picture.

In the large enterprise, there may be multiple such portfolios. This article describes, in summary form, the basic workings of a SAFe portfolio.

## Details

The SAFe *Portfolio Level* encapsulates the people and processes necessary to build systems and solutions that the Enterprise needs to meet its strategic objectives. The primary elements of the portfolio are Value Streams (one or more), each of which provides funding for the people and other resources necessary to build the Solutions that deliver the value. Each value stream is a long-lived series of system definition, development, and deployment steps used to build and deploy systems that provide a continuous flow of value to the business or Customer.

## Key Concepts

### Connection to the Enterprise

The portfolio has a bidirectional connection to the enterprise. Strategic Themes provide specific, itemized business objectives that connect the portfolio to the evolving enterprise business strategy. They provide business context for decision-making within the portfolio, affecting investments in value streams and serving as inputs to the Portfolio, solution, and Program Backlogs. However, strategic themes are not created by the business in isolation. Rather, key portfolio stakeholders participate in that process and thereby are among the cornerstones of strategy formation.

The other direction of the arrow, from the portfolio to the enterprise, indicates the constant feedback of *portfolio context* to the enterprise. This includes key performance indicators (KPIs) as well as qualitative assessments of the current solution's fitness for market purpose, along with any strengths, weaknesses, opportunities, and threats that are present at the portfolio level.

### Program Portfolio Management

Activities at the portfolio level and governance for the portfolio investment are provided for by Program Portfolio Management (PPM). PPM represents the highest-level fiduciary (investment and return) and content (what gets built) authority in the framework. There, the responsibilities for *strategy and investment funding, program management,* and *governance* rest with those business managers and executives who understand the enterprise business strategy, technology, and financial constraints and define and implement the portfolio solution strategy. They are typically assisted in these duties by a Program Management Office (PMO), which shares responsibility for guiding program execution and governance.

One of the primary PPM responsibilities is the allocation of investment funding to the value streams. Budgets are developed and administered with a Lean-Agile budgeting approach, *Beyond Project Cost Accounting*, which provides for fast and empowered decision-making, with appropriate fiduciary control. Each "partition" in the pie-shaped graphic represents a budget for a specific value stream. Within that budget allocation, value stream managers are generally empowered to develop solutions in whatever ways make the most economic and business sense. With this process, the enterprise exercises its fiduciary responsibility by driving investment to the agreed-to business priorities.

### Managing the Flow of Portfolio Epics

Another responsibility of the portfolio level is the discovery, definition, and administration of major initiatives that are required by the business but are crosscutting in nature. Business Epics capture and reflect the new business capabilities that can only be provided by cooperation among value streams. Epic Enablers reflect the architectural and other technical initiatives that are necessary to enable the new Capabilities.

To manage this flow of work, and to make sure it is visible to all stakeholders, SAFe provides a Portfolio Kanban system. The Kanban system makes the work visible and provides work-in-process limits to help ensure that demand is metered to the actual value stream capacities.

The portfolio backlog is the highest-level backlog in the framework, and it serves as a holding stage for epics that make it through the Kanban systems and await implementation. It contains the approved and prioritized epics necessary to help the portfolio achieve market differentiation, operational efficiencies, or better-integrated solutions. Epic Owners take the responsibility for managing epics, at least until implementation is ensured.

The Enterprise Architect has significant portfolio duties as well. This role has the requisite knowledge to work across value streams and programs and help provide strategic technical direction that can optimize portfolio outcomes. Aspects of this strategy can include recommendations for epic enablers that harmonize development and delivery technology stacks, interoperability of solutions, APIs, and hosting strategies. The Enterprise Architect often may act as an Epic Owner for enabler epics.

---

**LEARN MORE**

[1] Leffingwell, Dean. *Agile Software Requirements: Lean Requirements Practices for Teams, Programs, and the Portfolio.* Addison-Wesley, 2011.

# Enterprise

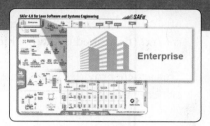

*A strategic inflection point is that moment when some combination of technological innovation, market evolution, and customer perception requires the company to make a radical shift or die.*

—Andy Grove, *Only the Paranoid Survive*

## Abstract

Each SAFe portfolio contains a set of Value Streams and the additional constructs necessary to provide funding and governance for the products, services, and Solutions that the *Enterprise* needs to fulfill some element of the business strategy. In the small to mid-size enterprise, one SAFe portfolio can typically be used to govern the entire technical solution set. In the larger enterprise (typically those with more than 500 – 1,000 technical practitioners), there can be multiple SAFe portfolios, one for each line of business:

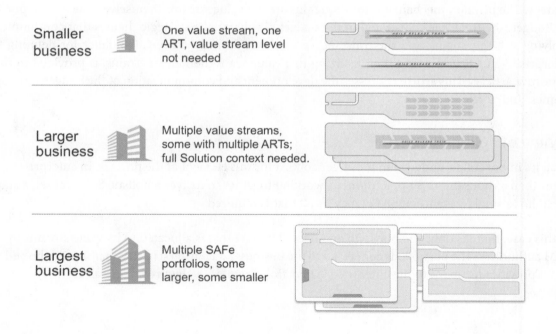

| | |
|---|---|
| **Smaller business** | One value stream, one ART, value stream level not needed |
| **Larger business** | Multiple value streams, some with multiple ARTs; full Solution context needed. |
| **Largest business** | Multiple SAFe portfolios, some larger, some smaller |

In either case, the portfolio is *not* the entire business, and it is important to ensure that the portfolio solution set evolves to meet the needs of the enterprise. SAFe provides three primary constructs for connecting the enterprise strategy to a portfolio. The first is *Budget*, i.e., the total funding provided to the portfolio for operating and capital expense. That provides the investment envelope in which the portfolio must operate. The second is a set of *Strategic Themes* that communicate certain aspects of strategic intent from the enterprise to the portfolio. The third is the constant feedback of *portfolio context* (described below), which provides governance and informs ongoing strategy formulation.

This article provides some general guidance by which the enterprise can define and communicate this critical information.

# Details

The SAFe Portfolio Level represents the highest level of concerns articulated in SAFe. Each program portfolio consists primarily of a set of Value Streams that deliver value. The portfolio level describes the constructs necessary—Lean-Agile budgeting, Program Portfolio Management (PPM), Portfolio Kanban system, Portfolio Backlog, Epics, and more—to govern portfolio investments and to guide the portfolio to the business objectives.

However, each portfolio exists for a single reason—that is, to fulfill its contribution toward realizing the overall *Enterprise* strategy. This is accomplished by aligning each portfolio's vision to the enterprise strategy. The primary mechanisms for doing this are the value streams themselves, the overall portfolio Budget (the total "pie" illustrated in the budget pie chart), the strategic themes that communicate evolving strategic intent, and the constant feedback via *portfolio context*. Guidance for defining the enterprise Value Streams, and then realizing this value via Agile Release Trains, is provided in their respective articles. This article addresses the development and communication of the budgets, strategic themes, and portfolio context.

## A View of a Single Enterprise SAFe Portfolio

First, it's important to understand the larger context for this element of the process. In enterprises with fewer than a thousand or so practitioners, working together to deliver a holistic Solution set, a single portfolio (a single instance of SAFe) may be all that is required.

In this case, there is only one portfolio and overall budget that is allocated to its value streams by the PPM authorities. The portfolio is connected to the business strategy by strategic themes and the budget, and it provides feedback to the enterprise via portfolio context, as Figure 1 illustrates.

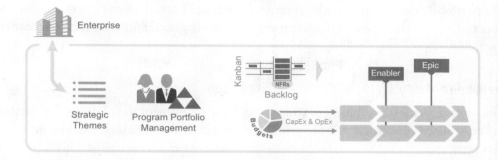

*Figure 1. Enterprise view of a single portfolio*

## Large Enterprises Will Have Multiple Instances of SAFe

However, SAFe is being successfully applied by many of the world's largest system and software builders. Many of these enterprises have thousands, and even tens of thousands, of IT, system, application, and solution development practitioners. (Some have more than 100,000.)

Of course, these practitioners are not all working on the same solutions, nor within the same value streams. More typically, IT and development are organized in support of the various lines of business, internal departments, Customer segments, or other business purposes. Most commonly, these business units have fewer than one thousand practitioners (though some have far more), each responsible for one SAFe portfolio.

To achieve the larger purpose, the enterprise will have multiple SAFe portfolios, each with its own budget and strategic themes, which reflect that unit's portion of the business strategy, as Figure 2 illustrates.

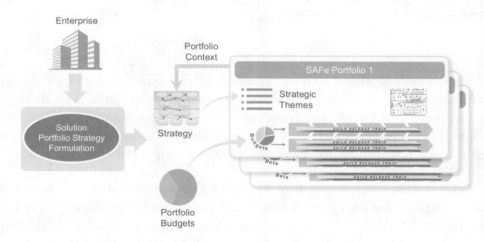

*Figure 2. Enterprise view of multiple SAFe portfolios*

Each SAFe portfolio exists in this broader enterprise context. That is the source of the business strategy that the portfolio must address, and it also provides the more general funding and governance model for all portfolios.

## Enterprise Strategy Drives Portfolio Strategy

Development of the enterprise business strategy, and the investment in solutions that enable it, is a somewhat centralized concern, as it is the primary responsibility of the executives and fiduciaries who have direct accountability for overall business performance. After all, portfolios don't form themselves or fund themselves; they exist solely to fulfill the larger enterprise purpose.

## Portfolio Context Informs Enterprise Strategy

However, strategy has emergent properties. It must also be based on the current business context, which, in turn, depends on the challenges and opportunities that exist in the current solution set, and in the local market conditions they address. To that end, development of strategy requires continuous collaboration, communication, and alignment—with and from—the downstream portfolios. In other words, it requires full and complete awareness of the portfolio context, which can include:

- **Key Performance Indicators (KPIs)** – It's incumbent on the portfolio to provide appropriate feedback on the allocated investment spend. This can include quantitative and financial measures, such as ROI, market share, Customer net promoter score, innovation accounting [2], and more.

- **Qualitative data** – Qualitative data can include Strengths, Weaknesses, Opportunities, and Threats (SWOT) analysis; and, most important, the accumulated solution, market, and business knowledge of the portfolio stakeholders. Any strategy that does not take this into account will be suboptimal.

## Strategy Formulation

Defining the portfolio budget and strategic themes is an exercise in strategy formulation (see the "Strategic Themes" article). Extensive collaboration is required. Philosophies of approach to strategy formulation are very broad. Current trends and influences in the tech sector include Geoffrey Moore's series of books [1] and *The Lean Startup* [2]. There are a variety of more specific strategy formulation approaches in vogue as well, including the Business Model Canvas, Lean Canvas [4], and more.

One such effective formulation is described in *Beyond Entrepreneurship* [3], by James Collins and William Lazier. The output of this process is a set of strategic themes that provide an ongoing "snapshot" of the enterprise strategy that communicates evolving strategic intent, as well as a budget, to the portfolio.

Figure 3 highlights the main aspects of that approach when adapted to the SAFe context; each aspect is discussed briefly in the sections below.

*Figure 3. Solution portfolio strategy formulation*

**Total Enterprise Budget and Investment in Program Portfolio** – Within the scope of the total operating budget (or allocation of people and other resources), a budgetary allocation is established for all technical solutions across all SAFe portfolios. In some cases, it may also provide guidelines for capital and operating expenses (see the "CapEx and OpEx" article).

**Enterprise Business Drivers** – Enterprise business drivers reflect the evolving enterprise strategy. Since the current business and solution portfolio context is largely understood, there is no need to repeat the obvious; these should reflect changes from current strategy. For example, business drivers such as "integrate the capabilities of the new acquisition into the suite" (a security company) and "move applications to the cloud" have been observed.

**Financial Goals** – The financial performance goals for the business should be clear, whether measured in revenue, profitability, market share, or other measures. Some of those financial elements will also be communicated to the portfolio.

**Mission, Vision, Core Values** – A clear and unifying mission, vision, and set of core values provide constancy of purpose and act as boundaries for strategy formulation.

**Competitive Environment** – Competitive analysis will help identify the largest threats and areas of opportunity.

**Portfolio Context and Distinctive Competence** – The best strategies are formed in the midst of full and complete portfolio context. This can be provided by the KPIs, SWOT analysis, and more. But strategic differentiation emphasizes what the enterprise is really good at, the business and technical DNA that brought the enterprise to its current place of success.

In accordance with Figure 3, portfolio budgets and strategic themes are an output of a process, one whereby the business fiduciaries and other stakeholders systematically analyze a set of inputs before arriving at conclusions, which in this case are the respective portfolio budgets and the strategic themes for each.

## Decentralize Execution

In accordance with SAFe Principle #9 – *Decentralize decision-making*, the formulation of business strategy is largely a centralized but collaborative concern, in which the business fiduciaries and key portfolio stakeholders play a central role. Execution of solution strategy, however, is decentralized to the portfolio and is supported by transparency, constant feedback, KPIs, and appropriate portfolio Metrics. Only these people have the local knowledge necessary to define, evolve, and budget for value streams and ARTs, to apply the Economic Framework, and to manage the development of the solutions necessary to address changing Customer needs and new market opportunities.

---

**LEARN MORE**

[1] Moore, Geoffrey. *Crossing the Chasm* (1991, 2014), *Inside the Tornado* (1995 and 2004), and *Escape Velocity* (2011). Harper Business Essentials.

[2] Ries, Eric. *The Lean Startup: How Today's Entrepreneurs Use Continuous Innovation to Create Radically Successful Businesses.* Random House, 2011.

[3] Collins, James and Lazier, William. *Beyond Entrepreneurship: Turning Your Business into a Great and Enduring Company.* Prentice Hall, 1992.

[4] Maurya, Ash. *Running Lean: Iterate from Plan A to a Plan That Works.* O'Reilly Media, 2012.

# Strategic Themes

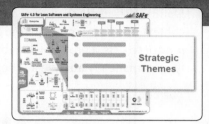

*Innovation distinguishes between a leader and a follower.*

—Steve Jobs

## Abstract

*Strategic Themes* are specific, itemized business objectives that connect a SAFe portfolio to the evolving Enterprise business strategy. They provide business context for decision-making within the portfolio and influence investments in Value Streams and serve as inputs to the Economic Framework, Budgets, Portfolio, Solution, and Program Backlog decisions.

Strategic themes need not restate the obvious, as most elements of a portfolio vision are understood by context; portfolio stakeholders generally know quite well what the portfolio is for, and they establish and manage their own mission and Visions. Rather, strategic themes provide the enterprise with the *differentiators* going forward from the current state to a future state. They help drive innovation and competitive differentiation that is achievable only via effective portfolio solutions. Strategic themes are best created as a result of a structured and collaborative strategic planning process—one that involves enterprise executives and fiduciaries as well as key stakeholders from each portfolio.

## Details

*Strategic Themes* are business objectives that provide strategic differentiators that highlight changes to the Enterprise strategy that affect a particular Solution portfolio. They provide one of the major communication protocols between the enterprise and its solution portfolios, as highlighted in Figure 1.

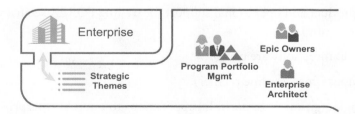

*Figure 1. Strategic themes connect a SAFe portfolio to the broader enterprise context*

Each solution portfolio plays a part in achieving the enterprise business strategy, is allocated a Budget for that purpose, and the portfolio Vision is guided, in part, by its strategic themes.

## Formulating Strategic Themes

Defining strategic themes is an exercise in strategy formulation, but in the individual SAFe portfolio context. In accordance with the guidance from the enterprise, strategic themes are an *output of a collaborative process*, a process whereby the enterprise portfolio stakeholders work with portfolio stakeholders to systematically analyze a set of inputs before arriving at conclusions, as is illustrated by Figure 2.

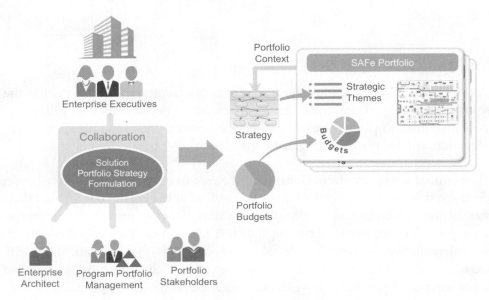

*Figure 2. Strategic themes collaboration*

Inputs to that process typically include the business mission, financial objectives and constraints, competitive environment, portfolio context, and more. (This is described further in "Enterprise.")

Some examples of strategic themes are:

- Appeal to a younger demographic (online retailer)

- Implement product and operational support for trading FOREX securities (securities company)

- Standardize on three software platforms

- Lower warehouse costs (online retailer)

- Establish single sign-on from portfolio applications to internal enterprise apps (independent software vendor)

Strategic themes are an important tool for communicating strategy to the entire portfolio. They provide a simple, memorable reference frame and should permeate the thinking of everyone involved in solution delivery.

## Strategic Themes Influence the Portfolio Vision

Strategic themes are primary inputs to the portfolio vision and serve as elements of the Economic Framework, affecting Value Streams and Agile Release Train budgets, the Portfolio Backlog, and individual ART Vision and Roadmap, as is illustrated in Figure 3.

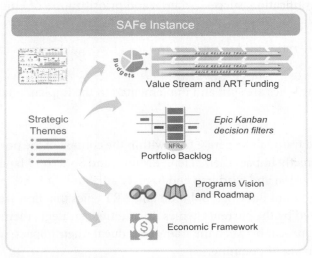

*Figure 3. Influence of strategic themes*

Each of these aspects is described below.

**Economic Framework**
Strategic themes may have a significant impact on the economic framework, where they can affect any of the major parameters, including development/cycle time, product cost, product value, development expense, and risk.

**Value Streams**
Strategic themes heavily influence value stream budgets, which provide the spending and personnel allocations necessary to accomplish the portfolio vision. In making these allocations, these questions should be considered:

- Do the current investments in value streams, and ARTs within the value streams, reflect the changes to the current business context?

- Are we investing the appropriate amounts in a) new products and services, b) extension of the capabilities of current products and services, and c) maintenance and support activities?

- What adjustments should be made given these new strategic themes?

**Portfolio Backlog**

Strategic themes provide decision-making filters in the Portfolio Kanban system, thereby influencing the portfolio backlog. Alignment to strategic themes:

- Impacts the identification, success criteria, and prioritization of Epics in the funnel and backlog states

- Warrants consideration and discussion in the lightweight business case in the analysis state

- May impact how Epics are split and implemented in the implementation state

**Vision and Priorities**

Lastly, value streams and trains also operate fully within the context of the portfolio vision, so evolving strategic themes may directly impact them. Here, Product and Solution Management applies strategic themes to influence the vision and roadmap and to drive attributes of WSJF prioritization for items in the Value Stream and Program Backlogs. Solution and ART epics that flow from the portfolio, or arise locally, are also influenced by the current themes. In addition, strategic themes provide an important means of conceptual alignment between the trains and, due to their impact, will often be presented by the Business Owners during PI Planning.

## Measuring Progress Against Strategic Themes

Strategic themes communicate differentiated strategic intent for the enterprise. Providing *success criteria* for strategic themes can provide a mechanism for understanding progress toward the intent. However, many desirable measures associated with the accomplishment of strategic intent are *trailing indicators*. Success factors such as ROI, new markets penetrated, etc., can take a long time to achieve. In their place, the enterprise needs feedback via early indicators, many of which are not financial in nature. Lean enterprises apply *innovation accounting* [1] to address this challenge. Innovation accounting is a thoughtful look at what early indicators are likely to produce the desired long-term results, followed by implementing the tooling, functionality, testing, or other mechanisms to collect that data.

In addition, certain success criteria can be investment or activity based. For example, an online retail store might want to "reach a younger demographic." In this case, success criteria could be a mix of investments, activities, and early indicators. A first learning Milestone might simply be to test the hypothesis of whether extending online capabilities to mobile platforms would appeal to the target audience; this could perhaps be measured simply with initial feedback from focus groups. Based on that, a second step might be to increase the budget for the mobile teams.

In parallel, a User Experience-oriented Epic could be used to capture the age of the user across all purchasing points, in order to start trending the data.

Strategic Theme success criteria provide learning milestones that allow the portfolio to understand the solutions involved, validate business and technical hypotheses, and, where necessary, pivot toward a better solution. The PI cadence offers an excellent timebox for experimenting with new approaches and gathering the feedback needed to show that investments in new strategic themes are likely to produce the desired, long-term results.

## LEARN MORE

[1] Ries, Eric. *The Lean Startup: How Today's Entrepreneurs Use Continuous Innovation to Create Radically Successful Businesses*. Crown Business, 2011.

# Program Portfolio Management

*Management is efficiency in climbing the ladder of success; leadership determines whether the ladder is leaning against the right wall.*

—Stephen Covey

## Abstract

*Program Portfolio Management* (PPM) represents the people who have the highest-level strategy and fiduciary decision-making responsibility in the framework. In larger Enterprises, there will be multiple SAFe portfolios, each helping to manage a set of initiatives, typically at the business unit or departmental level. Each SAFe portfolio has a PPM function, where the responsibilities for *Strategy and Investment Funding, Program Management,* and *Governance* rest with those business managers and executives who understand the enterprise business strategy, technology, and financial constraints and have the ultimate responsibility for defining and implementing their portion of the overall enterprise strategy. They are often assisted in these duties by a Project or Program Management Office (PMO), which shares responsibility for guiding program execution and governance.

Enterprises may use different titles and roles to fulfill these functions, or perhaps there are no official names or departments for some; nevertheless, effective fulfillment of the responsibilities is necessary for success.

## Details

*Program Portfolio Management* represents those individuals who have the primary responsibility for *Strategy and Investment Funding, Program Management,* and *Governance* within a specific SAFe portfolio, as illustrated in Figure 1.

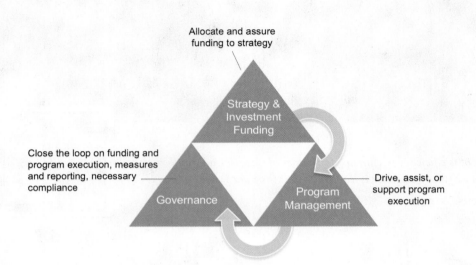

*Figure 1. Primary responsibilities of Program Portfolio Management*

Organizations may use different titles and roles to fulfill these responsibilities or there may not be an official department for PPM. What we call this group or the roles within it is a secondary concern; however, effective fulfillment of the responsibilities is necessary for success.

## Responsibilities of Program Portfolio Management

PPM has the responsibility to participate in the establishment and communication of the strategic themes that guide the Enterprise's investments and strategy, determine the relevant Value Streams and allocate Budgets to them, define and prioritize crosscutting Portfolio Backlog Epics, and report to the business on investment spend and progress via Key Performance Indicators (KPIs) and other aspects of *portfolio context* (for more on portfolio context, see "Enterprise").

During the transition to Lean-Agile, the PPM function may need to fulfill these responsibilities for both Agile and traditional waterfall programs, as Figure 2 illustrates.

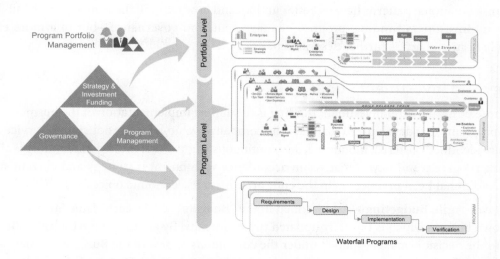

*Figure 2. PPM responsibilities may need to cover both Agile and waterfall programs*

## Lean-Agile Program Portfolio Management

Effective fulfillment of these responsibilities is a prerequisite for business success. However, historical use of the waterfall model, coupled with the somewhat natural inclination to institute top-down control over software development, has caused the industry to adopt certain behaviors and mindsets that can seriously inhibit the adoption of more effective Lean and Agile paradigms. These legacy mindsets, such as "widget engineering," "maximize utilization," and "just get it done," are discussed at length in [1] and [2].

SAFe describes a set of seven *transformational patterns* that can be used to move the organization to *Lean-Agile Program Portfolio Management*, as illustrated in Figure 3.

| From Traditional Approach | To Lean-Agile Approach |
|---|---|
| #1 Centralized control | Decentralized decision-making |
| #2 Project overload | Demand management; continuous value flow |
| #3 Detailed project plans | Lightweight, epic-only business cases |
| #4 Centralized annual planning | Decentralized, rolling-wave planning |
| #5 Work breakdown structure | Agile estimating and planning |
| #6 Project-based funding and control | Lean-Agile budgeting and self-managing Agile Release Trains |
| #7 Waterfall milestones | Objective, fact-based measures and milestones |

*Figure 3. Seven transformational patterns for Lean-Agile Program Portfolio Management*

These transformational patterns help us better understand how to fulfill the primary responsibilities—strategy and investment funding, program management, and governance—but in a more effective Lean-Agile fashion. Each is further described below.

## Strategy and Investment Funding

The purpose of strategy and investment funding is to support implementation of the business strategy through programs that develop and maintain the company's value-added products and services. Value streams are identified, fostered, monitored, and continuously improved. Investment funding is allocated to ongoing programs and new initiatives in accordance with business strategy and current strategic themes. Additional Lean practices help the enterprise meet its economic objectives:

- **Lean-Agile Budgeting** – As described in the "Budgets" article, each Value Stream has its own budget, which is typically updated twice annually. By allocating the budget authority to the decision-makers—albeit under the continuous review of the Business Owners— it is no longer necessary to establish a "project" for each new initiative. This avoids overhead and enables the train to make fast and local decisions as needed, within the constraints of the allocated budget. Due to their large scope, epics still require some level of PPM approval and oversight.

- **Demand Management and Continuous Value Flow** – Overloading any system decreases throughput. If demand isn't managed at the portfolio level, the invisible killer of "too much WIP" will limit velocity and quality as teams and individuals thrash from initiative to initiative. Bringing visibility to existing program work and understating Agile program velocities helps manage WIP and ensure efficient product development flow. This is managed and supported by implementation of the Portfolio Kanban system and maintenance and visibility of the portfolio backlog.

- **Epics and Lightweight Business Cases** – In order to provide visibility and economic justification for upcoming, crosscutting work, epics are defined and analyzed, each supported by a lightweight business case. Developed by Epic Owners, lightweight business cases provide for reasoning, analysis, and prioritization while avoiding over-specificity.

## Program Management

Program management supports and guides successful program execution. While this responsibility lies primarily within the Agile Release Trains and the Value Stream Engineers (VSEs) and Release Train Engineer (RTE), the PPM function can help develop, harvest, and apply successful program execution patterns across the portfolio. In many organizations, the VSEs and RTE are part of the PMO, where they can share best practices and common program measures and reporting. In other cases, they report into the development organization.

However, in either case, as compared to traditional organizations, Agile program management delegates many of the traditional functions, including:

- **Self-Managing Agile Release Trains** – Traditional project and program chartering and management activities are replaced by value stream-based, self-managing, and self-organizing Agile Release Trains, each of which provides a continuous flow of value to its stakeholders.

- **Decentralized, Rolling-Wave Planning** – Centralized planning is replaced with decentralized, program, and team-based rolling-wave planning, via the routine, cadence-based PI Planning activity.

- **Agile Estimating and Planning** – The formerly too-detailed business cases, too-early requirements specificity, and too-detailed work breakdown structures are replaced with Agile estimating and planning, using the currency of Story points, applied consistently through the team, program, value stream, and portfolio.

## Governance

Governance functions still exist in Agile, otherwise there would be no portfolio-level feedback on investment spend, nor program reporting, nor any means to assuredly communicate and validate important security, regulatory, standards, quality, and Release requirements. Governance can be looked at in terms of providing portfolio context and life-cycle governance.

**Portfolio Context**

Portfolio context includes:

- **Key Performance Indicators** – KPIs can include quantitative and financial measures, such as ROI, market share, Customer net promoter score, innovation accounting, and more. Many additional, portfolio, value stream, and program metrics are described in the "Metrics" article.

- **Qualitative Data** – Qualitative data can include Strengths, Weaknesses, Opportunities, and Threats (SWOT) analysis, and, most importantly, the accumulated solution, market, and business knowledge of the portfolio stakeholders.

**Life-Cycle Governance**

The guidance of SAFe Principles (namely, Principle #4 – *Build incrementally with fast, integrated learning cycles* and Principle #5 – *Base milestones on objective evaluation of working systems*), along with support from PPM, should encourage and facilitate incremental development and fast Customer feedback. In place of traditional milestones, Agile Milestones include Program Increments and incremental Releases, as illustrated in Figure 4.

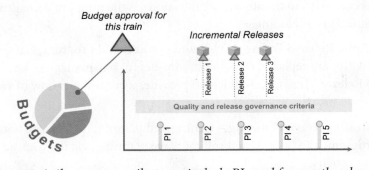

*Figure 4. Agile program milestones include PIs and frequently releasable solutions*

By far the most meaningful internal milestones are the above releases and cadence-based PIs, with continuous improvement facilitated by quantitative metrics, Customer feedback, and the Inspect and Adapt retrospective cycle.

**LEARN MORE**

[1] Leffingwell, Dean. *Agile Software Requirements: Lean Requirements Practices for Teams, Programs, and the Enterprise.* Addison-Wesley, 2011.

[2] Thomas, Joseph and Steven Baker. "Establishing an Agile Portfolio to Align IT Investments with Business Needs." DTE Energy, 2008.

# Epic Owners

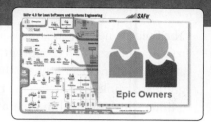

*To be in hell is to drift; to be in heaven is to steer.*
  —George Bernard Shaw

## Abstract

In SAFe, Epics drive much of the economic value for the Enterprise. Epics are containers for significant initiatives that are large and typically crosscutting, crossing multiple Value Streams and ARTs. They are investment intensive and far ranging in impact. To this end, the formulation and analysis of cost, impact, and opportunity of an epic are serious matters. To this end, epics require a lightweight business case and financial approval before implementation.

Due to their scope, implementing them is no small feat either, as they must be parsed into smaller chunks (e.g., Value Stream, Program Epics, or Capabilities, Features, etc.) and make their way into the backlogs of each affected release train.

To address this, we describe the role of the *Epic Owner*, which is a role, not a title. It falls to those who take the responsibility of shepherding a Portfolio Epic through the Portfolio Kanban system, developing the business case, and, when the epic is approved, working directly with the key stakeholders on the affected value streams to help realize the implementation.

## Details

### Summary Role Description

The *Epic Owner* is responsible for driving individual Epics from identification through the analysis process of the Portfolio Kanban system and on to the "go" / "no-go" decision-making process of Program Portfolio Management. When the epic is accepted for implementation, the Epic Owner works with the Agile Release Train development teams and Product Management to initiate the development activities necessary to realize the business benefits of the epic. Once successfully initiated, the Epic Owner may have some ongoing responsibilities for stewardship and follow-up.

Perhaps more likely, as the Features and Capabilities that define the epics are eventually incorporated into Program Backlogs for routine incorporation into the Solution (refer to the "Epics" and "Enablers" articles for discussion of splitting epics), the Epic Owner can return to other duties or take responsibility for additional emerging epics. Thereafter, implementation can be safely assumed, as the ARTs have the full responsibility for solution delivery, including the new elements.

The Epic Owner *role* in SAFe is just that—a responsibility assumed by an individual—not a job title. The role may be assumed by a program manager, Product Manager, project manager, Enterprise Architect, architect or engineer at the Value Stream or even Program Levels, business analyst, or any other program stakeholder suited to the responsibility. Typically, an Epic Owner works with one or two epics at a time, which fall within their area of expertise and current business mission.

## Responsibilities

The Epic Owner has the responsibilities outlined in the paragraphs below.

### Prior to Approval: Preparing the Epic

The Epic Owner's responsibilities begin early in the life cycle of the epic:

- Work with stakeholders and subject matter experts to define the epic and its potential benefits, establish the cost of delay, and identify business sponsors
- Work with development teams to size the epic and provide input for economic prioritization based on WSJF
- Define epic success criteria
- Shepherd the epics through the Portfolio Kanban system and create the lightweight business case [1]
- Prepare to present the business case to Program Portfolio Management for a "go" / "no-go" decision

### Presenting the Epic

The Epic Owner has the primary responsibility for presenting the merits of the epic to Program Portfolio Management. However, approval should *not* be ensured, as most every software enterprise has opportunities far exceeding capacity. An effective winnowing process may well determine the marketplace winners and losers. That is one of the many reasons the business cases are *lightweight*, so as to not create too great an emotional investment on the part of those responsible for analysis. Specific potential epics can and should be rejected in lieu of more favorable opportunities. [1]

### After Approval: Implementation

If the epic is approved, then the implementation work begins:

- Work with Product Management and Solution Management to split the epic into Value Stream and/or Program Epics and Features and prioritize them in the backlogs

- Provide guidance to the release train on the epic context of the target features

- Participate in PI Planning, System Demo, and Solution Demo whenever there is critical activity related to the epic

- Work with Agile Teams that perform research spikes and create proof of concepts, mock-ups, etc.

- Coordinate and synchronize epic-related activities with functions in sales, marketing, and other business units

- Understand and report on progress of the epic with key stakeholders

## The Collaborative Nature of the Epic Owner Role

An Epic Owner can only be effective through close collaboration with other groups in the Enterprise. They help fill in the gaps that often occur in organizations when high-level initiatives descend from the top of the organization to implementation. Key participants in the collaboration are highlighted in Figure 1.

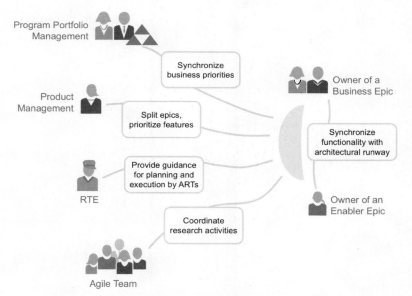

*Figure 1. The collaborative nature of the Epic Owner role*

Ensuring the holistic vision, appropriate economic prioritization, and consistency of epic-driven features is achievable only through close work with these key stakeholders.

---

**LEARN MORE**

[1] Leffingwell, Dean. *Agile Software Requirements: Lean Requirements Practices for Teams, Programs, and the Enterprise.* Addison-Wesley, 2011.

---

# Enterprise Architect

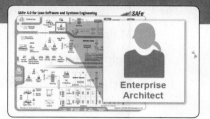

*All men can see these tactics whereby I conquer, but what none can see is
the strategy out of which victory is evolved.*

—*Sun Tzu*

## Abstract

In systems of Enterprise scale, poor strategic technical planning, communication, and visibility can
cause poor overall business systems performance, making significant redesign of multiple systems
necessary. Poor economics and poor business systems performance are likely results. To prevent this,
enterprise-class systems are well served by having some amount of intentional Architectural Runway
built into their larger systems, and the larger system of systems, to support current and near-term
business needs. In addition, some architectural governance—for example, to drive common usability
and system behavioral constructs across the enterprise's Solutions—is beneficial. To address parts of
this problem, SAFe highlights the role of System and Solution Architects in providing much of this
guidance at the Program and Value Stream Levels.

At the Portfolio Level, the challenge is even larger. Mergers and acquisitions, changes in underlying
technologies, emerging standards, competitive changes, and other factors often drive enterprises in
directions that are outside the purview of Agile programs. Enter the SAFe *Enterprise Architect* as a
responsible authority with the requisite knowledge to work across value streams and programs and help
provide strategic technical direction that can optimize enterprise outcomes. Aspects of this strategy
can include recommendations for development and delivery technology stacks, interprogram system
collaboration, interoperability of solutions, APIs, and hosting strategies. These strategies are most
effective when Enterprise Architects foster incremental implementation while maintaining a solid
connection to the team's work.

## Details

### Summary Role Description

The *Enterprise Architect* works with business stakeholders and Solution and System Architects to drive
holistic technology implementation across Value Streams.

The Enterprise Architect relies on continuous feedback, fosters adaptive design and engineering practices, and drives collaboration of programs and teams around a common technical vision.

## Responsibilities

The Enterprise Architect is focused primarily on the following responsibilities:

- Maintain a high-level, holistic vision of Enterprise Solutions and development initiatives
- Help define key technical initiatives that support Budgets via Enabler Epics
- Participate in the strategy for building and maintaining the enterprise Architectural Runway
- Understand and communicate strategic themes and other key business drivers for architecture to System Architects and nontechnical stakeholders
- Drive architectural initiatives in the Portfolio Kanban system and participate in Epic analysis where applicable
- Influence common modeling, design, and coding practices
- Collect, generate, and analyze innovative ideas and technologies that are applicable across the enterprise
- Facilitate the reuse of ideas, components, and proven patterns
- Synchronize the following across solutions whenever applicable:
  - System and data security and quality
  - Production infrastructure
  - Solution User Experience governance
  - Scalability, performance, and other NFRs

## Enterprise Architecture Strategy

The enterprise's ability to embrace organizational change is a key competitive advantage, and the *Enterprise Architectural strategy* is a principal constituent. Figure 1 illustrates five key aspects of such a strategy.

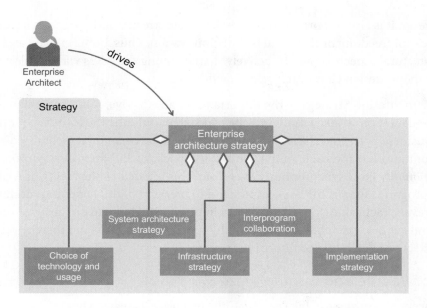

*Figure 1. Five elements of enterprise architecture strategy*

1. **Choice of technology** – The choice of technologies that will best support current Budgets is one key element of the strategy. Supporting activities include research and prototyping, understanding applicability and scope, and assessing maturity of innovative new technologies.

2. **System/Solution Architecture Strategy** – The Enterprise Architect works closely with Solution and System Architects to ensure that individual program and product strategies align with enterprise objectives. Emergent solutions to local problems should be consistent with the strategy. When that is not the case, the decision should be made explicitly, and the contraindicator may well influence enterprise strategy.

3. **Development and Deployment Infrastructure Strategy** – Development and deployment infrastructure is unnoticed when it fulfills its function properly. However, the strategy for building and maintaining the infrastructure is a key challenge, one that overlaps with System Architect responsibilities. Some of these include the reuse of configuration patterns, common physical infrastructure, knowledge sharing between value streams, Agile Release Trains (ARTs), and—especially—System Teams. In addition, some of the development and deployment infrastructure will likely overlap with internal IT systems, and the Enterprise Architect can help provide direction there as well.

4. **Interprogram Collaboration** – Various and differing aspects of architecture work happen in different teams and programs. Thus it is helpful to ensure that common technology, common design practices, and common infrastructure are used where applicable.

However, it is also important to ensure that value streams and programs have sufficient degrees of freedom, or there will be little innovation. Thus, both *common* and *variable* architectural aspects should be actively shared among the ARTs via joint design workshops, design Communities of Practice, etc.

5. **Implementation Strategy** – The importance of an effective, Agile, incremental implementation strategy can hardly be overstated. Building the technical foundation for Business Epics into the architectural runway must be an incremental process based on continuous technical learning and fast feedback, such that *architecture and business functionality* grow synchronously over time. This is aided by the ability of Agile Teams and programs to refactor as necessary and to preserve multiple possible design options wherever practical. Achievement comes in part through the use of abstraction and generalization, which helps avoid binding specificity too early and thereby preserves architectural flexibility for future business needs.

## Respect for People and Gemba Kaizen

The Lean concept of *"Go and see"* (aka *gemba*—"the real place") creates a healthy environment in which everyone operates on facts, not assumptions. This is particularly important for Enterprise Architects, who operate one (or two!) steps removed from day-to-day development activities. Thus the Enterprise Architect is well served by maintaining personal connections to each value stream, ART, and architect at these levels; receiving feedback on current enterprise-wide initiatives; participating in value stream or program-level design CoPs; and attending demos whenever critical redesign or foundation work is in process. Developers and testers will *better trust the strategy* that is driven by a person who knows their current challenges and context. In the same way, the Enterprise Architect will better trust the teams that provide full visibility of current context.

---

**LEARN MORE**

[1] Leffingwell, Dean. *Agile Software Requirements: Lean Requirements Practices for Teams, Programs, and the Enterprise.* Addison-Wesley, 2011.

[2] Bloomberg, Jason. *The Agile Architecture Revolution.* Wiley, 2013.

[3] Coplien, James and Gertrud Bjørnvig. *Lean Architecture for Agile Software Development.* Wiley, 2010.

# Portfolio Kanban

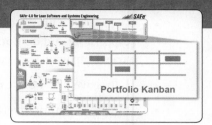

*I urge everyone—no matter how big their portfolio—to truly understand every suggestion they're given before acting.*

   —*Suze Orman*

## Abstract

SAFe suggests the development and implementation of Kanban systems throughout the content hierarchy—Portfolio, Value Stream, Program, and Team. While these Kanban systems operate in a similar manner, and they interoperate, they are largely separate systems, they serve separate purposes, and they operate at different levels of abstraction. This article summarizes the implementation of the highest-level such system, the *Portfolio Kanban* system for Epics. This system controls much of the economics of the portfolio.

Implementation and management of the portfolio Kanban system is under the auspices of Program Portfolio Management. Implementing such a system requires a material understanding of Lean and Agile development practices as applied to Portfolio Level practices. It also requires an understanding of the productive capacity of each Agile Release Train, the velocity of each, and the availability of each for new developments and business-as-usual support activities. When these are understood, the Enterprise can start to reason about portfolio level initiatives in a logical and pragmatic way, with full knowledge of the actual implementation context.

## Details

The SAFe Portfolio management Kanban system is used primarily to address the flow of Epics, those large, crosscutting initiatives that affect the course of action for Value Streams and the Agile Release Trains (ARTs) that realize them. Therefore the capture, analysis, approval, and release of epics into implementation is a material decision for the portfolio, one that requires participation of a number of key stakeholders, including Program Portfolio Management (PPM), and representation from the affected value streams and ARTs.

SAFe applies a *Portfolio Kanban* system in this context for a number of reasons:

- Make the strategic business initiative backlog fully visible

- Bring structure and visibility to the analysis and decision-making that moves these initiatives into implementation

- Provide WIP limits to ensure that the teams responsible for analysis undertake it responsibly and do not create expectations for implementation or time frames that far exceed capacity and reality

- Help drive collaboration among the key stakeholders in the business

- Provide a quantitative, transparent basis for economic decision-making for these, the most important business decisions

## A Kanban System for Epics

All Kanban systems are designed for a specific purpose; this one is made to capture, analyze, approve, and track epics. This particular system might appear as depicted in Figure 1 below.

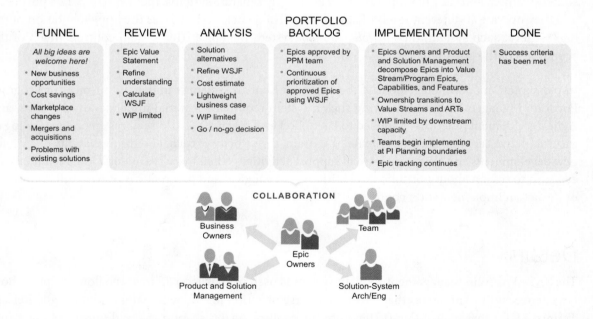

*Figure 1. Portfolio Kanban system and typical collaborators*

This portfolio Kanban system describes a number of stages that an epic passes through on the way to implementation (or rejection), and the collaboration that is required for each stage:

1. **Funnel** – This is the capture state, where all new "big" ideas are welcome.

2. **Review** – In this stage the preliminary estimates of opportunity, effort, and cost of delay are established.

3. **Analysis** – This is where the more thorough work is done to establish viability, measurable benefit, development and deployment impact, and potential availability of resources. A lightweight business case is developed. The epic is approved or rejected at the end of this state.

4. **Portfolio Backlog** – Epics that have made it through the portfolio Kanban with "go" approval wait in the Portfolio Backlog until capacity is available.

5. **Implementation** – When capacity becomes available, epics are transitioned to the relevant Program and Value Stream Kanbans, where implementation begins. Epics can subsequently be tracked at the portfolio level using the reports described in Metrics.

6. **Done** – The epic is done when it has met its success criteria.

Note: Because all Kanban systems are purpose-built, designing and implementing them is an evolving process within the context of each. In addition, such systems have additional mechanisms, such as capacity allocation in support of business epics versus Enablers, classes of service for work of various types based on cost of delay, use of swim lanes, methods for analyzing flow and seeing bottlenecks, adjusting WIP limits, and more. Such discussions are outside the scope of this article and may be found in the Guidance article "Improving Flow with Kanban".

## Description of the System

**1. Funnel**

The Funnel queue is the "capture" queue, where all new "big ideas" are welcome. They can come from any source; they may be business or technical concerns. Typical drivers include:

- The portfolio strategic themes
- Unanticipated changes in the marketplace, business acquisitions, mergers, emergence of new competitors, etc.
- The need for substantive Solution cost savings or operational efficiencies
- Problems with existing solutions that hinder business performance

In this queue, epics need no business case or estimates. Epics can be stated in any format, typically as just a short keyword or phrase, such as "Self-service for all auto loans." Tooling is trivial—a document, spreadsheet, or, better, a visual system on the wall will typically suffice. Since the investment of effort on items in this queue is minor, the queue is not WIP-limited. All ideas are captured for consideration. Funnel epics are discussed on a periodic cadence established by Program Portfolio Management. Epics that meet the decision criteria are promoted to the Review queue.

## 2. Review

Epics that reach the Review queue warrant further investment of time. In this queue, epics are roughly sized and some estimate of value is established. Time investment is controlled to the discussion level, with perhaps some very preliminary investigation. The epic will be elaborated in the Epic Value Statement format (see the "Epics" article). Since the investment is increasing, this queue is WIP-limited to curtail the number of active items in process. Sources of business benefit are identified and items are prioritized using WSJF. Epics that rise to the top are pulled into the Analysis queue as soon as space is available.

## 3. Analysis

Epics that make it into this queue deserve a more rigorous analysis and require further investment. An Epic Owner takes responsibility for the ongoing work. An active collaboration is initiated among the Enterprise Architects, System Architects, Agile Teams, Product and Solution Management, and key stakeholders on the potentially affected Agile Release Trains. Solution, design, and implementation alternatives are explored. Options for internal development and/or outsourcing are considered. A lightweight business case, with a "go" / "no-go" recommendation, is developed.

Items in this queue use scarce resources and, more important, imply a substantial upcoming investment. Therefore the capacity of the business analysts and of the development teams and Enterprise Architects, as well as the desired throughput rates for all items in this queue, combine to limit it according to WIP considerations. Promotion from Analysis to the portfolio backlog queue is an important economic decision for the Enterprise that can be made only by the appropriate authority, based on the developed business case. Epics that meet the "go" criteria are promoted to the portfolio backlog queue.

## 4. Portfolio Backlog

Items that have reached the portfolio backlog state have received a "go" decision from the appropriate authority, usually some subset of Program Portfolio Management. These epics are reviewed on a periodic basis (see below), and this queue represents a low-cost holding pattern for upcoming implementation work. Epics from this queue are promoted to the Implementing queue when there is sufficient capacity from one or more value streams or Agile Release Trains.

## 5. Implementation

As capacity becomes available, epics are pulled into the relevant value stream and program Kanbans, where they usually undergo further analysis. They are split into Capabilities and Features, and acceptance criteria are established. When ready, these new capabilities and features are presented at relevant PI Planning boundaries, including the Pre-PI Planning events in larger value streams. Actual implementation by the development teams then begins. The evolution of the solution in regular Program Increments (PIs) offers an excellent vantage point for objective evaluation of progress. Epics can be tracked to completion via appropriate metrics.

While the responsibility for implementation rests with the development teams, Epic Owners remain available on a "pull" basis and share responsibility until the teams have achieved a sufficient understanding of the work.

**6. Done**

The epic is considered done when it has meet all of its success criteria. However, due to the scope of epics, "completion to original intent" is not always the desired case, so it's likely that some identified capabilities and features are eventually discarded. In either case, the epic reaches a done state, and this marks the exit timing for the Cumulative Flow Diagram, if applied at this level.

## Driving the Portfolio Work Flow with the PI Cadence

Many PPM teams use epic "review and specification workshops" to advance epics from left to right in the system. Such workshops typically involve portfolio stakeholders and content and technical authorities from the value stream or ART level. Together, the team reasons about the implications of solution strategies, identifies ways to split epics into epics/capabilities/features at the lower levels, and makes the decisions necessary to move an epic forward to the next state, hold it where it is, or reject it from the system. During this process, epics are validated against strategic themes and moved from Funnel to Review, and from Review to Analysis as WSJF and other data suggest. The lightweight business case is developed and reviewed. Finally a "go" / "no-go" decision is reached. Approved epics then move to the portfolio backlog where they await implementation capacity.

These workshops may or may not occur on a cadence, though cadence is preferred. However, the timing of implementation is driven by the cadence of the affected value streams and ARTs, so they must occur frequently enough to be able to provide input to each value stream/ART ahead of their target PI planning processes.

**LEARN MORE**

[1] SAFe Guidance article, "Improving Flow with Kanban."

[2] Leffingwell, Dean. *Agile Software Requirements: Lean Requirements Practices for Teams, Programs, and the Enterprise*. Addison-Wesley, 2011.

[3] Anderson, David. *Kanban: Successful Evolutionary Change for Your Technology Business*. Blue Hole Press, 2010.

# Portfolio Backlog

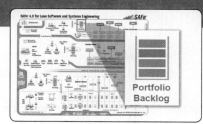

*Innovation comes from the producer, not the customer.*
 —W. Edwards Deming

## Abstract

The *Portfolio Backlog* is the highest-level backlog in SAFe. It provides a holding mechanism for the upcoming Business and Enabler Epics required to create a holistic *portfolio* solution set that provides the competitive differentiation and/or operational efficiencies necessary to address the strategic themes and facilitate business success.

Epics that make it to the portfolio backlog have made their way through the Portfolio Kanban system, where they have been reviewed, analyzed, and approved for implementation. Epics are estimated in the analysis step. Estimating, in turn, supports the need for portfolio level forecasting, which gives the Enterprise a sense of the future sufficient enough to support effective planning and execution.

## Details

The *Portfolio Backlog* holds and prioritizes Epics that have been approved for implementation. These epics have made it through the Portfolio Kanban system with "go" approval, as is illustrated in Figure 1.

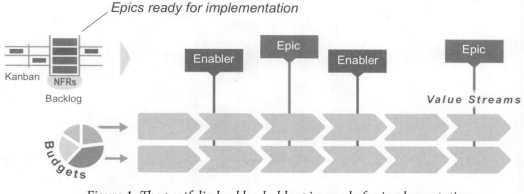

*Figure 1. The portfolio backlog holds epics ready for implementation*

Driven by significant concerns such as business opportunities, mergers and acquisitions, technological change, etc., these epics represent the approved initiatives that are typically used to bind various Agile Release Trains together to do things like share common infrastructure (ex: "migrate to JBoss app server") or implement common business behaviors (ex: "implement single sign-on across all products in the suite"). This provides the governance needed to create a harmonized and more value-added solution to the Customers of multiple Agile Release Trains or Value Streams.

Under the auspices of Program Portfolio Management, the portfolio backlog serves as a final gateway between these ideas and implementation. It provides a low-cost holding area (not much maintenance is required) and brings visibility to upcoming Business and Enabler Epics that have been approved, but await implementation capacity. Epics in the portfolio backlog are reviewed periodically and scheduled for implementation based on the availability of capacity in the affected Agile Release Trains.

## Portfolio Backlog Input

Due to their scope and typically crosscutting nature, epics usually require substantial investment and have considerable impact on both the development programs and business outcomes. Therefore, in order to reach the portfolio backlog, epics must first make their way through the Portfolio Kanban, where they are analyzed to determine feasibility and potential ROI. Epics that reach this boundary are in a mature state, in that they have been identified, elaborated, estimated, and analyzed as necessary to achieve a "go" recommendation from PPM.

## Managing the Portfolio Backlog

However, as Figure 2 illustrates, each is not the only epic in the backlog, and additional reasoning must be applied before scheduling for implementation. This includes logic considerations for sequencing, and ranking the epics relative to each other, typically by one final, WSJF prioritization. In this case, business and enabler epics are typically compared only against each other, inside the capacity allocation for each type. Those that rise to the top are then ready for implementation and are *pulled* from the portfolio backlog when trains have available capacity.

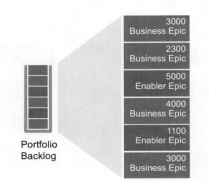

*Figure 2. Business and enabler epics in the portfolio backlog*

Note: The lightweight business case that precedes the portfolio backlog has a more robust prioritization process; this is just a final consideration, whereby the epic is compared to other epics that have also made it through the process. However, in addition to job size, an understanding of available program capacity must enter into consideration, because the *job duration* (denominator in WSJF) is heavily dependent on the level of resources available for implementation.

## Forecasting

SAFe enhances enterprise adaptability, providing faster response to changing market opportunities. And Agile delivery seems to work best when we *fix the date* and *float the scope*. This supports frequent incremental delivery and avoids the inevitable quality trade-offs when all aspects—scope, time, and resources—are fixed. Yet, in the enterprise, Agile, or not, *some sense of the future is required*:

- The enterprise, its partners, and Customers need to plan for upcoming Releases
- Visions must define, and track to the evolving enterprise strategy
- Roadmaps capture strategic intent in forecasted deliverables

Therefore, the ability to do effective Agile forecasting is a key economic driver, and a key ability of the Lean-Agile enterprise.

### Forecasting Requires Estimating

As we've described in other parts of SAFe, Agile Teams use story points and relative estimating to quickly arrive at estimates for size and duration for user stories. At the program level, Product Managers and System Architects—working with Product Owners and teams wherever appropriate—can use historical data to fairly quickly estimate the size of Features in story points as well. And whenever the economics justify further investment in estimating, teams can break larger features into Stories to get a more granular view.

Further, as we've illustrated in Figure 2, feature estimates, which are identified during the Kanban analysis step, can then be rolled up into epic estimates in the portfolio backlog, so that the economics of a potential epic are understood before implementation begins.

Finally and most importantly, given knowledge of program velocities, portfolio managers and other planners can use capacity allocation to estimate how long a portfolio epic might take under various scenarios. This provides a reasonable model for longer-term planning and forecasting, as Figure 3 illustrates.

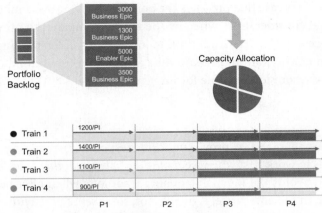

*Figure 3. Portfolio forecasting with epics size estimates, capacity allocation, and program velocities*

While, Agile or not, there is no crystal ball for high-fidelity estimation of large-scale software programs, SAFe does provide mechanisms for estimating and planning that have shown themselves to be more reliable than those historically applied with waterfall development methods.

## Moving to Implementation

As resources become available within the affected programs, prioritized epics are moved from the portfolio backlog to implementation. The Epic Owner shepherds this process forward and works with Product Management and System Architect/Engineering to split the epics into program epics and features and to prioritize those features in the respective program backlogs. Once this occurs, the epic is no longer part of the portfolio backlog, as it has been converted to features in the program backlog, but reporting on the epic progress is still appropriate, as is illustrated in the "Metrics" article.

---

**LEARN MORE**

[1] Leffingwell, Dean. *Agile Software Requirements: Lean Requirements Practices for Teams, Programs, and the Enterprise.* Addison-Wesley, 2011, chapter 23.

# Budgets

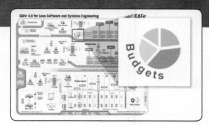

*Agile software development and traditional cost accounting don't match.*
   —*Rami Sirkia and Maarit Laanti*

## Abstract

Each SAFe portfolio exists for a purpose, to realize some set of technical Solutions that enable the business strategy. To enable this, each portfolio must execute within an approved operating *Budget*, as the operating costs for solution development are a primary factor in overall economic success. This article describes the basic mechanics for how SAFe portfolio budgets, once established, are administered and governed within a SAFe portfolio.

However, many traditional enterprises quickly ascertain that the drive for business agility via Lean-Agile development is in inherent conflict with current methods of budgeting and project cost accounting. The result may be that the move to Lean-Agile development—and the potential business benefits—are compromised or, worse, simply unachievable.

To address this, SAFe provides strategies for Lean-Agile budgets that directly address this challenge without the overhead of traditional project funding. With this model, fiduciaries have control of spend, yet programs are empowered for rapid decision-making and flexible value delivery. In this way, enterprises can have the best of both worlds: a development process that is far more responsive to market needs, along with professional and accountable management of technology spending.

## Details

Every SAFe Portfolio operates within the context of a known and approved investment spend. This is the basic fiduciary governance for development and deployment of IT, software and hardware, products, services, Solutions, and any other product or service offerings within a SAFe portfolio. As described in the "Enterprise" article, each portfolio, and thereby all portfolios in total, operate within a *Budget* that is an outcome of the strategic planning process, as is illustrated in Figure 1.

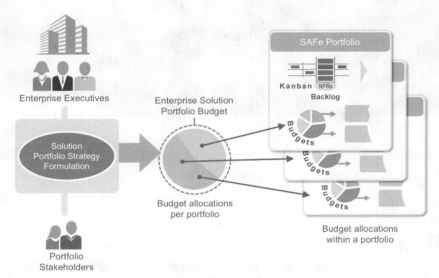

*Figure 1. Budgeting overview*

This is the traditional process, and it is still relevant in providing governance over investment spend for the solution portfolio.

Thereafter, however, the Lean enterprise operates far differently, and that is the focus of this article. SAFe recommends a dramatically different approach to budgeting within the portfolio, one that reduces overhead and costs associated with traditional cost accounting and empowers Decentralized Decision-Making.

No longer do portfolio level personnel plan the work for others, nor do they track the cost of the work at the project level. Instead, the Lean enterprise moves to a new paradigm: *Lean-Agile Budgeting: Beyond Project Cost Accounting.* This paradigm provides effective fiduciary control over total investment spend, but with far less overhead and friction and much higher throughput, as summarized in Figure 2.

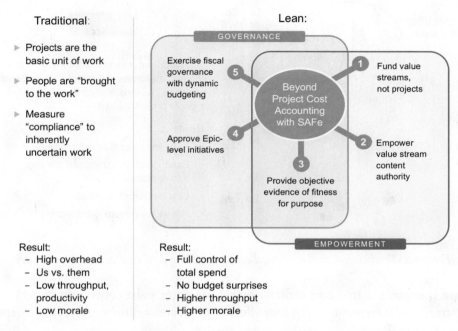

**Traditional:**

▷ Projects are the basic unit of work

▷ People are "brought to the work"

▷ Measure "compliance" to inherently uncertain work

Result:
- High overhead
- Us vs. them
- Low throughput, productivity
- Low morale

**Lean:**

GOVERNANCE

Exercise fiscal governance with dynamic budgeting ⑤

Approve Epic-level initiatives ④

Beyond Project Cost Accounting with SAFe

① Fund value streams, not projects

② Empower value stream content authority

③ Provide objective evidence of fitness for purpose

EMPOWERMENT

Result:
- Full control of total spend
- No budget surprises
- Higher throughput
- Higher morale

*Figure 2. Empowerment and governance with Lean-Agile budgeting*

Figure 2 illustrates that five major steps to this future state:

1. Fund Value Streams, not projects

2. Empower value stream content authority

3. Provide continuous objective evidence of fitness for purpose

4. Approve Epic-level initiatives

5. Exercise fiscal governance with dynamic budgeting

Each of these is discussed in the sections below.

## The Problem of Traditional Project Cost Accounting

But first, in order to embrace a new solution, it's important to understand the problems caused by the common project approach to technology funding.

**Problem #1 – Cost-center budgeting creates multiple challenges**

For most enterprises, prior to moving to Lean-Agile development, the budgeting process appears as in Figure 3.

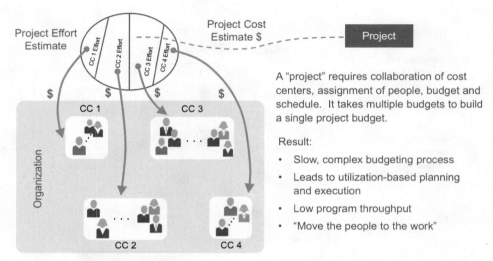

*Figure 3. Traditional project-based cost budgeting and cost accounting model*

The enterprise is organized into cost centers; each cost center must contribute project spending or people (the primary cost element) to the new effort. This creates a number of problems, including:

- The project budget process is slow and complicated; it takes many individual budgets (one per cost center) to create the *project* budget

- It drives teams to make fine-grained decisions far too early in the cone of uncertainty. Their hand is forced; if they can't identify all the tasks, how can they estimate how many people are needed, and for how long?

- The assignment of personnel is a temporary thing; the organization assumes people will come back into the cost center for future assignment. If they don't, other planned projects will suffer.

- The model drives cost center managers to make sure everyone is fully allocated. However, *running product development at 100% utilization is an economic disaster* [2]. The result is high variability to plan.

- The model prevents individuals and teams from working together longer than just the one project. This retards knowledge acquisition, team performance, and employee engagement. And collocation is out of the question.

**Problem #2 – Project-based constraints hinder adaptability, impede positive economic outcomes**
Once the project is initiated, the challenges continue. The actual needs of the business and the project-specific fact patterns change quickly. However, the projects cannot flex to the changing priorities, because their budgets and personnel are *fixed* for the project term, as Figure 4 illustrates.

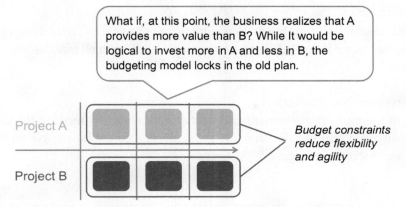

*Figure 4. Project funding inhibits the ability to react to change*

The result is that the organization is unable to flex to the changing business needs without the overhead of re-budgeting and reallocating personnel. Overhead kicks in; economics suffer. The Cost of Delay (the cost of not doing the thing you should be doing) increases.

**Problem #3 – Delays happen; things get even uglier**

But we are not done. Product development cannot innovate without takings risks [2]. By its very nature, development is extremely difficult to estimate because it contains a large degree of technical uncertainty. And everyone knows that most things take longer than planned. Moreover, even when things go really well, stakeholders may want more of a specific feature. That takes longer, too. Again, project-based funding hinders forward progress, culture, and transparency, as Figure 5 illustrates.

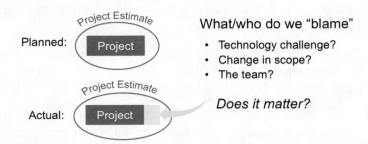

*Figure 5. When "overruns" happen, project accounting and re-budgeting increases Cost of Delay, negatively impacts culture*

When a schedule overruns for any reason, it is necessary to analyze the variances, re-budget, and re-plan. Resources are scrambled, and reassignments of personnel occur. Other projects are negatively impacted. The "blame game" sets in, pitting project manager against project manager and financial analysts against the teams. Any project overrun has budget impact. The casualties are transparency, productivity, and morale.

## Beyond Project Cost Accounting with SAFe

Clearly, traditional cost accounting is a serious inhibitor to the goal of faster delivery and better economic outcomes. But, as we indicated, a solution presents itself, each element of which is described in the sections below.

### 1. Fund Value Streams, Not Projects

The first step is to increase empowerment and decrease overhead by moving the day-to-day spend decisions (and associated resource decisions) to those closer to the solution. We do this by allocating budgets to each value stream, as Figure 6 illustrates.

*Figure 6. Operating budgets (allocated spend, personnel, and other resources)
are defined for each value stream*

This is a major step, and it delivers many benefits to the Lean enterprise:

- Value stream (VS) stakeholders, including the Value Stream Engineer (VSE) and Program Portfolio Management, are empowered to allocate the budget to whatever personnel and resources make sense based on the current backlog and Roadmap context

- Since value streams, and the Agile Release Trains that realize them, are long lived, the people involved work together for an extended period of time, increasing esprit de corps, knowledge, competency, and productivity

- Value streams provide resource pooling, so when things change, people in the value stream can flex to the current context. They can move from team to team, and even from ART to ART, potentially without requiring permissions above the VS/ART level.

- The budget is still controlled. In most cases, the expenses across a Program Increment (PI) are fixed or easy to forecast, so all stakeholders know the anticipated spend for the upcoming period, *regardless of what features get worked on*. And when a feature takes longer than planned, there is no impact on the budget and personnel decisions are a local—not budget or program—concern, as Figure 7 illustrates.

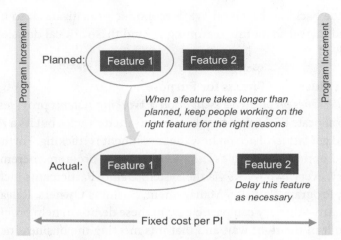

*Figure 7. The budget for a PI is fixed. When things take longer than anticipated, resources are not moved and the budget is not affected.*

## 2 . Empower Value Stream Content Authority

Step #1 is a giant step forward. Budget aside, however, the enterprise must still be assured that the value streams are building the right thing. That's one of the reasons projects were created to begin with. SAFe provides for this—not with projects, but via the empowerment and responsibilities of Solution and Product Management. And to provide visibility to everyone, all upcoming work is made, contained, and prioritized in the solution and Program Backlogs, as is illustrated in Figure 8.

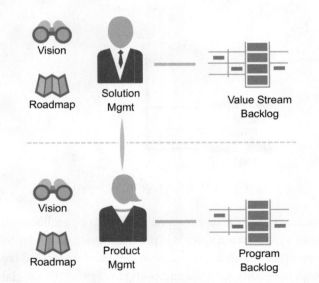

*Figure 8. Transparent content decision-making authority by Solution and Product Management*

Work is pulled from the backlogs based on WSJF economic prioritization, so fiduciaries are assured that there is sound and logical economic reasoning behind these critical decisions, and that the right stakeholders are involved.

### 3. Provide Objective Evidence of Fitness for Purpose

Principle #5 – *Base milestones on objective evaluation of working systems* provides the next piece of the puzzle. It's one thing to allocate the budget in value stream–sized chunks, but it's a reasonable expectation that all involved should get fast *feedback* on how the investment is tracking. Fortunately, SAFe provides regular, cadence-based opportunities to assess progress every program increment, via the Solution Demo and, if necessary, every two weeks via the System Demo. Participants include key stakeholders such as the Customer, Program Portfolio Management, Business Owners, Release Management, and the teams themselves. Any fiduciary can participate in these demos to help provide assurance that the right thing is being built in the right way, and that it is meeting the business needs of the Customer, one program increment at a time.

### 4. Approve Epic Level Initiatives

While the value stream is funded in the large, there is an exception to that rule. That is, by their very definition, epics are large enough and impactful enough to require additional approval. Often the initiatives impact multiple value streams and ARTs, and costs may run into many millions of dollars. That is why they all require vetting through the system and a lightweight business case, whether they arise at the portfolio, value stream, or Program Level, as Figure 9 illustrates.

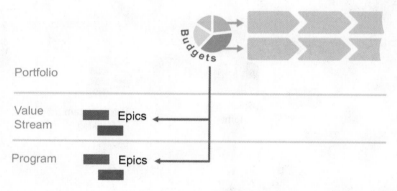

*Figure 9. Epics require approval*

Portfolio epics may be funded by a budgetary reserve, or perhaps by reallocation of personnel or budgets from another value stream. Value stream epics and program epics may arise locally, or they may occur as a result of portfolio level epics. Upon approval, however, they are funded from value streams. In any case, epics are large enough to require analysis and both strategic and financial-level decision-making. That's what makes an epic an epic.

## 5. Exercise Fiscal Governance with Dynamic Budgeting

Finally, while value streams are largely self-organizing and self-managing, they do not cause their own existence, nor fund themselves. To that end, Program Portfolio Management has the authority to set and adjust the value stream budgets within the portfolio. In order to respond to change, however, funding will vary over time based on business dynamics, as Figure 10 illustrates.

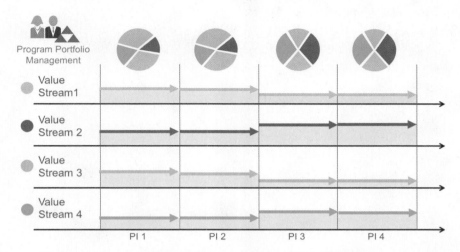

*Figure 10. Value stream budgets are adjusted dynamically over time*

Nominally, these budgets can be adjusted twice annually. Less frequently than that, and spending is fixed for too long a time, limiting agility. More frequently, and the enterprise may seem to be very Agile, but people are standing on shifting sand. That creates too much uncertainty and an inability to commit to any near-term course of action.

## LEARN MORE

[1] Special thanks to Rami Sirkia and Maarit Laanti for an original white paper on this topic, which you can find at www.scaledagileframework.com/original-whitepaper-lean-agile-financial-planning-with-safe/

[2] Reinertsen, Donald. *Principles of Product Development Flow: Second Generation Lean Product Development.* Celeritas Publishing, 2009.

# CapEx and OpEx

*Lean-Agile Leaders need to understand an Enterprise's current software development capitalization practice, as well as how to apply these principles in Agile development. Otherwise, the transformation to Agile may be blocked or, alternately, the company may not be able to correctly account for development expense.*

—Authors

CapEx & OpEx

## Abstract

Enterprises provide funding to a SAFe portfolio to support development of the technical Solutions that enable the enterprise to meet its business and financial objectives. These Budgets may include both Capital Expense (*CapEx*) and Operating Expense (*OpEx*) elements. In accordance with accounting standards, enterprises may capitalize (CapEx) some percentage of the labor involved in creating software for sale or internal use.

While software capitalization practices are well established in many enterprises, they are typically based on waterfall development, in which case up-front requirements and design phase gates may represent the events that can trigger CapEx treatment. In Agile development, however, these are typically not relevant stage gates. The enterprise is then faced with a new problem, which is how to apply effective treatment of these costs in an Agile development paradigm. If finance is unable to reconcile the change in method, then one of two things may happen: 1) They will block Agile development and mandate continued work under waterfall development, or 2) they will expense all Agile development labor costs—neither of which optimizes economics over time.

This article provides some strategies that SAFe enterprises can use to categorize labor costs in Agile development, some of which may be subject to CapEx treatment. However, this is an emerging field of understanding and there are many viewpoints. References 2, 3, and 4 at the end of this article provide additional perspectives.

*Disclaimer: The authors have no formal training nor accreditation in accounting. The treatment of software costs and potential for capitalization treatment varies by country, by industry (for example, while many companies in the U.S. are subject to one set of rules, suppliers to the U.S. federal government have an entirely different set of rules), and even by individual company policy. Moreover, even when subject to the FASB guidelines, under the general GAAP "principle of conservatism," some companies choose not to capitalize software development costs at all (see Ref 5 for an example).*

*The responsibility for appropriate implementation of financial accounting for capitalization of development costs rests with each enterprise. Lean-Agile change agents should engage early with business and financial stakeholders to establish an understanding of how the new way of working may affect accounting procedures.*

## Details

Enterprises provide funding to a SAFe Portfolio to enable the development and management of a set of Solutions. Within the portfolio, allocation of funding to individual Value Streams is under the auspices of Program Portfolio Management, who allocate the funding necessary for each value stream in a portfolio. A Budget for a SAFe portfolio may include both *CapEx* and *OpEx* elements:

- OpEx records the ongoing costs of running a product, business, or service. These costs include salaries and burden for operating personnel, sales, and marketing, general and administrative costs, training, supplies and maintenance, rent, and other expenses related to operating a business or an asset of the business. These costs are recorded and expensed in the period in which they occur.

- CapEx most typically reflect the monies required to purchase, upgrade, or fix tangible physical assets, such as computing equipment, machinery, or other property. In this case, the cost of purchase is put on the balance sheet as an asset, then expensed on the income statement over the useful life of that asset. In addition, in some cases, some of the labor costs associated with *development* of intangible assets, such as patents and *software*, may also be subject to CapEx treatment. In this case, CapEx may include salaries and direct burden, contract labor, materials, supplies, and other items directly related to the solution development activities.

Portfolio stakeholders must understand both CapEx and OpEx so that they are included as part of the Economic Framework for each value stream. Otherwise, money may not be spent in the right category, and/or the financial results of the portfolio will not be as intended. In particular, capitalization of some of the costs of software development can have a material effect on financial reporting. That is the topic of the remainder of this article.

## Accounting for Software Development Costs

Rules for capitalization of software assets vary by country and industry. In the U.S., the U.S. Financial Accounting Standards Board (FASB) provides guidance for Generally Accepted Accounting Principles (GAAPs) for U.S. companies that report financials in the public interest, including those that report publicly under U.S. Securities and Exchange Commission regulations. Similar organizations exist in other countries; for example, the U.K. Financial Reporting Council (FRC) provides policies that are largely similar to those of FASB. In addition, the U.S. Federal Government has different standards within the governance of the Federal Accounting Standards Advisory Board.

For U.S. companies operating in the private and public reporting sectors, U.S. FASB 86 [Ref 1] provides guidelines for accounting for the costs of computer software to be sold, leased, or otherwise marketed. FASB 86 states that costs incurred internally in creating a computer software product must be expensed when incurred as research and development, until technological feasibility has been established. Thereafter, software production costs may be capitalized and subsequently reported at the lower of either the unamortized cost or the net realizable value. Capitalized costs are amortized based on current and future revenue for each product, with an annual minimum equal to the straight-line amortization over the remaining estimated economic life of the product. For these purposes, a software product is defined as either a new product or a new initiative that changes the functionality of an existing one.

## Software Classifications Under FASB 86

There are three primary classifications of software development under FASB 86:

1. **Software for Sale** – Software developed for sale as a stand-alone or integrated product, typically by independent software vendors (ISVs)

2. **Software for Internal Use** – Software developed solely for internal purposes or in support of business processes within an enterprise, which is further described in SOP 98-1 (also see subtopic ASE 350-40 for fees paid in Cloud Computing)

3. **Embedded Software** – Software as a component of a tangible product that is needed to enable that product's essential functionality

Capitalization standards are treated differently within these categories, so the relevant guidelines must be taken into consideration.

## Capitalization vs. Expense Criteria

In general, in order to capitalize development costs, FASB 86 requires that a product must meet the following criteria:

- The product has achieved technical feasibility
- Management has provided written approval to fund the development effort

- Management has committed the resources to development
- Management is confident that the product will be successfully developed and delivered

Before capitalization of software can begin, finance departments typically require documented evidence that these specific activities have been completed. Once these criteria are met, further development costs may be subject to capitalization, as described in Table 1:

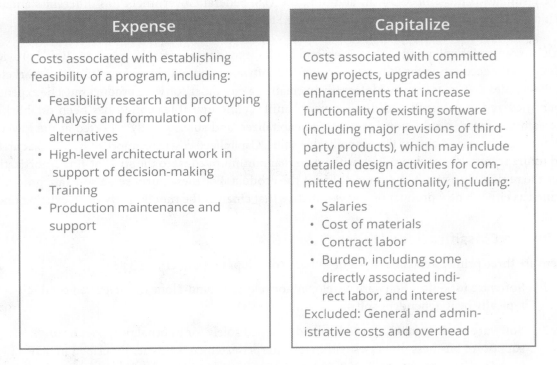

| Expense | Capitalize |
| --- | --- |
| Costs associated with establishing feasibility of a program, including:<br><br>• Feasibility research and prototyping<br>• Analysis and formulation of alternatives<br>• High-level architectural work in support of decision-making<br>• Training<br>• Production maintenance and support | Costs associated with committed new projects, upgrades and enhancements that increase functionality of existing software (including major revisions of third-party products), which may include detailed design activities for committed new functionality, including:<br><br>• Salaries<br>• Cost of materials<br>• Contract labor<br>• Burden, including some directly associated indirect labor, and interest<br>Excluded: General and administrative costs and overhead |

*Table 1. Categories of expensed and potentially capitalized costs*

## Capitalization Triggers in Waterfall Development

Historically, capitalization has been applied in the context of waterfall/stage-gate development. Waterfall development has a well-defined "up-front phase" during which requirements are developed, the design is produced, and feasibility is established. For those projects that receive further approval, the requirements and design milestones often serve as stage gates for starting capitalization, as can be seen in Figure 1.

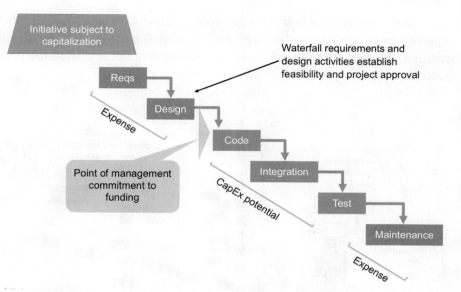

*Figure 1. Early waterfall phases establish feasibility and trigger management commitment to funding*

## Agile Development Capitalization Strategies in SAFe

In Agile, however, requirements and design emerge continuously, so there is no formal gate to serve as an official prelude to capitalization. However, that does not mean that projects fund themselves. Instead, the SAFe enterprise organizes around long-lived flows of value in value streams, which are implemented by the personnel and other resources of an Agile Release Train (ART), which operates on a fixed Program Increment cadence.

The majority of the work of most ARTs is typically focused on building and extending software assets that are past the point of feasibility analysis. They do this in large part by developing new Features for the solution. Since features "increase the functionality of existing software," the Stories associated with those features constitute much of the work of the ART personnel, and therefore the labor for same may be subject to potential capitalization.

The ARTs are also directly involved with establishing business and technical feasibility of the various portfolio initiatives (Epics) that work their way through the Portfolio Kanban. This work is somewhat analogous to the early stages of waterfall development and is typically expensed up until the "go" recommendation, at which time new feature development begins.

This means that both types of work are typically present in any program increment (and, by extension, any relevant accounting period). Much of this work is "new feature work" that increases the functionality of existing software.

Other work includes innovation and exploration efforts. These may be initiated from the portfolio Kanban—as part of the research and feasibility for potential new portfolio-level epics—or it may arise locally. In addition, maintenance, infrastructure work, etc., also occur during the period. Figure 2 illustrates these concepts.

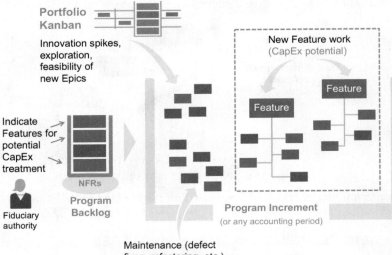

*Figure 2. Anatomy of a PI; many types of work occur in a given period*

## Categorization of Features for OpEx and CapEx

The work of implementing new projects and enhancing existing products is encapsulated in the creation of new *Features* for the solution, which, by their very definition, enhance functionality. This work can be easily identified and tracked for potential CapEx treatment. To do so, accounting fiduciaries work with Product Management to identify such features in the Program Backlog. Those selected are "typed" for potential CapEx treatment; that creates the basic tracking mechanism for effort. Thereafter, teams associate new stories with those features and perform the essential work of realizing the behavior of the features by implementing stories in the new code base.

## Applying Stories to CapEx and OpEx Treatment

Most stories contribute directly to new functionality of the feature; the effort for those stories may be subject to CapEx treatment. Other stories, such as Enabler stories for infrastructure, exploration, defects, refactors, and any other work, may not be. Agile Lifecycle Management (ALM) tooling can support the definition, capture, and work associated with implementing stories. By associating stories with features when applicable (typically called "parenting") in the tooling, the work related to feature development can be identified for potential CapEx treatment. Various query facilities in the ALM tool can help automate the needed summary calculations. Table 2 indicates three of the possible mechanisms for calculating the percentage of work that may be a candidate for CapEx treatment.

| By Story **Hours** | By Story **Points** | By Story **Count** |
|---|---|---|
| ← Increasing granularity, increasing overhead | | |
| Individuals record actual hours for **ALL** Stories in the timebox | Teams record actual points for **ALL** Stories in the timebox | Individuals record nothing additional |
| $X$ = total hours recorded to Stories that are parented by typed Features | $X$ = Story points for Stories that are parented by typed Features | $X$ = total Stories parented by typed Features |
| $Y$ = total hours invested in the period | $Y$ = total Story points in the period | $Y$ = total Stories in the period |
| Potential CapEx \$ = $(X/Y)$ x total period cost | | |

*Table 2. Possible mechanisms for tracking effort associated with CapEx stories*

### By Story Hours

The most granular means for capturing labor effort is to have individuals on the team record actual hours against each story. Although there is some overhead, many teams do this anyway because of traditional time-tracking requirements for job costing, billing, estimating, and other needs. However, this should not be the default mode for CapEx, as it incurs overhead and thereby reduces value delivery velocity. The rest of the calculation is straightforward: The CapEx potential percentage is simply the percentage of hours recorded for CapEx features, divided by the total of all hours invested in any period. After converting hours worked to cost, the enterprise can quickly assess the total cost that may be subject to CapEx treatment.

Note: During planning, some Agile Teams break stories into tasks and estimate and update task hours accordingly. This method requires only that actual total team hours be recorded to the story; tasking is not mandatory.

### By Story Points

Story points are the ubiquitous estimating and tracking currency for work in Scrum. (Note: This method may or may not pertain to SAFe teams applying Kanban, as Kanban teams do not always use story points.) Scrum teams estimate stories in story points and update their estimates to actuals to improve future estimates. While story points are relative, not absolute, units of measure, they are all that is necessary, as the enterprise needs only to know the percentage of story points allocated to stories that have CapEx potential, over the total story points delivered in any accounting period. Conversion to actual costs is handled in the same way as for the story hours method above. This is a low-friction, low-overhead method that does not generally create any additional burden on teams, other than the need to be sure to update estimates to actuals for each story completed. Again, ALM tooling typically supports the recording and automated calculation of such measures.

Note: In order to compensate for the relative nature of story points, which can vary from team to team, SAFe suggests a means for normalizing story point estimating across teams as part of the common economic underpinning for an ART, as described in SAFe Scrum.

**By Story Count**

The methods above provide a fairly granular means of encoding work to potentially capitalizable efforts. But there is work involved in entering and capturing the data, and that extra work does not, by itself, deliver end user value. Given the scope of the typical ART in the enterprise, there may be an easier way.

In a single PI, it is not unusual for an ART to implement many hundreds of stories (example: 10 teams, 10 stories per iteration, over 4 iterations, yields 400 stories per PI) of various types and sizes. Sizing a story is not biased by an understanding of the potential for CapEx treatment of a story (the teams need not even be aware of the difference), and therefore stories sizes will average out over time. In addition, over time the CapEx and associated depreciation schedules resolve to expense all development anyway. Thus near-term perfection is not necessarily the goal, as it is probably false precision anyway and may come at too high a cost. This yields a suggestion that simply counting stories by type is a fair proxy for the amount of effort devoted to potential CapEx stories. In a manner similar to those outlined for the story points and story count methods, this percentage can then be used to determine the CapEx potential in a given accounting period. Some Agilists have reported that this percentage approach is being applied on new Lean-Agile development initiatives (sometimes based even more simply on initial capacity allocation; see the "Program and Value Stream Backlogs" article). While appropriately subject to occasional audit, this provides an essentially friction-free approach that allows teams to focus exclusively on value delivery.

## What Specific Labor Efforts May Be Subject to CapEx Treatment?

There is one final aspect left to discuss: What specific labor elements may be applied to CapEx treatment? Again, the answer is highly specific to the actual enterprise. However, within the Agile development world, the following guidelines are often applied:

- The salaries of software developers, testers, User Experience, subject matter experts, and other Agile Team members who are directly involved in refining, implementing, and testing stories may be subject to CapEx, as is largely consistent with existing waterfall practices

- In addition, Product Owners and Scrum Masters are part of the team and directly contribute to story definition and implementation. This "indirect" labor is directly associated with new value delivery and, as such, may be appropriate for CapEx treatment. This can be accomplished by adding an additional average cost burden on a CapEx story.

- Further, not all work for a feature is performed solely by Agile Team members. System Architects, System Teams, and DevOps contributors also contribute to the features under development, and some portion of their cost may be subject to CapEx as well.

- Finally, in the larger value streams, additional roles contribute to value creation via Pre- and Post-PI Planning, creation and maintenance of Solution Intent, and the Solution Demo. While further removed from the specific implementation activities, all of these activities and roles provide value, so their potential for CapEx treatment is at the discretion of the enterprise.

## LEARN MORE

[1] FASB 86 Summary at fasb.org/summary/stsum86.shtml.

[2] Reed, Pat, and Walt Wyckoff. *Accounting for Capitalization of Agile Labor Costs*. Agile Alliance, February 2016.

[3] Greening, Dan. *Why Should Agilists Care About Capitalization?* InfoQ, January 29, 2013.

[4] Connor, Catherine. *The Top 10 Pitfalls of Agile Capitalization*. Rally, February 2016.

[5] Footnote from a U.S. public reporting software company's Form 10-K filing, highlighting a policy of not capitalizing software development expense: "Research and development expenses primarily consist of personnel and related costs of our research and development staff, including salaries, benefits, bonuses, payroll taxes, stock-based compensation, and costs of certain third-party contractors, as well as allocated overhead. Research and development costs related to the development of our software products are generally expensed as incurred. Development costs that have qualified for capitalization are not significant."

# Value Streams

*Sustainably shortest lead time. Best possible quality and value to people and society.*

—*House of Lean*

## Abstract

*Value Streams* are the primary SAFe construct for understanding, organizing, and delivering value. Each value stream is a long-lived series of steps that an enterprise uses to provide a continuous flow of value to a Customer. The primary role of a SAFe Portfolio is to finance and nurture a set of Solutions development activities (a *development value stream*) that either deliver end user value directly or support other business (operational) value streams. Identifying and optimizing value streams is a critical skill of the Lean-Agile Enterprise.

Organizing around value delivers substantial benefits to the organization, including faster learning, shorter time to market, higher quality, higher productivity, and solutions that are better fit for the intended purpose. In SAFe, organizing around value is accomplished by first understanding the value streams, and then organizing SAFe Agile Release Trains (ARTs) to realize them. Realizing value streams via ARTs is the "art" and science of SAFe.

In addition, value streams lend themselves to systematic analysis and improvement by value stream mapping, which is used to identify and address delays and non-value-added activities, thereby helping to accomplish the *shortest sustainable lead time*.

## Details

Lean and Agile methods both focus intensely on continuous value delivery, whereby value is achieved only when the end user, Customer, or internal business process receives the business benefit of some new Solution or Capability. In Lean, identifying and understanding the various flows of value is the most critical step—indeed, the starting point—for improving overall Enterprise performance. After all, if the enterprise doesn't have a clear picture of what it delivers and how it delivers it, how could it possibly improve?

This brief background gives SAFe its primary impetus in organizing development Portfolios around flows of value called *Value Streams*.

*A value stream is a long-lived series of steps used to deliver value, from concept or Customer order to delivery of a tangible result for the Customer.*

Figure 1 illustrates the anatomy of a value stream.

*Figure 1. Anatomy of a value stream*

The flow of value is *triggered* by some important event, perhaps a Customer purchase order or new feature request. It ends when some value has been delivered—a shipment, Customer purchase, or solution deployment. The steps in the middle are the activities the enterprise uses to accomplish this feat. A value stream contains the people who do the work, the *systems* they develop or operate, and the flow of information and materials. The time from the trigger to the value delivery is the *lead time*. Shortening the lead time shortens the time to market. That is the focus.

## Types of Value Streams

In the context of SAFe, systems builders must be aware that there are often two types of value streams present in the enterprise. *Operational value streams* show the steps used to provide goods or services to a Customer, be they internal or external [2]. This is how the company makes its money. Development value streams show the steps used to develop new products, systems, or services capabilities. Sometimes these are the same, as when a solution provider develops a product for sale and feeds distribution directly (example: a small SaaS company). In that case there is only one value stream, as development and operations are the same.

However, particularly in the context of the large IT shop, understanding both types of value streams is critical, as the development value stream feeds the operational value stream, as is illustrated in Figure 2.

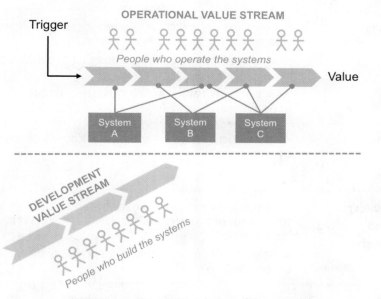

*Figure 2. Development value streams build the systems that operational value streams use to deliver value*

While the primary purpose of SAFe is providing guidance for the people who build the systems, Lean systems builders first understand the ultimate flow of value so that they can build and optimize systems to accelerate the end result. To this end, identifying value streams is one of the first steps in implementing SAFe. Further, many of the critical requirements for the development value streams, including not just functionality but also system and Enterprise Architecture, are driven directly by the operational value streams.

## Identifying Value Streams

For some organizations, identifying value streams is a simple task. Many are simply the products, services, or solutions they develop and sell. As the enterprise gets larger, however, the task becomes more complicated. Value flows through various applications and services and across many parts of the distributed organization, to many internal and external Customers of many different types. In the larger IT shop, for example, value may move across multiple departments and organizations and across many deployed systems. In such cases, *finding the value stream* is an important analytical and business context-based activity that provides the most basic foundation for the Lean-Agile transformation.

### Questions to Identify Value Streams

Understanding the actual flow of value in an enterprise is a challenge that can only be addressed in the specific business context. A series of questions, such as those in Table 1, can help discover the value streams.

| General questions | • What are the larger software, system, or solution-based objectives that differentiate the business in the market? |
|---|---|
| | • How do the external Customers describe or perceive the flow of value they receive? |
| | • What current initiatives have a significant number of devs and testers working together now? |
| Questions for the independent software vendor | • What products, systems, services, applications, or solutions does the enterprise sell? |
| Questions for builders of embedded and cyber-physical systems | • What products and systems does the enterprise sell? What are the larger subsystems or components? What key system operational capabilities are being enabled? |
| | • What critical Nonfunctional Requirements are being implemented or enhanced? |
| Questions for IT | • What key business processes are enabled? |
| | • What internal departments are supported? |
| | • What internal or external Customers do those departments serve? How do those departments describe the value they receive from IT? |
| | • What key process, cost, KPI, or business improvement initiatives are targeted? |

*Table 1. Some questions to help identify value streams in an enterprise*

## Value Stream Definition Template

Once identified, each value stream can be further characterized for more complete understanding. Table 2 provides a template, along with an operational value stream example.

| Name | Customer order |
|---|---|
| Description | Provides Customers with a fast, consistent ordering experience from mobile or web |
| Customer(s) | Small- to medium-size business |
| Triggers | New Customer order or order update |
| Inputs | New order detail (with Customer information) |
| Outputs | Shipment request to shipping, billing information to finance |
| Includes | Internal Customer-order work flows and personnel, SAP order management, help desk, mobile and web order entry applications |

*Table 2. Value stream definition template with an operational value stream example*

**Development Value Streams Cross Boundaries**

Once the value streams are identified, the next step is to start to understand how to form Agile Release Trains to realize them. The ARTs contain all the people and other assets needed to enhance the flow of value. First, the analyst must understand where in the organization that value is created, because that is where the people, processes, and systems are. When doing so, it becomes obvious that development value streams cross many boundaries. Enterprises are organized the way they are for many reasons: history, functional convenience, efficiency of centralization, acquisitions, geography, and more. As a result, it's quite possible that no one really understands the complete series of events necessary to continually develop and enhance the systems that help deliver the value. Further, attempts to improve tend to focus on functional, local improvements, the result of which may be optimization of one function or step but sub-optimization of the end-to-end flow.

It is the long-lived nature of a value stream that triggers different thinking in the Lean organization. To address this, enterprises apply systems thinking and come to understand how various parts of the system need to work together to accomplish improved flow. Typically, larger organizations are organized functionally; in addition, people are distributed in multiple geographies and multiple countries. But value moves across these boundaries, as Figure 3 illustrates.

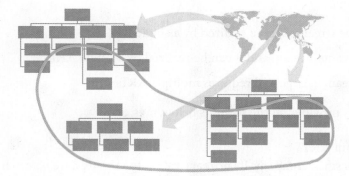

*Figure 3. Value flows across functional, organizational, and geographic boundaries*

## Budgeting for Development Value Streams

Identifying the value streams and understanding the flow through the organization is an important step in improving value delivery. It also unlocks the opportunity to implement Lean-Agile budgeting, which can substantially reduce overhead and friction and further accelerate flow.

In support of this, each portfolio in SAFe contains a set of development value streams, each of which has its own budget. Program Portfolio Management helps manage the budget for each train in accordance with Lean-Agile budgeting principles. Over time, budgets for each value stream are adjusted as necessary, based on changing business conditions.

This is further described in the "Budgets" article. Figure 4 shows the independent budgets for different development value streams.

*Figure 4. Each development value stream is allocated its own budget*

## Realizing Development Value Streams with Agile Release Trains

Once the flow of value—and the location of the people and systems that deliver that value—is understood, the enterprise can start to consider how to apply Agile Release Trains to enhance the flow. ARTs are virtual organizations, teams of Agile Teams, that are organized for the explicit purpose of working across boundaries to accelerate delivery. The "Agile Release Train" article describes the nature and purpose of ARTs. One significant conclusion is that ARTs work most efficiently when they are composed of a maximum of 100 – 150 people. Given that constraint, there are three possible value-stream-to-ART organizational outcomes:

1. Multiple value streams can be realized by a single ART

2. There is one value stream, and it can be realized by a single ART

3. The value stream is large and requires multiple ARTs

An example of each is provided in the sections below.

**Multiple Value Stream ART**

Consider the case of a small company. Its primary value streams are a website, which is made available to the public for free, and courseware it sells to monetize the business. The courseware is triggered by new content developed and posted to the website. At the time of the example, the business is able to realize its vision with fewer than 50 people in total. In this case, while there are two fairly different value streams, they can be accomplished with a single ART, as is illustrated in Figure 5.

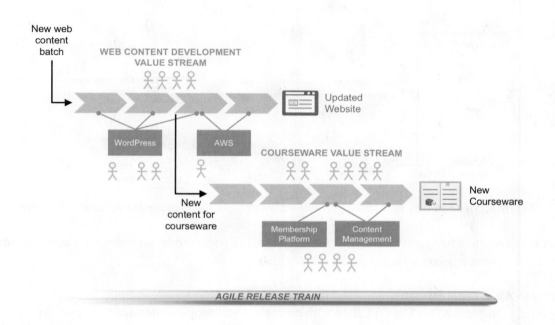

*Figure 5. Small, independent software vendor with two value streams and a single ART*

The top value stream is triggered by new content knowledge, which manifests itself in an updated website and new courseware.

Note: In the larger enterprise this is not the typical case. And even in this case, the company could have supported this with two small ARTs, but then they would have created cross-ART dependencies that would have had to be managed outside the basic ART planning and governance process. Moreover, the company found that reasoning the flow of value in each value stream gave them the insights they needed for accurate delivery. Therefore combining them into one value stream, "framework and courseware," didn't seem helpful. Another example of this model is a much larger company that shipped more than 100 high-tech products; they employed about 600 people in development. In this case they organized their ARTs around sets of products, grouped by those that had the greatest commonalities and dependencies. However, each product still delivered its individual end-user value and was budgeted appropriately.

**Single Value Stream ARTs**

The second example is a medium-size manufacturer who builds automated guided vehicles for multiple marketplaces. One significant market is the amusement parks industry (see the Baja Adventure Ride example). They have fewer than 200 people on staff, but they are reliant on a Supplier for the track system. In this case, they have two value streams: One is the Vehicle and the Supplier-provided Track, and the other is the Ride Management System. Each of these two value streams is realized by a single ART. The Ride Management System is considered a separate value stream, since it operates under a separate divisional budget, and that group sells variants of that system to other industrial applications as well. This is illustrated in Figure 6.

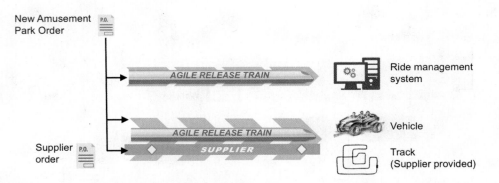

*Figure 6. Medium-size manufacturer with value streams, two release trains, and a Supplier*

Each new system is fairly custom, so the value streams are triggered by an order for a new adventure ride. In turn, that triggers an order to the rail Supplier.

**Multiple-ART Value Stream**

The third example is a "Big Data" IT shop with more than 900 people in development and deployment, and hundreds more in operations. They produce mapping data and algorithms for vehicles and mobile devices. They consider themselves a single value stream but organize development around six ARTs, as shown in Figure 7.

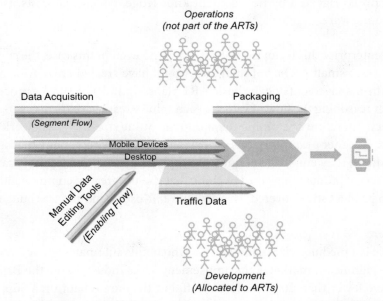

*Figure 7. Big Data IT shop with a single value stream organized into six ARTs*

In this case, while the enterprise value stream includes all the operations people involved in preparing, editing, normalizing, and mastering the data, the ARTs consist only of the development teams and supporting roles.

## Coordinating Agile Release Trains Within Value Streams

Figure 7 raises an interesting question. Assuming that there are some dependencies among the ARTs, how does the enterprise coordinate these activities to create a single, holistic solution set? This can require an extensive degree of cooperation; a common Value Stream Backlog; implementation of new, crosscutting capabilities; additional system integration; additional roles and responsibilities; special considerations for Pre-, Post-, and PI Planning activities; different degrees and types of DevOps support; and even more. This is one of the primary challenges of the larger Lean-Agile enterprise. Fortunately, coordinating multiple Agile Release Trains within a value stream is the entire subject of the "Introduction to the Value Stream Level" article.

## Coordinating Value Streams Within a Portfolio

Of course, many significant portfolios contain multiple value streams. While, by design, they should be as independent as possible, there is likely to be some nominal coordination required to ensure that the enterprise moves forward with each value stream in lockstep with the enterprise objectives. This is the topic of the "Coordination" article.

## Reducing Time to Market with Value Stream Mapping

Finally, there is another significant benefit to identifying the value streams and organizing release trains around them. Each value stream provides an identifiable and measurable flow of value to a Customer. As such, it can be systematically improved to increase delivery velocity and quality. For example, what if the ride management system value stream/ART of Figure 6 was always the critical path, and even when the vehicle was ready for shipment the ride management software was not? That would be a high Cost of Delay!

In this case, the ride management ART would apply value stream mapping [3] to identify the steps and flow through the system, and they might describe a flow such as that illustrated in Figure 8.

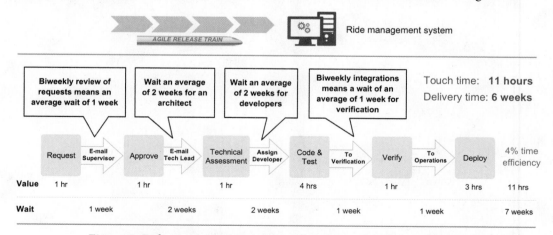

*Figure 8. Ride management system value stream mapping example*

The teams would quickly see that the amount of value-added touch time is only a small portion of the overall time it takes to deliver the end result. After all, it only took them 11 hours of work to create the new feature. And yet it couldn't be delivered for *seven weeks*. The majority of the time is spent in handoffs and delays. They have been working hard, and apparently efficiently from the touch time, yet the overall flow through the system could not meet the demand. Coding and testing faster won't help. Rather, the teams must take the systems view and focus on the *delays*.

*Reducing delays in the value stream is always the fastest way to reduce time to market.*

## LEARN MORE

[1] Ward, Allen. *Lean Product and Process Development*. Lean Enterprise Institute, 2014.

[2] Martin, Karen and Mike Osterling. *Value Stream Mapping*. McGraw Hill, 2014.

[3] Poppendieck, Mary and Tom Poppendieck. *Implementing Lean Software Development: From Concept to Cash*. Addison-Wesley, 2007.

# Epics

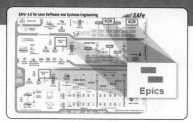

*A system must be managed. It is management's job to direct the efforts of all components toward the aim of a system.*

—W. Edwards Deming

## Abstract

*Epics* are containers for significant initiatives that help guide value streams toward the larger aim of the portfolio. In so doing, they drive much of the economic value for the enterprise. Epics are large and typically crosscutting, crossing multiple Value Streams and Agile Release Trains (ARTs). They are investment intensive and far ranging in impact; formulation and analysis of cost, impact, and opportunity is a serious matter. To this end, Epics require a lightweight business case and financial approval before implementation. There are two kinds of epics: Business epics and Enabler epics, and they may appear at the Portfolio, Value Stream, and Program level.

Most of this article is devoted to describing the definition, articulation, and implementation of portfolio epics as they are the largest and most impactful. Portfolio epics are developed and managed through the Portfolio Kanban, where they are processed through various states of maturity until they are either rejected or approved, in which case they move to the Portfolio Backlog to await implementation. This process assumes reasoned economic analysis of the business drivers behind the epic, its technical impact, and strategies for incremental implementation.

Value stream and program epics require similar treatment. They are also described in this article.

## Details

### Portfolio Epics

The largest *Epics*, portfolio business epics and Enabler Epics, capture the largest crosscutting initiatives that occur within a Portfolio. Business epics directly deliver business value; enabler epics are used to evolve the Architectural Runway to support upcoming business epics. These epics are initially captured in the Portfolio Kanban and move through this system under work-in-process (WIP) limits.

This helps ensure that those doing the work have the time necessary to conduct responsible analysis. Equally important, the Kanban system helps manage expectations for reasonable scoping and time frames for implementation of new business ideas. The final decision for actual implementation of each epic is subject to the authority of Program Portfolio Management (PPM). As resources become available, decision-makers can select from the best of a number of possible business opportunities, as there will typically be multiple analyzed epics in the backlog at any time. Epics that are approved go to the Portfolio Backlog, where they await implementation capacity.

Figure 1 provides an *Epic Value Statement* template that can be used to capture, organize, and communicate key information about an epic. This expression is developed in the Kanban *Review* state and is intended to provide just enough information to have a meaningful discussion about the proposed initiative.

| Forward-Looking Position Statement | |
|---|---|
| For | &lt;customers&gt; |
| who | &lt;do something&gt; |
| the | &lt;solution&gt; |
| is a | &lt;something–the "how"&gt; |
| that | &lt;provides this value&gt; |
| Unlike | &lt;competitor, current solution, or non-existing solution&gt; |
| our solution | &lt;does something better–the "why"&gt; |
| **Scope** | |
| Success criteria: | .<br>. |
| In scope: | .<br>. |
| Out of scope: | .<br>. |
| NFRs: | .<br>. |

*Figure 1. Epic value statement template format*

## Analysis

Epics are the most significant initiatives within the portfolio, so they must be carefully analyzed before being committed to implementation. Epic Owners take responsibility for this important task, while Enterprise Architects shepherd enabler epics that support technical considerations for business epics. The most worthy epics from the backlog are passed to analysis when space becomes available in that queue. There, effort and economic impact are better defined, WSJF prioritization is refined, cost estimates are established, and a lightweight business case is developed.

Analysis efforts can include:

- Workshops with business stakeholders to understand and describe business benefits of the business epic

- Workshops with Architects or Systems Engineering, from the Value Stream and Program Levels, and Agile Team to understand implementation effort and impact on current solutions; other relevant SMEs can be involved

- Implementation of spikes, research and exploration activities by the teams

- Developing concrete examples to resolve ambiguities (*specification by example*)

- Defining the *success criteria* for an epic

The result of the analysis phase is a lightweight business case that captures the results of the analysis, including a refined description, success criteria, estimates of implementation time and cost, and program impact. An example format is provided in Figure 2 below. The business case is then used by the appropriate authorities to make a "go" / "no-go" decision for the epic.

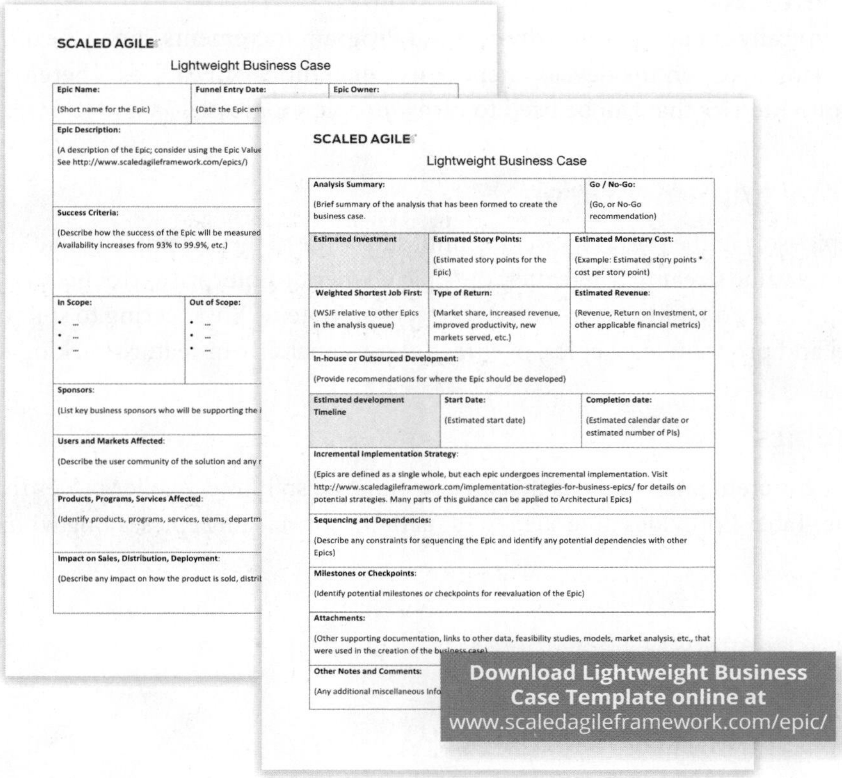

*Figure 2. Epic lightweight business case*

## Success Criteria

The epic value statement and lightweight business case both include *epic success criteria*, which can be used to validate that implementation is complete and successful. By their very nature, portfolio epics are large and tend to be abstract, so defining success criteria is a capstone to establishing a shared understanding among stakeholders of what the epic really implies for the business.

**Be Careful about Absolute Success Criteria**

However, epics are unique from Capabilities and Features, as it is often not necessary to complete epics, and that is why teams have to be so careful with success criteria. Due to their scope and impact, it is sometimes the case that implementing some—*but not all*—of an epic achieves the bulk of the economic value, and in accordance with WSJF, there may be a point at which some other investment would produce a greater economic return than completing the epic as anticipated.

For an example from experience, we discovered that an epic of "migrate all applications to use JBoss Webserver" would have been better stated as "migrate all applications to Jboss webserver—*except those applications approaching end of life*."

**Measuring Progress**

Since epics typically cut across value streams and Program Increments, it may be difficult to assess how progress is being made on the development of its Capabilities or Features. Therefore, SAFe provides a set of portfolio Metrics that can be used to measure epic progress.

## Incremental Implementation

Approved epics stay in the portfolio backlog until such time as there is implementation capacity available in one or more value streams. Thereafter, the Epic Owner or Enterprise Architect has the responsibility to work with the Product Managers and Architects or Systems Engineering to split the epics into value stream level and program level epics, or directly into capability or feature backlog items.

## Splitting Epics

Implementing incrementally means that an epic must be split into smaller pieces that represent incremental value. Table 1 provides nine suggested methods for splitting epics, along with examples for each.

| 1. **Solution / Subsystem / Component Epics** often affect multiple solutions, subsystems, or large components. In such cases, splitting by these aspects can be an effective implementation technique. | |
|---|---|
| *Multiple user profiles* | *... Multiple profiles in the opt-out website*<br>*... Multiple profiles in the admin system* |

| 2. **Success Criteria** The epic success criteria often provide hints as to how to incrementally achieve the anticipated business value. | |
|---|---|
| *Implement new artifact in search results*<br>Locations Success criteria:<br>a) Locations should provide additional filtering method when other disambiguation methods aren't useful;<br>b) Provide detailed location of a person | *... Provide state information in the search results (criterion [a] is partially satisfied, as states alone already provide some good filtering capability)*<br>*... Implement compound location: State and City (entire success criteria are satisfied)* |

| 3. **Major Effort First** Sometimes an epic can be split into several parts, where most of the effort will go toward implementing the first one. | |
|---|---|
| *Implement single sign-on across all products in the suite* | *... Install PINGID protocol server and test with mock identity provider*<br>*... Implement SSO management capability in our simplest product*<br>*... Implement SSO in our most complex product*<br>*... Proliferate as quickly as backlog capacity allows* |

| 4. **Simple/Complex** Capture that simplest version as its own epic, and then add additional program epics for all the variations and complexities. | |
|---|---|

| 5. **Variations in Data** Data variations and data sources are another source of scope, complexity, and implementation management. | |
|---|---|
| *Internationalize all end-user facing screens* | *... in Spanish*<br>*... in Japanese*<br>*... prioritize the rest by then-current market share* |

| 6. **Market Segment / Customer / Class of User** Segmenting the market or Customer base is another way to split an epic. Do the one that has higher business impact first. | |
|---|---|
| *Implement opt-in functionality* | *... For current partners*<br>*... For all major marketers* |

| 7. **Defer Solution Qualities (NFRs)** Sometimes the initial implementation isn't all that hard and the major part of the effort is in making it fast—or reliable—or more precise—or more scalable, so it may be feasible to achieve the solution qualities (Nonfunctional Requirements) incrementally. | |
|---|---|

| 8. **Risk Reduction/Opportunity Enablement** Given their scope, epics can be inherently risky; use risk analysis and do the riskiest parts first. | |
|---|---|
| *Implement filtering search results by complex user-defined expression* | *... Implement negative filtering*<br>*... Implement complex filtering expressions with all logical operations* |

| 9. **Use Case Scenarios** Use cases [1] can be used in Agile to capture complex user-to-solution or solution-to-solution interaction; split according to specific scenarios or user goals of the use case. | |
|---|---|
| *Transitive people-search functionality* | (goal 1 ~) *Find connection to a person*<br>(goal 2 ~) *Find connection to a company*<br>(goal 3 ~) *Distinguish strong and weak connections* |

*Table 1. Methods for splitting epics*

## Approving the Investment in Epics

Epics play another important role in the system that constitutes SAFe. Specifically, epics, by their very definition, require financial approval from the portfolio stakeholders, even in the context of an approved value stream budget. The ability to even implement Lean-Agile budgeting—to fund the value streams directly and empower value stream stakeholders to allocate spend to their initiatives—is dependent on certain checks and balances in the system. One of these is that large spend items still require visibility approval, even if the value stream budget can support it. Epics play a key role in that process as they consume significant amounts of resources and often represent changes in technical or business strategy. It behooves everyone—those empowering, and those empowered—to collaborate and approve such large spend items. Refer to the "Budgets" article for further discussion.

## Program and Value Stream Epics

The above discussion describes the most impactful kind of epic, portfolio epics. Many of these epics generate value stream epics and, correspondingly, program epics as well. In addition, many large initiatives (epics) arise at the local value stream or program level. While largely a local concern, their financial, people, and other resource impacts are large enough in scope to warrant a lightweight business case and discussion and financial approval from PPM. That's what makes an epic an epic. However, the splitting, implementation, and management practices for value stream and program epics is primarily a local concern. Methods for managing the epics at these levels are discussed in the article on Program and Value Stream Kanban systems.

---

**LEARN MORE**

[1] Leffingwell, Dean. *Agile Software Requirements: Lean Requirements Practices for Teams, Programs, and the Enterprise.* Addison-Wesley, 2011.

# Part 8
# Guidance

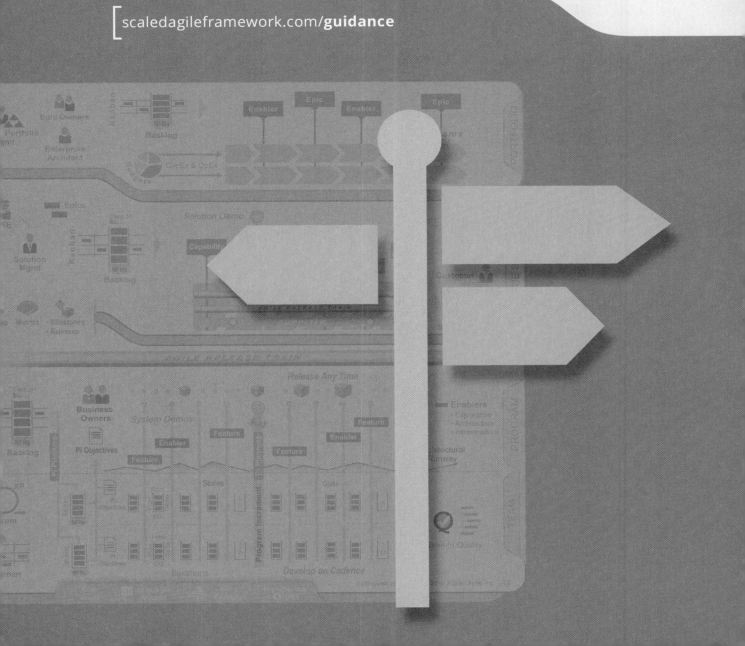

scaledagileframework.com/**guidance**

# Continuous Integration

*The epiphany of integration points is that they control product development. They are the leverage points to improve the system. When timing of integration points slip, the project is in trouble.*

—Dantar Oosterwal, *The Lean Machine*

## Abstract

*Continuous Integration (CI)* is perhaps the most essential technical practice for an ART and Value Stream. CI is a quality heartbeat that reduces risk and establishes fast, sustainable development. If teams focus solely on features and component development, accumulated assumptions and unintended interactions in the system create waste, which exhibits itself as delays and delivery variability. But with early and often CI, teams take a system view that keeps the development process in control and enhances predictability.

However, continuous integration in complex, heterogeneous systems—those that contain mechanical subsystems, software, electrical and electronic subsystems, subassemblies from suppliers, and so forth—is difficult. Lean systems builders need a balanced approach, which allows the teams to build quality in and receive fast feedback from the integrated increments. This often requires economic trade-offs between frequency and scope of integration and testing. Proper infrastructure and continuous improvement of CI practices, along with automation techniques and design for testability, facilitates fast feedback and helps ARTs achieve ever higher velocity.

## Details

Complexity in large solutions results in part from the inter-dependencies between components, the crosscutting nature of the solution's capabilities, and unintended interactions among solution elements. It is simply impossible to envision all those potential behaviors up front. While proactive identification and management of such dependencies is required, integrating and testing the collaborating components together, as a solution, is the only practical way to fully validate the solution.

### Feature and Component Level Continuous Integration

An Agile Team creates value only when the team members frequently integrate and test the results of their combined work. If integration does not happen frequently, there is no way to ensure the different roles and functions on the team are actually able to produce a consistent output—the team increment.

Therefore in SAFe, it is highly recommended that the members of an Agile Team integrate their work at least once per iteration, with a preference toward a more frequent rhythm.

This integration and testing effort is part of every iteration and should be properly planned for, by either including the effort as a part of story estimates (included in the story's definition of done), or having separate backlog items in the iteration backlog for integration and testing activities. One way or the other, the effort should be part of the team's velocity, otherwise the team will fail to establish a sustainable pace—the most basic prerequisite for development predictability at scale.

## ART Integration

While critical, *local* integration and testing isn't enough. Even a simple change to a "tested" component may have unintended consequences that may ripple through the rest of the system, as Figure 1 illustrates.

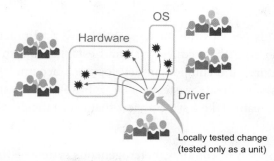

*Figure 1. Local integration and testing is necessary, but insufficient*

Worse, it may create a false sense of security ("wishful thinking", one of the key wastes of Lean) that the system is actually working. Without a full system view, significant problems can accumulate quickly as teams build more and more functionality on top of unvalidated work, with exponential growth of problems.

Frequent integration and testing, at least once every iteration, provides the necessary means to evaluate progress and discover problems while they are still easy to fix. This produces the *System Increment*—an integrated, functioning set of features and components, the subject of the System Demo—that can be reviewed by the teams themselves and by Product Owners and other key stakeholders. Even more importantly, it illustrates the real, tangible value of the increment.

## Solution Integration

Large solutions require an additional level of integration for learning and to understand the solution's progress across multiple release trains within a value stream. The solution demo event is where the results of all the development efforts from multiple Agile Release Trains—along with the contributions from suppliers and other value stream participants—are made visible to the Customers and other stakeholders. This is the most critical time for a fully integrated, solution-level demonstration; a time for objective evaluation and stakeholder and Customer feedback.

The solution integration and demo are the joint responsibility of the System Teams at the ART and Value Stream Levels, as illustrated in Figure 2 below. These big systems can be hard to integrate. In order to be able to routinely demonstrate a solution increment, teams must typically invest in integration, testing, and supporting infrastructure. Even then, the extent of integration and testing may be less than 100% and may need to vary across multiple early integration points, as illustrated in Figure 2.

To assist, teams can leverage virtualization, environment emulation, mocks, stubs, reduced test suites, etc. In addition, some effort for integration and demonstration, and time to invest in the supporting environment, may need to be explicitly allocated during Pre-PI Planning.

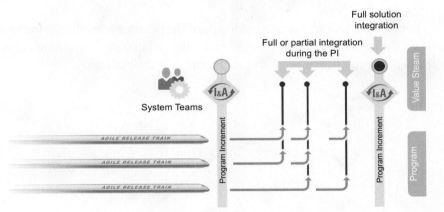

*Figure 2. Solution integration*

**Synchronize with Supplier and Solution Context**

Suppliers play a key role in SAFe due to their unique capabilities and solutions. They can have a large impact on lead time and value delivery. In order for both organizations to achieve optimal results, close collaboration and *trust* are required. This is facilitated by the following recommended practices:

- Plan the integration points

- Adopt cadence whenever appropriate; establish milestones on objective evaluation of the working solution

- Collaborate with parent system's and Supplier ART's system teams

- Build and maintain consistent integration and testing infrastructure

- Participate in the Pre- and Post-PI Planning and Solution Demos and invite Suppliers to attend

- Establish collaboration and synchronization between Architecture/Systems Engineering at all levels

- Synchronize the solution with solution context to ensure the as-built solution is compatible with the deployment environment

## Challenges and Trade-offs

Each ART's goal is to be able to fully integrate features across all teams in each iteration. However, that can be difficult due to solution complexity and heterogeneity, availability of specialty testing personnel, laboratories, equipment, third-party components, etc. Given this, teams may feel that achieving the integrated iteration goal is not realistic, at least initially. But that cannot be an excuse for discontinuous, late-in-the cycle integration and testing.

When such trade-offs are required, teams need to adjust the practice accordingly, but in a manner so as to still achieve a reliable, fast feedback mechanism. Figure 3 illustrates a trade-off curve that can help teams think through the optimum scope and extent of CI in their context.

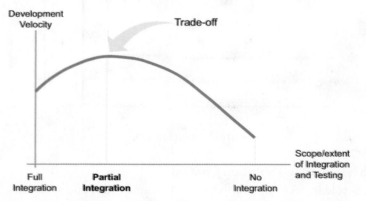

*Figure 3. Trade-off curve for integration and testing*

These trade-offs are achievable due to the fact that different parts of the solution have different levels of coupling, and some capabilities have various degrees of impact on different system elements. Also, different components contribute differently to the overall cost of integration and testing. Some are simply easier to integrate and test than others. Below are some suggestions for how to achieve most of the benefits, even if full, fast CI isn't immediately practical.

- **Integrate different aspects at different frequencies** – For example, the Baja Ride control System Teams might integrate their software multiple times per iteration, and potentially every day. A full vehicle integration, however, might be feasible only every few weeks, or perhaps at a Program Increment boundary.

- **Integrate all assets, but run deprecated tests** – Full validation, including running all regression tests, may be too slow or costly, but based on history, teams can usually determine that a majority of the problems can be found with a few vertical tests. The full regression suite is then reserved for less frequent intervals.

- **Use of emulated environments, stubs, and mocks** – Some components, equipment, third-party subsystems, etc. may not be readily available to test frequently in a real environment. Instead, teams build emulators, mocks, and stubs to simulate the rest of the system environment.

It is also important to note that frequent integration represents a special challenge for groups that are in the initial transition to leaner methods. They just haven't done it previously, nor have they yet built the infrastructure necessary to do so. But the goal is clear, so the current state cannot be an excuse to simply reduce the scope or extent of integration. Most of these challenges should disappear in a near-future state, but *only if the teams start now*.

## Enabling Continuous Integration

Building complex solutions in a Lean and Agile manner is a journey gated in large part by continuous integration capabilities. The following section provides some suggestions for how to move forward quickly.

### Common Cadence

Integration points are easier when all the teams are moving in the same, consistent rhythm. That's why all iterations are aligned on the same PI boundaries. While it may be necessary to allow some minor shifts of integration/testing effort past the iteration end point, the timelier, the better. If full CI can't be accomplished in the course of the iteration, teams can make near term trade-offs, while continuously improving their techniques and infrastructure.

### Infrastructure

Effective continuous integration depends on availability of the execution environments, CI and test tools, mocks and emulators, etc. Some of the infrastructure is built and supported by the System Team. Other aspects are more efficiently managed by the teams themselves, allowing them to more quickly understand the performance of the system at all times.

Infrastructure is of course, an investment, and as such must be evaluated against the anticipated return. An organization that doesn't yet have the Lean culture of Built-in Quality may struggle to understand the positive future impact of infrastructure enhancements. Therefore, new investments in development time, as well as equipment, may be considered simply a source of expense or delay. But Lean-Agile Leaders take the long view and make the investments necessary today to increase velocity for the marathon ahead.

**Engineering Techniques in Support of CI**

Continuous integration is easier when the system is designed with those concerns in mind. *Designing for Testability*—a technique that originates from hardware development—calls for better modularity, and separation of concerns, as well as the use of primary interfaces and physical test points. Set-Based Design can also help provide a clearer separation of some solution elements (via interfaces, protocols) that can be fixed for testing, while preserving flexibility.

The frequency of integration and testing is a primary determinate of quality. However, the cost of doing so may be a concern, especially if much of the work is performed manually. Automation of the process, or selected parts, lowers these costs and increases productivity. When accompanied by some of the other techniques discussed above, automation can significantly change the shape of the Figure 1 trade-off curve.

**Support of the System Team**

The System Team carries a lot of this responsibility. But it is not the only group of people, nor the ones solely responsible, for the quality of the ART increment. Integration and Testing is therefore a *role collaboration*, with a constant exchange of knowledge within the ART and value stream.

If Agile Teams are kept out of the integration loop, they will continue to deliver inconsistent increments. Similarly, if the teams do not provide the System Team with the ever-changing solution context, it will quickly lead to gaps in expectations and discrepancies in environments and configurations.

## CI Is a Culture

Many continuous integration discussions revolve around tooling, and tooling is a critical element. However, continuous integration is a cultural change, a new mindset that requires new responsibilities at all levels. Below are three suggestions for implementing a successful CI culture:

- **Integrate often** – The more frequently teams integrate, the quicker they find problems. The harder it is to do, the more often they need to do it—eliminating impediments and adding automation along the way—resulting in faster learning cycles and less rework.

- **Make integration results visible** – When the integration process breaks, everybody should know how and why it broke. And when it's fixed, they should know what fixed it, too.

- **Fixing a failed integration attempt is the top priority** – If teams simply keep working in the presence of a failed integration effort, it negates the gains and can even create apathy for the effort. To stress this, many teams use flashing lights when a build is broken, and highly visible indicators of percentages of the time the system is broken. Attention is then directed immediately to fixing the problems before new functionality is added, thereby accelerating learning and decreasing the impact of the underlying issue.

# Test-First

*We never have enough time for testing, so let's just write the test first.*
—Kent Beck

## Abstract

Agile testing differs from the big-bang, test-at-the-end approach of traditional development. Instead, code is developed and tested in small increments, often with the development of the test itself preceding the development of the code. In this way, tests serve to elaborate and better define the intended system behavior before the system is coded. Quality is built in from the beginning. This just-in-time approach to elaboration of the intended system behavior also mitigates the need for lengthy, detailed requirements, specifications, and sign-offs that are often used in traditional software development to control quality. Even better, these tests, unlike traditional requirements, are automated wherever possible. Even when they're not, they provide a definitive statement of what the system *actually does*, rather than a statement of early thoughts about what it was *supposed* to do.

This article describes a comprehensive approach to Agile testing, and *testing first*, based on Brian Marick's four-quadrant Agile Testing Matrix. Quadrants 1 and 2 define the tests that support the development of the system and its intended behavior; they are described in this article. Quadrants 3 and 4 are more fully described in the "Releases" and "Nonfunctional Requirements" articles, respectively.

Note: Of course, not all these tests can be written or executed *first*, but the authors believe that *Test-First* captures the proper sentiment.

## Details

Agile testing is a continuous process, not a one-time or end-game event. It is integral to Lean and Built-in-Quality. Simply, Agile Teams and ARTs can't go fast without endemic quality, and they can't achieve endemic quality without continuous testing and, wherever possible, "testing first."

### The Agile Testing Matrix

XP proponent and Agile Manifesto signer Brian Marick helped pioneer Agile testing by describing a matrix that guides reasoning about such tests. This matrix was further developed in *Agile Testing* [1] and extended for the scaled Agile paradigm in *Agile Software Requirements* [2].

Figure 1 describes and extends the original matrix with guidance on *what to test* and *when*.

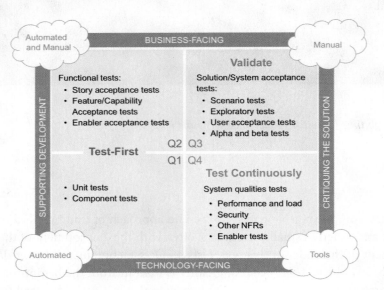

*Figure 1. Agile Testing Matrix*

- The *horizontal axis* of the matrix contains *business-* or *technology*-facing tests. Business-facing tests are understandable by the user and are described using business language. Technology-facing tests are written in the language of the developer and are used to evaluate whether the code delivers the behaviors the developer intended.

- The *vertical axis* contains tests *supporting development* (evaluating internal code) or critiquing the solution (evaluating the system against the user's requirements).

Classification into these four quadrants (Q1 – Q4) enables a comprehensive testing strategy that helps ensure quality:

- **Q1** contains unit and component tests. These automated tests are written by developers and run before and after code changes, to confirm that the system works as intended. Automating their execution reduces the overhead of executing a large number of tests in different development or test environments.

- **Q2** contains functional tests (user acceptance tests) for Stories, Features, and Capabilities, to validate that they work the way the Product Owner (or Customer/user) intended. Feature- and Capability-level acceptance tests validate the aggregate behavior of many user stories. Teams automate these tests whenever possible and only use manual tests when absolutely necessary.

- **Q3** contains system-level acceptance tests to validate that the aggregate behavior of the system meets usability and functionality requirements, including various scenarios that may be encountered in actual use.

These can include exploratory testing, user acceptance testing, scenario-based testing, final usability testing, and more. These tests are often done manually because they involve users and testers using the system in actual or simulated deployment and usage scenarios. These tests are used for final system validation and are required before delivery to the end user.

- **Q4** contains system qualities tests to verify that the system meets its Nonfunctional Requirements (NFRs), as exhibited in part by Enablers tests. They are typically supported by a suite of automated testing tools, such as load and performance, designed specifically for this purpose. Since any system changes can violate conformance with NFRs, they must be run continuously, or at least whenever is reasonably practical.

Quadrants 1 and 2 test the functionality of the system. When these tests are developed before the code is committed, that is described as *Test-first*. Test-first methods include both Test-Driven Development (TDD) and Acceptance Test-Driven Development (ATDD). Both methods use test automation to support continuous integration, team velocity, and development effectiveness. Quadrants 1 and 2 are described below; Quadrants 3 and 4 are described in the companion articles "Releases" and "Nonfunctional Requirements," respectively.

## Test-Driven (Test-First) Development

Beck [3] and others have defined a set of XP practices described under the umbrella label of Test-Driven Development, or TDD. The focus is on writing the unit test before writing the code, as described below:

1. Write the test first. Writing the test first ensures that the developer understands the required behavior of the new code.

2. Run the test, and watch it fail. Because there is as yet no code to be tested, this may seem silly initially, but this accomplishes two useful objectives: It tests the test itself and any test harnesses that hold the test in place, and it illustrates how the system will fail if the code is incorrect.

3. Write the minimum amount of code that is necessary to pass the test. If the test fails, rework the code or the test as necessary until a module is created that routinely passes the test.

In XP, this practice was primarily designed to operate in the context of unit tests, which are developer-written tests (also code) that test the classes and methods that are used. These are a form of "white-box testing" because they test the internals of the system and the various code paths that may be executed. Pair work is used extensively as well; when two sets of eyes have seen the code *and* the tests, it's probable that the module is of high quality. Even when not pairing, the test is "the first other set of eyes" that see the code, and developers note that they often refactor the code in order to pass the test as simply and elegantly as possible. This is quality at the source—one of the main reasons that SAFe relies on TDD.

### Unit Tests

Most TDD is done in the context of unit testing, which prevents QA and test personnel from spending most of their time finding and reporting on code-level bugs. This allows additional focus on more system-level testing challenges where more complex behaviors are found, based on the interactions of the unit code modules. In support of this, the open source community has built unit testing frameworks to cover most languages, including Java, C, C#, C++, XML, HTTP, and Python. Now there are unit-testing frameworks for most languages and coding constructs a developer is likely to encounter. These frameworks provide a harness for the development and maintenance of unit tests and for automatically executing unit tests against the system under development.

Because the unit tests are written before or concurrently with the code, and because the unit testing frameworks include test execution automation, unit testing can be accomplished within the Iteration. Moreover, the unit test frameworks hold and manage the accumulated unit tests, so regression testing automation for unit tests is largely free for the team. Unit testing is a cornerstone practice of software agility, and any investments a team makes toward more comprehensive unit testing will be well rewarded in quality and productivity.

### Component Tests

In a like manner, component testing is used to test larger-scale components of the system. Many of these are present in various architectural layers, where they provide services needed by features or other components. Testing tools and practices for implementing component tests vary according to the nature of the component. For example, unit testing frameworks can hold arbitrarily complex tests written in the framework language (Java, C, C#, and so on), so many teams use their unit testing frameworks to build component tests. They may not even think of them differently, as it's simply part of their testing strategy. In other cases, developers may use other testing tools or write fully customized tests in any language or environment that is most productive for them to test these larger system behaviors. These test are automated as well, where they serve as a primary defense against unanticipated consequences of refactoring and new code.

## Acceptance Test-Driven Development

Quadrant 2 of the Agile Testing Matrix shows that test-first applies as well to testing stories and features and capabilities as it does to unit testing. After all, the goal is to have the system work as intended, not to simply have the code do as intended. This is called *Acceptance Test-Driven Development* (ATDD), and whether it is adopted formally or informally, many teams simply find it more efficient to *write the acceptance test first*, before developing the code.

Pugh [4] notes that the emphasis here can be viewed more as expressing requirements in unambiguous terms than as a focus on the test per se. He further notes that there are three alternative labels to this requirement detailing process: ATDD, Specification by Example, and Behavior-Driven Design.

There are some slight differences to these three versions, but they all emphasize understanding requirements prior to implementation. In particular, specification by example suggests that the Product Owner should be sure to provide examples, as they often do not write the acceptance tests themselves.

Whether its viewed as a form of requirements expression or as a test, the understanding that results is the same. The acceptance tests serve to record the decisions made in the conversation (see the 3Cs in the "Writing Good Stories" section of the "Stories" article) between the team and the Product Owner, so that the team understands the specifics of the intended behavior the story represents.

### Functional Tests

Story acceptance tests are functional tests intended to ensure that the implementation of each new user story delivers the intended behavior. The testing is performed during the course of an iteration. If all the new stories work as intended, then it's likely that each new increment of software will ultimately satisfy the needs of the users.

Feature and capability acceptance testing is performed during the course of a Program Increment. The tools used are generally the same, but these tests operate at the next level of abstraction, typically testing how some number of stories work together to deliver a larger value to the user. Of course, there can easily be multiple feature acceptance tests associated with a more complex feature, and the same goes for stories. In this manner, there is strong verification that the system works as intended at the feature, capability, and story levels.

The following are characteristics of functional tests:

- Written in the language of the business

- Developed in a conversation between the developers, testers, and the Product Owner

- Black-box tests that verify only the outputs of the system and meet conditions of satisfaction, without concern for how the result is achieved

- Implemented during the course of the iteration in which the story is implemented

Although everyone can write tests, the Product Owner, as Business Owner/Customer proxy, is generally responsible for the efficacy of the tests. If a story does not pass its test, the teams get no credit for that story and it is carried over into the next iteration, when the code and/or the test are reworked until the story passes the test.

Features, capabilities, and stories cannot be considered done until they pass one or more acceptance tests. Stories realize the intended features and capabilities. There can be more than one test associated with a particular feature, capability, or story.

## Automating Acceptance Testing

Because acceptance tests run at a level above the code, there are a variety of approaches to executing them, including handling them as manual tests. However, manual tests pile up very quickly ("the faster you go, the faster they grow, the slower you go"), and eventually, the number of manual tests required to run a regression slows down the team and introduces major delays in value delivery.

To avoid this, teams know that they have to automate most of their acceptance tests. They use a variety of tools to do so, including the target programming language (Perl, Groovy, Java) or natural language as supported by specific testing frameworks, such as Robot Framework or Cucumber; or perhaps they use table formats as supported by the Framework for Integrated Testing (FIT). The preferred approach is to take a high level of abstraction that works directly against the business logic of the application, thereby preventing encumbrance by the presentation layer or other implementation details.

## Acceptance Test Template/Checklist

An ATDD checklist can help the team consider a simple list of things to do, review, and discuss each time a new story appears. *ASR* [2] provides an example of such a story acceptance-testing checklist.

---

### LEARN MORE

[1] Crispin, Lisa, and Janet Gregory. *Agile Testing: A Practical Guide for Testers and Agile Teams*. Addison-Wesley, 2009.

[2] Leffingwell, Dean. *Agile Software Requirements: Lean Requirements Practices for Teams, Programs, and the Enterprise*. Addison-Wesley, 2011.

[3] Beck, Kent. *Test-Driven Development*. Addison-Wesley, 2003.

[4] Pugh, Ken. *Lean-Agile Acceptance Test-Driven Development: Better Software Through Collaboration*. Addison-Wesley, 2011.

# Agile Contracts

*. . . select a winning contractor and then expect them to deliver on the requirements within the specified timeframe and budget. However, this traditional approach almost always led to failures—each a spectacular waste of taxpayer dollars.*

—Jason Bloomberg, Forbes, Fixing Scheduling with Agile at the VA [1]

## Abstract

Builders of large-scale systems must continually align with Customers and other stakeholders on what is being built. They must do so in the midst of frequent and continuous changes. Discoveries made during development, evolving Customer needs, changing technologies, and competitors' innovations can cause divergence of outcomes, or misalignment with expectations. Traditionally, requirement and design decisions were made up front to ensure that the Customer was getting what they wanted, and that was the basis for the contract. But these early requirements and design decisions constrained systems builders and reduced their ability to adapt to emerging information that could have helped them design a Solution that delivered better economic and competitive value for their Customers. The contract held them back. Thus the attempt to manage risk via early requirement specificity often backfired, to the detriment of all stakeholders.

To avoid this problem, other contract approaches with more shared risk and reward evolved, and, in many cases, they worked better. Even then, however, the legacy thinking of fixed requirements tended to influence agreements and expectations.

What's needed is a more Agile approach to contracts, one that benefits both parties in the near and the long term. This article describes the current state, then provides guidance for one such *Agile Contract* approach, the SAFe Managed-Investment Contract.

## Details

### Traditional Approaches to Systems Building Contracts

Traditionally, enterprises have used a variety of approaches to work with vendors in the outsourced procurement of complex systems. A continuum of approaches exist, ranging from "firm fixed price" to "time and materials," with almost every point in between. Figure 1 characterizes these various approaches, and the means by which risk is shared between the parties.

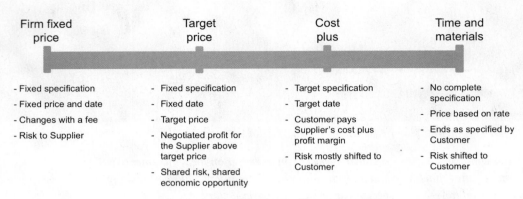

*Figure 1. A range of traditional contract types*

Despite a wide range of approaches, neither extreme delivers the best overall economic value, as discussed in the sections below.

### Firm Fixed-Price Contracts

On the left end of the scale are firm fixed-price contracts, which are common in industry today. The appeal of this approach is the assumption that the buyer will get exactly what they want and are willing to pay for, as Figure 2 illustrates.

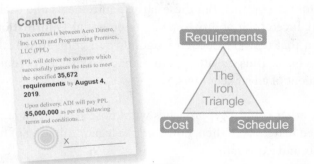

*Figure 2. Firm fixed-price contracts create the "iron triangle"*

In addition, it provides an opportunity for competitive bids, which may be required in many cases. Competitive bids can potentially provide economic advantages, as the bid should go to the Supplier with the highest degree of competence and efficiency.

However, there are many downsides to this approach:

- It assumes that the buyer's needs are well known far in advance of implementation

- Those needs must be reflected in requirements specifications and early design details. This triggers Big Up-Front Design (BUFD), waterfall-based development, and waterfall-based contracts.

- The contract is typically awarded to the lowest-cost bidder. That may or may not be the highest long-term economic value for the buyer.

Moreover, in order to get a fixed bid, critical decisions are made far too early in the cone of uncertainty (see Principle #3 – *Assume variability; preserve options*). The parties have entered into the "iron triangle" of fixed scope, schedule, and cost. But as facts change, both the buyer's and Supplier's hands are tied to the contract, *which now defines a thing no one wants to build or buy exactly as stated*. Much of the rest of the time is spent negotiating contract changes, and there is much waste in the process.

Worst of all, once the agreement is entered, each party has an *opposing* economic interest:

- It is to the buyer's short-term benefit to get as much out of the Supplier as possible, for as little money as possible
- It is in the Supplier's best interest to deliver the minimum value necessary to meet the contractual obligations

The net result is the contract type often sets up a *win-lose* scenario, which thereafter influences the entire business relationship between the parties, typically to the detriment of both.

**Time and Materials Contracts**

Given the above, it's clear why many in the industry want to move to the right on the spectrum. But the far right, time and materials—which might appear to be extremely Agile on the surface—has its challenges as well. The buyer has only trust to count on. Trust is a precious commodity indeed, and we lean on it in Lean, but misunderstandings, changes in market or technical conditions, and changes in buyer or Supplier economic models can force trust to take a back seat. And after all, it's in the Supplier's best economic interest to keep being paid for as long as possible. This can drag contracts out longer than necessary. Coupling this approach to a stage-gate process, whereby real progress can only be known at the end, compounds the problem.

Challenges can exist on the buyer's side as well. For example, when interviewed during a project post-mortem, Stephen W. Warren, executive in charge and CIO of the Department of Veterans Affairs Office of Information and Technology, noted that "according to the project manager, 'the project was never in crisis' since they were spending the entire budget every year, and thus were able to renew their funding for the next year. Their measure of success at the time was whether the project would continue to get funding, rather than whether it was able to deliver the necessary functionality." [1]

## A Collaborative Approach to Agile Contracts

Since neither end point on Figure 1 provides much assurance, perhaps the range in the middle is the sweet spot? Possibly, but even then the biases of traditional contracts, whether from the left or right, will likely creep into these agreements and expectations.

What's needed is a different approach, one that "trusts but verifies" that the systems builders are building the right thing in the right way, provides regular and objective governance for the buyer, and yet allows systems builders to have confidence in their Customers as well as in implied future economic commitments.

Characteristics of such an Agile contract type would include the ability to:

- Optimize the economic value for both parties in the long term as well as the short term
- Exploit variability via fixed versus variable requirements and adaptive response to new knowledge
- Provide complete and continuous visibility plus objective evidence of solution fitness
- Provide a measured approach to investment that can vary over time and stop when sufficient value has been achieved
- Provide the systems builder with near-term confidence of funding, and sufficient notice when funding winds down or stops
- Motivate both parties to build the best solution possible within agreed-to economic boundaries

## SAFe Managed-Investment Contracts

Given all of the above, the industry can benefit by moving toward a more Agile contracts paradigm, one where the optimum economics benefit both the buyer and the systems builder. The Lean-Agile constructs in SAFe can provide one such approach, the *SAFe Managed-Investment Contract*, which is described below.

### Precommitment

Prior to engaging in any significant investment contract for developing a complex system with many unknowns, some due diligence is required. In this case, the Customer and Supplier work together to come to terms on the basis of the contract. This is the precommitment phase, illustrated in Figure 3 on the next page.

During this phase the Customer has specific responsibilities, including understanding the basic constructs and responsibilities of this form of Agile contract, and defining and communicating the larger program mission statement to the Supplier (or potential Suppliers).

The Supplier does their initial homework as well. This often includes a first analysis of potential feasibility, and alignment of the buyer's solution needs with the Supplier's core competence. It also demands some understanding of the potential resources that will be required over the initial contract periods, and maybe even a rough cost estimate. However, these responsibilities are largely routine, and they can be assumed for the most part.

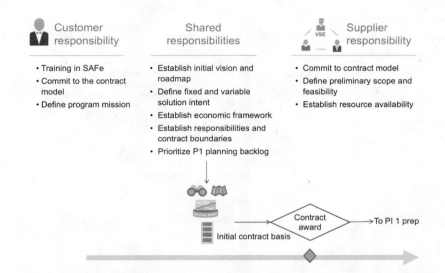

*Figure 3. SAFe Managed-Investment Contract precommitment phase*

The shared responsibilities in the middle, however, start the Customer and Supplier down a path to a more measured investment, one supported by continuous objective evidence of fitness for use. These responsibilities include:

- Establishing the initial vision and roadmap

- Defining the initial fixed and variable Solution Intent

- Prioritizing the initial program backlog for PI 1 planning

- Establishing execution responsibilities

- Establishing the economic framework, including economic trade-off parameters, the Program Increment funding commitment (number of PIs committed), initial funding levels, and other contractual terms

With respect to the PI funding commitment, in some cases the Supplier may need to provide a preliminary estimate for completion. In other cases, a pay-as-you-go approach may be suitable. Based on the agreements, the Customer will agree to fund the Supplier at certain rates for the early PIs. This is the initial commitment period. The length is based on context, but two PIs or so (20 weeks) may be a reasonable starting point.

Depending on context, the Customer may have such discussions with multiple potential Suppliers. If significant technical feasibility is involved, this can often be done under some form of feasibility contract, whereby the Supplier is compensated for the efforts to get to commitment. Alternately, this may be simply business as usual for the Supplier, with these precommitment investments a part of normal presales. At some point, however, the Customer can move on to award the contract.

## Contract Execution

Thereafter development begins, as is illustrated in Figure 4.

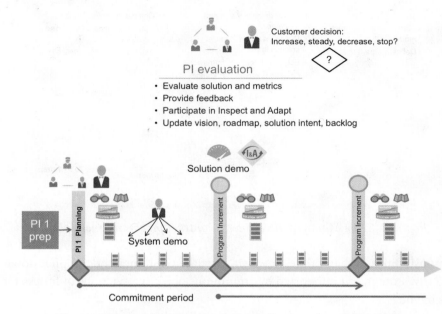

*Figure 4. SAFe Managed-Investment Contract execution phase*

A description of the activity timeline follows.

- **PI 1 preparation** – Both Supplier and Customer will invest some time and effort in preparing content and logistics for the first PI planning session. (Note: In some cases, it might be suitable that PI 1 planning is part of the precommitment phase, though this route clearly requires significant investment by both parties.)

- **PI 1 planning** – The first PI planning event is seminal to the program. There, Customer and Supplier stakeholders plan the first PI in Iteration-level detail.

- **PI 1 execution** – Depending on context, Customers participate at various levels in iteration execution; as a minimum, however, direct Customer engagement is usually required for each System Demo. For large Value Streams, however, the multiplicity of system demos may be replaced by a more fully integrated Solution Demo, which can occur more frequently than at PI boundaries.

- **PI evaluation** – Thereafter, each PI marks a critical milestone for both the Customer and Supplier. At each milestone, the solution demo is held and the Solution is evaluated. Agreed-to Metrics are compiled and analyzed, and decisions for the next PI are made.

The Inspect and Adapt session is used to assess progress and to plan improvements for the upcoming PI. At that point, the Customer may decide to keep funding steady state, to increase it, or to decrease it—or even begin to wind down, based on whether sufficient value *has* or has not been achieved. Thereafter, the next PI planning commences, with the input scope based on the outcome of that decision.

This process continues until the Solution has delivered the value the Customer requires, at which point the Customer starts winding down Supplier funding commitments in accordance with the agreement.

---

### LEARN MORE

[1] Bloomberg, Jason. "Fixing scheduling with Agile at the VA." *Forbes*. October 23, 2014.

[2] Jemilo, Drew. *Agile Contracts: Blast Off to a Zone of Collaborative Systems Building*. Agile 2015.

# Glossary of SAFe Terms

### Agile Architecture

Agile architecture is a set of values and practices that support the active evolution of the design and architecture of a system, concurrent with the implementation of new business functionality. With this approach, the architecture of a system, even a large one, evolves over time while simultaneously supporting the needs of current users. This avoids Big Up-Front Design (BUFD) and the starting and stopping of stage-gated methods.

### Agile Release Train

The Agile Release Train is a long-lived team of Agile Teams, typically consisting of 50 – 125 individuals. The ART aligns teams to a common mission and provides for a regular cadence for planning, development, and retrospective. Trains provide continuous product development flow, and each train has the dedicated resources necessary to continuously define, build, and test valuable and evaluate-able capabilities every two weeks.

### Agile Teams

The Agile Team is a cross-functional group of five to nine individuals who have the ability and authority to define, build, and test solution value—all in a short-iteration timebox. The team includes the individuals necessary to successfully deliver this value, supported by specialists where applicable.

### Architectural Runway

Architectural runway provides one of the means by which SAFe implements the concepts of Agile architecture. This runway provides the necessary technical basis for developing business initiatives and implementing new features and capabilities. An architectural runway exists when the enterprise's platforms have sufficient existing technological infrastructure to support the implementation of the highest-priority, near-term features without excessive, delay-inducing redesign.

### Budgets

SAFe provides strategies for Lean-Agile budgeting that funds value streams instead of projects. This empowers value streams with their own dedicated budget for rapid decision-making and flexible value delivery, while Program Portfolio Management (PPM) retains control of total spending, which is adjusted over time.

### Built-in Quality

Built-in quality is one of the four core values of SAFe. The enterprise's ability to deliver new functionality with the fastest sustainable lead time, along with the ability to be able to react to rapidly changing business conditions, is dependent on built-in quality.

### Business Epic

See *Epic*.

## Business Owners

Business Owners are a small group of stakeholders (typically three to five) who have the ultimate fiduciary, governance, efficacy, and ROI responsibility for the value delivered by a specific release train. Business Owners typically have management responsibility for Customer relationships, development, solution quality, deployment, operations, Product Management, and architecture.

## Capability

Capabilities are similar to features; however, they account for higher-level behaviors of the solution, which often spans multiple ARTs. Capabilities are maintained in the value stream backlog and are sized to fit in a program increment, so that each PI delivers solution value.

## CapEx and OpEx

A value stream budget may include both CapEx and OpEx elements. CapEx typically captures the expenses required to purchase, upgrade, or fix tangible physical assets or other property used to support solution building. In some cases, CapEx may also capture elements of the costs of labor for development of certain intangible assets. OpEx costs typically include salaries and overhead, contract labor, materials, supplies, and other items directly related to solution development activities.

## Communities of Practice

A Community of Practice (CoP) is an informal group of team members and other experts, acting within the context of a program or enterprise, that has a mission of sharing practical knowledge in one or more relevant domains.

## Continuous Integration

Continuous integration is a practice whereby team members integrate and validate their work frequently; in the case of software, this can occur at least daily or even multiple times per day. Where possible, integration is verified by automated build and test environments that quickly identify integration problems and defects.

## Coordination

See *Value Stream Coordination*.

## Core Values

SAFe respects and reflects four core values: alignment, built-in quality, transparency, and program execution.

## Customer

The Customer is whoever consumes the work of a value stream. Customers are the ultimate arbiters of value delivered. Whether internal or external to the development organization, they are an integral part of the development value stream.

## Develop on Cadence

Basing routine development activities on a fast, synchronous cadence—a regular, predictive rhythm of important events—helps manage the inherent variability in systems development. This is a fundamental premise of SAFe. Its effects can be seen directly on the Big Picture, with the fast cadence of synchronized, short iterations followed by the further integration of those iterations into larger program increments.

## DevOps

DevOps is a mindset, culture, and set of technical practices that stresses communication, collaboration, and close cooperation among Agile development teams and other technology professionals who are necessary for developing, testing, deploying, and maintaining software and systems.

## Economic Framework

An economic framework is a set of decision rules that aligns everyone to the financial objectives of the mission, including budget considerations driven from the program portfolio. SAFe's first Lean-Agile principle is to take an economic view; the economic framework captures the essential economic elements for successful solution development.

## Enabler Capability

Enabler capabilities occur at the value stream level, where they capture work of that type. As these enablers are a type of capability, they share the same attributes, including a statement of benefits and acceptance criteria, and they must be structured so as to fit within a single PI.

## Enabler Epic

Enabler epics are a type of epic, and as such are written using the value statement format defined for epics. They tend to cut across value streams and PIs. They require a lightweight business case to support their implementation. They are identified and tracked through the portfolio Kanban system.

## Enabler Feature

Enabler features occur at the program level, where they capture work of that type. As these enablers are a type of feature, they share the same attributes, including a statement of benefits and acceptance criteria, and are structured so as to fit within a single PI.

## Enabler Story

Enabler stories, as a type of story, must fit in iterations. However, while they may not require user voice format, they have acceptance criteria to clarify their requirements and support demonstration and testing.

## Enablers

Enablers encapsulate the exploration and the architectural and infrastructure development activities necessary to support some future solution capability. They occur at all levels of the framework and are described as enabler epics, enabler capabilities, enabler features, and enabler stories, depending on their level.

## Enterprise

The enterprise represents the business entity that has the ultimate strategy, fiduciary, and governance authority for the value streams that constitute a SAFe portfolio. Each SAFe portfolio exists in the broader enterprise context; that is the source of the business strategy that the portfolio must address. The enterprise also provides the general governance model for all portfolios.

## Enterprise Architect

The Enterprise Architect works with business stakeholders and Solution and System Architects to drive holistic technology implementation across value streams. The Enterprise Architect relies on continuous feedback, fosters adaptive design and engineering practices, and drives collaboration of programs and teams around a common technical vision.

## Epic

Epics are significant initiatives that help guide value streams toward the larger aim of the portfolio. They are investment intensive and far ranging in impact. They require a formulation and analysis of cost, impact, and opportunity in a lightweight business case, as well as financial approval before implementation. There are two kinds of epics: business epics and enabler epics, and they may appear at the portfolio, value stream, and program levels.

## Epic Owners

Epic Owners have the responsibility of shepherding epics through the portfolio Kanban system. They develop the business case and, when approved, work directly with the key stakeholders on the affected trains to help realize the implementation.

## Feature

A feature is a service provided by the system that fulfills stakeholder needs. Each is developed by a single Agile Release Train. They are maintained in the program backlog and are sized to fit in a program increment so that each PI delivers conceptual integrity. Each feature includes a statement of benefits and defined acceptance criteria.

## Implementing 1-2-3

Implementing SAFe 1-2-3 is a proven, successful pattern for SAFe implementation. It describes three basic steps: 1) train implementers and Lean-Agile change agents; 2) train all executives, managers, and leaders; 3) train teams and launch Agile Release Trains.

## Innovation and Planning Iteration

SAFe provides for periodic innovation and planning iterations, which serve a variety of purposes. They provide an estimating buffer for meeting objectives, a dedicated time for inspect and adapt and PI Planning activities, a cadence-based opportunity for innovation, time for continuing education, time for working on the technical infrastructure and other impediments, and time for backlog refinement.

## Inspect and Adapt

Inspect and Adapt (I&A) is a regular event, held at the end of each PI, that provides time to demonstrate the solution; get feedback; and then reflect, problem-solve, and identify improvement actions. The improvement items can then be immediately incorporated into PI planning.

## Iteration Execution

In SAFe, iterations have a fixed, two-week timebox. Agile Teams take items from the iteration backlog and define, build, and test them into the system baseline during this two-week period.

## Iteration Goals

Iteration goals are a high-level summary of the business and technical goals that the team and Product Owner agree to accomplish in an iteration. In SAFe, iteration goals are integral to the effective coordination of an Agile Release Train as a self-organizing, self-managing team of teams.

## Iteration Planning

Iteration planning is the ceremony during which all team members plan the upcoming iteration. The output of the meeting includes the iteration backlog, consisting of the stories and acceptance criteria committed to in the iteration; a statement of iteration goals; and a commitment by the team to the work needed to achieve those goals.

### Iteration Retrospective

The iteration retrospective is a short team meeting held at the end of an iteration, wherein team members gather in a private, safe environment to discuss the efficacy of their practices and define improvements for the upcoming period.

### Iterations

Iterations (*sprints* in Scrum) are a strict timebox in which teams deliver incremental value in the form of working, tested software and systems. Each iteration has a standard pattern: plan the iteration; commit to a goal; execute; demo the work to the key stakeholders; and, finally, hold a retrospective, wherein the team analyzes and determines actions necessary to improve their performance.

### Lean-Agile Leaders

Lean-Agile Leaders are lifelong learners, managers, teachers, and coaches who help teams build better software systems through understanding and exhibiting the values, principles, and practices of Lean, systems thinking, and Agile software development. Lean-Agile Leaders adhere to the principles of Lean-Agile leadership.

### Lean-Agile Mindset

By applying the Agile Manifesto and Lean thinking, a Lean-Agile mindset provides a comprehensive approach to Lean-Agile development that focuses on understanding and optimizing the flow of value from concept to delivery. SAFe's House of Lean is based on delivering value in the sustainably shortest lead time, respect for people and culture, flow, innovation, and relentless improvement—supported by a foundation of Lean-Agile leadership.

### Metrics

The primary measure in SAFe is the objective measurement of working solutions. This is determined empirically, by demonstration throughout and at the end of every iteration and program increment. There are a number of additional intermediate and long-term measures as well, metrics that teams, programs, and portfolios can use to measure progress.

### Milestones

Milestones mark specific progress points on the development timeline, and they can be invaluable in measuring and monitoring the progress and risk of a program. As opposed to phase-gate milestones, SAFe milestones are based on PIs, planned learning points, and fixed dates.

### Model-Based Systems Engineering

Model-Based Systems Engineering (MBSE) is the application of modeling and modeling tools to the requirements, design, analysis, and verification activities in solution development. MBSE provides a cost-effective way to learn about system characteristics prior to and during construction, and it helps manage the complexity and cost of large-system documentation.

### Nonfunctional Requirements

Nonfunctional requirements describe system attributes such as security, reliability, performance, maintainability, scalability, and usability. They can also be constraints or restrictions on the design of the system.

## PI Planning

PI planning is the seminal, cadence-based, face-to-face planning event that serves as the heartbeat of the Agile Release Train. It is integral and essential to SAFe.

## Portfolio Backlog

The portfolio backlog is the highest-level backlog in SAFe. It provides a holding mechanism for the upcoming business and enabler epics required to create a portfolio solution set, a set that provides the competitive differentiation and operational efficiencies necessary to address the strategic themes and facilitate business success.

## Portfolio Business Epic

Portfolio business epics capture the largest crosscutting, business-facing initiatives that occur within a portfolio.

## Portfolio Kanban

The SAFe portfolio Kanban system is used primarily to identify and manage the flow of epics that affect the course of action for value streams and the Agile Release Trains (ARTs) that realize them.

## Portfolio Level

The SAFe portfolio level is the highest level of concern in SAFe. It provides the basic constructs for organizing the Lean-Agile enterprise around the flow of value via one or more value streams, each of which develops the systems and solutions necessary to meet the strategic intent.

## Pre- and Post-PI Planning

The pre- and post-PI planning meetings allow ARTs and Suppliers in large value streams to build an aligned plan for the next PI. The pre- and post-PI planning meetings serve as a wrapper for program level PI planning, where the actual, detailed planning takes place.

## Product Management

Product Management is responsible for identifying Customer needs. They own the ART vision and roadmaps, pricing, licensing, ROI, and the program backlog. They drive PI objectives and release content via prioritized features and acceptance criteria, and they accept features into the baseline.

## Product Owner

The Product Owner is the team member responsible for defining stories and prioritizing the team backlog. The Product Owner is also a member of the extended Product Manager/Product Owner team, understanding and contributing to the program backlog, vision, and roadmap.

## Program Backlog

The program backlog is the single, definitive repository for all the upcoming work anticipated to advance the Agile Release Train solution. The backlog consists primarily of features intended to address user needs and deliver business benefits; it also includes the enabler features necessary to build the architectural runway.

## Program Epics

Program epics are initiatives that are large enough to warrant analysis and a lightweight business case, but they are constrained to a single Agile Release Train. Unlike features, which are small enough to fit inside a single PI, program epics could take several PIs to develop. They can be a result of value stream or portfolio epics, or they may arise locally as ARTs reason about initiatives that represent larger effort and value.

## Program Increment

A Program Increment (PI) is the larger development timebox that uses cadence and synchronization to facilitate planning, limit WIP, provide for aggregation of newsworthy value for feedback, and ensure consistent program level retrospectives. It is composed of multiple development iterations and an innovation and planning iteration. Due to its scope, the PI also provides the cadence for portfolio level and roadmap considerations.

## Program Kanban

The program Kanban helps ensure that features are analyzed prior to reaching an iteration boundary. They are estimated and prioritized appropriately, and feature acceptance criteria are established.

## Program Level

The program level is where people and other resources are applied to some important, long-lived enterprise mission. Programs in SAFe are delivered by long-lived Agile Release Trains, which deliver a portion (in some cases all) of a value stream.

## Program PI Objectives

The aggregation of each team's PI objectives becomes the program PI objectives, which are approved and assigned business value by the Business Owners. If value stream level PI planning is needed, then the programs' PI objectives are synthesized and aggregated to become value stream PI objectives.

## Program Portfolio Management

Program Portfolio Management (PPM) represents the function that has the highest-level strategy and fiduciary decision-making responsibility in an enterprise portfolio. The PPM function has responsibility for strategy and investment funding, program management, and governance.

## Release

The goal of Lean-Agile is frequent delivery of valuable, working, and fully tested solution increments. This is accomplished via a stream of releases, each of which has been validated and approved for final efficacy of use and is accompanied by the documentation necessary to ensure successful application.

## Release Any Time

SAFe provides a separation of concerns that provides development teams with the cadence and synchronization tools they need to manage complexity and rapid change in their environment, while allowing for either synchronous (occurring on the PI boundary) or asynchronous (occurring any time) releases of value to the market.

## Release Management

Release Management is a function that assists with planning, managing, and governing releases. This function has the authority and responsibility to help guide the value stream toward the business goals. It may contain dedicated individuals, or it may simply be a role that various Lean-Agile leaders play in the portfolio.

## Release Train Engineer

The Release Train Engineer (RTE) facilitates Agile Release Train processes and execution. The RTE escalates impediments, helps manage risk, helps ensure value delivery, and drives continuous improvement.

## Roadmap

The roadmap communicates planned Agile Release Train and value stream deliverables and milestones over a timeline. The roadmap includes committed deliverables and visibility into the forecasted deliverables of the next few PIs. It is developed and updated by Solution and Product Management as the vision and delivery strategy evolve.

## SAFe Principles

SAFe is based on nine immutable, underlying Lean and Agile principles. These are the fundamental tenets, the basic truths and economic underpinnings that drive the roles and practices that make SAFe effective.

## Scrum Master

The SAFe Scrum Master is a servant leader and coach for the Agile Team. Primary responsibilities include ensuring that the process is being followed; educating the team in Scrum, XP, and SAFe; eliminating impediments; and fostering the environment for high-performing team dynamics, continuous flow, and relentless improvement.

## ScrumXP

ScrumXP is a lightweight yet disciplined and productive process for cross-functional, self-organized teams to operate within the context of SAFe. A ScrumXP team consists of five to nine people, collocated wherever possible. ScrumXP teams use Scrum project management practices and XP-inspired technical practices, and they visualize and measure the flow of value.

## Set-Based Design

Set-Based Design is a practice that maintains multiple requirements and design options for a longer period in the development cycle. Empirical data is used to narrow focus based on the emergent knowledge.

## Shared Services

Shared Services represent specialty roles that are necessary for the success of an Agile Release Train or value stream but that cannot be dedicated full time to any specific train. These may include security specialists, information architects, DBAs, technical writers, quality assurance, IT operations personnel, and more.

## Solution

A solution is either a final product delivered to the ultimate economic buyer or, alternately, a set of systems that enable an operational value stream within the organization.

## Solution Architect/Engineering

SAFe Solution Architect/Engineering represents the individuals and teams who have the technical responsibility for the overall architectural and engineering design of the solution. They help align the value stream and Agile Release Trains to a common technological and architectural vision.

## Solution Context

Solution context identifies critical aspects of the target solution environment and its impact on the usage, installation, operation, and support of the solution itself. It impacts development priorities and infrastructure, test environments, solution capabilities, features, and nonfunctional requirements. It also establishes focus for DevOps and similar deployment considerations.

## Solution Demo

The solution demo is the apex event of the PI cycle for a value stream. The results of all the development efforts from multiple ARTs—along with the contributions from Suppliers—are integrated, evaluated, and made visible to the Customers and other stakeholders. This demo provides a regular cadence for objective evaluation of the solution and for gathering stakeholder and Customer feedback.

## Solution Intent

Solution intent represents the repository for storing, managing, and communicating knowledge of the solution that the systems builders are developing, as well as technical information about how they are going to build it. It includes specifications, designs, and tests for the current state of the solution, as well intended changes. It can be realized in many forms, from documents, spreadsheets, and whiteboard sessions to formal requirements and modeling tools.

## Solution Management

Solution Management is the value stream content authority. They have primary responsibility for development and prioritization of the value stream backlog. They work with Customers to understand their needs, create the vision and roadmap, define requirements, and guide work through the value stream Kanban.

## Spanning Palette

The spanning palette is not an artifact per se; rather, it comprises various roles and artifacts that may be applicable at any level of the framework. It is used to customize the framework implementation to a specific context. For a more complete discussion, see the "Program Level" article.

## Stories

Stories are the primary artifact used to define system behavior in Agile development. Stories are not requirements; they are short, simple descriptions of a small piece of desired functionality, usually told from the user's perspective and written in the user's language. Each story is intended to support implementation of a small, vertical slice of system functionality, supporting highly incremental development.

## Strategic Themes

Strategic themes are specific, itemized business objectives that connect the SAFe portfolio to the enterprise business strategy. They provide business context for decision-making within the portfolio, affecting the economic framework and investments in value streams and ARTs. They serve as inputs to the budget, portfolio, solution, and program backlog decisions.

## Supplier

Suppliers develop and deliver components and subsystems that help Lean-Agile organizations deliver value to their Customers. Suppliers possess unique and distinctively competent skills and solutions and are experts in their technology; they can provide a high leverage point for fast and economical delivery.

## System Architect/Engineering

System Architect/Engineering aligns the ARTs to a common technological and architectural vision of the solution under development. They participate in defining the system and subsystems, validate technology assumptions, and evaluate alternatives. They support system development through providing, communicating, and evolving the larger technological and architectural view of the solution.

## System Demo

The system demo is a primary mechanism for evaluating the full ART system and gaining feedback from the stakeholders. It occurs at the end of every iteration and provides an integrated, aggregate view of the new features that have been delivered by all the teams on the train in the most recent iteration. It provides the ART with a fact-based measure of current, system-level progress within the program increment.

## System Team

The System Team is a special Agile Team on the ART or value stream (sometimes both) that is chartered to provide assistance in building and using the Agile development environment infrastructure, including continuous integration and test automation, integrating assets from Agile Teams, and performing end-to-end solution testing. They often participate in demonstrating solutions in the system demo.

## Team Backlog

The team backlog represents the collection of all the things a team needs to do to advance their portion of the system. It contains user and enabler stories that originate from the program backlog, as well as stories that arise locally from the team's specific context.

## Team Demo

The team demo is used to measure the team's progress by showing working stories to the Product Owner and other team members and stakeholders, and to get their feedback at the end of each iteration. Teams demonstrate every story, spike, refactor, and new nonfunctional requirement in this demo.

## Team Kanban

Team Kanban is a method that facilitates the flow of value by visualizing work flow, establishing work-in-process limits, measuring throughput, and continuously improving the process. Kanban is particularly useful for System Teams, DevOps, and maintenance teams, and for other situations in which a response mandate, fast-changing priorities, and lower value of planning lead them to this choice.

## Team Level

The team level describes the organization, artifact, role, activities, and process model for the Agile Teams who power the Agile Release Train.

## Team PI Objectives

Team PI objectives are a summarized description of the specific business and technical goals that an Agile Team intends to achieve in the upcoming PI. Their purpose is to validate understanding of business and technical intent; focus alignment on outcomes rather than on process or tactical concerns; and summarize data in a way that enhances communication, alignment, and visibility.

## Test-First

Test-first is the practice of developing and testing a system in small increments, often with the development of the test itself preceding the development of the code or component. In this way, tests serve to elaborate and better define the intended system behavior before the system is built, thereby enhancing quality.

## User Experience

While Agile Teams have responsibility for implementing the solution, including the user-facing elements, User Experience (UX) designers support a consistent user experience across the components and systems of the larger solution.

### Value Stream Backlog

The value stream backlog is the definitive repository for all the upcoming work anticipated to advance the solution. The backlog consists of upcoming capabilities, which can span multiple ARTs, as well as enablers that advance learning and build the architectural runway.

### Value Stream Coordination

Value stream coordination provides guidance for managing dependencies across value streams in a portfolio.

### Value Stream Engineer

The Value Stream Engineer facilitates value stream processes and execution. He escalates impediments, manages risk, and helps ensure value delivery and continuous improvement.

### Value Stream Epics

Value stream epics are initiatives that are large enough to warrant analysis and a lightweight business case (see the "Epics" article) but are constrained to a single value stream. Unlike capabilities, which are defined to be small enough to fit inside a single program increment, value stream epics could take several PIs to develop. They can arise as a result of portfolio epics, or they may arise locally as value streams plan larger initiatives.

### Value Stream Kanban

The value stream Kanban helps ensure that value stream epics and capabilities are reasoned about and analyzed prior to reaching a PI boundary, that they are prioritized appropriately, and that acceptance criteria have been established to guide a high-fidelity implementation.

### Value Stream Level

The value stream level supports builders of large and complex solutions that typically require multiple ARTs, as well as the contributions of Suppliers. This level is most often used by enterprises that face the largest systems challenges, building large-scale, multidisciplinary software and cyber-physical systems.

### Value Stream PI Objectives

During the post-PI planning meeting, ART objectives are further summarized at the value stream level and become value stream objectives. This is the top level of PI objectives in SAFe, and they communicate to stakeholders what the value stream, as a whole, will deliver in the upcoming PI.

### Value Streams

Value streams are the primary SAFe construct for understanding, organizing, and delivering value. Each value stream is a long-lived series of steps that an enterprise uses to provide a continuous flow of value to a Customer. Value streams are realized by Agile Release Trains.

### Vision

The Vision describes a future view of the solution to be developed, reflecting Customer and stakeholder needs as well as features and capabilities that are proposed to address those needs. It provides the larger, contextual overview and purpose of the solution under development. Vision appears on the spanning palette and can be applied at any level in the framework.

## Weighted Shortest Job First (WSJF)

Weighted Shortest Job First (WSJF) is an economic model for prioritizing "jobs" based on product development flow. WSJF is calculated as the cost of delay divided by job duration. In SAFe, "jobs" are the epics, features, and capabilities that are developed by ARTs. There are three primary elements to the cost of delay: 1) user business value, 2) time criticality, and 3) risk reduction opportunity enablement value.

# Bibliography

SAFe is based on our own work; the work of the contributors and SPCs worldwide; and an incredible body of knowledge about Agile, Lean thinking, Lean product development, systems thinking, organizational change management, human potential, business strategy, management philosophy, and more. Each of the books and articles in the bibliography below have contributed materially to the authors' perspectives and are integral to what makes SAFe safe.

- Adkins, Lyssa. *Coaching Agile Teams: A Companion for ScrumMasters, Agile Coaches, and Project Managers in Transition*. Addison-Wesley, 2010.

- Adzic, Gojko. *Impact Mapping: Making a Big Impact with Software Products and Projects*. Provoking Thoughts, 2012.

- Ambler, Scott. "Agile Architecture: Strategies for Scaling Agile Development." Agile Modeling, 2012. www.agilemodeling.com/essays/agileArchitecture.htm.

- Ambler, Scott W. and Mark Lines. *Disciplined Agile Delivery: A Practitioner's Guide to Agile Software Delivery in the Enterprise*. IBM Press, 2012.

- Anderson, David J. *Kanban: Successful Evolutionary Change for Your Technology Business*. Blue Hole Press, 2010.

- Aoki, Katsuki and Thomas Taro Lennerfors. "New, Improved Keiretsu." *Harvard Business Review*. September 2013.

- Appelo, Jurgen. *Management 3.0: Leading Agile Developers, Developing Agile Leaders*. Addison-Wesley, 2011.

- Bain, Scott. *Emergent Design: The Evolutionary Nature of Professional Software Development*. Addison-Wesley, 2008.

- Beck, Kent. *Test-Driven Development: By Example*. Addison-Wesley, 2002.

- Beck, Kent and Cynthia Andres. *Extreme Programming Explained: Embrace Change*. Addison-Wesley, 2004.

- Beck, Kent and Martin Fowler. *Planning Extreme Programming*. Addison-Wesley, 2001.

- Bloomberg, Jason. *The Agile Architecture Revolution: How Cloud Computing, REST-Based SOA, and Mobile Computing Are Changing Enterprise IT*. Wiley, 2013.

- Bloomberg, Jason. "Fixing Scheduling with Agile at the VA." *Forbes*. October 23, 2014.

- Boehm, Barry and Richard Turner. *Balancing Agility and Discipline: A Guide for the Perplexed*. Addison-Wesley, 2003.

- Bradford, David L. and Allan R. Cohen. *Managing for Excellence: The Guide to Developing High Performance in Contemporary Organizations*. Wiley, 1997.

- Brooks, Frederick P., Jr. *The Mythical Man-Month*. Addison-Wesley, 1995.

- Brown, Tim. *Change by Design: How Design Thinking Transforms Organizations and Inspires Innovation*. Harper Business, 2009.

- Byrne, Art and James P. Womack. *The Lean Turnaround: How Business Leaders Use Lean Principles to Create Value and Transform Their Company*. McGraw-Hill Education, 2012.

- Christensen, Clayton M. *The Innovator's Dilemma: When New Technologies Cause Great Firms to Fail*. Harvard Business Review Press, 2013.

- Cockburn, Alistair. *Agile Software Development: The Cooperative Game*. Addison-Wesley, 2006.

- Cockburn, Alistair. *Crystal Clear: A Human-Powered Methodology for Small Teams*. Addison-Wesley, 2004.

- Cockburn, Alistair. "Using Both Incremental and Iterative Development." *STSC CrossTalk* 21 (2008): 27 – 30.

- Cohn, Mike. *Agile Estimating and Planning*. Prentice Hall, 2005.

- Cohn, Mike. *Succeeding with Agile: Software Development Using Scrum*. Addison-Wesley, 2009.

- Cohn, Mike. *User Stories Applied: For Agile Software Development*. Addison-Wesley, 2004.

- Collins, James C. and William C. Lazier. *Beyond Entrepreneurship: Turning Your Business into an Enduring Great Company*. Prentice Hall, 1995.

- Coplien, James and Gertrud Bjørnvig. *Lean Architecture: for Agile Software Development*. Wiley, 2010.

- Crispin, Lisa and Janet Gregory. *Agile Testing: A Practical Guide for Testers and Agile Teams*. Addison-Wesley, 2009.

- Davanzo, Sarah. "Business Trend: 'E-Shaped' People, Not 'T-Shaped.'"www.culturecartography.wordpress.com/2012/07/26/business-trend-e-shaped-people-not-t-shaped.

- Davies, Rachel and Liz Sedley. *Agile Coaching*. Pragmatic Bookshelf, 2009.

- Deming, W. Edwards. *The New Economics for Industry, Government, Education*. The MIT Press, 2000.

- Deming, W. Edwards. *Out of the Crisis*. MIT Center for Advanced Educational Services, 1982.

- Denne, Mark and Jane Cleland-Huang. *Software by Numbers: Low-Risk, High-Return Development*. Prentice Hall, 2003.

- Derby, Esther and Diana Larsen. *Agile Retrospectives: Making Good Teams Great*. Pragmatic Bookshelf, 2006.

- Drucker, Peter F. *The Essential Drucker: The Best of Sixty Years of Peter Drucker's Essential Writings on Management*. HarperBusiness, 2008.

- Drucker, Peter F. *Landmarks of Tomorrow*. Harper & Brothers, 1959.

- Duvall, Paul M., Steve Matyas, and Andrew Glover. *Continuous Integration: Improving Software Quality and Reducing Risk*. Addison-Wesley, 2007.

- Eckstein, Jutta. *Agile Software Development in the Large: Diving into the Deep*. Dorset House, 2004.

- Edmonds, S. Chris. *The Culture Engine: A Framework for Driving Results, Inspiring Your Employees, and Transforming Your Workplace*. Wiley, 2014.

- Evans, Eric. *Domain-Driven Design: Tackling Complexity in the Heart of Software*. Addison-Wesley, 2003.

- Fowler, Martin. "Refactoring." www.refactoring.com.

- Fowler, Martin et al. *Refactoring: Improving the Design of Existing Code*. Addison-Wesley, 1999.

- Gladwell, Malcolm. *The Tipping Point: How Little Things Can Make a Big Difference*. Little, Brown and Company, 2000.

- Goldratt, Eliyahu M. *The Goal: A Process of Ongoing Improvement*. North River Press, 2014.

- Gower, Bob and Rally Software. *Agile Business: A Leader's Guide to Harnessing Complexity*. Rally Software (Telemachus Press), 2013.

- Hackman, Richard and Greg Oldham. *Work Redesign*. Prentice Hall, 1980.

- Hammer, Michael and James Champy. *Reengineering the Corporation: A Manifesto for Business Revolution*. HarperBusiness, 2006.

- Heath, Chip and Dan Heath. *Switch: How to Change Things When Change Is Hard*. Broadway Books, 2010.

- Highsmith, Jim. *Agile Project Management: Creating Innovative Products*. Addison-Wesley, 2009.

- Humble, Jez and David Farley. *Continuous Delivery: Reliable Software Releases Through Build, Test, and Deployment Automation*. Addison-Wesley, 2010.

- Humble, Jez, Joanne Molesky, and Barry O'Reilly. *Lean Enterprise: How High Performance Organizations Innovate at Scale*. O'Reilly Media, 2015.

- Iansiti, Marco. "Shooting the Rapids: Managing Product Development in Turbulent Environments." *California Management Review* 38 (1995): 37 – 58.

- International Council on Systems Engineering. "What Is Systems Engineering?" www.incose.org/AboutSE/WhatIsSE.

- Jeffries, Ron, Ann Anderson, and Chet Hendrickson. *Extreme Programming Installed*. Addison-Wesley, 2000.

- Jemilo, Drew. *Agile Contracts: Blast Off to a Zone of Collaborative Systems Building*. Agile 2015.

- Kennedy, Michael N. *Product Development for the Lean Enterprise: Why Toyota's System Is Four Times More Productive and How You Can Implement It*. CreateSpace Independent Publishing Platform, 2003.

- Kim, Gene, Kevin Behr, and George Spafford. *The Phoenix Project: A Novel About IT, DevOps, and Helping Your Business Win*. IT Revolution Press, 2013.

- Kniberg, Henrik. *Scrum and XP from the Trenches*. lulu.com, 2015.

- Kniberg, Henrik and Anders Ivarsson. "Scaling Agility @ Spotify with Tribes, Squads, Chapters, and Guilds." https://dl.dropboxusercontent.com/u/1018963/Articles/SpotifyScaling.pdf. October 2012.

- Kniberg, Henrik. *Lean from the Trenches: Managing Large-Scale Projects with Kanban*. Pragmatic Bookshelf, 2011.

- Koskela, Lasse. *Test Driven: TDD and Acceptance TDD for Java Developers*. Manning Publications, 2007.

- Kotter, John P. *Leading Change*. Harvard Business Review Press, 2012.

- Krebs, Jochen. *Agile Portfolio Management*. Microsoft Press, 2008.

- Labovitz, George H. and Victor Rosansky. *The Power of Alignment: How Great Companies Stay Centered and Accomplish Extraordinary Things*. Wiley, 1997.

- Ladas, Corey. *Scrumban: Essays on Kanban Systems for Lean Software Development*. Modus Cooperandi Press, 2009.

- Laloux, Frederic. *Reinventing Organizations*. Nelson Parker, 2014.

- Larman, Craig and Bas Vodde. *Practices for Scaling Lean & Agile Development: Large, Multisite, and Offshore Product Development with Large-Scale Scrum*. Addison-Wesley, 2010.

- Larman, Craig and Bas Vodde. *Scaling Lean & Agile Development: Thinking and Organizational Tools for Large-Scale Scrum*. Addison-Wesley, 2008.

- Leffingwell, Dean. *Agile Software Requirements: Lean Requirements Practices for Teams, Programs, and the Enterprise*. Addison-Wesley, 2011.

- Leffingwell, Dean. *Scaling Software Agility: Best Practices for Large Enterprises*. Addison-Wesley, 2007.

- Leffingwell, Dean and Don Widrig. *Managing Software Requirements: A Use Case Approach* (second edition). Addison-Wesley, 2003.

- Lencioni, Patrick M. *The Five Dysfunctions of a Team: A Leadership Fable*. Jossey-Bass, 2002.

- Liker, Jeffrey K. *The Toyota Way: 14 Management Principles from the World's Greatest Manufacturer*. McGraw-Hill Education, 2004.

- Liker, Jeffrey and Thomas Y. Choi. "Building Deep Supplier Relationships." *Harvard Business Review*. December 2004.

- Liker, Jeffrey and Gary L. Convis. *The Toyota Way to Lean Leadership: Achieving and Sustaining Excellence Through Leadership Development*. McGraw-Hill, 2011.

- Manifesto for Agile Software Development. www.agilemanifesto.org.

- Martin, Karen and Mike Osterling. *Value Stream Mapping: How to Visualize Work and Align Leadership for Organizational Transformation*. McGraw-Hill Education, 2013.

- Martin, Robert C. *Clean Code: A Handbook of Agile Software Craftsmanship*. Prentice Hall, 2008.

- Maurya, Ash. *Running Lean: Iterate from Plan A to a Plan That Works*. O'Reilly Media, 2012.

- McChrystal, Stanley et al. *Team of Teams: New Rules of Engagement for a Complex World*. Portfolio, 2015.

- Middleton, Peter and James Sutton. *Lean Software Strategies: Proven Techniques for Managers and Developers*. Productivity Press, 2005.

- Moore, Geoffrey. *Crossing the Chasm*. Harper Business Essentials, 1991, 2014.

- Moore, Geoffrey. *Escape Velocity*. Harper Business Essentials, 2011.

- Moore, Geoffrey. *Inside the Tornado*. Harper Business Essentials, 1995, 2004.

- Nonaka, Ikujiro and Hirotaka Takeuchi. *The Knowledge-Creating Company: How Japanese Companies Create the Dynamics of Innovation*. Oxford University Press, 1995.

- Oosterwal, Dantar P. *The Lean Machine: How Harley-Davidson Drove Top-Line Growth and Profitability with Revolutionary Lean Product Development*. AMACOM, 2010.

- Orsini, Joyce Nilsson (ed.). *The Essential Deming: Leadership Principles from the Father of Quality*. McGraw-Hill Education, 2012.

- Patton, Jeff and Peter Economy. *User Story Mapping: Discover the Whole Story, Build the Right Product*. O'Reilly Media, 2014.

- Pink, Daniel H. *Drive: The Surprising Truth About What Motivates Us*. Riverhead Hardcover, 2009.

- Poppendieck, Mary and Tom Poppendieck. *Implementing Lean Software Development: From Concept to Cash*. Addison-Wesley, 2006.

- Poppendieck, Mary and Tom Poppendieck. *Lean Software Development: An Agile Toolkit*. Addison-Wesley, 2003.

- Pugh, Ken. *Lean-Agile Acceptance Test-Driven Development: Better Software Through Collaboration*. Addison-Wesley, 2011.

- Reinertsen, Donald G. *Managing the Design Factory: A Product Developer's Toolkit*. Free Press, 1997.

- Reinertsen, Donald G. *The Principles of Product Development Flow: Second Generation Lean Product Development*. Celeritas Publishing, 2009.

- Ries, Eric. *The Lean Startup: How Today's Entrepreneurs Use Continuous Innovation to Create Radically Successful Businesses*. Crown Business, 2011.

- Rother, Mike. *Toyota Kata: Managing People for Improvement, Adaptiveness, and Superior Results*. McGraw-Hill Education, 2009.

- Rubin, Ken. "Agile in a Hardware/Firmware Environment: Draw the Cost of Change Curve." www.innolution.com/blog/agile-in-a-hardware-firmware-environment-draw-the-cost-of-change-curve.

- Rubin, Kenneth S. *Essential Scrum: A Practical Guide to the Most Popular Agile Process*. Addison-Wesley, 2012.

- Schwaber, Ken. *Agile Project Management with Scrum*. Developer Best Practices, 2004.

- Schwaber, Ken. *The Enterprise and Scrum*. Microsoft Press, 2007.

- Schwaber, Ken and Mike Beedle. *Agile Software Development with Scrum*. Pearson, 2001.

- Senge, Peter M. *The Fifth Discipline: The Art & Practice of the Learning Organization*. Doubleday, 2006.

- Shalloway, Alan, Scott Bain, Ken Pugh, and Amir Kolsky. *Essential Skills for the Agile Developer: A Guide to Better Programming and Design*. Addison-Wesley, 2011.

- Shalloway, Alan, Guy Beaver, and James R. Trott. *Lean-Agile Software Development: Achieving Enterprise Agility*. Addison-Wesley, 2009.

- Shimokawa, Koichi and Takahiro Fujimoto (eds.). *The Birth of Lean*. Lean Enterprise Institute, 2009.

- Sliger, Michele and Stacia Broderick. *The Software Project Manager's Bridge to Agility*. Addison-Wesley, 2008.

- Surowiecki, James. *The Wisdom of Crowds*. Anchor, 2005.

- Sutherland, Jeff and Ken Schwaber. Scrum Guides. scrumguides.org.

- Tabaka, Jean. *Collaboration Explained: Facilitation Skills for Software Project Leaders*. Addison-Wesley, 2006.

- Takeuchi, Hirotaka and Ikujiro Nonaka. *Hitotsubashi on Knowledge Management*. Wiley, 2004.

- Takeuchi, Hirotaka and Ikujiro Nonaka. "The New, New Product Development Game." *Harvard Business Review*, January 1, 1986.

- Thomas, Joseph and Steven Baker. "Establishing an Agile Portfolio to Align IT Investments with Business Needs." DTE Energy, 2008. www.jctnet.us/Professional/Agile/CD-ThomasBaker-EstablishAgilePortfolio-Paper.pdf.

- Toyota Global. www.toyota-global.com/sustainability/society/partners/supplier_csr_en.pdf.

- Trompenaars, Fons and Ed Voerman. *Servant-Leadership Across Cultures: Harnessing the Strengths of the World's Most Powerful Management Philosophy*. McGraw-Hill, 2009.

- Wake, William. *Refactoring Workbook*. Addison-Wesley, 2003.

- Ward, Allen C. and Durward K. Sobek II. *Lean Product and Process Development*. Lean Enterprise Institute, 2014.

- Womack, James P. and Daniel T. Jones. *Lean Thinking: Banish Waste and Create Wealth in Your Corporation*. Productivity Press, 2003.

- Womack, James P., Daniel T. Jones, and Daniel Roos. *The Machine That Changed the World: The Story of Lean Production—Toyota's Secret Weapon in the Global Car Wars That Is Revolutionizing World Industry*. Free Press, 2007.

# Index

team level, 129–131

Iterations. *See also* PDCA cycles.
  abstract, 109
  adjusting, 111
  in the Big Picture, 109–111
  checking, 111
  definition, 515
  details, 109–111
  executing, 110
  PDCA cycle, 109–111
  planning, 110
  team level, 109–111

## J

Jeffries, Ron, 136

Job duration, WSJF (Weighted Shortest Job First), 185–186

Job sequencing based on cost of delay, economic framework, 348, 349

Job size as a proxy for duration, WSJF (Weighted Shortest Job First), 186

Just-in-time story elaboration, PO (Product Owner), 84

## K

Kanban. *See also* Team Kanban.
  average lead time, 101–102
  CFDs (Cumulative Flow Diagrams), 101–102
  classes of service, 102–103
  description, 100
  improving flow, 102–103
  measuring flow, 101–102
  Portfolio Kanban Board, 308–309
  program, 517
  Program Kanban Board, 315
  as a pull system, 99
  swim lanes, 102–103
  Team Kanban Board, 320
  throughput, 101–102
  Value Stream Kanban Board, 313
  visualizing flow, 100–101
  WIP limits, 100–101

Kettering, Charles, 255

KPIs (key performance indicators)
  enterprise, 420
  PPM (Program Portfolio Management), 433

## L

Labor efforts, as CapEx (capital expense), 469–471

Lazier, William, 420

Leaders, training, 39

*Leading SAFe 4.0, Leading the Lean-Agile Enterprise with the Scaled Agile Framework*, 39

Lean Portfolio Metrics, 307–308

*The Lean Startup*, 420

Lean-Agile approach to System Architect/Engineering, 173–175

Lean-Agile budgeting, economic framework, 348

*Lean-Agile Budgeting: Beyond Project Cost Accounting*, 454–455

Lean-Agile change agents, training, 38, 39

Lean-Agile Leaders. *See also specific leaders.*
  abstract, 11
  in the Big Picture, 11–15
  definition, 2, 515
  details, 11–15
  philosophy of SAFe, 11
  in System Architect/Engineering, 174
  traits of, 174

Lean-Agile Leaders, desirable behaviors
  decentralized decision-making, 12
  developing people, 12
  emphasizing lifelong learning, 12
  leading change, 11
  minimizing constraints, 12
  motivating knowledge workers, 12

Lean-Agile mindset. *See also* Agile Manifesto.
  abstract, 27
  Big Picture, 27–32
  definition, 515
  details, 27–33
  foundation of, 30
  leadership philosophy, 30
  training leaders in, 3

Lean-Agile mindset, House of Lean
  definition, 27
  flow, 29
  four pillars, 28–30
  goal, 28
  innovation, 29–30
  relentless improvement, 30, 81
  respect for people and culture, 28–29

Lean-Agile practices, suppliers, 390

Learning cycles, MBSE models, 360

Learning milestones, 326–327

Licensing, 38

Life-cycle governance, PPM (Program Portfolio Management), 433–434

Lightweight business cases, PPM (Program Portfolio Management), 432

URLs (Uniform Resource Locators). *See* Web addresses; Websites.

Usability. *See* UX (User Experience) design.

User Experience (UX) design. *See* UX (User Experience) design.

User stories, 134

User-business value, cost of delay factor, 184

UX (User Experience) design
abstract, 291
in the Big Picture, 291–294
centralized guidance and implementation, 293–294
characteristics of, 292
definition, 520
design criteria, 293
designers on the ART, 161, 293–294
details, 291–294
distributed, governed development, 294
interfaces, specifying, 367
as potential bottleneck, 294
roles and responsibilities, 291–292
spanning palette, 291–294
testing criteria, 293

## V

Value, optimizing, 195–196

Value centric stories, 134

Value delivery, optimizing, 107

Value stream, importance of DevOps, 273–274

Value stream backlogs
abstract, 193
in the Big Picture, 193–197
capacity allocation, 195–196
definition, 516, 521
details, 193–197
Little's Law, 197
PI planning, 195
pre- and post-PI planning meetings, 386
prioritizing, 194
program level, 193–197
queues, 197
refining, 194
solution integrity, optimizing, 195–196
value, optimizing, 195–196
wait times, 197

Value stream coordination
abstract, 343
in the Big Picture, 343–346
cadence, 344–345
content management, 345–346
definition, 521
deployment, 346
details, 343–346

enterprise architecture, 345–346
new portfolio work levels, 345
portfolio roadmap, 346
program management, 345–346
release, 346
synchronization, 344–345
value stream level, 343–346

Value Stream Engineer (VSE). *See* VSE (Value Stream Engineer).

Value stream epics, definition, 521

Value stream increment, PI (Program Increment), 211–212

Value stream Kanban
in the Big Picture, 187–191
definition, 521
epic specification workshop, 191
PI planning, 191
program level, 187–191
program/value stream backlog refinement, 191
solution/system demo, 191
supporting ceremonies, 191

Value Stream Kanban Board, 313

Value stream level
Agile architecture, 371–378
in the Big Picture. *See* Big Picture, value stream level.
coordination of dependencies, 343–346
Customers, 395–399
definition, 2, 521
description, 6
economic framework, 347–349
MBSE (Model-Based Systems Engineering), 359–364
pre- and post-PI planning, 383–388
Set-Based Design, 365–369
solution context, 405–409
solution demo, 379–382
solution intent, 351–358
solutions, 401–404
suppliers, 389–394
value stream coordination, 343–346
web address, 337

Value stream level backlogs
abstract, 193
in the Big Picture, 193–197
capacity allocation, 195–196
definition, 516, 521
details, 193–197
Little's Law, 197
PI planning, 195
pre- and post-PI planning meetings, 386
prioritizing, 194
queues, 197
refining, 194
solution integrity, optimizing, 195–196
value, optimizing, 195–196
wait times, 197

# SAFe® KEY RESOURCES

Guidance Articles / News & Updates / Case Studies / Videos & Presentations, Principles, Glossary, and more!

## scaledagileframework.com

scaledagileframework.com/**case-studies**

scaledagileframework.com/**implementing**

scaledagileframework.com/**posters**

scaledagileframework.com/**videos-and-presentations**

scaledagileframework.com/**glossary**

scaledagileframework.com/**safe-lean-agile-principles**

scaledagileframework.com/**blog**

Implementation Partners / Training & Certification / Course Calendar / Scaled Agile Insider Newsletter, and more!

## scaledagile.com

scaledagile.com/**find-training**

scaledagile.com/**partner-directory**

scaledagile.com/**implementing-safe**

scaledagile.com/**leading-safe**

scaledagile.com/**advanced-scrum-master**

scaledagile.com/**leading-safe-video**

scaledagile.com/**insider**

# SAFe® CERTIFICATIONS

## There's a certification for everyone on the SAFe Learning Path

| **SAFe Program Consultant 4.0 (SPC4)** | **SAFe Agilist (SA)** | **SAFe Practitioner (SP)** | **SAFe Advanced Scrum Master (SASM)** |
|---|---|---|---|

The SAFe Program Consultant 4.0 (SPC4) certification is for those who will be directly involved in a SAFe adoption. This includes practitioners, change agents, and consultants responsible for implementing Agile programs and portfolios as part of a Lean-Agile change initiative. SPC4s train SAFe Agilists (SA), SAFe Practitioners (SP), and Product Managers/Product Owners (PM/PO). **Take Implementing SAFe 4.0 with SPC4 Certification to certify.**

The SAFe Agilist (SA) certification program teaches enterprise leadership Lean-agile principles, how to execute and release value through Agile Release Trains (ARTs), how to build an Agile Portfolio, and how to lead a Lean-Agile transformation at enterprise scale. It is designed for executives, managers, consultants, and Agile change agents responsible for leading or supporting a Lean-Agile change initiative in a large software or systems-dependent enterprise. **Take a Leading SAFe 4.0 course to certify.**

The SAFe Practitioner (SP) certification teaches teams how to work in an Agile environment using Scrum, Kanban, and XP. Using real-world activities, the teams learn how to become Agile Teams, build their backlog, and plan and execute iterations. Agile teams learn about their ART and their role in planning, executing, and improving with other teams. This class prepares teams to execute the iterations in a Program Increment (PI), including all meetings at the Team and Program level. **Take a SAFe 4.0 for Teams course to certify.**

This course prepares current Scrum Masters for their leadership role at the Team and Program level in a SAFe enterprise. The course covers facilitation of cross-team interactions in support of the program execution and relentless improvement. It enhances the Scrum paradigm with an introduction to scalable engineering and DevOps practices; the application of Kanban to facilitate the flow of value; and supporting interactions with architects, product management, and other critical stakeholders in the larger program and enterprise contexts. **Take a SAFe 4.0 Advanced Scrum Master course to certify.**

---

**Find a SAFe training class near you at:**
## scaledagile.com/**calendar**

SAFe training and certification is offered worldwide through Scaled Agile and our Global Partner Network.

**Not sure which course is right for you? Go to:**
## scaledagile.com/**which-course**

*"You don't have to be perfect to start SAFe because you learn as you go—learning is built in. Before SAFe, I would not know how to help my teams but now I have many tools to enable the teams. My job is really fun and the bottom line is I have never enjoyed my job more!"*
**—Manager, Fortune 500 Enterprise**

# Psychology Applied to Teaching

# Students!
# Information for HM Video Cases and Online Resources That Accompany This Book

Are you interested in what *really* happens in the classroom? Do you want to know how teachers handle challenging situations? Watch the Houghton Mifflin Video Cases and see how new and experienced teachers apply concepts and strategies in real K–12 classrooms. These 4- to 6-minute video clips cover a variety of different topics that today's teachers face, and allow you to experience real teaching in action.

**To access the Houghton Mifflin Video Cases and other premium, online resources, look for your passkey which is packaged with your new text.**

## Enhance Your Learning Experience

Houghton Mifflin Video Cases are integrated into your new copy of Snowman/McCown/Biehler's, *Psychology Applied to Teaching* throughout the text and assignments. The cases include video clips and a host of related materials to provide a comprehensive learning experience.

Reflect on the teacher's approach and assess how you might handle the situation by considering the **Viewing Questions.**

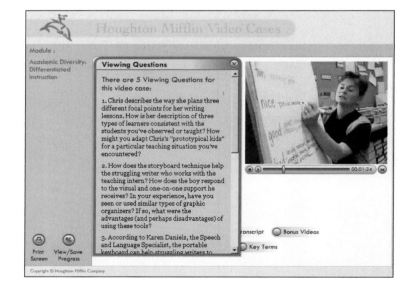

Read detailed **interviews with the teachers** as they explain their approach, how they engage students, and how they resolve issues.

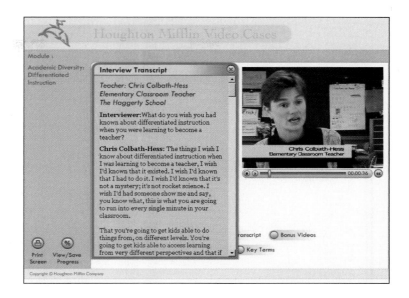

View **handouts and materials used in the class,** and gain ideas for your own portfolio.

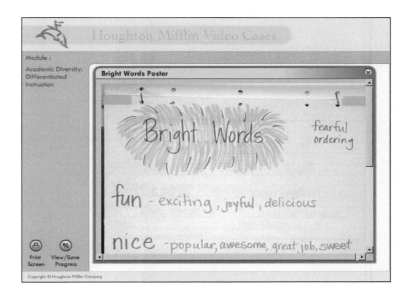

# Psychology Applied to Teaching

Twelfth Edition

Jack Snowman
*Southern Illinois University*

Rick McCown
*Duquesne University*

Robert Biehler

WADSWORTH
CENGAGE Learning™

Australia • Brazil • Japan • Korea • Mexico • Singapore • Spain • United Kingdom • United States

# WADSWORTH
## CENGAGE Learning

**Psychology Applied to Teaching, Twelfth Edition**
Snowman, McCown, and Biehler

Education Editor: Chris Shortt

Developmental Editor: Lisa Mafrici

Assistant Editor: Caitlin Cox

Editorial Assistant: Linda Stewart

Media Editor: Ashley Cronin

Marketing Manager: Kara Parsons

Marketing Communications Manager:
   Martha Pfeiffer

Print Buyer: Rebecca Cross

Production Service:
   S4Carlisle Publishing Services

Cover Designer: Patti Hudepohl

Cover Image: © Nancy Louie, iStockphoto

Compositor: S4Carlisle Publishing Services

For product information and technology assistance, contact us at **Cengage Learning Customer & Sales Support, 1-800-354-9706.**

For permission to use material from this text or product, submit all requests online at **www.cengage.com/permissions.** Further permissions questions can be e-mailed to **permissionrequest@cengage.com.**

ISBN 13: 978-0-495-81214-2
ISBN 10: 0-495-81214-5

**Wadsworth**
10 Davis Drive
Belmont, CA 94002-3098
USA

Cengage Learning is a leading provider of customized learning solutions with office locations around the globe, including Singapore, the United Kingdom, Australia, Mexico, Brazil, and Japan. Locate your local office at **www.cengage.com/global.**

Cengage Learning products are represented in Canada by Nelson Education, Ltd.

To learn more about Wadsworth, visit **www.cengage.com/wadsworth**
Purchase any of our products at your local college store or at our preferred online store **www.ichapters.com**

Printed in Canada
1 2 3 4 5 6 7 13 12 11 10 09

# Brief Contents

# Contents

## 3 Theories of Psychosocial and Cognitive Development        51

## Part II   Student Differences and Diversity

## 4   Culture and Cognition                                                                   93

# 5 Understanding Student Differences 127

# 6 Accommodating Student Diversity 154

## Part III   Learning and Thinking

### 7   Behavioral Learning Theory: Operant Conditioning     190

## 8 Information-Processing Theory 212

## 9 Constructivist Learning Theory, Problem Solving, and Transfer 235

## 10 Social Cognitive Learning 269

## Part IV Creating a Positive Environment for Learning and Teaching

## 11 Leading Classroom Learning 311

## 12 Motivation and Perceptions of Self | 340

## **13** Approaches to Instruction                                                                       **371**

## Part V   Assessing Students' Capabilities

## 14   Understanding Standardized Assessment                    410

## 15 Assessment of Classroom Learning 442

## 16 Becoming a Better Teacher by Becoming a Reflective Teacher 475

# Preface to the Twelfth Edition

This edition of *Psychology Applied to Teaching*, like those that preceded it, can be characterized by two words: change and continuity. Although these two terms carry opposing meanings, in the context of this book they complement each other.

Change is inescapable in educational psychology for several reasons. First, the theories on which this field rests are relatively young and so are still evolving. Second, new types of research and new ways of conducting research continue to be formulated. Third, new issues that affect and concern educators continually come to the fore. We have done our best to address each of these changes and hope, as a result, that students will be better able to understand the forces that shape contemporary education.

Yet, in the face of these changes, this book has been dedicated, ever since its first edition, to the same basic goal: providing a practical, student-oriented approach to educational psychology. The book is written to be used in three ways: (1) as a text that provides basic information, organized and presented so that it will be understood, remembered, and applied; (2) as a source of practical ideas about instructional techniques for student teachers and beginning teachers; and (3) as a means for teachers to improve their effectiveness as they gain experience in the classroom.

## Major Features of This Edition

Because of its central role in American society, education is a dynamic enterprise. Tens of thousands of people—including classroom teachers, school administrators, state education officials, politicians, and educational and psychological researchers—are constantly searching for and trying out new ideas to increase student learning and achievement. This is especially true of educational and psychological researchers. Since the previous edition of this text, many new developments have occurred in social, emotional, and cognitive development; learning processes; motivation; classroom assessment and management; standardized testing; bilingual education; inclusion of students with disabilities; and the use of computer-based technology to support student learning and achievement. The Twelfth Edition of *Psychology Applied to Teaching* is extensively revised and updated, incorporating new developments in all its domains.

Noteworthy themes of this edition include:

- **Advances in social cognitive theory.** Because of the many recent developments in social cognitive research, particularly with respect to self-regulated learning, Chapter 10 now includes extensive coverage of learning strategies and tactics and how students can be taught to create and use them.
- **Emphasis on critical issues** in educational psychology. All the editions of *Psychology Applied to Teaching* have framed the crucial issues in contemporary education in ways that encourage students to consider the research and make informed judgments. In each chapter's critically acclaimed Take a Stand! feature, we model this behavior for students by stating where we stand on a critical issue and specifying the reasons for that stance.
- **Emphasis on educational technology.** Each chapter contains at least one section, and sometimes several, on how technology can be used to address the main themes and concepts of that chapter. These sections are now highlighted so that they are easy to find. For example, the reader will find discussions of how such technology tools as multimedia, hypermedia, tutorial programs, simulation

programs, telecommunications, and the World Wide Web can be used to foster cognitive development, address individual differences, promote greater multicultural understanding, make learning easier for students with disabilities, promote learning and problem solving for all students, increase motivation for learning, help teachers manage their classrooms, and aid in assessment of students. These sections are highlighted with tabbed pages. In addition, all chapters provide addresses for websites that contain useful supplementary information and links to other relevant sites. Marginal icons direct readers to the textbook's student website, HM TeacherPrepSPACE, which provides connections to extended web resources.

■ **Emphasis on classroom applications.** *Psychology Applied to Teaching* was the first educational psychology textbook to provide numerous specific examples and guidelines for applying psychological concepts and research findings to classroom teaching. We want to ensure that new teachers are prepared for the realities of the classroom. That orientation and emphasis on bridging the gap from preservice to practice to foster teachers' lifelong career success not only continues but is also augmented by Chapter 13, "Approaches to Instruction," which links the writing of instructional objectives with five approaches to instruction that flow from different conceptions of learning.

■ **Emphasis on diverse learners.** To help prospective and new teachers understand and cope with the wide range of student diversity they will almost certainly face, we provide extensive treatment of this issue in two chapters: Chapter 4, "Culture and Cognition" and Chapter 5, "Understanding Student Differences." In addition, and where appropriate, we discuss aspects of student diversity in other chapters.

■ **Emphasis on real-life contexts.** Included in every chapter are references to Video Cases that students can view at HM TeacherPrepSPACE student website. Each case shows an actual classroom scene in which the teacher describes his or her actions and explains why they were taken. After each reference to a Video Case, readers are prompted by questions that help them relate the Video Case to the content of the chapter.

■ **Reflective teaching.** Thinking about what one does as a teacher and why has been shown to be an important characteristic of effective teachers. *Psychology Applied to Teaching* tries to foster in students an appreciation of this skill in several ways. The concept of reflective teaching, its importance, and the role that a personal journal can play in helping one become a more reflective teacher are introduced in Chapter 1. This theme is picked up again in Chapter 16, in which students learn how to construct a personal journal and how useful this activity is to practicing teachers. Also in Chapter 16, the master teacher draws conclusions and shows how important reflection is in a teaching career. Another feature students will encounter in Chapters 2 through 15 is the Pause and Reflect feature in which they are asked to respond to a question about classroom learning and instruction that is based on that chapter's content.

## Major Changes to Each Chapter

The following lists highlight some, though not all, of the major changes made to each chapter.

### Chapter 1: Applying Psychology to Teaching

■ A new and broader definition of educational psychology.

■ Attention to recent efforts by the Carnegie Foundation for the Advancement of Teaching and the American Psychological Association to help teachers value and use research-based practices in their classrooms.

■ New research that demonstrates the positive relationship between undergraduate coursework in education and psychology and competence as a teacher and the greater effectiveness of certified versus noncertified teachers.

### Chapter 2: Age-Level Characteristics

- New findings on the nature of friendships among preschool and kindergarten children.
- Current research on how accurately preschool and kindergarten children assess their competence for particular tasks.
- New material on how the developmental needs of primary grade children are being undercut by the elimination of recess by some schools.
- New material on the effects of bullying among primary grade students.
- New findings about the effects of early and late maturation among middle school boys and girls.
- Current data on obesity, sexual behavior, depression, and suicide among high school students.

### Chapter 3: Theories of Psychosocial and Cognitive Development

- New material on identity formation and how life events can affect cycles in one's identity status.
- New research that relates variability in children's thinking to persistence in problem solving.
- New research on how technology supports Vygotsky's theory of cognitive development.
- New research on the relationship between gender differences and moral reasoning.

### Chapter 4: Culture and Cognition

- New research on the status of the achievement gap between low-SES minority students and middle-SES White students, its likely causes, and possible solutions.
- Current research on the relationship between amount of homework and achievement for students at different grade levels.
- New research on how technology is being used to raise achievement among low-SES minority students.

### Chapter 5: Understanding Student Differences

- New research relevant to multiple intelligences that shows how learning outside of school can transfer to learning in the classroom.
- New material on how technology can be used to support various learning styles.
- The newly formulated "gender similarities hypothesis" as context for new research on gender differences in achievement and cognition

### Chapter 6: Accommodating Student Diversity

- New research on the effect of tracking among high school students with limited English proficiency.
- New material on the 2004 reauthorization of IDEA (also known as the *Individuals with Disabilities Education Improvement Act*) that went into effect in October of 2006.
- New material on the disproportionate numbers of minority students placed in special education as an argument in support of the policy of inclusion.
- Current figures on the percentage of students receiving special education services.

### Chapter 7: Behavioral Learning Theory: Operant Conditioning

- New research on the effect of computer-based instruction on learning, including integrated learning systems.
- New statistics on the use of corporal punishment.

### Chapter 8: Information-Processing Theory

- Greater emphasis on metacognition, on the relationships between cognitive development and information processing in the developmental trends of

metacognition, and on how those trends affect classroom teaching designed to enhance metacognitive abilities.
- A new chapter structure that changes the concept of strategic learning from an information-processing account to an aspect of self-regulated learning (see Chapter 10).

### Chapter 9: Constructivist Learning Theory, Problem Solving, and Transfer
- New material on the similarity between well-structured problems and performance goals and between ill-structured problems and learning goals.
- New material that builds on self-regulation and the role that personally valued goals play in providing opportunities for young children to gain experience in solving ill-structured problems.

### Chapter 10: Social Cognitive Theory
- Because of the rapid development of social cognitive theory, particularly with respect to the large volume of recent research on self-regulated learning, this chapter now includes a main section devoted exclusively to this topic. The nature of self-regulated learning is described in terms of formulating strategies and using tactics, and suggestions are given as to how students can be taught to acquire and display these skills.
- New research on the relationship between self-efficacy and achievement and the effects of providing students with self-regulated strategy instruction.
- New research on how contemporary computer-based instructional programs have been designed to provide students with cognitive and metacognitive feedback.

### Chapter 11: Leading Classroom Learning
- Updated statistics on violence and school safety.
- New material on the Smart and Good High Schools project of Lickona and Davidson as a schoolwide program to reduce violence and increase discipline.
- Current research on the effectiveness of the Resolving Conflict Creatively program.
- Current research on the use of virtual classes and schools as a way to keep students from dropping out of school.

### Chapter 12: Motivation and Perceptions of Self
- New research on self-efficacy and attributions as contributors to intrinsic motivation.
- New section on Mihaly Csikszentmihalyi's concept of "flow" and its relationship to academic engagement.

### Chapter 13: Approaches to Instruction
- Description of a major revision to Bloom's Taxonomy.
- New research on the effectiveness of scaffolded instruction among primary grade students.
- New research on how teachers can help students become self-directed learners.
- New research on the effectiveness of microcomputer-based laboratories (MBLs).
- Current research on how computer-based technology can be used to support project-based learning.
- New material on the relationship of Nel Noddings's writings about creating a caring atmosphere in classrooms and schools to the humanistic approach to education.
- Current research on how cooperative learning arrangements improve students' problem-solving performance.

### Chapter 14: Understanding Standardized Assessment
- New section on misconceptions about the nature and uses of standardized tests.
- The section on high-stakes testing has been expanded to include the five main requirements of No Child Left Behind (NCLB); additional problems with

implementing NCLB that have arisen in recent years; additional criticisms of high-stakes testing; current research on NCLB's effect on achievement, on how teachers teach, on the curriculum, and on the dropout rate; the extent to which the school choice and supplemental instructional services features of NCLB are being used; and additional recommendations for improving high-stakes testing.

■ The technology section contains new material on using web-based programs and resources to prepare students for high-stakes assessments, the pros and cons of using computer-based testing to assess mastery of standards, and the use of computer adaptive testing by some states and school districts.

### Chapter 15: Assessment of Classroom Learning
■ New research on the validity of performance assessments.
■ Updates on the use of technology in the assessment of student learning.

### Chapter 16: Becoming a Better Teacher by Becoming a Reflective Teacher
■ New material on the effectiveness of reflective teaching techniques.

### Special Features of the Text
The pedagogic features introduced in earlier editions have been improved and augmented to make this Twelfth Edition even more useful and effective.

***New* Houghton Mifflin Video Case Boxed Features**  As described later in the preface, this edition includes the integration of HM Video Cases to illustrate key topics in the text. Thirty-seven Video Cases appear on the textbook website, and they are correlated to the text with a boxed feature and questions for reflection.

**Take a Stand!**  In this era of accountability, teachers are frequently criticized and called on to defend their profession and their practices. Although many veteran teachers do this quite confidently and effectively, the novice teacher often feels ill prepared to engage the public. The Take a Stand! feature provides students with brief models of how one can articulate a compelling position on an educational issue. In Chapters 2 through 15, the senior author draws on his thirty years of experience and knowledge of the research literature to take a strong but supportable stand on an issue that relates to the chapter content. Further, the feature encourages students to do the same—to articulate and discuss their own opinions on key issues. At the textbook's website this feature is extended with additional resources and pedagogy. This feature became an immediate hit with instructors after its introduction in the Eleventh Edition.

**Key Points**  At the beginning of each chapter, Key Points are listed under major headings. They also appear in the margins of pages opposite sections in which each point is discussed. The Key Points call attention to sections of the text that are considered to be of special significance to teachers and thus serve as instructional objectives.

**Suggestions for Teaching in Your Classroom**  Most chapters include summaries of research findings and principles relating to a particular topic. These are followed by detailed descriptions of various ways in which the information and concepts might be applied in classrooms. Numerous examples of applications at different grade levels are supplied; readers are urged to select applications that will fit their own particular personality, style, and teaching situation and to record their ideas in a Reflective Journal. The Suggestions for Teaching are intended to be read while the book is used as a text and referred to by future teachers and in-service teachers after they have completed coursework. For ease in reference, these suggestions are printed on a colored background and tabbed.

**Pause and Reflect**  Knowing how difficult it is for students to meaningfully grasp the abstract concepts that make up educational psychology and how important it is for them to begin to develop the habit of reflective thinking, this feature was designed to help students make connections between one idea and another and between theory and actual classroom practice. As students read each chapter, they will encounter several Pause and Reflect features that ask them to stop and think about a concept or issue raised in the chapter or to consider how their own experiences relate to what they are reading.

**Journal Entries**   This feature is intended to help students prepare and use a Reflective Journal when they teach. Readers are urged to use the journal entries, which appear in the margins, to prepare a personal set of guidelines for reference before and during the student teaching experience and during the first years of teaching. A guide for setting up and using a Reflective Journal is included in Chapter 16, "Becoming a Better Teacher by Becoming a Reflective Teacher."

**Links to the HM TeacherPrepSPACE student website**   Because a wealth of material is available on the website that supplements the text, this edition includes marginal icons to suggest points at which the reader may want to refer to the website.

**Glossary**   A glossary of key terms and concepts is provided at the back of the book as an aid in reviewing for examinations or classroom discussion.

## Instructional Components That Accompany the Text

**Houghton Mifflin Video Cases**   Available online and organized by topic, each case is a 3- to 5-minute module consisting of video and audio files presenting actual classroom scenarios that depict the complex problems and opportunities teachers face every day. The video and audio clips are accompanied by "artifacts" that provide background information and allow preservice teachers to experience true classroom dilemmas in their multiple dimensions. A DVD containing all sixty Video Cases is available on request to all textbook adopters.

**Instructor's Resource Manual**   The Instructor's Resource Manual (IRM) has been rewritten in its entirety for this edition. The IRM was written by Rick McCown and four other full-time faculty colleagues who teach educational psychology at Duquesne University's School of Education. The IRM provides an organizing framework that enables instructors to select and access the instructional components that accompany the text much more efficiently than in the past. In addition to facilitating instructors' decisions regarding the use of the available instructional components, the IRM provides activities and formative assessments to enhance student engagement during class sessions. The formative assessments in the IRM are those that experienced educational psychology instructors have found to be effective in engaging aspiring teachers in a variety of classroom activities, activities that both check their comprehension and understanding of key concepts and help them construct factual, conceptual, procedural, and metacognitive knowledge. The IRM is available entirely online, which we have found aids planning and allows instructors to import easily those organizational tools, activities, and assessments they wish to use in class.

**HM Testing**   This Test Bank has been thoroughly revised by Jack Snowman. It includes test items consisting of multiple-choice items in alternate forms, short-answer questions, and essay questions. Consistent with this text's long-standing emphasis on mastery, each multiple-choice and short-answer question reflects a Key Point and either the Knowledge, Comprehension, Application, or Analysis level of Bloom's Taxonomy. Feedback booklets allow instructors to point out misconceptions in students' reasoning.

**HM TeacherPrepSPACE™ websites**   Helping today's instructors and students learn how to use technology meaningfully is a primary strength of this text. As a corollary, a dedicated, interactive website for both instructors and students is available; it can be accessed at **http://login.cengage.com.** The site, updated by Jack Snowman and Rick McCown, offers a wide variety of study aids (including ACE practice tests, interactive glossary flashcards, and new concept maps), project ideas, technology links, site-based cases, Video Cases, lesson plans, PowerPoint slides, and more. Students can access HM TeacherPrepSPACE content at any time via the Internet. Some content may be passkey protected. Although the marginal icons in the text remind students to use the student website, we cannot possibly cross-reference all of our online material. We hope that both instructors and students will explore the student website and make full use of it in their classrooms.

**Houghton Mifflin Teacher Education Website**   Houghton Mifflin's general education website for students (go to **http://login.cengage.com**) provides additional pedagogic support and resources for beginning and experienced professionals in education, including the unique *Project-Based Learning Space*. This page links to five extended problem-based projects and provides background theory about project-based learning.

## Acknowledgments

Authors write books to share what they have learned and, in the case of this book, to facilitate the learning of those who aspire to teach. Unless the book is published, however, learning can neither be shared nor facilitated. Our publisher has been partnering with authors to share and facilitate learning for more than 150 years. Their mission statement follows:

> At Houghton Mifflin Education, we are dedicated to the preparation and training of educators. To this end, we provide quality content, technology, and services to ensure that new teachers are prepared for the realities of the classroom. Our aim is to bridge the gap from preservice to practice to foster teachers' lifelong career success.

We are proud that *Psychology Applied to Teaching* has shared and facilitated learning through twelve editions and that it has been a Houghton Mifflin text since the first edition.

In addition to the authors and the publisher, many others have played a significant role in shaping the book. A number of reviewers made constructive suggestions and provided thoughtful reactions at various stages in the development of this edition. Thanks go out to the following individuals for their help:

Sue E. Anderson
  Jamestown College
Jane Benjamin
  Mansfield University
Li Cao
  State University of West Georgia
Veronica Galvan Carlan
  Private Consultant
Lorraine A. Cavaliere
  Gwynedd-Mercy College
W. Pitt Derryberry
  Western Kentucky University
Sue Diel
  Friends University

Jeffrey Kaplan
  University of Central Florida
Edward Lonky
  State University of New York,
  Oswego
Joe D. Nichols
  Indiana University-Purdue University
  at Fort Wayne
Frank A. Pullo
  Wilkes University
Lorae Roukema
  Campbell University
Miriam Sailers
  Spring Arbor University

Because all teachers—at various points along the way—have been shaped by those who taught them, teachers are living legacies. As it happens, we (Jack and Rick) share a legacy. We were, and continue to be, influenced and inspired by the same teacher. Our teacher brought us both to the study of educational psychology, opened the door, invited us in, and has in the course of his teaching made us his colleagues. Our teacher is a good man and that helps make him a good teacher. Our teacher's name is Donald J. Cunningham, and we thank him. Our acknowledgment carries also the hope that he is pleased with the legacy he entrusted to us.

The work of writing a book requires spending a lot of time inside one's own head, but that time commitment makes demands also on the author's family. For their understanding and their support, Jack thanks his wife, Rickey, and Rick thanks his wife, Nona.

# Applying Psychology to Teaching

*HM TeacherPrepSPACE*

*HM TeacherPrepSPACE student website* offers many helpful resources. Go to *login.cengage.com* to preview this chapter's Concept Maps and Chapter Themes.

## KEY POINTS

These key points will help you learn the important information in this chapter. To help you study, they also appear in the margins of the pages, next to the text where they are discussed.

### What Is Educational Psychology?

- Educational psychologists study how students learn in classrooms

### How Will Learning About Educational Psychology Help You Be a Better Teacher?

- Teaching is complex work because it requires a wide range of knowledge and skills
- Research in educational psychology offers many useful ideas for improving classroom instruction
- Teachers who have had professional training are generally more effective

### The Nature and Values of Science

- Unsystematic observation may lead to false conclusions
- Grade retention policies are influenced by unsystematic observation
- Scientific methods: sampling, control, objectivity, publication, replication

### Complicating Factors in the Study of Behavior and Thought Processes

- Research focuses on a few aspects of a problem
- Complexity of teaching and learning limits uniform outcomes
- Differences of opinion result from selection and interpretation of data
- Accumulated knowledge leads researchers to revise original ideas

### Good Teaching Is Partly an Art and Partly a Science

- Teaching as an art: beliefs, emotions, values, flexibility
- Research provides a scientific basis for "artistic" teaching
- Good teachers combine "artistic" and "scientific" characteristics

### Reflective Teaching: A Process to Help You Grow from Novice to Expert

- Reflective teachers think about what they do and why
- Reflective teachers have particular attitudes and abilities

A s you begin to read this book, you may be asking yourself, "What will this book tell me about teaching that I don't already know?" The answer to that question depends on several factors, including your previous experiences with teaching and the number of psychology courses you have taken. Because you have been actively engaged in the process of formal education for a number of years, you already know a great deal about learning and teaching. You have had abundant opportunities to observe and react to more than one hundred teachers. You have probably read several hundred texts, finished all kinds of assignments, used a variety of software programs, taken hundreds of examinations, and worked with different types of people. Undoubtedly you have also established strong likes and dislikes for certain subjects and approaches to teaching.

Yet despite your familiarity with education from the student's point of view, you probably have had limited experience with education from the teacher's point of view. Therefore, a major purpose of this book is to help you take the first steps in what will be a long journey to becoming an expert teacher.

Throughout this book, we will describe many different psychological theories, concepts, and principles and illustrate how you might apply them to teaching. The branch of psychology that specializes in understanding how different factors affect the classroom behavior of both teachers and students is **educational psychology**. In the next several sections, we will briefly describe the nature of this field of study and highlight the features of this book that will help you understand psychological principles and apply them in your classroom. ●

# WHAT IS EDUCATIONAL PSYCHOLOGY?

Educational psychologists study how students learn in classrooms

Most educational psychologists, us included, would define their field as a scientific discipline that is concerned with understanding and improving how students acquire a variety of capabilities through formal instruction in classroom settings. David Berliner (2006), for example, described educational psychology as a scientific discipline that uses psychological concepts and research methods to understand how the various characteristics of students, teachers, learning tasks, and educational settings interact to produce the everyday behaviors common in school settings. This description of educational psychology suggests that you will need to understand your own psychological makeup and such aspects of the learner as physical, social, emotional, and cognitive development; cultural, social, emotional, and intellectual differences; learning and problem-solving processes; self-esteem; motivation; testing; and measurement in order to formulate effective instructional lessons.

We recognize that you may have some doubts right now both about your ability to master all of this material and the necessity to do so. To help you learn as much of this material as possible, we have incorporated into each chapter a number of helpful features that are described at the end of this chapter. But first let's examine why the learning you will do in educational psychology is a worthwhile goal.

### HM *TeacherPrepSPACE*

The importance of these topics to classroom learning has been underscored by the American Psychological Association (APA). In November 1997, the APA's Board of Educational Affairs proposed that efforts to improve education be based on a set of fourteen learner-centered psychological principles. These principles, derived from decades of research and practice, highlight the importance of learning processes, motivation, development, social processes, individual differences, and instructional practices in classroom learning. These are the same topics and principles that have long been emphasized by *Psychology Applied to Teaching*. A description of and rationale for each principle can be found on the following APA website: **http://apa.org/ed/cpse/LCPP.pdf.**

# HOW WILL LEARNING ABOUT EDUCATIONAL PSYCHOLOGY HELP YOU BE A BETTER TEACHER?

There's no question that knowledge of psychological concepts and their application to educational settings has the potential to help you be a better teacher. Whether that potential is ever fulfilled depends on how willing you are to maintain an open mind and a positive attitude. We say this because many prospective and practicing teachers have anything but a positive attitude when it comes to using psychological knowledge in the classroom. One teacher, for example, notes that "educational psychology and research are relatively useless because they rarely examine learning in authentic

*The information in this book can help you be a better teacher for three reasons: teaching is a complex activity that requires a broad knowledge base; many instructional practices are supported by research; and teachers who are knowledgeable about that research are better teachers.*

classroom contexts" (Burch, 1993). As you read through the next few paragraphs, as well as the subsequent chapters, you will see that criticisms like this are easily rebutted. We offer a three-pronged argument (teaching is a complex enterprise, research can inform teachers, and professional coursework contributes to competence) to explain how educational psychology can help you be a better teacher, whether you plan to teach in an elementary school, a middle school, or a high school.

## Teaching Is a Complex Enterprise

The first part of our argument is that teaching is not the simple, straightforward enterprise some people imagine it to be; in fact, it ranks in the top quartile on complexity for all occupations (Rowan, 1994), and the U.S. Department of Labor includes teachers in the same occupational group as engineers, architects, computer scientists, and lawyers (U.S. Department of Labor, 2001). There are many reasons for this complexity. In increasing ways, teachers have daily responsibility for diverse populations of students with varied and sometimes contradictory needs. But perhaps most fundamental, the complexity of teaching derives from its decision-making nature. Teachers are constantly making decisions—before and after instruction as well as on the spot. If you are to be informed and effective, these decisions should be based on a deep reservoir of knowledge and a wide range of skills.

> Teaching is complex work because it requires a wide range of knowledge and skills

The view that teaching is a complex activity that requires in-depth knowledge in a number of areas has been recognized by the National Board for Professional Teaching Standards (**www.nbpts.org**). This is an independent, nonprofit organization of educators, administrators, and political and business leaders whose mission is to establish clear and measurable standards for what accomplished teachers should know and be able to do and to identify those teachers through a voluntary system of certification. The board's standards are based on the following five propositions (National Board for Professional Teaching Standards, 2003):

1. Teachers are committed to students and their learning.
2. Teachers know the subjects they teach and how to teach those subjects to students.
3. Teachers are responsible for managing and monitoring student learning.
4. Teachers think systematically about their practice and learn from experience.
5. Teachers are members of learning communities.

In general, the standards require teachers to be knowledgeable about learning and development, individual differences, motivation, self-concept, assessment, classroom management, and various approaches to instruction, all of which are covered in this textbook. Although the complexity inherent in teaching makes it a difficult profession to master, making progress toward that goal is also one of teaching's greatest rewards.

To help you prepare to take on such challenges and become an effective teacher, educational psychology offers many useful ideas. It does not, in most cases, provide specific prescriptions about how to handle particular problems; rather, it gives you general principles that you can use in a flexible manner. Fortunately, the research literature contains a wealth of these ideas.

## Research That Informs Teachers

> Research in educational psychology offers many useful ideas for improving classroom instruction

The second part of our argument pertains to the potential usefulness of educational psychology research. Contrary to the opinion ventured by the anonymous teacher quoted previously, the research literature contains numerous studies that were conducted under realistic classroom conditions and offer useful ideas for improving instruction. There is consistent classroom-based support for the following instructional practices (Berliner & Casanova, 1996; Cruickshank, 1990; Marzano, Pickering, & Pollock, 2005), all discussed in later chapters of this text:

1. Using more advanced students to tutor less advanced students
2. Giving positive reinforcement to students whose performance meets or exceeds the teacher's objectives and giving corrective feedback to students whose performance falls short of the teacher's objectives
3. Communicating to students what is expected of them and why
4. Requiring students to respond to higher-order questions
5. Providing students with cues about the nature of upcoming tasks by giving them introductory information and telling them what constitutes satisfactory performance
6. Teaching students how to monitor and improve their own learning efforts and offering them structured opportunities to practice independent learning activities
7. Knowing the misconceptions that students bring to the classroom that will likely interfere with their learning of a particular subject matter
8. Creating learning situations in which students are expected to organize information in new ways and formulate problems for themselves
9. Accepting responsibility for student outcomes rather than seeing students as solely responsible for what they learn and how they behave
10. Showing students how to work in small, cooperative learning groups

The federal government and other policymaking organizations have acknowledged the importance of applying research on learning and learning-related issues to teaching. As part of the federal No Child Left Behind Act of 2001 (a revision of the earlier Elementary and Secondary Education Act), all schools that receive federal funds to create and maintain programs (such as safe and drug-free schools and Title I) must document how those programs are supported by scientifically-based research. This legislation also authorizes the National Science Foundation to create a network of Science of Learning Centers. (For a list of award winners from 2003 through 2006, go to **www.nsf.gov/funding/pgm_summ.jsp?pims_id=5517&from=fund** and click on "Abstracts of Recent Awards Made Through This Program".) These centers have an interdisciplinary focus, combining, for example, the work of researchers in psychology, education, computer science, linguistics, and sociology on various learning-related issues. The knowledge gained from these efforts will then be used to shape curriculum development and assessment (Azar, 2002). Teachers for a New Era, a program funded by the Carnegie Corporation to facilitate the development of exemplary teacher education programs, has as one of its three organizing principles that prospective teachers will develop respect for research-based evidence (Cochran-Smith, 2005). The American Psychological Association created the Applications of Psychological Science to Teaching and Learning Task Force and the Coalition for Psychology in the Schools and Education to help K–12 teachers use research-based practices that enhance classroom learning (American Psychological Association, 2006).

## Coursework and Competence

The third part of our argument that educational psychology can help you be a better teacher concerns the courses you are currently taking, particularly this educational psychology course. Many researchers have asked, "How do the courses teachers take as students relate to how capable they perceive themselves to be as teachers?" One means that researchers have used to determine the answer has been to ask beginning teachers to rate how prepared they feel to handle a variety of classroom tasks.

On the plus side, studies of beginning teachers (e.g., Maloch, Fine, & Flint, 2002/2003; Ruhland & Bremer, 2002) report that most believe that their teacher education programs adequately have prepared them to deal with most classroom challenges, and they are confident of their ability to be effective teachers. One recent

Teachers who have had professional training are generally more effective

*The students of teachers who were trained in teacher education programs and certified by their states score higher on standardized achievement tests than do the students of noncertified teachers.*

study (Brouwer & Korthagen, 2005) found that students who graduated from teacher education programs that emphasized integrating theory and practice (by alternating classroom work with practice teaching) and gradually increasing the complexity of student teaching activities (by having students first do observations, then teach partial lessons, whole lessons, and a series of lessons), and who rated that experience most favorably, rated themselves as more competent at the outset of their teaching careers. On the negative side, many teachers have reported that they feel uncomfortable in areas such as motivating students to learn, working with culturally diverse students, teaching exceptional students, managing the classroom, and teaching students how to use computers (e.g., Houston & Williamson, 1992/1993; Leyser, Frankiewicz, & Vaughn, 1992; Ruhland & Bremer, 2002; Scales, 1993). The importance of these topics and skills to effectiveness as a teacher was underscored in a survey of school principals (Torff & Sessions, 2005). When asked to specify which of five factors was most frequently associated with teacher ineffectiveness, classroom management skills received the highest average rating from 242 principals. In second, third, and fourth places were lesson implementation skills, rapport with students, and lesson planning skills, respectively. Being deficient in subject matter knowledge was perceived to be the least important cause of teachers' ineffectiveness. This textbook will address all of these issues, with special emphasis on most of those about which teachers have reported discomfort. Our belief is that this course and this book will be one important means for helping you feel prepared to enter your first classroom.

Another way to gauge the value of teacher-education coursework is to look at the effectiveness of certified versus noncertified teachers. Several studies (see American Educational Research Association, 2004; Berry, Hoke, & Hirsch, 2004; Darling-Hammond & Youngs, 2002; Laczko-Kerr & Berliner, 2003; Wayne & Youngs, 2003; and Wilson, Floden, & Ferrini-Mundy, 2002 for summaries of this research) found that the students of certified teachers scored higher on standardized achievement tests than did the students of noncertified teachers even though the noncertified teachers were judged to have had a good understanding of their subject matter. The literature on instructional quality also shows that well-trained teachers know how to manage classrooms, develop lessons that directly address state standards, motivate students, assess student work accurately, work with special-needs students, and productively use technology.

# THE NATURE AND VALUES OF SCIENCE

The primary purpose of this book is to offer suggestions on how psychology (the scientific study of behavior and mental processes) might be applied to teaching. This text is based on the premise that information reported by scientists can be especially useful for those who plan to teach. Some of the reasons for this conviction become apparent when the characteristics of science are examined and compared with the limitations of casual observation.

## Limitations of Unsystematic Observation

Unsystematic observation may lead to false conclusions

Those who make unsystematic observations of human behavior may be easily misled into drawing false conclusions. For instance, they may treat the first plausible explanation that comes to mind as the only possible explanation. Or they may mistakenly apply a generalization about a single episode to superficially similar situations. In the process, they may fail to realize that an individual's reactions in a given situation are due primarily to unrecognized idiosyncratic factors that may never occur again or that the behavior of one person under certain circumstances may not resemble that of other persons in the same circumstances. In short, unsystematic observers are especially prone to noting only evidence that fits their expectations and ignoring evidence that does not.

Grade retention policies are influenced by unsystematic observation

A clear example of the limitations of unsystematic observation is the practice of retaining children for a second year in a given grade because of poor achievement. Grade retention has long been assumed to be an effective way of dealing with individual differences in learning rate, emotional development, and socialization skills. The average retention rate for students in kindergarten through twelfth grade in the United States was a little over 5 percent for the 2003–2004 school year, with the highest rate (16.9 percent) occurring among students from low-income families (U.S. Department of Education, 2006). Retention is an expensive tactic since the average school spent $8,044 per student during the 2002–2003 school year (Hill & Johnson, 2005). To some extent, retention rates are related to the growth of state learning standards and high-stakes testing programs (which we discuss in Chapter 14 on standardized tests); school districts are often required to retain students whose test scores fall below a certain level.

This widespread and expensive use of retention continues even though most research clearly shows that it has negative effects. Retained students are 40 to 50 percent more likely than nonretained students to drop out of school. Moreover, low-achieving children who are promoted learn at least as much, if not more, the following year, have a stronger self-concept, and are better adjusted emotionally than similar children who are retained, even when the retention occurs as early as kindergarten (Duffrin, 2004a; Hong & Raudenbush, 2005; Jimerson, 2001; Jimerson & Kaufman, 2003; Jimerson, Anderson, & Whipple, 2002; Meisels & Liaw, 1993;

## pause & reflect

Imagine that you are a second-grade teacher. Your principal suggests that one of your students who performed poorly this year repeat second grade next year. Given what you know about the research on retention, how would you respond?

Nagaoka & Roderick, 2004; Rodney, Crafter, Rodney, & Mupier, 1999). Yet grade retention continues to be recommended by some parents, schools, administrators, and teachers because they believe that repeating a grade should be beneficial to a student, and people tend to overgeneralize from the exceptional case in which the outcome was positive (Duffrin, 2004b; Graue & DiPerna, 2000; Owings & Kaplan, 2001; Thomas, 2000). The reason retention does not work is simple: it does not address the causes of students' poor performance. These students typically begin school with more poorly developed academic skills, more serious health problems, and less stable home environments than their peers. In addition, retained students receive the same type of instruction and material the second time around. In short, retention is an attempt by policymakers, administrators, and some teachers to fit a short-term and relatively inexpensive solution to a long-term problem. The best way to minimize, if not avoid, the use of retention is to provide developmentally, cognitively, and culturally appropriate forms of instruction (Darling-Hammond & Falk, 1997). The major goal of this text is to help you know how to provide such instruction as a teacher.

### Strengths of Scientific Observation

Those who study behavior and mental processes scientifically are more likely to acquire trustworthy information than a casual observer is, and they are likely to apply what they learn more effectively because they follow the scientific procedures of sampling, control, objectivity, publication, and replication. In most cases, researchers study a representative sample of subjects so that individual idiosyncrasies are canceled out. An effort is made to note all plausible hypotheses to explain a given type of behavior, and each hypothesis is tested under controlled conditions. If all factors but one can be held constant in an experiment, the researcher may be able to trace the impact of a given condition by comparing the behaviors of those who have been exposed to it and those who have not.

| Scientific methods: sampling, control, objectivity, publication, replication

Scientific observers make special efforts to be objective and guard against being misled by predetermined ideas, wishful thinking, or selected evidence. Observations are made in a carefully prescribed, systematic manner, which makes it possible for different observers to compare reactions.

Complete reports of experiments—including descriptions of subjects, methods, results, and conclusions—are published in professional journals. This dissemination allows other experimenters to replicate a study to discover if they obtain the same results. The existence of reports of thousands of experiments makes it possible to discover what others have done. This knowledge can then serve as a starting point for one's own speculations.

## COMPLICATING FACTORS IN THE STUDY OF BEHAVIOR AND THOUGHT PROCESSES

Although the use of scientific methods makes it possible to overcome many of the limitations of unscientific observation, the application of knowledge acquired in a scientific manner to classroom settings is subject to several complicating factors. We want you to be aware of these so that you do not think we are insisting that science can cure all your classroom problems.

### The Limited Focus of Research

Human behavior is complex, changes with age, and has many causes. A student may perform poorly on a history exam, for example, for one or more of the following reasons: poorly developed study skills, inattentiveness in class, low interest in the subject, a poorly written text, low motivation to achieve high grades, vaguely worded exam questions, and difficulty with a particular type of exam question (compare-and-contrast essays, for example).

| Research focuses on a few aspects of a problem

To understand how these factors affect performance on school-related tasks, research psychologists study at most only a few of them at a time under conditions that may not be entirely realistic. Imagine that a researcher is interested in comparing simulation software with drill or tutorial software in terms of their effect on conceptual understanding. The researcher may recruit subjects who are equivalent in terms of social class, prior knowledge of the topic of the reading passage, and age; randomly assign them to one of two experimental groups; give them either a simulation program or a drill program to use; and then examine each group's responses to several types of comprehension items. As a consequence of such focused approaches, most research studies provide specific information about a particular aspect of behavior. More comprehensive knowledge, however, is acquired by combining and interrelating separate studies that have looked at different aspects of a common problem.

## The Complexity of Teaching and Learning

David Berliner (2002), a leading educational researcher, considers the scientific study of education to be "the hardest-to-do science of them all" for at least two reasons. First, it is difficult to implement research findings and programs uniformly because schools and classrooms differ from one another along such lines as quality and quantity of personnel, teaching methods, budget, leadership, and community support. Thus, a program or technique may work just as the research says it should in one district or teacher's class, but not in other classes or districts.

> Complexity of teaching and learning limits uniform outcomes

Second, the outcomes of schooling that teachers, students, and parents typically value are the result of complex interactions among numerous variables. This is true for both cognitive (thinking) outcomes and affective (emotional) outcomes. Achievement may, for example, be the result of interactions among student characteristics (such as prior knowledge, interests, and socioeconomic levels), teacher characteristics (type of training, ideas about learning, interests, and values, for example), curriculum materials, socioeconomic status of the community, and peer influences. Consequently, students exposed to the same materials and teaching methods are likely to vary in how much and what they learn.

Such differences in student outcomes are largely a result of the fact that ideas are not given from one person to another like so many packages but rather are actively *constructed* by each person (Brooks & Brooks, 2001; Schifter, 1996; Wheatley, 1991). Because different factors come into play for different people and the same factors affect people differently, two people can read the same passage yet construct entirely different interpretations of its meaning. This concept, known as *constructivism*, is so fundamental to human behavior and to learning that we will return to it again and again in this text.

*Understanding and managing the teaching/learning process is a challenge for researchers and teachers because it is affected by numerous variables that interact with one another.*

Because of these differences in context and individual characteristics, researchers rarely find that a particular instructional technique, program, or set of learning materials produces the same effect for all students. Consequently, the most useful research findings are those that stem from such questions as these:

- Who (males or females; high-, average-, or low-achieving students; ethnic minority or majority students; younger or older students) is likely to benefit most from this technique, program, or type of material?
- Under what conditions are the strongest results likely to be obtained?
- For what types of outcomes (such as multiple-choice tests, essay tests, performance tests) are the strongest results likely to be obtained?

## Selection and Interpretation of Data

The amount of scientific information available on behavior and mental processes is so extensive that no individual could examine or interpret all of it. Accordingly, researchers learn to be highly selective in their reading. In addition, conclusions about the meaning of scientific results vary from one researcher to another. As you read this book, you will discover that there are differences of opinion among psychologists regarding certain aspects of development, motivation, and intelligence. Opposing views may be based on equally scientific evidence, but the way in which the evidence is selected and interpreted will vary. The fact that a topic is studied scientifically does not necessarily mean that opinions about interpretations of the data will be unanimous.

Differences of opinion result from selection and interpretation of data

## New Findings Mean Revised Ideas

Scientific information is not only voluminous and subject to different interpretations; it is also constantly being revised. A series of experiments may lead to the development of a new concept or pedagogical technique that is highly successful when it is first tried out. Subsequent studies, however, may reveal that the original research was incomplete, or repeated applications of a technique may show that it is less effective once the novelty has worn off. But frequent shifts of emphasis in education also reflect the basic nature of science. A quality of science that sets it apart from other intellectual processes is that the discoveries by one generation of scientists set the stage for far-reaching discoveries by the next. More researchers are studying aspects of psychology and education now than at any previous time in history, and thousands of reports of scientific research are published every month.

Accumulated knowledge leads researchers to revise original ideas

As our knowledge accumulates, it is inevitable that interpretations of how children learn and how we should teach will continue to change. We know more about development, learning, and teaching today than ever before, but because of the nature of some of the factors just discussed and the complexity of human behavior, our answers are tentative and incomplete.

You should be aware, of course, that fads occur in education (just as they occur in other fields). Occasionally national or international events cause changes in our political and social climate that often result in pressures on education to "do something." And when large numbers of educators embrace a new practice without waiting for or paying attention to research findings, fads develop. One of our objectives in writing this text is to demonstrate the importance of basing your practices on principles that have some research support. If you do so, you can avoid contributing to fads.

Over the past few pages, we have asked you to consider some of the values of science, the strengths of scientific observation, and a few of the factors that complicate the scientific study of behavior and lead to frequent changes of emphasis in teaching techniques. These considerations help explain why this book stresses how psychology might be applied to teaching; they also support the

## pause & reflect

Think of a popular instructional practice. Would you classify it as a fad or as the outgrowth of scientific knowledge? Why? How can you tell the difference?

position that information reported by scientists can be especially valuable for those who plan to teach. At the same time, our intention has been to acquaint you with a few of the limitations and sometimes unsettling by-products of science.

The science of psychology has much to offer educators, but a scientific approach to teaching does have its limits. Because teaching is a dynamic *decision-making process*, you will be greatly aided by a systematic, objective framework for making your decisions. Research on teaching and learning can give you that framework. But for the reasons just cited, research cannot give you a prescription or a set of rules that specify how you should handle every situation. Often you will have to make on-the-spot, subjective decisions about how to present a lesson, explain a concept, handle mass boredom, or reprimand a student. This contrast between an objective, systematic approach to planning instruction and the need to make immediate (yet appropriate) applications and modifications of those plans calls attention to a question that has been debated for years: Is teaching primarily an art or a science—or a combination of both?

## GOOD TEACHING IS PARTLY AN ART AND PARTLY A SCIENCE

Some educators have argued that teaching is an art that cannot be practiced or even studied in an objective or scientific manner because of its inherent unpredictability (Eisner, 2002; Flinders, 1989; Hansgen, 1991; Rubin, 1985). Selma Wasserman (1999), who taught public school and college for many years, recounts how her teacher-education program prepared her for her first day as a public school teacher:

> Learning the "correct answers" not only had not equipped me for the complex and confusing world of the classroom but, even worse, had led me down the garden path. Implicit in what I had learned was that teaching was merely a matter of stockpiling certain pieces of information about teaching. If I only knew what the answers were, I would be prepared to face the overwhelming and exhausting human dilemmas that make up life in classrooms. Unfortunately, I had been swindled. My training in learning the answers was as useless as yesterday's pizza. I was entering a profession in which there are few, if any, clear-cut answers, a profession riddled with ambiguity and moral dilemmas that would make Solomon weep. Even more of a handicap was that I became desperate in my search for the answers—certain that they were out there, somewhere, if only I could find them. (p. 466)

Wasserman's account suggests that there are no authoritative sources that will provide teachers with fail-safe prescriptions for the myriad problems they will face. Good teaching is as much the result of one's beliefs, values, and emotions as of one's formal knowledge. A few examples of beliefs that support good teaching are that teaching is one of society's most valuable and rewarding activities, that teaching must be done as well as possible every day, that it is important to get students excited about learning, and that there is no such thing as an unteachable student.

*Part of the art of teaching is knowing when to introduce an unusual assignment or activity that captures students' interest.*

When Wasserman states that teaching is not a matter of clear-cut answers, she is urging teachers to be flexible. Flexibility, which can be thought of as a "feel" for doing the right thing at the right time, can take many forms. First, it means being able to choose from among all the techniques and information at your disposal to formulate effective lesson plans that take the diverse needs and interests of all your students into consideration. It means knowing, for example, when to present a formal lesson and when to let students discover things for themselves, when to be demanding and when to make few demands, when and to whom to give direct help, and when and to whom to give indirect help.

Second, flexibility entails the communication of emotions and interest in a variety of ways. David Flinders (1989) describes a teacher who, when talking to students, would lean or step in their direction and maintain eye contact. At various times, she would raise her eyebrows, nod her head, smile, and bring the index finger of her right hand to her lips, indicating serious consideration of the student's comments. In their book *Acting Lessons for Teachers: Using Performance Skills in the Classroom* (2006), Robert Tauber and Cathy Sargent Mester describe the importance for successful teaching of such acting skills as voice animation (variations in pitch, volume, voice quality, and rate), body animation (facial expressions, gestures), and use of classroom space.

## pause & reflect

The effective teacher as artist communicates enthusiasm. At some point, however, you may be asked to teach a grade level or subject for which you have little enthusiasm, or you may grow bored teaching the same grade level or subject year after year. How will you fulfill the role of teacher-artist in these situations?

Third, flexibility includes the ability to improvise. When a lesson plan falls flat, the flexible teacher immediately thinks of an alternative presentation that recaptures the students' interest. Expert teachers actually plan improvisation into their lessons. Instead of writing out what they intend to do in great detail, they formulate general mental plans and wait to see how the students react before filling in such details as pacing, timing, and number of examples (Moshavi, 2001; Westerman, 1991). Obviously this type of high-wire act requires a great deal of experience and confidence.

Fourth, flexibility involves the willingness and resourcefulness to work around impediments. Teaching does not always occur under ideal circumstances, and teachers must sometimes cope with inadequate facilities, insufficient materials, interruptions, and other difficulties.

Teacher educator Sharon Feiman-Nemser (2003) underscored the importance of flexibility to the art of teaching by noting what experienced educators said when asked what beginning teachers most needed to learn. One recommended that new teachers focus on helping students understand the essence of each lesson, even if that means going beyond or ignoring guidelines in a teacher's manual. Another noted that because teachers are essentially on stage, they need to develop a performing self that they are comfortable with. A third observation was that new teachers need to learn how to size up situations and think on their feet. In sum, **teaching as an art** involves beliefs, emotions, values, and flexibility. Because these characteristics are intangible, they can be very difficult, if not impossible, to teach. Teachers must find these qualities within themselves.

The argument for **teaching as a science** is equally persuasive. Although many educational psychologists agree that the science of teaching, as such, does not exist, they contend that it is possible and desirable to have a scientific basis for the art of teaching (e.g., Gage & Berliner, 1998; Hiebert, Gallimore, & Stigler, 2002; Kosunen & Mikkola, 2002). By drawing on established research findings, both prospective and practicing teachers can learn many of the prerequisites that make artistic teaching possible. Also, as Robert Slavin (1989) persuasively argues, working from a scientific basis helps teachers avoid the pitfall of subscribing to the latest fad.

The case for teaching as a science rests on the existence of a usable body of research findings. Research has identified dozens of instructional practices that improve student achievement. For example, at least twenty-four separate studies have found that giving teachers more instructional time—that is, giving students more time to learn—leads to higher achievement (Walberg, 1990; Wang, Haertel, & Walberg, 1993). (This finding is often used to support proposals for a longer school

*Teaching as an art: beliefs, emotions, values, flexibility*

*Research provides a scientific basis for "artistic" teaching*

year.) Other studies have demonstrated the benefits of alerting students to important material through the use of objectives and pretests, engaging students in a task through the use of questions and homework, and providing corrective feedback and reinforcement with written comments, verbal explanations, and praise.

As useful as the scientific literature is, there is at least one other major contributor to a teacher's knowledge base: classroom experience. Although the knowledge that teachers gain from teaching actual lessons often lacks the broad generalizability that is characteristic of scientific knowledge, it does have the following advantages:

- It is linked to a particular task and goal (such as teaching students how to discover the various themes embedded in a reading passage).
- It is sufficiently detailed, concrete, and specific that other teachers can use the same techniques with the same or highly similar material.
- It typically combines knowledge of the task, knowledge of teaching methods, and knowledge of students' characteristics (Hiebert et al., 2002).

Look back at the heading of this section. Notice that it reads "Good Teaching Is Partly an Art and Partly a Science," not "Teaching as an Art Versus Teaching as a Science." Our choice of wording indicates our belief that good teaching is a skillful blend of artistic and scientific elements. The teacher who attempts to base every action on scientific evidence is likely to come across as rigid and mechanical—perhaps even indecisive (when the scientific evidence is lacking or unclear). The teacher who ignores scientific knowledge about teaching and learning and makes arbitrary decisions runs the risk of using methods that are ineffective.

> Good teachers combine "artistic" and "scientific" characteristics

### pause & reflect

How do good teachers strike a balance between the art and the science of teaching? Are they born with the right personality? Are they the products of good teacher-education programs? If both factors play a role, which is more important?

## VIDEO CASE    ◀◀ ▶ ▶▶

HM

### Teaching as a Profession:
### What Defines Effective Teaching

*Watch the video clip, study the artifacts in the case, and reflect on the following questions:*

1. This section of the chapter explains that teaching is both art and science. How did the teachers in the video case combine both artistic and scientific approaches to teaching?

2. Give some specific examples from the video case that illustrate how teachers employed the attribute of flexibility that is described in the chapter.

## REFLECTIVE TEACHING: A PROCESS TO HELP YOU GROW FROM NOVICE TO EXPERT

> Reflective teachers think about what they do and why

The blending of artistic and scientific elements can be seen in discussions of what is called **reflective teaching** (see, for example, Eby, Herrell, & Hicks, 2002; Ellis, 2001; Henderson, 2001; and McEntee et al., 2003). Reflective teachers are constantly engaged in thoughtful observation and analysis of their actions in the classroom before, during, and after interactions with their students.

Prior to instruction, reflective teachers may think about such things as the types of knowledge and skills students in a democratic society need to learn, the kind of classroom atmosphere and teaching techniques that are most likely to produce this learning, and the kinds of assessments that will provide clear evidence that these goals are being accomplished (a topic that we discuss at some length in the chapters on assessment and testing). Jere Brophy and Janet Alleman (1991) illustrate the importance of thinking about long-range goals by pointing out how the choice of goals affects content coverage and how content coverage affects teachers' choice of classroom activities. If, for example, one goal is for students to acquire problem-solving skills, students would likely be engaged in activities that call for inquiring, reasoning, and decision making. Debates, simulations, and laboratory experiments are just three examples of activities that might be used to meet such a goal. If the goal is for students to memorize facts and information, students will likely be given activities that call for isolated memorization and recall. Worksheets and drill-and-practice exercises are typically used to meet this type of goal. The point here is that effective teachers are reflective: they think about these issues as a basis for drawing up lesson plans.

As they interact with students, reflective teachers are highly aware of how students are responding to what they are doing and are prepared to make minor but significant changes to keep a lesson moving toward its predetermined goal. Consider an elementary school classroom in which some students are having difficulty understanding the relationship between the orbits of the planets around the sun and their position in the night sky. The teacher knows there is a problem: some students have a puzzled expression on their faces, and others cannot describe this phenomenon in their own words. Realizing that some students think in more concrete terms than others, the teacher decides to push the desks to the sides of the room and have the students simulate the planets by walking through their orbits. All in the moment, this teacher engages in thoughtful observation, spontaneous analysis, and flexible, resourceful problem solving.

For events that cannot be handled on the spot, some period of time outside of school should be set aside for reflection. This is the time to assess how well a particular lesson met its objective, wonder why some students rarely participate in class discussions, ponder the pros and cons of grouping students by ability, and formulate plans for dealing with these concerns.

To become a reflective teacher, you will need to acquire several attitudes and abilities. Three of the most important attitudes are an introspective orientation, an open-minded but questioning attitude about educational theories and practices, and

| Reflective teachers have particular attitudes and abilities

*Reflective teachers set aside time to think about what they do in class, why they do it, and how their methods affect student performance.*

the willingness to take responsibility for your decisions and actions. These attitudes need to be combined with the ability to view situations from the perspectives of others (students, parents, principal, other teachers), the ability to find information that allows an alternative explanation of classroom events and produces more effective instructional methods, and the ability to use compelling evidence in support of a decision (Eby et al., 2002; Ross, Bondy, & Kyle, 1993). In short, to become a reflective teacher, you need both the willingness and ability to reveal and challenge your assumptions about teaching and learning. We hasten to add that although reflection is largely a solitary activity, you should discuss your concerns with colleagues, friends, students, and parents to get different perspectives on the nature of a problem and possible alternative courses of action.

As you can probably see from this brief discussion, the reflection process is likely to work well when teachers have command of a wide range of knowledge about the nature of students, the learning process, and the instructional process. By mastering much of the content of this text, you will be well prepared to make productive use of the time you devote to reflection.

Another factor that has been shown to contribute to teacher reflectivity is journal writing. Keeping a written journal forces you to express with some clarity your thoughts and beliefs about the causes of classroom events, how you feel about those events, and what you might do about them (Bennett & Pye, 2000; Good & Whang, 2002; McVarish & Solloway, 2002). Thus, one potentially helpful way you might begin developing this reflective capacity is to follow our suggestion for compiling a Reflective Journal. In the final chapter of this book, we describe how you might set up this journal.

## pause & reflect

The reflective teacher sets aside regular blocks of time to think about teaching activities and make new plans. Most teachers complain about having insufficient time to reflect and plan. What would you do to make more time available?

## SPECIAL FEATURES OF THIS BOOK

This book has several distinctive features that are intended to be used in rather specialized ways: Key Points, Suggestions for Teaching in Your Classroom, Take a Stand!, Houghton Mifflin Video Cases, one or more sections of every chapter that are devoted to discussing applications of technology to teaching, references to numerous websites that relate to various aspects of teaching and learning, Pause and Reflect questions, and Journal Entries. In addition, your compilation of a separate component to accompany this book—the Reflective Journal—is recommended. This journal makes use of the text's Journal Entries and the Suggestions for Teaching.

### Key Points

*HM TeacherPrepSPACE*

The textbook's student website includes additional study aids, such as Thought Questions and Glossary Flashcards for glossary terms.

At the beginning of each chapter, you will find a list of *Key Points*. The Key Points also appear within the body of the chapter, printed in the margins. These points have been selected to help you learn and remember sections of each chapter that are of special significance to teachers. (These sections may be stressed on exams, but they were originally selected because they are important, not because they can serve as the basis for test items.) To grasp the nature of the Key Points, turn back to the opening page of this chapter, which lists points stressed under the chapter's major headings. Then flip through the chapter to see how the appearance of the Key Points in the margins calls attention to significant sections of the text.

### Suggestions for Teaching in Your Classroom

In most of the chapters, you will find summaries of research that serve as the basis for related principles or conclusions. These sets of principles or conclusions are the foundation for *Suggestions for Teaching in Your Classroom*. Suggestions are usually followed by examples illustrating how they might be applied. In most cases, examples are provided for both elementary and secondary grades because there usually are differences in the way a principle might be applied in dealing with younger and with older students.

Many research articles and textbooks provide only vague guidelines for classroom use and no concrete examples. But when new research-based ideas are presented in a concrete and usable form, teachers are much more likely to try them out (Gersten & Brengelman, 1996). This is why *Psychology Applied to Teaching* places so much emphasis on concrete suggestions for teaching. But as useful as our suggestions might be, you cannot use them as prescriptions. Every school building and every group of students is different. You have to learn how to adapt the suggestions in this book and any other books that you will read to the particular dynamics of each class. This is the essence of being a reflective teacher.

## Take a Stand!

Earlier in this chapter we discussed why the scientific study of behavior and thought processes in a classroom setting is a complex undertaking. Such factors as the limited focus of research, the complexity of teaching and learning, and the revision of ideas due to new findings make it difficult at times to draw definitive conclusions about why students behave as they do and how teachers might respond. But there are other instances when the evidence is sufficiently deep and consistent, or the logic so compelling, that we feel confident taking a stand on an issue and believe you can as well, be it publicly or privately.

For each of the following chapters, we identify one of these instances with the Take a Stand! label, and we state our beliefs succinctly. You may, of course, disagree with our conclusion and decide to take either no stand or a different stand. That's fine, and we commend you for being an independent and critical thinker so long as your decision is based on additional evidence and logical thinking.

In the student website, one section is devoted to the issues highlighted in the Take a Stand! features. Here, you can find additional material related to these important topics. We invite you to take advantage of this resource, because exploring a controversial issue is a good way to both broaden and sharpen your thinking.

*HM TeacherPrepSPACE*

At the textbook's student website, the Take a Stand! section can help you develop your own positions on major issues.

## Houghton Mifflin Video Cases

In each chapter you will find one or two (sometimes more) video cases. Available online and organized by topic, each "case" is a three- to five-minute module consisting of video and audio files presenting actual classroom scenarios that depict the complex problems and opportunities teachers face every day. The video and audio clips are accompanied by "artifacts" to provide background information and allow you to experience true classroom dilemmas in their multiple dimensions. After each video case, you are asked to reflect on questions related to the chapter.

## Emphasis on the Role of Technology in Learning and Instruction

Throughout this book, we discuss the role of technology in relation to all the major aspects of learning and instruction. In addition, the **Student Website** that accompanies this book provides many technology-oriented resources as well as other useful material for developing your skills as a teacher.

When we use the term *technology*, we are referring to devices that extend and amplify people's ability to store, transform, retrieve, and communicate information. Although this broad definition encompasses a wide array of devices (such as calculators, slide and movie projectors, videocassette and audiotape recorders, videodisc players, and computers), our focus will be largely on computers because of their widespread use and potential to transform teaching and learning.

**HM** *TeacherPrepSPACE*

Go to the textbook's student website for links to important web pages.

As with any other instructional method, material, or medium that has been enthusiastically received, however, you should strive to keep things in proper perspective. There is no doubt about the computer's ability to help students and teachers analyze, sort, transform, and present information in a variety of formats or about the ability of the World Wide Web to connect students to other individuals and information sources. But as Richard Mayer (2001), a leading educational psychology researcher, has noted, educational technology is simply a medium of instruction, not a method of instruction. It is Mayer's belief, and ours, that teachers should embed technology within a learner-centered approach to teaching—that is, within an approach based on an understanding of how students develop and learn.

Mayer's view of technology as a medium rather than a method is supported by a two-year study of how three teachers used laptop computers in their classrooms (Windschitl & Sahl, 2002). The findings indicated that the teachers used the computers in very different ways. Of the three teachers, only one had a preexisting commitment to a student-centered, constructivist approach to teaching. She was more inclined than the other teachers, for example, to allow students to choose and explore specific issues within a broad topic area. She saw laptop computers as a way for students to access the same world of information used by adults and as a tool to help them formulate sophisticated ideas. One of the other teachers was more strongly committed to a teacher-centered philosophy and used technology only to support that approach. Because she believed that her role was to help students acquire basic skills, her use of computers was more limited, revolving around drill-and-practice exercises. In essence, she saw computer technology as a way to present one's work rather than as a way to further one's learning.

As you examine the technology resources and ideas mentioned in this book, you should be thinking about the ways in which they might enhance the learning environment of your own classroom. To help you do this, we encourage you to examine the National Educational Technology Standards that have been proposed for four grade levels by the International Society for Technology in Education (ISTE, 2000). For each grade level, Table 1.1 lists two of the six standards and their respective competencies. The complete list of technology standards and competencies for students as well as standards for teachers and administrators (**www.cnets.iste.org/ currstands**), and a list of states that have adopted the standards (**http://cnets.iste .org/getdocs.html**), can be found on the ISTE website.

# VIDEO CASE   ◀◀ ▶ ▶▶

### An Expanded Definition of Literacy: Meaningful Ways to Use Technology

*Watch the video clip, study the artifacts in the case, and reflect on the following questions:*

1. Describe a few specific examples from the video case that illustrate meaningful ways to use technology.

2. Can you provide examples of a few different kinds of technologies from the video case that match the technology standards listed in Table 1.1?

## Pause and Reflect

As you have seen several times in this chapter, from time to time we pose a question that invites you to think about issues raised in the text and how you will handle them in your own teaching. You can use these questions either for personal reflection or for discussion with classmates and practicing teachers.

| Table 1.1 | Examples of Technology Standards and Competencies for Students |
|---|---|

| Grade Level | Standards | Competencies |
|---|---|---|
| **PreK–2** | Basic Operations and Concepts | Use input devices (e.g., mouse, keyboard, remote control) and output devices (e.g., monitor, printer) to successfully operate computers, VCRs, audiotapes, and other technologies. |
| | Technology Communications Tools | Gather information and communicate with others using telecommunications, with support from teachers, family members, or student partners. |
| **3–5** | Social, Ethical, and Human Issues | Discuss common uses of technology in daily life and the advantages and disadvantages those uses provide. |
| | Technology Problem-Solving and Decision-Making Tools | Evaluate the accuracy, relevance, appropriateness, comprehensiveness, and bias of electronic information sources. |
| **6–8** | Technology Productivity Tools | Use content-specific tools, software, and simulations (e.g., environmental probes, graphing calculators, exploratory environments, web tools) to support learning and research. |
| | Technology Research Tools | Select and use appropriate tools and technology resources to accomplish a variety of tasks and solve problems. |
| **9–12** | Social, Ethical, and Human Issues | Identify capabilities and limitations of contemporary and emerging technology resources and assess the potential of these systems and services to address personal, lifelong learning, and workplace needs. |
| | Technology Productivity Tools | Investigate and apply expert systems, intelligent agents, and simulations in real-world situations. |

SOURCE: International Society for Technology in Education (2000).

## Journal Entries

*HM TeacherPrepSPACE*

You can find additional Reflective Journal Questions at the textbook's student website.

Within the margins of each chapter, you will find numerous instances of the phrase *Journal Entry*. These marginal headings are related to the material just opposite in the text. They are intended to serve as suggested wordings for the headings of pages in a Reflective Journal that we strongly encourage you to keep. In the final chapter, we describe the beneficial effects of reflection and journal writing on teaching, and we describe how you can use the suggested Journal Entries to organize your first Reflective Journal. If you do not have time to begin your journal while taking the course, we hope you will go through the book a second time, after you finish this course, for the purpose of developing a custom-designed journal.

## HOW THIS BOOK WILL HELP PREPARE YOU TO MEET INSTRUCTIONAL STANDARDS

We live in an age of standards and accountability, particularly in education. Just as students, teachers, and administrators are held accountable for students' meeting various learning standards, prospective and beginning teachers are increasingly expected to demonstrate that they have met a set of knowledge standards that are believed to be the foundation of high-quality instruction. Among the standards that govern the preparation and licensing of teachers, two that are particularly prominent are the Praxis II, a standardized test, and a set of ten instructional principles and related standards called the INTASC (Interstate New Teacher Assessment and Support Consortium) standards. In this section, we briefly discuss the content of the Praxis II and the INTASC standards and show you how *Psychology Applied to Teaching* will help prepare you to meet the standards.

## Praxis II and *Psychology Applied to Teaching*

As part of recent educational reform efforts, many state boards of education and teacher education programs require that as a condition for licensure, beginning teachers demonstrate that they are knowledgeable about the psychological and educational factors that are likely to affect how well their students will perform in the classroom. A popular instrument used for this purpose is the Praxis II, published by the Educational Testing Service (ETS). The Principles of Learning and Teaching section of the Praxis II assesses a beginning teacher's knowledge of topics that are typically covered in an educational psychology course.

Because *Psychology Applied to Teaching* (PAT) is closely aligned with the Principles of Teaching and Learning section of the Praxis II and emphasizes classroom applications, we believe PAT will help prepare you to do well on this important assessment. On this book's front endpapers, you will find a table that lists the topics and subtopics covered by the Principles of Learning and Teaching test (also available on the ETS website at **www.ets.org/praxis**), along with the chapter numbers and pages in PAT where discussions of these topics can be found.

## INTASC and *Psychology Applied to Teaching*

*HM TeacherPrepSPACE*

*To review this chapter's content and help yourself prepare for licensing exams, see the ACE practice tests and PowerPoint slides at the textbook's student website.*

In the early 1990s, the Interstate New Teacher Assessment and Support Consortium (INTASC) published a set of ten instructional principles and related standards to guide the preparation of beginning teachers. These principles and standards represent the core knowledge, dispositions, and skills that INTASC believes are essential for all beginning teachers, regardless of their specialty or grade level. The INTASC standards are also designed to be compatible with the certification program for highly skilled veteran teachers developed by the National Board for Professional Teaching Standards.

An important part of the philosophy behind the INTASC standards is the belief that well-trained teachers have the knowledge, dispositions, and skills to help all students achieve at acceptable levels. That notion has also been a major part of the philosophy of *Psychology Applied to Teaching*. To help you see how the content of *Psychology Applied to Teaching* corresponds to the INTASC knowledge standards, we have included a correlation table on the book's back endpapers.

# Age-Level Characteristics

## HM TeacherPrepSPACE

**HM TeacherPrepSPACE student website** offers many helpful resources. Go to **login.cengage.com** to preview this chapter's Concept Maps and Chapter Themes.

*These key points will help you learn the important information in this chapter. To help you study, they also appear in the margins of the pages, next to the text where they are discussed.*

### Preschool and Kindergarten (Three, Four, and Five Years)

- Large-muscle control better established than small-muscle control and eye-hand coordination
- Play patterns vary as a function of social class, gender, and age
- Gender differences in toy preferences and play activities noticeable by kindergarten
- By age four, children have a theory of mind: aware of own mental processes and that others may think differently
- Peer comparisons help four- and five-year-olds more accurately judge their capabilities

### Primary Grades (1, 2, and 3; Six, Seven, and Eight Years)

- Primary grade children have difficulty focusing on small print
- Accident rate peaks in third grade because of confidence in physical skills
- Rigid interpretation of rules in primary grades
- To encourage industry, use praise, avoid criticism
- Awareness of cognitive processes begins to emerge

### Elementary School (Grades 4 and 5; Nine and Ten Years)

- Boys slightly better at sports-related motor skills; girls better at flexibility, balance, rhythmic motor skills
- Peer group norms for behavior begin to replace adult norms
- Self-image becomes more generalized and stable; is based primarily on comparisons with peers
- Delinquents have few friends, are easily distracted, are not interested in schoolwork, lack basic skills
- Elementary grade students reason logically but concretely

### Middle School (Grades 6, 7, and 8; Eleven, Twelve, and Thirteen Years)

- Girls' growth spurt occurs earlier, and so they look older than boys of same age
- Early-maturing boys likely to draw favorable responses
- Late-maturing boys may feel inadequate
- Early-maturing girls may suffer low self-esteem
- Late-maturing girls likely to be popular and carefree
- Average age of puberty: girls, eleven; boys, fourteen
- Discussion of controversial issues may be difficult because of strong desire to conform to peer norms
- Teenagers experience different degrees of emotional turmoil
- Environment of middle schools does not meet needs of adolescents, leading to lower levels of learning
- Self-efficacy beliefs for academic and social tasks become strong influences on behavior

### High School (Grades 9, 10, 11, and 12; Fourteen, Fifteen, Sixteen, and Seventeen Years)

- Factors related to initiation of sexual activity vary by gender, race
- Parents influence values, plans; peers influence immediate status
- Girls more likely than boys to experience anxiety about friendships
- Depression most common among females, minorities
- Depression may be caused by negative cognitive set, learned helplessness, sense of loss
- Depression and unstable family situation place adolescents at risk for suicide
- Political thinking becomes more abstract, less authoritarian, more knowledgeable

The theories described in the next chapter will call attention to the course of psychosocial, cognitive, and moral development. Although these types of behavior are important, they represent only a small part of the behavior repertoire of a child or adolescent. This chapter, which is organized by age and grade levels, will present an overview of types of behavior that are not directly related to any particular theory. In selecting points for emphasis, we used one basic criterion: Does this information about development have potential significance for teachers?

To organize the points to be discussed, we have divided the developmental span into five levels, corresponding to common grade groupings in schools:

*Preschool and kindergarten.* Ages three through five
*Primary grades.* Grades 1 through 3; ages six through eight

*Elementary grades.* Grades 4 and 5; ages nine and ten

*Middle school.* Grades 6 through 8; ages eleven through thirteen

*High school.* Grades 9 through 12; ages fourteen through seventeen

Because the way grades are grouped varies, you may find yourself teaching in a school system in which the arrangement described in this chapter is not followed. In that case, simply refer to the appropriate age-level designations and, if necessary, concentrate on two levels rather than one.

At each of the five levels, behaviors are discussed under four headings: physical, social, emotional, and cognitive characteristics. Following each characteristic are implications for teachers. To help you establish a general conception of what children are like at each level, brief summaries of the types of behavior stressed by the theorists discussed in the next chapter are listed in a table in each section (Tables 2.1, 2.2, 2.3, 2.4, and 2.7). ●

# PRESCHOOL AND KINDERGARTEN (THREE, FOUR, AND FIVE YEARS)

## Physical Characteristics: Preschool and Kindergarten

**JOURNAL ENTRY**
Active Games

1. *Preschool children are extremely active. They have good control of their bodies and enjoy activity for its own sake.* Provide plenty of opportunities for children to run, climb, and jump. Arrange these activities, as much as possible, so that they are under your control. If you follow a policy of complete freedom, you may discover that thirty improvising three- to five-year-olds can be a frightening thing. In your Reflective Journal, you might note some specific games and activities that you could use to achieve semicontrolled play.

**JOURNAL ENTRY**
Riot-Stopping Signals and Activities

2. *Because of an inclination toward bursts of activity, kindergartners need frequent rest periods. They themselves often don't recognize the need to slow down.* Schedule quiet activities after strenuous ones. Have rest time. Realize that excitement may build up to a riot level if the attention of "catalytic agents" and their followers is not diverted. In your journal, you might list some signals for calling a halt to a melee (for example, playing the opening chords of Beethoven's Fifth Symphony on the piano) or for diverting wild action into more or less controlled activity (marching around the room to a brisk rendition of "Stars and Stripes Forever").

**JOURNAL ENTRY**
Allowing for Large-Muscle Control

3. *Preschoolers' large muscles are more developed than those that control fingers and hands. Therefore, preschoolers may be quite clumsy at, or physically incapable of, such skills as tying shoes and buttoning coats.* Avoid too many small-motor activities, such as pasting paper chains. Provide big brushes, crayons, and tools. In your journal, you might note other activities or items of king-sized equipment that would be appropriate for the children's level of muscular development.

Large-muscle control better established than small-muscle control and hand-eye coordination

4. *Young children find it difficult to focus their eyes on small objects. Therefore, their eye-hand coordination may be imperfect.* If possible, minimize the necessity for the children to look at small things. (Incomplete eye development is the reason for large print in children's books.) This is also important to keep in mind if you are planning to use computers or software programs; highly graphic programs requiring a simple point-and-click response are most appropriate for very young students.

5. *Although children's bodies are flexible and resilient, the bones that protect the brain are still soft.* Be extremely wary of blows to the head in games or fights between children. If you notice an activity involving such a blow, intervene immediately; warn the class that this is dangerous and explain why.

6. *Gender differences in physical development and motor skill proficiency are usually not noticeable until kindergarten and are fairly small in magnitude.* Differences that do manifest themselves are due in part to biological endowment and in part to

| ■ **Table 2.1** | Applying Theories of Development to the Preschool and Kindergarten Years |
|---|---|

**Psychosocial development:** initiative vs. guilt. Children need opportunities for free play and experimentation, as well as experiences that give them a sense of accomplishment.

**Cognitive development:** preoperational thought. Children gradually acquire the ability to conserve and decenter but are not capable of operational thinking and are unable to mentally reverse operations.

**Moral development:** morality of constraint, preconventional. Rules are viewed as unchangeable edicts handed down by those in authority. Punishment-obedience orientation focuses on physical consequences rather than on intentions.

**General factors to keep in mind:** Children are having their first experiences with school routine and interactions with more than a few peers and are preparing for initial academic experiences in group settings. They need to learn to follow directions and get along with others.

differences in socialization (Berk, 2006). Consequently, you may want to encourage all children to participate in tasks that emphasize gross motor skills and tasks that emphasize fine motor skills.

## Social Characteristics: Preschool and Kindergarten

1. *Most children have one or two best friends, but these friendships may change rapidly. Preschoolers tend to be quite flexible socially; they are usually willing and able to play with most of the other children in the class. Favorite friends tend to be of the same gender, but many friendships between boys and girls develop.* Young children generally interact with most of the other children in their preschool and kindergarten classes but think of their friends as those with whom they share toys and play the most. These "friendships" can dissolve quickly, however, if one child hits the other, refuses to share a toy, or is not interested in playing (Berk, 2006; Kail, 2007). Whereas some children prefer to play alone or observe their peers, others lack the skills or confidence to join others. In those cases, you might want to provide some assistance.

2. *Younger children exhibit different types of play behavior, which may vary as a function of social class and gender.* Kenneth Rubin, Terence Maioni, and Margaret Hornung

*Young children engage in a variety of types of play. These play patterns may vary as a function of social class and gender.*

(1976) observed and classified the free play of preschoolers according to their level of social and cognitive participation. The four levels of social participation they observed were taken from the pioneering work of Mildred Parten (1932) and are as follows:

*Solitary play*. Children play alone with toys that are different from those used by other children within speaking distance of them. They make no attempt to interact with others.

*Parallel play*. Children play beside but not really with other children. They use the same toys in close proximity to others but in an independent way.

*Associative play*. Children engage in rather disorganized play with other children. There is no assignment of activities or roles; individual children play in their own ways.

*Cooperative play*. Children engage in an organized form of play in which leadership and other roles are assigned. The members of the group may cooperate in creating some project, dramatize some situation, or engage in some sort of coordinated enterprise.

The four levels of cognitive participation they observed were taken from the work of Sara Smilansky (1968), who based them on Piaget's work, and are as follows:

*Functional play*. Making simple, repetitive muscle movements with or without objects

*Constructive play*. Manipulating objects to construct or create something

*Dramatic play*. Using an imaginary situation

*Games with rules*. Using prearranged rules to play a game

> Play patterns vary as a function of social class, gender, and age

Rubin et al. found that children of lower socioeconomic status (SES) engaged in more parallel and functional play than their middle-class peers, whereas middle-class children displayed more associative, cooperative, and constructive play. Girls engaged in more solitary- and parallel-constructive play and in less dramatic play than did boys. Boys engaged in more solitary-functional and associative-dramatic play than did girls.

Other forms of play described by researchers include pretend play (mimicking the behavior of parents, siblings, and peers), exercise play (running, climbing, jumping, and other large-muscle activities), and rough-and-tumble play (mostly wrestling types of activities, as well as pretend fighting) (Bukatko & Daehler, 2004; Smith, 2005).

3. *Preschool and kindergarten children show definite preferences for gender of play peers and for pair versus group play.* A three-year study (Fabes, Martin, & Hanish, 2003) of more than two hundred preschool children (average age 4.25 years) found the following play preferences:

- Same-sex play occurred more often than mixed-sex play.
- Girls were more likely than boys to play in pairs rather than groups, and boys were more likely than girls to play in groups rather than pairs. When girls did play in groups, they were more likely than boys to play in a group in which they were not the only member of their sex.
- When boys played with each other, whether in pairs or groups, they were more likely than girls who played with each other to engage in active-forceful play. This tendency was less apparent when a boy played in a group that was otherwise made up of all girls. But when a girl played in a group whose other members were boys, her level of active-forceful play tended to increase.

> Gender differences in toy preferences and play activities noticeable by kindergarten

4. *Awareness of gender roles and gender typing is evident.* By the time children enter kindergarten, most of them have developed an awareness of gender differences and of masculine and feminine roles (Wynn & Fletcher, 1987). This awareness of **gender roles** shows up very clearly in the toys and activities that boys and girls prefer. Boys are more likely than girls to play outdoors, to engage in rough-and-tumble play, and

*HM TeacherPrepSPACE*

Want to try an interactive quiz on gender roles? Go to the textbook's student website.

**JOURNAL ENTRY**
Encouraging Girls to Achieve, Boys to Be Sensitive

to behave aggressively. Boys play with toy vehicles and construction toys, and they engage in action games (such as football). Girls prefer art activities, doll play, and dancing (Carter, 1987). By age six, some children associate job titles that are considered to be gender neutral, such as doctor, librarian, and flight attendant, with either males (in the case of doctors) or females (in the case of librarians and waiters) (Liben, Bigler, & Krogh, 2002). Such strong gender typing in play activities occurs in many cultures, including non-Western ones, and is often reinforced by the way parents behave: they model what their culture has defined as gender-appropriate roles and encourage boys to be active and independent and girls to be more docile (Lancey, 2002). Peers may also reinforce these tendencies. A boy or girl may notice that other children are more willing to play when he or she selects a gender-appropriate toy.

Therefore, if you teach preschool children, you may have to guard against a tendency to respond too soon when little girls ask for help. If they *need* assistance, of course you should supply it; but if preschool girls can carry out tasks on their own, you should urge them to do so. You might also remind yourself that girls often need to be encouraged to become more achievement oriented and boys to become more sensitive to the needs of others.

## Emotional Characteristics: Preschool and Kindergarten

1. *Kindergarten children tend to express their emotions freely and openly. Anger outbursts are frequent.* It is probably desirable to let children at this age level express their feelings openly, at least within broad limits, so that they can recognize and face their emotions. In *Between Parent and Child* (1965; Ginott, Ginott, & Goddard, 2003) and *Teacher and Child* (1972), Haim Ginott offers some specific suggestions on how a parent or teacher can help children develop awareness of their feelings. His books may help you work out your own philosophy and techniques for dealing with emotional outbursts.

   Suppose, for example, that a boy who was wildly waving his hand to be called on during share-and-tell time later knocks down a block tower built by a girl who monopolized sharing time with a spellbinding story of a kitten rescued by firefighters. When you go over to break up the incipient fight, the boy angrily pushes you away. In such a situation, Ginott suggests you take the boy to a quiet corner and engage in a dialogue such as this:

   *You:* It looks as if you are unhappy about something, Connor.

   *Boy:* Yes, I am.

   *You:* Are you angry about something that happened this morning?

   *Boy:* Yes.

   *You:* Tell me about it.

   *Boy:* I wanted to tell the class about something at sharing time, and Lily talked for three hours, and you wouldn't let me say anything.

   *You:* And that made you mad at Lily and at me?

   *Boy:* Yes.

   *You:* Well, I can understand why you are disappointed and angry. But Lily had an exciting story to tell, and we didn't have time for anyone else to tell what they had to say. You can be the very first one to share something tomorrow morning. Now how about doing an easel painting? You always do such interesting paintings.

**JOURNAL ENTRY**
Helping Students Understand Anger

   Ginott suggests that when children are encouraged to analyze their own behavior, they are more likely to become aware of the causes of their feelings. This awareness, in turn, may help them learn to accept and control their feelings and find more acceptable means of expressing them. But because these children are likely to be in Piaget's preoperational stage of intellectual development, bear in mind that this approach may not be successful with all of them. The egocentric orientation of four- to five-year-olds makes it difficult for them to reflect on the thoughts of self or others. Anger outbursts are more likely to occur when children are tired, hungry, or exposed to too much adult interference. If you take such conditions into account and try to alleviate them (by providing a nap or a snack, for example), temper tantrums may be minimized.

**JOURNAL ENTRY**
Ways to Avoid Playing Favorites

2. *Jealousy among classmates is likely to be fairly common, as kindergarten children have much affection for the teacher and actively seek approval. When there are thirty individuals competing for the affection and attention of just one teacher, some jealousy is inevitable.* Try to spread your attention around as equitably as possible, and when you praise particular children, do it in a private or casual way. If one child is given lavish public recognition, it is only natural for the other children to feel resentful. Think back to how you felt about teachers' pets during your own school years. If you have observed or can think of other techniques for minimizing jealousy, jot them down in your journal.

## Cognitive Characteristics: Preschool and Kindergarten

By age four, children have a theory of mind: aware of own mental processes and that others may think differently

1. *By age four, many children begin to develop a theory of mind.* Children's **theory of mind** concerns the ability of children around the age of four to be aware of the difference between thinking about something and experiencing that same thing and to predict the thoughts of others. Being able to make this distinction is critical to understanding such aspects of social life as surprises, secrets, tricks, mistakes, and lies.

By three years of age, most children realize the difference between thinking about something and actually experiencing that same something. But a significant change occurs around age four when children begin to realize that thoughts may be false. In one study described by Janet Astington (1998), a box that children knew normally contained candy was filled instead with pencils. When three-year-olds opened the box and discovered the pencils, they were asked what a friend would think was in the box before it was opened. They replied that the friend would know (just as they now did) that there were pencils inside. When they were asked later what they thought was in the box before it was opened, they replied "pencils" rather than "candy," indicating an inability to recall that their belief had changed. But four-year-olds understood that the friend would be misled by the fact that pencils had replaced the candy. The four-year-olds also remembered that they themselves had expected the box to contain candy. So, beginning at age four, children start to realize that the actions of people are based on how they *think* the world is.

Talking about different viewpoints will help children understand that people have beliefs about the world, that different people believe different things, and that beliefs may change when new information is acquired. Astington (1998) offers the following example of how teachers can foster the development of children's theory of mind:

> In a 1st-grade classroom that I recently observed, the teacher often talked about her own thought processes, saying, for example, "I just learned something new" when she found out that one student had a pet rabbit at home. When she was surprised or made a mistake, she talked about her own wrong beliefs, and at story-time, she had the children talk about the motivations and beliefs of story characters. Her style of talk helped the class focus not just on the thought content, but also on the thinking process—yet the term *theory of mind* was unknown to this teacher. (p. 48)

**JOURNAL ENTRY**
Handling Sharing

2. *Kindergartners are quite skillful with language. Most of them like to talk, especially in front of a group.* Providing a sharing time gives children a natural opportunity for

talking, but many will need help in becoming good listeners. Some sort of rotation scheme is usually necessary to divide talking opportunities between the gabby and the silent extremes. You might provide activities or experiences for less confident children to talk about, such as a field trip, a book, or a film. In your journal, you might note some comments to use if students start to share the wrong thing (such as a vivid account of a fight between their parents) or if they try to one-up classmates (for example, "Your cat may have had five kittens, but *our* cat had a *hundred* kittens"). For titillating topics, you might say, "There are some things that are private, and it's better not to talk about them to others."

**Peer comparisons help four- and five-year-olds more accurately judge their capabilities**

3. *Many preschool and kindergarten children do not accurately assess their competence for particular tasks.* Preschool and kindergarten children typically think of themselves as being much more competent than they actually are, even when their performance lags behind that of their peers. They do not differentiate between effort and ability as factors that affect performance. Although this limitation in self-assessment is influenced, at least in part, by the characteristics of preoperational-stage thinking, it can also be the result of classroom environments that are relatively unstructured, that emphasize free play, and that de-emphasize peer-peer comparisons. Israeli children who grew up on a kibbutz, a communal form of living in which child rearing occurs as much within a peer group as within one's nuclear family, used peer comparison to construct a sense of their own competence about a year earlier than did urban children who spent most of their time within their own families (Butler, 2005).

Despite this limitation in self-assessed competence, research suggests that under the right conditions even some four-year-olds can draw accurate conclusions about how well or poorly they have completed a task. In one study, children between the ages of four and five were asked to do a simple maze-type task (tracing a winding path between an illustrated child and a house) under one of two conditions: either in the presence of another child's work or in comparison with their own earlier attempt at the same task. About 40 percent of those who had another child's work available were able to use that to accurately assess their own performance. Most of the rest of this group could gauge their own performance by using the goal as a basis for comparison ("I only got halfway to the house"). Children in the second group, however, were unable to use their prior performance on the maze to judge whether their current performance was any better or worse, even when shown both attempts. Self-assessment of competence under this condition does not typically appear until somewhere between seven and eight years of age (Butler, 2005).

**JOURNAL ENTRY**
Encouraging Competence

4. *Competence is encouraged by interaction, interest, opportunities, urging, limits, admiration, and signs of affection.* Studies of young children rated as highly competent (Burchinal, Peisner-Feinberg, Pianta, & Howes, 2002; Clawson & Robila, 2001; Schweinhart, Weikart, & Hohmann, 2002) show that to encourage preschoolers to make the most of their abilities, adults should

- Interact with the child often and in a variety of ways.
- Show interest in what the child does and says.
- Provide opportunities for the child to investigate and experience many things.
- Permit and encourage the child to do many things.
- Urge the child to try to achieve mature and skilled types of behavior.
- Establish firm and consistent limits regarding unacceptable forms of behavior, explain the reasons for these as soon as the child is able to understand, listen to complaints if the child feels the restrictions are too confining, and give additional reasons if the limits are still to be maintained as originally stated.
- Show that the child's achievements are admired and appreciated.
- Communicate love in a warm and sincere way.

Diana Baumrind's (1971, 1991a) analysis of four types of child-rearing approaches shows why such techniques contribute to competence in children.

Baumrind found that parents of competent children are **authoritative parents.** They have confidence in their abilities as parents and therefore provide a model of competence for their children to imitate. When they establish limits and explain reasons for restrictions, they encourage their children to set standards for themselves and to think about why certain procedures should be followed. And because these parents are warm and affectionate, children value their positive responses as rewards for mature behavior. The children of authoritative parents tend to be self-motivated. They stand up for what they believe, yet are able to work productively with others.

**Authoritarian parents,** by contrast, make demands and wield power, but their failure to take into account the child's point of view and their lack of warmth lead to resentment and insecurity on the part of the child. Children of authoritarian parents may do as they are told, but they are likely to do so out of compliance or fear, not out of a desire to earn love or approval. They also tend to be other-directed rather than inner-directed.

**Permissive parents,** as defined by Baumrind, are disorganized, inconsistent, and lack confidence, and their children are likely to imitate such behavior. Permissive parents make few demands of their children, allow them to make many of their own decisions, do not require them to exhibit mature behavior, and tend to avoid confrontations with their children. As a result, such children are markedly less assertive and intellectually skilled than are children from authoritative homes.

Finally, **rejecting-neglecting parents** do not make demands on their children or respond to their emotional needs. They do not structure the home environment, are not supportive of their children's goals and activities, and may actively reject or neglect their child-rearing responsibilities. Children of rejecting-neglecting parents are the least socially and intellectually competent of the four types.

You might refer to these observations not only when you plan how to encourage competence but also when you think about the kind of classroom atmosphere you hope to establish.

## pause & reflect

Given the characteristics of preschool and kindergarten children, what classroom atmosphere and instructional tactics would you use to foster learning and enjoyment of school?

# PRIMARY GRADES (1, 2, AND 3; SIX, SEVEN, AND EIGHT YEARS)

## Physical Characteristics: Primary Grades

**JOURNAL ENTRY**
Building Activity into Class Work

1. *Primary grade children are still extremely active. Because they are frequently required to participate in sedentary pursuits, energy is often released in the form of nervous habits—for example, pencil chewing, fingernail biting, and general fidgeting.* To minimize fidgeting, avoid situations in which your students must stay glued to their desks for long periods. Have frequent breaks, and try to work activity (such as bringing papers to your desk) into the lessons themselves. When children use computer software that contains sound effects, distribute headphones to ensure that they concentrate on their own work and to minimize distractions between students.

One of the effects of the current emphasis on preparing students to meet state learning standards is the reduction or elimination of recess time, even for kindergarten and primary grade students. One survey, for example, found that 30 percent of kindergarten classrooms did not have a recess period (Pellegrini & Bohn, 2005). Are educators acting wisely in seeking to reduce the number and length of breaks young children receive in order to focus more intensively on teaching academic skills? Not according to cognitive development theory and research.

As we will note in the next chapter, Piaget believed that children's ability to think beyond their own perspective is greatly facilitated by peer interaction because such interactions involve other points of view that must be comprehended and accommodated. During the school day, these types of interactions occur most frequently during such unstructured activities as recess. A second theoretical perspective, called the *cognitive immaturity hypothesis*, maintains that giving young students unstructured breaks reduces cognitive interference from preceding instruction and increases attention to subsequent instruction. Research findings support the accuracy of these theoretical positions. For example, the opportunity for kindergarten students to play with peers during recess was a significant predictor of first-grade achievement. Second, children (especially boys) who received a recess break earlier rather than later in the morning were more attentive after the break than before (Pelligrini & Bohn, 2005).

2. *Children still need rest periods; they become fatigued easily as a result of physical and mental exertion.* Schedule quiet activities after strenuous ones (story time after recess, for example) and relaxing activities after periods of mental concentration (art after spelling or math).

3. *Large-muscle control is still superior to fine coordination. Many children, especially boys, have difficulty manipulating a pencil.* Try not to schedule too much writing at one time. If drill periods are too long, skill may deteriorate, and children may develop a negative attitude toward writing or toward school in general.

4. *Many students may have difficulty focusing on small print or objects. Quite a few children may be farsighted because of the shallow shape of the eye.* Try not to require too much reading at one stretch. Be on the alert for children rubbing their eyes or blinking, signs of eye fatigue. When you are preparing class handouts, be sure to print in large letters or use a large-size computer font. Until the lens of the eye can be easily focused, young children have trouble looking back and forth from near to far objects.

   Although many children at this age have had extensive exposure to computer games and video games and therefore have begun to develop greater eye-hand coordination with images on screen, it's still appropriate to select software programs that incorporate easy-to-see graphics and easy-to-click buttons to avoid frustration.

5. *Children tend to be extreme in their physical activities. They have excellent control of their bodies and develop considerable confidence in their skills. As a result, they often underestimate the danger involved in their more daring exploits. The accident rate is at a peak in the third grade.* You might check on school procedures for handling injuries, but also try to prevent reckless play. During recess, for example, encourage class participation in "wild" but essentially safe games (such as relay races involving stunts) to help the children get devil-may-care tendencies out of their systems. In your journal, you might list other games to use for this purpose.

| |
| --- |
| Primary grade children have difficulty focusing on small print |

| |
| --- |
| Accident rate peaks in third grade because of confidence in physical skills |

| **Table 2.2** | Applying Theories of Development to the Primary Grade Years |
| --- | --- |

**Psychosocial development:** industry vs. inferiority. Students need to experience a sense of industry through successful completion of tasks. Try to minimize and correct failures to prevent development of feelings of inferiority.

**Cognitive development:** transition from preoperational to concrete operational stage. Students gradually acquire the ability to solve problems by generalizing from concrete experiences.

**Moral development:** morality of constraint, preconventional. Rules are viewed as edicts handed down by authority. Focus is on physical consequences, meaning that obeying rules should bring benefit in return.

**General factors to keep in mind:** Students are having first experiences with school learning, are eager to learn how to read and write, and are likely to be upset by lack of progress. Initial attitudes toward schooling are being established. Initial roles in a group are being formed, roles that may establish a lasting pattern (for example, leader, follower, loner, athlete, or underachiever).

JOURNAL ENTRY
Safe But Strenuous Games

6. *Bone growth is not yet complete. Therefore, bones and ligaments can't stand heavy pressure.* If you notice students indulging in strenuous tests of strength (punching each other on the arm until one person can't retaliate, for example), you might suggest that they switch to competition involving coordinated skills. During team games, rotate players in especially tiring positions (for example, the pitcher in baseball).

## Social Characteristics: Primary Grades

The characteristics noted here are typical of both primary and elementary grade students and underlie the elementary level characteristics described in the next section.

1. *Children become somewhat more selective in their choice of friends and are likely to have a more or less permanent best friend.* Friendships are typically same-sex relationships marked by mutual understanding, loyalty, cooperation, and sharing. Competition between friends should be discouraged because it can become intense and increase their dissatisfaction with each other. Although friends disagree with each other more often than with nonfriends, their conflicts are shorter, less heated, and less likely to lead to a dissolving of the relationship (Hartup, 1989; Ross & Spielmacher, 2005).

Rigid interpretation of rules in primary grades

2. *Primary grade children often like organized games in small groups, but they may be overly concerned with rules or get carried away by team spirit.* Keep in mind that, according to Piaget, children at this age practice the morality of constraint: they find it difficult to understand how and why rules should be adjusted to special situations. When you divide a class into teams, you may be amazed at the amount of rivalry that develops (and the noise level generated). One way to reduce both the rivalry and the noise is to promote the idea that games should be fun. Another technique is to rotate team membership frequently. If you know any especially good but not excessively competitive team games, note them in your journal. You might also consult *Cooperative Learning: Theory, Research, and Practice* (2nd ed., 1995), by Robert Slavin, for descriptions of several team learning games that emphasize cooperation.

JOURNAL ENTRY
Enjoyable Team Games

3. *Quarrels are still frequent. Words are used more often than physical aggression, but many boys (in particular) may indulge in punching, wrestling, and shoving.* Occasional fights are to be expected. If certain children, especially the same pair, seem to be involved in one long battle, you should probably try to effect a truce. But when you can, give children a chance to work out their own solutions to disagreements; social conflict is effective in spurring cognitive growth (Howe, Rinaldi, Jennings, & Petrakos, 2002; Murphy & Eisenberg, 2002; Tudge & Rogoff, 1989).

JOURNAL ENTRY
Handling Feuds and Fights

Although occasional quarrels and minor physical aggression will likely have only temporary effects on students, you should keep an eye out for students who are frequent targets of insults, threats, physical aggression, and exclusion from the peer group. Research has shown that third- and fourth-graders who were frequently victimized by classmates had lower scores on standardized achievement tests, lower grades, and higher levels of depression than their nonvictimized peers both at the time the incidents occurred and a year later (Schwartz, Gorman, Nakamoto, & Toblin, 2005).

## Emotional Characteristics: Primary Grades

To encourage industry, use praise, avoid criticism

1. *Students are sensitive to criticism and ridicule and may have difficulty adjusting to failure.* Young children need frequent praise and recognition. Because they tend to admire or even worship their teachers, they may be crushed by criticism. Provide positive reinforcement as frequently as possible, and reserve your negative reactions for nonacademic misbehavior. Scrupulously avoid sarcasm and ridicule. Remember that this is the stage of industry versus inferiority; if you make a child feel inferior, you may prevent the development of industry.

*Most primary grade students eagerly strive to obtain "helping" jobs around the classroom. Accordingly, you may wish to arrange a rotating schedule for such jobs.*

**JOURNAL ENTRY**
Spreading Around
Responsibilities

2. *Most primary grade children are eager to please the teacher.* They like to help, enjoy responsibility, and want to do well in their schoolwork. The time-honored technique for satisfying the urge to help is to assign jobs (eraser cleaner, wastebasket emptier, paper distributor, and the like) on a rotating basis. In your journal, you might note other techniques—for example, were there any particular responsibilities you enjoyed as a student?

3. *Children are becoming sensitive to the feelings of others.* Unfortunately, this permits them to hurt others deeply by attacking a sensitive spot without realizing how devastating their attack really is. It sometimes happens that teasing a particular child who has reacted to a gibe becomes a group pastime. Be on the alert for such situations. If you are able to make a private and personal appeal to the ringleaders, you may be able to prevent an escalation of the teasing, which may make a tremendous difference in the way the victim feels about school.

## Cognitive Characteristics: Primary Grades

1. *Children understand that there are different ways to know things and that some ways are better than others.* When an observation can be explained with either a possible (that is, a theoretical) explanation or an evidence-based explanation, preschoolers fail to see one as more compelling than the other, but primary grade children usually prefer the explanation based on evidence. This is the beginning of scientific thinking (Kuhn, 2002). In one study described by Deanna Kuhn (1999, 2002), preschoolers viewed a set of pictures depicting two individuals running a race. They were asked to indicate who won the race and to explain what led them to that conclusion. One of the runners was wearing a fancier running shoe, and some of the children said that was the reason he beat his opponent. But because this same individual was also holding a trophy and exhibiting a wide grin in the last picture, some children cited that fact as evidence that the boy won the race. By the time they reach the primary grades, virtually all children understand that a fact-based explanation is superior to a theory-based explanation and so point to the second picture as the reason for their conclusion.

Awareness of cognitive
processes begins to emerge

2. *Primary grade children begin to understand that learning and recall are caused by particular cognitive processes that they can control.* Not until children are about seven or eight years of age do they begin to realize that learning and memory

stem from cognitive processes that are under their conscious control. When learning words, for example, younger children may need to be prompted or directed to group the words by category because they do not realize that such a technique aids recall. Likewise, they may not recognize their lack of comprehension when they read difficult or unfamiliar material and may need to be prompted to think about how well they are understanding what they read. By the primary grades, this awareness and monitoring of one's learning processes, called *metacognition*, begins to emerge (Schneider, 2002). We will return to the subject in Chapter 8, "Information-Processing Theory."

**JOURNAL ENTRY**
Assigning Short and Varied Tasks

3. *Because of continuing neurological development and limited experience with formal learning tasks, primary grade children do not learn as efficiently as older children do.* Therefore, you should assign primary grade children relatively short tasks and switch periodically from cognitively demanding activities to less demanding ones. Providing youngsters with periodic breaks, such as recess, increases their ability to attend to and perform well on subsequent classroom tasks. The nature of the recess activity does not seem to be important. It can be physical activity in a schoolyard or playing games in class (Pellegrini & Bjorklund, 1997).

4. *Talking aloud to oneself reaches a peak between the ages of six and seven and then rapidly declines.* Don't be surprised or concerned if you observe students talking to themselves, either when they are by themselves or when they are with classmates. This is a well-documented phenomenon that Vygotsky called private speech. Vygotsky described private speech as a transition between speaking with others and thinking to oneself. Private speech is first noticeable around age three and may constitute anywhere from 20 to 60 percent of a child's utterances between the ages of six and seven. By age eight, however, it all but disappears and is replaced by silent, or inner, speech (Berk, 1994; Bukatko & Daehler, 2004; Feigenbaum, 2002).

As its name implies, private speech is not intended to communicate a message to someone else, nor does it always take the form of complete sentences. One important purpose of private speech, which may consist of single words or phrases, is to help children clarify their thinking and solve difficult problems, such as those that arise in the course of doing math problems or reading unfamiliar material. For example, a child may count on her fingers out loud while working on a math problem and then say, "The answer's ten." Observations of first and second graders found that those who talked to themselves while doing math problems did better at math the following year than did students who exhibited little private speech. Another interesting finding is that students who exhibit the greatest use of self-guiding private speech are more likely to have authoritative mothers (Berk, 1994).

## ELEMENTARY SCHOOL (GRADES 4 AND 5; NINE AND TEN YEARS)

### Physical Characteristics: Elementary Grades

1. *Both boys and girls become leaner and stronger.* In general, there is a decrease in the growth of fatty tissue and an increase in bone and muscle development. In a year's time, the average child of this age will grow about 2 to 3 inches and gain about 5 to 7 pounds. As a result, the typical child will tend to have a lean and gangly look. Although the average nine-year-old boy is slightly taller and heavier than the average nine-year-old girl, this difference all but disappears a year later. And from age eleven until about fourteen and a half, girls are slightly heavier and taller than boys. Because secondary sex characteristics have not yet appeared, boys and girls can be mistaken for one another. This is particularly likely to happen when girls have close-cropped hair, boys have very long hair, and both genders wear gender-neutral clothing (Berk, 2006; Bukatko & Daehler, 2004; Hetherington & Parke, 1993).

| **Table 2.3** | Applying Theories of Development to the Elementary Grade Years |
|---|---|

**Psychosocial development:** industry vs. inferiority. Keep students constructively busy; try to play down comparisons between best and worse learners.

**Cognitive development:** concrete operational. Except for the most intellectually advanced students, most will need to generalize from concrete experiences.

**Moral development:** morality of constraint; transition from preconventional to conventional. A shift to viewing rules as mutual agreements is occurring, but "official" rules are obeyed out of respect for authority or out of a desire to impress others.

**General factors to keep in mind:** Initial enthusiasm for learning may fade as the novelty wears off and as the process of perfecting skills becomes more difficult. Differences in knowledge and skills of fastest and slowest learners become more noticeable. "Automatic" respect for teachers tends to diminish. Peer group influences become strong.

2. *Obesity can become a problem for some children of this age group.* Because nine- and ten-year-olds have more control over their eating habits than younger children do, there is a greater tendency for them to overeat, particularly junk food. When this eating pattern is coupled with a relatively low level of physical activity (mainly because of television watching, computer use, and playing video games) and a genetic predisposition toward obesity, children become mildly to severely overweight. In the last half of the 1970s, 6.5 percent of children from six to eleven years of age were judged to be overweight. By 2002, the percentage had more than doubled to 15.8 percent. Not only do overweight children put themselves at risk for cardiovascular problems and Type II diabetes later in life, but they also become targets for ridicule and ostracism in the present from peers (Eberstadt, 2003; Kelly & Moag-Stahlberg, 2002; National Center for Health Statistics, 2005; Sweeting & West, 2001).

3. *Although small in magnitude, gender differences in motor skill performance are apparent.* Boys tend to outperform girls on tasks that involve kicking, throwing, catching, running, broad jumping, and batting. Girls surpass boys on tasks that require muscular flexibility, balance, and rhythmic movements. These differences may be due in part to gender-role stereotyping. That is, because of socialization differences, girls are more likely to play hopscotch and jump rope, whereas boys are more likely to play baseball and basketball.

   One benefit of attaining mastery over large and small muscles is a relatively orderly classroom. Fourth and fifth graders can sit quietly for extended periods and concentrate on whatever intellectual task is at hand (Berk, 2006; Hetherington & Parke, 1993). Another benefit is that children enjoy arts and crafts and musical activities.

4. *This is a period of relative calm and predictability in physical development.* Growth in height and weight tends to be consistent and moderate, hormonal imbalances are absent, disease occurs less frequently than at any other period, and bodily coordination is relatively stable (Berk, 2006; Hetherington & Parke, 1993).

**Social Characteristics: Elementary Grades**

1. *The peer group becomes powerful and begins to replace adults as the major source of behavior standards and recognition of achievement.* During the early school years, parents and teachers set standards of conduct, and most children try to live up to them. But by grades 4 and 5, children are more interested in getting along with one another without adult supervision. Consequently, children come to realize that the rules for behavior within the peer group are not quite the same as the rules for behavior within the family or the classroom. Because children of this age are increasingly concerned with being accepted by their peer group and do not have enough self-assurance to oppose group norms, there is a noticeable increase, by both boys and girls, in gossip about others (Ross & Spielmacher, 2005).

Boys slightly better at sports-related motor skills; girls better at flexibility, balance, rhythmic motor skills

**JOURNAL ENTRY**
Minimizing Gender Differences in Motor Skill Performance

Peer group norms for behavior begin to replace adult norms

**JOURNAL ENTRY**
Moderating the Power of Peer Group Norms

*Elementary grade boys tend to be better than girls on motor skill tasks that involve large muscle movement, whereas elementary grade girls tend to perform better than boys on motor skill tasks that involve muscular flexibility, balance, and rhythmic movements.*

2. *Friendships become more selective and gender based.* Elementary grade children become even more discriminating than primary grade children in the selection of friends and playmates. Most children choose a best friend, usually of the same gender. These relationships, based usually on common ideas, outlooks, and impressions of the world, may last through adolescence. Although children of this age will rarely refuse to interact with members of the opposite sex when directed to do so by parents and teachers, they will avoid the opposite sex when left to their own devices (Ross & Spielmacher, 2005).

## Emotional Characteristics: Elementary Grades

1. *During this period, children develop a more global, integrated, and complex self-image.* Researchers who study self-perceptions (e.g., Harter, 1990, 1999; Marsh & Hattie, 1996) distinguish among the concepts of self-description, self-esteem, and self-concept:

   - A **self-description** is simply the way in which people describe themselves to others. Self-descriptive statements are largely, but not entirely, free of evaluative judgments. Examples of self-descriptions are "I am eleven years old," "I am tall for my age," and "I am an outgoing person."
   - **Self-esteem** (or self-worth, as it is sometimes called) refers to the overall or global evaluation people make of themselves. It is indicated by such statements as "I believe that I am a worthwhile person" and "I am pretty happy with myself."
   - **Self-concept** refers to the evaluative judgments people make of themselves in specific domains, such as academic performance, social interactions, athletic performance, and physical appearance. It is indicated by such statements as "I have a good head for math," "I have a hard time making friends," and "My big nose makes me look ugly."

   Taken together, self-descriptions, self-esteem, and self-concept constitute a person's **self-image** or self-portrait. By middle childhood each of these aspects of self-image is present; children can make an accurate self-description, construct a global evaluation of themselves, and specify their positive and negative attributes in specific domains.

Self-image becomes more generalized and stable; is based primarily on comparisons with peers

There are several important facts to keep in mind about the formulation of a child's self-image. First, in the elementary grades it is more generalized or integrated than is the case for primary grade children because it is based on information gained over time, tasks, and settings. A child may think of herself as socially adept not just because she is popular at school but because she has always been well liked and gets along well with adults, as well as peers, in a variety of situations. It is this generalized quality that helps make self-portraits relatively stable.

Second, comparison with others is the fundamental basis of a self-image during the elementary grades. This orientation is due in part to the fact that children are not as egocentric as they were a few years earlier and are developing the capability to think in terms of multiple categories. It is also due to the fact that competition and individualism are highly prized values in many Western cultures. Consequently, children will naturally compare themselves with one another ("I'm taller than my friend") as well as with broad-based norms ("I'm tall for my age") in an effort to determine who they are. This social comparison process can have detrimental effects on a student's academic self-image when most of his classmates are more able learners (Marsh & Craven, 2002).

**JOURNAL ENTRY**
Ways to Improve Students' Self-Image

Third, in the elementary grades the self is described for the first time in terms of emotions (pride, shame, worry, anger, happiness) and how well they can be controlled. Fourth, a child's sense of self is influenced by the information and attitudes that are communicated by such significant others as parents, teachers, and friends and by how competent the child feels in areas in which success is important. The implications of this fact will be discussed in many of the remaining chapters of the text.

Because major developmental changes usually do not occur during the elementary grades, a child's self-image will remain fairly stable for a few years if there are no major changes in the child's home or social environment. But as you will see later in this chapter, the developmental changes that typically occur during the middle school and high school grades often produce dramatic changes in the sense of self (Alasker & Olweus, 2002).

## pause & reflect

The primary and elementary years correspond to Erikson's stage of industry versus inferiority. The implication is that educators should encourage a sense of industry and competence in each student. On a scale of 1 to 10, how well do you think schools accomplish this goal? What major factors account for your rating?

2. *Disruptive family relationships, social rejection, and school failure may lead to delinquent behavior.* Gerald Patterson, Barbara DeBaryshe, and Elizabeth Ramsey (1989) marshal a wide array of evidence to support their belief that delinquent behavior is the result of a causal chain of events that originates with dysfunctional parent-child relationships. In their view, poor parent-child relationships lead to behavior problems, which lead to peer rejection and academic failure, which lead to identification with a deviant peer group, which results in delinquent behavior. Parents of such children administer harsh and inconsistent punishment, provide little positive reinforcement, and do little monitoring and supervising of each child's activities.

Delinquents have few friends, are easily distracted, are not interested in schoolwork, lack basic skills

Because these children have not learned to follow adult rules and regulations but have learned how to satisfy their needs through coercive behavior, they are rejected by their peers, are easily distracted when doing schoolwork, show little interest in the subjects they study, and do not master many of the basic academic skills necessary for subsequent achievement. Attempts at short-circuiting this chain of events stand a greater chance of success if they begin early and are multifaceted. In addition to counseling and parent training, mastery of basic academic skills is important.

## Cognitive Characteristics: Elementary Grades

| Elementary grade students reason logically but concretely

1. *The elementary grade child can think logically, although such thinking is constrained and inconsistent.* In terms of Piaget's stages, upper elementary grade children are concrete operational stage thinkers. Most will have attained enough mastery of logical schemes that they can understand and solve tasks that involve such processes as class inclusion (understanding the superordinate-subordinate relationships that make up hierarchies), seriation, conservation, and symbolic representation (reading maps, for example), provided that the content of the task refers to real, tangible ideas that the child has either experienced or can imagine. But general and abstract ideas often escape the elementary age child. For example, sarcasm, metaphor, and allegory are usually lost on concrete stage thinkers.

2. *On tasks that call for simple memory skills, elementary grade children often perform about as well as adolescents or adults. But on tasks that require more complex memory skills, their performance is more limited.* When tasks call for recognizing previously learned information, such as vocabulary words or facts about a person or event, or for rehearsing several items for immediate use, elementary grade children can perform about as well as older students. Relatively simple memory processes, such as recognition or rote repetition, approach their maximum levels by this point in cognitive development. But the same is not true for tasks that require such advanced memory processes as elaboration and organization. When asked to sort a set of pictures into categories, for example, elementary grade children create fewer and more idiosyncratic categories (which are generally less

*Although elementary grade children understand the logical basis for tasks such as classification, seriation, and conservation, they can solve such tasks only if they are based on concrete objects and ideas.*

effective for later recall of the items in the category) than do older children or adults (Kail, 2007). Also bear in mind that elementary grade children need constant practice on a variety of tasks before they use such memory processes consistently and efficiently (Schneider, 2002).

# MIDDLE SCHOOL (GRADES 6, 7, AND 8; ELEVEN, TWELVE, AND THIRTEEN YEARS)

In this section, we use the term *adolescent* for the first time. Although it may strike you as odd to think of eleven- and twelve-year-olds as adolescents, developmental psychologists typically apply this term to individuals as young as ten years of age. The reason they do is that the onset of puberty is taken as the primary characteristic that defines the passage from middle childhood to adolescence (Balk, 1995; Steinberg, 2005). Although a variety of terms are used to denote the initial period of change that marks the adolescent years (ages ten to fourteen), we use two of the more popular: *early adolescent* and *emerging adolescent*.

## Physical Characteristics: Middle School

Girls' growth spurt occurs earlier, and so they look older than boys of same age

**JOURNAL ENTRY**
Helping Students Adjust to the Growth Spurt

Early-maturing boys likely to draw favorable responses

1. *Physical growth tends to be both rapid and uneven.* During the middle school years, the average child will grow 2 to 4 inches per year and gain 8 to 10 pounds per year. But some parts of the body, particularly the hands and feet, grow faster than others. Consequently, middle school children tend to look gangly and clumsy. Because girls mature more rapidly than boys, their **growth spurt** begins at about age ten and a half, reaches a peak at about age twelve, and is generally complete by age fourteen. The growth spurt for boys begins on average at about age twelve and a half, peaks at about age fourteen, and is generally complete by age sixteen. The result of this timing difference in the growth spurt is that many middle school girls look considerably older than boys of the same age. After the growth spurt, however, the muscles in the average boy's body are larger, as are the heart and lungs (Steinberg, 2005).

   After reviewing research on early and later maturation, Laurence Steinberg (2005) concludes that differences in physical maturation are likely to produce specific differences in later behavior (see Table 2.5). Because of their more adult-like appearance, **early-maturing boys** are likely to be more popular with peers, have more positive self-concepts, and have more friends among older peers. But

| **Table 2.4** | Applying Theories of Development to the Middle School Years |
| --- | --- |

**Psychosocial development:** transition from industry vs. inferiority to identity vs. role confusion. Growing independence leads to initial thoughts about identity. There is greater concern about appearance and gender roles than about occupational choice.

**Cognitive development:** beginning of formal operational thought for some. There is increasing ability to engage in mental manipulations and test hypotheses.

**Moral development:** transition to morality of cooperation, conventional level. There is increasing willingness to think of rules as flexible mutual agreements; yet "official" rules are still likely to be obeyed out of respect for authority or out of a desire to impress others.

**General factors to keep in mind:** A growth spurt and puberty influence many aspects of behavior. An abrupt switch occurs (for sixth graders) from being the oldest, biggest, most sophisticated students in elementary school to being the youngest, smallest, least knowledgeable students in middle school. Acceptance by peers is extremely important. Students who do poor schoolwork begin to feel bitter, resentful, and restless. Awareness grows of a need to make personal value decisions regarding dress, premarital sex, and code of ethics.

| **Table 2.5** | The Impact of Early and Late Maturation | |
|---|---|---|
| **Maturational Stage** | **Characteristics as Adolescents** | **Characteristics as Adults** |
| Early-maturing boys | Self-confident, high in self-esteem, likely to be chosen as leaders (but leadership tendencies more likely in low-SES boys than in middle-class boys), more likely to socialize with older peers and engage in substance abuse, delinquent behavior | Self-confident, responsible, cooperative, sociable. But also more rigid, moralistic, humorless, and conforming |
| Late-maturing boys | Energetic, bouncy, given to attention-getting behavior, poor body image, lower self-esteem, lower aspirations for educational achievement, not popular | Impulsive and assertive. But also insightful, perceptive, creatively playful, able to cope with new situations |
| Early-maturing girls | Not popular or likely to be leaders, more likely to date older boys, lower self-esteem, lacking in poise (but middle-class girls more confident than those from low-SES groups), more likely to date, smoke, and drink earlier, greater likelihood of eating disorders and depression | Self-possessed, self-directed, able to cope, emotionally stable, wide range of interests |
| Late-maturing girls | Confident, outgoing, assured, popular, likely to be chosen as leaders | Likely to experience difficulty adapting to stress, less agreeable, more likely to exhibit fluctuating moods |

SOURCES: Hetherington & Parke (1993); Livson & Peskin (1980); Steinberg (2005); Weichold, Silbereisen, & Schmitt-Rodermund (2003).

---

Late-maturing boys may feel inadequate

Early-maturing girls may suffer low self-esteem

Late-maturing girls likely to be popular and carefree

**JOURNAL ENTRY**
Helping Early and Late Maturers Cope

**Average age of puberty:** girls, eleven; boys, fourteen

---

friendships with older adolescents put early-maturing boys at greater risk for delinquency, drug and alcohol abuse, truancy, and increased sexual activity. As adults, early maturers were more likely to be responsible, cooperative, self-controlled, conforming, and conventional. **Late-maturing boys,** by contrast, are likely to have relatively lower self-esteem and stronger feelings of inadequacy. But later in adolescence, they show higher levels of intellectual curiosity, exploratory behavior, and social initiative. As adults, late-maturing boys are more impulsive, assertive, insightful, and inventive.

Because **early-maturing girls** are taller and heavier than their peers and don't have a thin and "leggy" fashion model look, they are likely to have lower self-esteem and are more likely to suffer from depression, anxiety, eating disorders, and panic attacks. They are more likely to be popular with boys, particularly older boys, and experience more pressure to date and become sexually active than their more normally developing peers. **Late-maturing girls,** whose growth spurt is less abrupt and whose size and appearance more closely reflect the feminine stereotype mentioned, share many of the characteristics (positive self-concept, popularity) of the early-maturing boy. Late-maturing girls are more likely to be seen by peers as attractive, sociable, and expressive.

If late-maturing boys in your classes appear driven to seek attention or inclined to brood about their immaturity, you might try to give them extra opportunities to gain status and self-confidence by succeeding in schoolwork or other nonathletic activities. If you notice that early-maturing girls seem insecure, you might try to bolster their self-esteem by giving them extra attention and by recognizing their achievements.

2. *Pubertal development is evident in practically all girls and in many boys.* From ages eleven through thirteen, most girls develop sparse pubic and underarm hair and exhibit breast enlargement. In boys, the testes and scrotum begin to grow, and lightly pigmented pubic hair appears (McDevitt & Ormrod, 2004).

3. *Concern and curiosity about sex are almost universal, especially among girls.* The average age of puberty for girls in the United States is eleven years (Steinberg, 2005); the range is from eight to eighteen years. For boys, the average age of puberty is fourteen years; the range is from ten to eighteen years. Because sexual

maturation involves drastic biological and psychological adjustments, children are concerned and curious. It seems obvious that accurate, unemotional answers to questions about sex are desirable. However, for your own protection, you should find out about the sex education policy at your school. Many school districts have formal programs approved by community representatives and led by designated educators. Informal spur-of-the-moment class discussions may create more problems than they solve.

## Social Characteristics: Middle School

1. *The development of interpersonal reasoning leads to greater understanding of the feelings of others.* Robert L. Selman (1980) has studied the development of **interpersonal reasoning** in children. Interpersonal reasoning is the ability to understand the relationship between motives and behavior among a group of people. The results of Selman's research are summarized in Table 2.6. The stages outlined there reveal that during the elementary school years, children gradually grasp the fact that a person's overt actions or words do not always reflect inner feelings. They also come to comprehend that a person's reaction to a distressing situation can have many facets. Toward the end of the elementary school years and increasingly during adolescence, children become capable of taking a somewhat detached and analytical view of their own behavior, as well as the behavior of others. By mid-adolescence, they can, for example, understand that offering unsolicited academic help to a classmate may embarrass that individual (Hoffman, 2000).

    Selman believes that teachers and therapists might be able to aid children who are not as advanced in role-taking skills as their age-mates by helping them become more sensitive to the feelings of others. If an eight-year-old boy is still functioning at the egocentric level, for example, he may fail to interpret the behavior of classmates properly and become a social isolate. Selman describes how one such boy was encouraged to think continually about the reasons behind his social actions and those of others and acquired sufficient social sensitivity to learn to get along with others.

    Discussion techniques Selman recommends can be introduced in a natural, rather than a formal, way. If you see a boy react with physical or verbal abuse

**JOURNAL ENTRY**
Ways to Promote Social
Sensitivity

---

**Table 2.6** | Stages of Interpersonal Reasoning Described by Selman

**Stage 0: egocentric level (about ages four to six).** Children do not recognize that other persons may interpret the same social event or course of action differently from the way they do. They do not reflect on the thoughts of self and others. They can label the overtly expressed feelings of others but do not comprehend cause-and-effect relations of social actions.

**Stage 1: social information role taking (about ages six to eight).** Children are able in limited ways to differentiate between their own interpretations of social interactions and the interpretations of others. But they cannot simultaneously think of their own view and those of others.

**Stage 2: self-reflective role taking (about ages eight to ten).** Interpersonal relations are interpreted in specific situations whereby each person understands the expectations of the other in that particular context. Children are not yet able to view the two perspectives at once, however.

**Stage 3: multiple role taking (about ages ten to twelve).** Children become capable of taking a third-person view, which permits them to understand the expectations of themselves and of others in a variety of situations as if they were spectators.

**Stage 4: social and conventional system taking (about ages twelve to over fifteen).** Each individual involved in a relationship with another understands many of the subtleties of the interactions involved. In addition, a societal perspective begins to develop. That is, actions are judged by how they might influence *all* individuals, not just those who are immediately concerned.

SOURCE: Adapted from discussions in Selman (1980).

when jostled by a playmate, for example, you might say, "You know, people don't always intentionally bump into others. Unless you are absolutely sure that someone has hurt you on purpose, it can be a lot pleasanter for all concerned if you don't make a big deal out of it."

Discussion of controversial issues may be difficult because of strong desire to conform to peer norms

2. *The desire to conform reaches a peak during the middle school years.* Early adolescents find it reassuring to dress and behave like others, and they are likely to alter their own opinions to coincide with those of a group. When you encourage student participation in class discussions, you may need to be alert to the tendency for students at these grade levels to be reluctant to voice minority opinions. If you want them to think about controversial issues, it may be preferable to invite them to write their opinions anonymously rather than voice them in front of the rest of the class.

## VIDEO CASE ◀◀ ▶ ▶▶

### Social and Emotional Development: The Influence of Peer Groups

*Watch the video clip, study the artifacts in the case, and reflect upon the following questions:*

1. Describe how the middle school students in this Video Case illustrate Selman's theory of interpersonal reasoning.

2. How do the students in this Video Case illustrate the "desire to conform"?

## pause & reflect

During the middle school years, the peer group becomes the general source for rules of behavior. Why? What advantages and disadvantages does this create?

Because early adolescents are often so concerned with receiving social approval from their peers, they may adapt their explanations of school performance to suit this purpose. This tendency was demonstrated by Jaana Juvonen (2000) in a study of fourth, sixth, and eighth graders. These students were asked to imagine that they had received a low score on an important exam and then to indicate how they would explain their performance to teachers and peers. The results may surprise you. The fourth and sixth graders were willing to explain their poor performance to both teachers and peers as being due to low ability rather than to low effort, whereas the eighth graders were much more likely to offer that explanation to their peers than to their teacher. This seems counterintuitive. Why would adolescents want to portray themselves to their peers as being dumb (to put it crudely)? The answer is that ability is seen by many adolescents as something beyond their control (see our account of Carol Dweck's work along this line in Chapter 12, "Motivation and Perceptions of Self"). They therefore conclude that ascribing poor performance to low ability rather than to low effort will result in expressions of sympathy rather than contempt ("It wasn't Matthew's fault that he got a low grade on the last math exam; he just doesn't have a head for numbers").

### Emotional Characteristics: Middle School

1. *The view of early adolescence as a period of "storm and stress" appears to be an exaggeration.* Starting with G. Stanley Hall, who wrote a pioneering two-volume text on adolescence in 1904, some theorists have described adolescence as a period of turmoil. Feelings of confusion, anxiety, and depression; extreme mood swings; and low levels of self-confidence are felt to be typical of this age group. Some of the reasons cited for this turbulence are rapid changes in height, weight, and

*Because of the importance of peer group values, middle school students often dress and behave similarly.*

Teenagers experience different degrees of emotional turmoil

body proportions; increases in hormone production; the task of identity formation; increased academic responsibilities; and the development of formal operational reasoning (Jackson & Bosma, 1990; Peterson, 1988; Susman, 1991).

Since the 1970s, however, a number of psychologists have questioned whether turmoil is universal during the emerging adolescent (and later) years (for example, see Jackson & Bosma, 1990; Peterson, 1988; Steinberg & Morris, 2001). Current evidence suggests that although many adolescents have social and emotional problems from time to time and experiment with risky behavior, most do not develop significant social, emotional, or behavioral difficulties. For example, although most adolescents will have been drunk at least once before high school graduation, relatively few will develop drinking problems or allow alcohol to adversely affect their academic or social lives. Those adolescents who do exhibit a consistent pattern of delinquency, substance abuse, and depression are likely to have exhibited these behaviors as children. In other words, problems displayed *during* adolescence are not necessarily problems *of* adolescence (Steinberg & Morris, 2001).

Some gender differences in psychological adjustment have been documented. Boys who exhibit problems during adolescence are more likely to have had similar problems in childhood, whereas girls are more likely to exhibit problems initially in adolescence. Achievement situations are more likely to produce anxiety responses in boys, whereas girls are more likely to become anxious in interpersonal situations. Finally, girls are more likely than boys to exhibit signs of depression.

2. *As a result of the continued influence of egocentric thought, middle school students are typically self-conscious and self-centered.* Because emerging adolescents are acutely aware of the physical and emotional changes that are taking place within them, they assume that everyone else is just as interested in, and is constantly evaluating, their appearance, feelings, and behavior. Consequently, they are deeply concerned about such matters as what type of clothing to wear for special occasions, with whom they should and should not be seen in public (they should never be seen with their parents at the mall, for example), and how they greet and talk with various people.

Another manifestation of adolescent egocentrism is the assumption that adults do not, indeed cannot, understand the thoughts and feelings of early adolescence.

It's as if the early adolescent believes she is experiencing things no one else has ever experienced before. Hence, a teen or preteen will likely say to a parent, "You just don't know what it feels like to be in love" (Wiles, Bondi, & Wiles, 2006).

## Cognitive Characteristics: Middle School

1. *Because of the psychological demands of early adolescence, middle school students need a classroom environment that is open, supportive, and intellectually stimulating.* Early adolescence is an unsettling time for students because of changes in their physical development, social roles, cognitive development, and sexuality. Another source of stress is coping with the transition from the elementary grades to a middle school (which often begins in sixth grade) or junior high (which typically begins in seventh grade). Partly because of these personal and environmental stresses, the self-concept, academic motivation, and achievement levels of adolescents decline, sometimes drastically. Are schools at all to blame for these problems? Perhaps they are. Several researchers (e.g., Clements & Seidman, 2002; Midgley, 2001; Roeser & Lau, 2002; Wigfield & Eccles, 2002a) provide persuasive evidence that these negative changes are due in part, perhaps in large part, to the fact that the typical school environment does not meet the needs of developing adolescents.

Their argument is based on an analysis of the psychological needs of early adolescence and the kinds of changes that take place in classroom organization, instruction, and climate as one moves from the last of the elementary grades to the first of the middle school or junior high grades. Although the typical middle school classroom is much improved in meeting students' needs for a sense of community, acceptance, and belonging, the environment continues to be largely incompatible with students' intellectual needs (Gentry, Gable, & Rizza, 2002; Midgley, 2001; Midgley, Middleton, Gheen, & Kumar, 2002; Wigfield & Eccles, 2002a). Common problems include these:

- Instead of providing students with opportunities to make decisions about such things as classroom rules, seating arrangements, homework assignments, and time spent on various tasks, teachers impose most of the requirements and limit the choices students can make. In one study, most middle school students

*Environment of middle schools does not meet needs of adolescents, leading to lower levels of learning*

*Early adolescents are faced with several developmental challenges. Consequently, middle school teachers should make a special effort to establish a supportive classroom atmosphere in which students can meet their social, emotional, and cognitive needs.*

### Meeting the Intellectual Needs of Middle School Students

Research from developmental and cognitive psychologists paints a consistent picture of middle school students. They can handle more abstract and complex tasks and work more independently of the teacher, and they have strong needs for both autonomy and social contact. Consequently, middle school teachers ought to minimize the use of lecture, independent seatwork, and competition for grades. Instead, teachers should design lessons around constructivist learning principles. For example, teachers should create assignments that relate to the issues and experiences adolescents are familiar with and care about, let students work cooperatively in small groups, provide whatever intellectual and emotional support students need to complete assignments, and foster the perception that the purpose of education is personal growth rather than competition for grades. Teachers who fail to provide this kind of environment may be doing more harm than good.

*HM TeacherPrepSPACE*

Do you agree that middle school teaching practices often leave much to be desired? As you consider this issue, check the additional resources available in the Take a Stand! section of the textbook's student website.

(grades 6 through 8) characterized their classroom activities as less interesting and enjoyable and as providing fewer opportunities for choice than did students in grades 3 through 5 (Gentry et al., 2002).

- Competition and social comparisons among students are increased as a result of such practices as whole-class instruction, ability grouping, normative grading (also called grading on the curve, a practice we discuss in Chapter 15, "Assessment of Classroom Learning"), and public evaluations of one's work. Small-group instruction is infrequent, and individualized instruction almost never occurs.

- Many classroom tasks in middle school or junior high involve low-level seatwork, verbatim recall of information, and little opportunity for discussion or group work. In one study of eleven junior high school science classes, the most frequent activity was copying information from the board or textbook onto worksheets. This emphasis on rote learning and recall has unfortunately been intensified in recent years by the growth of statewide learning standards, standardized testing, and accountability. We say "unfortunately" because this type of testing and approach to accountability discourages teachers from using instructional methods that foster meaningful learning.

- Students perceive their relationships with their teachers as being less friendly, supportive, and caring than those in earlier grades.

When middle schools fail to provide students with an intellectually challenging yet emotionally safe classroom environment, one negative consequence is an effect on motivation. Theorists like Carol Dweck describe achievement goals as being either *mastery* or *performance* in nature. Students who subscribe to a mastery goal are primarily interested in understanding ideas and their interrelationships, acquiring new skills, and refining them over time. Students who subscribe to a performance goal are primarily interested in demonstrating their ability to finish first (however that is defined) and avoiding situations in which a relative lack of ability would be apparent. Mastery goals have been associated with positive feelings about one's ability, potential, the subject matter, and school and with the use of effective learning strategies (which we describe in Chapter 10, "Social Cognitive Theory").

The most recent evidence suggests that as students move from the elementary grades to the middle grades, there is a shift in their values and practices that leads to more of an emphasis on performance goals. Some researchers blame this change on teaching practices. For example, middle grade teachers are more inclined to post papers and exams with the highest scores, to grade on a curve, to accord special privileges to high achievers, and to remind students of the importance of getting high grades and producing mistake-free papers. Such an environment tells students that meaningful learning is not necessarily expected and that support of learning will not be provided (Midgley, 2001). Students then are motivated to focus on their scores and grades rather than on what they can learn.

2. *Self-efficacy becomes an important influence on intellectual and social behavior.* As we mentioned in point 1 under "Social Characteristics," middle school children become capable of analyzing both their own views of an interpersonal interaction and those of the other person. This newfound analytic ability is also turned inward, resulting in evaluations of one's intellectual and social capabilities. Albert Bandura (1986), a learning theorist whom we will discuss later in the book, coined the term **self-efficacy** to refer to how capable people believe they are at dealing with one type of task or another. Thus a student may have a very strong sense of self-efficacy for math ("I know I can solve most any algebraic equation"), a moderate degree of self-efficacy for certain athletic activities ("I think I play baseball and basketball about as well as most other kids my age"), and a low sense of self-efficacy for interpersonal relationships ("I'm just not good at making friends").

These self-evaluative beliefs influence what activities students choose and for how long they will persist at a given task, particularly when progress becomes difficult. Students with a moderate to strong sense of self-efficacy will persist at a task long enough to obtain the success or corrective feedback that leads to expectations of future success. Students with a low sense of self-efficacy, however, tend to abandon tasks at the first sign of difficulty, thereby establishing a pattern of failure, low expectations of future success, and task avoidance. Because self-efficacy beliefs grow out of personal performance, observation of other people doing the same thing, and verbal persuasion, you can help students develop strong feelings of self-efficacy by following the suggestions we will make in later chapters about modeling and imitation, learning strategies, and effective forms of instruction.

> Self-efficacy beliefs for academic and social tasks become strong influences on behavior

# HIGH SCHOOL (GRADES 9, 10, 11, AND 12; FOURTEEN, FIFTEEN, SIXTEEN, AND SEVENTEEN YEARS)

## Physical Characteristics: High School

1. *Most students reach physical maturity, and virtually all attain puberty.* Although almost all girls reach their ultimate height, some boys may continue to grow even after graduation from high school. Tremendous variation exists in height and weight and in rate of maturation. Approximately 13 percent of students are considered to be overweight (Centers for Disease Control, 2006). As noted earlier, late-maturing boys seem to have considerable difficulty adjusting to their

---

**Table 2.7**    Applying Theories of Development to the High School Years

**Psychosocial development:** identity vs. role confusion. Concerns arise about gender roles and occupational choice. Different identity statuses become apparent.

**Cognitive development:** formal operational thought for many students. There is increasing ability to engage in mental manipulations, understand abstractions, and test hypotheses.

**Moral development:** morality of cooperation, conventional level. There is increasing willingness to think of rules as mutual agreements and to allow for intentions and extenuating circumstances.

**General factors to keep in mind:** Achievement of sexual maturity has a profound effect on many aspects of behavior. Peer group and reactions of friends are extremely important. There is concern about what will happen after graduation, particularly for students who do not intend to continue their education. Awareness grows of the significance of academic ability and importance of grades for certain career patterns. There is a need to make personal value decisions regarding use of drugs, premarital sex, and code of ethics.

slower rate of growth. There is still concern about appearance, although it may not be as strong as during the middle school years. Glandular changes leading to acne may be a source of worry and self-consciousness to some students. The most significant glandular change accompanying puberty is arousal of the sex drive.

2. *Many adolescents become sexually active, although the long-term trend is down.* From 1991 through 2005 sexual intercourse among high school students decreased across the board, as shown in Table 2.8. Still, in the latter year, 63 percent of students reported having engaged in sexual intercourse by the end of grade 12.

The factors that are significantly related to initiation of sexual activity among high school students vary by gender and race. White males and females with low educational goals and below-average grades are more likely to have sexual intercourse at an earlier age as compared with peers who have higher goals and grades. The factors that were most strongly related to initiation of sexual activity for African American female students were having a mother with twelve or more years of education (presumably, mothers with more education spend less time at home caring for their children), spending less time with one's mother, and being uninvolved in church activities. The factors that predicted onset of sexual activity for African American male students were low grade-point average, living in a one-parent family, limited contact with the father, and lack of participation in family decision making. In addition, the onset of sexual activity is associated with subsequent declines in educational goals and achievement and an increased risk of substance abuse (Hallfors et al., 2002; Ramirez-Valles, Zimmerman, & Juarez, 2002; Schvaneveldt, Miller, Berry, & Lee, 2001).

These findings illustrate the pressing need for sex education during the high school years. In particular, adolescents need to understand the distinction between sex and mature love. A major characteristic of mature love is that "the well-being of the other person is just a little bit more important than the well-being of the self" (Gordon & Gilgun, 1987, p. 180).

3. *Although the birthrate for unmarried adolescents has fallen in recent years, it remains unacceptably high, as is the rate of sexually transmitted*

| Factors related to initiation of sexual activity vary by gender, race |

**pause & reflect**

What are the advantages and disadvantages of sex education in school? For help with your answer, visit the websites of the National Campaign to Prevent Teen Pregnancy (**www.teenpregnancy.org**) and the Sexuality Information and Education Council of the United States (**www.siecus.org**).

| **Table 2.8** | Trends in Sexual Activity Among High School Students | |
|---|---|---|
| | **Percentage Who Reported Ever Having Sexual Intercourse** | |
| | **1991** | **2005** |
| **Gender** | | |
| Females | 50.8 | 45.7 |
| Males | 57.4 | 47.9 |
| **Grade Levels** | | |
| Ninth grade | 39.0 | 34.3 |
| Tenth grade | 48.2 | 42.8 |
| Eleventh grade | 62.4 | 51.4 |
| Twelfth grade | 66.7 | 63.1 |
| **Ethnic Groups** | | |
| Black | 81.4 | 67.6 |
| Hispanic | 53.1 | 51.0 |
| White | 50.0 | 43.0 |

SOURCE: Centers for Disease Control (2002a, 2006).

*Because many adolescents are sexually active, there is a strong need for sex education in the schools.*

*diseases.* In 1991, the birthrate for teens of ages fifteen to nineteen was 61.8 births per 1,000. By 2000, that figure had declined to 47.7. Pregnancy rates for teens fifteen to nineteen years old have also declined. In 1990 the pregnancy rate was 117 per 1,000, but it slid to 83.6 per 1,000 in 2000 (Alan Guttmacher Institute, 2004). This decline is attributed to a combination of increased abstinence and contraception. Even so, pregnancy rates and birthrates in the United States are considerably higher than in Canada and many European countries because American teens are less likely than their Canadian and European counterparts to use contraception (Boonstra, 2002). Among the many factors related to these trends in adolescent sexual behavior, one has clear educational implications: Adolescents who were retained at least once and were behind schedule in their schooling were more likely to have unprotected sex than adolescents who had not been retained (Abma & Sonenstein, 2001).

The relatively high levels of sexual activity and low levels of regular contraception among adolescents are particularly worrisome because they put adolescents at risk for contracting **sexually transmitted diseases (STDs).** According to one report (Panchaud, Singh, Feivelson, & Darroch, 2000), STDs among adolescents in the United States are considerably more prevalent than in most other developed countries. The rates for syphilis, gonorrhea, and chlamydia, for example, are 6.4 per 100,000 adolescents, 571.8 per 100,000, and 1,138 per 100,000, respectively.

The worst of the STDs is, of course, acquired immune deficiency syndrome (AIDS) because there is no known cure. Although the number of AIDS cases among adolescents is currently low, it will rise in the future, potentially becoming a major problem. The percentage of adolescents who test positive for human immunodeficiency virus (HIV, the viral cause of AIDS) ranges from about 2 percent to 6 percent (MacKay, Fingerhut, & Duran, 2000). Because HIV has a long incubation period, AIDS symptoms may not show up for several years. Consequently, the proportion of today's teens who will be diagnosed with AIDS in their twenties will be more than the 2 percent to 6 percent figure just cited.

## Social Characteristics: High School

Parents influence values, plans; peers influence immediate status

1. *Parents and other adults are likely to influence long-range plans; peers are likely to influence immediate status.* When adolescents look for models and advice on such social matters as dress, hairstyle, speech patterns, friendships, and leisure activities, the peer group is likely to have the greatest influence (as a visit to any high school will reveal). Peer values can also influence academic performance (Dornbusch & Kaufman, 2001). When the issues are which courses to take in school and what different careers are like, teachers, guidance counselors, and parents are likely to have more influence over decision making than peers. For questions about values, ethics, and future plans, the views of parents are usually sought. The influence of peer groups is strongest during early and middle childhood (Steinberg, 2005).

Not surprisingly, most conflicts between parents and their adolescent children are about such peer-influenced issues as personal appearance, friends, dating, hours, and eating habits (Hill, 1987). This general pattern may be modified, however, by type of parenting style. The adolescent children of parents who have an authoritarian style (see Diana Baumrind's work on parenting styles in the section on the cognitive characteristics of preschool and kindergarten children) have a stronger tendency than other adolescents to make decisions that are consistent with peer group advice. The adolescent children of parents who have an authoritative style, on the other hand, are more likely to make decisions that are consistent with parental advice (Steinberg & Morris, 2001). Perhaps this is why the influence of parents appears to be greatest when there are mutual affection and respect between parent and child (Baumrind, 1991b; Hill, 1987).

Girls more likely than boys to experience anxiety about friendships

2. *Girls seem to experience greater anxiety about friendships than boys do.* Factors that cause girls to become concerned about the reactions of others will be summarized in the next chapter. Adolescent girls tend to seek intimacy in friendships. Boys, in contrast, often stress skills and interests when they form friendships, and their tendencies to be competitive and self-reliant may work against the formation of close relationships with male companions. Because adolescent girls often wish to form an intimate relationship with another girl, they are more likely than boys to experience anxiety, jealousy, and conflicts regarding friendships with same-sex peers. You should not be surprised, therefore, if secondary school girls are much more preoccupied with positive and negative aspects of friendships than boys are (Hardy, Bukowski, & Sippola, 2002; Pleydon & Schner, 2001; Steinberg, 2005).

3. *Many high school students are employed after school.* During the school months of 1999–2000, 68.2 percent of sixteen-year-olds worked part-time at some point during the school year. For seventeen- and eighteen-year-olds the percentages increased to 78.9 and 84.8, respectively. Some students may have worked for only a week or two, but the average number of weeks worked was 23.4 for sixteen-year-olds, 33.8 for seventeen-year-olds, and 34.2 for eighteen-year-olds (Bureau of Labor Statistics, 2003).

   The pros and cons of after-school employment have been vigorously debated. On the positive side, it is thought to enhance self-discipline, a sense of responsibility, self-confidence, and attitudes toward work. On the negative side, part-time employment leaves less time for homework, participation in extracurricular activities, and development of friendships; it may also lead to increased stress, lower grades, and lower career aspirations. Most experts agree that students who work more than 20 hours per week are likely to have lower grades than students who work less or not at all (Steinberg, 2005).

## Emotional Characteristics: High School

1. *Many psychiatric disorders either appear or become prominent during adolescence. Included among these are eating disorders, substance abuse, schizophrenia, depression, and suicide.* Eating disorders are much more common in females than in males. *Anorexia nervosa* is an eating disorder characterized by a preoccupation with body weight and food, behavior directed toward losing weight, peculiar patterns of handling food, weight loss, intense fear of gaining weight, and a distorted perception of one's body. This disorder occurs predominantly in females (more than 90 percent of the cases) and usually appears between the ages of fourteen and seventeen (American Psychiatric Association, 2000).

   *Bulimia nervosa* is a disorder in which binge eating (uncontrolled rapid eating of large quantities of food over a short period of time), followed by self-induced vomiting, is the predominant behavior. Binges are typically followed by feelings of guilt, depression, self-disgust, and fasting. As with anorexia, over 90 percent of individuals with bulimia are female (American Psychiatric Association, 2000).

   Adolescents who engage in *substance abuse* (tobacco, alcohol, and illegal drugs) not only jeopardize their physical and emotional health but also increase their risk of doing poorly in school or of dropping out of school. A 1999 survey of high school students found that:

   • More than one-third reported smoking on one or more of the previous thirty days, and about 17 percent reported smoking on twenty or more of the previous thirty days.

   • About one-half reported drinking in the previous thirty days. Twenty-eight percent of female students and 35 percent of male students engaged in binge drinking.

*HM TeacherPrepSPACE*

How well do you understand adolescent drinking behavior? Try the interactive quiz on the textbook's student website.

- Forty-seven percent had used marijuana at least once during their lifetimes, and 27 percent had used marijuana one or more times in the preceding thirty days.
- Ten percent reported using some form of cocaine at least once during their lifetimes, and 4 percent reported using cocaine in the preceding thirty days (MacKay et al., 2000).

*Schizophrenia*, a thinking disorder characterized by illogical and unrealistic thinking, delusions, and hallucinations, is relatively rare among adolescents, affecting less than 0.25 percent of all thirteen- to nineteen-year-olds. Yet it is the most frequently occurring psychotic disorder, and the number of cases diagnosed between the ages of twelve and eighteen is steadily increasing. Early symptoms include odd, unpredictable behavior; difficulty communicating with others; social withdrawal; and rejection by peers (Beiser, Erickson, Fleming, & Iacono, 1993; Conger & Galambos, 1997; Gilberg, 2001).

2. *The most common type of emotional disorder during adolescence is depression.* The most common forms of **depression**, from least to most serious, are *depressed mood*, *depressive syndrome*, and *clinical depression*. Depressed mood is primarily characterized by feelings of sadness or unhappiness, although emotions such as anxiety, fear, guilt, anger, and contempt are frequently present, as well (Peterson et al., 1993). In 2005, 36.7 percent of high school females and 20.4 percent of high school males reported feeling so sad and hopeless almost every day for two or more weeks in a row that they stopped engaging in some usual activities. The percentages of White, Black, and Latino students who gave this response were 25.8, 28.4, and 36.2, respectively (Centers for Disease Control, 2006). As you can see from these data, more girls than boys report having emotional responses indicative of depression, as do minority students, particularly those of Latino origin.

Common symptoms of depression include feelings of worthlessness, crying spells, and suicidal thoughts, threats, and attempts. Additional symptoms include moodiness, social isolation, fatigue, hypochondria, and difficulty in concentrating (Cicchetti & Toth, 1998; Peterson et al., 1993). Depression in adolescents precedes substance abuse (MacKay et al., 2000). High school students who experience such symptoms typically try to ward off their depression through restless activity or flight to or from others. They may also engage in problem behavior or delinquent acts carried out in ways that make it clear they are appealing for help. (A depressed fifteen-year-old boy may carry out an act of vandalism, for instance, at a time when a school authority or police officer is sure to observe the incident.)

Aaron Beck (1972) suggests that depression consists of a *cognitive set* made of negative views of oneself, the world, and the future. Martin Seligman (1975) proposes that depression is caused by *learned helplessness*, which leads to feelings of having no control over one's life. Irving Weiner (1975) emphasizes that depression typically involves a *sense of loss* that may have many causes. Depression may stem from the abrupt end of a personal relationship through death, separation, or broken friendship. An individual may undergo a sharp drop in self-esteem as a result of failure or guilt. Or a person may experience a loss of bodily integrity following illness, incapacitation, or disfigurement. For female adolescents, increases in sex hormones, specifically testosterone and estradiol, have also been linked to depression (Angold, Worthman, & Costello, 2003).

Although many techniques exist for changing a negative self-concept to a positive view of self, one effective approach to minimizing depression is to help as many of your students as possible to experience success as they learn. Techniques to accomplish that goal will be discussed in subsequent chapters of this book.

3. *If depression becomes severe, suicide may be contemplated.* In 2005, 16.9 percent of high school students had seriously considered attempting suicide during the previous twelve months, 13 percent had made a suicide plan, and 8.4 percent had made one or more attempts. Many more females than males considered attempting suicide (21.8 percent versus 12 percent, respectively) and made one or more attempts (10.8 percent versus 6 percent).

---

*Marginal notes:*

Depression most common among females, minorities

Depression may be caused by negative cognitive set, learned helplessness, sense of loss

**JOURNAL ENTRY**
Helping Students Overcome Depression

*Many high school students, girls in particular, experience periods of depression, loneliness, and anxiety. Because severe depression often precedes a suicide attempt, teachers should refer students they believe to be depressed to the school counselor.*

Depression and unstable family situation place adolescents at risk for suicide

Latino teens are more likely than White or Black teens to consider a suicide attempt (17.9 percent, 16.9 percent, and 12.2 percent, respectively) and to make a suicide attempt (11.3 percent, 7.3 percent, and 7.6 percent, respectively) (Centers for Disease Control, 2006). As of 2003, the death rate from suicide in the fifteen- to twenty-four-year age group was highest for American Indian/Alaskan Native males (27.2 per 100,000 residents) and females (8.3 per 100,000 residents) and lowest for Asian or Pacific Islander males (9.0 per 100,000 residents) and Black females (2.0 per 100,000 residents) (National Center for Health Statistics, 2005).

The single most important signal of a youth at risk for suicide is depression. Along with the common symptoms noted earlier under point 2, other signs of depression and potential suicide include poor appetite, weight loss, changes in sleeping patterns, difficulty in concentrating, academic problems, poor self-concept, withdrawing from friends and/or social activities, giving away prized possessions, lack of interest in personal appearance, and feelings of loneliness. These symptoms take on added significance when accompanied by a family history of suicide or parents who commit abuse or use drugs and alcohol excessively. The factors that usually trigger a suicide include a shameful or humiliating experience, such as perceived failure at school or rejection by a romantic partner or parent (Fisher, 2006; Perkins & Hartless, 2002; Sofronoff, Dalgliesh, & Kosky, 2005).

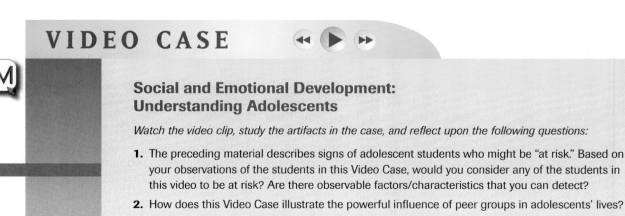

## VIDEO CASE ◄◄ ► ►►

### Social and Emotional Development: Understanding Adolescents

*Watch the video clip, study the artifacts in the case, and reflect upon the following questions:*

**1.** The preceding material describes signs of adolescent students who might be "at risk." Based on your observations of the students in this Video Case, would you consider any of the students in this video to be at risk? Are there observable factors/characteristics that you can detect?

**2.** How does this Video Case illustrate the powerful influence of peer groups in adolescents' lives?

If you notice that a student in one of your classes seems extremely depressed, take the trouble to ask if there is anything you can do to provide support and seek the advice of the school counselor. To encourage students to discuss their concerns with you, suggest that they read books written for adolescents that address suicide in a direct and forthright manner (Fisher, 2006). Your interest and sympathy may prevent a suicide attempt. Also, be aware that recent prevention efforts include school-based programs. These programs, which are run by a mental health professional or an educator (or both), are typically directed to high school students, their parents, and their teachers. They usually include a review of suicide statistics, a list of warning signs, a list of community mental health resources and how to contact them, and a discussion of how to refer a student or peer to counseling.

## Cognitive Characteristics: High School

1. *High school students become increasingly capable of engaging in formal thought, but they may not use this capability.* These students are more likely than younger students to grasp relationships, mentally plan a course of action before proceeding, and test hypotheses systematically. Without supervision and guidance, however, they may not use such capabilities consistently. Accordingly, you might take advantage of opportunities to show students at these grade levels how they can function as formal thinkers. Call attention to relationships and to ways that previously acquired knowledge can be applied to new situations. Provide specific instruction in techniques of problem solving. (Ways you might do this will be discussed in Chapter 9, "Constructivist Learning Theory, Problem Solving, and Transfer.") Although some students may ignore your advice, others will probably take it more seriously. Despite the constant attempts of adolescents to appear totally self-sufficient and independent, they still view parents and teachers as knowledgeable authority figures when it comes to school achievement (Amiram, Bar-Tal, Alona, & Peleg, 1990).

> Political thinking becomes more abstract, less authoritarian, more knowledgeable

2. *Between the ages of twelve and sixteen, political thinking becomes more abstract, liberal, and knowledgeable.* Joseph Adelson (1972, 1986) used an interview approach to obtain information about the development of political thought during the adolescent years. At the start of the interviews, the participants were requested to imagine that one thousand people had ventured to an island in the Pacific for the purpose of establishing a new society. The respondents were then asked to explain how these people might establish a political order; devise a legal system; establish a balance among rights, responsibilities, personal liberty, and the common good; and deal with other problems of public policy.

The analysis of the interview responses showed no significant gender differences in the understanding of political concepts and no significant differences attributable to intelligence and social class, although brighter students were better able to deal with abstract ideas and upper-class students were less likely to be authoritarian. The most striking and consistent finding was the degree to which the political thinking of the adolescent changed in the years between ages twelve and sixteen. Adelson concluded that the most significant changes were (1) an increase in the ability to deal with such abstractions as freedom of speech, equal justice under law, and the concept of community; (2) a decline in authoritarian views; (3) an increase in the ability to imagine the consequences of current actions; and (4) an increase in political knowledge.

Increased ability to deal with abstractions is a function of the shift from concrete to formal operational thought. When thirteen-year-olds were asked, "What is the purpose of laws?" a typical answer was, "So people don't steal or kill" (Adelson, 1972, p. 108). A fifteen- or sixteen-year-old, by contrast, was more likely to say, "To ensure safety and enforce the government" (p. 108).

When considering punishment for crimes, younger children (Piaget's moral realists) hold the conviction that laws are immutable and that punishment should be stern. But by age fourteen and fifteen, the adolescents whom Adelson interviewed were more likely to consider circumstances and individual rights and to recommend rehabilitation rather than punishment.

If you will be teaching courses in social studies, you may find this information useful in lesson planning. It may also help you understand why students may respond to discussions of political or other abstract matters in different ways.

# SELECTING TECHNOLOGIES FOR DIFFERENT AGE LEVELS

As this chapter and the next one indicate, your teaching approaches will be influenced by the developmental level of your students. Your incorporation of educational technology will be no different. For kindergarten and primary grade teachers, tools to enhance student literacy are likely to be a priority. Elementary, middle school, and high school teachers will be more interested in tools that promote thinking, problem solving, and communication.

## Using Technology to Reduce Egocentrism

As we will point out in the next chapter, primary to elementary grade children are limited by egocentrism in their ability to think logically. Egocentrism, as you may recall, is the inability to understand the world from any perspective but your own. According to Jean Piaget, who first proposed the concept, the main factor that contributes to the decline of egocentrism is exposure to different points of view through social interaction. Because these interactions do not have to be face-to-face, it is quite possible that sharing experiences and points of view by computer may produce the same result.

One way to accomplish these exchanges is through Kidlink (**www.kidlink.org**), a nonprofit organization that helps teachers and students arrange electronic exchanges with students from around the world. The goal of Kidlink is to help children understand themselves, identify and define life goals, and collaborate with peers. Joyce Burtch, a middle school teacher, has described how she created a program through Kidlink for her students, including three students with moderate neurological and physical impairments (Burtch, 1999).

The Virtual Classroom Program at J. Percy Page High School in Edmonton, Canada, illustrates how students and teachers can use technology to establish interactions with students and professionals from all over the globe. Through the use of Canada's high-speed communications network, students from Page High School have participated in real-time videoconferences with students from other parts of Canada, as well as Switzerland, Ireland, and Germany, on such topics as the global water crisis, technology and privacy, cultural differences and world conflict, and gene technology. During these videoconferences, students at one school make presentations, often accompanied by slide shows or film, and engage in discussion and debate with students from the other school (or schools, as more than two classrooms at a time can participate). In addition, students can listen to and ask questions of prominent professionals from a wide range of disciplines (Andrews & Marshall, 2000).

A similar project that had implications for egocentrism reduction occurred between fifth-grade students in Italy and Greece. Each group of students wrote the beginning of a fairy tale that contained a moral issue and posted it to a website. The fifth graders from the other country downloaded the partially written story, discussed it in class, wrote an ending, and then posted the completed story to the website. The group that started the story then downloaded it, discussed it among themselves, wrote a final draft, and posted a summary of their discussion on the website. The comments made by the students reflected a strong effort to come to grips with the perspective of the other group (Ligorio, Talamo, & Pontecorvo, 2005).

For schools that do not have the luxury of arranging real-time videoconferences, written asynchronous exchanges via e-mail have proven useful for accomplishing the same goal. One advantage of e-mail exchanges is that children who are outgoing and fluent speakers are less likely to discourage others from participating. In a test of this idea, fifth and sixth graders from two schools in the Netherlands worked on a biology project for several weeks, both among themselves and with students from the other school, by periodically exchanging e-mails about various aspects of the project. The researchers found that over the course of the study, the students became more reflective and aware of the different views of their peers (De Vries, Van der Meij, Boersma, & Pieters, 2005).

## Effect of Technology on Cognitive and Interpersonal Reasoning

Electronic conferencing, by allowing students to assume roles, can promote the development of interpersonal reasoning. For instance, middle school and high school students who assume the roles of famous historical characters on sensitive environmental issues exhibit higher levels of dialogue and interpersonal reasoning than would be expected by Selman's (1980) developmental scheme (Bonk & Sugar, 1998).

Another type of program that allows students to interact electronically with experts and explorers around the world is **adventure learning.** For instance, students from various schools might get together for virtual field trips to places such as the Statue of Liberty for insights on immigration policies or the Civil War battlefield at Gettysburg for demonstrations of military tactics (Siegel & Kirkley, 1998). They also might communicate electronically with explorers traversing the Arctic tundra or the Amazon rain forest. While on virtual field trips, students are electronically transported to the actual site to view historical reenactments, listen to experts, ask questions, and electronically correspond with peers across the nation.

Adventure-learning explorations can be incorporated into the **problem-based learning** (PBL) approach, a technique that promotes formal operational thought by emphasizing real-world problem solving. We discuss PBL in Chapter 13, "Approaches to Instruction." Two adventure-learning websites that you might want to take a look at are the Global Online Adventure Learning Site at **www.goals.com/index.htm** and ThinkQuest's Ocean AdVENTure site at **http://library.thinkquest.org/18828.**

*HM TeacherPrepSPACE*

To review this chapter, try the ACE practice tests and PowerPoint slides on the textbook's student website.

# 3

# Theories of Psychosocial and Cognitive Development

## HM *TeacherPrepSPACE*

**HM TeacherPrepSPACE student website** offers many helpful resources. Go to **login.cengage.com** to preview this chapter's Concept Maps and Chapter Themes.

**KEY POINTS**

*These key points will help you learn the important information in this chapter. To help you study, they also appear in the margins of the pages, next to the text where they are discussed.*

## Erikson: Psychosocial Development

- Erikson's theory encompasses the life span, highlights the role of the person and culture in development
- Personality development based on epigenetic principle
- Personality grows out of successful resolution of psychosocial crises
- 2 to 3 years: autonomy vs. shame and doubt
- 4 to 5 years: initiative vs. guilt
- 6 to 11 years: industry vs. inferiority
- 12 to 18 years: identity vs. role confusion
- Role confusion: uncertainty as to what behaviors others will react to favorably
- Students' sense of industry hampered by unhealthy competition for grades
- Identity: accepting one's body, having goals, getting recognition
- Psychosocial moratorium delays commitment
- Adolescents exhibit a particular process, called an identity status, for establishing an identity
- Individuals in identity diffusion avoid thinking about jobs, roles, values
- Individuals in foreclosure unquestioningly endorse parents' goals and values
- Individuals in moratorium uncertain about identity
- Individuals who have reached identity achievement status have made their own commitments
- Criticisms of Erikson's theory: based largely on personal experience, not applicable to many cultures, gender-biased

## Piaget: Cognitive Development

- Organization: tendency to systematize processes
- Adaptation: tendency to adjust to environment
- Scheme: organized pattern of behavior or thought
- Assimilation: new experience is fitted into existing scheme
- Accommodation: scheme is created or revised to fit new experience
- Equilibration: tendency to organize schemes to allow better understanding of experiences
- Sensorimotor stage: schemes reflect sensory and motor experiences
- Preoperational stage: child forms many new schemes but does not think logically
- Perceptual centration, irreversibility, egocentrism: barriers to logical thought
- Egocentrism: assumption that others see things the same way

- Concrete operational stage: child is capable of mentally reversing actions but generalizes only from concrete experiences
- Formal operational stage: child is able to deal with abstractions, form hypotheses, engage in mental manipulations
- Adolescent egocentrism: adolescents preoccupied with their own view of the world and how they appear to others
- Piaget: cognitive development more strongly influenced by peers than by adults
- Instruction can accelerate development of schemes that have begun to form
- Piaget's theory underestimates children's abilities
- Most adolescents are not formal operational thinkers
- Sequence of stages uniform across cultures but rate of development varies

## Vygotsky: Cognitive Development

- How we think influenced by current social forces and historical cultural forces
- Psychological tools aid and change thought processes
- Cognitive development strongly influenced by those more intellectually advanced
- Teachers should help students learn how to use psychological tools
- Cognitive development promoted by instruction in zone of proximal development
- Scaffolding techniques support student learning

## Using Technology to Promote Cognitive Development

- Computer-based simulations promote exploration and visual representations of abstract ideas, and correct misconceptions
- Computer programs can act as expert collaborative partners

## Piaget, Kohlberg, and Gilligan: Moral Development

- Morality of constraint (moral realism): rules are sacred, consequences determine guilt
- Morality of cooperation (moral relativism): rules are flexible, intent important in determining guilt
- Preconventional morality: avoid punishment, receive benefits in return
- Conventional morality: impress others, respect authority
- Postconventional morality: mutual agreements, consistent principles
- Criticisms of Kohlberg's theory: moral development difficult to accelerate, moral dilemmas not relevant to daily life, relies on macromoral issues, ignores characteristics other than moral reasoning
- Although slight differences do exist, both males and females use both caring and justice orientations to resolve real-life moral dilemmas
- Moral knowledge does not always result in moral behavior

In the opening chapter, we pointed out that individuals vary in how they perceive and think about the world around them. This commonplace observation implies that you need to be aware of the major ways in which students differ from one another in order to design potentially effective lessons. What may work well for one part of your class may not work quite so well for another part. The lesson that was a huge success with last year's class may be a disaster with this year's group if you fail to take into account critical differences between the two classes. The five chapters in Part I introduce you to how students may differ from one another in psychosocial development, cognitive development, age, mental ability, thinking style, achievement, ethnic background, and social class. You will also discover how those differences affect classroom learning.

Human development is a complex topic to discuss; in addition to analyzing many different forms of behavior, we must trace the way each type of behavior changes as a child matures. Authors of books on development have adopted different strategies for coping with this challenge. Some have described theories that outline stages in the emergence of particular forms of behavior. Others have summarized significant types of behavior at successive age levels. Still others have examined specific types of behavior, noting age changes for every topic. Each approach has advantages and disadvantages.

Developmental theories call attention to the overall sequence, continuity, and interrelatedness of aspects of development, but they typically account for only limited facets of behavior. Texts organized in terms of age levels make readers aware of varied aspects of children's behavior at a given age but sometimes tend to obscure how particular types of behavior emerge and change. And although texts organized according to types of behavior do not have the limitation of the age-level approach, they may make it difficult for the reader to grasp the overall pattern of behavior at a particular stage of development.

In an effort to profit from the advantages and to minimize the disadvantages of each approach, this chapter and the previous present discussions of development that combine all three. This chapter focuses on Erik Erikson's psychosocial stages, Jean Piaget's cognitive stages, and Lev Vygotsky's views on the role of social interaction. It also describes Piaget's ideas about moral development, Lawrence Kohlberg's extension of Piaget's work, and Carol Gilligan's criticism and modification of Kohlberg's theory. Chapter 2 describes age-level characteristics of students at five levels: preschool, primary school, elementary school, middle school, and high school. Discussion at each age level focuses on four types of behavior: physical, social, emotional, and cognitive. The information in these chapters will help you adapt teaching techniques to the students who are in the age range that you expect to teach, as well as develop expectations of student behavior across age ranges. The patterns of behavior described in these chapters are ones that typical children and adolescents exhibit.

The following three chapters are devoted to individual differences and how to deal with them. Chapter 4, "Culture and Cognition," describes the characteristics of students from different ethnic and social class backgrounds. Chapter 5, "Understanding Student Differences," discusses the nature of variability and how students vary with respect to gender, mental ability, and cognitive style. And Chapter 6, "Accommodating Student Diversity," describes types of students who vary from their classmates to such an extent that they may require special kinds of education. ●

## ERIKSON: PSYCHOSOCIAL DEVELOPMENT

Of all the developmental theories that we could have chosen to discuss, why did we decide to open this chapter with Erik Erikson's theory of psychosocial development? There are several reasons for this choice:

- Erikson described psychological growth from infancy through old age. Thus, one can draw out instructional implications for every level of education from preschool through adult education.
- Erikson's theory portrays people as playing an active role in their own psychological development through their attempts to understand, organize, and integrate their everyday experiences.

Erikson's theory encompasses the life span, highlights the role of the person and culture in development

- This theory highlights the important role that cultural goals, aspirations, expectations, requirements, and opportunities play in personal growth, a theme discussed in Chapter 5 (Newman & Newman, 2003).

  Although Erikson (1902–1994) studied with Sigmund Freud, he concluded that Freud's tendency to stay in Vienna and interact with only a small, select group of individuals prevented the founder of psychoanalysis from fully appreciating how social and cultural factors (for example, values, attitudes, beliefs, and customs) influence behavior, perception, and thinking. Erikson decided to formulate a theory of development based on psychoanalytic principles but taking into account such influences.

## Basic Principles of Erikson's Theory

Personality development based on epigenetic principle

**Epigenetic Principle** Erikson based his description of personality development on the **epigenetic principle,** which states that in fetal development, certain organs of the body appear at certain specified times and eventually "combine" to form a child. Erikson hypothesized that just as the parts of the body develop in interrelated ways in a human fetus, so the personality of an individual forms as the ego progresses through a series of interrelated stages. All of these ego stages exist in some form from the very beginning of life, and each has a critical period of development.

Personality grows out of successful resolution of psychosocial crises

**Psychosocial Crisis** In Erikson's view, personality development occurs as one successfully resolves a series of turning points, or psychosocial crises. Although the word *crisis* typically refers to an extraordinary event that threatens well-being, Erikson had a more benign meaning in mind. Crises occur when people feel compelled to adjust to the normal guidelines and expectations that society has for them but are not altogether certain that they are prepared to carry out these demands fully. For example, Western societies expect children of elementary and middle school age to develop a basic sense of industry, mostly through success in school. Adolescents are expected to come to terms with such questions as, "Who am I?" and "Where am I going?" (Newman & Newman, 2003).

As you will see in the next section, Erikson described these crises in terms of opposing qualities that individuals typically develop. For each crisis, there is a desirable quality that can emerge and a corresponding unfavorable characteristic. Erikson did not mean to imply that a healthy individual develops only positive qualities. He emphasized that people are best able to adapt to their world when they possess both the positive and negative qualities of a particular stage, provided the positive quality is significantly stronger than the negative quality. In the first stage, for example, it is important that the child learn trust, but a person who never experienced a bit of mistrust would struggle to understand the world. In Erikson's view, difficulties in development and adjustment arise when the negative quality outweighs the positive for any given stage or when the outcome for most stages is negative (Newman & Newman, 2003).

As you read through the following brief descriptions of the stages of psychosocial development, keep in mind that a positive resolution of the issue for each stage depends on how well the issue of the previous stage was resolved. An adolescent who strongly doubts her own capabilities, for example, may have trouble making the commitments required for identity development in adulthood (Fadjukoff, Pulkkinen, & Kokko, 2005; Marcia, 1991, 2002).

## Stages of Psychosocial Development

The following designations, age ranges, and essential characteristics of the stages of personality development are proposed by Erikson in *Childhood and Society* (1963).[1]

---

[1] All quotations in "Stages of Psychosocial Development" are drawn from Chapter 7 of *Childhood and Society*.

**Trust Versus Mistrust (Birth to One Year)**    The basic psychosocial attitude for infants to learn is that they can trust their world. The parents' "consistency, continuity, and sameness of experience" in satisfying the infant's basic needs fosters truth. Such an environment will permit children to think of their world as safe and dependable. Conversely, children whose care is inadequate, inconsistent, or negative will approach the world with fear and suspicion.

2 to 3 years: autonomy vs. shame and doubt

**Autonomy Versus Shame and Doubt (Two to Three Years; Preschool)**    Just when children have learned to trust (or mistrust) their parents, they must exert a degree of independence. If toddlers are permitted and encouraged to do what they are capable of doing at their own pace and in their own way—and with judicious supervision by parents and teachers—they will develop a sense of autonomy (willingness and ability to direct one's behavior). But if parents and teachers are impatient and do too many things for young children or shame young children for unacceptable behavior, these children will develop feelings of self-doubt.

4 to 5 years: initiative vs. guilt

**Initiative Versus Guilt (Four to Five Years; Preschool to Kindergarten)**    The ability to participate in many physical activities and to use language sets the stage for initiative, which "adds to autonomy the quality of undertaking, planning, and 'attacking' a task for the sake of being active and on the move." If four- and five-year-olds are given freedom to explore and experiment and if parents and teachers take time to answer questions, tendencies toward initiative will be encouraged. Conversely, if children of this age are restricted and made to feel that their activities and questions have no point or are a nuisance to adults and older siblings, they will feel guilty about acting on their own.

6 to 11 years: industry vs. inferiority

**Industry Versus Inferiority (Six to Eleven Years; Elementary to Middle School)**    A child entering school is at a point in development when behavior is dominated by intellectual curiosity and performance. "He now learns to win recognition by producing things. . . . He develops a sense of industry." If children at this stage are encouraged to make and do things well, helped to persevere, allowed to finish tasks, and praised for trying, industry results. If the children's efforts are unsuccessful or if they are derided or treated as bothersome, feelings of inferiority result. Children who feel inferior may never learn to enjoy intellectual work and take pride in doing at least one kind of thing really well. At worst, they may believe they will never excel at anything.

12 to 18 years: identity vs. role confusion

Role confusion: uncertainty as to what behaviors others will react to favorably

**Identity Versus Role Confusion (Twelve to Eighteen Years; Middle Through High School)**    The goal at this stage is development of the roles and skills that will prepare adolescents to take a meaningful place in adult society. The danger at this stage is **role confusion:** having no clear conception of appropriate types of behavior that others will react to favorably. If adolescents succeed (as reflected by the reactions of others) in integrating roles in different situations to the point of experiencing continuity in their perception of self, identity develops. In common terms, they know who they are. If they are unable to establish a sense of stability in various aspects of their lives, role confusion results.

**Intimacy Versus Isolation (Young Adulthood)**    To experience satisfying development at this stage, the young adult needs to establish close and committed intimate relationships and partnerships with other people. The hallmark of intimacy is the "ethical strength to abide by such commitments, even though they may call for significant sacrifices and compromises." Failure to do so will lead to a sense of isolation.

**Generativity Versus Stagnation (Middle Age)**    "Generativity . . . is primarily the concern of establishing and guiding the next generation." Erikson's use of the term *generativity* is purposely broad. It refers, of course, to having children and raising them. In addition, it refers to the productive and creative efforts in which adults take part (e.g., teaching) that have a positive effect on younger generations. Those unable or unwilling to "establish" and "guide" the next generation become victims of stagnation and self-absorption.

**Integrity Versus Despair (Old Age)**   Integrity is "the acceptance of one's one and only life cycle as something that had to be and that, by necessity, permitted of no substitutions. . . . Despair expresses the feeling that the time is now short, too short for the attempt to start another life and to try out alternate roads to integrity."

Of Erikson's eight stages, the two you should pay particular attention to are industry versus inferiority and identity versus role confusion, because they are the primary psychosocial issues that students must resolve during their elementary, middle school, and high school years. If you are committed to helping students learn as much as possible, you need to have a basic understanding of these two stages so that your lesson plans and instructional approaches help students achieve a strong sense of industry and identity. The next two sections briefly describe the major factors that contribute to students' sense of industry and their grasp of who they are and what they might become.

## Helping Students Develop a Sense of Industry

Between kindergarten and sixth grade, most children are eager to demonstrate that they can learn new skills and successfully accomplish assigned tasks. One factor that has long been known to have a detrimental effect on one's sense of industry is competition for a limited number of rewards. If you have ever taken a class where the teacher graded exams or projects "on a curve," you are familiar with the most common form that such competition takes in schools. What the teacher does is compare each student's score with the score of every other student in that class. The few students who achieve the highest scores receive the top grade, regardless of the actual level of their scores. Then a predetermined number of B's, C's, D's, and F's are awarded. Because the resulting distribution of grades looks something like the outline of a bell, it is often referred to as a "bell-shaped curve" (which explains the origin of the term "grading on the curve").

There are at least two reasons that this practice may damage a student's sense of industry:

1. Grading on the curve limits the top rewards to a relatively small number of students regardless of each student's actual level of performance. If the quality of instruction is good and students learn most of what has been assigned, the range of scores will be relatively small. Consider the impact to your sense of industry if you respond correctly to 85 percent of the questions on an exam but earn only a grade of C. The same problem exists when, for whatever reasons, all students perform poorly. How much pride can you have in a grade of A or B when you know it is based on a low success rate? The senior author of this book endured a college chemistry class in which the top grade on an exam went to a student who answered only 48 percent of the questions correctly.

2. Curve grading also guarantees that some students have to receive failing grades regardless of their actual level of performance. Students who are forced into this unhealthy type of competition (there are acceptable forms of competition, which we describe in Chapter 13) may develop a sense of inadequacy and inferiority that will hamper them for the rest of their school career.

The solution to this problem is to base grades on realistic and attainable standards that are worked out ahead of time and communicated to the students. In Chapter 15 on assessment, we describe how to do this. Also, in Chapter 13, we describe several instructional approaches that will likely have a beneficial impact on students' sense of industry because they all promote learning and a sense of accomplishment. In general, they establish a classroom atmosphere in which students feel accepted for who they are and

Students' sense of industry hampered by unhealthy competition for grades

## pause & reflect

Suppose you were an elementary school teacher. What kinds of things would you do to help your students attain a sense of industry rather than inferiority? How would you help them feel more capable and productive? What would you avoid doing?

## Take a Stand!

### Promote Industry; Stamp Out Inferiority

For some educators, parents, and educational policymakers, an important purpose of education is to sort children into ability categories by forcing them to compete for a limited number of top grades. We strongly oppose such an approach and urge you to do the same because it promotes a sense of inferiority in most students by interfering with the development of such important characteristics

as self-efficacy, self-worth, self-regulated learning skills, and intrinsic motivation. The evidence in support of this stand can be found in most of the subsequent chapters in this book. Instead, emphasize to students and others that a more relevant and useful goal is to help all students develop the attitudes, values, and cognitive skills that lead to high levels of meaningful learning.

*HM TeacherPrepSPACE*

Do you agree that grading on a curve can promote a sense of inferiority for those who do not earn the top grades? Go to the textbook's student website and select the Take a Stand! section to find out more about this and other controversial issues.

---

understand that the teacher is as interested in their success as they are. These goals are accomplished by providing clear expectations as to what students should be able to do after a unit of instruction, designing lessons that are logical and meaningful, and using teaching methods that support effective learning processes.

## Helping Students Formulate an Identity

The most complex of Erikson's stages is identity versus role confusion; he wrote more extensively about this stage than any other. Because this stage is often misunderstood, let's use Erikson's own words to describe the concept of **identity:** "An optimal sense of identity . . . is experienced merely as

> Identity: accepting one's body, having goals, getting recognition

a sense of psychosocial well-being. Its most obvious concomitants are a feeling of being at home in one's body, a sense of 'knowing where one is going' and an inner assuredness of anticipated recognition from those who count" (1968, p. 165). As you may know from your own experience or the experiences of others, the process of identity formation is not always smooth, and it does not always follow the same path. But by being aware of the problems and uncertainties that adolescents may experience as they try to develop a sense of who they are, you can help them positively resolve this major developmental milestone.

## pause & reflect

American high schools are often criticized for not helping adolescents resolve identity problems. Do you agree? Why? How could schools improve?

**Taking a Psychosocial Moratorium**   One aspect of identity formation that often causes difficulty for adolescents is defining the kind of work they want to do—in other words, choosing a career. For individuals who are unprepared to make a career choice, Erikson suggested the possibility of a **psychosocial moratorium.** This is a period marked by a delay of commitment. Such a postponement occurred in Erikson's own life: after leaving high school, he spent several years wandering around Europe without making any firm decision about the sort of job he would seek. Under ideal circumstances, a psychosocial moratorium should be a period of adventure and exploration, having a positive, or at least neutral, impact on the individual and society.

> Psychosocial moratorium delays commitment

## Adolescent Identity Statuses

> Adolescents exhibit a particular process, called an identity status, for establishing an identity

Erikson's observations on identity formation have been usefully extended by James Marcia's notion of **identity statuses** (1966, 1980, 1991, 2002). Identity statuses, of which there are four, are styles or processes "for handling the psychosocial task of establishing a sense of identity" (Waterman & Archer, 1990, p. 35). Marcia (1980) developed this idea as a way to test scientifically the validity of Erikson's notions about identity.

Marcia established the four identity statuses after he had conducted semistructured interviews with a selected sample of male youths. The interviewees were asked their thoughts about a career, their personal value system, their sexual attitudes, and their religious beliefs. Marcia proposed that attainment of a mature identity depends on two variables: crisis and commitment. "Crisis refers to times during

*Identity, as Erikson defines it, involves acceptance of one's body, knowing where one is going, and recognition from those who count. A high school graduate who is pleased with his or her appearance, has already decided on a college major, and is admired by parents, relatives, and friends is likely to experience a sense of psychosocial well-being.*

adolescence when the individual seems to be actively involved in choosing among alternative occupations and beliefs. Commitment refers to the degree of personal investment the individual expresses in an occupation or belief" (1967, p. 119). Subsequent research has shown that exploring and making commitments to interpersonal relationships also contribute to identity formation (Allison & Schultz, 2001; Marcia, 2001, 2002).

After analyzing interview records with these two criteria in mind, Marcia established four identity statuses, described in Table 3.1, that vary in their degree of crisis and commitment:

- Identity diffusion
- Foreclosure
- Moratorium
- Identity achievement

The moratorium and identity achievement statuses are generally thought to be more developmentally mature than the foreclosure and identity diffusion statuses because individuals exhibiting moratorium and identity achievement have either evaluated alternatives and made a commitment or are actively involved in obtaining and evaluating information in preparation for a commitment (Marcia, 2001). Support for the hypothesized superiority of the identity achievement status was provided by Anne Wallace-Broscious, Felicisima Serafica, and Samuel Osipow (1994). They found that high school students who had attained the identity achievement status scored higher on measures of career planning and career certainty than did students in the moratorium or diffusion statuses.

As you read the brief descriptions of each identity type in Table 3.1, keep a few points in mind. First, the more mature identity statuses are slow to evolve and are found in a relatively small percentage of individuals. Among one sample of sixth, seventh, and eighth graders, 12 percent were in the moratorium status and 9 percent had reached the identity achievement status (Allison & Schultz, 2001). Among adults, only about 33 percent undergo the exploration and identity construction process that characterizes the achievement status (Marcia, 1999).

Second, an identity status is not a once-and-for-all accomplishment; identity can continue to undergo developmental change in adulthood (Fadjukoff, Pulkkinen, & Kokko, 2005). If an ego-shattering event (loss of a job, divorce) occurs later in life, individuals who have reached identity achievement, for example, may find themselves uncertain about old values and behavior patterns and once again in crisis. But for most individuals, a new view of oneself is eventually created. This cycling between certainty and doubt as to who one is and where one fits in society may well occur in each of the last three of Erikson's stages and is often referred to as a MAMA (moratorium-achievement-moratorium-achievement) cycle (Marcia, 1999, 2001, 2002).

| Table 3.1 | James Marcia's Identity Statuses | | |
| --- | --- | --- | --- |
| **Identity Status** | **Crisis** | **Commitment** | **Characteristics** |
| Identity diffusion | Not yet experienced. Little serious thought given to occupation, gender roles, values. | Weak. Ideas about occupation, gender roles, values are easily changed as a result of positive and negative feedback. | Not self-directed; disorganized, impulsive, low self-esteem, alienated from parents; avoids getting involved in school work and interpersonal relationships. |
| Foreclosure | Not experienced. May never suffer doubts about identity issues. | Strong. Has accepted and endorsed the values of his or her parents. | Close-minded, authoritarian, low in anxiety; has difficulty solving problems under stress; feels superior to peers; strong identification with and more dependent on parents and other authority figures for guidance and approval than in other statuses. |
| Moratorium | Partially experienced. Has given some thought to identity-related questions. | Weak. Has not achieved satisfactory answers. | Anxious, dissatisfied with school; changes major often, daydreams, engages in intense but short-lived relationships; may temporarily reject parental and societal values. |
| Identity achievement | Fully experienced. Has considered and explored alternative positions regarding occupation, gender roles, values. | Strong. Has made self-chosen commitments to at least some aspects of identity. | Introspective; more planful, rational, and logical in decision making than in other identity statuses; high self-esteem; works effectively under stress; likely to form close interpersonal relationships. Usually the last identity status to emerge. |

SOURCES: Bilsker & Marcia (1991); Cramer (2001); Hoegh & Bourgeois (2002); Kroger (1996); MacKinnon & Marcia (2002); Marcia (1999, 2002); Vondracek, Schulenberg, Skorikov, Gillespie, & Wahlheim (1995).

Individuals in identity diffusion avoid thinking about jobs, roles, values

Individuals in foreclosure unquestioningly endorse parents' goals and values

Individuals in moratorium uncertain about identity

Individuals who have reached identity achievement status have made their own commitments

Finally, because identity is an amalgam of commitments from a number of different domains, only a small percentage (about 20 percent) of adolescents will experience a triumphant sense of having "put it all together." To cite just one example, an adolescent is more likely to have made a firm occupational choice than to be decisive about gender role or religious values (Waterman, 1988).

**Cultural, Ethnic, and Gender Factors in Identity Status**   Although the foreclosure status is the historical norm for adolescents in Western societies, things can and do change. For example, individuals in moratorium were more numerous during the 1960s and 1970s than during the 1980s. This was a time of great social and cultural upheaval (opposition to the war in Vietnam, civil rights demonstrations, the women's movement), and many adolescents reacted to the uncertainty produced by these changes by not making a commitment to occupational, sexual, and political values (Scarr, Weinberg, & Levine, 1986; Waterman, 1988). Also, recent evidence indicates that adolescents are now more likely to be in a moratorium status or an identity achievement status, or in transition between these two statuses, than in the foreclosure status common to earlier generations (Branch & Boothe, 2002; Forbes & Ashton, 1998; Watson & Protinsky, 1991).

Gender differences in identity status are most apparent in the areas of political ideology, family and career priorities, and sexuality. With respect to political beliefs, males are more likely to exhibit a foreclosure process and females a diffusion process. With respect to family and career priorities and sexuality, males are likely to be foreclosed or diffuse, whereas females are likely to express an identity achievement or a moratorium status. These findings indicate that female adolescents are more likely than males to make developmentally advanced decisions in the areas of family and career roles and sexuality. A likely explanation has to do with how the female gender role has and has not changed over the past twenty years. Although most females now work outside the home, they are still expected to have primary responsibility for child rearing (Stier, Lewin-Epstein, Braun, 2001).

A relevant question to ask about Marcia's identity statuses, particularly if you plan to teach in a foreign country or instruct students with different cultural backgrounds, is whether these identity statuses occur only in the United States. The answer appears to be no. Researchers in such diverse countries as Korea, India, Nigeria, Japan, Denmark, Holland, Colombia, and Haiti report finding all four statuses, although the percentage of adolescents and young adults in each status does vary by culture (Portes, Dunham, & Del Castillo, 2000; Scarr et al., 1986).

## Criticisms of Erikson's Theory

Although Erikson's theory has in general been supported by research (Steinberg & Morris, 2001), several aspects have been criticized. For example, although Erikson occasionally carried out research investigations, most of his conclusions were based on personal and subjective interpretations that have been only partly substantiated by controlled investigations of the type that most psychologists value. As a result, there have been only limited checks on Erikson's tendency to generalize from limited experiences. Some of his observations on identity, for example, reflect his own indecision about occupational choice (Sorell & Montgomery, 2001).

Criticisms of Erikson's theory: based largely on personal experience, not applicable to many cultures, gender-biased

Other criticisms focus on Erikson's contention that one's identity is achieved by actively exploring alternatives regarding one's career, ideological beliefs, and interpersonal relationships and then making choices. This is not, in all likelihood, a universal practice. In some societies and cultures, these decisions are, for the most part, made by adults and imposed on adolescents (Marcia, 1999, 2001; Sorell & Montgomery, 2001). There appear to be two basic societal conditions that make it possible for individuals to explore and construct an identity: the willingness to tolerate an extended adolescence that makes a minimal contribution to society, and a certain level of societal wealth. In addition, individuals need to have developed secure attachments to parents and other influential individuals (successful resolution of the trust versus mistrust stage) and a high level of cognitive development (Hoegh & Bourgeois, 2002; Marcia, 1999). The absence of these last two conditions may account for the fact that by adulthood, only about 33 percent of individuals have undergone the exploration and construction processes that characterize the moratorium and achievement statuses.

Some critics, such as Carol Gilligan (1982, 1988), argue that Erikson's stages reflect the personality development of males more accurately than that of females. Gilligan believes that the process and timing of identity formation are different for each gender. Beginning in about fourth grade (the industry versus inferiority stage), girls are as concerned with the nature of interpersonal relationships as they are with achievement, whereas boys focus mainly on achievement. And during adolescence, many young women seem to work through the crises of identity *and* intimacy simultaneously, whereas most young men follow the sequence that Erikson described: identity versus role confusion, then intimacy versus isolation (Gilligan, 1982; Ochse & Plug, 1986; Sorrell & Montgomery, 2001).

If you keep these reservations in mind, you are likely to discover that Erikson's observations (as well as the identity statuses that Marcia described) clarify important aspects of development. Suggestions for Teaching that draw on Erikson's observations follow. (These suggestions might also serve as the nucleus of a section in your reflective journal. Possible journal entries are indicated in the margins, and more can be found on the book's website.)

# Suggestions for Teaching in Your Classroom

## Applying Erikson's Theory of Psychosocial Development

**1** **Keep in mind that certain types of behaviors and relationships may be of special significance at different age levels.**

**JOURNAL ENTRY**
Ways to Apply Erikson's Theory
(Preschool and Kindergarten)

**2** **With younger preschool children, allow plenty of opportunities for free play and experimentation to encourage the development of autonomy, but provide guidance to reduce the possibility that children will experience doubt. Also avoid shaming children for unacceptable behavior.**

**3** **With older preschool children, encourage activities that permit the use of initiative and provide a sense of accomplishment. Avoid making children feel guilty about well-motivated but inconvenient (to you) questions or actions.**

**JOURNAL ENTRY**
Ways to Apply Erikson's Theory
(Elementary Grades)

**4** **During the elementary and middle school years, help children experience a sense of industry by presenting tasks that they can complete successfully.**

Arrange such tasks so that students will know they have been successful. To limit feelings of inferiority, play down comparisons, and encourage cooperation and self-competition. Also try to help jealous children gain satisfaction from their own behavior. (Specific ways to accomplish these goals are described in several later chapters.)

**JOURNAL ENTRY**
Ways to Apply Erikson's Theory
(Secondary Grades)

**5** **At the secondary school level, keep in mind the significance of each student's search for a sense of identity.**

The components of identity that Erikson stressed are acceptance of one's appearance, knowledge about where one is going, and recognition from those who count. Role confusion is most frequently caused by failure to formulate clear ideas about gender roles and by indecision about occupational choice.

The American school system, particularly at the high school level, has been described as a place where individual differences are either ignored or discouraged and negative feedback greatly outweighs positive feedback (Johnson, Farkas, & Bers, 1997; Steinberg, 1996; Toch, 2003). Because you are important to your students, you can contribute to their sense of positive identity by recognizing them as individuals and praising them for their accomplishments. If you become aware that particular students lack recognition from peers because of abrasive qualities or ineptness and if you have the time and opportunity, you might also attempt to encourage social skills.

You might be able to reduce identity problems resulting from indecisiveness about gender roles by having class discussions (for example, in social science courses) centering on changes in attitudes regarding masculinity, femininity, and family responsibilities. You can, for example, encourage boys to become more sensitive to the needs of others and girls to be more achievement oriented. This approach to gender-role development that combines traditional "masculine" and "feminine" behaviors is called **psychological androgyny** (Karniol, Gabay, Ochion, & Harari, 1998; Steinberg, 2005).

Another forum for such discussion is an online bulletin board or class website. Online writing can be conducive to explorations of sensitive issues because it provides a slightly slower, more thoughtful pace and also offers an equal voice to male and female students, even those who feel shy about speaking in class. An online discussion that is carefully moderated by an experienced teacher can both model and explore the territory of psychological androgyny (Woodhill & Samuels, 2004).

Working with your school counselor, you may in some cases be able to help students make decisions about occupational choice by providing them with information (gleaned from classroom performance and standardized test results) about their intellectual capabilities, personality traits, interests, and values. Or you may be able to help students decide whether to apply for admission to college instead of entering the job market after high school graduation.

**6** **Remember that the aimlessness of some students may be evidence that they are engaging in a psychosocial moratorium. If possible, encourage such individuals to focus on short-term goals while they continue to search for long-term goals.**

There are many ways to enable students to work toward short-term goals, particularly in your classroom. These will be described in detail in later chapters that deal with approaches to instruction and motivation.

**7** **Remain aware that adolescents may exhibit characteristics of different identity status types.**

Some may drift aimlessly; others may be distressed because they realize they lack goals and values. A few high school students may have arrived at self-chosen commitments; others may have accepted the goals and values of their parents.

If you become aware that certain students seem depressed or bothered because they are unable to develop a satisfactory set of personal values, consult your school psychologist or counselor. In addition, you might use the techniques just summarized to help these students experience at least a degree of identity achievement. Perhaps the main value of the identity status concept is that it calls attention to individual differences in the formation of identity. Because students in the foreclosure status will pose few, if any, classroom problems, you must keep in mind that foreclosure is not necessarily desirable for the individual student. Also, those experiencing identity diffusion or moratorium may be so bothered by role confusion that they are unwilling to carry out even simple assignments unless you supply support and incentives.

**HM TeacherPrepSPACE**

If you would like more suggestions for your journal, check the Reflective Journal Questions at the textbook's student website.

# PIAGET: COGNITIVE DEVELOPMENT

## Basic Principles of Piaget's Theory

Jean Piaget (1896–1980) earned his doctorate in biology in 1918 and began a program of research that has been called "the master plan" to address the question, "How does knowledge develop?" (Smith, 2002, p. 515). His theory of intellectual development, reflective of his basic interest in biology as well as knowledge, continues to spur research on the problem of how knowledge develops.

Piaget postulated that human beings inherit two basic tendencies: **organization** (the tendency to systematize and combine processes into coherent general systems) and **adaptation** (the tendency to adjust to the environment). For Piaget, these tendencies governed both physiological and mental functioning. Just as the biological process of digestion transforms food into a form that the body can use, so intellectual processes transform experiences into a form that the child can use in dealing with new situations. And just as biological processes must be kept in a state of balance (through homeostasis), intellectual processes seek a balance through the process of equilibration (a form of self-regulation that all individuals use to bring coherence and stability to their conception of the world).

**Organization**    *Organization* refers to the tendency of all individuals to systematize or combine processes into coherent (logically interrelated) systems. When we think of tulips and roses as subcategories of the more general category *flowers*, instead of as two unrelated categories, we are using organization to aid our thinking process. This organizational capacity makes thinking processes efficient and powerful and allows a better fit, or adaptation, of the individual to the environment.

**Schemes**    Children formulate organized patterns of behavior or thought, known as **schemes,** as they interact with their environment, parents, teachers, and age-mates. Schemes can be behavioral (throwing a ball) or cognitive (realizing that there are many different kinds of balls). Whenever a child encounters a new experience that does not easily fit into an existing scheme, adaptation is necessary.

**Adaptation**    The process of creating a good fit or match between one's conception of reality (one's schemes) and the real-life experiences one encounters is called *adaptation*. According to Piaget, adaptation is accomplished by two subprocesses: **assimilation** and **accommodation.** A child may adapt by either interpreting an experience so that it fits an existing scheme (assimilation) or changing an existing scheme to incorporate the experience (accommodation).

Imagine a six-year-old who goes to an aquarium for the first time and calls the minnows "little fish" and the whales "big fish." In both cases, the child is assimilating—attempting to fit a new experience into an existing scheme (in this case, the conception that all creatures that live in the water are fish). When her parents point out that even though whales live in the water, they are mammals, not fish, the six-year-old begins to accommodate—to modify her existing scheme to fit the new experience she has encountered. Gradually (accommodations are made slowly, over repeated experiences), a new scheme forms that contains nonfish creatures that live in the water.

**Relationships Among Organization, Adaptation, and Schemes**    To give you a basic understanding of Piaget's ideas, we have talked about them as distinct elements. But the concepts are all related. In their drive to be organized, individuals try to have a place for everything (accommodation) so they can put everything in its place (assimilation). The product of organization and adaptation is the creation of new schemes that allow individuals to organize at a higher level and adapt more effectively.

**Equilibration, Disequilibrium, and Learning**    Piaget believed that people are driven to organize their schemes in order to achieve the best possible adaptation to their environment. He called this process **equilibration.** But what motivates people's drive toward equilibration? It is a state of *disequilibrium*, or a perceived discrepancy between an existing scheme and something new. In other words, when people encounter something that is inconsistent with or contradicts what they already know or believe, this experience produces a disequilibrium that they are driven to eliminate (assuming they are sufficiently interested in the new experience to begin with).

*Activities that encourage children to create new ideas or schemes through experimentation, questioning, discussion, and discovery often produce meaningful learning because of the inherent drive toward equilibration.*

A student may wonder why, for example, tomatoes and cucumbers are referred to as fruits in a science text since she has always referred to them as vegetables and has distinguished fruits from vegetables on the basis of sweetness. This discrepancy may cause the student to read the text carefully or ask the teacher for explanation. Gradually the student reorganizes her thinking about the classification of fruits and vegetables in terms of edible plant roots, stems, leaves, and ovaries so that it is more consistent with the expert view. These processes are two sides of the learning coin: for equilibration to occur, disequilibrium must already have occurred. Disequilibrium can occur spontaneously within an individual through maturation and experience, or it can be stimulated by someone else (such as a teacher).

**Constructing Knowledge**  Meaningful learning, then, occurs when people *create* new ideas, or knowledge (rules and hypotheses that explain things), from existing information (for example, facts, concepts, and procedures). To solve a problem, we have to search our memory for information that can be used to fashion a solution. Using information can mean experimenting, questioning, reflecting, discovering, inventing, and discussing. This process of creating knowledge to solve a problem and eliminate a disequilibrium is referred to by Piagetian psychologists and educators as **constructivism** (Brooks & Brooks, 2001; Elkind, 2005; Haney & McArthur, 2002; Yager, 2000). It is a powerful notion that will reappear in later chapters and in other forms. (The Pause and Reflect features in each chapter are intended to stimulate constructivist thinking, as is the manner in which we encourage you to set up and use your journal for reflective thinking and teaching.)

## Stages of Cognitive Development

Organization and adaptation are what Piaget called *invariant functions*. This means that these thought processes function the same way for infants, children, adolescents, and adults. Schemes, however, are not invariant. They undergo systematic change at particular points in time. As a result, there are real differences between the ways younger children and older children think and between the ways children and adults think. The schemes of infants and toddlers, for example, are sensory and motor in nature. They are often referred to as *habits* or *reflexes*. In early childhood, schemes gradually become more mental in nature; during this period, they are called *concepts* or *categories*. Finally, by late adolescence or early adulthood, schemes are complex and result in what we call *strategic* or *planful* behavior.

On the basis of his studies, Piaget concluded that schemes evolve through four stages. The *rate* at which a particular child proceeds through these stages varies, but Piaget believed the *sequence* is the same in all children.

Piaget's four stages are described in the following sections. To help you grasp the sequence of these stages, Table 3.2 briefly outlines the range of ages to which they generally apply and their distinguishing characteristics.

Although Piaget used this "stage" or stair-step metaphor to describe the pattern of cognitive development, don't be misled into thinking that children jump from one stage to the next. In trying to understand certain concepts or solve certain problems, children may on some occasions use a more advanced kind of thinking but on other occasions revert to an earlier, less sophisticated form. Over time, the more advanced concepts and strategies supplant the less sophisticated ones. Because of this variability in how children think, some developmental psychologists (e.g., Siegler, 1996) prefer to use the metaphor of overlapping waves rather than stages to characterize the nature of cognitive development. But because Piaget spoke in terms of stages, we will as well.

| Sensorimotor stage: schemes reflect sensory and motor experiences

**Sensorimotor Stage (Infants and Toddlers)**    Up to the age of two, children acquire understanding primarily through sensory impressions and motor activities. Therefore, Piaget called this the *sensorimotor stage*. Because infants are unable to move around much on their own during the first months of postnatal existence, they develop schemes primarily by exploring their own bodies and senses. After toddlers learn to walk and manipulate things, however, they get into everything and build up a sizable repertoire of schemes involving external objects and situations.

An important cognitive development milestone, *object permanence*, occurs between the fourth and eighth months. Prior to this point, the phrase "out of sight, out of mind" is literally true. Infants treat objects that leave their field of vision as if they no longer exist. When they drop an object from their hands or when an object at which they are looking is covered, for example, they do not search for it. As object permanence develops, children's intentional search behaviors become increasingly apparent.

Most children under age two are able to use schemes they have mastered to engage in mental as well as physical trial-and-error behavior. By age two, toddlers' schemes have become more mental in nature. You can see this in the way toddlers imitate the behavior of others. They imitate people they have not previously observed, they imitate the behavior of animals, and, most important, they imitate even when the model is no longer present (this is called *deferred imitation*). These types of imitative behaviors show toddlers' increasing ability to think in terms of symbols.

| **Table 3.2** | Piaget's Stages of Cognitive Development | |
|---|---|---|
| **Stage** | **Age Range** | **Characteristics** |
| Sensorimotor | Birth to two years | Develops schemes primarily through sense and motor activities. Recognizes permanence of objects not seen. |
| Preoperational | Two to seven years | Gradually acquires ability to conserve and decenter but not capable of operations and unable to mentally reverse actions. |
| Concrete operational | Seven to eleven years | Capable of operations but solves problems by generalizing from concrete experiences. Not able to manipulate conditions mentally unless they have been experienced. |
| Formal operational | Eleven years and older | Able to deal with abstractions, form hypotheses, solve problems systematically, engage in mental manipulations. |

Preoperational stage: child forms many new schemes but does not think logically

Perceptual centration, irreversibility, egocentrism: barriers to logical thought

**Preoperational Stage (Preschool and Primary Grades)** The thinking of preschool and primary grade children (roughly two to seven years old) centers on mastery of symbols (such as words), which permits them to benefit much more from past experiences. Piaget believed that many symbols are derived from mental imitation and involve both visual images and bodily sensations (notice how the schemes of this stage incorporate and build on the schemes of the previous stage). Although the thinking at this stage is much more sophisticated than that of one- and two-year-olds, preschool children are limited in their ability to use their new symbol-oriented schemes. From an adult perspective, their thinking and behavior are illogical.

When Piaget used the term *operation*, he meant an action carried out through logical thinking. *Preoperational*, then, means prelogical. The main impediments to logical thinking that preschoolers have to overcome are *perceptual centration, irreversibility*, and *egocentrism*. You can see these impediments at work most clearly when children attempt to solve **conservation** problems—those that test their ability to recognize that certain properties stay the same despite a change in appearance or position.

One of the best-known conservation problems is conservation of continuous quantity. A child is taken to a quiet place by an experimenter, who then pours water (or juice or beans or whatever else) into identical short glasses until the child agrees that each contains an equal amount. Then the water is poured from one of these glasses into a tall, thin glass, and the child is asked, "Is there more water in this glass [the experimenter points to the tall glass] or this one [the short glass]?" Immediately after the child answers, the experimenter asks, "Why do you think so?" If the child's response is evasive or vague, the experimenter continues to probe until the child's underlying thought processes become clear.

In carrying out this experiment (and many others similar to it) with children of different ages, Piaget discovered that children below the age of six or so maintain that there is more water in the tall, thin glass than in the short, squat glass. Although they agree at the beginning of the experiment that the water in the two identical glasses is equal, young children stoutly insist that after the water has been poured, the taller glass contains more. When asked, "Why do you think so?" many preschool children immediately and confidently reply, "Because it's taller." Children over the age of six or so, by contrast, are more likely to reply, "Well, it *looks* as if there's more water in this one because it's taller, but they're really the same."

One reason preoperational stage children have difficulty solving conservation problems (as well as other problems that require logical thinking) is **perceptual centration:** the strong tendency to focus attention on only one characteristic of an object or aspect of a problem or event at a time. The young child focuses only on the height of the water in the two containers and ignores the differences in width and volume. Another way to put this is to say that the child has not yet mastered **decentration**—the ability to think of more than one quality at a time—and is therefore not inclined to contemplate alternatives.

The second impediment to logical thinking is **irreversibility.** This means that young children cannot mentally pour the water from the tall, thin glass back into the short, squat one (thereby proving to themselves that the glasses contain the same amount of water). For the same reason, these youngsters do not understand the logic behind simple mathematical reversals (4 + 5 = 9; 9 − 5 = 4).

Egocentrism: assumption that others see things the same way

The third major impediment is **egocentrism.** When applied to preschool children, *egocentric* does not mean selfish or conceited. It means that youngsters find it difficult, if not impossible, to take another person's point of view. In their conversations and in experimental situations in which they are asked to describe how something would look if viewed by someone else, preschool children reveal that they often have difficulty seeing things from another person's perspective (Piaget & Inhelder, 1956). They seem to assume that others see things the same way they see them. As a result, attempts to explain the logic behind conservation are usually met with quizzical looks and the insistence (some would mistakenly call it stubbornness) that the tall, thin glass contains more water.

**Concrete Operational Stage (Elementary to Early Middle School)**    Through formal instruction, informal experiences, social contact, and maturation, children over the age of seven gradually become less influenced by perceptual centration, irreversibility, and egocentrism (DeVries, 1997). Schemes are developing that allow a greater understanding of such logic-based tasks as conservation (matter is neither created nor destroyed but simply changes shape or form or position), class inclusion (the construction of hierarchical relationships among related classes of items), and seriation (the arrangement of items in a particular order).

But operational thinking is limited to objects that are actually present or that children have experienced concretely and directly. For this reason, Piaget described the stage from approximately seven to eleven years as that of *concrete operations*. The nature of the concrete operational stage can be illustrated by the child's mastery of different kinds of conservation.

By the age of seven, most children are able to explain correctly that water poured from a short, squat glass into a tall, thin glass is still the same amount of water. Being able to solve the water-pouring problem, however, does not guarantee that a seven-year-old will be able to solve a similar problem involving two balls of clay. A child who has just explained why a tall glass of water contains the same amount as a short one may inconsistently maintain a few moments later that rolling one of two equally sized balls of clay into an elongated shape causes the rolled one to appear as if it contains more clay.

Children in the primary and early elementary grades tend to react to each situation in terms of concrete experiences. The tendency to solve problems by generalizing from one situation to a similar situation does not occur with any degree of consistency until the end of the elementary school years.

Nevertheless, children in the concrete operational stage are often more capable of learning advanced concepts than most people realize. According to the National Research Council (2000), for example, the fundamental abilities that elementary students (K–4) are expected to acquire include asking questions about objects, conducting simple observations, using simple equipment (such as a magnifying glass) to gather data and extend the senses, and constructing and communicating explanations.

**Formal Operational Stage (Middle School, High School, and Beyond)**    When children *do* reach the point of being able to generalize and engage in mental trial and error by thinking up hypotheses and testing them in their heads, they are at the stage of *formal operations*, according to Piaget. The term *formal* reflects the ability to respond to the *form* of a problem rather than its content and to *form* hypotheses. For example, the formal operational thinker can read the analogies "5 is to 15 as 1 is to 3" and "penny is to dollar as year is to century" and realize that despite the different content, the form of the two problems is identical (both analogies are based on ratios). In the same way, the formal thinker can understand and use complex language forms: proverbs ("Strike while the iron is hot"), metaphor ("Procrastination is the thief of time"), sarcasm, and satire.

We can see the nature of formal operational thinking and how it differs from concrete operational thinking by looking at a simplified version of Piaget's rod-bending experiment. Adolescents are given a basin filled with water, a set of metal rods of varying lengths, and a set of weights. The rods are attached to the edge of the basin and the weights to the ends of the rods. The subject's task is to figure out how much weight is required to bend a rod just enough to touch the water. Let's say that our hypothetical subject picks out the longest rod in the set (which is 9 inches long), attaches it to the edge of the basin, and puts just enough weight on the end of it to get it to touch the water. This observation is then recorded. Successively shorter rods are selected, and the same procedure is carried out. At some point, the subject

---

Concrete operational stage: child is capable of mentally reversing actions but generalizes only from concrete experiences

**pause & reflect**

From Piaget's point of view, why is it incorrect to think of children as "small adults"?

Formal operational stage: child is able to deal with abstractions, form hypotheses, engage in mental manipulations

*Students who are within Piaget's formal operational stage of cognitive development are capable of solving problems by systematically using abstract symbols to represent real objects.*

comes to the 4-inch rod. This rod does not touch the water even when all of the weights have been attached to it. There are, however, three more rods, all of which are shorter than the last one tested.

This is where the formal and concrete operators part company. The formal operational thinker reasons that if all of the available weights are not sufficient to bend the 4-inch rod enough to touch the water, the same will be true of the remaining rods. In essence, the rest of the experiment is done mentally and symbolically. The concrete operational thinker, however, continues trying out each rod and recording each observation independent of the others. Although both subjects reach the same conclusion, the formal operator does so through a more powerful and efficient process.

But remember that new schemes develop gradually. Although adolescents can sometimes deal with mental abstractions representing concrete objects, most twelve-year-olds solve problems haphazardly, using trial and error. It is not until the end of the high school years that adolescents are likely to approach a problem by forming hypotheses, mentally sorting out solutions, and systematically testing the most promising leads.

Some interpreters of Piaget (e.g., Wadsworth, 1996) note that a significant aspect of formal thought is that it causes the adolescent to concentrate more on possibilities than on realities. This is the ability that Erikson and others (e.g., Kalbaugh & Haviland, 1991) suggest is instrumental in the emergence of the identity crisis. At the point when older adolescents can become aware of all the factors that have to be considered in choosing a career and can imagine what it might be like to be employed, some may feel so threatened and confused that they postpone the final choice. Yet the same capability can also help resolve the identity crisis because adolescents can reason about possibilities in a logical manner. An adolescent girl, for example, may consider working as a pediatrician, teacher, or child psychologist in an underprivileged environment because she has always enjoyed and sought out activities that allowed her to interact with children and has also been concerned with the effects of deprivation on development.

Although mastery of formal thought equips the older adolescent with impressive intellectual skills, it may also lead to a tendency for the burgeoning formal thinker to become preoccupied with abstract and theoretical matters. Barry Wadsworth makes this point in the following way:

> If motivated to do so, and if in possession of the necessary content, adolescents with formal reasoning can reason as logically as adults. The tools for an evaluation of intellectual arguments are formed and fully functional. One of the major affective differences between the thought of the adolescent and that of the adult is that, initially in their use of formal operations, adolescents apply a criterion of pure logic in evaluating reasoning about human events. If it is logical it is good, right, and so on. This is the nature of their egocentrism. Adolescents lack a full appreciation of the way in which the world is ordered. With the capability for generating endless hypotheses, an adolescent believes that what is best is what is logical. He or she does not yet differentiate between the logical world as she thinks it to be and the "real" world. (1996, p. 124)

This inability to differentiate between the world as the adolescent thinks it should be and the world as it actually is was referred to by David Elkind (1968) as **adolescent egocentrism.** This occurs when high school students use their emerging formal operational capabilities to think about themselves and the thinking of others. Because adolescents are preoccupied with themselves and how they appear to others, they assume that peers and adults are equally interested in what they think and do. This is why, in Elkind's view, the typical adolescent is so self-conscious. The major difference between the egocentrism of childhood and that of adolescence is summed up in Elkind's observation: "The child is egocentric in the sense that he is unable to take another person's point of view. The adolescent, on the other hand, takes the other person's point of view to an extreme degree" (1968, p. 153).

Elkind believes that adolescent egocentrism also explains why the peer group becomes such a potent force in high school:

> Adolescent egocentrism . . . accounts, in part, for the power of the peer group during this period. The adolescent is so concerned with the reactions of others toward him, particularly his peers, that he is willing to do many things which are opposed to all of his previous training and to his own best interests. At the same time, this egocentric impression that he is always on stage may help to account for the many and varied adolescent attention-getting maneuvers. (1968, p. 154)

Although the concept of adolescent egocentrism is widely accepted among researchers, ascribing its cause to formal operational thinking gets mixed support. Some studies have found a relationship, while other studies have not (Rycek, Stuhr, & McDermott, 1998; Vartanian, 2000).

## The Role of Social Interaction and Instruction in Cognitive Development

**How Social Interaction Affects Cognitive Development**    When it comes to social experiences, Piaget clearly believed that peer interactions do more to spur cognitive development than do interactions with adults. The reason is that children are more likely to discuss, analyze, and debate the merits of another child's view of some issue (such as who should have which toy or what the rules of a game should be) than they are to take serious issue with an adult. The balance of power between children and adults is simply too unequal. Not only are most children quickly taught that adults know more and use superior reasoning, but also the adult always gets to have the last word: argue too long, and it's off to bed with no dessert. But when children interact with one another, the outcome is more dependent on how well each child uses her wits (Light & Littleton, 1999).

It is the need to understand the ideas of a peer or playmate in order to formulate responses to those ideas that leads to less egocentrism and the development of new, more complex mental schemes. Put another way, a strongly felt sense of cognitive

---

*Adolescent egocentrism: adolescents preoccupied with their own view of the world and how they appear to others*

*Piaget: cognitive development more strongly influenced by peers than by adults*

conflict automatically impels the child to strive for a higher level of equilibrium. Formal instruction by an adult expert simply does not have the same impact regardless of how well designed it might be. That is why parents and teachers are often surprised to find children agreeing on some issue after having rejected an adult's explanation of the very same thing. Thus, educational programs that are patterned after Piaget's ideas usually provide many opportunities for children to interact socially and discover through these interactions basic ideas about how the world works (Crain, 2000; Rogoff, 1990; Tudge & Winterhoff, 1993). In Chapter 13, "Approaches to Instruction," we describe in detail a systematic way to accomplish this goal: cooperative learning. Proof of the feasibility of this approach can be found in several summaries and analyses of the effects of cooperative learning (see, e.g., Johnson & Johnson, 1995; Qin, Johnson, & Johnson, 1995; and Slavin, 1995).

**How Instruction Affects Cognitive Development**    Although Piaget believed that formal instruction by expert adults will not significantly stimulate cognitive development, not all psychologists have been willing to accept this conclusion at face value. Over the past thirty years, dozens of experiments have been conducted to determine whether it is possible to teach preoperational stage children to understand and use concrete operational schemes or to teach students in the concrete operational stage to grasp formal operational reasoning.

The typical conclusion of psychologists who have analyzed and evaluated this body of research ranges from uncertainty to cautious optimism (see, e.g., Case, 1975; Good & Brophy, 1995; Nagy & Griffiths, 1982; Sprinthall, Sprinthall, & Oja, 1998). The uncertainty results from shortcomings in the way some studies were carried out and disagreements about what constitutes evidence of true concrete operational thinking or formal operational thinking.

The cautious optimism comes from the work of Michael Shayer and others (Adey, Shayer, & Yates, 2001; Shayer, 1999) in England. They found that schools that participated in a science instruction program called CASE (Cognitive Acceleration through Science Education), which combined aspects of the cognitive developmental theories of Piaget and Vygotsky, had a much greater percentage of thirteen- and fourteen-year-olds at or above the early formal operational stage than did non-CASE schools. Furthermore, after two years in the program, CASE students scored higher on national tests of mathematics, science, and English than did students in the non-CASE schools. CASE programs have also been implemented to help preoperational stage children acquire concrete operational schemes (Robertson, 2001) and to help teachers accelerate the cognitive development of students with various learning impediments (Simon, 2002).

| | The safest conclusion that can be drawn from this literature (see, for example, Sigelman & Shaffer, 1991; Sprinthall et al., 1998) is that children who are in the process of developing the schemes that will govern the next stage of cognitive functioning can, with good-quality instruction, be helped to refine those schemes a bit faster than would normally be the case. For example, teachers can teach the principle of conservation by using simple explanations and concrete materials and allowing children to manipulate the materials. This means that teachers should nurture the process of cognitive growth at any particular stage by presenting lessons in a form consistent with but slightly more advanced than the students' existing schemes. The objective here is to help students assimilate and accommodate new and different experiences as efficiently as possible. |

*Instruction can accelerate development of schemes that have begun to form*

## Criticisms of Piaget's Theory

*Piaget's theory underestimates children's abilities*

**Underestimating Children's Capabilities**    Among the thousands of articles that have been published in response to Piaget's findings are many that offer critiques of his work. Some psychologists argue that Piaget underestimated children's abilities not only because he imposed stringent criteria for inferring the presence of particular cognitive abilities, but also because the tasks he used were often complex and far removed from children's real-life experiences (Case, 1999). The term *preoperational*, for instance, stresses what is absent rather than what is present. Over the past two decades, researchers have focused more on what preoperational children *can* do. The results (summarized by Kamii, 2000; Siegler, 1998) suggest that preschoolers' cognitive abilities are more advanced in some areas than Piaget's work suggests.

**Overestimating Adolescents' Capabilities**    Other evidence suggests that Piaget may have overestimated the formal thinking capabilities of adolescents. Norman Sprinthall and Richard Sprinthall (1987) reported that only 33 percent of a group of high school seniors could apply formal operational reasoning to scientific problem solving. Research summarized by Michael Shayer (1997) indicates that only 20 percent of children exhibit well-developed formal operational thinking by the end of adolescence. According to these studies, formal reasoning seems to be the exception, not the rule, throughout adolescence.

A study of French adolescents (Flieller, 1999) reported similar percentages but also sought to determine if a new pattern had emerged. Of a group of ten- to twelve-year-olds who were tested on formal operational tasks in 1972, only 9 percent were at the beginning of that stage and only 1 percent were mature formal operators. The percentages for a group of ten- to twelve-year-olds tested in 1993 were just slightly higher: 13 percent and 3 percent, respectively. Significantly larger differences were noted, however, between two groups of thirteen- to fifteen-year-olds. Among those tested in 1967, 26 percent were early formal operators and 9 percent were mature formal operators. But among those tested in 1996, 40 percent were early formal operators and 15 percent were mature formal operators. The author of this study suggested that the increase in formal operational thinking among thirteen- to fifteen-year-olds may be attributable in part to teaching practices (such as creating tables to display information and using tree diagrams to clarify grammatical structure) that foster the development of formal operational schemes.

**Vague Explanations for Cognitive Growth**    Piaget's theory has also been criticized for its vagueness in specifying the factors that are responsible for cognitive growth. Why, for example, do children give up conserving responses in favor of nonconserving responses at a particular age?

Robert Siegler (1996) has suggested an explanation: He believes that variability in children's thinking plays an influential role. For example, it is not uncommon to hear children use on successive occasions different forms of a given verb, as in "I *ate* it," "I *eated* it," and "I *ated* it." Similar variability has been found in the use of memory strategies (five-year-old and eight-year-old children do not always rehearse information they want to remember), addition rules, time-telling rules, and block-building tasks. Siegler's explanation is that variability gives the child a range of plausible options about how to deal with a particular problem. The child then tries them out in an attempt to see which one produces the best adaptation. Note the use of the qualifying word *plausible*. Most children do not try out any and all possible solutions to a problem. Instead they stick to possibilities that are logically consistent with underlying principles of the problem. Once children have acquired a logical explanation for solving problems, they learn more and persist longer (Siegler & Svetina, 2006).

**Cultural Differences**    Questions have also been raised as to whether children from different cultures develop intellectually in the manner Piaget described. The answer at this point is both yes and no. The sequence of stages appears to be universal, but the rate of development may vary from one culture to another (Dasen & Heron, 1981; Hughes & Noppe, 1991; Leadbeater, 1991; Rogoff & Chavajay, 1995).

Although children in Western industrialized societies (like the United States) usually are not given baby-sitting responsibilities until they are at least ten years old

*Most adolescents are not formal operational thinkers*

*Sequence of stages uniform across cultures but rate of development varies*

because their high level of egocentrism prevents them from considering the needs of the other child, Mayan children in Mexican villages as young as age five play this role because their culture stresses the development of cooperative behavior (Sameroff & McDonough, 1994).

Research conducted during the 1970s found that individuals living in non-Western cultures who had little formal education did not engage in formal operational thinking. Although these same people used concrete operational schemes when tested with the kinds of tasks Piaget used, they usually did so at a later age than the Swiss children Piaget originally studied. This result was attributed to their lack of schooling, which left them unfamiliar with the language and conventions of formal testing. When concrete operational tasks were conducted with materials that were part of these people's everyday lives (such as asking children from Zambia to reproduce a pattern with strips of wire rather than with paper and pencil), they performed as well as Western children who drew the patterns on paper (Rogoff & Chavajay, 1995).

Now that you are familiar with Piaget's theory of cognitive development, you can formulate specific classroom applications. You might use the Suggestions for Teaching for the grade level you expect to teach as the basis for a section in your journal.

## pause & reflect

Noting that American schoolchildren score lower than many European and Asian children on standardized achievement tests, critics argue that U.S. formal schooling should begin earlier than age five and should focus on basic reading and math skills. In light of research on Piaget's theories, what do you think of this proposal?

# Suggestions for Teaching in Your Classroom

## Applying Piaget's Theory of Cognitive Development

### GENERAL GUIDELINES

**1** **Focus on what children at each stage can do, and avoid what they cannot meaningfully understand.**

This implication must be interpreted carefully, as recent research has shown that children at the preoperational and concrete operational levels can do more than Piaget believed. In general, however, it is safe to say that since preoperational stage children (preschoolers, kindergartners, most first and some second graders) can use language and other symbols to stand for objects, they should be given many opportunities to describe and explain things through the use of speech, artwork, body movement, role play, and musical performance. Although you can introduce the concepts of conservation, seriation, class inclusion, time, space, and number, attempts at mastering them should probably be postponed until children are in the concrete operational stage.

Concrete operational stage children (grades 3–6) can be given opportunities to master such mental processes as ordering, seriating, classifying, reversing, multiplying, dividing, subtracting, and adding by manipulating concrete objects or symbols. Although a few fifth and sixth graders may be capable of dealing with abstractions, most exercises that involve theorizing, hypothesizing, or generalizing should be done with concrete objects or symbols.

Formal operational stage children (grades 7 through high school) can be given activities that require hypothetical-deductive reasoning, reflective thinking, analysis, synthesis, and evaluation.

**2**  **Because individuals differ in their rates of intellectual growth, gear instructional materials and activities to each student's developmental level.**

**3**  **Because intellectual growth occurs when individuals attempt to eliminate a disequilibrium, instructional lessons and materials that introduce new concepts should provoke interest and curiosity and be moderately challenging in order to maximize assimilation and accommodation.**

**4**  **Although information (facts, concepts, procedures) can be efficiently transmitted from teacher to student through direct instruction, knowledge (rules and hypotheses) is best created by each student through the mental and physical manipulation of information.**

Accordingly, lesson plans should include opportunities for activity, manipulation, exploration, discussion, and application of information. Small-group science projects are one example of how to implement this goal.

**5**  **Because students' schemes at any given time are an outgrowth of earlier schemes, point out to them how new ideas relate to their old ideas and extend their understanding. Memorization of information for its own sake should be avoided.**

**6**  **Begin lessons with concrete objects or ideas, and gradually shift explanations to a more abstract and general level.**

## PRESCHOOL, ELEMENTARY, AND MIDDLE SCHOOL GRADES[2]

**JOURNAL ENTRY**
Ways to Apply Piaget's Theory
(Preschool, Elementary, and
Middle Grades)

**1**  **Become thoroughly familiar with Piaget's theory so that you will be aware of how your students organize and synthesize ideas.**

You may gain extra insight if you analyze your own thinking, since you are likely to discover that in some situations, you operate at a concrete rather than an abstract level.

**2**  **If possible, assess the level and the type of thinking of each child in your class. Ask individual children to perform some of Piaget's experiments, and spend most of your time listening to each child explain her reactions.**

**3**  **Remember that learning through activity and direct experience is essential. Provide plenty of materials and opportunities for children to learn on their own.**

**4**  **Arrange situations to permit social interaction, so that children can learn from one another.**

Hearing others explain their views is a natural way for students to learn that not everyone sees things the same way. The placement of a few advanced thinkers with less mature thinkers is more likely to facilitate this process than is homogeneous grouping.

**5**  **Plan learning experiences to take into account the level of thinking attained by an individual or group.**

---

[2] These guidelines are adapted from Elkind (1989); Ginsburg and Opper (1988); Kamii (2000); Singer and Revenson (1996); and Wadsworth (1996).

Encourage children to classify things on the basis of a single attribute before you expose them to problems that involve relationships among two or more attributes. Ask many questions, and give your students many opportunities to explain their interpretations of experiences so that you can remain aware of their level of thinking.

**6** **Keep in mind the possibility that students may be influenced by egocentric speech and thought.**

Consider the possibility that each child may assume that everyone else has the same conception of a word that he or she has. If confusion becomes apparent or if a child becomes impatient about failure to communicate, request an explanation in different terms. Or ask several children to explain their conception of an object or a situation.

### MIDDLE SCHOOL AND SECONDARY GRADES[3]

**JOURNAL ENTRY**
Ways to Apply Piaget's Theory
(Middle School and Secondary Grades)

**1** **Become well acquainted with the nature of concrete operational thinking and formal thought so that you can recognize when your students are resorting to either type or a combination of the two.**

**2** **To become aware of the type of thinking that individual students use, ask them to explain how they arrived at solutions to problems.**

Do this as part of your classroom curriculum or in response to experimental situations similar to those that Piaget devised.

**3** **Teach students how to solve problems more systematically (suggestions for doing this will be provided in later chapters), and provide opportunities for hands-on science experiments.**

**4** **Keep in mind that some high school students may be more interested in possibilities than in realities.**

If class discussions become unrealistically theoretical and hypothetical, call attention to facts and practical difficulties. If students are contemptuous of unsuccessful attempts by adults to solve school, local, national, and international problems, point out the complexity of many situations involving conflicts of interest, perhaps by having students develop arguments for both sides.

**HM TeacherPrepSPACE**

If you would like more suggestions for your journal, check the Reflective Journal Questions at the textbook's student website.

**5** **Allow for the possibility that younger adolescents may go through a period of egocentrism that will cause them to act as if they are always on stage and to be extremely concerned about the reactions of peers.**

# VYGOTSKY: COGNITIVE DEVELOPMENT

From the time Piaget's work first became known to large numbers of American psychologists in the early 1960s until the 1980s, it was the dominant explanation of cognitive development. Not that Piaget didn't have his critics. As the previous section made clear, many psychologists challenged one aspect or another of his work. But there were no competing explanations of cognitive development. Beginning in the early 1980s, however, the ideas of Russian psychologist Lev Vygotsky began to appear in the psychological literature with increasing frequency. Vygotsky, who died from tuberculosis in 1934, was a contemporary of Piaget who had very different

---

[3] Many of these suggestions are derived from points made in Chapter 2 of *Adolescence* (Steinberg, 2005).

views about the major forces that shape learning and thinking, particularly with respect to the roles of culture, social interaction, and formal instruction (Rowe & Wertsch, 2002).

## How One's Culture Affects Cognitive Development

How we think influenced by current social forces and historical cultural forces

Vygotsky's theory of cognitive development is often referred to as a sociocultural theory because it maintains that how we think is a function of both social and cultural forces. If, for example, you were given a list of nouns (such as *plate, box, peach, knife, apple, hoe, cup,* and *potato*) and told to create groupings, you would probably put *plate, knife,* and *cup* in a group labeled utensils and *peach, apple,* and *potato* in a group labeled food. Why? Is there something inherently compelling about those groupings? Not really.

We could just as logically have put *plate, knife,* and *apple* in a group, because we can use the first two to eat the third. But we are more likely to put objects in taxonomic categories than in functional categories because we have been taught by others who organize ideas taxonomically most of the time. And why do we think that way? Because we are the product of a culture that prizes the ability of its members to think at the most abstract levels (which is why Piaget saw formal operations as the most advanced stage of thinking).

Typically, then, parents and schools shape children's thought processes to reflect that which the culture values. So even when individuals are by themselves, what they think and do is the result of cultural values and practices, some of which may stretch back over hundreds or thousands of years, as well as recent social contacts (Wertsch & Tulviste, 1996).

Psychological tools aid and change thought processes

**The Importance of Psychological Tools**    Vygotsky believed that the most important things a culture passes on to its members (and their descendants) are what he called *psychological tools*. These are the cognitive devices and procedures with which we communicate and explore the world around us. They both aid and change our mental functioning. Speech, writing, gestures, diagrams, numbers, chemical formulas, musical notation, rules, and memory techniques are some examples of common psychological tools (Gredler & Shields, 2004).

Early explorers, for example, created maps to help them represent where they had been, communicate that knowledge to others, and plan future trips. Today we use the same type of tool to navigate efficiently over long distances or within relatively compact but complex environments (like large cities). Another example is the use of multiplication. If asked to solve the multiplication problem $343 \times 822$, you would, in all likelihood, quickly and easily come up with the answer, 281,946, by using the following procedure:

$$
\begin{array}{r}
343 \\
\times\ 822 \\
\hline
686 \\
686\phantom{0} \\
2744\phantom{00} \\
\hline
281,946
\end{array}
$$

But you could have produced the same answer by adding 343 to itself 821 times. Why would you automatically opt for the first procedure? Because the culture in which you operate has, through the medium of formal instruction, provided you with a psychological tool called multiplication as a means of more efficiently and accurately solving certain types of complex mathematical problems (Wertsch, 1998).

Children are introduced to a culture's major psychological tools through social interactions with their parents and later through more formal interactions with classroom teachers. Eventually these social interactions are internalized as cognitive processes that are autonomously invoked. As Vygotsky so elegantly put it, "Through others we become ourselves" (Tudge & Scrimsher, 2003, p. 218).

## How Social Interaction Affects Cognitive Development

The difference between Vygotsky's views on the origin and development of cognitive processes and those of other cognitive developmental psychologists is something like the old question, "Which came first: the chicken or the egg?" Influenced by Piaget, many developmental psychologists argue that as children overcome cognitive conflict through the internal processes of assimilation, accommodation, and equilibration, they become more capable of higher-level thinking, and so come to understand better the nature of the world in which they live and their place in it. In other words, cognitive development makes social development possible (see our discussion of Robert Selman's work on the social development of children in Chapter 5).

Cognitive development strongly influenced by those more intellectually advanced

Vygotsky, however, believed that just the opposite was true. He saw social interaction as the primary cause of cognitive development. Unlike Piaget, Vygotsky believed that children gain significantly from the knowledge and conceptual tools handed down to them by those who are more intellectually advanced, whether they are same-age peers, older children, or adults.

Consider, for example, a simple concept like *grandmother*. In the absence of formal instruction, a primary grade child's concept of grandmother is likely to be narrow in scope because it is based on personal experience ("My grandmother is seventy years old, has gray hair, wears glasses, and makes the best apple pie"). But when children are helped to understand the basic nature of the concept with such instructional tools as family tree diagrams, they understand the notion of grandmother (and other types of relatives) on a broader and more general basis. They can then use this concept to compare family structures with friends and, later, to do genealogical research (Tappan, 1998; Tudge & Scrimsher, 2003).

In order for social interactions to produce advances in cognitive development, Vygotsky argued, they have to contain a process called *mediation*. Mediation occurs when a more knowledgeable individual interprets a child's behavior and helps transform it into an internal and symbolic representation that means the same thing to the child as to others (Light & Littleton, 1999; Tudge & Winterhoff, 1993; Wertsch & Tulviste, 1996). Perhaps the following example will help clarify this point: Imagine a child who reaches out to grasp an object that is beyond her reach. A nearby parent thinks the child is pointing at the object and says, "Oh, you want the box of crayons," and retrieves the item for the child. Over time, what began as a grasping action becomes transformed, through the mediation of an adult, into an internalized sign ("I want you to give that object to me") that means the same thing to the child as it does to the adult (Driscoll, 2005). Thus, a child's potential level of mental development can be brought about only by introducing the more advanced thought processes of another person.

## How Instruction Affects Cognitive Development

Vygotsky drew a distinction between the type of information that preschool children learn and the type of information that children who attend school learn (or should learn). During early childhood, children acquire what Vygotsky called **spontaneous concepts.** That is, they learn various facts and concepts and rules (such as how to speak one's native language and how to classify objects in one's environment), but they do so for the most part as a by-product of such other activities as engaging in play and communicating with parents and playmates. This kind of knowledge is unsystematic, unconscious, and directed at the child's everyday concrete experiences. Hence, Vygotsky's use of the term *spontaneous*.

Teachers should help students learn how to use psychological tools

Schooling, however, should be directed to the learning of what Vygotsky called **scientific concepts.** Scientific concepts are the psychological tools that allow us to manipulate our environment consciously and systematically. Vygotsky believed that the proper development of a child's mind depends on learning how to use these

*Jean Piaget believed that children's schemes develop more quickly when children interact with one another than when they interact with adults. But Lev Vygotsky believed that children learn more from the instructional interactions they have with those who are more intellectually advanced, particularly if the instruction is designed to fall within the child's zone of proximal development.*

psychological tools, and this will occur only if classroom instruction is properly designed. This means providing students with explicit and clear verbal definitions as a first step. The basic purpose of instruction, then, is not simply to add one piece of knowledge to another like pennies in a piggy bank but to stimulate and guide cognitive development (Crain, 2000; Rogoff, 1990).

Contemporary psychologists have extended Vygotsky's notions of spontaneous and scientific concepts. They use the term **empirical learning** to refer to the way in which young children acquire spontaneous concepts. The hallmark of empirical learning is that the most observable characteristics of objects and events are noticed and used as a basis for forming general concepts. The main limitation of this approach is that salient characteristics are not necessarily critical or defining characteristics, and it is the latter that form the basis of correct concept formation. For example, in the absence of formal instruction, children come to believe that any utterance that has two or more words is a sentence, that whales are fish, and that bamboo is not a type of grass.

**Theoretical learning,** on the other hand, involves using psychological tools to learn scientific concepts. As these general tools are used repeatedly with a variety of problems, they are gradually internalized and generalized to a wide variety of settings and problem types. Good-quality instruction, in this view, is aimed at helping children move from the very practical empirical learning to the more general theoretical learning and from using psychological tools overtly, with the aid of an adult, to using these tools mentally, without outside assistance (Karpov & Bransford, 1995).

Here's an example that compares the efficacy of the empirical and theoretical approaches: Two groups of six-year-old children were taught how to write the twenty-two letters of the Russian alphabet. Group 1 was taught using the empirical approach. The teacher gave the students a model of each letter, showed them how to write each one, and gave a verbal explanation of how to write each letter. The students then copied each letter under the teacher's supervision. When they produced an acceptable copy of a letter, they were taught the next letter. Group 2 was taught using the theoretical approach. First, students were taught to analyze the shape of each letter so they could identify where the direction of the contour of each line changed. Then they were to place dots in those locations outlining the change in contour. Finally, they were to reproduce the pattern of dots on another part of the page and connect the dots with a pencil.

The speed with which the children in each group learned to produce the letters of the alphabet accurately differed by quite a large margin. The average student in the empirical group needed about 170 trials to learn the first letter and about 20 trials to write the last letter. The number of trials taken to learn all twenty-two letters was about 1,230. The average student in the theoretical group required only about 14 trials to learn how to write the first letter correctly, and from the eighth letter on needed only 1 trial per letter. The number of trials needed to learn all twenty-two letters for the second group was about 60. Furthermore, these students were able to use the general method they were taught to help them learn to write the letters of the Latin and Arabic alphabets (Karpov & Bransford, 1995).

**Instruction and the Zone of Proximal Development**   This discussion of empirical and theoretical learning illustrates Vygotsky's belief that well-designed instruction is like a magnet. If it is aimed slightly ahead of what children know and can do at the present time, it will pull them along, helping them master things they cannot learn on their own. We can illustrate this idea with an experiment that Vygotsky (1986) described. He gave two eight-year-olds of average ability problems that were a bit too difficult for them to solve on their own. (Although Vygotsky did not specify what types of problems they were, imagine that they were math problems.) He then tried to help the children solve the problems by giving them leading questions and hints. He found that one child, with the hints, was able to solve problems designed for twelve-year-olds, whereas the other child, who also received the hints, could reach only a nine-year-old level.

> Cognitive development promoted by instruction in zone of proximal development

Vygotsky referred to the difference between what a child can do on his own and what can be accomplished with some assistance as the **zone of proximal development (ZPD)**. The size of the first eight-year-old's zone is 4 (that is, the eight-year-old could, with help, solve the problem designed for a child four years older), whereas the second child has a zone of 1 (he could solve the problem designed for a child one year older). According to Vygotsky, students with wider zones are likely to experience greater cognitive development when instruction is pitched just above the lower limit of their ZPD than will students with narrower zones because the former are in a better position to capitalize on the instruction. The ZPD, then, encompasses those abilities, attitudes, and patterns of thinking that are in the process of maturing and can be refined only with assistance (Tappan, 1998, 2005; Tudge & Scrimsher, 2003).

> Scaffolding techniques support student learning

Helping students answer difficult questions or solve problems by giving them hints or asking leading questions is an example of a technique called **scaffolding.** Just as construction workers use external scaffolding to support their building efforts, Vygotsky recommended that teachers similarly support learning in its early phases. The purpose of scaffolding is to help students acquire knowledge and skills they would not have learned on their own. As the student demonstrates mastery over the content in question, the learning aids are faded and removed. Scaffolding techniques that are likely to help students traverse their ZPD include prompts, suggestions, checklists, modeling, rewards, feedback, cognitive structuring (using such devices as theories, categories, labels, and rules for helping students organize and understand ideas), and questioning (Gallimore & Tharp, 1990; Ratner, 1991). As students approach the upper limit of their ZPD, their behavior becomes smoother, more internalized, and more automatized. Any assistance offered at this level will likely be perceived as disruptive and irritating.

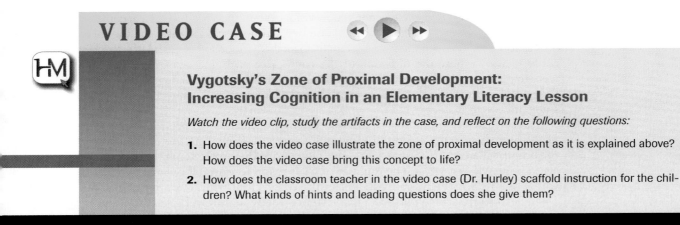

**VIDEO CASE**   ◄◄  ▶  ►►

**Vygotsky's Zone of Proximal Development:
Increasing Cognition in an Elementary Literacy Lesson**

*Watch the video clip, study the artifacts in the case, and reflect on the following questions:*

1. How does the video case illustrate the zone of proximal development as it is explained above? How does the video case bring this concept to life?

2. How does the classroom teacher in the video case (Dr. Hurley) scaffold instruction for the children? What kinds of hints and leading questions does she give them?

Mark Tappan (1998) has proposed the following four-component model that teachers can use to optimize the effects of their scaffolding efforts and help students move through their ZPD:

1. *Model desired academic behaviors.* Children can imitate many behaviors that they do not have the capability to exhibit independently, and such experiences stimulate them to act this way on their own.

2. *Create a dialogue with the student.* A child's understanding of concepts, procedures, and principles becomes more systematic and organized as a result of the exchange of questions, explanations, and feedback between teacher and child within the child's ZPD. As with modeling, the effectiveness of this dialogue is determined, at least in part, by the extent to which the teacher and student are committed to creating and maintaining a relationship in which each makes an honest effort to satisfy the needs of the other.

3. *Practice.* Practice speeds up the internalizing of thinking skills that students observe and discuss with others.

4. *Confirmation.* To confirm others is to bring out the best in them by focusing on what they can do with some assistance, and this process helps create a trusting and mutually supportive relationship between teacher and student. For example, you might say to a student, "I know this assignment seems difficult right now and that you have had some problems in the past with similar assignments, but with the help I'm willing to offer, I'm certain you'll do good-quality work."

Vygotsky's notion of producing cognitive development by embedding instruction within a student's ZPD is an attractive one and has many implications for instruction. In the chapter on social cognitive theory, for example, we will describe how this notion was used to improve the reading comprehension skills of low-achieving seventh graders.

## USING TECHNOLOGY TO PROMOTE COGNITIVE DEVELOPMENT

Piaget and Vygotsky believed that people use physical, mental, and social experiences to construct personal conceptions (schemes) of what the world is like. Although there are numerous opportunities throughout the course of each day to watch what other people do, try out ideas, and interact with others, we are normally limited to the physical and social stimuli that make up our immediate environment. Factors such as distance, time, and cost keep us from wider-ranging interactions.

Technology, however, greatly reduces these limitations and thus has the potential to expand the range of our experiences.

## Technology Applied to Piaget

There are at least two main ways in which technology can be used in schools to support Piaget's original ideas about cognitive development: (1) as a simulation tool, or microworld, for displaying knowledge and repairing misconceptions and errors in thinking, and (2) as a source for same-age peers to debate issues, thereby fostering cognitive conflict and disequilibrium. A review of twenty-seven controlled evaluation studies suggests that both uses of technology have increased at the elementary and secondary levels (Kulik, 2003a).

Computers provide many routes to knowledge and can help restructure common student misconceptions (for example, that the seasons are caused by the closeness of the earth to the sun or that electrical current is equal in all parts of a circuit). One way technology can overcome such misconceptions is to create explorable **microworlds,** or simulated learning environments, that allow students to get a sense of how things work in the real world (Healy & Hoyles, 2001; Kordaki & Potari, 2002). One such microworld, the Geometer's Sketchpad, allows students to transform objects with unusual shapes into squares so their areas can be calculated and directly compared. In one eighth-grade classroom, students used the Sketchpad to calculate in square miles the areas of the fifty states and create formulas to express relationships among them (such as AK = TX + OK + NM + CO, meaning Alaska is as big as Texas, Oklahoma, New Mexico, and Colorado combined) (Bay, Bledsoe, & Reys, 1998).

Another microworld, the Conservation of Area and Its Measurement (C.AR.ME), provides a set of geometric tools to help students create different ways to represent the concept of area measurement. A group of high school students created eleven ways to represent the measurement of area using C.AR.ME (Kordaki & Potari, 2002). A third microworld, Probability Explorer, allows students to design probability experiments that relate to such real-world activities as weather forecasting; it is intended to help students refine their intuitive understanding of chance (Drier, 2001). As these examples illustrate, microworlds foster cognitive development by encouraging student exploration, student control, and visual representation of abstract ideas.

*Computer-based simulations promote exploration and visual representations of abstract ideas, and correct misconceptions*

*Computer-based technology can be used to promote cognitive development in ways that are consistent with both Piaget's and Vygotsky's views.*

**HM** *TeacherPrepSPACE*

To explore microworlds, see the textbook's student website.

Computer programs can act as expert collaborative partners

A **microcomputer-based laboratory (MBL)** can also be used to build on existing knowledge and correct misconceptions. In an MBL, one or more sensors are attached to a microcomputer to generate graphs of such physical phenomena as temperature, sound, motion, and electromotive force (Peña & Alessi, 1999; Trumper & Gelbman, 2000, 2002).

In a review of twenty MBL studies, Mary Nakhleh (1994) found that MBL applications show promise in altering or restructuring students' faulty understandings of key science concepts. Because MBLs provide an immediate link between a hands-on, concrete experience and a symbolic representation of that experience (a graph), their use may facilitate the shift from concrete to formal operational thinking (Trumper & Gelbman, 2000).

A second fundamental way to put Piaget's ideas into practice is to use technology to promote cognitive conflict and disequilibrium. Remember that, according to Piaget, cognitive development is contingent on students' confronting others who have contradictory thoughts and claims, thereby creating internal tension and conflict. When students notice a discrepancy or a contradiction of what they believe, they are motivated to find more information and move back to a state of equilibrium. One way to accomplish this goal is to have students debate with peers over a computer network.

## Technology Applied to Vygotsky

As with Piaget, there are at least two ways to link educational technology with the ideas of Vygotsky by using the computer: (1) as an expert peer or collaborative partner to support skills and strategies that can be internalized by the learner and (2) as a tool to link learners to more knowledgeable peers and experts, who establish a master-novice apprenticeship and scaffold the student's learning.

As you'll recall, Vygotsky believed that children gain significantly from the knowledge and conceptual tools handed down to them by those who are more intellectually advanced. Roy Pea (1985, 2004) and Gavriel Salomon (1988) were among the first to suggest that the computer might play the same role as more capable tutors with such tasks as writing an essay and reading a book. Basically, the computer is programmed to provide prompts and expert guidance during reading and writing tasks. These supports, or scaffolds, are gradually faded as students become more competent at regulating their own behavior. According to some researchers (Cotterall & Cohen, 2003; Donovan & Smolkin, 2002), such support is vital in writing, because young children often lack the cognitive resources and skills to move beyond simple knowledge telling in their compositions. Salomon, who helped develop both the Reading Partner and Writing Partner software tools, found that they improved children's reading comprehension, essay writing, effort, and awareness of useful self-questioning strategies (Salomon, Globerson, & Guterman, 1989; Zellermayer, Salomon, Globerson, & Givon, 1991). Some studies of the same period did not always report such positive results (Bonk & Reynolds, 1992; Daiute, 1985; Reynolds & Bonk, 1996). However, as educators and researchers have gained experience with technologically based learning environments, Vygotsky's ideas have become better understood in that context and therefore more effectively applied (Alavi & Leidner, 2001; Borthick, Jones, & Wakai, 2003). For example, Yelland and Masters (2007) found that within technological environments, children can support each other's learning, and the scaffolding that occurs in such environments supports learners cognitively, affectively, and technologically. Indeed, within the context of technologically driven learning environments, the technology itself, if it is designed to be supportive of the learner, is sometimes referred to as a scaffold (De Lisi, 2006).

The second technology-based technique that has been derived from Vygotsky's view of cognitive development is the **cognitive apprenticeship** (Bonk & Cunningham, 1998; Brown, Collins, & Duguid, 1989). Like the traditional master-apprentice relationship in the skilled crafts and trades, a mentor works closely with a learner to

# VIDEO CASE ◀◀ ▶ ▶▶

## Middle School Reading Instruction: Integrating Technology

*Watch the video clip, study the artifacts in the case, and reflect on the following questions:*

**1.** How does the online chatroom depicted in this video case illustrate Piaget's theory of cognitive conflict that is described in the chapter?

**2.** Describe the way that the online discussion group supports Vygotsky's theories of master-novice apprenticeship and scaffolding.

develop the learner's cognitive skills. Also like the traditional apprenticeship, mentors provide students with real-life tasks to perform under realistic conditions. The learner moves from newcomer to expert by first observing the mentor and then participating in some tasks. Gradually there is a shift in responsibility for solving the task from the expert or teacher to the student as the student moves from the fringes of the community to a more central role within it. As that happens, new skills are tested and, it is hoped, internalized.

When this master-apprentice relationship occurs on a computer network, it is typically called **telementoring** (Duff, 2000; Rea, 2001). The education and technology literature is filled with examples of telementoring in K–12 education. For instance, international weather projects such as the Kids as Global Scientists project (Mistler-Jackson & Songer, 2000), the Collaborative Visualization project (Edelson, Pea, & Gomez, 1996), and the Global Learning and Observations to Benefit the Environment program (Barab & Luehmann, 2003; Finarelli, 1998) all involve students in genuine scientific data collection and reporting. The collaborative relationships that students establish with peers and mentors create in students a strong sense of participation in what is called a community of practice. The website of the International Telementor Program (**www.telementor.org**) provides volunteer mentors from around the world to teachers and students.

Richard Ruopp et al. (1993) documented how an electronic community of physics teachers, in a project called Labnet was able to use MBLs to get students to share and compare their experimental findings across sites, while simultaneously providing a vehicle for teacher pooling of talents and discussion of lesson plans. Such a project is a prime example of two-tiered scaffolding (Gaffney & Anderson, 1991): consultants and experts scaffolded teachers, who in turn scaffolded students. With the rise in telecommunications and collaborative technologies for the Internet, the possibilities for working online with specialists, practitioners, or content experts continue to increase.

## PIAGET, KOHLBERG, AND GILLIGAN: MORAL DEVELOPMENT

### Piaget's Analysis of the Moral Judgment of the Child

Because he was intrigued by all aspects of children's thinking, Piaget became interested in moral development. He began his study of morality by observing how children played marbles. (He first learned the game himself, so that he would be able to understand the subtleties of the conception.) Piaget discovered that interpretations of rules followed by participants in marble games changed with age.

*Using Technology to Promote Cognitive Development*

**Age Changes in Interpretation of Rules**   Four- to seven-year-olds just learning the game seemed to view rules as interesting examples of the social behavior of older children. They did not understand the rules but tried to go along with them. Seven- to ten-year-olds regarded rules as sacred pronouncements handed down by older children or adults. At about the age of eleven or twelve, children began to see rules as agreements reached by mutual consent. Piaget concluded that younger children see rules as absolute and external.

Although children ranging from the age of four to about ten do not question rules, they may frequently break them because they do not understand them completely. After the age of eleven or so, children become increasingly capable of grasping why rules are necessary. At that point, Piaget concluded, they tend to lose interest in adult-imposed regulations and take delight in formulating their own variations of rules to fit a particular situation. Piaget illustrated this point by describing how a group of ten- and eleven-year-old boys prepared for a snowball fight (1965, p. 50). They divided themselves into teams, elected officers, decided on rules to govern the distances from which the snowballs could be thrown, and agreed on a system of punishments for those who violated the rules. Although they spent a substantial amount of playtime engaging in such preliminary discussions, they seemed to thoroughly enjoy their newly discovered ability to make up rules to supplant those that previously had been imposed on them by their elders.

**Moral Realism Versus Moral Relativism**   The way children of different ages responded to rules so intrigued Piaget that he decided to use the interview method to obtain more systematic information about moral development. He made up pairs of stories and asked children of different ages to discuss them. Here is a typical pair of stories:

A: There was a little boy called Julian. His father had gone out and Julian thought it would be fun to play with father's ink-pot. First he played with the pen, and then he made a little blot on the tablecloth.

B: A little boy who was called Augustus once noticed that his father's ink-pot was empty. One day that his father was away he thought of filling the ink-pot so as to help his father, and so that he should find it full when he came home. But while he was opening the ink-bottle he made a big blot on the table cloth. (1965, p. 122)

After reading these stories, Piaget asked, "Are these children equally guilty? Which of the two is naughtier, and why?" As was the case with interpretations of rules, Piaget found that younger children reacted to these stories differently from older children.

The younger children maintained that Augustus was guiltier than Julian because he had made a bigger inkblot on the tablecloth. They took no account of the fact that Julian was misbehaving and that Augustus was trying to help his father. Older children, however, were more likely to base their judgment of guilt on the intent of each child.

Piaget referred to the moral thinking of children up to the age of ten or so as the **morality of constraint,** but he also called it *moral realism*. The thinking of children of eleven or older Piaget called the **morality of cooperation.** He also occasionally used the term *moral relativism*. Piaget concluded that the two basic types of moral reasoning differ in several ways. We summarize these differences in Table 3.3.

## pause & reflect

Remember our definition of *decentration* in the earlier discussion of Piaget's theory. How do you think the young child's lack of decentration might affect her moral reasoning?

## Kohlberg's Description of Moral Development

Just as James Marcia elaborated Erikson's concept of identity formation, Lawrence Kohlberg elaborated Piaget's ideas on moral thinking. Kohlberg believed that (1) moral reasoning proceeds through fixed stages, and (2) moral development can be accelerated through instruction.

Morality of constraint (moral realism): rules are sacred, consequences determine guilt

Morality of cooperation (moral relativism): rules are flexible, intent important in determining guilt

| Table 3.3 | Morality of Constraint Versus Morality of Cooperation | |
|---|---|---|
| **Morality of Constraint (Typical of Six-Year-Olds)** | **Morality of Cooperation (Typical of Twelve-Year-Olds)** | |
| Holds single, absolute moral perspective (behavior is right or wrong) | Is aware of different viewpoints regarding rules | |
| Believes rules are unchangeable | Believes rules are flexible | |
| Determines extent of guilt by amount of damage | Considers the wrongdoers' intentions when evaluating guilt | |
| Defines moral wrongness in terms of what is forbidden or punished | Defines moral wrongness in terms of violation of spirit of cooperation | |

(Notice that these first four differences call attention to the tendency for children below the age of ten or so to think of rules as sacred pronouncements handed down by external authority.)

| | | |
|---|---|---|
| Believes punishment should stress atonement and does not need to "fit the crime" | Believes punishment should involve either restitution or suffering the same fate as one's victim | |
| Believes peer aggression should be punished by an external authority | Believes peer aggression should be punished by retaliatory behavior on the part of the victim* | |
| Believes children should obey rules because they are established by those in authority | Believes children should obey rules because of mutual concerns for rights of others | |

(Notice how these last three differences call attention to the tendency for children above the age of ten or so to see rules as mutual agreements among equals.)

*Beyond the age of twelve, adolescents increasingly affirm that reciprocal reactions, or "getting back," should be a response to good behavior, not bad behavior.

SOURCES: Freely adapted from interpretations of Piaget (1932) by Kohlberg (1969) and Lickona (1976).

*HM TeacherPrepSPACE*

For an interactive exploration of Kohlberg's moral dilemmas, see the textbook's student website.

**Kohlberg's Use of Moral Dilemmas**   As a graduate student at the University of Chicago in the 1950s, Lawrence Kohlberg became fascinated by Piaget's studies of moral development. He decided to expand on Piaget's original research by making up stories involving moral dilemmas that would be more appropriate for older children. Here is the story that is most often mentioned in discussions of his work:

> In Europe a woman was near death from cancer. One drug might save her, a form of radium that a druggist in the same town had recently discovered. The druggist was charging $2,000, ten times what the drug cost him to make. The sick woman's husband, Heinz, went to everyone he knew to borrow the money, but he could only get together about half of what it cost. He told the druggist that his wife was dying and asked him to sell it cheaper or let him pay later, but the druggist said "No." The husband got desperate and broke into the man's store to steal the drug for his wife. Should the husband have done that? Why? (1969, p. 376)

**Kohlberg's Six Stages of Moral Reasoning**   After analyzing the responses of ten- to sixteen-year-olds to this and similar moral dilemmas, Kohlberg (1963) eventually developed a description of six stages of moral reasoning. Be forewarned, however, that Kohlberg later revised some of his original stage designations and that descriptions of the stages have also been modified since he first proposed them. In different discussions of his stages, therefore, you may encounter varying descriptions. The outline presented in Table 3.4 is a composite summary of the sequence of moral development as described by Kohlberg, but you should expect to find differences if you read other accounts of his theory.

The scoring system Kohlberg developed to evaluate a response to a moral dilemma is extremely complex. Furthermore, the responses of subjects are lengthy and may feature arguments about a particular decision. To help you understand a bit more about each Kohlberg stage, the following list offers simplified examples of responses to a dilemma such as that faced by Heinz. For maximum clarity, only brief typical responses to the question, "Why shouldn't you steal from a store?" are mentioned.

**Preconventional morality: avoid punishment, receive benefits in return**

*Stage 1: punishment-obedience orientation.* "You might get caught." (The physical consequences of an action determine goodness or badness.)

*Stage 2: instrumental relativist orientation.* "You shouldn't steal something from a store, and the store owner shouldn't steal things that belong to you." (Obedience to laws should involve an even exchange.)

**Conventional morality: impress others, respect authority**

*Stage 3: good boy–nice girl orientation.* "Your parents will be proud of you if you are honest." (The right action is one that will impress others.)

*Stage 4: law-and-order orientation.* "It's against the law, and if we don't obey laws, our whole society might fall apart." (To maintain the social order, fixed rules must be obeyed.)

**Postconventional morality: mutual agreements, consistent principles**

*Stage 5: social contract orientation.* "Under certain circumstances laws may have to be disregarded—if a person's life depends on breaking a law, for instance." (Rules should involve mutual agreements; the rights of the individual should be protected.)

---

| **Table 3.4** | Kohlberg's Stages of Moral Reasoning |
| --- | --- |

**LEVEL 1: PRECONVENTIONAL MORALITY.** (Typical of children up to the age of nine. Called *preconventional* because young children do not really understand the conventions or rules of a society.)

**Stage 1 Punishment-obedience orientation.** The physical consequences of an action determine goodness or badness. Those in authority have superior power and should be obeyed. Punishment should be avoided by staying out of trouble.

**Stage 2 Instrumental relativist orientation.** An action is judged to be right if it is instrumental in satisfying one's own needs or involves an even exchange. Obeying rules should bring some sort of benefit in return.

**LEVEL 2: CONVENTIONAL MORALITY.** (Typical of nine- to twenty-year-olds. Called *conventional* since most nine- to twenty-year-olds conform to the conventions of society because they are the rules of a society.)

**Stage 3 Good boy–nice girl orientation.** The right action is one that would be carried out by someone whose behavior is likely to please or impress others.

**Stage 4 Law-and-order orientation.** To maintain the social order, fixed rules must be established and obeyed. It is essential to respect authority.

**LEVEL 3: POSTCONVENTIONAL MORALITY.** (Usually reached only after the age of twenty and only by a small proportion of adults. Called *postconventional* because the moral principles that underlie the conventions of a society are understood.)

**Stage 5 Social contract orientation.** Rules needed to maintain the social order should be based not on blind obedience to authority but on mutual agreement. At the same time, the rights of the individual should be protected.

**Stage 6 Universal ethical principle orientation.** Moral decisions should be made in terms of self-chosen ethical principles. Once principles are chosen, they should be applied in consistent ways.*

* In an article published in 1978, several years after Kohlberg had originally described the six stages, he described the last stage as an essentially theoretical ideal that is rarely encountered in real life.

SOURCE: Based on descriptions in Kohlberg (1969, 1976, 1978).

*Stage 6: universal ethical principle orientation.* "You need to weigh all the factors and then try to make the most appropriate decision in a given situation. Sometimes it would be morally wrong *not* to steal." (Moral decisions should be based on consistent applications of self-chosen ethical principles.)

**Criticisms and Evaluations of Kohlberg's Theory**   Is Kohlberg's contention that moral reasoning proceeds through a fixed universal sequence of stages accurate? Based on analysis of research on moral development, Martin Hoffman (1980) believes that although Kohlberg's sequence of stages may not be true of every individual in every culture, it may provide a useful general description of how moral reasoning develops in American society. Carol Gilligan (1979), whose position we will discuss in detail later, has proposed two somewhat different sequences that reflect differences in male and female socialization.

What about Kohlberg's view that moral development can be accelerated through direct instruction? Is this another "mission impossible," as some critics contend? Alan Lockwood (1978), after summarizing the findings of almost a dozen studies on acceleration of moral reasoning, concludes that the strongest effects (about half a stage increase in reasoning) occurred among individuals whose reasoning reflected stages 2 and 3. The effect of the instruction varied considerably from one subject to another. Some individuals showed substantial increases in reasoning; others showed no change. A comprehensive review of research on this topic by André Schlaefli, James Rest, and Stephen Thoma (1985) revealed similar conclusions. The authors found that moral education programs produced modest positive effects. They also found that the strongest effects were obtained with adult subjects.

Paul Vitz (1990) criticizes Kohlberg's use of moral dilemmas on the grounds that they are too far removed from the kinds of everyday social interactions in which children and adolescents engage. He prefers instead the use of narrative stories, both fictional and real accounts of others, because they portray such basic moral values as honesty, compassion, fairness, and hard work in an understandable context. Others (e.g., Rest, Narvaez, Bebeau, & Thoma, 1999) have criticized the fact that Kohlberg relied on the ability of his participants to explain clearly how they solved such hypothetical dilemmas as Heinz's. Individuals not adept at self-reflection or without the vocabulary to express their thoughts clearly either would not be recruited into such studies or would have little to contribute.

Another criticism concerns the type of moral issue that most interested Kohlberg. Kohlberg's theory deals primarily with what are called macromoral issues. These are broad social issues such as civil rights, free speech, the women's movement, and wilderness preservation. The focus is on how the behavior of individuals affects the structure of society and public policy. At this level, a moral person is one who attempts to influence laws and regulations because of a deeply held principle. For some psychologists (e.g., Rest et al., 1999), a limitation of Kohlberg's theory is that it does not adequately address micromoral issues. *Micromoral issues* concern personal interactions in everyday situations, examples of which include courtesy (not interrupting someone before that person has finished speaking), helpfulness (giving up your seat on a crowded bus or train to an elderly person), remembering significant events of friends and family, and being punctual for appointments. For micromoral issues, a moral person is one who is loyal, dedicated, and cares about particular people.

Finally, Kohlberg's work has also been criticized because it places such a strong emphasis on the role of reasoning in moral behavior but says little about the nature of people who behave in moral ways. Studies of adolescents who exhibit high levels of moral commitment and action (such as volunteering to work for social service agencies and community soup kitchens) show that these individuals have a self-concept that distinguishes them from other adolescents. They describe themselves in terms of moral characteristics and goals, have a greater sense of stability, and emphasize the importance of personal beliefs and personal philosophy. Yet these same adolescents

Criticisms of Kohlberg's theory: moral development difficult to accelerate, moral dilemmas not relevant to daily life, relies on macromoral issues, ignores characteristics other than moral reasoning

did not differ from their peers on measures of moral judgment—their scores ranged from stage 3 to stage 5. It appears that advanced levels of moral reasoning may be only weakly related to moral behavior (Arnold, 2000).

**Educational Implications of Kohlberg's Theory**    Carol Harding and Kenneth Snyder (1991) believe that teachers can make productive use of contemporary films to illustrate moral dilemmas. Film is an attractive medium to students, and several types of moral dilemmas are often portrayed in the space of about two hours. To highlight the dilemma of the rights of the individual versus the rights of others in a community, Harding and Snyder recommend the films *Platoon* and *Wall Street*. *Platoon* is a story about the Vietnam War and contains scenes of American soldiers burning villages and abusing villagers who are suspected of having ties to or of being the enemy. In response to such scenes, students can be asked such questions as, "Should the enemy in war be granted certain rights, or is personal survival more important?"

The Tom Snyder educational software company offers a series of computer-based programs titled Decisions, Decisions, in which students identify and discuss moral dilemmas such as protecting the environment or using drugs. Students discuss each situation and as a group choose a response. Each response is stored by the program and in turn affects the development and outcome of the following situations to illustrate that events do not occur in isolation and that all decisions have consequences.

If films or computer programs are not available but you occasionally wish to engage your students in a discussion of moral dilemmas, the daily newspaper is an excellent source of material. Biology teachers, for example, can point to stories of the conflicts produced by machines that keep comatose patients alive or by medical practices based on genetic engineering. Civics or government teachers could use news items that reflect the dilemma that arises when freedom of speech conflicts with the need to curtail racism.

## pause & reflect

*Wall Street* is a story about a corporate raider who uses borrowed money to take control of public companies and then sells off the assets (thereby eliminating people's jobs) to enrich himself. In your opinion, how does this reflect a moral dilemma? What types of questions might be asked about *Wall Street*?

## pause & reflect

How would you respond to a parent or colleague who argued that students have better things to do in class than discuss ways of resolving moral dilemmas?

## Gilligan's View of Identity and Moral Development

Carol Gilligan (1982, 1988) argues that Erikson's view of identity development and Kohlberg's view of moral development more accurately describe what occurs with adolescent males than with adolescent females. In her view, Erikson's and Kohlberg's ideas emphasize separation from parental authority and societal conventions. Instead of remaining loyal to adult authority, individuals as they mature shift their loyalty to abstract principles (for example, self-reliance, independence, justice, and fairness). This process of detachment allows adolescents to assume a more equal status with adults. It's almost as if adolescents are saying, "You have your life, and I have mine; you don't intrude on mine, and I won't intrude on yours."

But, Gilligan argues, many adolescent females have a different primary concern. They care less about separation and independence and more about remaining loyal to others through expressions of caring, understanding, and sharing of experiences. Detachment for these female adolescents is a moral problem rather than a sought-after developmental milestone. The problem for them is how to become autonomous while also being caring and connected.

Given this view, Gilligan believes that adolescent females are more likely to resolve Erikson's identity versus role confusion and intimacy versus isolation crises concurrently rather than consecutively. The results of at least one study (Ochse & Plug, 1986) support this view. With respect to Kohlberg's theory, Gilligan argues that because females are socialized to value more highly the qualities of understanding, helping, and cooperation with others than that of preserving individual rights, and because this latter orientation is reflected most strongly in Kohlberg's two conventional stages (stages 3 and 4), females are more likely to be judged to be at a lower level of moral development than males.

Stephen Thoma (1986) has offered a partial answer to Gilligan's criticism. After reviewing more than fifty studies on gender differences in moral development, he drew three conclusions:

1. The effect of gender on scores from the Defining Issues Test (the DIT is a device that uses responses to moral dilemmas to determine level of moral reasoning) was very small. Less than one-half of 1 percent of the differences in DIT scores was due to gender differences.
2. Females almost always scored higher. This slight superiority for females appeared in every age group studied (middle school, high school, college, adults).
3. Differences in DIT scores were strongly associated with differences in age and level of education. That is, individuals who were older and had graduated from college were more likely to score at the postconventional level than those who were younger and had less education.

Thoma's findings suggest that females are just as likely as males to use justice and fairness concepts in their reasoning about *hypothetical* moral dilemmas.

But there is one aspect of Gilligan's criticism that cannot be answered by Thoma's analysis of existing research. She argues that when females are faced with their own real-life moral dilemmas (abortion, civil rights, environmental pollution) rather than hypothetical ones, they are more likely to favor a caring-helping-cooperation orientation than a justice-fairness-individual rights orientation.

Perhaps the best approach that educators can take when they involve students in discussions of moral issues is to emphasize the utility of *both* orientations. The recent research on gender differences supports that females use both orientations to think about issues of right and wrong, and so do males. Emphasizing both orientations when classroom discussions focus on matters of right and wrong is one way of acknowledging student diversity. It also makes sense given a more recent review of many studies of gender differences in moral orientation. Jaffee, Hyde, and Shibley (2000) found that females as a group use a caring orientation to a slightly greater extent than the justice orientation. They found also that males as a group tend to use

Although slight differences do exist, both males and females use caring and justice orientations to resolve real-life moral dilemmas.

*Carol Gilligan believes that Erikson's theory of identity development and Kohlberg's theory of moral development do not accurately describe the course of identity formation and moral reasoning in females. She believes that adolescent females place a higher value on caring, understanding, and sharing of experiences than they do on independence, self-reliance, and justice.*

a justice orientation slightly more often. Jaffee, Hyde, and Shibley found small differences between very large groups.

## Does Moral Thinking Lead to Moral Behavior?

**The Hartshorne and May Studies**   Hugh Hartshorne and Mark May (1929, 1930a, 1930b) observed thousands of children at different age levels reacting in situations that revealed their actual moral behavior. The researchers also asked the children to respond to questions about hypothetical situations to reveal how much they understood about right and wrong behavior. Elementary school children, for example, were allowed to correct their own papers or record their own scores on measures of athletic skill without being aware that accurate measures were being made independently by adult observers. The children were also asked what they thought was the right thing to do in similar situations.

> Moral knowledge does not always result in moral behavior

A comparison of the two sets of data made it possible to determine, among other things, whether children practiced what they preached. What Hartshorne and May discovered was that many children who were able to describe right kinds of behavior in hypothetical situations indulged in wrong behavior in real-life situations. Children reacted in specific rather than consistent ways to situations that called for moral judgment. Even a child who was rated as among the most honest in a group would behave in a dishonest way under certain circumstances. A boy who was an excellent student but an indifferent athlete, for example, would not cheat when asked to correct his own paper, but he would inflate scores on sports skills.

Another significant, and dismaying, discovery that Hartshorne and May made was that children who went to religious education classes or belonged to such organizations as the Boy Scouts or Girl Scouts were just as dishonest as children who were not exposed to the kind of moral instruction provided by such organizations. Hartshorne and May concluded that one explanation for the ineffectiveness of moral instruction in the 1920s was that too much stress was placed on having children memorize values such as the Ten Commandments or the Boy Scout oath and law. The two researchers suggested that it would be more effective to invite children to discuss real-life moral situations as they occurred. Instead of having children chant, "Honesty is the best policy," for example, Hartshorne and May urged teachers to call attention to the positive consequences of honest acts. If a student in a school reported that he had found money belonging to someone else, the teacher might praise the child and ask everyone in the class to think about how relieved the person who had lost the money would be to get it back.

Recent research shows that Hartshorne and May's basic finding is still valid. Approximately 90 percent of high school students and 70 percent of college students admitted to engaging in academic cheating. At both grade levels, males cheated more often than females. Moreover, cheating was judged to be more or less acceptable depending on the reason. Cheating was deemed more justifiable if it resulted in passing a class and getting a job that would help one's family. It was also seen as more justifiable if it was done to avoid disappointing one's parents, to avoid academic probation, or because the instructor had treated the student unfairly (Jensen, Arnett, Feldman, & Cauffman, 2002). As we will see in later chapters in the book, students' perceptions of their teachers can prove critical. In terms of cheating, students who perceive their teacher as less than effective facilitators of learning are more likely to cheat than students who view their instructors as effective teachers (Murdock, Miller, & Kohlhardt, 2004).

The insights on moral reasoning that Piaget, Kohlberg, and Gilligan offered are important for aspiring teachers. But as Hartshorne and May pointed out eight decades ago—and as contemporary researchers are still finding—there are gaps between moral reasoning and moral action or behavior. Mark Tappan (2006) has recently advocated a "sociocultural" approach to the study of moral development.

You'll recall that Vygotsky's views on cognitive development helped to define the sociocultural approach. Tappan's approach makes use of the theoretical insights that we have considered in this section and, most important, attempts to connect reasoning and behavior in order to understand actions. Tappan's theoretical work may prove very helpful in judging the effectiveness of moral education programs aimed at improving not only students' ability to reason morally but to act in morally responsible ways.

**Research on Character Education Programs**  Many parents, educators, and political leaders believe that today's students lack the moral values possessed by previous generations. Concerned adults cite violence in schools and widespread drug abuse, among other problems, as evidence of such a decline.

One commonly voiced solution to these problems is for the schools to institute moral education programs (also called character education programs). After reviewing the research on the effectiveness of character education programs, James Leming (1993) drew the following conclusions:

- Telling students what they should or should not do, through either slogans ("Just say no") or conduct codes, is unlikely to have significant or lasting effects on character.
- Helping students think about how to resolve moral dilemmas in higher-level ways does not automatically result in increases in morally acceptable behavior.
- An individual's social environment plays an important role in the learning and exhibiting of virtuous behavior. When students have clear rules with which to guide their behavior, accept those rules as appropriate and worthwhile, and are rewarded for complying with those rules, they are more likely to exhibit morally acceptable behavior.
- Producing changes in moral behavior requires a commitment to a well-conceived, long-term program.

As part of character education programs or as an independent activity, many social critics recommend that children either read or have read to them stories with a moral theme (sometimes called virtue stories). Being exposed to such stories is supposed to help children develop a strong set of traditional moral values, such as honesty, trustworthiness, responsibility, and loyalty. Darcia Narvaez (2002) points out that such a claim, whether its advocates realize it, rests on five assumptions that are not supported by contemporary research findings on learning:

***Assumption 1: Reading Is a Passive Activity***  The picture that emerges from thousands of research studies is that reading comprehension is not passive. Rather, it is the result of considerable cognitive activity. Children attempt to create a coherent, meaningful representation of a text by integrating the information in a text with prior knowledge.

***Assumption 2: All Readers Extract the Same Information from a Text***  Because of individual differences in prior knowledge, interests, and reading skills, each reader constructs a somewhat unique representation of what a text is about. Furthermore, texts with unfamiliar ideas are likely to be recalled less well and have more distortions than texts with more familiar ideas.

***Assumption 3: All Readers Understand the Author's Point***  Once again, because of individual differences in prior knowledge, interests, and familiarity with the ideas presented in a text, some readers will "get" an author's point while others will construct something entirely different. (If you have ever argued with someone about the point of a movie or novel, you can appreciate this phenomenon.) Research on summarizing text passages shows that before the age of ten, children can accurately recount much of what they read but have great difficulty synthesizing that information to identify the author's main point.

***Assumption 4: Moral Themes Are Readily Accessible to Readers***    Because children have different conceptions (moral schemas, or prior moral knowledge) of how to get along with others and why such behavior is important, moral themes in a text are not necessarily accessible. As we noted earlier, people may base moral judgments on a variety of criteria, including personal interests (morally correct behavior is that which benefits me), maintaining norms (morally correct behavior is that which fosters law and order), and ideals (morally correct behavior is that which is consistent with higher-order principles). Older or more intellectually advanced children are more likely to grasp moral themes that reflect maintenance of norms and ideals than are younger or less advanced children. A recent study (Williams et al., 2002), although not done with morality stories, reinforces this point. Second and third graders who were trained to identify and comprehend story themes did better than noninstructed children, but they were unable to apply these themes to real-life situations or to identify and apply themes for which they received no instruction.

***Assumption 5: Moral Themes Are Just Another Type of Information Conveyed by a Text***    Because moral themes vary in their complexity and abstractness, and because children's comprehension of such themes develops through predictable stages, moral themes cannot be treated as the equivalent to fact-based information.

Despite the fact that character education programs have not received strong support in the research literature (probably because many programs are poorly designed and/or implemented), they are popular among parents and educators, and some appear to produce positive effects.

Whether or not your school has a character education program, there are certainly ways you can influence the moral development of your students. The following Suggestions for Teaching in Your Classroom section provides several ideas. But before you use any techniques of moral education in your classes, it is wise to check with your principal. In some communities, parents have insisted that they, not teachers, should take the responsibility for moral instruction.

# Suggestions for Teaching in Your Classroom

## Encouraging Moral Development

**JOURNAL ENTRY**
Ways to Encourage Moral Development

*HM TeacherPrepSPACE*

For additional journal entries, see the Reflective Journal Questions at the textbook's student website.

1    Recognize that younger children respond to moral conflicts differently from older children.

2    Try to take the perspective of students, and stimulate their perspective-taking abilities.

3    Develop an awareness of moral issues by discussing a variety of real and hypothetical moral dilemmas and by using daily opportunities in the classroom to heighten moral awareness. (Moral education should be an integral part of the curriculum; it should not take place during a "moral education period.")

Here is a hypothetical moral dilemma that a first-grade teacher presented to her class:

> Mark was going to the movies when he met his friend Steven. Although Steven wanted to go to the movie with Mark, he had spent all of his allowance and wouldn't be getting any more until after the movie left town. Both boys were 12 years old but looked much younger. If they lied about their ages, they could both see the movie for the amount of money that Mark had. Mark was unsure if he should lie about his age. Steven said, "It's your money, so it's your decision." What should Mark do?

The responses of the students illustrate both the punishment-obedience orientation (stage 1) and the instrumental relativist orientation (stage 2) of Kohlberg's preconventional level of morality:

Ms. KITTLE: *Okay, what do you think Mark should do?*

JOHN: *Him and Steven should tell them how old they are.*

EMILY: *They shouldn't lie about their age.*

Ms. KITTLE: *Why do you think they shouldn't lie?*

TINA: *Because if they did lie, they'd get a spanking.*

JOHN: *Mark shouldn't lie about his age because it leads to a mess.*

Ms. KITTLE: *What kind of mess?*

JOHN: *His mother might find out.*

SARA: *The father too.*

ERIN: *They'd get punished.*

Ms. KITTLE: *So you all think Mark and Steven shouldn't lie because they might get caught and be punished. What if no one catches them—would it be right to lie then?*

MOST: *Yes!*

BILLY: *No, it's not. The manager of the show might catch them.*

Ms. KITTLE: *But what if no one catches them?*

BILLY: *Then it's all right.*

Ms. KITTLE: *Who thinks it would still be wrong to lie, even if Mark and Steven wouldn't get caught? (Five children raise their hands.)*

TROY: *They'd still get in a mixed-up mess.*

Ms. KITTLE: *How?*

TROY: *Somebody might tell somebody that they lied.*

Ms. KITTLE: *He might, that's true. But would it still be wrong even if Steven didn't tell anybody?*

TROY: *Yes.*

Ms. KITTLE: *Why, Troy?*

TROY: *I don't know—but it is.*

EMILY: *It's not nice to lie.*

TROY (IN A RUSH): *Yeah, and it's not fair to other people, either!*

Ms. KITTLE: *Who wouldn't it be fair to?*

TROY: *The others in the show. They had to pay full price.*

Ms. KITTLE: *You mean if other twelve-year-old kids had to pay the full price for their tickets, then it's not fair for Mark and Steven to get in cheaper?*

TROY: *Right. (Lickona, 1998)*

**4** **Create a classroom atmosphere that will enhance open discussion. For example, arrange face-to-face groupings, be an accepting model, foster listening and communication skills, and encourage student-to-student interaction.**

Richard Hersh, Diana Paolitto, and Joseph Reimer (1979) offer the following specific suggestions for supervising classroom discussions:

- *Highlight the moral issue to be discussed.* Example: Describe a specific real or hypothetical moral dilemma.
- *Ask "why?" questions.* Example: After asking students what they would do if they were faced with the moral dilemma under discussion, ask them to explain why they would act that way.
- *Complicate the circumstances.* Example: After students have responded to the original dilemma, mention a factor that might complicate matters—for example, the involvement of a best friend in the dilemma.
- *Use personal and naturalistic examples.* Example: Invite students to put themselves in the position of individuals who are confronted by moral dilemmas described in newspapers or depicted on television.

*HM TeacherPrepSPACE*

To solidify your understanding of this chapter, use the ACE practice tests and PowerPoint slides at the textbook's student website.

# 4 Culture and Cognition

## KEY POINTS

*These key points will help you learn the important information in this chapter. To help you study, they also appear in the margins of the pages, next to the text where they are discussed.*

### The Rise of Multiculturalism

- Cultural pluralism assumes that societies should maintain different cultures, that every culture within a society should be respected, that individuals have the right to participate in society without giving up cultural identity
- U.S. becoming more culturally diverse because of changes in immigration, birthrates
- Ethnocentrism: belief that one's own culture is superior to other cultures

### Ethnicity and Social Class

- Culture: how a group of people perceives, believes, thinks, behaves
- Ethnic group members differ in verbal and nonverbal communication patterns
- Ethnic group members may hold different values
- Ethnic group members may favor different learning arrangements and processes
- Poverty rates higher for ethnic families of color than for Whites
- Minority children often score lower on tests, drop out of school sooner
- Achievement gap between low-SES minority students and White students due to living conditions, family environment, characteristics of the student, and classroom environment
- Low-SES children more likely to live in stressful environment that interferes with studying

- Classroom atmosphere, teachers' approaches connected with achievement levels of low-SES students
- Teacher expectancy (Pygmalion) effect: impact of teacher expectations leads to self-fulfilling prophecy
- Limited effect of teacher expectancy on IQ scores
- Strong effect of teacher expectancy on achievement, participation
- Teacher expectancies influenced by social class, ethnic background, achievement, attractiveness, gender

### Multicultural Education Programs

- Multicultural education can be approached in different ways
- Multicultural programs aim to promote respect for diversity, reduction of ethnocentrism and stereotypes, improved learning
- Multicultural lessons organized around key concepts
- Peer tutoring improves achievement
- Cooperative learning: students work together in small groups
- Cooperative learning fosters better understanding among ethnically diverse students
- Mastery learning: most students can master the curriculum
- Multicultural understanding can be promoted by electronically linking students from different cultural backgrounds

### Bilingual Education

- Transition programs focus on rapid shift to English proficiency
- Maintenance programs focus on maintaining native-language competence
- Two-way bilingual education programs feature instruction in both languages
- Bilingual education programs produce moderate learning gains

Previously in this text, we pointed out that if your instructional plans are to be effective, they have to take into account what your students are like. In previous chapters, we described students in terms of their age-related differences in psychosocial, cognitive, and moral development, and we discussed how students typically are similar to and different from one another in terms of physical, social, and cognitive characteristics. In this chapter, we will turn to two other important ways in which students differ: cultural background and language. In Chapter 6, we will discuss still another dimension of diversity: the concepts of ability and disability.

**Culture** is a term that describes how a group of people perceives the world; formulates beliefs; evaluates objects, ideas, and experiences; and behaves. It can be thought of as a blueprint that guides the ways in which individuals within a group do such important things as communicate with others (both verbally and nonverbally), handle time and space, express emotions, and approach work and play. The concept of culture typically includes ethnic group but can also encompass religious beliefs and socioeconomic status (Banks, 2006; Gollnick & Chinn, 2002).

Different groups of people vary in their beliefs, attitudes, values, and behavior patterns because of differences in cultural norms. (By *norms,* we mean the perceptions, beliefs, and behaviors that characterize most members of a group.) Students who were raised with mainstream American values, for example, find acceptable the practice of working individually and competing with others for academic rewards. Most Native Americans and Asians, in contrast, have been taught to de-emphasize competition and individual accomplishment in favor of cooperation and group solidarity (Sadker & Sadker, 2005).

To provide the appropriate classroom and school conditions that will help your students from different cultural backgrounds master a common curriculum, you must come to understand and take into account your students' differing cultural backgrounds. A culturally aware teacher will emphasize the ways in which American society has been enriched by the contributions of many different ethnic groups (and place special emphasis on those ethnic groups to which the students belong) and will not schedule a major exam or field trip for a day when certain students are likely to be out of school in observance of a religious holiday.

The approach to teaching and learning that we will describe in this chapter, one that seeks to foster an understanding of and mutual respect for the values, beliefs, and practices of different cultural groups, is typically referred to as **multicultural education**. Because culturally diverse children often come to school with different language backgrounds, another related issue is bilingual education, described at the end of this chapter.

# THE RISE OF MULTICULTURALISM

## From Melting Pot to Cultural Pluralism

More than most other countries, the United States is made up of numerous ethnic groups with widely diverse histories, cultural backgrounds, and values. In addition to the hundreds of thousands of Blacks who were brought to the United States as slaves, the United States was peopled by many waves of immigrants, mostly from Europe but also from Asia and Latin America. Throughout the eighteenth and nineteenth centuries, the United States needed large numbers of people to settle its western frontier, build its railroads, harvest its natural resources, and work in its growing factories. As Table 4.1 indicates, approximately 33 million people immigrated to the United States between 1820 and 1920.

Throughout this period, the basic view of American society toward immigrants was that they should divest themselves of their old customs, views, allegiances, and rivalries as soon as possible and adopt English as their primary language, along with mainstream American ideals, values, and customs. This assimilation of diverse ethnic groups into one national mainstream was known as the **melting pot** phenomenon, a term and viewpoint popularized in a 1909 play by Israel Zangwill, *The Melting Pot*. The main institution responsible for bringing about this assimilation was the public school (Banks, 2006; Ornstein & Levine, 2006).

The notion of America as a great melting pot was generally accepted until the social unrest of the late 1960s and early 1970s. As an outgrowth of urban riots and the civil rights movement, minority ethnic groups argued not only for bilingual education programs in public schools but also for ethnic studies. Since the early 1970s, factors such as discrimination, the desire to maintain culturally specific ideas and practices, and continued immigration from different parts of the world have served to maintain, if not accelerate, this trend toward cultural diversity—or **cultural pluralism,** to use the preferred term. Cultural pluralism rests on three beliefs: (1) that a society should strive to maintain the different cultures that reside within it; (2) that each culture within a society should be respected by others; and (3) that individuals within a society have the right to participate in all aspects of that society without having to give up their cultural identity (Sleeter & Grant, 2007).

> Cultural pluralism assumes that societies should maintain different cultures, that every culture within a society should be respected, and that individuals have the right to participate in society without giving up cultural identity

## The Changing Face of the United States

Given recent changes in birthrates and immigration patterns and population projections for the next thirty to fifty years, one could argue that the decline of the melting pot philosophy and the rise of cultural pluralism and multicultural education will only accelerate in the years ahead. Consider the following statistics.

| Table 4.1 | Number of Immigrants to the United States, by Decade | | |
|---|---|---|---|
| **Years** | **Number** | **Years** | **Number** |
| 1820–1830 | 151,824 | 1911–1920 | 5,735,811 |
| 1831–1840 | 599,125 | 1921–1930 | 4,107,209 |
| 1841–1850 | 1,713,251 | 1931–1940 | 528,431 |
| 1851–1860 | 2,598,214 | 1941–1950 | 1,035,039 |
| 1861–1870 | 2,314,824 | 1951–1960 | 2,515,479 |
| 1871–1880 | 2,812,191 | 1961–1970 | 3,321,677 |
| 1881–1890 | 5,246,613 | 1971–1980 | 4,493,314 |
| 1891–1900 | 3,687,564 | 1981–1990 | 7,338,062 |
| 1901–1910 | 8,795,386 | 1991–2000 | 9,095,417 |
| | | Total | 66,089,431 |

SOURCE: U.S. Office of Immigration Statistics (2006).

Between 1996 and 2005, 84 percent of legal immigrants to the United States came from non-European countries. Most of these immigrants came from Asia (principally the Philippine Islands, China, and India) and the Americas (principally Mexico and South America) and settled in the major cities of California, New York, Texas, and Florida. In the ten-year period from 1991 to 2000, about 9.1 million legal immigrants arrived in the United States, an all-time U.S. immigration record for a decade. The first decade of the twenty-first century may well top that figure, as 4.9 million individuals legally entered the United States from 2001 through 2005 (U.S. Office of Immigration Statistics, 2006). Adding to the change produced by immigration itself is the fact that immigrant mothers have a higher average birthrate than native-born mothers. As of 2004, native-born women averaged 56.7 births per 1,000, whereas foreign-born women averaged 83.7 per 1,000 (U.S. Census Bureau, 2005b).

These immigration and birthrate patterns are expected to have a significant effect over the next two decades on the makeup of the school-age population (see Figure 4.1).

**Figure 4.1** Projected Change in Percentage of School-Age Children for Four Ethnic Groups Between 2010 and 2025

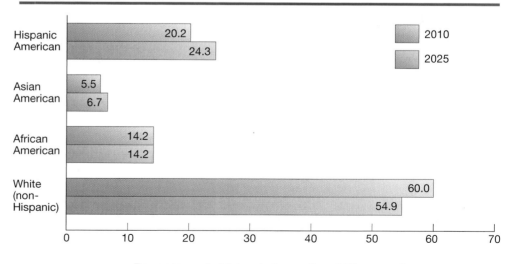

Percentage of children between 5 and 18 years of age

*Because of rounding errors, percentages for each year do not add up to exactly 100 percent.

SOURCE: U.S. Census Bureau (2002).

U.S. becoming more culturally diverse because of changes in immigration, birthrates

According to Census Bureau projections, the populations of Latino and Asian American schoolchildren will increase rapidly, raising their combined percentage of the school-age population to about 30 percent. Black school-age children will also increase in numbers, although their proportion of the overall school population will remain at 14 to 15 percent. The proportion of White non-Hispanic schoolchildren will fall from 60 percent to just under 55 percent. As these figures make clear, not only is the United States rapidly on its way to becoming an even more ethnically diverse nation than ever before, but certain areas of the country (for example, southern California, Texas, southern Florida, New York) already have very large minority populations.

Much of the rest of this chapter will focus on characteristics of certain groups of students. But for you and your students to benefit from your knowledge of cultural diversity, you must view it in the proper perspective. The perspective we encourage you to adopt has three aspects, which are described in the following Suggestions for Teaching in Your Classroom.

# Suggestions for Teaching in Your Classroom

## Taking Account of Your Students' Cultural Differences

### 1 Recognize that differences are not necessarily deficits.

Ethnocentrism: belief that one's own culture is superior to other cultures

**JOURNAL ENTRY**
Minimizing Ethnocentric Tendencies

Students who subscribe to different value systems and exhibit different communication patterns, time orientations, learning modes, motives, and aspirations should not be viewed as incapable (García, 2002). Looking on ethnic and social class differences as deficits usually stems from an attitude called *ethnocentrism*. This is the tendency of people to think of their own culture as superior to the culture of other groups. You may be able to moderate your ethnocentric tendencies and motivate your students to learn by consciously using instructional tactics that are congruent with the different cultural backgrounds of your students.

### 2 Recognize that the groups we and others describe with a general label are frequently made up of subgroups with somewhat different characteristics.

These subgroups, in fact, may use different labels to refer to themselves. Among Native Americans, for example, Navajos differ from the Hopi in physical appearance, dress, and hairstyle. Individuals who are called Hispanic may trace their ancestry to one of a dozen or more countries and often refer to themselves as either Chicano, Latino, Mexicano, of Mexican descent, or of Spanish descent (P. Schmidt, 2003; Okagaki, 2006). One teacher, despite eighteen years' experience, found herself ill prepared to teach children on a Chippewa-Cree reservation partly because she knew relatively little about the history, culture, and community in which she taught (Starnes, 2006). Learn as much as you can about the subgroups your students come from, and keep these specific qualities in mind as you teach.

**3** **Above all, remember that each student is a unique person. Although descriptions of various ethnic groups and subgroups may accurately portray some general tendencies of a large group of people, they may apply only partly or not at all to given individuals.**

## pause & reflect

How can you use the concept of constructivism (discussed earlier in this book) to help students overcome any ethnocentrism they may have and understand the beliefs and practices of other cultures?

Rather than thinking of culture as a set of perceptions, thoughts, beliefs, and actions that are inherent in all individuals who nominally belong to a culture (perhaps because of surname or country of origin), you will be far better served in working with students and their parents if you take the time to understand the extent to which individuals participate in the practices of their cultural communities. For example, some Latino students may prefer cooperative learning arrangements because such behavior is the norm at home and in their community, whereas others may prefer to work independently because that behavior is more typical for them (Gutiérrez & Rogoff, 2003). And although many Latino students earn lower grades and test scores than their White peers, there are also many who do not fit this pattern. Researchers have found that Latino students who spoke English at home, who came from two-parent families, who spent more time on homework than their peers, and who had parents who supervised their homework not only significantly outscored their Latino peers who did not share these characteristics but also scored at the same level as White students who shared the same characteristics (Ramirez & Carpenter, 2005).

# ETHNICITY AND SOCIAL CLASS

Culture: how a group of people perceives, believes, thinks, behaves

As we pointed out in the opening paragraphs of this chapter, culture refers to the ways in which a group of people perceives, thinks about, and interacts with the world. It provides a set of norms that guide what we say and how we say it, what we feel, and what we do in various situations. Two significant factors that most readily distinguish one culture from another are ethnicity and social class.

## The Effect of Ethnicity on Learning

An **ethnic group** is a collection of people who identify with one another on the basis of one or more of the following characteristics: country from which one's ancestors came, race, religion, language, values, political interests, economic interests, and behavior patterns (Banks, 2006; Gollnick & Chinn, 2002). Viewed separately, the ethnic groups in the United States, particularly those of color, are numerical minorities; collectively, however, they constitute a considerable portion of American society (Banks, 2006). Most Americans identify with some ethnic group (Blacks, Chinese Americans, Latinos, German Americans, Irish Americans, and Italian Americans, to name but a few). As a teacher, you need to know how your students' ethnicity can affect student-teacher relationships.

Christine Bennett (2007) identifies five aspects of ethnicity that are potential sources of student-student and student-teacher misunderstanding: verbal communication, nonverbal communication, time orientation, social values, and instructional formats and learning processes.

**Verbal Communication Patterns** Problems with verbal communication can occur in a number of ways. First, classroom discussions may not go as planned if teachers have students who do not understand—or feel overly confined by—the mainstream convention of "you take a turn and then somebody else takes a turn." For example, in Latino families in which there are several siblings and the parenting style is authoritarian, children may be reluctant to enter into a teacher-led discussion in class. Because teachers, like parents, are viewed as authority figures, many children consider it disrespectful to offer their opinions. They are there to learn what the teacher tells them. But as with their siblings at home, they may be quite active in small-group discussions composed entirely of peers (García, 2002).

Second, because of differences in cultural experiences, some students may be reluctant to speak or perform in public, whereas others may prefer exchanges that resemble a free-for-all shouting match. Some American Indian children, for example, prefer to work on ideas and skills in private. A public performance is given only after an acceptable degree of mastery is attained (Bennett, 2007; Vasquez, 1990). This practice is not as unique to American Indian culture as it might seem at first glance. Music lessons and practices are typically done in private, and public performances are not given until a piece or program is mastered.

| Ethnic group members differ in verbal and nonverbal communication patterns

**Nonverbal Communication**   A form of nonverbal communication that mainstream American culture highly values is direct eye contact. Most people are taught to look directly at the person to whom they are speaking, as this behavior signifies honesty on the part of the speaker and interest on the part of the listener. Among certain American Indian, Latino, and Asian cultures, however, averting one's eyes is a sign of deference to and respect for the other person, whereas looking at someone directly while being corrected is a sign of defiance. Thus an Asian American, Latino, or American Indian student who looks down or away when being questioned or corrected about something is not necessarily trying to hide guilt or ignorance or to communicate lack of interest (Bennett, 2007; Howe, 1994; Pewewardy, 2002).

**Time Orientation**   Mainstream American culture is very time oriented, and people who know how to organize their time and work efficiently are praised and rewarded. We teach our children to value such statements as "Time is money" and "Never put off until tomorrow what you can do today." Nowhere else is this time orientation more evident than in our schools. Classes begin and end at a specified time regardless of whether one is interested in starting a project, pursuing a discussion, or finishing an experiment. But for students whose ethnic cultures are not so time bound (Latinos and American Indians, for example), such a rigid approach to learning may be upsetting. Indeed, it may also be upsetting to some students who reflect the mainstream culture (Bennett, 2007; Pewewardy, 2002).

| Ethnic group members may hold different values

**Social Values**   Two values that lie at the heart of mainstream American society are competition ("Competition brings out the best in people") and rugged individualism ("People's accomplishments should reflect their own efforts"). Because schools tend to reflect mainstream beliefs, many classroom activities are competitive and done on one's own for one's personal benefit. However, students from some ethnic groups, such as Mexican Americans, are more likely to have been taught to value cooperative relationships and family loyalty. These students may thus prefer group projects; they may also respond more positively to praise that emphasizes family pride rather than individual glory (Bennett, 2007; Vasquez, 1990).

| Ethnic group members may favor different learning arrangements and processes

**Instructional Formats and Learning Processes**   Finally, ethnic groups may differ in terms of the instructional formats and learning processes they prefer. The dominant instructional format, especially at the middle school and high school levels, is one in which all students work from the same text, workbook, and worksheets., Rows of chairs face the front of the room, and the teacher governs exchanges with students by talking, asking questions, and listening to answers (Sleeter & Grant,

2007). This approach to teaching may be somewhat incompatible with the learning conditions that students from other cultural backgrounds favor. For example, native Hawaiian children's achievement improved when teachers switched from whole-class instruction and independent seatwork to small-group learning centers, because the latter approach was more similar to the children's out-of-school social structure (Okagaki, 2001). Black students also seem to favor learning tasks that allow for interpersonal interaction, multiple activities, and the use of multiple sensory modalities (such as combining body movement with sound) (Sleeter & Grant, 2007). One way of teaching math to students with these preferences might be to engage them with problems that involve buying, trading, or borrowing.

Aspects of American Indian culture also call for flexibility in instructional formats and processes. Because longer periods of silence between speakers are more customary in Navajo than in Anglo-American culture, teachers need to wait longer for students to answer questions (Okagaki, 2001). Furthermore, because Navajo students are taught by their culture to treat serious learning as private, they may not fully participate in such traditionally Western activities as tests, debates, and contests (Okagaki, 2001; Soldier, 1997). Choctaw children are less likely than other children to speak individually in class, and to speak in shorter sentences when they do speak, but they are more likely to participate in choral responding (two or more students responding to the teacher simultaneously) because of their cultural emphasis on group processes (Okagaki, 2001). Bobby Ann Starnes, who taught on a Chippewa-Cree reservation in northern Montana, found that her students learned best when she used such instructional techniques and approaches as collaborative learning arrangements, open-ended questioning, inductive reasoning, whole-to-part sequencing of lessons, emphasis on visual learning strategies, and emphasizing students' cultural identity (Starnes, 2006).

With respect to learning processes, some researchers have found that many American Indians prefer visual imagery and drawing to verbal propositions as a way to represent knowledge mentally, and many have a preference for the field-dependent and reflective cognitive styles (Guild, 1994; Pewewardy, 2002). Additional evidence that the cultural backgrounds of students influence the learning process they use comes from the work of Nola Purdie and John Hattie (1996). They sought to determine whether there was any truth to the common perception that Japanese students tend to be literal learners who emphasize memorizing at the expense of their own views and interpretations. People who believe this description attribute it to the emphasis in Japanese culture on subordination of individual viewpoints to the group's perceptions and goals.

*Students from different ethnic groups often prefer different instructional formats and learning processes. Black students, for example, may favor cooperative learning over lecture/recitation, whereas American Indian students may dislike debates and contests.*

Purdie and Hattie found that the Japanese students they interviewed chose memorizing as their preferred learning process, whereas a similar group of Australian students gave it a very low preference rating (eighteenth out of twenty-four options). A group of Japanese students who had been living in Australia for almost three years at the time of the study fell in between these two extremes. These differences in learning processes may be related to differences in attitudes toward learning. Western students place a higher value on working independently, competing with others, and completing tasks efficiently (and Australian students can be considered Western in these respects). Japanese students, by contrast, place a higher value on working cooperatively with others, complying with authority, and being thorough in their approach to tasks (Li, 2002).

These findings suggest that although cultural background does influence choice of learning activity, the effects of culture seem to diminish as one becomes more accustomed to and comfortable with the values and practices of another culture.

## The Effect of Social Class on Learning

The social class from which a student comes plays an influential role in behavior. **Social class** is an indicator of an individual's or a family's relative standing in society. It is determined by such factors as annual income, occupation, amount of education, place of residence, types of organizations to which family members belong, manner of dress, and material possessions. The first three factors are used by the federal government to determine the closely related concept of **socioeconomic status (SES).** The influence of social class is such that the members of working-class Latino and Irish American families may have more in common than the members of an upper-middle-SES Latino family and those of a working-class Latino family (Gollnick & Chinn, 2002).

Keep in mind as you read the next several pages that although we often mention the impact of social class on Black, Latino, and American Indian students, the effects are often the same for low-SES Whites (see, for example, Evans & English, 2002).

Because of the severe and long-lasting historic pattern of discrimination experienced by ethnic groups of color in the United States, many members of these groups have fewer years of education, less prestigious occupations, and lower incomes than the average White person. In 2004, 17.8 percent of American children under age eighteen lived in families with incomes below the poverty level. Although most such children are White (meaning of European ancestry), Figure 4.2 shows that the poverty rates among Black, American Indian, and Hispanic American families are usually about three times higher than those for White children (U.S. Census Bureau, 2006).

*Poverty rates higher for ethnic families of color than for Whites*

**Graduation Rates and Achievement Levels**   How do such differences in social class influence learning and performance in school? One major effect is that significantly fewer Black, Latino, and American Indian adolescents graduate from high school than do Whites, thereby shortening their years of education and earning potential. Whereas 74.9 percent of Whites graduate from high school, only 50.2 percent of Blacks, 53.2 percent of Latinos, and 51.1 percent of American Indians do so (Swanson, 2004). Investigations into the reasons that minority students fail to complete school have found that social class factors, economic factors, school environment factors, and individual factors may all play a role. Compared with White students who graduate, minority students have lower levels of motivation, lower self-esteem, and weaker academic skills; they are also more impulsive. In addition, students who do not graduate nearly always report a sense of alienation from school because of low teacher expectations, expressions of racial or ethnic group prejudice from teachers and students, and unfair discrimination. Students required to repeat

**pause & reflect**

What steps might you take to reduce or eliminate the sense of alienation that causes many minority students to drop out of school?

**Figure 4.2** Percentage of Families Within Ethnic Groups Living Below Poverty Level in 2004

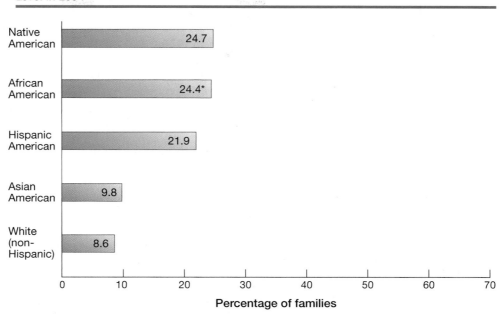

*The average from 2003 and 2004.

SOURCES: U.S. Census Bureau (2005a, 2006).

grades (recall our discussion of this topic earlier in the text) are among the most likely to drop out of school and not graduate.

During their time in school, many minority students achieve at significantly lower levels than do White students. Compared with White high school sophomores and seniors, Black, Latino, and American Indian students score lower on standardized tests of vocabulary, reading, writing, mathematics, and science (Ornstein & Levine, 2006). This achievement gap has been found even among Black students who are members of relatively affluent middle-SES families (Ogbu, 2003; Rothstein, 2004). These differences appear early. Results from the National Assessment of Educational Progress, as well as state tests, reveal that the reading, writing, mathematics, and science skills of Black and Latino children are substantially below those of White children as early as the fourth grade. Although the achievement gap has been gradually narrowing over the past several years in reading (Black and Latino students have improved at a faster rate than have White students), the same has not been the case for math, and so much work remains to be done (Coley, 2003; Davison, Seo, Davenport, Butterbaugh, & Davison, 2004; Education Trust, 2004; Okagaki, 2006; Perie, Moran, & Lutkus, 2005).

The long-standing achievement gap between low-SES (and some middle-SES) minority students and their White classmates is perhaps the most researched and discussed effect of social class on learning (e.g., Bell, 2002/2003; Denbo, 2002; Hrabowski, 2002/2003; Ladson-Billings, 2002; Lee, 2002; Lee & Bowen, 2006; Nieto, 2002/2003; Ogbu, 2003; Rothstein, 2004; Singham, 2003; Sirin, 2005). The exact reasons for the gap relate to a number of interweaving factors, including living conditions, family environment, characteristics of the student, and classroom environment. As you read the following sections about these factors, think about how they combine and reinforce one another—and about what you as a teacher can do to minimize their effect.

**Health and Living Conditions**  Many low-SES Americans do not receive satisfactory health care (Stinson, 2003). For example, there is a greater incidence of premature

---

Minority children often score lower on tests, drop out of school sooner

Achievement gap between low-SES minority students and White students due to living conditions, family environment, characteristics of the student, and classroom environment

births, birth defects, and infant mortality among low-SES children as compared with middle-SES children (Umar, 2003). Because poor children do not receive medical or dental care regularly, accurate statistics on general health are difficult to compile. It seems reasonable to assume, however, that the same inadequate nutrition and health care that leads to elevated infant mortality rates probably also leads to higher rates of illness in later years.

Another health-related factor in the development and intellectual performance of low-SES children is lead poisoning. Because many of these children live in homes that were painted prior to the discontinuation of lead-based paint, their ingestion of paint dust and chips leads to elevated levels of lead in the blood. Exposure to lead, even in small amounts, is associated with low standardized test scores, attention deficits, and disruptive behavior in children. Almost 37 percent of Black children and 17 percent of Mexican American children between the ages of one and five have lead levels in their blood that are associated with cognitive impairments and behavioral problems. These impairments need not be permanent, however: medication can reduce the level of lead in the blood, leading to an improvement in the children's academic performance (Jackson, 1999).

| Low-SES children more likely to live in stressful environment that interferes with studying

Furthermore, many low-SES students, especially those in urban areas, live in relatively small, and sometimes overcrowded, apartments. Adequate study space is often nonexistent, and parental supervision is spotty or absent. In their neighborhoods, street crime is a constant threat (Levine & Levine, 1996). An additional burden for approximately 25 percent of Black and Latino primary grade children is changing schools due to a change in residence by the family. The challenge of new peers, instructional methods, and curricula may exacerbate whatever learning problems these students already have (Evans, 2005).

**Family Environment**    Low-SES students are more likely than middle-SES students to grow up in one-parent families. Sixty-two percent of Black students live with one parent versus 25 percent of White students, with the father usually being the missing parent (Evans, 2005). Like many other risk factors, the effect of a one-parent family on the academic performance of a child is not straightforward. It depends on such factors as the duration and cause of the separation, the age and sex of the child, and the type of interactions the child has with the remaining parent. But although one-parent families may not negatively affect a child's performance in school, two-parent families are likely to be more effective because both parents have the potential to exert a positive influence (Levine & Levine, 1996).

*On average, ethnic minority and low-SES students do not perform as well as other groups in school because of such factors as poor health care, an unstable family environment, low motivation, negative attitudes toward school, and negative classroom environments.*

Some studies show that parents' support for their children's schooling varies by social class and ethnic group. For example, White and Asian American adolescents are more likely than Latino or Black adolescents to get support for academic achievement from parents as well as friends (Lee & Bowen, 2006; Okagaki, 2001, 2006).

Moreover, compared with the parents of low-SES children, the parents of middle-SES children in the United States expose their children to a wider variety of experiences. They tend to buy their children more books, educational toys and games, to take them on more trips that expand their knowledge of the world, and to talk to them more. (Because low-SES parents speak about 600 words per hour to their children, whereas middle- and upper-middle-SES parents speak about 2,100 words per hour to their children, many Black and Latino children start school with a vocabulary of about 5,000 words, whereas the average White student has a vocabulary of about 20,000 words.) These experiences accumulate and make school learning more familiar and easy than it would otherwise be. A child who has not had such experiences is likely to be at a disadvantage when placed in competitive academic situations (Evans, 2005; Hart & Risley, 1995; Levine & Levine, 1996). Furthermore, there has been increasing concern about the development of a technological underclass of children whose families cannot afford to provide access to computers and online services at home. In 2004, 66 percent of children whose average family income was under $35,000 per year had Internet access at home, whereas 84 percent of children whose average family income was over $50,000 had such access (Henry J. Kaiser Family Foundation, 2004).

Overall, the interactions that occur between low-SES parents and their children tend to lack the characteristic of mediation (a concept we introduced earlier in the book in connection with Vygotsky's theory of cognitive development). When mediation occurs, someone who is more intellectually advanced than the learner presents, explains, and interprets stimuli in a way that produces a more meaningful understanding than the learner could have obtained working alone.

To illustrate this process, imagine a child walking alone through a hands-on science museum looking at the various exhibits, occasionally pushing the buttons of interactive displays, and listening to some of the prerecorded messages. What the child learns from this experience is likely to be a haphazard collection of isolated fragments of information that are not meaningful. Now imagine another child of the same age looking at and interacting with the same exhibits but accompanied by a parent or older sibling who wants this to be a meaningful learning experience. The parent or sibling points out specific aspects of the displays, names them, describes their purpose, and explains how they work. This child is more likely than the first child to construct a set of cohesive, interrelated, and meaningful knowledge structures (Ben-Hur, 1998).

**Students' Motivation, Beliefs, and Attitudes**   Many low-SES students (as well as some middle-SES students) may not be strongly motivated to do well in school because of one or more of several variables. One is lower levels of a characteristic called *need for achievement*. A need for achievement (which is discussed more fully in Chapter 12, "Motivation and Perceptions of Self") is a drive to accomplish tasks and is thought to be one of the main reasons that people vary in their willingness to invest time and energy in the achievement of a goal. Research suggests that low-SES Black students score lower than comparable groups of White students on tests of need for achievement, but this racial difference is considerably smaller among middle-SES samples (Cooper & Dorr, 1995).

Other studies have found that some minority students, especially males, tend to develop beliefs and attitudes that inhibit strong academic performance:

• Black and Latino adolescents are more likely than Asian American or White adolescents to believe that they can get a good job without first getting a good education.

Asian American, White, and Latino adolescents who are doing well in school, on the other hand, see getting a good education as a prerequisite to getting a good job (Ogbu, 2003; Okagaki, 2001).

- Ethnic and racial minority middle school females appear to place a higher value on academic achievement than do ethnic and racial minority middle school males. When ethnic and racial minority females from a low-income urban elementary and middle school were asked to identify classmates whom they admired, respected, and wanted to be like, about 60 percent of second- and fourth-grade students and 66 percent of seventh-grade students selected a high-achieving classmate. Ethnic and racial minority males from the same schools responded similarly, but only through fourth grade. Whereas 51 percent of second graders and 52 percent of fourth graders chose a high-achieving classmate, only 21 percent of seventh-grade males made that choice. Average achievers were selected by about 56 percent of seventh-grade males, and low achievers by about 23 percent. Data from other studies indicate that although Black males recognize the importance of working hard, many of them adopt an indifferent attitude toward high levels of school achievement.
- Personal experiences with racial discrimination (or even the suspicion that one has been discriminated against) have been linked to decreased perceptions of mastery, mistrust of teachers and school rules, and negative attitudes toward school (Graham & Hudley, 2005).

This decline in achievement-related values and attitudes on the part of minority male adolescents, which is sometimes referred to as an aversion to "acting White," has been corroborated by the observations of teachers, who made such comments as "They can do the work but they just don't seem to care" and "In the peer culture, one risks rejection by exerting effort in school" (Graham & Taylor, 2002). In addition, research finds that Black students with a B+ or higher grade-point average (GPA) and Latino students with a C+ or higher GPA were less popular with their peers than were Black and Latino students with lower grades (Fryer & Torelli, 2005). This inability to establish what might be called an academic identity appears to be related to a sense that one is not part of the larger school community, that school does not meet one's needs, that one is incapable of meeting academic demands, and that schoolwork is not part of who one wants to be (Fryer & Torelli, 2005; Jackson, 2003; Okagaki, 2006).

The frustration that is created by peers who do not share one's academic values was described by a Black female student who was attending a student conference of the Minority Student Achievement Network:

> I'm a member from Amherst, Massachusetts, and it is predominantly White. . . . I'm able to get along with the White kids, but it's the Black kids that I find I have a hard time relating to . . . . In class, they're always thinking, "There goes that girl, trying to be smart, trying to 'act White.'" It seems like I can't relate to them, and I'm Black myself. How is that supposed to make me feel? I'm trying to fit in both worlds, and it's like I have no place. (Ash, 2000, p. 6)

The relationship of low self-esteem to low achievement is dramatic but not always simple. In one study (van Laar, 2000), many Black high school and college students scored as high on measures of self-esteem as did Whites even though the Black students had lower levels of achievement. This seeming paradox results from minority students' belief that because of discrimination, they will not have available to them the same opportunities for employment and career advancement that are available to White students. Being able to blame the environment rather than oneself allows one to maintain a healthy sense of self-esteem. This perception may also play a role in minorities' lower need for achievement, the characteristic we discussed at the beginning of this section.

**Classroom Environment**   Although teachers cannot work magical changes in a student's social class, health, family, or peer group, they can, as the following study illustrates, do a great deal to encourage learning among students of all social classes. First-grade children who were judged to be at-risk for academic failure, either because their mothers had below-average levels of education or because they demonstrated such maladaptive classroom behaviors as aggression, defiance, lack of sustained attention, and poor ability to follow instructions, scored at about the same level on a standardized achievement test as their not-at-risk peers when they experienced high levels of emotional and instructional support from their teachers. By contrast, at-risk children whose teachers were judged to provide lower levels of emotional and instructional support scored significantly below their not-at-risk peers (Hamre & Pianta, 2005).

> Classroom atmosphere, teachers' approaches connected with achievement levels of low-SES students

Other studies have found high levels of achievement among low-SES students to be associated with the following attitudes and approaches among teachers (Burris & Welner, 2005; Denbo, 2002; Hamre & Pianta, 2005; Mathis, 2005; Rolón, 2002/2003):

- Awareness of child's needs, moods, interests, and capabilities
- Classroom atmosphere characterized by pleasant conversations, spontaneous laughter, and exclamations of excitement
- Teachers' high but realistic expectations for their students
- Mastery goals (an approach discussed later in this chapter and in Chapter 12)
- Never accepting low-quality work
- The use of scaffolded instruction (as discussed in Chapter 3, "Theories of Psychosocial and Cognitive Development")
- Aligning instruction with standards (discussed more fully in Chapter 13, "Approaches to Instruction")
- Using formative evaluation (discussed more fully in Chapter 15, "Assessment of Classroom Learning")
- Eliminating ability grouping (in the elementary and middle school grades) and tracking (in the high school grades) systems and using heterogeneously grouped classes supplemented by extra support classes and after-school help. One New York high school that did this increased its graduation rate for Black/Latino and White students from 32 percent and 88 percent, respectively, to 82 percent and 97 percent (Burris & Welner, 2005). We discuss ability grouping and tracking more fully in the Chapter 6, "Accommodating Student Diversity."

Teachers' expectations for their students are so important that we devote the next section to this subject.

## The Effect of Ethnicity and Social Class on Teachers' Expectations

So far we have described how students' ethnic and social class backgrounds influence their approach to and success with various learning tasks. Now we would like to tell you how those and other characteristics often affect (consciously and unconsciously) the expectations that teachers have for student performance and how those expectations affect the quantity and quality of work that students exhibit. This phenomenon has been extensively studied since 1968 and is known variously as the *Pygmalion effect*, the *self-fulfilling prophecy*, and the **teacher expectancy effect**. By becoming aware of the major factors that influence teachers' perceptions of and actions toward students, you may be able to reduce subjectivity to a minimum, particularly with students whose cultural backgrounds are very different from your own.

> Teacher expectancy (Pygmalion) effect: impact of teacher expectations leads to self-fulfilling prophecy

The teacher expectancy effect basically works as follows:

1. On the basis of such characteristics as race, SES, ethnic background, dress, speech pattern, and test scores, teachers form expectancies about how various students will perform in class.

2. They subtly communicate those expectancies to the students in a variety of ways.
3. Students come to behave in a way that is consistent with what the teacher expects.

**pause & reflect**

How have your experiences with members of ethnic or racial minority groups been similar to or different from what you have heard and read about those groups? Which source (personal experience or ideas derived from others) most affects your expectations for minority students?

This phenomenon was first proposed by Robert Rosenthal and Lenore Jacobson in their 1968 book, *Pygmalion in the Classroom*. They described an experiment in which first- through sixth-grade teachers were led to believe that certain children had untapped potential and were "likely to show unusual intellectual gains in the year ahead" because of their scores on a new kind of ability test. In fact, the test was composed of standard items, and the designated students were chosen at random. Nevertheless, Rosenthal and Jacobson reported that the students who were labeled potential achievers showed significant gains in intelligence quotient (IQ) and that the reason for these gains was that their teachers expected more of these students. The authors referred to this phenomenon as the *Pygmalion effect* because they felt that teacher expectations had influenced the students to become intelligent in the same way that the expectations of the mythical Greek sculptor Pygmalion caused a statue he had carved to come to life.

**Research on the Effects of Teachers' Expectancies**    Given the obvious implications of the teacher expectancy effect for shaping student behavior, researchers wasted no time investigating its validity and limits (see Spitz, 1999, for an excellent summary and analysis of the original and subsequent research, and Rosenthal, 2002, for the views of the senior author of *Pygmalion* on the original study). Despite the dramatic results that Rosenthal and Jacobson reported, subsequent research showed that the effect of teacher expectancy on IQ scores was essentially limited to first- and second-grade students, was moderate in strength at those grade levels, and occurred only when it was induced within the first two weeks of the school year (Raudenbush, 1984). Apparently, once teachers have had an opportunity to observe and interact with their students, they view these experiences as more credible and informative than the results of a mental ability test.

| Limited effect of teacher expectancy on IQ scores

But research that has investigated the effect of teacher expectancy on classroom achievement and participation has generally found sizable positive *and* negative effects (Brophy, 1983; Chen & Bargh, 1997; Good & Nicholls, 2001; Jussim, Eccles, & Madon, 1997; Rosenthal, 1985). In addition, it appears that teacher expectations are more likely to maintain already existing tendencies than to alter well-established behaviors drastically. For example, primary grade teachers react differently to students in the fast-track reading group than to students in the slow-track group. When working with the more proficient readers, teachers tend to smile, lean toward the students, and establish eye contact more often, and they tend to give criticism in friendlier, gentler tones than they use in the slow-track group. They often overlook the oral reading errors of proficient readers, and when they give corrections, they do so at the end of the sentence or other meaningful unit rather than in the middle of such units. And they ask comprehension questions more often than factual questions as a means of monitoring students' attention to the reading selection.

| Strong effect of teacher expectancy on achievement, participation

In contrast, teachers correct less proficient readers more often and in places that interrupt meaningful processing of the text, give these students less time to decode difficult words or to correct themselves, and ask low-level factual questions as a way of checking on students' attention. Teachers' body posture is often characterized by frowning, pursing the lips, shaking the head, pointing a finger, and sitting erect. Offering unsolicited help and giving enthusiastic praise to Black students may lead at least some of those students to infer that they have lower levels of academic ability. In sum, through a variety of subtle ways, teachers communicate to students that they expect them to perform well or poorly and then create a situation that is consistent with the expectation. As a result, initial differences between good and poor readers either remain or widen over the course of the school career (Graham & Hudley, 2005; Wuthrick, 1990).

**Factors That Help Create Expectancies**   In addition to documenting the existence of teacher expectancy effects and the conditions under which they occur, researchers have sought to identify the factors that might create high or low teacher expectations. Here are some important factors taken from analyses by Thomas Good and Sharon Nicholls (2001), Gloria Ladson-Billings (1994), Vonnie McLoyd (1998), and Sonia Nieto (2004):

- Middle-SES students are expected to receive higher grades than low-SES students, even when their IQ scores and achievement test scores are similar.
- Black students are given less attention and are expected to learn less than White students, even when both groups have the same ability.
- Teachers tend to perceive children from poor homes as less mature, less capable of following directions, and less capable of working independently than children from more advantaged homes.
- Teachers who think of intelligence as a fixed and stable capacity are more likely to formulate negative and positive expectations of students than are teachers who think of intelligence as a collection of skills that can be shaped.
- Teachers are more influenced by negative information about students (for example, low test scores) than they are by neutral or positive information.
- High-achieving students receive more praise than low-achieving ones.
- Attractive children are often perceived by teachers to be brighter, more capable, and more social than unattractive children.
- Teachers tend to approve of girls' behavior more frequently than they approve of boys' behavior.

It is important to bear in mind that these factors (plus others such as ethnic background, knowledge of siblings, and impressions of parents) usually operate in concert to produce an expectancy. The following Suggestions for Teaching in Your Classroom will give you some ideas for combating the damaging effects of teacher expectancies, as well as other problems often faced by low-SES and minority students.

> Teacher expectancies influenced by social class, ethnic background, achievement, attractiveness, gender

# Suggestions for Teaching in Your Classroom

## Promoting Classroom Achievement for All Students

**1 Use every possible means for motivating educationally disadvantaged students to do well in school.**

A good place to start in thinking about how to teach such students is with the opinions of the students themselves. According to the responses of almost four hundred low-income, inner-city middle school and high school students, good teachers do the following:

- Push students to learn by such actions as not accepting excuses for missed or late work, constantly checking homework, giving rewards, and keeping parents informed.

- Maintain an orderly and well-run classroom in which disruptions are kept to a minimum. (You will find more detailed information on how to create such an environment in Chapter 11, "Leading Classroom Learning.")
- Make themselves always available to provide a student with help in whatever form the student prefers. Some students, for example, want help after school, some during class, some individually, some by working with peers, and some through whole-class question-and-answer sessions. Some students may ask for help only if they are sure that no one besides the teacher knows they are receiving it.
- Strive to have all students understand the material by not rushing through lessons and by offering explanations in a clear step-by-step fashion and in various ways.
- Use a variety of instructional tactics, such as group work, lecture, textbook reading, worksheets, whole-class instruction, and hands-on activities.
- Make an effort to understand students' behavior by trying to understand the personalities and after-school lives of students (Corbett & Wilson, 2002).

The perceptions of these students are remarkably consistent with a set of five teaching standards that is based on Vygotsky's theory of cognitive development and that was designed with low-SES, ethnic minority students in mind (Doherty, Hilberg, Epaloose, & Tharp, 2002; Tharp, Estrada, Dalton, & Yamauchi, 2000). The five standards are as follows:

- *Joint Productive Activity:* The teacher works with small groups of students on a joint project, modeling language, skills, and problem-solving strategies.
- *Language and Literacy Development:* The teacher designs activities that involve extended language use and development of content vocabulary and assists students through questioning, rephrasing, and modeling.
- *Contextualization:* The teacher relates new information to what students already know by situating problems and issues in familiar home and community contexts.
- *Challenging Activities:* The teacher gives students challenging objectives to master and provides feedback about their progress.
- *Instructional Conversation:* The teacher and small groups of students discuss their views about the relevance of learning certain topics.

We need to say a last word about homework as a way to promote achievement. The amount of homework assigned to students over the past fifteen years has increased, largely because of the need for increasing numbers of students to achieve state-mandated standards and comply with the provisions of the No Child Left Behind Act of 2001. Educators believed that increasing the amount of homework assigned to students would lead to higher grades and test scores. Does it? Not surprisingly, the main conclusion to be drawn from the research literature (see, for example, Cooper, 2001; Cooper, Robinson, & Patall, 2006; and Muhlenbruck, Cooper, Nye, & Lindsay, 2000) is that it depends on the student's grade level. Compared with peers who did no homework, there was no benefit for elementary grade students and only a modest benefit for middle school students. The greatest benefit occurred among high school students.

**2** **Use a variety of instructional techniques to help educationally disadvantaged students master both basic and higher-order knowledge and skills.**

Research from the 1970s (Brophy & Evertson, 1976) found that the classroom and standardized test performances of educationally disadvantaged students improves when teachers follow these seven guidelines:

- Eliminate distractions and maximize the amount of time students actually spend working on a task
- Establish high expectations and a classroom climate that supports achievement
- Break tasks down into small, easy-to-manage pieces, and arrange the pieces in a logical sequence
- Have students work on specific exercises in small groups

**JOURNAL ENTRY**
Using Productive Techniques
of Teaching

- Ask direct questions that have direct answers
- Provide frequent opportunities for practice and review
- Provide timely corrective feedback

Designing classroom instruction along these guidelines has both benefits and costs. The benefits are that students spend more time on-task, success tends to be more consistent, and more students reach a higher level of mastery of content knowledge and skills. The main cost is the lack of transfer that usually occurs when knowledge and skills are learned as isolated segments in a nonmeaningful context. A second cost is that students have few opportunities to interact with one another.

If teachers combine the seven guidelines just mentioned with current learning theory and research (Gordon, Rogers, Comfort, Gavula, & McGee, 2001; Knapp & Shields, 1990; Knapp, Shields, & Turnbull, 1995; Means & Knapp, 1991; as well as later chapters of this book), they may be able to raise the basic skill level of educationally disadvantaged students *and* improve their ability to transfer what they have learned to meaningful and realistic contexts. To accomplish this goal, a teacher should also do the following:

- Provide opportunities for students to apply ideas and skills to real-life or realistic situations in order to make the lesson more meaningful. For example, after collecting and analyzing information, students might write letters to the mayor or city council requesting more streetlights for increased safety at night or improvements to basketball courts and baseball fields.
- Allow students the opportunity to discuss among themselves the meaning of ideas and their potential applications. In making a request of a government official, students should be encouraged to discuss which arguments are likely to be most effective and how they would respond should the official turn their proposal down.
- Embed basic skills instruction within the context of complex and realistic tasks. Letter-writing campaigns, for example, can be used to practice such basic English skills as vocabulary acquisition, spelling, punctuation, and grammar.
- Point out how classroom tasks relate to students' out-of-school experiences. One example is to draw attention to the basic similarities between poetry and rap music.
- Model for and explain to students the various thinking processes that are activated and used when one engages in a complex task. As you will see when you read Chapter 10, "Social Cognitive Theory," effective learners approach tasks strategically, which is to say they analyze the task, formulate a plan for dealing with it, use a variety of specific learning skills, and monitor their progress. These are fundamental learning processes that are almost never made explicit to students.
- Gradually ease students into the process of dealing with complex and realistic tasks. There is no question that the approach described in this list carries with it more risk of failure than was the case for the structured, small-scale approach of the 1970s. But much of this risk can be minimized by *scaffolding*, which we described in Chapter 3. As you may recall, in scaffolding, the teacher initially provides a considerable amount of support through explanations, demonstrations, and prompts of various types. As students demonstrate their ability to carry out more of a task independently, the scaffolding is withdrawn.

**3** **Be alert to the potential dangers of the teacher expectancy effect. Concentrate on individuals while guarding against the impact of stereotyping.**

Myrna Gantner (1997), an eighth-grade teacher in an inner-city middle school near the Mexican border, learned the following lessons about treating her Latino students as individuals:

- Treat Latino students the same as you would treat any other student. When teachers believe that inner-city Latino students are less capable than other students, they tend to give them less time and attention. Students quickly notice these differences and may respond with lower-quality work and more disruptive behavior.

- Don't prejudge students. If you believe that most Latino children use drugs, belong to gangs, or have limited academic ability, students will eventually become aware of your prejudice and act accordingly. Gantner's students said they were most appreciative of teachers who were interested in them as individuals, had high expectations for them, and showed them how to achieve their goals.
- Don't ridicule or make fun of students' limited English proficiency. The best way to acquire proficiency in a second language is to use it frequently. Students will be less inclined to do so if they think teachers and other students will laugh at their mistakes.

**4** **Remember that in addition to being a skilled teacher, you are also a human being who may at times react subjectively to students.**

**JOURNAL ENTRY**
Ways to Minimize Subjectivity

Try to control the influence of such factors as name, ethnic background, gender, physical characteristics, knowledge of siblings or parents, grades, and test scores. If you think you can be honest with yourself, you might attempt to describe your prejudices so that you will be in a position to guard against them. (Do you tend to be annoyed when you read descriptions of the exploits of members of a particular religious or ethnic group, for example?) Try to think of a student independently of his or her siblings and parents.

# MULTICULTURAL EDUCATION PROGRAMS

The concept of multicultural education has been around for some time. Many of the elements that constitute contemporary programs were devised seventy to eighty years ago as part of a then-current emphasis on international education (Gollnick & Chinn, 2002). In this section, we will give you some idea of what it might be like to teach today from a multicultural perspective by describing the basic goals, assumptions, and characteristics of modern programs.

## Assumptions and Goals

The various arguments in favor of multicultural education that are made by its proponents (for example, Banks, 1994, 2002, 2006; Bennett, 2007; García, 2002; Gollnick & Chinn, 2002; Ogbu, 1992; Singer, 1994) stem from several assumptions. These assumptions and the goals that flow from them appear in Table 4.2.

## Basic Approaches and Concepts

Multicultural education can be approached in different ways

**Approaches**    James Banks (2002, 2006), a noted authority on multicultural education, describes four approaches to multicultural education. Most multicultural programs, particularly those in the primary grades, adopt what he calls the *contributions approach*. In this approach, ethnic historical figures whose values and behaviors are consistent with American mainstream culture (for example, Booker T. Washington, Sacajawea) are studied, whereas individuals who have challenged the dominant view (such as W. E. B. Du Bois, Geronimo) are ignored.

A second approach, which incorporates the first, is called the *ethnic additive approach*. Here, an instructional unit composed of concepts, themes, points of view, and individual accomplishments is simply added to the curriculum. The perspective from which an ethnic group's contributions are viewed, however, tends to be that of the mainstream.

| Table 4.2 | Common Assumptions and Goals of Multicultural Education Program |
| --- | --- |
| **Assumptions of Multicultural Education** | **Goals of Multicultural Education** |
| U.S. culture has been formed by the contributions of different cultural groups | Promote understanding of the origins and lack of validity of ethnic stereotypes (e.g., Blacks are violent, Jews are stingy, Asian Americans excel at math and science, Latinos are hot tempered) |
| Individuals must have self-esteem and group esteem to work productively with people from other cultures | Teachers should give all students a sense of being valued and accepted by expressing positive attitudes, using appropriate instructional methods, and formulating fair disciplinary policies and practices |
| Learning about the achievements of one's cultural group will raise self- and group esteem | Promote self-acceptance and respect for other cultures by studying the impact ethnic groups have had on American society |
| American society benefits from positive interactions among members of different cultural groups | Reduce ethnocentrism and increase positive relationships among members of different ethnic groups by understanding the viewpoints and products of these groups |
| Academic performance is enhanced when teachers incorporate various cultural values and experiences into instructional lessons | Help students master basic reading, writing, and computation skills by embedding them in a personally meaningful (i.e., ethnically related) context |

*Multicultural programs aim to promote respect for diversity, reduction of ethnocentrism and stereotypes, improved learning*

## pause & reflect

Think about the four approaches to multicultural education described in this section. What advantages and disadvantages do you see for each approach? Which approach would you use? Why?

In a third approach, which Banks calls the *transformation approach*, the assumption is that there is no one valid way of understanding people, events, concepts, and themes. Rather, there are multiple views, and each has something of value to offer. For example, the view of the early pioneers who settled the American West could be summed up by such phrases as "How the West Was Won" and "The Westward Movement." But the Native American tribes who had lived there for thousands of years may well have referred to the same event as "How the West Was Taken" or "The Westward Plague." You may recognize that the transformation approach is based on the principle of constructivism (discussed in earlier chapters). Because this approach requires the concrete operational schemes described in Chapter 3, it is typically introduced at the middle school level.

Finally, there is the *decision making and social action approach*. It incorporates all of the components of the previous approaches and adds the requirement that students make decisions and take actions concerning a concept, issue, or problem being studied.

*Multicultural lessons organized around key concepts*

**Concepts** Regardless of which approach you use, Banks (2002) suggests that multicultural units and lessons be organized around a set of key concepts that incorporate a range of facts, generalizations, and subject-matter disciplines. These concepts can be used to analyze a particular ethnic group or to compare and contrast groups. The following set of key concepts and associated questions illustrates what Banks has in mind:

*Immigration:* From what country or countries did this group originate? When and in what numbers did this group immigrate to the United States?

*Culture:* What ethnic elements (for example, values, customs, perspectives) are present in the group's culture today? How is the group's culture reflected in its music, literature, and art?

*In order for children to understand and appreciate different cultural values and experiences, those values and experiences have to be integrated into the curriculum and rewarded by the teacher.*

*Identity:* To what extent does the group see itself as separate and apart from other groups in society because of its unique history?

*Perspectives:* To what extent do most members of the group hold the same view on an issue of importance to it?

*Ethnic institutions:* What educational, commercial, religious, and social organizations were formed by members of the group to help satisfy its needs?

*Demographic, social, political, and economic status:* How can the current status of the group be described in terms of numbers, political influence, and income?

*Racism and discrimination:* In what ways has this group been subjected to racism and discrimination?

*Intraethnic diversity:* How do members of the group differ from each other in terms of such major characteristics as geographical location, social class, religion, and political affiliation?

*Acculturation:* To what extent has the group influenced and been influenced by the mainstream society?

## pause & reflect

Why are these concepts so important that Banks labels them key concepts?

### Characteristics of Effective Multicultural Teachers

Although Banks's ideas about how to structure multicultural education programs are well conceived, they require the efforts of effective teachers for their potential benefits to be realized. Eugene García (2002), on the basis of his own research and that of others, identifies several characteristics that contribute to the success some teachers have in teaching students from culturally diverse backgrounds. Briefly stated, the effective multicultural teacher does the following:

1. Provides students with clear objectives.
2. Continuously communicates high expectations to the student.
3. Monitors student progress and provides immediate feedback.
4. Has several years of experience in teaching culturally diverse students.
5. Can clearly explain why she uses specific instructional techniques (such as the ones described in the next section).
6. Strives to embed instruction in a meaningful context. For example, a topic from one subject, such as controlling crop-damaging insects with insecticide, could be

*Advocates of multicultural education believe that ethnic minority students learn more effectively when some of their learning materials and assignments contain ethnically related content.*

extended to other subjects (examining the effects of insecticide on human health, graphing crop yields sprayed with various types and amounts of insecticides).

7. Provides opportunities for active learning through small-group work and hands-on activities. One teacher, for example, created writing workshops in which students wrote, revised, edited, and published their products for others to read.

8. Exhibits a high level of dedication. Effective multicultural teachers are among the first to arrive at school and among the last to leave, work on weekends, buy supplies with their own money, and are constantly looking for opportunities to improve their instructional practices.

9. Enhances students' self-esteem by having classroom materials and practices reflect students' cultural and linguistic backgrounds.

10. Has a strong affinity for students. Effective multicultural teachers describe their culturally diverse students in such terms as "I love these children like my own" and "We are a family here."

## VIDEO CASE ◄◄ ▶ ►►

### Culturally Responsive Teaching: A Multicultural Lesson for Elementary Students

*Watch the video, study the artifacts in the case, and reflect upon the following questions:*

1. Does the "Coming to America" lesson shown in this Video Case meet any of the goals listed in Table 4.2? If so, which ones?

2. Do you find Mrs. Hurley to be an effective multicultural teacher? How does she meet the criteria listed?

## Instructional Goals, Methods, and Materials

**Instructional Goals**  Teachers whose classes have a high percentage of children from ethnic minority and low-SES backgrounds often assume that they need to emphasize mastery of basic skills (such as computation, spelling, grammar, and word decoding) because minority and low-SES students are often deficient in those skills. Although this approach does improve children's performance on tests of basic skills, some educators argue that it does so at the expense of learning higher-level skills and that it is possible for students from poverty backgrounds to acquire both basic and higher-level skills.

Michael Knapp, Patrick Shields, and Brenda Turnbull (1995) conducted a study to investigate this issue. They examined teaching practices in almost 140 first- through sixth-grade classrooms in fifteen elementary schools that served large numbers of children from low-SES families to determine whether the assumption that low-SES children can acquire both basic and higher-level skills is true. Over a two-year period, these authors studied classrooms in which the learning of basic skills was paramount, as well as classrooms that emphasized higher-level and more meaningful outcomes. Teachers in the first group made extensive use of drill and practice, tasks that were limited in their demands, and tasks that could be completed quickly. Teachers in the second group used classroom discussions to let students work out the reasons behind mathematical procedures or explore alternative solutions to math problems, required students to read longer passages and gave them opportunities to discuss what they had read, taught them reading comprehension strategies, and gave them more extended writing assignments.

Knapp and his colleagues found that children whose instruction emphasized conceptual understanding and problem solving performed better on mathematics, reading comprehension, and writing test items that measured advanced skills than their counterparts whose instruction focused on mastery of basic skills. And their performance on basic skill items was either no worse or better than that of students whose teachers emphasized the learning of basic skills.

**Instructional Methods**   The three instructional tactics that are recommended most often by proponents of multicultural education are peer tutoring, cooperative learning, and mastery learning. Although each of these techniques can be used with any group of students and for almost any purpose, they are so well suited to the goals of multicultural education that the phrase "culturally responsive teaching" has been used to describe them (Wlodkowski & Ginsberg, 1995).

| Peer tutoring improves achievement

***Peer Tutoring***   As its name implies, **peer tutoring** involves the teaching of one student by another. The students may be similar in age or separated by one or more years. (The latter arrangement is usually referred to as *cross-age tutoring*.) The theoretical basis of peer tutoring comes from Jean Piaget's notions about cognitive development. Recall from our discussion of Piaget earlier in the book that cognitive growth depends on the presence of a disequilibrating stimulus that the learner is motivated to eliminate. When children with different cognitive schemes (because of differences in age, knowledge, or cultural background) are forced to interact with each other, cognitive conflict results. Growth occurs when children try to resolve this conflict by comparing and contrasting each other's views.

Researchers have consistently found that peer tutoring (also referred to as peer-assisted learning) aids achievement for a wide range of students and subject matters. An analysis of eighty-one studies published between 1974 and 2000 found that on average students who received peer tutoring scored at the 63rd percentile on a measure of achievement, whereas students who did not receive peer tutoring scored at the 50th percentile. The strongest effects were obtained for younger students (grades 1–3), urban students, ethnic minority students, and low-SES students. Also, stronger effects were produced by studies in which students rather than teachers were responsible for such self-management behaviors as setting goals, selecting rewards, and administering rewards (Rohrbeck, Ginsburg-Block, Fantuzzo, & Miller, 2003). Peer tutoring also has positive effects on nonachievement outcomes. An analysis of thirty-six studies by the same researchers (Ginsburg-Block, Rohrbeck, & Fantuzzo, 2006) found positive effects for social outcomes (such as ability to make friends and cooperativeness) and self-concept for the same groups. Because peer tutoring involves working cooperatively either in pairs or small groups, American Indian and Latino students are particularly likely to be comfortable with its use.

Cooperative learning: students work together in small groups

***Cooperative Learning*** Closely related to peer tutoring is cooperative learning. The general idea behind **cooperative learning** is that by working in small, heterogeneous groups (of four or five students total) and by helping one another master the various aspects of a particular task, students will be more motivated to learn, will learn more than if they had to work independently, and will forge stronger interpersonal relationships than they would by working alone.

David Johnson and Roger Johnson (1998), who have been researching the effects of cooperative learning for over twenty-five years, make a basic observation about the relevance of cooperative learning to the goals of multicultural education programs: students cannot learn everything they need to know about cultural diversity from reading books and articles. A deeper understanding of the nature and value of diversity is gained by learning how to work cooperatively with individuals from different cultural backgrounds.

Cooperative learning fosters better understanding among ethnically diverse students

Robert Slavin (1995), a leading exponent of cooperative learning, reports that cooperative learning produced significantly higher levels of achievement than did noncooperative arrangements in sixty-three of ninety-nine studies (64 percent). The results for the student team learning programs have been the most consistently positive. Of particular relevance to this chapter are the findings that students who cooperate in learning are more likely to list as friends peers from different ethnic groups and are better able to take the perspective of a classmate than are students who do not work in cooperative groups.

Cooperative learning is a generally effective instructional tactic that is likely to be particularly useful with Latino, Black, and American Indian students. These cultures value a communal orientation that emphasizes cooperation and sharing. Thus these students may be more prepared than other individuals to work productively as part of a group by carrying out their own responsibilities, as well as helping others do the same (Bennett, 2007; Nieto, 2004; Soldier, 1989). One study found that small groups of Black fifth-grade students who were told that they had to help one another learn a reading passage recalled more of the text than did similar students who worked either in pairs or individually (Dill & Boykin, 2000). We will have more to say about cooperative learning and its effects on learning in Chapter 13.

Mastery learning: most students can master the curriculum

***Mastery Learning*** The third frequently recommended instructional tactic, **mastery learning,** is an approach to teaching and learning that assumes that most students can master the curriculum if certain conditions are established: that students (1) have sufficient aptitude to learn a particular task, (2) have sufficient ability to understand instruction, (3) are willing to persevere until they attain a certain level of mastery, (4) are allowed whatever time is necessary to attain mastery, and (5) are provided with good-quality instruction.

Mastery learning proponents assume that all of these conditions can be created if they are not already present. Aptitude, for example, is seen as being partly determined by how well prerequisite knowledge and skills have been learned. And perseverance can be strengthened by the deft use of creative teaching methods and various forms of reward for successful performance. The basic mastery learning approach is to specify clearly what is to be learned, organize the content into a sequence of relatively short units, use a variety of instructional methods and materials, allow students to progress through the material at their own rate, monitor student progress in order to identify budding problems and provide corrective feedback, and allow students to relearn and retest on each unit until mastery is attained (Block, Efthim, & Burns, 1989; Gentile & Lalley, 2003).

Like the research on peer tutoring and cooperative learning, the research on mastery learning has generally been positive. On the basis of a comprehensive review of this literature, Chen-Lin Kulik, James Kulik, and Robert Bangert-Drowns (1990) conclude that mastery learning programs produce moderately strong effects on achievement. The average student in a mastery learning class scored at the 70th percentile on a classroom examination, whereas the average student in a conventional class scored at the 50th percentile. The positive effect of mastery learning was slightly more pronounced for lower-ability students. As compared with students in conventional classes, those in mastery classes had more positive feelings about the subjects they studied and the way in which they were taught.

**Textbooks**   Let's assume that you have decided to incorporate a multicultural orientation into your classroom lessons. Can you count on the history or social studies textbook that your school district has chosen to provide adequate coverage of this topic? Probably not. Jesus Garcia (1993) examined how various ethnic groups have been portrayed in elementary and high school social studies and history textbooks. Although contemporary textbooks provide broader coverage of various ethnic groups than did earlier textbooks, Garcia concludes that their coverage is still superficial. Discussions of Blacks, for example, include such topics as slavery, Reconstruction, the civil rights movement, Black organizations, free Blacks in colonial America, and the development of Black churches. But none of these topics is discussed in great depth. The same conclusion was drawn about the treatments of Irish, Italian, Jewish, and Polish Americans.

The implication for teachers who believe that their classroom should have a strong multicultural emphasis is that their school's textbooks should probably be viewed as just a starting point. The teacher who is committed to providing students a strong multicultural experience will have to seek out high-quality supplementary materials.

## A Rationale for Multicultural Education

Some people seem to believe that multicultural education programs represent a rejection of basic American values and that this opposition to traditional values is the only rationale behind such programs. We feel this belief is mistaken on both counts. We see multicultural programs as being consistent with basic American values (such as tolerance of differences and equality of opportunity) and consider them to be justified in several ways.

1. *Multicultural programs foster teaching practices that are effective in general as well as for members of a particular group.* For example, expressing an interest in a student through occasional touching and smiling and allowing the child to tutor a younger student are practices likely to benefit most students, not just those of Latino origin.
2. *All students may profit from understanding different cultural values.* For example, the respect for elders that characterizes American Indian and Asian American cultures is likely to become increasingly desirable as the percentage of elderly Americans increases over the years. Similarly, learning the American Indian value of living in harmony with nature may come to be essential as we run out of natural resources and attempt to alleviate environmental pollution (Triandis, 1986).
3. *The United States is becoming an increasingly multicultural society, and students thus need to understand and know how to work with people of cultures different from their own.*
4. *Multicultural education programs expose students to the idea that "truth" is very much in the eye of the beholder.* From a European perspective, Christopher Columbus did indeed discover a new world. But from the perspective of the Arawak Indians who were native to the Caribbean, Columbus invaded territories that they had occupied for thousands of years. Similarly, one can describe the history of the United States as one in which continual progress toward democratic ideals has been made or as one in which progress has been interrupted by conflict, struggle, violence, and exclusion (Banks, 1993).
5. *Multicultural programs can encourage student motivation and learning.* These programs demonstrate respect for a child's culture and teach about the contributions that the student's group has made to American society. Proponents argue that these features both personalize education and make it more meaningful. Conversely,

when children perceive disrespect for their cultural background, the result can be disastrous. Consider the following comment by a Mexican-American student who realized for the first time that his teachers viewed him as both different and inferior:

> One recreation period, when we were playing our usual game of soccer, I took time out to search for a rest room. I spotted a building on the north side of the playground and ran for it. As I was about to enter, a teacher blew her whistle very loudly, freezing me on the spot. She approached me and demanded to know where I was going, who I was, and what I was doing on that side of the playground. I was dumbfounded and afraid to respond, so she took me by the ear and escorted me back across the playground to the south side. Her parting remark was a stern admonition not to cross the line and to stay with all the other Mexicans.
>
> At that very moment I stopped, turned, and looked at the school as if for the first time. I saw a white line painted across the playground. On one side were the white children playing; on my side were the Mexicans. Then I looked at the building, which was divided in half. The office was in the center, with two wings spreading north and south—one wing for whites and the other for Mexicans. I was overwhelmed with emotions that I could not understand. I was hurt, disappointed, and frustrated. But more than anything else, I was profoundly angry. (Mendoza, 1994, p. 294)

## VIDEO CASE ◄◄ ▶ ►►

### Diversity: Teaching in a Multiethnic Classroom

*Watch the video, study the artifacts in the case, and reflect upon the following questions:*

1. How does the Video Case illustrate the point that all students may benefit from understanding different cultural values?

2. Describe how multicultural lessons like the Kamishibai project promote student motivation and learning.

6. *The rationale for multicultural education that we have provided has been reinforced by numerous studies that document the disappointing academic performance of a significant number of minority-group students.* As we mentioned earlier, Black, Latino, and American Indian students tend to score lower than White students on standardized tests of vocabulary, reading, writing, mathematics, and science (Ornstein & Levine, 2006), and these differences appear as early as the fourth grade. Although such problems are not easy to solve, the inclusion of ethnically related content and activities in the curriculum helps make classroom assignments more meaningful and encourages minority students to master reading, writing, computational, and reasoning skills (Banks, 2002; Vasquez, 1990).

## Bridging the Cultural and SES Gap with Technology

As we stated earlier, a basic purpose of multicultural education is to give students the opportunity to learn about the characteristics of people from different cultures and to try to understand how those individuals view the world. For schools that draw from an ethnically, racially, and socioeconomically diverse population, acquiring firsthand experience with the history, beliefs, and practices of different cultures is not likely to be a major problem. But schools that draw from more homogeneous populations

*Computer-based technology helps students learn more about other cultures and social classes by providing access to various reference sources and individuals from almost anywhere in the world.*

Multicultural understanding can be promoted by electronically linking students from different cultural backgrounds

*HM TeacherPrepSPACE*

For quick links to relevant websites, go to the Weblinks section of the textbook's student website.

have traditionally been limited to such resources as books, magazines, and videotapes. This limitation on multicultural education is being surmounted, however, by the ability of technology to bring the world to the student, and in a very real sense.

Telecommunication projects allow students from different places and varied backgrounds to interact with one another, sharing ideas and experiences and learning new points of view. These exchanges can lead to a greater respect for diversity (Kontos & Mizell, 1997; Salmon & Akaran, 2001). Kerry Freedman and Meihui Liu (1996), for instance, found that despite clear differences in attitudes and communication patterns, telecommunication projects among nonnative Asian American students, American Indian students on a reservation, and White rural students encouraged more questioning and interaction than occurred in face-to-face settings. Discussions of lifestyle, local stores, city services, handgun problems, and explorations of the concept of diversity were eye-opening for these students. Michaele Salmon and Susan Akaran (2001) describe an e-mail exchange program between kindergarten students from New Jersey and first-grade Eskimo children from Alaska that produced greater respect for and understanding of each other's culture.

Another noteworthy program is the International Education and Resource Network (iEARN; **www.iearn.org**), which developed from the AT&T Learning Network (Riel, 1993, 1996). iEARN is a nonprofit organization, made up of more than fifteen thousand schools in a hundred different countries, that allows teachers and students to work together online on various education projects. One way for students and teachers to work on a common project is through Interactive Forums. In these electronic spaces, teachers and students meet other participants and get involved in ongoing projects. Another way to accomplish this goal is Learning Circles—interactive, project-based partnerships among a small number of schools located around the world. Each Learning Circle session lasts fourteen weeks.

The 4Directions Project is another significant example. Developed by a consortium of nineteen American Indian schools in ten states and eleven public and private universities and organizations, the project allows isolated far-flung members of American Indian schools to share local customs and values with other American Indian tribes around the country. The students display their projects and achievements and participate in virtual communities through Internet teleconferencing. Although the 4Directions website (**http://4directions.org**) was created to facilitate communication among American Indian communities, the project welcomes other schools to participate in the project or use its resources (Allen et al., 1999). The Resources page contains several features, including culturally relevant lesson plans for eight subject areas and a virtual tour of the National Museum of the American Indian.

Earlier in this chapter, we indicated that many students from low-SES homes are considered to be at risk for educational failure because of adverse conditions surrounding their physical, social, emotional, and cognitive development. Technology may be an effective tool in combating this problem, as it has demonstrated its effectiveness at raising the achievement levels of at-risk, low-SES students. In one study (Cole & Hilliard, 2006), a group of low-SES third-grade students from an inner-city school who were two or more grade levels behind in reading were given eight weeks of reading instruction using a web-based program called *Reading Upgrade*. This program uses music and video within an interactive environment to maintain student attention to and interest in lessons that focus on decoding, phonemic awareness, fluency, and comprehension. The *Reading Upgrade* group significantly outscored a similar group of students who received conventional reading instruction without the aid of computers; they gained the equivalent of one grade level on measures of decoding, fluency, and comprehension in just eight weeks.

In another study (Page, 2002), half of the third- and fifth-grade low-SES students in five schools worked in technology-enriched classrooms while the other students worked on the same lessons without the aid of technology. For a unit on the planets and constellations within the Milky Way galaxy, for example, students in the technology-enriched classrooms would gather information for a report from science software or the World Wide Web and then prepare a slide show presentation using PowerPoint. For other lessons they might have videoconferences with same-grade students from other schools. Although there were no differences between the two groups on a standardized test of reading, students in the technology-enriched classes did score higher than their peers who did not use technology on a standardized test of mathematical skills and a test of self-esteem. In addition, there was considerably more student-to-student interaction and less teacher-to-student interaction in the technology-enriched classes.

Bear in mind, however, that although virtually all schools now have Internet-connected computers, access to such technology is not equal across school districts. In 2003, the number of students per Internet-connected computer for schools with the lowest poverty concentration was 4.2, whereas the number of students per Internet-connected computer for schools with the highest poverty concentration was 5.1 (Parsad & Jones, 2005). In some schools, insufficient technology resources may hinder the efforts we have described in this section.

Now that you are familiar with the nature and goals of multicultural education programs and some of the instructional tools that are available to you, the following Suggestions for Teaching should help you get started.

# Suggestions for Teaching in Your Classroom

## Promoting Multicultural Understanding and Classroom Achievement

### 1 Use culturally relevant teaching methods.

To fulfill the goals of multicultural education, teachers should practice what is referred to as either culturally relevant pedagogy (Ladson-Billings, 2002) or culturally responsive pedagogy (Nieto, 2002/2003). This approach to instruction is based on two premises. First, all students, regardless of their ethnic, racial, and social class backgrounds, have assets they can use to aid their learning. Second, teachers need to be aware of and meet students' academic needs in any number of ways. In other words, simply adopting a multicultural basal reader is not culturally responsive pedagogy. In addition to adopting multicultural reading material, you should do everything possible to help all students learn to read. For example, successful teachers of Latino students in Arizona and California have high expectations for students, make their expectations clear, never accept low-quality work, scaffold students' learning, and use Spanish for instruction or allow students to speak Spanish among themselves when working in pairs or groups (Rolón, 2002/2003).

Gloria Ladson-Billings (2002), who has written extensively about working with minority and at-risk students, provides several examples of culturally relevant or responsive teaching. A second-grade teacher allowed her students to bring in lyrics from rap songs that both she and the students deemed to be inoffensive. The students performed the songs, and the teacher and students discussed the literal and figurative meanings of the words and such aspects of poetry as rhyme scheme, alliteration, and onomatopoeia. The students acquired an understanding of poetry that exceeded both the state's and school district's learning standards. Another teacher invited the parents of her students to conduct "seminars" in class for two to four days, one to two hours at a time. One parent who was famous for the quality of her sweet potato pie taught the students how to make one. In addition, the students were required to complete such related projects as a written report on George Washington Carver's research on the sweet potato, a marketing plan for selling pies, and a statement of the kind of education and experience one needed to become a cook or chef. Similar seminars were done by a carpenter, a former professional basketball player, a licensed practical nurse, and a church musician, all of whom were parents or relatives of the students.

**2** **Help make students aware of the contributions that specific ethnic groups have made to the development of the United States and the rest of the world.**

**JOURNAL ENTRY**
Ways to Promote Awareness of
Contributions of Ethnic Minorities

As we noted earlier, James Banks (2002) has identified four approaches to multicultural education, the first of which is the contributions approach. This approach emphasizes the contributions that prominent individuals of various ethnic groups have made to the United States, as well as each group's major holidays, celebrations, and customs. One suggestion for implementing this approach is to invite family members of students (and other local residents) of different ethnic backgrounds to the classroom. Ask them to describe the values subscribed to by members of their group and explain how those values have contributed to life in the United States and the rest of the world.

**3** **Use instructional techniques and classroom activities that are consistent with the value system of students who share a particular cultural background and that encourage students to learn from and about one another's cultures.**

Students from Latino cultures place a high value on the concept of collectivism, or the interdependence of family members. From an early age, children are taught to think first about fostering the success of any group to which they belong by seeking to work cooperatively with others (Rothstein-Fisch, Greenfield, & Trumbull, 1999). To capitalize on this value, consider doing some or all of the following:

- Assign two or three children rather than just one to a classroom task, such as cleaning up after an art period, and allow them to help one another if necessary.
- Increase the use of choral reading with students whose English proficiency is limited so they can practice their decoding and pronunciation skills without being the center of attention.

- After distributing a homework assignment, allow students to discuss the questions but not to write down the answers. Those who are more proficient in English and have better-developed intellectual skills can help their less skilled classmates better understand the task. One third-grade teacher who used this technique was surprised to find that every student completed the assignment.

Bear in mind, however, that students whose families have recently immigrated to the United States may not be familiar or comfortable with such student-centered techniques. In some cultures, for example, students are taught not to speak unless asked a direct question by the teacher, not to volunteer answers without being asked (so as not to appear boastful or conceited), and never to question what the teacher says, even when they know it to be wrong. These students will need time to become used to such practices as working with other students and asking the teacher for additional explanations (Miller & Endo, 2004).

**4** **At the secondary level, involve students in activities that explore cultural differences in perceptions, beliefs, and values.**

A well-conceived multicultural education program cannot, and should not, avoid or minimize the issue of cultural conflict. There are at least two reasons for helping students examine this issue. One is that conflict has been a constant and salient aspect of relationships among cultural groups. Another is that cultural conflicts often produce changes that benefit all members of a society (a prime example is the civil rights movement of the 1960s, with its boycotts, marches, and demonstrations).

Cultural conflicts arise from differences in perceptions, beliefs, and values. American culture, for example, places great value on self-reliance. Americans generally respect and praise individuals who, through their own initiative, persistence, and ingenuity, achieve substantial personal goals, and they tend to look down on individuals who are dependent on others for their welfare. Consequently, American parents who are financially dependent on their children, even though the children may be prosperous enough to support them, would probably feel ashamed enough to hide the fact. The same situation in China would likely elicit a different reaction because of different values about self-reliance and family responsibilities. Chinese parents who are unable to provide for themselves in their old age but have children successful enough to support them might well brag about it to others (Appleton, 1983).

One technique for exploring cultural conflict is to have students search through newspapers and news magazines for articles that describe clashes. Ask them to identify the source of the conflict and how it might be positively resolved. Another technique is to involve students in games that simulate group conflict. Class members can, for example, play the role of state legislators who represent the interests of diverse ethnic groups and who have been lobbied to change the school funding formula so that poorer school districts receive more money (Appleton, 1983). The use of both simulations and the discussion of newspaper articles will probably work best at the high school level because adolescents are better able than younger students to understand the abstract concepts involved in these activities.

**JOURNAL ENTRY**
Ways to Help Students Explore
Conflicts Between Cultures

**5** **Involve students, especially at the secondary level, in community service activities.**

Service-learning programs, found in many school systems, serve several purposes. First, they afford students the opportunity to broaden the knowledge they acquire in school by working to solve real problems in a community setting. Second, they help students develop a sense of civic and social responsibility. Third, they help students become more knowledgeable about career options. And fourth, they provide a useful and needed service to the community (Billig, 2000). To cite one example of a service-learning program with a multicultural perspective, a group of college

Suggestions for Teaching in Your Classroom

students advocated and helped draft legislation that would address the needs of poor Latina female heads of households (Weah, Simmons, & Hall, 2000). More detailed information about service-learning programs and organizations can be found on the website of the Corporation for National and Community Service (www.learnandserve.org).

*HM TeacherPrepSPACE*

Would you like more suggestions for your journal? See the Reflective Journal Questions at the textbook's student website.

### 6  Make every effort to contact and work with the parents of ethnic minority students.

Linda Holman (1997) is the principal of an elementary school in El Paso, Texas. In her school, 43 percent of the 700 students have limited English proficiency and are recent immigrants to the United States. To help students and their parents make a successful transition to a new country and school system, Holman makes the following suggestions:

- During the first week of the school year, hold parent-teacher-child conferences. Be willing to hold these meetings in the parents' home and during the evening hours if necessary.
- Recruit bilingual parent volunteers to help teachers and staff members talk with parents and students.
- In discussing classroom tasks and student performance with parents, avoid technical terminology and acronyms. Not only does this result in fewer misunderstandings, but it also lessens the sense of inferiority that some parents feel.
- Encourage parents to work with their children in their native language in order to build a strong foundation for second-language learning.

Lee Little Soldier (1997) makes the same recommendation about meeting with parents of American Indian students. He states that parents may at first be intimidated by the atmosphere of the school. Offering to work with them in the comfort of their home indicates the school's interest in the family, as well as the child.

## BILINGUAL EDUCATION

As we mentioned earlier, the 1990s set a U.S. record for the number of immigrants during a decade. Just over 11 million legal immigrants arrived in the United States between 1991 and 2002. Not surprisingly, many of the school-age children of these families have either limited or no English proficiency. For 2004, about 5.3 percent (or 2.8 million) of K–12 students were classified as having limited English proficiency (LEP). About 29 percent of these students lived in homes in which Spanish was the primary language spoken at home. This was an increase in LEP students of about 100 percent since 1979 (U.S. Department of Education, 2006).

To address the needs of these students, the federal government provides financial support for the establishment of bilingual education programs. Because language is viewed as an important part of a group's culture, many school districts integrate bilingual education with multicultural education. In this section, we will examine the nature and effectiveness of bilingual education programs.

Before we consider different approaches to bilingual education, there are three general points we would like you to keep in mind.

1. Bilingual programs have become an emotionally charged and politicized topic (Macedo, 2000; Porter, 2000; Rothstein, 1998; Thompson, DiCerbo, Mahoney, & MacSwan, 2002; Pérez, 2004). Educators, parents, and legislators have strong opinions regarding the amount of time and resources that should be devoted to helping students master native-language skills and whether such programs should include

cultural awareness goals. Some people favor moving students into all-English classes as quickly as possible, whereas others believe that students should have a firm grasp of their native language *and* English before attempting to make the transition to regular classes. Although research on this issue is helpful because it informs us about what *is*, such research cannot tell us what we should do about what we know.

2. Some language-minority students may suffer from problems that bilingual education alone cannot solve, such as the multiple difficulties associated with low SES.

3. No one approach to bilingual education is likely to be equally effective for all language-minority students. What works well for some low-SES Puerto Rican children may not work well for middle-SES Cuban children, and vice versa.

## Goals and Approaches

Most bilingual education programs have a common long-term goal, but they differ in their approach to that goal. The goal is to help minority-language students acquire as efficiently as possible the English skills they will need to succeed in school and society. The approaches to that goal usually fall into one of three categories: *transition*, *maintenance*, or *two-way bilingual*.

**Transition Programs**    Programs that take a transition approach teach students wholly (in the case of non-English-proficient students) or partly (in the case of limited-English-proficient students) in their native language so as not to impede their academic progress, but only until they can function adequately in English. At that point, they are placed in regular classes, in which all of the instruction is in English. To make the transition time as brief as possible, some programs add an English-as-a-second-language (ESL) component. ESL programs typically involve pulling students out of their regular classes and providing them with full-time intensive instruction in English (Gersten, 1999; Mora, Wink, & Wink, 2001; Thomas & Collier, 1999).

> Transition programs focus on rapid shift to English proficiency

**Maintenance Programs**    Programs that take a maintenance approach try to maintain or improve students' native-language skills. Instruction in the students' native language continues for a significant time before transition to English. Supporters of maintenance programs point to the results of psychological and linguistic studies that suggest that a strong native-language foundation supports the subsequent learning

> Maintenance programs focus on maintaining native-language competence

*Some bilingual education programs emphasize using the student's native language competence to help the student learn English as quickly as possible. Other programs emphasize the maintenance or improvement of both the student's native language and English.*

of both English and subject-matter knowledge. In addition, many proponents of multicultural education favor a maintenance approach because they see language as an important part of a group's cultural heritage (Mora et al., 2001; Robledo & Cortez, 2002).

**Two-Way Bilingual Programs**   Some bilingual education scholars (e.g., Calderón & Minaya-Rowe, 2003; Pérez, 2004; Thomas & Collier, 1997/1998, 1999) are critical of both transitional and maintenance bilingual education programs because they are remedial in nature and because students who participate in such programs tend to be perceived as inferior in some respect. These educators favor what is generally known as **two-way bilingual (TWB) education** (although the terms *bilingual immersion* and *dual language* are also used). In a TWB program, subject-matter instruction is provided in two languages to all students. This approach is typically used when English is the primary language of about half the students in a school and the other language (usually Spanish) is the primary language of the other half of the students.

> Two-way bilingual education programs feature instruction in both languages

TWB programs are used in 333 schools in twenty-nine states in the United States (Center for Applied Linguistics, 2006). Although most of these programs are English-Spanish, other programs include Korean, French, Cantonese, Navajo, Japanese, Arabic, Portuguese, Russian, and Mandarin Chinese as the minority language. TWB programs differ from traditional transition and ESL programs in that they begin as early as kindergarten and continue throughout the elementary school years in order to maintain facility in the student's native language while building facility in the nonnative language.

Canada and Miami, Florida, have two of the oldest and largest TWB programs. Canada has always had a large French-speaking population, mostly in the province of Québec. Because many parents wanted their children to be proficient in both English and French, Canadian schools in the 1960s began a K–12 program. In kindergarten and first grade, 90 percent of the instruction is in French and the remaining 10 percent is in English. From grade 2 through grade 5, the proportion gradually shifts to 50/50. By grade 6, most students can work equally well on any subject matter in either language.

The impetus for a TWB program in the Miami area was the large number of residents who emigrated from Cuba. As with all other two-way programs, students whose primary language is Spanish *and* students whose primary language is English participate in the program together. Unlike the Canadian model, which has a strong immersion component in the early grades (80 to 90 percent of the instruction is in French), teachers in Miami's program teach in Spanish for half the day and in English for the other half of the day at all grade levels.

TWB programs typically include the following features:

- At least six years of bilingual instruction
- High-quality instruction in both languages
- Separation of the two languages for instruction (for example, by time of day, day of the week, or even by week)
- Use of the minority language for teaching and classroom discussion at least 50 percent of the time
- A roughly balanced percentage of students for whom each language is primary
- Use of peer tutoring

Despite the growth and success of TWB programs, some states have eliminated all bilingual education programs. In 1998, Californians voted to eliminate their state's bilingual education program and provide instead a one-year English-immersion program, in which language-minority students are taught only in English. In 2000, voters in Arizona approved a similar proposition (Thompson et al., 2002). An English-immersion program was approved in Massachusetts in 2002 but was later amended to allow TWB programs to continue to operate (Saltzman, 2003).

## VIDEO CASE ◄◄ ▶ ►►

### Bilingual Education:
### An Elementary Two-Way Immersion Program

*Watch the video, study the artifacts in the case, and reflect upon the following questions:*

**1.** The two teachers in this Video Case work together closely to teach students in two different languages. In your opinion, what are the pros and cons of this approach to bilingual education?

**2.** What are some of the specific challenges that teachers in a two-way program (such as the one depicted in the Video Case) might face?

### Research Findings

The question of whether bilingual education programs facilitate the learning of non-English-speaking students is one that has been vigorously debated (see, for example, Beaumont, de Valenzuela, & Trumbull, 2002; Cummins, 1999; Krashen, 1999; Meier, 1999; Pérez, 2004). Nevertheless, the weight of the evidence to date seems to support the following conclusions:

> Bilingual education programs produce moderate learning gains

- In comparison with immersion (English-only) programs, participation in bilingual education programs produces small to moderate gains in reading, language skills, mathematics, and total achievement when measured by tests in English. When measured by tests administered in the student's native language, participation in bilingual education leads to significantly better performance on tests of listening comprehension, reading, writing, total language, mathematics, social studies, and attitudes toward school and self. Thus, increasing the amount of time devoted to instruction in English (as is done in immersion programs) does not necessarily lead to higher levels of achievement (Cummins, 1999; Slavin & Cheung, 2005; Willig, 1985). Early analysis of California's immersion program indicates that although LEP students improved their scores on the Stanford-9 (a standardized achievement test), the scores of non-LEP students increased by a similar amount. Consequently, the achievement gap between LEP and non-LEP students remained unchanged (Thompson et al., 2002).

- ESL programs appear to have positive effects on reading comprehension skills and grade-point average. ESL students recognize cognate vocabulary (related words) fairly well (although there is a wide range of proficiency for this outcome), demonstrate the ability to monitor their comprehension, and use prior knowledge to help them understand and remember what they read (Fitzgerald, 1995). Also, Mexican American students who had more years of ESL/bilingual education than their peers had higher grades (Padilla & Gonzalez, 2001).

- Students who participate in TWB programs score at or above grade level on subject-matter tests and score higher on reading and mathematics tests than LEP students who are taught only in English (Pérez, 2004; Slavin & Cheung, 2005). Perhaps for this reason, the bilingual-immersion program in New York City became so popular that students who wanted to participate had to be selected by lottery (Genesee & Cloud, 1998; Thomas & Collier, 1997/1998).

## TECHNOLOGY AND BILINGUAL EDUCATION

Multimedia, hypermedia, e-mail, and other technologies are enhancing opportunities for bilingual students and LEP students to more efficiently acquire English-language

## Take a Stand!

### Bilingual Education: Plus les choses changent, plus elles restent les mêmes

The preceding French phrase translates to "The more things change, the more they remain the same." So it is with the current dispute over the goals and methods of bilingual education. In the early part of the twentieth century, prior to World War I, bilingual public schools were not uncommon, particularly in areas with large numbers of German immigrants. After the war, however, public financing of bilingual schools was abruptly withdrawn, partly as a reaction against Germany (which lost the war and was seen as the aggressor) and partly because of increasing nationalism and isolationism. American society strongly endorsed a one country/one culture policy and stressed once again the idea of America as a melting pot. As a result, English-immersion programs for immigrant students became the norm.

But during and after World War II, as now, American students' deficiencies in foreign-language fluency became noticeable and a source of concern.

This situation contributed to the first Bilingual Education Act in 1965, which emphasized the maintenance of one's native language, as well as mastery of English.

As a future educator whose decisions will rest partly on scientific evidence, we suggest that you ignore as much as possible both the pro and con arguments about bilingual education that appear to be based on biases and political beliefs. Focus instead on what the research has to say. Our reading of the current research leads us to conclude that bilingual education, particularly in the form of two-way bilingual programs, benefits both limited-English-proficient and native English-speaking students. Given the ease with which technology allows students from different countries to communicate and work collaboratively, as well as the trend toward international commerce, programs that increase students' bilingual fluency should be encouraged and strongly supported.

### HM TeacherPrepSPACE

Have you ever taken part in bilingual education? What is your position on expanding its use in U.S. schools? For more material on this subject, go to the Take a Stand! section of the textbook's student website.

### HM TeacherPrepSPACE

*To review this chapter, go to the ACE practice tests and PowerPoint slides at the textbook's student website.*

skills and other subject matter. Former ESL teacher Jan Lacina describes, for example, how Internet chat sessions, discussion boards, and computer programs can be used to help students refine their language skills. Chat rooms and discussion boards have the advantage of letting students review and possibly revise what they have written before sending it off and may be particularly beneficial for students who are shy or are anxious about mispronunciations (Lacina, 2004/2005). A computer program that may be worth investigating is the Soliloquy Reading Assistant (**www.soliloquylearning.com**). Students read aloud into a headset microphone, and the program provides audio and visual help for words the student mispronounces or has trouble pronouncing.

There are also numerous Web resources that support bilingual instruction. One site that serves both teachers and students is **www.eslcafe.com**. A menu called "Stuff for Students" contains the following pages: Help Center (a discussion forum), Hint-of-the Day, Idioms, Phrasal Verbs, Pronunciation Power, Quizzes, Slang, and Student Forums. The website Science Fair Assistant (**www.iteachilearn.com/teach/tech/science.htm**), written in both English and Spanish, is designed to help children in grades K–8 find experiments and ideas for a science project. Finally, a number of publications describe how to use websites in creating lessons to improve LEP students' listening, oral proficiency, reading comprehension, and writing skills (e.g., Feyten et al., 2002).

# 5 Understanding Student Differences

## KEY POINTS

These key points will help you learn the important information in this chapter. To help you study, they also appear in the margins of the pages, next to the text where they are discussed.

### The Nature and Measurement of Intelligence

- Intelligence test scores most closely related to school success, not job success, marital happiness, or life happiness
- IQ scores can change with experience, training
- Intelligence involves more than what intelligence tests measure
- Triarchic theory: part of intelligence is ability to achieve personal goals
- Multiple intelligences theory: intelligence composed of eight distinct forms of intelligence
- Individuals with a high level of a particular intelligence may use it in different ways
- Factors other than high levels of a particular intelligence influence interests, college major, career choice

### Using the New Views of Intelligence to Guide Instruction

- Triarchic theory suggests that instruction and assessment should emphasize all types of ability
- Various technology tools may strengthen different intelligences

### Learning Styles

- Learning styles are preferences for dealing with intellectual tasks in a particular way

- Impulsive students prefer quick action; reflective students prefer to collect and analyze information before acting
- Field-independent students prefer their own structure; field-dependent students prefer to work within existing structure
- Legislative style prefers to create and plan; executive style prefers to follow explicit rules; judicial style prefers to evaluate and judge
- Teachers should use various instructional methods to engage all styles of learning at one time or another
- Teachers should use various test formats to expand students' repertoire of learning styles and measure accurately what students have learned

### Gender Differences and Gender Bias

- Evidence that boys score higher on tests of visual-spatial ability and math reasoning and that girls score higher on tests of memory and language skills is being called into question
- Gender bias: responding differently to male and female students without having sound educational reasons for doing so
- Gender bias can affect course selection, career choice, and class participation of male and female students
- Academic success, encouragement, models influence women to choose careers in science, math
- Loss of voice: students suppress true beliefs about various topics in the presence of parents, teachers, and classmates of opposite sex
- Females and males have equal access to computers, but small differences exist in how they are used

---

S it back for a few minutes, and think about some of your friends and classmates over the past twelve years. Make a list of their physical characteristics (height, weight, visual acuity, and athletic skill, for example), social characteristics (outgoing, reserved, cooperative, sensitive to the needs of others, assertive), emotional characteristics (self-assured, optimistic, pessimistic, egotistical), and intellectual characteristics (methodical, creative, impulsive, good with numbers, terrible at organizing ideas). Now analyze your descriptions in terms of similarities and differences. In all likelihood, they point to many ways in which your friends and classmates have been alike but to even more ways in which they have differed from one another. Indeed, although human beings share many important characteristics, they also differ from one another in significant ways (and we tend to notice the differences more readily than the similarities).

Now imagine yourself a few years from now, when your job as a teacher is to help every student learn as much as possible despite all the ways in which students differ from one another. By fourth grade, for example, the range of achievement in some classes is greater than four grade levels. Some children's reading or math skills may be at the second-grade level, whereas other children may be functioning at the sixth-grade level. By sixth grade, about one-third of all children will be working one grade level or more below the average student in class

(Biemiller, 1993). In one study of a group of first graders from a suburban school district, the number of words correctly read from a list of one hundred words ranged from none to one hundred. By the middle grades, the least capable students will have read about one hundred thousand words, the average student will have read about one million words, and the most capable students will have read between ten and fifty million words (Roller, 2002).

The variability among any group of students is one reason that teaching is both interesting and challenging. Richard Snow, who has written extensively about individual differences in education, has summarized this challenge as follows:

> At the outset of instruction in any topic, students of any age and in any culture will differ from one another in various intellectual and psychomotor abilities and skills, in both general and specialized prior knowledge, in interests and motives, and in personal styles of thought and work during learning. These differences, in turn, appear directly related to differences in the students' learning progress. (1986, p. 1029)

Although it usually will be essential for you to plan lessons, assignments, and teaching techniques by taking into account typical characteristics, you will also have to expect and make allowances for differences among students. The practice of using different learning materials, instructional tactics, and learning activities with students who vary along such dimensions as intelligence, learning style, gender, ethnicity, and social class is commonly referred to as *differentiated instruction* (see, e.g., Benjamin, 2005; Gregory & Chapman, 2002). The aim is for all students to meet the same goals.

In Chapters 4 and 6, we examine five broad characteristics that distinguish one group of students from another and have a demonstrated effect on learning. In this chapter, we focus on differences in mental ability (usually referred to as *intelligence*), learning styles, and gender. In Chapter 4, we explore two related characteristics that are becoming more important every year: cultural and socioeconomic background. Teachers and researchers have demonstrated a strong interest in all five characteristics in recent years, and much has been written about them. ●

# THE NATURE AND MEASUREMENT OF INTELLIGENCE

## The Origin of Intelligence Testing

The form and content of contemporary intelligence tests owe much to the pioneering work of French psychologist Alfred Binet. In 1904, Binet was appointed to a commission of experts charged by the minister of public instruction for the Paris school system with figuring out an accurate and objective way of distinguishing between children who could profit from normal classroom instruction and those who required special education. Because the point of this project was to predict degree of future academic success, Binet created a set of questions and tasks that reflected the same cognitive processes as those demanded by everyday classroom activities. Thus Binet's first scale measured such processes as memory, attention, comprehension, discrimination, and reasoning.

In 1916, Lewis Terman of Stanford University published an extensive revision of Binet's test. This revision, which came to be known as the Stanford-Binet, proved to be extremely popular. One reason for its popularity was that Terman, following the 1912 suggestion of a German psychologist named William Stern, expressed a child's level of performance as a global figure called an intelligence quotient (IQ). Stern's original formula divided a child's mental age, which was determined by performance on the test, by the child's chronological age and multiplied the resulting figure by 100 to eliminate fractional values (Seagoe, 1975).

| Intelligence test scores most closely related to school success, not job success, marital happiness, or life happiness

We have provided this abbreviated history lesson to illustrate two important points:

1. The form and function of contemporary intelligence tests have been directly influenced by the task Binet was given a century ago. Intelligence test items are

*Individually administered intelligence tests (such as the one shown here) are usually given to determine eligibility for a special class. They were designed to predict, and are moderately good predictors of, academic performance.*

**HM TeacherPrepSPACE**

Do you want to take a sample intelligence test? Go to the textbook's student website.

still selected on the basis of their relationship to school success. Thus predictions about job success, marital bliss, happiness in life, or anything else made on the basis of an IQ score are attempts to make the test do something for which it was not designed. As some psychologists have pointed out, this type of test might better have been called a test of scholastic aptitude or school ability rather than a test of intelligence.

2. Stern and Terman's use of the IQ as a quantitative summary of a child's performance was not endorsed by Binet, who worried that educators would use a summary score as an excuse to ignore or get rid of uninterested or troublesome students. Binet's intent was "to identify in order to help and improve, not to label in order to limit" (Gould, 1981, p. 152).

Later in this section, we will see that Binet's concern was well placed. First, however, we will turn to a more detailed consideration of what intelligence tests do and do not measure.

## What Traditional Intelligence Tests Measure

In 1904, British psychologist Charles Spearman noticed that children given a battery of intellectual tests (such as the memory, reasoning, and comprehension tests that Binet and Terman used) showed a strong tendency to rank consistently from test to test: children who scored high (or average or below average) on memory tests tended to score high (or average or below average) on reasoning and comprehension tests. Our use of the words *tendency* and *tended* indicates, of course, that the rankings were not identical. Some children scored well on some tests but performed more poorly on others.

Spearman explained this pattern by saying that intelligence is made up of two types of factors: a general factor (abbreviated as *g*) that affects performance on all intellectual tests and a set of specific factors (abbreviated as *s*) that affects performance on only specific intellectual tests. Spearman ascribed to the *g* factor the tendency for score rankings to remain constant over tests. That the rankings varied somewhat from test to test, he said, resulted from individual differences in specific factors. Not surprisingly, Spearman's explanation is called the *two-factor theory of intelligence*.

When you examine such contemporary intelligence tests as the Stanford-Binet Intelligence Scale–IV (Thorndike, Hagen, & Sattler, 1986), the Wechsler Intelligence Scale for Children–IV (Wechsler, 2003), and the Wechsler Adult Intelligence Scale–II (Wechsler, 1997), you will notice that the items in the various subtests differ greatly from one another. They may involve performing mental arithmetic, explaining the meanings of words, reproducing a pictured geometric design with blocks, or selecting from a larger set three pictures that share a common characteristic and form a group. These varied items are included because, despite their apparent differences, they relate strongly to one another and to performance in the classroom. In other words, intelligence tests still reflect Binet's original goal and Spearman's two-factor theory. In practice, the examiner can combine the scores from each subtest into a global index (the IQ score), offer a prediction about the tested individual's degree of academic success for the next year or so, and make some judgments about specific strengths and weaknesses.

## Limitations of Intelligence Tests

So where does all this leave us in terms of trying to decide what traditional intelligence tests do and do not measure? Four points seem to be in order:

1. The appraisal of intelligence is limited by the fact that it cannot be measured directly. Our efforts are confined to measuring the overt manifestations (responses to test items) of what is ultimately based on brain function and experience.

2. The intelligence we test is a sample of intellectual capabilities that relate to classroom achievement better than they relate to anything else. That is why, as stated

earlier, many psychologists prefer the terms *test of scholastic aptitude* or *test of school ability.*

| IQ scores can change with experience, training

3. Because current research demonstrates that the cognitive abilities measured by intelligence tests can be improved with systematic instruction (Sternberg, 2002a, 2002b, 2003), intelligence test scores should not be viewed as absolute measures of ability. Many people—parents, especially—fail to grasp this fact. An IQ score is not a once-and-for-all judgment of how bright a child is. It is merely an estimate of how successful a child is in handling certain kinds of problems at a particular time on a particular test as compared with other children of the same age.

4. Because IQ tests are designed to predict academic success, anything that enhances classroom performance (such as a wider range of factual information or more effective learning skills) will likely have a positive effect on intelligence test performance. This means that IQ scores are not necessarily permanent. Research on the stability of IQ scores shows that, although they do not change significantly for most people, they can change dramatically for given individuals and that changes are most likely to occur among individuals who were first tested as preschoolers (Weinert & Hany, 2003). This last point is often used to support early intervention programs such as Head Start and Follow-Through.

## pause & reflect

Imagine that a colleague tells you about one of her students, who has a C+ average and received an IQ score of 92 (low average) on a recent test. Your colleague says that because the student is working up to his ability level, he should not be encouraged to set higher goals because that would only lead to frustration. Your colleague then asks for your opinion. How do you respond?

Because traditional theories of intelligence and their associated IQ tests view intelligence as being composed of a relatively small set of cognitive skills that relate best to academic success, and because the results of such tests are used primarily to place students in special programs, contemporary theorists have proposed broader conceptions of intelligence that have more useful implications for classroom instruction.

## Contemporary Views of Intelligence

**David Wechsler's Global Capacity View**   As David Wechsler (1975) persuasively points out, intelligence is not simply the sum of one's tested abilities. Wechsler defines **intelligence** as the global capacity of the individual to act purposefully, think rationally, and deal effectively with the environment. Given this definition, which many psychologists endorse, an IQ score reflects just one facet of a person's global capacity: the ability to act purposefully, rationally, and effectively on academic tasks in a *classroom* environment. However, people display intelligent behavior in other settings (at work, home, and play, for example), and other characteristics contribute to intelligent behavior (such as persistence, realistic goal setting, the productive use of corrective feedback, creativity, and moral and aesthetic values). A true assessment of intelligence would take into account behavior related to these other settings and characteristics.

| Intelligence involves more than what intelligence tests measure

In fact, recent research (Perkins, Tishman, Ritchhart, Donis, & Andrade, 2000) has shown that in everyday settings, intelligent behavior is related to the ability to recognize occasions that call for various capabilities and the motivation to actually use those capabilities. For example, in a situation that has the potential to become confrontational and hostile, intelligence might involve being open-minded and using a sense of humor. If this sounds to you like a description of the well-known concept of wisdom, Robert Sternberg, a leading intelligence theorist and researcher whose work we describe in the next section, would agree. He defines wisdom as the use of one's abilities for the benefit of oneself and others by either adapting to one's environment, shaping it to better suit one's needs, or selecting a more compatible environment in which to function (Keane & Shaughnessy, 2002).

Assessment of intelligence in everyday settings would be highly subjective and would take a great deal of time. That is one reason that current intelligence tests assess only a small sample of cognitive abilities. But if recent formulations of intelligence by Robert Sternberg and Howard Gardner become widely accepted, future intelligence tests may be broader in scope than those in use today. Even before such tests are devised, these theories serve a useful purpose by reminding us that intelligence is multifaceted and can be expressed in many ways.

**Robert Sternberg's Triarchic Theory**   Like David Wechsler, Robert Sternberg (2002a, 2002b, 2003) believes that most of the research evidence supports the view that intelligence has many facets, or dimensions, and that traditional mental ability tests measure just a few of these facets. Sternberg's **triarchic theory of intelligence** (which he also refers to as the *theory of successful intelligence*) has, as its name suggests, three main parts (see Figure 5.1):

- *Practical ability* involves applying knowledge to everyday situations, using knowledge and tools, and seeking relevance.
- *Creative ability* involves inventing, discovering, imagining, and supposing.
- *Analytical ability* involves breaking ideas and products into their component parts, making judgments, evaluating, comparing and contrasting, and critiquing.

Because these abilities need information on which to operate, memory ability underlies each of them (Grigorenko, Jarvin, & Sternberg, 2002).

Sternberg's work is a break with tradition in two respects. First, it includes an aspect of intelligence that has been—and still is—largely overlooked: how people use practical intelligence to adapt to their environment. Second, Sternberg believes that each of these abilities can be improved through instruction and that students learn best when all three are called into play.

> Triarchic theory: part of intelligence is ability to achieve personal goals

In describing the nature of practical intelligence, Sternberg argues that part of what makes an individual intelligent is the ability to achieve personal goals (for example, graduating from high school or college with honors, working for a particular company in a particular capacity, or having a successful marriage). One way to accomplish personal goals is to understand and adapt to the values that govern behavior in a particular setting. For example, if most teachers in a particular school

**Figure 5.1**   The Three Components of Sternberg's Triarchic Theory

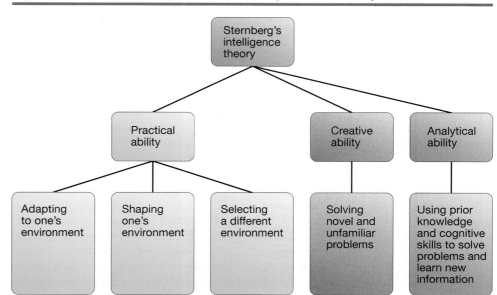

SOURCE:  Adapted from Sternberg (1985); Sternberg, Ferrari, Clinkenbeard, & Grigorenko (1996).

*Robert Sternberg's theory maintains that intelligence is composed of practical ability, creative ability, and analytical ability.*

(or executives in a particular company) place a high value on conformity and cooperation, the person who persistently challenges authority, suggests new ideas without being asked, or operates without consulting others will, in all likelihood, receive fewer rewards than those who are more willing to conform and cooperate. According to Sternberg's theory, this person would be less intelligent.

Where a mismatch exists and the individual cannot adapt to the values of the majority, the intelligent person explores ways to make the values of others more consistent with his own values and skills. An enterprising student may try to convince her teacher, for example, that short-answer questions are better measures of achievement than essay questions or that effort and classroom participation should count just as much toward a grade as test scores. Finally, where all attempts at adapting or attempting to change the views of others fail, the intelligent person seeks out a setting in which his behaviors are more consistent with those of others. For instance, many gifted and talented students will seek out private alternative schools where their particular abilities are more highly prized.

Sternberg's basic point is that intelligence should be viewed as a broad characteristic of people that is evidenced not only by how well they answer a particular set of test questions but also by how well they function in different settings. The individual with average test scores who knows how to get people to do what she wants is, in this view, at least as intelligent as the person who scores at the 99th percentile of a science test.

Elena Grigorenko, Linda Jarvin, and Robert Sternberg (2002) conducted three experiments to test the educational applicability of the triarchic theory. In each study, instructional lessons and materials were designed to improve the analytical, creative, and practical thinking skills of middle and high school students, as well as their vocabulary and reading comprehension skills. As an example of an analytical task, students read a story about a pioneer family and then drew a family tree diagram to show how the characters were related and a timeline to show when key events occurred. As an example of a creative task, students looked for examples in another story of how the author appealed to the human senses and then tried to describe what one would hear, see, and smell in such settings as a park, a pizza restaurant, and a zoo. As an example of a practical task, after reading a story about a family's Christmas celebration, students discussed all the steps involved in preparing a meal for a large group of people and how you might solve such problems as overcooking the main course.

The first study was done with two sets of inner-city fifth graders in each of two consecutive years. For each group, the study lasted about five months. Half the students in each set were exposed to triarchically based instruction and half were exposed to instruction that emphasized the learning and recall of factual information. Using stories from their basal reader, students in the experimental (triarchic) group completed classroom and homework tasks that emphasized the use of analytical, creative, and practical abilities. Students in the control group completed tasks that emphasized recall. As predicted, the experimental students significantly outscored the control students on tests of vocabulary and reading comprehension skills that tapped analytical, creative, and practical thinking skills, as well as on a standardized reading test.

The second study investigated the effect of a six-week triarchic reading program on high-achieving, low-socioeconomic-status (SES), inner-city sixth graders. As in the first study, the triarchic and control groups read passages both in class and at home and answered questions that emphasized analytical, creative, and practical thinking skills. On the posttest, the triarchic group outscored the control group on analytical, creative, and practical measures.

The third study investigated the effect of a six-week triarchic program on inner-city high school students' analytical, creative, and practical vocabulary and comprehension skills. Unlike the second study, which was a standalone reading program, the triarchic instruction in this study was integrated into students' English, social sciences, French, physical sciences, history, and art classes. Although students in the triarchic group scored higher on the vocabulary and comprehension skills posttest, their scores and those of the control group were not significantly different. Despite this one disappointing result, the research to date indicates that triarchically based instruction produces significant gains in students' vocabulary and reading comprehension skills, as well as their analytical, creative, and practical thinking skills (Sternberg & Grigorenko, 2004).

**Howard Gardner's Multiple Intelligences Theory**   Howard Gardner's conception of intelligence, like Sternberg's, is broader than traditional conceptions. It is different from Sternberg's, however, in that it describes eight separate types of intelligence. Accordingly, Gardner's work is referred to as the **theory of multiple intelligences** (or *MI theory*). The intelligences that Gardner describes are *logical-mathematical, linguistic, musical, spatial, bodily-kinesthetic, interpersonal* (understanding of others), *intrapersonal* (understanding of self), and *naturalist* (the ability to notice the characteristics that distinguish one plant, mineral, or animal from another and to create useful classification schemes called *taxonomies*) (Gardner, 1999). Table 5.1 describes each of these intelligences and provides examples of the kind of person who best represents each one.

> Multiple intelligences theory: intelligence composed of eight distinct forms of intelligence

Because these intelligences are presumed to be independent of one another, an individual would likely exhibit different levels of skill in each of these domains. One student, for example, may show evidence of becoming an outstanding trial lawyer, novelist, or journalist because his linguistic intelligence produces a facility for vividly describing, explaining, or persuading. Another student may be able to manipulate aspects of sound (such as pitch, rhythm, and timbre) to produce musical experiences that people find highly pleasing. And the student who is adept at understanding her own and others' feelings and how those feelings relate to behavior would be exhibiting high intrapersonal and interpersonal intelligence. Like Sternberg's work, Gardner's theory cautions us against focusing on the results of IQ tests to the exclusion of other worthwhile behaviors.

Gardner's MI theory has become extremely popular among educators. As usually happens with such ideas, they are often misinterpreted. A number of misconceptions have arisen:

1. *Misconception: A person who has a strength in a particular intelligence will excel on all tasks within that domain.* Not so. A student with a high level of linguistic intelligence may be quite good at writing insightful essays on various topics but

| Table 5.1 | Gardner's Eight Intelligences | |
|---|---|---|
| **Intelligence** | **Core Components** | **End States** |
| Logical-mathematical | Sensitivity to, and capacity to discern, logical or numerical patterns; ability to handle long chains of reasoning | Scientist Mathematician |
| Linguistic | Sensitivity to the sounds, rhythms, and meanings of words; sensitivity to the different functions of language | Poet Journalist |
| Musical | Abilities to produce and appreciate rhythm, pitch, and timbre; appreciation of the forms of musical expression | Violinist Composer |
| Spatial | Capacities to perceive the visual-spatial world accurately and to perform transformations on one's initial perceptions | Sculptor Navigator |
| Bodily-kinesthetic | Abilities to control one's body movements and handle objects skillfully | Dancer Athlete |
| Interpersonal | Capacities to discern and respond appropriately to the moods, temperaments, motivations, and desires of other people | Therapist Salesperson |
| Intrapersonal | Access to one's own feelings and the ability to discriminate among them and draw on them to guide behavior; knowledge of one's own strengths, weaknesses, desires, and intelligences | Person with detailed, accurate self-knowledge |
| Naturalist | Ability to recognize and classify the numerous plants and animals of one's environment and their relationships on a logical, justifiable basis; talent of caring for, taming, and interacting with various living creatures | Botanist Entomologist |

SOURCE: Gardner (1999); Gardner & Hatch (1989).

be unable to produce a good poem. Another student may excel at the kind of direct, fact-oriented style of writing that characterizes good newspaper reporting but be limited in her ability to write a long, highly analytical essay.

**Individuals with a high level of a particular intelligence may use it in different ways**

Instead of focusing on how much intelligence students have, we need to attend to the different ways in which students make the most of their intelligences. For example, Thomas Hatch (1997), an associate of Gardner, describes how three children, all of whom were judged to have a high level of interpersonal intelligence, used that ability in different ways. One child was very adept at organizing the classroom activities of his classmates. The second was able to resolve conflicts among his classmates far better than anybody else in that class. The third child shunned leadership and was sometimes excluded from group activities but excelled at forming friendships among his peers. He was so good at this that he was able to make friends with one of the least popular students in class.

**Factors other than high levels of a particular intelligence influence interests, college major, career choice**

2. *Misconception: Ability is destiny.* If a child exhibits a high level of linguistic intelligence, she will not necessarily choose to major in English or journalism or seek a

# VIDEO CASE    ◀◀ ▶ ▶▶

## Multiple Intelligences:
## Elementary School Instruction

*Watch the video clip, study the artifacts in the case, and reflect upon the following questions:*

1. Which of Gardner's eight intelligences, as described in Table 5.1, are depicted in this Video Case? How do specific students within the Video Case illustrate these intelligences?

2. How does the teacher in this Video Case use MI theory to teach traditional academic skills and subject matter? Do you think his approach is effective? Why or why not?

*Contemporary theories typically view intelligence as being composed of several types of capabilities. Howard Gardner's theory of multiple intelligences, for example, describes several different ways of expressing intelligent behavior.*

job as a writer. Not only do intelligences change over time in how they are used, but decisions about a college major and career are influenced by many other factors. The student who wrote such interesting stories as a child may grow up to be a college professor who excels at writing journal articles and textbooks or a noted politician or a successful business leader (Hatch, 1997).

3. *Misconception: Every child should be taught every subject in eight different ways in order to develop all of the intelligences.* MI theory does not indicate or even suggest that such a step is necessary in order for learning to occur. In fact, it may be counterproductive if students are turned off by lessons that appear forced and contrived. And as a practical matter, there simply isn't enough time in the day to teach every lesson eight ways (Gardner, 1999; Hatch, 1997).

Although there have been no systematic evaluations to date of Gardner's theory, a fair amount of anecdotal evidence exists. An elementary school in Turkey, for example, has designed its curriculum around MI theory. One part involves "exploratories." On Friday afternoons students spend one hour in an area of the classroom in which they can engage in an activity that draws on their strongest intelligence. They then spend a second hour in one of five other exploratory areas. Over the course of five weeks, they rotate through all of the exploratory areas, thereby developing their weaker intelligences (Saban, 2002).

Karen Rubado (2002), a middle grades alternative school teacher, describes how she used MI theory to improve the self-concept and achievement of students who had failed in regular classes and had given up. Through a variety of activities (such as questionnaires, using each intelligence in practice exercises, classifying school activities according to each intelligence), she helped these students understand that they could be smart in different ways and that, in varying degrees, they possessed all eight intelligences. There were noticeable increases in students' motivation, self-esteem, and achievement.

## pause & reflect

Assuming that Robert Sternberg and Howard Gardner are correct in thinking that people can be intelligent in ways other than the traditional analytical, linguistic, and logical-mathematical modes, why do you think schools have been so reluctant to address other abilities?

## USING THE NEW VIEWS OF INTELLIGENCE TO GUIDE INSTRUCTION

The various theories of intelligence that were formulated during the first half of the twentieth century are of limited value to educators because they do not allow teachers to match instructional approaches and learning assessments to abilities. For example, because traditional intelligence tests, such as the Stanford-Binet or the Wechsler Intelligence Scale for Children–IV, are designed to rank students according to how they score rather than to assess how they think, their basic educational use is to determine eligibility for programs for the gifted and talented, learning disabled, and mentally disabled. What sets the theories of Sternberg and Gardner apart is their belief in a broad view of intelligence that can inform instructional practice and improve student performance (Green & Tanner, 2005; Sternberg & Zhang, 2005). As we have shown, the preliminary evidence suggests that these beliefs have merit. What follows are a few illustrations of how you can use their ideas in your classroom.

> Triarchic theory suggests that instruction and assessment should emphasize all types of ability

**Sternberg's Triarchic Theory**   Based on his triarchic theory, Sternberg proposes a teaching and assessment model (Sternberg, 1996, 1997a; Sternberg et al., 1996). He suggests that for any grade level and for any subject, teaching and testing can be designed to emphasize the three abilities in his triarchic theory—analytical, creative, and practical—as well as memory. To take into account individual differences, instruction and testing should involve all four abilities. At some point, each student has an opportunity to excel because the task and related test match the student's ability. Table 5.2 shows how language arts, mathematics, social studies, and science can be taught so as to emphasize all four of these abilities. Notice that Sternberg does not suggest that *all* instruction and assessment match a student's dominant ability. Some attempts need to be made to strengthen abilities that are relatively weak.

As was mentioned earlier and as can be seen from the research we have reviewed, Sternberg's triarchic theory of intelligence has become known more recently as a theory of "successful intelligence." Using the framework of successful intelligence, Sternberg and his colleagues have addressed how teachers can successfully interact with other teachers, with parents, and with principals and other administrators (Stemler, Elliott, Grigorenko, & Sternberg, 2006). Their framework suggests future research designed to describe more clearly the nature of effective teaching and successful schools. Sternberg's ideas are likely to be around for a while and to remain influential. You are likely to encounter his ideas not only as you prepare to teach your own students but also as you engage in continuing professional development as a practicing teacher.

| **Table 5.2** | Teaching Different Subjects from a Triarchic Perspective | | | |
|---|---|---|---|---|
| | **Memory** | **Analysis** | **Creativity** | **Practicality** |
| Language arts | Remember the name of Tom Sawyer's aunt. | Compare the personality of Tom Sawyer with that of Huckleberry Finn. | Write a very short story with Tom Sawyer as a character. | Describe how you could use Tom Sawyer's power of persuasion. |
| Mathematics | Remember the mathematical formula Distance = Rate × Time. | Solve a mathematical word problem using the $D = R \times T$ formula. | Create your own mathematical word problem using the $D = R \times T$ formula. | Show how to use the $D = R \times T$ formula to estimate driving time from one city to another. |
| Social studies | Remember a list of factors that led up to the U.S. Civil War. | Compare, contrast, and evaluate the arguments of those who supported slavery versus the arguments of those who opposed it. | Write a page of a journal from the viewpoint of either a Confederate or a Union soldier. | Discuss the applicability of the lessons of the Civil War to countries today. |
| Science | Name the main types of bacteria. | Analyze the means the immune system uses to fight bacterial infections. | Suggest ways to cope with the increasing immunity bacteria are showing to antibiotic drugs. | Suggest three steps that individuals might take to reduce the chances of bacterial infection. |

SOURCE: Adapted from Sternberg (1997a).

**Gardner's Multiple Intelligences Theory**  Gardner's general recommendation for applying MI theory in the classroom is essentially the same as Sternberg's. He believes that teachers should use MI theory as a framework for devising alternative ways to teach subject matter. Some children learn a subject best when it is presented in a particular format or emphasizes a particular type of ability, whereas other children learn well when the subject is taught under different conditions (Checkley, 1997).

MI theory should lead to increased transfer of learning to out-of-school settings. Because MI theory helps students mentally represent ideas in multiple ways, they are likely to develop a better understanding of the topic and be able to use that knowledge in everyday life. For the same reason, MI theory also suggests that learning in out-of-school settings should lead to increased transfer of learning in school subjects. For example, musical experiences—both listening to music and taking music lessons—have been shown to have a positive relationship with scores on a variety of cognitive measures, including IQ tests (Schellenberg, 2006a). Listening to music that one enjoys enhances performance on a variety of cognitive performance measures for both adults and children. For preschool-age children, listening to music enhances creativity (Schellenberg, 2006b). Taking music lessons is positively related to academic ability, even when other factors, such as family income, parental education, and participation in activities other than music, are taken into account (Schellenberg, 2006a).

Because MI theory stresses different ways of learning and expressing one's understanding, it fits well with the current emphasis on performance assessment (described in Chapter 14, "Understanding Standardized Assessment," and Chapter 15, "Assessment of Classroom Learning"). For example, instead of using just multiple-choice questions to measure linguistic competence, teachers can ask students to play the role of newspaper editor and write an editorial in response to a current issue.

As we mentioned earlier, it is a mistake to think that every lesson has to be designed to involve all eight intelligences. But with a little thought, many lessons can be designed to include two or three. For example, a high school algebra teacher combined kinesthetic and logical-mathematical abilities to teach a lesson on graphing. Instead of using in-class paper-and-pencil exercises, this teacher took the students outside to the school's courtyard. Using the large cement pavement squares as a grid and the grooves between the squares as X and Y coordinates, she had the students stand at various junctures and plot their own locations. Similarly, as part of a primary grade lesson on birds and their nesting habits, students designed and built birdhouses and then noted whether the birds used them, thereby using spatial, bodily-kinesthetic, and logical-mathematical abilities (Campbell, 1997).

## Using Technology to Develop Intelligence

Because contemporary theories view intelligence as being made up of modifiable cognitive skills, you shouldn't be overly surprised that there are technology implications for the development of intelligence. In fact, technology education can support higher-level thinking such as metaphorical and analogical thinking; it provides students opportunities to "think outside the box" and, by doing so, to develop their cognitive capabilities (Lewis, 2005). Robert Sternberg (1997c), author of the triarchic theory, expressed that sentiment when he said, "Technology can enable people to better develop their intelligence—no question about it" (p. 13). The following study (Howard, McGee, Shin, & Shia, 2001) provides one example of how technology can facilitate certain aspects of intelligence from a triarchic perspective.

Ninth-grade students were administered the Sternberg Triarchic Abilities Test and classified as being relatively stronger either in analytical, creative, or practical thinking. They then learned how to conduct and communicate the results of scientific research by working in groups of three with a computer simulation program called Astronomy

Village (modeled after the famous Kitt Peak Observatory in Arizona). To assess both their understanding of the content and their problem-solving ability, students were given scenarios and related questions to answer such as the following:

*Scenario:* You are a member of a research team that has been asked to calculate the distance to a particular star. A famous astronomer has suggested that the star is relatively close to Earth (within 25 light years).

*Content comprehension question:* Put an X in the boxes next to the five concepts that are most important to finding the distance to that star.

*Problem-solving question:* You have been asked to meet with the press to discuss how the team will proceed with this research. Assume that the people who will be reading your explanation have little or no knowledge of astronomy. Write your explanation so that it is easy enough for anyone to understand. Make sure you provide specific details of the procedures you will follow to measure the distance. You may want to use drawings to illustrate your thinking.

As expected, students who had relatively strong analytical or practical abilities scored significantly higher on the content comprehension questions than did students who were relatively strong in creative ability. The explanation given by the authors was that analytically-oriented students did well because this is the type of question they are most used to seeing in school and have the most success answering. Students high in practical ability did well because the simulation appealed to their preference for real-life tasks. But a different pattern emerged for the problem-solving items. Students who had relatively strong creative or practical ability scored significantly higher on these items than did students who were relatively strong in analytical ability. Presumably, the unfamiliarity of the astronomy problems provided students high in creative ability an opportunity to use this form of thinking. Because students with high practical ability did well on both types of questions, simulation types of computer programs appear to be a particularly good match for them.

Like Robert Sternberg, Howard Gardner believes that technology has a role to play in fostering the development of intelligence (or, from his perspective, intelligences). For example, he notes that computer programs allow students who cannot read music or play an instrument to create musical compositions and that CD-ROMs, videodiscs, and hypermedia can engage several intelligences (Weiss, 2000). **Hypermedia** is a marriage of **multimedia** (a communication format integrating several types of media such as text, graphics, animation, sound, images, and video) and **hypertext** (a system of linking text in a nonlinear way, thereby enabling users to jump from one section of text to another section of the same document or to other documents, often through highlighted words). With hypermedia, the learner can explore facts, concepts, or knowledge domains and immediately traverse to interesting links or appealing presentation formats. Most websites use hypermedia, and so do computerized encyclopedias and many other types of educational software.

*Various technology tools may strengthen different intelligences*

For many educators, technology holds great promise in addressing the MI theory promoted by Gardner (McKenzie, 2002). For instance, web-based conferencing might promote students' interpersonal intelligence. Programs that make it easy to do concept mapping, flowcharts, photo editing, and three-dimensional imaging are closely tied to visual-spatial intelligence (Lach, Little, & Nazzaro, 2003; McKenzie, 2002). Idea generation and prewriting software tools, such as Sunbuddy Writer, Imagination Express, and Inspiration, can assist verbal intelligence (Quenneville, 2001). Computer programming with tools such as LOGO might help students' problem-solving and logical-mathematical intelligence (Gillespie & Beisser, 2001; Suomala & Alajaaski, 2002). Other software addresses musical intelligence (for instance, by enabling students to see musical scores as the notes are played) and bodily-kinesthetic intelligence (by offering a visual breakdown of an athletic skill such as a tennis swing). Clearly, there are technology tools for all the aspects of intelligence that Sternberg and Gardner described.

As a teacher, these tools allow you a great deal of flexibility. With the many options that hypermedia applications offer, you can allow students to choose ways of learning that match their own strongest abilities, or you can have students use software that helps them improve in areas in which they are weak.

## LEARNING STYLES

Whether one conceives of intelligence as having one major component or several, psychologists agree that it is an *ability*. Typically, it is better to have more of an ability than less of it. In recent years, psychologists have also studied how students use their abilities, and this line of research has led to the concept of a *learning style*. Unlike abilities, styles are value neutral—that is, all styles are adaptive under the right circumstances.

> Learning styles are preferences for dealing with intellectual tasks in a particular way

A **learning style** can be defined as a consistent preference over time and subject matter for perceiving, thinking about, and organizing information in a particular way (Sternberg & Grigorenko, 2001; Zhang & Sternberg, 2006). Some students, for example, prefer to think about the nature of a task, collect relevant information, and formulate a detailed plan before taking any action, whereas others prefer to run with the first idea they have and see where it leads. Some students prefer to work on several aspects of a task simultaneously, whereas others prefer to work on one aspect at a time in a logical sequence.

Notice that styles are referred to as *preferences*. They are not fixed modes of behavior that we are locked into. When the situation warrants, we can, at least temporarily, adopt different styles, although some people are better than others at switching styles.

In the psychological literature on styles, a distinction is drawn between cognitive styles and learning styles. Because learning style is considered to be the more inclusive concept and because the implications for instruction are the same, we will use the term *learning style*. Among the many learning style dimensions that have been investigated, we will examine three. Two of these (reflectivity-impulsivity and field dependence–field independence) were formulated over forty years ago and have a long history of research. The third (mental self-government) is more recent in origin and contains some original elements but also includes styles that have been the subject of much research.

### Reflectivity and Impulsivity

One of the first learning style dimensions to be investigated was reflectivity-impulsivity. During the early 1960s, Jerome Kagan (1964a, 1964b) found that some students seem to be characteristically **impulsive,** whereas others are characteristically **reflective.** Impulsive students are said to have a fast conceptual tempo. When faced with a task for which there is no ready solution or a question for which the answer is uncertain, the impulsive student responds more quickly than students who are more reflective. In problem-solving situations, the impulsive student collects less information, does so less systematically, and gives less thought to various solutions than do more reflective students. Reflective students, in contrast, prefer to spend more time collecting information (which means searching one's memory as well as external sources) and analyzing its relevance to the solution before offering a response (Morgan, 1997).

> Impulsive students prefer quick action; reflective students prefer to collect and analyze information before acting

Kagan discovered that when tests of reading and inductive reasoning were administered in the first and second grades, impulsive students made more errors than reflective students did. He also found that impulsiveness is a general trait; it appears early in a person's life and is consistently revealed in a great variety of situations.

### Field Dependence and Field Independence

Another very popular learning style dimension, known as field dependence–field independence, was proposed by Herbert Witkin (Witkin, Moore, Goodenough, &

*During the elementary years it becomes apparent that students approach tasks in different ways. This preference for doing things in a particular way is often referred to as a cognitive style. Some students, for example, are impulsive thinkers who tend to react quickly when asked a question; other students are reflective thinkers who prefer to mull over things before answering.*

Field-independent students prefer their own structure; field-dependent students prefer to work within existing structure

Cox, 1977) and refers to the extent to which a person's perception and thinking about a particular piece of information are influenced by the surrounding context. For example, when some individuals are shown a set of simple geometric figures and asked to locate each one (by outlining it with a pencil) within a larger and more complex display of intersecting lines, those with a field-dependent style take significantly longer to respond and identify fewer of the figures than individuals with a field-independent style. The former are labeled **field dependent** because their perception is strongly influenced by the prevailing field. The latter are called **field independent** because they are more successful in isolating target information despite the fact that it is embedded within a larger and more complex context.

When we talk about individuals who have a field-dependent style and compare them with individuals who have a field-independent style, we do not mean to imply that there are two distinctly different types of individuals. That is like saying that people are either tall or short. Just as people's heights range over a measured span, students can vary in the extent to which they are field dependent or field independent. In fact, relatively few individuals exhibit a pure field-dependent or field-independent style (Morgan, 1997).

In school, the notes that field-dependent students take are more likely to reflect the structure and sequence of ideas as presented by the teacher or textbook author, whereas the notes of field-independent students are more likely to reflect their own ideas about structure and sequence. When reading, field-independent students are more likely than field-dependent students to analyze the structure of the story. The significance of this difference in approach is clearly seen with materials and tasks that are poorly structured. Field-independent students usually perform better in these situations because of their willingness to create a more meaningful structure.

The positive effect of field independence on achievement is particularly noticeable in the sciences because of their emphasis on analyzing objects and ideas into their component parts, reorganizing ideas into new configurations, and identifying potential new uses of that information. Biology students, for example, need to be able to identify tissues, organs, and systems that are difficult to see at first glance because they are embedded in the surrounding tissue of an organism.

In social situations, field-dependent people, in comparison with field-independent people, spend more time looking directly at the faces of others; are more aware of prevailing attitudes, values, and behaviors; prefer to be in the company of other people; and are generally thought of as more tactful, considerate, socially outgoing, and affectionate than field-independent individuals (Fehrenbach, 1994; Morgan, 1997; Witkin et al., 1977). Not surprisingly, in one study kindergarten children gave field-dependent teachers higher ratings than field-independent teachers. They also preferred teachers whose styles matched their own (Saracho, 2001).

## Mental Self-Government Styles

Robert Sternberg (1994), whose ideas on intelligence we discussed earlier in this chapter, has proposed an interesting learning style theory that is roughly modeled on the different functions and forms of civil government. Sternberg's **styles of mental self-government** theory has attracted considerable research and has, to date, been validated as a useful approach to understanding learning styles in a variety of settings (Zhang, 2005). In Sternberg's theory, thirteen mental self-government styles fall into one of five categories: functions, forms, levels, scope, and leaning. Within these categories, there are legislative, executive, and judicial functions; monarchic, hierarchic, oligarchic, and anarchic forms; global and local levels; internal and external scopes; and liberal and conservative leanings. Most individuals have a preference for one style within each category.

In Table 5.3 we briefly describe the main characteristics of each style and suggest an instructional activity consistent with it. If you are wondering how to identify these styles, Sternberg offers a simple solution: Teachers can simply note the type of instruction that various students prefer and the test types on which they perform best.

Evidence that these styles can apply to various cultures comes from Hong Kong, where instructional methods tend to emphasize rote learning and to be more regimented than is the case in many U.S. schools. High school students in Hong Kong who expressed a preference for the legislative, liberal, and judicial styles tended to have lower grades than did students who preferred the conservative and executive styles (Zhang & Sternberg, 2001).

## Using Awareness of Learning Styles to Guide Instruction

Because the typical classroom contains two dozen or more students who collectively exhibit several styles, teachers must be flexible and learn to use a variety of teaching and assessment methods so that, at some point, every student's style is addressed (recall our discussion of the teacher-as-artist earlier in the book). An impulsive boy, for example, may disrupt a class discussion by blurting out the first thing that pops into his head, thereby upstaging the reflective types, who are still in the process of formulating more searching answers. To minimize this possibility, you may want to have an informal rotation scheme for recitation or sometimes require that everyone sit and think about a question for two or three minutes before answering. To give the impulsive style its place in the sun, you might schedule speed drills or question-and-answer sessions covering previously learned basic material.

To motivate students with a legislative style, have them describe what might have happened if a famous historical figure had acted differently than he or she did. For example, how might World War II have ended if President Harry Truman had decided *not* to drop the atomic bomb on Japan? To motivate students with a judicial style, have them compare and contrast the literary characters Tom Sawyer (from Mark Twain's novel of the same name) and Holden Caulfield (from J. D. Salinger's novel *Catcher in the Rye*).

---

Legislative style prefers to create and plan; executive style prefers to follow explicit rules; judicial style prefers to evaluate and judge

Teachers should use various instructional methods to engage all styles of learning at one time or another

## pause & reflect

Analyze yourself in terms of the learning styles discussed in this chapter. Recall classroom situations that made you comfortable because they fit your style(s) and classroom situations in which you were uncomfortable because of a mismatch of style. Now imagine the students who will fill your classroom. Should you even try to design your lessons and assessments so that they match the styles of most students at least some of the time? If so, how will you do that?

| Table 5.3 | Matching Instructional Activities to Sternberg's Mental Self-Government Styles | |
|---|---|---|
| **Styles** | **Characteristics** | **Instructional Activities** |
| Legislative | Prefers to formulate rules and plans, imagine possibilities, and create ideas and products. | Require students to design science projects, write stories, imagine how historical figures might have done things differently, organize work groups. |
| Executive | Prefers to follow rules and guidelines. | Present well-organized lectures, require students to prepare book reports, work out answers to problems. |
| Judicial | Prefers to compare things and make evaluations about quality, worth, effectiveness. | Require students to compare literary characters, critique an article, evaluate effectiveness of a program. |
| Monarchic | Prefers to work on one task at a time or to use a particular approach to tasks. | Assign one project, reading assignment, or homework assignment at a time. Allow ample time to complete all aspects of the assignment before assigning another. |
| Hierarchic | Prefers to have several tasks to work on, deciding which one to do first, second, and so on, and for how long. | Assign several tasks that vary in length, difficulty, and point value and are due at various times over several weeks. |
| Oligarchic | Prefers to have several tasks to work on, all of which are treated equally. | Assign several tasks that are equivalent in length, difficulty, and point value. |
| Anarchic | Prefers an unstructured, random approach to learning that is devoid of rules, procedures, or guidelines. | Assign tasks and problems that require nonconventional thinking and methods, self-directed form of study. |
| Global | Prefers to have an overall view of a task before beginning work. | Require students to scan a reading assignment to identify major topics, create an outline before writing, formulate a plan before beginning a complex task. |
| Local | Prefers to identify and work on the details of a particular part of a task before moving to another part. | Present a detailed outline or overview of a lecture or project. Require students to identify and interrelate particular details of each part of a reading assignment. |
| Internal | Prefers to work alone. | Require seatwork, projects, and assignments that do not depend on others for completion. |
| External | Prefers to work with others. | Assign group projects or reports, encourage study groups, create discussion groups. |
| Liberal | Prefers to work out own solution to problems. | Assign projects for which students must work out solution procedures. For example, identify and report on proposed legislation that concerns the environment. |
| Conservative | Prefers to do things according to established procedures. | Assign homework or projects that specify the steps, procedures, or rules for accomplishing the task. |

SOURCE: Adapted from Sternberg (1994).

---

Teachers should use various test formats to expand students' repertoire of learning styles and measure accurately what students have learned

When you design your classroom assessments, keep in mind that multiple-choice tests, for example, match up nicely with the executive and conservative styles, whereas students with a legislative style are more likely to perform better on projects and performances. Try to use a variety of assessment methods on each test and across all the tests given during a term. You may also want to consider letting students choose the type of assessment they prefer. Another reason for using various teaching techniques and testing formats is that it may stimulate students to expand their own repertoire of learning styles (Sternberg, 1994). Recent research suggests that, although students display learning style preferences, they can learn through a variety of instructional tasks (Krätzig & Arbuthnot, 2006). Table 5.3 can serve as a guide for varying your instructional tasks and, consequently, expanding your students' repertoires.

## Using Technology to Accommodate Learning Styles

Just as technology can be used to strengthen different forms of intelligence, so can it target different learning styles. For example, students with an impulsive cognitive style often perform at lower-than-desirable levels because they don't always follow directions or fully attend to a model's behavior. Although teachers are limited in how much time they can spend reteaching material, computers are not. Consequently, a computer program called VISPRO (for Visualizing Processes) was designed to model the writing of letters and numbers for preschool and kindergarten children who have an impulsive cognitive style. The child clicks on one of several letters at the bottom of the screen, the program draws the letter, and the image remains on the screen for two or three seconds for the child to study. The child then writes the letter on paper, using the direction and shape modeled by the program. The child can study the formation of a particular letter as often as desired by simply clicking on its icon at the bottom of the screen (Bornas, Servera, & Llabrés, 1997).

Aside from specific programs, such as VISPRO, the range of technological tools (Internet, telecommunications, multimedia, hypermedia, etc.) can be used at all grade levels to address the varied learning styles that students bring to the classroom. Amy Benjamin is a veteran teacher who has written a number of books that focus on differentiating instruction in middle and high school classrooms. She argues that technology not only is an effective tool for accommodating student differences but also offers a unique opportunity for collaboration among novice and veteran teachers. Speaking to veteran teachers, she writes, "Our young colleagues, like our students, are used to e-communications and e-learning. . . . We know about classroom management, they know about technology. . . . As never before, novices and veteran teachers have much to offer each other" (2005, p. 5). As you encounter veteran teachers and learn how they accommodate student differences, consider that technology enables learners to engage information in different ways, and consider how you might collaborate with your veteran colleagues in the service of student learning.

# GENDER DIFFERENCES AND GENDER BIAS

At the beginning of this chapter, we asked you to think about the ways in which friends and classmates over the past twelve or so years may have differed from one another. In all likelihood, you thought about how those people differed cognitively, socially, and emotionally. And with good reason. As we have seen so far in this chapter and in preceding ones, students' academic performance is strongly influenced by their cognitive, social, and emotional characteristics. But there is another major characteristic you may have ignored: gender. Although it may not be obvious, there are noticeable differences in the achievement patterns of males and females and in how they are taught. As Myra Sadker and David Sadker (1994) point out, "Sitting in the same classroom, reading the same textbook, listening to the same teacher, boys and girls receive very different educations" (p. 1). Just how different is the subject of the next few sections.

## Gender Differences in Cognition and Achievement

A large body of research shows that there are reliable gender differences in cognitive functioning and achievement. On some tests, boys outscore girls, and on other tests girls have the upper hand (Halpern & LaMay, 2000; Marsh & Yeung, 1998; Royer,

Tronsky, Chan, Jackson, & Marchant, 1999; Wigfield, Battle, Keller, & Eccles, 2002). Although these differences are statistically significant (meaning they are probably not due to chance), they tend to be modest in size—about 10 to 15 percentile ranks. As research on gender differences has continued, it appears that the differences that were found in earlier studies may be due to factors that go beyond cognitive abilities (Spelke, 2005).

Generally, research on gender differences has found that males tend to outscore females on the following tests:

Evidence that boys score higher on tests of visual-spatial ability and math reasoning and that girls score higher on tests of memory and language skills is being called into question

- *Visual-spatial ability.* This category includes tests of spatial perception, mental rotation, spatial visualization, and generation and maintenance of a spatial image. A substantial body of research exists indicting that male superiority in visual-spatial ability appears during the preschool years and persists throughout the life span. More recent research suggests that the male advantage in spatial tasks is true only for children from middle- and high-SES groups. When males and females from low-SES groups are compared, no difference exists (Levine, Vasilyeva, Lourenco, Newcombe, & Huttenlocher, 2005).
- *Mathematical reasoning.* This difference, thought to be related to males' superior visual-spatial skill, may have more to do with social influences on academic and career choices than with cognitive abilities. When such influences are taken into account, more recent analyses of gender differences do not always show that males are superior to females (Halpern, Wai, & Saw, 2005).
- *College entrance.* Tests such as the Scholastic Achievement Test (SAT) are designed to predict grade-point average after the freshman year of college. The overall superiority of males in this category may be related to differences in mathematical experiences, which may give them increased opportunity to develop mathematical reasoning.

Research shows that females tend to outscore males on the following tests:

- *Memory.* This is a broad category that includes memory for words from word lists, working memory (the number of pieces of information that one is aware of and that are available for immediate use), name-face associations, first-last name associations, memory for spatial locations, and episodic memory (memories for the events in one's own life). This difference appears to persist throughout the life span.
- *Language use.* This is another broad category that encompasses tests of spelling, reading comprehension, writing, onset of speech, and rate of vocabulary growth. Gender differences in language use appear anywhere between one and five years of age and grow larger over time. For example, the average difference in the size of males' and females' vocabulary at sixteen, twenty, and twenty-four months of age is 13, 51, and 115 words, respectively. On tests of reading comprehension, the gender gap also grows larger over time. By the senior year of high school, girls outscore boys by almost 10 percentile ranks. The superior scores that girls get on tests of writing are due in large part to the fact that their essays are better organized, more grammatically correct, and more logical. It is worth noting that although these writing skills would strike most people as being reflective of intelligence, they are not part of standardized tests of intelligence.

Just as gender differences appear on tests of cognitive skills, the same differences appear in academic performance. A 1999 study of mathematics achievement among eighth graders in thirty-eight countries concluded that most of the participating countries, including the United States, were making progress toward gender equity in mathematics education, but the study found a few notable differences between the genders (Mullis et al., 2001). Among the major findings were the following:

- In most countries, the mathematics achievement differences between boys and girls were statistically nonsignificant. Boys significantly outscored girls in only four countries: Israel, the Czech Republic, Iran, and Tunisia.

- There was, however, a modest overall significant difference in favor of boys.
- A slightly higher percentage of boys had scores above the median (the midpoint of a distribution) and above the 75th percentile.

Although gender differences have been found and documented in the research literature over many years, recent research that takes into account a number of social and cultural factors is calling many of the "well-established" findings into question. Even so, gender differences have been and continue to be found.

Why do gender differences in cognition and achievement exist? No one knows for sure, although hormonal differences, differences in brain structure, differences in cognitive processes, and socialization differences are all thought to play a role. Despite increased awareness of how society reinforces gender-role stereotyping and measures taken to ensure greater gender equity, girls and boys continue to receive different messages about what is considered to be appropriate behavior. One source of influence that is being intensively studied is the peer group. During the middle childhood years (roughly ages six through nine), boys and girls are often under more pressure from their peers to exhibit gender-typed behaviors, in order to maintain the group's identity, than they are from their parents. But these observations do not answer the question of causation. Are gender differences the result of social pressures to participate in some activities and not others, or are socialization patterns the result of biological differences, or do both factors play a role? We simply do not know yet.

In addition to gender differences on tests of cognitive skills and in academic performance, students' emotional reactions to grades show gender differences. A study of more than nine hundred fourth-, fifth-, and sixth-grade children (Pomerantz, 2002) showed that the girls on average received higher grades than the boys in language arts, social studies, science, and mathematics. But, somewhat perversely, girls expressed greater worry about academic performance, higher levels of general anxiety, and higher levels of depression. The girls' perceived self-competence was lower than that of the boys for social studies, science, and math. The difference between boys and girls in levels of internal distress was smaller among students who received A's and B's and larger among students who received C's and D's. To put this picture in stark terms, girls achieve higher grades than boys but don't seem to be able to enjoy the fruits of their labors as much. Why this is the case is not clear. One possibility is that girls are more concerned than boys with pleasing teachers and parents. Thus failure or lower-than-expected achievement is interpreted as disappointing those on whom they depend for approval. Another possibility is that girls are more likely than boys to use academic performance as an indicator of their abilities, spurring them to higher levels of learning, as well as higher levels of internal distress because of the possibility of failure. Boys may be better able to maintain higher levels of self-confidence by denying the link between performance and ability.

A more recent study by Angela Duckworth and Martin Seligman (2006) offers an alternative, but related, explanation for the existence of gender differences in cognition and achievement. They note that throughout the school-age years, girls earn higher grades than boys in all major subjects, even though girls do not perform better than boys on achievement or IQ tests. In a study of eighth graders in an urban magnet school, Duckworth and Seligman found that, as a group, females demonstrated more self-discipline than their male counterparts. In this study, eighth-grade girls earned higher grade-point averages (GPAs) than boys but did only slightly better on an achievement test and less well on an IQ test. After extensive analyses, Duckworth and Seligman (2006) concluded that part of the reason girls had higher GPAs was that they were more self-disciplined. The more researchers learn about gender differences, the more a number of factors beyond cognitive and perceptual abilities seem either to account for those differences or to suggest that such differences are less significant than once thought.

Although you should be aware of the gender differences we have mentioned and should take steps to try to reduce them, you should also keep the following points in mind. First, there are many tasks for which differences do not exist. In fact, a recent review of research on gender differences, supported by the National Science Foundation, advanced the "gender similarities hypothesis" over the hypothesis of "gender differences" (Hyde, 2005). Second, some differences do not appear until later in development. For example, boys and girls have similar scores on tests of mathematical problem solving until adolescence, when boys begin to pull ahead. Third, what is true in general is not true of all individuals. Some boys score higher than most girls on tests of language use, and some girls score higher than most boys on tests of mathematical reasoning (Halpern, 1997; Halpern et al., 2005; Wigfield et al., 2002). Finally, as Robert Sternberg and Howard Gardner have argued, virtually all cognitive skills can be improved to some degree with the aid of well-designed instruction.

## Gender Bias

Gender bias: responding differently to male and female students without having sound educational reasons for doing so

If you asked your class a question and some students answered without waiting to be called on, how do you think you would react? Do you think you would react differently to male students than to female students? Do not be so sure that you would not. Studies have found that teachers are more willing to listen to and accept the spontaneous answers of male students than female students. Female students are often reminded that they are to raise their hands and be recognized by the teacher before answering. Boys also receive more extensive feedback than do girls, but they are punished more severely than girls for the same infraction. These consistent differences in responses to male and female students when there is no sound educational reason for them are the essence of **gender bias**.

Why do teachers react so differently to males and females? Probably because they are operating from traditional gender-role stereotypes: they expect boys to be more impulsive and unruly and girls to be more orderly and obedient (American Association of University Women, 1999; Matthews, Binkley, Crisp, & Gregg, 1998).

Exposure to gender bias apparently begins early in a child's school life. Most preschool programs stress the importance of following directions and rules (impulse control) and contain many activities that facilitate small-muscle development and language skills. Because girls are typically better than boys in these areas before they go to preschool, the typical preschool experience does not help girls acquire new academically related skills and attitudes. For example, preschool-age girls are usually not as competent as boys at large-motor activities (such as jumping, climbing, throwing, and digging) or investigatory activities (such as turning over rocks or pieces of wood to see what is under them). Lest you think that climbing, digging, and investigating one's environment are trivial behaviors, bear in mind that they are critical to the work of scientists who do field research (for example, botanists, geologists, anthropologists, and oceanographers), occupations in which women are significantly underrepresented. Perhaps the designers of preschool curricula should make a greater effort to include these more male-oriented activities (American Association of University Women, 1999).

Other students can be the source of gender bias as easily as the teacher can be. The authors of one study (Matthews et al., 1998) observed a fifth-grade classroom for four months and made the following observations:

- The class was divided into six small groups to work on ideas for a drug prevention program. Five of the groups chose a boy to deliver their report.
- On another occasion, the students worked in groups to create a machine that would produce both sounds and action. After each group demonstrated its machine, they called on other students to provide a name for it. Boys were called on thirty-one times, whereas girls were called on thirteen times.
- After a science lab, a girl complained that the boys said that the way in which the girls were weighing items and comparing the weights was wrong. Another girl remarked that the boys did not want the girls to touch any of the equipment. On hearing this, one of the boys said that he thought the girls might drop or damage something.

- Boys were more likely than girls to name a boy as the best student in mathematics and science, whereas the girls usually named a girl as the best in English.
- Boys usually named another boy as the one who contributed most to class discussions, whereas girls named both boys and girls.

## How Gender Bias Affects Students

Gender bias can affect course selection, career choice, and class participation of male and female students

Gender bias can affect students in at least three ways: the courses they choose to take, the careers they consider, and the extent to which they participate in class activities and discussions.

**Course Selection**     There are modest but noticeable differences in the percentage of high school boys and girls who take math and science courses. In 1998, a larger percentage of girls than boys took algebra II (63.7 versus 59.8 percent) and trigonometry (9.7 versus 8.2 percent). Although there was no difference in the percentages of boys and girls who took geometry and precalculus, slightly more boys than girls took calculus (11.2 versus 10.6 percent). The pattern for science courses was similar. A larger percentage of girls than boys took biology (94.1 versus 91.4 percent), advanced placement or honors biology (18 versus 14.5 percent), and chemistry (63.5 versus 57.1 percent), whereas more boys than girls took physics (31.7 versus 26.2 percent) and engineering (7.1 versus 6.5 percent) (Bae, Choy, Geddes, Sable, & Snyder, 2000).

**Career Choice**     As you may be aware because of numerous stories in the media, relatively few girls choose careers in science or mathematics. Wigfield and colleagues

### pause & reflect

Can you recall any instances of gender bias from teachers or friends? If so, do you think it had any effect on your choice of career?

(2002) found that a much smaller percentage of women than men held positions in such math- and science-oriented professions as chemistry and biological science (about 31 percent), engineering (about 18 percent), computer systems analysis (about 27 percent), and drafting/surveying/mapping (about 17 percent). On the other hand, a much greater percentage of women than men were found in such nonmath and nonscience fields as educational administration (63 percent), educational and vocational counseling (69 percent), social work (68 percent), and public relations (68 percent).

Several factors are thought to influence the choice male and female students make to pursue a career in science or engineering. One is familiarity with and interest in the tools of science. In one study of middle school science classes in which instructors who were committed to increasing girls' active participation emphasized hands-on experiences, gender differences were still noted. Boys spent more time than girls manipulating the equipment, thereby forcing girls to participate in more passive ways (Jovanovic & King, 1998).

A second factor is perceived self-efficacy (how confident one feels in being able to meet the demands of a task). In the middle school science classes just mentioned (Jovanovic & King, 1998), even though end-of-year science grades were equal for girls and boys, only girls showed a significant decrease in their perception of their science ability over the school year. A 1996 survey found that although fourth-grade boys and girls were equally confident about their math abilities, by twelfth grade only 47 percent of girls were confident about their math skills, as compared with 59 percent of the boys (Bae et al., 2000).

A third factor is the competence-related beliefs and expectations communicated by parents and teachers. Girls who believe they have the ability to succeed in male-dominated fields were encouraged to adopt these beliefs by parents and teachers (Wigfield et al., 2002).

Academic success, encouragement, models influence women to choose careers in science, math

Supporting evidence that factors such as self-efficacy influence career choice comes from a recent study of fifteen women with established careers in math, science, or technology. Because there have always been women who have successfully carved

*Women who choose a career in math or science are likely to be those who do well in science classes, are encouraged to pursue math or science careers by parents or teachers, and have respected models available to emulate.*

out careers in math or science, Amy Zeldin and Frank Pajares (2000) wanted to know what sets them apart from equally qualified women who choose other fields. Zeldin and Pajares found that these fifteen women had very high levels of self-efficacy for math and science that could be traced to three sources: (1) early and consistent academic success, (2) encouragement to pursue math and science careers from such influential others as parents and teachers, and (3) the availability of respected models (both male and female) whom they could observe and model themselves after. All three sources working in concert appear necessary to persuade women to consider a career in math, science, or technology.

**Class Participation**    As we pointed out earlier, many children tend to adopt the gender role that society portrays as the more appropriate and acceptable. Through the influence of parenting practices, advertising, peer norms, textbooks, and teaching practices, girls are reinforced for being polite, helpful, obedient, nonassertive, quiet, and aware of and responsive to the needs of others. Boys are reinforced for being assertive, independent, aggressive, competitive, intellectually curious, and achievement oriented. When females look at the world around them, they see relatively few women in positions of power and influence, relatively few women interviewed by the media for their opinions or expertise on various issues, and boys either ignoring or not taking seriously the suggestions and opinions offered by girls. The result, according to Carol Gilligan and others, is that adolescent girls learn to suppress their true personalities and beliefs. Instead of saying what they really think about a topic, they say either that they have no opinion or what they think others want to hear. Gilligan refers to this behavior as **loss of voice** (Harter, Waters, & Whitesell, 1997).

To measure the extent of loss of voice in different contexts, Susan Harter, Patricia Waters, and Nancy Whitesell gave questionnaires to several hundred students of both genders in grades 6 through 12. The questionnaire items asked students to rate how honestly they voiced their ideas when they were in the presence of teachers, male classmates, female classmates, parents, and close friends. Their main findings were as follows:

- Males and females are most likely to speak their minds when they are with close friends and classmates of the same gender and are less likely to do so when they are in the presence of members of the opposite gender, parents, and teachers.
- Loss of voice did not increase between grades 6 and 12.

Loss of voice: students suppress true beliefs about various topics in the presence of parents, teachers, and classmates of opposite sex

**Eliminate Gender Bias**

Gender bias, or treating male students differently from female students when such differences are neither warranted nor desirable, should have no place in any teacher's classroom. Because such biases are typically based on stereotypes and prejudices (the type of nonsystematic data we criticized in Chapter 1, "Applying Psychology to Teaching"), they are likely to have the negative impact on students' attitudes toward school, motivation for learning, classroom participation, course selection, and career choice that researchers have documented.

One way to avoid this undesirable practice is to think about the normally unconscious assumptions you make about the capabilities, motives, and interests of males and females, perhaps because of your own socialization. And when students, colleagues, or parents make broad-based, stereotypical statements such as "Girls aren't interested in electronics" or "Boys don't like to display their emotions," respond by saying, "Oh, which girl [or boy]?" to get across the point that any given individual can deviate from whatever average trends might exist.

*HM TeacherPrepSPACE*

Do you believe that all teachers need to take specific steps to combat gender stereotypes? Look into the additional resources on this issue at the Take a Stand! section at the textbook's student website.

- Equal numbers of males and females reported suppressing their true thoughts in certain circumstances.
- Girls who strongly identified with the stereotypical female gender role were more likely than androgynous females (those who exhibit behaviors that are characteristic of both gender roles) to suppress their true thoughts when interacting with their teachers and male classmates. This difference between feminine and androgynous females disappeared with close friends and parents.
- Androgynous males and females who said they were frequently encouraged and supported by teachers for expressing their views were most likely to speak their minds in classroom and other settings.

These findings have major implications for the way in which teachers address female students, particularly those who have adopted a strong feminine gender role, and for the use of constructivist approaches to teaching (discussed in detail in Chapter 13, "Approaches to Instruction"). Because constructivism relies heavily on free and open discussion to produce its effects, teachers need to monitor carefully the verbal exchanges that occur among students and to intervene when necessary to ensure that all students feel that their opinions are getting a fair and respectful hearing.

## Working Toward Gender Equity in the Classroom

Although much of the literature on gender bias highlights the classroom obstacles that make it difficult for girls to take full advantage of their talents, gender equity is about producing an educational experience that will be equally meaningful for students of both genders. Several authors (Bailey, 1996; Jobe, 2002/2003; Taylor & Lorimer, 2002/2003) suggest the following techniques to benefit both genders:

1. Use work arrangements and reward systems that will encourage all students to value a thorough understanding of a subject or task and that emphasize group success as well as individual accomplishment. In Chapter 13, "Approaches to Instruction," we will describe how a technique called cooperative learning does just this.
2. Emphasize concrete, hands-on science, math, and technology activities.
3. Incorporate math, science, and technology concepts into such other subjects as music, history, art, and social studies.
4. Talk about the practical, everyday applications of math and science. Although girls seem more interested in science when they understand how such knowledge transfers to everyday life, so do many boys. Nobody suffers when the curriculum is made more meaningful and relevant.
5. Emphasize materials that highlight the accomplishments and characteristics of women (such as Hillary Rodham Clinton, Oprah Winfrey, Sandra Day O'Connor, and Condoleeza Rice) and women's groups.
6. From the titles listed on the website **www.guysread.com,** create a reading list that appeals to boys.

Charles Rop (1998) describes how Anna Kasov, a veteran high school teacher, teaches introductory chemistry. In high school and college, Kasov found science to be a male-dominated profession that did not go out of its way to make women students feel comfortable or accepted.

As Kasov and others have pointed out, science becomes more interesting for all students, but for girls in particular, when they understand its relevance. The following quotation from Kasov about her own college experience is instructive:

> One of the things that I vividly remember is sitting in this lecture going through these biochemical cycles. I wondered where this happens—in the cell, in the nucleus, in the mitochondria? The guy didn't even bother to tell us. We were counting ATPs somewhere and I thought, "This is so stupid. I have no idea what this has to do with anything." (Rop, 1998, p. 60)

Consequently, Kasov recommends giving girls opportunities to manipulate technology, deemphasizing competition in favor of collaborative problem solving, showing how the products of chemical research affect the everyday lives of people, and integrating chemical concepts with other subjects, such as history, literature, and the arts.

## VIDEO CASE  ◄◄ ▶ ►►

### Gender Equity in the Classroom: Girls and Science

*Watch the video clip, study the artifacts in the case, and reflect upon the following questions:*

1. How does the Girls and Science program depicted in this Video Case try to address the problem of gender bias?

2. Describe some of the strategies used by the group leaders to promote gender equity and student interest in the material. Are these strategies effective?

## Gender Differences and Technology: Overcoming the Gap

In the 1980s, when desktop computers first started appearing in classrooms, surveys showed that females were less likely than males to use a computer at both school and home. That difference has now disappeared. A 2001 national survey of children and adolescents between the ages of five and seventeen found that about 80 percent of males and females reported using a computer at school and about 65 percent of both sexes reported using a computer at home (DeBell & Chapman, 2003).

Although there is no overall difference between males and females in computer use, small gender differences still exist in the ways in which computers are used. Among students who actually use computers at home, more females than males use computers for word processing (52.8 versus 46.8 percent), e-mail (55 versus 50.5 percent), and completing school assignments (69.2 versus 66.5 percent). The largest difference in favor of the males was for the category of playing games (92.7 versus 88.8 percent) (DeBell & Chapman, 2003).

Males are also more likely to have appropriate computer-using role models than females, for at least two reasons. First, female teachers express less confidence in using computers in the classroom than do male teachers. Second, about 80 percent of computer coordinators at the secondary level are men. In the primary and elementary grades, about 75 percent of computer coordinators are women (Volman & van Eck, 2001). Among the steps that can be taken to continue to reduce the gender gap is to use *telementoring* to put female students in touch with women

*Females and males have equal access to computers, but small differences exist in how they are used*

professionals, especially in occupations in which women are underrepresented (Duff, 2000).

The Suggestions for Teaching that follow will help you better respond to differences in intelligence, learning styles, and gender.

# Suggestions for Teaching in Your Classroom

## Addressing Student Differences

**1** **Design lessons and test items that call for memory, analytical, creative, and practical abilities.**

Robert Sternberg (1997a) has pointed out that many teachers tend to emphasize memory and analytical abilities, which is fine for students—male or female—who are good at memorizing facts or breaking things down into their component parts and explaining how the parts relate to each other. But students whose abilities are in the creative or practical areas may appear to be less capable than they really are. You can get a better idea of each student's strengths and weaknesses and how well students have learned the subject matter you just taught by using a variety of instructional cues and test items.

To emphasize students' memory abilities when you teach and test, use prompts such as:

"Who said . . .?"
"Summarize the ideas of . . ."
"Who did . . .?"
"When did . . .?"
"How did . . .?"
"Describe . . ."

To emphasize students' analytical abilities, use prompts such as:

"Why in your judgment . . .?"
"Explain why . . ."
"Explain what caused . . ."
"Critique . . ."

To emphasize creative abilities, use prompts such as:

"Imagine . . ."
"Design . . ."
"Suppose that . . ."
"What would happen if . . .?"

To emphasize practical thinking, ask students to:

"Show how you can use . . ."
"Implement . . ."
"Demonstrate how in the real world . . ."

**JOURNAL ENTRY**
Encouraging the Development of
Multiple Intelligences

**2** **Design lessons that emphasize different intelligences.**

As Howard Gardner and others point out, most of the tasks that we ask students to master reflect the linguistic and logical-mathematical forms of intelligence. But there are other ways that students can come to know things and demonstrate what they have learned. Potentially, lesson plans for any subject can be designed that incorporate each of Gardner's eight intelligences. Here are a few examples suggested by Thomas Armstrong (1994) and David Lazear (1992).

### Elementary Grades: Punctuation Marks

Bodily-kinesthetic: Students use their bodies to mimic the shape of various punctuation marks.

Musical: Students make up different sounds or songs for each punctuation mark.

Interpersonal: In small groups of four to six, students teach and test one another on proper punctuation usage.

### Middle School Grades: American History

Linguistic: Students debate the pros and cons of key historical decisions (such as Abraham Lincoln's decision to use military force to prevent the Confederate states from seceding from the Union, the Supreme Court decision in *Plessy v. Ferguson* that allowed separate facilities for Blacks and Whites, or President Harry Truman's decision to drop the atomic bomb on Japan).

Musical: Students learn about and sing some of the songs that were popular at a particular point in the country's history.

Spatial: Students draw murals that tell the story of a historical period.

### High School Grades: Boyle's Law (Physics)

Logical-mathematical: Students solve problems that require the use of Boyle's law: for a fixed mass and temperature of gas, the pressure is inversely proportional to the volume, or $P \times V = K$.

Bodily-kinesthetic: Students breathe air into their mouths, move it to one side of their mouths (so that one cheek is puffed out), indicate whether the pressure goes up or down, distribute it to both sides of their mouths, and indicate again whether the pressure goes up or down.

Intrapersonal: Students describe times in their lives when they felt they were either under a lot of psychological pressure or little pressure and whether they felt as if they had either a lot of or a little psychological space.

**JOURNAL ENTRY**
Allowing for Differences in Cognitive Style

### 3  Recognize that different styles of learning call for different methods of instruction.

Robert Sternberg's work on styles of mental self-government calls for the same approach to instruction and testing as does his work on intellectual abilities: use a variety of instructional methods and testing formats. Not only will you have a more accurate picture of what students know, but you will also be helping them learn how to shift styles to adapt to changing conditions. For example, students with a judicial style have a preference for "why" questions (for example, Why did the United States go to war with Iraq in 2003?), whereas students with a legislative style have a preference for "suppose" or "what if" questions (for example, If you were President George W. Bush, would you have gone to war with Iraq?). Table 5.3 indicates which of Sternberg's learning styles are most compatible with particular methods of instruction.

**JOURNAL ENTRY**
Taking Steps to Eliminate Gender Bias

### 4  Help students become aware of the existence of gender bias.

The following techniques have all been used by teachers to demonstrate that males often receive preferential treatment in our society in somewhat subtle ways (Bailey, 1996; Rop, 1998; Rutledge, 1997):

- Have students count how often in the space of a month male and female athletes are mentioned in the sports section of the local paper, and have the students create a graph depicting the difference.
- Have students survey similar-aged friends and classmates about the size of their allowance and report the results by gender.

- Have students review several textbooks and record how often men and women are mentioned.
- Have students keep a record of who participates in class discussions, how often they speak, for how long, and how they respond to comments made by male versus female classmates.

**JOURNAL ENTRY**
Encouraging Girls to Excel in Math and Science

**5** **Encourage girls to consider pursuing a career in science.**

Anna Kasov, the high school chemistry teacher we mentioned earlier, offers the following suggestions to teachers interested in encouraging adolescent girls to consider a career in science:

- Invite female scientists to class to talk about science as a career, or arrange for an electronic exchange through e-mail.
- Have students read articles written by female scientists, contact the authors with questions about the articles, and report the findings to the class.
- Contact recent female graduates who are majoring in science in college, and ask them to talk to the class about their experiences.

**HM** *TeacherPrepSPACE*

For additional suggestions for your journal, see the Reflective Journal Questions on the textbook's student website

**6** **Recognize that you will not be able to address the various abilities and cognitive styles of all of your students all of the time.**

Although this chapter has described three major ways in which students differ from one another and explained why it is important to gear instruction to these differences (the goal of differentiated instruction), we do not want you to get the impression that you should strive to accommodate the unique needs of each student every minute of the day. When you have twenty-five or more students in a class, such a goal is nearly impossible. But that does not mean you should make no attempt to get to know and work with students as individuals, either. You might, for example, adopt the practice of Lori Tukey (2002), a sixth-grade teacher. She allowed students themselves to provide basic instruction on various aspects of writing. Each student listed aspects of writing, such as spelling, punctuation, and organization, that he or she wanted to improve. Then those who were proficient at one or more of these aspects were identified as "experts" to whom other students could go for help. This tactic gave the teacher enough extra time to work individually with each student twice a month.

**HM** *TeacherPrepSPACE*

*To solidify your understanding of this chapter, go to the textbook's student website and use the ACE practice tests and PowerPoint slides.*

# 6 Accommodating Student Diversity

## HM TeacherPrepSPACE

**HM TeacherPrepSPACE student website** offers many helpful resources. Go to **login.cengage.com** to preview this chapter's Concept Maps and Chapter Themes.

## KEY POINTS

*These key points will help you learn the important information in this chapter. To help you study, they also appear in the margins of the pages, next to the text where they are discussed.*

### Ability Grouping

- Ability grouping assumes intelligence is inherited, reflected in IQ, and unchangeable and that instruction will be superior
- No research support for between-class ability grouping
- Joplin Plan and within-class ability grouping for math and science produce moderate increases in learning
- Between-class ability grouping negatively influences teaching goals and methods
- Joplin Plan and within-class ability grouping may allow more focused instruction

### The Individuals with Disabilities Education Act (IDEA)

- Before placement, student must be given complete, valid, and appropriate evaluation
- IEP must include objectives, services to be provided, criteria for determining achievement
- Students with disabilities must be educated in least restrictive environment
- Mainstreaming: policy of placing students with disabilities in regular classes
- Inclusion policy aims to keep students with disabilities in regular classroom for entire day
- Students with learning disabilities, speech impairments, mental retardation, or emotional disturbance most likely to be served under IDEA
- Multidisciplinary assessment team determines whether student needs special services
- Classroom teacher, parents, several specialists prepare IEP

### Students with Mental Retardation

- Students with mild retardation may frustrate easily, lack confidence and self-esteem

- Students with mild retardation tend to oversimplify, have difficulty generalizing
- Give students with mild retardation short assignments that can be completed quickly

### Students with Learning Disabilities

- Learning disabilities: disorders in basic processes that lead to learning problems not due to other causes
- Students with learning disabilities have problems with perception, attention, memory, metacognition
- Symptoms of ADHD include inattention, hyperactivity, and impulsivity
- Help students with learning disabilities to reduce distractions, attend to important information

### Students with Emotional Disturbance

- Emotional disturbance: poor relationships, inappropriate behavior, depression, fears
- Term *behavior disorder* focuses on behavior that needs to be changed, objective assessment
- Students with behavior disorders tend to be either aggressive or withdrawn
- Foster interpersonal contact among withdrawn students
- Use techniques to forestall aggressive or antisocial behavior

### Students Who Are Gifted and Talented

- Gifted and talented students show high performance in one or more areas
- Minorities underrepresented in gifted classes because of overreliance on test scores
- Gifted and talented students differ from their nongifted peers intellectually and emotionally
- Separate classes for gifted and talented students aid achievement but may lower academic self-concept of some students

### Using Technology to Assist Exceptional Students

- Federal legislation has led to the development of various assistive technologies

---

Prior to the twentieth century, few educators had to deal with the challenge of teaching extremely diverse groups of students. Most communities were fairly small, and students in a given school tended to come from similar backgrounds. Many children, especially those of low socioeconomic status (SES), attended school irregularly or not at all. In 1900, for example, only 8.5 percent of eligible students attended high school (Boyer, 1983), and these students were almost entirely from the upper and middle classes (Gutek, 1992). In addition, children with mental, emotional, or physical disabilities were sent to special schools, educated at home, or not educated at all. In comparison with today's schools, earlier student populations were considerably less diverse.

In Chapter 4, you read about the varieties of cultural and socioeconomic diversity among today's students. This chapter focuses on another dimension of diversity: the twin (but often somewhat fuzzy) concepts of ability and disability. Before explaining how educators attempt to meet the needs of diverse students, we take a brief look at historical developments that helped shape current educational practices.

## HISTORICAL DEVELOPMENTS

### The Growth of Public Education and Age-Graded Classrooms

By 1920, public education in the United States was no longer a small-scale and optional enterprise, largely because of three developments. First, by 1918, all states had passed compulsory attendance laws. Second, child labor laws had been enacted by many states, as well as by Congress in 1916, to eliminate the hiring of children and adolescents in mines and factories. Third, large numbers of immigrant children arrived in the United States from 1901 through 1920. The result was a vast increase in the number and diversity of children attending elementary and high school.

Educators initially dealt with this growth in student variability by forming age-graded classrooms. Introduced in the Quincy, Massachusetts, schools in the mid-1800s, these classrooms grouped all students of a particular age together each year to master a certain portion of the school's curriculum (Gutek, 1992). The main assumptions behind this approach were that teachers could be more effective in helping students learn and that students would have more positive attitudes toward themselves and school when classrooms were more homogeneous than heterogeneous (Oakes, 2005; Peltier, 1991). Regardless of whether these assumptions were well founded (an issue we will address shortly), they were (and still are) so widely held by educators that two additional approaches to creating even more homogeneous groups were eventually implemented: ability grouping and special class placement.

### Ability-Grouped Classrooms

Ability grouping involved the use of standardized mental ability or achievement tests to create groups of students who were considered very similar to each other in learning ability. In elementary and middle schools, students typically were (and frequently still are) placed in low-, average-, or high-ability groups. At the high school level, students were placed into different tracks that were geared toward such different post-high school goals as college, secretarial work, and vocational school.

Ability grouping was another means for school authorities to deal with the large influx of immigrant students. Because many of these children were not fluent in English and had had limited amounts of education in their native countries, they scored low on standardized tests when compared with American test norms. In addition, many of these children came from poor homes and were in poor health. At the time, their assignment to a low-ability group seemed both logical and appropriate (Wheelock, 1994).

In the next major part of this chapter, we will look at current applications of ability grouping, which now takes several forms and is still used to reduce the normal range of variability in cognitive ability and achievement found in the typical classroom.

### Special Education

For children whose abilities and disabilities fell within the normal range, age grading and ability testing were seen as workable approaches to creating more homogeneous classes. However, compulsory attendance laws also brought to school many children with mild to severe mental and physical disabilities. These students were deemed incapable of profiting from any type of normal classroom instruction and so were assigned to special schools. Unfortunately, as Alfred Binet feared, the labeling of a student as "mentally retarded" or "physically disabled" often resulted in a vastly inferior education. Early in the twentieth century, special schools served as convenient dumping grounds for all kinds of children who could not adapt to the regular classroom (Vallecorsa, deBettencourt, & Zigmond, 2000).

In the latter two-thirds of this chapter, we will detail the varied types and degrees of special class placement for children whose intellectual, social, emotional, or physical development falls outside (above as well as below) the range of normal variation. In discussing this approach, we pay particular attention to Public Law (PL) 101-476, the Individuals with Disabilities Education Act (IDEA), which was enacted to counter past excesses of special class placement and to encourage the placement of children with disabilities in regular classes.

# ABILITY GROUPING

Ability grouping is a widespread practice (Brewer, Rees, & Argys, 1995; Dornbusch & Kaufman, 2001; Loveless, 1998). In the elementary grades, virtually all teachers form separate groups within their classrooms for instruction in reading, and many do so for mathematics as well. At the middle school level, approximately two-thirds to three-fourths of schools assign students to different self-contained classes in one or more subjects on the basis of standardized test scores. This proportion rises to about 85 percent at the high school level, where students are assigned to different classes (e.g., honors, college preparatory, basic) on a subject-by-subject basis (Dornbusch & Kaufman, 2001). At the middle and high school levels, the term *tracking* rather than *ability grouping* is typically used. In this section, we will describe the most common ways in which teachers group students by ability, examine the assumptions that provide the rationale for this practice, summarize research findings on the effectiveness of ability grouping, and look at alternative courses of action.

## Types of Ability Groups

Four approaches to ability grouping are popular among educators today: between-class ability grouping, regrouping, the Joplin Plan, and within-class grouping. You may be able to recall a few classes in which one or another of these techniques was used. If not, you will no doubt encounter at least one of them during your first year of teaching.

**Between-Class Ability Grouping**   The goal of **between-class ability grouping** is for each class to be made up of students who are homogeneous in standardized intelligence or achievement test scores. Three levels of classes are usually formed: high, average, and low. Students in one ability group typically have little or no contact with students in other ability groups during the school day. Although each group covers the same subjects, a higher group does so in greater depth and breadth than lower groups. At the high school level, as we mentioned, this approach is often called *tracking.*

**Regrouping**   The groups formed under a **regrouping** plan are more flexible in assignments and narrower in scope than between-class groups. Students of the same age, ability, and grade but from different classrooms come together for instruction in a specific subject, usually reading or mathematics. If a student begins to outperform the other members of the group significantly, a change of group assignment is easier because it involves just that particular subject.

*In ability grouping, students are selected and placed in homogeneous groups with other students who are considered to have very similar learning abilities.*

Regrouping has two major disadvantages, however. First, it requires a certain degree of planning and cooperation among the teachers involved. They must agree, for example, to schedule reading and arithmetic during the same periods. Second, many teachers are uncomfortable working with children whom they see only once a day for an hour or so.

**Joplin Plan**   The **Joplin Plan** is a variation of regrouping. The main difference is that regroupings take place across grade levels. For example, all third, fourth, and fifth graders whose grade-equivalent scores in reading are 4.6 (fourth grade, sixth month) would come together for reading instruction. The same would be done for mathematics. The Joplin Plan has the same advantages and disadvantages as simple regrouping, and it is the basis for a successful reading program called Success for All (Kulik, 2003b).

**Within-Class Ability Grouping**   The most popular form of ability grouping, occurring in almost all elementary school classes, **within-class ability grouping** involves the division of a single class of students into two or three groups for reading and math instruction. Like regrouping and the Joplin Plan, within-class ability grouping has the advantages of being flexible in terms of group assignments and being restricted to one or two subjects. In addition, it eliminates the need for cooperative scheduling. One disadvantage of this approach is that the teacher needs to be skilled at keeping the other students in the class productively occupied while working with a particular group.

## pause & reflect

You probably experienced ability grouping in one form or another at the elementary and secondary levels. Think about whether it might have been between-class grouping, regrouping, the Joplin Plan, or within-class grouping. Could you tell which group you were in? Did you have feelings about being in that group?

## Assumptions Underlying Ability Grouping

Ability grouping assumes intelligence is inherited, reflected by IQ, and unchangeable and that instruction will be superior

When ability grouping was initiated early in the twentieth century, much less was known about the various factors that affect classroom learning. Consequently, educators simply assumed certain things to be true. One of those assumptions was that intelligence, which affects the capacity to learn, was a fixed, inherited trait and that little could be done to change the learning capacity of individuals. A second assumption was that intelligence was adequately reflected by an intelligence quotient (IQ) score. A third assumption was that all students would learn best when grouped with those of similar ability (Marsh & Raywid, 1994; Ornstein & Levine, 2006). Although many educators still believe these assumptions are true, the research evidence summarized here and elsewhere in this book casts doubt on their validity.

## Evaluations of Ability Grouping

Because ability grouping occurs in virtually all school districts, its effects have been intensively studied (Abrami, Lou, Chambers, Poulsen, & Spence, 2000; Applebee, Langer, Nystrand, & Gamoran, 2003; Hoffer, 1992; Kulik, 2003b; Callahan, 2005; Lloyd, 1999; Lou, Abrami, & Spence, 2000; Marsh & Raywid, 1994; Raudenbush, Rowan, & Cheong, 1993; Yonezawa, Wells, & Serna, 2002). The main findings of these analyses are as follows:

| No research support for between-class ability grouping

1. There is little to no support for between-class ability grouping. Students assigned to low-ability classes generally performed worse than comparable students in heterogeneous classes. Students assigned to average-ability classes performed at about the same level as their nongrouped peers. High-ability students sometimes performed slightly better in homogeneous classes than in heterogeneous classes. A report by the Carnegie Corporation on educating adolescents (Jackson & Davis, 2000) noted: "Instruction in tracked classes thus falls short on measures of both equity and excellence. Tracking affects students unequally, both by grouping minorities and economically disadvantaged students in lower tracks and by providing unequal educational opportunities to students. Instruction in lower-track classes is typically far from excellent, often depending on rote memorization and recall, isolated facts, worksheets, and a slow pace" (p. 66). A study conducted in California of high school students learning English as a second language supports the Carnegie report. The academic track in which the high school students were placed was a better predictor of a variety of academic performances—including grades and scores on standardized achievement tests—than was the students' proficiency in English. Lower-track placement meant also that students took fewer classes that would qualify them for college admission (Callahan, 2005).

2. Research on the effect of regrouping for reading or mathematics is inconclusive. Some of the relatively few studies that have been done on this form of ability grouping suggest that it can be effective if the instructional pace and level of the text match the student's actual achievement level rather than the student's nominal grade level. In other words, a fifth grader who scores at the fourth-grade level on a reading test should be reading out of a fourth-grade reading book.

| Joplin Plan and within-class ability grouping for math and science produce moderate increases in learning

3. The Joplin Plan yields moderately positive effects compared with instruction in heterogeneous classes.

4. Within-class ability grouping in mathematics and science in grades 1 through 12 has produced modestly positive results (about eight percentile ranks) compared with whole-class instruction and an even smaller positive effect (about four percentile ranks) when compared with mixed-ability groups. Average-achieving students benefit most from being placed in homogeneous-ability groups, whereas low-achieving students benefit most from being placed in mixed-ability groups. Because within-class ability grouping for reading is an almost universal practice at every grade level, researchers have not had the opportunity to compare its effectiveness with whole-class reading instruction. Nevertheless, it would be reasonable to expect much the same results for reading as were found for mathematics and science (see Saleh, Lazonder, & De Jong, 2004).

Research also shows that some within-class grouping practices are more effective than others. The largest positive effects were found in classrooms that had the following two conditions: (1) students were assigned to groups not only on the basis of ability but also on the basis of other factors that contributed to group cohesiveness and (2) cooperative learning techniques were used that included the features of positive interdependence and individual accountability (Abrami et al., 2000; Lou et al., 2000). (See Chapter 13, "Approaches to Instruction," for a discussion of these and other features of cooperative learning.)

5. Students in homogeneously grouped classes scored the same as students in heterogeneously grouped classes on measures of self-esteem.

6. Students in high-ability classes had more positive attitudes about school and higher educational aspirations than did students in low-ability classrooms.

7. Between-class ability grouping affected the quality of instruction received by students in several ways:

> Between-class ability grouping negatively influences teaching goals and methods

   a. The best teachers were often assigned to teach the highest tracks, whereas the least experienced or weakest teachers were assigned to teach the lowest tracks.

   b. Teachers of high-ability classes stressed critical thinking, self-direction, creativity, and active participation, whereas teachers of low-ability classes stressed working quietly, following rules, and getting along with classmates. This effect was particularly noticeable in math and science.

   c. Teachers of low-ability groups covered less material and simpler material than did teachers of high-ability groups.

   d. Teachers of low-ability students expected and demanded less of them than did teachers of high-ability students.

Despite the evidence against between-class ability grouping, ethnic minority and low-SES students are frequently assigned to the lowest tracks, where they fall further behind White, middle-SES students. This situation has prompted accusations of discrimination, and some districts have responded by adopting policies that specifically allow low-track minority students to enroll in honors courses. However, this technique (sometimes called a "freedom of choice program") does not necessarily increase minority students' participation in higher-level courses. An examination of this practice in four middle schools and six high schools indicates that it is largely ineffective in encouraging ethnic minority/low-SES students to enroll in honors classes (Yonezawa et al., 2002). The major reasons for the failure of freedom of choice programs are as follows:

a. In some of the schools studied, low-track students (who were mostly low-income and minority students) were not always informed that they could request honors classes.

b. In some cases, the requests of low-track students were delayed by such tactics as not being able to get an appointment with a counselor. In fact, some counselors tried to dissuade students from taking an honors or high-track class.

c. Only after requesting a high-track class did students learn that they needed to have taken prerequisite courses or had to have a minimum grade-point average. In one case, a counselor administered an abbreviated reading comprehension test before allowing students to enroll in advanced courses.

d. Because of their previous academic placement and history, low-track students felt they did not have the ability or confidence to succeed in advanced classes. They had, in essence, come to identify themselves as "low-track" or "slow."

e. Some students were uninterested in advanced classes because that action would have separated them from their friends and a familiar culture. Others believed that they simply would not be accepted by the other (mostly White, middle-SES) students.

## To Group or Not to Group?

The findings just summarized suggest three courses of action. The first course is to discontinue the use of full-day, between-class ability groups or tracks. Despite the fact that most middle and high schools continue to use this form of ability grouping, students do not learn more or feel more positively about themselves and school. This is a case in which even widely held beliefs must be modified or eliminated when the weight of evidence goes against them.

> Joplin Plan and within-class ability grouping may allow more focused instruction

The second course of action is to use only those forms of ability grouping that produce positive results: within-class grouping and the Joplin Plan, especially for reading

## Take a Stand!

### Ability Grouping and Tracking: A Practice That Fails to Deliver What It Promises

At the beginning of this book, we stated that an advantage of using scientific methods to study education was that it helped us avoid drawing false conclusions about an idea or practice because of subjective and unsystematic thinking. When people substitute personal values and experience for systematic research findings, educational decisions that are detrimental to students are usually the result. So it is with between-class ability grouping and rigid tracking systems at the middle school and high school levels. Many educators fervently believe that teachers are more effective and students learn more when classrooms are more homogeneous in ability than heterogeneous. But almost all of the research

conducted on ability grouping and tracking over the past several decades refutes these beliefs. Consequently, this is a practice that should rarely, if ever, be used. Among other detriments, it destroys the motivation of students and stunts their intellectual growth.

We believe that teachers should speak out forcefully against between-class ability grouping and in favor of the effective instructional practices that can be used with all students, especially cooperative learning and peer tutoring. When the opportunity arises, let your colleagues know that the assumptions they carry about the benefits of ability grouping are not supported by the scientific literature.

*HM TeacherPrepSPACE*

Do you share the authors' opposition to ability grouping and tracking? Do you think such practices aided or hindered your own educational progress? Explore this subject further at the Take a Stand! section at the textbook's student website.

and mathematics. We do not know why these forms of ability grouping work. It is assumed (Tieso, 2003) that the increase in group homogeneity allows for more appropriate and potent forms of instruction (for example, greater effort by the teacher to bring lower-achieving groups up to the level of higher-achieving groups). If this assumption is correct, within-class ability grouping and the Joplin Plan must be carried out in such a way that homogeneous groups are guaranteed to result. The best way to achieve similarity in cognitive ability among students is to group them on the basis of past classroom performance, standardized achievement test scores, or both. The least desirable (but most frequently used) approach is to base the assignments solely on IQ scores.

The third course of action is to dispense with all forms of ability grouping, a practice called *detracking*. Detracking practices vary widely. Without a concerted effort to meet the educational needs of all students, detracking may lead to slightly lower performance of average and above-average students (Loveless, 1999). When implemented well, however, detracking has been shown to support learning of all students in heterogeneous classrooms (Rubin, 2006).

In keeping with the concept of differentiated instruction mentioned earlier in the book, teachers can use a variety of organizational and instructional techniques that will allow them to cope with a heterogeneous class, or they can use these same techniques in conjunction with the Joplin Plan or within-class grouping. For instance, you might use with all students instructional techniques that are associated with high achievement. These would include:

- Making clear presentations
- Displaying a high level of enthusiasm
- Reinforcing students for correct responses
- Providing sufficient time for students to formulate answers to questions

## VIDEO CASE  ◄◄ ▶ ►►

### Inclusion: Grouping Strategies for Inclusive Classrooms

*Watch the video, study the artifacts in the case, and reflect upon the following questions:*

1. In the Video Case, we see a class that groups students in a heterogeneous fashion. Discuss the pros and cons of this grouping strategy.

2. Describe some of the strategies that the teachers in the Video Case use to ensure that all students participate in their various learning groups.

- Prompting correct responses
- Providing detailed feedback about the accuracy of responses
- Requiring a high level of work and effort
- Organizing students into small, heterogeneous learning groups and using cooperative learning techniques

Other ideas include optional honors activities, pullout (meaning programs that occur outside the classroom), challenge classes that are available to all students, study skills classes for low-achieving students, and small-group projects (Oakes & Wells, 1998).

# THE INDIVIDUALS WITH DISABILITIES EDUCATION ACT (IDEA)

Many of the criticisms and arguments marshaled against ability grouping have come to be applied as well to special classes for students with disabilities. In addition, the elimination of racially segregated schools by the U.S. Supreme Court in the case of *Brown v. Board of Education* (1954) established a precedent for providing students with disabilities with an equal opportunity for a free and appropriate education (Ornstein & Levine, 2006). As a result, influential members of Congress were persuaded in the early 1970s that it was time for the federal government to take steps to correct the perceived inequities and deficiencies in our educational system. The result was a landmark piece of legislation, Public Law 94-142, the Education for All Handicapped Children Act of 1975. This law was revised and expanded in 1986 as the Handicapped Children's Protection Act (PL 99-457) and again in 1990 as the Individuals with Disabilities Education Act (IDEA, PL 101-476).

IDEA was then amended in 1997 to broaden and clarify a number of its provisions ("Individuals with Disabilities," 1997). The 1990 version of IDEA, for example, said nothing about the participation of children with disabilities in standardized testing programs. The 1997 amendment, however, states that children with disabilities must be provided with whatever modifications are necessary (for instance, large print for children who have visual impairments, extended time limits for children with learning disabilities) to allow them to take part in state- and districtwide assessments. If a child with a disability does not participate in a standardized assessment, school district officials must explain why they feel such an assessment is inappropriate and how that child will be assessed (Ysseldyke, Algozzine, & Thurlow, 2000). The Individuals with Disabilities Education Improvement Act of 2004 (IDEA, PL 108-446) is called IDEA 2004. IDEA 2004 enhanced opportunities for parental involvement in the education of children with disabilities, echoing the requirements of the No Child Left Behind Act of 2001 that school districts provide parents with training and materials to help their children's achievement (Dardig, 2005). The final regulations governing the implementation of IDEA 2004 were issued in August of 2006 and went into effect in October of that year.

## Major Provisions of IDEA

**A Free and Appropriate Public Education**   The basic purpose of IDEA is to ensure that all individuals from birth through age twenty-one who have an identifiable disability, regardless of how severe, receive at public expense supervised special education and related services that meet their unique educational needs. These services can be delivered in a classroom, at home, in a hospital, or in a specialized institution and may include physical education and vocational education, as well as instruction in the typical academic subjects ("Individuals with Disabilities," 1997).

**Preplacement Evaluation**   Before a child with a disability can be placed in a program that provides special education services, "a full and individual evaluation of the

Before placement, student must be given complete, valid, and appropriate evaluation

child's educational needs" must be conducted. Such an evaluation must conform to the following rules:

1. Tests must be administered in the child's native language.
2. A test must be valid for the specific purpose for which it is used.
3. Tests must be administered by trained individuals according to the instructions provided by the test publisher.
4. Tests administered to students who have impaired sensory, manual, or speaking skills must reflect aptitude or achievement rather than the impairment.
5. No single procedure (such as an IQ test) can be the sole basis for determining an appropriate educational program. Data should be collected from such nontest sources as observations by other professionals (such as the classroom teacher), medical records, and parental interviews.
6. Evaluations must be made by a multidisciplinary team that contains at least one teacher or other specialist with knowledge in the area of the suspected disability.
7. The child must be assessed in all areas related to the suspected disability ("Individuals with Disabilities," 1997).

When you deal with students whose first language is not English, it is important to realize that standardized tests are designed to reflect cultural experiences common to the United States and that English words and phrases may not mean quite the same thing when translated. Therefore, these tests may not be measuring what they were developed to measure. In other words, they may not be valid. The results of such assessments should therefore be interpreted very cautiously (Kubiszyn & Borich, 2007).

**Individualized Education Program**    Every child who is identified as having a disability and who receives special education services must have an **individualized education program (IEP)** prepared. The IEP is a written statement that describes the educational program that has been designed to meet the child's unique needs. The IEP must include the following elements:

| IEP must include objectives, services to be provided, criteria for determining achievement |

1. A statement of the child's existing levels of educational performance
2. A statement of annual goals, including short-term instructional objectives
3. A statement of the specific special education and related services to be provided to the child and the extent to which the child will be able to participate in regular educational programs
4. The projected dates for initiation of services and the anticipated duration of the services
5. Appropriate objective criteria and evaluation procedures and schedules for determining, on at least an annual basis, whether short-term objectives are being achieved ("Individuals with Disabilities," 1997)

The IEP is to be planned by a multidisciplinary team composed of the student's classroom teacher in collaboration with a person qualified in special education, one or both of the student's parents, the student (when appropriate), and other individuals at the discretion of the parents or school. (An example of an IEP is depicted later in this chapter in Figure 6.1.)

| Students with disabilities must be educated in least restrictive environment |

**Least Restrictive Environment**    According to the 1994 Code of Federal Regulations that governs the implementation of IDEA, educational services must be provided to children with disabilities in the **least restrictive environment** that their disability will allow. A school district must identify a continuum of increasingly restrictive placements (instruction in regular classes, special classes, home instruction, instruction in hospitals and institutions) and, on the basis of the multidisciplinary team's evaluation, select the least restrictive setting that will best meet the student's special educational needs. This provision is often referred to as **mainstreaming** because the goal of the law is to have as many children with disabilities as

| Mainstreaming: policy of placing students with disabilities in regular classes |

*The least restrictive environment provision of IDEA has led to mainstreaming—the policy that children with disabilities should attend regular classes to the maximum extent possible. Some special education proponents argue that full-time regular classroom placement should be the only option for such students.*

possible, regardless of the severity of the disability, enter the mainstream of education by attending regular classes with nondisabled students. In recent years, mainstreaming has frequently evolved into *inclusion,* a practice we discuss later in this chapter.

## The Policy of Inclusion

Although IDEA calls for children with disabilities to be placed in the least restrictive environment, the law clearly allows for more restrictive placements than those of the regular classroom "when the nature or severity of the disability is such that education in regular classes with the use of supplementary aids and services cannot be achieved satisfactorily" ("Individuals with Disabilities," 1997, p. 61). Nevertheless, there has been a movement in recent years to eliminate this option. Known as **inclusion** or **full inclusion,** this extension of the mainstreaming provision has become one of the most controversial outgrowths of IDEA.

As most proponents use the term, *inclusion* means keeping special education students in regular classrooms and bringing support services to the children rather than the other way around. *Full inclusion* refers to the practice of eliminating all pullout programs *and* special education teachers and of providing regular classroom teachers with training in teaching special-needs students so that they can teach these students in the regular classroom (Kirk, Gallagher, & Anastasiow, 2003; Smelter, Rasch, & Yudewitz, 1994; Smith, 2004).

Inclusion policy aims to keep students with disabilities in regular classroom for entire day

**The Debate About Inclusion**    The proponents of inclusion and full inclusion often raise four arguments to support their position:

1.  Research suggests that special-needs students who are segregated from regular students perform more poorly academically and socially than comparable students who are mainstreamed (Kavale, 2002).
2.  Given the substantial body of evidence demonstrating the propensity of children to observe and imitate more competent children (see, for example, Schunk, 1987), it can be assumed that students with disabilities will learn more by interacting with

nondisabled students than by attending homogeneous classes (Sapon-Shevin, 1996, 2003).

3. The Supreme Court in *Brown v. Board of Education* declared the doctrine of separate but equal to be unconstitutional. Therefore, pullout programs are a violation of the civil rights of children with special needs because these programs segregate them from their nondisabled peers in programs that are assumed to be separate but equal (Kavale, 2002; Mock & Kauffman, 2002; Skrtic, Sailor, & Gee, 1996).

4. Disproportionate numbers of minority students are placed in special education (Artiles, Klingner, & Tate, 2006; Harry & Klingner, 2006). As one example, according to the National Research Council (2002), Black students are disproportionately placed in special education categories, such as "mental retardation" and "learning disabilities" (these and other types of special needs are described later in this chapter). Black students who are placed in special education achieve at lower levels and are less likely to leave special education placements than their White counterparts (U.S. Department of Education, 2004). The gap in special education not only mirrors the "achievement gap" discussed in Chapter 4 but also results in Black students with special needs being separated from the curriculum that nondisabled peers experience (Blanchett, 2006). This harkens back to the violations of segregation addressed in *Brown v. Board of Education* (see Oakes, 2005) and can also contribute to a lack of tolerance among groups (Sapon-Shevin, 2003).

The opponents of inclusion often cite cases of special-needs students disrupting the normal flow of instruction or of teachers being inadequately prepared to assist learners with special needs (Kavale, 2002; Mock & Kauffman, 2002).

**Research Findings**    The evidence that bears on the inclusion issue is a combination of anecdotes (reports about individual cases) and experiments that compare inclusive to noninclusive practices for special-needs students. It seems to indicate, at least for now, that inclusion works well for some students but produces modest or no benefits for others. On the basis of this evidence (Kavale, 2002; MacMillan, Gresham, & Forness, 1996; Mock & Kauffman, 2002; Raison, Hanson, Hall, & Reynolds, 1995; Stevens & Slavin, 1995; Zigmond et al., 1995), three conclusions seem warranted:

1. Inclusion may not be an appropriate course of action for every child with a disability.
2. Inclusion will likely work best when the presence of a disabled student stimulates the teacher to improve the general quality of classroom instruction and when well-trained support staff, such as teacher aides and inclusion facilitators, are available (Choate, 2003; Ruder, 2000).
3. For students who are mainstreamed, IEPs should be written so as to reflect better what a given student probably can and cannot accomplish.

It also seems that successful inclusion programs may take many years to implement. For example, two researchers (McLeskey & Waldron, 2002) who helped an elementary school district institute an inclusion program found that students with disabilities made at least as much academic progress in regular classes as they did in special education classes and that teachers, administrators, and parents were satisfied with the inclusive program. But the transformation required a considerable amount of effort and about twelve years to accomplish.

## What IDEA Means to Regular Classroom Teachers

By the time you begin your teaching career, the original legislation governing the delivery of educational services to the disabled, PL 94-142, will have been in effect for about thirty years. Each state was required to have established laws and policies for implementing the various provisions by 1978. The first guiding principle to follow, therefore, is *find out what the local ground rules are.* You will probably be told during orientation meetings about the ways IDEA is being put into effect in your state and local school district. But if such a presentation is not given or is incomplete, it would be wise to ask about guidelines you should follow. Your second guiding principle, then, should be *when in doubt, ask*. With these two caveats in mind, consider some questions you may be asking yourself about the impact of IDEA as you approach your first teaching job.

# VIDEO CASE    ◄◄ ▶ ►►

## Foundations: Aligning Instruction with Federal Legislation

*Watch the video, study the artifacts in the case, and reflect upon the following questions:*

1. After reading about the inclusion debate and listening to the school professionals in this Video Case, discuss your thoughts and position on this important educational issue.

2. Based on both the teacher interviews in this Video Case and the material you just read about the regular classroom teacher's responsibilities under IDEA, which of these responsibilities do you think are most important? Explain your answer.

**What Kinds of Disabling Conditions Are Included Under IDEA?**   According to the U.S. Department of Education (2005), during the 2002–2003 academic year, 5.66 million children and youths from ages six through seventeen (about 11.6 percent of the total number of individuals in this age group) received special education services under IDEA.

For individuals between the ages of three and twenty, IDEA recognizes twelve categories of disability. A thirteenth category, developmental delay, applies only to children from ages three through nine and is optional for state programs. The first twelve categories described in the legislation are listed as follows in alphabetical order, with brief definitions of each type:

*Autism.* Significant difficulty in verbal and nonverbal communication and social interaction that adversely affects educational performance.

*Deaf-blindness.* Impairments of both hearing and vision, the combination of which causes severe communication, developmental, and educational problems. The combination of these impairments is such that a child's educational and physical needs cannot be adequately met by programs designed for only deaf children or only blind children.

*Hearing impairment.* Permanent or fluctuating difficulty in understanding speech that adversely affects educational performance.

*Mental retardation.* Significant subaverage general intellectual functioning accompanied by deficits in adaptive behavior (how well a person functions in social environments).

*Multiple disabilities.* Two or more impairments (such as mental retardation—blindness and mental retardation—orthopedic, but not deaf-blindness) that cause such severe educational problems that a child's needs cannot be adequately met by programs designed solely for one of the impairments.

*Orthopedic impairments.* Impairment in a child's ability to use arms, legs, hands, or feet that significantly affects that child's educational performance.

*Other health impairments.* Conditions such as asthma, hemophilia, sickle cell anemia, epilepsy, heart disease, and diabetes that so limit the strength, vitality, or alertness of a child that educational performance is significantly affected.

*Emotional disturbance.* Personal and social problems exhibited in an extreme degree over a period of time that adversely affect a child's ability to learn and get along with others (prior to the 1997 amendments to IDEA, this category was called "serious emotional disturbance").

*Specific learning disability.* A disorder in one or more of the basic psychological processes involved in understanding or using language that leads to learning problems not traceable to physical disabilities, mental retardation, emotional disturbance, or cultural-economic disadvantage.

*Speech or language impairment.* A communication disorder such as stuttering, impaired articulation, or a language or voice impairment that adversely affects educational performance.

*Traumatic brain injury.* A brain injury due to an accident that causes cognitive or psychosocial impairments that adversely affect educational performance.

*Visual impairment including blindness.* A visual impairment so severe that even with corrective lenses a child's educational performance is adversely affected.

> Students with learning disabilities, speech impairments, mental retardation, or emotional disturbance most likely to be served under IDEA

The percentages of each type of student who received special educational services during the 2002–2003 school year are indicated in Table 6.1. As you can see, the children with disabilities who most commonly received services (85 percent of the total) were those classified as having a specific learning disability, a speech or language impairment, mental retardation, or an emotional disturbance.

**What Are the Regular Classroom Teacher's Responsibilities Under IDEA?**
Regular classroom teachers may be involved in activities required directly or indirectly by IDEA in four possible ways: referral, assessment, preparation of the IEP, and implementation and evaluation of the IEP.

*Referral*   Most referrals for assessment and possible special instruction are made by a child's teacher or his or her parents because they are the ones most familiar with the quality of the child's daily work and progress as compared with other children.

| Table 6.1 | Students Receiving Special Education Services, 2002–2003 | |
|---|---|---|
| **Disabling Condition** | **Percentage of Total School Enrollment[a]** | **Percentage of Students with Disabilities Served** |
| Specific learning disabilities | 5.59 | 48.3 |
| Speech or language impairments | 2.26 | 19.5 |
| Mental retardation | 1.07 | 9.2 |
| Emotional disturbance | 0.93 | 8.0 |
| Other health impairments | 0.78 | 6.7 |
| Multiple disabilities | 0.24 | 2.0 |
| Autism | 0.23 | 2.0 |
| Hearing impairments | 0.14 | 1.2 |
| Orthopedic impairments | 0.14 | 1.2 |
| Visual impairments | 0.05 | 0.4 |
| Traumatic brain injury | 0.04 | 0.3 |
| Deaf-blindness | 0.00 | 0.0 |
| Total | 11.58 | 98.8[b] |

[a]Percentages are based on children with disabilities ages 6–17 as a percentage of total school enrollment for kindergarten through twelfth grade.

[b]Percentages do not add to 100 percent because of rounding.

SOURCE: U.S. Department of Education (2005).

*The decision as to whether a child qualifies for special education services under IDEA is made largely on the basis of information supplied by the multidisciplinary assessment team. Classroom teachers typically contribute information about the child's academic and social behavior.*

**Assessment**　The initial assessment procedures, which must be approved by the child's parents, are usually carried out by school psychologists who are certified to administer tests. If the initial conclusions of the school psychologist support the teacher's or parents' perception that the student needs special services, the **multidisciplinary assessment team** required under IDEA will be formed. Because the 1997 amendment of IDEA requires that classroom teachers be part of the multidisciplinary assessment team, you should be prepared to provide such information as the quality of the child's homework and test scores, ability to understand and use language, ability to perform various motor functions, alertness at different times of the day, and interpersonal relationships with classmates (Kubiszyn & Borich, 2007; Smith, 2004).

> Multidisciplinary assessment team determines whether student needs special services

**Preparation of the IEP**　At least some, if not all, of the members of the assessment team work with the teacher (and the parents) in preparing the IEP. The necessary components of an IEP were described earlier, and they are illustrated in Figure 6.1.

> Classroom teacher, parents, several specialists prepare IEP

**Implementation and Evaluation of the IEP**　Depending on the nature and severity of the disability, the student may spend part or all of the school day in a regular classroom or be placed in a separate class or school. If the student stays in a regular classroom, the teacher will be expected to put into practice the various instructional techniques listed in the IEP. Because the IEP is planned by a multidisciplinary team, you will be given direction and support in providing regular class instruction for students who have a disabling condition as defined under IDEA. The classroom teacher may also be expected to determine whether the listed objectives are being met and to furnish evidence of attainment. Various techniques of instruction, as well as approaches to evaluation that stress student mastery of individualized assignments, will be discussed in several of the chapters that follow.

The types of atypical students you will sometimes be expected to teach in your classroom will vary. Some will be special education students who are being mainstreamed for part of the school day. Others, although different from

## pause & reflect

Many teachers say that although they agree with the philosophy behind IDEA, they feel that their training has not adequately prepared them to meet the needs of students with disabling conditions. Would you say the same about your teacher education program? Why? What might you do to prepare yourself better?

**Figure 6.1** Example of an Individualized Education Program (IEP)

| INDIVIDUAL EDUCATIONAL PLAN | Description of Services to Be Provided |
|---|---|

**INDIVIDUAL EDUCATIONAL PLAN**    11/2008
                                    DATE

STUDENT: Last Name         First          Middle   5.3   8 - 4 - 98
                                                   Grade Level   Birthdate/Age

School of Attendance   Home School

School Address                    School Telephone Number

**Child Study Team Members**

                                          L D Teacher
        Homeroom         Case Manager      Parents
Name        Title        Name                 Title
        Facilitator
Name        Title        Name                 Title
        Speech
Name        Title        Name                 Title

**Summary of Assessment results**

IDENTIFIED STUDENT NEEDS: _Reading from last half of_
_____DISTAR II - present performance level_

LONG TERM GOALS: _To improve reading achievement level_
_by at least one year's gain. To improve math_
_achievement to grade level. To improve_
_language skills by one year's gain._

SHORT TERM GOALS: _Master Level 4 vocabulary and reading_
_skills. Master math skills in basic curriculum._
_Master spelling words from Level 3 list. Complete_
_units 1-9 from Level 3 curriculum._

MAINSTREAM MODIFICATIONS: _____

White Copy—Cumulative Folder          Goldenrod Copy—Case Manager
Pink Copy—Special Teacher             Yellow Copy—Parent

**Description of Services to Be Provided**

| Type of Service | Teacher | Starting Date | Amt. of time per day | OBJECTIVES AND CRITERIA FOR ATTAINMENT |
|---|---|---|---|---|
| SLD level III | LD Teacher | 11-11-96 | 2½ hrs | Reading: will know all vocabulary through the "Honeycomb" level. Will master skills as presented through Distar II. Will know 1 2 3 second-symbols presented in "Sound Way to Reading." Math: will pass all tests at Basic 4 level. Spelling: 5 words each week from level 3 lists Language: will complete Units 1 – 9 of the 4th grade language program. Will also complete supplemental units from "Language Step by Step." |

| Mainstream Classes | Teacher | Amt. of time per day | OBJECTIVES AND CRITERIA FOR ATTAINMENT |
|---|---|---|---|
|  |  | 3½ hrs | Out of seat behavior: Sit attentively and listen during mainstream class discussions. A simple management plan will be implemented if he does not meet this expectation. Mainstream modifications of Social Studies: will keep a folder in which he expresses through drawing the topics his class will cover. Modified district Social Studies curriculum. No formal testing will be made. |

The following equipment and other changes in personnel, transportation, curriculum methods, and educational services will be provided: _Distar II Reading Program, Spelling Level 3, "Sound Way to Reading" Program, Vocabulary tapes_

Substantiation of least restrictive alternatives: _The planning team has determined academic needs are best met with direct SLD support in reading, math, language, and spelling_

ANTICIPATED LENGTH OF PLAN _1 yr._ The next periodic review will be held: _May 2009_
                                                                   DATE/TIME/PLACE

☐ I approve this program placement and the above IEP
☐ I do not approve this placement and/or the IEP
☐ I request a conciliation conference

                                          PARENT/GUARDIAN

Form 2011                                 Principal or Designee

---

typical students in some noticeable respect, will not qualify for special education services under IDEA. The remainder of this chapter will describe students from both categories and techniques for teaching them. Students with mental retardation, learning disabilities, and emotional disturbance often require special forms of instruction, and we will focus on these categories. In addition, though not mentioned in IDEA, students who are gifted and talented require special forms of instruction, as we will also discuss.

## STUDENTS WITH MENTAL RETARDATION

### Definition of Mental Retardation

The American Association on Mental Retardation (AAMR) defines **mental retardation** as "a disability characterized by significant limitations both in intellectual functioning and in adaptive behavior as expressed in conceptual, social, and practical adaptive skills. This disability originates before age 18" (American Association on Mental Retardation, 2002).

An individual whose score is two or more standard deviations below the mean (a score of 70 to 75 or below) on a standardized test of intelligence is considered to have a significant limitation in intellectual functioning. If you're not sure what a standard deviation is, take a look now at Chapter 14, "Understanding Standardized Assessment," in which we discuss this statistical concept. As with intellectual functioning, a significant limitation in adaptive behavior is said to exist when an individual scores at least two standard deviations below the mean on standardized tests of adaptive skills.

As a result of legal challenges to IQ testing and special class placement, as well as to the trend toward mainstreaming, students classified as "mildly" retarded who were once separated are more likely now to be placed in regular classes. In a mainstreamed environment, it is most unlikely that you will encounter a great many mainstreamed children classified as "moderately" or "severely" retarded because of the specialized forms of care and instruction they need. (If you do encounter children with moderate or severe mental retardation, there will likely be someone to help with the child's learning needs.) You may, however, be asked to teach one or more of the higher-scoring children with mild retardation for at least part of the day.

## Characteristics of Children with Mild Retardation

Students who have below-average IQ scores follow the same general developmental pattern as their peers with higher IQ scores, but they differ in the rate and degree of development.[1] Accordingly, students with low IQ scores may possess characteristics typical of students with average IQ scores who are younger than they are. One general characteristic of such students, therefore, is that they often appear immature compared with their age-mates. Immature students are likely to experience frustration frequently when they find they are unable to do things their classmates can do, and many students with mild retardation tend to have a low tolerance for frustration and a tendency toward low self-esteem, low confidence, and low motivation. These feelings, in conjunction with the cognitive deficits outlined in the next paragraph, sometimes make it difficult for the child with mild retardation to make friends and get along with peers of average ability.

The cognitive characteristics of children with mild retardation include a tendency to oversimplify concepts, limited ability to generalize, smaller memory capacity, shorter attention span, the inclination to concentrate on only one aspect of a learning situation and to ignore other relevant features, the inability to formulate learning strategies that fit particular situations, and delayed language development. These children also show a limited amount of *metacognition*, that is, knowledge about how one learns and the factors that affect learning. (This concept will be discussed more fully in Chapter 8, "Information-Processing Theory.")

Several of these cognitive deficits often operate in concert to produce or contribute to the learning problems of students with mild retardation. Consider, for example, the problem of generalization (also known as transfer). This refers to the ability of a learner to take something that has been learned in one context, such as paper-and-pencil arithmetic skills, and use it to deal with a similar but different task, such as knowing whether one has received the correct change after making a purchase at a store. Students with mild mental retardation may not spontaneously exhibit transfer because (1) their metacognitive deficits limit their tendency to look for signs of similarity between two tasks, (2) their relatively short attention span prevents them from noticing similarities, and (3) their limited memory capacity and skills lessen their ability to recall relevant knowledge.

These characteristics can be understood more completely if they are related to Jean Piaget's description of cognitive development. Middle and high school students with mild retardation may never move beyond the level of concrete operations. They may be able to deal with concrete situations but find it difficult to grasp abstractions,

*Students with mild retardation may frustrate easily, lack confidence and self-esteem*

*Students with mild retardation tend to oversimplify, have difficulty generalizing*

---

[1] Many of the points in this section are based on a discussion of characteristics of mentally retarded children in *Exceptional Children and Youth* (2006), by Nancy Hunt and Kathleen Marshall; *Exceptional Children: An Introduction to Special Education* (2003), by William L. Heward; *Educating Exceptional Children* (2006), by Samuel Kirk, James Gallagher, and Nicholas Anastasiow; and *Introduction to Special Education* (2004), by Deborah Deutsch Smith.

generalize from one situation to another, or state and test hypotheses. Younger children with retardation tend to classify things in terms of a single feature.

The following Suggestions for Teaching take into account the characteristics just described, as well as points made by Nancy Hunt and Kathleen Marshall (2006, pp. 188–195); William L. Heward (2003, pp. 220–226); Samuel Kirk, James Gallagher, and Nicholas Anastasiow (2006, pp. 186–198); and Deborah Deutsch Smith (2004, pp. 206–212).

# Suggestions for Teaching in Your Classroom

## Instructing Students with Mild Retardation

**1** **As much as possible, try to avoid placing students with mild retardation in situations that are likely to lead to their frustration. When, despite your efforts, such students indicate that they are close to their limit of frustration tolerance, encourage them to engage in relaxing change-of-pace pursuits or in physical activities.**

Because children with retardation are more likely to experience frustration than their more capable peers, try to minimize the frequency of such experiences in the classroom. Probably the most effective way to do this is to give students with mild retardation individual assignments so that they are not placed in situations in which their work is compared with that of others. No matter how hard you try, however, you will not be able to eliminate frustrating experiences, partly because you will have to schedule some all-class activities and partly because even individual assignments may be difficult for a child with mild retardation to handle. If you notice that such a student appears to be getting more and more bothered by an inability to complete a task, you might try to divert attention to a less demanding form of activity or allow the student to take a short break by sharpening pencils or going for a drink of water.

**JOURNAL ENTRY**
Helping Students with Mild Retardation Deal with Frustration

**2** **Do everything possible to encourage a sense of self-esteem.**

Children with mild retardation are prone to devalue themselves because they are aware that they are less capable than their classmates at doing many things. One way to combat this tendency toward self-devaluation is to make a point of showing that you have positive feelings about less capable students. You might, for example, say something like "I'm so glad you're here today. You make the classroom a nicer place to be in." If you indicate that you have positive feelings about an individual, that person is likely to acquire similar feelings about herself.

As you saw in Chapter 4, many teachers, usually inadvertently, tend to communicate low expectations to some of their students. To avoid committing the same error, you might do one or more of the following: make it clear that you will allow plenty of time for all students to come up with an answer to a question, repeat the question and give a clue before asking a different question, remind yourself to give frequent personal attention to students with mild retardation, or try to convey to these students the expectation that they *can* learn. Perhaps the best overall strategy to use in building self-esteem is to help children with retardation successfully complete learning tasks. Suggestions 3 through 5 offer ideas you might use.

**JOURNAL ENTRY**
Combating the Tendency to Communicate Low Expectations

**JOURNAL ENTRY**
Giving Students with Mild
Retardation Simple Assignments

Give students with mild
retardation short assignments
that can be completed quickly

**3** **Present learning tasks that contain a small number of elements, at least some of them familiar to students, and that can be completed in a short period of time.**

Because students with mild retardation tend to oversimplify concepts, try to provide learning tasks that contain only a few elements, at least some of which they have previously learned. For example, you might ask middle or secondary school social studies students with mild retardation to prepare a report on the work of a single police officer, as opposed to preparing an analysis of law enforcement agencies (which might be an appropriate topic for the most capable student in the class). Also, because students with retardation tend to have a short attention span, short assignments are preferable to long ones.

**4** **Try to arrange what is to be learned into a series of small steps, each of which leads to immediate feedback.**

Again because of their short attention span, students with mild retardation may become distracted or discouraged if they are asked to concentrate on demanding tasks that lead to a delayed payoff. Therefore, it is better to give a series of short activities that produce immediate feedback than to use any sort of contract approach or the equivalent, in which the student is expected to engage in self-directed effort leading to a remote goal.

Students who lack confidence, tend to think of one thing at a time, are unable to generalize, and have a short memory and attention span usually respond quite positively to programmed instruction and certain forms of computer-assisted instruction (described more completely in Chapter 7, "Behavioral Learning Theory"). Some computer programs offer a systematic step-by-step procedure that emphasizes only one specific idea per step or frame. They also offer immediate feedback. These characteristics closely fit the needs of children who are mildly retarded. You might look for computer programs in the subject or subjects you teach or develop your own materials, perhaps in the form of a workbook of some kind.

**5** **Teach simple techniques for improving memory, and consistently point out how use of these techniques leads to more accurate recall.**

In Chapter 10, "Social Cognitive Theory," we describe a set of memory aids called *mnemonic devices*. Used for thousands of years by scholars and teachers in different countries, most are fairly simple devices that help a learner organize information, encode it meaningfully, and generate cues that allow it to be retrieved from memory when needed. The simplest mnemonic devices are rhymes, first-letter mnemonics (also known as acronyms), and sentence mnemonics. For example, a first-letter mnemonic or acronym for the Great Lakes is *HOMES: H*uron, *O*ntario, *M*ichigan, *E*rie, *S*uperior.

**6** **Devise and use record-keeping techniques that make it clear that students have completed assignments successfully and are making progress.**

**JOURNAL ENTRY**
Giving Students with Mild
Retardation Proof of Progress

Students who are experiencing difficulties in learning are especially in need of tangible proof of progress. When, for instance, they correctly fill in blanks in a programmed workbook and discover that their answers are correct, they are encouraged to go on to the next question. You might use the same basic approach in more general ways by having students with mild retardation keep their own records showing their progress. (This technique might be used with all students in a class.) For example, you could make individual charts for primary grade students. As they successfully complete assignments, have them color in marked-off sections, stick on gold stars or the equivalent, or trace the movement of animal figures, rockets, or something else toward a destination.

# STUDENTS WITH LEARNING DISABILITIES

By far the greatest number of students who qualify for special education under IDEA are those classified as having **learning disabilities**. According to the U.S. Department of Education (2005) figures, the number of students identified as learning disabled increased from approximately 800,000 in 1976–1977 to 2,735,116 in 2002–2003. In the 1976–1977 school year, students with learning disabilities accounted for about 24 percent of the disabled population. By the 2002–2003 school year, that estimate had grown to nearly 50 percent. Especially because so many students are now classified as learning disabled, it is important to define and explore the characteristics of students with learning disabilities.

## Characteristics of Students with Learning Disabilities

According to IDEA, an individual who has a specific learning disability can be described as follows:

> Learning disabilities: disorders in basic processes that lead to learning problems not due to other causes

1. The individual has a *disorder in one or more of the basic psychological processes*. These processes refer to intrinsic prerequisite abilities such as memory, auditory perception, and visual perception.
2. The individual has *difficulty in learning*, specifically in the areas of speaking, listening, writing, reading (word recognition skills and comprehension), spelling, and mathematics (calculation and reasoning).
3. The problem is *not due primarily to other causes*, such as visual or hearing impairments, motor disabilities, mental retardation, emotional disturbance, or economic, environmental, or cultural disadvantage.

In addition to problems with cognitive processing and learning, many students with a learning disability (as well as students with mild mental retardation and students with emotional disturbance) have more poorly developed social skills than their nondisabled peers. Such students are more likely to ignore the teacher's directions, cheat, use profane language, disturb other students, disrupt group activities, and start fights. Consequently, they are often rejected by the rest of the class, which contributes to lowered self-esteem and poor academic performance (Gresham & MacMillan, 1997).

Some people dismiss the notion of a learning disability as a fiction because, they say, everyone at one time or another has misread numbers, letters, and words; confused pronunciations of words and letters; and suffered embarrassing lapses of attention and memory. But students with learning disabilities really are different from others—mostly in degree rather than in kind. Although the individual without a disability may occasionally exhibit lapses in basic information processing, the individual with a learning disability does so consistently and with little hope of self-correction. The important point to keep in mind is that you need to know what a student with a learning disability (as well as a low-achieving student without a learning disability) can and cannot do so that you can effectively remediate those weaknesses (Spear-Swerling & Sternberg, 1998).

## Identifying Students with Learning Disabilities

The major criterion used by most school districts to identify children with learning disabilities is at least an average score on a standardized test of intelligence and a significantly below average score (one standard deviation or more) on a standardized achievement test. In other words, districts typically look for a discrepancy between achievement and IQ scores.

Because about 80 percent of children with learning disabilities have difficulty with reading (Meyer, 2000), a considerable amount of research has been done to determine whether a discrepancy between IQ and reading comprehension scores is a valid indicator of a learning disability. One approach to this problem has been

*Students with a learning disability learn more slowly than other students because of difficulties in perception, attention, and memory.*

to compare children who exhibit the discrepancy we just described with children whose IQ and reading scores are both below average. Researchers often refer to students in the first group as IQ-discrepant and students in the second group as IQ-consistent. Two analyses of almost four dozen studies that have examined this issue (Meyer, 2000; Steubing et al., 2002) conclude that IQ-consistent students are indistinguishable from IQ-discrepant students in terms of reading skills (such as phonological awareness and word naming) and behavior (such as social skills and fine motor skills).

This research casts doubt on the usefulness of the discrepancy criterion. Learning disabilities certainly exist, but educators may need to develop a more sophisticated means of identifying them.

## Problems with Basic Psychological Processes

The fundamental problem that underlies a learning disability is, as the law states, "a disorder in one or more basic psychological processes." Although this phrase is somewhat vague, it generally refers to problems with how students receive information, process it, and express what they have learned. Specifically, many students with learning disabilities have deficits in perception, attention, memory encoding and storage, and metacognition.

Some students with learning disabilities have great difficulty perceiving the difference between certain sounds (*f* and *v*, *m* and *n*, for example) or letters (*m* and *n*, or *b*, *p*, and *d*, for example). As a result, words that begin with one letter (such as *v*ase) are sometimes perceived and pronounced as if they begin with another letter (as in *f*ase). As you can no doubt appreciate from this simple example, this type of deficit makes learning to read and reading with comprehension long and frustrating for some students.

Many students with learning disabilities also have difficulty with attention and impulse control: focusing on a task, noticing important cues and ideas, and staying with the task until it is completed. The source of the distraction may be objects and activities in the classroom, or it may be unrelated thoughts. In either case, the student misses much of what the teacher says or what is on a page of text or misinterprets directions.

Because so many students with learning disabilities have problems with perception and attention, they also have problems with accurate recall of information. Accurate recall is heavily dependent on what is stored in memory in the first place and

Students with learning disabilities have problems with perception, attention, memory, metacognition

where information is stored in memory (Hunt & Marshall, 2006), so students who encode partial, incorrect, or unimportant information have memory problems.

Like students with mild retardation, many students with learning disabilities have a deficit in metacognitive skills (Hunt & Marshall, 2006). As a result, their learning activities are chaotic, like those of young children. For example, they may begin a task before they have thought through all of the steps.

Students with learning disabilities tend to be characterized as passive and disorganized: passive in the sense that they take few active steps to attend to relevant information, store it effectively in memory, and retrieve it when needed; and disorganized in the sense that their learning activities are often unplanned and subject to whatever happens to capture their attention at the moment.

Given these problems with basic processes, researchers have studied ways to help students structure the way they learn. For example, one approach to improving the reading skills of students with learning disabilities that shows some promise is teaching students how to use reading comprehension strategies (Gersten, Fuchs, Williams, & Baker, 2001). One such program that was tested on middle school students with reading disabilities (Bryant et al., 2000) contained the following components:

1. *Word identification:* Students used a first-letter mnemonic to help them recall the seven steps involved in decoding multisyllabic words.
2. *Partner reading:* To improve reading fluency (reading whole words in text accurately and at an appropriate speed), pairs of students modeled fluent reading for one another and helped each other decode unfamiliar words.
3. *Collaborative strategic reading:* This technique is aimed at improving reading comprehension and combines two proven instructional techniques, reciprocal teaching and cooperative learning (we discuss both techniques in detail in later chapters). Students first learn how to use the four comprehension-aiding techniques that are part of reciprocal teaching: (a) previewing a reading passage to help students make predictions about what they will read and already know about the topic, (b) monitoring reading to identify and fix comprehension failures, (c) identifying main ideas, and (d) asking questions and reviewing. Students then apply the techniques by working either in pairs or small cooperative groups.

Compared with pretest scores, students achieved higher posttest scores on word identification, reading fluency, and reading comprehension tests. The differences for word identification and reading fluency were statistically significant (meaning they were not likely due to chance).

## Attention–Deficit/Hyperactivity Disorder

Many children who have a learning disability are also diagnosed as having **attention-deficit/hyperactivity disorder (ADHD).** Estimates of the extent to which these two conditions co-occur range from 25 to 40 percent (Lerner, 2003). Approximately 3.3 percent of six- to eleven-year-old children have ADHD alone, with boys outnumbering girls by at least three to one (Bowman, 2002). In addition, some studies have found that as many as 30 percent of children with ADHD exhibit aggressive behaviors (such as fighting, stealing, lying, and vandalism) that are consistent with the psychiatric diagnosis of conduct disorder (Connor, 2002). The co-occurrence of ADHD and conduct disorder (called *comorbidity*) is seen more frequently among children from urban homes than middle-SES suburban homes and is associated with significant social, behavioral, and academic problems (Bloomquist & Schnell, 2002).

Symptoms of ADHD include inattention, hyperactivity, and impulsivity

The American Psychiatric Association recognizes three types of children with ADHD: (1) children who are predominantly inattentive, (2) children who are predominantly hyperactive and impulsive, and (3) children who exhibit a combination of all three behaviors. For a student to be judged as having ADHD, the symptoms have to appear before the age of seven; they have to be displayed in several settings, such as at home, at school, and at play; and they have to persist over time (American

Psychiatric Association, 2000). Although ADHD is not mentioned in IDEA as a separate disability category, services for children with ADHD can be funded under the "specific learning disabilities" category, the "emotionally disturbed" category, or the "other health impaired" category of IDEA (Lerner, 2003).

In general, the treatments for ADHD fall into one of the following three categories (Lerner, 2003; Purdie, Hattie, & Carroll, 2002):

1. *Prescribed stimulant medication:* The most popular class of drugs prescribed for children with ADHD is psychostimulants. The psychostimulants that are prescribed most often are Ritalin, Dexedrine, Cylert, and Adderall. The effect of these medications is highly specific. Some children do better on one drug, others on another, and still others do not respond to any of them.

2. *School-based psychological/educational programs:* These programs typically involve either behavior management, cognitive behavioral therapy, or classroom environment restructuring. Behavior management programs (which we describe in more detail in Chapter 7, "Behavioral Learning Theory") involve the systematic use of reinforcement and punishment to increase the frequency of desired behaviors and decrease the frequency of undesired behaviors. Cognitive behavior therapy programs involve teaching students to remind themselves to use effective learning skills, monitor their progress, and reinforce themselves. Classroom environment restructuring programs use such techniques as reducing classroom noise, assigning students permanent seats, seating students with ADHD at the front of the class, and providing frequent breaks between tasks.

3. *Multimodal programs:* Multimodal programs involve combinations of one or more of the preceding treatments, typically stimulant medications and cognitive behavioral programs.

An analysis of seventy-four research studies (Purdie et al., 2002) found, not surprisingly, that an overall best treatment for ADHD does not exist. Rather, different treatments had stronger effects depending on the outcome that was being examined. For example, stimulant medications were more effective than other treatments in minimizing impulsivity, hyperactivity, and attentional deficits; multimodal programs were most effective in reducing classmates' dislike and fostering more effective prosocial skills and positive peer interactions; and school-based programs were most effective in aiding the growth of cognitive skills.

The following Suggestions for Teaching will give you some ideas about how to help students with learning disabilities and ADHD improve their learning skills and feel better about themselves.

# Suggestions for Teaching in Your Classroom

## Instructing Students with Learning Disabilities and ADHD

**JOURNAL ENTRY**
Helping Students with Learning Disabilities Improve Basic Learning Processes

**1** **Structure learning tasks to help students with learning disabilities and ADHD compensate for weaknesses in psychological processes.**

Because of their weaknesses in basic psychological processes, students with learning disabilities and ADHD are often distractible, impulsive, forgetful, disorganized, poor at comprehension, and unaware of the factors that affect learning. Research findings indicate that the most effective instructional approach in such cases is one that combines direct instruction with strategy instruction (both methods are described in Chapter 13, "Approaches to Instruction"). This combined approach has produced substantial improvements in reading comprehension, vocabulary, word recognition, memory, writing, cognitive processing, and self-concept (Swanson & Hoskyn, 1998).

The following examples are consistent with an instructional approach that is based on both direct instruction and strategy instruction.

### EXAMPLES

- For students who have difficulty distinguishing between similar-looking or -sounding stimuli (such as letters, words, or phrases), point out and highlight their distinguishing characteristics. For example, highlight the circular part of the letters *b, p,* and *d* and place a directional arrow at the end of the straight segment to emphasize that they have the same shape but differ in their spatial orientation. Or highlight the letters *t* and *r* in the words *though, thought,* and *through* to emphasize that they differ from each other by the absence or presence of one letter.

- For students who are easily distracted, instruct them to place only the materials being used on top of the desk or within sight.

- For students who seem unable to attend to important stimuli such as significant sections of a text page, show them how to underline or outline in an effort to distinguish between important and unimportant material. Or suggest that they use a ruler or pointing device under each line as they read so that they can evaluate one sentence at a time. To help them attend to important parts of directions, highlight or write keywords and phrases in all capitals. For especially important tasks, you might want to ask students to paraphrase or repeat directions verbatim.

- For students who have a short attention span, give brief assignments, and divide complex material into smaller segments. After each short lesson segment, provide both immediate positive feedback and tangible evidence of progress. (Many sets of published materials prepared for use with students with learning disabilities are designed in this way.)

- To improve students' memory for and comprehension of information, teach memorization skills and how to relate new information to existing knowledge schemes to improve long-term storage and retrieval. Also, make frequent use of simple, concrete analogies and examples to explain and illustrate complex, abstract ideas. (We will describe several techniques for enhancing memory and comprehension in Chapter 10, "Social Cognitive Theory.")

- To improve organization, suggest that students use a notebook to keep a record of homework assignments, a checklist of materials needed for class, and a list of books and materials they need to take home for studying and homework.

- To improve general awareness of the learning process, emphasize the importance of thinking about the factors that could affect one's performance on a particular task, of forming a plan before actually starting to work, and of monitoring the effectiveness of learning activities.

- Consider the variety of learning environments available through multimedia software programs. Some students with learning disabilities may respond better to a combination of visual and auditory information, whereas others may learn best in a hands-on setting. Multimedia programs provide options to address these different styles and also allow the student to control the direction and pace of learning. Examples of such programs can be found on the Special Needs page of the website of the Educational Software Directory (**www.educational-software-directory.net**).

> Help students with learning disabilities to reduce distractions, attend to important information

*HM TeacherPrepSPACE*

For additional journal suggestions, see the Reflective Journal Questions.

**2** **Capitalize on the resources in your classroom to help students with learning disabilities and ADHD improve academically, socially, and emotionally.**

Although you and the resource teacher will be the main sources of instruction and support for mainstreamed students, recognize that other sources of classroom support are almost always available. The other students in your class, for example, can supplement your instructional efforts. As we pointed out in Chapter 4, peer tutoring typically produces gains in achievement and improvements in interpersonal relationships and attitudes toward subject matter. These effects have been documented for students with learning disabilities as well as for low-achieving students without learning disabilities (Fuchs, Fuchs, Mathes, & Simmons, 1997). And do not overlook the benefits of having students with learning disabilities play the role of tutor. Giving students with disabilities the opportunity to tutor either a low-achieving classmate in a subject that is not affected by the student's disability or a younger student in a lower grade can produce a noticeable increase in self-esteem.

Another way to make use of the other students in your class is through cooperative learning. This technique was described in Chapter 4 and is explored in more detail in Chapter 13, "Approaches to Instruction." Like peer tutoring, which it incorporates, it also produces gains in achievement, interpersonal relationships, and self-esteem.

Finally, make use of the various ways in which information can be presented to students and in which students can respond. In addition to text material and lecturing, you can use films, computer-based presentations, picture charts, diagrams, and demonstrations. In addition to having students demonstrate what they have learned through paper-and-pencil tests and other written products, you can have them make oral presentations, produce pictorial products, create an actual product, or give a performance. Hands-on activities are particularly useful for students with ADHD.

# STUDENTS WITH EMOTIONAL DISTURBANCE

## Estimates of Emotional Disturbance

In the 2005 report to Congress on the implementation of IDEA, the Department of Education noted that 453,827 students between the ages of six and seventeen were classified as emotionally disturbed in the 2002–2003 school year. This figure accounted for 8 percent of all schoolchildren classified as disabled and slightly less than 1 percent of the general school-age population. Not everyone agrees that these figures accurately reflect the scope of the problem. Other scholars believe that 3 to 5 percent of all school-age children qualify for special education services under IDEA's emotional disturbance criteria (Heward, 2003).

## Definitions of Emotional Disturbance

Two reasons that estimates of **emotional disturbance** vary are the lack of clear descriptions of such forms of behavior and different interpretations of the descriptions that do exist. Children with *emotional disturbance* are defined in IDEA in this way:

(I)  The term means a condition exhibiting one or more of the following characteristics over a long period of time and to a marked degree that adversely affects a child's educational performance:

> (A)  An inability to learn that cannot be explained by intellectual, sensory, or health factors;
>
> (B)  An inability to build or maintain satisfactory interpersonal relationships with peers and teachers;
>
> (C)  Inappropriate types of behavior or feelings under normal circumstances;
>
> (D)  A general pervasive mood of unhappiness or depression; or
>
> (E)  A tendency to develop physical symptoms or fears associated with personal or school problems.

(II)  The term includes schizophrenia. The term does not apply to children who are socially maladjusted, unless it is determined that they have a serious emotional disturbance. (Office of the Federal Register, 1994, pp. 13–14)

> Emotional disturbance: poor relationships, inappropriate behavior, depression, fears

Several special education scholars (Kirk et al., 2006, pp. 253–255; Heward, 2003, p. 284; Smith, 2004, pp. 260–261) point out the difficulties caused by vague terminology in distinguishing between students who have emotional disturbance and students who do not. The phrase *a long period of time*, for example, is not defined in the law (although many special education experts use six months as a rough rule of thumb). Indicators such as *satisfactory interpersonal relationships, a general pervasive mood*, and *inappropriate types of behavior or feelings under normal circumstances* are difficult to measure objectively and can often be observed in non-disturbed individuals. Because long-term observation of behavior is often critical in making a correct diagnosis of emotional disturbance, you can aid the multidisciplinary assessment team in this task by keeping a behavioral log of a child you suspect may have this disorder.

That many educators and psychologists use such terms as *emotionally disturbed, socially maladjusted*, and *behavior disordered* synonymously makes matters even more confusing. The term **behavior disorder** has many adherents and has been adopted by several states for two basic reasons. One reason is that it calls attention to the actual behavior that is disordered and needs to be changed. The second reason is that behaviors can be directly and objectively assessed. Although there are subtle differences between the terms *emotionally disturbed* and *behavior disorder*, they are essentially interchangeable, and you can probably assume that those who use them are referring to children who share similar characteristics. Because of the nature of bureaucracies, however, it may be necessary for anyone hoping to obtain special assistance for a child with what many contemporary psychologists would call a behavior disorder to refer to that child as *emotionally disturbed*, as that is the label used in IDEA.

> Term *behavior disorder* focuses on behavior that needs to be changed, objective assessment

## Characteristics of Students with an Emotional Disturbance

The most frequently used classification system of emotional disturbance (or behavior disorder) involves two basic patterns: externalizing and internalizing (Heward, 2003; Wicks-Nelson & Israel, 2003).

> Students with behavior disorders tend to be either aggressive or withdrawn

- *Externalizing* students are often aggressive, uncooperative, restless, and negativistic. They tend to lie and steal, defy teachers, and be hostile to authority figures. Sometimes they are cruel and malicious.
- *Internalizing* students, by contrast, are typically shy, timid, anxious, and fearful. They are often depressed and lack self-confidence.

*Students who have an emotional disturbance tend to be either aggressive or withdrawn. Because aggressive students disrupt classroom routines, teachers need to focus on classroom design features and employ behavior management techniques to reduce the probability of such behaviors.*

Teachers tend to be more aware of students who display aggressive disorders because their behavior often stimulates or forces reactions. The withdrawn student, however, may be more likely to develop serious emotional problems such as depression and may even be at risk of suicide during the adolescent years. The following Suggestions for Teaching will help you teach both the withdrawn student and the aggressive student.

# Suggestions for Teaching in Your Classroom

## Instructing Students with Emotional Disturbance

### 1 Design the classroom environment and formulate lesson plans to encourage social interaction and cooperation.[2]

Foster interpersonal contact among withdrawn students

Students whose emotional disturbance manifests itself as social withdrawal may stay away from others on purpose (perhaps because they find social contacts threatening), or they may find that others stay away from them (perhaps because they have poorly developed social skills). Regardless of the cause, the classroom environment and your instructional activities can be designed to foster appropriate interpersonal contact.

**EXAMPLES**

**JOURNAL ENTRY**
Activities and Materials That Encourage Cooperation

- Preschool and elementary school teachers can use toys and materials, as well as organized games and sports, that encourage cooperative play and have a reduced focus on individual performance. Activities might include dress-up games or puppet plays; games might include soccer, variations of It (such as tag), and kickball or softball modified such that everyone on the team gets a turn to kick or bat before the team plays in the field.

- Elementary and middle school teachers can use one or more of several team-oriented learning activities. *Cooperative Learning* (1995) by Robert Slavin provides details on using such activities as student teams–achievement divisions, jigsaw, and team-accelerated instruction.

### 2 Prompt and reinforce appropriate social interactions.

Prompting and positive reinforcement are basic learning principles that will be discussed in Chapter 7, "Behavioral Learning Theory." Essentially, a prompt is a stimulus that draws out a desired response, and positive reinforcement involves giving the student a positive reinforcer (something the student wants) immediately after a desired behavior. The aim is to get the student to behave that way again. Typical reinforcers are verbal praise, stickers, and small prizes.

**EXAMPLE**

- You can set up a cooperative task or activity: "Marc, I would like you to help Carol and Raquel paint the scenery for next week's play. You can paint the trees and flowers, Carol will paint the grass, and Raquel will do the people." After several minutes, say something like, "That's good work. I am really pleased at how well the three of you are working together." Similar comments can be made at intervals as the interaction continues.

---

[2] Most of these suggestions are derived from points made in Chapters 7, 8, and 9 of *Strategies for Addressing Behavior Problems in the Classroom* (5th ed., 2006), by Mary Margaret Kerr and C. Michael Nelson.

### 3 Train other students to initiate social interaction.

In all likelihood, you will have too many classroom responsibilities to spend a great deal of time working directly with a withdrawn child. It may be possible, however, using the steps that follow, to train other students to initiate contact with withdrawn students.

**JOURNAL ENTRY**
Getting Students to Initiate Interaction with a Withdrawn Child

**EXAMPLE**

- First, choose a student as a helper who interacts freely and well, can follow your instructions, and can concentrate on the training task for at least ten minutes. Second, explain that the goal is to get the withdrawn child to work or play with the helping student but that the helper should expect rejection, particularly at first. Role-play the actions of a withdrawn child so that the helper understands what you mean by rejection. Emphasize the importance of making periodic attempts at interaction. Third, instruct the helper to suggest games or activities that appeal to the withdrawn student. Fourth, reinforce the helper's attempts to interact with the withdrawn child.

### 4 Design the classroom environment to reduce the probability of disruptive behavior.

Use techniques to forestall aggressive or antisocial behavior

The best way to deal with aggressive or antisocial behavior is to nip it in the bud. This strategy has at least three related benefits. One benefit of fewer disruptions is that you can better accomplish what you had planned for the day. A second benefit is that you are likely to be in a more positive frame of mind than if you spend half the day acting as a referee. A third benefit is that because of fewer disruptions and a more positive attitude, you may be less inclined to resort to permissible or even impermissible forms of physical punishment (which often produces undesirable side effects).

**EXAMPLES**

- With student input, formulate rules for classroom behavior and penalties for infractions of rules. Remind all students of the penalties, particularly when a disruptive incident seems about to occur, and consistently apply the penalties when the rules are broken.

- Place valued objects and materials out of reach when they are not needed or in use.

- Minimize the aggressive student's frustration with learning by using some of the same techniques you would use for a child with mild retardation: break tasks down into small, easy-to-manage pieces; provide clear directions; and reinforce correct responses.

### 5 Reinforce appropriate behavior, and, if necessary, punish inappropriate behavior.

In suggestion 2, we described the use of positive reinforcement to encourage desired behavior. Reinforcement has the dual effect of teaching the aggressive student which behavior is appropriate and reducing the frequency of inappropriate behavior as it is replaced by desired behavior. Disruptive behavior will still occur, however. Three effective techniques for suppressing it while reinforcing desired behaviors are contingency contracts, token economies and fines, and time-out. Each of these techniques will be described in Chapter 7.

### 6 Use group contingency-management techniques.

You may want to reward the entire class when the aggressive student behaves appropriately for a certain period of time. Such rewards, which may be free time, special classroom events, or certain privileges, should make the aggressive student the hero and foster better peer relationships.

# STUDENTS WHO ARE GIFTED AND TALENTED

Students who learn at a significantly faster rate than their peers or who possess superior talent in one or more areas also need to be taught in special ways if they are to make the most of their abilities. Unlike students with mental retardation, learning disabilities, and emotional disturbance, however, students with superior capabilities are not covered by IDEA. Instead, the federal government provides technical assistance to states and local school districts for establishing programs for superior students. Although most states have such programs, some experts in special education (Colangelo & Davis, 2003b; Gallagher, 2003) feel that school systems are not given the resources they need to meet the needs of all gifted and talented students adequately. The Suggestions for Teaching that follow a bit later reflect this situation. All of the suggestions are inexpensive to implement and require few additional personnel.

A definition of the term **gifted and talented** was part of a bill passed by Congress in 1988:

> The term *gifted and talented children and youth* means children and youth who give evidence of high performance capability in areas such as intellectual, creative, artistic, or leadership capacity, or in specific academic fields, and who require services or activities not ordinarily provided by the school in order to fully develop such capabilities.

Gifted and talented students show high performance in one or more areas

## Identification of Gifted and Talented Students

Eligibility for gifted and talented programs has traditionally been based on standardized test scores, particularly IQ tests. It was not uncommon in years past for students to have to achieve an IQ score of at least 130 to be admitted to such programs. But criticisms about the narrow range of skills covered by such tests (and their heavy reliance on multiple-choice items) have led most states to de-emphasize or eliminate the use of traditional intelligence tests and a numerical cutoff score for identification (Reid, Romanoff, & Algozzine, 2000; Renzulli, 2002).

Evidence that alternative assessments can do a better job of identifying gifted and talented children does exist. In one study (Reid et al., 2000), 434 second-grade students who were recommended for a gifted education program were tested with both traditional and nontraditional measures. The traditional assessment was a nonverbal test of analogical reasoning. The nontraditional assessment, which combined aspects of both Gardner's and Sternberg's theories of intelligence, was a set of linguistic, logical-mathematical, and spatial problem-solving tasks that called for analytical, synthetic, and practical thinking. For example, students were given a bag of small items, each of which had to be used as the basis of a five-minute story. For another task, students were given a set of colored cardboard pieces and told to make a variety of objects, such as an animal, a building, something that moves, and whatever they wanted. On the basis of analogical reasoning scores, about 17 percent of the sample would have been recommended for placement in the gifted program. That percentage rose to 40 percent when scores from the problem-solving assessment were used. Another interesting statistic was that almost 70 percent of the students recommended on the basis of their problem-solving performances would not have been recommended on the basis of their analogical reasoning scores.

Joseph Renzulli (2002), a leading researcher of giftedness and gifted education, believes that the concept of giftedness should be expanded beyond the dimensions examined in the study we just described to include students who can channel their assets into constructive social actions that benefit others. As an example, he describes Melanie, a fifth-grade girl, who befriended Tony, a visually impaired first-grade boy who was ignored by most other students and teased by a few others. Melanie persuaded some of the school's most popular students to sit with Tony in the lunchroom, and she recruited other students to create and illustrate large-print books on topics of interest to Tony. Over the course of several months, Tony was accepted by many of the school's students, and his attitude toward school markedly improved. According to Howard Gardner's multiple intelligences theory, Melanie's gift likely stems from an above-average interpersonal (and possibly intrapersonal) intelligence. In the adult world, two examples of this type of person are Mother Teresa and Martin Luther King Jr.—and, as Renzulli points out, no one really cares what their test scores or grade-point averages were.

Broadening the definition and instruments used to assess giftedness will serve diversity goals as well. Students from many minority cultures are underrepresented in programs for the gifted and talented. In fact, there is a general ignorance of characteristics that are more highly valued by a minority culture than by the majority culture. Some American Indian tribes, for example, de-emphasize the concept of giftedness because it runs counter to their belief that the welfare and cohesion of the group are more important than celebrating and nurturing the talents of any individual. The members of other tribes may place as much value on a child's knowledge of tribal traditions, storytelling ability, and artistic ability as they do on problem-solving ability and scientific reasoning (Callahan & McIntire, 1994). A child's giftedness may therefore be evident only when examined from the perspective of a particular culture. This may explain why only 2 percent of American Indians can be found in classes for the gifted and talented (Winner, 1997).

> Minorities underrepresented in gifted classes because of overreliance on test scores

## Characteristics of Gifted and Talented Students

In one sense, gifted and talented students are like any other group of students. Some are healthy and well coordinated, whereas others are not. Some are extremely popular and well liked, but others are not. Some are well adjusted; others are not (Kirk et al., 2006). Some formulate strong identities (Marcia's identity achievement status) and are successful later in life, whereas others are not (Zuo & Cramond, 2001). But as a group, gifted and talented students are often noticeably different (Dai, Moon, & Feldhusen, 1998; Piechowski, 1997; Winner, 1997). Here are some of the main characteristics that many gifted and talented students share:

- They excel on tasks that involve language, abstract logical thinking, and mathematics.
- They are faster at encoding information and retrieving it from memory.
- They are highly aware of how they learn and the various conditions that affect their learning. As a result, they excel at transferring previously learned information and skills to new problems and settings.
- They exhibit such high levels of motivation and task persistence that the phrase "rage to master" is sometimes used to describe their behavior. Their motivation to learn is partly due to high levels of self-efficacy and appropriate attributions. That is, they believe they have the capability to master those tasks and subject matters they choose to tackle and that their success is the result of both high ability and hard work.
- They tend to be more solitary and introverted than average children.
- They tend to have very intense emotional lives. They react with intense feelings, such as joy, regret, or sorrow, to a story, a piece of music, or a social encounter. They also tend to be emotionally sensitive and sometimes surpass adults in their ability to notice and identify with the feelings of others.

> Gifted and talented students differ from their nongifted peers intellectually and emotionally

For the most part, gifted and talented students see themselves as they were just described. In comparison with intellectually average students, they have a moderately stronger academic self-concept but score at about the same level on measures of physical and social self-concepts (Hoge & Renzulli, 1993).

Researchers who favor broadening the traditional definition of giftedness add other characteristics to the mix. Joseph Renzulli (2002), for example, believes that people like Melanie (the student who befriended an unpopular boy) possess characteristics such as optimism, courage, passion, energy, sensitivity to others, and a sense of vision; characteristics that are often found in people who achieve positions of leadership (see also Sternberg, 2005). In a longitudinal study, Wai, Lubinski, and Benbow (2005) found that students who were identified at age thirteen as intellectually precocious tended to be recognized for their creativity and achievements twenty years later. Furthermore, when the preferences of the youth were taken into account, the nature and quality of accomplishments were well predicted.

## Instructional Options

Gifted and talented students constantly challenge a teacher's skill, ingenuity, and classroom resources. While trying to instruct the class as a whole, the teacher is faced with the need to provide more and more interesting and challenging materials and ideas to gifted students. In this section, we will examine three possible ways to engage these students.

**Accelerated Instruction**   Accelerated instruction is often suggested as one way to meet the academic needs of gifted and talented students. For many people, the phrase *accelerated instruction* means allowing the student to skip one or more grades, which, although not as common as in years past, does occasionally occur. But there are at least three other ways of accomplishing the same goal: (1) the curriculum can be compressed, allowing gifted and talented students to complete the work for more than one grade during the regular school year; (2) the school year can be extended by the use of summer sessions; and (3) students can take college courses while still in high school.

Whatever the form of accelerated instruction, this is always a hotly debated topic, with pros and cons on each side. Two often quoted advantages for giving gifted students the opportunity to work on complex tasks are that it keeps them from becoming bored

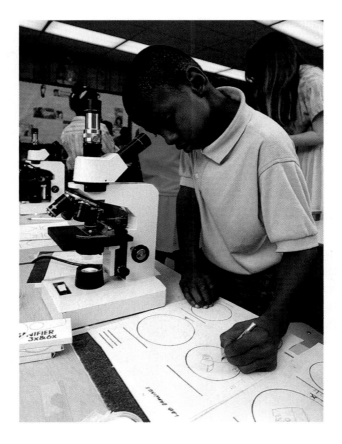

*Because gifted and talented students understand and integrate abstract ideas more quickly than do their nongifted classmates, they are capable of successfully completing tasks that older students routinely carry out.*

with school and that it produces more positive attitudes toward learning. On the negative side, two frequent arguments are that a gifted student may have trouble with the social and emotional demands of acceleration and that acceleration produces an undesirable sense of elitism among gifted students. Research evidence supports the presumed academic benefits of acceleration and fails to confirm the predicted negative social and emotional outcomes (Gallagher, 2003; Kulik, 2003b). As with all other informed educational decisions, the unique needs of the individual and the situation must be considered before the best course of action can be determined.

**Gifted and Talented Classes and Schools**   Some public school districts offer separate classes for gifted and talented students as either an alternative to accelerated instruction or as something that follows accelerated instruction. In addition, so-called magnet schools are composed of students whose average level of ability is higher than that found in a typical elementary, middle, or high school. Finally, many states sponsor high-ability high schools, particularly in mathematics and science.

Recent findings suggest that such placements do not produce uniformly positive results and should be made only after the characteristics of the student and the program have been carefully considered. In terms of achievement, the typical gifted student can expect to score moderately higher (at about the 63rd percentile) on tests than comparable students who remain in heterogeneous classes (Kulik & Kulik, 1991). But the effects of separate class or school placement on measures of academic self-concept have been inconsistent; some researchers find them to be higher than those of students who remain in heterogeneous classes, whereas other researchers have found either no differences or declines (Hoge & Renzulli, 1993; Kulik & Kulik, 1991; Marsh & Craven, 2002).

> Separate classes for gifted and talented students aid achievement but may lower academic self-concept of some students

**Enrichment and Differentiated Instruction**   Because of the potential negative effects of grade skipping, the limited availability of special classes and schools, and the fact that such classes and schools are not good options for some gifted and talented students, teachers may find themselves with one or two gifted and talented students in a regular classroom. A solution for meeting the special needs of these students (as well as those with disabilities) is a practice often referred to as *differentiated instruction*, a technique we have mentioned earlier. Basically, this means using different learning materials, instructional methods, assignments, and tests to accommodate differences in students' abilities, learning styles, prior knowledge, and cultural background (Benjamin, 2005; Gregory, 2003; Gregory & Kuzmich, 2005).

One scheme for delivering differentiated instruction to gifted and talented learners has been developed by Joseph Renzulli and Sally Reis (Reis & Renzulli, 1985; Renzulli, Gentry, & Reis, 2003; Renzulli & Reis, 1985). Based on their view that giftedness is a combination of above-average cognitive ability, creativity, and task commitment, Renzulli and Reis describe three levels of curriculum enrichment for gifted and talented learners:

*Type I enrichment:* Exploratory activities that are designed to expose students to topics, events, books, people, and places not ordinarily covered in the regular curriculum. The basic purpose of these activities is to stimulate new interests. Among the many suggestions Renzulli and Reis offer are having students view and write reports on films and videos (such as *The Eagle Has Landed: The Flight of Apollo 11*) and having local residents make presentations on their occupations or hobbies.

*Type II enrichment:* Instructional methods and materials aimed at the development of such thinking and feeling processes as thinking creatively, classifying and analyzing data, solving problems, appreciating, and valuing.

## pause & reflect

Relatively little money is spent on programs for the gifted and talented compared with the amounts made available for the disabled. Defenders of this arrangement sometimes argue that because gifted students have a built-in advantage, we should invest most of our resources in services for those with disabilities. Do you agree or disagree? Why?

*Type III enrichment:* Activities in which students investigate and collect data about a real topic or problem. For example, a student may decide to document the history of her school, focusing on such issues as changes in size, instructional materials and methods, and curriculum.

Numerous sites on the Internet are devoted to long-distance education, enrichment, and tutoring. You might explore the Global Network Academy (**www.gnacademy.org**), which offers online courses in a wide range of areas. The website of the Talent Identification Program at Duke University contains information about online teaching and learning opportunities and various telementoring programs (**www.tip.duke.edu**). The following Suggestions for Teaching provide further ideas for working with gifted and talented students.

## VIDEO CASE ◄◄ ▶ ►►

**Academic Diversity:
Differentiated Instruction**

*Watch the video, study the artifacts in the case, and reflect upon the following questions:*

**1.** What did the teacher in this Video Case do to make the lesson work for all of her students? Describe some of the strategies and tools that she used.

**2.** Based on reading the chapter and watching the Video Case, what do you think would be most challenging for a classroom teacher about "doing" differentiated instruction?

# Suggestions for Teaching in Your Classroom

## Instructing Gifted and Talented Students

**1** **Consult with gifted and talented students regarding individual study projects, perhaps involving a learning contract.**

**JOURNAL ENTRY**
Individual Study for Students
Who Are Gifted and Talented

One of the most effective ways to deal with gifted students is to assign individual study projects. These may involve a contract approach, in which you consult with students on an individual basis and agree on a personal assignment that is to be completed by a certain date.

Such assignments should probably be related to some part of the curriculum. If you are studying Mexico, for example, a gifted student could devote free time to a special report on some aspect of Mexican life that intrigues him. In making these assignments, you should remember that even very bright students may not be able to absorb, organize, and apply abstract concepts until they become formal thinkers. Thus, until early middle school years, it may be preferable to keep these assignments brief rather than comprehensive.

To provide another variation of the individual study project, you could ask the gifted student to act as a research specialist and report on questions that puzzle the class. Still another individual study project is the creation of an open-ended, personal yearbook. Any time a gifted student finishes the assigned work, she might be allowed to write stories or do drawings for such a journal.

When possible, unobtrusive projects are preferable. Perhaps you can recall a teacher who rewarded the fast workers by letting them work on a mural (or the equivalent) covering the side board. If you were an average student, you can probably attest that the sight of the class "brains" having the time of their lives was not conducive to diligent effort on the part of the have-nots sweating away at their workbooks. Reward assignments should probably be restricted to individual work on unostentatious projects.

### 2 Encourage supplementary reading and writing.

**JOURNAL ENTRY**
Providing Gifted and Talented Students with Opportunities for Additional Reading and Writing

Encourage students to spend extra time reading and writing. A logical method of combining both skills is the preparation of book reports. It is perhaps less threatening to call them book *reviews* and emphasize that you are interested in personal reaction, not a précis or an abstract. Some specialists in the education of the gifted have suggested that such students be urged to read biographies and autobiographies. The line of reasoning here is that potential leaders might be inspired to emulate the exploits of a famous person. Even if such inspiration does not result, you could recommend life stories simply because they are usually interesting.

Other possibilities for writing are e-mail exchanges with other students, siblings at college, or friends in different areas. Or a student may write a review of a website that she has discovered. If the appropriate software and support are available, students could be encouraged to create home pages or websites for themselves, either on a topic mutually selected with the teacher or on their personal interests (the latter would be much like a yearbook entry).

### 3 Have gifted students act as tutors.

Depending on the grade, subject, and personalities of those involved, gifted students might be asked to act occasionally as tutors, lab assistants, or the equivalent. Some bright students will welcome such opportunities and are capable of providing instruction in such a way that their peers do not feel self-conscious or humiliated. Others may resent being asked to spend school time helping classmates or may lack skills in interpersonal relationships. If you do decide to ask a gifted student to function as a tutor, it would be wise to proceed tentatively and cautiously.

## USING TECHNOLOGY TO ASSIST EXCEPTIONAL STUDENTS

Federal legislation has led to the development of various assistive technologies

There is perhaps no other area in education today in which technology is making as significant an impact as in the field of special education, and this is largely due to the use of assistive technology. Mandated by IDEA for any need related to the learning or development of a child with a disability, **assistive technology** is defined in IDEA as "any item, piece of equipment, or product system, whether acquired commercially off the shelf, modified, or customized, that is used to increase, maintain, or improve functional capabilities of a child with a disability" ("Individuals with Disabilities," 1997, Section 602[1]).

Assistive technology tools may range from less expensive low-tech equipment such as adapted spoons, joysticks, taped stories, adaptive switches, head-pointing devices, captioned programming, and communication boards (message display devices that contain vocabulary choices from which the child can select an answer) to commercially developed high-tech devices such as screen magnifiers, speech synthesizers and digitizers, voice-recognition devices, touch screens, alternative computer keyboards, word prediction programs, and special reading software (Beck, 2002; Duhaney & Duhaney, 2000).

## Technology for Students with Hearing Impairments

Hearing-impaired students can be assisted with technology tools in a number of ways, including closed captioning, audio amplification, and cochlear implants. Closed captioning (presenting spoken words as text on a screen) occurs most often in connection with television programs. But this technology can also be used in classrooms to help hearing-impaired students follow a teacher's lectures or explanations. A system called RAPIDTEXT allows 120–225 words per minute to be typed (using a stenographic keyboard) and sent to a student's computer monitor. Another way to accomplish the same goal is through audio amplification. The teacher wears a small microphone and transmitter whose signal is amplified and sent to a student who wears a lightweight receiver (Duhaney & Duhaney, 2000). A third option for students with severe to profound hearing loss is a cochlear implant. This system involves several external components (microphone, speech processor, transmitter, power pack) and a surgically implanted receiver-stimulator. Cochlear implants can also be combined with audio amplification systems (Moore & Teagle, 2002). The website for Gallaudet University, a well-known school for the deaf in Washington, D.C., includes a page that describes its Technology Access Program (**tap.gallaudet.edu**).

As helpful as the preceding devices are, one thing they are not is a magic bullet. They cannot, for example, overcome students' lack of learning skills. A group of mainstreamed high school hearing-impaired students who were given class notes from a speech-to-text support service simply read them (which is what most non–hearing-impaired students would do) rather than using them in conjunction with other study methods (Elliott, Foster, & Stinson, 2002).

## Technology for Students with Visual Impairments

Closed captioning and audio amplification are popular among deaf students; speech synthesizers and magnification devices offer similar liberating assistance to those who are visually impaired. With speech synthesis, the user can select a word, sentence, or chunk of information from any written or scanned text and hear it pronounced by a speech synthesizer. For example, the Kurzweil Reader scans printed material and converts it into high-quality speech. The Braille 'n Speak is a note taking system that also relies on speech synthesis. As students type on a seven-key keyboard, their input is converted into standard text that can either be read aloud or stored in the system's memory. In addition to devices that magnify the content of computer screens, head-mounted magnifiers allow students to see over various distances (Duhaney & Duhaney, 2000; Griffin, Williams, Davis, & Engleman, 2002).

Software programs called screen readers (such as Job Access with Speech, Windows-Eyes, and WinVision) allow individuals with visual impairments to have the contents of a screen read to them by a speech synthesis program. The websites of the National Federation of the Blind (**www.nfb.org**) and the American Printing House for the Blind (**www.aph.org**) describe screen readers and other software and hardware devices that are available for individuals with visual impairments.

## Technology for Students with Orthopedic Impairments

For students who have physical limitations, pointing devices that are held in the mouth, attached to the head, or voice activated may provide the needed device control. Students with more limited fields of motion but acceptable fine motor skill may also benefit from condensed or mini keyboards that position the keys more closely

*HM TeacherPrepSPACE*

For links to the websites mentioned in this section, plus other important web resources, go to the textbook's student website.

together and require less strength to use. For students with less fine motor control, touch-sensitive expanded keyboards offer more space between keys and are often programmed to accept overlay plastic sheets for different applications or user needs (Duhaney & Duhaney, 2000). Free programs (called freeware) and inexpensive ones (called shareware) for helping individuals with physical and other disabilities use computers more effectively can be found at the Virtual Assistive Technology Center website (**vatc.freeservers.com**).

## Technology for Students with Speech or Language Impairments

Technology can also help individuals with communication impairments. Using computer software with a speech synthesizer and expanded keyboard, Teris Schery and Lisa O'Connor (1997) demonstrated positive effects of computer training in vocabulary, early grammar skills, and social communication among toddlers with Down syndrome as well as young children with severe language and behavioral disabilities. In a small pilot study, they later discovered that parent volunteers briefly trained in using this software can be more effective than a professional speech pathologist. Computer programs designed to help students with speech or language impairments acquire language and communication skills can be found on the websites of Apple Computer (**www.apple.com/education/accessibility/disabilities/language**) and the International Society for Augmentative and Alternative Communication (**www.isaac-online.org**).

## Technology for Students with Learning Disabilities

As we saw earlier in this chapter, learning disabled (LD) students typically have problems with reading, writing, and mathematics. But research has shown that the severity of these troubles can be reduced by using software programs designed for students with learning problems. For instance, in one study, LD students who responded to the demands of a computerized study guide (read a passage as many times as possible within a fifteen-minute period, respond silently to study guide questions at least twice, and then take a fifteen-item multiple-choice test) achieved higher scores than LD students who were not exposed to the program. In another study, a videodisc program helped LD students achieve higher scores on a test of math fractions. In a third study, students who worked on a hypermedia study guide for social studies scored higher on factual and inferential questions than students who experienced a lecture covering the same material (Maccini, Gagnon, & Hughes, 2002). Finally, software that allowed for a synchronized visual and auditory presentation of text helped college students with ADHD to read for longer periods of time with less stress and fatigue (Hecker, Burns, Elkind, Elkind, & Katz, 2002).

In the area of writing, there are many tools for students with learning disabilities that can help them—and other students—with basic sentence generation, transcription, and revision. Spelling, style, and grammar checkers can help raise student focus from mechanical demands and surface-level concerns to higher-level text cohesion and integration issues. Word prediction software can help students write more coherent and meaningful sentences by offering a choice of several words based on what the student has already written (Duhaney & Duhaney, 2000). Something as simple as an e-pal program (an electronic version of a pen pal) can improve certain aspects of LD students' writing. In one study (Stanford & Siders, 2001), sixth, seventh, and eighth graders with learning disabilities either exchanged e-mails with college students, exchanged written letters with college students, or wrote to an imaginary pen pal. At the end of eight weeks, students in the e-pal group wrote longer and more complex letters than students in the other two groups. However, technology by itself does not improve the writing of LD students. Instead, sound instructional practices such as peer tutoring on the word-processed text raise the quality and number of student revisions and overall quality of their writing (MacArthur, 1994). Additional information about resources and teaching strategies for students with learning disabilities can be found on the student website.

## Technology for Gifted and Talented Students

Gifted students can also benefit from advances in instructional technology, such as distance education. Stanford University, for instance, has been experimenting with providing year-round accelerated instruction in mathematics, physics, English, and computer science to gifted high school students through the Education Program for Gifted Youth (EPGY) (Ravaglia, Alper, Rozenfeld, & Suppes, 1998; Ravaglia, Sommer, Sanders, Oas, & DeLeone, 1999). In addition to digitized lectures and online quizzes, students in EPGY can contact the instructors using e-mail, telephone project staff, attend discussion sessions at Stanford, and try out various physics experiments at home. Given all these supports, it is not surprising that students have done exceedingly well in this program (Tock & Suppes, 2002). The website for EPGY can be found at **http://epgy.stanford.edu**.

An online enrichment activity that can be used for any student, including the gifted and talented, is a web quest (Ridgeway, Peters, & Tracy, 2002). This is an inquiry-oriented activity in which most or all of the information that students need is drawn from the Web. An excellent source of web quests is the WebQuest Page of San Diego State University (**webquest.sdsu.edu**). Here you will find dozens of activities arranged by grade level and by subject matter within each grade level.

*HM TeacherPrepSPACE*

*To review this chapter, see the ACE practice tests and PowerPoint slides at the textbook's student website.*

# 7

# Behavioral Learning Theory: Operant Conditioning

## HM TeacherPrepSPACE

**HM TeacherPrepSPACE student website** offers many helpful resources. Go to **login.cengage.com** to preview this chapter's Concept Maps and Chapter Themes.

## KEY POINTS

*These key points will help you learn the important information in this chapter. To help you study, they also appear in the margins of the pages, next to the text where they are discussed.*

### Operant Conditioning

- Operant conditioning: voluntary response strengthened or weakened by consequences that follow
- Positive reinforcement: strengthen a target behavior by presenting a positive reinforcer after the behavior occurs
- Negative reinforcement: strengthen a target behavior by removing an aversive stimulus after the behavior occurs
- Punishment: weaken a target behavior by presenting an aversive stimulus after the behavior occurs
- Time-out: weaken a target behavior by temporarily removing a positive reinforcer after the behavior occurs
- Extinction: weaken a target behavior by ignoring it
- Spontaneous recovery: extinguished behaviors may reappear spontaneously
- Generalization: responding in similar ways to similar stimuli
- Discrimination: responding in different ways to similar stimuli
- Complex behaviors are shaped by reinforcing closer approximations to terminal behavior
- Fixed interval schedules: reinforce after regular time intervals

- Variable interval schedules: reinforce after random time intervals
- Fixed ratio schedules: reinforce after a set number of responses
- Variable ratio schedules: reinforce after a different number of responses each time

### Educational Applications of Operant Conditioning Principles

- Skinner's approach to instruction: clear goals, logical sequencing of material, self-pacing
- Types of CBI programs include drill and practice, simulations, tutorials
- Tutorial and simulation programs produce higher achievement than conventional instruction
- ILS: comprehensive, self-paced learning system
- Behavior modification: shape behavior by ignoring undesirable responses, reinforcing desirable responses
- Premack principle: required work first, then chosen reward
- Token economy is a flexible reinforcement system
- Contingency contracting: reinforcement supplied after student completes mutually agreed-on assignment
- Time-out works best with disruptive, aggressive children
- Research unclear about strength of negative effects of corporal punishment

### Using Computer-Based Instruction in Your Classroom

- Need to make informed choices of software
- CBI no substitute for high-quality teaching

---

Now that you are familiar with how students develop from preschool through high school, with some of the major ways in which students differ from one another, and with the main ways in which schools try to address student variability, it is time to examine what is perhaps the most fundamental and important aspect of schooling: the learning process. Because the primary reason that we have schools is to help children acquire the knowledge and skills that adults consider necessary for successful functioning in society, the instructional and curricular decisions that teachers make should be based on an understanding of how people learn. But as with most of the other topics in

this text, learning is a complex phenomenon that has been studied from different perspectives.

This chapter is devoted to what is generally called behavioral learning theory. More precisely, the chapter describes a theory called operant conditioning and some of its implications. Operant conditioning focuses on the environmental factors that influence the types of behaviors people exhibit and the extent to which they are likely to exhibit those behaviors in the future. As you will see, this theory underlies many computer-based instructional applications. Subsequent chapters will examine the roles that other people and our own thought processes play in learning.

# OPERANT CONDITIONING

In 1913, with the publication of an article titled "Psychology as the Behaviorist Views It," the influential American psychologist John Watson argued that psychology would quickly lose credibility as a science if it focused on internal mental and emotional states that could not be directly observed or accurately measured. The solution was to study what could be directly observed and objectively and accurately measured: the external stimuli that people experienced and what people did in response—in a word, behavior.

From that point until the late 1960s, behavioral theories of one sort or another dominated the psychology of learning. Although they are considerably less popular today, they still offer many useful ideas for classroom teachers.

## Basic Nature and Assumptions

Behavioral learning theories culminated in the work of B. F. Skinner. Skinner put together a theory that not only successfully combines many different ideas but also serves as the basis for a variety of applications to human behavior. Skinner's theory, **operant conditioning,** takes as its starting point the fact that many of the voluntary responses of animals and humans are strengthened when they are reinforced (followed by a desirable consequence) and weakened when they are either ignored or punished. In this way, organisms learn new behaviors and when to exhibit them and "unlearn" existing behaviors. The term *operant conditioning* refers to the fact that organisms learn to "operate" on their environment (make a particular response) in order to obtain or avoid a particular consequence. Some psychologists use the term *instrumental* because the behavior is instrumental in bringing about the consequence.

> Operant conditioning: voluntary response strengthened or weakened by consequences that follow

Most of the experiments on which the principles of operant conditioning are based involved an ingenious apparatus that Skinner invented, which is appropriately referred to as a *Skinner box.* This is a small enclosure that contains only a bar (or lever) and a small tray. Outside the box is a hopper holding a supply of food pellets that are dropped into the tray when the bar is pressed under certain conditions.

A hungry rat is placed in the box, and when in the course of exploring its new environment the rat approaches and then presses the bar, it is rewarded with a food pellet. The rat then presses the bar more frequently than it did before being rewarded. If food pellets are supplied under some conditions when the bar is pushed down—for example, when a tone is sounded—but not under others, the rat learns to discriminate one situation from the other, and the rate of bar pressing drops noticeably when the tone is not sounded. If a tone is sounded that is very close in frequency to the original tone, the rat generalizes (treats the two tones as equivalent) and presses the bar at the same rate for both. But if the food pellets are not given after the rat presses the bar, that behavior stops, or is extinguished.

The Skinner box's prominent role in operant conditioning experiments reflects Skinner's view of psychology as a natural science. Several important assumptions underlie this view:

- *Assumption 1.* Underlying all natural sciences is the assumption that natural phenomena (such as weather patterns, earthquakes, and human behavior) may appear on the surface to be random but really operate according to set laws. What psychology needed, in Skinner's view, was the means by which a researcher could control the environment to observe the lawful and hence predictable influence of environmental factors on behavior.
- *Assumption 2.* A science develops most effectively when scientists study some phenomenon at its simplest, most fundamental level. What is learned at this level can then be used to understand more complex processes.

- *Assumption 3.* Principles of learning that arise from experiments with animals *should* apply to humans. Note the conditional phrasing of this sentence. Although Skinner accepted the usefulness of animal research, he was always careful to point out that such principles needed to be tested again at the human level.
- *Assumption 4.* A change in an organism's behavior pattern is the only basis for concluding that learning has occurred. Although he admitted the existence of such internal processes as thoughts, motives, and emotions, Skinner had two objections to including them in his theoretical system. First, such processes have no place in the scientific study of learning because they cannot be directly observed or measured. Second, he believed that his experiments with rats in the Skinner box show that learning is caused not by internal processes but by the environmental consequences that follow behavior.

## Basic Principles of Operant Conditioning

To repeat the basic idea behind operant conditioning: all behaviors are accompanied by certain consequences, and these consequences strongly influence (some might say determine) whether these behaviors are repeated and at what level of intensity. In general, the consequences that follow behavior are either pleasant and desirable or unpleasant and aversive. Depending on conditions that we will discuss shortly, these consequences either increase (strengthen) or decrease (weaken) the likelihood that the preceding behavior will recur under the same or similar circumstances.

When consequences strengthen a preceding behavior, *reinforcement* has taken place. When consequences weaken a preceding behavior, *punishment* and *extinction* have occurred. There are two forms of reinforcement and two forms of punishment. This section describes both forms of reinforcement, both forms of punishment, extinction, and several related principles that can be applied to aspects of human learning.

### pause & reflect

Operant conditioning holds that we learn to respond or not respond to certain stimuli because our responses are followed by desirable or aversive consequences. How many of your own behaviors can you explain in this fashion? Why, for example, are you reading this book and pondering these questions?

> Positive reinforcement: strengthen a target behavior by presenting a positive reinforcer after the behavior occurs

**Positive Reinforcement**   Although the term *positive reinforcement* may be unfamiliar to you, the idea behind it probably is not. If you can recall spending more time studying for a certain subject because of a compliment from the teacher or a high grade on an examination, you have experienced positive reinforcement. Specifically, **positive reinforcement** involves strengthening a target behavior—that is, increasing and maintaining the probability that a particular behavior will be repeated—by presenting a stimulus (called a *positive reinforcer*) immediately after the behavior has occurred. Praise, recognition, and the opportunity for free play are positive reinforcers for many (but not all) students.

The term *positive* as Skinner used it refers to the act of presenting a stimulus (think of positive as *adding* here); it does not refer to the pleasant nature of the stimulus itself. You will understand better why this distinction is very important as we consider the other form of reinforcement.

> Negative reinforcement: strengthen a target behavior by removing an aversive stimulus after the behavior occurs

**Negative Reinforcement**   People frequently have difficulty understanding the concept of negative reinforcement, most often confusing it with punishment, so we will examine it carefully here. The goal of **negative reinforcement** is the same as that of positive reinforcement: to *increase* the strength of a particular behavior. The method, however, is different. Instead of supplying a desirable stimulus, *one removes an unpleasant and aversive stimulus* whenever a target behavior is exhibited. As you study this definition, pay special attention to the removing action. Just as positive refers to adding, negative refers to the act of *removing* a stimulus. By removing something unwanted, you encourage the student to learn new behaviors.

*Students are likely to be motivated to learn if they are positively reinforced for completing a project or task. Awards and praise from the teacher and one's peers are strong positive reinforcers for many students.*

In everyday life, negative reinforcement occurs quite frequently. A child picks up his clothes or toys to stop his parents' nagging. A driver uses a seat belt to stop the annoying buzzer sound. Later in the chapter, we will describe how educators use negative reinforcement. We will also discuss its desirability relative to positive reinforcement.

| Punishment: weaken a target behavior by presenting an aversive stimulus after the behavior occurs |

**Punishment**   There are three procedures that reduce the likelihood that a particular behavior will be repeated. The first is **punishment,** also known as Type I punishment, or presentation punishment. Punishment is defined by operant psychologists as the presentation of an aversive stimulus (such as scolding, paddling, ridiculing, or making a student write five hundred times "I will not chew gum in class") that reduces the frequency of a target behavior. From an operant perspective, you can claim to have punished someone else only if the target behavior is actually reduced in frequency. (Note that whether these methods of punishment do achieve their goal and are effective and whether they are ethical are other issues—ones that we will discuss later in this chapter.)

Many people confuse negative reinforcement with punishment. Both involve the use of an aversive stimulus, but the effects of each are opposite. Remember that negative reinforcement strengthens a target behavior, whereas punishment weakens or eliminates a behavior.

| Time-out: weaken a target behavior by temporarily removing a positive reinforcer after the behavior occurs |

**Time-Out**   The second procedure that decreases the frequency of or eliminates a target behavior is another form of punishment, **time-out.** But instead of presenting an aversive stimulus, time-out *temporarily removes the opportunity to receive positive reinforcement.* (Time-out is sometimes called Type II punishment, or removal punishment.) For instance, a student who frequently disrupts classroom routine to get attention may be sent to sit in an empty room for five minutes. Removal from a reinforcing environment (as well as the angry tone of voice and facial expression that normally accompany the order to leave the classroom) is usually looked on as an aversive consequence by the individual being removed. An athlete who is suspended from competition is another example of this form of punishment.

| Extinction: weaken a target behavior by ignoring it |

**Extinction**   A third consequence that weakens undesired behavior is extinction. **Extinction** occurs when a previously reinforced behavior decreases in frequency, and eventually ceases altogether, because reinforcement is withheld. Examples of extinction include a mother's ignoring a whining child or a teacher's ignoring a student who spontaneously answers a question without waiting to be called on. Both extinction and time-out are most effective when combined with other consequences, such as positive reinforcement. To help yourself define and remember the distinguishing characteristics of positive reinforcement, negative reinforcement, punishment, and extinction, study Figure 7.1.

**Spontaneous Recovery**   When used alone, extinction is sometimes a slow and difficult means of decreasing the frequency of undesired behavior because extinguished behaviors occasionally reappear without having been reinforced, an occurrence known as **spontaneous recovery.** Under normal circumstances, however, the time between spontaneous recoveries lengthens, and the intensity of the recurring behavior becomes progressively weaker. If the behavior undergoing extinction is not terribly disruptive and if the teacher (or parent, counselor, or supervisor) is willing to persevere, these episodes can sometimes be tolerated on the way to more complete extinction.

> Spontaneous recovery: extinguished behaviors may reappear spontaneously

**Generalization**   When an individual learns to make a particular response to a particular stimulus and then makes the same or a similar response in a slightly different situation, **generalization** has occurred. For example, students who were positively reinforced for using effective study skills in history go on to use those same skills in chemistry, social studies, algebra, and other subjects. Or, to use a less encouraging illustration, students ignore or question a teacher's every request and direction because they have been reinforced for responding that way to their parents at home. The less similar the new stimulus is to the original, however, the less similar the response is likely to be.

> Generalization: responding in similar ways to similar stimuli

**Discrimination**   When inappropriate generalizations occur, as in the preceding example, they can be essentially extinguished through discrimination training. In **discrimination** individuals learn to notice the unique aspects of seemingly similar situations (for example, that teachers are not parents, although both are adults) and to respond differently to each situation. Teachers can encourage this process by reinforcing only the desired behaviors (for instance, attention, obedience, and cooperation) and withholding reinforcement following undesired behaviors (such as inattention or disobedience).

> Discrimination: responding in different ways to similar stimuli

*The time-out procedure recommended by behavior modification enthusiasts involves weakening an undesirable form of behavior (such as shoving on the playground) by temporarily removing positive reinforcement (by having the misbehaving student remain in a corner of the classroom for five minutes while the rest of the class continues to enjoy another activity).*

**Figure 7.1** Conditions That Define Reinforcement, Punishment, and Extinction

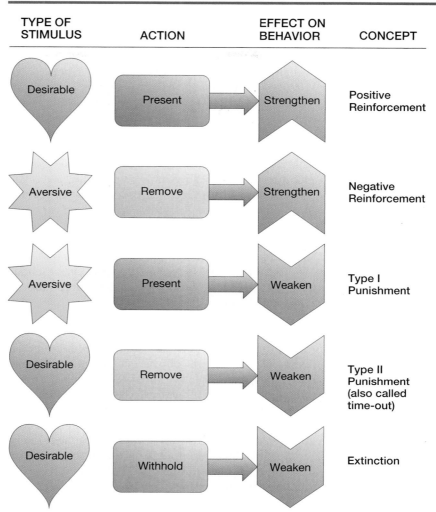

| TYPE OF STIMULUS | ACTION | EFFECT ON BEHAVIOR | CONCEPT |
|---|---|---|---|
| Desirable | Present | Strengthen | Positive Reinforcement |
| Aversive | Remove | Strengthen | Negative Reinforcement |
| Aversive | Present | Weaken | Type I Punishment |
| Desirable | Remove | Weaken | Type II Punishment (also called time-out) |
| Desirable | Withhold | Weaken | Extinction |

**Shaping**   Up to now, we have not distinguished relatively simple learned behaviors from more complex ones. A bit of reflection, however, should enable you to realize that many of the behaviors human beings learn (such as playing a sport or writing a term paper) are complex and are acquired gradually. The principle of **shaping** best explains how complex responses are learned.

In shaping, actions that move progressively closer to the desired *terminal behavior* (to use Skinner's term) are reinforced. Actions that do not represent closer approximations of the terminal behavior are ignored. The key to success is to take one step at a time. The movements must be gradual enough so that the person or animal becomes aware that each step in the sequence is essential. This process is typically called *reinforcing successive approximations to the terminal behavior*.

At least three factors can undermine the effectiveness of shaping:

- Too much positive reinforcement for early, crude responses may reduce the learner's willingness to attempt a more complex response.
- An expectation of too much progress too soon may decrease the likelihood of an appropriate response. If this results in a long period of nonreinforcement, what has been learned up to that point may be extinguished. For example, expecting a student to work industriously on a homework assignment for ninety minutes just after you have shaped forty-five minutes of appropriate homework behavior is probably

*Complex behaviors are shaped by reinforcing closer approximations to terminal behavior*

too big a jump. If what you demand is beyond the student's capability, the student may revert to her original level of performance owing to the lack of reinforcement.

- Delay in the reinforcement of the terminal behavior allows time for additional, unrelated behaviors to occur. When the reinforcement eventually occurs, it may strengthen one or more of the more recent behaviors rather than the terminal behavior.

**Schedules of Reinforcement**    If you have been reading this section on basic principles carefully, you may have begun to wonder whether the use of operant conditioning principles, particularly positive reinforcement, requires you as the teacher to be present every time a desired response happens. If so, you might have some justifiable reservations about the practicality of this theory. The answer is yes, up to a point, but after that, no. As we have pointed out, when you are trying to get a new behavior established, especially if it is a complex behavior that requires shaping, learning proceeds best when every desired response is positively reinforced and every undesired response is ignored. This is known as a *continuous reinforcement* schedule.

Once the behavior has been learned, however, positive reinforcement can be employed on a noncontinuous, or intermittent, basis to perpetuate that behavior. There are four basic *intermittent reinforcement* schedules: fixed interval (FI), variable interval (VI), fixed ratio (FR), and variable ratio (VR). Each schedule produces a different pattern of behavior.

Fixed interval schedules: reinforce after regular time intervals

***Fixed Interval Schedule***    In this schedule, a learner is reinforced for the first desired response that occurs after a predetermined amount of time has elapsed (for example, five minutes, one hour, or seven days). Once the response has occurred and been reinforced, the next interval begins. Any desired behaviors that are made during an interval are ignored. The reinforced behavior occurs at a lower level during the early part of the interval and gradually rises as the time for reinforcement draws closer. Once the reinforcer is delivered, the relevant behavior declines in frequency and gradually rises toward the end of the next interval.

FI schedules of reinforcement occur in education when teachers schedule exams or projects at regular intervals. The grade or score is considered to be a reinforcer. As you are certainly aware, it is not unusual to see little studying or progress occur during the early part of the interval. However, several days before an exam or due date, the pace quickens considerably.

Variable interval schedules: reinforce after random time intervals

***Variable Interval Schedule***    If you would like to see a more consistent pattern of behavior, you might consider using a variable interval schedule. With a VI schedule, the length of time between reinforcements is essentially random but averages out to a predetermined interval. Thus four successive reinforcements may occur at the following intervals: one week, four weeks, two weeks, five weeks. The average interval is three weeks. Teachers who give surprise quizzes or call on students to answer oral questions on the average of once every third day are invoking a variable interval schedule.

Fixed ratio schedules: reinforce after a set number of responses

***Fixed Ratio Schedule***    Within this schedule, reinforcement is provided whenever a predetermined number of responses are made. A rat in a Skinner box may be reinforced with a food pellet whenever it presses a lever fifty times. A factory worker may earn $20 each time he assembles five electronic circuit boards. A teacher may reinforce a student with praise for every ten arithmetic problems correctly completed. FR schedules tend to produce high response rates because the faster the learner responds, the sooner the reinforcement is delivered. However, a relatively brief period of no or few responses occurs immediately after the reinforcer is delivered.

Variable ratio schedules: reinforce after a different number of responses each time

***Variable Ratio Schedule***    Like a variable interval schedule, this schedule tends to eliminate irregularities in response rate, thereby producing a more consistent rate. This is accomplished through reinforcement after a different number of responses from one time to the next according to a predetermined average. If you decided to use a VR fifteen schedule, you might reinforce a desired behavior after twelve, seven, twenty-three, and eighteen occurrences, respectively (that is, after the twelfth, nineteenth, forty-second, and sixtieth desired behaviors). Because the occurrence of reinforcement is so unpredictable, learners tend to respond fairly rapidly for long periods of time. If you need proof, just watch people play the slot machines in gambling casinos.

# EDUCATIONAL APPLICATIONS OF OPERANT CONDITIONING PRINCIPLES

In the late 1940s, when Skinner's daughter was in elementary school, he observed a number of instructional weaknesses that concerned him. These included the excessive use of aversive consequences to shape behavior (students studying to avoid a low grade or embarrassment in the classroom), an overly long interval between students taking tests or handing in homework and getting corrective feedback, and poorly organized lessons and workbooks that did not lead to specific goals. Skinner became convinced that if the principles of operant conditioning were systematically applied to education, all such weaknesses could be reduced or eliminated.

That belief, which he then reiterated consistently until his death in 1990 (see, for example, Skinner, 1984), is based on four prescriptions that come straight from his laboratory research on operant conditioning:

1. Be clear about what is to be taught.
2. Teach first things first.
3. Allow students to learn at their own rate.
4. Program the subject matter.

This straightforward formulation became the basis for two educational applications: an approach to teaching that we now call computer-based instruction and a set of procedures for helping students learn appropriate classroom behaviors referred to as behavior modification. The next few sections will describe the nature of these applications and assess the extent to which they improve classroom learning.

## Computer–Based Instruction

**Does Computer–Based Technology Aid Learning?**  When desktop computers and the instructional programs that were created for them were introduced into public schools in the early 1980s, many educators and psychologists believed that students would learn significantly more through this medium than through traditional teacher-led, text-based instruction. This new approach to instruction was referred to as either **computer-based instruction (CBI)** or **computer-assisted instruction (CAI).**

Instructional programs designed for computers generally fall into one of three categories:

- **Drill-and-practice programs:** These programs provide students with sets of relatively simple exercises and problems, such as adding fractions and recognizing parts of speech, so they can practice knowledge and skills learned earlier.
- **Simulation programs:** Also called microworlds or problem-solving programs, these artificial environments mimic the real world in which students have to use previously learned knowledge to solve problems. A microworld program that we describe in more detail in a later chapter requires students to design a plant that will grow in the particular climate of each of five alien worlds.
- **Tutorial programs:** These programs mimic what a teacher does in class by teaching students new information and skills in a methodical, step-by-step approach.

*HM TeacherPrepSPACE*

How well do you understand reinforcement? Try this chapter's Netlab at the textbook's student website.

Skinner's approach to instruction: clear goals, logical sequencing of materials, self-pacing

Types of CBI programs include drill and practice, simulations, tutorials

Showing students the steps involved in solving algebraic equations is an example of this type of program.

The research that has been done on the effectiveness of these varieties of CBI paints an interesting picture.

***Research on the Effects of CBI***   Computer-based instruction is such a widely researched topic that several authors from time to time have attempted to summarize what has been learned about one aspect or another of this matter. In the typical experiment, one group of students receives instruction either partly or entirely via computer while an equivalent group receives either conventional instruction (a text assignment supplemented by classroom lecture and discussion) or an alternative form of CBI. Here is a brief summary of the main findings from several of these analyses:

> Tutorial and simulation programs produce higher achievement than conventional instruction

1. Studies conducted during the 1970s and 1980s on the effect of tutorial programs produced a positive average effect of 0.36 of a standard deviation. This meant that the typical student who learned from a computer-based tutorial scored 14 percentile ranks higher on an achievement test than the typical conventionally-taught student. For studies on tutorial programs conducted during the 1990s, the effect was even stronger. CBI-taught students scored 22 percentile ranks higher than their conventionally taught peers (Kulik, 2003a).
2. The average effect of simulation programs on achievement for studies conducted during the 1990s was a positive average effect of 0.32 of a standard deviation. Students who worked on simulation programs scored 13 percentile ranks higher than their conventionally taught peers (Kulik, 2003a).
3. An analysis of fifty-two studies published between 1983 and 2003 also found a moderate positive effect for CBI. Students who received CBI outscored those who received traditional instruction by an average of 21 percentile ranks, or a little more than a half of a standard deviation (Liao, 2007).
4. Students whose beginning reading skills (e.g., phonological awareness, word reading, text reading, reading/listening) were supported by CBI outscored students

*Computer-based instruction has been shown to produce moderate increases in learning, particularly for tutorial and simulation programs.*

whose instruction was not computer based on reading tests by about 10 percentile ranks (Blok, Oostdam, Otter, & Overmaat, 2002). Interestingly, the findings of this review were about the same as those from reviews conducted ten to fifteen years earlier. Despite the introduction of more sophisticated computer programs in recent years (providing verbal feedback, for example), their effect on the learning of beginning reading skills has remained fairly constant.

5. As we mentioned in earlier chapters, hypermedia is a program format that combines hypertext (a system of links that allow users to jump from one section of text to another or from one document to another in whatever order they desire) and multimedia (the combination of several forms of media, such as text, graphics, animation, sound, pictures, and video). Although hypermedia programs were expected to boost student learning greatly, their effects to date have been more modest. They appear to have no effect on student comprehension of information, and lower-ability students tend to be overwhelmed by the decision making such programs call for and by the need to keep track of which links one has visited. Hypermedia does, however, help higher-ability students search through lengthy and multiple information sources rapidly in order to locate target information (Dillon & Gabbard, 1998).

6. An analysis of data collected from tens of thousands of students in thirty-one countries found that performance in school was positively related to the use of a computer at home for accessing the Web, to the availability of educational software at home, and to moderate computer use at school. Both low and high levels of use at school were associated with lower levels of achievement (Bielefeldt, 2005).

## VIDEO CASE  ◄◄ ▶ ►►

### Integrating Technology to Improve Student Learning: A High School Science Simulation

*Watch the video, study the artifacts in the case, and reflect upon the following questions:*

1. Is Mr. Bateman's biology lesson and use of technology in class a good example of Skinner's approach to instruction?

2. According to current educational research, computer-based simulation programs like the one depicted in this Video Case greatly improve student achievement in science. Using the Video Case and the text's discussion of behavioral theory, explain why this might be true.

***Integrated Learning Systems*** In recent years, some software packages have combined tutorial programs based on operant conditioning principles with programs that keep track over time of student performance and provide feedback to both the student and the teacher. These packages are called **integrated learning systems (ILS)** (Kulik, 2003a; Mazyck, 2002; Underwood, Cavendish, Dowling, Fogelman, & Lawson, 1996). Technology experts estimate that ILS may be used by as many as 25 percent of all school districts and, because of their high cost ($60,000 and up), account for about 50 percent of all technology-related expenditures by schools (Brush, Armstrong, Barbrow, & Ulintz, 1999; Kulik, 2003a; Mazyck, 2002).

| ILS: comprehensive, self-paced learning system

Such systems present information in a more sequenced and comprehensive fashion than traditional CBI programs. Integrated learning systems can, in fact, cover the content for entire K–8 mathematics, reading, language arts, and science curricula. Some systems include an English-language curriculum to address the needs of schools with high levels of limited-English-proficient students. Integrated learning systems allow students to go through tutorials at their own pace; they also administer tests, track student progress across grade levels, and present students with appropriate remediation or enrichment activities.

A review of sixteen studies published since 1990 resulted in a mixed conclusion (Kulik, 2003a). The seven studies that examined the effect of an ILS on mathematics achievement alone produced a positive average effect of 0.40 of a standard deviation. This means that the typical ILS-taught student scored 16 percentile ranks higher on a math test than did the typical conventionally taught student. The remaining nine studies examined the effect of an ILS on both mathematics achievement and reading comprehension. For these studies, the effect on math was positive but quite small, just 0.17 of a standard deviation, and the effect for reading was almost zero (meaning that ILS-taught and conventionally taught students scored about the same on a reading test). Why the difference in the two groups of studies? One possible, if not likely, reason is that ILS that covered both subjects tried to do so in less time than would have been allotted for either subject alone (Kulik, 2003a).

***Evaluation of Computer-Based Instruction***   How can we sum up the varieties of CBI or CAI that have evolved from operant conditioning principles? Overall, the research findings suggest that CBI is not the equivalent of a wonder drug, but, when properly designed and used, it can effectively supplement a teacher's attempts to present, explain, apply, and reinforce knowledge and skills. Simulation programs seem to be particularly useful for helping students understand scientific concepts and procedures.

These findings also reaffirm what we suggested in the opening chapter about good teaching being partly an art and partly a science. Whenever you as a teacher apply any psychological principle in your classroom, you will need to ask yourself: For whom is this instructional technique likely to be beneficial? With what materials? For what outcome? We will return to the issue of using CBI in your classroom at the end of this chapter.

## pause & reflect

Many educators feel that operant conditioning presents a cold, dehumanizing picture of human learning and ignores the role of such factors as free will, motives, and creativity. Do you feel that way while reading this chapter? Do you think positive attributes of operant conditioning balance out possible negative aspects?

Behavior modification: shape behavior by ignoring undesirable responses, reinforcing desirable responses

## Behavior Modification

Although applied in many ways, the term **behavior modification** basically refers to the use of operant conditioning techniques to (as the phrase indicates) modify behavior. Because those who use such techniques attempt to manage behavior by making rewards contingent on certain actions, the term *contingency management* is also sometimes used.

After Skinner and his followers had perfected techniques of operant conditioning in modifying the behavior of animals, they concluded that similar techniques could be used with humans. In this section we will briefly discuss several techniques that teachers may use to strengthen or weaken specific behaviors. Techniques applied in education to strengthen behaviors include shaping, token economies, and contingency contracts. Techniques that aim to weaken behaviors include extinction and punishment.

**Shaping**   You may want to take a few minutes now to review our earlier explanation of shaping. Most attempts at shaping important classroom behaviors should include at least the following steps (Miltenberger, 2004; Walker, Shea, & Bauer, 2007):

1. Select the target behavior.
2. Obtain reliable baseline data (that is, determine how often the target behavior occurs in the normal course of events).
3. Select potential reinforcers.
4. Reinforce successive approximations of the target behavior each time they occur.

5. Reinforce the newly established target behavior each time it occurs.
6. Reinforce the target behavior on a variable reinforcement schedule.

To illustrate how shaping might be used, imagine that you are a third-grade teacher (or a middle or high school teacher) with a chronic problem: one of your students rarely completes more than a small percentage of the arithmetic (or algebra) problems on the worksheets you distribute in class, even though you know the student possesses the necessary skills. To begin, you decide that a reasonable goal would be for the student to complete at least 85 percent of the problems on a given worksheet. Next, you review the student's work for the past several weeks and determine that, on average, he completed only 25 percent of the problems per worksheet. Your next step is to select positive reinforcers that you know or suspect will work.

Reinforcers come in a variety of forms. Most elementary school teachers typically use such things as stickers, verbal praise, smiles, and classroom privileges (for example, feeding the gerbil, cleaning the erasers). Middle school and high school teachers can use letter or numerical grades, material incentives (such as board games and computer games, as long as school policy and your financial resources allow it), and privately given verbal praise.

With certain reservations, public forms of recognition can also be used. The reservations include the following:

- Because many adolescents are acutely self-conscious, any public display of student work or presentation of awards should be made to several students at the same time to avoid possible embarrassment (Emmer, Evertson, Clements, & Worsham, 2006).
- Awards should be made without letter grades.
- Awards should be given with an awareness that public displays of recognition are not appropriate or comfortable for all cultures.

One popular shaping technique that has stood the test of time involves having students list favorite activities on a card. Then they are told that they will be able to indulge in one of those activities for a stated period of time after they have completed a set of instructional objectives. This technique is sometimes called the **Premack principle** after psychologist David Premack (1959), who first proposed it. It is also called *Grandma's rule* because it is a variation of a technique that grandmothers have used for hundreds of years ("Finish your peas, and you can have dessert").

| Premack principle: required work first, then chosen reward

Once you have decided on a sequence of objectives and a method of reinforcement, you are ready to shape the target behavior. For example, you can start by reinforcing the student for completing five problems (25 percent) each day for several consecutive days. Then you reinforce the student for completing five problems and starting a sixth (a fixed ratio schedule). Then you reinforce the student for six completed problems, and so on. Once the student consistently completes at least 85 percent of the problems, you provide reinforcement after every fifth worksheet on the average (a variable ratio schedule).

Although you control the classroom environment while students are in school, this accounts for only about half of their waking hours. Accordingly, parents might supplement your efforts at shaping behavior. The first step in a home-based reinforcement program is obtaining the parents' and student's formal agreement to participate. Then you typically send home a brief note or form on a regular basis (daily, weekly) indicating whether the student exhibited the desired behaviors. For example, in response to the items "Was prepared for class" and "Handed in homework," you would circle "yes" or "no." In response to a homework grade or test grade, you would circle the appropriate letter or percentage-correct designation. The parents are then responsible for providing the appropriate reinforcement or punishment (temporary loss of a privilege, for example). Home-based reinforcement programs are readily learned by parents and are effective in reducing undesired behaviors (e.g., Benoit, Edwards, Olmi, Wilczynski, & Mandal, 2001; Mackay, McLaughlin, Weber, & Derby, 2001). Overall, this procedure has been successful in both reducing disruptive classroom behavior and increasing academic performance (longer time on tasks and higher test scores, for example). Some studies suggest that it may not be necessary to target both areas, as improved academic performance often results in decreased disruptiveness (Kelley & Carper, 1988).

**Token Economies** A second technique used to strengthen behavior in the classroom, the **token economy,** was introduced first with people who had been hospitalized for emotional disturbances and then with students in special education classes. A token is something that has little or no inherent value but that can be used to "purchase" things that do have inherent value. In society, money is our most ubiquitous token. Its value lies not in what it is made of but in what it can purchase—a car, a house, or a college education. By the same token (if you will excuse the pun), students can accumulate check marks, gold stars, or happy faces and "cash them in" at some later date for any one of several reinforcers. Such instructional activities as doing math worksheets, working at the computer, engaging in leisure reading, and playing academic games have proven to be effective reinforcers in token economies (Higgins, Williams, & McLaughlin, 2001). Token economies have even been proven effective in getting college students to increase their degree of in-class participation (Boniecki & Moore, 2003).

| Token economy is a flexible reinforcement system

One reason for the development of the token economy approach was the limited flexibility of more commonly used reinforcers. Candies and cookies, for instance, tend to lose their reinforcing value fairly quickly when supplied continually. It is not always convenient to award free time or the opportunity to engage in a highly preferred activity immediately after a desired response. And social rewards may or may not be sufficiently reinforcing for some individuals. Tokens, however, can always be given immediately after a desirable behavior, can be awarded according to one of the four schedules mentioned earlier, and can be redeemed for items or activities that have high reinforcing value.

Token economies, especially when combined with classroom rules, appropriate delivery of reinforcers, and response cost (a concept we describe a bit later in the chapter), are effective in reducing such disruptive classroom behaviors as talking out of turn, being out of one's seat, fighting, and being off-task. Reductions of 50 percent

*One useful method for positively reinforcing desired behavior is a token economy—supplying students with objects that have no inherent value but that can be accumulated and redeemed for more meaningful reinforcers.*

or more in such behaviors are not uncommon. Token economies are also effective in improving academic performance in a variety of subject areas (Higgins et al., 2001; Kehle, Bray, Theodore, Jenson, & Clark, 2000; Naughton & McLaughlin, 1995). Token economies have been used successfully with individual students, groups of students, entire classrooms, and even entire schools.

**Contingency Contracting**  A third technique teachers use to strengthen behavior is **contingency contracting.** A contingency contract is simply a more formal method of specifying desirable behaviors and consequent reinforcement. The contract, which can be written or verbal, is an agreement worked out by two people (teacher and student, parent and child, counselor and client) in which one person (student, child, client) agrees to behave in a mutually acceptable way and the other person (teacher, parent, counselor) agrees to provide a mutually acceptable form of reinforcement. For example, a student may contract to sit quietly and work on a social studies assignment for thirty minutes. When the student is done, the teacher may reinforce the child with ten minutes of free time, a token, or a small toy.

Contracts can be drawn up with all members of a class individually, with selected individual class members, or with the class as a whole. As with most other contracts, provisions can be made for renegotiating the terms. Moreover, the technique is flexible enough to incorporate the techniques of token economies and shaping. It is possible, for example, to draw up a contract that provides tokens for successive approximations to some target behavior (Bushrod, Williams, & McLaughlin, 1995).

**Extinction, Time-Out, and Response Cost**  The primary goal of behavior modification is to strengthen desired behaviors. Toward that end, techniques such as shaping, token economies, and contingency contracts are likely to be very useful. There will be times, however, when you have to weaken or eliminate undesired behaviors because they interfere with instruction and learning. For these occasions, you might consider some form of extinction. Research has demonstrated that extinction is effective in reducing the frequency of many types of problem behaviors (Miltenberger, 2004).

The most straightforward approach is to ignore the undesired response. If a student bids for your attention by clowning around, for instance, you may discourage repetition of that sort of behavior by ignoring it. It is possible, however, that classmates will not ignore the behavior but laugh at it. Such response-strengthening reactions from classmates will likely counteract your lack of reinforcement. Accordingly, you need to observe what happens when you try to extinguish behavior by not responding. Another complication that you should consider before trying extinction is that a student's behavior may progress from being mildly annoying to so disruptive that it interferes with your ability to teach. If you are then forced to attend to the disruptive student, you will, in all likelihood, have reinforced that disruptive behavior (Obenchain & Taylor, 2005).

If other students are reinforcing a youngster's undesired behavior or if a behavior becomes disruptive, you may want to apply the time-out procedure. Suppose a physically active third-grade boy seems unable to keep himself from shoving classmates during recess. If verbal requests, reminders, or warnings fail to limit shoving, the boy can be required to take a five-minute time-out period immediately after he shoves a classmate. He must sit alone in the classroom for that period of time while the rest of the class remains out on the playground. Time-out is an effective means of reducing or eliminating undesired behaviors, particularly those that are aggressive or disruptive, for both regular and mainstreamed children (Miltenberger, 2004; Walker et al., 2007). The rules for the procedure should be clearly explained, and after being sentenced to time-out (which should last no more than five minutes), a child should be given reinforcement for agreeable, helpful behavior—for example, "Thank you for collecting all the playground balls so nicely, Tommy."

Another technique, **response cost,** is similar to time-out in that it involves the removal of a stimulus. It is often used with a token economy. With this procedure, a

---

Contingency contracting: reinforcement supplied after student completes mutually agreed-on assignment

Time-out works best with disruptive, aggressive children

# VIDEO CASE    ◄◄ ▶ ►►

## Classroom Management:
## Handling a Student with Behavior Problems

*Watch the video, study the artifacts in the case, and reflect upon the following questions:*

**1.** Which basic principles of operant conditioning did Mrs. Henry use when trying to help the troubled student in the Video Case? Explain your answer.

**2.** Give some examples of positive reinforcement that the teachers could use with this student (in order to decrease his negative behavior).

certain amount of positive reinforcement (for example, 5 percent of previously earned tokens) is withdrawn every time a child makes an undesired response. Anyone who has been caught exceeding the speed limit and been fined at least $50 can probably attest to the power of response cost as a modifier of behavior. As with extinction and time-out, research confirms that response cost helps reduce a variety of problem behaviors (such as getting off-task, not following directions, and engaging in disruptive behavior) for a wide range of children (Miltenberger, 2004).

**Punishment**    Punishment is one of the most common behavior modification techniques, particularly when it takes the form of corporal punishment. It is also one of the most controversial. One factor that makes this issue controversial is that many parents (about 94 percent, according to one estimate) believe in corporal punishment and spank their children, whereas lobbying groups (such as End Physical Punishment of Children and the National Coalition to Abolish Corporal Punishment in Schools) work to persuade state and federal officials to pass laws that outlaw the practice (Gershoff, 2002).

### pause & reflect

Skinner argued that society too frequently uses aversive means to shape desired behavior (particularly punishment) rather than the more effective positive reinforcement. As you think about how your behavior has been shaped, would you agree or disagree? Why do you think we use punishment so frequently?

A second factor is that researchers have different views about what the existing research means. For example, Elizabeth Gershoff (2002) analyzed eighty-eight studies conducted over the past sixty years and concluded that corporal punishment was strongly associated with such negative behaviors and experiences as low internalization of moral rules, aggression, delinquent and antisocial behavior, low-quality parent-child relationships, and being the recipient of physical abuse. The definition of corporal punishment used by Gershoff was "the use of physical force with the intention of causing a child to experience pain but not injury for the purposes of correction or control of the child's behavior" (p. 540).

Gershoff's conclusions were challenged by Diana Baumrind, Robert Larzelere, and Philip Cowan (2002) on several grounds, one of which concerned the definition Gershoff chose to work from. These researchers argued that Gershoff's findings were due in part to the fact that the definition she used allowed her to include studies whose forms of punishment were more severe than most parents administer. Baumrind et al. advocated limiting the analysis to studies in which the form of corporal punishment used was the more common mild to moderate spanking. They defined spanking as a "subset of the broader category of corporal punishment that is a) physically non-injurious; b) intended to modify behavior; and c) administered with an opened hand to the extremities or buttocks" (p. 581). A reanalysis of those studies examined by Gershoff that were more consistent with this narrower definition produced a considerably weaker (but still positive) relationship between spanking and aggressive behavior. For this reason, as well as limitations in many of the studies, Baumrind et al. (2002) concluded that a blanket condemnation of spanking cannot be made on the basis of the existing research (although it may be made on other bases).

A final word of caution before leaving this topic. As Elizabeth Gershoff pointed out, the studies she reviewed were correlational in nature. That is, researchers simply sought to determine whether a relationship exists between corporal punishment and aggressive behaviors exhibited by children. Consequently, one cannot draw the conclusion from this research that spanking children *causes* them to be more aggressive. It is just as plausible, until additional research proves otherwise, that children who are inherently more aggressive than others cause their parents and other adults to administer more corporal punishment. Another possibility is that a third variable, such as inconsistent discipline, is responsible for both increased use of corporal punishment and aggressive behavior in children.

| Research unclear about strength of negative effects of corporal punishment

Corporal punishment is currently banned in twenty-eight states by either state law or state department of education regulation. Two states, Ohio and Utah, have limited bans. The remaining twenty states either explicitly permit schools to punish students physically or are silent on the matter. In states that allow corporal punishment, local school districts may regulate, but not prohibit, its use. Where states have not addressed the issue, local districts may regulate the use of corporal punishment or ban it altogether. The use of corporal punishment in schools has consistently fallen over the past 27 years. In 1976, approximately 3.5 percent of schoolchildren received some form of corporal punishment. By 2003 the percentage had fallen to 0.6 (National Coalition to Abolish Corporal Punishment in Schools, 2005).

## Take a Stand!

### Positive Reinforcement Versus Punishment as a Classroom Management Tool

Common sense suggests that when one pedagogical technique is shown to be largely effective for achieving a particular objective and a second technique is shown to be largely ineffective, the former would be used by at least a sizable minority of teachers while the latter would be ignored by most. Well, common sense does not always prevail, particularly in the case of using positive reinforcement and punishment as classroom management tools. As we've documented on these pages, few teachers use positive reinforcement in their classrooms despite its demonstrated effectiveness in promoting desired behaviors. Various forms of punishment, which have numerous disadvantages, are more popular.

One reason for this contrary state of affairs undoubtedly has to do with the decline in popularity of operant conditioning theory in educational psychology textbooks and courses. It is not unusual these days for students in teacher-education programs to have learned little or nothing about operant conditioning principles and their classroom applications. As a result, many teachers fall into what is called the negative reinforcement trap. Here's how it works: A student's misbehavior instinctively

elicits a punishing response from a teacher because punishment can be administered quickly and easily and often produces a rapid (albeit temporary) suppression of the undesired behavior. Let's say the teacher sends the offending student to the principal's office. Having obtained at least temporary relief, the teacher is now more inclined to send the next misbehaving student to the office. Now let's examine this situation from the student's perspective. Some students may misbehave because they find the work boring or, even worse, threatening because of a fear of failure. Sending such a student out of the room removes the student from a punishing environment. This is a form of negative reinforcement, which increases the likelihood that the student will engage in subsequent misbehavior.

The best way to deal with this problem is to avoid it in the first place by using a combination of effective teaching methods and positive reinforcement, an approach that is referred to in the literature as positive behavior support (see Gettiger & Stoiber, 2006; Marquis et al., 2000). In our Suggestions for Teaching section, we discuss several ways in which positive reinforcement can be used appropriately and effectively.

*HM TeacherPrepSPACE*

Have you seen the type of situation described here during your own schooling? What do you think about it? For more on this topic, go to the Take a Stand! section of the textbook's student website.

**Should You Use Behavior Modification?** This may seem a strange question to ask given the number of pages we have just spent covering behavior modification methods. Obviously, we feel that the results of decades of research on these techniques justify their use by teachers. Nevertheless, there are criticisms of behavior modification that are not adequately addressed by research findings and that you should carefully consider.

One criticism is that many students, including those in the primary grades, will eventually catch on to the fact that they get reinforced only when they do what the teacher wants them to do. Some may resent this and misbehave out of spite. Others may weigh the amount of effort required to earn a favorable comment or a privilege and decide the reinforcer is not worth the trouble. Still others may develop a "What's in it for me?" attitude. That is, some students may come to think of learning as something they do only to earn an immediate reinforcer. The potential danger of using behavior modification over an extended period of time is that learning may come to an abrupt halt when no one is around to supply reinforcement (Kohn, 1993). (This point will be addressed in the chapter on social cognitive theory.)

A second major criticism is that behavior modification methods, because of their potential power, may lend themselves to inappropriate or even unethical uses. For example, teachers may shape students to be quiet and obedient because it makes their job easier, even though such behaviors do not always produce optimum conditions for learning.

In response to these criticisms, Skinner and other behavioral scientists (see Chance, 1993; Flora, 2004; Maag, 2001, for example) argue that if we do not systematically use what we know about the effects of stimuli and consequences on behavior, we will leave things to chance. In an uncontrolled situation, some fortunate individuals will have a favorable chain of experiences that will equip them with desirable attitudes and skills, but others will suffer an unfortunate series of experiences that will lead to difficulties and disappointment. In a controlled situation, it may be possible to arrange experiences so that almost everyone acquires desirable traits and abilities. What behavioral psychologists seem to be saying is that educators could be accused of being unethical for not making use of an effective learning tool. The challenge, of course, is to use it wisely. The following Suggestions for Teaching in Your Classroom will give you additional ideas for putting operant conditioning principles into practice.

# Suggestions for Teaching in Your Classroom

## Applying Operant Conditioning in the Classroom

### 1 Remain aware that behavior is the result of particular conditions.

**JOURNAL ENTRY**
Checking on Causes of Behavior

Unlike the controlled environment of a Skinner box, many causes of behavior in a real-life classroom may not be observable or traceable. You might as well accept the fact, therefore, that quite often you are going to be a haphazard shaper of behavior. Nevertheless, there will be times when you and your students may benefit if you say to yourself, "Now, there have to be some causes for that behavior. Can I figure out what they are and do something about changing things for the better? Am I doing something that is leading to types of behavior that are making life difficult for some or all of us in the room?" When you are engaging in such speculations, keep in mind that reinforcement strengthens behavior. And check to see whether you are inadvertently rewarding students for misbehavior (by calling attention to them, for example, or by failing to reinforce those who engage in desirable forms of behavior).

**EXAMPLES**

- If you become aware that it takes a long time for your students to settle down at the beginning of a period and that you are reacting by addressing critical remarks specifically to those who dawdle the longest, ignore the dawdlers and respond positively to those who are ready to get to work.

- Let's say that you have given students thirty minutes to finish an assignment. To your dismay, few of them get to work until almost the end of the period, and you find that you have to do a lot of nagging. When you later analyze why this happened, you conclude that you actually encouraged the time-killing behavior because of the way you set up the lesson. The next time you give a similar assignment, tell the students that as soon as they complete it, they can have class time to work on homework and that you will be available to give help or advice to those who want it.

### 2 Use reinforcement, and use it appropriately to strengthen behaviors you want to encourage.

Why would we remind you to do something as obvious as reinforce behaviors you want students to acquire and exhibit in the future? Wouldn't you do that almost automatically? Well, we certainly hope so, but statistics suggest otherwise. A large team of researchers headed by Jon Goodlad (1984) observed the classroom behavior of 1,350 teachers and 17,163 students in thirty-eight schools from seven sections of the country. What they found may surprise you. Teachers' praise of student work occurred about 2 percent of the observed time in the primary grades and about 1 percent of the time in high school.

Once you have resolved to reinforce desired behavior systematically, you need to be sure that you do it appropriately. Although reinforcement is a simple principle that can be readily understood at an intuitive level, it has to be used in the right way to produce desired results. Paul Chance (1992) offers seven guidelines for the effective use of positive reinforcement:

**JOURNAL ENTRY**
Ways to Supply Reinforcement

- Use the weakest reward available to strengthen a behavior. In other words, do not use material rewards when you know that praise will be just as effective a reinforcer. Save the material rewards for that special behavior for which praise or other reinforcers may not be effective.
- When possible, avoid using rewards as incentives. What Chance means is not to get into the habit of automatically telling the student that if she does what you want, you will provide a specific reward. Instead, sometimes ask the student to do something (like work quietly or help another student), and then provide the reinforcer.
- Reward at a high rate in the early stages of learning, and reduce the frequency of rewards as learning progresses.
- Reward only the behavior you want repeated. Although you may not realize it, students are often very sensitive to what is and is not being reinforced. If you decide that one way to encourage students to be more creative in their writing is to tell them not to worry about spelling and grammar errors, then do not be surprised to see many misspelled words and poorly constructed sentences. Or if you decide to reward only the three highest scorers on a test, reasoning that competition brings out the best in people, be prepared to deal with the fact that competition also brings out some of the worst in people (like cheating and refusing to help others).
- Remember that what is an effective reinforcer for one student may not be for another. For some students, comments such as "Very interesting point," "That's right," or "That was a big help" will strengthen the target behavior. But for others, something less overt, such as smiling encouragingly, may be just right.
- Set standards so that success is a realistic possibility for each student. You may have students whose English proficiency is limited or who have disabilities related to learning and intellectual functioning. One way to deal with such diversity is to reward students for making steady progress from whatever their baseline level of performance was at the beginning of the term.
- An often-mentioned goal of teachers is to have students become intrinsically motivated or to take personal pride and satisfaction in simply doing something well. You can use natural instructional opportunities to point this out—for

*One of the basic principles of instruction derived from operant conditioning experiments is that teachers should provide elementary grade students with immediate reinforcement for correct responses.*

example, explore with students how satisfying it is to write a clear and interesting story as they are writing.

**3**   **Take advantage of knowledge about the impact of different reinforcement schedules to encourage persistent and permanent learning.**

**a. When students first attempt a new kind of learning, supply frequent reinforcement. Then supply rewards less often.**

When students first try a new skill or type of learning, praise almost any genuine attempt, even though it may be inept. As they become more skillful, reserve your praise for especially good performances. Avoid a set pattern of commenting on student work. Make favorable remarks at unpredictable intervals.

**b. If you want to encourage periodic spurts of activity, use a fixed interval schedule of reinforcement.**

Occasionally, you will want to encourage students to engage in spurts of activity, as steady output might be too demanding or fatiguing. In such cases, supply reinforcement at specified periods of time. For example, when students are engaging in strenuous or concentrated activity, circulate and provide praise and encouragement by following a set pattern that will bring you in contact with each student at predictable intervals.

**4**   **Give students opportunities to make overt responses, and provide prompt feedback.**

**a. Require students to make frequent, overt, and relevant responses.**

The tendency of teachers is to talk, and for large chunks of time. Those who advocate a programmed approach to teaching recommend that teachers limit the amount of information and explanation they give to students and substitute opportunities for students to respond overtly. In addition, the responses should be directly related to the objectives. If your objectives emphasize the application of concepts and principles, then most of the responses students are asked to make should be about applications. The reason for this suggestion is that the delivery of corrective feedback and other forms of positive reinforcement can be increased when students make frequent responses, thereby accelerating the process of shaping.

**EXAMPLES**

- Instead of lecturing for twenty to thirty minutes at a time about the development of science and technology in the twentieth century, present information in smaller chunks, perhaps eight to ten minutes at a time, and then ask students to describe how an everyday product or service grew out of a particular scientific principle.
- Periodically ask students to summarize the main points of the material you presented over the past several minutes.

**JOURNAL ENTRY**
Ways to Supply Immediate
Feedback

**b.  Provide feedback so that correct responses will be reinforced and students will become aware of and correct errors.**

Research clearly shows that students who study material about a topic, answer a set of questions about that material, and are then told whether their responses are correct and why score significantly higher on a subsequent test of that material than do students who receive no feedback. The difference was about three-fourths of a standard deviation, meaning that the average student who received no feedback scored at the 50th percentile, whereas the average student who received feedback scored at the 77th percentile. Here are a couple of examples of how you can provide timely and useful feedback to students (Bangert-Drowns, Kulik, Kulik, & Morgan, 1991).

**EXAMPLES**

- Immediately after students read a chapter in a text, give them an informal quiz on the key points you listed. Then have them pair off, exchange quizzes, and correct and discuss them.
- As soon as you complete a lecture or demonstration, ask individual students to volunteer to read to the rest of the class what they wrote about the points they were told to look for. Indicate whether the answer is correct; if it is incorrect or incomplete, ask (in a relaxed and non-threatening way) for additional comments. Direct students to amend and revise their notes as they listen to the responses.

**5  When students must struggle to concentrate on material that is not intrinsically interesting, use special forms of reinforcement to motivate them to persevere.**

**JOURNAL ENTRY**
Ways to Encourage Perseverance

For a variety of reasons, some students may have an extraordinarily difficult time concentrating on almost anything. And, as we all know, to master almost any skill or subject, we have to engage in a certain amount of tedious effort. Accordingly, you may sometimes find it essential to use techniques of behavior modification to help students stick to a task. If and when that time comes, you might follow these procedures.

**a.  Select, with student assistance, a variety of reinforcers.**

A behavior modification approach to motivation appears to work most successfully when students are aware of and eager to earn a payoff. Because students react differently to rewards and because any reward is likely to lose effectiveness if used to excess, it is desirable to list several kinds of rewards and permit students to choose. Some behavior modification enthusiasts (for example, Alberto & Troutman, 2006) even recommend that you make up a *reinforcement preference list* for each student. If you allow your students to prepare individual reinforcement menus themselves, they should be instructed to list school activities they really enjoy doing. It would be wise, however, to stress that the students' lists must be approved by you so that they will not conflict with school regulations or interfere with the rights of others. A student's reward menu might include activities such as reading a book of one's choice, working on an art or craft project, or viewing a videotape or DVD in another room.

**b. Establish, in consultation with individual students, an initial contract of work to be performed to earn a particular reward.**

Once you have established a list of payoffs, you might consult with students (on an individual basis, if possible) to establish a certain amount of work that must be completed for students to obtain a reward selected from the menu. (Refer to Chapter 13 on instructional approaches for Robert Mager's suggestions for preparing specific objectives.) To ensure that students will earn the reward, the first contract should not be too demanding. For example, it might be something as simple as, "Successfully spell at least seven out of ten words on a list of previously misspelled words" or "Correctly answer at least six out of ten questions about the content of a textbook chapter."

**c. Once the initial reward is earned, establish a series of short contracts leading to frequent, immediate rewards.**

The results of many operant conditioning experiments suggest that the frequency of reinforcement is of greater significance than the amount of reinforcement. Therefore, having students work on brief contracts that lead to frequent payoffs immediately after the task is completed is preferable to having them work toward a delayed, king-sized reward.

# USING COMPUTER-BASED INSTRUCTION IN YOUR CLASSROOM

We mentioned earlier that under the right conditions, computers can effectively supplement classroom instruction. If you are now thinking that you might like to use CBI in your own classroom, you should consider the multiple ways computers can be used and how you can get the most out of them for your own students.

## Getting the Most Out of Computer-Based Instruction

Need to make informed choices of software

We would like to make two points about how you can optimize your use of computer-based instruction. First, recognize that out of the thousands of instructional programs that are on the market, most have such significant shortcomings in their design that they are not worth using. Thus you will have to be an informed consumer, either by conducting your own evaluations of instructional software (not as difficult a job as you might think) or by consulting sources whose evaluations can be trusted. Here are the names and addresses of several websites to help get you started:

The Educational Software Selector (TESS): **www.epie.org/epie_tess.htm**
California Learning Resource Network: **clrn.org/home**
Learning Resources and Technology Resources: **lrt.ednet.ns.ca**
Software Evaluation Tool and Resources: **kathyschrock.net/1computer**
World Village Educational Reviews: **www.worldvillage.com/softwarereviews/ educational.html**

CBI no substitute for high-quality teaching

Second, as enthusiastic as you and others may be about the potential of CBI, recognize that it cannot substitute for high-quality classroom teaching. There is a set of skills all teachers need to master in order to integrate computers successfully in a classroom. As we noted early in this text, and as Larry Cuban (1986) points out in a provocative book about the relationship between teachers and machines, successful teaching often depends on the ability of a live teacher to establish a positive emotional climate (by communicating interest, excitement, expectations, and

**HM TeacherPrepSPACE**

To review this chapter, see the ACE practice tests and PowerPoint slides at the textbook's student website.

caring), to monitor student actions and reactions (by "reading" students' verbal and nonverbal communications), and to orchestrate the sequence and pace of instructional events (by making additions, deletions, and modifications in lesson plans). This is one reason that Cuban (2001), in another provocative book, concludes that computers have been oversold as a means to raise teacher and student productivity. If one thinks of the computer as simply another tool to work with, then each type of computer program—drills, tutorials, simulations, integrated learning systems—requires teachers to plan learning activities, interact with students, provide encouragement and feedback, and design assessments. Although acquiring these skills may be a challenge, many teachers feel that being able to give their students meaningful access to such powerful learning tools is a significant reward (Grabe & Grabe, 2007).

| Table 7.1 | Major Types of CBI Programs | |
|---|---|---|
| **Type of Program** | **Purpose** | **Main Features*** |
| Drill and practice | Practice knowledge and skills learned earlier to produce fast and accurate responses | • Presents many problems, questions, and exercises.<br>• Checks answers and provides feedback.<br>• Provides cues when student is not sure of correct responses.<br>• Keeps track of errors.<br>• Adjusts difficulty level of problems and questions to the proficiency level of the student. |
| Tutorial | Teach new information (e.g., facts, definitions, concepts) and skills | • New material presented in linear or branching format.<br>• Linear programs require all students to begin with first frame and work through subsequent frames in given sequence. Incorrect responses minimized by brief answers, small steps, and frequent prompts.<br>• Branching programs allow students to respond to different sets of frames depending on correctness of responses. For incorrect responses, program provides supplementary material that attempts to reteach.<br>• Dialogue programs mimic teacher-student interactions by presenting material, evaluating responses, and adjusting subsequent instruction by presenting either more difficult or easier material. |
| Problem-solving programs: Simulations and games | Teach new information and skills and provide an opportunity to apply what was learned in a meaningful context that would otherwise be unavailable because of cost, physical danger, and time constraints | • Student uses newly learned and existing information to solve a realistic problem.<br>• Settings may be realistic (e.g., piloting a plane), historical/adventure (e.g., guiding a wagon train across the Oregon Trail), or imaginary (e.g., colonizing a new world).<br>• Students practice creating and testing hypotheses on effects of different variables on achieving a goal. |

*Not all programs contain all of the listed features.

SOURCES: Grabe & Grabe (2007).

# 8 Information-Processing Theory

## KEY POINTS

*These key points will help you learn the important information in this chapter. To help you study, they also appear in the margins of the pages, next to the text where they are discussed.*

### The Information-Processing View of Learning

- Information processing: how humans attend to, recognize, transform, store, retrieve information

### A Model of Information Processing

- Sensory register: stimuli held briefly for possible processing
- Recognition: noting key features and relating them to stored information
- Attention: focusing on a portion of currently available information
- Information in long-term memory influences what we attend to
- Short-term memory: about seven bits of information held for about twenty seconds
- Maintenance rehearsal: hold information for immediate use
- Elaborative rehearsal: use stored information to aid learning
- Organizing material reduces number of chunks, provides recall cues
- Meaningful learning occurs when organized material is associated with stored knowledge

- Long-term memory: permanent storehouse of unlimited capacity
- Information in long-term memory organized as schemata
- Students remember much of what they learn in school, especially if mastery and active learning are emphasized

### Suggestions for Teaching in Your Classroom

- Unpredictable changes in environment usually command attention
- Attention span can be increased with practice
- Distributed practice: short study periods at frequent intervals
- Serial position effect: tendency to remember items at beginning and end of a long list
- Concrete analogies can make abstract information meaningful

### Metacognition

- Metacognition: our own knowledge of how we think
- Insight into one's learning processes improves with age

### Technology as an Information-Processing Tool

- Multimedia and hypermedia programs that make appropriate use of animation and interactivity improve learning

---

In Chapter 7, "Behavioral Learning Theory," we noted that operant conditioning emphasizes the role of external factors in learning. Behavioral psychologists focus on the nature of a stimulus to which a student is exposed, the response that the student makes, and the consequences that follow the response. They see no reason to speculate about what takes place in the student's mind before and after the response. The extensive Suggestions for Teaching in Your Classroom presented in Chapter 7 serve as evidence that conclusions and principles based on analyses of external stimuli, observable responses, and observable consequences can be of considerable value to teachers.

But cognitive psychologists, meaning those who study how the mind works and influences behavior, are convinced that it is possible to study nonobservable behavior, such as thought processes, in a scientific manner. Some cognitive psychologists focus on how people use what they know to solve different kinds of problems in different settings; their work will be discussed in Chapter 9, "Constructivist Learning Theory, Problem Solving, and Transfer." Many cognitive psychologists are especially interested in an area of study known as **information-processing theory,** which seeks to understand how people acquire new information, how they store information and recall it from memory, and how what they already know guides and determines what and how they will learn.

Information-processing theory became a popular approach to the study of learning because it provided psychologists with a framework for investigating the role of a variable that behaviorism had ignored: the nature of the learner. Instead of being viewed as relatively passive organisms that respond in fairly predictable ways to environmental stimuli, learners were now seen as highly active interpreters and manipulators of environmental stimuli. The stage was set for psychology to study learning from a broader and more complicated perspective—namely, as an *interaction* between the learner and the environment.

# THE INFORMATION-PROCESSING VIEW OF LEARNING

Information processing: how humans attend to, recognize, transform, store, retrieve information

Information-processing theory rests on a set of assumptions of which three are worth noting.

1. Information is processed in steps, or stages. The major steps typically are attending to a stimulus, recognizing it, transforming it into some type of mental representation, comparing it with information already stored in memory, assigning meaning to it, and acting on it in some fashion (Searleman & Herrmann, 1994). At an early processing stage, human beings *encode* information (represent it in thought) in somewhat superficial ways (as when they represent visual and auditory stimuli as true-to-life pictures and sounds) and at later stages in more meaningful ways (as when they grasp the gist of an idea or its relationship to other ideas).
2. There are limits on how much information can be processed at each stage. Although the absolute amount of information human beings can learn appears to be limitless, it must be acquired gradually.
3. The human information-processing system is interactive. Information already stored in memory influences and is influenced by perception and attention. We see what our prior experiences direct us to see, and, in turn, what we see affects what we know.

Thus, according to the information-processing view, learning results from an interaction between an environmental stimulus (the *information* that is to be learned) and a learner (the one who *processes*, or transforms, the information). What an information-processing psychologist wants to know, for instance, is what goes on in a student's mind as a teacher demonstrates how to calculate the area of a triangle or as the student reads twenty pages of a social studies text. In the sense that contemporary information processing emphasizes the use of existing knowledge schemes to interpret new information and build new knowledge structures, it can be considered a *constructivist* view of learning (Winne, 2001). (See Chapter 9 for a full description of the nature of the theory and the viewpoints most associated with it.)

We believe that you ought to read this chapter very carefully because the information-processing decisions you make affect when you learn, how much you learn, how well you learn—indeed, whether you learn at all. To give you an appreciation of the information-processing approach to learning and how it can help teachers and students do their jobs, the next section will describe several basic cognitive processes and their role in how people store and retrieve information. Later in the chapter we will describe research on selected learning tactics and discuss the nature of strategic learning.

# A MODEL OF INFORMATION PROCESSING

Information-processing psychologists assume that people process new information in stages, that there are limits on how much information can be processed at each stage, and that previously learned information affects how and what people currently learn. Consequently, many psychologists think of information as being held in and transferred among three memory stores: a sensory register, a short-term store, and a long-term store. Each store varies as to the processes required to move information into and out of it, how much information it can hold, and for how long it can hold information. A symbolic representation of these memory stores and their associated processes appears in Figure 8.1. Called a *multi-store* model, it is based on the work of several theorists (for example, Atkinson & Shiffrin, 1968; Norman & Rumelhart, 1970).

Note that our use of the term *memory stores* is not meant to suggest specific locations in the brain where information is held; it is simply a metaphorical device for classifying different memory phenomena. Nevertheless, studies of neurological functioning using techniques such as positron emission tomography (PET) scans (e.g., Haier, 2001; Owen, McMillan, Laird, & Bullmore, 2005) suggest that different types of tasks do activate different parts of the brain. For example, verbal memory tasks are correlated with heightened activity in the thalamus. Another interesting finding is that as people become more proficient at a task, activity decreases in the cortex, suggesting that the brain becomes more efficient at processing information. But as interesting as findings such as these are, research on neurological functioning during learning and memory tasks is in its infancy, and educators should be highly skeptical of "brain-based" educational materials and instructional methods (Jorgenson, 2003).

Shortly after the introduction of multi-store models, information-processing theorists divided themselves into two groups. In one camp are those who believe that a multi-store model is the best way to explain a variety of memory phenomena. In the other camp are those who favor a theoretically leaner, single-memory system. Although this debate has yet to be firmly resolved, the multi-store model is seen as having enough validity that it can be productively used to organize and present much of what is known about how humans store, process, and retrieve information from memory (Searleman & Herrmann, 1994; Spear & Riccio, 1994; Winne, 2001).

As shown in Figure 8.1, *control processes* govern both the manner in which information is encoded and its flow between memory stores. These processes include *recognition, attention, maintenance rehearsal, elaborative rehearsal* (also called *elaborative encoding*), and retrieval. Each control process is associated primarily with a particular memory store.

The control processes are an important aspect of the information-processing system for two reasons. First, they determine the quantity and quality of information that the learner stores in and retrieves from memory. Second, it is the learner who

**Figure 8.1**  A Model of Information Processing

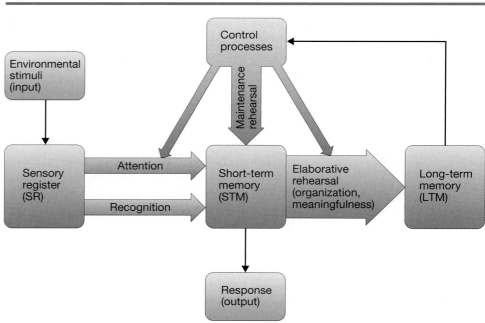

decides whether, when, and how to employ them. That the control processes are under our direct, conscious control will take on added importance when we discuss educational applications a bit later. Before we get to applications, however, we need to make you more familiar with the three memory stores and the control processes specifically associated with each of them.

## The Sensory Register and Its Control Processes

**The Sensory Register**   A description of how human learners process information typically begins with environmental stimuli. Our sense receptors are constantly stimulated by visual, auditory, tactile, olfactory, and gustatory stimuli. These experiences are initially recorded in the **sensory register (SR),** the first memory store. It is called the sensory register because the information it stores is thought to be encoded in the same form in which it is originally perceived—that is, as raw sensory data.

Sensory register: stimuli held briefly for possible processing

The purpose of the SR is to hold information just long enough (about one to three seconds) for us to decide whether we want to attend to it further. Information not selectively attended to and recognized decays or disappears from the system. At the moment you are reading these words, for example, you are being exposed to the appearance of letters printed on paper, sounds in the place where you are reading, and many other stimuli. The sensory register might be compared to an unending series of instant-camera snapshots or videotape segments, each lasting from one to three seconds before fading away. If you recognize and attend to one of the snapshots, it will be "processed" and transferred to short-term memory.

**The Nature of Recognition**   The process of **recognition** involves noting key features of a stimulus and relating them to already stored information. This process is interactive in that it depends partly on information extracted from the stimulus itself and partly on information stored in long-term memory. The ability to recognize a dog, for example, involves noticing those physical features of the animal that give it "dogness" (for example, height, length, number of feet, type of coat) and combining the results of that analysis with relevant information from long-term memory (such as that dogs are household pets, are walked on a leash by their owners, and are used to guard property).

Recognition: noting key features and relating them to stored information

To the degree that an object's defining features are ambiguous (as when one observes an unfamiliar breed of dog from a great distance) or that a learner lacks relevant prior knowledge (as many young children do), recognition and more meaningful processing will suffer. Recognition of words and sentences during reading, for example, can be aided by such factors as clear printing, knowledge of spelling patterns, knowledge of letter sounds, and the frequency with which words appear in natural language. The important point to remember is that recognition and meaningful processing of information are most effective when we make use of all available sources of information (Driscoll, 2005).

One implication of this information-processing view is that elementary school students need more structured learning tasks than middle school or high school students. Because of their limited store of knowledge in long-term memory and narrow ability to relate what they do know logically to the task at hand, younger students should be provided with clear, complete, explicit directions and learning materials (Doyle, 1983; Palmer & Wehmeyer, 2003).

**The Impact of Attention**   The environment usually provides us with more information than we can deal with at one time. From the multitude of sights, sounds, smells, and other stimuli impinging on us at a given moment, we notice and record in the sensory register only a fraction. At this point, yet another reduction typically occurs. We may process only one-third of the already-selected information recorded in the SR. We continually focus on one thing at the expense of something else. This selective focusing on a portion of the information currently stored in the sensory register is what we call **attention**.

Attention: focusing on a portion of currently available information

As with any other human characteristic, there are individual differences in attention. Some people can concentrate on a task while they are surrounded by a variety of sights and sounds. Others need to isolate themselves in a private study area. Still others have difficulty attending under any conditions. What explains these differences? Again, information from long-term memory plays an influential role. According to Ulric Neisser, "Perceivers pick up only what they have schemata for, and willy-nilly ignore the rest" (1976, p. 79). In other words, we choose what we will see (or hear) by using our prior knowledge and experiences (i.e., schemata) to anticipate the nature of incoming information. Students daydream, doodle, and write letters rather than listen to a lecture because they anticipate hearing little of value.

Information in long-term memory influences what we attend to

Moreover, these anticipatory schemata are likely to have long-lasting effects. If someone asked you now to read a book about English grammar, you might recall having been bored by diagramming sentences and memorizing grammatical rules in elementary school. If that was the case, you might not read the grammar text very carefully. A basic challenge for teachers is to convince students that a learning task will be useful, enjoyable, informative, and meaningful. Later in this chapter, we will present some ideas as to how this might be accomplished.

## Short-Term Memory and Its Control Processes

**Short-Term Memory**   Once information has been attended to, it is transferred to **short-term memory (STM),** the second memory store. Short-term memory can hold about seven unrelated bits of information for approximately twenty seconds. Although this brief time span may seem surprising, it can be easily demonstrated. Imagine that you look up and dial an unfamiliar phone number and receive a busy signal. If you are then distracted by something or someone else for fifteen to twenty seconds, chances are you will forget the number. Short-term memory is often referred to as *working memory* because it holds information we are currently aware of at any given moment and is the place where various encoding, organizational, and retrieval processes occur.

Short-term memory: about seven bits of information held for about twenty seconds

Working memory is increasingly being viewed as a critical component in our information-processing system. In the view of one researcher, working memory capacity may be equivalent to Spearman's *g* factor (intelligence as a general mental capability) and "is more highly related to learning, both short-term and long-term, than is any other cognitive factor" (Kyllonen, 1996, p. 73). Two other researchers (Hambrick & Engle, 2003), noting that working memory capacity predicts performance in various comprehension and reasoning tasks, argue that working memory capacity is important when tasks require concentration and effort. In other words, the ability to attend to the relevant elements of the task at hand and ignore unimportant stimuli helps explain why some people learn more quickly and effectively than others. This view is supported by a study of how college students process textbook material. Those who scored higher than their peers on a test of working memory capacity were more likely to use demanding but effective cognitive processes (such as making predictions as they read and reflecting on their level of understanding) and recalled more information (Linderholm & van den Broek, 2002).

**Rehearsal**   A severe limitation of short-term memory is how quickly information disappears or is forgotten in the absence of further processing. This problem can be dealt with through *rehearsal*. Most people think of rehearsal as repeating something over and over either in silence or out loud. The usual purpose for such behavior is to memorize information for later use, although occasionally we simply want to hold material in short-term memory for immediate use (for example, to redial a phone number after getting a busy signal). Rehearsal can serve both purposes, but not in the same way. Accordingly, cognitive psychologists have found it necessary and useful to distinguish two types of rehearsal: maintenance and elaborative.

Maintenance rehearsal: hold information for immediate use

**Maintenance rehearsal** (also called *rote rehearsal* or *repetition*) has a mechanical quality. Its only purpose is to use mental and verbal repetition to hold information in short-term memory for some immediate purpose. Although this is a useful and often-used capability (as in the telephone example), it has no effect on long-term memory storage.

Elaborative rehearsal: use stored information to aid learning

**Elaborative rehearsal** (also called *elaborative encoding*) consciously relates new information to knowledge already stored in long-term memory. Elaboration occurs when we use information stored in long-term memory to add details to new information, clarify the meaning of a new idea, make inferences, construct visual images, and create analogies (King, 1992b). In these ways, we facilitate both the transfer of information to long-term memory and its maintenance in short-term memory. For example, if you wanted to learn the lines for a part in a play, you might try to relate the dialogue and behavior of your character to similar personal experiences you remember. As you strive to memorize the lines and actions, your mental "elaborations" will help you store your part in long-term memory so that you can retrieve it later.

Elaborative rehearsal, whereby information from long-term memory is used in learning new information, is the rule rather than the exception. Mature learners don't often employ maintenance rehearsal by itself. The decision to use one or the other, however, depends on the demands you expect the environment to make on you. If you need to remember things for future use, use elaborative rehearsal; if you want to keep something in consciousness just for the moment, use rote rehearsal.

It is important for you to keep in mind that younger children may not use rehearsal processes in the same way as more mature learners. Kindergarten students rarely engage in spontaneous rehearsal. By the age of seven, however, children typically use simple rehearsal strategies. When presented with a list of items, the average seven-year-old rehearses each word by itself several times. From the age of ten, rehearsal becomes more like that of an adult. Several items may be grouped together and rehearsed as a set.

So far, we have explained the effect of elaborative rehearsal in terms of relating new information to information already stored in long-term memory. That's fine as a very general explanation. But to be more precise, we need to point out that elaborative rehearsal is based on *organization* (as in the preceding example, in which several items were grouped together on some basis and rehearsed as a set) and *meaningfulness* (as in the earlier example, in which lines in a play were related to similar personal experiences).

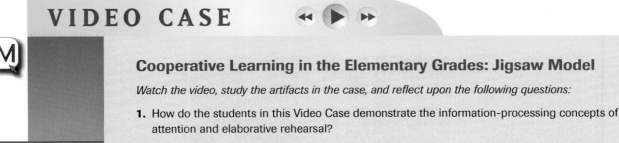

# VIDEO CASE

## Cooperative Learning in the Elementary Grades: Jigsaw Model

*Watch the video, study the artifacts in the case, and reflect upon the following questions:*

1. How do the students in this Video Case demonstrate the information-processing concepts of attention and elaborative rehearsal?

2. What are some ways that students in this Video Case demonstrate how their prior knowledge (information in long-term memory) influences their preparation in expert groups, their peer teaching to their home groups, and their assessments?

**Organization**    Quite often the information we want to learn is complex and inter-related. We can simplify the task by organizing multiple pieces of information into a few "clumps," or "chunks," of information, particularly when each part of a chunk helps us remember other parts (Cowan, 2005). The value of organizing material was illustrated by an experiment (Bower, Clark, Lesgold, & Winzenz, 1969) in which two groups of participants were asked to learn 112 words in four successive lists but under different conditions. One group was given each of the four lists for four trials in the hierarchical or "blocked" arrangement displayed in Figure 8.2. The other group was given the same lists and the same hierarchical tree arrangement, but the words from each list were randomly arranged over the four levels of the hierarchy.

As you can see, through the first three trials, the first group recalled more than twice as many words as the second and achieved perfect recall scores for the last two trials.

**Figure 8.2** Hierarchical Arrangement of Words Produces Superior Recall

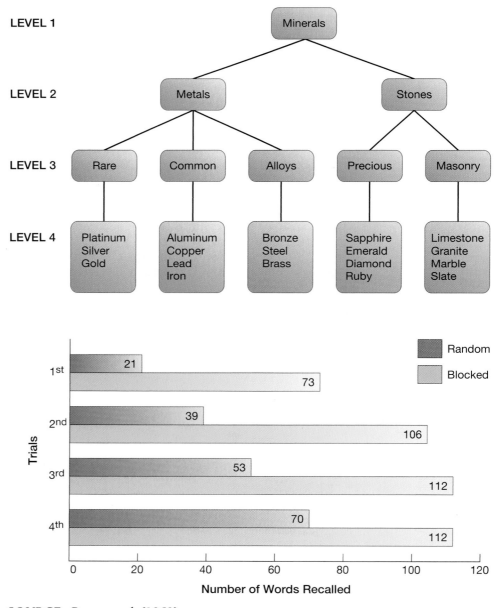

SOURCE:  Bower et al. (1969)

Organizing material reduces number of chunks, provides recall cues

The organized material was much easier to learn not only because there were fewer chunks to memorize but also because each item in a group served as a cue for the other items. When you decide to store pertinent material from this chapter in your long-term memory in preparation for an exam, you will find the job much easier if you organize what you are studying. To learn the various parts of the information-processing model under discussion, for instance, you might group the ideas being described under the various headings used in this chapter.

**Meaningfulness**   The meaningfulness of new information that one is about to learn has been characterized as "potentially the most powerful variable for explaining the learning of complex verbal discourse" (Johnson, 1975, pp. 425–426). According to David Ausubel (Ausubel, Novak, & Hanesian, 1978), **meaningful learning** occurs when a learner encounters clear, logically organized material and consciously tries to relate the new material to ideas and experiences stored in long-term memory. To understand learning theory principles, for example, you might imagine yourself using them to teach a lesson to a group of students. Or you might modify a previously constructed flowchart on the basis of new information. The basic idea behind meaningful learning is that the learner actively attempts to associate new ideas to existing ones (Driscoll, 2005). As another example, many of the "Pause and Reflect" questions in this book are designed to foster meaningful encoding by getting you to relate text information to relevant prior experience.

Meaningful learning occurs when organized material is associated with stored knowledge

Lev Vygotsky, the Russian psychologist we mentioned in Chapter 3 on stage theories of development, emphasized the role of teachers, parents, siblings, and other kinds of expert tutors in meaningful learning. Vygotsky pointed out that some of what we learn about the world in which we live comes from direct, unfiltered contact with stimuli. Touch a hot stove, and you get burned. Insult or ridicule a friend, and you are likely to have one fewer friend at the end of the day. The limitation of this kind of learning, which Vygotsky called *direct* learning, is that one is likely to miss the general lesson or principle that underlies the event. Consequently, Vygotsky favored *mediated* learning. A mediator is an individual, usually older, more knowledgeable, and skilled, who selects stimuli to attend to, directs attention to certain aspects of the chosen stimulus, and explains why things are the way they are and why things are done in a certain way. Thus parents explain to their children why it is not acceptable to hit or tease playmates, and teachers explain to students why it is necessary for them to learn how to use the concepts and rules of English grammar, plane geometry, and the like (Kozulin & Presseisen, 1995).

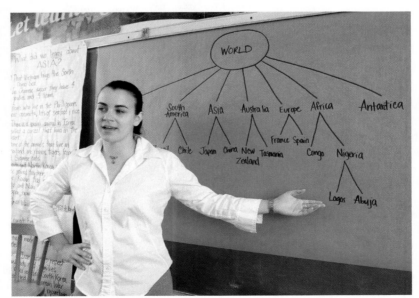

*To help students encode information, teach them how to group objects and ideas according to some shared feature.*

From a Vygotskian perspective, the main goal of instruction is to provide learners with the psychological tools they will need to engage in *self*-mediation. If individuals are to function effectively once they leave school, they have to learn how to look beyond the immediate situation and see how they can use new knowledge and skills in future situations. Psychologists refer to this process as transfer of learning; we will discuss it at length in Chapter 9 on constructivism and problem solving.

This brief description of meaningfulness and its role in learning contains a strong implication for teaching in culturally diverse classrooms. You can foster meaningful learning for students from other cultures by pointing out similarities between ideas presented in class and students' culture-specific knowledge. For example, you might point out that September 16 has the same significance to people of Mexican origin as July 4 has to U.S. citizens because the former date commemorates Mexico's revolution against and independence from Spain.

**Visual Imagery Encoding**    Generating mental images of objects, ideas, and actions is a particularly powerful form of elaborative encoding. Like pictures, images can be said to be worth a thousand words because they contain a wealth of information in a compact, organized, and meaningful format. Consider Benjamin Banneker, who has been called the first Black intellectual. Banneker was a self-taught mathematician, astronomer, and surveyor (Cothran, 2006). He predicted a solar eclipse in 1789, published tides tables, and was appointed by President George Washington to the commission that established the boundaries of Washington, D.C. His accomplishments suggest that mental imagery was critical to his thinking. Other notable individuals, such as Albert Einstein (physics), Michael Faraday (physics), James D. Watson (biochemistry), and Joan Didion (literature), have described how mental imagery played a significant role in their thinking and problem-solving efforts (Shepard, 1978).

Research has consistently shown that directing students to generate visual images as they read lists of words or sentences, several paragraphs of text, or lengthy text passages produces higher levels of comprehension and recall as compared with students who are not so instructed. Also, text passages that contain many concrete words and phrases are more easily understood and more accurately recalled than passages that contain more abstract than concrete ideas (Clark & Paivio, 1991). In one study (Sadoski, Goetz, & Rodriguez, 2000), the beneficial effect of concreteness was

*According to Russian psychologist Lev Vygotsky, meaningful learning is most likely to occur when a more knowledgeable and skilled individual explains to a less knowledgeable individual why things are the way they are, as when one points out the reasons behind various rules and procedures, the causes of different events, and the motives for people's behaviors.*

obtained for several passage types (such as expository text, persuasive text, stories, and narratives). The more concrete the passage was, the more it was rated comprehensible by students, and students who read concrete passages recalled 1.7 times as much information as students who read abstract passages. As we will see in Chapter 10, concreteness and visual imagery are an integral part of several effective study skills.

The theory that these findings support is Allan Paivio's dual coding theory (Clark & Paivio, 1991; Reed, 2006; Vekiri, 2002). According to the **dual coding theory,** concrete material (such as pictures of familiar objects) and concrete words (such as *horse, bottle, water*) are remembered better than abstract words (such as *deduction, justice, theory*) because the former can be encoded in two ways—as images and as verbal labels—whereas abstract words are encoded only verbally. This makes retrieval easier because a twice-coded item provides more potential retrieval cues than information that exists in only one form.

Before you go on to read about long-term memory, look at Table 8.1, which summarizes some important points about the control processes of short-term memory and the implications for teachers. Later in the chapter, our Suggestions for Teaching in Your Classroom sections will help you put these ideas into practice.

## Long-Term Memory

Long-term memory: permanent storehouse of unlimited capacity

We have already referred in a general way to the third memory store, **long-term memory (LTM),** which is perhaps the most interesting of all. On the basis of neurological, experimental, and clinical evidence, most cognitive psychologists believe that the storage capacity of LTM is unlimited and that it contains a permanent record of everything an individual has learned, although some doubt exists about the latter point (see, for example, Schunk, 2004).

The neurological evidence comes from the work of Wilder Penfield (1969), a Canadian neurosurgeon who operated on more than one thousand patients who experienced epileptic seizures. To determine the source of the seizures, Penfield electrically stimulated various parts of the brain's surface. During this procedure,

| **Table 8.1** | Implications for Instruction: How Findings About the Control Processes of Short-Term Memory Should Influence Your Teaching |
|---|---|
| **Research Finding** | **Implications** |
| *Recognition* involves relating a stimulus to information from long-term memory. | Compared with older students, elementary school students have less knowledge stored in long-term memory, and therefore they need structured learning tasks in which one step leads clearly to the next. |
| *Attention* is influenced by previous experience stored in long-term memory—we notice what we expect to be important. | Teachers should develop techniques for capturing students' attention and convincing them that the information being presented will be important to them. |
| *Rehearsal* prevents the quick disappearance of information from short-term memory. Most children do not begin to rehearse on their own until about age seven. | All children, especially younger ones, can benefit from being taught rehearsal techniques. |
| *Organization* of material into chunks makes it much easier to remember. | Teachers can aid students by presenting material in logical chunks and by showing students how to organize information on their own. |
| *Meaningful learning* occurs when the learner relates new information to prior ideas and experiences. | Teachers should mediate learning by relating new information to students' cultural knowledge and by helping students to learn techniques of self-mediation. |
| *Visual imagery* is easier to recall than abstractions. | Teachers should help students develop learning skills that incorporate visual imagery and other memory-aiding techniques. |

many patients reported vivid images of long-dormant events from their past. It was as if a neurological videotape had been turned on.

The experimental evidence, although less dramatic, is just as interesting, and it too has its origins in the early days of information-processing theory. In a typical memory study (such as Tulving & Pearlstone, 1966), participants receive a list of nouns to learn. After giving participants ample opportunity to recall as many of the words as possible, researchers provide retrieval cues—for instance, category labels such as "clothing," "food," or "animals." In many cases cued participants quickly recall additional items. Experiments on how well people recognize previously seen pictures have produced some startling findings. Thirty-six hours after viewing over 2,500 pictures, a group of college students correctly identified an average of about 2,250, or 90 percent (Standing, Conezio, & Haber, 1970). In fact, it has been estimated that if 1 million pictures could be shown, recognition memory would still be 90 percent or better (Standing, 1973). Finally, psychiatrists and psychotherapists have reported many case histories of individuals who have been helped to recall seemingly forgotten events through hypnosis and other techniques (Erdelyi & Goldberg, 1979).

**How Information Is Organized in Long-Term Memory**    As you have seen, long-term memory plays an influential role throughout the information-processing system. The interests, attitudes, skills, and knowledge of the world that reside there influence what we perceive, how we interpret our perceptions, and whether we process information for short-term or long-term storage. In most instances, retrieval of information from long-term memory is extremely rapid and accurate, like finding a book in a well-run library. Accordingly, we can conclude that information in long-term memory must be organized. The nature of this organization is a key area in the study of memory. The insights it provides help to illuminate the encoding and retrieval processes associated with long-term memory.

Many cognitive psychologists believe that our store of knowledge in long-term memory is organized in terms of **schemata** (which is plural for *schema* and is related in meaning to Jean Piaget's *scheme*). A schema is typically defined as an abstract structure of information. It is abstract because it summarizes information about many different cases or examples of something, and it is structured because it represents how its own informational components are interrelated. Schemata give us expectations about objects and events (dogs bark, birds fly, students listen to their

Information in long-term memory organized as schemata

*Because people interpret new information and experiences on the basis of existing memory schemes, and because no two people's schemes are identical, each person is likely to represent the same idea or experience in a unique fashion.*

teachers and study industriously). When our schemata are well formed and a specific event is consistent with our expectation, comprehension occurs. When schemata are poorly structured or absent, learning is slow and uncertain (Bruning, Schraw, Norby, & Ronning, 2004; Moreno, 2006; Schunk, 2004). The following example should make this notion of schemata more understandable.

For almost everyone raised in the United States, the word *classroom* typically calls to mind a scene that includes certain people (teacher, students), objects (desks, chalkboard, books, pencils), rules (attend to the teacher's instructions, stay in the classroom unless given permission to leave), and events (reading, listening, writing, talking, drawing). This is a generalized representation, and some classrooms may contain fewer or more of these characteristics. However, as long as students and teachers share the same basic classroom schema, each will generally know what to expect and how to behave in any classroom. It is when people do not possess an appropriate schema that comprehension, memory, and behavior problems arise.

This notion was first investigated during the early 1930s by Sir Frederick Bartlett (1932), an English psychologist. In one experiment, Bartlett had participants read and recall a brief story, titled "The War of the Ghosts," that was based on North American Indian folklore. Because Bartlett's participants had little knowledge of American Indian culture, they had difficulty accurately recalling the story; they omitted certain details and distorted others. The distortions were particularly interesting because they reflected an attempt to interpret the story in terms of the logic and beliefs of Western culture. Similar studies, conducted more recently with other kinds of reading materials, have reported similar results (Derry, 1996). The conclusion that Bartlett and other researchers have drawn is that remembering is not simply a matter of retrieving a true-to-life record of information. People often remember their *interpretations* or *constructions* of something read, seen, or heard (Lampinen & Odegard, 2006). In addition, when they experience crucial gaps in memory, they tend to fill in these blanks with logical reconstructions of what they think must have been. People then report these reconstructions as memories of actual events (Derry, 1996).

These experiments vividly demonstrate the interactive nature of memory. What we know influences what we perceive and how we interpret and store those perceptions. And because our memories of specific events or experiences are assembled, constructed, and sometimes reassembled by the brain over time, accurate and complete recall of information we once stored is not always possible. As a teacher, then, you should pay deliberate attention to how your students use their background knowledge, helping them to use it as accurately and completely as possible to process new information.

**How Well Do We Remember What We Learn in School?** Conventional wisdom (which is often wrong, by the way) holds that much of the information that we learn in school is forgotten soon after a unit of instruction or course has ended. You may have felt the same way yourself on more than one occasion. But is this belief true? To

*HM TeacherPrepSPACE*

Interested in finding out about your own memory? Go to the textbook's student website.

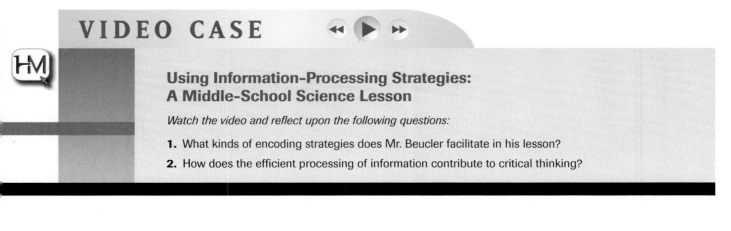

# VIDEO CASE ◄◄ ▶ ►►

## Using Information-Processing Strategies: A Middle-School Science Lesson

*Watch the video and reflect upon the following questions:*

**1.** What kinds of encoding strategies does Mr. Beucler facilitate in his lesson?

**2.** How does the efficient processing of information contribute to critical thinking?

### Students Are Learners, Not Just Performers

Visit a school in the last two months of winter and you will see teachers preparing their students to perform as well as they possibly can on the state exams in April and May. Ask teachers why they are so focused on the state exams, and they will tell you that the administration has made student performance on the state exams a top priority. Ask the administrators why student performance on the state exams deserves so much time and energy, and they will tell you that poor student performance on the exams can decrease property values in the community, can mean the replacement—at considerable expense—of an entire curriculum, can even cost teachers and administrators their jobs. As you will see in Chapter 14, "Understanding Standardized Assessment," a lot is riding on students' performance on the state exams. And so teachers guide students through the material they expect to be on the tests; teachers go over and over it in an effort to ensure that every student gets every possible test item correct. The teachers lead the students through seemingly endless drill and practice. (Some teachers—and some students—

call it "drill and kill.") The teachers work very hard, the students work very hard, and the administrators feel the pressure and keep the pressure on.

Days and weeks of drill and practice, focused on rote learning that serves only to make students perform better on a test, go against what research tells us about effective learning. By focusing on discrete information or skills, students have few opportunities to draw on their prior knowledge, to learn in authentic settings, to explore and investigate in order to understand new information in meaningful contexts. Research shows us that prior knowledge is critical for student learning. Drilling students to perform can kill learning. We believe educational professionals must be held accountable, but they should be held accountable for student learning, not just test performance. If we are content simply to focus on performance, then let's continue to devote each winter to test preparation. But if we value our students as learners instead of performers, then the time has come to end the winter of our discontent. And we should do it now.

#### HM TeacherPrepSPACE

Does the authors' position accord with your own experience? That is, did you feel as if you were learning material solely for the purpose of answering questions correctly on a state-mandated test and not for any future meaningful use? If so, how can you prepare your students for these exams and still make the learning experience relevant to their lives? Explore this issue further at the Take a Stand! section of the textbook's student website.

---

answer this question, George Semb and John Ellis (1994) reviewed the results of fifty-six research articles published between 1930 and 1993. Their main findings are very consistent with the information-processing principles that you have read about and should at least partially reassure you that you haven't been wasting your time all these years:

- More than seven out of ten studies reported less than a 20 percent loss of what was learned when measured with a recognition task. Half of the studies reported less than a 20 percent loss of what was learned when measured with free recall.
- Subject matter that had a higher-than-average level of unfamiliar facts and associations (such as zoology, anatomy, and medical terminology) and for which students would have little relevant prior knowledge (such as electricity, mechanics, and linguistics) was associated with increased levels of forgetting.
- Most of the forgetting of information occurred within four weeks after the end of a unit of instruction. Additional declines in recall occurred more slowly.
- Less forgetting occurred among students who learned the material to a high level either by being required to achieve a high score on an exam before moving on to the next unit of instruction, by having to teach it to less knowledgeable students, or by taking advanced courses.
- Less forgetting occurred in classes in which students were more actively involved in learning (as in a geography field trip on which students had to observe, sketch, record, and answer questions).

Students remember much of what they learn in school, especially if mastery and active learning are emphasized

The instructional implications that flow from these findings include an emphasis on mastery learning, peer tutoring, frequent testing with corrective feedback, and forms of instruction that actively involve students in learning. In addition, the Suggestions for Teaching in Your Classroom that begin on page 226 point out several ways in which you can help your students improve their information processing.

## METACOGNITION

The discussion up to this point has focused on a general explanation of how people attend to, encode, store, and retrieve information. In a word, we have described some of the major aspects of thinking. During the past few decades, researchers have inquired into how much knowledge individuals have about their own thought processes and what significance this knowledge has for learning. The term that was coined to refer to how much we know of our own thought processes is *metacognition*. As we will see, it plays a very important role in learning.

## The Nature and Importance of Metacognition

The notion of metacognition was proposed by developmental psychologist John Flavell (1976) to explain why children of different ages deal with learning tasks in different ways. For example, when seven-year-olds are taught how to remember pairs of nouns using both a less effective technique (simply repeating the words) and a more effective technique (imagining the members of each pair doing something together), most of these children will use the less effective technique when given a new set of pairs to learn. Most ten-year-olds, however, will opt to use the more effective method (Kail, 1990). The explanation for this finding is that the seven-year-old has not had enough learning experiences to recognize that some problem-solving methods are better than others. To the younger child, one means is as good as another. This lack of metacognitive knowledge makes true strategic learning impossible for young children.

One way to grasp the essence of metacognition is to contrast it with cognition. The term *cognition* is used to describe the ways in which information is processed—that is, the ways it is attended to, recognized, encoded, stored in memory for various lengths of time, retrieved from storage, and used for one purpose or another. **Metacognition** refers to our knowledge about those operations and how they might best be used to achieve a learning goal. As Flavell put it:

> I am engaging in metacognition . . . if I notice that I am having more trouble learning A than B; if it strikes me that I should double-check C before accepting it as a fact; if it occurs to me that I had better scrutinize each and every alternative in any multiple-choice type task situation before deciding which is the best one; if I become aware that I am not sure what the experimenter really wants me to do; if I sense that I had better make a note of D because I may forget it; if I think to ask someone about E to see if I have it right. Such examples could be multiplied endlessly. (1976, p. 232)

Metacognition: our own knowledge of how we think

*Metacognition refers to the knowledge we have about how we learn. It is a key component of our ability to regulate our learning processes.*

# Suggestions for Teaching in Your Classroom

## Helping Your Students Become Efficient Information Processors

**1** **Develop and use a variety of techniques to attract and hold attention, and give your students opportunities to practice and refine their skills in maintaining attention.**

### a. Be aware of what will capture your students' attention.

The ability to capture your students' attention is affected by characteristics of the information itself and the learners' related past experiences. Learners are more likely to attend to things they expect to find interesting or meaningful. It is also true that human beings are sensitive to abrupt, sudden changes in their environment. Thus anything that stands out, breaks a rhythm, or is unpredictable is almost certain to command students' attention.

**EXAMPLES**

- Print key words or ideas in extra-large letters on the board.
- Use colored chalk to emphasize important points written on the board.
- When you come to a particularly important part of a lesson, say, "Now really concentrate on this. It's especially important." Then present the idea with intensity and emphasis.
- Start off a lesson with unexpected remarks, such as, "Imagine that you have just inherited a million dollars and . . . ."

### b. To maintain attention, emphasize the possible utility of learning new ideas.

Although it is possible to overdo attempts at making the curriculum relevant, it never hurts to think of possible ways of relating school learning to the present and future lives of students. When students realize that the basic purpose of school is to help them adapt to their environment, they are more likely to pay close attention to what you are trying to do.

**EXAMPLE**

- Teach basic skills—such as arithmetic computation, arithmetic reasoning, spelling, writing, and reading—as part of class projects that relate to students' natural interests (for example, keeping records of money for newspaper deliveries; measuring rainfall, temperature, and wind speed; writing letters to local television stations to express opinions on or request information about television shows).

### c. Teach students how to increase their span of attention.

Remember that paying attention is a skill that many students have not had an opportunity to refine. Give your students plenty of opportunities to practice and improve their ability to maintain attention.

**EXAMPLES**

- Institute games that depend on maintaining attention, such as playing Simon Says, keeping track of an object hidden under one of several boxes (the old shell game), or determining whether two pictures are identical or different. At first, positively reinforce students for all correct responses. Then reinforce only for improvements in performance. Remind students that their success is a direct result of how well they pay attention.

---

**JOURNAL ENTRY**
Techniques for Maintaining Attention

Unpredictable changes in environment usually command attention

---

**JOURNAL ENTRY**
Techniques for Capturing Attention

---

Attention span can be increased with practice

---

**JOURNAL ENTRY**
Techniques for Increasing Attention Span

- Read a short magazine or newspaper story and ask students to report who, what, where, when, and why.

**2  Point out and encourage students to recognize that certain bits of information are important and can be related to what they already know.**

Attention is one control process for the sensory register; the other is recognition. Sometimes the two processes can be used together to induce students to focus on important parts of material to be learned. Sometimes you can urge your students to recognize key features or familiar relationships on their own.

**EXAMPLES**

- Say "This math problem is very similar to one you solved last week. Does anyone recognize something familiar about this problem?"
- Say "In this chapter, the same basic point is made in several different ways. As you read, try to recognize and write down as many variations on that basic theme as you can."
- Give students opportunities to express ideas in their own words and relate new knowledge to previous learning.
- Have students practice grouping numbers, letters, or classroom items according to some shared feature, such as odd numbers, multiples of five, letters with circles, or things made of wood.

**3  Use appropriate rehearsal techniques, including an emphasis on meaning and chunking.**

**JOURNAL ENTRY**
Ways to Use Chunking to
Facilitate Learning

The power of chunking information into meaningful units was demonstrated in a study conducted with a single college student of average memory ability and intelligence (Ericsson, Chase, & Faloon, 1980). Over twenty months, he was able to improve his memory for digits from seven to almost eighty. Being a track and field buff, he categorized three- and four-digit groups as running times for imaginary races. Thus 3,492 became "3 minutes and 49.2 seconds, near world record time." Number groups that could not be encoded as running times were encoded as ages. These two chunking techniques accounted for almost 90 percent of his associations.

The main purpose of chunking is to enhance learning by breaking tasks into small, easy-to-manage pieces. To a large degree, students who are ten and older can learn to do this for themselves if you show them how chunking works. In addition, you can help by not requiring students to learn more than they can reasonably handle at one time. If you have a list of fifty spelling words to be learned, it is far better to present ten words a day, five days in a row, during short study periods than to give all fifty at once. This method of presentation is called **distributed practice.** A description of the positive effect of distributed practice on classroom learning and an explanation of why educators do not make greater use of it have been offered by Frank Dempster (1988).

**Distributed practice: short study periods at frequent intervals**

In distributed practice, it is usually necessary to divide the material into small parts, which seems to be the best way for students to learn and retain unrelated material (for example, spelling words). This approach makes use of the **serial position effect,** which is people's tendency to learn and remember the words at the beginning and end of a long list more easily than those in the middle. By using short lists, you in effect eliminate the hard-to-memorize middle ground.

**Serial position effect: tendency to remember items at beginning and end of a long list**

Distributed practice may not be desirable for all learning tasks. If you ask students to learn roles in a play, short rehearsals might not be effective because students may have a difficult time grasping the entire plot. If you allow enough rehearsal time to run through a whole act, your students will be able to relate one speech to another and comprehend the overall structure of the play. When students learn by way of a few rather long study periods, spaced infrequently, psychologists call it **massed practice.**

You might also tell your students about the relative merits of distributed versus massed practice. Robert Bjork (1979) has pointed out that most students not only are unaware of the benefits of distributed study periods but also go to considerable lengths to block or mass the study time devoted to a particular subject, even when that tactic is a hindrance rather than a help.

### 4  Organize what you ask your students to learn, and urge older students to organize material on their own.

At least some items in most sets of information that you ask your students to learn will be related to other items, and you will find it desirable to call attention to interrelationships. The Bower et al. (1969) experiment described earlier in which one group of students was given a randomly arranged set of items to learn and another group was presented the same items in logically ordered groups illustrates the value of organization. By placing related items in groups, you reduce the number of chunks to be learned and also make it possible for students to benefit from cues supplied by the interrelationships between items in any given set. And by placing items in logical order, you help students grasp how information at the beginning of a chapter or lesson makes it easier to learn information that is presented later.

**JOURNAL ENTRY**
Organizing Information into
Related Categories

### EXAMPLES

- If students are to learn how to identify trees, birds, rocks, or the equivalent, group items that are related (for example, deciduous trees and evergreen trees). Call attention to distinctive features and organizational schemes that have been developed.

- Print an outline of a chapter on the board, or give students a duplicated outline, and have them record notes under the various headings. Whenever you give a lecture or demonstration, print an outline on the board. Call attention to the sequence of topics, and demonstrate how various points emerge from or are related to other points.

### 5  Make what students learn more meaningful by presenting information in concrete, visual terms.

Concrete analogies can make abstract information meaningful

To avoid blank stares and puzzled expressions from students when you explain an idea in abstract terms, try using representations that can more easily be visualized. Concrete analogies, for example, offer one effective way to add meaning to material. Consider someone who has no knowledge of basic physics but is trying to understand a passage about the flow of electricity through metal. For this person, statements about crystalline lattice arrays, free-floating electrons, and the effects of impurities will mean very little. However, such abstract ideas can be explained in more familiar terms. You might compare the molecular structure of a metal bar to a Tinker Toy arrangement, for example, or liken the effect of impurities to placing a book in the middle of a row of falling dominoes. Such analogies increase recall and comprehension (Royer & Cable, 1975, 1976).

You should also consider using what are called graphical displays. These are visual-symbolic spatial representations of objects, concepts, and their relationships. Examples of graphical displays include diagrams, matrices, graphs, concepts maps, and charts.

**JOURNAL ENTRY**
Ways to Present Information
Concretely

According to Allan Paivio's dual coding theory, the use of graphical displays leads to higher levels of learning because they increase the concreteness of information, thereby allowing it to be encoded in memory in both a visual and a language format. Evidence from both cognitive and neuroscience research supports the idea that information can be stored in long-term memory in both visual and linguistic forms. Another theory, called the visual argument hypothesis, holds that graphical representations aid learning because the spatial arrangement of the items that make up the display allows for a visual form of chunking, thereby decreasing the demands on working memory. Support for the visual argument hypothesis comes from research that shows that students who are given graphic organizers are better able to integrate information and draw inferences about relationships than are students who are given plain text (Vekiri, 2002).

**EXAMPLES**

- When you explain or demonstrate, express complex and abstract ideas in several different ways. Be sure to provide plenty of examples.
- Use illustrations, diagrams, and concept maps.
- Make sure the type of visual display used is consistent with the goal of a lesson. For example, when the goal is to understand a cause-and-effect relationship, diagrams that show relationships among objects or concepts should be used, but when the goal is to learn about changes over time, as in plant or animal growth, animation would be a better choice than a static display.

Metacognition is obviously a very broad concept. It covers everything an individual can know that relates to how information is processed. To get a better grasp of this concept, you may want to use the three-part classification scheme that Flavell (1987) proposed:

- *Knowledge-of-person variables:* for example, knowing that you are good at learning verbal material but poor at learning mathematical material, or knowing that information not rehearsed or encoded is quickly forgotten.
- *Knowledge-of-task variables:* for instance, knowing that passages with long sentences and unfamiliar words are usually harder to understand than passages that are more simply written.
- *Knowledge-of-strategy variables:* for example, knowing that one should skim through a text passage before reading it to determine its length and difficulty level.

Lev Vygotsky believed that children acquire metacognitive knowledge and skills most effectively through direct instruction, imitation, and social collaboration in the following way:

1. Children are told by more experienced and knowledgeable individuals what is true and what is false, what is right and what is wrong, how various things should and should not be done, and why. ("Jason, don't touch that stove. It's hot and will give you a painful burn if you touch it.")
2. As opportunities arise, children use this knowledge to regulate their own behavior (saying out loud, "Hot stove. Don't touch.") as well as the behavior of others. If you have ever seen young children play "house" or "school" and faithfully mimic the dictates of their parents or teacher, then you have seen this process at work.
3. Children regulate their own behavior through the use of inner speech. ("Hot stove. Don't touch" is said to oneself, not said aloud.)

Vygotsky's analysis strongly suggests that providing children with opportunities to regulate their own and others' behavior, as in peer tutoring, is an excellent way to help them increase their metacognitive knowledge and skills and to improve the quality of their learning. In Chapter 10, we will describe one such program, reciprocal teaching. Programs such as reciprocal teaching have produced high levels of learning, motivation, and transfer (Karpov & Haywood, 1998; Kim, Baylor, & PALS Group, 2006).

Recent research indicates significant differences in what younger and older children know about metacognition. What follows is a discussion of some of these differences.

## Age Trends in Metacognition

Two reviews of research on metacognition (Duell, 1986; Kail, 1990) examined how students of different ages use memorization techniques and how well they understand what they are doing. Following are some of the key conclusions of the reviews:

- In terms of diagnosing task difficulty, most six-year-olds know that more familiar items are easier to remember than less familiar items and that a small set of items is easier to recall than a large set of items. What six-year-olds do not yet realize is that the amount of information they can recall immediately after they study it is limited.

- Similar findings have been obtained for reading tasks. Most second graders know that interest, familiarity, and story length influence comprehension and recall. However, they are relatively unaware of the effect of how ideas are sequenced, the introductory and summary qualities of first and last paragraphs, and the relationship between reading goals and tactics. Sixth graders, by contrast, are much more aware of the effects of these variables on comprehension and recall.

- Most young children know very little about the role their own capabilities play in learning. For example, not until about nine years of age do most children realize that their recall right after they study something is limited. Consequently, children through the third grade usually overestimate how much they can store in and retrieve from short-term memory.

- There are clear developmental differences in how well students understand the need to tailor learning tactics to task demands. For example, four- and six-year-old children in one study cited by Robert Kail (1990) did not alter how much time they spent studying a set of pictures when they were told that a recognition test would follow either three minutes later, one day later, or one week later. Eight-year-olds did use that information to allocate less or more study time to the task.

- In terms of monitoring the progress of learning, most children younger than seven or eight are not very proficient at determining when they know something well enough to pass a memory test. Also, most first graders typically don't know what they don't know. When given multiple opportunities to study and recall a lengthy set of pictures, six-year-olds chose to study pictures they had previously seen and recalled, as well as ones they hadn't. Third graders, by contrast, focused on previously unseen pictures.

Insight into one's learning processes improves with age

The general conclusion that emerges from these findings is that the youngest school-age children have only limited knowledge of how their cognitive processes work and when to use them. Consequently, primary grade children do not systematically analyze learning tasks, formulate plans for learning, use appropriate techniques of enhancing memory and comprehension, or monitor their progress because they do not (some would say cannot) understand the benefits of doing these things. But as children develop and gain more experience with increasingly complex academic tasks, they experience growth in executive functions, or control processes (see Figure 8.1). Through such growth, they acquire a greater awareness of metacognitive knowledge and its relationship to classroom learning (H. L. Swanson, 2006). In this process, teachers can assist their students and guide them toward maximum use of their metacognitive knowledge.

With some effort and planning, a teacher can make logically organized and relevant lessons. However, this is only half the battle, because students must then attend to the information, encode it into long-term memory, and retrieve it when needed. Helping students to use the attention, encoding, and retrieval processes discussed in the previous sections is not always easy. The sad fact is that most children and adults are inefficient learners (Bond, Miller, & Kennon, 1987; Brown, Campione, & Day, 1981; Covington, 1985; Peverly, Brobst, Graham, & Shaw, 2003; Selmes, 1987; Winne & Jamieson-Noel, 2002, 2003). Their attempts at encoding rarely go beyond rote rehearsal (for example, rereading a textbook chapter), simple organizational schemes (outlining), and various cueing devices (underlining or highlighting), and they have a poor sense of how well prepared they are to take a test.

In Chapter 10, we address learning strategies and tactics that can help overcome information-processing difficulties. Before considering how we can help students become strategic learners, we suggest ways in which you can encourage your students to develop their metacognitive skills.

Our major suggestion is that you encourage your students to develop their metacognitive skills and knowledge by thinking about the various conditions that affect how they learn and remember. The very youngest students (through third grade) should be told periodically that such cognitive behaviors as describing, recalling, guessing, and understanding mean different things, produce different results, and vary in how well they fit a task's demands. For older elementary school and middle school students, explain the learning process, and focus on the circumstances in which different learning tactics are likely to be useful. Then have students keep a diary or log in which they note when they use learning tactics, which ones, and with what success. Look for cases in which good performance corresponds to frequent reported use of tactics and positively reinforce those individuals. Encourage greater use of tactics among students whose performance and reported use of them are below average.

Although this same technique can be used with high school and college students, they should also be made aware of the other elements that make up strategic learning. Discuss the meaning of and necessity for analyzing a learning task, developing a learning plan, using appropriate tactics, monitoring the effectiveness of the plan, and implementing whatever corrective measures might be called for.

Next we examine several ways in which you can use computer-based technology to improve your students' information-processing skills for a variety of learning tasks.

# TECHNOLOGY AS AN INFORMATION-PROCESSING TOOL

Although computer-based technology may have had its roots in behavioral learning theory, as you saw in the chapter on that subject, current technology is more likely to reflect an information-processing perspective. The programs and devices described in this section influence how we access, filter, represent, and evaluate knowledge. As the limitations of human memory and the difficulty of creating learning strategies have been clarified, computer-based technology has been called on to help overcome these constraints and reduce the cognitive processing burden of complex tasks. For instance, technology might help someone better grasp an idea for a musical composition, see the structure of her writing plans, or watch chemical molecules react.

In this section, we will examine technological tools that help students process and represent information, so that they can acquire important knowledge and skills from different subject areas, and provide multiple representations of knowledge to regulate their own thinking. We consider technology tools for writing, reading, science and math, and art and music, as well as multimedia and hypermedia tools.

## Technology Tools for Writing

Because of its flexibility, technology can be used in a variety of ways to make writing less threatening and to increase both the quantity and quality of students' writing. In classrooms where computers are networked, teachers can use a technique called Electronic Read Around. Sitting at separate computers, each student writes on a topic the teacher gives. Each student then clicks on an icon representing another student's computer, reads what that student wrote, and provides feedback in a different font at the end of the document. This process is repeated until each student has read and commented on every other student's text. Students then use the comments to revise and edit their own pieces (Stràssman & D'Amore, 2002).

One of the most important parts of the writing process is the prewriting phase. This is the point at which authors generate, evaluate, and organize their ideas. For

*HM TeacherPrepSPACE*

For quick links to websites mentioned here, go to the textbook's student website.

novice writers, which most students are, the prospect of having to do this entirely on one's own can be quite anxiety provoking. For many students it is comforting to have a friend available as a sounding board. This can be easily accomplished through the use of online synchronous chats (basically, instant messaging). A student can share ideas in real time with one or more classmates on the topic they are writing about. Not only does this give students additional opportunities to write, but the chat writing doesn't have to follow the same grammatical conventions as formal writing assignments (Strassman & D'Amore, 2002).

The World Wide Web is yet another technology resource teachers can use to make writing more attractive to students. One approach that shows promise is the use of weblogs (commonly referred to as blogs). Weblogs can take the form of a personal journal in which the writer makes periodic entries for others to read, or they can be like bulletin boards in which the online audience responds both to what the author has written and to the comments of others (Weiler, 2003). To learn more about weblogs and how to start one, visit the Weblogs in Education site (**www.schoolblogs.com**). Two other websites that provide opportunities for collaborative writing projects are Kidforum (**www.kidlink.org/KIDFORUM/collaborative_writing.htm**) and Through Our Eyes (**www.kidlink.org/KIDPROJ**).

## Technology Tools for Reading

As with writing, the use of electronic support systems to increase students' reading skills has increased around the world (Lai, Chang, & Ye, 2006 Llabo, 2002). In comparison with primary grade students who read a print version of a story, students who listened to a story from a CD-ROM storybook significantly increased their sight word vocabulary, reading level, and ability to retell the story accurately and completely (Matthew, 1996; McKenna, Cowart, & Watkins, 1997). When third graders had to read a CD-ROM story themselves but were able to use such other features as clicking on words and illustrations to obtain pronunciations and definitions, their retelling scores did not differ from those of children who read a print version, but they did score significantly higher on comprehension questions (Doty, Popplewell, & Byers, 2001).

## Technology Tools for Science and Math

In mathematics and science, Marcia Linn (1992) and other prominent researchers have argued that students should spend less time manually calculating and plotting data and more time using technology to summarize and interpret data, look for trends, and predict relationships. To help teachers put this philosophy into practice, Linn and others created the Web-based Inquiry Science Environment (WISE) Project (**wise.berkeley.edu**). Based largely on constructivist learning principles and fifteen years of classroom research, the WISE website contains a variety of science projects that teachers can adapt to local curricula and to state and national standards. The overarching goal of the WISE learning environment is to help students make connections among science ideas rather than learn by rote isolated facts whose relevance is not understood and that are soon forgotten. For each project, students have to locate relevant information on the Web, record and organize their findings in an electronic notebook, and participate in online discussions to refine their procedures and conclusions. The Houses in the Desert project, for example, requires pairs of middle school students to design a desert house that will be comfortable to live in. Using resources available on the Web, students have to, among other things, analyze the suitability of various materials for walls, roofs, and windows and perform a heat-flow analysis. The WISE site also allows students to compare climate data in a desert with climate data from their own community (Linn & Slotta, 2000).

For mathematics and physics, the Calculator-Based Laboratory (CBL) from Texas Instruments provides "a data-collection system that uses probes, such as temperature, light, and voltage probes, to gather data into a graphing calculator" (Nicol,

1997, p. 86). The current version is the CBL 2. CBLs convert information from sensors and probes into data that can be understood and graphed by the calculator. Students taking a math class might use this tool to represent and manipulate quadratic equations in algebra, visualize statistics and other information in geometry classes, and better understand derivatives and inequalities in calculus (Engebretsen, 1997; O'Neal, 2001).

Math teachers can also use the Web to help students understand the connections among math topics and to other disciplines. For example, data from the website of the National Center for Health Statistics (**www.cdc.gov/nchs**) on the number of births in the United States for various time periods can be used to teach such concepts as absolute and relative yearly increases and decreases. These same data can also be used to analyze the relationship between birthrates and other societal trends, such as immigration patterns. Connections between oscillating functions in math and the tides, planetary movements, and average monthly temperatures can be made with data from the websites of the National Oceanic and Atmospheric Administration (**www.noaa.gov**) and the National Geophysical Data Center (**www.ngdc.noaa.gov**). These relationships can be made more concrete, and hence more meaningful, by using graphing calculators and spreadsheets to create graphic representations (Alagic & Palenz, 2006; Drier, Dawson, & Garofalo, 1999).

## Technology Tools for Art and Music

As you may be aware, computer tools are also being used in the fine and performing arts. Art education, for instance, benefits from electronic tools such as the draw and paint modules of AppleWorks and Microsoft Works that quickly erase or alter ideas. Students can use these tools to mimic the branching, spiraling, and exploding structures of nature (as seen, for example, in trees, vines, and flowers) (Lach et al., 2003), and they can create abstract patterns by repeating, changing the horizontal and vertical orientation, and changing the alignment of a basic pattern (Yoerg, 2002). With these tools, students can also draw objects in two-point perspective (Patterson, 2002) and create stylized portraits by using shadows, contour lines, stippling, and cross-hatching (Mathes, 2002).

For the music classroom, there are tools such as digital oscilloscopes that help students understand relationships between pitch and wavelength. In addition, CD technology can be used to present graphical representations of notes as they are played, sections of which can be saved and compared with other verses of the same song or with other songs, thereby helping students understand themes and patterns in music. Moreover, computer tools such as a musical instrument digital interface (MIDI) and formal instrumental music tuition (FIMT) allow students to compose at the keyboard, play a musical instrument and record it on a computer, and play one part of a multi-instrument piece while the program plays the other instruments (Peters, 2001; Reninger, 2000; Seddon & O'Neill, 2006). Students can explore concepts of pitch, duration, sound combination, repetition, and melody and engage in the process of musical thinking.

## Multimedia Tools

As mentioned in previous chapters, multimedia encyclopedias, databases, and libraries provide students with a wide variety of information resources. Multimedia tools offer multiple views (text, photographs, digitized video, animation, sound) on difficult concepts that can enrich student understanding of the topic. The use of multimedia tools is related to such information-processing concepts as meaningful learning, the dual coding of information, the use of visual imagery, and elaborative rehearsal (Mayer & Moreno, 2002). Like the mind, multimedia tools provide more than one way to retrieve or visit information; the richer or more dense the network or web of connections, the more likely one will comprehend the meaning.

## Hypermedia Tools

Hypermedia technology exists when multimedia information can be nonsequentially accessed, examined, and constructed by users, thereby enabling them to move from one information resource to another while controlling which options to take (Grabe & Grabe, 2007). There are clear advantages to hypermedia, such as the richness of the network of ideas, the compact storage of information, the rapid nonlinear access to information, the flexible use of information, and learner control over the system. Not surprisingly, it has been suggested that hypermedia tools radically alter the way people read, write, compute, and perhaps even think (Yang, 2001).

A hypermedia science program that students are likely to find attractive is Scholastic's *The Magic School Bus Explores in the Age of the Dinosaurs*. Designed for first through fifth graders, the program allows students to explore multiple locations in different parts of the world (for example, Argentina, Arizona, Colorado, Tanzania, Mongolia) and in three prehistoric time periods (Triassic, Jurassic, and Cretaceous). The program offers a dozen games and activities that involve dinosaurs. *Habitat Management and Monitoring* is one of three interactive science modules developed for high school students by the U.S. Environmental Protection Agency and Purdue University.

**Research on Multimedia and Hypermedia Technology**   One of the features of multimedia programs that supposedly contributes to their effectiveness as a learning tool is the use of animation. Drawing from the numerous studies that he and his associates have conducted on this topic, Richard Mayer (Mayer & Moreno, 2002) concludes that animation in multimedia programs produces gains in learning when on-screen text is presented next to the animation that it describes rather than somewhere else on the screen. Animation is even more effective when it is accompanied by simultaneous, conversational narration rather than by text. Extraneous words, sounds, and video should be excluded. You can put these findings to practical use by using them to evaluate multimedia programs your school district already owns or is considering buying.

Another attractive feature of many multimedia and hypermedia programs is interactivity. Interactive programs let children decide when to move to the next screen and the sequence in which they view information. Although many pro and con claims are made for interactivity, research evidence on its effects is just starting to appear.

In one study (Ricci & Beal, 2002), a group of first-grade children listened to and watched the story of the ugly duckling on a computer. They could move to the next page in the story at will by clicking on an arrow or produce additional animation and sound effects by clicking on any or all of the computer screen's "hotspots." They could, for example, click on a pond reed and see costumed ants march across the foreground accompanied by music. A second group of students passively watched and listened to the story as it appeared on the screen. A third group saw and heard on their own computer screens whatever was being produced by the children in the interactive group. A fourth group sat in front of a darkened computer screen and just listened to the story. Children in the first three groups scored higher than children in the fourth group on memory for story detail, comprehension, and ability to draw inferences. These results demonstrated that the interactivity feature had no detrimental effect on the story memory or inferential reasoning of children in group one despite the fact that some of them clicked on dozens of hotspots over the course of the story.

When students select topics and associated terms for a Web search and then evaluate the results, they are engaged in metacognition: making decisions about what information to read, thinking about knowledge interrelationships, and engaging in extensive self-questioning and note taking (Gunn & Hepburn, 2003; Hoffman, Wu, Krajcik, & Soloway, 2003; MaKinster, Beghetto, & Plucker, 2002). When they create databases of related ideas or link information in multiple formats, they are making decisions and elaboratively encoding the information. These are important metacognitive skills.

Multimedia and hypermedia programs that make appropriate use of animation and interactivity improve learning

*HM TeacherPrepSPACE*

*To review this chapter, see the ACE practice tests and PowerPoint slides at the student website.*

# 9 Constructivist Learning Theory, Problem Solving, and Transfer

**KEY POINTS**

*These key points will help you learn the important information in this chapter. To help you study, they also appear in the margins of the pages, next to the text where they are discussed.*

## Meaningful Learning Within a Constructivist Framework

- Constructivism: creating a personal interpretation of external ideas and experiences
- Bruner: discover how ideas relate to each other and to existing knowledge
- Construction of ideas strongly influenced by student's prior knowledge
- Construction of ideas aided by discussion and debate
- Cognitive constructivism emphasizes role of cognitive processes in meaningful learning
- Social constructivism emphasizes role of culture and social interaction in meaningful learning
- Constructivism aided by cognitive apprenticeship, realistic tasks, multiple perspectives
- Constructivist-oriented teaching encourages creating new views; uses scaffolding, realistic tasks, and class discussion

## The Nature of Problem Solving

- Well-structured problems: clearly stated, known solution procedures; known evaluation standards
- Ill-structured problems: vaguely stated, unclear solution procedures; vague evaluation standards
- Issues: ill-structured problems that arouse strong feelings
- Problem finding depends on curiosity, dissatisfaction with status quo
- Problem framing depends on knowledge of subject matter, familiarity with problem types
- Inert knowledge due to learning isolated facts under limited conditions
- Studying worked examples is an effective solution strategy

- Solve simpler version of problem first; then transfer process to harder problem
- Break complex problems into manageable parts
- Work backward when goal is clear but beginning state is not
- Backward fading: a procedure that helps students develop problem-solving capability by reasoning from the solution back to first steps
- Solve a similar problem and then apply the same method
- Create an external representation of the problem
- Evaluate solutions to well-structured problems by estimating or checking

## Suggestions for Teaching in Your Classroom

- Comprehension of subject matter critical to problem solving

## Transfer of Learning

- Early view of transfer based on degree of similarity between two tasks
- Positive transfer: previous learning makes later learning easier
- Negative transfer: previous learning interferes with later learning
- Specific transfer due to specific similarities between two tasks
- General transfer due to use of same cognitive strategies
- Near transfer: previously learned knowledge and skills used relatively soon on highly similar task
- Far transfer: previously learned knowledge and skills used much later on dissimilar tasks and under different conditions
- Low-road transfer: previously learned skill automatically applied to similar current task
- High-road transfer: formulate rule from one task and apply to related task
- Low-road and high-road transfer produced by varied practice at applying skills, rules, memory retrieval cues

## Technology Tools for Knowledge Construction and Problem Solving

- Technology tools are available to help students construct knowledge, become better problem solvers

When you begin to teach, you may devote a substantial amount of class time to having students learn information discovered by others. But the acquisition of a storehouse of facts, concepts, and principles is only part of what constitutes an appropriate education. Students must also learn how to *find, evaluate,* and *use* what they need to know to accomplish whatever goals they set for themselves. In other words, students need to learn how to be effective problem solvers.

One justification for teaching problem-solving skills in *addition* to ensuring mastery of factual information is that life in technologically oriented countries is marked by speedy change. New products, services, and social conventions are rapidly introduced and integrated into our lifestyles. Microcomputers, the Internet, cellular telephones, anticancer drugs, and in vitro fertilization, to name just a few examples, are relatively recent innovations that significantly affect the lives of many people.

But change, particularly rapid change, can be a mixed blessing. Although new products and services such as those just mentioned can make life more convenient, efficient, and enjoyable, they can also make it more complicated and problematic. The use of robots to perform certain jobs, for example, promises increased efficiency and productivity (which contribute to our standard of living), but it also threatens the job security of thousands of workers. Advances in medical care promise healthier and longer lives, but they introduce a host of moral, ethical, legal, and economic problems.

The educational implication that flows from these observations is clear: if we are to benefit from our ability to produce rapid and sometimes dramatic change, our schools need to invest more time, money, and effort in teaching students how to be effective problem solvers. As Lauren Resnick, a past president of the American Educational Research Association, argues:

> We need to identify and closely examine the aspects
> of education that are most likely to produce ability
> to adapt in the face of transitions and breakdowns.
> Rather than training people for particular jobs—a task
> better left to revised forms of on-the-job training—
> school should focus its efforts on preparing people to

be good *adaptive learners*, so that they can perform effectively when situations are unpredictable and task demands change. (1987, p. 18)

Resnick's argument, which echoes many others, is not without some justification. A survey by the American Management Association (Greenberg, Canzoneri, & Joe, 2000) found that 38 percent of job applicants lacked sufficient skills for the positions they sought. Rather than blaming "a 'dumbing down' of the incoming workforce," the authors attributed the problem to "the higher skills required in today's workplace" (p. 2).

Good problem solvers share two general characteristics: a well-organized, meaningful fund of knowledge and a systematic set of problem-solving skills. Historically, cognitive learning theories have been particularly useful sources of ideas for imparting both. In this chapter, then, we will examine the issue of meaningful learning from the perspective of a cognitive theory that we introduced previously in the book: constructivism. We will then go on to describe the nature of the problem-solving process and what you can do to help your students become better problem solvers. We will conclude by describing the circumstances under which learned capabilities are applied to new tasks, a process known as transfer of learning. ●

# MEANINGFUL LEARNING WITHIN A CONSTRUCTIVIST FRAMEWORK

| Constructivism: creating a personal interpretation of external ideas and experiences

**Constructivism,** as you may recall, holds that meaningful learning occurs when people actively try to make sense of the world—when they construct an interpretation of how and why things are—by filtering new ideas and experiences through existing knowledge structures (referred to in previous chapters as schemes). For example, an individual who lives in a country that provides, for little or no cost, such social services as medical care, counseling, education, job placement and training, and several weeks of paid vacation a year is likely to have constructed a rather different view of the role of government in people's lives from that of someone who lives in a country with a more market-oriented economy. To put it another way, meaningful learning is the active creation of knowledge structures (such as concepts, rules, hypotheses, and associations) from personal experience. In this section, we'll take a brief look at an early constructivist-oriented approach to learning, examine the nature of the constructivist model, and then put it all in perspective by considering the limits, as well as the advantages, of the constructivist viewpoint.

## Jerome Bruner and Discovery Learning: An Early Constructivist Perspective

Constructivist explanations of learning are not new. Over the past seventy-five years, they have been promoted by such notable scholars as John Dewey, Jean Piaget, Lev

Vygotsky, and Jerome Bruner. One of Bruner's contributions from the 1960s was the concept of **discovery learning.**

Bruner argued that too much school learning takes the form of step-by-step study of verbal or numerical statements or formulas that students can reproduce on cue but are unable to use outside the classroom. When students are presented with such highly structured materials as worksheets and other types of drill-and-practice exercises, Bruner argues, they become too dependent on other people. Furthermore, they are likely to think of learning as something done only to earn a reward.

Instead of using techniques that feature preselected and prearranged materials, Bruner believes teachers should confront children with problems and help them seek solutions either independently or by engaging in group discussion. True learning, says Bruner, involves "figuring out how to use what you already know in order to go beyond what you already think" (1983, p. 183). Like Piaget, Bruner argues that conceptions that children arrive at on their own are usually more meaningful than those proposed by others and that students do not need to be rewarded when they seek to make sense of things that puzzle them.

| Bruner: discover how ideas relate to each other and to existing knowledge

Bruner does not suggest that students should discover every fact or principle or formula they may need to know. Discovery is simply too inefficient a process to be used that widely, and learning from others can be as meaningful as personal discovery (Mayer, 2004). Rather, Bruner argues that certain types of outcomes—understanding the ways in which ideas connect with one another, the possibility of solving problems on our own, and how what we already know is relevant to what we are trying to learn— are the essence of education and can best be achieved through personal discovery.

# VIDEO CASE ◀◀ ▶ ▶▶

## Elementary School Language Arts: Inquiry Learning

*Watch the video, study the artifacts in the case, and reflect upon the following questions:*

**1.** How does this Video Case illustrate the concepts of constructivism and discovery learning?

**2.** How does the classroom teacher in this Video Case encourage students to construct their own knowledge? What strategies and instructional approaches does she use?

## Constructivism Today

**Facets of Constructivism**   Contemporary constructivist theory has several variations, two of which we will describe shortly. But despite their differences, all the variations incorporate the following four facets.

| Construction of ideas strongly influenced by student's prior knowledge

1.  *To constructivists, meaningful learning is the active creation of knowledge structures from personal experience.* Each learner builds a personal view of the world by using existing knowledge, interests, attitudes, goals, and the like to select and interpret currently available information (Brooks & Brooks, 2001; Shapiro, 2002). As Rochel Gelman (1994) points out, this assumption highlights the importance of what educational psychologists call entering behavior—the previously learned knowledge and skill that students bring to the classroom.

The knowledge that learners bring with them to a learning task has long been suspected of having a powerful effect on subsequent performance. In 1978, David Ausubel wrote on the flyleaf of his textbook, *Educational Psychology: A Cognitive View,* "If I had to reduce all of educational psychology to just one principle, I would say this: the most important single factor influencing learning is what the learner already knows. Ascertain this and teach him accordingly" (Ausubel, Novak, & Hanesian, 1978). Research findings appear to have borne out Ausubel's contention. A review of 183 studies (Dochy, Segers, & Buehl, 1999) concluded that a strong relationship exists between prior knowledge and performance. Almost all of the studies (91 percent) reported a positive effect of prior knowledge on performance, and in some circumstances most of the variation (60 percent) in students' scores on a test was a function of what learners knew about the topic prior to instruction.

2. *The essence of one person's knowledge can never be totally transferred to another person because knowledge is the result of a personal interpretation of experience, which is influenced by such factors as the learner's age, gender, race, ethnic background, and knowledge base.* When knowledge is transferred from one person to another, some aspects of it are invariably "lost in translation." The area of musical performance provides an apt illustration of this aspect of constructivism. Although a piano teacher can tell a student volumes about how and why a piece should be performed in a particular way, the teacher cannot tell the student everything. The interpretation of a composition is constructed from such factors as the performer's knowledge of the composer's personality and motives, the nature of the instrument or instruments for which the composition was written, and the nature of the music itself. Because performers assign different meanings to such knowledge, different (yet equally valid) interpretations of the same composition result. Think, for example, of the many different ways in which you have heard "The Star-Spangled Banner" sung.

3. *Even though knowledge is personal, people often agree about what is true.* This third facet follows directly from the second. Does constructivism necessarily mean that everyone walks around with a personal, idiosyncratic view of the world and that consensus is impossible? A few minutes of reflection should tell you that the answer is no. And if you recall what you read in the chapter on culture and congnition, you will recognize that the cultures and societies to which people belong channel and place limits on the views people have of the world around them. Consequently, individuals make observations, test hypotheses, and draw conclusions that are largely consistent with one another (Duffy & Cunningham, 1996; Hung, 2002).

Of course, there are many instances in which people cannot reconcile their views and so agree to disagree. For example, in January 2002, President George W. Bush signed into law the reauthorization of the Elementary and Secondary Education Act, more popularly known as No Child Left Behind (NCLB). Although everyone agrees on what the law requires (e.g., all children in grades 3 through 8 scoring at the proficient level or above on tests of math and reading/language arts by 2014, with negative consequences for schools and districts that fail to show progress toward these goals), there is sharp disagreement about the true purpose of this legislation and its likely effects on students and teachers. Some see it as an effective means of school reform, whereas others see it as an attempt to undercut the autonomy and vitality of public education. In matters such as these, truth is where it always is for the constructivist: in the mind of the beholder.

**Construction of ideas aided by discussion and debate**

4. *Additions to, deletions from, or modifications of individuals' knowledge structures come mainly from the sharing of multiple perspectives.* Systematic, open-minded discussions and debates are instrumental in helping individuals create personal views (Hay & Barab, 2001; Paavola, Lipponen, & Hakkarainen, 2004). As we have seen in previous chapters, scholars form and reform their positions on aspects of theory or research as a result of years of discussion and debate with colleagues. The debate between the Piagetians and the Vygotskians (discussed in Chapter 3 on stage theories of development) is a good example of this facet of constructivism. Consequently, students need to be provided with conditions that allow them to share and discuss multiple perspectives on information and experiences.

*Most constructivist theories take one of two forms: cognitive constructivism or social constructivism. The former emphasizes the effect of one's cognitive processes on meaningful learning, whereas the latter emphasizes the effect of other people's arguments and points of view on meaningful learning.*

Cognitive constructivism emphasizes role of cognitive processes in meaningful learning

Social constructivism emphasizes role of culture and social interaction in meaningful learning

**Two Variations on a Constructivist Theme**   One view of meaningful learning that we have described, Jean Piaget's, holds that it is the natural result of an intrinsic drive to resolve inconsistencies and contradictions—that is, always to have a view of the world that makes sense in the light of what we currently know. One contemporary variation of constructivism, **cognitive constructivism,** is an outgrowth of Piaget's ideas because it focuses on the cognitive processes that take place within individuals. In other words, an individual's conception of the truth of some matter (for example, that both birds and airplanes can fly because they use the same aeronautical principles) is based on her ability, with guidance, to assimilate information effectively into existing schemes and develop new schemes and operations (the process Piaget called *accommodation*) in response to novel or discrepant ideas (Fosnot, 1996; Windschitl, 2002).

The constructivist variation known as **social constructivism** holds that meaningful learning occurs when people are explicitly taught how to use the psychological tools of their culture (such as language, mathematics, and approaches to problem solving) and are then given the opportunity to use these tools in authentic, real-life activities to create a common, or shared, understanding of some phenomenon (McInerney, 2005). Students are encouraged to engage in open-ended discussion with peers and teachers about such things as the meaning of terms and procedures, the relationships among ideas, and the applicability of knowledge to specific contexts. This process is often referred to by social constructivists as *negotiating meaning.* This view has its roots in the writings of such individuals as the psychologist Lev Vygotsky and the educational philosopher John Dewey (Perkins, 1999; Shapiro, 2002; Windschitl, 2002).

Although the cognitive and social constructivist perspectives emphasize different aspects of learning, they are not incompatible. The cognitive approach does not deny the value of learning in group activities, and the social approach does not deny the value of working independently of others. As one constructivist observed, "learning is an act of both individual interpretation and negotiation with other individuals" (Windschitl, 2002, p. 142). For example, people who play musical instruments in an orchestra practice both in a group and by themselves because some things are best learned in isolation (aspects of technique, such as breathing, fingering, or bowing) and others are best learned as part of the orchestra (discussing how various techniques best express the composer's intent). In athletics, too, certain skills are practiced alone, whereas others are practiced with others (Anderson, Greeno, Reder, & Simon, 2000). Both perspectives also subscribe to the belief that "learning is an active process that is student-centered in the sense that, *with the teacher's help*, learners select and transform information, construct hypotheses, and make decisions" (Chrenka, 2001, p. 694; italics added).

Table 9.1 summarizes the characteristics of cognitive and social constructivism and the basic instructional approaches that flow from each of these variations. The main conditions that support an individual's attempt to construct personally meaningful knowledge are detailed in the next section.

| Table 9.1 | Cognitive and Social Constructivist Approaches to Learning and Teaching | |
| --- | --- | --- |
| **Approach** | **Basic Characteristics** | **Instructional Implications** |
| Cognitive constructivism | • Existing knowledge schemes and operations are modified by the addition (assimilation) of new ideas that are judged to be related. New knowledge schemes and operations are created (accommodation) to adapt to ideas and procedures that are inconsistent with existing schemes.<br>• Assimilation and accommodation processes are assumed to be innate and supported by opportunities to interact with peers and the physical environment. | • Teacher challenges students' current conceptions by presenting new ideas that do not quite fit (inducing disequilibrium).<br>• Students work individually and together to construct new, more effective schemes.<br>• Emphasis is on constructing personal meaning by developing new schemes. |
| Social constructivism | • Learning initially occurs in the presence of and is influenced by more knowledgeable others.<br>• The knowledge and skills that are acquired through the guidance of others are connected to existing schemes and gradually internalized, allowing the learner to become increasingly self-regulated and independent. | • Teacher helps students through scaffolded instruction to construct ideas using realistic, open-ended tasks.<br>• Under teacher guidance, students work collaboratively to construct new conceptions.<br>• Emphasis is on constructing and internalizing shared meaning. |

Constructivism aided by cognitive apprenticeship, realistic tasks, multiple perspectives

**Conditions That Foster Constructivism**    The fostering conditions that constructivists typically mention include a cognitive apprenticeship between student and teacher, a use of realistic problems and conditions, and an emphasis on multiple perspectives.

*Cognitive Apprenticeship*    The first condition, that of a cognitive apprenticeship, will be illustrated in Chapter 10 on social cognitive theory when we will describe the reciprocal teaching program of Annemarie Palincsar and Ann Brown (1984). Its main feature is that the teacher models a cognitive process that students are to learn and then gradually turns responsibility for executing the process over to students as they become more skilled. As you may recall from our earlier discussions—in Chapter 3, for example—providing such environmental supports as modeling, hints, leading questions, and suggestions and then gradually removing them as the learner demonstrates increased competence is called *scaffolding*. Cognitive apprenticeships also occur in less formal circumstances, as when a child joins an existing peer group (such as a play group), at first mostly watches what the other children do, and then gradually, with little explicit direction from the others, participates in one or more aspects of the task.

*Situated Learning*    In the second condition, often called **situated learning** (or situated cognition), students are given learning tasks set in realistic contexts. A realistic context is one in which students must solve a meaningful problem by using a variety of skills and information. The rationale for this condition is twofold:

1. Learning is more likely to be meaningful (related to previously learned knowledge and skills) when it is embedded in a realistic context (Duffy & Cunningham, 1996; Hung, 2002).
2. Traditional forms of classroom learning and instruction, which are largely decontextualized in the sense that what students learn is relevant only to taking tests and performing other classroom tasks, leads to a condition that has been referred to as **inert knowledge.** That is, students fail to use what they learned earlier (such as mathematical procedures) to solve either real-life problems (such as calculating the square footage of the walls of a room in order to know how many rolls of

wallpaper to buy) or other school-related problems because they don't see any relationship between the two (Perkins, 1999). But as we point out later in this chapter when we discuss transfer of learning, some have argued that too strong an emphasis on situated cognition may create the same kind of problem (Bereiter, 1997; Cooper & Harries, 2005).

As an example of situated learning, the game of baseball can be used as a vehicle for middle school or high school students to apply aspects of science, mathematics, and sociology. Students could be asked to use their knowledge of physics to explain how pitchers are able to make the ball curve left or right or drop down as it approaches home plate. They could be asked to use their mathematical skills to figure out how far home runs travel. They could also be asked to read about the Negro Leagues and Jackie Robinson and discuss why it took until the late 1940s for major league baseball to begin integration.

A more formal way of implementing situated learning is to use problem-based learning (PBL) (Hung, 2002). Unlike a traditional approach to instruction in which students first learn a body of knowledge and then use that knowledge to solve problems, PBL presents students with complex, authentic problems (such as creating a water management plan for the desert southwest) and requires them to identify and locate the information they need to solve the problem. In other words, students decide what they need to know in order to solve the problem (Angeli, 2002; Soderberg & Price, 2003; Uyeda, Madden, Brigham, Luft, & Washburne, 2002). In Chapter 13, "Approaches to Instruction," we describe how PBL can be used with computer-based technology.

***Multiple Perspectives***   The third condition that fosters constructivism is students' viewing ideas and problems from multiple perspectives. The rationale, again, is twofold: most of life's problems are multifaceted, and the knowledge base of experts is a network of interrelated ideas. The complex process of becoming an effective teacher is a good example of the need for multiple perspectives, including the perspectives of other teachers (Chan & Pang, 2006). As we mentioned at the beginning of the book, being an effective teacher requires the mastery of many skills and disciplines so that classroom problems can be analyzed and attacked from several perspectives.

The following section provides an example of a constructivist-oriented teaching lesson, and Table 9.2 notes the major characteristics of a constructivist classroom.

***An Example of Constructivist Teaching***   A fifth-grade teacher wanted his students to understand that the mathematical concept of pi expresses the relationship between the circumference of a circle and its diameter. On the first day of school he gave students writing tablets divided into three columns. He told them that over the next three weeks they were to identify circular objects of all sizes outside of school and measure how many inches each one was across its center and around its perimeter (he purposely avoided using the terms diameter and circumference at this point). The first measurement was to be recorded in the first column of the tablet and the second measurement in the second column. Over the next three weeks the students measured all manner of round things (such as coins, tires, and dishes), all the time wondering why they were doing this project and what the teacher's explanation would be. When the class met on the day of the project's deadline, the students were both surprised and disappointed that the teacher did not offer an explanation. Instead, he had the students look over their two columns of numbers and said, "Now tell me what you can see that is interesting about these two sets of numbers."

Gradually, the students noticed that the measurements of the circumference were always larger than the measurements of the diameter. He then asked, "How much bigger are the numbers in the second column, the distance around the circle, in relation to the numbers in the first column, the distance across the circle?" Once again, students

| Table 9.2 | Characteristics of a Constructivist Classroom |
| --- | --- |

- Teaching and learning start from a student's current understanding of a subject. Therefore, a teacher's first task is to determine the completeness and accuracy of what students currently know about key topics.
- Teachers help students create realistic learning experiences that will lead students to elaborate on and restructure current knowledge. Teachers believe that meaningful learning involves discovering, questioning, analyzing, synthesizing, and evaluating information.
- Students frequently engage in complex, meaningful, problem-based activities whose content and goals are negotiated with the teacher.
- Students have frequent opportunities to debate and discuss substantive issues.
- A primary goal of instruction is for students to learn to think for themselves. Consequently, teachers use a variety of indirect teaching methods, such as modeling the thinking processes they want students to use; providing prompts, probes, and suggestions; providing heuristics (a topic discussed later in this chapter); and using technology to organize and represent information.
- Students engage in such high-level cognitive processes as explaining ideas, interpreting texts, predicting phenomena, and constructing arguments based on evidence.
- In addition to assessing student learning with written exams, teachers also require students to write research reports, make oral presentations, build models, and engage in problem-solving activities.
- Student progress is assessed continually rather than just at the end of a unit and the end of a semester.
- Subject-matter disciplines and their knowledge bases are seen as continually undergoing revision.

SOURCES: Brooks & Brooks (2001); Gabler, Schroeder, & Curtis (2003); Windschitl (2002).

wondered when the teacher would simply tell them the answer. But with a bit of coaxing, students began to guess, until one girl realized that the answer to the question could be gained by dividing the larger number by the smaller one. The students did so, recorded their answers in the third column of their tablet, and were astounded to realize that the answer was always the same (3.14) regardless of the size of the circles.

In a much more meaningful way than would have occurred had the students simply memorized the fact that pi is the ratio of the circumference of a circle to its diameter, the students learned, as one put it, "No matter how big a circle is, the distance around it is always a little more than three times the distance across it." They also learned that discovering ideas is fun and that mathematics has a basis in the real world (Funk, 2003).

> Constructivist-oriented teaching encourages creating new views; uses scaffolding, realistic tasks, and class discussion

The essence of a constructivist-oriented lesson is to provide students with realistic problems that cannot be solved with their current level of understanding and, by allowing them to interact mainly among themselves, to work out new understandings. It's important to emphasize the social nature of this approach. The experiences and ideas of others become springboards for further experimentation and discussion.

## Putting Constructivism in Perspective

Although constructivism has much to offer teachers, like any other theory, it does have its limitations, and there may be problems with its implementation (Kirschner, Sweller, & Clark, 2006; Matthews, 2002). Here are a few you should keep in mind:

- Because of constructivism's emphasis on guiding rather than telling, accepting different perspectives on issues and solutions to problems, modifying previous conceptions in the light of new information, and creating an atmosphere that encourages active participation, it is almost impossible to create highly detailed lesson plans. Much of what teachers do depends on how students respond. Teaching from this perspective will place a premium on your teacher-as-artist abilities.
- Teaching from a constructivist perspective is more time-consuming and places higher demands on learners as compared with a typical lecture format (de Jong & van Joolingen, 1998; Perkins, 1999).

- Constructivism is not the only orientation to learning and teaching that you will ever need (nor is any other theory, for that matter). You need to know which theory or approach best fits which purposes and circumstances. Sometimes memorization of factual information is essential, and sometimes an instructional objective can be accomplished more efficiently (and just as effectively) with a clear and well-organized lecture (Airasian & Walsh, 1997).

The extent to which teachers engage in constructivist teaching practices is determined in large part by how completely they accept its underlying principles (e.g., knowledge is temporary, knowledge is the result of discussions among students and between students and the teacher, students have input into the curriculum, learning is grounded in real-life tasks and settings to make it relevant to students' lives). Teachers who believe that they, and not the students, should decide what gets learned and how and that their primary responsibility is to prepare students for high-stakes tests are less likely to use a constructivist approach (Haney & McArthur, 2002).

## VIDEO CASE ◀◀ ▶ ▶▶

### Middle School Science Instruction: Inquiry Learning

*Watch the video, study the artifacts in the case, and reflect upon the following questions:*

1. Does Robert Cho's science class meet the criteria for a constructivist classroom?

2. Based on this Video Case and the discussion on constructivism in this section of the text, why do you think that teaching using a constructivist approach is more time-consuming for teachers (as opposed to other teaching methods)? Cite some possible reasons.

Assuming you do accept some constructivist principles and that you acknowledge that there is a beneficial role for instructional support within constructivist classrooms (Hardy, Jonen, Möller, & Stern, 2006), there are many techniques you can use to foster meaningful learning within a constructivist framework. Several computer-based approaches are described at the end of this chapter. One that does not rely on computer technology but that is particularly well suited to developing, comparing, and understanding different points of view, is the classroom discussion (Brookfield & Preskill, 2005; Brown & Renshaw, 2000; Rabow, Charness, Kipperman, & Radcliffe-Vasile, 1994). Because this format also allows students to deal with realistic problems that are often complex and ambiguous and to exercise cognitive skills taught by the teacher, it is an excellent general-purpose method for helping students construct a meaningful knowledge base. It is also an effective way to improve the quality of students' writing. A study of discussion-based approaches to literature instruction in middle and high school classrooms (involving almost one thousand students) found that higher levels of discussion-based instruction about reading assignments were associated with more abstract and elaborated reports, analyses, and essays based on the readings (Applebee, Langer, Nystrand, & Gamoran, 2003).

Let's turn our attention to some specific Suggestions for Teaching that describe how to use discussion and other techniques to emphasize meaningful learning in your classroom.

# Suggestions for Teaching in Your Classroom

## Using a Constructivist Approach to Meaningful Learning

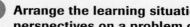 **Arrange the learning situation so that students are exposed to different perspectives on a problem or an issue.**

This is the crux of the discovery approach and the constructivist view of learning. The basic idea is to *arrange* the elements of a learning task and *guide* student actions so that students discover, or construct, a personally meaningful conception of a problem or issue (as opposed to someone else's conception). In some cases, you may present a topic that is a matter of opinion or that all students are sure to know something about. In other cases, you might structure the discussion by exposing all participants to the same background information.

**a. Ask students to discuss familiar topics or those that are matters of opinion.**

**EXAMPLES**

- "What are some of the techniques that advertising agencies use in television commercials to persuade us to buy certain products?"
- "What do you think is the best book you ever read, and why do you think so?"

**b. Provide necessary background information by asking all students to read all or part of a book, take notes on a lecture, view a film, conduct library research, or conduct research on the Internet.**

**EXAMPLES**

- After the class has read *Great Expectations,* ask, "What do you think Dickens was trying to convey when he wrote this novel? Was he just trying to tell a good story, or was he also trying to get us to think about certain kinds of relationships between people?"
- "After I explain some of the principles of electrical currents, I'm going to ask you to suggest rules for connecting batteries in series and in parallel. Then we'll see how well your rules work."

**2 Structure discussions by posing a specific question, presenting a provocative topic-related issue, or asking students to choose topics or subtopics.**

It is important to structure a discovery session by giving students something reasonably specific to discuss; otherwise, they may simply engage in a disorganized and desultory bull session. You might supply direction in the following ways:

**a. In some cases, encourage students to arrive at conclusions already reached by others.**

Thousands of books provide detailed answers to such questions as, "What is human about human beings? How did they get that way? How can they be made more so?" But constructivists believe that answers mean more when they are constructed by the individual, not supplied ready-made by others. As you look over lesson plans, therefore, you might try to put together some questions for students to answer by engaging in discussion rather than by reading or listening to what others have already discovered. In searching for such topics, you might take into account the techniques that Bruner described. Here is a list of those techniques, together with an example of each one. Keep in mind that students often acquire a deeper understanding of ideas and issues when they have had appropriate previous experience:

- *Emphasize contrast.* In an elementary school social studies unit on cultural diversity, say, "When you watch this film on Mexico, look for customs and ways of living that differ from ours. Then we'll talk about what these differences are and why they may have developed."
- *Stimulate informed guessing.* In a middle school unit on natural science, you might say, "Suppose we wanted to figure out some kind of system to classify trees so that we could later find information about particular types. What would be the best way to do it?" After students have developed a classification scheme, show them schemes that specialists have developed.
- *Encourage participation.* In a high school political science class, illustrate the jury system by staging a mock trial. (Note that the use of a simulation satisfies the constructivist criterion of realistic tasks and contexts.)
- *Stimulate awareness.* In a high school English class, ask the students to discuss how the author developed the plot.

**JOURNAL ENTRY**
Similar Applications You
Could Use

**b. In other cases, present a controversial topic for which there is no single answer.**

Discussions might center on provocative issues about which there are differences of opinion. One caution here is to avoid topics (such as premarital sex or legalized abortion) that parents may not want discussed in school, either because they are convinced it is their prerogative to discuss them with their children or because they feel that students may be pressured to endorse your opinion because you assign grades. You should not avoid controversy, but neither should you go out of your way to agitate students and their parents.

Another caution is to avoid selecting issues that provoke more than they instruct. You may be tempted to present a highly controversial topic and then congratulate yourself at the end of the period if most students engaged in heated discussion. But if they simply argued enthusiastically about something that had nothing to do with the subject you are assigned to teach, you cannot honestly claim to have arranged an instructive exchange of ideas.

**EXAMPLES**

- In a middle school science class, ask students to list arguments for and against attempting to alter the genetic code of human beings.
- In a high school political science class, ask students to list arguments for and against democratic forms of government.

**3** **If time is limited and if only one topic is to be covered, ask students to form a circle and have an all-class discussion.**

**JOURNAL ENTRY**
Ways to Supervise Discussion
Sessions

You may sometimes wish to have the entire class discuss a topic. Such discussions are most likely to be successful if all students have eye contact with one another. The simplest way to achieve this is to ask all students to form a circle. Next, invite responses to the question you have posed. As students make remarks, serve more as a moderator than as a leader. Try to keep the discussion on the topic, but avoid directing it toward a specific predetermined end result. If one or more students tend to dominate the discussion, say something like, "Kim and Carlos have given us their ideas. Now I'd like to hear from the rest of you." If an aggressive student attacks or belittles something that a classmate says, respond with something like, "It's good to *believe* in a point of view, but let's be friendly as we listen to other opinions. This is supposed to be a discussion, not an argument or a debate."

Factors that lead to successful or unsuccessful discussions are often idiosyncratic, but there are certain procedures you might follow to increase the likelihood of success.

### a. Ask questions that stimulate students to apply, analyze, synthesize, and evaluate.

When you first structure a discussion session, but also while it is under way, take care to ask questions likely to elicit different points of view. If you ask students to supply information (for example, "When did Charles Dickens write *Great Expectations?*"), the first correct response will lead to closure. You may end up asking a series of questions leading to brief answers—the equivalent of a fill-in exam. When you seek to encourage students to construct personally meaningful interpretations of the issues or to develop skills as deductive thinkers, it is preferable to ask questions that are likely to tap higher levels of thinking.

#### EXAMPLES

- "You just learned how to calculate the area of a circle. Think of as many different ways as you can of how you might be able to use that bit of knowledge if you were a do-it-yourself homeowner." (Application)

- "Last month we read a novel by Dickens; this month we read a play by Shakespeare. What are some similarities in the way each author developed the plot of his story?" (Synthesis)

### b. Allow sufficient time for initial responses, and then probe for further information (if appropriate).

Recent research has found that many teachers fail to allow enough time for students to respond to questions. Quite often, instructors wait only one second before repeating the question, calling on another student, or answering the question themselves. When teachers wait at least three seconds after asking a question, students are more likely to participate; their responses increase in frequency, length, and complexity; and their achievement improves. There are changes in teacher behavior as well. As a function of waiting longer, teachers ask more complex questions and have higher expectations for the quality of students' responses (Ormrod, 2004).

One possible explanation for improved student recitation when teachers wait longer for a response is that reflective thinkers have an opportunity to figure out what they want to say. But even impulsive thinkers probably welcome a few more seconds of thinking time. It seems logical to expect that snap answers will be more superficial than answers supplied after even a few seconds of reflection.

In addition to giving students ample time to make an initial response, you should encourage them to pursue an idea. If it seems appropriate, probe for further information or clarification of a point by asking students who give brief or incomplete answers to explain how or why they arrived at a conclusion or to supply additional comments.

#### EXAMPLE

- "Well, Keesha, I'm sure a gardener might sometimes need to figure the area of a circle, but can you give a more specific example? If you can't think of one right away, put up your hand as soon as you can describe a specific situation in which it would help to know the area of a circular patch of lawn or soil."

### c. When selecting students to speak in class, use techniques likely to sustain steady but nonthreatening attention. At the same time, guard against the temptation to call primarily on bright, articulate, assertive students.

The way you moderate student contributions may not only determine how successful the discussion will be but may also influence how students feel about themselves and each other. Jacob Kounin (1970) points out that when a teacher first names a student and then asks a question, the rest of the class may tend to turn its attention to other things. The same tendency to tune out may occur if a teacher follows a set pattern of calling on students (for example, by going around a circle). To keep all the students on their toes, you might ask questions first and then, in an unpredictable sequence, call on those who volunteer to speak, frequently switching from one part of the room to another. Guard against the temptation to call primarily on students you expect to give good or provocative answers. Repeatedly ignoring students who may be a bit inarticulate or unimaginative may cause them and their classmates to conclude that you think they are incompetent. These students may then lose interest in and totally ignore what is taking place.

**4  Use guided experiences to satisfy both constructivist principles and state learning standards.**

**JOURNAL ENTRY**
Techniques for Satisfying
Constructivist Principles and
State Learning Standards

Because constructivism is strongly student-centered and emphasizes high-level outcomes, it is sometimes perceived as being incompatible with the need for teachers to prepare students for high-stakes tests that are based on state learning standards. But through the use of guided experiences, teachers can do both. The trick is to embed standards in learning experiences that students care about. Geoffrey Caine, Renate Nummela Caine, and Carol McClintic (2002) describe how this was done for eighth-grade classes studying the U.S. Civil War.

To satisfy state learning standards, students needed to learn such things as the nature of slavery, the causes of the war, important dates and the sequence of events, major battles, and significant individuals who affected the course of the war. The first step was to teach students how to listen to one another and express disagreements in a nonjudgmental way.

An introductory event was then used to spark students' interest in the topic. They were read a story about a woman who disguised herself as a man, enlisted in the Union Army, and worked as a coal handler on a canal boat. They were then shown a short segment from the motion picture *Gettysburg* in which Confederate soldiers marched directly into cannon and rifle fire. The last part of the introduction involved telling students that over four hundred women disguised themselves as men and participated in the war and that the fifty-one thousand soldiers who were killed during the three-day battle of Gettysburg exceeded the number of U.S. soldiers who were killed during the entire Vietnam War. When invited to raise questions, the students wanted to know such things as why women fought in the war, how it was that nobody knew they were women, why the North and South went to war, and why soldiers would walk into enemy gunfire.

The students were assigned to groups based on the similarity of the questions they raised and were told to seek answers from library resources, the Internet, and interviews with war veterans. The teachers used the subsequent reports each group made to the class and the discussions that followed to ensure that such standards-related issues as the different groups involved in the war and the nature of slavery were introduced and discussed.

**5  If abundant time is available and if a controversial or subdivided topic is to be discussed, divide the class into groups of about five.**

**JOURNAL ENTRY**
Techniques for Arranging
Small-Group Discussions

A major limitation of any kind of discussion is that only one person can talk at a time. You can reduce this difficulty by dividing the class into smaller groups before asking them to exchange ideas. A group of about five seems to work best. If only two or three students are interacting with one another, the exchange of ideas may be limited. If there are more than five, not all members will be able to contribute at frequent intervals.

Raymond Brown and Peter Renshaw (2000) describe an approach to small-group classroom discussion based on the following five principles derived from Vygotsky's sociocultural theory of cognitive development:

1. Students should present their ideas with sufficient clarity that other students can distinguish relevant from irrelevant ideas.
2. Relevant ideas can be rejected by others only if their validity can be questioned on the basis of past experience or logical reasoning.
3. Ideas that contradict one another or that belong to mutually exclusive points of view must be resolved through group argument.
4. All members understand and agree that the group will strive to reach a consensus on an issue by each member actively contributing to arguments that lead to a solution.
5. The group will present its arguments to the other members of the class.

# THE NATURE OF PROBLEM SOLVING

As with most of the other topics covered in this book, an extensive amount of theorizing and research on problem solving has been conducted over the years. We will focus our discussion on the types of problems that students are typically required to deal with, the cognitive processes that play a central role in problem solving, and various approaches to teaching problem solving in the classroom.

Let's begin by asking what we mean by the terms *problem* and *problem solving*. Most, if not all, psychologists would agree that "a problem is said to exist when one has a goal and has not yet identified a means for reaching that goal" (Gagné, Yekovich, & Yekovich, 1993, p. 211). **Problem solving,** then, is the identification and application of knowledge and skills that result in goal attainment (Martinez, 1998). Although this definition encompasses a wide range of problem types, we will focus on three types that students frequently encounter both in and out of school.

## Three Common Types of Problems

In the first category are the well-structured problems of mathematics and science—the type of problems that students from kindergarten through middle school are typically required to solve. **Well-structured problems** are clearly formulated, can be solved by recall and application of a specific procedure (called an *algorithm*), and result in a solution that can be evaluated against a well-known, agreed-on standard (Hamilton & Ghatala, 1994)—for example:

$$5 + 8 =$$
$$732 - 485 =$$
$$8 + 3x = 40 - 5x$$

What constitutes a problem to be solved varies with the age and experience of the learner and the nature of the problem itself (Martinez, 1998). The second of the mathematical examples is likely to be a genuine problem for some first or second graders who are used to seeing subtraction exercises arrayed vertically (minuend on top, subtrahend beneath, horizontal line under the subtrahend). Fifth graders, however, who have had experience with arithmetic assignments in a variety of formats, would be able to retrieve and use the correct algorithm automatically. Because the fifth graders know the means to reach their goal, they do not face a problem-solving task according to our definition, but just a type of exercise or practice.

In the second category are the ill-structured problems often encountered in everyday life and in disciplines such as economics or psychology. **Ill-structured problems**

Well-structured problems: clearly stated, known solution procedures; known evaluation standards

Ill-structured problems: vaguely stated, unclear solution procedures; vague evaluation standards

*Well-structured problems have a clear structure, can be solved by using a standard procedure, and produce solutions that can be evaluated against an agreed-on standard. They are the type of problem that students are asked to solve most frequently.*

Issues: ill-structured problems that arouse strong feelings

are more complex, provide few cues pointing to solution procedures, and have less definite criteria for determining when the problem has been solved (Hamilton & Ghatala, 1994). Examples of ill-structured problems are how to identify and reward good teachers, how to improve access to public buildings and facilities for persons with physical disabilities, and how to increase voter turnout for elections.

The third category includes problems that are also ill structured but that differ from the examples just mentioned in two respects. First, these problems tend to divide people into opposing camps because of the emotions they arouse. Second, the primary goal, at least initially, is not to determine a course of action but to identify the most reasonable position. These problems are often referred to as **issues** (Ruggiero, 1988, 2007). Examples of issues are capital punishment, gun control, and nondenominational prayer in classrooms. High school students typically have more opportunities than younger students to deal with ill-structured problems and issues of the type cited above. That does not mean, however, that younger students have no opportunities to deal with ill-structured problems or issues. Consider self-regulated learning, which will be discussed in the next chapter. Goal orientation plays a role in the development of self-regulated learning and self-efficacy. Performance goals provide clear, easily specified outcomes; they are similar to well-structured problems. Learning goals, however, are more similar to ill-structured problems or issues. Suppose you have young students who desire to become politicians or firefighters. They will see value in establishing goals that will help them learn the knowledge and skills they need to become politicians or firefighters. Generating personally valued goals (Miller & Brickman, 2004) can be opportunities for younger students to solve ill-structured problems.

## Helping Students Become Good Problem Solvers

Despite the differences that exist among well-structured problems, ill-structured problems, and issues, recent theory and research suggest that good problem solvers employ the same general approach when solving one or another of these problem types (Bransford & Stein, 1993; Gagné et al., 1993; Krulik & Rudnick, 1993; Nickerson, 1994; Pretz, Naples, & Sternberg, 2003; Ruggiero, 1988, 2007). This approach consists of five steps or processes:

1. Realize that a problem exists.
2. Understand the nature of the problem.

3. Compile relevant information.
4. Formulate and carry out a solution.
5. Evaluate the solution.

Well-structured problems may call only for the implementation of steps 2, 4, and 5, but the other two problem types require all five steps. We will discuss each of these steps in the next few pages, along with some specific techniques that you can use to help your students become good problem solvers.

**Step 1: Realize That a Problem Exists**     Most people assume that if a problem is worth solving, they won't have to seek it out; it will make itself known. Like most other assumptions, this one is only partly true. Well-structured problems are often thrust on us by teachers, in the form of in-class exercises or homework, or by supervisors at work. Ill-structured problems and issues, however, often remain hidden from most people. It is a characteristic of good problem solvers that they are more sensitive to the existence of problems than most of their peers (Pretz et al., 2003).

> **Problem finding depends on curiosity, dissatisfaction with status quo**

The keys to problem recognition, or *problem finding* as it is sometimes called, are curiosity and dissatisfaction. You need to question why a rule, procedure, or product is the way it is or to feel frustrated or irritated because something does not work as well as it might. The organization known as Mothers Against Drunk Driving, for example, was begun by a woman who, because her daughter had been killed in a traffic accident by a drunk driver, was dissatisfied with current, ineffective laws. This organization has been instrumental in getting state legislatures to pass laws against drunk driving that mandate more severe penalties.

Problem finding does not come readily to most people, possibly because schools emphasize solving well-structured problems and possibly because most people have a natural tendency to assume that things work as well as they can. Like any other cognitive process, however, problem recognition can improve with instruction and practice. Students can be sensitized in a number of ways to the absence or flaws and shortcomings of products, procedures, rules, or whatever else. We will make some specific suggestions about improving problem recognition and the other problem-solving processes a bit later in Suggestions for Teaching in Your Classroom: Teaching Problem-Solving Techniques.

**Step 2: Understand the Nature of the Problem**     The second step in the problem-solving process is perhaps the most critical. The problem solver has to construct an *optimal* representation, or understanding, of the nature of a problem or issue. The preceding sentence stresses the word *optimal* for two reasons. First, most problems can be expressed in a number of ways. Written problems, for example, can be recast as pictures, equations, graphs, charts, or diagrams. Second, because the way we represent the problem determines the amount and type of solution-relevant information we recall from long-term memory, some representations are better than others. For obvious reasons, problem-solving researchers often refer to this process as **problem representation** or **problem framing** (Derry et al., 2005; Giaccardi, 2005).

> **Problem framing depends on knowledge of subject matter, familiarity with problem types**

To achieve an optimal understanding of a problem, an individual needs two things: a high degree of knowledge of the subject matter (facts, concepts, and principles) on which the problem is based and familiarity with that particular type of problem. This background will allow the person to recognize important elements (words, phrases, and numbers) in the problem statement and patterns of relationships among the problem elements. This recognition will activate one or more solution-relevant schemes from long-term memory. It is this level of knowledge of subject matter and problem types that distinguishes the high-quality problem representations of the expert problem solver from the low-quality representations of the novice. Experts typically represent problems in terms of one or more basic patterns or underlying principles, whereas novices focus on limited or superficial surface features of problems.

To give you a clearer idea of the nature and power of an optimal problem representation, consider the following situation. When novices are given a set of physics problems to solve, they sort them into categories on the basis of some noticeable feature. For example, they group together all problems that involve the use of an inclined plane or all the ones that involve the use of pulleys. Then novices search their memories for previously learned information. The drawback to this approach is that although two or three problems may involve the use of an inclined plane, their solutions may depend on the application of different laws of physics. Experts, in contrast, draw on their extensive and well-organized knowledge base to represent groups of problems according to a common underlying principle, such as conservation of energy or Newton's third law (Gagné et al., 1993; Pretz et al., 2003).

An important aspect of the problem-solving process is the ability to activate relevant schemes (organized collections of facts, concepts, principles, and procedures) from long-term memory when they are needed. The more relevant and powerful the activated scheme is, the more likely it is that an effective problem solution will be achieved. But as many observers of education have pointed out, acquiring this ability is often easier said than done. John Bransford argues that standard educational practices produce knowledge that is *inert*. As mentioned earlier in the chapter, inert knowledge can be accessed only under conditions that closely mimic the original learning context (Bransford, Sherwood, Vye, & Rieser, 1986). Richard Feynman, a Nobel Prize–winning physicist, made the same observation in describing how his classmates at the Massachusetts Institute of Technology failed to recognize the application of a previously learned mathematical formula: "They didn't put two and two together. They didn't even know what they 'knew.' I don't know what's the matter with people: they don't learn by understanding; they learn by some other way—by rote, or something. Their knowledge is so fragile!" (1985, p. 36). To overcome this limitation of inert and fragile knowledge, teachers need to present subject matter in a highly organized fashion, and students need to learn more about the various conditions under which their knowledge applies.

*Inert knowledge due to learning isolated facts under limited conditions*

**Step 3: Compile Relevant Information**  For well-structured problems that are relatively simple and familiar (such as arithmetic drill problems), this step in the problem-solving process occurs simultaneously with problem representation. In the process of defining a problem, we very quickly and easily recall from long-term memory all the information needed to achieve a solution. As problems and issues become more complex, however, we run into two difficulties: the amount of information relevant to the solution becomes too great to keep track of mentally, and there is an increasing chance that we may not possess all the relevant information. As a result, we are forced to compile what we know in the form of lists, tables, pictures, graphs and diagrams, and so on, and to seek additional information from other sources.

The key to using oneself as an information source is the ability to accurately retrieve from long-term memory information that will aid in the solution of the problem. We need to think back over what we have learned in other somewhat similar situations, make a list of some other form of representation of those ideas, and make a judgment as to how helpful that knowledge might be. Techniques for ensuring accurate and reliable recall were discussed in Chapter 8 on information-processing theory.

In addition to relying on our own knowledge and experience to solve problems, we can draw on the knowledge and experience of friends, colleagues, and experts. The main purpose of soliciting the views of others about solutions to problems and positions on issues is to identify the reasons and evidence those people offer in support of their positions. This skill of asking questions and analyzing responses is quite useful in debates and classroom discussions of controversial issues.

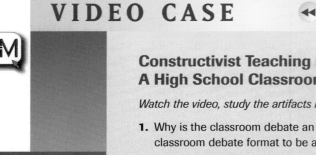

VIDEO CASE    ◄◄ ► ►►

## Constructivist Teaching in Action: A High School Classroom Debate

*Watch the video, study the artifacts in the case, and reflect upon the following questions:*

1. Why is the classroom debate an excellent example of constructivism in action? Do you find the classroom debate format to be an example of social constructivism or cognitive constructivism?

2. How does the classroom teacher in this Video Case arrange the elements of this lesson and guide students so that their constructivist learning experience is effective? Please cite specific examples.

---

**HM TeacherPrepSPACE**

Want to test your own problem-solving process? See the Netlabs at the textbook's student website.

Studying worked examples is an effective solution strategy

Solve simpler version of problem first; then transfer process to harder problem

Break complex problems into manageable parts

**Step 4: Formulate and Carry Out a Solution**   When you feel that you understand the nature of a problem or issue and possess sufficient relevant information, you are ready to attempt a solution. The first step is to consider which of several alternative approaches is likely to be most effective. The literature on problem solving mentions quite a few solution strategies. Because these solution strategies are very general in nature—they can apply to different kinds of problems in different content areas and offer only a general approach to solving a problem—they are referred to as *heuristics* (Martinez, 1998). We will discuss seven **heuristics** that we think are particularly useful.

- *Study worked examples.* This approach may strike you as so obvious that it hardly merits attention, but it is worth mentioning for two reasons. First, obvious solution strategies are the ones that are most often overlooked. Second, it is a very effective solution strategy (Sweller, van Merriënboer, & Paas, 1998). The beneficial effect is thought to be due to the learners' acquisition of a general problem schema. To get the most out of this heuristic, use multiple examples and different formats for each problem type and encourage learners to explain to themselves the problem-solving strategy illustrated by the examples (Atkinson, Derry, Renkl, & Wortham, 2000).

- *Work on a simpler version of the problem.* This is another common and very effective approach. Geometry offers a particularly clear example of working on a simpler problem. If you are having difficulty solving a problem of solid geometry (which involves three dimensions), work out a similar problem in plane geometry (two dimensions) and then apply the solution to the three-dimensional example (Nickerson, 1994; Polya, 1957). Architects and engineers employ this approach when they construct scaled-down models of bridges, buildings, experimental aircraft, and the like. Scientists do the same thing by creating laboratory simulations of real-world phenomena.

- *Break the problem into parts.* The key to this approach is to make sure you break the problem into manageable parts. Whether you can do this will depend largely on how much subject-matter knowledge you have. The more you know about the domain from which the problem comes, the easier it is to know how to break a problem into logical, easy-to-handle parts.

  At least two benefits result from breaking a problem into parts: (1) it reduces the amount of information you have to keep in short-term memory to a manageable level, and (2) the method used to solve one part of the problem can often be used to solve another part. Bransford and Stein (1993) use the following example to illustrate how this approach works.

*To figure out the solution to a problem, good problem solvers often work first on a simpler version of the problem.*

*Problem:* What day follows the day before yesterday if two days from now will be Sunday?

1. What is today if two days from now will be Sunday? (Friday)
2. If today is Friday, what is the day before yesterday? (Wednesday)
3. What day follows Wednesday? (Thursday)

| Work backward when goal is clear but beginning state is not |

- *Work backward.* This is a particularly good solution strategy to use whenever the goal is clear but the beginning state is not. Bransford and Stein (1993) offer the following example. Suppose you arranged to meet someone at a restaurant across town at noon. When should you leave your office to be sure of arriving on time? By working backward from your destination and arrival time (it takes about ten minutes to find a parking spot and walk to the restaurant; it takes about thirty minutes to drive to the area where you would park; it takes about five minutes to walk from your office to your car), you would more quickly and easily determine when to leave your office (about 11:15) than if you had worked the problem forward.

| Backward fading: a procedure that helps students develop problem-solving capability by reasoning from the solution back to first steps |

- *Backward fading.* Students vary in how much they know about the subject matter on which the problems are based, and students with more prior knowledge do better on problem-solving tests when they are given problem-solving instruction and practice than when they are given worked examples to study (Atkinson et al., 2000). For these reasons, a good procedure to use with all students is something called *backward fading.* Backward fading is basically a combination of studying worked examples, working backward, and practicing solving problems. First, a completely worked-out example (such as one that requires three steps to complete) is provided. Then a similar problem is presented with only the first two steps worked out. The last step has to be completed by the learner. A third problem provides the solution to the first step and requires the learner to determine the solution for steps two and three. Finally, the fourth problem requires the learner to solve all three steps. Compared with peers who saw ordinary worked examples and practiced solving problems, a group of college students who were exposed to the backward fading procedure scored significantly better on problems that were both similar to and different from the practice problems (Atkinson, Renkle, & Merrill, 2003).

Solve a similar problem and then apply the same method

- *Solve an analogous problem.* If you are having difficulty solving a problem, possibly because your knowledge of the subject matter is incomplete, it may be useful to think of a similar problem about a subject in which you are more knowledgeable. Solve the analogous problem, and then use the same method to solve the first problem. In essence, this is a way of making the unfamiliar familiar.

  Although solving analogous problems is a very powerful solution strategy, it can be difficult to employ, especially for novices. In our previous discussion of understanding the problem, we made the point that novices represent problems on the basis of superficial features, whereas experts operate from knowledge of underlying concepts and principles. The same is true of analogies. Most of us know that DNA is somehow related to the image of a "twisted ladder" called the *double helix*, but there is much more to mapping the human genome than visualizing a twisted ladder. Novices are more likely than experts to use superficial analogies (Gick, 1986). Analogous problems are discussed in the upcoming Suggestions for Teaching.

Create an external representation of the problem

- *Create an external representation of the problem.* This heuristic is doubly useful because it also aids in problem framing. Many problems can be represented as pictures, equations, graphs, flowcharts, and the like. The figures in the next Suggestions for Teaching section illustrate how a pictorial or symbolic form of representation can help one both understand and solve the problem (Martinez, 1998).

**Step 5: Evaluate the Solution**    The last step in the problem-solving process is to evaluate the adequacy of the solution. For relatively simple, well-structured problems in which the emphasis is on producing a correct response, two levels of evaluation are available:

Evaluate solutions to well-structured problems by estimating or checking

- The problem solver can ask whether, given the problem statement, the answer makes sense. For example, if the problem reads $75 \times 5 = ?$ and the response is 80, a little voice inside the problem solver's head should say that the answer cannot possibly be right. This signal should prompt a reevaluation of the way the problem was represented and the solution procedure that was used (for example, "I misread the times sign as a plus sign and added when I should have multiplied").
- The problem solver can use an alternative algorithm to check the accuracy of the solution. This is necessary because an error in carrying out an algorithm can produce an incorrect response that is still in the ballpark. For example, a common error in multiple-column subtraction problems is to subtract a smaller digit from a larger one regardless of whether the small number is in the minuend (top row) or the subtrahend (bottom row) (Mayer, 1987), as in

$$\begin{array}{r} 522 \\ -\,418 \\ \hline 116 \end{array}$$

## pause & reflect

Critics of American education argue that students are poor problem solvers because they receive little systematic instruction in problem-solving processes. How would you rate the instruction you received in problem solving? In terms of the five steps discussed on the preceding pages, which ones were you taught? What can you do to ensure that your students become good problem solvers?

Because this answer is off by only 12 units, it "looks right." The flaw can be discovered, however, by adding the answer to the subtrahend to produce the minuend.

The evaluation of solutions to ill-structured problems is likely to be more complicated and time-consuming for at least two reasons. First, the evaluation should occur both before and after the solution is implemented. Although many flaws and omissions can be identified and corrected beforehand, some will slip through. There is much to be learned by observing the effects of our solutions. Second, because these ill-structured problems are complex, often involving a dozen or more variables, some sort of systematic framework should guide the evaluation. Vincent Ruggiero suggests a four-step procedure (1988, pp. 44–46):

1. Ask and answer a set of basic questions. Imagine, for example, that you have proposed a classroom incentive system (a token economy, perhaps) to enhance student motivation. You might ask such questions as, How will this program be implemented? By whom? When? Where? With what materials? How will the materials be obtained?
2. Identify imperfections and complications. Is this idea, for example, safe, convenient, efficient, economical, and compatible with existing policies and practices?
3. Anticipate possible negative reactions from other people. For instance, might parents or the school principal object?
4. Devise improvements.

The next section contains guidelines and examples that will help you improve the problem-solving skills of your students.

# Suggestions for Teaching in Your Classroom

## Teaching Problem-Solving Techniques

### 1 Teach students how to identify problems.

Because the notion of finding problems is likely to strike students as an unusual activity, you may want to introduce this skill in gradual steps. One way to start is to have students list different ways in which problems can be identified. Typical responses are to scan newspaper and magazine articles, observe customer and employee behavior in a store, watch traffic patterns in a local area, and interview local residents, including, for instance, teachers, business owners, police, clergy, or government officials. A next step is to have students carry out these suggested activities in order to gain an understanding of the status quo and to find out how people identify problems. They may learn, for example, that a principal periodically has lunch with a teacher in order to learn of conditions that decrease the teacher's effectiveness.

### 2 Teach students how to represent problems.

Problem representation involves transforming the words that express a problem into an internal representation of those words. To do this, students must understand the concepts embedded in the problem statement and the relationships among those concepts. Consequently, the ability to construct a good representation of a problem is based on a command of the subject matter surrounding the problem and familiarity with the particular type of problem.

As the work of Jerome Bruner and David Ausubel indicates, students need to acquire a genuine understanding of many of the associations, discriminations, concepts, and rules of a discipline before they can effectively solve problems in that subject-matter area. Too often, students are taught to state principles on cue, but they reveal by further responses that they do not understand what they are saying. The recommendations we make in this book about presenting information in an organized fashion and in meaningful contexts will go a long way toward helping students understand the subject matter on which problems are based; see the specific suggestions in Chapter 8 and Chapter 13.

Comprehension of subject matter critical to problem solving

The classic illustration of what can occur when information is not learned meaningfully was given over a century ago by William James in his *Talks to Teachers*:

> A friend of mine, visiting a school, was asked to examine a young class in geography. Glancing at the book, she said: "Suppose you should dig a hole in the ground, hundreds of feet deep, how should you find it at the bottom—warmer or colder than on top?" None of the class replying, the teacher said: "I'm sure they know, but I think you don't ask the question quite rightly. Let me try." So, taking the book, she asked: "In what condition is the interior of the globe?" and received the immediate answer from half the class at once: "The interior of the globe is in a condition of igneous fusion." (1899, p. 150)

If these students had genuinely understood concepts and principles regarding the composition of the earth (such as the relationship between igneous fusion and heat), instead of having simply memorized meaningless phrases, they would have been able to answer the original question.

Once you are satisfied that students meaningfully understand the elements of a problem, you can demonstrate methods to represent those elements and how they interrelate. One frequent recommendation is to use visual forms of problem representation (concept maps, Venn diagrams, flowcharts, and drawings, for example). Visual representations of ideas foster comprehension because of their concreteness. The following two examples illustrate how a Venn diagram (a set of intersecting circles) and a flow diagram can represent a particular type of problem.

### EXAMPLE PROBLEM

The government wants to contact all druggists, all gun store owners, and all parents in a town without contacting anyone twice. Based on the following statistics, how many people must be contacted?

| | |
|---|---:|
| Druggists | 10 |
| Gun store owners | 5 |
| Parents | 3,000 |
| Druggists who own gun stores | 0 |
| Druggists who are parents | 7 |
| Gun store owners who are parents | 3 |

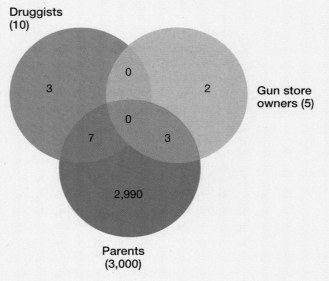

### Solution Using Venn Diagram

As the Venn diagram illustrates, the total number of people who must be contacted is 2,990 + 7 + 3 + 3 + 2 = 3,005 (adapted from Whimbey & Lochhead, 1999, p. 104).[1]

---

[1] Excerpts and diagrams in this section are from "Solution Using Venn Diagram," adapted from A. Whimbey and J. Lochhead, *Problem Solving and Comprehension*, Sixth Edition (Mahwah, NJ: Lawrence Erlbaum Associates, Inc., Publishers), pp. 104, 128. © 1999 reprinted by permission.

**EXAMPLE PROBLEM**

Sally loaned $7.00 to Betty. But Sally borrowed $15.00 from Estella and $32.00 from Joan. Moreover, Joan owes $3.00 to Estella and $7.00 to Betty. One day the women got together at Betty's house to straighten out their accounts. Which woman left with $18.00 more than she came with?

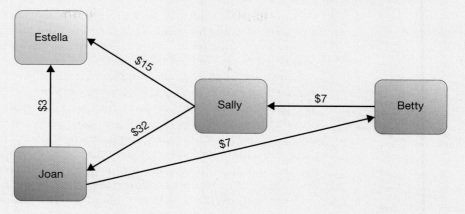

### Solution Using Flow Diagram

Verbal reasoning problems that describe transactions can take the form of a flow diagram, as shown here. From the diagram, it is clear that Estella left with $18.00 more than she came with (adapted from Whimbey & Lochhead, 1999, p. 128).

**3** **Teach students how to compile relevant information.**

Good problem solvers start with themselves when compiling information to solve a problem or evidence to support a position on an issue. They recognize the importance of recalling earlier-learned information (metacognitive knowledge) and are adept at doing so (cognitive skill). Poor problem solvers, by contrast, lack metacognitive knowledge, cognitive skills, or both. If their deficiency is metacognitive, they make little or no effort to recall solution-relevant memories, even when the information was recently learned, because they do not understand the importance of searching long-term memory for potentially useful knowledge. Even if a student poor in problem solving recognizes the value of searching long-term memory for relevant information, he may still be handicapped because of inadequate encoding and retrieval skills.

To minimize any metacognitive deficiency, make sure your instruction in problem-solving methods emphasizes the importance of retrieving and using previously learned knowledge. To minimize retrieval problems, make sure you recall and implement the Suggestions for Teaching in Your Classroom sections that we offered in Chapter 8.

If a student does not possess all the relevant information needed to work out a solution or analyze an issue, you will have to guide her toward individuals and sources that can help. In referring students to individuals, select people who are judged to be reasonably knowledgeable about the subject, are careful thinkers, and are willing to share their ideas (Ruggiero, 1988, 2007). As an example, consider the issue of whether certain books (such as the novels *Catcher in the Rye*, by J. D. Salinger, *I Know Why the Caged Bird Sings* by Maya Angelou, *Native Son* by Richard Wright, and *Tom Sawyer* by Mark Twain) should be banned from a school's reading list. In interviewing a knowledgeable person, students might ask questions such as the following because they allow some insight into the individual's reasoning process and the evidence used to support his position:

- What general effects do you think characters in novels who rebel against adult authority have on a reader's behavior?
- Are certain groups of people, such as middle and high school students, likely to be influenced by the motives and actions of such characters? Why do you think so?

- Does a ban on certain books violate the authors' right to free speech?
- Does a book ban violate the principle of academic freedom? Why?
- Is it the proper role of a school board to prevent or discourage students from exposure to certain ideas during school hours?

If a reasonably informed person is not available, recognized authorities can often be interviewed by phone. If a student chooses this tactic, Ruggiero suggests calling or writing in advance for an appointment, preparing questions in advance, and asking permission to tape-record the interview.

Obviously, in addition to or in lieu of personal interviews, students can find substantial information in a good library. For example, you can steer them toward books by recognized authorities, research findings, court cases, and interviews with prominent individuals in periodicals. Although the Internet potentially contains a vast amount of information on any topic, warn students about using material gathered there indiscriminately. As with any other medium, there are more and less reliable sources, and only material from reputable sources should be gathered. One additional benefit is that an extra layer of problem-solving activity is introduced when students must decide how to gather and evaluate online information.

**HM** *TeacherPrepSPACE*

Check the Reflective Journal Questions at the textbook's student website for ideas to address in your journal writing.

### 4  Teach several methods for formulating problem solutions.

Previously, we mentioned six methods for formulating a problem solution: study worked examples, work on a simpler version of the problem, break the problem into parts, work backward, solve an analogous problem, and create an external representation of the problem. We encourage you to check out some sources as demonstrations of worked problems and as opportunities for you to practice your own problem-solving skills so that you will be well prepared to teach each of these six methods.

### 5  Teach students the skills of evaluation.

Solutions to well-structured problems are usually evaluated through the application of an estimating or checking routine. Such procedures can be found in any good mathematics text. The evaluation of solutions to ill-structured problems and analyses of issues, however, is more complex and is less frequently taught. Ruggiero (1988, 2007) discusses the following ten habits and skills as contributing to the ability to evaluate complex solutions and positions:

- Being open-minded about opposing points of view.
- Selecting proper criteria of evaluation. Violations of this skill abound. A current example is the use of standardized achievement test scores to evaluate the quality of classroom instruction.
- Understanding the essence of an argument. To foster this skill, Ruggiero recommends that students be taught how to write a *précis*, which is a concise summary of an oral argument or a reading passage.
- Evaluating the reliability of sources.
- Properly interpreting factual data (for example, recognizing that an increase in a state's income tax rate from 4 to 6 percent is an increase not of 2 percent but of 50 percent).
- Testing the credibility of hypotheses. On the basis of existing data, hypotheses can range from highly improbable to highly probable.
- Making important distinctions (for instance, between preference and judgment, emotion and content, appearance and reality).
- Recognizing unstated assumptions (for example, that because two events occur close together in time, one causes the other; that what is clear to us will be clear to others; that if the majority believes something, it must be true).
- Evaluating the validity and truthfulness of one's arguments (by, for example, checking that conclusions logically follow from premises and that conclusions

have not been influenced by such reasoning flaws as either-or thinking, over-generalizing, or oversimplifying).
- Recognizing when evidence is insufficient.

All of these ten skills can be modeled and taught in your classroom.

# TRANSFER OF LEARNING

Throughout this chapter and preceding ones, we have indicated that classroom instruction should be arranged in such a way that students independently apply the knowledge and problem-solving skills they learn in school to similar but new situations. This capability is the main goal of problem-solving instruction and is typically valued very highly by educators (De Corte, 2003; Haskell, 2001). Referred to as **transfer of learning,** it is the essence of being an autonomous learner and problem solver, both in and out of school (Pugh & Bergin, 2005). In this section, we will examine the nature of transfer and discuss ways in which you can help bring it about.

## The Nature and Significance of Transfer of Learning

**The Theory of Identical Elements**    During the early 1900s, it was common practice for high school students and colleges to require that students take such subjects as Latin, Greek, and geometry. Because they were considered difficult topics to learn, mastery of them was expected to improve a student's ability to memorize, think, and reason. These enhanced abilities were then expected to facilitate the learning of less difficult subjects. The rationale behind this practice was that the human mind, much like any muscle in the body, could be exercised and made stronger. A strong mind, then, would learn things that a weak mind would not. This practice, known as the *doctrine of formal discipline*, constituted an early (and incorrect) explanation of transfer (Barnett & Ceci, 2002; Haag & Stern, 2003).

Early view of transfer based on degree of similarity between two tasks

In 1901, Edward Thorndike and Robert Woodworth proposed an alternative explanation of how transfer occurs. They argued that the degree to which knowledge and skills acquired in learning one task can help someone learn another task depends on how similar the two tasks are (if we assume that the learner recognizes the similarities). The greater the degree of similarity is between the tasks' stimulus and response elements (as in riding a bicycle and riding a motorcycle), the greater the amount of transfer will be. This idea became known as the **theory of identical elements** (Cox, 1997).

**Positive, Negative, and Zero Transfer**    In time, however, other psychologists (among them Ellis, 1965; Osgood, 1949) identified different types of transfer and the conditions under which each type prevailed. A useful distinction was made among positive transfer, negative transfer, and zero transfer (Ormrod, 2004).

Positive transfer: previous learning makes later learning easier

The discussion up to this point has been alluding to **positive transfer,** defined as a situation in which prior learning aids subsequent learning. According to Thorndike's analysis, positive transfer occurs when a new learning task calls for essentially the same response that was made to a similar, earlier-learned task. The accomplished accordion player, for instance, probably will become a proficient pianist faster than someone who knows how to play the drums or someone who plays no musical instrument at all, all other things being equal. Similarly, the native English speaker who is also fluent in French is likely to have an easier time learning Spanish than is someone who speaks no foreign language.

Negative transfer: previous learning interferes with later learning

**Negative transfer** is defined as a situation in which prior learning interferes with subsequent learning. It occurs when two tasks are highly similar but require different responses. A tennis player learning how to play racquetball, for example, may encounter problems at first because of a tendency to swing the racquetball racket as if it were a tennis racket. Primary grade children often experience negative transfer when they encounter words that are spelled alike but pronounced differently (as in "I will *read* this story now since I *read* that story last week").

**Zero transfer** is defined as a situation in which prior learning has no effect on new learning. It can be expected when two tasks have different stimuli and different responses. Learning to conjugate Latin verbs, for example, is not likely to have any effect on learning how to find the area of a rectangle.

**Specific and General Transfer** The preceding description of positive transfer, although useful, is somewhat limiting because it is unclear whether transfer from one task to another is due to specific similarities or to more general similarities. Psychologists (as described by Ellis, 1978) decide whether transfer is due to specific or general factors by setting up learning tasks such as the following for three different but equivalent groups of learners.

|         | Initial Task  | Transfer Task |
| ------- | ------------- | ------------- |
| Group 1 | Learn French  | Learn Spanish |
| Group 2 | Learn Chinese | Learn Spanish |
| Group 3 | Learn Spanish |               |

Specific transfer due to specific similarities between two tasks

General transfer due to use of same cognitive strategies

If on a Spanish test, group 1 scores higher than group 2, the difference is attributed to **specific transfer** of similarities between French and Spanish (such as vocabulary, verb conjugations, and sentence structure). If groups 1 and 2 score the same but both outscore group 3, the difference is attributed to nonspecific transfer, or **general transfer,** of similarities between the two tasks since Chinese shares no apparent specific characteristics with French or Spanish, both Romance languages. In this case, it is possible that learners use cognitive strategies—such as imagery, verbal elaboration, and mnemonic devices—when learning a foreign language and that these transfer to the learning of other foreign languages. Such nonspecific transfer effects have also been demonstrated for other classroom tasks, such as problem solving and learning from text (Ellis, 1978; Royer, 1979).

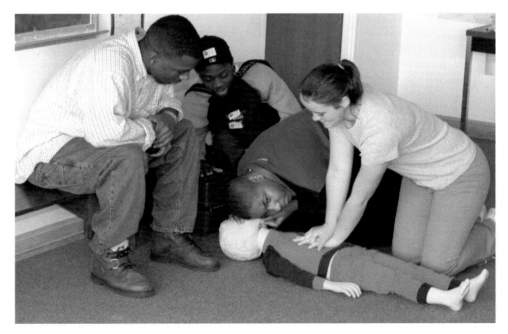

*If teachers want students to apply what they learn in the classroom in other settings in the future, they should create tasks and conditions that are similar to those that students will encounter later.*

Support for specific transfer, as well as for the identical elements theory, comes from a study of college students in Germany who had taken either French or Latin when they were in seventh grade as their second foreign language. At the time of the study, these students were enrolled in an intensive beginners' course in Spanish. On a written test that required the students to translate a passage into Spanish, those who had taken French several years earlier made significantly fewer grammar and vocabulary errors than did students who had taken Latin (Haag & Stern, 2003).

**Near and Far Transfer**   Another common distinction, similar to the specific-general distinction, is based on the perceived similarity of the original learning task to the transfer task. **Near transfer** refers to situations in which the knowledge domains are highly similar, the settings in which the original learning and transfer tasks occur are basically the same, and the elapsed time between the two tasks is relatively short. **Far transfer** occurs when the knowledge domains and settings are judged to be dissimilar and the time between the original learning and transfer tasks is relatively long (Barnett & Ceci, 2002). Thus using math skills one acquired over the past several weeks to solve the problems at the end of the current chapter in a textbook is an example of near transfer. Using those same skills several years later to determine which of several investment options is most likely to produce the highest rate of return is an example of far transfer.

> Near transfer: previously learned knowledge and skills used relatively soon on highly similar task

> Far transfer: previously learned knowledge and skills used much later on dissimilar tasks and under different conditions

You may have noticed our use of such imprecise and subjective terms as "highly similar," "basically the same," "relatively long," and "judged to be dissimilar." This is done for a good reason. At present, there is no way to precisely measure the similarity between a learning task and a transfer task. The best we can do is identify the major dimensions that two tasks share (such as subject matter, physical setting, time between two tasks, and the conditions under which each is performed) and subjectively decide that the two dimensions are sufficiently similar or dissimilar to warrant the label *near transfer* or *far transfer*. Sometimes this approach produces a high degree of agreement, but at other times one person's far transfer is another person's near transfer (Barnett & Ceci, 2002).

## Contemporary Views of Specific/Near and General/Far Transfer

Gavriel Salomon and David Perkins (1989) combine aspects of specific and near transfer and general and far transfer under the labels *low-road transfer* and *high-road transfer*, respectively.

**Low-Road Transfer**   **Low-road transfer** refers to a situation in which a previously learned skill or idea is almost automatically retrieved from memory and applied to a highly similar current task. For example, a student who has mastered the skill of two-column addition and correctly completes three-column and four-column addition problems with no prompting or instruction is exhibiting low-road transfer. Another example is a student who learns how to tune up car engines in an auto shop class and then almost effortlessly and automatically carries out the same task as an employee of an auto repair business. As you may have suspected, low-road transfer is basically a contemporary version of Thorndike and Woodworth's identical elements theory (Cox, 1997).

> Low-road transfer: previously learned skill automatically applied to similar current task

Two conditions need to be present for low-road transfer to occur:

1. Students have to be given ample opportunities to practice using the target skill.
2. Practice has to occur with different materials and in different settings. The more varied the practice is, the greater is the range of tasks to which the skill can be applied.

If, for example, you want students to be good note takers, give them instruction and ample practice at taking notes from their biology, health, and English textbooks. Once they become accomplished note takers in these subjects, they will likely apply this skill to other subjects in an almost automatic fashion.

In essence, what we are describing is the behavioral principle of generalization. Because the transfer task is similar in one or more respects to the practice task and tends to occur in similar settings, low-road transfer is similar to specific and near transfer.

**High-Road Transfer**    **High-road transfer** refers to the ways people transfer prior knowledge and skills over longer time periods to new situations that look rather different from the original task. High-road transfer involves the conscious, controlled, somewhat effortful formulation of an "abstraction" (that is, a rule, a schema, a strategy, or an analogy) that allows a connection to be made between two tasks. For example, an individual who learns to set aside a certain number of hours every day to complete homework assignments and study for upcoming exams formulates the principle that the most efficient way to accomplish a task is to break it down into small pieces and work at each piece according to a set schedule. As an adult, the individual uses this principle to deal successfully with complex tasks at work and at home.

> High-road transfer: formulate rule from one task and apply to related task

As another example, imagine a student who, after much observation and thought, has finally developed a good sense of what school is and how one is supposed to behave there. This student has developed a school schema. Such a schema would probably be made up of actors (teachers and students), objects (desks, chalkboards, books, pencils), and events (reading, listening, writing, talking, drawing). Because this is an idealized abstraction, actual classrooms may contain fewer or greater numbers of these characteristics in varying proportions. Even so, with this schema, a student could walk into any instructional setting (another school classroom, a training seminar, or a press briefing, for example) and readily understand what was going on, why it was going on, and how one should behave. Of course, with repeated applications of schemata, rules, strategies, and the like, the behaviors become less conscious and more automatic. What was once a reflection of high-road transfer becomes low-road transfer.

> **HM TeacherPrepSPACE**
>
> For help in remembering the key terms introduced in this chapter, you may want to use the interactive flashcards at the textbook's student website.

Several researchers (e.g., Bereiter, 1997; Salomon & Perkins, 1989) refer to this deliberate, conscious, effortful formulating of a general principle or schema that can be applied to a variety of different-looking but fundamentally similar tasks as *mindful abstraction*. The *mindful* part of the phrase indicates that the abstraction must be thought about and fully understood for high-road transfer to occur. That is, people must be aware of what they are doing and why they are doing it. This is essentially training in metacognition. Recall our earlier discussion in this chapter of inert knowledge and Richard Feynman's observations of how his classmates at the Massachusetts Institute of Technology failed to recognize the application of a previously learned mathematical formula because it was initially learned for use only in that course. Carl Bereiter (1997) argues that when learning is too strongly situated in a particular context, as in the case of Feynman's MIT classmates, high-road transfer is impeded.

## Take a Stand!

### If You Want Transfer, Then Teach for Transfer

From the elementary grades through graduate school, you will find teachers who believe that it is perfectly acceptable to provide students with basic explanations and examples of concepts and procedures during classroom instruction and then test them on their ability to answer more advanced questions or solve more difficult problems. Their intuitively appealing rationale is that if the students are paying attention in class, carefully reading the textbook, and diligently doing the assigned homework, they will be able to make the jump from the simpler, lower-level classroom examples to the more difficult and advanced test items.

We hope you have learned from the discussion of transfer in this chapter that nothing could be further from the truth. Students have to be exposed to the same types of concepts, problems, and procedures during instruction that they will be held accountable for on an exam, and they may even have to be prompted on the exam to use the knowledge they were taught. In other words, *if you want transfer, then teach for transfer*. Give your students opportunities to use what they learn in new situations. If you expect transfer to occur spontaneously, like so many other teachers, you will be disappointed most of the time.

> **HM TeacherPrepSPACE**
>
> What are your own experiences with teachers who expect transfer to occur automatically? To investigate this subject further, see the Take a Stand! section of the textbook's student website.

**Teaching for Low-Road and High-Road Transfer**   As we noted at the beginning of this section, transfer of previously learned knowledge and skill to new tasks and settings is a goal that is high on almost every teacher's list. Yet one study of classroom activity found that only 7 percent of tasks required students to use information they had learned previously (Bennett, Desforges, Cockburn, & Wilkinson, 1984). Perhaps most teachers feel they simply don't know how to teach for transfer. That need not be your fate. The following guidelines (based on Cox, 1997; De Corte, 2003; Halpern, 1998; Salomon & Perkins, 1989) should produce greater levels of both low-road and high-road transfer:

1. Provide students with multiple opportunities for varied practice to help them develop a rich web of interrelated concepts.
2. Give students opportunities to solve problems that are similar to those they will eventually have to solve, and establish conditions similar to those they will eventually face.
3. Teach students how to formulate, for a variety of tasks, general rules, strategies, or schemes that they can use in the future with a variety of similar problems.
4. Give students cues that will allow them to retrieve from memory earlier-learned information that can be used to make current learning easier.
5. Teach students to focus on the beneficial effects of creating and using rules and strategies to solve particular kinds of problems.

*Low-road and high-road transfer produced by varied practice at applying skills, rules, memory retrieval cues*

## TECHNOLOGY TOOLS FOR KNOWLEDGE CONSTRUCTION AND PROBLEM SOLVING

Previously in the book, we noted that one use of computers in schools is as a learning and problem-solving tool. This use of computer-based technology supports a constructivist approach to learning and is often called learning *with* computers (Jonassen, 2000; Jonassen, Howland, Moore, & Marra, 2003). Students learn with computers when computers support knowledge construction, exploration, learning by doing, learning by conversing, and learning by reflecting.

David Jonassen (Jonassen, 2000; Jonassen et al., 2003) uses the term *mindtools* to refer to computer applications that lend themselves to these types of activities. Mindtools include databases, semantic networks (concept mapping programs), spreadsheets, expert systems (artificial intelligence), microworlds, search engines, visualization tools, hypermedia, and computer conferencing. Rather than using computer programs just to present and represent information, which is what drill and tutorial programs do, mindtools allow learners to construct, share, and revise knowledge in more open-ended environments. In effect, learners become producers, designers, and "authors of knowledge" (Lehrer, 1993). In the sections that follow, we briefly examine applications of computer-based technology that support the constructivist view of learning.

*Technology tools are available to help students construct knowledge, become better problem solvers*

### Multimedia Simulations

A basic principle of constructivism is that meaningful learning involves learning by doing, as opposed to learning just by reading and/or listening. Because actual hands-on experience is not always feasible, computer-based simulation programs can be used as the next best thing. But learning by doing, particularly in the absence of instructor guidance, or scaffolding, has been criticized as being inefficient because of the large number of mistakes that students make.

One study (Mayer, Mautone, & Prothero, 2002) tested this contention by examining the effect of different types of instructor scaffolding on undergraduate students' performance in a multimedia geology simulation. The simulation places students on an unknown planet and requires them to identify the geological features (such as canyons, mountain ridges, craters, or islands) that are present on a certain part of the planet's surface. The catch is that the students cannot directly see these features but have to infer their existence by creating what are called profile lines. Profile lines provide information about distance, elevation of the target feature, and the surrounding area. Students then use this information to visualize the unknown feature. This process is analogous to geologists' using sonar waves to identify underground or underwater features. In the study, the students were given either written instructions, a verbal explanation of how to use a strategy summary sheet for identifying each geologic feature, pictorial sketches of each feature, or both the summary sheet and the sketches.

Students who received either sketches of the features they were asked to identify or both sketches and guidance about which steps to take in drawing and interpreting profile lines identified more features than did students who received just written instructions. The authors likened this effect to the positive effect of providing students with worked examples. These results suggest that simulations will work best when accompanied by careful and appropriate scaffolding.

The learning-by-doing feature of multimedia simulation programs attains perhaps its fullest expression in virtual reality environments. By wearing a head-mounted display and earphones and being able to physically move through the environment by walking around a room, learners feel as if they are actually "in" the environment in which the simulation occurs. For this reason, virtual reality environments are also called high-immersion environments. By contrast, standard multimedia simulations, in which students sit in front of a computer screen and explore an environment by moving the computer's mouse, are considered to be low-immersion environments. Because of virtual reality's high-immersion features, it is thought to produce higher levels of motivation and learning than the standard multimedia simulation. Of the few experimental tests of this claim, one was conducted by Roxana Moreno and Richard Mayer (2002).

The simulation used in this study took undergraduate students to five alien planets, each of which had a different climate, and required them to design a plant (choosing from various roots, stems, and leaves) that would grow well under the prevailing conditions. They were given prompts and feedback by the computer in the form of either speech or on-screen text. Students in the high-immersion condition wore a head-mounted display and earphones and explored each planet's environment by walking around the room in which the experiment was conducted. Students in the low-immersion condition sat in front of a computer wearing headphones (to hear the spoken feedback) and navigated around each environment by using the mouse.

Although students in the high-immersion condition rated the experience as being more lifelike and involving, their performance on tests of retention (the number of types of roots, stems, and leaves recalled) and transfer (designing plants for conditions that were different from those on the five planets) was equivalent to that of students in the low-immersion condition. Because there is as yet insufficient research on the relative benefits of virtual reality, it is too soon to conclude that this technology has no place in the classroom. In fact, more recent efforts have examined the relative benefits of guidance and reflection in multimedia learning environments (Moreno & Mayer, 2005). Once again using plant design, Moreno and Mayer found that providing students with corrective explanations of their answers produced greater transfer and fewer misconceptions while solving problems and engaging in multimedia learning.

## Computer-Supported Intentional Learning Environments

Marlene Scardamalia and Carl Bereiter (1996, p. 10) ask us to "imagine a network of networks—people from schools, universities, cultural institutions, service organizations, businesses—simultaneously building knowledge within their primary groups while advancing the knowledge of others. We might call such a community network a knowledge-building society." Since the 1980s these researchers have developed and tested aspects of such a network with the Computer-Supported Intentional Learning Environments (CSILE) project (Scardamali & Bereiter, 1991).

The CSILE project is built around the concept of intentional learning (Scardamalia & Bereiter, 1991). In an intentional learning environment, students learn how to set goals, generate and interrelate new ideas, link new knowledge to old, negotiate meaning with peers, and relate what they learned to other tasks. The product of these activities, like the product of any scientific inquiry, is then made available to other students (Watkins, 2005).

The CSILE project allows students to create informational links, or "notes," in several ways (for example, text notes, drawings, graphs, pictures, timelines, and maps). CSILE also contains designated "cooperation" icons that encourage students to reflect on how their work links to others, as well as idea browsing and linking tools for marking notes that involve or intend cooperation. Using this database system, students comment on the work of others, read responses to their hypotheses, or search for information posted by their peers under a particular topic title. For instance, a search for the word *whales* would call up all the work of students who assigned that word as a keyword in their CSILE contributions. In such a decentralized, free-flowing environment, no longer must the teacher initiate all discussion and coordinate turn taking (Hewitt, 2002; Scardamalia & Bereiter, 1991, 1996). Jim Hewitt (2002) describes how a sixth-grade teacher used CSILE to gradually transform his instructional approach from being teacher directed and task centered to being collaborative and knowledge centered.

Studies show that students who use CSILE perform better on standardized language and reading tests, ask deeper questions, are more elaborate and coherent in their commentaries, demonstrate more mature beliefs about learning, and engage in discussions that are more committed to scientific progress (Scardamalia & Bereiter, 1996). The availability of a cooperation icon seems to foster greater peer commenting and cooperative efforts (Scardamalia & Bereiter, 1991), and students who make more conceptual progress with CSILE tend to be more problem- than fact-oriented (Oshima, Scardamalia, & Bereiter, 1996).

A version of CSILE for the Web, called Knowledge Forum, is also available. The goal of Knowledge Forum is to have students mimic the collaborative knowledge-building process that characterizes the work of expert learners. Consequently, students must label their contribution to a communal database topic prior to posting it by using such labels as *My Theory, I Need to Understand, New Information, This Theory Cannot Explain, A Better Theory,* and *Putting Our Knowledge Together.* So, if in the course of helping to build a knowledge base about human vision, a student wrote, "I need to understand why we have two eyes instead of one or three," another member of this community could post a New Information note that discussed the relationship between binocular vision and depth perception. The resulting knowledge base would then be subject to modifications and additions from others. You can obtain more information about Knowledge Forum at **www.knowledgeforum.com**.

## Learning Through Collaborative Visualization

As indicated in previous chapters, the emergence of computer networks has fostered global scientific data collection and sharing. Now, less skilled young learners can be apprenticed into fields such as meteorology and environmental science through social interaction with experts and peers in a learning community. Many science projects illustrate how to embed learning in real-world contexts by having students collect such data as rainfall, wind speed, and environmental pollutants and share their findings with peers. Such projects exemplify both the situated learning and social constructivist ideas outlined earlier in this chapter.

One such project was called Learning Through Collaborative Visualization (CoVis). One of the primary goals of CoVis was to foster project-based science learning, or "collaboratories" (Edelson, Pea, & Gomez, 1996, p. 158), which use computer networks so that students can access practicing environmental scientists and scientific tools. The belief was that science is learned through participation and "learning-in-doing," not through preparation by someone else. The project included e-mail, news group discussions, listservs (Internet sites on which individuals exchange information and ask questions about a specific topic), remote screen sharing, and communication with peers and scientists using both video and audio conferencing. Students' collaborative investigations might include such topics as weather forecasting, ozone depletion trends, global warming, and severe storms. Unlike conventional instruction, CoVis used computer visualization tools to represent real-time data (for example, temperature as color, wind as vectors, and atmospheric pressure as contours).

Research on CoVis revealed mixed success with the telecommunications tools, as some were easier and more practical to use than others (Gomez, Fishman, & Pea, 1998). This research also indicated that teachers need assistance in developing assessment devices for student work and that students may need some help adapting to this new type of learning environment. Case studies also found dramatic differences in adaptation and inventive use of CoVis between schools of low and high socioeconomic status (Shrader, Lento, Gomez, & Pea, 1997).

Although the CoVis program ended in 1998, its website (**www.covis.northwestern .edu**) serves as an archive for CoVis materials. Research on ideas spawned by CoVis is now being conducted by the Center for Learning Technologies in Urban Schools (LeTUS; **www-personal.umich.edu/~fishman/research**). You can download a visualization program called WorldWatcher from the website of the GEODE Initiative (**www.worldwatcher.northwestern.edu**), which grew out of CoVis.

## Jasper Woodbury and Anchored Instruction

Another project that attempts to foster constructivist principles while overcoming the inert knowledge problem comes from a group of researchers at Vanderbilt University called the Cognition and Technology Group at Vanderbilt (CTGV). For more than a decade, CTGV researchers have devised and tested an interesting set of instructional materials that incorporate constructivist principles based on ideas of anchored instruction. **Anchored instruction** involves creating tasks that situate and focus student learning in interesting real-world contexts with many subproblems or issues (for example, making a business plan for the dunking booth at a school's fun fair; Barron et al., 1995). Anchoring problems in a larger context helps students gain a meaningful understanding of the problems and perceive both critical aspects of problems and different points of view (Cognition and Technology Group at Vanderbilt, 1990; Lee, Lee, & Lau, 2006).

The Adventures of Jasper Woodbury is a videodisc-based series designed to promote mathematical problem solving, reasoning, and effective communication among middle school students using anchored instruction. There are three stories for each of four topics (complex trip planning, statistics and business plans, geometry, and algebra) in the series. Each story is a fifteen- to twenty-minute adventure that involves Jasper Woodbury and other characters. At the end of each story, the characters are faced with a problem that students must solve before they are allowed to see how the characters in the video solved the problem. Each episode was designed to be consistent with the learning standards recommended by the National Council of Teachers of Mathematics (Cognition and Technology Group at Vanderbilt, 1993).

In the course of solving the problem posed in the video, students become involved in activities such as generating subgoals, identifying

## pause & reflect

This chapter argues that if teachers want transfer, they should teach for transfer. Go to the Adventures of Jasper Woodbury website and read the summaries of the adventures for any of the subject areas. Are these materials likely to produce transfer? Why?

**Technology Tools for Knowledge Construction and Problem Solving**

relevant information, cooperating with others, discussing the advantages and disadvantages of possible solutions, and comparing perspectives (Cognition and Technology Group at Vanderbilt, 1992a, 1992b). Information about the twelve adventures, the theory behind the Jasper series, research findings, and how the videodiscs can be ordered can be found on the Jasper Woodbury website (**www.peabody.vanderbilt.edu/projects/funded/jasper/jasperhome.html**).

A study of nineteen fifth-grade classrooms that had adopted a constructivist orientation to teaching mathematics reported strong positive effects for those classrooms that used Jasper. Students who worked with the program outscored their non-Jasper peers on the Problem Solving and Data Interpretation, Mathematics Concepts and Estimation, and Mathematics Computation subtests of the Iowa Tests of Basic Skills, with the largest difference occurring on the Problem Solving and Data Interpretation subtest (Hickey, Moore, & Pellegrino, 2001).

Because it is based on constructivist learning principles, the Jasper Woodbury series was designed to be a collaborative problem-solving activity. The benefits of working with other students versus working alone were tested on a group of academically talented sixth graders who viewed the "Journey to Cedar Creek" episode (Barron, 2000). Students who worked in groups of three scored significantly higher than students who worked alone on measures of general planning, subproblem planning, and solutions to subproblems. As a test of near transfer, all students then worked individually on a similar version of the "Cedar Creek" episode. Students who initially worked in teams achieved significantly higher scores than students who worked alone on general planning and subproblem solutions, though not on subproblem planning.

Despite these positive findings, students do not always formulate effective solutions to the problems. The most frequent error students made in solving Jasper problems is overlooking such important solution elements as expenses, amount of time needed to carry out the plan, and the degree of risk incurred by the plan. If you use the Jasper series, you should be prepared to model for students how to analyze such complex problems and formulate an appropriate solution plan (Vye et al., 1997).

The CTGV researchers have extended their anchored instruction research to create a videodisc-based Scientists in Action series meant to help students experience and better understand actual science work (Sherwood, Petrosino, Lin, & Cognition and Technology Group at Vanderbilt, 1998). This series differs from the Jasper Woodbury series in several ways:

- Challenges are posed at several points during the course of the story rather than at the end. When the video resumes, students can compare their solutions with what the scientists on the video actually did.
- Although some of the information needed to solve the problem is presented in the video, much of it is available in ancillary materials (such as topographic maps and actual data from experiments on water quality) that the characters in the video refer to.
- There are links to other curriculum areas, especially social issues related to science.
- The stories are designed so that the hypothesis most students are expected to generate will be wrong (such as the source of river pollution). The video then provides additional data that allows students to revise their original hypothesis. This procedure is used to mimic more closely the way science is done in the real world.

**HM** *TeacherPrep***SPACE**

Use the Weblinks section of the textbook's student website for convenient links to sites mentioned in this section.

For more information on the four episodes that make up this series, visit the Scientists in Action website (**www.vanderbilt.edu/educ2040/sia/bb_teacher_home**).

A third project by this group, the Tenth Planet Literacy Series, is a multimedia program that also uses anchored instruction to support children's decoding, writing, and recording of their own books (see Secules, Cottom, Bray, & Miller, 1997).

The Tenth Planet series can be purchased from Sunburst Technology. The company's website (**http://store.sunburst.com**) contains information about the series and its cost.

## Constructivist-Oriented Websites

Dozens of websites provide constructivist-oriented inquiry and problem-solving activities for students of all ages. In this section, we briefly describe three of them to give you an idea of what is available.

National Geographic offers an Xpeditions website (**www.nationalgeographic .com/xpeditions**) that has numerous resources and activities to help students learn about geographic concepts and issues. In "A Reason for the Season," students are given basic information about the rotation of the earth around the sun, the tilt in the earth's axis, the summer and winter solstices, and the autumnal and vernal equinoxes, and they are then challenged to figure out why the seasons change. The site includes teacher-tested lesson plans sorted by geography standard and grade level.

ThinkQuest (**www.thinkquest.org**) is an international academic competition for students aged nine to nineteen. Students work in teams in one of three age divisions to research a topic in science, mathematics, literature, the social sciences, or the arts and publish their findings as a website that teachers and students around the world can use. As part of the Supportive Inquiry-Based Learning Environment (SIBLE) Project, researchers at Northwestern University have created a set of five software tools called Progress Portfolio that help students document and reflect on their progress as they work through computer- and web-based science simulations and explorations. These tools allow students to save and print information that is currently on their computer screen, annotate their work with "sticky notes," create worksheet-like pages, organize work into folders or tables, and present work in a PowerPoint-like slide show. The Progress Portfolio program can be downloaded from the Progress Portfolio website (**www.progressportfolio .northwestern.edu**).

*HM **TeacherPrepSPACE***

*For help in reviewing this chapter, see the ACE practice tests and the PowerPoint slides at the textbook's student website.*

Technology Tools for Knowledge Construction and Problem Solving

# 10 Social Cognitive Theory

## KEY POINTS

*These key points will help you learn the important information in this chapter. To help you study, they also appear in the margins of the pages, next to the text where they are discussed.*

### The Triadic Reciprocal Causation Model

- Triadic reciprocal causation model: behavior is the result of interactions among personal characteristics, behavior, environmental factors

### Self-Control, Self-Regulation, and Self-Efficacy

- Self-control: controlling one's behaviors in a particular setting in the absence of reinforcement or punishment
- Self-regulation: consistently using self-control skills in new situations
- Self-regulation is important because students are expected to become increasingly independent learners as they progress through school
- Self-efficacy: how capable one feels to handle particular kinds of tasks
- Self-efficacy beliefs influence use of self-regulating skills
- Self-efficacy influenced by past performance, verbal persuasion, emotions, observing models
- Self-efficacy influences goals and activities, cognitive processes, perseverance, emotions
- Self-regulated learners set goals, create plans to achieve those goals
- Self-regulated learners focus on task, process information meaningfully, self-monitor
- Self-regulated learners evaluate their performance, make appropriate attributions for success and failure, reinforce themselves

### Helping Students Become Self-Regulated Learners

- Self-regulated learning: thoughts, feelings, and actions purposely generated and controlled to maximize a learning outcome
- Strategy: plan to achieve a long-term goal

- Tactic: specific technique that helps achieve immediate objective
- Rote rehearsal not a very effective memory tactic
- Acronym: word made from first letters of items to be learned
- Acrostic: sentence made up of words derived from first letters of items to be learned
- Loci method: visualize items to be learned stored in specific locations
- Keyword method: visually link pronunciation of foreign word to English translation
- Mnemonic devices meaningfully organize information, provide retrieval cues
- Self-questioning improves comprehension, knowledge integration
- Taking notes and reviewing notes aid retention and comprehension
- Learning strategy components: metacognition, analysis, planning, implementation, monitoring, modification
- Self-regulation skills learned best in four-level process: observation, emulation, self-control, self-regulation
- People learn to inhibit or make responses by observing others

### Research on Social Cognitive Theory

- Self-efficacy, self-regulation related to each other and to achievement
- Observing a peer model improves students' self-efficacy for math problem solving and math problem-solving ability
- Observing a peer model improves the quality of students' writing more than simply practicing writing
- Reciprocal teaching: students learn comprehension skills by demonstrating them to peers

### Using Technology to Promote Self-Regulated Learning

- Computer programs that include models can improve students' problem-solving skills
- Computer programs that let students control access to information work best with those who have some self-regulatory skills

---

In Chapters 7 and 8, we examined two very different descriptions of how learning occurs. Operant conditioning focuses exclusively on the role of observable, external events on learning new behaviors and strengthening or weakening existing ones. According to this theory, people are exposed to stimuli, they make some sort of response, and the reinforcing or punishing consequences that do or do not follow influence the probability that those responses will be made again. Consequently, operant conditioning requires that people make observable responses in order for others to conclude that learning has occurred. The strength of operant conditioning is the insight it provides about how environmental consequences affect learning. Its main weakness is that it offers no insights into what people do with that information.

Information-processing theory, on the other hand, focuses almost exclusively on the role of internal processes in learning. In this view, people are exposed to stimuli, and whether and how they attend to, encode, store, and retrieve that information influences what they know and can do. But information-processing theory has very little to say about how the social setting in which behavior occurs influences what people learn.

This chapter will examine a third approach that shares common ground with operant conditioning and information-processing theory but goes beyond both. Known initially as *social learning theory* and more recently as **social cognitive theory,** this explanation of learning was based on the premise that neither spontaneous behavior nor reinforcement was necessary for learning to occur. New behaviors could also be learned by observing and imitating a model. The current version of social cognitive theory incorporates elements of both operant conditioning and information processing, and it emphasizes how behavioral and personal factors interact with the social setting in which behavior occurs.

Albert Bandura (1986, 1997, 2001, 2002) is generally considered to be the driving force behind social cognitive theory. His goal is to explain how learning results from interactions among three factors: (1) personal characteristics, such as the various cognitive processes covered in the chapter on information processing, as well as self-perceptions and emotional states; (2) behavioral

patterns; and (3) the social environment, such as interactions with others. Bandura calls the process of interaction among these three elements **triadic reciprocal causation.** This impressive-sounding mouthful is not as difficult to understand as it sounds. *Triadic* simply means having three elements, and *reciprocal* indicates that the elements influence one another. The entire term means that one's internal processes, behavior, and social environment (the "triadic" part of the term) can affect one another (the "reciprocal" part) to produce learning (the "causation" part). To simplify our writing and your reading, we will refer to Bandura's triadic reciprocal causation model as the *triadic model.*

Bandura and others (e.g., Schunk, 1998, 2001; Zimmerman, 1990, 2000) are particularly interested in using social cognitive theory to describe how people become *self-controlled* and *self-regulated* learners. Consequently, we'll begin our exploration of social cognitive theory by taking a more detailed look at the triadic model. Then we'll explain the meaning of and differences between self-control and self-regulation.

## THE TRIADIC RECIPROCAL CAUSATION MODEL

The triadic model holds that a person's behavior is always the result of interactions among personal characteristics, behavioral patterns, and environmental factors. Bandura and others describe these three elements as follows:

- *Personal characteristics* include mental and emotional factors such as goals and anxiety. They also include metacognitive knowledge, which (as you learned in Chapter 8 on information-processing theory) refers to understanding of one's own cognitive processes, such as knowledge of the role of analysis, planning, and monitoring in learning. Personal characteristics further include *self-efficacy*, that is, beliefs about one's ability to successfully carry out particular tasks. Self-efficacy is a concept we introduced in the Chapter 2 on age-level characteristics, and a later section of this chapter will discuss it in detail.

- *Behavioral patterns* include self-observation (such as using personal journals to note how various factors influence learning, motivation, and self-efficacy); self-evaluation; making changes in behavior to overcome or reduce perceptions of low self-efficacy, anxiety, and ineffective learning strategies; and creating productive study environments.

- *Environmental factors* refer to an individual's social and physical environment. They include such things as the nature of a task, reinforcing and punishing consequences, explanations and modeling of various skills by others, and verbal persuasion from others to exhibit particular behaviors.

As shown in Figure 10.1, Bandura portrays these relationships in a triangular arrangement with bidirectional arrows (Bandura, 1997; Zimmerman, 1990).

To grasp the interactive nature of the triadic model, consider the following two examples. The components of the model are represented by the letter *P* for personal

> Triadic reciprocal causation model: behavior is the result of interactions among personal characteristics, behavior, environmental factors

**Figure 10.1** The Triadic Reciprocal Causation Model

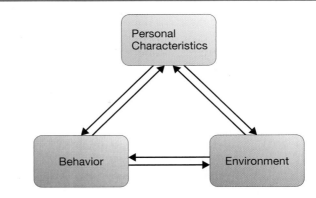

SOURCE: Bandura (1997).

characteristic, *B* for behavioral pattern, or *E* for environmental factor. In each example, notice how the elements influence one another.

1. A student's high self-efficacy for mathematical problem solving (P) leads the student to work on mathematical problems (B) rather than painting a picture. High self-efficacy also makes the student likely to persist in the face of difficulty (B). At the same time, the act of successfully working on mathematical tasks (B) raises the student's self-efficacy for solving mathematical problems (P).

2. A teacher introduces a new science topic by describing the theory and research that contributed to the current state of knowledge in this area (B). But when students show signs of confusion or boredom (E), thereby making the teacher uncomfortable and dissatisfied (P), the teacher tries a different approach (B).

Bear in mind, however, that things do not operate as simply as Figure 10.1 suggests. As the activity and setting change, the strength of certain P-B-E connections can be expected to change. If, for example, you happen to be in a setting, such as school, in which rules and regulations place limits on behavior, the behavioral aspect of the model is likely to have less impact than if you are allowed more freedom of expression. Also, some relationships may be stronger than others at particular points in time (Schunk, 1998; Zimmerman, 1990).

Social cognitive theory assumes that people, and not environmental forces, are the predominant cause of their own behavior (recall that operant conditioning assumes that one's choices and actions are strongly influenced, if not determined, by environmental stimuli and consequences). Bandura uses the term **personal agency** to refer to the potential control we have over our own behavior, and he believes that our capacity for personal agency grows out of our skills of self-control and self-regulation (Martin, 2004).

## SELF-CONTROL, SELF-REGULATION, AND SELF-EFFICACY

| Self-control: controlling one's behaviors in a particular setting in the absence of reinforcement or punishment |

*Self-control* is the ability to control one's actions in the absence of external reinforcement or punishment. Some examples of self-control are inhibiting inappropriate behavior, rewarding oneself for acceptable behavior, and choosing to wait longer for a larger reward rather than taking an immediate but smaller reward. A student who has been taught by the teacher to start a new task after finishing a seatwork assignment and who does that when the teacher is not present is exhibiting self-control.

Self-regulation: consistently using self-control skills in new situations

*Self-regulation* involves the consistent and appropriate application of self-control skills to new situations. It is the product of interactions among the three components that make up Bandura's triadic model: personal characteristics, behavioral patterns, and environmental factors. Self-regulating individuals set their own performance standards, evaluate the quality of their performance, and reinforce themselves when their performance meets or exceeds their internal standards (Zimmerman, 1990, 2000; Zimmerman & Kitsantas, 2005). A teacher who modifies a particular day's lesson plan to capitalize on students' interest in a major news story, monitors students' reaction to the new lesson, compares her students' and her own performance against an internal standard, and rewards herself if she feels that standard has been met is illustrating the essence of self-regulation.

Self-regulation is both a cyclical and a dynamic process. It is cyclical because the results of prior performance are used to guide and refine current efforts. It is dynamic because personal, behavioral, and environmental factors are constantly changing. Consequently, skilled self-regulated learners monitor their use of cognitive processes, their affective states, their environmental conditions, and the quality of their performance and make whatever modifications are called for in order to maximize the probability of achieving their goal (Zimmerman, 2000). We will examine the self-regulation cycle in more detail later in this chapter.

Self-regulation is a critically important capability for students to acquire for at least three reasons:

Self-regulation is important because students are expected to become increasingly independent learners as they progress through school

1. As students get older, and especially when they get into the middle and high school grades, they are expected to assume greater responsibility for their learning than was the case in earlier grades, and so they receive less prompting and guidance from teachers and parents.

2. As students move through the primary, elementary, middle school, and high school grades, they have to learn and be tested over increasingly larger amounts of more complex material. With less parental and teacher supervision, the temptation to put off studying or to do it superficially increases. Unfortunately, the damaging long-term consequences of poorly regulated academic behavior (low grades and diminished opportunities for higher education and employment) are not immediately apparent.

3. Because of the rapid pace of change in today's world, individuals increasingly need to be self-directed, autonomous learners not just during their school years but over their lifetimes (Zimmerman, 1990, 2002).

## pause & reflect

Should the development of self-regulated learning skills be left to parents and out-of-school experiences, or should this be a primary goal of our education system? If the latter, when should it begin?

Although the skills of self-control and self-regulation are important to academic success, some students are more successful than others in acquiring and using these skills. The characteristic that is most strongly related to and best explains differences in self-regulation is perceived self-efficacy, a concept we mentioned several times earlier in this chapter. In the next section, we further describe self-efficacy and its relationship to self-regulation.

## The Role of Self-Efficacy in Self-Regulation

Self-efficacy: how capable one feels to handle particular kinds of tasks

Unlike self-esteem, which we described in an earlier chapter as the overall, or global, evaluation that people make of themselves, **self-efficacy** refers to how capable or prepared we believe we are to handle particular kinds of tasks (Bandura, 1997, 2001, 2002). For example, a student may have a high level of self-efficacy for mathematical reasoning—a feeling that she can master any math task she might encounter in a particular course—but have a low level of self-efficacy for critical analysis of English literature.

Self-efficacy beliefs occupy a central role in social cognitive theory because of their widespread and significant effects. They help influence whether people think optimistically or pessimistically, act in ways that are beneficial or detrimental to achieving goals, approach or avoid tasks, engage tasks with a high or low level of motivation, persevere for a short or lengthy period of time when tasks are difficult, and are motivated or demoralized by failure. These beliefs are often called the single most important factor that affects the strength of a person's sense of agency.

Bandura argues that self-efficacy is more influential than expected rewards or punishments or actual skills because it is based on a belief that one can or cannot produce the behaviors that are required to bring about a particular outcome. Students with the same level of mathematical skill may, for example, have different attitudes about mathematics and perform differently on tests of mathematical problem solving because of differences in their self-efficacy beliefs (Bandura, 2001; Martin, 2004).

Students who believe they are capable of successfully performing a task are more likely than students with low levels of self-efficacy to use such self-regulating skills as concentrating on the task, creating strategies, using appropriate tactics, managing time effectively, monitoring their own performance, and making whatever adjustments are necessary to improve their future learning efforts. By contrast, students who do not believe they have the cognitive skills to cope with the demands of a particular subject are unlikely to do much serious reading or thinking about the subject or to spend much time preparing for tests. Such students are often referred to as lazy, inattentive, lacking initiative, and dependent on others. They often find themselves in a vicious circle as their avoidance of challenging tasks and dependence on others reduces their chances of developing self-regulation skills and a strong sense of self-efficacy (Bandura, 1997; Schunk, 1998).

Self-efficacy can be affected by one or more of several factors and, in turn, can affect one or more of several important self-regulatory behaviors (see Figure 10.2).

**Factors That Affect Self-Efficacy**  Four factors that affect self-efficacy are shown on the "Antecedents" side of Figure 10.2.

> Self-efficacy beliefs influence use of self-regulating skills

**Figure 10.2** Antecedents and Effects of Self-Efficacy

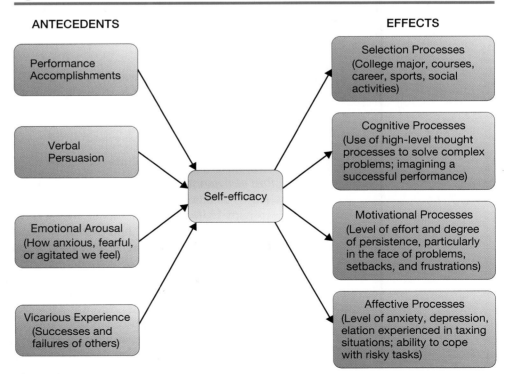

ANTECEDENTS

- Performance Accomplishments
- Verbal Persuasion
- Emotional Arousal (How anxious, fearful, or agitated we feel)
- Vicarious Experience (Successes and failures of others)

Self-efficacy

EFFECTS

- Selection Processes (College major, courses, career, sports, social activities)
- Cognitive Processes (Use of high-level thought processes to solve complex problems; imagining a successful performance)
- Motivational Processes (Level of effort and degree of persistence, particularly in the face of problems, setbacks, and frustrations)
- Affective Processes (Level of anxiety, depression, elation experienced in taxing situations; ability to cope with risky tasks)

Self-efficacy influenced by past performance, verbal persuasion, emotions, observing models

1. *Performance accomplishments.* One obvious way in which we develop a sense of what we can and cannot do in various areas is by thinking about how well we have performed in the past on a given task or a set of closely related tasks. If, for example, my friends are always reluctant to have me on their team for neighborhood baseball games, and if I strike out or ground out far more often than I hit safely, I will probably conclude that I just do not have whatever skills it takes to be a competitive baseball player. Conversely, if my personal history of performance in school includes mostly grades of A and consistent rank among the top ten students, my sense of academic self-efficacy is likely to be quite high.

2. *Verbal persuasion.* A second source of influence mentioned by Bandura—verbal persuasion—is also fairly obvious. We frequently try to convince a child, student, relative, spouse, friend, or coworker that he or she has the ability to perform some task at an acceptable level. Perhaps you can recall feeling somewhat more confident about handling some task (such as college classes) after having several family members and friends express their confidence in your ability.

3. *Emotional arousal.* A third source of influence is more subtle. It is the emotions we feel as we prepare to engage in a task. Individuals with low self-efficacy for science may become anxious, fearful, or restless prior to attending chemistry class or to taking an exam in physics. Those with high self-efficacy may feel assured, comfortable, and eager to display what they have learned. Some individuals are acutely aware of these emotional states, and their emotions become a cause as well as a result of their high or low self-efficacy.

4. *Vicarious experience.* Finally, our sense of self-efficacy may be influenced by observing the successes and failures of individuals with whom we identify. This is what Bandura refers to as vicarious experience. If I take note of the fact that a sibling or neighborhood friend who is like me in many respects but is a year older has successfully adjusted to high school, I may feel more optimistic about my own adjustment the following year. We will have more to say a bit later in this chapter about the role of observing and imitating a model.

## pause & reflect

On the basis of your own experience, do you agree that personal experience is the most important factor affecting self-efficacy? What steps can you take to raise the probability that your students will experience more successes than failures?

Of these four factors, personal accomplishment is the most important because it carries the greatest weight. As important as it is to feel calm and be free of crippling fear or anxiety; to have parents, peers, and teachers express their confidence in us; and to have successful models to observe, actual failures are likely to override the other influences. In other words, our feelings, the comments of others, and the actions of models need to be confirmed by our own performance if they are to be effective contributors to self-efficacy.

**Types of Behaviors Affected by Self-Efficacy**   Bandura has identified four types of behaviors that are at least partly influenced by an individual's level of self-efficacy. These are shown on the "Effects" side of Figure 10.2.

Self-efficacy influences goals and activities, cognitive processes, perseverance, emotions

1. *Selection processes.* By the term *selection processes*, we mean the way the person goes about selecting goals and activities. Individuals with a strong sense of self-efficacy, particularly if it extends over several areas, are more likely than others to consider a variety of goals and participate in a variety of activities. They may, for example, think about a wide range of career options, explore several majors while in college, take a variety of courses, participate in different sporting activities, engage in different types of social activities, and have a wide circle of friends.

2. *Cognitive processes.* Individuals with high self-efficacy, compared with their peers who are low in self-efficacy, tend to use higher-level thought processes (such as analysis, synthesis, and evaluation) to solve complex problems. Thus, in preparing a classroom report or a paper, students with low self-efficacy may do little more than repeat a set of facts found in various sources; often this behavior stems from their belief that they are not capable of more. In contrast, students with

*A person's self-efficacy for a particular task is influenced primarily by past performance but also by encouragement from others, emotional reactions, and observing others.*

high self-efficacy often discuss similarities and differences, inconsistencies and contradictions, and make evaluations about the validity and usefulness of the information they have found. Another cognitive difference is that people high in self-efficacy are more likely to visualize themselves being successful at some challenging task, whereas individuals low in self-efficacy are more likely to imagine disaster. This leads to differences in the next category of behaviors—motivation.

3. *Motivational processes.* Those who rate their capabilities as higher than average can be expected to work harder and longer to achieve a goal than those who feel less capable. This difference should be particularly noticeable when individuals experience frustrations (poor-quality instruction, for example), problems (coursework being more difficult than anticipated), and setbacks (a serious illness).

4. *Affective processes.* Finally, when faced with a challenging task, the individual with high self-efficacy is more likely to experience excitement, curiosity, and an eagerness to get started rather than the sense of anxiety, depression, and impending disaster that many individuals with low self-efficacy feel.

Before leaving this discussion of self-efficacy, we would like to make one last point about its role in self-regulated behavior. As important as self-efficacy is, you should realize that other factors play a role as well. In addition to feeling capable of successfully completing a particular task, students also need to possess basic knowledge and skills, anticipate that their efforts will be appropriately rewarded, and value the knowledge, skill, or activity that they have been asked to learn or complete (Schunk, 1998).

As we noted earlier, students (as well as adults) vary in how extensively and how well they regulate their thoughts, feelings, and behavior as they pursue goals. To help students with poorly developed self-regulation skills become better learners, you need to know what a well-formed self-regulatory system includes. In the next section we describe a system of self-regulatory processes that has been proposed by Barry Zimmerman (2000, 2002), a leading social cognitive theorist and researcher.

## The Components of a Self-Regulatory System

Self-regulatory processes and their related beliefs can be grouped into one of three categories, each of which comes into play at different points in time in the course of pursuing a goal (see Figure 10.3). First are the *forethought* processes and self-beliefs that occur prior to beginning a task. Next are the *performance* processes that are activated during the course of a task. Third are the *self-reflection* processes that occur after a response or series of responses have been made. Because self-reflection influences subsequent forethought processes, this system is cyclical in nature. Consequently,

**Figure 10.3** Phases and Categories of the Self-Regulation Cycle

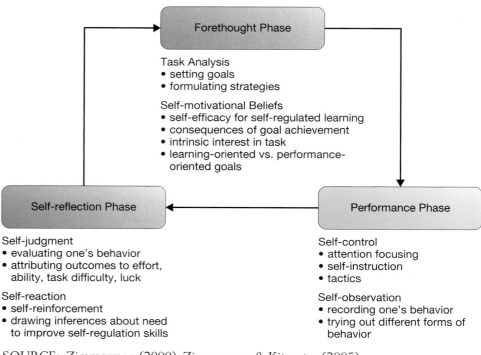

Forethought Phase

Task Analysis
- setting goals
- formulating strategies

Self-motivational Beliefs
- self-efficacy for self-regulated learning
- consequences of goal achievement
- intrinsic interest in task
- learning-oriented vs. performance-oriented goals

Self-reflection Phase

Self-judgment
- evaluating one's behavior
- attributing outcomes to effort, ability, task difficulty, luck

Self-reaction
- self-reinforcement
- drawing inferences about need to improve self-regulation skills

Performance Phase

Self-control
- attention focusing
- self-instruction
- tactics

Self-observation
- recording one's behavior
- trying out different forms of behavior

SOURCE: Zimmerman (2000); Zimmerman & Kitsantas (2005).

Zimmerman (2000, 2002; Zimmerman & Kitsantas, 2005) refers to these processes as occurring in phases.

As you know from earlier chapters, children acquire their cognitive skills gradually. So in addition to describing the main self-regulatory processes that come into play at each phase, we will also note the developmental limitations you can expect to see if you teach primary grade children.

**Forethought Phase**    The forethought phase is subdivided into the categories of task analysis and self-motivational beliefs. Task analysis includes the self-regulatory processes of *goal setting* and *strategic planning*. When setting goals, self-regulated learners do not just specify one or more long-term goals, especially those that take time to achieve. Instead, for each long-term goal, they establish a series of near-term subgoals that are achievable and provide evidence of progress. For example, to accomplish the long-term goal of achieving a grade of A in physics, a self-regulating student will set subgoals that pertain to number of hours spent per week studying, working sample problems at the end of the textbook chapter, doing homework as accurately as possible, and seeking help when problems arise. As we point out later in this chapter, planning is a necessary self-regulatory skill because the circumstances under which one learns are constantly changing. Thus self-regulated learners constantly assess themselves and the nature and demands of a learning task in order to select those methods that are most likely to lead to goal attainment.

As we also point out later, possessing these skills is of little value if one isn't motivated to use them. This is why the self-motivational beliefs category is part of this phase. Included here are self-efficacy beliefs, outcome expectations, intrinsic interest, and goal orientation. In the context of this discussion, self-efficacy pertains to how capable people believe themselves to be about using self-regulatory processes. Outcome expectations refer to what one believes will be the consequences of achieving a goal (such as praise, prestige, increased responsibility). Intrinsic interest can maintain motivation for self-regulated learning in situations in which external

*Self-regulated learners set goals, create plans to achieve those goals*

rewards are either unavailable or unattractive. Goal orientations (which we discuss in Chapter 12, "Motivation and Perceptions of Self") can be learning oriented or performance oriented. Individuals who have a learning orientation are interested in learning primarily for its internal rewards (better understanding of the world in which one lives, increased competence) and are more apt to be motivated to use self-regulation processes than are performance-oriented individuals whose goal is to achieve a higher score or grade than others.

***Developmental Limitations***   In the forethought phase, young children are likely to be more limited than older children in their ability to do the following:

- Attend to a model, such as a teacher, for long periods of time
- Distinguish relevant model behaviors and verbalizations from less relevant ones
- Encode a model's behavior as generalized verbal guidelines
- Formulate and maintain well-defined long-term goals (Schunk, 2001)

**Performance Phase**   This phase contains several self-regulatory processes, and again they divide into two categories: the self-control category and the self-observation category. Self-control processes help learners focus on the task and meaningfully process the information they are trying to learn. *Attention focusing*, for example, involves ignoring distractions, executing a task at a slower than normal pace, and not thinking about prior mistakes or failed efforts. *Self-instruction* involves describing to oneself, either silently or out loud, how to carry out the steps of a task or process. *Tactics* (or *task strategies*) include the many memory-directed and comprehension-directed techniques that we discuss later in this chapter.

| Self-regulated learners focus on task, process information meaningfully, self-monitor

Self-observation processes, also known as self-monitoring, increase awareness of one's performance and the conditions that affect it. These processes include *self-recording* and *self-experimentation*. Two frequently used methods of self-recording are written journals and logbooks. When done consistently, self-recording can reveal desirable and undesirable behavioral patterns that correspond to particular environmental conditions, such as putting off homework or studying for an exam in favor of socializing with friends. The results of self-recording can lead learners to self-experimentation, or trying out different forms of behavior. For instance, a student might change the time and place of study or the techniques that are used to see whether these changes produce better results.

***Developmental Limitations***   For the performance phase, you can expect primary grade children to be limited in their ability to do the following:

- Ignore both external and internal distractions (such as self-doubts and thoughts of prior difficulties)
- Perform the steps of a task more slowly and deliberately in order to avoid making mistakes
- Provide themselves with verbal reminders of the steps needed to carry out a task
- Select appropriate tactics for a particular task (Schunk, 2001)

**Self-Reflection Phase**   As with the first two phases, this phase is composed of two categories, self-judgment and self-reaction, each of which involves two self-regulatory processes.

| Self-regulated learners evaluate their performance, make appropriate attributions for success and failure, reinforce themselves

The first of the self-judgment processes is *self-evaluation*. Whenever we label our performance as good or bad, acceptable or unacceptable, satisfactory or unsatisfactory, we are engaging in self-evaluation. There are basically four ways in which students can make these self-evaluative judgments:

1. *Students can adopt what is called a mastery criterion.* This system uses a graded scale that was created by someone with extensive knowledge about the range of performances for that skill or topic; the scale ranges from novice to expert.

By using a mastery criterion, learners know where they stand with respect to an absolute standard of performance and whether they are making progress with additional study and practice.

2. *Students can compare their current performance against their own previous performance.*
3. *Students can use a normative standard.* This involves comparing one's performance against the performances of others, such as classmates. Normative standards emphasize how one compares with others rather than one's absolute level of performance.
4. *Students can use a collaborative standard.* This method applies to situations in which an individual is part of a group effort. The student would make a positive self-evaluation if he or she had fulfilled those responsibilities identified as necessary for the group to succeed in its endeavor.

*Causal attributions*, which we also cover in Chapter 12, are the second self-judgment process. They involve ascribing a major cause to a behavior. A student's successes and failures can be attributed to effort, ability, task difficulty, and luck, among other factors. Students who attribute their successes to effort and ability and their failures to insufficient effort are more likely to engage in self-regulated learning behaviors than are students who attribute success to good luck or easy tasks and failure to bad luck or low ability.

The self-reaction category is composed of *self-satisfaction* and *adaptive inferences.* Self-satisfaction is the positive feeling we get when we know we have done a job well and achieved whatever goal we established at the outset. Think of it as **self-reinforcement,** which is the label used for it in Figure 10.3. Adaptive inferences are the conclusions that learners draw about the need to improve their self-regulatory skills. Learners can, however, make defensive rather than adaptive inferences. These individuals see no need to improve their self-regulatory skills because they have little interest in the task at hand or feel incapable of developing the skills necessary to successfully carry out the task. Consequently, they resort to such maladaptive behaviors as helplessness, procrastination, task avoidance, apathy, and disengagement in an effort to protect themselves from the aversive effects of anticipated failure.

***Developmental Limitations***    For the self-reflection phase, expect primary grade children to be limited in their ability to do the following:

- Compare themselves to peers as a basis for judging their own capabilities. Young children's beliefs about their capabilities are more likely to be influenced by teacher feedback than by comparisons to peers' performance. For older students, the reverse is true.
- Make appropriate attributions for their successes and failures. In the primary grades the concepts of effort and ability are not clearly distinguished, and so effort

## VIDEO CASE    ◄◄ ▶ ▶▶

HM

### Performance Assessment:
### Student Presentations in a High School English Class

*Watch the video, study the artifacts in the case, and reflect upon the following questions:*

1. How do the class presentations in this Video Case allow students to practice their self-regulation skills?

2. Explain how the peer assessment component of this literature lesson illustrates the self-reflection phase of Zimmerman's model.

is viewed as the primary cause of success and failure. Older students, however, are more likely to ascribe success primarily to ability and failure primarily to insufficient ability.

- Accurately assess the level of their own capabilities. Primary grade children are likely to overestimate what they can do if they have learned only some aspects of a skill or if they use incorrect learning or problem-solving skills that accidentally produce an acceptable outcome. Conversely, young children can underestimate their competence when they are uncertain about the correctness of their responses (Schunk, 2001).

Now that we've laid out the basic structure of social cognitive theory and described its major focus (self-regulated behavior), we can turn our attention to how the concepts of self-regulation apply to classroom learning.

## HELPING STUDENTS BECOME SELF-REGULATED LEARNERS

### What Is Self-Regulated Learning?

As we have suggested in the preceding sections, the concept of self-regulation can be directly applied to learning academic material in and out of classrooms. **Self-regulated learning** (which is also referred to as intentional learning; see, for example, Sinatra & Pintrich, 2003) refers to any thoughts, feelings, or actions that are purposely generated and controlled by a student to maximize learning of knowledge and skills for a given task and set of conditions. Self-regulated learning involves, among other things, analyzing the characteristics of learning tasks, using various techniques for learning new information, using various techniques for remaining calm and confident, estimating how much time it will take to complete a task, monitoring one's progress, knowing when and from whom to seek help, and feeling a sense of pride and satisfaction about accomplishing one's learning goals (Paris & Paris, 2001; Schunk, 2001; Zimmerman, 2000; Zimmerman & Kitsantas, 2005).

> Self-regulated learning: thoughts, feelings, and actions purposely generated and controlled to maximize a learning outcome

Not surprisingly, self-regulated learners are also referred to as *self-directed*, *autonomous*, or *strategic* learners. An example of a self-regulating student is one who does the following:

- Prepares for an upcoming exam by studying for two hours each night for several nights instead of trying to cram all the studying into one or two nights (thereby applying the principle of distributed practice, discussed in Chapter 8, "Information-Processing Theory")
- Uses memory-directed tactics, such as mnemonic devices, to accurately store and recall information for test items that will demand verbatim recall
- Uses comprehension-directed tactics, such as concept maps and self-questioning, to deal with test items that will require comprehension, analysis, and synthesis of information
- Creates self-tests to monitor the effectiveness of study efforts and takes some time off from studying if the results of a self-test are satisfactory

### How Well Prepared Are Students to Be Self-Regulated Learners?

We would like to be able to report that most students possess the self-regulated learning skills just listed, but, unfortunately, we cannot. Although evidence exists that students are more likely to use effective learning skills as they get older (Schneider, Knopf, & Stefanek, 2002) and that some students behave strategically by using different learning skills for different tasks (Hadwin, Winne, Stockley, Nesbit, & Woszczyna, 2001), many do not do so either systematically or consistently. Their

*Students who are self-regulated learners tend to achieve at high levels by using appropriate cognitive and metacognitive skills for particular tasks in the right way and at the right time.*

attempts at encoding rarely go beyond rote rehearsal (for example, rereading a textbook chapter), simple organizational schemes (outlining), and various cuing devices (underlining or highlighting), and they have a poor sense of how well prepared they are to take a test (Bond, Miller, & Kennon, 1987; Brown, Campione, & Day, 1981; Covington, 1985; Peverly, Brobst, Graham, & Shaw, 2003; Selmes, 1987; Winne & Jamieson-Noel, 2002, 2003). Because of its complexity, you can expect expertise in self-regulated learning (SRL) to develop gradually over many years. One estimate, based on research on the development of related skills, is that most students will need about 85 percent of the approximately twelve thousand hours they spend in school through twelfth grade in order to become highly proficient in SRL (Winne & Stockley, 1998).

In one study (Schneider et al., 2002), 7 percent of twelve-year-olds used an effective organizing technique to learn and recall a set of pictures, but those same individuals used no discernible strategy for the same task at age eighteen. In another study (Hyönä, Lorch, & Kaakinen, 2002), only 20 percent of a group of college students noted text features that signaled transitions and important information (such as headings, topic sentences, and sentences that end paragraphs and sections), constructed a mental representation of the topic, and related it to earlier parts of the text.

One reason for this state of affairs is that students are rarely taught how to make the most of their cognitive capabilities. In one study, sixty-nine kindergarten through sixth-grade teachers gave strategy instruction only 9.5 percent of the time they were observed. Rationales for strategy use were given less than 1 percent of the time, and 10 percent of the teachers gave no strategy instructions at all. Moreover, the older the students were, the less likely they were to receive strategy instruction (Moely et al., 1992). A similar study of eleven middle school teachers eight years later produced the same findings. Teaching behaviors that reflected strategy instruction occurred only 9 percent of the time (Hamman, Berthelot, Saia, & Crowley, 2000).

Findings such as these are surprising, not to mention disappointing, as it is widely recognized that the amount of independent learning expected of students increases consistently from elementary school through high school and into college. The rest of this chapter will try to convince you that it need not be this way, at least for your students. In the next

## pause & reflect

Many teachers have said that they would like to teach their students more about the nature and use of learning processes but that they don't have time because of the amount of subject material they must cover. What can you do to avoid this pitfall?

section, we describe two related yet different cognitive skills that students will need to learn how to use if they are to become proficient self-regulated learners: strategies and tactics.

## The Nature of Learning Tactics and Strategies

Strategy: plan to achieve a long-term goal

Tactic: specific technique that helps achieve immediate objective

A **learning strategy** is a general *plan* that a learner formulates for achieving a somewhat distant academic goal (such as getting an A on the next exam). Like all other strategies, it specifies what will be done to achieve the goal, where it will be done, and when it will be done. A **learning tactic** is a specific *technique* (such as a memory aid or a form of note taking) that a learner uses to accomplish an immediate objective (such as to understand the concepts in a textbook chapter and how they relate to one another).

As you can see, tactics have an integral connection to strategies. They are the learning tools that move you closer to your goal. Thus they have to be chosen so as to be consistent with the goals of a strategy. If you had to recall verbatim the Preamble to the U.S. Constitution, for example, would you use a learning tactic that would help you understand the gist of each stanza or one that would allow accurate and complete recall? It is surprising how often students fail to consider this point. Because understanding the different types and roles of tactics will help you better understand the process of strategy formulation, we will discuss tactics first.

## Types of Tactics

Most learning tactics can be placed in one of two categories based on the tactic's primary purpose:

- *Memory-directed tactics*, which contain techniques that help produce accurate storage and retrieval of information
- *Comprehension-directed tactics*, which contain techniques that aid in understanding the meaning of ideas and their interrelationships (Levin, 1982)

Because of space limitations, we cannot discuss all the tactics in each category. Instead, we have chosen to discuss a few briefly that are either very popular with students or have been shown to be reasonably effective. The first two, *rehearsal* and *mnemonic devices*, are memory-directed tactics. Both can take several forms and are used by students of almost every age. The last three, *self-questioning, note taking,* and **concept mapping,** are comprehension-directed tactics and are used frequently by students from the upper elementary grades through college.

Rote rehearsal not a very effective memory tactic

**Rehearsal**   The simplest form of rehearsal—rote rehearsal—is one of the earliest tactics to appear during childhood, and almost everyone uses it on occasion. It is not a particularly effective tactic for long-term storage and recall because it does not produce distinct encoding or good retrieval cues (although, as discussed earlier, it is a useful tactic for purposes of short-term memory). The consensus among researchers (Schlagmüller & Schneider, 2002; Schneider & Bjorklund, 1998) is that most five- and six-year-olds do not spontaneously rehearse but can be prompted to do so. Seven-year-olds sometimes use the simplest form of rehearsal. By eight years of age, youngsters start to rehearse several items together as a set instead of rehearsing single pieces of information one at a time. A slightly more advanced version, *cumulative rehearsal,* involves rehearsing a small set of items for several repetitions, dropping the item at the top of the list and adding a new one, giving the set several repetitions, dropping the item at the head of the set and adding a new one, rehearsing the set, and so on.

By early adolescence, rehearsal reflects the learner's growing awareness of the organizational properties of information. When given a list of randomly arranged words from familiar categories, thirteen-year-olds will group items by category to form rehearsal sets. This version of rehearsal is likely to be the most effective because of the implicit association between the category members and the more general category label. If at the time of recall the learner is given the category label or can generate it spontaneously, the probability of accurate recall of the category members increases significantly.

**Mnemonic Devices**    A **mnemonic device** is a memory-directed tactic that helps a learner transform or organize information to enhance its retrievability. Such devices can be used to learn and remember individual items of information (a name, a fact, a date), sets of information (a list of names, a list of vocabulary definitions, a sequence of events), and ideas expressed in text. These devices range from simple, easy-to-learn techniques to somewhat complex systems that require a fair amount of practice. Because they incorporate visual and verbal forms of elaborative encoding, their effectiveness is due to the same factors that make imagery and category clustering successful: organization and meaningfulness.

Although mnemonic devices have been described and practiced for over two thousand years, they were rarely made the object of scientific study until the 1960s (see Yates, 1966, for a detailed discussion of the history of mnemonics). Since that time, mnemonics have been frequently and intensively studied by researchers, and several reviews of mnemonics research have been done (for example, Bellezza, 1981; Carney & Levin, 2002; Levin, 1993; Snowman, 1986). Table 10.1 provides descriptions, examples, and uses of five mnemonic devices: rhymes, acronyms, acrostics, the loci method, and the keyword method.

*Acronym: word made from first letters of items to be learned*

*Acrostic: sentence made up of words derived from first letters of items to be learned*

*Loci method: visualize items to be learned stored in specific locations*

*Keyword method: visually link pronunciation of foreign word to English translation*

*Mnemonic devices meaningfully organize information, provide retrieval cues*

***Why Mnemonic Devices Are Effective***    Mnemonic devices work so well because they enhance the encodability and retrievability of information. First, they provide a context (such as acronyms, sentences, mental walks) in which apparently unrelated items can be organized. Second, the meaningfulness of material to be learned is enhanced through associations with more familiar meaningful information (for example, memory pegs or loci). Third, they provide distinctive retrieval cues that must be encoded with the material to be learned. Fourth, they force the learner to be an active participant in the learning process (Morris, 1977).

An example of these mnemonic benefits can be seen in a study conducted with college students (Rummel, Levin, & Woodward, 2003). You may find this study particularly relevant because the students used a variation of the keyword mnemonic to learn about a topic you covered in a previous chapter—theories of intelligence. Students assigned to the mnemonic condition were asked to read an eighteen-hundred-word passage that discussed the contributions of five psychologists to the measurement of intelligence and seven psychologists to the development of theories of intelligence. After each paragraph they encountered a mnemonic illustration that linked the theorist's surname to his major contribution. For example, after the paragraph about Charles Spearman, students saw a drawing of a man holding a "primary" hunting spear along with several specialized spears on the ground to represent Spearman's theory that intelligence is composed of one general and several specialized factors. Students assigned to the non-mnemonic condition encountered a summary sentence after each paragraph instead of an illustration. After reading the passage, all students were asked to write two short essays in which they compared and contrasted the work of each theorist and summarized the major aspects of each theory. They then took a three-column matching test in which they had to match each theorist's name with that person's major contribution and other information about that person's work. A second matching test was taken one week later. On the essay test, the two groups had equivalent scores on structural coherence and correct chronological sequence, but the mnemonic students scored considerably higher on correctly associating each theorist's name with his major accomplishment. On the matching test, the mnemonic group outscored the non-mnemonic group by a wide margin for matching names and major facts on both the immediate test and the delayed test.

***Why You Should Teach Students How to Use Mnemonic Devices***    Despite the demonstrated effectiveness of mnemonic devices, many people argue against teaching

| Table 10.1 | Five Types of Mnemonic Devices | | |
|---|---|---|---|
| **Mnemonic** | **Description** | **Example** | **Uses** |
| Rhyme | The items of information that one wants to recall are embedded in a rhyme that may range from one to several lines. A rhyme for recalling the names of the first 40 U.S. presidents, for example, contains 14 lines. | • Thirty days hath September, April, June, and November<br>• Fiddlededum, fiddlededee, a ring around the moon is $\pi \times d$. If a hole in your sock you want repaired, use the formula $\pi r$ squared (to recall the formulas for circumference and area). | Recalling specific items of factual information |
| Acronym | The first letter from each to-be-remembered item is used to make a word. Often called the first-letter mnemonic. | • HOMES (for the names of the Great Lakes—Huron, Ontario, Michigan, Erie, Superior) | Recalling a short set of items, particularly abstract items, in random or serial order |
| Acrostic | The first letter from each to-be-remembered item is used to create a series of words that forms a sentence. The first letter of each word in the sentence corresponds to the first letters of the to-be-remembered items. | • Kindly Place Cover Over Fresh Green Spring Vegetables (for the taxonomic classification of plants and animals—Kindgom, Phylum, Class, Order, Family, Genus, Species, and Variety)<br>• A Rat In The House May Eat The Ice Cream (to recall the spelling of the word *arithmetic*) | Recalling items, particularly abstract ones, in random or serial order |
| Method of loci | Generate visual images of and memorize a set of well-known locations that form a natural series (such as the furniture in and the architectural features of the rooms of one's house). Second, generate images of the to-be-learned items (objects, events, or ideas), and place each in a separate location. Third, mentally walk through each location, retrieve each image from where it was placed, and decode into a written or spoken message. *Loci* (pronounced *low-sigh*) is the plural of *locus*, which means "place." | • To recall the four stages of Piaget's theory: For sensorimotor stage, picture a car engine with eyes, ears, nose, and a mouth. Place this image in your first location (fireplace mantel). For preoperational stage, picture Piaget dressed in a surgical gown scrubbing up before an operation. Place this image in your second location (bookshelf). For concrete-operational stage, picture Piaget as a surgeon cutting open a piece of concrete. Place this image in your third location (chair). For formal-operational stage, picture Piaget as an operating room surgeon dressed in a tuxedo. Place this image in your fourth location (sofa). | Can be used by children, college students, and elderly people to recall lists of discrete items or ideas from text passages. Works equally well for free recall and serial recall, abstract and concrete items. |
| Keyword | Created to aid the learning of foreign language vocabulary but is applicable to any task in which one piece of information has to be associated with another. First, isolate some part of the foreign word that, when spoken, sounds like a meaningful English word. This is the keyword. Then create a visual image of the keyword. Finally, form a compound visual image between the keyword and the translation of the foreign word. | • Spanish word *pato* (pronounced *pot-o*) means "duck" in English. Keyword is *pot*. Imagine a duck with a pot over its head or a duck simmering in a pot.<br>• English psychologist Charles Spearman proposed that intelligence was composed of two factors—*g* and *s*. Keyword is "spear." Imagine a spear being thrown at a gas (for *g* and *s*) can. | For kindergarten through fourth grade, works best when children are given keywords and pictures. Can be used to recall cities and their products, states and their capitals, medical definitions, and famous people's accomplishments. |

SOURCES: Atkinson (1975); Atkinson & Raugh (1975); Bellezza (1981); Carney, Levin, & Levin (1994); Raugh & Atkinson (1975); Yates (1966).

them to students. They feel that students should learn the skills of critical thinking and problem solving rather than ways to recall isolated bits of verbatim information reliably. When factual information is needed, one can always turn to a reference source. Although we agree with the importance of teaching students to be critical thinkers and problem solvers, we feel this view is shortsighted for three reasons.

- It is very time-consuming to be constantly looking things up in reference books.
- The critique of mnemonic training ignores the fact that effective problem solving depends on ready access to a well-organized and meaningful knowledge base. Indeed, people who are judged to be expert in a particular field have an impressive array of factual material at their fingertips.
- Critics of mnemonics education focus only on the "little idea" that mnemonic usage aids verbatim recall of bits of information. The "big idea" is that students come to realize that the ability to learn and remember large amounts of information is an acquired capability. Too often students (and adults) assume that an effective memory is innate and requires high intelligence. Once they realize that learning is a skill, students may be more inclined to learn how to use other tactics and how to formulate broad-based strategies.

**Self- and Peer-Questioning**   Because students are expected to demonstrate much of what they know by answering written test questions, self-questioning can be a valuable learning tactic. The key to using questions profitably is to recognize that different types of questions make different cognitive demands. Some questions require little more than verbatim recall or recognition of simple facts and details. If an exam is designed to stress factual recall, then it may be helpful for a student to generate such questions while studying. Other questions, however, assess comprehension, application, or synthesis of main ideas or other high-level information.

To ensure that students fully understood how to write comprehension-aiding questions, Alison King (1992b) created a set of question stems (see Table 10.2) that

| **Table 10.2**   Self-Questioning Stems |
| --- |
| What is a new example of . . . ? |
| How would you use . . . to . . . ? |
| What would happen if . . . ? |
| What are the strengths and weaknesses of . . . ? |
| What do we already know about . . . ? |
| How does . . . tie in with what we learned before? |
| Explain why . . . . |
| Explain how . . . . |
| How does . . . affect . . . ? |
| What is the meaning of . . . ? |
| Why is . . . important? |
| What is the difference between . . . and . . . ? |
| How are . . . and . . . similar? |
| What is the best . . . , and why? |
| What are some possible solutions to the problem of . . . ? |
| Compare . . . and . . . with regard to . . . . |
| How does . . . cause . . . ? |
| What do you think causes . . . ? |

SOURCE: From King, A. (1992b). "Facilitating Elaborative Learning Through Guided Student-Generated Questioning," *Educational Psychologist, 27*(1), 111–126. Reprinted by permission of Lawrence Erlbaum Associates, Inc.

were intended to help students identify main ideas and think about how those ideas related to each other and to what the student already knew. When high school and college students used these question stems, they scored significantly better on tests of recall and comprehension of lecture material than did students who simply reviewed the same material. King (1994, 1998) also demonstrated that pairs of fourth- and fifth-grade students who were taught how to ask each other high-level questions and respond with elaborated explanations outperformed untrained students on tests that measured both comprehension and the ability to integrate text information with prior knowledge.

Self-questioning is a highly recommended learning tactic because it has a two-pronged beneficial effect:

Self-questioning improves comprehension, knowledge integration

- It helps students to understand better what they read. In order to answer the kinds of question stems King suggested, students have to engage in such higher-level thinking processes as translating ideas into their own words ("What is the meaning of . . . ?" "Explain why . . . ."), looking for similarities and differences ("What is the difference between . . . and . . . ?" "How are . . . and . . . similar?"), thinking about how ideas relate to one another ("Compare . . . and . . . with regard to . . . .") and to previously learned information ("How does . . . tie in with what we learned before?"), and evaluating the quality of ideas ("What are the strengths and weaknesses of . . . ?").
- It helps students to monitor their comprehension. If too many questions cannot be answered or if the answers appear to be too superficial, this provides clear evidence that the student has not achieved an adequate understanding of the passage.

Studies that have examined the effect of responding to question stems report very strong effects. The average student who responded to question stems while reading a passage scored at the 87th percentile on a subsequent teacher-made test, whereas the average student who did not answer questions scored only at the 50th percentile. Differences of this magnitude do not appear in research studies very often and, in this case, argue strongly for providing students with question stems and teaching them how to construct their own questions and answers (Rosenshine, Meister, & Chapman, 1996). Discussion of the conditions that underlie effective self-questioning instruction can be found in articles by Bernice Wong (1985), Zemira Mevarech and Ziva Susak (1993), and Alison King (2002).

Taking notes and reviewing notes aid retention and comprehension

**Note Taking**   As a learning tactic, note taking comes with good news and bad. The good news is that note taking can benefit a student in two ways. First, the process of taking notes while listening to a lecture or reading a text leads to better retention and comprehension of the noted information than just listening or reading does. For example, Andrew Katayama and Daniel Robinson (2000) found that college students who were given a set of partially completed notes for a text passage and told to fill in the blank spaces scored higher on a test of application than students who were given a complete set of notes. Second, the process of reviewing notes produces additional chances to recall and comprehend the noted material. The bad news is that we know very little about the specific conditions that make note taking an effective tactic.

This uncertainty as to what constitutes a good set of notes probably explains the results Alison King (1992a) obtained in a comparison of self-questioning, summarizing, and note taking. One group of students was given a set of question stems, shown how to generate good questions with them, and allowed to practice. A second group was given a set of rules for creating a good summary (identify a main idea or subtopic and related ideas, and link them together in one sentence), shown how to use them to create good summaries, and allowed to practice. A third group, however, was told simply to take notes as group members normally would in class. Both the self-questioning and summarizing groups scored significantly higher on both an immediate and a one-week-delayed retention test.

**Concept Mapping**    This is a technique that helps students identify, visually organize, and represent the relationships among a set of ideas. We mention concept maps again and provide an example in Chapter 13, "Approaches to Instruction." Considerable research documents the positive effect of concept mapping on students' recall and comprehension when compared with just reading text, especially for students with low verbal ability or low prior knowledge (Nesbit & Adesope, 2006; Novak, 1998; O'Donnell, Dansereau, & Hall, 2002; Romance & Vitale, 1999). Creating concept maps is more beneficial than studying those prepared by others, and they have a stronger effect among middle school students than they do among high school students (Nesbit & Adesope, 2006).

**Conclusions Regarding Learning Tactics**    On the basis of this brief review, we draw two conclusions. One is that students need to be systematically taught how to use learning tactics to make connections among ideas contained in text and lecture, as well as between new and previously learned information. No one expects students to teach themselves to read, write, and compute. So why should they be expected to teach themselves how to use a variety of learning tactics?

The second conclusion is that learning tactics should not be taught as isolated techniques, particularly to high school students. If tactics are taught that way, most students probably will not keep using them for very long or recognize that as the situation changes, so should the tactic. Therefore, as we implied earlier, students should be taught how to use tactics as part of a broader learning strategy.

## Using Learning Strategies Effectively

**The Components of a Learning Strategy**    As noted, a learning strategy is a plan for accomplishing a learning goal. It consists of six components: metacognition, analysis, planning, implementation of the plan, monitoring of progress, and modification. To give you a better idea of how to formulate a learning strategy of your own, following is a detailed description of each of these components (Snowman, 1986, 1987):

| Learning strategy components: metacognition, analysis, planning, implementation, monitoring, modification

1. *Metacognition.* In the absence of some minimal awareness of how we think and how our thought processes affect our academic performance, a strategic approach to learning is simply not possible. At the very least, we need to know that effective learning requires an analysis of the learning situation, formulation of a learning plan, skillful implementation of appropriate tactics, periodic monitoring of our progress, and modification of things that go wrong. In addition, we need to know why each of these steps is necessary, when each step should be carried out, and how well prepared we are to perform each step. Without this knowledge, students who are taught one or more of the learning tactics mentioned earlier do not keep up their use for very long, nor do they apply the tactics to relevant tasks.
2. *Analysis.* To analyze the task and obtain relevant information, the strategic learner can play the role of an investigative journalist, asking questions that pertain to *what, when, where, why, who,* and *how.* In this way, the learner can identify important aspects of the material to be learned (*what, when, where*), understand the nature of the test that will be given (*why*), recognize relevant personal learner characteristics (*who*), and identify potentially useful learning activities or tactics (*how*).
3. *Planning.* Once satisfactory answers have been gained from the analysis phase, the strategic learner then formulates a learning plan by hypothesizing something like the following: "I know something about the material to be learned (I have to read and comprehend five chapters of my music appreciation text within the next three weeks), the nature of the test criterion (I will have to compare and contrast the musical structure of symphonies that were written by Beethoven, Schubert, and Brahms), my strengths and weaknesses as a learner (I am good at tasks that

*Students can formulate strategic learning plans that identify and analyze the important aspects of a task. Then they can tailor these plans to their own strengths and weaknesses as learners.*

involve identifying similarities and differences, but I have difficulty concentrating for long periods of time), and the nature of various learning activities (skimming is a good way to get a general sense of the structure of a chapter; mnemonic devices make memorizing important details easier and more reliable; note taking and self-questioning are more effective ways to enhance comprehension than simple rereading). Based on this knowledge, I should divide each chapter into several smaller units that will take no longer than thirty minutes to read, take notes as I read, answer self-generated compare-and-contrast questions, use the loci mnemonic to memorize details, and repeat this sequence several times over the course of each week."

4. *Implementation of the plan.* Once the learner has formulated a plan, each of its elements must be implemented *skillfully.* A careful analysis and a well-conceived plan will not work if tactics are carried out poorly. Of course, a poorly executed plan may not be entirely attributable to a learner's tactical skill deficiencies. Part of the problem may be a general lack of knowledge about what conditions make for effective use of tactics (as is the case with note taking).

5. *Monitoring of progress.* Once the learning process is under way, the strategic learner assesses how well the chosen tactics are working. Possible monitoring techniques include writing out a summary, giving an oral presentation, working practice problems, and answering questions.

6. *Modification.* If the monitoring assessment is positive, the learner may decide that no changes are needed. If, however, attempts to memorize or understand the learning material seem to be producing unsatisfactory results, the learner will need to reevaluate and modify the analysis. This will cause changes in both the plan and the implementation.

We must emphasize three points about the nature of a learning strategy. The first is that learning conditions constantly change. Subject matters contain different types of information and structures, teachers use different instructional methods and have different styles, exams differ in the kinds of demands they make, and the interests, motives, and capabilities of students change over time. Accordingly, strategies must be *formulated* or constructed anew as one moves from task to task rather than *selected* from a bank of previously formulated strategies. The true strategist, in other words, exhibits a characteristic that is referred to as *mindfulness* (Alexander, Graham, &

## Take a Stand!

### Teach Students How to Be Self-Regulated Learners

A perennial complaint among educators is that many students lack the skills and knowledge to function as self-regulated learners. This is a strange complaint as everyone from politicians to parents endorses the goals of self-directed learning and lifelong learning. Like motherhood and apple pie, they are easy goals to endorse because nobody could be against them. But when it comes to putting one's resources where one's rhetoric is, much of this support disappears like the morning mist. The following reasons account for a large part of this inconsistency:

1. Many people (including teachers, parents, and students) believe that self-regulation is a natural process that students will figure out and master if they just work at it long and hard enough. This leads to the ubiquitous but mostly useless advice to "study harder."

2. School is thought of as a place where students acquire bodies of information about various subject matters and the so-called basic skills of reading, writing, and computing. There is simply not enough room in the curriculum to teach students how to be self-directed learners.

3. Teachers and administrators are held accountable for how well students score on state-mandated tests. Consequently, school curricula and classroom instruction emphasize those skills and bodies of knowledge that relate most directly to state learning standards and test items, and SRL skills are either ignored or take a back seat.

If this situation is to change, everyone involved in education needs to realize that there is nothing more basic than learning how to be a self-regulated learner. These skills allow students to become proficient at reading, writing, and computing and to direct their learning long after they finish school. Consequently, SRL skills should be as much a part of the curriculum as the three Rs.

The place to start is the individual classroom. At the very least, you should teach students that a relationship exists between the cognitive processes they use and the outcomes they observe, how and when to use various learning tactics, how to determine whether learning is proceeding as planned, and what to do if it is not.

#### HM TeacherPrepSPACE

What's your response to this argument? Is SRL so "basic" that teachers ought to teach it? At the textbook's student website, you can find out more about this important issue.

---

Harris, 1998). A mindful learner is aware of the need to be strategic, attends to the various elements that make up a learning task, and thinks about how to use the leaning skills he possesses to greatest effect.

The second point is that the concept of a learning strategy is obviously complex and requires a certain level of intellectual maturity. Thus you may be tempted to conclude that although *you* could do it, learning to be strategic is beyond the reach of most elementary, middle school, and high school students. Research evidence suggests otherwise, however. A study of high school students in Scotland, for example, found that some students are sensitive to contextual differences among school tasks and vary their approach to studying accordingly (Selmes, 1987). Furthermore, as we will show in the next section, research in the United States suggests that elementary school youngsters can be trained to use many of the strategy components just mentioned.

Finally, because strategic learners tailor their learning processes to the perceived demands of a task, teachers need to clearly convey to students such critical information as what tasks or parts of tasks (such as certain parts of a reading assignment) are sufficiently important that they will test students on them and what form the tests will take. Students, in turn, need to accurately perceive those demands (Beishuizen & Stoutjesdijk, 1999). A study conducted in the Netherlands (Broekkamp, van Hout-Wolters, Rijlaarsdam, & van den Bergh, 2002) shows that this process occurs less frequently than one would desire. The study examined how twenty-two history teachers and their eleventh-grade students rated the importance of sections of an eight-thousand-word textbook passage on U.S. presidents. In brief, here is what the researchers found:

1. There was only limited agreement among teachers about which sections of the text students should focus on in preparation for a test.
2. There was only limited agreement among students, as well as between students and their teacher, as to which sections of the text were most important.

In other words, teachers had only limited success in communicating to students what parts of the passage were more important than others, and students were as apt to focus on the less important parts as the more important ones.

These findings suggest that teachers should provide students with clear and comprehensive information about the relative importance of various parts of a reading passage, instruct students in how to identify the important parts of a reading passage, and avoid dwelling on or overemphasizing aspects of a reading assignment that they have no intention of testing students on.

## Modeling and Self-Regulated Learning

What little students know about the nature and use of self-regulatory skills has usually been acquired through direct instruction (by teachers, parents, and peers) and trial-and-error learning. But there is another way to strengthen self-efficacy beliefs and learn how to use self-regulatory skills: observing and imitating the behavior of a skilled model. This form of learning is often referred to as **observational learning** or **modeling.**

The notion that learning occurs by watching and imitating the behavior of others has been acknowledged and valued for thousands of years. Social cognitive theory, with its belief that the student's environment interacts with personal characteristics and behavior, has stressed the role of observational learning in schools.

Observational learning can play an especially strong role in the acquisition of self-regulatory skills. Specifically, evidence suggests that these skills are learned most efficiently and effectively when they are acquired according to the following four-level model: observation, emulation, self-control, and self-regulation (Zimmerman, 2000, 2002; Zimmerman & Kitsantas, 2002, 2005). In the description that follows, note how the high levels of support and guidance (or *scaffolding*, to use the constructivist terminology) that are present for the observation and emulation levels are reduced at the self-control level and eliminated at the self-regulation level. Table 10.3 summarizes the cognitive and behavioral requirements of the learner and the source of the learner's motivation for each level.

> Self-regulation skills learned best in four-level process: observation, emulation, self-control, self-regulation

**Observation**   At the observation level, learners pick up the major features of a skill or strategy, as well as performance standards, motivational beliefs, and values, by watching and listening as a model exhibits the skill and explains the reasons for his behavior: for example, a model who persists at trying to solve a problem and expresses the belief that he is capable of solving the problem. What would motivate

| **Table 10.3** | A Social Cognitive Model of Self-Regulated Skill Learning | |
|---|---|---|
| **Level** | **Main Requirement of the Learner** | **Source of Motivation** |
| Observation | Attend to actions and verbalizations of the model and discriminate relevant from irrelevant behaviors | Vicarious: note rewards received by the model and anticipate receiving similar rewards for exhibiting similar behavior |
| Emulation | Exhibit the general form of the modeled behavior | Direct: feedback from the model and/or others |
| Self-control | Learn to exhibit the modeled behavior automatically through self-directed practice (focus on the underlying rule or process that produces the behavior and compare the behavior with personal standards) | Self-satisfaction from matching the standards and behavior of the model |
| Self-regulation | Learn to adapt the behavior to changes in internal and external conditions (such as the reactions of others) | Self-efficacy beliefs; degree of intrinsic interest in the skill |

SOURCES: Zimmerman (2000, 2002); Zimmerman & Kitsantas (2002).

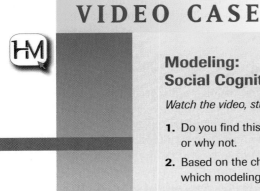

# VIDEO CASE ◄◄ ▶ ►►

## Modeling:
## Social Cognitive Theory in a High School Chemistry Lesson

*Watch the video, study the artifacts in the case, and reflect upon the following questions:*

1. Do you find this teacher's use of modeling/observational learning to be effective? Explain why or why not.

2. Based on the character and the Video Case, give some ideas of subject areas or lessons in which modeling/observational learning would work especially well.

a student to observe and then try to emulate a model's behavior? At least four factors do so:

1. Students are more likely to closely attend to a model and retain what has been observed if they are unfamiliar with the task at hand or if they feel incapable of carrying out the task.

2. Students attend to models they admire, respect, and perceive as having knowledge, skills, and attributes that they themselves would like to have. The popular conception, by the way, that older children and adolescents look primarily to sports or music stars rather than family members as models is not supported by research. In response to the question "What persons are your personal model?" about 46 percent of a large sample (over one thousand) of European children and adolescents listed either their mother or father, and 31 percent listed a relative. Music and sports stars were named by only 15 percent and 12 percent of respondents, respectively (Bucher, 1997).

3. Students attend to models whose behavior they judge to be acceptable and appropriate. Thus students will often model a peer's behavior.

4. Students are more likely to imitate a model's behavior if they see that the model is reinforced for exhibiting the behavior and anticipate that they will be similarly reinforced (Schunk, 2001). This type of reinforcement is referred to as **vicarious reinforcement.** A middle school student, for example, who observes an admired classmate being praised by the teacher for promptly completing an assignment may strive to work quickly and diligently on the next assignment in anticipation of receiving similar praise.

**Emulation**    At the emulation level, learners reproduce the general form of the model's behavior. Because learners rarely copy the exact behaviors of a model, the term *emulation* is used here instead of the word *imitation*. The learner's response can be refined by the model's use of guidance, feedback, and direct reinforcement (such as praise from the model). Social cognitive theorists identify four types of emulation effects that result from observing models: inhibition, disinhibition, facilitation, and true observational learning.

| People learn to inhibit or make responses by observing others

*Inhibition* occurs when we learn not to do something that we already know how to do because a model we are observing refrains from behaving in that way, is punished for behaving in that way, or does something different from what we intended to do. Consider the following example: A ten-year-old is taken to her first symphony concert by her parents. After the first movement of Beethoven's Fifth Symphony, she is about to applaud but notices that her parents are sitting quietly with their hands in their laps. She does the same.

*Disinhibition* occurs when we learn to exhibit a behavior that is usually disapproved of by most people because a model does the same without being punished.

*Social cognitive theory holds that one way students acquire self-regulated learning skills is by observing and imitating the behavior of admired models, such as teachers, siblings, and peers.*

For example, a student attends his school's final football game of the season. As time expires, thousands of students run onto the field and begin tearing up pieces of turf to take home as a souvenir. Noticing that the police do nothing, the student joins in.

An early, and now classic, experiment on disinhibition was conducted by Bandura in the early 1960s (Bandura, Ross, & Ross, 1961). A child was seated at a table and encouraged to play with a toy. The model sat at a nearby table and either played quietly with Tinkertoys for ten minutes or played with the Tinkertoys for a minute and then played aggressively with an inflatable clown "Bobo" doll for several minutes, punching, kicking, and sitting on it and hitting it with a hammer. In a subsequent unstructured play situation, children who did not observe a model, as well as those who observed a nonaggressive model, displayed little aggression. By contrast, children exposed to the aggressive model behaved with considerably more aggression toward the Bobo doll and other toys.

*Facilitation* occurs whenever we are prompted to do something that we do not ordinarily do because of insufficient motivation rather than social disapproval. For example, a college student attends a lecture on reforming the American education system. Impressed by the lecturer's enthusiasm and ideas, the student vigorously applauds at the end of the presentation. As several members of the audience stand and applaud, the student stands as well.

The last of the four types of emulation effects, *true observational learning*, occurs when we learn a new behavioral pattern by watching and imitating the performance of someone else. A teenage girl learning how to hit a topspin forehand in tennis by watching her instructor do the same is an example of true observational learning.

## pause & reflect

Can you recall a teacher you admired so much that you emulated some aspect of her behavior (either then or later)? How might you have the same effect on your students?

**Self-Control**   The self-control level is marked by the learner's being able to exhibit the modeled behavior in the absence of the model. Self-control is achieved through self-directed practice. The learner focuses on the underlying rule or process that produces the behavior and compares the behavior with personal standards. At this level, the learner's motivation comes from a sense of self-satisfaction at matching the standards and behavior of the model.

**Self-Regulation**   The self-regulation level is attained when learners can adapt the modeled behavior to changes in internal and external conditions (such as a low level of interest in a topic or negative reactions of others). The motivation for self-regulated behavior comes from one's perceived self-efficacy and degree of intrinsic interest in the modeled behavior.

Before leaving this description of SRL and examining some of the relevant research, we would like you to keep the following point in mind: self-regulation is possible only in an environment that allows students the opportunity to make choices. Teachers who specify in great detail what students will do, when they will do it, where they will do it, and how they will do it will see very little development and use of SRL processes (Schunk, 2004).

# RESEARCH ON SOCIAL COGNITIVE THEORY

Although social cognitive theory offers a compelling explanation of learning, its value to teachers and others depends on the extent to which its concepts and their proposed relationships are supported by research findings. The research that we summarize in this section falls into three broad categories: (1) correlational studies that have examined the relationships among self-efficacy, self-regulation, and achievement, (2) experimental studies that have examined the effect of modeling on self-efficacy, self-regulation, and achievement, and (3) experimental studies that have examined the effect of instruction on self-regulated learning skills.

## Relationships Among Self-Efficacy, Self-Regulation Processes, and Achievement

| Self-efficacy, self-regulation related to each other and to achievement

Social cognitive theory holds that self-efficacy and self-regulation processes should be positively related to each other and that both should be positively related to achievement. A number of studies, including the following, support these relationships.

- For eight- and nine-year-olds (but not for five-, six-, or seven-year-olds), self-efficacy for reading was positively and significantly related to reading comprehension (Chapman & Tunmer, 1995).
- Among an ethnically diverse sample of fifth, eighth, and eleventh graders, perceived self-efficacy for defining words and solving mathematical problems was significantly and positively related to the use of such self-regulatory processes as reviewing notes, seeking peer assistance, and organizing and transforming information (Zimmerman & Martinez-Pons, 1990).
- Seventh-grade students with higher levels of perceived self-efficacy for performing well on English and science assignments were more likely to use self-regulatory processes and earn higher scores on exams, quizzes, essays, and lab reports than were students with lower levels of perceived self-efficacy. Also, students who reported greater use of self-regulatory processes earned higher scores than did students who reported less use of self-regulatory processes (Pintrich & De Groot, 1990).
- Another study (Klassen, 2004) examined whether seventh-grade Canadian students who were born in India or whose fathers were born in India had different mathematics efficacy beliefs than Canadian students who were born in Canada or the United States or whose fathers were born in Canada or the United States. Specifically, it was expected that the efficacy beliefs of Indian students would be more strongly influenced by social persuasion and vicarious experience because of their culture's emphasis on group identity, group solidarity, and responsibility to the group, whereas the efficacy beliefs of Canadian students would be more strongly influenced by past performance and emotional arousal because of the Western emphasis on self, independence, and individual initiative.

The study turned up points of similarity and difference between the two groups. For both groups of students, higher self-efficacy ratings were significantly related to higher math performance, and past performance predicted math efficacy beliefs. On the other hand, the Indian students' efficacy beliefs were, in keeping with their cultural emphasis, more strongly influenced by social persuasion and social comparisons.

- Tenth-grade students who were assigned to complete either a well-structured assignment or an ill-structured assignment (we defined and illustrated these concepts in the previous chapter) filled out a self-efficacy questionnaire at six points during the course of the assignment that assessed both their self-efficacy for learning (for example, "I'm confident I'm learning the basic ideas in this project" and "I know which mental techniques would best meet the needs of this project") and self-efficacy for performance (such as, "I expect to do well on this project" and "I believe I will receive an excellent grade on this project"). The well-structured task required students to choose a form of cancer and write a report about it that included its causes, symptoms, and treatments; an assessment of their risk for that form of cancer; and a list of behaviors that would likely reduce their risk for that form of cancer. Students who were assigned to the ill-structured task were required to role-play members of a task force who were asked by the government how to best combat cancer and to explain their conclusions in a written report. This exercise was designed to stimulate critical thinking about how government should fund treatment versus preventative measures.

  Consistent with the prediction from social cognitive theory that the nature of a task affects students' perception of the task's difficulty and their self-efficacy, students' self-efficacy for learning and their task performance were higher for the well-structured task than for the ill-structured task. The researchers also found that at the outset of the task, regardless of whether it was well-structured or ill-structured, self-efficacy for performance was significantly higher than self-efficacy for learning, but the difference disappeared by the end of the task (Lodewyk & Winne, 2005).

## Effects of Modeling on Self-Efficacy, Self-Regulation, and Achievement

In social cognitive theory, modeling is seen as an effective means of enhancing self-efficacy, teaching students how to use self-regulation skills, and increasing achievement, particularly when the observer is similar to the model or when the observer strongly identifies with the model (Schunk & Zimmerman, 1997). Support for the theory has come from a number of studies, particularly ones that focus on skills in mathematics and writing.

**Improving Students' Mathematical Problem-Solving Skills** Mathematical problem-solving ability is a difficult skill for many students to master, and it has a prominent place in the curriculum (it is one of the three R's). For these reasons, it has often been studied by social cognitive researchers who are interested in the effects of modeling. The research we describe in this section is just a sample of what has appeared in the literature in the past several years.

***Effect of Peer Models*** A study conducted with ten-year-olds (Schunk & Hanson, 1985) tested the hypothesis that children become increasingly likely to attend to and emulate a model as the perceived similarity between the observer and the model increases. Children who were having difficulty learning to do subtraction-with-regrouping problems (also known as borrowing problems) were assigned to one of four groups. One group watched a videotape of a same-sex peer being taught how to solve such problems by a teacher. Because the peer model quickly solved a set of similar problems without making any errors, he or she was referred to as a mastery model. A second group also watched a videotape of a same-sex peer being taught by a teacher and then working on a set of similar problems. Because this model made mistakes at first but overcame them and then performed flawlessly, he or she was referred to as a peer-coping model. The peer models in both groups verbalized the subtraction operations, along with high self-efficacy statements. A third group watched a videotape of a teacher explaining and carrying out the subtraction operations. The fourth group did not view a model.

All the children were then given step-by-step written instructions in how to solve subtraction-with-regrouping problems. Because of the greater similarity between the students and the peer-coping model, it was expected that students who observed such a model would perform better than students who observed a mastery model. Although there was no difference between the mastery- and coping-model groups on a posttest, both had significantly higher levels of self-efficacy for solving subtraction problems and solved significantly more problems correctly than did children who either observed the adult model or worked solely from written instructions.

Observing a peer model improves students' self-efficacy for math problem solving and math problem-solving ability

***Effect of Perceived Similarity in Learning Ability***    Another study that tested the similarity hypothesis (Schunk, Hanson, & Cox, 1987) did so by examining the effect of perceived similarity in learning ability (coping versus mastery) and gender (same sex versus opposite sex). Children in grades 4, 5, and 6 whose arithmetic achievement was below the 35th percentile were assigned to one of the following conditions: male mastery model, male coping model, female mastery model, female coping model. The mastery and coping models exhibited the same behaviors as the mastery and coping models in the study of ten-year-olds just described. The children in each group watched a videotape in which each of six fractions skills was modeled by a teacher and then performed by a peer under the supervision of the teacher. The teacher demonstrated how to do a problem and then asked the model to do a similar one. The model verbalized the procedure and was then told by the teacher that the solution was correct.

Students in all four groups were then given written instructions on each of six days that explained how to solve each of the six types of fractions problems they had seen the model solve. The students were then given several similar problems that they had to solve on their own. An adult was always present to answer questions. The main result was that children who observed a coping model, regardless of whether the model was male or female, reported significantly higher levels of self-efficacy for learning to solve fractions problems and solved significantly more problems correctly than did children who observed a mastery model.

***Effect of Self-Modeling***    A further study (Schunk & Hanson, 1989) took the similarity hypothesis to its logical conclusion by having students use themselves as their model. Children in grades 4, 5, and 6 whose arithmetic achievement was below the 35th percentile were assigned to either a peer-model, self-model, peer-model + self-model, or no-model condition. Children in the first and third groups watched a videotape in which each of six fractions skills was modeled by a teacher and then by three same-sex peers under the supervision of the teacher. The teacher demonstrated how to do a problem and then asked a model to do a similar one. The model verbalized the procedure and was then told by the teacher that the solution was correct.

Students in all four groups were then given written instructions for six days on how to solve different types of fractions problems (with an adult present to answer questions) and were videotaped working out similar problems at a chalkboard. After days 4, 5, and 6, children in the self-model and peer-model + self-model conditions watched the videotape of their performance from the previous day (thereby serving as their own model). Although there were no differences among the three modeling conditions, students in all three scored significantly higher than the students in the no-model condition on measures of self-efficacy for solving fractions problems and numbers of fractions problems solved correctly.

***Effect of Learning-Goal Orientation***    Earlier in this chapter we outlined a set of self-regulatory processes that are activated either before a task is begun, during a task, or after the task has been completed. One process that comes into play prior to engaging in a task and that is assumed to affect students' self-efficacy and performance is whether a student has a learning goal or a performance goal (Zimmerman, 2000). *Learning goals* focus on acquiring specific knowledge and skills, whereas *performance goals* focus just on completing the task. One study (Schunk, 1996) tested the effects of learning-goal orientation on learning six fractions skills (one per day for six days) for a group of average-achieving fourth-grade students.

Each day's lesson began with a statement from the teacher that established the goal. Students assigned to the learning-goal condition were told: "While you're working it helps to keep in mind what you're trying to do. You'll be trying to learn how to solve fractions problems where the denominators are the same and you have to add the numerators." Students assigned to the performance-goal condition were told: "While you're working it helps to keep in mind what you're trying to do. You'll be trying to solve fractions problems where the denominators are the same and you have to add the numerators." To ensure that the students in both groups understood the goal of each session (notice that their instructions differed by only a few words), the teacher asked them to repeat the instructions and indicate whether they had any questions. This was followed by a ten-minute explanation and demonstration by the teacher of the fractions skill the students would be learning that day, ten minutes of guided practice, and twenty-five minutes of independent practice. At the end of day 6, students judged their ability to solve fractions problems and indicated the extent to which they were pleased with their progress in learning fractions skills.

The main finding was that students in the learning-goal group exhibited a significantly higher level of self-efficacy for solving fractions problems—and solved significantly more problems correctly—than did the students in the performance-goal group. In addition, students in the learning-goal group had higher self-evaluation and self-satisfaction scores.

**Improving Students' Writing Skills**    Writing skills are also frequently used by researchers to investigate the effects of modeling. Writing is particularly important in the middle school years because writing tasks are more complex than in earlier years and play a larger role in classroom performance. Students who feel poorly prepared to carry out writing tasks tend to be more anxious about them and to spend less time on them (Klassen, 2002). As with the studies we summarized on mathematical problem solving, the research summarized next is just a sample.

***Modeling for Strategy Development***    As we noted earlier in the chapter, self-regulation skills make significant contributions to achievement, especially when students reach the middle school grades, and modeling can be an effective way to help students acquire these skills. A recent study (Harris, Graham, & Mason, 2006) investigated the feasibility of providing self-regulated strategy instruction in the primary grades. Second-grade students who had scored significantly below average on a writing test were assigned to one of three groups: self-regulated strategy development (SRSD), self-regulated strategy development plus peer support (SRSD + PS), and comparison. In five steps, pairs of students in the two SRSD groups were taught a general planning strategy for writing stories and persuasive essays. The strategy involved picking an idea to write about, organizing one's thoughts, and writing the story or essay. To help the students remember these three elements, they were taught the mnemonic POW. They were also taught specific techniques to help them organize their story and persuasive essay ideas. For example, to help them write good stories, they were taught to ask themselves such questions as: Who are the main characters? When does the story take place? What do the main characters want to do? How does the story end?

The first instructional step involved teaching students the three elements of the planning, or POW, strategy; the specific techniques for writing either stories or essays; discussing why each of the POW elements and the specific writing techniques were important; discussing the characteristics of a good story or essay; and providing examples of each part of the writing strategy. The only difference between the SRSD and SRSD + PS conditions occurred at this point. Each pair of students in the SRSD + PS condition was told that they had to help each other correctly use the planning strategies and writing techniques described.

Step 2 involved teaching students that their goal was to include all the necessary parts of a story or essay that were identified in step 1 and to monitor whether their story or essay contained all of these parts by using a visual aid (a rocket that was divided into several parts, each of which was colored in when a story or essay part was completed).

In step 3, the teacher modeled the POW strategy, using the visual aid and overt self-instruction. The latter involved asking oneself such questions as "What do I have to do here?" "What comes next?" and "Does that make sense?" and telling oneself such things as "I did that part really well!" and "I'm almost finished."

In step 4, the students, with instructor support, established their writing goal, planned the story or essay, and wrote the story using the elements introduced in steps 1 and 2. Working in pairs, the students read their stories to each other and discussed how the strategies helped them write better.

In step 5, students wrote their stories or essays independently.

Students assigned to the comparison condition received their normal writing instruction from their classroom teacher.

Students in the two SRSD conditions significantly outscored their peers in the comparison condition in a number of ways. On a posttest administered at the end of the instructional sequence, they spent more time planning their stories and essays, and they wrote essays that were longer, more complete, and of a higher quality. These advantages carried over to the classroom, where the two SRSD groups continued to produce not only better quality persuasive essays than the comparison students but also better quality narrative and information papers as well (for which they had received no specific training). Furthermore, students in the SRSD + PS condition wrote persuasive papers for their classroom teacher that were higher in quality than those produced by students in the SRSD-only condition.

***Observing Weak and Strong Models***    In another test of the model-observer similarity principle (Braaksma, Rijlaarsdam, & van den Bergh, 2002), eighth-grade students in a Dutch school who were classified as having either low, medium, or high verbal ability observed a weak peer model and a strong peer model write an argumentative passage.

Argumentative passages contain an opinion (such as "It is better to live in a city than in a village"), one or more supporting arguments (for example, a city offers more choices for shopping and going to school, cities are more conducive to personal growth, and there are more job opportunities in a city), one or more subordinate arguments (for example, cities are more conducive to personal growth because there is a wider range of people to meet and there are more cultural events to attend), and connective words such as *because* and *and* that logically relate the supporting arguments to the opinion and the subordinate arguments to each other and to the supporting argument.

In the study, the weak models omitted critical aspects of an argumentative passage and produced passages that were less coherent than those produced by the strong models. Both weak and strong models verbalized their thought processes: planning what to write and then checking to make sure that it was complete and made sense. One group of students was asked to identify the model who performed less well and to explain why this was the less competent model. A second group was asked to identify which model performed better and to explain why this was the more competent model.

Students with low verbal ability who were asked to identify and evaluate the weak model received higher scores on the argumentative passages they wrote than did students with low verbal ability who either were asked to identify and evaluate the strong model or who just practiced writing argumentative passages. Students with high verbal ability who wrote argumentative passages after identifying and evaluating the strong model or who merely practiced writing argumentative passages received higher scores than did their peers with high verbal ability who identified and evaluated the weak model. Both groups, in other words, seemed to respond better to models they perceived as similar to themselves.

***Modeling Versus Practice*** Most people have come to believe, partly because of their own experience and partly because of supporting research, that practice makes perfect. But one study (Couzijn, 1999) provides support for the contention of social cognitive theory that observing a model can be more effective than rote practice in helping students acquire new skills.

A group of ninth-grade students worked through a four-part self-instructional course on argumentative writing. After each part, they participated in one of the following four exercises: (1) working individually on writing exercises, (2) watching a videotape of two students of the same age doing writing exercises while thinking aloud, (3) watching a peer doing writing exercises while thinking aloud and then watching another peer verbally analyze the writer's passage, or (4) writing an argumentative passage and then observing a peer analyze the passage while thinking aloud. All students were then asked to write argumentative passages (e.g., "Do you think students should give grades to their teachers?") that were scored for putting the issue in context, text structure, argumentation structure, and presentation of argument (e.g., use of paragraphing, markers, and connectors).

As expected, students in groups (2), (3), and (4)—all the students exposed to modeling of one sort or another—produced better quality argumentative passages than did students who simply practiced their writing.

> Observing a peer model improves the quality of students' writing more than simply practicing writing

## Effects of Instruction on Self-Regulated Learning Skills

### pause & reflect

A major problem in training students to use learning strategies and tactics is getting the youngsters to spend the time and effort required. Suppose some students expressed a lack of interest, saying their own methods were just as effective (although you knew they were not). How would you convince these students otherwise?

> Reciprocal teaching: students learn comprehension skills by demonstrating them to peers

Research clearly shows that training students to use various tactics and strategies is a worthwhile use of the teacher's time. In one study, students who were trained to use a single mnemonic technique outperformed untrained students by a wide margin on subsequent tests of memory (68th percentile versus 50th percentile, respectively). The effect was particularly noticeable among primary grade and low-achieving students. A similar advantage was found for students who had been taught to use a variety of tactics and were tested for memory and low-level comprehension (75th percentile versus the control group's 50th percentile). Although the weakest effect was found in studies in which students were taught a general strategy rather than specific tactics, these students nevertheless performed significantly better than students who were left to their own devices (70th percentile versus 50th percentile, respectively) (Hattie, Biggs, & Purdie, 1996).

A particularly effective strategy-training program is the *reciprocal teaching* (RT) program of Annemarie Palincsar and Ann Brown (1984). As the title of this program indicates, students learn certain comprehension skills by demonstrating them to each other. Palincsar and Brown trained a small group of seventh graders whose reading comprehension scores were at least two years below grade level to use the techniques of summarizing, self-questioning, clarifying, and predicting to improve their reading comprehension. They chose these four methods because students can use them to improve *and* monitor comprehension.

During the early training sessions, the teacher explained and demonstrated the four methods while reading various passages. The students were then given gradually increasing responsibility for demonstrating these techniques to their peers, with the teacher supplying prompts and corrective feedback as needed. Eventually, each student was expected to offer a good summary of a passage, to pose questions about important ideas, to clarify ambiguous words or phrases, and to predict upcoming events, all to be done with little or no intervention by the teacher. (This approach to strategy instruction is based on Vygotsky's zone of proximal development concept that we mentioned previously in the book.)

Palincsar and Brown (1984) found that the RT program produced two general beneficial effects. First, the quality of students' summaries, questions, clarifications, and predictions improved. Early in the program, students produced overly detailed summaries and many unclear questions. But in later sessions, concise summaries and questions dealing explicitly with main ideas were the rule. For example, questions on main ideas increased from 54 percent to 70 percent. In addition, the questions were increasingly stated in paraphrase form rather than as verbatim statements. Second, the RT-trained students, who had begun the sessions well below grade level, scored as high as a group of average readers on tests of comprehension (about 75 percent correct for both groups) and much better than a group taught how to locate information that might show up in a test question (75 percent correct versus 45 percent correct).

Subsequent research on the effectiveness of RT under both controlled and realistic conditions has continued to produce positive findings across a broad age spectrum (fourth grade through college). On average, students using RT have scored at the 62nd percentile on standardized reading comprehension tests (compared with the 50th percentile for the average control student) and at the 81st percentile on reading comprehension tests that were created by the experimenters (Alfassi, 1998; Carter, 1997; Kim, Baylor, & PALS Group, 2006; Rosenshine & Meister, 1994a).

In a comparison of strategies designed to improve reading comprehension (Mason, 2004), half of a sample of fifth-grade students with poor reading comprehension skills were taught how to think before reading, while reading, and after reading (TWA for short). Students were taught to think prior to reading about the author's purpose in writing the story, what relevant information they already possessed about the subject, and what they wanted to learn from the passage. While they were reading they were asked to think about reading at an optimal speed, making connections between prior knowledge and the information in the passage, and rereading parts of the passage they felt they did not understand. After reading, they were asked to think about the main idea and create a summary of the passage and what they learned from the passage. Consistent with social cognitive theory, the elements of this technique were taught through a combination of modeling, direct instruction, and guided practice. The remaining students were taught a questioning technique called *reciprocal questioning* (parts of which were incorporated into Palincsar and Brown's reciprocal teaching strategy). The heart of reciprocal questioning, or RQ, is the following five-step procedure: (1) the teacher and students silently read a passage; (2) the teacher closes his or her book; (3) the students ask the teacher questions, which the teacher answers; (4) the students close their books; and (5) the teacher asks the students questions, which the students answer. As with the TWA strategy, RQ was taught using modeling, direct instruction, and guided practice.

Students who were taught the TWA strategy outscored their peers who were taught RQ on ability to orally and accurately state the main idea of the fifteen passages they had read, to summarize a given paragraph of each passage, and to retell what they had read. The oral retellings of the students using TWA were of a higher quality and contained more information and main idea units than the retellings of the students who used RQ. Strangely, this advantage did not carry over to parallel written tests of reading comprehension.

An excellent example of how social cognitive theory (as well as such related theories as cognitive development and motivation) has been thoroughly integrated into a school curriculum is the Benchmark School in Media, Pennsylvania (Pressley, Gaskins, Solic, & Collins, 2006). Benchmark is a private school that serves students between the ages of six and twelve who have experienced several years of academic failure largely because of such self-regulatory deficits as poor attention, poor listening, working too fast, poor frustration tolerance, organizational difficulties, and lack of willingness to expend effort. To overcome these problems, Benchmark teachers use a variety of techniques derived from social cognitive and other theories, including modeling of cognitive processes, teaching reading comprehension techniques, encouraging the use of background knowledge, teaching note-taking skills, teaching students how to analyze and break down large tasks into smaller, easier-to-manage parts, teaching reflection and monitoring techniques, and consistently using positive reinforcement.

As a result of these and other characteristics of the school, Benchmark students at the end of the 2003–2004 school year scored on average at the 77th percentile on the reading section of a standardized achievement test, whereas they had scored at the 34th percentile two years earlier. In addition, almost all students graduate from high school (or earn their GEDs) and attend college.

Now that you are familiar with social cognitive theory and research, it is time to examine several Suggestions for Teaching derived from these principles and research findings.

# Suggestions for Teaching in Your Classroom

## Applying Social Cognitive Theory in the Classroom

**1** **Include the development of self-regulated learning skills in your objectives and lesson plans.**

The research that we summarized clearly shows that SRL skills make a significant contribution to students' achievement. Consequently, their development should be included in your instructional objectives and lesson plans. You can help students become more effective self-regulated learners by incorporating the following elements into your classroom instruction (Ley & Young, 2001; Randi & Corno, 2000; Schunk, 2001).

**a. Emphasize the importance of SRL skills to learning and when they should be used.**

**JOURNAL ENTRY**
Teaching Self-Regulated
Learning Skills

In all likelihood, you will want students to attain some degree of proficiency in goal setting, planning, use of tactics and strategies, monitoring of one's actions and progress, self-evaluation, and self-reinforcement. When teaching planning skills, for example, point out that students who are good planners know the conditions under which they learn best and choose or arrange environments that eliminate or decrease distractions. To raise students' awareness of the value of a good learning environment, you can have them keep a log of how much time they spend studying in various places and at various times, what internal and external distractions they experience, and how they deal with those distractions. On the basis of this information, they can draw conclusions about when and under what circumstances they best learn. To help students choose or create a hospitable learning environment, you can prepare and distribute a checklist of desirable features. Likely features of a good learning environment would include: relative quiet, good lighting and ventilation,

*Teachers can help students acquire and refine self-regulated learning skills by providing direct instruction in such skills as goal setting, planning, using learning tactics, monitoring, and self-evaluation.*

comfortable furniture, and the absence of other people, of a television set, and of alternative reading material such as comic books or magazines.

Self-regulated learners commonly use many types of memory and comprehension tactics. You can help students appreciate the value of these skills by using such techniques as mnemonic devices, outlines, concept maps, previews, graphs, flowcharts, and tables as you teach and by explaining how they are used and the ways in which they aid learning. To increase the probability that students will use such techniques themselves, teach them how to make outlines before they write essays, and show them how to create concept maps, graphs, flowcharts, and tables after they have read a section of text.

**b. Model SRL skills, including the standards you use to evaluate your performance and reinforce yourself.**

You can enhance the learning of SRL skills by having students observe and imitate what you and other skilled learners do. As noted, when you demonstrate a skill or process, you should first explain what you are going to do. Then take time to describe why you are going to do it and how you will evaluate the quality of your performance. Then demonstrate the behavior, evaluate your performance, and, if you feel your behavior has met your standards, verbally administer some self-praise. The importance of modeling thought processes that are normally hidden from observation was noted by Margaret Metzger (1998), a high school English teacher. To help students better understand the process of literary interpretation and criticism, she recommended a procedure in which she led some students through a discussion of a story while other students observed and took notes on the process.

**c. Provide guided practice and corrective feedback for the SRL skills you want students to learn.**

As we noted earlier in this chapter, self-observation or self-monitoring is an important SRL skill that plays a role at several points in the learning process. Self-regulating students are very proficient at monitoring their progress in meeting goals, the effectiveness of their learning strategies and tactics, and the quality of their achievements. They do this by comparing their performance both to internal standards and external feedback. Once you have explained and demonstrated self-monitoring, give students structured opportunities to practice this skill and provide feedback.

**JOURNAL ENTRY**
Helping Students Practice and
Refine Self-Regulated Learning
Skills

To familiarize students with the process of self-monitoring, you can require them to keep a log or journal in which they (a) state goals, (b) note how they prepare for and address the demands of projects, homework, and other tasks, and (c) assess the extent to which they have achieved one or more goals. Students could record, for example, how much time they spent on a task, the types of tactics they used, the number of problems they worked, and the extent to which they felt they understood the material.

External feedback should be constructive regardless of whether the basic message contains good news or bad news. On one hand, when you point out mistakes or omissions students have made on assignments and tests, focus on the cognitive processes students may have misused or omitted and provide suggestions for correcting such problems in the future. On the other hand, when the quality of a student's work has improved over time, point that out and relate it to one or more cognitive processes.

**2** **Teach students how to use both memory and comprehension tactics and to take notes.**

**a. Teach students how to use various forms of rehearsal and mnemonic devices.**

**JOURNAL ENTRY**
Ways to Teach Memory Tactics

We have at least two reasons for recommending the teaching of rehearsal. One is that maintenance rehearsal is a useful tactic for keeping a relatively small amount of information active in short-term memory. The other is that maintenance rehearsal is one of a few tactics that young children can learn to use. If you do decide to teach rehearsal, we have two suggestions. First, remind young children that rehearsal is something that learners consciously decide to do when they want to remember things. Second, remind students to rehearse no more than seven items (or chunks) at a time.

Upper elementary grade students (fourth, fifth, and sixth graders) can be taught advanced forms of maintenance rehearsal, such as cumulative rehearsal, and forms of elaborative rehearsal, such as rehearsing sets of items that form homogeneous categories. As with younger students, provide several opportunities each week to practice these skills.

As you prepare class presentations or encounter bits of information that students seem to have difficulty learning, ask yourself if a mnemonic device would be useful. You might write up a list of the devices discussed earlier and refer to it often. Part of the value of mnemonic devices is that they make learning easier. They are also fun to make up and use. Moreover, rhymes, acronyms, and acrostics can be constructed rather quickly. You might consider setting aside about thirty minutes two or three times a week to teach mnemonics. First, explain how rhyme, acronym, and acrostic mnemonics work and then provide examples of each (see Table 10.1). Once students understand how the mnemonic is supposed to work, have them construct mnemonics to learn various facts and concepts. You might offer a prize for the most ingenious mnemonic.

**b. Teach students how to formulate comprehension questions.**

**JOURNAL ENTRY**
Ways to Teach Comprehension
Tactics

We concluded earlier that self-questioning could be an effective comprehension tactic if students were trained to write good comprehension questions and given opportunities to practice the technique. We suggest you try the following instructional sequence:

1. Discuss the purpose of student-generated questions.
2. Point out the differences between knowledge-level questions and different types of comprehension-level questions (such as analysis, synthesis, and evaluation). An excellent discussion of these types can be found in the *Taxonomy of Educational Objectives, Handbook I: Cognitive Domain* (Bloom, Englehart, Furst, Hill, & Krathwohl, 1956).

3. Explain and illustrate the kinds of responses that should be given to different types of comprehension-level questions.
4. Provide students with a sample paragraph and a set of high-level question stems. Have students formulate questions and responses either individually or in pairs.
5. Provide corrective feedback.
6. Give students short passages from which to practice.
7. Provide corrective feedback (André & Anderson, 1978/1979; King, 1994).

c. **Teach students how to take notes.**

**JOURNAL ENTRY**
Teaching Students How to Take Notes

Despite the limitations of research on note taking mentioned earlier, three suggestions should lead to more effective note taking.

• Provide students with clear, detailed objectives for every reading assignment. The objectives should indicate what parts of the assignment to focus on and how that material should be processed (whether memorized verbatim, reorganized and paraphrased, or integrated with earlier reading assignments).
• Inform students that note taking is an effective comprehension tactic when used appropriately. Think, for example, about a reading passage that is long and for which test items will demand analysis and synthesis of broad concepts (as in "Compare and contrast the economic, social, and political causes of World War I with those of World War II"). Tell students to concentrate on identifying main ideas and supporting details, to paraphrase this information, and to record similarities and differences.
• Provide students with practice and corrective feedback in answering questions that are similar to those on the criterion test.

**3** **Establish the foundation for self-regulated learning in kindergarten and the primary grades.**

**JOURNAL ENTRY**
Providing a Foundation for Self-Regulated Learning Skills in the Primary Grades

As we noted earlier, becoming a proficient self-regulated learner requires thousands of hours of instruction and experience spread over many years. Consequently, the foundation for SRL should be established in kindergarten and the primary grades. Observations of teachers in kindergarten through third grade (Perry, VandeKamp, Mercer, & Nordby, 2002) provide some insight as to how this might be accomplished. In general, teachers whose classrooms were rated as high-SRL classrooms emphasized student choice of activities, support in meeting academic challenges

*Research findings demonstrate that note taking in one form or another is an effective tactic for improving comprehension of text and lecture material. Consequently, students should be taught the basic principles that support effective note taking.*

(a technique we referred to earlier in the book as scaffolding), and evaluation of one-self and classmates in a nonthreatening, mastery-oriented environment. Here are some specific examples of how SRL-oriented instruction was carried out.

**EXAMPLES**

● Prior to an oral reading of the story *The Three Little Pigs*, students were allowed to decide whether to track the text with their fingers or their eyes.

● When a student had trouble decoding a word during an oral story reading, the teacher asked the other children in the group to suggest a solution. They then tried each suggestion to see which one worked.

● Students were asked to create an alternative story ending for *The Three Little Pigs*. To help them meet this challenge, the teacher allowed students to share their ideas with a classmate and, later, with the teacher. The teacher recorded each child's idea on chart paper so everyone in class could see everyone else's ideas.

● Kindergarten and first-grade children who had trouble writing out their ideas for a writing assignment were encouraged to start with drawings as a way to plan and organize their ideas.

● In preparation for student/parent–teacher conferences, students were asked to select samples of their work to share with parents and reflect on what they could do now that they could not do earlier in the school year.

● To help second-grade students choose and carry out a research topic, the teacher asked them to answer three questions: Am I interested in this topic? Can I find books about this topic? Can I read the books by myself, or will I need help from a friend or an adult?

**4** **When teaching SRL skills, bear in mind the developmental limitations of younger students.**

If basic instruction in SRL skills is to begin as early as kindergarten, teachers need to acknowledge that, because young children are more limited cognitively than older children, they will require more support and guidance. Dale Schunk (2001) suggests that teachers of primary and early elementary grade children do the following:

• Keep demonstrations and explanations of various skills and behaviors relatively short.

• As you or someone else models a skill, point out which aspects of the model's behaviors are more important than others.

• Set a series of short-term goals, each of which can be accomplished after a limited amount of instruction.

• Design your lessons to minimize interruptions and distractions and periodically tell students that you believe they are capable learners.

• Periodically remind students to carry out a task more slowly and think about the skills needed to complete the task.

• Provide verbal feedback about children's capabilities (e.g., "You're good at reading").

• Help students make appropriate attributions for success and failure by reminding them that effort is the primary cause of success and insufficient effort is the primary cause of failure. If you mention that ability also plays a role in performance, emphasize that ability is a set of learnable skills and not a fixed cognitive capacity.

• Provide students with clear guidelines for determining the appropriateness of their behavior and point out when they have and have not satisfied those guidelines.

**5** **Embed instruction in SRL in interesting and challenging classroom tasks.**

Judi Randi and Lyn Corno (2000) suggest that if teachers want to teach their students SRL skills, they should embed their instruction in a classroom task that both illustrates and requires students to use SRL skills. One such task, which they describe in detail, is to analyze a story about a hero who has to undertake a dangerous journey and rely on personal resources in order to accomplish a goal. This is often called a journey tale. Two well-known examples from Greek literature are the *Odyssey* and *Jason and the Argonauts*. The students are then asked to draw parallels between the self-regulatory skills used by the story's hero and their own journeys as learners. For instance, just as Odysseus created a plan to escape from the Cyclops's cave, students should first think about the steps they will need to take to accomplish a goal.

### 6   Help students develop a sense of self-efficacy for SRL.

**JOURNAL ENTRY**
Ways to Help Students Develop Self-Efficacy for Self-Regulated Learning

As this chapter has suggested, self-efficacy, the belief that one can meet the demands of a particular task, is related to SRL in a reciprocal way. It contributes to the development of SRL skills and is also strengthened by their use. Students who are confident that they are capable of learning SRL skills are more likely than others to invest time and effort in self-regulation. In addition, students who believe that their SRL skills make them more effective learners are more likely to have higher levels of self-efficacy than students without such skills (Schunk & Miller, 2002). You can help students develop a strong sense of self-efficacy for SRL by emphasizing mastery of SRL skills, by providing successful models of SRL with whom students identify, and by telling students that you believe they are capable of being self-regulated learners. Here are a few suggestions for accomplishing this goal.

**EXAMPLES**

- For a variety of tasks, require students to set a moderately difficult short-term goal (such as receiving a grade of B+ on the next writing assignment) and specify how they intend to reach the goal. If the goal or the means to reach it is unrealistic (for instance, getting a grade of A on all writing assignments for the school year) or too general (studying harder for the next test), remind them that appropriate goals are specific, short-term, and moderately difficult, and then have them write new goals and means.

- Have students practice self-monitoring by writing down the steps they took to accomplish a task and the effect each step had on achieving the goal.

*HM TeacherPrepSPACE*

See the textbook's student website for additional suggestions for your journal.

- Have a student who is popular with most classmates and possesses good SRL skills describe how he or she approaches tasks and prepares for exams. Another option is to create cooperative learning groups in which at least two of the students have strong SRL skills, and require all students to verbalize the processes they use to cope with the demands of various parts of the task.

- When students exhibit improved performance on a task, remind them that this is due to their use of particular SRL skills and that they are better prepared than previously to cope with the demands of future classroom tasks.

### 7   Use such effective strategy training programs as reciprocal teaching, but be prepared to make adaptations to fit your particular circumstances.

As an instructional tool, RT has at least two positive characteristics: it is defined by a set of clear components and procedures, and it has been demonstrated to improve reading comprehension in numerous studies. But as a three-year study of seventeen elementary grade teachers demonstrated, you may encounter some obstacles to implementing a textbook version of RT that will cause you to make some modifications in how you use it (Hacker & Tenent, 2002).

In the study, only three teachers implemented RT as it is described in the literature. The remaining fourteen teachers felt compelled to implement a modified form of the technique because of the problems they encountered. Here are the main obstacles encountered by many of the teachers and their solutions:

1. *Strategy use problems:* Students' use of the four comprehension techniques of RT was infrequent or of low quality. For example, most of the questions

posed by students were superficial and fact-oriented, predictions were not logical, and clarifying comments were rarely made.

*Solutions:* Many teachers spent a great deal of time teaching students (through explicit instruction and modeling) how to formulate high-quality questions and tried to stimulate use of clarifying by having students identify words and sentences they did not understand.

2. *Dialogue problems:* Discussions among the students of the proper use of the four reading skills and the content of the reading passages were both limited and of low quality, largely due to their limited cooperative learning skills, but also because some students were shy about speaking in front of peers.

*Solutions:* Using whole-class instruction and modeling, teachers taught students how to be good listeners, to take turns talking, to reach a consensus about the details and meaning of a passage, and to give constructive feedback to one another.

3. *Scaffolding problems:* Because of the previously mentioned problems with strategy use and dialogue, some teachers continued to provide a high level of support to students long beyond the point suggested by the literature on reciprocal teaching. The amount and duration of scaffolding were related to the age and reading ability of the students. Younger students and those with weaker reading skills required more scaffolding.

*Solutions:* Teachers provided additional scaffolding through whole-class instruction; reading partnerships; modeling; allowing students more time to learn the elements of RT; writing predictions, clarifications, and summaries; and direct instruction of group skills.

This study points to an interesting conclusion and lesson. The conclusion is that RT may well require more training, practice, and time than the literature suggests. The lesson, which echoes a basic theme of the first chapter of this book, is that even when a solid scientific basis exists for a particular technique, an effective implementation often requires those improvisational skills referred to as the art of teaching.

## USING TECHNOLOGY TO PROMOTE SELF-REGULATED LEARNING

As we noted earlier, teaching students to become proficient self-regulated learners will require thousands of hours of instruction spread over many years. With the many instructional responsibilities teachers have, you stand a better chance of contributing to this goal if you can use technology to supplement and reinforce your efforts. The studies we summarize in this section suggest that, with certain qualifications, this is a real possibility.

### Modeling

Modeling, as we saw earlier in this chapter, is an effective way to help students acquire important SRL skills. But what if a teacher does not have sufficient time to perform this function or cannot always supply the modeling just when students need it? Might not a computer-based video model serve as an effective substitute? This was the driving question behind a study conducted with sixth-grade students (Pedersen & Liu, 2002).

The students, divided into three groups, worked on a computer-based hypermedia problem-solving simulation over the course of fifteen 45-minute class periods.

Called *Alien Rescue*, the simulation had students play the role of scientists on an international space station whose mission was to rescue alien life forms. They encountered a ship that contained six species of aliens, survivors of a distant solar system that was destroyed by the explosion of a nearby star. The life-support system of the alien ship had been damaged, and its members were in suspended animation. The students' task was to figure out which planets or moons of our solar system might serve as suitable homes for each of the alien species by using existing databases and a simulation within the program that let them design and launch probes. They recorded their notes and solutions in an online notebook.

The students were assigned to one of three conditions:

- In the modeling condition, students watched video segments of an expert scientist solving the same problem for one of the alien species. At four points in the program the model explained what he was trying to accomplish and how he used various tools, such as the online notebook and the probe design room. He also modeled such cognitive processes as self-questioning, making connections, identifying missing information, forming hypotheses, and taking notes in a list format.
- In the direct instruction condition, students received the same information, but without modeling. The scientist explained the function of various tools and provided tips about how to work effectively (e.g., "If I were building a probe, I would use my mission statement to help me decide what to include on my probe").
- In the help condition, the scientist explained the function of various tools but provided no advice or modeling on how to use them.

Although the students in each group worked at their own computers, they were encouraged to share information with classmates and ask one another for help.

The students in the modeling condition significantly outscored those in the direct instruction and help conditions on several measures. They were more apt to take notes in list format, to separate their notes into sections by topic, and to consult their notes. They designed fewer probes, but this was expected because they spent more time thinking about and designing probes that were consistent with their mission statements. The modeling group also attained significantly higher scores than the other two groups for the quality of their problem solutions.

A follow-up study (Pedersen & Liu, 2002/2003), also done with sixth graders and using the same simulation and conditions, found that students in the modeling condition were more likely to transfer some of their problem-solving skills, such as asking more appropriate questions and fewer inappropriate questions, to a similar problem (finding an alternative habitat for an endangered salamander) than were students in the direct instruction and help conditions.

## Providing Cognitive and Metacognitive Feedback

As you undoubtedly know from your own experience, although we do mention it in later chapters, efficient and effective learning of new skills requires timely feedback. Because teachers may not always be in a position to offer feedback precisely when it is needed, computer programs have been created to fill this need. One such program, *Summary Street*, was designed to help students improve their ability to summarize text by giving them many opportunities to summarize different types of text, by providing feedback, and by having them revise their summaries (with more feedback) as often as necessary until they meet the standards built into the program. Eighth-grade students who worked with *Summary Street* for four weeks showed greater improvement both in the amount of relevant information contained in their summaries and in the quality of their summaries than did a comparable group of students who summarized the same passages but did not receive feedback. Furthermore, low- and medium-performing students made the largest improvements (Franzke, Kintsch, Caccamise, Johnson, & Dooley, 2005).

Using Technology to Promote Self-Regulated Learning

Computer programs that include models can improve students' problem-solving skills

As we noted earlier in the chapter, self-regulated learners monitor their thinking as they work through a task in order to ensure a high level of learning. Teachers and parents often help students develop and strengthen this skill by reminding them to think about key operations, such as appropriately defining the problem or issue at hand and recalling relevant prior knowledge. This type of support is often referred to as *metacognitive feedback*. The type of feedback students usually receive, called *results feedback*, takes the form of such cautionary and positive statements as "Try again," "Check once more," and "Very good, wonderful job!"

One study (Kramarski & Zeichner, 2001) compared computer-provided instruction and metacognitive feedback with computer-provided instruction and results feedback on eleventh graders' mathematical problem solving. As students in the metacognitive feedback group worked through the program, the computer would prompt them to think about the nature of the problem, the relevance of prior knowledge, and the use of appropriate problem-solving techniques by posing such questions as "What is the problem all about?" "What are the similarities and differences between the problem at hand and problems you have solved in the past?" and "What tactics or principles are appropriate for solving this problem and why?" Students in the results feedback group received comments such as "Think about it, you made a mistake," "Try again," "Check it once more," "Very good," and "Wonderful job!"

On a twenty-seven-item test that required students to explain the reasoning that led them to solve the problem as they did, students who received metacognitive feedback significantly outscored students who received results feedback. The explanations of the metacognitive-feedback group were of a significantly higher quality (they included both algebraic formulas and verbal arguments) than the explanations of the results-feedback group.

## Providing Scaffolded Instruction

Earlier in the book we described Vygotsky's theory of cognitive development and his recommendation that teachers use various instructional aids, called scaffolds, to help students acquire the knowledge and self-regulatory skills that they would probably not otherwise acquire. But as busy as most classrooms are, it is not always possible for teachers to maximize the use of scaffolded instruction. Many advocates of computer-based instruction believe that computer programs that have various types of scaffolds built into them can accomplish what some teachers cannot. A study designed to assess that belief (Brush & Saye, 2001) examined the extent to which eleventh-grade students used the features of a hypermedia database called Decision Point! that contained both information about the civil rights movement in the United States during the 1960s and several types of scaffolds designed to encourage students to make optimal use of the database.

Each student was assigned to a four-person group. The students in each group were told to assume that they were civil rights leaders in 1968 shortly after the assassination of Martin Luther King Jr. They were asked to develop a solution to the following problem: What strategies should be used to continue pursuing the goal of the civil rights movement? Using the Decision Point! database, each group was assigned to gather relevant information on particular aspects of the civil rights movement (e.g., the legal system, desegregation, voting rights, the Student Non-Violent Coordinating Committee, and the rejection of integration).

The Decision Point! database contained four types of scaffolds. The first was a set of interactive essays. Each essay provided an overview of an historical event, such as the March on Washington to secure voting rights for all Blacks, with hyperlinks to related documents within the database. If you have seen online encyclopedias in which certain names, places, events, and concepts of an essay are highlighted and linked to related documents, you can visualize how these interactive essays worked. The second scaffold was a set of recommended documents for each event.

The program suggested that students first examine eight to ten recommended documents for an event before exploring any other information sources. The third scaffold was a student guide that provided categories that might be used by a professional historian to organize and synthesize information about an event (such as groups involved in the event, goals of each group, and strategies used by each group). The final scaffold was a journal in which students could note the effectiveness of their daily information-gathering strategies, the problems they had encountered, and the progress they had made toward completing the task. The purpose of the journal was to help students monitor their efforts.

Of the four scaffolds designed into the database, the interactive essays were used the most. Each group examined at least one of the essays, and two of the four groups read the essays for each event they were assigned. A third group examined all but one of the essays. The hyperlinks, however, were used much less frequently. Only 39 percent of the total number of documents available were accessed. Although students ignored most of the available documents, the ones they did examine were usually those recommended by the program. Consequently, this was felt to be a somewhat effective scaffold. Only two groups used the student guide scaffold to summarize their analyses for each event they were assigned to research. Moreover, the students' responses to this scaffold were judged to be inadequate. Most contained just a single phrase or sentence for each category. The student journals were used least of all. No group completed a journal for each day of data collection, and the entries were brief and superficial.

The results of this study provide limited support for embedding self-regulatory scaffolds in computerized databases. Students are most likely to use those scaffolds that they perceive to be most relevant to the successful completion of a task and ignore those that appear less relevant or require more time to complete than they have available. As the next set of studies indicates, it is also possible that students declined to use most of the scaffolds in the Decision Point! program because they lacked other self-regulatory qualities such as persistence and self-efficacy.

## The Effect of Self-Regulated Learning Skills on Computer-Based Instruction

From the earliest days of computer-based instruction, the designers of instructional programs have disagreed over the issue of how much control to give students. Some programs offer students no choices; the program provides the same material to all students in the same sequence, under the same conditions, and at the same rate. Other programs allow students to choose which material they will examine, for how long, and in what sequence. Although the learner control option has been strongly promoted by many designers, research findings have been inconclusive. One reason for these mixed results is that the relative benefits of program versus learner control are likely to be partly a function of the level of students' SRL learning skills (Eom & Reiser, 2000; Young, 1996).

This hypothesis was tested with a group of seventh-grade students who received a computer-based lesson on the use of four techniques used in advertising: bandwagon, testimonials, transfer, and uniqueness (Young, 1996). The bandwagon technique tries to persuade people to buy a product by claiming that most people use it, thereby implying that nonusers are not as smart or up-to-date as everyone else. Testimonials are endorsements of a product by a well-known person. The transfer technique is similar to testimonials except that the famous person does not explicitly endorse the product but is simply associated with it. The uniqueness technique emphasizes how popular or special people will be by using the advertised product.

On the basis of their responses to an SRL questionnaire, the students were divided into high and low self-regulated learning skills (SRLS) groups. Half of each group was assigned to a program control (PC) condition in which the instructional events occurred in the same sequence for everybody. The other half of each group was assigned to a learner control (LC) condition in which students could decide what material they wanted to see, the sequence in which they wanted to see it, and whether or not they wanted to review the instruction. The lesson for each condition consisted of two definitions (one a paraphrase of the other) of each advertising technique, one example and one nonexample, and two practice questions. The practice items presented an advertisement, and students were asked to indicate whether or not it was an example of a particular technique, such as a testimonial. This was followed by a review session in which students responded to multiple-choice questions similar to those they would encounter on the posttest.

As expected, students in the LC condition with high SRLS scores significantly outscored their low-SRLS peers on the posttest (73.2 percent correct versus 37 percent correct). But both high- and low-SRLS students scored at about the same level in the PC condition (64.7 percent correct versus 67.7 percent correct). Another interesting finding concerned the number of instructional elements that students in the LC condition chose to view. Out of a maximum of twenty-four (two definitions, two examples, and two practice items per technique), both high- and low-SRLS students viewed only about ten items. Yet high-SRLS students in this condition achieved the highest average posttest score (73.2 percent correct).

A very similar study (Eom & Reiser, 2000) that used the same instructional materials and procedures was conducted a few years later with sixth- and seventh-grade students and produced similar results. High self-regulators in the PC and LC conditions scored about the same on the posttest (65 percent and 58 percent, respectively). Low self-regulators in the PC condition achieved higher scores than did low self-regulators in the LC condition (66 percent and 37 percent, respectively). In addition, students in the PC condition, regardless of whether they were high or low self-regulators, spent significantly more time viewing the instructional materials, which may account for the generally higher posttest scores by those in the PC groups. As Young (1996) found, students in the LC condition viewed about 50 percent of the available twenty-four instructional events.

Taken together, these two studies strongly suggest that the use of computer programs that allow learner control should be limited to students who have acquired many of the self-regulatory skills described in this chapter. It also implies that if teachers want to use such programs, they should first help students acquire SRL skills.

> Computer programs that let students control access to information work best with those who have some self-regulatory skills

## The Effect of Self-Efficacy on Computer-Based Instruction

Use of the World Wide Web as an information-gathering and problem-solving resource is becoming increasingly popular in schools. But social cognitive theory suggests that successful use of the Web for this purpose will require high levels of self-efficacy and self-regulation because of the large number of independent decisions students must make. Because self-efficacy is task-specific, it stands to reason that the following types of self-efficacy will play a role in web-based instruction (WBI): self-efficacy for learning the subject matter, self-efficacy for using the Web, and, because WBI requires learners to locate and analyze information with little or no teacher guidance, self-efficacy for self-regulated learning. The effect of these forms of self-efficacy on achievement and Web use was investigated among high school sophomores in Korea (Joo, Bong, & Choi, 2000).

Before beginning the study, students were given measures of self-efficacy for SRL, academic self-efficacy, Internet self-efficacy, and cognitive strategy use. The students were then given worksheets for three topics (common diseases of the organs in our body, smoking and health, drugs and prevention) that contained questions to be answered and blank tables to be completed. Each worksheet listed the addresses of websites that were likely to contain useful information. The students were responsible for locating whatever information the site contained that would help them fill out the worksheet. In addition, they could use commercial search engines to identify other sites that contained relevant information. Following the third session, students took two tests: a written exam of multiple-choice and short-answer questions that covered the three topics and a performance test in which students had to access two websites and locate information pertaining to given questions.

Several gender differences were found that are consistent with the research findings we described in Chapter 5, "Understanding Student Differences." Female students scored significantly higher than male students on the self-efficacy for SRL and cognitive strategy use measures. The fact that the females also significantly outscored the males on the written exam suggests that higher levels of self-efficacy for SRL and greater use of SRL skills account for the finding that females typically earn higher grades than males. Consistent with research findings reported earlier in this chapter, self-efficacy for SRL was highly correlated with academic self-efficacy and strategy use. Finally, previous experience with computers and self-efficacy for SRL were both related significantly to self-efficacy for Internet use, which in turn was related significantly to performance on the Web search test.

## Conclusions About Computer Technology and Self-Regulated Learning

The studies we have summarized, and many others, indicate that computer-based instructional programs can play a productive role in the development and support of students' SRL skills. They can provide students with concrete examples of self-regulation skills and explanations of how those skills relate to achieving a goal. They can support and strengthen the skill of self-monitoring by reminding students at critical points to think about the nature of the problem being solved, similar problems encountered in the past, and appropriate problem-solving tactics. They can also provide a variety of scaffolds.

In short, technology can do for SRL many of the things that teachers do, giving teachers more time to work individually with students who need additional help. But (and to repeat a point we made earlier in the book), the use of technology to promote SRL has its limits. Without teacher guidance and oversight, some students will profit from such open-ended tools as hypermedia simulations, databases, and the World Wide Web, whereas others will likely feel overwhelmed and confused. If you use these tools to promote SRL and other goals, one of the first things you will need to do is determine students' current levels of SRL ability and self-efficacy.

*HM TeacherPrepSPACE*

*For help reviewing this chapter, look at the ACE practice tests and PowerPoint slides at the textbook's student website.*

# 11 Leading Classroom Learning

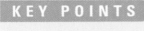

## KEY POINTS

*These key points will help you learn the important information in this chapter. To help you study, they also appear in the margins of the pages, next to the text where they are discussed.*

### Authoritarian, Permissive, and Authoritative Approaches to Classroom Management

● Authoritative approach to classroom management superior to permissive and authoritarian approaches

### Preventing Problems: Techniques of Classroom Management

● Ripple effect: group response to a reprimand directed at an individual
● Teachers who show they are "with it" head off discipline problems
● Being able to handle overlapping activities helps maintain classroom control
● Teachers who continually interrupt activities have discipline problems
● Keeping entire class involved and alert minimizes misbehavior
● Identify misbehavers; firmly specify constructive behavior
● Well-managed classroom: students complete clear assignments in busy but pleasant atmosphere
● Effective teachers plan how to handle classroom routines
● During first weeks, have students complete clear assignments under your direction
● Manage behavior of adolescents by making and communicating clear rules and procedures

### Suggestions for Teaching in Your Classroom: Techniques of Classroom Management

● Establish, call attention to, and explain class rules the first day
● Establish a businesslike but supportive classroom atmosphere

### Techniques for Dealing with Behavior Problems

● Use supportive reactions to help students develop self-control
● Give criticism privately; then offer encouragement
● I-message: tell how you feel about an unacceptable situation
● Determine who owns a problem before deciding on course of action

### Suggestions for Teaching in Your Classroom: Handling Problem Behavior

● Be prompt, consistent, reasonable when dealing with misbehavior

### Violence in American Schools

● Incidents of crime and serious violence occur relatively infrequently in public schools and have been decreasing in recent years
● Male aggressiveness due to biological and cultural factors
● Middle school and junior high boys with low grades may feel trapped
● Misbehavior of high school students may reveal lack of positive identity
● Classroom disruptions can be significantly reduced by various approaches
● Violence less likely when schoolwide programs teach students constructive ways to handle conflicts

---

**B**y now you have no doubt begun to realize what we pointed out at the beginning of the book: teaching is a complex enterprise. It is complex for the following reasons:

• Students vary in their physical, social, emotional, cognitive, and cultural characteristics.
• Learning occurs gradually and only with extensive and varied practice.
• Different students learn at different rates.
• Systematic preparations have to be made to ensure that students master the objectives that teachers lay out.
• Different students, or groups of students, are often working on different tasks at any point in time.

• Student behaviors are somewhat unpredictable.
• Students are motivated to learn (or not learn) by different factors.
• Learning can be measured and evaluated in a variety of ways.

If not managed properly, an endeavor as complex as teaching can easily become chaotic. When that happens, students are likely to become confused, bored, uninterested, restless, and perhaps even disruptive. But a well-managed classroom is not what many people think: students working silently at their desks (or in front of their computers), speaking only when spoken to, and providing verbatim recitations of what the teacher and textbook said.

Such a classroom is incompatible with the contemporary views of learning and motivation described in the preceding chapters. If some of your goals are for students to acquire a meaningful knowledge base, become proficient problem solvers, and learn how to work productively with others, then you have to accept the idea that these goals are best met in classrooms that are characterized by a fair amount of autonomy, physical movement, and social interaction (Emmer & Stough, 2001).

To help you accomplish these goals *and* keep student behavior within manageable bounds, we describe in this chapter a general approach to classroom management that is related to an effective parenting style, various techniques that you can use to prevent behavior problems from occurring, and a set of techniques for dealing with misbehavior once it has occurred. In addition, we analyze the issue of school violence, summarize approaches to reducing its frequency, and note how technology has been used to encourage underachieving and disruptive students to stay in school. ●

## AUTHORITARIAN, PERMISSIVE, AND AUTHORITATIVE APPROACHES TO CLASSROOM MANAGEMENT

You may recall from Chapter 2 on age-level characteristics that Diana Baumrind (1971, 1991a) found that parents tend to exhibit one of four styles in managing the behavior of their children: authoritarian, permissive, authoritative, or rejecting-neglecting. The first three of these styles have been applied to a teacher's actions in the classroom. We will quickly review Baumrind's categories and then take a brief look at how teachers' approaches to management can be characterized by these styles, too.

*Authoritarian* parents establish rules for their children's behavior and expect them to be blindly obeyed. Explanations of the reason a particular rule is necessary are almost never given. Instead, rewards and punishments are given for following or not following rules. *Permissive* parents represent the other extreme. They impose few controls. They allow their children to make many basic decisions (such as what to eat, what to wear, when to go to bed) and provide advice or assistance only when asked. *Authoritative* parents provide rules but discuss the reasons for them, teach their children how to meet them, and reward children for exhibiting self-control. Authoritative parents also cede more responsibility for self-governance to their children as the children demonstrate increased self-regulation skills. This style, more so than the other two, leads to children's internalizing the parents' norms and maintaining intrinsic motivation for following them in the future.

You can probably see the parallel between Baumrind's work and classroom management. Teachers who adopt an authoritarian style are likely to have student compliance rather than autonomy as their main goal ("Do what I say because I say so") and make heavy use of rewards and punishments to produce that compliance. Teachers who adopt a permissive style are likely to rely heavily on students' identifying with and respecting them as their main approach to classroom management ("Do what I say because you like me and respect my judgment"). Teachers who adopt an authoritative style are likely to want their students to learn to eventually regulate their own behavior. By explaining the rationale for classroom rules and adjusting those rules as students demonstrate the ability to govern themselves appropriately, authoritative teachers hope to convince students that adopting the teacher's norms for classroom behavior as their own will lead to the achievement of valued academic goals ("Do what I say because doing so will help you learn more"). The students of authoritative teachers better understand the need for classroom rules and tend to operate within them most of the time (McCaslin & Good, 1992).

Two studies support the extension of Baumrind's parenting styles to classroom teachers. In one, middle school students who described their teachers in terms that

Authoritative approach to classroom management superior to permissive and authoritarian approaches

reflect the authoritative style (for example, the teacher sets clear rules and explains the penalty for breaking them, trusts students to carry out certain tasks independently, treats all students fairly, does not criticize students for not having the right answer, and has high expectations for academic achievement and behavior) scored higher on measures of motivation, prosocial behavior, and achievement than did students who described their teachers in more authoritarian terms (Wentzel, 2002). The other study demonstrated that a teacher's decision to either support student autonomy or be more controlling of what students do in class is very much a function of the environment in which they work. When teachers have curriculum decisions and performance standards imposed on them for which they will be held accountable and when they feel that students are not highly motivated to learn, their intrinsic motivation for teaching suffers. This lowered intrinsic motivation, in turn, leads them to be less supportive of student autonomy and more controlling (Pelletier, Séguin-Lévesque, & Legault, 2002).

The next part of this chapter will describe guidelines you might follow to establish and maintain an effective learning environment.

## PREVENTING PROBLEMS: TECHNIQUES OF CLASSROOM MANAGEMENT

### Kounin's Observations on Group Management

Interest in the significance of classroom management was kindled when Jacob Kounin wrote a book titled *Discipline and Group Management in Classrooms* (1970). Kounin noted that he first became interested in group management when he reprimanded a college student for blatantly reading a newspaper in class. Kounin was struck by the extent to which the entire class responded to a reprimand directed at only one person, and he subsequently dubbed this the **ripple effect**. Chances are you can recall a situation in which you were diligently working away in a classroom and the teacher suddenly became quite angry at a disruptive classmate. If you felt a bit tense after the incident (even though your behavior was blameless) and tried to give the impression that you were a paragon of student virtue, you have had personal experience with the ripple effect.

Once his interest in classroom behavior was aroused, Kounin supervised a series of observational and experimental studies of student reactions to techniques of teacher control. In analyzing the results of these various studies, he came to the conclusion that the following classroom management techniques appear to be most effective:

*Ripple effect: group response to a reprimand directed at an individual*

**pause & reflect**

Would you use the ripple effect deliberately? Why or why not?

*Teachers who show they are "with it" head off discipline problems*

1. *Show your students that you are "with it."* Kounin coined the term **withitness** to emphasize that teachers who prove to their students that they know what is going on in a classroom usually have fewer behavior problems than teachers who appear to be unaware of incipient disruptions. An expert at classroom management will nip trouble in the bud by commenting on potentially disruptive behavior before it gains momentum. An ineffective teacher may not notice such behavior until it begins to spread and then perhaps hopes that it will simply go away.

   At first glance Kounin's suggestion that you show that you are with it might seem to be in conflict with operant conditioning's prediction that nonreinforced behavior will disappear. If the teacher's reaction is the only source of reinforcement in a classroom, ignoring behavior may cause it to disappear. In many cases, however, a misbehaving student gets reinforced by the reactions of classmates. Therefore, ignoring behavior is much less likely to lead to extinction of a response in a classroom than in controlled experimental situations.

**JOURNAL ENTRY**
Learning to Deal with
Overlapping Situations

> Being able to handle
> overlapping activities helps
> maintain classroom control

**JOURNAL ENTRY**
Learning to Handle Momentum

> Teachers who continually
> interrupt activities have
> discipline problems

**JOURNAL ENTRY**
Ways to Keep the Whole Class
Involved

2. *Learn to cope with overlapping situations.* When he analyzed videotapes of actual classroom interactions, Kounin found that some teachers seemed to have one-track minds. They were inclined to deal with only one thing at a time, and this way of proceeding caused frequent interruptions in classroom routine. One primary grade teacher whom Kounin observed, for example, was working with a reading group when she noticed two boys on the other side of the room poking each other. She abruptly got up, walked over to the boys, berated them at length, and then returned to the reading group. By the time she returned, however, the children in the reading group had become bored and listless and were tempted to engage in mischief of their own.

Kounin concluded that withitness and skill in handling overlapping activities seemed to be related. An expert classroom manager who is talking to children in a reading group, for example, might notice two boys at the far side of the room who are beginning to scuffle with each other. Such a teacher might in midsentence tell the boys to stop and make the point so adroitly that the attention of the children in the reading group does not waver.

3. *Strive to maintain smoothness and momentum in class activities.* This point is related to the previous one. Kounin found that some teachers caused problems for themselves by constantly interrupting activities without thinking about what they were doing. Some teachers whose activities were recorded on videotape failed to maintain the thrust of a lesson because they seemed unaware of the rhythm of student behavior (that is, they did not take into account the degree of student inattention and restlessness but instead moved ahead in an almost mechanical way). Others flip-flopped from one activity to another. Still others would interrupt one activity (for example, a reading lesson) to comment on an unrelated aspect of classroom functioning ("Someone left a lunch bag on the floor"). There were also some who wasted time dwelling on a trivial incident (making a big fuss because a boy lost his pencil). And a few teachers delivered individual, instead of group, instruction ("All right, Charlie, you go to the board. Fine. Now, Rebecca, you go to the board"). All of these types of teacher behavior tended to interfere with the flow of learning activities.

4. *Try to keep the whole class involved, even when you are dealing with individual students.* Kounin found that some well-meaning teachers had fallen into a pattern of calling on students in a predictable order and in such a way that the rest of the

*Jacob Kounin found that teachers who were "with it" could deal with overlapping situations, maintained smoothness and momentum in class activities, used a variety of activities, kept the whole class involved, and had few discipline problems.*

class served as a passive audience. Unless you stop to think about what you are doing during group recitation periods, you might easily fall into the same trap. If you do, the "audience" is almost certain to become bored and may be tempted to engage in troublemaking activities just to keep occupied.

Some teachers, for example, call on students to recite by going around a circle, or going up and down rows, or following alphabetical order. Others call on a child first and then ask a question. Still others ask one child to recite at length (read an entire page, for example). All of these techniques tend to spotlight one child in predictable order and cause the rest of the class members to tune out until their turn comes. You are more likely to maintain interest and limit mischief caused by boredom if you use techniques such as the following:

- Ask a question, and after pausing a few seconds to let everyone think about it, pick out someone to answer it. With subsequent questions, call on students in an unpredictable order so that no one knows when he or she will be asked to recite. (If you feel that some students in a class are very apprehensive about being called on, even under relaxing circumstances, you can either ask them extremely easy questions or avoid calling on them at all.)
- If you single out one child to go to the board to do a problem, ask all other students to do the same problem at their desks, and then choose one or two at random to compare their work with the answers on the board.
- When dealing with lengthy or complex material, call on several students in quick succession (and in unpredictable order) and ask each to handle one section. In a primary grade reading group, for example, have one child read a sentence; then pick someone at the other side of the group to read the next sentence, and so on.
- Use props in the form of flashcards, photocopied or computer-printed sheets, or workbook pages to induce all students to respond to questions simultaneously. Then ask students to compare answers. One ingenious elementary school teacher whom Kounin observed had each student print the ten digits on cards that could be inserted in a slotted piece of cardboard. She would ask a question such as "How much is 8 and 4?" and then pause a moment while the students arranged their answers in the slots and then say, "All show!"

5. *Introduce variety and be enthusiastic, particularly with younger students.* After viewing videotapes of different teachers, Kounin and his associates concluded that some teachers seemed to fall into a deadly routine much more readily than others. They followed the same procedure day after day and responded with the same, almost reflexive comments. At the other end of the scale were teachers who introduced variety, responded with enthusiasm and interest, and moved quickly to new activities when they sensed that students either had mastered or were satiated by a particular lesson. It seems logical to assume that students will be less inclined to sleep, daydream, or engage in disruptive activities if they are exposed to an enthusiastic teacher who varies the pace and type of classroom activities.

6. *Be aware of the ripple effect.* When criticizing student behavior, be clear and firm, focus on behavior rather than on personalities, and try to avoid angry outbursts. If you take into account the suggestions just made, you may be able to reduce the amount of student misbehavior in your classes. Even so, some behavior problems are certain to occur. When you deal with these, you can benefit from Kounin's research on the ripple effect. On the basis of observations, questionnaires, and experimental evidence, he concluded that "innocent" students in a class are more likely to be positively impressed by the way the teacher handles a misbehavior if the following conditions exist:

- The teacher identifies the misbehaver and states what the unacceptable behavior is. ("Jorge! Don't flip that computer disk at Jamal.")
- The teacher specifies a more constructive behavior. ("Please put the computer disk back in the storage box.")

- The teacher explains why the deviant behavior should cease. ("If the computer disk gets broken or dirty, no one else will be able to use it, and we'll have to try to get a new one.")
- The teacher is firm and authoritative and conveys a no-nonsense attitude. ("All infractions of classroom rules will result in an appropriate punishment—no ifs, ands, or buts.")
- The teacher does not resort to anger, humiliation, or extreme punishment. Kounin concluded that extreme reactions did not seem to make children behave better. Instead, anger and severe reprimands upset them and made them feel tense and nervous. ("Roger, I am deeply disappointed that you used obscene language in your argument with Michael. Such behavior is simply unacceptable in my classroom.")
- The teacher focuses on behavior, not on personality. (Say, "Ramona, staring out the window instead of reading your textbook is unacceptable behavior in my classroom" rather than "Ramona, you're the laziest student I have ever had in class.")

## VIDEO CASE ◀◀ ▶ ▶▶

### Classroom Management: Best Practices

*Watch the video, study the artifacts in the case, and reflect upon the following questions:*

1. Can you give an example of "withitness" from this Video Case?

2. In this Video Case, several teachers provide their philosophies of and approaches to classroom management. Which statements align most closely with your own philosophies of classroom management? Are there any that you disagree with? Explain your answers.

## University of Texas Studies of Group Management

Stimulated by Kounin's observations, members of the Research and Development Center for Teacher Education at the University of Texas at Austin instituted a series of studies on classroom management. The basic procedure followed in most studies was to first identify very effective and less effective teachers by using a variety of criteria (often stressing student achievement) and then analyze in detail classroom management techniques that very effective teachers used. In some studies (Brophy, 1979; Good, 1982), basic characteristics of well-managed classrooms were described. They can be summarized as follows:

1. Students know what they are expected to do and generally experience the feeling that they are successful doing it.
2. Students are kept busy engaging in teacher-led instructional activities.
3. There is little wasted time, confusion, or disruption.
4. A no-nonsense, work-oriented tone prevails, but at the same time there is a relaxed and pleasant atmosphere.

> Well-managed classroom: students complete clear assignments in busy but pleasant atmosphere

These conclusions relate to information presented in earlier chapters. The first point can be interpreted as supporting the use of instructional objectives that are stated in such a way that students know when they have achieved them. The next three points stress student productivity under teacher guidance. These outcomes are more likely when teachers use procedures that behavioral and cognitive psychologists have recommended.

Another set of studies carried out by the Texas researchers led to two recent books on group management—one for elementary school teachers (Evertson, Emmer, &

Worsham, 2006) and the other for middle school and high school teachers (Emmer, Evertson, Clements, & Worsham, 2006). You may wish to examine the appropriate book for your grade level, but for now we will provide the following summary of basic keys to management success stressed in both volumes:

**Effective teachers plan how to handle classroom routines**

1. On the first day with a new class, very effective teachers clearly demonstrate that they have thought about classroom procedures ahead of time. They have planned first-day activities that make it possible for classroom routine to be handled with a minimum of confusion. They also make sure students understand why the procedures are necessary and how they are to be followed.
2. A short list of basic classroom rules is posted or announced (or both), and students are told about the penalties they will incur in the event of misbehavior.

**During first weeks, have students complete clear assignments under your direction**

3. During the first weeks with a new group of students, effective teachers have students engage in whole-group activities under teacher direction. Such activities are selected to make students feel comfortable and successful in their new classroom.
4. After the initial orientation period is over, effective teachers maintain control by using the sorts of techniques that Kounin described: they show they are with it, cope with overlapping situations, maintain smoothness and momentum, and avoid ignoring the rest of the class when dealing with individual students.
5. Effective teachers give clear directions, hold students accountable for completing assignments, and give frequent feedback.

## Managing the Middle, Junior High, and High School Classroom

Most of the classroom management techniques and suggestions we have discussed so far are sufficiently general that they can be used in a variety of classroom settings and with primary through secondary grade students. Nevertheless, teaching preadolescents and adolescents is sufficiently different from teaching younger students that the management of the middle school, junior high, and high school classroom requires a slightly different emphasis and a few unique practices.

Classroom management has to be approached somewhat differently in the secondary grades (and in those middle schools in which students change classes several times a day) because of the segmented nature of education for these grades. Instead of being in charge of the same twenty-five to thirty students all day, most junior high or high school teachers (and some middle school teachers) are responsible for as many as five different groups of twenty-five to thirty students for about fifty minutes each. This arrangement results in a wider range of individual differences, a greater likelihood that these teachers will see a wide range of behavior problems, and a greater concern with efficient use of class time.

Because of the special nature of adolescence, relatively short class times, and consecutive classes with different students, middle school, junior high, and high school teachers must concentrate their efforts on preventing misbehavior. Edmund Emmer, Carolyn Evertson, Barbara Clements, and Murray Worsham (2006), in *Classroom Management for Middle and High School Teachers*, discuss how teachers can prevent misbehavior by carefully organizing the classroom environment, establishing clear rules and procedures, and delivering effective instruction.

According to Emmer and his associates, the physical features of the classroom should be arranged to optimize teaching and learning. They suggest an environment in which (1) the arrangement of the seating, materials, and equipment is consistent with the kinds of instructional activities the teacher favors; (2) high-traffic areas, such as the teacher's desk and the pencil sharpener, are kept free of congestion; (3) the teacher can easily see all students; (4) frequently used teaching materials and student supplies are readily available; and (5) students can easily see instructional presentations and displays.

In too many instances, teachers spend a significant amount of class time dealing with misbehavior rather than with teaching and learning, either because students are

*Because middle school, junior high, and high school students move from one teacher to another every fifty minutes or so, it is important to establish a common set of rules that govern various activities and procedures and to clearly communicate the reasons for those rules.*

never told what is expected of them or because rules and procedures are not communicated clearly. Accordingly, Emmer and associates suggest that classroom rules be specifically stated, discussed with students on the first day of class, and, for seventh, eighth, and ninth grades, posted in a prominent place. Sophomores, juniors, and seniors should be given a handout on which the rules are listed. A set of five to eight basic rules should be sufficient. Some examples of these basic rules follow:

Bring all needed materials to class.
Be in your seat and ready to work when the bell rings.
Respect and be polite to all people.
Do not talk or leave your desk when someone else is talking.
Respect other people's property.
Obey all school rules.

You may also want to allow some degree of student participation in rule setting. You can ask students to suggest rules, arrange for students to discuss why certain classroom rules are necessary, and perhaps allow students to select a few rules. This last suggestion should be taken up cautiously, however. Because middle school and secondary teachers teach different sets of students, having a different set of rules for each class is bound to cause confusion for you and hard feelings among some students. You may find yourself admonishing a student for breaking a rule that applies to a different class, and some students will naturally want to know why they cannot do something that is allowed in another class.

Manage behavior of adolescents by making and communicating clear rules and procedures

In addition to rules, various procedures need to be formulated and communicated. Procedures differ from rules in that they apply to a specific activity and are usually directed at completing a task rather than completing a behavior. To produce a well-run classroom, you will need to formulate efficient procedures for beginning-of-the-period tasks (such as taking attendance and allowing students to leave the classroom), use of materials and equipment (such as the computer, dictionary, and pencil sharpener), learning activities (such as discussions, seatwork, and group work), and end-of-the-period tasks (such as handing in seatwork assignments, returning materials and equipment, and making announcements).

Much of what Jacob Kounin, Carolyn Evertson, and Edmund Emmer mention in relation to the characteristics of effective instruction has been described in previous

# VIDEO CASE ◄◄ ▶ ►►

## Secondary Classroom Management: Basic Techniques

*Watch the video, study the artifacts in the case, and reflect upon the following questions:*

**1.** How does Mr. Turner achieve successful classroom management with his high school students? What specific strategies from the textbook do you see in action?

**2.** Examine the arrangement of Mr. Turner's secondary-level classroom (i.e., arrangement of student desks, location of equipment, etc.). How do these factors influence Mr. Turner's management of the classroom?

chapters. For example, they recommend that short-term (daily, weekly) and long-term (semester, annual) lesson plans be formulated and coordinated, that instructions and standards for assignments be clear and given in a timely manner, that feedback be given at regular intervals, and that the grading system be clear and fairly applied. As the next section illustrates, technology can help you carry out these tasks efficiently and effectively.

## Technology Tools for Classroom Management

A large part of classroom management involves such routine tasks as taking attendance, completing forms, maintaining student records, tracking student progress, and settling disputes. Although effectively carrying out such tasks is part of what makes a classroom well managed, they can be both tedious and time-consuming. Fortunately, technology tools now exist to help teachers keep records of student progress, organize teaching notes, create lesson plans and timelines, send individualized notes to students, update attendance records, and generate electronic study guides (McNally & Etchison, 2000). Computer technology can help teachers create test question banks and individual tests (including alternate forms), as well as record, calculate, and graph student grades (Cardwell, 2000). Moreover, teachers can employ database, word processing, and spreadsheet files to maintain class rosters, develop seating charts, create professional-looking handouts and worksheets, and note missing student work (McNally & Etchison, 2000).

**Integrated Learning Systems**    The message of the first section of this chapter is that an ounce of prevention is worth a pound of cure. In other words, clear classroom rules, good classroom management practices, and effective instruction are likely to prevent more instances of classroom disruption than heavy-handed, arbitrary punishment. And as we mentioned in the chapter on operant conditioning, an integrated learning system may be a useful tool for helping teachers achieve this goal. These systems, which are also referred to as curriculum courseware and management systems, provide a type of individualized instruction. They adjust the difficulty level and content of lessons to each student's pattern of progress, allow students to progress at their own rate, and provide teachers with continuous assessment reports that are keyed to state and professional organization learning standards.

In addition to keeping teachers continually updated on students' progress, these reports can be used to group students according to strengths and weaknesses for additional classroom instruction (Herr, 2000). As one fifth-grade teacher said, "Thanks to the management system, I clearly became more of a facilitator of learning, rather than the 'sage on the stage.' It did not replace my role as teacher; it simply made my job easier and expanded my role in ways I never thought possible" (Herr, 2000, p. 4).

**New Classroom Roles for Teachers**   What happens to the classroom management duties of teachers when schools adopt technology? Carolyn Keeler's (1996) study of thirteen elementary classrooms engaged in a schoolwide computer implementation project revealed that students were more on-task, self-managed, and engaged than before. As technology tools provided greater insight into student thought processes, the teachers became more interested in individual students and their progress. Given the perceived improvements in student motivation and behavior, as well as increases in student responsibility for their own learning, these teachers stated that they would most likely not return to the instructional techniques that they used earlier. In effect, technology significantly changed the teaching-learning environment of this school.

The following Suggestions for Teaching will help you become an effective manager of student behavior in the classroom.

# Suggestions for Teaching in Your Classroom

## Techniques of Classroom Management

### 1 Show you are confident and prepared the first day of class.

The first few minutes with any class are often crucial. Your students will be sizing you up, especially if they know you are a new teacher. If you act scared and unsure of yourself, you will probably be in for trouble. Even after years of experience, you may find that confronting a roomful of strange students for the first time is a bit intimidating. You will be the center of attention and may feel the equivalent of stage fright. To switch the focus of attention and begin identifying your students as individuals rather than as a threatening audience, you might consider using this strategy. Hand out four- by six-inch cards as soon as everyone is seated, and ask your students to write down their full names, the names they prefer to be called, what their hobbies and favorite activities are, and a description of the most interesting experience they have ever had. (For primary grade students who are unable to write, substitute brief oral introductions.)

As they write, you will be in a position to make a leisurely scrutiny of your students as individuals. Recognizing that you are dealing with individuals should reduce the tendency to feel threatened by a group. Perhaps you have read about singers who pick out a single sympathetic member of the audience and sing directly to that person. The sea of faces as a whole is frightening; the face of the individual is not. Even if you are not bothered by being the center of attention, you might still consider using this card technique to obtain information that you can use to learn names rapidly and to individualize instruction. Whatever you do during the first few minutes, it is important to give the impression that you know exactly what you are doing. The best way to pull that off is to be thoroughly prepared.

### 2 Think ahead about how you plan to handle classroom routine, and explain basic procedures the first few minutes of the first day.

**JOURNAL ENTRY**
Planning How to Handle
Routines

The Texas researchers found that very effective teachers demonstrated from the first moment with a new group of students that they knew how to handle the details of their job. They also conveyed the impression that they expected cooperation. To demonstrate that you are a confident, competent instructor, you should plan exactly how you will handle classroom routines. You will pick up at least some ideas about the details of classroom management during student-teaching experiences, but it might be worth asking a friendly experienced teacher in your school for advice about tried-and-true procedures that have worked in that particular school.

Try to anticipate how you will handle such details as taking attendance, assigning desks, handing out books and materials, permitting students to go to the restroom, and so forth. If you don't plan ahead, you will have to come up with an improvised policy on the spur of the moment, and that policy might turn out to be highly inefficient or in conflict with school regulations.

### 3 Establish class rules, call attention to them, and explain why they are necessary.

Establish, call attention to, and explain class rules the first day

Some teachers list standard procedures on a chart or bulletin board; others simply state them the first day of class or hand out a flyer to students. Either technique saves time and trouble later because all you have to do is refer to the rule when a transgression occurs. The alternative to this approach is to interrupt the lesson and disturb the whole class while you make a hurried, unplanned effort to deal with a surprise attack. Your spur-of-the-moment reaction may turn out to be clumsy and ineffective.

When you introduce rules the first day, take a positive, nonthreatening approach. If you spit rules out as if they were a series of ultimatums, students may feel you have a chip on your shoulder, which the unwritten code of the classroom obligates them to try knocking off. Whatever your approach, encourage understanding of the reasons for the rules. You can make regulations seem desirable rather than restrictive if you discuss why they are needed. Reasonable rules are much more likely to be remembered and honored than pronouncements that seem to be the whims of a tyrant.

#### EXAMPLES

- "During class discussion, please don't speak out unless you raise your hand and are recognized. I want to be able to hear what each person has to say, and I won't be able to do that if more than one person is talking."

- "During work periods, I don't mind if you talk a bit to your neighbors. But if you do it too much and disturb others, I'll have to ask you to stop."

- "If you come in late, go to your desk by walking along the side and back of the room. It's disturbing—and not very polite—to walk between people who are interacting with each other."

### 4 Begin class work the first day with an instructional activity that is clearly stated and can be completed quickly and successfully.

When selecting the very first assignment to give to a new class, refer to the suggestions for preparing instructional objectives proposed by Robert Mager and Norman Gronlund (see Chapter 13, "Approaches to Instruction"), and arrange a short assignment that students can complete successfully before the end of the period. Clearly specify what is to be done, and perhaps state the conditions and criteria for determining successful completion. In addition, mention an activity (such as examining the assigned text) that students should engage in after they have completed the assignment. In the elementary grades, you might give a short assignment that helps students review material covered in the preceding grade. At the secondary level, pick out an initial assignment that is short and interesting and does not depend on technical knowledge.

#### EXAMPLES

- "Your teacher from last year told me that most of you were able to spell all of the words on the list I am going to read. Let's see if you can still spell those words. If you have trouble with certain ones, we can work together to come up with reminders that will help you remember the correct spelling."

- "The first chapter in our natural science text for this fall is about birds. I want you to read the first ten pages, make a list of five types of birds that are described, and prepare your own set of notes about how to recognize them. At 10:30, I am going to hold up pictures of ten birds, and I want you to see if you can correctly identify at least five of them."

- In a high school history class, ask students to write a brief description of a movie they have seen that depicted historical events. Then ask them to indicate whether they felt the film interpretation was accurate.

**5**  **During the first weeks with a new group of students, have them spend most of their time engaging in whole-class activities under your direction.**

The very effective teachers observed by the Texas researchers followed the strategy just described, which makes sense when you stop to think about it. You can't expect students to adjust to the routine of a new teacher and classroom in just a few days. Accordingly, it would be wise to make sure students have settled down before asking them to engage in relatively unstructured activities such as discovery learning. Furthermore, group discussions or cooperative-learning arrangements usually work out more successfully when the participants have a degree of familiarity with one another and a particular set of background factors (such as a chapter in a textbook). Thus, during the first weeks with a new class, prepare instructional objectives that ask students to complete assignments under your direction. Postpone using the other techniques just mentioned until later in the report period.

**6**  **Give clear instructions, hold students accountable for carrying them out, and provide frequent feedback.**

All three of these goals can be achieved by making systematic use of instructional objectives (as described in Chapter 13, "Approaches to Instruction") and by putting into practice the model of instruction described throughout this book.

**7**  **Continually demonstrate that you are competent, well prepared, and in charge.**

As students work to achieve instructional objectives, participate in group discussions, or engage in any other kind of learning activity, show them that you are a competent classroom manager. Arrange periods so that there will be a well-organized transition from one activity to the next, maintain smoothness and momentum, and don't waste time. Use a variety of teaching approaches so that you please most of your students at least some of the time. Show you are with it by being alert for signs of mischief or disruptive behavior, and handle such incidents quickly and confidently by using the techniques described later in this chapter.

**8**  **Be professional but pleasant, and try to establish a businesslike but supportive classroom atmosphere.**

Establish a businesslike but supportive classroom atmosphere

If you establish classroom routines in a competent fashion and keep your students busy working to achieve clearly stated instructional objectives, you should be able to establish a no-nonsense, productive atmosphere. At the same time, you should strive to make your room an inviting and pleasant place to be. Keep in mind the points made in previous chapters regarding the importance of self-esteem, self-efficacy, and interpersonal relationships. Put yourself in the place of students thrust into a strange classroom with an unfamiliar instructor. Try to identify with your students so that you can appreciate how they feel if they do or say something embarrassing or have difficulty with class work.

One of the best ways to get students to respond positively to you and make them feel welcome in your classroom is to learn their names as quickly as possible (even if you have five sections of secondary school students to teach). To accomplish this feat, refer to the cards mentioned in point 1. Use the information that students have provided, perhaps supplemented by your own notes about or sketches of distinctive physical and facial features, to establish associations between names and faces. Before and after every class period the first few days, flip through your pile of cards, try to picture the appearance of the students, and practice using their names. Refer to the description of mnemonic devices in Chapter 10 on social cognitive theory. A high-tech alternative is to take their photographs with a digital camera and make a set of prints after you have secured the permission of your building principal and the students' parents. Once you have learned a student's name, use it as often as possible to maintain the memory trace. Greet students by name as they come in the door, use their names when asking them to recite or carry out some task, and speak to them personally when you hand back assignments.

# TECHNIQUES FOR DEALING WITH BEHAVIOR PROBLEMS

If you follow the procedures just discussed, you should be able to establish a well-managed classroom. Even if you do everything possible to prevent problems from developing, however, you are still likely to have to deal with disruptive behavior. Therefore, techniques for handling disruptive behavior, the extent of disciplinary problems, and some of the factors that lead to misbehavior are topics that merit attention.

## Influence Techniques

In *Mental Hygiene in Teaching* (1959), Fritz Redl and William Wattenberg describe a list of behavior management interventions called *influence techniques*. This list was modified by James Walker, Thomas Shea, and Anne Bauer in *Behavior Management: A Practical Approach for Educators* (2007). In the following sections and subsections, based on the ideas of both sets of individuals, we will offer specific examples, roughly reflecting a least-direct to most-direct ordering. Some of these examples are also drawn from personal experience and from reports by students and teachers. You might use the Journal Entries to pick out or devise techniques that seem most appropriate for your grade level or that you feel comfortable about.

The value of these techniques is that they appeal to self-control and imply trust and confidence on the part of the teacher. However, they may become ineffective if they are used too often, and that is why we describe so many different techniques. The larger your repertoire is, the less frequently you will have to repeat your various gambits and ploys.

**Planned Ignoring**   As we pointed out in Chapter 7 on behavioral learning theory, you might be able to extinguish inappropriate attention-seeking behaviors by merely ignoring them. Such behaviors include finger snapping, body movements, book dropping, hand waving, and whistling. If you plan to use this technique, make sure the student is aware that he is engaging in the behavior and that the behavior does not interfere with the efforts of other students.

**Example**

- Carl has recently gotten into the habit of tapping his pencil on his desk as he works on an assignment as a way to engage you in a conversation that is unrelated to the work. The next several times Carl does this, do not look at him or comment on his behavior.

*Signals such as staring at a misbehaving student or putting a finger to one's lips are examples of the influence techniques suggested by Redl and Wattenberg.*

Use supportive reactions to help students develop self-control

**Signals**    In some cases, a subtle signal can put an end to budding misbehavior. The signal, if successful, will stimulate the student to control herself. (Note, however, that this technique should not be used too often and that it is effective only in the early stages of misbehavior.)

**Examples**

- Clear your throat.
- Stare at the offender.
- Stop what you are saying in midsentence and stare.
- Shake your head (to indicate no).
- Say, "Someone is making it hard for the rest of us to concentrate" (or the equivalent).

**Proximity and Touch Control**    Place yourself close to the misbehaving student. This makes a signal a bit more apparent.

**Examples**

- Walk over and stand near the student.
- With an elementary grade student, it sometimes helps if you place a gentle hand on a shoulder or arm.

**Interest Boosting**    If the student seems to be losing interest in a lesson or assignment, pay some additional attention to the student and the student's work.

**Example**

- Ask the student a question, preferably related to what is being discussed. (Questions such as, "Ariel, are you paying attention?" or "Don't you agree, Ariel?" invite wisecracks. *Genuine* questions are preferable.) Go over and examine some work the student is doing. It often helps if you point out something good about it and urge continued effort.

**Humor**    Humor is an excellent all-around influence technique, especially in tense situations. However, remember that it should be *good*-humored humor—gentle and benign rather than derisive. Avoid irony and sarcasm.

**Example**

- "Shawn, for goodness sake, let that poor pencil sharpener alone. I heard it groan when you used it just now."

Perhaps you have heard someone say, "We're not laughing at you; we're laughing *with* you." Before you say this to one of your students, you might take note that one second grader who was treated to that comment unhinged the teacher by replying, "I'm not laughing."

**Helping over Hurdles**    Some misbehavior undoubtedly occurs because students do not understand what they are to do or lack the ability to carry out an assignment.

**Examples**

- Try to make sure your students know what they are supposed to do.
- Arrange for students to have something to do at appropriate levels of difficulty.
- Have a variety of activities available.

**Program Restructuring**    At the beginning of this book, we noted that teaching is an art because lessons do not always proceed as planned and must occasionally be changed in midstream. The essence of this technique is to recognize when a lesson or activity is going poorly and to try something else.

**JOURNAL ENTRY**
Using Alternative Activities to
Keep Students on Task

**Examples**

- "Well, class, I can see that many of you are bored with this discussion of the pros and cons of congressional term limits. Let's turn it into a class debate instead, with the winning team getting fifty points toward its final grade."
- "I had hoped to complete this math unit before the Christmas break, but I can see that most of you are too excited to give it your best effort. Since today is the last day before the break, I'll postpone the lesson until school resumes in January. Let's do an art project instead."

**Antiseptic Bouncing**    Sometimes a student will get carried away by restlessness, uncontrollable giggling, or the like. If you feel that this is nonmalicious behavior and due simply to lack of self-control, ask the student to leave the room. (You may have recognized that antiseptic bouncing is virtually identical to the *time-out* procedure described by behavior modification enthusiasts.)

**Examples**

- "Nancy, please go down to the principal's office and sit on that bench outside the door until you feel you have yourself under control."
- Some high schools have "quiet rooms": supervised study halls that take extra students any time during a period, no questions asked.

**Physical Restraint**    Students who lose control of themselves to the point of endangering other members of the class may have to be physically restrained. Such restraint should be protective, not punitive; that is, don't shake or hit. This technique is most effective with younger children; such control is usually not appropriate at the secondary level.

**Example**

- If a boy completely loses his temper and starts to hit another child, lead him gently but firmly away from the other students, or sit him in a chair, and keep a restraining hand on his shoulder.

**Direct Appeals**    When appropriate, point out the connection between conduct and its consequences. This technique is most effective if done concisely and infrequently.

**Examples**

- "We have a rule that there is to be no running in the halls. Scott forgot the rule, and now he's down in the nurse's office having his bloody nose taken care of. It's too bad Mr. Harris opened his door just as Scott went by. If Scott had been walking, he would have been able to stop in time."
- "If everyone would stop shouting, we'd be able to get this finished and go out to recess."

Give criticism privately; then
offer encouragement

**Criticism and Encouragement**    On those occasions when it is necessary to criticize a particular student, do so in private if possible. When public criticism is the only possibility, do your best to avoid ridiculing or humiliating the student. Public humiliation may cause the child to resent you or to hate school, to counterattack, or to withdraw. Because of the ripple effect, it may also have a negative impact on innocent students (although nonhumiliating public criticism has the advantage of setting an example for other students). One way to minimize the negative after-effects of criticism is to tack on some encouragement in the form of a suggestion as to how the backsliding can be replaced by more positive behavior.

**Examples**

- If a student doesn't take subtle hints (such as stares), you might say, "LeVar, you're disturbing the class. We all need to concentrate on this." It sometimes adds punch if you make this remark while you are writing on the board or helping some other student.

- Act completely flabbergasted, as though the misbehavior seems so inappropriate that you can't comprehend it. A kindergarten teacher used this technique to perfection. She would say, "Adam! Is that you?" (Adam has been belting Lucy with a shovel.) "I can't believe my eyes. I wonder if you would help me over here." Obviously, this gambit can't be used too often, and the language and degree of exaggeration have to be altered a bit for older students. But indicating that you expect good behavior and providing an immediate opportunity for the backslider to substitute good deeds can be very effective.

**Defining Limits**   In learning about rules and regulations, children go through a process of testing the limits. Two-year-olds particularly, when they have learned how to walk and talk and manipulate things, feel the urge to assert their independence. In addition, they need to find out exactly what the house rules are. (Does Mommy *really* mean it when she says, "Don't take the pots out of the cupboard"? Does Daddy *really* mean it when he says, "Don't play with that hammer"?) Older children do the same thing, especially with new teachers and in new situations. The technique of defining limits includes not only establishing rules (as noted earlier) but also enforcing them.

**Examples**

- Establish class rules, with or without the assistance of students, and make sure the rules are understood.
- When someone tests the rules, show that they are genuine and that there *are* limits.

**Postsituational Follow-Up**   Classroom discipline occasionally has to be applied in a tense, emotion-packed atmosphere. When this happens, it often helps to have a postsituational discussion—in private if an individual is involved, with the whole class if it was a groupwide situation.

**Examples**

- In a private conference: "Leila, I'm sorry I had to ask you to leave the room, but you were getting kind of carried away."
- "Well, everybody, things got a bit wild during those group work sessions. I want you to enjoy yourselves, but we practically had a riot going, didn't we? And that's why I had to ask you to stop. Let's try to hold it down to a dull roar tomorrow."

**Marginal Use of Interpretation**   Analysis of behavior can sometimes be made while it is occurring rather than afterward. The purpose here is to help students become aware of potential trouble and make efforts to control it.

**Example**

- To a restless and cranky prelunch class, you might say, "I know that you're getting hungry and that you're restless and tired, but let's give it all we've got for ten minutes more. I'll give you the last five minutes for some free visiting time."

## I-Messages

In *Teacher and Child*, Haim Ginott offers a cardinal principle of communication: "Talk to the situation, not to the personality and character" (1972, p. 84). Instead of making derogatory remarks about the personalities of two boys who have just thrown bread at each other, Ginott suggests that as a teacher you deliver an **I-message** explaining how you feel. Don't say, "You are a couple of pigs"; say, "I get angry when I see bread thrown around. This room needs cleaning." According to

Ginott, guilty students who are told why a teacher is angry will realize the teacher is a real person, and this realization will cause them to strive to mend their ways.

Ginott offers several examples of this cardinal principle of communication in Chapter 4 of *Teacher and Child*. And in Chapter 6 he offers some observations on discipline:

- Seek alternatives to punishment.
- Try not to diminish a misbehaving student's self-esteem.
- Try to provide face-saving exits.

Despite the fact that Ginott's work is over thirty years old, its usefulness is demonstrated by the fact that his ideas appear regularly in recent books and articles on classroom management (Cangelosi, 2004; DiGiulio, 2000; Palmer, 2001).

**Determine who owns a problem before deciding on course of action**

**JOURNAL ENTRY**
Speculating About Problem Ownership

**pause & reflect**

Ginott and Gordon both recommend that when responding to misbehavior, teachers speak about the behavior and not the character of the student. How often have you seen this done? If it strikes you as a good approach, what steps will you take to use it as often as possible with your own students?

**Problem Ownership**    In *TET: Teacher Effectiveness Training* (1974), Thomas Gordon suggests that teachers try to determine who owns a problem before they decide how to handle that problem. If a student's misbehavior (such as disrupting the smooth flow of instruction with inappropriate comments or joking remarks) results in the teacher's feeling annoyed, frustrated, or angry at not being able to complete a planned lesson, the teacher owns the problem and must respond by doing something to stop the disruptive behavior. But if a student expresses anger or disappointment about some classroom incident (getting a low grade on an exam), that student owns the problem.

Gordon suggests that failure to identify problem ownership may cause teachers to intensify difficulties unwittingly, even as they make well-intended efforts to diminish them. If a student is finding it difficult to concentrate on schoolwork because her needs are not satisfied, the situation will not be ameliorated if the teacher orders, moralizes, or criticizes. According to Gordon, such responses act as roadblocks to finding solutions to student-owned problems because they tend to make the student feel resentful and misunderstood.

Some practical suggestions for handling problem behavior appear in the following Suggestions for Teaching in Your Classroom.

# Suggestions for Teaching in Your Classroom

## Handling Problem Behavior

**1** **Have a variety of influence techniques planned in advance.**

You may save yourself a great deal of trouble, embarrassment, and strain if you plan ahead. When first-year teachers are asked which aspects of teaching bother them most, classroom control is almost invariably near the top of the list. Perhaps a major reason is that problems of control frequently erupt unexpectedly, and they often demand equally sudden solutions. If you lack experience, your shoot-from-the-hip reactions may be ineffective. Initial attempts at control that are ineffective tend to

Suggestions for Teaching in Your Classroom

*Teachers who excel at classroom management have at their disposal a variety of influence techniques that they consistently and immediately apply to prevent or deal with misbehavior. In each case, they use a technique that is appropriate to the severity of the misbehavior.*

reinforce misbehavior, and you will find yourself trapped in a vicious circle. You can avoid this sort of trap if you devise specific techniques ahead of time. Being familiar with several of the techniques mentioned in the preceding section will prepare you for the inevitable difficulties that arise.

If you find yourself forced to use prepared techniques too often, some self-analysis is called for. How can you prevent so many problems from developing? Frequent trouble is an indication that you need to work harder at motivating your class. Also, check on your feelings when you mete out punishment. Teachers who really like students and want them to learn consider control techniques a necessary evil and use them only when they will provide a better atmosphere for learning. If you find yourself looking for trouble or perhaps deliberately luring students into misbehaving, or if you discover yourself gloating privately or publicly about an act of punishment, stop and think. Are you using your power to build up your ego or giving vent to personal frustration rather than paying attention to your students' needs?

### 2  Be prompt, consistent, and reasonable.

Be prompt, consistent, reasonable when dealing with misbehavior

No attempt to control behavior will be effective if it is remote from the act that provokes it. If a troublemaker is to comprehend the relationship between behavior and counterreaction, one must quickly follow the other. Don't postpone dealing with misbehaving students or make vague threats to be put into effect sometime in the future (such as not permitting the students to attend an end-of-the-year event). By that time, most students will have forgotten what they did wrong. They then feel resentful and persecuted and may conclude that you are acting out of sheer malice. A frequent reaction is more misbehavior in an urge to get even. (In such situations, guilty students are not likely to remember that you are the one doing the evening up.) However, retribution that is too immediate and applied when a student is still extremely upset may also be ineffective. At such times, it is often better to wait a bit.

Being consistent about classroom control can save a lot of time, energy, and misery. Strictness one day and leniency the next, or roughness on one student and gentleness with another, invite all students to test you every day just to see whether this is a good day or a bad day or whether they can get away with something more frequently than others do. Establishing and enforcing class rules is an excellent way to encourage yourself to be consistent.

Harshness in meting out retribution encourages, rather than discourages, more extreme forms of misbehavior. If students are going to get into a lot of trouble for even a minor offense, they will probably figure they should get their money's worth. Several hundred years ago in England, all offenses—from picking pockets to murder—were punishable by death. The petty thief quickly became a murderer; it was a lot easier (and less risky) to pick the pocket of a dead man and, since the punishment was the same, eminently more sensible. The laws were eventually changed to make punishment appropriate to the degree of the offense. Keep this in mind when you dispense justice.

**3** **Avoid threats.**

If at all possible, avoid a showdown in front of the class. In a confrontation before the whole group, you are likely to get desperate. You may start out with a "Yes, you will"–"No, I won't" sort of duel and end up making a threat on the spur of the moment. Frequently, you will not be able to make good on the threat, and you will lose face. It's far safer and better for everyone to settle extreme differences in private. When two people are upset and angry with each other, they look silly at best and completely ridiculous at worst. You lose a great deal more than a student does when this performance takes place in front of the class. In fact, a student may actually gain prestige by provoking you successfully.

Perhaps the worst temptation of all is to try getting back at the entire class by making a blanket threat of a loss of privilege or detention. It hardly ever works and tends to lead to a united counterattack by the class. One elementary school teacher had the reputation of telling her students at least once a year that they would not be allowed to participate in the Spring Play-Day if they didn't behave. By the time students reached this grade, they had been tipped off by previous students that she always made the threat but never carried it out. They behaved accordingly.

**4** **Whenever you have to deal harshly with a student, make an effort to reestablish rapport.**

If you must use a drastic form of retribution, make a point of having a confidential conference with your antagonist as soon as possible. Otherwise, she is likely to remain an antagonist for the rest of the year. It's too much to expect chastised students to come to you of their own volition and apologize. You should set up the conference and then explain that the punishment has cleared the air as far as you are concerned. You shouldn't be surprised if a recalcitrant student doesn't respond with signs or words of gratitude. Perhaps some of the causes of misbehavior lie outside school, and something you did or said may have been merely the last straw. Even if you get a sullen reaction, at least indicate your willingness to meet punished students more than halfway.

At the elementary level, you can frequently make amends simply by giving the child some privilege—for example, passing out papers or being hall monitor at recess. One teacher made it a point to praise a child for some positive action shortly after a severe reprimand.

**5** **If you decide that a problem is owned by a student, try to help the student solve the problem by using active listening.**

As we noted earlier, when a student experiences a problem (such as feeling upset about an argument with a friend or feeling anxious about an upcoming exam) that interferes with the student's classroom performance but does not interfere with the teacher's ability to instruct, the student owns the problem. Thomas Gordon (1974) believes that it is a mistake for teachers to tell such students that they must or should change their attitude and behavior, because this suggests that there is something

**JOURNAL ENTRY**
Being Prompt, Consistent, and Reasonable in Controlling the Class

**JOURNAL ENTRY**
Ways to Reestablish Rapport

wrong with the student and that she is at fault for having the problem. Instead, he suggests active listening, as in the following example:

STUDENT: *"It's just that I don't know what kind of a test you're going to give and I'm afraid it'll be an essay type."*
TEACHER: *"Oh, you're worried about the kind of test we are going to have."*
STUDENT: *"Yes, I don't do well on essay tests."*
TEACHER: *"I see, you feel you can do better on objective tests."*
STUDENT: *"Yeah, I always botch up essay tests."*
TEACHER: *"It'll be a multiple-choice test."*
STUDENT: *"What a relief! I'm not so worried now." (Gordon, 1974, p. 69)*

### 6  When you have control, ease up some.

It is extremely difficult, if not impossible, to establish a controlled atmosphere after allowing anarchy. Don't make the mistake of thinking you will be able to start out without any control and suddenly take charge. It may work, but in most cases you will have an armed truce or a cold war on your hands. It is far better to adopt the authoritative approach of starting out on the structured side and then easing up a bit after you have established control.

### 7  Follow the advice of a master teacher.

Margaret Metzger is a veteran high school English teacher whose sensible and practical views on modeling and clearly communicating one's goals to students were mentioned in earlier chapters. She has also written, in the form of an open letter to new teachers, an insightful and compelling distillation of her experiences in learning the art of classroom management (Metzger, 2002). Metzger's recommendations for managing the behavior of adolescents also illustrate a point we have made in previous chapters: successful teachers formulate practices that are consistent with, if not inspired by, research-based findings. Although we offer a summary of Metzger's recommendations, this is an article we urge you to read in its entirety and refer to repeatedly during your first few years of teaching.

Metzger (2002) divides her suggestions into two lists: "simple principles of survival," created during her early years of teaching, and "more complex principles," which grew out of her experiences during her middle teaching years. Here, in summary form, are both lists.

## SIMPLE PRINCIPLES OF SURVIVAL

1. *Use a light touch.* Don't immediately resort to a highly aversive technique to control students' behavior. Instead, try such simpler methods as whispering instead of yelling, using humorous statements, changing locations, talking to students privately, calling students by name, smiling a lot, and ignoring some infractions.
2. *Let students save face.* Instead of describing a student's misbehavior and issuing a reprimand, which takes time and interrupts the flow of a lesson, indicate that you've noticed the misbehavior and use such quick and somewhat humorous phrases as "It's a good thing I like you," "Here's the deal: I'll pretend I didn't see that, and you never do it again," "Consider yourself scolded," "Am I driving you over the edge?" and "That's inappropriate."
3. *Insist on the right to sanity.* To avoid becoming a burnout candidate, don't try to address all misbehaviors. Instead, make a list of possible classroom infractions and rank them. Decide which behaviors have to be addressed immediately, which can wait until some later time, and which can be ignored. Margaret Metzger, for example, decided to ignore students who came late to class. She was often so busy trying to get the class under way (returning papers, talking with students about makeup work) that she wasn't always in a position to notice who arrived late.

4. *Get help.* Learn who among the school staff (administrators, guidance counselors, truant officer, other teachers) are able and willing to help you solve certain discipline problems.

5. *Get out of the limelight.* This is Metzger's way of saying that you shouldn't feel as if you have to actively lead the class all period, every period. Learn to make appropriate use of student presentations, seatwork, movies, and group work.

## MORE COMPLEX PRINCIPLES

1. *Ask questions.* Teachers often assume, incorrectly, that they have all the information they need to understand why one or more students misbehaved. Rather than make this assumption, take the time to ask students for an explanation. As Metzger says, "Sometimes you feel you have already spent too much time on the disruptive students. Frankly, you don't want to talk to them. Too bad. Do it" (2002, p. 80). Administrators, other teachers, and the students' parents can also be useful sources of information.

2. *Give adult feedback.* If students are engaging in behaviors that you find disruptive or that indicate a serious underlying problem, don't mince words. Tell them directly. Here are two examples offered by Metzger:

   - "Your posture, your mumbling under your breath, and your tardiness all show disrespect. If you hate this class, you should talk to me about it. If you like this class, you should know that you are giving misleading signals." (p. 80)
   - "You have complained about everything we have done for the past two months. I now see you as a constant whiner. You probably don't want to give this impression, and it's getting on my nerves. So for the next two months, let's have a moratorium on complaining. You can start whining again in January. Does this seem fair?" (p. 80)

3. *Respect the rights of the whole class.* Try to remember that most of your students follow the rules and are just as deserving of your attention as those who do not.

4. *Ask students to do more.* This echoes a suggestion we have made several times in earlier chapters. Often the best-behaved classes are those in which the work is interesting, relevant to students' lives, and challenging.

5. *Bypass or solve perennial problems.* There will always be students who forget to bring a pencil or book to class. Rather than erupt every time this problem arises, take steps to eliminate it. For several dollars a year, you can buy a supply of pencils and allow students to borrow one for class. For students who forget to bring their books, you can keep a few extra copies on hand. To ensure that students return at the end of class what they have borrowed, you may need to require that they leave with you something that they will not leave the classroom without, such as a shoe or a watch.

Metzger (2002) also advises teachers to reflect on themselves as a factor in classroom management by asking the following questions: "Does race or gender influence my response? Does this interaction remind me of another one? What from my background is being triggered? Am I tired, grouchy, or distracted? What else is going on in my life? Who is watching? Is the problem mine or the student's? Has the student hit some raw nerve in me? Why am I threatened by the behavior? Why do I lack resilience on this matter? Am I being inflexible? Am I being authoritative or authoritarian?" (pp. 81–82).

Metzger ends her article with a copy of a twenty-five-point memo that she gives to all students at the beginning of each semester and that reflects her philosophy of classroom management. Read it.

If you would like to compare your current understanding of classroom management against the views of a veteran middle school teacher, take the brief six-item quiz created by Kim Chase (2002) that appears in the December 2002 issue of *Phi Delta Kappan.*

**JOURNAL ENTRY**
Techniques for Becoming an Expert Classroom Manager

**HM TeacherPrepSPACE**

For additional ideas for your journal writing, see the Reflective Journal Questions on the textbook's student website.

# VIOLENCE IN AMERICAN SCHOOLS

## How Safe Are Our Schools?

You have probably read or heard reports about the frequency of crime in the United States, particularly among juveniles. According to figures compiled by the Office of Juvenile Justice and Delinquency Prevention (Snyder & Sickmund, 2006), 15 percent of all juveniles (any individual below the age of eighteen) were arrested for committing serious violent crimes. The good news about this figure is that it represents a 32 percent decline from 1994.

Because the kinds of behaviors one observes in schools tend to reflect trends in society at large, it is natural that a certain amount of violent behavior occurs on school grounds and during school hours. However, schools are still relatively safe places. One basis for that claim is that the most common types of school-based conflicts fall into a few time-honored categories: verbal harassment (name calling, insults, teasing), verbal arguments, and physical fights (hitting, kicking, scratching, and pushing). Most of the fights do not involve serious injury or violations of law (DeVoe et al., 2005). Second, a recent government report found relatively low levels of violence and crime (DeVoe et al., 2005). Here are the main findings from that report:

> Incidents of crime and serious violence occur relatively infrequently in public schools and have been decreasing in recent years

- From July 1, 2001, through June 30, 2002, seventeen school-age students (ages five through nineteen) were murdered at school. This translates to less than one homicide per million students for that one-year period.
- In 2003, 150,000 students between ages twelve and eighteen were the victims at school of such nonfatal violent crimes as rape, sexual assault, robbery, and aggravated assault. This figure translates to six crimes per thousand students. By contrast, twice as many of these crimes, or twelve per thousand students, occurred away from school. Between 1992 and 2003, the rate of nonfatal violent crimes at school decreased from forty-eight per thousand students to twenty-eight per thousand students.
- In 2003, 9.2 percent of high school students were threatened or injured with a weapon within a twelve-month period.
- The percentage of students ages twelve through eighteen who reported being bullied increased from 5 percent in 1999 to 7.2 percent (6.5 percent for girls, 7.8 percent for boys) in 2003.
- The percentage of students ages twelve through eighteen who reported avoiding school activities or one or more places at school for their own safety decreased from 6.9 percent in 1999 to 5 percent in 2003.
- The percentage of teachers threatened with injury by a student decreased from 12 percent during the 1993–1994 school year to 9 percent during the 1999–2000 school year. The percentage of teachers who were physically attacked during that same time period remained constant at about 4 percent. During the 1999–2000 school year, three times as many elementary grade teachers (6 percent) as secondary grade teachers (2 percent) were physically attacked by students.

These findings suggest that overall crime rates in schools are decreasing, that students feel increasingly safe at school, and that most teachers and students are likely to be physically safe in their own classrooms and school buildings. Nevertheless, school violence can occur in any school and at any time. Accordingly, you should be aware of the various explanations of school violence and the steps that can be taken to reduce its frequency.

## Analyzing Reasons for Violence

> Male aggressiveness due to biological and cultural factors

**Biological Factors** One of the clear-cut gender differences that has been repeatedly supported by consistent evidence is that males are more aggressive than females (Bloomquist & Schnell, 2002; Connor, 2002; Englander, 2003). Although the cause of this difference cannot be traced precisely, it is likely due in part to one or more of the following neurological, hormonal, and physiological factors: overactive behavioral activation systems and underactive behavioral inhibition systems (both of which are located in the frontal lobes of the brain), below-average levels of neurotransmitters, higher than average levels of testosterone, elevated levels of lead in the bloodstream, and a higher tolerance for pain (Bloomquist & Schnell, 2002; Connor, 2002).

**Gender-Related Cultural Influences**  As noted in the discussion of age-level characteristics in an earlier chapter, there is evidence that young girls in our society are encouraged to be dependent and to be eager to please adults, whereas young boys are encouraged to assert their independence (Carter, 1987; Englander, 2003; Lancey, 2002). Furthermore, it appears that boys are more likely than girls to be reinforced by aggressive and antisocial peers for assertive and illegal forms of behavior (Bloomquist & Schnell, 2002). These gender-related cultural influences may partly account for the fact that boys are more likely than girls to engage in such overt aggressive behaviors as fighting, bullying, robbery, and sexual assault and, particularly in the later elementary and middle school years, such covert aggressive behaviors as stealing, lying, vandalism, and setting fires. Girls, on the other hand, are more likely than boys to engage in what is called relational aggression—the withholding or termination of friendships and other social contacts and spreading rumors in order to hurt another girl's feelings (Bloomquist & Schnell, 2002; Connor, 2002).

The same reasoning may well apply to disruptive behavior in the classroom. A boy who talks back to the teacher or shoves another boy in a skirmish in the cafeteria is probably more likely to draw a favorable response from peers than is a girl who exhibits the same behavior. This cultural difference adds to the physiological factors that predispose boys to express frustration and hostility in physical and assertive ways.

**Academic Skills and Performance**  Boys also seem more likely than girls to experience feelings of frustration and hostility in school. For a variety of reasons (more rapid maturity, desire to please adults, superiority in verbal skills), girls earn higher grades, on the average, than boys do. A low grade almost inevitably arouses feelings of resentment and anger. In fact, any kind of negative evaluation is a very direct threat to a student's self-esteem. Thus a middle school, junior high, or high school boy who has received an unbroken succession of low grades and is unlikely to graduate may experience extreme frustration and anger. Even low-achieving students are likely to be aware that their chances of getting a decent job are severely limited by the absence of a high school diploma.

| Middle school and junior high boys with low grades may feel trapped |

Older high school boys can escape further humiliation by dropping out of school, but middle school and junior high boys cannot legally resort to the same solution, which may partially explain why, as of 2003, the crime rate at school is slightly higher among sixth, seventh, and eighth graders than among high school students (DeVoe et al., 2005).

**Interpersonal Cognitive Problem-Solving Skills**  Children who get along reasonably well with their peers do so in part because they are able to formulate realistic plans to satisfy their social goals and can think of several possible solutions to interpersonal problems. The former skill is referred to as *means-ends thinking*, and the latter is called *alternative-solution thinking*. Students who are deficient in these two interpersonal cognitive problem-solving skills are more likely than others to show an inability to delay gratification, to have difficulty making friends, to have emotional blow-ups when frustrated, to show less sympathy to others in distress, and to exhibit verbal and physical aggression (Shure, 1999).

| Misbehavior of high school students may reveal lack of positive identity |

**Psychosocial Factors**  Other explanations of disruptive classroom behavior are supplied by Erik Erikson's and James Marcia's observations on identity, which we discussed in the chapter on stage theories of development. A teenager who has failed to make a clear occupational choice, who is confused about gender roles, or who does not experience acceptance "by those who count" may exhibit what Erikson called a negative identity. Instead of striving to behave in ways that parents and teachers respond to positively, teenagers with negative identities may deliberately engage in opposite forms of behavior (Lowry, Sleet, Duncan, Powell, & Kolbe, 1995).

This hypothesis has been supported by a study of two thousand middle and high school students. Those classified as having a diffusion identity status (no serious thought given or commitment made to occupational and gender roles) were much more likely than adolescents classified as having an achievement status to exhibit behaviors characteristic of both a conduct disorder and attention-deficit/hyperactivity disorder (Adams et al., 2001).

**School Environment**   So far we have mentioned the role of biological, gender-related, cultural, academic, cognitive, and psychosocial factors in school violence. Each of these explanations places the responsibility for violent behavior largely or entirely on the individual. Other explanations focus instead on schools that are poorly designed and do not meet the needs of their students. Violent behavior, in this view, is seen as a natural (though unacceptable) response to schools that are too large, impersonal, and competitive; that do not enforce rules fairly or consistently; that use punitive ways of resolving conflict; and that impose an unimaginative, meaningless curriculum on students (Lowry et al., 1995; Bloomquist & Schnell, 2002).

## Reducing School Violence and Misbehavior

**Classroom Interventions**   Because most teachers work with two dozen or more students, some of whom have disabilities, and typically have no assistance, classroom interventions that are designed to prevent misbehavior and keep small disruptions from escalating into serious problems need to be both effective and easy to implement.

One such intervention, which has been shown to work with mainstreamed students with behavior disorders as well as with regular students, combines two classroom

---

> **pause & reflect**
>
> Do you agree with the argument that school violence can be caused by a non-meaningful, unimaginative curriculum and an impersonal school environment? If so, what can you do to make the subjects you teach lively, interesting, and useful? What ideas for making your school a more welcoming and pleasant place for students can you share with colleagues and administrators?

Classroom disruptions can be significantly reduced by various approaches

*Some experts on school violence argue that impersonal and punitively oriented schools produce higher-than-average levels of school violence.*

management techniques mentioned earlier in this chapter, three behavior modification techniques that we described in Chapter 7 on operant conditioning, and a reinforcement contingency that allows the other students in the class to be rewarded when the target students exhibit desired behaviors (Kehle et al., 2000). The components of this program include the following:

- *Classroom rules.* A relatively short list of five or six rules is posted where all students can see it. These rules are stated in a positive manner, are measurable, and specify basic expected behavior (for example, "Raise your hand if you need to leave your seat or the room," "Wait for permission to speak," and "Keep hands and feet to yourself").
- *Teacher movement.* The teacher circulates among the students to detect problem behaviors and reinforce desired behaviors.
- *Reinforcement.* Target students who exhibit desired behavior should be reinforced immediately, as frequently as possible, in an enthusiastic manner, and with eye contact.
- *Token economy.* As soon as the target students have followed all class rules for a specified period of time, they are awarded points. After a certain number of points have been accumulated, they can be redeemed for a tangible reinforcer. Among the tangible reinforcers are several highly desired objects (such as stickers or sports trading cards) called mystery motivators. When the student has accumulated enough points to redeem them for a tangible reinforcer, he spins an arrow that is attached to the center of a cardboard circle. The circle is divided into pie-shaped segments, each of which contains the name of a particular reinforcer. One segment is labeled "mystery motivator." Whichever segment the arrow lands on is the reinforcer the student receives. If the arrow lands on the mystery motivator segment, the student withdraws a slip of paper from an envelope that contains the names of several highly desirable reinforcers.
- *Response cost.* Students can lose points as a consequence of not following any of the posted rules.
- *Group contingency.* To keep the other students from feeling resentful toward the reinforced students and to capitalize on the power of peer pressure, something called a dependent group contingency is applied. When the target students receive their mystery motivator, the rest of the students in the class receive the same reward.

This intervention has produced declines in the frequency of disruptive behavior (such as making noises, talking out of turn, and wandering around the classroom) of as much as 50 percent (Kehle et al., 2000).

A very different approach to classroom management is called Judicious Discipline (Landau & Gathercoal, 2000). This program teaches students that they have both rights and responsibilities with respect to their behavior. That is, they are free to behave in various ways provided their behaviors do not threaten the safety, health, or academic well-being of classmates. To help students determine the appropriateness of their behavior, they are taught to ask themselves three questions that have to do with time, place, and manner: "Is this the appropriate time for what is happening? Is this the appropriate place for what I am doing? Is this the best manner?" The principles behind this approach and its application are reinforced during class meetings, during which the teacher and students discuss problems that have occurred and how they can be addressed. The guidelines for class meetings include the following:

- At least some of the topics are suggested by students.
- The students and teacher sit in a circle so that everyone has eye contact.
- Students' names are never used during a class meeting; just the issue or issues are discussed.
- Although all students attend class meetings, no student is obligated to actively participate.
- Immediately following the meeting, the teacher and students take a few minutes to record their thoughts in a journal.

Research on Judicious Discipline shows that it is associated with decreases in dropout rates, violence, and referrals to the principal's office, and increases in daily attendance.

## VIDEO CASE  ◄◄ ▶ ►►

### Elementary Classroom Management: Basic Techniques

*Watch the video, study the artifacts in the case, and reflect upon the following questions:*

**1.** Would you describe Ms. Moylan's classroom management style as authoritarian, permissive, or authoritative? Provide specific examples from the Video Case to support your answer.

**2.** What elements of the well-managed classroom do you see in this Video Case?

**Schoolwide Programs to Reduce Violence and Improve Discipline**  Although classroom interventions such as the ones described in the previous section can make life less threatening and more enjoyable for individual teachers and their students, they do not address disruptive behavior elsewhere in a school, and they may conflict with other teachers' procedures. Consequently, some educators have designed violence-reduction programs that can be implemented throughout an entire school. This section describes four such approaches.

*Unified Discipline*  In a program called Unified Discipline (Algozzine & White, 2002; White, Algozzine, Audette, Marr, & Ellis, 2001), teachers, administrators, and other school personnel create a uniform approach to managing disruptive behavior. The goal of Unified Discipline is to create a consensus about the following program elements:

- *Attitudes.* The school staff members agree that all students can improve their behavior, that learning to manage one's behavior is an important part of an education, that corrections for misbehavior should be administered in a professional manner, and that becoming angry with students for misbehaving undermines a teacher's instructional effectiveness.
- *Expectations.* The school staff members agree to the rules for student behavior and to use the program's correction procedures in the same way whenever a student breaks a rule.
- *Rules.* The rules that govern student behavior are typically divided into categories. One school, for example, created a three-level system. Class III rules pertained to such behaviors as physically assaulting another person, bringing a weapon to school, and selling drugs, tobacco, or alcohol. Class II rules pertained to behaviors such as fighting, ignoring adult requests, and vandalism. Class I rules pertained to behaviors such as disrupting others and using inappropriate language. The rules that govern classroom behavior have to be, of course, appropriate to the students' grade level. One group of kindergarten through second-grade teachers decided that students had to follow all teacher directions promptly, speak in an appropriate voice, keep body parts to themselves, and stay in their assigned places. Teachers in grades 3 through 5 decided that students had to follow all teacher directions promptly, stay on-task, be prepared for class, raise their hands to be recognized, and respect the rights and property of others.
- *Correction procedures.* As with rules, correction procedures vary somewhat by grade level. In the lower grades of one school, a first offense results in the

teacher's putting a green ticket in a pocket with the student's name on it. The pocket is stapled to a poster board. A second offense results in a yellow ticket. At the third offense, the student receives a red ticket and has to sit in an exclusion area of the classroom for several minutes. For a fourth offense, the student gets a blue ticket and is sent to another room for a time-out of about twenty minutes. In the upper grades, students receive a verbal correction for a first offense, a loss of privilege for a second offense, and a time-out for a third offense. For students of all ages, teachers respond to infractions by stating the misbehavior, stating the rule that was violated, stating the consequence, and encouraging the student to follow the rule in the future.

- *Roles*. The principal's role is to support teachers when they follow the Unified Discipline procedures and, for the most serious offenses, make decisions about consequences based on a student's needs, history, and the circumstances surrounding the misbehavior (a refreshing change from the mindless uniform punishments dictated by "zero tolerance" policies). The teachers' role is to support the principal and not engage in second-guessing with other teachers, students, or parents.

In one elementary school, the Unified Discipline program resulted in a 20 percent decrease in referrals of students to the principal's office during the first year and decreases of 50 percent or more in subsequent years, fewer violations of classroom rules, and increases in the amount of time students spent on-task (Algozzine & White, 2002).

### Smart and Good High Schools

Despite reports in the media of such troubling behaviors among high school students as cheating, drug use, alcohol abuse, bullying, and disrespect toward teachers, some high schools are successful in helping their students develop positive character traits. Thomas Lickona and Matthew Davidson (2005) studied the operations of twenty-four high schools that had been identified by at least one organization (such as the Department of Education or the Coalition of Essential Schools) as being exemplary in an effort to determine how they helped students develop their characters. This collection of schools was quite diverse in terms of size (three hundred students on the small end and forty-three hundred students on the large end), type (public, private, and charter), and setting (urban, suburban, and rural).

Lickona and Davidson (2005) defined character as being composed of two main parts: *performance character*

---

## Take a Stand!

### Show Zero Tolerance for Zero Tolerance Policies

Zero tolerance policies mandate specific, nonnegotiable punishments, usually suspension from school, for specific offenses. These policies are typically aimed at curbing such serious offenses as fighting, sexual harassment, or bringing weapons or drugs to school. They are extremely popular, with as many as 75 percent of all schools having such policies. But, as we have pointed out many times in this book, popular ideas or practices are not always good ones. We believe that zero tolerance policies have more disadvantages than advantages and simply give the appearance that serious problems are being addressed. Here are several reasons why we believe educators should not support zero tolerance policies:

- The same punishment is handed out for violations that seem to be the same but that involve very different behaviors and motives. Under the terms of a zero tolerance antidrug policy, do we really want to expel from school both the child who shares a zinc cough drop with a classmate and the child who brings marijuana to school?

- Zero tolerance policies do not teach students those behaviors that will produce positive reinforcement. This is why Skinner was adamantly opposed to the use of punishment as a means of modifying students' behavior.

- They result in more students being expelled from school than would otherwise be the case. For some students, being banished from an environment that they find aversive is positively reinforcing and encourages them to continue to exhibit those behaviors that produce suspension.

- Many research studies have failed to find a relationship between such policies and significant reductions in school violence.

- In some cases in which students were automatically expelled from school, extenuating circumstances should have led to a different decision.

- More often than not, courts will support an administrator's decision to suspend a student where the circumstances warrant, making zero tolerance policies redundant.

*HM TeacherPrepSPACE*

What are your views of zero tolerance policies? Have you seen them applied in your community? To explore this issue further, go to the Take a Stand! section of the textbook's student website.

and *moral character*. Performance character includes such components as diligence, a strong work ethic, a positive attitude, and perseverance and contributes to successful academic performance. Moral character includes such components as integrity, respect, cooperation, and justice and contributes to productive, fulfilling personal relationships. High schools that help students develop these two aspects of character are, in their words, "Smart and Good High Schools" (xv).

The high schools that Lickona and Davidson identified as being Smart and Good employed a variety of devices to help students become (1) lifelong learners and critical thinkers, (2) diligent and capable performers, (3) socially and emotionally skilled, (4) more attuned to the ethical implications of their behaviors, (5) respectful and responsible, (6) self-disciplined, (7) contributors to their community, and (8) oriented toward creating a purposeful life. Whether such schools are judged to be more successful than other schools at reducing undesirable student behaviors has yet to be determined.

*One approach to reducing school violence is to train students to mediate disputes between other students.*

| Violence less likely when schoolwide programs teach students constructive ways to handle conflicts

***Resolving Conflict Creatively Program***    A somewhat different approach to decreasing physical violence, particularly between students, is the Resolving Conflict Creatively Program (RCCP), created by Linda Lantieri in 1985. The goal of the program is to teach students how to use nonviolent conflict resolution techniques in place of their more normal and more violent methods. Students are trained by teachers to monitor the school environment (such as the playground, the cafeteria, and the hallways) for imminent or actual physical confrontations between students. For example, picture two students who are arguing about a comment that struck one as an insult. As the accusations and counteraccusations escalate, one student threatens to hit the other. At that moment, one or two other students who are wearing T-shirts with the word *mediator* printed across the front and back intervene and ask if the two students would like help in resolving their problem. The mediating students may suggest that they all move to a quieter area where they can talk. The mediators then establish certain ground rules, such as that each student gets a turn to talk without being interrupted and that name calling is not allowed.

RCCP was designed as a primary prevention program. This means that all students, even those not prone to violence, are taught how to prevent disagreements from becoming violent confrontations. In schools in which the program has been implemented, teachers have noted less physical violence in their classrooms, fewer insults and verbal putdowns, and greater spontaneous use of conflict resolution skills (Lantieri, 1995).

Nevertheless, educators noticed that the program did not produce desirable results with all students. So during the 1997–1998 school year, an intervention component was added for children who exhibit behaviors that are associated with violent behavior in later years. School counselors and RCCP-trained teachers, working with groups of fifteen to twenty children, engaged the students in activities that were designed to increase a sense of social responsibility (caring and cooperative behaviors, for example) and to develop such interpersonal skills as active listening. The capstone of this thirty-week program was the social action project. The group had to decide on and implement a community service project, such as fixing dinner for a family in need of assistance, making Easter baskets for the mentally disabled residents of a nearby center, or collecting books and art materials for a children's hospital. An evaluation of this new component reported improvements in listening skills, anger management skills, ability to share with others, relationships with teachers and students, self-esteem, and attitudes toward school (Lantieri, 1999). RCCP has been adopted by four hundred schools in the United States and by schools in Brazil, England, and Puerto Rico (Roerden, 2001). An evaluation of RCCP conducted in more than three hundred fifty

## pause & reflect

If you were a primary or elementary grade teacher and had to choose between a program such as Don't Strike Back and a peer mediation program such as the Resolving Conflict Creatively Program, which one would you choose? Why?

New York City classrooms reported gains in interpersonal negotiation strategies, prosocial behavior, and mathematics achievement and decreases in aggressive behavior, but only in those classes in which teachers provided more instruction in RCCP techniques than the average teacher did (Brown, Roderick, Lantieri, & Aber, 2004).

Additional information about RCCP, the states and school districts in which it has been implemented, and whom to contact can be found on the following website: **www.esrnational.org/about-rccp.html**.

## Using Technology to Keep Students in School

As we pointed out previously, students who exhibit poor academic performance and believe that their teachers don't care about them are prone to engage in disruptive and violent behavior. They are also at risk for dropping out of school. In 2004, 10.3 percent of sixteen- to twenty-four-year-olds were classified as dropouts (were out of school and had not earned a diploma or alternative credential). The percentages for White, Black, and Latino youths were 6.8 percent, 11.8 percent, and 23.8 percent, respectively (U.S. Department of Education, 2006). Although these dropout rates have steadily fallen over the past twenty-five years, some believe that creative uses of technology may cause them to fall even faster. Here are a few examples of how some schools have used technology to reduce student absenteeism and the dropout rate:

- The Hueneme School District in Hueneme, California, created a "smart classroom" to help retain students who are at risk of dropping out. Students in this program were given experience in computerized robotics, computer-aided manufacturing, desktop publishing, and aeronautics and pneumatic technology. Average daily attendance for this program was close to 100 percent (Cardon & Christensen, 1998).
- The Azusa Unified School District in Azusa, California, made extensive use of an integrated learning system to encourage student attendance and retention. Students spent four class periods each day working at their computer terminals on English, reading, social studies, mathematics, and science. By the end of the program's second year, the average daily attendance was 96 percent, and 93 percent of students remained in the program from one year to the next (Cardon & Christensen, 1998).
- Virtual schools, a growing phenomenon that is also referred to as distance education or distance learning, are courses or entire programs (particularly at the high school level) that are available on the Web and that may help students with high absentee rates—such as the children of migrant workers, students whose school districts don't offer desired courses, and students who are home-schooled—to take courses and complete their schooling (Roblyer, 2006). During the 2002–2003 school year, about 328,000 public school students were enrolled in virtual classes (Setzer & Lewis, 2005), and as of the 2005–2006 school year, twenty-two states had established at least one virtual school (Swanson, 2006). Although such programs are praised for the flexibility they offer, they are also criticized because low-income students may have limited Internet access, because computer failures result in lost time and assignments, and because the lack of face-to-face interaction makes learning more difficult for some students (Podoll & Randle, 2005; Roblyer, 2006). What little research exists suggests that, overall, students who take courses online learn about as much as students who take the same courses in actual classrooms. What is not known at this point is why some students succeed in a virtual school environment whereas others do not (Bernard et al., 2004; Rice, 2006).

*HM TeacherPrepSPACE*

*To review this chapter, see the ACE practice tests and PowerPoint slides at the textbook's student website.*

Technology for Classroom Assessment

# 12 Motivation and Perceptions of Self

**HM TeacherPrepSPACE student
website** offers many helpful resources. Go
to **login.cengage.com** to preview this
chapter's Concept Maps and Chapter
Themes.

## KEY POINTS

*These key points will help you
learn the important information in
this chapter. To help you study,
they also appear in the margins of
the pages, next to the text where
they are discussed.*

### The Behavioral View of Motivation

- Behavioral view of motivation: reinforce desired behavior
- Extrinsic motivation occurs when learner does something to earn external rewards
- Intrinsic motivation occurs when learner does something to experience inherently satisfying results
- Excessive use of external rewards may lead to temporary behavior change, materialistic attitudes, decreased intrinsic motivation
- Intrinsic motivation enhanced when reward provides positive feedback, is available to all who qualify
- Intrinsic motivation undermined by forcing students to compete for limited supply of rewards
- Give rewards sparingly, especially on tasks of natural interest

### The Social Cognitive View of Motivation

- Social cognitive view of motivation: observe and imitate admired models; raise self-efficacy
- Self-efficacy affects choice of goals, expectations of success, attributions for success and failure

### Other Cognitive Views of Motivation

- Cognitive development view of motivation: strive for equilibration; master the environment
- Need for achievement revealed by desire to attain goals that require skilled performance
- High-need achievers prefer moderately challenging tasks
- Low-need achievers prefer very easy or very hard tasks
- Unsuccessful students attribute success to luck, easy tasks; failure, to lack of ability
- Successful students attribute success to effort, ability; failure, to lack of effort

- Students with incremental beliefs tend to have mastery goals and are motivated to meaningfully learn, improve skills
- Students with entity beliefs tend to have performance goals and are motivated to get high grades, avoid failure
- Personal interest marked by intrinsic desire to learn that persists over time; situational interest is context dependent and short term
- Flow experienced as intense engagement or absorbed concentration
- Often difficult to arouse cognitive disequilibrium
- Need for achievement difficult to assess on basis of short-term observations
- Faulty attributions difficult to change

### The Humanistic View of Motivation

- People are motivated to satisfy deficiency needs only when those needs are unmet
- Self-actualization depends on satisfaction of lower needs, belief in certain values
- When deficiency needs not satisfied, person likely to make bad choices
- Encourage growth choices by enhancing attractions, minimizing dangers
- Teachers may be able to satisfy some deficiency needs but not others

### The Role of Self-Perceptions in Motivation

- Self-esteem is global judgment we make of self; self-concept is judgment we make of self in specific domains; self-efficacy is belief in our ability to carry out a specific action
- Academic self-concept and achievement can positively affect each other
- Design instruction to improve both academic self-concept and achievement

### Motivating Students with Technology

- Technology can be used to support both extrinsic and intrinsic motivation
- Technology increases intrinsic motivation by making learning more interesting and meaningful

Teaching is very much like putting together a puzzle. You first have to identify the pieces and then figure out how to construct them into a meaningful whole. This book is designed to help you identify the relevant pieces that make up the effective teaching puzzle and give you some ideas for using them in a coordinated fashion. Earlier in the text, for example, you learned the importance of understanding how students develop socially, emotionally, and cognitively; what students are like at different ages; and how they differ from one another. You will also be introduced to those pieces of the puzzle that pertain to the learning process and how different views of learning can be used to guide the type of instruction you provide. The puzzle pieces in this part deal with the importance of establishing a classroom environment that will motivate students to learn and of maintaining that positive atmosphere over time.

In this chapter, we address the question of why students strive (or don't strive) for academic achievement—that is, what motivates students? The importance of motivation was vividly pointed out by Larry Cuban, a Stanford University professor of education who returned to teach a high school class for one semester after a sixteen-year absence. Of this experience, he says, "If I wanted those students to be engaged intellectually, then every day—and I *do* mean *every* day—I had to figure out an angle, a way of making connections between whatever we were studying and their daily lives in school, in the community, or in the nation" (1990, pp. 480–481).

The senior author of this book remembers an instance from his days as a school psychologist that reinforces Cuban's observation. A teacher referred a ten-year-old student for testing and possible placement in a special education class (this was before the advent of inclusive classrooms) because the student's classroom performance, particularly in math, was very poor. On almost every test and homework assignment he received grades of F or D. Two pieces of evidence led to the conclusion that this student suffered more from lack of motivation than from intellectual deficits. First, his score on an individually administered intelligence test was average. Second, and most significant, he made pocket money in the evenings by keeping score for several bowling teams at the neighborhood bowling alley. Obviously, there was nothing wrong with this student's ability to learn or with his arithmetic skills!

*Motivation* can be defined as the selection, persistence, intensity, and direction of behavior (Elliot & Covington, 2001). In practical terms, motivation is simply the willingness of a person to expend a certain amount of effort to achieve a particular goal under a particular set of circumstances. Nevertheless, many teachers have at least two major misconceptions about motivation that prevent them from using this concept with maximum effectiveness. One misconception is that some students are unmotivated. Strictly speaking, that is not an accurate statement. As long as a student chooses goals and expends a certain amount of effort to achieve them, she is, by definition, motivated. What teachers really mean is that students are not motivated to behave in the way teachers would like them to behave. In other words, their motivation is negatively, rather than positively, oriented. The second misconception is that one person can directly motivate another. This view is inaccurate because motivation comes from within a person. What you *can* do, with the help of the various motivation theories discussed in this chapter, is create the circumstances that *influence* students to do what you want them to do (Keane & Shaughnessy, 2002).

Many factors determine whether the students in your classes will be motivated or not motivated to learn. You should not be surprised to discover that no single theoretical interpretation of motivation explains all aspects of student interest or lack of it. Different theoretical interpretations do, however, shed light on why some students in a given learning situation are more likely to want to learn than others (Pressley, Gaskins, Solic, & Collins, 2006). Furthermore, each theoretical interpretation can help you develop techniques for motivating students in the classroom. ●

# THE BEHAVIORAL VIEW OF MOTIVATION

Earlier in the text we noted that some psychologists explain learning from a theoretical perspective that focuses exclusively on the effects of observable stimuli, responses, and consequences on our propensity to exhibit particular behaviors. This approach is called operant conditioning, and its application to motivation has focused on the effect of reinforcement.

## The Effect of Reinforcement

In Chapter 7 on behavioral learning theory, we discussed Skinner's emphasis on the role of reinforcement in learning. After demonstrating that organisms tend to repeat actions that are reinforced and that behavior can be shaped by reinforcement, Skinner developed the technique of programmed instruction to make it possible for students to be reinforced for every correct response. Supplying the correct answer—and being informed by the program that it *is* the correct answer—motivates the student to go on to the next frame, and as the student works through the program, the desired terminal behavior is progressively shaped.

Following Skinner's lead, many behavioral learning theorists devised techniques of behavior modification. Students are motivated to complete a task by being promised a reward of some kind. Many times, the reward takes the form of praise or a grade. Sometimes it is a token that can be traded in for some desired object, and at other times the reward may be the privilege of engaging in a self-selected activity.

Operant conditioning interpretations of learning help reveal why some students react favorably to particular subjects and dislike others. For instance, some students may enter a required math class with a feeling of delight, whereas others may feel that they have been sentenced to prison. Skinner suggests that such differences can be traced to past experiences. He would argue that the student who loves math has been shaped to respond that way by a series of positive experiences with math. The math hater, in contrast, may have suffered a series of negative experiences.

| Behavioral view of motivation: reinforce desired behavior

## Limitations of the Behavioral View

Although approaches to motivation based on positive reinforcement are often useful, you should be aware of the disadvantages that can come from overuse or misuse of such techniques. Most of the criticisms of the use of reinforcement as a motivational incentive stem from the fact that it represents **extrinsic motivation**. That is, the learner decides to engage in an activity (such as participate in class, do homework, study for exams) to earn a reward that is not inherently related to the activity (such as praise from the teacher, a high grade, or the privilege of doing something different). By contrast, students under the influence of **intrinsic motivation** study a subject or acquire a skill because it produces such inherently positive consequences as becoming more knowledgeable, competent, and independent.

| Extrinsic motivation occurs when learner does something to earn external rewards

| Intrinsic motivation occurs when learner does something to experience inherently satisfying results

Although extrinsic motivation is widespread in society (individuals are motivated to engage in many activities because they hope to win certificates, badges, medals, public recognition, prizes, or admiration from others), this approach has at least three potential dangers (Covington, 2002; Kohn, 1999):

### pause & reflect

What percentage of your behavior do you think stems from intrinsic motivation? From extrinsic motivation? Is it possible to change this ratio? How?

1. Changes in behavior may be temporary. As soon as the extrinsic reward has been obtained, the student may revert to such earlier behaviors as studying inconsistently, turning in poor-quality homework, and disrupting class with irrelevant comments and behaviors.
2. Students may develop a materialistic attitude toward learning. They may think (or say), "What tangible reward will I get if I agree to learn this information?" If the answer is "none," they may decide to make little or no effort to learn it.
3. Giving students extrinsic rewards for completing a task may lessen whatever intrinsic motivation they may have for that activity.

| Excessive use of external rewards may lead to temporary behavior change, materialistic attitudes, decreased intrinsic motivation

This last disadvantage, which is referred to as the *undermining effect*, has been extensively investigated by researchers (Akin-Little, Eckert, Lovett, & Little, 2004; Deci, Koestner, & Ryan, 1999; Jenson, Olympia, Farley, & Clark, 2004). It appears that giving students rewards may indeed decrease their intrinsic motivation for a task, but only under certain conditions. Under other conditions, external rewards may enhance intrinsic motivation. Figure 12.1 summarizes recent research on this subject. Notice, in particular, that intrinsic motivation falls when students must compete for a limited supply of rewards. In contrast, intrinsic motivation rises when the reward consists of positive verbal feedback and is available to all who meet the standard.

| Intrinsic motivation enhanced when reward provides positive feedback, is available to all who qualify

Making students compete against each other for limited rewards (the "grading on the curve" practice we first mentioned in our discussion of Erik Erikson's psychosocial

**Figure 12.1** Conditions Determining Effect of External Rewards on Intrinsic Motivation

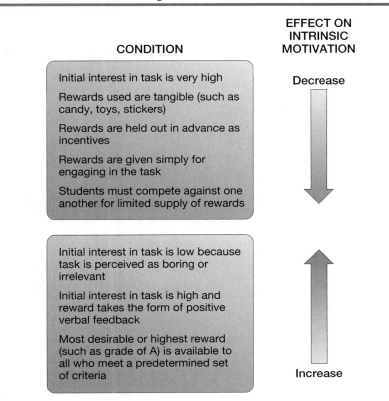

SOURCES: Cameron (2001); Cameron, Banko, & Pierce (2001); Covington (2002); Deci, Koestner, & Ryan (2001); Elliot & Covington (2001).

| |
|---|
| Intrinsic motivation undermined by forcing students to compete for limited supply of rewards |

theory of development) is particularly damaging to intrinsic motivation because of its impact on self-worth. Whether intended or not, children in our society base their sense of self-worth on their accomplishments. When we artificially limit opportunities to attain the highest level of accomplishment, intrinsic motivation declines in an effort to protect one's sense of worth (Covington, 2002).

| |
|---|
| Give rewards sparingly, especially on tasks of natural interest |

Taken as a whole, these results strongly suggest that teachers should avoid the indiscriminate use of rewards for influencing classroom behavior, particularly when an activity seems to be naturally interesting to students. Instead, rewards should be used to provide students with information about their level of competence on tasks they have not yet mastered and to encourage them to explore topics in which their initial interest is low.

## THE SOCIAL COGNITIVE VIEW OF MOTIVATION

| |
|---|
| Social cognitive view of motivation: observe and imitate admired models; raise self-efficacy |

Social cognitive theorists, such as Albert Bandura, Dale Schunk, and Barry Zimmerman, emphasize two factors that strongly influence motivation to learn: (1) the models to which people are exposed and (2) people's sense of self-efficacy, or how capable they believe they are to handle a particular task.

### Power of Persuasive Models

One factor that positively affects students' self-efficacy and motivation to learn certain behaviors is the opportunity to see other people exhibiting those behaviors and to observe the consequences that occur. Social cognitive theorists refer to this as

*When students admire and identify with classmates who are positively reinforced for their behavior, the observing students' self-efficacy and motivation to exhibit the same behavior may be strengthened.*

observation, imitation, and vicarious reinforcement. As we pointed out in discussing social cognitive theory in Chapter 13, *vicarious* reinforcement means that we expect to receive the same reinforcer that we see someone else get for exhibiting a particular behavior.

A student who observes an older brother or sister reaping benefits from earning high grades may strive to do the same with the expectation of experiencing the same or similar benefits. A student who notices that a classmate receives praise from the teacher after acting in a certain way may decide to imitate such behavior to win similar rewards. A student who identifies with and admires a teacher may work hard partly to please the admired individual and partly to try becoming like that individual. Both vicarious reinforcement and direct reinforcement can raise an individual's sense of self-efficacy for a particular task, which, in turn, leads to higher levels of motivation.

## The Importance of Self-Efficacy

An individual's sense of self-efficacy can affect motivation to learn through its influence on the learning goal one chooses, the outcome one expects, and the reasons (or attributions) one gives to explain successes and failures.

**Choice of Learning Goal**   Analyses of learning goals suggest that a student may choose a task mastery goal, a performance-approach goal, a performance-avoidance goal, or a combination of task mastery and performance-approach goals (Britner & Pajares, 2006; Elliot & Thrash, 2001; Pintrich & Schunk, 2002; Urdan & Mestas, 2006; Urdan, Ryan, Anderman, & Gheen, 2002).

- *Task mastery goals* involve doing what is necessary to learn meaningfully the information and skills that have been assigned. Students with high levels of self-efficacy choose this goal more often than do students with low levels of self-efficacy. In pursuit of task mastery goals, students with high efficacy will use a variety of encoding techniques, do more organizing of information to make it meaningful, review and practice more frequently, monitor their understanding more closely, formulate more effective learning strategies, and treat mistakes as part of learning.
- *Performance-approach goals* involve demonstrating to teachers and peers one's superior intellectual ability by outperforming most others in class. If the best way

to accomplish this goal is to do assignments neatly and exactly according to directions, or to memorize large amounts of information to get a high grade on a test without necessarily understanding the ideas or how they relate to one another, then these tactics will be used. Students who adopt performance-approach goals often do well on tests, but they are less likely than students who adopt mastery goals to develop a strong interest in various subjects. On the other hand, students who choose performance goals tend to have high levels of self-efficacy.

- *Performance-avoidance goals* involve reducing the possibility of failure so as not to appear less capable than other students. Students can reduce their chances of failure by avoiding novel and challenging tasks or by cheating. They can also engage in *self-handicapping behaviors*, such as putting off homework or projects until the last minute, studying superficially for an exam, and getting involved in many in-school and out-of-school nonacademic activities. The purpose of self-handicapping is to be able to blame poor performance on the circumstances rather than on one's ability. Students most likely to choose performance-avoidance goals are boys and those with low grades and low academic self-efficacy.

Teachers may unwittingly encourage self-handicapping behaviors, even in students whose sense of self-efficacy is at least adequate, by using a norm-referenced grading system. Because students are compared with one another to determine the top, middle, and low grades, this system encourages students to attribute their grades to a fixed ability. Students who have doubts about their ability are then more likely to engage in self-handicapping behaviors (Urdan, Midgley, & Anderman, 1998).

**Outcome Expectations**   A second way in which self-efficacy can affect motivation is in terms of the outcomes that students expect. Those with high levels of self-efficacy more often expect a positive outcome. As a result, they tend to be more willing to use the more complex and time-consuming learning skills and to persist longer in the face of difficulties. (It is possible, however, for a student to have a relatively high level of self-efficacy but expect a relatively low grade on a test because the student believes the teacher is prejudiced or grades unfairly.) Those with lower levels of self-efficacy are more likely to expect a disappointing outcome, tend to use simpler learning skills, and are likely to give up more quickly when tasks demand greater cognitive efforts (Pintrich & Schunk, 2002).

Self-efficacy affects choice of goals, expectations of success, attributions for success and failure

**Attributions**   A third way in which self-efficacy influences motivation is through the reasons students cite to explain why they succeeded or failed at a task. Those with a high level of self-efficacy for a subject are likely to attribute failure to insufficient effort (and so vow to work harder the next time) but credit their success to a combination of ability and effort. Their peers who are lower in self-efficacy are likely to explain their failures by saying that they just don't have the ability to do well, but they will chalk their successes up to an easy task or luck. As we point out a bit further on in this chapter, this latter attribution pattern undercuts motivation (Pintrich & Schunk, 2002).

## OTHER COGNITIVE VIEWS OF MOTIVATION

In addition to social cognitive theorists, researchers who take other cognitive approaches to learning have done extensive studies of motivation. The views described in this section emphasize how the following five characteristics affect students' intrinsic motivation to learn: the inherent need to construct an organized and logically consistent knowledge base, one's expectations for successfully completing a task, the factors that one believes account for success and failure, one's beliefs about the nature of cognitive ability, and one's interests.

You should also be aware that intrinsic motivation for school learning is fairly well developed by about nine years of age (fourth grade) and becomes increasingly stable through late adolescence. Thus it is important to develop intrinsic motivation in students in the primary grades, as well as to identify students with low levels of academic motivation (Gottfried, Fleming, & Gottfried, 2001).

## Cognitive Development and the Need for Conceptual Organization

The cognitive development view is based on Jean Piaget's principles of equilibration, assimilation, accommodation, and schema formation, which we discussed in the chapter on stage theories of development. Piaget proposes that children possess an inherent desire to maintain a sense of organization and balance in their conception of the world (equilibration). A sense of equilibration may be experienced if a child assimilates a new experience by relating it to an existing scheme, or the child may accommodate by modifying an existing scheme if the new experience is too different.

| Cognitive development view of motivation: strive for equilibration; master the environment

In addition, individuals will repeatedly use new schemes because of an inherent desire to master their environment. This explains why young children can, with no loss of enthusiasm, sing the same song, tell the same story, and play the same game over and over and why they repeatedly open and shut doors to rooms and cupboards with no apparent purpose. It also explains why older children take great delight in collecting and organizing almost everything they can get their hands on and why adolescents who have begun to attain formal operational thinking will argue incessantly about all the unfairness in the world and how it can be eliminated (Stipek, 2002).

## The Need for Achievement

Have you ever decided to take on a moderately difficult task (such as taking a course on astronomy even though you are a history major and have only a limited background in science) and then found that you had somewhat conflicting feelings about it? On the one hand, you felt eager to start the course, confident that you would be pleased with your performance. But on the other hand, you also felt a bit of anxiety because of the small possibility of failure. Now try to imagine the opposite situation. In reaction to a suggestion to take a course outside your major, you refuse because the probability of failure seems great, whereas the probability of success seems quite small.

| Need for achievement revealed by desire to attain goals that require skilled performance

In 1964, John Atkinson proposed that such differences in achievement behavior are due to differences in something called the *need for achievement*. Individuals with a high need for achievement have a stronger expectation of success than they do a fear of failure for most tasks and therefore anticipate a feeling of pride in accomplishment. When given a choice, high-need achievers seek out moderately challenging tasks because they offer an optimal balance between challenge and expected success. By contrast, individuals with a low need for achievement avoid such tasks because their fear of failure greatly outweighs their expectation of success, and they therefore anticipate feelings of shame. When faced with a choice, they typically choose either relatively easy tasks because the probability of success is high or very difficult tasks because there is no shame in failing to achieve a lofty goal. Atkinson's theory was an early version of what is currently called *expectancy-value theory*. An individual's level of motivation for a particular task is governed by that person's expectation of success and the value placed on that success (Wigfield & Eccles, 2002b).

| High-need achievers prefer moderately challenging tasks

| Low-need achievers prefer very easy or very hard tasks

Atkinson's point about taking fear of failure into account in arranging learning experiences has been made by William Glasser in *Choice Theory in the Classroom* (2001) and *The Quality School* (1998). Glasser argues that for people to succeed at life in general, they must first experience success in one important aspect of their lives. For most children, that one important part should be school. Erik Erikson made the same point by maintaining that the primary psychosocial task for school-age children is to successfully resolve the issue of industry versus inferiority.

## Explanations of Success and Failure: Attribution Theory

Some interesting aspects of success and failure are revealed when students are asked to explain why they did or did not do well on some task. The four most commonly given reasons stress ability, effort, task difficulty, and luck. To explain a low score on a math test, for example, different students might make the following statements:

"I just have a poor head for numbers." (lack of ability)
"I didn't really study for the exam." (lack of effort)
"That test was the toughest I've ever taken." (task difficulty)
"I guessed wrong about which sections of the book to study." (luck)

Because students *attribute* success or failure to the factors just listed, research of this type contributes to what is referred to as **attribution theory**. We have already touched on this topic in discussing self-efficacy.

Students with long histories of academic failure and a weak need for achievement typically attribute their success to easy questions or luck and their failures to lack of ability. Ability is a stable attribution (that is, people expect its effect on achievement to be pretty much the same from one task to another), whereas task difficulty and luck are both external attributions (in other words, people feel they have little control over their occurrence). Research has shown that stable attributions, particularly concerning ability, lead to expectations of future success or failure and that internal attributions (those under personal control) lead to pride in achievement or to shame following failure. Because low-achieving students attribute failure to low ability, they see future failure as more likely than future success. In addition, ascribing success to factors beyond one's control diminishes the possibility of taking pride in achievement and placing a high value on rewards. Consequently, satisfactory achievement and reward may have little effect on the failure-avoiding strategies that poor students have developed over the years (Elliott & Bempechat, 2002).

Success-oriented students (high-need achievers), in contrast, typically attribute success to ability and effort and failure to insufficient effort. Consequently, failure does not diminish expectancy of success, feelings of competence, or reward attractiveness for these students. They simply resolve to work harder in the future. This attribution pattern holds even for academically gifted students who might be expected to focus on ability because they excel at most tasks and are well aware of their superior capabilities. Citing effort as a factor in their success or failure is thought to be more motivating than citing just ability because effort is a modifiable factor that allows one to feel in control of one's destiny (Dai, Moon, & Feldhusen, 1998).

The typical attribution pattern of high-achieving students highlights an important point: both effort and ability should be credited with contributing to one's success. Students who attribute their success mostly to effort may conclude that they have a low level of ability because they have to work harder to achieve the same level of performance as others (Tollefson, 2000).

*Unsuccessful students attribute success to luck, easy tasks; failure, to lack of ability*

*Successful students attribute success to effort, ability; failure, to lack of effort*

## pause & reflect

Do you fit the pattern of most successful students, attributing success to effort and ability and failure to lack of effort? If so, how did you get this way? Is there anything you can draw from your own experiences to help students develop this pattern?

## Beliefs About the Nature of Cognitive Ability

Children's motivation for learning is affected by their beliefs about the nature of ability. During the primary and elementary grades, children create and refine their conception of ability. By the time they reach middle school, most children start to think of themselves and others as belonging to particular categories in terms of ability.

**Changes in Beliefs About Ability** According to Carol Dweck (2002a, 2002b), a leading theorist and researcher on this subject, noticeable changes in children's ability conceptions occur at two points in time: between seven and eight years of age and between ten and twelve years of age. Compared with kindergarten and early primary grade children, seven- and eight-year-olds are more likely to do the following:

- Show an increased interest in the concept of ability and take greater notice of peer behaviors that are relevant to achievement comparisons.
- Distinguish ability from such other characteristics as social skills, likeability, and physical skills and believe that the same person can have different levels of ability for different academic skills (such as reading, writing, and mathematics).
- Think of ability as a more internal and less observable characteristic that is defined normatively (that is, by comparing oneself to others).
- Think of ability as a characteristic that is stable over time and can therefore be used to make predictions about future academic performance.
- Engage in self-criticism related to ability and compare their performance with that of others.

Compared with seven- and eight-year-olds, ten- to twelve-year-old children are more likely to do the following:

- Distinguish between effort and ability as factors in performance. Consequently, some are more likely to say of two students who receive the same grade on a test or assignment that the one who exerted more effort has less ability.
- Evaluate their academic ability more accurately, although more begin to underestimate their ability.
- Think of ability as being both a stable characteristic and a fixed capacity that explains the grades they currently receive and will receive in the future. It is not uncommon to hear older children and adolescents talk about peers who do or do not have "it" (Anderman & Maehr, 1994). Consequently, students who believe their ability in a particular subject is below average seek to avoid additional courses in that subject. Girls, especially high-achieving ones, are more likely than boys to adopt this view of ability, and this may partly explain their greater reluctance to take advanced science and math classes in high school.
- Value performance goals (getting the highest grade possible) over learning goals (making meaningful connections among ideas and how they relate to the world outside of school).

Why these changes occur, and why they occur in some individuals but not others, is not entirely known, but comparing the performance of a student with the performance of every other student in a class to determine who gets which grades (the practice of grading on the curve that we mentioned earlier) is suspected of playing a major role. One casualty of this belief, as we've indicated, is motivation for learning (Lepper, Corpus, & Iyengar, 2005).

**Types of Beliefs About Ability**    According to the work of Dweck (2002a) and others (e.g., Quihuis, Bempechat, Jiminez, & Boulay, 2002), students can be placed into one of three categories based on their beliefs about the nature of cognitive ability:

1. *Entity theorists.* Some students subscribe solely to what is called an entity theory; they talk about intelligence as if it were a thing, or an entity, that has fixed characteristics.
2. *Incremental theorists.* Other students subscribe solely to what is called an incremental theory, believing that intelligence can be improved gradually by degrees or increments as they refine their thinking skills and acquire new ones. Entity and incremental theorists hold to their respective views for all subjects.
3. *Mixed theorists.* Students in this group subscribe to both entity and incremental theories, depending on the subject. A mixed theorist may, for example, be an entity theorist for math but an incremental theorist for science, whereas the opposite (or some other) pattern may prevail for another student.

Students with incremental beliefs tend to be motivated to acquire new and more effective cognitive skills and are said to have *mastery goals*. They seek challenging

Students with incremental beliefs tend to have mastery goals and are motivated to meaningfully learn, improve skills

*Students who believe that intelligence is a collection of cognitive skills that can be refined are likely to adopt mastery goals and attribute failure to insufficient effort, whereas students who believe that intelligence is an unchangeable capacity are likely to adopt performance goals and attribute failure to low ability.*

Students with entity beliefs tend to have performance goals and are motivated to get high grades, avoid failure

tasks and do not give up easily, because they see obstacles as a natural part of the learning process. They often tell themselves what adults have told them for years: "think carefully," "pay attention," and "try to recall useful information that you learned earlier." They seem to focus on the questions, "How do you do this?" and "What can I learn from this?" Errors are seen as opportunities for useful feedback. Not surprisingly, they are more likely than entity theorists to attribute failure to insufficient effort and ineffective learning skills.

Students who believe that intelligence is an unchangeable entity are primarily motivated to appear smart to others by getting high grades and praise and by avoiding low grades, criticism, and shame. Such students are said to have *performance goals*. When confronted with a new task, their initial thought is likely to be, "Am I smart enough to do this?" They may forgo opportunities to learn new ideas and skills if they think they will become confused and make mistakes, and they tend to attribute failure to low ability rather than insufficient effort.

However, among students who subscribe to the entity theory, there is a difference between those with high confidence in their ability and those with low confidence. High-confidence entity theorists are likely to demonstrate such mastery-oriented behaviors as seeking challenges and persisting in the face of difficulty. Those with low confidence, in contrast, may be more interested in avoiding failure and criticism—even after achieving initial success—than in continuing to be positively reinforced for out-performing others. Because of their anxiety over the possibility of failure, these low-confidence entity theorists are less likely than students who have an incremental view of ability to exhibit subsequent motivation for a task (Rawsthorne & Elliot, 1999). If avoidance is not possible, they become discouraged at the first sign of difficulty. This, in turn, produces anxiety, ineffective problem solving, and withdrawal from the task (as a way to avoid concluding that one lacks ability and thereby maintain some self-esteem). According to attribution theory, entity theorists should continue this pattern, because success is not attributed to effort, but failure is attributed to low ability.

## The Effect of Interest on Intrinsic Motivation

Interest can be described as a psychological state that involves focused attention, increased cognitive functioning, persistence, and emotional involvement (Ainley,

Hidi, & Berndorff, 2002; Hidi & Ainley, 2002; Renninger & Hidi, 2002; Schraw & Lehman, 2001). A person's interest in a topic can come from personal and/or situational sources:

Personal interest marked by intrinsic desire to learn that persists over time; situational interest is context dependent and short term

- *Personal interest* (also referred to as individual or topic interest) is characterized by an intrinsic desire to understand a topic, a desire that persists over time and is based on preexisting knowledge, personal experience, and emotion.
- *Situational interest* is more temporary and is based on context-specific factors, such as the unusualness of information or its personal relevance. For example, baseball teams that qualify for or win League Championship or World Series after many years of not doing so (think Chicago Cubs or Boston Red Sox) often spark temporary interest in the players and the games among people who live in those cities. Similarly, people who buy a company's stock often become interested, albeit temporarily, in the company's activities.

The degree of personal interest a student brings to a subject or activity has been shown to affect intrinsic motivation for that task. Such students pay greater attention to the task, stay with it for a longer period of time, learn more from it, and enjoy their involvement to a greater degree (Schraw & Lehman, 2001).

It is possible, of course, that situational interest in a topic can grow into a personal interest. Consider, for example, a high school student who knows nothing of how information is stored in and retrieved from memory but learns about it when she has to read a chapter on memory in her psychology textbook. Fascinated with the description of various forms of encoding and retrieval cues because of her own problems with being able to recall information for tests accurately, she searches for additional books and articles on the topic and even thinks about majoring in psychology in college (Renninger & Hidi, 2002; Schraw & Lehman, 2001).

**Factors That Influence Personal Interest**    A long-term interest in a particular subject or activity may be influenced by one or more of the following factors (Bergin, 1999; Hidi, 2001; Hidi & Ainley, 2002; Schraw & Lehman, 2001):

- *Ideas and activities that are valued by one's culture or ethnic group.* As we discussed in the chapter on cultural diversity, culture is the filter through which groups of people interpret the world and assign values to objects, ideas, and activities. Thus, inner-city male youths are likely to be strongly interested in playing basketball and following the exploits of professional basketball players, whereas a rural midwestern male of the same age is likely to be interested in fishing and hunting.
- *The emotions that are aroused by the subject or activity.* Students who experience extreme math anxiety, for example, are less likely to develop a strong interest in math-related activities than those who experience more positive emotions.
- *The degree of competence one attains in a subject or activity.* People typically spend more time pursuing activities that they are good at than activities at which they do not excel.
- *The degree to which a subject or activity is perceived to be relevant to achieving a goal.* As noted in the chapter on approaches to instruction, many students fail to perceive such relevance, partly because teachers rarely take the time to explain how a topic or lesson may affect students' lives.
- *Level of prior knowledge.* People are often more interested in topics they already know something about than in topics they know nothing about.
- *A perceived hole in a topic that the person already knows a good deal about.* A person who considers himself to be well informed about the music of Mozart would likely be highly interested in reading the score of a newly discovered composition by Mozart.

**Factors That Influence Situational Interest**    Some of the factors that spark a spontaneous and short-term interest in a topic or activity include (Bergin, 1999;

Hidi, 2001; Hidi & Ainley, 2002; Schraw & Lehman, 2001; Schraw, Flowerday, & Lehman, 2001):

- *A state of cognitive conflict or disequilibrium.* Teachers can sometimes spark students' interest in a topic by showing or telling them something that is discrepant with a current belief. Consider, for example, a high school class on government. The teacher has a lesson planned on government spending and wants to avoid the usual lack of interest that this topic produces. One tactic would be to ask students if they believe that the money they contribute to social security from their part-time jobs (or the full-time jobs they will eventually have) is placed in an account with their name on it, where it remains until they become eligible for benefits in their mid-sixties. Most will probably believe something like that. The teacher could then tell them that the contributions they make today are actually used to pay the benefits of current retirees and that their social security benefits will come from the social security taxes levied on a future generation of workers.
- *Well-written reading material.* Texts and other written materials that are logically organized and engaging are rated as more interesting by students and produce higher levels of comprehension than more poorly written material.
- *The opportunity to work on a task with others.* As we saw earlier in the book, cooperative arrangements are highly motivating and produce high levels of learning.
- *The opportunity to engage in hands-on activities.*
- *The opportunity to observe influential models.*
- *The teacher's use of novel stimuli.*
- *The teacher's use of games and puzzles.*

These findings have a number of clear instructional implications. Given that some students may develop a strong interest in a topic as a result of a classroom activity or assignment and that this initial interest may grow into a personal interest and the adoption of mastery goals, a general recommendation is for teachers to do what constructivist learning theory implies: involve students in a variety of subject matters and meaningful activities (Hidi & Harackiewicz, 2000). If you think about it, the purpose of exposing students to a wide variety of topics during their school years is not simply to provide them with basic knowledge of all of those topics but also to increase the likelihood that students will encounter those topics in situations that engage them, perhaps to the point at which topics grow into personal interests. Many of us have "discovered" our personal interests, and indeed our careers, as a result of situational interest growing into personal interest.

The section on Suggestions for Teaching in Your Classroom offers further recommendations.

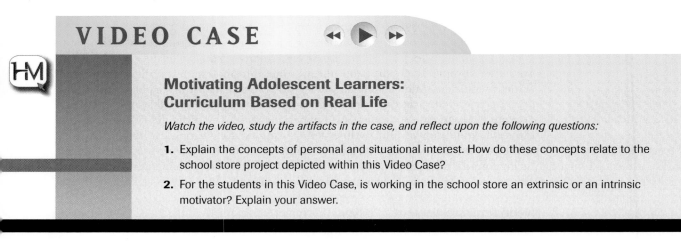

# VIDEO CASE

## Motivating Adolescent Learners: Curriculum Based on Real Life

*Watch the video, study the artifacts in the case, and reflect upon the following questions:*

1. Explain the concepts of personal and situational interest. How do these concepts relate to the school store project depicted within this Video Case?

2. For the students in this Video Case, is working in the school store an extrinsic or an intrinsic motivator? Explain your answer.

Flow experienced as intense engagement or absorbed concentration

**Flow and Engagement**    The concept of "flow" has been championed for more than three decades by Mihaly Csikszentmihalyi. Flow is the mental state of high engagement in an activity. It is characterized by intense concentration, sustained interest, and enjoyment of the activity's challenge (Csikszentmihalyi, 1975, 1996, 2000, 2002). If you have ever been engaged in an activity (e.g., playing a video game, reading a novel, working on a problem, or writing a paper) that captured your interest so completely that you lost track of time and had trouble breaking away from the activity, you have experienced something like the state of flow. Factors that influence either personal or situational interest can result in students experiencing flow and developing intrinsic motivation.

Research has used the concept of flow as a way of investigating the effects of student engagement in classrooms. Rathunde and Csikszentmihalyi (2005) compared the academic experiences of nearly three hundred middle school students divided into two groups: those who were enrolled in a program that took advantage of the factors that influence both personal and situational interest (called a "Montessori" middle school program) and students in a traditional middle school program. The students in the two groups were matched on a number of demographic factors to help ensure that any differences between the groups were most likely due to the kind of program they attended. The study produced two major findings. First, the students in both types of middle school programs reported very similar experiences while engaged in nonacademic activities at school. Second, when engaged in academic activities, the Montessori students reported more flow experiences, more energetic engagement in the academic activities, and greater intrinsic motivation than the students in the traditional middle school.

Another study by Csikszentmihalyi and his colleagues used the concept of flow to examine how high school students spent their time in school and the conditions under which the students felt engaged. They studied a longitudinal sample of more than five hundred high school students from across the United States. The high school students reported increased engagement in academic activities when both the challenge of the activity and their own skill were high, when the instruction was perceived as relevant, and when the students felt control over the learning environment. In more concrete terms, the high school students were more engaged in individual and group learning activities than in listening to lectures, watching videos, or taking exams (Shernoff, Csikszentmihalyi, Schneider, & Shernoff, 2003). The researchers concluded that a sense of flow (i.e., intense engagement) is more likely when students feel a sense of control over their own learning and when the learning activities challenge students at a level appropriate to their skills.

## Limitations of Cognitive Views

Often difficult to arouse cognitive disequilibrium

**Cognitive Development**    Although cognitive development theory, with its emphasis on people's need for a well-organized conception of the world, can be useful as a means for motivating students, it has a major limitation: it is not always easy or even possible to induce students to experience a cognitive disequilibrium sufficient to stimulate them to seek answers. This is particularly true if an answer can be found only after comparatively dull and unrewarding information and skills are mastered. (How many elementary school students, for example, might be expected to experience a self-impelled urge to learn English grammar or acquire skill in mathematics?) You are likely to gain some firsthand experience with the difficulty of arousing cognitive disequilibrium the first time you ask students to respond to what you hope will be a provocative question for class discussion. Some students may experience a feeling of intellectual curiosity and be eager to clarify their thinking, but others may stare out the window or surreptitiously do homework for another class.

Need for achievement difficult to assess on basis of short-term observations

**Need for Achievement**    Perhaps the major problem that teachers have in using Atkinson's theory of need for achievement is the lack of efficient and objective instruments for measuring its strength. Although you could probably draw reasonably accurate conclusions about whether a student has a high or low need for achievement by watching that student's behavior over time and in a variety of situations, you may not be in a position to make extensive observations. And the problem with short-term observations is that a student's achievement orientation may be affected by more or less chance circumstances.

Faulty attributions difficult to change

**Attribution Theory and Beliefs About Ability**    The major implication of the idea that faulty attributions are at least partly responsible for sabotaging students' motivation to learn is that students must be taught to make more appropriate attributions. But this is likely to be a substantial undertaking requiring a concerted, coordinated effort. One part of the problem in working with students who attribute failure to lack of ability is that ability tends to be seen as a stable factor that is relatively impervious to change. The other part of the problem is that the same students often attribute their success to task difficulty and luck, two factors that cannot be predicted or controlled because they are external and random.

An additional limitation is that attribution training is not likely to be fully effective with elementary school children. For them, two individuals who learn the same amount of material are equally smart despite the fact that one person has to work twice as long to achieve that goal. Older children and adolescents, however, have a better grasp of the concept of efficiency; they see ability as something that influences the amount and effectiveness of effort (Stipek, 2002).

Now that you are familiar with some of the approaches to motivation, it is time to consider Suggestions for Teaching in Your Classroom that show how these ideas can be converted into classroom practice.

# Suggestions for Teaching in Your Classroom

## Motivating Students to Learn

**①  Use behavioral techniques to help students exert themselves and work toward remote goals.**

**JOURNAL ENTRY**
Using Behavior Modification Techniques to Motivate

Techniques you might use for this purpose were described in Chapter 7 on behavioral and social learning theories. They include verbal praise, shaping, modeling, symbolic reinforcers (smile faces, stars, and the like), and contingency contracting.

**a.  Give praise as positive reinforcement, but do so effectively.**

Think about the times when you've been praised for a job well done, particularly when you weren't sure about the quality of your work. In all likelihood, it had a strong, maybe even dramatic, effect on your motivation. That being the case, you might think that effective positive reinforcement in the form of verbal praise is a common occurrence in the classroom. But you would be wrong. Extensive observations of classroom life reveal that verbal praise is rarely given (Goodlad, 1984) and is often given in ways that limit its effectiveness (Brophy, 1981). Jere Brophy recommends that teachers use praise in the following ways:

- As a spontaneous expression of surprise or admiration. ("Why, Juan! This report is really excellent!")

- As compensation for criticism or as vindication of a prediction. ("After your last report, Lily, I said I knew you could do better. Well, you have done better. This is really excellent.")
- As an attempt to impress all members of a class. ("I like the way Nguyen just put his books away so promptly.")
- As a transition ritual to verify that an assignment has been completed. ("Yes, Maya, that's very good. You can work on your project now.")
- As a consolation prize or as encouragement to students who are less capable than others. ("Well, Josh, you kept at it, and you got it finished. Good for you!")

In an effort to help teachers administer praise more effectively, Brophy drew up the guidelines for effective praise listed in Table 12.1.

### b.  Use other forms of positive reinforcement.

In addition to verbal praise, you can make use of such other forms of positive reinforcement as modeling, symbolic reinforcers, and contingency contracts.

#### EXAMPLES

- Arrange for students to observe that classmates who persevere and complete a task receive a reinforcer of some kind. (But let this occur more or less naturally. Also, don't permit students who have finished an assignment to engage in attention-getting or obviously enjoyable self-chosen activities; those who are still working on the assignment may become a bit resentful and therefore less inclined to work on the task at hand.)
- Draw happy faces on primary grade students' papers, give check marks as students complete assignments, write personal comments acknowledging good work, and assign bonus points.

### Table 12.1    Guidelines for Effective Praise

| Effective Praise | Ineffective Praise |
|---|---|
| 1. Is delivered contingently | 1. Is delivered randomly or unsystematically |
| 2. Specifies the particulars of the accomplishment | 2. Is restricted to global positive reactions |
| 3. Shows spontaneity, variety, and other signs of credibility; suggests clear attention to the student's accomplishment | 3. Shows a bland uniformity, which suggests a conditional response made with minimal attention |
| 4. Rewards attainment of specified performance criteria (which can include effort criteria, however) | 4. Rewards mere participation, without consideration of performance process or outcomes |
| 5. Provides information to students about their competence or the value of their accomplishments | 5. Provides no information at all or gives students information about their status |
| 6. Orients students toward better appreciation of their own task-related behavior and thinking about problem solving | 6. Orients students toward comparing themselves with others and thinking about competing |
| 7. Uses students' own prior accomplishments as the context for describing new accomplishments | 7. Uses the accomplishments of peers as the context for describing students' present accomplishments |
| 8. Is given in recognition of noteworthy effort or success at tasks that are difficult (for *this* student) | 8. Is given without regard to the effort expended or the meaning of the accomplishment (for *this* student) |
| 9. Attributes success to effort and ability, implying that similar successes can be expected in the future | 9. Attributes success to ability alone or to external factors such as luck or easy task |
| 10. Leads students to expend effort on the task because they enjoy the task or want to develop task-relevant skills | 10. Leads students to expend effort on the task for external reasons—to please the teacher, win a competition or reward, etc. |
| 11. Focuses students' attention on their own task-relevant behavior | 11. Focuses students' attention on the teacher as an external authority figure who is manipulating them |
| 12. Fosters appreciation of and desirable attributions about task-relevant behavior after the process is completed | 12. Intrudes into the ongoing process, distracting attention from task-relevant behavior |

SOURCE:  Brophy (1981).

- Develop an individual reward menu, or contract, with each student based on the Premack principle (Grandma's rule), which we discussed earlier in the book. After passing a spelling test at a particular level, for example, each student might be given class time to work on a self-selected project.

- When making use of such motivational techniques, you might do your best to play down overtones of manipulation and materialism. Point out that rewards are used in almost all forms of endeavor to induce people to work toward a goal. Just because someone does something to earn a reward does not mean that the activity should never be indulged in for intrinsic reasons. For example, athletes often compete to earn the reward of being members of the best team, but they still enjoy the game.

**2** **Make sure that students know what they are to do, how to proceed, and how to determine when they have achieved goals.**

Many times students do not exert themselves in the classroom because they say they don't know what they are supposed to do. Occasionally, such a statement is merely an excuse for goofing off, but it may also be a legitimate explanation for lack of effort. Recall that knowing what one is expected to do is important information in the construction of a learning strategy. You should use the techniques described in Chapter 13, "Approaches to Instruction," to take full advantage of the values of instructional objectives. In terms of motivation, objectives should be clear, understood by all members of the class, and attainable in a short period of time.

For reasons illustrated by behavioral theorists' experiments with different reinforcement schedules, students are more likely to work steadily if they are reinforced at frequent intervals. If you set goals that are too demanding or remote, lack of reinforcement during the early stages of a unit may derail students, even if they started out with good intentions. Whenever you ask students to work toward a demanding or remote goal, try to set up a series of short-term goals.

**JOURNAL ENTRY**
Ways to Arrange Short-Term Goals

**EXAMPLE**

- One way to structure students' learning efforts is to follow the suggestions offered by Raymond Wlodkowski for drawing up a personal contract. He recommends that such a contract should contain four elements. A sample contract from Wlodkowski (1978, p. 57) is presented here, with a description of each element in brackets.

Date _____

**1.** Within the next two weeks I will learn to multiply correctly single-digit numbers ranging between 5 and 9, for example, $5 \times 6$, $6 \times 7$, $7 \times 8$, $8 \times 9$, $9 \times 5$. [What the student will learn]
**2.** When I feel prepared, I will ask to take a mastery test containing 50 problems from this range of multiplication facts. [How the student can demonstrate learning]
**3.** I will complete this contract when I can finish the mastery test with no more than three errors. [The degree of proficiency to be demonstrated]
**4.** My preparation and study will involve choosing work from the workbook activities, number games, and filmstrip materials. [How the student will proceed]

Signed _____

**3** **Encourage low-achieving students to attribute success to a combination of ability and effort and failure to insufficient effort.**

Should you decide to try to alter the attributions of a student who is having difficulty with one or more subjects, here are three suggestions based on an analysis of twenty attribution training studies (Robertson, 2000):

- Make sure the student has the ability to succeed on a task before telling the student to attribute failure to insufficient effort. Students who try hard but lack the cognitive skills necessary for success are likely to become convinced not only that they lack the ability but also that they will never become capable of success on that type of task.

- Tell students that having the ability for a subject is the same as knowing how to formulate and use a learning strategy for that subject. Thus success is attributable to an appropriate strategy (which is controllable), whereas failure is attributable to insufficient effort at formulating the strategy (also controllable).
- Combine attribution training with strategy instruction for students who don't understand the relationship between strategy use and success and failure.

**4  Encourage students to think of ability as a set of cognitive skills that can be added to and refined, rather than as a fixed entity that is resistant to change, by praising the processes they use to succeed.**

**JOURNAL ENTRY**
Ways to Promote an Incremental View of Intelligence

The work that Carol Dweck (2002a, 2002b) has done on students' beliefs about ability clearly shows that those who adopt an entity view are more likely to develop a maladaptive approach to learning than are students who adopt an incremental view. One way to help students develop incremental rather than entity beliefs is to praise them for their effort and use of effective skills rather than for their ability after doing well on a task.

Many parents and teachers believe they are strengthening a student's motivation for learning by praising their ability with such comments as, "You did very well on this test; you certainly are smart" or "You're really good at this." Dweck's research shows that this type of praise encourages students to develop entity beliefs that impede their motivation. A better alternative is to offer what Dweck calls process praise. Examples of process praise are: "That's a really high score; you must have worked really hard at these problems"; "Now that you've mastered this skill, let's go on to something a bit harder that you can learn from"; and "You did a fine job on this paper because you started early and used the writing skills we practiced in class."

**5  Encourage students to adopt appropriate learning goals.**

As we noted earlier, students may adopt task mastery goals, performance-approach goals, or performance-avoidance goals. To briefly review, students who have task mastery goals are motivated to use effective learning tactics to acquire new knowledge and skills even if it means an occasional disappointing performance. Students who adopt performance-approach goals, on the other hand, are principally motivated to outscore others on exams and assignments in order to demonstrate their ability. Students who adopt performance-avoidance goals are principally motivated to avoid failure and appear less capable than their peers by engaging in such behaviors as self-handicapping, avoiding novel and challenging tasks, and cheating. To help students maintain high levels of motivation and achievement, you should establish conditions that encourage the adoption of mastery goals (Midgley, Middleton, Gheen, & Kumar, 2002). The problem with performance-approach goals is that they suppress intrinsic interest in tasks and encourage students to equate failure with low ability. Performance-avoidance goals have many obvious problems, including the reinforcement of low self-efficacy and stunted intellectual growth.

**a.  Help students develop mastery learning goals.**

The following suggestions (Urdan & Midgley, 2001) were designed with middle school students in mind but are just as applicable to both lower and higher grades:

- Group students by topic, interests, or their own choice rather than by ability.
- Use a variety of assessment techniques (discussed in Chapter 15, "Assessment of Classroom Learning") rather than just one, and make the top grade potentially achievable by all students by evaluating performance according to a predetermined set of criteria.
- Provide students with feedback about their progress rather than feedback about how they scored relative to the rest of the class.
- Recognize students who demonstrate progress rather than focusing just on students who have achieved the highest grades.

- Provide students with opportunities to choose what projects they will do, what electives they will take, and for how long they wish to study a particular subject rather than having these decisions made exclusively by administrators and teachers.
- Treat mistakes as a part of learning, encourage students to take academic risks, and allow students to redo work that does not meet some minimum satisfactory standard.
- Provide students with complex and challenging tasks that require comprehension and problem solving rather than tasks that require little more than rote learning and verbatim recall.
- Use cross-age tutoring, peer tutoring, and enrichment activities rather than grade retention with students who are falling behind.
- Use cooperative-learning methods rather than competition. Because so much has been written about the use of cooperative-learning techniques and their demonstrated effectiveness in raising motivation and learning, we discuss this recommendation in more detail next.

**b. Use cooperative-learning methods.**

As we pointed out in previous chapters, cooperative-learning methods have proven effective in increasing motivation for learning and self-esteem, redirecting attributions for success and failure, fostering positive feelings toward classmates, and increasing performance on tests of comprehension, reasoning, and problem solving (Johnson & Johnson, 1995; Johnson et al., 1995; Slavin, 1995). Accordingly, you may want to try one or more of the cooperative learning techniques described by David Johnson and Roger Johnson (Johnson et al., 1994), Robert Slavin (1995), and Kath Murdoch and Jeni Wilson (2004). To familiarize you with these methods, we will briefly describe the Student Teams–Achievement Divisions (STAD) method that Slavin and his associates at Johns Hopkins University devised.

STAD is one of the simplest and most flexible of the cooperative-learning methods, having been used in grades 2 through 12 and in such diverse subject areas as math, language arts, social studies, and science. As with other cooperative-learning methods, students are assigned to four- or five-member groups, with each group mirroring the makeup of the class in terms of ability, background, and gender. Once these assignments are made, a four-step cycle is initiated:

1. *Teach.* The teaching phase begins with the presentation of material, usually in a lecture-discussion format. Students should be told what it is they are going to learn and why it is important.
2. *Team study.* During team study, group members work cooperatively with teacher-provided worksheets and answer sheets.
3. *Test.* Each student *individually* takes a quiz. Using a scoring system that ranges from 0 to 30 points and reflects degree of individual improvement over previous quiz scores, the teacher scores the papers.
4. *Recognition.* Each team receives one of three recognition awards, depending on the average number of points the team earned. For example, teams that average 15 to 19 improvement points receive a GOODTEAM certificate, teams that average 20 to 24 improvement points receive a GREATTEAM certificate, and teams that average 25 to 30 improvement points receive a SUPERTEAM certificate.

The cooperative learning method Teams-Games-Tournaments is similar to STAD except that students compete in academic tournaments instead of taking quizzes.

Another popular cooperative learning technique, Jigsaw, was created by Elliott Aronson. The class is divided into groups of about five or six, each group works on the same project, and each member of a group is solely responsible for a particular part of the project. For a project on energy consumption in the United States, for example, one student of each group may be responsible for researching and reporting to the other group members on how the price of oil is determined. Another student in each group may report on the factors that determine the size and efficiency of automobiles, still another on the status of alternative energy sources, and so on. To control for the fact that some students may not listen attentively to or may criticize the reports of others in the group because of preexisting animosities (Maria thinks Brandon is a jerk because he insulted her friend last week), they are reminded that they will be taking an exam based on the content of each person's report. So it is in Maria's interest to lay aside her dislike of Brandon because he is the only source of part of the information she will be tested on. Before reporting to the other members of their group, the students from each group with identical assignments get together to share information, discuss ideas, and rehearse their presentations. They are referred to as the "expert" group. Research on Jigsaw shows improvements in listening, interpersonal relationships, and achievement when compared with traditional instruction (Aronson, 2002).

**6  Maximize factors that appeal to both personal and situational interest.**

**a.** **Find out what your students' interests are and design as many in-class and out-of-class assignments as possible around those interests.**

**b.** **Try to associate subjects and assignments with pleasurable rather than painful experiences by using such techniques as cooperative learning and constructivist approaches to teaching, as well as providing students with the information-processing tools they need to master your objectives.**

**c.** **Link new topics to information students are already likely to have or provide relevant background knowledge in creative yet understandable ways.**

**d.** **Select reading materials that are logically organized and written in an engaging style.**

**7  Try to make learning interesting by emphasizing activity, investigation, adventure, social interaction, and usefulness.**

More than thirty years ago, May Seagoe suggested an approach to motivation that is based on students' interests and is consistent with many of the motivation theories and technology tools mentioned in this chapter. Among the "points of appeal that emerge from studies of specific interests," she lists the following:

> (a) the opportunity for overt bodily activity, for manipulation, for construction, even for observing the movement of animals and vehicles of various sorts; (b) the opportunity for investigation, for using mental ingenuity in solving puzzles, for working problems through, for creating designs, and the like; (c) the opportunity for adventure, for vicarious experiences in make believe, in books, and in the mass media; (d) the opportunity for social assimilation, for contacts with others suitable to the maturity level of the child (ranging from parallel play to discussion and argument), for social events and working together, for human interest and humanitarianism, and for conformity and display; and (e) the opportunity for use of the new in real life, making the new continuous with past experience and projecting it in terms of future action. (1970, p. 25)

One approach that incorporates most or all of these features and that can be used with preschool and primary grade children is the project approach. Lillian Katz and Sylvia Chard (2000) define a project as an in-depth study of a particular topic that one or more children undertake, that extends over a period of days or weeks, and that involves children seeking answers to questions that they formulate by themselves or

*May Seagoe found that students respond with interest to school situations that are active, investigative, adventurous, social, and useful. Having members of a fifth-grade class play the roles of state government officials is an activity that includes almost all these features.*

in consultation with the teacher. Projects may involve an initial discussion that captures the students' interest (for example, discussing how a house is built); dramatic play; drawing, painting, and writing; group discussions; field trips; construction activities; and investigation activities. As many researchers (e.g., Collier, 1999) have noted, class projects for all grade levels can be designed to make use of various forms of technology. Because projects are based on children's natural interests and involve a wide range of activities, they are more likely to be intrinsically motivating.

Diane Curtis (2002) describes a fifth-grade project that helped students fulfill state curriculum standards in social studies, math, writing, and technology. Building on their interest in architecture, the students completed a project on several of the major memorial buildings in Washington, D.C. (such as those honoring Presidents Washington and Jefferson, as well as the Vietnam War Memorial). They gathered information from books, the World Wide Web, and architects about the memorials, drew computer models of them, created a timeline of construction, and researched the contributions of Jefferson and others to the writing of the U.S. Constitution. This was followed by a field trip to the U.S. capital and a presentation of their work to community members.

One potential drawback to the use of projects is the amount of time they take. To help teachers overcome that barrier, several websites offer project-based programs that provide curriculum materials, assignments, resources, and contact with experts. See, for example:

> **www.jasonproject.org**
> **www.learner.org/jnorth**
> **www.thinkquest.org**
> **http://quest.classroom.com**

As you think about how you are going to organize your lesson plans for each day and each period, you might ask yourself: "Are there ways that I can incorporate activity, investigation, adventure, social interaction, and usefulness into this presentation?" "Are there projects that I can assign to students, particularly as cooperative groups, that incorporate most of these features?" Here are some examples of techniques you might use.

**ACTIVITIES**

- Have several students go to the board. Give a rapid-fire series of problems to be solved by those at the board, as well as those at their desks. After five problems, have another group of students go to the board, and so on.
- Think of ways to move out of the classroom legitimately every now and then. Teach geometry, for instance, by asking the class to take several balls of string and lay out a baseball diamond on the side lawn of the school.

*HM TeacherPrepSPACE*

For quick links to websites mentioned here, use the Weblinks section of the textbook's student website.

**JOURNAL ENTRY**
Ways to Make Learning Active

## INVESTIGATIONS

**JOURNAL ENTRY**
Ways to Promote Investigation

- In elementary grade classrooms (and in some middle school and high school classrooms), set up a variety of learning centers with themes such as library, games, social science, cultural appreciation, and computer use and organize these with intriguing displays and materials. For example, your social science center could be stocked with maps, charts, and documents. Your computer center might include educational software such as CD-ROMs and database programs; student-created publications made with desktop publishing or word processing programs; a computer with Internet access; and lists of appropriate and interesting online sites.

- In middle school and high school classrooms, you might arrange centers that pertain to different aspects of a single subject. In a science class, for example, you might have an appreciation center stressing aesthetic aspects of science, a display center calling attention to new developments in the field, a library center consisting of attractive and provocative books, and so on.

## ADVENTURES

**JOURNAL ENTRY**
Ways to Make Learning Seem Adventurous

- Occasionally, use techniques that make learning entertaining and adventurous. Such techniques might be particularly useful when you introduce a new topic. You might employ devices used by advertisers and the creators of *Sesame Street,* for instance. Use intensity, size, contrast, and movement to attract attention. Make use of color, humor, exaggeration, and drama to introduce a new unit. Take students by surprise by doing something totally unexpected.

- The night before you introduce a new unit, redecorate part of the room. Then ask the class to help you finish it.

- Arrange a "Parade of Presidents" in which each student selects a president of the United States and presents a State of the Union message to the rest of the class, with the rest of the class taking the part of members of Congress.

- Hand out a duplicated sheet of twenty questions based on articles in each section of a morning newspaper. Students compete against each other to discover how many of the questions they can answer in the shortest period of time. Typical questions: "Why is the senator from Mississippi upset?" "Who scored the most points in the UCLA–Notre Dame basketball game?" "What city suffered widespread flood damage?"

## SOCIAL INTERACTIONS

**JOURNAL ENTRY**
Ways to Make Learning Social

- Have students pair off and ask each other questions to prepare for an exam. Do the same with difficult-to-learn material by suggesting that pairs cooperate—for example, in developing mnemonic devices or preparing flashcards—to help each other master information.

- Organize an end-of-unit extravaganza in which individuals and groups first present or display projects and then celebrate by having refreshments.

## USEFULNESS

**JOURNAL ENTRY**
Ways to Make Learning Useful

- Continually point out that what is being learned can be used outside class. Ask students to keep a record of how they use in real life what they learn in class.

- Develop exercises that make students aware that what they are learning has transfer value. Have students in an English class write a job application letter; have math students balance a checkbook, fill out an income tax form, or work out a yearly budget; have biology students think about ways they can apply what they have learned to avoid getting sick.

# THE HUMANISTIC VIEW OF MOTIVATION

*HM TeacherPrepSPACE*

For interactive Netlabs on motivation, go to the textbook's student website.

Abraham Maslow earned his Ph.D. in a psychology department that supported the behaviorist position. After he graduated, however, he came into contact with Gestalt psychologists (a group of German psychologists whose work during the 1920s and 1930s laid the foundation for the cognitive theories of the 1960s and 1970s), prepared for a career as a psychoanalyst, and became interested in anthropology. As a result of these various influences, he came to the conclusion that American psychologists who endorsed the behaviorist position had become so preoccupied with overt behavior and objectivity that they were ignoring other important aspects of human existence (hence, the term *humanistic* to describe his views). When Maslow observed the behavior of especially well-adjusted persons—or *self-actualizers*, as he called them—he concluded that healthy individuals are motivated to seek fulfilling experiences.

## Maslow's Theory of Growth Motivation

Maslow describes seventeen propositions, discussed in Chapter 1 of *Motivation and Personality* (1987), that he believes would have to be incorporated into any sound theory of *growth motivation* (or *need gratification*). Referring to need gratification as the most important single principle underlying all development, he adds that "the single, holistic principle that binds together the multiplicity of human motives is the tendency for a new and higher need to emerge as the lower need fulfills itself by being sufficiently gratified" (1968, p. 55).

Maslow elaborates on this basic principle by proposing a five-level hierarchy of needs. *Physiological* needs are at the bottom of the hierarchy, followed in ascending order by *safety, belongingness* and *love, esteem,* and *self-actualization* needs (see Figure 12.2). This order reflects differences in the relative strength of each need. The lower a need is in the hierarchy, the greater is its strength, because when a lower-level need is activated (as in the case of extreme hunger or fear for one's physical safety), people will stop trying to satisfy a higher-level need (such as esteem or self-actualization) and focus on satisfying the currently active lower-level need (Maslow, 1987).

The first four needs (physiological, safety, belongingness and love, and esteem) are often referred to as **deficiency needs** because they motivate people to act only when they are unmet to some degree. Self-actualization, by contrast, is often called a **growth need** because people constantly strive to satisfy it. Basically, **self-actualization** refers to the need for self-fulfillment—the need to develop all of one's potential talents and capabilities. For example, an individual who felt she had the capability to write novels, teach, practice medicine, and raise children would not feel self-actualized until she had accomplished all of these goals to some minimal degree. Because it is

> People are motivated to satisfy deficiency needs only when those needs are unmet

**Figure 12.2** Maslow's Hierarchy of Needs

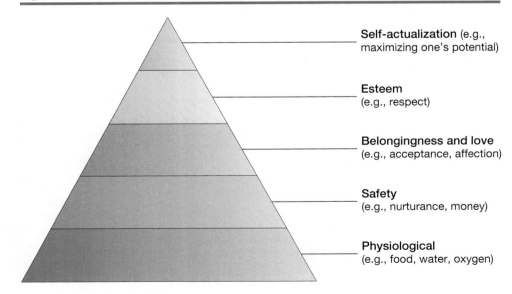

Self-actualization (e.g., maximizing one's potential)

Esteem (e.g., respect)

Belongingness and love (e.g., acceptance, affection)

Safety (e.g., nurturance, money)

Physiological (e.g., food, water, oxygen)

SOURCE: Maslow (1943).

at the top of the hierarchy and addresses the potential of the whole person, self-actualization is discussed more frequently than the other needs.

Maslow originally felt that self-actualization needs would automatically be activated as soon as esteem needs were met, but he changed his mind when he encountered individuals whose behavior did not fit this pattern. He concluded that individuals whose self-actualization needs became activated and met held in high regard such values as truth, goodness, beauty, justice, autonomy, and humor (Feist & Feist, 2001).

In addition to the five basic needs that compose the hierarchy, Maslow describes cognitive needs (such as the needs to know and to understand) and aesthetic needs (such as the needs for order, symmetry, or harmony). Although not part of the basic hierarchy, these two classes of needs play a critical role in the satisfaction of basic needs. Maslow maintains that such conditions as the freedom to investigate and learn and fairness, honesty, and orderliness in interpersonal relationships are critical because their absence makes satisfaction of the five basic needs impossible. (Imagine, for example, trying to satisfy your belongingness and love needs or your esteem needs in an atmosphere characterized by dishonesty, unfair punishment, and restrictions on freedom of speech.)

**Self-actualization depends on satisfaction of lower needs, belief in certain values**

## pause & reflect

Maslow states that for individuals to be motivated to satisfy self-actualization needs, deficiency needs have to be satisfied first. Has this been true in your experience? If not, what was different?

### Implications of Maslow's Theory

The implications of Maslow's theory of motivation for teaching are provocative. One down-to-earth implication is that a teacher should do everything possible to see that the lower-level needs of students are satisfied so that students are more likely to function at the higher levels. Students are more likely to be primed to seek satisfaction of the esteem and self-actualization needs, for example, if they are physically comfortable, feel safe and relaxed, have a sense of belonging, and experience self-esteem. William Glasser (1998), whose ideas we mentioned earlier in this chapter, states that low-achieving students have told him they would like to get better grades but don't make more of an effort because, in their eyes, teachers don't care about them or what they do.

**When deficiency needs not satisfied, person likely to make bad choices**

Only when the need for self-actualization is activated is a person likely to choose wisely when given the opportunity. Maslow emphasizes this point by making a distinction between *bad choosers* and *good choosers*. When some people are allowed freedom to choose, they seem to make wise choices consistently. Most people, however, frequently make self-destructive choices. An insecure student, for example, may choose to attend a particular college more on the basis of how close it is to home than on the quality of its academic programs.

*Theorists such as Abraham Maslow, who argue that deficiency needs such as belongingness and self-esteem must be satisfied before students will be motivated to learn, call attention to the importance of positive teacher-student relationships in the classroom.*

Growth, as Maslow sees it, is the result of a never-ending series of situations offering a free choice between the attractions and dangers of safety and those of growth. If a person is functioning at the level of growth needs, the choice will ordinarily be a progressive one. Maslow adds, however, that "the environment (parents, therapists, teachers) . . . can help by making the growth choice positively attractive and less dangerous, and by making the regressive choice less attractive and more costly" (1968, pp. 58–59). This point can be clarified by a simple diagram Maslow uses to illustrate a situation involving choice (1968, p. 47).

|  | |  |
|---|---|---|
| Enhance the dangers | | Enhance the attraction |
| **Safety** | ←— Person —→ | **Growth** |
| Minimize the attractions | | Minimize the dangers |

> Encourage growth choices by enhancing attractions, minimizing dangers

This diagram emphasizes that if you set up learning situations that impress students as dangerous, threatening, or of little value, they are likely to play it safe, make little effort to respond, or even try to avoid learning. If, however, you make learning appear appealing, minimize pressure, and reduce possibilities for failure or embarrassment, your students are likely to be willing, if not eager, to do an assigned task.

### Limitations of Maslow's Theory

Although Maslow's speculations are thought provoking, they are also sometimes frustrating. Quite often, you may not be able to determine precisely which of a student's needs are unsatisfied. Even if you *are* quite sure that a student lacks interest in learning because he feels unloved or insecure, you may not be able to do much about it. A girl who feels that her parents do not love her or that her peers do not accept her may not respond to your efforts. And if her needs for love, belonging, and esteem are not satisfied, she is less likely to be in the mood to learn.

> Teachers may be able to satisfy some deficiency needs but not others

Then again, there will be times when you can be quite instrumental in helping to satisfy certain deficiency needs. The development of self-esteem, for example, is closely tied to successful classroom achievement for almost all students. Although you may not be able to feed students when they are hungry or protect them from physical danger, you can always take steps to help them learn more effectively.

## THE ROLE OF SELF-PERCEPTIONS IN MOTIVATION

Current interest in the effects of self-perceptions on school motivation and achievement runs high and seems to have been prompted by such developments as a better understanding of the nature of self-concept and self-esteem, Albert Bandura's introduction of the self-efficacy concept, advances in the measurement of self-perceptions, and the consistent finding of a positive relationship among self-perceptions, motivation, and school achievement (Trautwein, Ludtke, Koller, & Baumert, 2006). Much of this interest can be traced to ideas published during the 1960s and 1970s by psychologists such as Abraham Maslow, Carl Rogers, and Arthur Combs. These individuals stressed that how students see and judge themselves and others plays an important part in determining how motivated they are and how much they learn.

In the next section we focus on the relationship of academic self-concept to motivation and learning. As we noted earlier in the book, self-concept is somewhat different from self-esteem, self-efficacy, and self-definition. Table 12.2 offers a quick review of these terms.

### The Role of Academic Self-Concept in Motivation and Learning

Over the years, researchers have consistently found a moderately positive relationship (called a correlation) between measures of academic self-concept and school achievement. Students who score relatively high on measures of academic self-concept tend

| Table 12.2 | Comparing Self-Definition, Self-Esteem, Self-Concept, and Self-Efficacy | |
|---|---|---|
| **Type of Self-Perception** | **Major Characteristics** | **Examples** |
| Self-definition | • The largely nonevaluative picture people have of themselves. | • "I am a sixth grader." <br> • "I am five feet one inches tall." <br> • "My favorite subject is history." |
| Self-esteem (self-worth) | • The global evaluative judgments people make of themselves. <br> • Self-description describes who you are; self-esteem indicates how you feel about that identity. | • "I am a good person." <br> • "I am happy with myself the way I am." <br> • "I feel inferior to most people." |
| Self-concept | • The evaluative judgments people make of their competence in specific areas or domains and their associated feelings of self-worth. <br> • Past-oriented. <br> • For older students, self-concepts may be hierarchically arranged. For example, academic self-concept = verbal self-concept + mathematical self-concept + science self-concept, etc. | • "I'm pretty good at sports." <br> • "I have always done well in math." <br> • "My academic skills are about average." <br> • "I get tongue-tied when I have to speak in public." |
| Self-efficacy | • The beliefs people have about their ability to carry out a specific course of action. <br> • Future-oriented. | • "I believe I can learn how to use a computer program." <br> • "I don't think I'll ever figure out how to solve quadratic equations." <br> • "I'm sure I can get at least a B in this course." |

SOURCES: Bong & Skaalvik (2003); Harter (1999); Kernis (2002); Marsh & Hattie (1996); Schunk & Pajares (2002).

---

> Self-esteem is global judgment we make of self; self-concept is judgment we make of self in specific domains; self-efficacy is belief in our ability to carry out a specific action

to have higher-than-average grades. But correlation does not imply causation. The fact that students with high academic self-concept scores tend to have high grades is not sufficient grounds for concluding that high academic self-concept causes high achievement. It is just as plausible that high achievement causes increased academic self-concept or that increases in both variables are due to the influence of a third variable. Recent work on the relationship between academic self-concept and achievement has begun to shed some light on what causes what.

> Academic self-concept and achievement can positively affect each other

On the basis of their own research with children in grades 2, 3, and 4 and of the research of others, Frédéric Guay, Herbert Marsh, and Michel Boivin (2003) propose the causal explanation depicted in Figure 12.3. These researchers maintain that academic self-concept and achievement have what are called reciprocal effects. That is, not only does prior achievement affect children's academic self-concept, but also the current strength of a child's academic self-concept influences subsequent achievement. In addition, prior achievement has a significant positive relationship with subsequent achievement, and prior self-concept has a significant positive relationship with subsequent self-concept.

Although the role of motivation was not directly tested in this study, related research suggests that the effect of academic self-concept on subsequent achievement is likely to be influenced by motivation. So a student with a strong academic self-concept for, say,

**Figure 12.3** Relationship Between Academic Self-Concept and Achievement

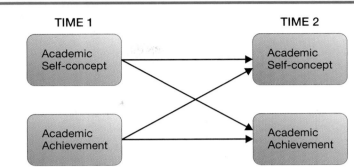

SOURCE: Adapted from Guay, Marsh, & Boivin (2003).

social studies is likely to be highly motivated to take additional courses in that subject and to use effective learning skills, which produce higher levels of achievement. At the same time, high levels of achievement strengthen the student's academic self-concept, which supports a high level of motivation, which supports high levels of achievement, and so on.

The instructional implication that flows from this research is fairly clear: teachers should design instructional programs that are aimed directly at improving both academic self-concept and achievement. The former can be accomplished by, for example, pointing out to students how well they have learned certain skills and bodies of knowledge, and the latter can be accomplished by teaching students the information-processing and self-regulation skills we discussed in the chapters on information-processing theory and social cognitive theory.

> Design instruction to improve both academic self-concept and achievement

## Limitations of the Self-Perceptions Approach

One problem with using students' views of themselves as a way of influencing their motivation and learning is the lack of useful, commercially prepared measures of self-efficacy and academic self-concept. Most of the available instruments assess global self-concept or global self-esteem. But the narrower the measure of self-perception is (such as math self-concept, science self-concept, and reading self-concept), the better it predicts motivation and achievement. One solution to this limitation is to prepare the same kinds of instruments that researchers use. This is not as difficult as it might seem.

*Students who have strong academic self-concepts often are more highly motivated and earn higher grades than students with weaker academic self-concepts.*

## Take a Stand!

### Increase Motivation by Maintaining High Self-Worth

There is no getting around the fact that classrooms are competitive places, largely because students know they are there to develop certain competencies and that some are better equipped to do so than others. Consequently, the decisions students make that affect their motivation to learn revolve around creating and maintaining a sense of self-worth. When a student pays attention to and imitates the behavior of high-achieving models, strives to develop high levels of self-efficacy in various subject areas, selects task mastery goals, attributes success and failure to appropriate combinations of effort and ability, believes that intellectual ability can be learned and refined, and strives to satisfy growth needs, the student is driven by the need to feel good about herself (self-esteem or self-worth).

The leading proponent of this view, Martin Covington, points out that students who believe they are less capable than others (in terms of acquiring the academic competencies demanded by parents, teachers, and society at large) will be less motivated to strive for high levels of achievement because of the increased risk of failure, and they will be more motivated to engage in such self-protective behaviors as reducing effort and self-handicapping.

You can establish the conditions that lead to high levels of motivation by following the many suggestions made in this and other chapters. In particular (and we know we have raised this issue before), do not turn your classroom into a cutthroat, survival-of-the-fittest contest for a limited supply of As, Bs, awards, and praise. Instead, help students acquire the skills they need to meet the learning standards established by you, your school district, and your state. Remember, your primary role in the classroom is to teach, not to sort.

#### HM TeacherPrepSPACE

Do you agree with the argument that teachers should "teach, not sort"? How will you apply your beliefs in your classroom? To delve further into this issue, see the Take a Stand! section of the textbook's student website.

Some researchers use a relatively small set of questions ("How good are you at math?" "If you were to rank all the students in your math class from the worst to the best, where would you put yourself?" "Compared with your other school subjects, how good are you at math?") and ask students to rate themselves on a 7-point scale that may range from "not at all good" to "very good" (Stipek, 2002).

Another problem is that whatever success you may have in changing a student's self-esteem and academic self-concept is likely to be slow in coming. This conclusion follows from two others. One is that changes in self-perception are best made by helping students become more effective learners than by constantly telling them they should feel good about themselves. The second conclusion is that learning how to use the cognitive skills that result in meaningful learning takes time because of their complexity and the doubts that some students will have about their ability to master these skills.

Now that you are familiar with approaches to motivation based on humanistic theories and on self-perceptions, consider the additional Suggestions for Teaching in Your Classroom that follow.

# Suggestions for Teaching in Your Classroom

## Satisfying Deficiency Needs and Strengthening Self-Perceptions

### 1 Make learning inviting to students.

Motivation researchers (e.g., Purkey & Novak, 1996; Tomlinson, 2002) maintain that students care about learning when they are invited to learn. Teachers extend such invitations when they do the following:

- Meet Maslow's safety and belonging needs. Examples of meeting students' safety and belonging needs include never ridiculing a student for lack of knowl-

**JOURNAL ENTRY**
Ways to Invite Students to Learn

edge or skills or letting other students do the same, praising students when they do well and inquiring about possible problems when they do not, relating lessons to students' interests, and learning students' names as quickly as possible.

- Provide opportunities for students to make meaningful contributions to their classroom. Examples here include having students help classmates master instructional objectives through short-term tutoring or cooperative learning arrangements and inviting students to use personal experiences and background as a way to broaden a lesson or class discussion. One classroom teacher created overhead transparencies of students' work for use as an instructional tool; this gave students the sense that they were a contributing part of a community (Gilness, 2003).
- Create a sense of purpose for the material students are required to learn. As we pointed out in Chapter 13, "Approaches to Instruction," students rarely ask "Why do I have to learn this?" (although it is uppermost in their minds), and teachers rarely offer an explanation without being prompted. One way to create purpose for a reading lesson is to engage the students in a discussion of an issue they are interested in that is at the heart of a story or novel they are about to read.
- Allow students to develop a sense of power about their learning. Students who believe that the knowledge and skills they are learning are useful to them now (using history as a tool for thinking about the present, for example), who know what constitutes good-quality work and believe themselves capable of producing it, and who know how to set goals and meet them are more likely than other students to believe they are in control of their learning.
- Create challenging tasks for students. Students who work hard, who feel they are being stretched, yet who succeed more often than not are more likely to enjoy learning and to approach future tasks with increased motivation than are students whose work is routine and consistently at a low level of difficulty.

**2** **Direct learning experiences toward feelings of success in an effort to encourage an orientation toward achievement, high self-esteem, and a strong sense of self-efficacy and academic self-concept.**

To feel successful, an individual must first establish goals that are neither so low as to be unfulfilling nor so high as to be impossible and then be able to achieve them at an acceptable level.

**a. Make use of objectives that are challenging but attainable and, when appropriate, that involve student input.**

**JOURNAL ENTRY**
Ways to Encourage Students to
Set Their Own Objectives

Although you will have primary responsibility for choosing the learning objectives for your students, you can use this process to heighten motivation by inviting your students to participate in selecting objectives or at least in thinking along with you as you explain why the objectives are worthwhile. This will tend to shift the emphasis from extrinsic to intrinsic motivation.

To help students suggest appropriate objectives, you may want to use the techniques recommended by Robert Mager (1997; discussed in Chapter 13). You might assist your students in stating objectives in terms of a time limit, a minimum number of correct responses, a proportion of correct responses, or a sample of actions.

**EXAMPLES**

- "How many minutes do you think you will need to outline this chapter? When you finish, we'll see that film I told you about."
- "George, you got six out of ten on this spelling quiz. How many do you want to try for on the retest?"

**JOURNAL ENTRY**
Ways to Help Students Master
Objectives

**b. Help students master your objectives.**

As you have seen, a student's past accomplishments on a particular task influence his or her self-efficacy and academic self-concept. Consequently, you should do whatever you can to help students achieve at an acceptable level. One important recommendation for helping students become better learners was made earlier: teach them how to create and use learning strategies. Another suggestion that will help them get the most out of their strategies is to assign moderately difficult tasks and provide the minimum amount of assistance necessary to complete the task successfully (think of Vygotsky's zone of proximal development and the concept of scaffolding).

Many of the motivational techniques we have suggested in this chapter can be enhanced by the appropriate use of technology. To conclude the chapter, we discuss research on the link between technology and motivation, and we survey a number of kinds of technology that have been shown to be useful.

**HM** *TeacherPrepSPACE*

See the Reflective Journal Questions at the textbook's student website for additional journal ideas.

# MOTIVATING STUDENTS WITH TECHNOLOGY

## Extrinsic Versus Intrinsic Motivation

Previously in this chapter, we contrasted the behavioral, or extrinsic, approach to motivation with various cognitive, or intrinsic, approaches. Our goal was not to demonstrate that one approach is inherently superior to the other but to point out how and when both approaches can profitably be used to support classroom learning. A parallel situation exists with regard to the motivating effects of technology. Behavioral psychologists, for example, argue that students who work on computer-based drill-and-practice programs are motivated by the immediate feedback they receive and the steady progress they make. Cognitive psychologists argue that involving students in fantasy environments or authentic tasks that are directed to audiences besides the teacher is intrinsically motivating because such programs and tasks give students a sense of confidence, personal responsibility, and control over their own learning (Hewitt, 2002; Hickey et al., 2001; Moreno & Mayer, 2002, 2005).

> Technology can be used to support both extrinsic and intrinsic motivation

Despite the differences in these two approaches to motivation, they are not mutually exclusive. Some of the most innovative and effective technological aids to learning combine both approaches. For example, the Jasper Woodbury series, which we mentioned in Chapter 9 on constructivist learning theory, tries to engage intrinsic motivation by giving students control over and responsibility for how they collect, analyze, and use the data presented by the program and by embedding the task in a realistic context. The accompanying extrinsic rewards include class announcements of accomplishments, student demonstrations of problem-solving strategies, teacher praise for correct problem solutions, and feedback and encouragement from peers in other schools about one's problem solutions (Barron, 2000; Cognition and Technology Group at Vanderbilt, 1996). Other types of extrinsic rewards that can be used in conjunction with other technology-based approaches to learning include membership in multimedia clubs, special computer events and fairs for parents or the community, and certificates of recognition.

## Using Technology to Increase Motivation to Learn

Now that we've established that computer-based technology can accommodate extrinsic and intrinsic approaches to motivation, we can look at whether it does, in fact, increase students' motivation to learn.

> Technology increases intrinsic motivation by making learning more interesting and meaningful

Critics of computer-based learning argue that any observed increases in student motivation are likely to be short term and due largely to the novelty of the medium. But several studies have demonstrated that the use of computer-based instruction increases students' intrinsic motivation and performance:

- Eighth graders who were judged to be candidates to drop out of school because of academic and social problems received two weeks of instruction on the Bill of

Rights. Those who were given a chance to create and present a multimedia project on the subject scored better on tests of both subject matter and attitudes toward learning than peers who engaged in traditional classroom projects (Woodul, Vitale, & Scott, 2000).

- High school seniors working in cooperative learning groups created PowerPoint presentations about poets of the Romantic period. Compared with previous classes, this group showed a much higher level of motivation for learning about this subject matter (Marr, 2000).

- In an example of the concept of flow, some students in one Nevada school were so motivated by their semester-long multimedia project on water use in their state that they came to school as early as 6 A.M. to work on it and stayed after 4 P.M. Students also conducted additional field studies to verify their work and spent weekends checking out possible sites for videotaping (Ebert & Strudler, 1996).

- High school students in Israel who were learning to use the LEGO/LOGO program exhibited the same enthusiasm for learning as did the Nevada students. LOGO is a computer programming language for moving objects in space, and LEGO is a set of plastic blocks, sensors, gears, and motors. With these components, the students designed and built such objects as robots, cars, and cranes. According to the researchers, "The laboratory became a second home to the pupils. They came to work on their projects during breaks and free hours, and even after school" (Doppelt & Barak, 2002, p. 26).

Computer-based or augmented programs are often used to improve students' literacy skills and motivation for reading and writing. For example, a technology-enhanced summer program designed to help low-achieving inner-city middle school children improve their reading and writing skills produced noticeable improvements in motivation. Students used data gathering tools, data management tools, and presentation tools to complete inquiry projects and present the results to an audience of parents, peers, and siblings. As the students shared their efforts with one another and noticed the impact of such features as computer graphics, web pages, PowerPoint slide shows, and videotaped interviews, they quickly and eagerly revised their own projects to incorporate one or more of these features (Owens, Hester, & Teale, 2002).

# VIDEO CASE   ◄◄ ▶ ►►

## Integrating Internet Research: High School Social Studies

*Watch the video, study the artifacts in the case, and reflect upon the following questions:*

1. Does the Civil Rights Scrapbook Project promote extrinsic motivation, intrinsic motivation, or both? What evidence can you cite based on observing the students in this Video Case?

2. If you were a student in this class, would you find this technology project motivating? Why or why not? What aspects of the lesson are especially motivating? What ideas do you have to make the lesson more motivating for students?

A survey of elementary grade teachers who published students' writing projects on a classroom website revealed a similar motivating effect. Students were more inclined to complete their projects and to do high-quality work when they knew it would be seen by a wider audience (Karchmer, 2001). According to one fourth-grade teacher:

Before the Internet, my children did not write as much, as writing without a purpose was not fulfilling. We have a purpose now and that makes the work more interesting for the children. They are really proud to see their work on the Internet . . . . I believe the students are being more careful with their language arts skills. Their errors are pretty easy to see, and they do not seem to have any problem with changing them. In paper and pencil writing, it is very difficult to get them to change what they are writing. (Karchmer, 2001, p. 459)

**HM TeacherPrepSPACE**

*To review this chapter, see the ACE practice tests and PowerPoint slides at the textbook's student website.*

E-mail is often used to heighten student interest and motivation through pen-pal projects that link students in different countries or locales or to coordinate inter-school projects. Celeste Oakes (1996) described how she used e-mail with her first-grade class in Nevada to correspond with students in Alaska, to ask questions of space shuttle astronauts, to collaboratively write stories with students from other schools, and to write letters to Santa Claus. Rebecca Sipe (2000) described a project in which her preservice teacher education undergraduates corresponded with tenth-grade English students, who helped the preservice students formulate realistic classroom beliefs and practices. Carole Duff (2000) described how female high school students use e-mail to get career advice, academic guidance, and personal support from a professional woman mentor.

# 13 Approaches to Instruction

*HM TeacherPrepSPACE*

*HM TeacherPrepSPACE student website* offers many helpful resources. Go to *login.cengage.com* to preview this chapter's Concept Maps and Chapter Themes.

## KEY POINTS

*These key points will help you learn the important information in this chapter. To help you study, they also appear in the margins of the pages, next to the text where they are discussed.*

### Devising and Using Objectives

- Goals are broad, general statements of desired educational outcomes
- Instructional objectives specify observable, measurable student behaviors
- Taxonomy: categories arranged in hierarchical order
- Cognitive taxonomy: knowledge, comprehension, application, analysis, synthesis, evaluation
- Taxonomy of affective objectives stresses attitudes and values
- Psychomotor taxonomy outlines steps that lead to skilled performance
- Most test questions stress knowledge, ignore higher levels of cognitive taxonomy
- Mager: state specific objectives that identify act, define conditions, state criteria
- Gronlund: state general objectives, list sample of specific learning outcomes
- Objectives work best when students are aware of them

### The Behavioral Approach to Teaching: Direct Instruction

- Direct instruction: focus on learning basic skills, teacher makes all decisions, keep students on-task, emphasize positive reinforcement
- Direct instruction involves structured, guided, and independent practice
- Direct instruction helps students learn basic skills

### The Cognitive Approach to Teaching: Facilitating Meaningful and Self-Directed Learning

- Information-processing approach: design lessons around principles of meaningful learning, teach students how to learn more effectively

- Tell students what you want them to learn and why, and how they will be tested
- Present organized and meaningful lessons
- Present new information in small chunks
- Constructivist approach: students discover how to be autonomous, self-directed learners
- Meaningful learning aided by exposure to multiple points of view
- Technology supports a cognitive approach to instruction by helping students code, store, and retrieve information

### The Humanistic Approach to Teaching: Student-Centered Instruction

- Maslow: help students develop their potential by satisfying their needs
- Rogers: establish conditions that allow self-directed learning
- Humanistic approach addresses needs, values, motives, self-perceptions
- Japanese classrooms marked by humanistic orientation, high scores on international math and science test

### The Social Approach to Teaching: Teaching Students How to Learn from Each Other

- Competitive reward structures may decrease motivation to learn
- Cooperative learning characterized by heterogeneous groups, positive interdependence, promotive interaction, individual accountability
- Cooperative learning effects likely due to stimulation of motivation, cognitive development, meaningful learning
- Students with low and average ability in mixed-ability groups outperform peers in homogeneous groups on problem-solving tests; students with high ability in homogeneous groups score slightly higher than peers in mixed-ability groups
- Successful technology applications are embedded in an active social environment

---

This chapter is concerned with helping you answer two questions: What are my objectives? (or What do I want students to know and be able to do after I complete a unit of instruction?) and How can I help students achieve those objectives? The ordering of these two questions is not arbitrary. Instructional planning should always begin with a description of what you want students to know and be able to do some weeks, or even months, after the beginning of an instructional unit. If you decide in advance what you want your students to achieve, you can

prepare lessons that logically lead to a particular result and also use evaluation techniques efficiently designed to determine what level of achievement has occurred.

Once you have a clear idea of what you are trying to accomplish with your students, you can consider how you are going to help get them there. Here is where you can use your knowledge of learning and motivation. After all, if the goal of teaching is to help students acquire and use a variety of knowledge and skills, what better way to do that than to use approaches and techniques that are consistent with what is known about how people learn and the conditions under which they learn best?

The theories that underlie the approaches to instruction described in this chapter emphasize different aspects of the learning process, and each has been supported by research. Thus no one theory is sufficiently comprehensive and powerful that you can rely exclusively on it as a guide for designing classroom instruction. To work effectively with the diversity of students you will almost certainly encounter, you will need to use a variety of instructional approaches and techniques. For some objectives and students, you may want to use a highly structured approach that is consistent with the principles of behavioral and social learning theories. For other objectives, you may want to focus on helping students develop more effective learning and problem-solving skills. You may also want students to work productively in groups and respond to you and to learning in positive ways and develop positive feelings about themselves as students. And you will probably also want to integrate computer-based technology with one or more of these approaches.

Lest you think that our recommendation of combining theories is an interesting but untested idea, this integrated approach has been put into practice by the staff of an alternative middle school in Rhode Island called the Urban Collaborative Accelerated Program (UCAP) (**http://infoworks.ride.uri.edu/2006/reports/school .asp**). The purpose of UCAP was to work with students who had been retained in a grade one or more times and were therefore at risk of dropping out of school. The most radical and striking characteristic of UCAP is the use of fifty criteria to determine whether students should be promoted to the next grade. This approach is quite consistent with the behavioral view that complex behaviors cannot be properly learned until more basic behaviors are mastered and that students must clearly and convincingly demonstrate those behaviors. It is also consistent with an approach to instruction and classroom assessment called mastery learning (which we discuss in Chapter 15 on classroom assessment). Other techniques that were used, and the approaches they represent, were: having teachers play the role of coach instead of information provider through lectures (constructivist approach, humanistic approach), the use of problem- and project-based learning (constructivist approach), and small-group learning and peer tutoring (social approach) (DeBlois, 2005). As of 2004, UCAP was meeting the achievement targets called for by No Child Left Behind and was classified by the state as a moderately performing and improving school. ●

# DEVISING AND USING OBJECTIVES

## Contrasting Objectives with Educational Goals

Goals are broad, general statements of desired educational outcomes

One way to help you understand the nature of instructional objectives is to contrast them with something with which they are often confused: educational goals. Goals are relatively broad statements of what political and educational leaders would like to see schools accomplish. Perhaps the best-known set of educational goals were those in the U.S. government's Goals 2000 program. Signed into law in 1994, Goals 2000 listed eight goals that the government hoped to achieve by the year 2000. (The current status of the Goals 2000 program is described on a website maintained by the U.S. Department of Education. It can be found at **www.ed.gov/G2K/index.html**.) Although a few of the goals were stated in measurable terms ("At least 90 percent of all students will graduate from high school"), others were much more vague in their wording, such as these:

- Students will acquire the thinking skills that will allow them to become responsible citizens, independent learners, and productive workers.
- All adults will be sufficiently literate, knowledgeable, and skilled to compete in a global economy and behave as responsible citizens.

Unfortunately, statements of this sort do not provide very useful guidelines for teachers charged with the responsibility for achieving the goals. What exactly is meant by "thinking skills" or being "sufficiently literate, knowledgeable, and skilled"? And will these terms mean the same thing to every teacher? Thinking skills, for example, could be interpreted to mean everything from memorization to problem solving.

Instructional objectives specify observable, measurable student behaviors

**Instructional objectives,** in contrast to these broad educational goals, specify the kinds of observable and measurable student behaviors that make it possible for the underlying goals to be achieved. To give teachers both a common vocabulary and a system for writing different kinds of objectives, psychologists have created organizational schemes called taxonomies.

## Taxonomies of Objectives

Awareness of the vagueness of educational goals stimulated a group of psychologists who specialized in testing to seek a better way to describe educational objectives. After experimenting with various ways to prepare lists of objectives that would be more useful to teachers than vaguely worded sets of goals, the test specialists decided to develop taxonomies of educational objectives.

Taxonomy: categories arranged in hierarchical order

A **taxonomy** is a classification scheme with categories arranged in hierarchical order. Because goals of education are extremely diverse, the decision was made to prepare taxonomies in three areas, or *domains:* cognitive, affective, and psychomotor. The taxonomy for the **cognitive domain** stresses knowledge and intellectual skills; the taxonomy for the **affective domain** concentrates on attitudes and values; and that for the **psychomotor domain** focuses on physical abilities and skills.

**Taxonomy for the Cognitive Domain**  The taxonomy for the cognitive domain was prepared by Benjamin S. Bloom, Max D. Englehart, Edward J. Furst, Walker H. Hill, and David R. Krathwohl (1956). It consists of six hierarchically ordered levels of instructional outcomes: knowledge, comprehension, application, analysis, synthesis, and evaluation. The taxonomy is described as a hierarchy because it was reasoned that comprehension relies on prior mastery of knowledge or facts, that application depends on comprehension of relevant ideas, and so on through the remaining levels. An abridged outline of the taxonomy for the cognitive domain follows:

Cognitive taxonomy: knowledge, comprehension, application, analysis, synthesis, evaluation

**Taxonomy of Educational Objectives: Cognitive Domain**

**1.0** *Knowledge.* Remembering previously learned information, such as facts, terms, procedures, and principles.

**2.0** *Comprehension.* Grasping the meaning of information by putting it into one's own words, drawing conclusions, or stating implications.

**3.0** *Application.* Applying knowledge to actual situations, as in taking principles learned in math and applying them to laying out a baseball diamond or applying principles of civil liberties to current events.

**4.0** *Analysis.* Breaking down objects or ideas into simpler parts and seeing how the parts relate and are organized. For example, discussing how the public and the private sectors differ or detecting logical fallacies in an argument.

**5.0** *Synthesis.* Rearranging component ideas into a new whole. For example, planning a panel discussion or writing a comprehensive term paper.

**6.0** *Evaluation.* Making judgments based on internal evidence or external criteria. For example, evaluating a work of art, editing a term paper, or detecting inconsistencies in the speech of a politician.

Although the cognitive domain taxonomy has served educators well for more than fifty years, research in the areas of cognitive psychology, curriculum and instruction, and assessment suggested to some that a change was in order. So in 2001 a revision was published by a group of scholars from these three areas (Anderson et al., 2001).

The revised taxonomy is organized as a two-dimensional table rather than as a cumulative hierarchy. The first dimension is called the Cognitive Process Dimension and contains mostly familiar concepts: Remember, Understand, Apply, Analyze, Evaluate, and Create. The second dimension is called the Knowledge Dimension and has four categories: Factual Knowledge, Conceptual Knowledge, Procedural Knowledge, and Metacognitive Knowledge. Each Knowledge category is composed of two

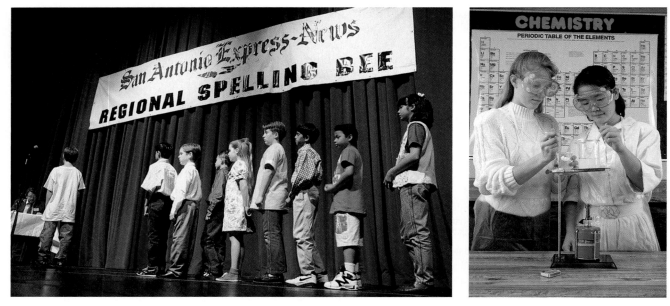

*Being familiar with the different taxonomies of objectives, such as the one for the cognitive domain, helps teachers plan lessons and create tests that require students to use different types of cognitive processes.*

or more types. Procedural Knowledge, for example, is composed of "Knowledge of subject-specific skills and algorithms," "Knowledge of subject-specific techniques and methods," and "Knowledge of criteria for determining when to use appropriate procedures."

The objectives that flow from the revised taxonomy reflect the intersection of these two dimensions. An objective that lies at the intersection of Apply and Conceptual Knowledge, for example, might be "The student will apply Vygotsky's principle of scaffolded instruction by teaching a struggling primary grade student how to multiply fractions."

Time will tell whether the revised taxonomy proves to be as popular and useful as the original.

**Taxonomy for the Affective Domain**   In addition to arranging instructional experiences to help students achieve cognitive objectives, virtually all teachers are interested in encouraging the development of attitudes and values. To clarify the nature of such objectives, a taxonomy for the affective domain was prepared (Krathwohl, Bloom, & Masia, 1964). Affective objectives are more difficult to define, evaluate, or encourage than cognitive objectives because they are often demonstrated in subtle or indirect ways. Furthermore, certain aspects of value development are sometimes considered to be more the responsibility of parents than of teachers. Finally, because values and attitudes involve a significant element of personal choice, they are often expressed more clearly out of school than in the classroom. The complete taxonomy for the affective domain stresses out-of-school values as much as, if not more than, in-school values.

The following abridgment concentrates on the kinds of affective objectives you are most likely to be concerned with as a teacher. You will probably recognize, though, that there is not much you can do to influence substantially the kinds of objectives described in the higher levels of the taxonomy because they represent a crystallization of values formed by experiences over an extended period of time.

| Taxonomy of affective objectives stresses attitudes and values |

**Taxonomy of Educational Objectives: Affective Domain**

1.0 *Receiving (attending).* Willingness to receive or attend.
2.0 *Responding.* Active participation indicating positive response or acceptance of an idea or policy.
3.0 *Valuing.* Expressing a belief or attitude about the value or worth of something.

4.0 *Organization.* Organizing various values into an internalized system.

5.0 *Characterization by a value or value complex.* The value system becomes a way of life.

**Taxonomy for the Psychomotor Domain**    Cognitive and affective objectives are important at all grade levels, but so are psychomotor objectives. Regardless of the grade level or subject you teach, at some point you are likely to want to help your students acquire physical skills of various kinds. In the primary grades, for example, you will want your students to learn how to print legibly. And in many subjects in middle school and high school, psychomotor skills (for example, driving a car, playing a violin, adjusting a microscope, manipulating a computer keyboard, operating a power saw, throwing a pot) may be essential. Recognition of the importance of physical skills prompted Elizabeth Simpson (1972) to prepare a taxonomy for the psychomotor domain. An abridged version of the taxonomy follows:

**Taxonomy of Educational Objectives: Psychomotor Domain**

1.0 *Perception.* Using sense organs to obtain cues needed to guide motor activity.

2.0 *Set.* Being ready to perform a particular action.

3.0 *Guided response.* Performing under the guidance of a model.

4.0 *Mechanism.* Being able to perform a task habitually with some degree of confidence and proficiency. For example, demonstrating the ability to get the first serve in the service area 70 percent of the time.

5.0 *Complex or overt response.* Performing a task with a high degree of proficiency and skill. For example, typing all kinds of business letters and forms quickly with no errors.

6.0 *Adaptation.* Using previously learned skills to perform new but related tasks. For example, using skills developed while using a word processor to do desktop publishing.

7.0 *Origination.* Creating new performances after having developed skills. For example, creating a new form of modern dance.

**Why Use Taxonomies?**    Using these taxonomies will help you avoid two common instructional failings: ignoring entire classes of outcomes (usually affective and psychomotor) and overemphasizing the lowest level of the cognitive domain. According to Benjamin S. Bloom, organizer and driving force of the team that prepared the first taxonomy,

> After the sale of over one million copies of the *Taxonomy of Educational Objectives—Cognitive Domain* [Bloom et al., 1956] and over a quarter of a century of use of this domain in preservice and in-service teacher training, it is estimated that over 90% of test questions that U.S. public school students are *now* expected to answer deal with little more than information. Our instructional material, our classroom teaching methods, and our testing methods rarely rise above the lowest category of the Taxonomy—knowledge. (1984, p. 13)

The next section describes how you can write and profitably use objectives.

## Ways to State and Use Objectives

Many psychologists have offered suggestions for writing and using objectives, but the following discussion is limited to recommendations made by two of the most influential writers on the subject: Robert F. Mager and Norman E. Gronlund.

**Mager's Recommendations for Use of Specific Objectives**    With the publication of a provocative and unorthodox little treatise titled *Preparing Instructional Objectives* (1962, 1997), Mager sparked considerable interest in the use of objectives. Mager emphasizes the importance of objectives by pointing out that

---

*Psychomotor taxonomy outlines steps that lead to skilled performance*

*Most test questions stress knowledge, ignore higher levels of cognitive taxonomy*

if you don't know where you're going, the best-made maps won't help you get there. . . . Without a way to communicate your instructional objectives to others:

- You wouldn't be able to decide which instructional content and procedures would help you to accomplish your objectives.
- You wouldn't be able to create measuring instruments (tests) that tell you whether your students had become competent enough to move on.
- And your students wouldn't be able to decide for themselves when to stop practicing. (1997, p. vi)

Mager then offers these suggestions for writing **specific objectives** of instruction:

1. Describe what you want learners to be doing when demonstrating achievement, and indicate how you will know they are doing it.
2. In your description, identify and name the behavioral act that indicates achievement, define the conditions under which the behavior is to occur, and state the criterion of acceptable performance.
3. Write a separate objective for each learning performance.

> **Mager: state specific objectives that identify act, define conditions, state criteria**

Here are some examples of the types of objectives Mager recommends:

> Correctly solve at least seven addition problems consisting of three two-digit numbers within a period of three minutes.
>
> Given pictures of ten trees, correctly identify at least eight as either deciduous or evergreen.
>
> Correctly spell at least 90 percent of the words on the list handed out last week.
>
> Given a computer and word processing program, set it up to type a business letter (according to the specifications provided) within two minutes.

Note that the criterion of acceptable performance can be stated as a time limit, a minimum number of correct responses, or a proportion of correct responses.

Mager's proposals were widely endorsed immediately after the publication of *Preparing Instructional Objectives*, but in time it became apparent that the very specific kinds of objectives he recommended were most useful in situations in which students were asked to acquire knowledge of factual information or to learn simple skills. Norman E. Gronlund concluded that a different type of objective was more appropriate for more complex and advanced kinds of learning.

*Mager recommends that teachers use objectives that identify the behavioral act that indicates achievement, define conditions under which the behavior is to occur, and state the criterion of acceptable performance.*

**Gronlund's Recommendations for Use of General Objectives**   Gronlund (2004) has developed a two-step procedure for writing a more general type of objective:

1. Examine what is to be learned with reference to lists of objectives such as those included in the three taxonomies. Use such lists to formulate **general objectives** of instruction that describe types of behavior students should exhibit in order to demonstrate what they have learned.

2. Under each general instructional objective, list up to five *specific learning outcomes* that provide a representative sample of what students should be able to do when they have achieved the general objective. Each learning outcome should begin with an *action verb* (such as *explain* or *describe*) that names the particular action the student is expected to take.

Gronlund: state general objectives, list sample of specific learning outcomes

To see how Gronlund's method differs from Mager's, imagine that you are teaching an educational psychology course and that you want to write objectives that reflect an understanding of the four stages of Piaget's theory of cognitive development. Figure 13.1 compares objectives you might develop using Gronlund's approach with objectives that follow Mager's method.

Gronlund gives several reasons for beginning with general objectives. First, most learning activities are too complex to be described in terms of a specific objective for every learning outcome, as Mager proposed. Second, the kind of specific objective Mager advocated may tend to cause instructors and students to concentrate on memorizing facts and mastering simple skills. As indicated earlier, these types of behaviors are at the lowest levels of the taxonomies of objectives. Third, specific objectives can restrict the flexibility of the teacher. Gronlund's objectives allow performance criteria to be kept separate from the objective so a teacher can revise performance standards as needed without having to rewrite the objective. This feature is useful if the same behavior is to be evaluated several times over the course of a unit of instruction, with successively higher levels of performance required. A fourth and final reason is that general objectives help keep you aware that the main target of your instructional efforts is the general outcome (such as comprehension, application, or analysis).

### pause & reflect

One criticism of writing objectives is that it limits the artistic side of teaching, locking teachers into a predetermined plan of instruction. Can you respond by recalling a teacher who provided objectives but was still enthusiastic, flexible, and inventive?

**Figure 13.1** Types of Objectives: Gronlund's and Mager's Approaches Compared

**Topic:** Piaget's Theory of Cognitive Development

| **Gronlund's Approach** | **Mager's Approach** |
|---|---|
| **General objective** | **Specific objectives** |
| The student will understand the characteristics of Piaget's four stages of cognitive development. | Given a list of Piaget's four stages of cognitive development, the student, within twenty minutes, will describe in his or her own words two problems that students at each stage should and should not be able to solve. |
| **Specific learning outcomes, stated with action verbs** | Given a videotape of kindergarteners presented with a conservation-of-volume problem, the student will predict the response of 90 percent of the students. |
| *Describe* in his or her own words the type of thinking in which students at each stage can and cannot engage. | Given a videotape of fifth-grade students presented with a class inclusion problem, the student will predict the response of 90 percent of the students. |
| *Predict* behaviors of students of different ages. | Given eight descriptions of instructional lessons, two at each of Piaget's four stages, the student will be able to explain in each case why the lesson would or would not succeed. |
| *Explain* why certain teaching techniques would or would not be successful with students of different ages. | |

To illustrate the differences between general objectives and specific outcomes, Gronlund has prepared lists of phrases and verbs that can be used in writing each type of objective for each of the levels of all three taxonomies of educational objectives. These lists can be found in Appendix C of Gronlund's *Writing Instructional Objectives for Teaching and Assessment* (2004).

## Aligning Assessment with Objectives and Instruction

Deciding in advance what you want your students to achieve by drawing from the various levels of the taxonomies and formulating instructional methods to help them master those objectives will be a largely wasted effort if you fail to recognize that the tests you create must also fit those objectives and methods.

As we discuss in Chapter 15 on assessment, there are several types of classroom assessment methods, each of which is most useful for measuring only *certain* outcomes. Multiple-choice, short-answer, and true-false tests are useful for measuring mastery of basic factual knowledge. For objectives that emphasize the comprehension, analysis, and synthesis levels of Bloom's Taxonomy, essay questions that call for students to summarize, compare, and contrast would be more useful. For objectives that reflect a constructivist orientation, paper-and-pencil tests are likely to be much less useful than requiring students to solve a complex problem, create a product over an extended period of time, or work productively with a small group of peers on a project. (This type of testing, called *performance assessment*, is discussed in Chapter 14, "Understanding Standardized Assessment," and Chapter 15, "Assessment of Classroom Learning.")

Here's a small example of how things can go wrong if you don't align your tests with both your objectives and your instructional methods. If you tell students that you want them to organize information into logical structures, integrate ideas into broad themes, and make connections with knowledge learned elsewhere, and you teach them how to think along those lines, but you load your tests with short-answer and multiple-choice items that require rote memorization, don't be surprised when students simply memorize facts. From their perspective, the content and level of the test items are the real objectives.

One final comment about alignment. In the first paragraph of this section, we referred to the tests you *create* rather than the tests you *use*. These two terms imply a subtle but important distinction. The best way to ensure alignment of objectives, teaching approach, and assessment is for you to be the creator of the assessment. If you use a test that somebody else has designed, such as a standardized test, it is almost a certainty that some of the items will not match your objectives or instructional approach.

## Evaluations of the Effectiveness of Objectives

Do students learn more when their teachers provide them with clearly written objectives? The answer is yes, but only under certain conditions. Reviews of research on the effectiveness of objectives (Faw & Waller, 1976; Klauer, 1984; Melton, 1978) lead to the following conclusions:

1. Objectives seem to work best when students are aware of them, treat them as directions to learn specific sections of material, and feel they will aid learning.
2. Objectives seem to work best when they are clearly written and the learning task is neither too difficult nor too easy.
3. Students of average ability seem to profit more from being given objectives than do students of higher or lower ability.
4. Objectives lead to an improvement in intentional learning (what is stressed as important) but to a decline in incidental learning (not emphasized by the teacher). General objectives of the type that Gronlund recommended seem to lead to more incidental learning than do specific objectives of the type that Mager recommended.

*HM TeacherPrepSPACE*

Need guidance in preparing lesson plans that align objectives, activities, and assessment? Check the sample lesson plans and template at the textbook's student website.

Objectives work best when students are aware of them

## pause & reflect

Based on this chapter and your own experience, do you agree that writing objectives and providing them to students are worthwhile uses of a teacher's time? If so, what steps will you take to make writing objectives a standard part of your professional behavior?

As we mentioned at the beginning of the chapter, once you have decided what it is you want your students to learn, you need to decide which approaches you will use to help them achieve those objectives. Our use of the term *approaches* is deliberate. To repeat what we said at the beginning of the chapter, different approaches to instruction are based on different theories of learning and motivation, and given the complexity of the learning process and the diversity of learners in most classrooms, no one theory can be used for all instructional purposes and for all students. So as you read through the next several sections, try to imagine how you might use each approach over the course of a school year.

## THE BEHAVIORAL APPROACH TO TEACHING: DIRECT INSTRUCTION

For behavioral psychologists, learning means acquiring new behaviors, and new behaviors are learned because of the role that external stimuli play. Thus a behavioral approach to teaching involves arranging and implementing those conditions that make it highly likely that a desired response will occur in the presence of a particular stimulus (such as reading a sentence fluently, accurately using the correct mathematical operations when faced with a long-division problem, and giving the correct English translation of a paragraph written in Spanish). Perhaps the most popular approach to teaching that is based on behavioral theory is direct instruction.

### The Nature of Direct Instruction

The underlying philosophy of **direct instruction** (sometimes called *explicit teaching*) is that if the student has not learned, the teacher has not effectively taught. This approach calls for the teacher to keep students consistently engaged in learning basic skills and knowledge through the design of effective lessons, corrective feedback, and opportunities for practice. It is most frequently used in the teaching of basic skills (for example, reading, mathematical computation, writing) and subject matter (for example, science, social studies, foreign language vocabulary) in the primary and elementary grades. It is also used to teach remedial classes at the middle school and high school levels. It is felt to be most useful for young learners, slow learners, and all learners when the material is new and difficult to grasp at first. Although there are several variations of direct instruction, the following represents a synthesis of descriptions offered by George Adams and Sigfried Engelmann (1996), Bruce Joyce and Marsha Weil (2004), Barak Rosenshine (1987), and Barak Rosenshine and Carla Meister (1994b).

The main characteristics of direct instruction include:

1. Focusing almost all classroom activity on learning basic academic knowledge and skills. Affective and social objectives, such as improved self-esteem and learning to get along with others, are either de-emphasized or ignored.
2. Having the teacher make all instructional decisions, such as how much material will be covered at one time, whether students work individually or in groups, and whether students work on mathematics during the morning and social studies during the afternoon.
3. Keeping students working productively toward learning new academic knowledge and skills (usually called being on-task) as much as possible.
4. Maintaining a positive classroom climate by emphasizing positive reinforcement and avoiding the use of aversive consequences.

Direct instruction: focus on learning basic skills, teacher makes all decisions, keep students on-task, emphasize positive reinforcement

*Teachers who subscribe to direct instruction emphasize efficient learning of basic skills through the use of structured lessons, positive reinforcement, and extensive practice.*

The goal of direct instruction is to have students master basic skills. Advocates of this method believe that students who mislearn information require substantially more time and effort to relearn concepts than would have been the case had they learned them correctly in the first place.

For obvious reasons, direct instruction is a highly structured approach to teaching and is often referred to as *teacher-directed* or *teacher-led instruction*.

## The Components of Direct Instruction

**JOURNAL ENTRY**
Using a Direct Instruction Approach

Bruce Joyce and Marsha Weil (2004) identify five general components, or phases, that make up direct instruction: orientation, presentation, structured practice, guided practice, and independent practice. These components are not derived just from theory. They reflect the techniques that effective teachers at all grade levels have been observed to use.

**Orientation**    During the orientation phase, the teacher provides an overview of the lesson, explains why students need to learn the upcoming material, relates the new subject either to material learned during earlier lessons or to their life experience, and tells students what they will need to do to learn the material and what level of performance they will be expected to exhibit.

**Presentation**    The presentation phase initially involves explaining, illustrating, and demonstrating the new material. As with all other forms of instruction based on operant conditioning, the lesson is broken down into small, easy-to-learn steps to ensure mastery of each step in the lesson sequence. Numerous examples of new concepts and skills are provided, and, consistent with social learning theory, the teacher demonstrates the kind of response students should strive for (such as a particular pronunciation of foreign vocabulary, a reading of a poem or story, the steps in mathematical operations, or how to analyze a novel for theme, character, or setting). To assist comprehension, and where appropriate, material can be presented pictorially (as slides, videotapes, on computer) or graphically (as a concept map, a timeline, or in table form). At the first sign of difficulty, the teacher gives additional explanations.

The last step of the presentation phase is to evaluate students' understanding. This is typically done through a question-and-answer session in which the questions call for specific answers, as well as explanations of how students formulated their answers. Some sort of system is used to ensure that all students receive an equal opportunity to respond to questions. Throughout the lesson, efforts are made to stay on-task and avoid nonproductive digressions.

Direct instruction involves structured, guided, and independent practice

**Structured, Guided, and Independent Practice**    The last three phases of the direct instruction model all focus on practice, although with successively lower levels of assistance. Joyce and Weil (2004) refer to these three phases as *structured practice, guided practice,* and *independent practice.* Because the level of teacher assistance is gradually withdrawn, you may recognize this progression as an attempt to apply the behavioral principle of shaping. You may also recognize it as the constructivist principle of scaffolding.

Structured practice involves the greatest degree of teacher assistance. The teacher leads the entire class through each step in a problem or lesson so as to minimize incorrect responses. Visual displays, such as overhead transparencies, are commonly used during structured practice as a way to illustrate and help students recall the components of a lesson. As the students respond, the teacher reinforces correct responses and corrects errors.

During guided practice, students work at their own desks on problems of the type explained and demonstrated by the teacher. The teacher circulates among the students, checking for and correcting any errors.

When students can correctly solve at least 85 percent of the problems given to them during guided practice, they are deemed ready for independent practice. At this point, students are encouraged to practice on their own either in class or at home. Although the teacher continues to assess the accuracy of the students' work and provide feedback, it is done on a more delayed basis.

## Getting the Most Out of Practice

Joyce and Weil (2004) offer the following suggestions to help make practice effective:

1. Shape student learning by systematically moving students from structured practice to guided practice to independent practice.
2. Schedule several relatively short but intense practice sessions, which typically produce more learning than fewer but longer sessions. For primary grade students, several five- to ten-minute sessions scattered over the day are likely to produce better results than the one or two thirty- to forty-minute sessions that middle school or high school students can tolerate.
3. Carefully monitor the accuracy of students' responses during structured practice to reinforce correct responses and correct unacceptable responses. The reason for this suggestion comes straight out of operant conditioning research. As you may recall from the chapter on behavioral learning theory, Skinner found that new behaviors are learned most rapidly when correct responses are immediately reinforced and incorrect responses are eliminated. When a learner makes incorrect responses that are not corrected, they become part of the learner's behavioral repertoire and impede the progress of subsequent learning.
4. To ensure the high degree of success that results in mastery of basic skills, students should not engage in independent practice until they can respond correctly to at least 85 percent of the examples presented to them during structured and guided practice.
5. Practice sessions for any lesson should be spread over several months. The habit of some teachers of not reviewing a topic once that part of the curriculum

has been covered usually leads to a lower quality of learning. Once again, distributed practice produces better learning than massed practice.

6. Space practice sessions close together during structured practice but further and further apart for guided practice and independent practice.

## Effectiveness of Direct Instruction

George Adams and Sigfried Engelmann (1996) conducted a review of thirty-seven studies of direct instruction and reported strong effects. On average, students who received direct instruction scored at the 81st percentile on an end-of-unit exam, whereas their conventionally taught peers scored at the 50th percentile.

More recent studies of direct instruction have been done in urban schools that enroll high percentages of minority students and students of low socioeconomic status (SES). These studies have produced positive but more modest results. For example, a version of direct instruction called the BIG Accommodation model (because instruction is organized around "big ideas") was implemented in a California middle school that served high-poverty neighborhoods. After one year, the percentage of seventh- and eighth-grade students who were reading at the fifth-grade level or lower declined, whereas the percentage reading at the sixth- and seventh-grade or higher levels increased. Similar results were obtained for math achievement scores. In percentage terms, the most dramatic increase occurred among limited-English-proficient learners. Before the program was implemented, only 10 percent scored at grade level (seventh grade or above) on reading and math tests. One year later that figure rose to about 36 percent. The largest gains in grade equivalent scores were made by White (2.1), American Indian (1.7), and Latino (1.6) students (Grossen, 2002).

| Direct instruction helps students learn basic skills

## Using Technology to Support Behavioral Approaches to Instruction

The computer-based approach to instruction that uses behavioral learning principles emphasizes specific performance objectives, breaking down learning into small steps, shaping student success, using immediate feedback and consistent rewards, and predefining assessment techniques. Learning is viewed much like an industrial assembly line: information is transferred efficiently from a computer program to a waiting student.

Most of the drill-and-practice computer-assisted instruction tools and integrated learning systems mentioned in the chapter on behavioral learning theory fit within this framework (Mazyck, 2002; Ysseldyke et al., 2003), as would multimedia technology if used simply to embellish a lecture with new pictures or sounds. Although this approach to the use of technology in instruction may be perceived as rote, boring, and dehumanizing, it can prove valuable if you are interested in accurate and efficient learning of basic facts and skills.

# THE COGNITIVE APPROACH TO TEACHING: FACILITATING MEANINGFUL AND SELF-DIRECTED LEARNING

The focus of cognitive learning theories is the mind and how it works. Hence, cognitive psychologists are primarily interested in studying those mental processes that expand our knowledge base and allow us to understand and respond to the world differently. In this section, we will lay out two approaches to instruction that are based on different forms of cognitive theory: information processing and constructivism. The information-processing approach to teaching involves implementing those conditions that help students effectively transfer information from the "outside" (a text or lecture, for example) to the "inside" (the mind), whereas the constructivist approach focuses on providing students opportunities to create their own meaningful view of reality.

## The Nature and Elements of an Information-Processing Approach

As we noted previously in the book, information-processing theory focuses on how human beings interpret and mentally manipulate the information they encounter. Research shows that, for information to be meaningfully learned, it must be attended to, its critical features must be noticed, and it must be coded in an organized and meaningful way so as to make its retrieval more likely (Joyce & Weil, 2004; Marx & Winne, 1987; Pressley, Woloshyn, & Associates, 1995).

Information-processing approach: design lessons around principles of meaningful learning, teach students how to learn more effectively

The approach to teaching that flows from information-processing theory has two main parts. First, design lessons and gear teaching behaviors to capitalize on what is known about the learning process. As you will see, this part of the information-processing approach has much in common with the behavioral approach that we just covered. Both approaches direct you to structure the classroom environment in a certain way (and to use some of the same tactics) to improve the effectiveness and efficiency of learning. Second—and this is what makes the information-processing approach unique—make students aware of how they learn and how they can use those processes to improve their classroom performance. Following are several suggestions for helping students become more effective processors of classroom instruction.

**JOURNAL ENTRY**
Using an Information-Processing Approach to Instruction

**Communicate Clear Goals and Objectives**   In previous chapters, we pointed out that motivation for learning is highest when students can relate new information to what they already know and to out-of-school experiences. The ability to make these links is what makes learning in general, and school learning in particular, meaningful. The first question that students ask themselves when they take a new course, encounter a new topic, or are asked to learn a new skill is, "Why do I have to learn this?"

Unfortunately, many teachers seem unaware of the need to explain clearly to students the immediate and larger purposes of learning most of a school's curriculum. Seymour Sarason (1993), who has written extensively and persuasively about the problems of education (including teacher education) and the need for reform, notes that "although that kind of question occurs to every child, I have never heard a student ask that question out loud, just as I have never observed a teacher address the issue" (p. 224). But some teachers do recognize the value of communicating clear goals. Margaret Metzger (1996), a veteran high school teacher, notes that teachers have to convince students that what they learn in school is important and relevant to their lives outside school, both now and in the future.

Tell students what you want them to learn and why, and how they will be tested

At the beginning of each lesson, tell students what you want them to accomplish, why you think it's important that they learn this knowledge or skill, and how you are going to assess their learning. If you intend to use paper-and-pencil tests, tell them what content areas will be covered, what kinds of questions you will include (in terms of the levels of Bloom's Taxonomy), and how many of each type of question will be on the test. Without this information, students will be unable to formulate a rational approach to learning and studying because they will be forced to guess about these features. They may, for example, take your general directive to "learn this material for the test" as a cue to memorize, when you expected them to be able to explain ideas in their own words. If you intend to use performance measures, tell students the conditions under which they will have to perform and what criteria you will use to judge their performance.

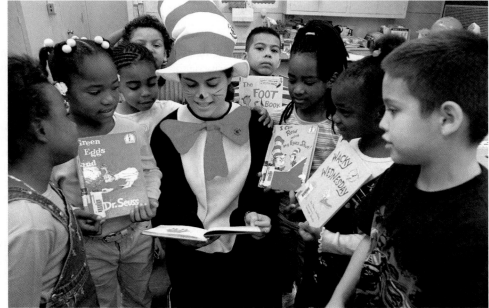

*One implication of the information-processing approach to instruction is to use attention-getting devices since information not attended to will not be learned.*

**Use Attention-Getting Devices**   Information-processing theory holds that material not attended to is not processed, and material that is not processed is not stored in memory. Consequently, you should use (but not overuse) a variety of attention-getting devices. The suggestion we just made to explain the purpose of a lesson, what students will be held accountable for learning, and how student learning will be assessed will likely capture the attention of some students. But once you are into a lesson, you may need to gain and maintain students' attention repeatedly.

The first Suggestions for Teaching in Your Classroom section ("Helping Your Students Become Efficient Information Processors") in Chapter 8, "Information-Processing Theory," mentioned a few devices for capturing students' attention. Here are several more:

- Orally emphasize certain words or phrases by raising or lowering your voice.
- Use dramatic gestures.
- Underline key words and phrases that you write on a chalkboard or whiteboard.
- When discussing the work of important people, whether in science, math, social studies, or history, dress up to look like the person and speak as you think the person might have spoken.

**Emphasize Organization and Meaningfulness**   Research studies have repeatedly found that students learn and recall more information when it is presented in an organized format and a meaningful context. Information is organized when the components that make it up are linked together in some rational way. If you teach high school physics, you can organize material according to major theories or basic principles or key discoveries, depending on your purpose. For history, you can identify main ideas and their supporting details or describe events as a chain of causes and effects. Just about any form of organization would be better than having students memorize names, dates, places, and other facts as isolated fragments of information.

A popular method for organizing and spatially representing the relationships among a set of ideas is *concept mapping* (as we noted earlier in Chapter 10, "Social Cognitive Theory"). This technique involves specifying the ideas that make up a

| Present organized and meaningful lessons

**Figure 13.2** Two Concept Maps Constructed from Identical Concepts

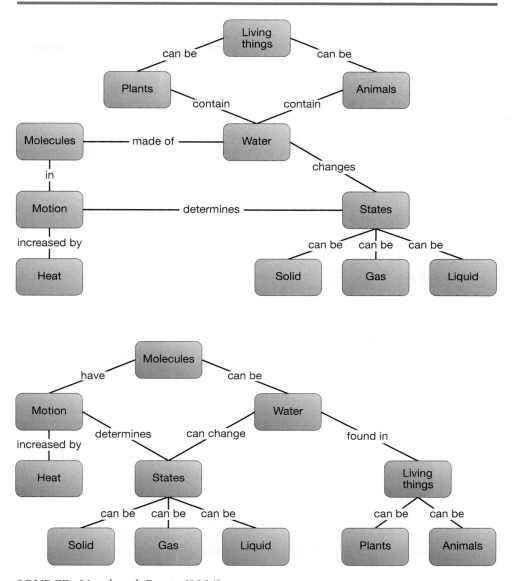

SOURCE: Novak and Gowin (1984).

topic and indicating with lines how they relate to one another. Figure 13.2 is a particularly interesting example of both organized knowledge and a constructivist view of learning. (We will take a further look at this latter angle when we discuss constructivist approaches.)

As we pointed out in Chapter 8, meaningful learning results in richer and more stable memory representations and occurs more readily when information can be related to familiar ideas and experiences. Several techniques are known to facilitate meaningful learning:

- Using some form of overview or introduction that provides a meaningful context for new material
- Using concrete examples and analogies to illustrate otherwise abstract ideas
- Using visually based methods of representing information, such as maps, graphs, three-dimensional models, and illustrations

- Stressing practical applications and relationships to other subjects (you may recall from a previous chapter that this tactic is used to help adolescent girls remain interested in science)

### Present Information in Learnable Amounts and Over Realistic Time Periods

When students struggle to master the information they are expected to learn, the problem sometimes arises simply from an excess of information being presented to them at once—that is, from too great an external demand. At other times, the student's working (short-term) memory is strained because of the nature of the task itself: for instance, if the task has several components that all have to be monitored. By taking the nature of the task into consideration, you can judge how much information to expect your students to learn in a given time.

For tasks in which a set of discrete elements must be learned in a one-at-a-time fashion, such as learning foreign language vocabulary or the symbols of chemical elements, the demand on working memory and comprehension is low because the elements are independent. Learning the meaning of one word or symbol has no effect on learning any of the others. As long as the external load on working memory is kept reasonable by limiting the number of words or symbols that students have to learn at any time, learning problems should be minimal.

Other tasks make greater demands on working memory because their elements interact. Learning to produce and recognize grammatically correct utterances ("The cat climbed up the tree" versus "Tree the climbed cat up the") is a task that places a higher demand on working memory because the meaning of all the words must be considered simultaneously in order to determine if the sentence makes sense. For such tasks, keeping the amount of information that students are required to learn at a low level is critically important because it leaves the student with sufficient working memory to engage in schema construction (Sweller et al., 1998).

| Present new information in small chunks

One instructional recommendation that flows from this analysis is the same as one of the recommendations for direct instruction: break lessons into small, manageable parts and don't introduce new topics until you have evidence that students have learned the presented material. A second recommendation is to build into lessons opportunities for students to write about, discuss, and use the ideas they are learning. By monitoring the accuracy of their responses, you will also have the information you need to judge whether it is time to introduce new ideas. Finally, arrange for relatively short practice sessions spread over several weeks rather than one or two long practice sessions, because distributed practice leads to better learning than massed practice.

### Facilitate Encoding of Information into Long-Term Memory

High-quality learning rarely occurs when students adopt a relatively passive orientation. As we pointed out in Chapter 8, many students do little more than read assigned material and record ideas in verbatim form. They spend little time thinking about how ideas within topics and between topics relate to one another or to concepts they have already learned. One reason is that many students simply do not know what else to do with information. Another reason is that teachers do little to support the kind of encoding that results in more meaningful forms of learning. Recall the study we mentioned that found that teachers in primary grades through middle school provided students with suggestions for processing information less than 10 percent of the time and with explanations for the suggestions they did give less than 1 percent of the time. To help your students encode information for more effective storage in and retrieval from long-term memory, incorporate the following techniques into your classroom instruction:

- Present information through such different media as pictures, videotape, audiotape, live models, and manipulation of physical objects.

## pause & reflect

In Chapter 8, on information-processing theory, we noted that elementary-grade teachers rarely give students instruction in how to process information effectively. One reason is that teacher-education programs typically provide little or no coursework on this subject. Is this true of your program? What can you do when you teach to make full use of information-processing principles?

- Use lots of examples and analogies (to foster elaboration).
- Prompt students to elaborate by asking them to put ideas in their own words, relate new ideas to personal experience, and create their own analogies.

**Practice What You Preach** As we pointed out in discussing social learning theory, a great deal of learning takes place by observing and emulating a model. Because teachers are generally perceived by students as being competent, in a high-status occupation, and having power, their behaviors are likely to be noticed and imitated. This is especially true when the behaviors that teachers model are important to a student's classroom success. If you are convinced that how students process information plays a major role in how well they learn that information, then you should clearly and explicitly demonstrate how to analyze a task, formulate a learning plan, use a variety of learning tactics (such as mnemonics, summarizing, self-questioning, note taking, concept mapping), monitor the effectiveness of those tactics, and make changes when the results are unsatisfactory.

## The Nature and Elements of a Constructivist Approach

In previous chapters, we noted that the essence of constructivist theory is that people learn best by creating their own understanding of reality. Using such characteristics as existing knowledge, attitudes, values, and experiences as filters, people interpret current experience in a way that seems to make sense to them at the time. As Figure 13.2 demonstrates by constructing two different concept maps from an identical set of concepts, knowledge can be organized in any number of ways, and the scheme one creates will reflect one's purpose or focal point. Thus some students understand that the Jane Austen novel *Sense and Sensibility* is as much a satire of the paternalistic class system of 1800s England as it is a love story, whereas other students see it only as a love story, and a boring one at that. The goal of constructivist-oriented teaching, then, is to provide a set of conditions that will lead students to construct a view of reality that both makes sense to them and addresses the essence of your objectives (Delgarno, 2001).

A brief description of five of the more prominent elements that help define a constructivist-oriented classroom follows. Although two of these elements reflect a social constructivist orientation, bear in mind that the goal of both cognitive and social constructivism is the same: to help students become more effective thinkers and problem solvers by helping them construct richer and more meaningful schemes. A social constructivist orientation simply gives greater weight to the role of social interaction in this process.

**JOURNAL ENTRY**
Using a Constructivist Approach to Instruction

**Provide Scaffolded Instruction Within the Zone of Proximal Development** To review quickly what we said previously in the book, the zone of proximal development is the difference between what a learner can accomplish without assistance and what can be accomplished with assistance. As an example, consider the case of a youngster who has been given her first bicycle. Because the child has no experience with balancing herself on a two-wheeled bike, her parents know she will fall quite a few times before learning how to balance, steer, and pedal at the same time. To avoid injury and loss of motivation, one parent holds the bike upright and helps the child steer in a straight line while she figures out how to monitor her balance and make the necessary adjustments. This is done initially at very low speeds, with the parent firmly holding the frame of the bike. Gradually, the child is allowed to pedal faster, and the parent loosens his grip on the bike. Eventually, the parent does little more than run alongside the bike, and then he withdraws altogether.

The value of scaffolding was demonstrated in a study (Hardy, Jonen, Möller, & Stern, 2006) in which third graders received either high or low levels of instructional support on a lesson about density and buoyancy (e.g., Why does a large iron ship float?). In the high-instructional-support condition, the teacher sequenced the material into consecutive units, decided when certain instructional materials and objects would be available, pointed out contradictory statements made by the students, and summarized their conclusions. In the low-instructional-support condition, students were given a variety of materials and objects and worked in small groups to conduct experiments. The teacher's major role in the low-support condition was to provide support for the process of investigation. When tested on their understanding of the concepts of density and buoyancy, both groups significantly outscored an uninstructed control group. But one year later, the high-support group demonstrated a better grasp of these concepts than did the low-support group.

This common example illustrates two related points about teaching from a constructivist perspective: instruction should demand more than what a student is capable of doing independently, and, because of these demands, instruction should be scaffolded. That is, teachers should provide just enough support, through such devices as explanations, modeling, prompting, offering clarifications, and verifying the accuracy of responses, that the learner can successfully complete the task. As students indicate that they have begun to internalize the basic ideas and procedures of the lesson, the scaffolding is gradually withdrawn (Brooks & Brooks, 2001; Shapiro, 2003).

| Constructivist approach: students discover how to be autonomous, self-directed learners

**Provide Opportunities for Learning by Discovery**   By its very nature, constructivism implies the need to let students discover things for themselves. But what things? According to Jerome Bruner, whose pioneering work we mentioned in Chapter 9, on constructivist learning theory, the process of discovery should be reserved for those outcomes that allow learners to be autonomous and self-directed. These include understanding how ideas connect with one another, knowing how to analyze and frame problems, asking appropriate questions, recognizing when what we already know is relevant to what we are trying to learn, and evaluating the effectiveness of our strategies. The case we cited in Chapter 9 of the fifth-grade teacher who wanted his students to understand the relationship between the circumference of a circle and its diameter is a good example of how these outcomes can be learned by guided discovery.

| Meaningful learning aided by exposure to multiple points of view

**Foster Multiple Viewpoints**   Given the basic constructivist premise that all meaningful learning is constructed and that everyone uses a slightly different set of filters

*Adopting a constructivist approach to teaching means arranging for students to work collaboratively in small groups on relevant problems and tasks, encouraging diverse points of view, and providing scaffolded instruction.*

with which to build his or her view of reality, what we refer to as knowledge is actually a consensus of slightly different points of view. Thus another element of a constructivist approach to teaching is to help students understand that different views of the same phenomena exist and that they can often be reconciled to produce a broader understanding.

The technique of **cooperative learning** is another way to expose students to peers who may have different views about the "right" way to do something or the "truth" of some matter and help them forge a broader understanding that is acceptable to all members of the group. Consider, for example, a group of college students who, as part of a science methods course, were asked to figure out how to generate electricity for a home using windmills, with the condition that batteries could not be used. Some members of the group were stumped because they couldn't figure out how to supply the house with a constant supply of electricity in the absence of a battery. Their inability to solve this problem was due to their narrow conception of an energy storage device—the kinds of batteries that are used to power such things as toys, flashlights, and cars. But other members of the group maintained that the function of a battery could be performed by any device that stored energy, such as a spring or a tank of hot water, thereby helping the rest of the group to see a different and broader truth (Brooks & Brooks, 2001). In the last major section of this chapter, we describe cooperative learning in considerable detail.

**Emphasize Relevant Problems and Tasks**  Can you recall completing a class assignment or reading a chapter out of a textbook that had no apparent relevance to anything that concerned you? Not very interesting or exciting, was it? Unfortunately, too many students perceive too much of schooling in that light. One constructivist remedy is to create interest and relevance by posing problems or assigning tasks that are both challenging and realistic. One basic purpose of emphasizing problems and tasks that are relevant to the lives of students is to overcome the problem of inert knowledge, mentioned in Chapter 9 on constructivism. Constructivists believe that the best way to prepare students to function effectively in real-life contexts is to embed tasks in contexts that come as close as possible to those of real life (Delgarno, 2001; Duffy & Cunningham, 1996).

Problems can be challenging either because the correct answer is not immediately apparent or because there is no correct answer. The ill-structured problems and issues that we described previously are, by their nature, challenging and realistic and do not have solutions that everyone perceives as being appropriate and useful. But if you assign students an ill-structured task to investigate, pose it in such a way that they will see its relevance. For example, instead of asking high school students to debate the general pros and cons of laws that restrict personal freedoms, have them interview their community's mayor, chief of police, business owners, and peers about the pros and cons of laws that specify curfews for individuals under a certain age and that prohibit such activities as loitering and the purchase of alcohol and tobacco. Because many adolescents consider themselves mature enough to regulate their own behavior, analyzing and debating laws that are intended to restrict certain adolescent behaviors is likely to produce a fair amount of disequilibrium.

**Encourage Students to Become Self-Directed Learners**  According to constructivist and humanistic theory (which we discuss later in this chapter), students should, under the right circumstances, be able to direct more of their learning than they typically do. One important condition that paves the way for students becoming more self-directed is the way in which teachers interact with students. Students in one study (Reeve & Jang, 2006) were more likely to feel as if they were in control of their own learning when teachers engaged in such behaviors as giving students time to work on a task in their own ways, giving students the opportunity to talk, encouraging students to complete tasks, listening to students, and being responsive to students' questions. By contrast, student autonomy was more likely to be negatively related to such teacher behaviors as giving students the solutions to problems or the answers to questions, giving students commands and directions, telling students they should or should not do something, and asking students such controlling questions as, "Can you do it the way I showed you?"

If you still believe, despite the findings cited in the preceding paragraph, that school-age children simply don't have the emotional maturity and cognitive skills necessary to direct more of their own learning, a program for eighth graders in Radnor, Pennsylvania, called *Soundings* has illustrated its feasibility (Brown, 2002). The program is built around a set of questions that students have identified as being of interest and importance to them. Students then help the teacher develop the curriculum, study methods, and assessments.

In line with humanistic theory, the first goal of every school year is the development of safe and trusting relationships among students and between the students and the teacher. This goal is accomplished by having pairs of students interview each other and then introduce the other student to the class; by having students interview the teacher; and by using cooperative games. Then the teachers, who act as coordinators of the students' efforts, train students to ask meaningful and insightful questions (for example, "Why do we eat breakfast?" "Who decided which foods would be breakfast foods?" "Do people in all cultures eat the same foods for breakfast?") that flow from two general questions: "What questions and concerns do you have about yourself?" and "What questions and concerns do you have about the world?"

Working in small groups, students examine their own questions as well as those of their classmates, identify common questions that will be the subject of a large-group discussion, and write their questions on large sheets that are posted on a wall and viewed by the other students in class. After viewing all the lists and discussing common themes and their importance, the students create a prioritized list of themes to study throughout the year (such as violence in our culture, medical issues affecting our lives, and surviving alien environments). Students then develop a timeline for studying the selected topics, block out time periods on the calendar, and join a small group that is interested in one of the topics.

## The Challenges to Being a Constructivist Teacher

Constructivist-oriented approaches to teaching run counter to the dominant didactic approach in which the teacher transmits established, accumulated knowledge to students through lecture and demonstration and students incorporate that knowledge largely through drill-and-practice exercises. Consequently, teachers interested in adopting a constructivist approach will have to successfully negotiate a set of challenges that Mark Windschitl (2002) describes as conceptual, pedagogical, cultural, and political.

The conceptual challenge is to fully understand the theoretical foundation on which constructivism rests and to reconcile current pedagogical beliefs with constructivist beliefs. This involves, for example, understanding the difference between cognitive and social constructivism and such concepts as cognitive apprenticeship, scaffolding, situated learning, and negotiated meaning. A solid grasp of constructivist theory will also help teachers avoid misconceptions: for instance, that direct instruction can never be used, that students must always be physically and socially active to learn, that all ideas and interpretations offered by students are equally valid, and that constructivist teaching avoids rigorous assessment practices.

The pedagogical challenge has several facets:

- Constructivist teachers need to understand how different students think, how complete each student's knowledge is about a subject, how accurate that knowledge is, and how aware students are about the state of their own knowledge.
- Teachers must know how to use a variety of methods to support understanding during problem-based activities. These methods include modeling; providing prompts,

probes, and suggestions that differ in their explicitness; providing problem-solving rules of thumb; and using technology to organize and represent information.

- Teachers must guide students to choose meaningful projects or issues to investigate that are sufficiently complex, intellectually challenging, and related to the theme of the particular subject under study.
- Teachers have to teach students how to work productively in collaborative activities even though some students may be uninterested in or even opposed to working with others.
- Teachers need to have a deep enough understanding of a subject to be able to guide students who become puzzled by an observation to an explanation (as in the case of students who wonder why seedlings grow taller under weaker light than under stronger light).
- Last, constructivist teachers need to know how to use a wide range of alternative assessment devices, such as interviews, observations, student journals, peer reviews, research reports, art projects, the building of physical models, and participation in plays, debates, and dances.

The cultural challenge pertains to the implicit classroom norms that govern the behavior of teachers and students. As noted, the dominant approach to instruction is a didactic one in which established facts and procedures are transmitted from an expert (the teacher) to novices (students). The classroom culture that flows from this model is one in which teachers talk most of the time while students sit, are quiet and attentive, do seatwork, and take tests. A constructivist classroom, on the other hand, is characterized by inquiry, collaboration among students, use of the teacher as a resource, explanations of points of view and solutions to problems to others, and attempts to reach consensus about answers and solutions. The major challenge for teachers is to recognize that their beliefs about what constitutes an ideal classroom are likely to have been shaped by their experiences as students in traditional classrooms.

The political challenge is to convince those who control the curriculum and influence teaching methods (school board members, administrators, other teachers, and parents) that constructivist teaching will satisfy state learning standards, is consistent with the content of high-stakes tests, and will help students meaningfully learn the key ideas that underlie various subjects. Should you run into this problem, you might cite a research study or two that supports constructivist teaching. For example, third graders in Germany whose teachers used a constructivist approach scored higher on a test of mathematical word problems and at the same level on a test of arithmetic computation problems as third graders whose teachers used the traditional direct-transmission approach (Staub & Stern, 2002).

The technology section that follows presents some additional ideas for embedding learning in realistic settings.

## Using Technology to Support Cognitive Approaches to Instruction

As educators begin to understand and address cognitive learning theories, the focus of computer technology is shifting from remediating learner skill deficiencies and rehearsing basic skills to finding ways to help the learner build, extend, and amplify new knowledge (Grabe & Grabe, 2007; Jonassen et al., 2003). Your willingness and readiness to use today's technology for this purpose is likely to be partly a function of the extent to which you use computer technology to meet personal and professional goals. Fourth- and eighth-grade teachers who reported higher levels of classroom technology use and personal computer use were more likely to use constructivist teaching practices than their peers who reported lower levels of technology use (Rakes, Fields, & Cox, 2006).

*Technology supports a cognitive approach to instruction by helping students code, store, and retrieve information*

**Helping Students Process Information**   An information-processing approach to instruction uses technology to minimize the cognitive demands of a task; to help learners form schemas, or patterns, of information; to extend or augment thinking in new directions; and to supply information overviews and memory cues (Grabe & Grabe, 2007). The programs for outlining and note taking mentioned in Chapter 8 on information-processing theory are consistent with this approach, as are electronic encyclopedias (for example, Grolier's *Multimedia Encyclopedia*), hypermedia databases that contain conceptual resources such as timelines, information maps, and overviews, and concept mapping software such as Inspiration that helps students organize their knowledge and ideas (Delgarno, 2001).

**Discovery and Exploratory Environments**   Computers are not just tools to transmit or represent information for the learner; they also provide environments that allow for discoveries and insights. In such an **exploratory environment,** students might explore exciting information resources on the Web, enter simulations or microworlds like LEGO-LOGO, browse and rotate objects in a hypermedia or web database, and use imaging technologies to explore inaccessible places (such as underwater canyons or planet surfaces).

For instance, the Geometric Supposer is an exploratory tool that students can use to construct, manipulate, and measure different geometric figures and relationships. High school juniors and seniors who used the Geometric Supposer for an academic year in their plane geometry course achieved significantly higher scores on a geometry test than a comparable group that covered the same topics without the aid of any computer programs (Funkhouser, 2002/2003). Another exploratory tool, GenScope, was designed to help students better understand the principles of genetics. High school students in technical biology and general life science courses who used the GenScope program performed significantly better than did students in classes without the program on a test of genetic reasoning (Hickey, Kindfield, Horwitz, & Christie, 2003).

**Guided Learning**   Although students can use modeling programs and simulations to plan experiments, take measurements, analyze data, and graph findings, there is still a need for teacher scaffolding and guidance in support of the learning process (Delgarno, 2001). In these **guided learning** environments, teachers might help students set goals, ask questions, encourage discussions, and provide models of problem-solving processes. Such teachers provide a clear road map of the unit at the beginning, clear expectations and sequencing of activities, continued reinforcement and guidance, teacher modeling, opportunities for students to practice problem-solving steps, reflection on learning, and regular checking and sharing of student progress. (Note how this approach combines elements of the behavioral and social cognitive approaches.)

One guided learning environment, the Higher Order Thinking Skills program (HOTS), focuses on higher-order thinking skills among at-risk youths in grades 4 through 8 (Pogrow, 1990, 1999, 2005). HOTS was designed around active learning, Socratic questioning, and reflection activities in using computers, and attempts to improve four key thinking processes: (1) metacognition, (2) inferential thinking, (3) transfer of learning, and (4) synthesis, or combining information from different sources into a coherent whole. Instead of the rote computer-based drills that these students would normally receive, they are prompted to reflect on their decision-making process while using computer tools. Teachers do not give away the answers but instead draw out key concepts by questioning students or telling them to go back and read the information on the computer screen. The developer of HOTS, Stanley Pogrow, calls this "controlled floundering," or leading students into frustration so that they have to reflect on the information on the screen to solve a problem. In effect, the learning dialogues and conversations between the teacher and student are the keys to learning here, not student use of the computer, as small-group discussion allows students to compare strategies and reflect on those that work. One reason for this program's emphasis on Socratic questioning and reflection is the finding, mentioned in Chapter 4 on culture and cognition, that the amount of discourse in low-SES households is often significantly less than in middle- and upper-SES households and that this factor is thought to contribute to these students' lower levels of achievement in school.

Pogrow (1999) reports that students in the HOTS program record year-to-year gains that are twice those of the national average on standardized tests of reading and math and three times those of control groups on tests of reading comprehension. Approximately 15 percent of HOTS students make the honor rolls in their schools. Gains in self-concept, as well as in thinking skills, have also been reported (Eisenman & Payne, 1997). Additional information on the HOTS program can be found at **www.hots.org**.

**HM** *TeacherPrep**SPACE***

For direct links to the HOTS site and others mentioned in this chapter, go to the Weblinks section at the textbook's student website.

**Problem- and Project-Based Learning**   Another way to implement constructivist trends in education is to use technology for **problem-based learning (PBL)**, an instructional method that requires learners to develop solutions to real-life problems. Computer-based problem-solving programs typically provide students with story problems, laboratory problems, or investigation problems. Story problem programs are usually tutorials and are very much like the math story problems you probably encountered in school. Laboratory problems are typically simulations of laboratory science problems, such as chemistry or biology. Investigation problems are set in realistic environments (microworlds) and may involve such varied subject areas as astronomy, social studies, environmental science, and anthropology (Jonassen et al., 2003). When using PBL with technology, students can plan and organize their own research while working collaboratively with others.

Although PBL has its roots in medical and business school settings, it has been successfully adapted to the elementary, middle school, and high school grades. Problem-solving programs that are based on constructivist principles and are most likely to foster meaningful learning will do the following:

- Encourage students to be active learners, engaging in such behaviors as making observations, manipulating objects, and recording the results of their manipulations
- Encourage students to reflect on their experiences and begin to construct mental models of the world
- Provide students with complex tasks that are situated in real-world settings
- Require students to state their learning goals, the decisions they make, the strategies they use, and the answers they formulate
- Require students to work in cooperative groups in which there is a considerable amount of social interaction (Hung, 2002; Jonassen et al., 2003)

Technology is also being used to support project-based learning. Project-based learning provides structure by giving students a project or a problem, along with project goals and deadlines. A study conducted in Holland with sixteen- and seventeen-year-old high school students illustrates this approach. The students were given five hours to write an essay of approximately 750 words on how the behavior of Dutch youths changed during the 1950s and 1960s. Although the students worked in pairs, they did so at their own computers and interacted by means of a chat facility and a shared draft of the essay that each one could edit. They were supplied with such computer-based resources as excerpts from textbooks, interpretations of historians, photos, tables, and interviews. Half the students (those in the explanatory condition) were asked to explain why the behavior of youths changed during the 1950s and 1960s, whereas the other half (those in the evaluative condition) were asked to judge whether those changes were revolutionary. As expected, the condition to which students were assigned shaped the content of their discussions. Students in the explanatory condition talked significantly more about the reasons for the change in behavior, and those in the evaluative condition talked more about their particular points of view (van Drie, van Boxtel, & van der Linden, 2006).

Another example of how computer-based technology can shape the way in which students work on projects comes from Israel. High school students who worked on

*Using Technology to Support Cognitive Approaches to Instruction*

computer-based electronics projects were more likely than students who worked on the same projects without the aid of a computer to create new ideas, improvise solutions to problems, and use more trial-and-error solutions to problems (Barak, 2005).

**Situated Learning**   As you may recall from Chapter 9, situated learning, or situated cognition, is the concept that knowledge is closely linked to the environment in which it is acquired. The more true to life the task is, the more meaningful the learning will be. Technology can play a key role in providing access to a wide variety of real-world learning situations. For instance, computer-based instructional technology such as CSILE, WISE, the GLOBE Program, and the WEB Project can apprentice students into real-life learning and problem-solving settings by providing access to authentic data and the tools to manipulate the data (Hung, 2001).

One project that embodied the concept of situated learning was conducted with elementary grade students in a Northern Ireland school and a Republic of Ireland school. Called the Author-on-Line Project, students in both schools read a book called *The Cinnamon Tree* by Aubrey Flegg and wrote a book report. The students then posted their reports on a portion of the Northern Ireland Network for Education website. As new reports appeared, they were read by all of the students and discussed. At this point, the author got involved by posting his reactions to each student's report. The students discussed his comments in class and, either individually or in small groups, composed a response. At one point the author adopted the persona of the book's main character, a thirteen-year-old girl, thereby giving the students the rather unique opportunity to interact with a fictional character (Clarke & Heaney, 2003). The senior author of this book can attest to the authentic and situated nature of this experience, as it parallels the exchanges he has with his editor.

# THE HUMANISTIC APPROACH TO TEACHING: STUDENT-CENTERED INSTRUCTION

The **humanistic approach** pays particular attention to the role of noncognitive variables in learning, specifically, students' needs, emotions, values, and self-perceptions. It assumes that students will be highly motivated to learn when the learning material is personally meaningful, when they understand the reasons for their own behavior, and when they believe that the classroom environment supports their efforts to learn, even if they struggle. Consequently, a humanistic approach to teaching strives to help students better understand themselves and to create a supportive classroom atmosphere that activates the inherent desire all human beings have to learn and fulfill their potential (Groeben, 1994; Maslow, 1987; Rogers, 1983).

The relevance of a humanistic approach to teaching may not be immediately apparent to everyone, but it is easy to support. First, we've known for some time that learning is as much influenced by how students feel about themselves as by the cognitive skills they possess. When students conclude that the demands of a task are beyond their current level of knowledge and skill (what we referred to in a previous chapter as a low sense of self-efficacy), they are likely to experience such debilitating emotions as anxiety and fear. Once these negative self-perceptions and emotions are created, the student has to divert time and energy from the task at hand to figuring out how to deal with them. And the solutions that students formulate are not always appropriate. Some may, for instance, decide to reduce their efforts and settle for whatever passing grade they can get. Others may give up entirely by cutting class, not completing homework assignments, and not studying for tests. A considerable amount of research from the health field has shown that people are more likely to use positive methods of coping with the stress of illness and disease when they perceive their environment to be *socially supportive*. The small amount of comparable research that exists on classroom learning suggests a similar outcome (Boekarts, 1993; Ryan & Patrick, 2001).

Second, this approach has the implicit support of teachers and parents. High on their list of desired educational outcomes is for students to develop positive feelings about themselves and about learning and to perceive school as a place where they will be supported in their efforts to develop new knowledge and skills.

## Pioneers of the Humanistic Approach

The humanistic approach to teaching was proposed during the 1960s principally by Abraham Maslow, Carl Rogers, and Arthur Combs.

**Maslow: Let Children Grow**   Abraham Maslow's approach to the study of human behavior was unique for its time (1960s). Whereas most of his colleagues studied the psychological processes of people who were having problems dealing with the demands and stresses of everyday life (as Sigmund Freud had done), Maslow decided that more could be learned by studying the behavior of especially well-adjusted people, whom he referred to as *self-actualizers*. Self-actualizers, be they children, adolescents, or adults, have an inherent need for experiences that will help them fulfill their potential.

In Chapter 15 of *Toward a Psychology of Being* (1968), Maslow describes forty-three basic propositions that summarize his views (a more detailed outline of Maslow's view is presented in Chapter 12, "Motivation and Perceptions of Self"). Some of the most significant of these propositions are as follows:

- Each individual is born with an essential inner nature.
- This inner nature is shaped by experiences and unconscious thoughts and feelings, but it is not *dominated* by such forces. Individuals control much of their own behavior.
- Children should be allowed to make many choices about their own development.
- Parents and teachers play a significant role in preparing children to make wise choices by satisfying their physiological, safety, love, belonging, and esteem needs, but they should do this by helping and letting children grow, not by attempting to shape or control the way they grow.

> Maslow: help students develop their potential by satisfying their needs

**Rogers: Learner–Centered Education**   Carl Rogers was a psychotherapist who pioneered a new approach to helping people cope more effectively with their problems. He called it *client-centered* (or *nondirective*) therapy, to stress the fact that the client, rather than the therapist, should be the central figure and that the therapist was not to tell the patient what was wrong and what should be done about it.

As he practiced this person-centered approach, Rogers came to the conclusion that he was most successful when he did not attempt to put up a false front of any kind; when he established a warm, positive, acceptant attitude toward his clients; and when he was able to sense their thoughts and feelings. Rogers concluded that these conditions set the stage for successful experiences with therapy because clients became more self-accepting and aware of themselves. Once individuals acquired these qualities, they were inclined and equipped to solve personal problems without seeking the aid of a therapist (Rogers, 1967).

In addition to functioning as a therapist, Rogers served as a professor. Upon analyzing his experiences as an instructor, he concluded that the person-centered approach to therapy could be applied just as successfully to teaching. He thus proposed the idea of **learner-centered education:** that teachers should try to establish the same conditions as do person-centered therapists. Rogers argues (1980) that the results of learner-centered teaching are similar to those of person-centered therapy: students become capable of educating themselves without the aid of direct instruction from teachers.

> Rogers: establish conditions that allow self-directed learning

**Combs: The Teacher as Facilitator**   Arthur Combs assumed that "all behavior of a person is the direct result of his field of perceptions at the moment of his behaving"

(1965, p. 12). From this assumption, it follows that the way a person perceives himself is of paramount importance and that a basic purpose of teaching is to help each student develop a positive self-concept. He observed, "The task of the teacher is not one of prescribing, making, molding, forcing, coercing, coaxing, or cajoling; it is one of ministering to a process already in being. The role required of the teacher is that of facilitator, encourager, helper, assister, colleague, and friend of his students" (1965, p. 16).

Combs elaborated on these points by listing six characteristics of good teachers:

1. They are well informed about their subject.
2. They are sensitive to the feelings of students and colleagues.
3. They believe that students can learn.
4. They have a positive self-concept.
5. They believe in helping all students do their best.
6. They use many different methods of instruction. (1965, pp. 20–23)

Taken together, the observations of Maslow, Rogers, and Combs lead to a conception of education in which teachers trust pupils enough to permit them to make many choices about their own learning. At the same time, teachers should be sensitive to the social and emotional needs of students, empathize with them, and respond positively to them. Finally, teachers should be sincere, willing to show that they too have needs and experience positive feelings about themselves and what they are doing.

## Teaching from a Humanistic Orientation

Humanistic approach addresses needs, values, motives, self-perceptions

Teachers who adopt a humanistic orientation seek to create a classroom atmosphere in which students believe that the teacher's primary goal is to understand the student's needs, values, motives, and self-perceptions and to help the student learn. This atmosphere is established primarily by the teacher's expressing genuine interest in and acceptance of the student and valuing the contribution each student makes to the progress of the class. The teacher avoids giving the impression that she would like the student better if only the student dressed more appropriately, had a more positive attitude toward learning, associated with a different group of peers, and so on. In this kind of setting, students will be more inclined to discuss openly their feelings about and problems with learning and related issues. The teacher is then in a position to help students figure out better approaches to their schoolwork and relationships with others. The teacher does not tell students what to do but guides them to the correct action. Because the students' perceptions and decisions are the central focus, this approach is often referred to as either *student-directed* or *nondirective* (Joyce & Weil, 2004; Tomlinson, 2002).

To illustrate this approach, consider the case of a student who is unhappy about a poor grade on a test. The instinctive reaction of most teachers would be to explain how to study and prepare for the next test. The humanistically oriented teacher instead asks the student to describe his interest in the subject matter, how capable a learner the student feels himself to be, how well the student understands the subject, under what conditions the student studies, whether the student feels the teacher's instruction to be clear and well organized, and so on. To help students understand their feelings and the role they play in learning, the teacher may disclose some of her own feelings. For example, the teacher may tell this hypothetical student, "When I've had a bad day and feel as if I've let my students down, I sometimes question my ability as a teacher. Is that how you feel?" Once these self-perceptions have been raised and clarified, the teacher encourages the student to suggest a solution to the problem (Joyce & Weil, 2004).

## pause & reflect

Can you recall any teachers who practiced humanistic techniques? Did you like these teachers? Did you feel you learned as much from them as from other teachers? Would you model yourself after such teachers?

## The Humanistic Model

**JOURNAL ENTRY**
Using a Humanistic Approach to Instruction

According to Bruce Joyce and Marsha Weil (2004), the nondirective model is made up of the following components:

1. *Defining the helping situation.* The topic that the student wants to discuss is identified, and the student is told that he or she is free to express any and all feelings that relate to the topic.
2. *Exploring the problem.* If the teacher has been able to establish the atmosphere of trust just described, it is assumed that students will be willing to describe the problem and any associated feelings. The teacher does not attempt to diagnose the student's problem but seeks to understand the situation as the student experiences it and then reflects this understanding back to the student. The teacher functions more as a resource, facilitator, and guide than as a director.
3. *Developing insight.* The student uses the information gained from exploring the problem to understand how various perceptions, emotions, beliefs, and behaviors cause various effects (such as a belief that one lacks ability, leading to incomplete homework assignments and lack of interest in the subject, or a need for affiliation that leads to more socializing than studying).
4. *Planning and decision making.* The teacher helps the student identify alternative behaviors and how they will be carried out.
5. *Integration.* The student reports on actions taken, their effects, and plans for future actions.

This approach to instruction strongly implies that students who believe their teachers care about them as people and want to help them maximize their learning are likely to be highly motivated. Nel Noddings (2003), an educational researcher who has written extensively about establishing a caring atmosphere in classrooms, describes this approach as one that seeks to produce happy students. She argues that

*Adopting a humanistic approach to teaching means identifying and meeting students' physical, social, emotional, and intellectual needs, as well as helping students understand how their perceptions, emotions, and behaviors affect their achievement.*

happiness should be, but rarely is, an explicit and high-priority goal of educators and educational policymakers (it already is for parents—they say so in overwhelming numbers in surveys of educational goals). In her view, happy classrooms

- satisfy the physical needs of children
- are clean and maintained, have reliable heating systems, are well lit, and are physically safe
- are those in which learning is an exciting, meaningful, and pleasurable experience
- are those in which children have an opportunity to learn through play
- avoid the use of sarcasm, humiliation, and fear
- capitalize on students' interests
- foster intellectual growth in every student
- foster the development of character
- foster interpersonal growth (learning how to get along with others)

## Research on Aspects of Humanistic Education

As we noted previously, Maslow believed that children's academic and personal growth is enhanced when various needs are met. One of those needs, belonging, has been the subject of considerable research. Belonging, which is also referred to as relatedness and sense of community, means the desire to get support from and be accepted by teachers and classmates and to have opportunities to participate in classroom planning, goal setting, and decision making.

According to some motivational theorists, belonging is one of three basic psychological needs (autonomy and competence are the other two) essential to human growth and development. Yet the need to belong receives less attention from educators than autonomy or competence does. One possible reason for this discrepancy is the belief that students' emotional needs are best met at home and in other out-of-school groups. This attitude does a disservice to students for two reasons: teachers play an important role in helping to satisfy the need to belong (a point we elaborate on in the following), and research has uncovered positive relationships between satisfaction of the need to belong and the following school-related outcomes (Anderman, 2002; Osterman, 2000):

- increased intrinsic motivation to learn
- a strong sense of competence
- a heightened sense of autonomy
- a stronger sense of identity
- the willingness to conform to classroom rules and norms
- positive attitudes toward school, class work, and teachers
- higher expectations of success
- lower levels of anxiety
- supportiveness of others
- higher levels of achievement

Feelings of rejection or exclusion from the group are associated with the following negative outcomes (Anderman, 2002; Osterman, 2000):

- higher levels of stress and health problems
- behavior problems in school
- lower interest in school
- lower achievement
- dropping out of school

Two studies offer persuasive evidence of the positive effect that a humanistic classroom environment can have on a variety of student behaviors. The first piece of evidence comes from an unusual source: an analysis of why Japanese students outscore U.S. students after fourth grade on an internationally normed standardized test of mathematics and science (the Third International Mathematics and Science Study). After observing ten science lessons taught in five Japanese public schools, Marcia Linn, Catherine Lewis, Ineko Tsuchida, and Nancy Butler Songer (2000) attributed the difference in part to a classroom atmosphere that Abraham Maslow and Carl Rogers would have endorsed.

Japanese classrooms marked by humanistic orientation, high scores on international math and science test

In addition to emphasizing cognitive development, elementary education in Japan also places a high value on children's social and ethical development. This is done by such tactics as (1) giving children various classroom responsibilities so they feel a valued part of the school, (2) emphasizing such qualities as friendliness, responsibility, and persistence, and (3) communicating to students that teachers value their presence in the classroom and the contributions they make. By fourth grade, Japanese children have been steeped in a school culture that emphasizes responsibility to the group, collaboration, and kindness. In addition, Linn et al (2000). found that almost every lesson began with an activity that was designed to spark the students' interest in the topic by connecting it to either their personal experiences or to previous lessons. The positive emotional attachment to school and the commitment to the values of hard work and cooperation that this approach produces are thought to play a strong role in how well students learn mathematics and science lessons.

The second piece of evidence (Ryan & Patrick, 2001) comes from a study of eighth-grade classroom environments and their effects on students. The environment created by each teacher was described along four lines:

1. Teacher support (students' perceptions of how strongly teachers valued and established personal relationships with them)
2. Promoting interaction among classmates (e.g., allowing students to share ideas, work together in small groups, give help during individual seatwork)
3. Promoting mutual respect and social harmony among classmates
4. Promoting performance goals (emphasizing competition and relative ability comparisons among classmates)

Each of these components was related to several outcome measures, including the four listed in Figure 13.3. The figure uses plus and minus signs to show the significant associations that the researchers reported. Notice that the first three environmental components—the ones that humanistic educators would favor—tended to increase desirable outcomes and decrease undesirable ones. The fourth, however—stressing competition and performance goals—raised students' off-task and disruptive behavior and decreased students' confidence in being able to interact with the teacher.

## Take a Stand!

### The Perennial Relevance of Humanistic Theory

As you know from reading this section, humanistic approaches to learning and teaching were formulated during the 1960s and 1970s. What you probably don't know is that they were every bit as popular at that time as, say, constructivist theories are today. But humanistic theories gradually fell from favor and eventually almost disappeared from sight. By the late 1980s, many textbooks had either drastically cut back or eliminated coverage of them, fewer papers on humanistic topics were delivered at major conferences, and fewer conceptual and research articles appeared in journals.

The reasons for the decline appeared to be threefold. First, information-processing theory, social cognitive theory, and constructivism ignited a torrent of research that promised, more than noncognitive conceptualizations, dramatic gains in achievement. Second, the humanistic theorists and researchers who came after Maslow, Rogers, and Combs were not of the same stature and did not have the same

impact on the field. Third, concerns about students' emotions, needs, and values seemed to many people to be frivolous, if not irrelevant, at a time when American students appeared to be inferior to earlier generations of students, as well as to students from other countries, in terms of standardized test scores. Teachers and students were urged to get back to basics!

In recent years, however, humanistic theory has staged something of a comeback. Current conceptualizations of classroom instruction recognize that students' needs and self-perceptions are every bit as important to understanding and improving classroom learning as the quality of their thinking. The research we have described on the effects of belongingness, teacher support, and social harmony among students exemplifies this trend. So if someone tries to convince you that humanistic theories are dead, tell them that humanistic approaches to education never die; they just hang around waiting to be acknowledged.

### HM TeacherPrepSPACE

What are your thoughts about humanistic education? Will you use its principles in your classroom? Explore the debate about humanistic teaching at the Take a Stand! section at textbook's student website.

**Figure 13.3** Results of the Ryan and Patrick Study of Eighth-Grade Classrooms

| | Outcomes | | | |
| --- | --- | --- | --- | --- |
| **Environment Created by Teacher** | Self-efficacy for interacting with teacher | Self-efficacy for academic performance | Use of self-regulated learning skills | Off-task and disruptive behavior |
| Teacher support for students | + | | + | – |
| Promoting interaction among classmates | + | | | |
| Promoting mutual respect and harmony | | + | + | |
| Promoting performance goals | – | | | + |

+ means significant increase; – means significant decrease.
Desirable outcomes indicated in **blue**, undesirable in **red**.

The results of these two studies on classroom atmosphere have strong implications for teachers in urban areas whose classrooms have a high percentage of minority students. Black students who were bused to school or were attending an urban school reported weaker feelings of belonging than students who were attending neighborhood or suburban schools (Anderman, 2002). But Black students in urban schools who said they liked going to school described their relationships with their teachers as supportive and caring (Baker, 1999). This suggests that teachers who take a humanistic approach can offset some of the negative emotions experienced by many minority students and help produce the positive outcomes we have just described.

### Using Technology to Support Humanistic Approaches to Instruction

Using technology to support a humanistic approach to teaching may seem like a contradiction in terms. But educational technology is becoming more learner centered in both its design and its use. Learner-centered technology tools can link concepts to everyday experiences, guide students in the problem-solving process, encourage learners to think more deeply, facilitate unique knowledge construction, and provide opportunities for social interaction and dialogue. For example, graphing calculators, hand-held computers, and microcomputer laboratory equipment allow students to depict data collected from a polluted stream or pond. Prompts embedded in a word processing program encourage reflection on one's report about that environmental problem. Finally, computer conferencing on the Web allows these same students to engage in discussions about their findings with same-age peers far beyond their own classroom. A key strength of emerging technology environments is that they place the responsibility for learning in the hands of learners, thereby enabling them to ask personally relevant questions, pursue needed knowledge, and generally be more self-directed.

## THE SOCIAL APPROACH TO TEACHING: TEACHING STUDENTS HOW TO LEARN FROM EACH OTHER

Classroom tasks can be structured so that students are forced to compete with one another, to work individually, or to cooperate with one another to obtain the rewards that teachers make available for successfully completing these tasks. Traditionally, competitive arrangements have been assumed to be superior to the other two in increasing motivation and learning. But reviews of the research literature by David Johnson and Roger Johnson (Johnson & Johnson, 1995; Johnson, Johnson, & Smith, 1995) found cooperative arrangements to be far superior in producing these benefits. In this section, we will describe competitive, individual, and cooperative learning arrangements; identify the elements that make up the major approaches to cooperative learning; and examine the effect of cooperative learning on motivation, achievement, and interpersonal relationships. We would also like to point out that cooperative learning methods are fully consistent with social constructivism because they encourage inquiry, perspective sharing, and conflict resolution.

## Types of Classroom Reward Structures

**Competitive Structures** Competitive goal structures are those in which one's grade is determined by how well everyone else in the group performs (a reward structure that is typically referred to as *norm referenced*). The traditional practice of grading on the curve predetermines the percentage of A, B, C, D, and F grades regardless of the actual distribution of test scores. Because only a small percentage of students in any group can achieve the highest rewards and because this accomplishment must come at some other students' expense, competitive goal structures are characterized by *negative interdependence*. Students try to outdo one another, view classmates' failures as an advantage, and come to believe that the winners deserve their rewards because they are inherently better (Johnson & Johnson, 1998; Johnson, Johnson, & Holubec, 1994; Johnson et al., 1995).

Some researchers have argued that competitive reward structures lead students to focus on ability as the primary basis for motivation. This orientation is reflected in the question, "Am I smart enough to accomplish this task?" When ability is the basis for motivation, competing successfully in the classroom may be seen as relevant to self-esteem (because nobody loves a loser), difficult to accomplish (because only a few can succeed), and uncertain (because success depends on how everyone else does). These perceptions may cause some students to avoid challenging subjects or tasks, give up in the face of difficulty, reward themselves only if they win a competition, and believe that their own successes are due to ability, whereas the successes of others are due to luck (Ames & Ames, 1984; Covington, 2000).

**Individualistic Structures** Individualistic goal structures are characterized by students working alone and earning rewards solely on the quality of their own efforts. The success or failure of other students is irrelevant. All that matters is whether the student meets the standards for a particular task (Johnson et al., 1994; Johnson et al., 1995). For example, thirty students working by themselves at computer terminals are functioning in an individual reward structure. According to Carole Ames and Russell Ames (1984), individual structures lead students to focus on task effort as the primary basis for motivation. This orientation is reflected in the statement, "I can do this if I try." Whether a student perceives a task as difficult depends on how successful she has been with that type of task in the past.

**Cooperative Structures** Cooperative goal structures are characterized by students working together to accomplish shared goals. What is beneficial for the other students in the group is beneficial for the individual and vice versa. Because students in cooperative groups can obtain a desired reward only if the other students in the group also obtain the same reward, cooperative goal structures are characterized by *positive interdependence*. Also, all groups may receive the same rewards, provided they meet the teacher's criteria for mastery. For example, a teacher might present a lesson on map reading, then give each group its own map and a question-answering

## pause & reflect

Have you ever experienced a competitive reward structure in school? Were your reactions positive or negative? Why? Would you use it in your own classroom? How and when?

Competitive reward structures may decrease motivation to learn

exercise. Students then work with each other to ensure that all know how to interpret maps. Each student then takes a quiz on map reading. All teams whose average quiz scores meet a preset standard receive special recognition (Johnson & Johnson, 1998; Joyce & Weil, 2004; Slavin, 1995). In the Suggestions for Teaching: Motivating Students to Learn section in Chapter 12, "Motivation and Perceptions of Self," we describe two particular cooperative learning techniques: Student Teams–Achievement Divisions and Jigsaw.

## pause & reflect

Have you ever experienced a cooperative reward structure in school? Were your reactions positive or negative? Why? Would you use it in your own classroom? How and when?

Cooperative structures lead students to focus on effort and cooperation as the primary basis of motivation. This orientation is reflected in the statement, "We can do this if we try hard and work together." In a cooperative atmosphere, students are motivated out of a sense of obligation: one ought to try, contribute, and help satisfy group norms (Ames & Ames, 1984). William Glasser points out that student motivation and performance tend to be highest for such activities as band, drama club, athletics, the school newspaper, and the yearbook, all of which require a team effort (Gough, 1987).

## Elements of Cooperative Learning

Over the past thirty years, different approaches to cooperative learning have been proposed by different individuals. The three most popular are those of David Johnson and Roger Johnson (Johnson et al., 1994), Robert Slavin (1994, 1995), and Shlomo Sharan and Yael Sharan (Sharan, 1995; Sharan & Sharan, 1999). To give you a general sense of what cooperative learning is like and to avoid limiting you to any one individual's approach, the following discussion is a synthesis of the main features of each approach.

**Group Heterogeneity**   The size of cooperative-learning groups is relatively small and as heterogeneous as circumstances allow. The recommended size is usually four to five students. At the very least, groups should contain both males and females and students of different ability levels. If possible, different ethnic backgrounds and social classes should be represented as well.

**Group Goals/Positive Interdependence**   A specific goal, such as a grade or a certificate of recognition, is identified for the group to attain. Students are told that they will have to support one another because the group goal can be achieved only if each member learns the material being taught (in the case of a task that culminates in an exam) or makes a specific contribution to the group's effort (in the case of a task that culminates in a presentation or a project).

**Promotive Interaction**   This element is made necessary by the existence of positive interdependence. Students are shown how to help one another overcome problems and complete whatever task has been assigned. This may involve episodes of peer tutoring, temporary assistance, exchanges of information and material, challenging of one another's reasoning, feedback, and encouragement to keep one another highly motivated. *Promotive* means simply that students promote each other's success.

Cooperative learning characterized by heterogeneous groups, positive interdependence, promotive interaction, individual accountability

**Individual Accountability**   This feature stipulates that each member of a group has to make a significant contribution to achieving the group's goal. This may be satisfied by requiring the group to achieve a minimal score on a test, by having the group's test score be the sum or average of each student's quiz scores, or by having each member be responsible for a particular part of a project (such as doing the research and writing for a particular part of a history report).

**Interpersonal Skills**   Positive interdependence and promotive interaction are not likely to occur if students do not know how to make the most of their face-to-face interactions. And you can safely assume that the interpersonal skills most students possess are probably not highly developed. As a result, they have to be taught such basic skills as leadership, decision making, trust building, clear communication, and conflict management. The conflict that arises over differences of opinion, for example, can be constructive if it is used as a stimulus to search for more information or to rethink one's conclusions. But it can destroy group cohesion and productivity if it results in students' stubbornly clinging to a position or referring to one another as "stubborn," "dumb," or "nerdy."

**Equal Opportunities for Success**   Because cooperative groups are heterogeneous with respect to ability and their success depends on positive interdependence, promotive interaction, and individual accountability, it is important that steps be taken to ensure that all students have an opportunity to contribute to their team. You can do this by awarding points for degree of improvement over previous test scores, by having students compete against comparable members of other teams in a game- or tournament-like atmosphere, or by giving students learning assignments (such as math problems) that are geared to their current level of skill.

**Team Competition**   This may seem to be an odd entry in a list of cooperative-learning components, especially in the light of the comments we already made about the ineffectiveness of competition as a spur to motivation and learning. But we're not being contradictory. The main problem with competition is that it is rarely used appropriately. When competition occurs between well-matched teams, is done in the absence of a norm-referenced grading system, and is not used too frequently, it can be an effective way to motivate students to cooperate with each other.

## Does Cooperative Learning Work?

The short answer to this question is yes. In the vast majority of studies, forms of cooperative learning have been shown to be more effective than noncooperative reward structures in raising the levels of variables that contribute to motivation, in raising achievement, and in producing positive social outcomes.

**Effect on Motivation**   One way in which cooperative learning contributes to high levels of motivation is in the proacademic attitudes that it fosters among group members. Slavin (1995) cites several studies in which students in cooperative-learning groups felt more strongly than did other students that their groupmates wanted them to come to school every day and work hard in class.

Probably because of such features as promotive interaction and equal opportunities for success, cooperative learning has been shown to have a positive effect on motivation-inducing attributions. That is, students in cooperative-learning groups were more likely to attribute success to hard work and ability than to luck (Slavin, 1995).

Although most of the reported effects of cooperative learning have been positive, negative results have occasionally appeared. Eleventh-grade students whose chemistry classes used a form of cooperative learning experienced declines in motivation, whereas students in the whole-class instruction group reported slight increases. The researchers attributed this finding to students being dissatisfied with the pace and amount of learning because of an upcoming high-stakes test (Shachar & Fischer, 2004).

**Effect on Achievement**   Slavin (1995) examined several dozen studies that lasted four or more weeks and used a variety of cooperative-learning methods. Overall, students in cooperative-learning groups scored about one-fourth of a standard deviation higher on achievement tests than did students taught conventionally. This translates to an advantage of ten percentile ranks (60th percentile for the average cooperative-learning student versus 50th percentile for the average conventionally taught student). But the beneficial effect of cooperative learning varied widely as a function of the particular method used. The best performances occurred with two techniques called Student Teams–Achievement Divisions and Teams-Games-Tournaments. (Both are described in Chapter 12 on motivation.) The cooperative-learning features that seem to be most responsible for learning gains are group goals and individual accountability.

David Johnson, Roger Johnson, and Karl Smith (1995) also reviewed much of the cooperative-learning literature but drew a somewhat different conclusion. They found that the test scores of students in the cooperative-learning groups were about two-thirds of a standard deviation higher than the test scores of students in competitive or individualistic situations. This translates to an advantage of twenty-five percentile ranks (75th versus 50th). It's not clear why Slavin's analysis produced a somewhat lower estimate of the size of the advantage produced by cooperative learning. It may be due in part to differences in the studies that each cited; Slavin focused on studies lasting at least four weeks. It may also be due to differences in the cooperative techniques that various researchers used.

A more current analysis of several studies done on students in grades 1–8 (Gillies, 2003) corroborated the findings of Johnson, Johnson, and Smith (1995). Students in cooperative groups who worked on problem-solving activities that required students to use all six cognitive processes represented in Bloom's Taxonomy scored significantly higher on a subsequent achievement test than did comparable peers who also worked in groups but received no training in group interaction.

**Effect on Social Interaction**    An important part of cooperative learning programs is teaching students how to productively interact with one another, including how to ask relevant, leading questions and how to give group members cogent arguments and justifications for the explanations and help they offer. A team of researchers (Veenman, Denessen, van den Akker, & van der Rijt, 2005) examined whether pairs of students trained to interact in this way would use these skills more frequently to solve math problems than would student pairs not taught these skills. The study produced a somewhat unusual result. Although students who received training made significantly more high-level, or elaborative, responses when asking for and giving help on the math task than did the untrained students, they did so less frequently than they had before the training. The researchers also found that students who had prior experience with cooperative learning, whether or not they received specific, supplementary training in how to productively ask questions and provide assistance to a classmate, scored higher on the math task than students who had no prior exposure to cooperative learning.

Lest someone argue that comparing students in cooperative learning groups with students who compete with one another or who work alone is tantamount to "stacking the deck," these positive social effects have also been observed when students who were put in cooperative groups and taught how to properly interact were compared with students who were placed in groups but received no training in how to productively interact and support one another. The former exhibited more cooperative behavior, provided more unsolicited explanations to peers, and provided more concrete examples and explanations than did the latter (Gillies, 2003).

In sum, students who learn cooperatively tend to be more highly motivated to learn because of the proacademic attitudes of groupmates, appropriate attributions for success and failure, and greater on-task behavior. They also score higher on tests of achievement and problem solving and tend to get along better with classmates of different racial, ethnic, and social class backgrounds. This last outcome should be of particular interest if you expect to teach in an area marked by cultural diversity.

## Why Does Cooperative Learning Work?

When researchers attempt to explain the widespread positive effects that are typically found among studies of cooperative learning, they usually cite one or more of the following explanations (Slavin, 1995).

**Cooperative learning effects likely due to stimulation of motivation, cognitive development, meaningful learning**

**Motivational Effect**   The various features of cooperative learning, particularly positive interdependence, are highly motivating because they encourage such achievement-oriented behaviors as trying hard, attending class regularly, praising the efforts of others, and receiving help from one's groupmates. Learning is seen as an obligation and a valued activity because the group's success is based on it and one's groupmates will reward it.

**Cognitive-Developmental Effect**   According to Lev Vygotsky, collaboration promotes cognitive growth because students model for each other more advanced ways of thinking than any would demonstrate individually. According to Jean Piaget, collaboration among peers hastens the decline of egocentrism and allows the development of more advanced ways of understanding and dealing with the world.

## VIDEO CASE   ◀◀ ▶ ▶▶

### Cooperative Learning: High School History Lesson

*Watch the video, study the artifacts in the case, and reflect upon the following questions:*

1. How does this Video Case illustrate Vygotsky's theory of cognitive growth through collaboration?

2. Do you think the teacher's ad hoc learning groups are as effective as cooperative learning groups that are thoroughly planned in advance? Please explain your answer.

**Cognitive Elaboration Effect**   As we saw in the previous discussion of information-processing theory, new information that is elaborated (restructured and related to existing knowledge) is more easily retrieved from memory than is information that is not elaborated. A particularly effective means of elaboration is explaining something to someone else.

## Teachers' Use of Cooperative Learning

**JOURNAL ENTRY**
Using a Social Approach to Instruction

As we have seen, cooperative learning is a topic about which much has been written and much research has been done. But until recently, no one had tried to assess the extent to which teachers actually use it and in what form. To fill that gap in the literature, Laurence Antil, Joseph Jenkins, Susan Wayne, and Patricia Vadasy (1998) interviewed twenty-one teachers from six elementary schools to assess the extent to which they used cooperative learning methods. All of the teachers claimed they were familiar with cooperative learning through preservice learning, student teaching, graduate classes, workshops, or other teachers. Seventeen of the teachers said they used it every day in a typical week. Most reported being attracted to cooperative learning because it enabled them to address both academic and social learning goals within a single approach. But even though teachers say they use cooperative learning, they aren't necessarily using it as it was intended.

Antil et al. argued that for an instructional approach to merit the label *cooperative learning*, it must include at least the conditions of positive interdependence and individual accountability. A more stringent definition would call for the inclusion of promotive interaction, group heterogeneity, and the development of interpersonal skills. Only five of the twenty-one teachers met the two-feature criterion, and only one reported using all five features. For example, instead of creating heterogeneous groups by putting students of different ability levels together, some teachers used random assignment, allowed students to select their teammates, or allowed students who sat near one another to form groups. Similar results were obtained from a study of 216 highly rated elementary and middle school teachers. Their actual use of such critical components as individual accountability, positive interdependence, and development of interpersonal skills was significantly less than what they would have preferred (Lopata, Miller, & Miller, 2003).

Why do teachers follow the spirit but not the letter of the cooperative learning model? Antil et al. offer several possibilities:

- Perhaps teachers find the models too complicated and difficult to put into practice. For example, in Slavin's model, individual accountability involves keeping a running log of students' weekly test scores, computing individual averages and improvement scores, totaling scores for each team based on members' improvement scores, and assigning group rewards.
- Teachers don't really believe the researchers' claims that certain elements of cooperative learning are essential for improved learning, perhaps because their classroom experience has led them to believe otherwise.
- Teachers interpret the research as providing suggestions or guidelines rather than prescriptions that must be followed, leaving them free to construct personal adaptations.
- Researchers rarely explicitly state that the demonstrated benefits of cooperative learning will occur only when certain conditions are met.

Another possibility not mentioned by Antil et al. is based on studies of how teachers implement other instructional tools, such as reciprocal teaching. Sometimes, unexpected and unfavorable classroom conditions force teachers into making alterations and compromises they might not make under more favorable circumstances (Hacker & Tenent, 2002).

**HM TeacherPrepSPACE**

The Thought Questions and Reflective Journal Questions at the textbook's student website can help you think about the issues raised in this chapter.

Do teachers' adaptations of the cooperative learning approaches advocated by researchers lead to inferior outcomes? Unfortunately, that's a question that has no definitive answer at this point, because there is little research on how effective cooperative learning is when some of its defining elements are omitted. But the following study, which looked at the effects of group heterogeneity on problem solving, suggests that you should stay as close as circumstances permit to the original features of cooperative learning.

Noreen Webb, Kariane Nemer, Alexander Chizhik, and Brenda Sugrue (1998) looked at seventh- and eighth-grade students who had been given three weeks of instruction on electricity concepts (such as voltage, resistance, and current) and electric circuits and who were judged as having either low ability, low-medium ability, medium-high ability, or high ability. These students were assigned to either homogeneous or heterogeneous groups and then allowed to work collaboratively to solve a hands-on physics test (create a circuit by using batteries, bulbs, wires, and resistors). Students with low and low-medium ability who worked in heterogeneous groups (that is, groups that included a student with either medium-high or high ability) outscored their peers in homogeneous groups on both the hands-on test and a subsequent paper-and-pencil test that students took individually. The difference was attributed to the active involvement of the students with lower ability in the problem-solving process. In response to the more relevant and accurate comments made by the students with high ability, the students with lower ability made and defended suggestions, asked questions, and paraphrased other students' suggestions.

A follow-up analysis of the performance of the top 25 percent of this sample was done to examine the effect of placing the students with highest ability in either

Students with low and average ability in mixed-ability groups outperform peers in homogeneous groups on problem-solving tests; students with high ability in homogeneous groups score slightly higher than peers in mixed-ability groups

homogeneous or heterogeneous groups (Webb, Nemer, & Zuniga, 2002). As in the original study, students were classified as having low, low-medium, medium-high, or high ability on the basis of preexperiment test scores. Students with high ability who worked in homogeneous groups (with just other students with high ability) earned significantly higher scores on the hands-on and paper-and-pencil tests than students with high ability who worked in groups that contained students with either medium-high or low-medium ability. But the performance of students with high ability in homogeneous groups was only slightly lower when they worked in groups that contained students with the lowest ability.

Now that you have read about the behavioral, cognitive, humanistic, and social approaches to instruction, take a few minutes to study Table 13.1. It summarizes the basic emphases of each approach and allows you to compare them for similarities and differences.

## Using Technology to Support Social Approaches to Instruction

**Social Constructivist Learning** Whereas the cognitive constructivist looks to find tools to help the child's mind actively construct relationships and ideas, the

| **Table 13.1** | Behavioral, Cognitive, Humanistic, and Social Approaches to Instruction |
|---|---|
| Behavioral (direct instruction) | Teacher presents information efficiently. Student accepts all information transmitted by teacher and textbook as accurate and potentially useful. Emphasis is on acquiring information in small units through clear presentations, practice, and corrective feedback and gradually synthesizing the pieces into larger bodies of knowledge. |
| Cognitive (information processing) | Teacher presents and helps students to process information meaningfully. Student accepts all information transmitted by teacher and textbook as accurate and potentially useful. Emphasis is on understanding relationships among ideas, relationships between ideas and prior knowledge, and on learning how to control one's cognitive processes effectively. |
| Cognitive (constructivist) | Teacher helps students to construct meaningful and adaptive knowledge structures by requiring them to engage in higher levels of thinking such as classification, analysis, synthesis, and evaluation; providing scaffolded instruction within the zone of proximal development; embedding tasks in realistic contexts; posing problems and tasks that cause uncertainty, doubt, and curiosity; exposing students to multiple points of view; and allowing students the time to formulate a consensus solution to a task or problem. |
| Humanistic | Teacher creates a classroom environment that addresses students' needs, helps students understand their attitudes toward learning, promotes a positive self-concept in students, and communicates the belief that all students have value and can learn. Goal is to activate the students' inherent desire to learn and grow. |
| Social | Teacher assigns students to small, heterogeneous groups and teaches them how to accomplish goals by working together. Each student is accountable for making a significant contribution to the achievement of the group goal. Because of its emphasis on peer collaboration, this approach is consistent with a social constructivist view of learning. |

Successful technology applications are embedded in an active social environment

social constructivist looks as well for tools that help children negotiate ideas and findings in a community of peers. For instance, some point out that it is not just the quality of a computer simulation or microworld that determines the degree to which students will become more like expert scientists; rather, the social activities and talk between students and teachers in that environment are also central to student learning (Roschelle, 1996). This contention is supported by a large number of studies. An analysis of the results from 122 studies found that students whose computer-based instruction took place in the context of small-group learning outscored students who worked alone at a computer by about six percentile ranks on individual tests of achievement. When the performance of the group as a whole was compared with that of students who worked alone, the difference increased to about twelve percentile ranks. In addition, students who worked on computer-based projects with other students exhibited more self-regulated learning behavior, greater persistence, and more positive attitudes toward group work and classmates as compared with students who worked on computers alone (Lou, Abrami, & d'Apollonia, 2001).

**Cooperative and Collaborative Learning**   Cooperative learning is fairly well structured, with assigned roles, tasks, and procedures to help students learn material covered in a classroom setting; a related concept, **collaborative learning,** allows the students themselves to decide on their roles and use their individual areas of expertise to help investigate problems (Veermans & Cesareni, 2005). As noted throughout this book, with the emergence of the World Wide Web and telecommunications technologies that enable students to publish and share their work internationally, there is no shortage of cooperative and collaborative learning opportunities (Burns, 2002). Networking technologies can be used for many cooperative and collaborative tasks—for example:

- collecting data for group science projects (Riel & Fulton, 2001)
- studying seashore organisms with input from a professional biologist (Veermans & Cesareni, 2005)
- interacting with scientists in the field (Riel & Fulton, 2001)
- describing the origin of and evidence surrounding such myths as the sunken city of Atlantis (Veermans & Cesareni, 2005)
- practicing reading and writing in a foreign language (Greenfield, 2003; LeLoup & Ponterio, 2003)
- giving peer and expert feedback on art, music, and writing assignments (Sherry & Billig, 2002)
- mentoring by adult experts in such subjects as math, science, and writing (Riel & Fulton, 2001)
- communicating with students in other countries (LeLoup & Ponterio, 2003)

## VIDEO CASE   ◄◄ ▶ ►►

### Multimedia Literacy: Integrating Technology into the Middle School Curriculum

*Watch the video, study the artifacts in the case, and reflect upon the following questions:*

**1.** Does the technology-based lesson in the Video Case promote social constructivist teaching and learning? Why or why not?

**2.** How does the teacher in the Video Case establish an effective cooperative-learning environment? Cite some specific examples based on your viewing of the case.

As noted in previous chapters, the emergence of computer networking technologies is creating many interesting opportunities for students to enter into virtual communities with peers from other schools and countries and to share and discuss various data and ideas. Students who participate in the GLOBE Program (**www.GLOBE.gov**), for example, collaborate with students from around the world on environmental science projects (Riel & Fulton, 2001). The WEB Project (**www.webproject.org**) allows students to interact with and receive feedback from adult experts about works in progress. Art and music students, for example, get suggestions from artists, multimedia designers, musicians, and composers (Sherry & Billig, 2002). Last, the 4Directions Project (**www.4directions.org**), which we mentioned in Chapter 4 on culture and cognition, allows American Indian students in ten states to interact with one another and with adult experts. They can, for example, discuss research ideas and career options with American Indian professionals (Allen, Resta, & Christal, 2002).

# 14 Understanding Standardized Assessment

## KEY POINTS

*These key points will help you learn the important information in this chapter. To help you study, they also appear in the margins of the pages, next to the text where they are discussed.*

### Standardized Tests

- Standardized tests: items presented and scored in standard fashion; results reported with reference to standards
- Basic purpose of standardized test is to obtain accurate, representative sample of some aspect of a person
- Standardized test scores are used to identify strengths and weaknesses, plan instruction, select students for programs
- Reliability: similarity between two rankings of test scores obtained from the same individual
- Validity: how accurately a test measures what users want it to measure
- Content validity: how well test items cover a body of knowledge and skill
- Predictive validity: how well a test score predicts later performance
- Construct validity: how accurately a test measures a theoretical attribute
- Meaningfulness of standardized test scores depends on representativeness of norm group
- Formal testing of young children is inappropriate because of rapid developmental changes
- Achievement tests measure how much of a subject or skill has been learned
- Diagnostic achievement tests designed to identify specific strengths and weaknesses
- Competency tests determine whether potential graduates possess basic skills
- Aptitude tests measure predisposition to develop additional capabilities in specific areas

- Norm-referenced tests compare one student with others
- Criterion-referenced tests indicate degree of mastery of objectives
- Percentile rank: percentage of scores at or below a given point
- Standard deviation: degree of deviation from the mean of a distribution
- z score: how far a raw score is from the mean in standard deviation units
- T score: raw score translated to a scale of 1–100 with a mean of 50
- Stanine score: student performance indicated with reference to a 9-point scale based on normal curve

### Using Standardized Tests for Accountability Purposes: High-Stakes Testing

- High-stakes testing: using test results to hold students and educators accountable for achievement
- NCLB requires standards, annual testing in math and reading, annual progress for all students, public reports, accountability system
- High-stakes tests expected to improve clarity of goals, quality control, teaching methods, and student motivation
- High-stakes tests criticized because of structural limitations, misinterpretation/misuse of results, narrow view of motivation, adverse side effects
- Research on effects of high-stakes testing limited and inconsistent

### Standardized Testing and Technology

- Websites of state departments of education, private companies provide services that help prepare students for state assessments
- Computer adaptive testing: computers determine sequence and difficulty level of test items

Because standardized assessment of scholastic aptitude and achievement is such a popular practice in the United States (as well as in many other countries), this chapter will focus on the nature of standardized tests, how they are used to assess student variability, and how these test results can be employed in putting together effective instructional programs for students. As you will see, the use of standardized tests is truly a double-edged sword: it has the potential to harm students as well as help them. ●

# STANDARDIZED TESTS

## Nature of Standardized Tests

The kinds of assessment instruments described in this chapter are typically referred to as **standardized tests**, although the term *published tests* is sometimes used (because they are prepared, distributed, and scored by publishing companies or independent test services). You have almost certainly taken several of these tests during your academic career, and so you are probably familiar with their appearance and general characteristics. They are called standardized tests for the following reasons:

- They are designed by people with specialized knowledge and training in test construction.
- Every person who takes the test responds to the same items under the same conditions.
- The answers are evaluated according to the same scoring standards.
- The scores are interpreted through comparison with the scores obtained from a group (called a norm group) that took the same test under the same conditions or (in the case of some achievement tests) through comparison with a predetermined standard.

> Standardized tests: items presented and scored in standard fashion; results reported with reference to standards

The basic purpose of giving a standardized test is to obtain an *accurate and representative sample* of how much of some characteristic a person possesses (such as knowledge of a particular set of mathematical concepts and operations). The benefit of getting an accurate measure from a test is obvious. When standardized tests are well designed, they are likely to be more accurate measures of a particular characteristic than nonstandardized tests. Standardized tests measure a *sample* of the characteristic, as a comprehensive measure would be too expensive, time-consuming, and cumbersome to administer (Walsh & Betz, 2001).

> Basic purpose of standardized test is to obtain accurate, representative sample of some aspect of a person

## Uses of Standardized Tests

Historically, educators have used standardized test scores, particularly achievement tests, for a variety of instructionally related purposes. Teachers, guidance counselors, and principals have used test data to identify general strengths and weaknesses in student achievement, to inform parents of their child's general level of achievement, to plan instructional lessons, to group students for instruction, and to recommend students for placement in special programs. To cite just one example, when a child moves to a different school, it is highly desirable for those in the new school to have some idea as to what the child knows about basic subjects. Standardized achievement tests do an effective job of providing information about the mastery of general subject matter and skills and thus can be used for planning, grouping, placement, and instructional purposes.

> Standardized test scores are used to identify strengths and weaknesses, plan instruction, select students for programs

When you read the test profiles that report how students in your classes have performed on standardized tests, you will get a general idea of some of your students' strengths and weaknesses. If certain students are weak in particular skill areas and you want to help them overcome those weaknesses, test results *may* give you *some* insights into possible ways to provide remedial instruction. If most of your students score below average in certain segments of the curriculum, you will know that you should devote more time and effort to presenting those topics and skills to the entire class. You can and should, of course, supplement what you learn from standardized test results with your own tests and observations in order to design potentially effective forms of remedial or advanced instruction.

## pause & reflect

If you are like most other people, you took a variety of standardized tests throughout your elementary and high school years. Do you think that those tests adequately reflected what you had learned and were capable of learning and therefore were always used in your best interest? What can you do to increase the chances that you will use test scores to help *your* students fulfill their potential?

*When properly used, standardized test scores can keep parents, students, and educators aware of a student's general level of achievement, and they can help teachers and administrators make decisions about placing students in special programs.*

## Criteria for Evaluating Standardized Tests

Like most other things, standardized tests vary in quality. To use test scores wisely, you need to be an informed consumer—to know what characteristics distinguish well-constructed from poorly constructed tests. Four criteria are widely used to evaluate standardized tests: reliability, validity, normed excellence, and examinee appropriateness. Each of these criteria will be explained individually.

**Reliability**    A basic assumption that psychologists make about human characteristics (such as intelligence and achievement) is that they are relatively stable, at least over short periods of time. For most people, this assumption seems to be true. Thus you should be able to count on a test's results being consistent, just as you might count on a reliable worker to do a consistent job time after time. This stability in test performance is known as **reliability**. You can think of reliability as the extent to which test scores are free of measurement errors that arise from such factors as test anxiety, motivation, correct guesses, and vaguely worded items, thereby producing a consistent performance over the course of a test or over repeated assessments of the same characteristic (Frisbie, 2005). It is one of the most important characteristics of standardized tests.

Reliability: similarity between two rankings of test scores obtained from the same individual

To illustrate the importance of reliability, imagine that you wish to form cooperative learning groups for mathematics. Because these types of groups should be composed of five to six students who differ on a number of characteristics, including achievement, you use the students' most recent scores from a standardized mathematics test to assign two high, two medium, and two low achievers to each group. One month later, the children are retested, and you now find that many of those who scored at the top initially (and whom you thought were very knowledgeable about mathematics) now score in the middle or at the bottom. Conversely, many students who initially scored low now have average or above-average scores. What does that do to your confidence in being able to form heterogeneous groups based on scores from this test? If you want to be able to differentiate among individuals consistently, you need to use an instrument that performs consistently.

Psychologists who specialize in constructing standardized tests assess reliability in a variety of ways:

- *Split-half reliability.* Psychologists administer a single test to a group of students, create two scores by dividing the test in half, and measure the extent to which the rankings change from one half to the other. This method gauges the internal consistency of a test.

- *Test-retest reliability.* Psychologists administer the same test to the same people on two occasions and measure the extent to which the rankings change over time.
- *Alternate-form reliability.* Psychologists administer two equivalent forms of a test to the same group of students at the same time and compare the results.

Regardless of which method is used to assess reliability, the goal is to create two rankings of scores and see how similar the rankings are. This degree of consistency is expressed as a correlation coefficient (abbreviated with a lowercase $r$) that ranges from 0 to 1. Well-constructed standardized tests should have correlation coefficients of about .95 for split-half reliability, .90 for test-retest reliability, and .85 for alternate-form reliability (Kubiszyn & Borich, 2007). Bear in mind, however, that a particular test may not report all three forms of reliability and that reliabilities for subtests and for younger age groups (kindergarten through second grade) are likely to be lower than these overall figures.

**Validity**    A second important characteristic of a test is that it accurately measures what it claims to measure. A reading comprehension test should measure just that—nothing more, nothing less. Whenever we speak of a test's accuracy in this sense, we are referring to its **validity**.

Because most of the characteristics we are interested in knowing something about (such as arithmetic skills, spatial aptitude, intelligence, and knowledge of the American Civil War) are internal and hence not directly observable, tests are indirect measures of those attributes. Therefore, any test-based conclusions we may draw about how much of a characteristic a person possesses, or any predictions we may make about how well a person will perform in the future (on other types of tests, in a job, or in a specialized academic program, for example), are properly referred to as *inferences*. So when we inquire about the validity of a test by asking, "Does this test measure what it claims to measure?" we are really asking, "How accurate are the inferences that I wish to draw about the test taker?" (Frisbie, 2005; Messick, 1989).

The degree to which these inferences can be judged accurate, or valid, depends on the type and quality of the supporting evidence that we can muster. Three kinds of evidence that underlie test-based inferences are content validity evidence, predictive validity evidence, and construct validity evidence.

***Content Validity Evidence***    This kind of evidence rests on a set of judgments about how well a test's items reflect the particular body of knowledge and skill (called a *domain* by measurement specialists) about which we want to draw inferences. If a test on the American Civil War, for example, contained no items on the war's causes, its great battles, or the years it encompassed, some users might be hesitant to call someone who had achieved a high score knowledgeable about this topic. Then again, other users might not be nearly so disturbed by these omissions (and the inference that would be drawn from the test score) if they considered such information to be relatively unimportant.

***Predictive Validity Evidence***    This evidence allows us to make probabilistic statements about how well students will behave in the future ("Based on his test scores, there is a strong likelihood that Yusef will do well in the creative writing program next year"). Many colleges, for example, require students to take the American College Testing Program (ACT) or the Scholastic Assessment Test (SAT) and then use the results (along with other information) to predict each prospective student's grade-point average at the end of the first year. All other things being equal, students with higher test scores are expected to have higher grade-point averages than students with lower test scores and thus stand a better chance of being admitted.

---

*Validity: how accurately a test measures what users want it to measure*

*Content validity: how well test items cover a body of knowledge and skill*

*Predictive validity: how well a test score predicts later performance*

Construct validity: how accurately a test measures a theoretical attribute

***Construct Validity Evidence***    This evidence indicates how accurately a test measures a theoretical description of some internal attribute of a person. Such attributes—for example, intelligence, creativity, motivation, and anxiety—are called *constructs* by psychologists.

To illustrate the nature of construct validity, we will use a hypothetical theory of intelligence called the Perfectly Valid theory. This theory holds that highly intelligent individuals should have higher-than-average school grades now and in the future, demonstrate superior performance on tasks that involve abstract reasoning, and be able to distinguish worthwhile from nonworthwhile goals. They may or may not, however, be popular among their peers. If the Perfectly Valid theory is accurate and if someone has done a good job of constructing an intelligence test based on this theory (the Smart Intelligence Test), people's scores on the Smart Test should vary in accordance with predictions derived from the Perfectly Valid theory. We should see, for example, a strong, positive relationship, or correlation, between intelligence quotient (IQ) scores and grade-point average but no relationship between IQ scores and measures of popularity. As more and more of this type of evidence is supplied, we can feel increasingly confident in drawing the inference that the Smart Intelligence Test is an accurate measure of the Perfectly Valid theory of intelligence.

# VIDEO CASE    ◄◄ ▶ ▶▶

HM

## Assessment in the Elementary Grades:
## Formal and Informal Literacy Assessment

*Watch the video, study the artifacts in the case, and reflect upon the following questions:*

1. In your own words, explain how the standardized test in the Video Case will benefit Myto and allow teachers to plan his instruction more effectively.

2. What factors might influence the reliability and validity of this standardized test?

**Normed Excellence**    For a test score to have any meaning, it has to be compared with some yardstick, or measure of performance. Standardized tests use the performance of a norm group as the measure against which all other scores are compared. A **norm group** is a sample of individuals carefully chosen so as to reflect the larger population of students for whom the test is intended. In many cases, the larger population consists of all elementary school children, all middle school children, or all high school children in the United States.

Meaningfulness of standardized test scores depends on representativeness of norm group

The norm group must closely match the larger population it represents on such major demographic variables as age, sex, race, ethnic group, region of country, family income, and occupation of head of household. These variables are considered major because they are strongly associated with differences in school performance. If, for example, the U.S. Census Bureau reports that 38 percent of all Latino males between the ages of six and thirteen live in the southwestern region of the country, a good test constructor testing in the Southwest will try to put together a norm group that contains the same percentage of six- to thirteen-year-old Latino males.

As you might suspect, problems of score interpretation arise when the major demographic characteristics of individuals who take the test are not reflected in the norm group. Suppose you were trying to interpret the score of a fourteen-year-old Black male on the EZ Test of Academic Achievement. If the oldest students in the norm group were twelve years of age and if Black children were not part of the norm group, you would have no way of knowing whether your student's score was below average, average, or above average, compared with the norm.

*Standardized achievement tests are given to assess how much of a particular subject students have learned, and aptitude tests are given to assess the level of a student's capabilities in a particular area.*

**Examinee Appropriateness**   Because developing a standardized test is a substantial undertaking that requires a considerable investment of money, time, and expertise, most tests of this type are designed for nationwide use. But the curricula in school districts in different types of communities and in different sections of the country vary to a considerable extent. Therefore, it is important to estimate how appropriate a given test is for a particular group of students. When you are estimating the content validity of a test, you should pay attention not only to how well the questions measure what they are supposed to measure but also to whether they are appropriate in terms of level of difficulty and of the vocabulary and characteristics of your students.

For example, the administration of readiness tests to preschool and kindergarten children to determine whether they are ready to begin school or should be promoted to first grade has been heavily criticized on the basis of examinee appropriateness. A major problem with the use of tests for the making of admission and retention decisions in the early grades is their low reliability. Young children change physically, socially, emotionally, and intellectually so rapidly that many of them score very differently when retested six months later (Bjorklund, 2005).

| Formal testing of young children is inappropriate because of rapid developmental changes

## Types of Standardized Tests

In this section we will examine two major categories of standardized tests—achievement tests and aptitude tests—each of which has several varieties. We will also examine two approaches to the interpretation of test scores: norm referenced and criterion referenced.

| Achievement tests measure how much of a subject or skill has been learned

**Achievement Tests**   One type of standardized test that you probably took during your elementary school years was the **single-subject achievement test**, designed to assess how much you had learned—that is, achieved—in a particular basic school subject. The very first standardized test you took was probably designed to evaluate aspects of reading performance. Then at intervals of two years or so, you probably worked your way tensely and laboriously through **achievement batteries** designed to assess your performance in reading as well as math, language, and perhaps other subjects. During your high school years, you may have taken one or more achievement batteries that evaluated more sophisticated understanding of basic reading-writing-arithmetic skills, as well as course content in specific subjects.

Diagnostic achievement tests designed to identify specific strengths and weaknesses

Competency tests determine whether potential graduates possess basic skills

At some point during your elementary school years, you may also have been asked to take a **diagnostic test**, a special type of single-subject achievement test intended to identify the source of a problem in basic subjects and perhaps in study skills as well.

Depending on when and where you graduated from high school, you may have been asked to take a **competency test** a few months before the end of your senior year. Competency tests came into use in the mid-1970s when it was discovered that many graduates of American high schools were unable to handle basic skills. In many school districts, therefore, students are asked to prove that they are competent in reading, writing, and arithmetic before they are awarded diplomas.

You may have earned some of your college credits by taking the College-Level Examination Program, a **special-purpose achievement test**. Depending on the state in which you choose to teach, you may be required to take and pass another special-purpose achievement test, the Praxis II, before being granted a teaching certificate.

**Aptitude Tests**    An aptitude is an underlying predisposition to respond to some task or situation in a particular way; it makes possible the development of more advanced capabilities (Snow, 1992). The word *aptitude* is derived from the Middle English *apte*, which meant "to grasp" or "to reach" and is related to the French *à propos*, which means "appropriate," "fitting," or "suited to a purpose."

Aptitude tests measure predisposition to develop additional capabilities in specific areas

For several decades, aptitudes have come to be identified entirely with cognitive predispositions, and **aptitude tests**, designed to indicate the level of knowledge and skill a student could acquire with effective instruction, have become increasingly common. Thus there are now a number of somewhat general tests of **scholastic aptitude** (the cognitive skills deemed most likely to predict a student's ability to cope with academic demands), such as the familiar SAT, and many specific tests of aptitude, such as tests of musical aptitude, mechanical aptitude, and spatial relations.

Some contemporary psychologists argue that we should stop trying to distinguish between aptitude (or ability) and achievement and should abandon the view that one's ability is the cause of one's achievement. Robert Sternberg (1998), for example, notes that the items that appear in various mental ability tests (such as vocabulary, reading comprehension, verbal analogies, arithmetic problem solving, and determining similarities) are often the focus of classroom instruction and are the same types of items that appear on many achievement tests. Second, he notes that achievement test scores are as good predictors of ability test scores as ability test scores are predictors of achievement test scores. Rather than thinking of such aptitudes as verbal reasoning, mathematical reasoning, spatial orientation, and musical aptitude as largely inherited capabilities that are responsible for the level of expertise one develops in a particular area, he prefers to think of aptitudes as various forms of *developing* expertise.

Norm-referenced tests compare one student with others

**Norm-Referenced Tests**    Most of the achievement and aptitude tests just described are referred to as **norm-referenced tests** because performance is evaluated with reference to norms—the performance of others—established when the final form of the test was administered to the sample of students who made up the standardization group. After taking an achievement battery in the elementary grades, for example, you were probably told that you had performed as well on reading comprehension questions as 80 percent (or whatever) of all of the students who took the test. If you take the Graduate Record Examination (GRE), you will be told how far from the average score of 500 you are (in terms of a score to be described shortly). Thus you will learn just where you stand in a distribution of scores arranged from lowest to highest. Tests that are constructed according to norm-referenced criteria tend to cover a broad range of knowledge and skill but have relatively few items for each topic or skill tested. But an alternative approach to reporting achievement scores, the criterion-referenced method, is frequently used.

Criterion-referenced tests indicate degree of mastery of objectives

**Criterion-Referenced Tests**    A different approach to reporting achievement test scores is used by **criterion-referenced tests**. When a test is scored in this manner, an individual's performance is not compared with the performance of others. Instead, students are evaluated according to how well they have mastered specific objectives in various well-defined skill areas. Because of this feature, you may find criterion-referenced tests more useful than norm-referenced tests in determining who needs how much additional instruction in what areas (provided, of course, that the test's objectives closely match your own).

The criterion-referenced approach is intended to reduce overtones of competition and to emphasize mastery of objectives at a rate commensurate with students' abilities. Tests that have criterion-referenced scoring systems tend to cover less ground than norm-referenced tests but contain more items for the objectives they do assess. Because norm-referenced and criterion-referenced scoring systems provide different types of information about student achievement, many testing companies provide both types of scores.

A relatively new development in criterion-referenced testing has occurred in several states. In an attempt to counter some of the disadvantages of traditional norm-referenced standardized testing, states such as Vermont and Kentucky have begun to rely partly or entirely on performance-based measures in their statewide assessment systems. We will offer some examples from these new tests later in this chapter.

## pause & reflect

Do you prefer norm-referenced or criterion-referenced tests? Why? Can you describe circumstances in which a norm-referenced test would be clearly preferable to a criterion-referenced test, and vice versa?

### Interpreting Standardized Test Scores

Scores on the most widely used standardized tests are typically reported on student profile forms that summarize and explain the results. Although most profiles contain sufficient information to make it possible to interpret scores without additional background, you should know in advance about the kinds of scores you may encounter, particularly because you may be asked to explain scores to students as well as to their parents.

**Grade Equivalent Scores**   The **grade equivalent score** interprets test performance in terms of grade levels. A student who makes a grade equivalent score of 4.7 on an achievement test, for example, got the same number of items right on this test as the average fourth grader in the standardization group achieved by the seventh month of the school year.

The grade equivalent score was once widely used at the elementary level, but because it may lead to misinterpretations, it is not as popular as it once was. One problem with grade equivalent scores is the tendency to misinterpret a score above a student's actual grade level as an indication that the student is capable of consistently working at that level. This kind of assumption might lead parents or perhaps teachers themselves to consider accelerated promotion. Remember that although such scores may show that a student did somewhat better on the test than the average student a grade or two above her, they do not mean that the student tested has acquired knowledge of all the skills covered in the grade that she would miss if she skipped a grade.

**Percentile Ranks**   Probably the most widely used score for standardized tests is the **percentile rank**. This score indicates the percentage of students who are at and below a given student's score. It provides specific information about relative position.

Students earning a percentile rank of 87 did as well as or better than 87 percent of the students in the particular normative group being used. They did not get 87 percent of the questions right—unless by coincidence—and this is the point parents are most likely to misunderstand. Parents may have been brought up on the percentages grading system, in which 90 or above was A, 80 to 89 was B, and so on down the line. If you report that a son or daughter has a percentile rank of 50, some parents are horror-struck or outraged, not understanding that the child's score on this test is

Percentile rank: percentage of scores at or below a given point

average, not a failure. In such cases, the best approach is to emphasize that the percentile rank tells the percentage of cases at or below the child's score. You might also talk in terms of a hypothetical group of 100; for example, a child with a percentile rank of 78 did as well as or better than 78 out of every 100 students who took the test.

Although the percentile rank gives simple and direct information on relative position, it has a major disadvantage: the difference in achievement among students clustered around the middle of the distribution is often considerably less than the difference among those at the extremes. The reason is that *most* scores are clustered around the middle of most distributions of large groups of students. The difference in raw score (number of items answered correctly) between students at percentile ranks 50 and 51 may be 1 point. But the difference in raw score between the student ranked 98 and one ranked 97 may be 10 or 15 points, because the best (and worst) students scatter toward the extremes. This quality of percentile ranks means that ranks on different tests cannot be averaged. To get around that difficulty, standard scores are often used.

| Standard deviation: degree of deviation from the mean of a distribution

**Standard Scores**    Standard scores are expressed in terms of a common unit: the **standard deviation**. This statistic indicates the degree to which scores in a group of tests (a distribution) differ from the average, or mean. (The *mean* is the arithmetical average of a distribution and is calculated by adding all scores and dividing the total by the number of scores.) The standard deviation is most valuable when it can be related to the normal probability curve. Figure 14.1 shows a normal probability curve indicating the percentage of cases to be found within three standard deviations above and below the mean. The horizontal axis indicates the score, ranging from low on the left to high on the right; the vertical axis represents the number of cases corresponding to each score. Notice, for example, that more than 68 percent of the cases fall between +1 SD (one standard deviation above the mean) and −1 SD (one standard deviation below the mean).

As you can see from the figure, the normal probability curve, or **normal curve** as it is usually known, is a mathematical concept that depicts a hypothetical bell-shaped distribution of scores. Such a perfectly symmetrical distribution rarely, if ever, occurs in real life. However, because many distributions of human characteristics and performance closely *resemble* the normal distribution, it is often assumed that such distributions are typical enough to be treated as "normal." Thus information that mathematicians derive for the hypothetical normal distribution can be applied to the approximately normal distributions that are found when human attributes are measured. When very large numbers of students are asked to take tests

**Figure 14.1** Normal Probability Curve

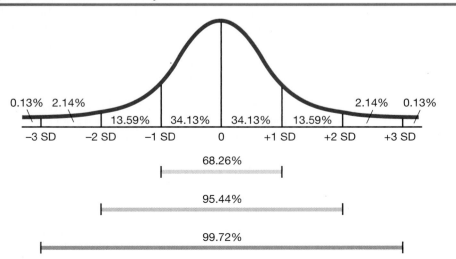

designed by specialists who go to great lengths to cancel out the impact of selective factors, it may be appropriate to interpret the students' scores on such tests with reference to the normal curve.

For purposes of discussion, and for purposes of acquiring familiarity with test scores, it will be sufficient for you to know about two of the standard scores that are derived from standard deviations. One, called a **z score**, tells how far a given raw score is from the mean in standard deviation units. A z score of $-1.5$, for example, would mean that the student was 1.5 standard deviation units below the mean. Because some z scores (such as the one in the example just given) are negative and involve decimals, **T scores** are often used instead. T scores range from 0 to 100 and use a pre-selected mean of 50 to get away from negative values. Most standardized tests that use T scores offer detailed explanations, either in the test booklet or on the student profile of scores, of how they should be interpreted. In fact, many test profiles adopt the form of a narrative report when explaining the meaning of all scores used.

To grasp the relationship among z scores, T scores, and percentile ranks, examine Figure 14.2. The diagram shows each scale marked off below a normal curve. It supplies information about the interrelationships of these various scores, provided that the distribution you are working with is essentially normal. In a normal distribution, for example, a z score of $+1$ is the same as a T score of 60 or a percentile rank of 84; a z score of $-2$ is the same as a T score of 30 or a percentile rank of about 2. (In addition, notice that the distance between the percentile ranks clustered around the middle is only a small fraction of the distance between the percentile ranks at the ends of the distribution.)

**Stanine Scores**   During World War II, U.S. Air Force psychologists developed a statistic called the **stanine score** (an abbreviation of "standard nine-point scale"). The name reflects the fact that this is a type of standard score, and it divides a population into nine groups. Each stanine is one-half of a standard deviation unit, as indicated in Figure 14.3.

When stanines were introduced on test profiles reporting the performance of public school children on standardized tests, they were often used to group students. (Students in stanines 1, 2, and 3 would be placed in one class; those in 4, 5, and 6 in another class; and so on.) For the reasons given in Chapter 6, "Accommodating Student

*z score: how far a raw score is from the mean in standard deviation units*

*T score: raw score translated to a scale of 1–100 with a mean of 50*

*Stanine score: student performance indicated with reference to a 9-point scale based on normal curve*

**Figure 14.2** Relationship Among z Scores, T Scores, and Percentile Ranks

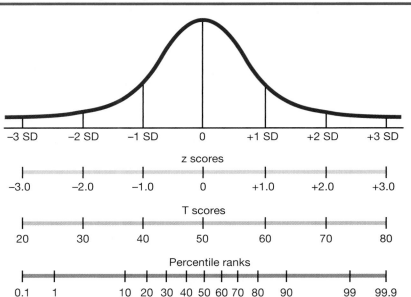

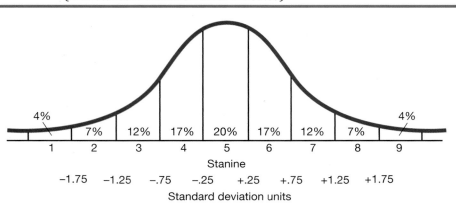

**Figure 14.3** Percentage of Cases in Each Stanine (with Standard Deviation Units Indicated)

**pause & reflect**

If you had to tell parents about the results of a standardized test, which type of score could you explain most clearly: raw score, percentile rank, z score, T score, or stanine score? Which do you think would be most informative for parents? For you? If you do not understand these tests completely, what can you do about this situation?

Diversity," and later in this chapter, such ability grouping has become a highly controversial issue in American schools. Consequently, stanine scores are now used just to indicate relative standing. They are easier to understand than z scores or T scores, as any child or parent can understand that stanines represent a 9-point scale with 1 as the lowest, 5 as the average, and 9 as the highest. Furthermore, unlike percentile ranks, stanine scores can be averaged. When it is desirable to have more precise information about relative standing, however, percentile ranks may be more useful, even though they cannot be averaged.

**Local and National Norms**   Percentile ranks and stanines are often used when local norms are prepared. As noted in our earlier description of how standardized tests are developed, the norms used to determine a student's level of performance are established by asking a representative sample of students to take the final form of the test. Inevitably, there will be differences between school systems (in texts used and the time during a school year or years when certain topics are covered, for instance). Accordingly, some test publishers report scores in terms of local as well as national norms. Each student's performance is thus compared not only with the performance of the members of the standardization group but also with the performance of all students in the same school system.

## Misconceptions About the Nature and Use of Standardized Tests

Although the concept of psychological and educational assessment is not a particularly difficult one to grasp, many members of the general public, including educators, draw incorrect inferences about what test scores mean because, for one reason or another, they have one or more of the following misconceptions (Braun & Mislevy, 2005):

1. **A test measures what its name implies.** This misconception can take a couple of forms. First, many people do not realize that a test measures a lot of things, some of which have nothing to do with its title. All test performances are influenced by, for example, familiarity with the testing situation, the type of test used, the way the test is administered, and how the test is scored. Second, a test measures a particular attribute according to how the person who constructed the test defined that attribute. Consequently, one person's intelligence test may assess certain

characteristics that another person's intelligence test chooses to ignore. A common result of holding this naïve belief is that people draw inferences from test scores that are not supported by the validity evidence for that test.

2. **All tests with the same title are the same.** Even though two tests are called seventh-grade science tests, this doesn't mean that they are interchangeable. Even if they have the same format (multiple-choice questions, for example), one may emphasize recall of factual material while the other may emphasize conceptual understanding or problem solving. The goal in assessment is to match a school district's objectives and standards with what a test measures.

3. **A test score accurately reflects what people know and can do.** No test provides a "true" score of an individual's knowledge and capabilities because all tests have built-in measurement error. Consequently, when people retake the same or an equivalent test, their scores vary. The best we can do is to say that a person's so-called true score probably lies between a lower and an upper boundary.

4. **Two tests that claim to measure the same thing can be made interchangeable.** For the reasons mentioned before, this is the exception rather than the rule. This is the reason that students in some school districts score well on the reading and math tests of the National Assessment of Educational Progress (NAEP) but more poorly on their state's tests of the same skills.

5. **Tests are scored by adding up the number of items people answer correctly.** Whereas this is true for unidimensional tests, or tests in which all items measure the same thing, it is not true for tests that measure different skills in different ways. A language test that measures knowledge of vocabulary and grammar, as well as reading comprehension and conversational fluency, should report separate scores for each capability.

6. **Scores of 70 percent correct, 80 percent correct, and 90 percent correct are equivalent to grades of C, B, and A, respectively.** This belief comes from the naïve assumption that all tests are basically the same. But because test items can be written at different levels of difficulty, two tests that measure the same knowledge base are likely to produce different scores when taken by the same students.

7. **Multiple-choice questions are useful only for measuring how well students can recognize and recall factual knowledge.** This belief undoubtedly stems from the fact that the vast majority of multiple-choice items that appear on tests are written at the knowledge level of Bloom's Taxonomy. But it is possible to write multiple-choice items that reflect the rest of the Taxonomy.

8. **One can tell if an item is good just by looking at it.** As with most things, the mere appearance of an item can be deceiving. Whether or not a test item is good, which is to say useful, depends largely on how well the form and cognitive demands of an item match both the instruction received by the student and the stated purpose of the test. An item for which students have not been adequately prepared or that measures factual knowledge when a test is advertised as measuring ability to apply knowledge is not a good item, at least for that particular test.

Earlier, we pointed out that standardized tests can be used in several ways to support the instructional goals of a school and a teacher. When teachers fully understand the characteristic being measured; when reliable, valid, and well-normed tests are readily available; and when teachers know how to interpret test results appropriately, this strategy for assessing individual differences can work quite well, particularly when it is supplemented with teacher observations and informal assessments. Effective remedial reading and math programs, for example, are based to a large extent on scores from diagnostic reading and math tests. But when tests are used for purposes other than those for which they were designed, misuses occur, and inappropriate decisions and controversy often result. In the next section, we'll take a look at the widespread and controversial practice of high-stakes testing: using standardized test scores to hold students, teachers, and administrators accountable for academic achievement.

# USING STANDARDIZED TESTS FOR ACCOUNTABILITY PURPOSES: HIGH-STAKES TESTING

## The Push for Accountability in Education

In 1983, the National Commission on Excellence in Education published a report titled *A Nation at Risk: The Imperative for Educational Reform*. The report painted a bleak picture of the quality of education in the United States. It noted, for example, that about 13 percent of all seventeen-year-olds were judged to be functionally illiterate, that standardized test scores had generally fallen below levels achieved twenty-five years earlier, and that many seventeen-year-olds were judged as being deficient in such higher-order thinking skills as drawing inferences from written material and writing a persuasive essay. To justify the amount of money being spent on education and to improve student outcomes, the report called for standardized tests to be used as a way of documenting students' achievement and spurring educators to focus on raising achievement in such basic areas as reading, math, and science.

Subsequent standardized test data, such as scores from the National Assessment of Educational Progress and the Third International Mathematics and Science Study, and reports on the numbers of students who were being promoted from grade to grade despite poor reading, writing, and math skills reinforced the perception that American students were poorly educated and had fallen behind students in many other countries. (For alternative interpretations of these findings, see Bracey, 2002, 2003; Berliner & Biddle, 1995.) State legislatures and state departments of education responded by mandating the establishment of learning standards, the administration of standardized tests to determine how well those standards are being met, and, in some cases, mechanisms for rewarding or punishing students, teachers, and administrators for acceptable or unacceptable scores. As of 2006, twenty-two states required high school students to pass an exit exam to receive a diploma (Kober et al., 2006).

High-stakes testing: using test results to hold students and educators accountable for achievement

Because standardized test scores, either by themselves or in conjunction with other data, are being used to determine whether students get promoted to the next grade or graduate from high school, whether teachers and administrators receive financial rewards or demotions, and whether school districts receive additional state funds or lose their accreditation, this practice is commonly referred to as high-stakes testing, and it has swept the nation. If you are in a teacher education program, you are likely to have firsthand experience with high-stakes testing through the Praxis series of exams or something similar. Created by the Educational Testing Service, Praxis exams are given by many colleges and universities to determine eligibility for entrance to teacher education programs and by states to determine eligibility for licensure.

## The Federal Initiative: No Child Left Behind (NCLB)

In December 2001, the U.S. Congress passed legislation proposed by President George W. Bush to implement testing of students in reading and mathematics in all public schools that receive federal funds. This legislation, a reauthorization of the Elementary and Secondary Education Act (ESEA), is commonly known as the No Child Left Behind (NCLB) Act. In addition to the accountability programs that states themselves put into place over the past several years, states and their school districts must now also adhere to the requirements of NCLB. You can read and download a copy of NCLB at the Department of Education's website (**www.ed.gov/policy/elsec/leg/esea02/index.html**).

NCLB requires standards, annual testing in math and reading, annual progress for all students, public reports, accountability system

**Requirements of NCLB**    The No Child Left Behind Act contains several requirements that states must meet (No Child Left Behind Act, 2001):

- *Standards*. States must establish what the law calls challenging content and achievement standards in mathematics, reading or language arts, and science, but

*To hold students accountable for learning certain subjects and skills at acceptable levels and to improve the quality of education, all states annually administer standardized achievement tests in several subject areas. These tests are linked to state learning standards.*

the legislation leaves it to each state to decide for itself the meaning of the word *challenging.*

- *Testing.* Annual testing of all students in grades 3 through 8 in math and reading/language arts and at least one assessment of students in grades 9 through 12 in the same two subjects. In 2007, states must also administer a science assessment at least once to students in grades 3 through 5, 6 through 9, and 10 through 12. Decisions about test format, length, and item type have been left to each state. Vermont's assessment program, for example, includes mathematics problem-solving portfolios, writing portfolios, and science performance tasks, in addition to the more familiar selected-response items (Vermont Department of Education, 2004). Kentucky's program also includes writing portfolios, as well as open-ended questions that require students to explain the reasoning behind their answers in reading, science, social studies, mathematics, and the humanities (Kentucky Department of Education, 2004).

- *Adequate Yearly Progress (AYP).* By 2014, all students must score at least at the "proficient" level (as defined by each state) of their state assessment in reading/language arts and math. To ensure that this goal is met, states must demonstrate each year that a certain additional percentage of all students have met that goal. This feature is referred to as adequate yearly progress, or AYP. Adequate yearly progress must be demonstrated by all groups of students, including racial and ethnic minorities, students of low socioeconomic status (SES), students with limited English proficiency, and students with disabilities.

The original wording of NCLB stated that schools would fail to meet the AYP requirement if too many students in *any* of the subgroups just mentioned failed to score at the minimally acceptable level (usually called "proficient" or "meets expectations") or if fewer than 95 percent of eligible students in all subgroups were tested. Because of complaints from many school districts, the U.S. Department of Education in early 2004 amended the 95 percent assessment requirement, so that schools can meet the law if they average a 95 percent participation rate over two or three years ("White House Is Easing Up," 2004).

Schools that fail to meet the AYP requirement not only must use different instructional approaches and programs but also must choose approaches and programs that have been shown to be effective by scientific research.

- *Reporting.* States and school districts must issue report cards to parents and the general public that describe how every group of students has performed on the annual assessment.
- *Accountability System.* School districts that fail to demonstrate AYP for two or more consecutive years are subject to the following sanctions:

  1. Schools that fail to achieve AYP for two consecutive years are identified as needing improvement, and students have the option of transferring to other schools in the district.
  2. Schools that fail to achieve AYP for three consecutive years are subject to the actions specified in point 1, and, additionally, students must be provided with supplemental instructional services (such as tutoring) by an outside provider.
  3. Schools that fail to achieve AYP for four consecutive years are subject to the actions in points 1 and 2, as well as either replacement of school staff, appointment of outside experts to advise the school, extension of the school day or year, or a change in the school's organizational structure.
  4. Schools that fail to achieve AYP for five consecutive years are subject to the actions specified in points 1, 2, and 3, along with restructuring of the school, which can mean replacing all or most of the school staff, state takeover of school operations, or conversion to a charter school.

- Schools that meet or exceed AYP for two or more consecutive years and that have made the greatest gains are designated "distinguished school" and may make financial awards to teachers.

Although NCLB mandates that students be tested in the areas of reading/language arts, math, and science and that they perform at a particular level, it has been left up to the states to decide which aspects of those subjects will be tested and how different levels of performance will be defined. This does not mean that states have free rein to do whatever they please; each state has an accountability plan for meeting the requirements of NCLB that has been approved by the federal government. States are free to amend these plans in the future, but changes have to be approved by the U.S. Department of Education. For example, Michigan's proposal not to test students with limited English proficiency who have been enrolled in U.S. schools for less than three years was not approved. Instead, Michigan will give these students reading and math tests that use a simpler level of English than the regular state exams (Olson, 2003a).

State assessment plans can be quite different from one another. For example, Iowa plans to use two commercially published norm-referenced tests to measure student progress, whereas Nebraska will use a combination of state and local assessments. Pennsylvania originally planned to use state and local assessments but ultimately decided to use just state tests because of the cost and interpretive difficulties associated with using different types of tests (Olson, 2003a).

**Problems with Implementing NCLB**    The No Child Left Behind law both is complex and has high stakes attached to it. Consequently, problems with its implementation, both potential and actual, have been noted. Here are a few of them:

- Because establishing high standards decreases the probability of meeting the AYP requirement, as well as the ultimate requirement of proficiency by all students in 2014, states may be tempted to weaken both their content and performance standards (Dillon, 2005; Fuller, Gesicki, Kang, & Wright, 2006; Popham, 2005).
- Setting the cut score that determines whether or not a student has reached the proficiency level is based on the judgment of educators and carries significant consequences. If the score is set too low, a state's accountability plan may not pass federal muster. If it is set too high, the school may have a difficult time demonstrating AYP. This difference in defining the standard for proficiency probably accounts for a good part of the difference between low- and high-scoring states. For example, in 2001 the percentage of students who scored at the proficient

level in math ranged from a low of 7 percent in Louisiana to a high of 92 percent in Texas. It is rather unlikely that the quality of instruction in Texas is that much better than the quality of instruction in Louisiana (Linn et al., 2002).

- Some states have negotiated with the U.S. Department of Education for a larger minimum subgroup size than the law specifies (Goldberg, 2005; Popham, 2005; Sunderman, 2006), for changes in how AYP is determined, and for the ability to set different proficiency targets for different subgroups (Sunderman, 2006). The result of these changes is a lack of common accountability standards.

- The law fails to acknowledge that many minority students, students with disabilities, and students with limited English proficiency have long-standing and deep-seated learning problems that will take years to remediate (Abedi & Dietel, 2004; Kim & Sunderman, 2005; Popham, 2004; Thomas, 2005). Although students with limited English proficiency can take state tests in their native languages, such tests are often not available or not properly aligned with state standards (Center on Educational Policy, 2005).

- Students who qualify for special education must, according to IDEA, have goals and objectives that match their learning levels incorporated into their individualized education programs (IEPs). But NCLB requires that these students meet the same standards as students without disabilities (Houston, 2005).

- Although NCLB requires schools that fail to meet AYP for three or more consecutive years to provide free tutoring to students, only 18 percent of eligible students received this service during the 2004–2005 school year. Students in small and rural school systems are less likely to receive tutoring than those in urban districts because of the lack of providers in those areas, of transportation to a tutoring provider, or of computers to access Internet-provided services (Goldberg, 2005; Richard, 2005). Although school districts that have failed to meet AYP goals are prohibited from providing their own tutoring services, the Department of Education in 2005 allowed the city of Chicago to do so in order to encourage more students to take advantage of the service. Several other large urban districts were said to be readying their own proposals for a similar exemption (Gewertz, 2005).

- Some state departments of education are struggling to provide the services that NCLB requires. Because of limited staff, particularly those with expertise in statistical analysis, and insufficient financial help from the federal government, many states are having difficulty carrying out such NCLB-mandated tasks as identifying failing schools, monitoring schools' improvement plans, and providing new administrators and teachers for schools that chronically fail to meet state standards. These problems will only get worse if, as current trends suggest, an increasing number of schools are labeled as failing (Tucker & Toch, 2004).

Because public education has many stakeholders (teachers, administrators, students, parents, legislators, and business leaders, for example) who differ in terms of their education-related attitudes, values, and ideals, the advent of high-stakes testing programs and NCLB has sparked a veritable flood of pro and con arguments. In the next two sections we summarize the major arguments that support and are critical of high-stakes testing.

## Arguments in Support of High-Stakes Testing Programs

| High-stakes tests expected to improve clarity of goals, quality control, teaching methods, and student motivation

High-stakes testing programs receive support because of their potential and actual beneficial effects on goal clarity, quality control, teaching skills and methods, and student motivation.

**Goal Clarity**   A major responsibility of teachers and a contributing factor to effective teaching is the ability to clearly communicate one's educational goals. A state's content and performance standards can help teachers clarify their goals and more clearly communicate those goals to students and parents (Falk, 2002; Hamilton & Stecher, 2004).

**Improved Quality Control**   NCLB and the state assessment programs that preceded it were implemented as a means to more closely monitor the quality of teaching and learning and to provide incentives for educators to make improvements. Here are a few ways in which high-stakes tests are thought to bring about improved quality control:

- Because high-stakes tests require results to be reported for groups of students that have traditionally been underserved (e.g., racial and ethnic minorities, students with disabilities and limited English proficiency), educators now monitor their academic progress as closely as they monitor the progress of regular students (Cizek, 2001a; Hershberg, 2005; Linn, 2003).
- States have markedly increased their collection of achievement data and improved the quality of their programs (Cizek, 2001a).
- Standardized tests with high stakes attached to them are an objective, efficient, and equitable way to hold teachers and students accountable for achieving a common set of standards (Clarke, Abrams, & Madaus, 2001; Hershberg, 2005).

**Beneficial Effects for Teaching**   High-stakes testing programs can have a beneficial effect on teaching in a number of ways:

- High-stakes tests have stimulated the designers of professional development seminars and workshops to emphasize teaching skills that are curriculum relevant and result oriented (Cizek, 2001a).
- Teachers are becoming more knowledgeable about the nature and uses of standardized testing (Cizek, 2001a).
- Motivated by the prospect of financial bonuses and helping their school district maintain its accreditation, teachers will search for and use more effective instructional methods and focus on material described in the standards (Clarke et al., 2001).
- Well-conceived learning standards deal with significant outcomes (e.g., asking questions and solving problems), reflect how students normally learn (actively in meaningful contexts), and are appropriate for the students' developmental stage. Standards that reflect these concerns are likely to lead educators to use inquiry forms of learning, to embed lessons in meaningful contexts, and to use various performance-based assessments, as well as paper-and-pencil assessments (Falk, 2002).
- NCLB does not specify a particular type of assessment instrument that schools have to use to determine AYP in math and reading. Although most states will use a standardized test devised either by their departments of education or an outside testing company, some have indicated that they will use locally constructed tests instead of or in addition to state-mandated tests. The benefit to teachers in those states is that locally produced tests are more likely to provide them with diagnostically useful information that they can use to improve students' achievement (Clarke et al., 2001; Neill, 2003).
- Teachers may collaborate with one another more often because NCLB mandates annual testing in grades 3 through 8 and threatens schools with sanctions if adequate yearly progress is not made (Winkler, 2003).

**Beneficial Effects for Students**   High-stakes tests may motivate students to improve their study skills and work harder to avoid the embarrassment and disruption of academic progress that comes from being retained in a grade or not being allowed to graduate from high school (Clarke et al., 2001).

## Arguments Critical of High-Stakes Testing Programs

High-stakes testing programs are frequently criticized because they do not adhere to a rigorous set of assessment guidelines such as those promoted by the American

High-stakes tests criticized because of structural limitations, misinterpretation/ misuse of results, narrow view of motivation, adverse side effects

Educational Research Association (2000) and because they are subject to misuse and misinterpretation. In this section we summarize these criticisms in terms of structural limitations, the way test scores are interpreted, the motivational basis on which these programs rest, and undesirable side effects.

**Structural Limitations** High-stakes testing programs are perceived to be more of a hindrance than an aid to educators because of the nature of the components that make them up and how those parts fit together.

- For the sake of objectivity, efficiency, and cost, state assessments are often narrow in scope, limited in range, and shallow in depth. They favor selected-response items, are limited in the subjects they cover, do not assess any given topic in great depth, and mostly assess what students know rather than what they can do with what they know (Brulle, 2005; Goldberg, 2005; Hershberg, 2005; Sadker & Zittleman, 2004). For example, under realistic conditions many writing projects pass through the stages of planning, drafting, revising, editing, and publishing. But because efficiency is highly valued in the construction of high-stakes tests, many writing tests assess only a student's ability to create a draft (Schuster, 2004).
- State assessments that are narrow in scope, limited in range, and shallow in depth may not provide teachers with the type of diagnostic information they need to improve the effect of their instruction. Telling a teacher that a student's score was in the "Needs Improvement" category on a reading test does not help that teacher make the next reading lesson more effective (Cizek, 2003; Goldberg, 2005; Neill, 2003; Popham, 2003, 2004). Teachers would be better served if they were told which standards a student has or has not mastered and if the standards were described with sufficient clarity so that teachers could draw reasonably accurate inferences about how to remediate the student's weaknesses.
- A test's content, and the learning standards on which the test is based, do not necessarily reflect the knowledge and skills that the majority of people value the most and believe are most important for students to learn (Goldberg, 2004; Sadker & Zittleman, 2004).
- States frequently adopt far more content standards than teachers can cover and students can master, and they are often worded so generally that it is difficult to be certain about the precise content or skill in question (Clarke et al., 2001; Popham, 2003).
- The abstract paper-and-pencil items that make up the bulk of state assessments may confuse many third graders, who are either in Piaget's preoperational stage or the early part of the concrete operational stage (Gould, 2003).
- Standardized tests, as well constructed as they may be, are subject to measurement error for one or more reasons. One common source of error is the use of a single type of test. Unfortunately, most high-stakes assessment programs do not measure achievement in different ways (Clarke et al., 2001; Gulek, 2003). Other sources of measurement error, particularly on reading/language arts tests, can come from so-called summer loss, from retaining students in their current grade, and from intensive test preparation. Students in high-poverty schools typically do not catch up to their reading levels of the previous June until October because they do less reading over the summer than their middle-SES peers. The lower reading scores these students achieve when tested in the spring lead to unwarranted charges of poor teaching. The test scores of students who are retained produce the opposite effect—an overestimate of school effectiveness. If a school district retains, say, 10 percent of its lowest achieving third graders, the average score of those students who were promoted to fourth grade will be somewhat inflated. Intensive test preparation can also be considered a source of test error because, as we note later in our discussion of undesirable side effects, although it may raise scores, it rarely improves the underlying characteristic that is being measured. In other words, there is usually little transfer from high-stakes tests for

which students have been intensively prepped to other tests that measure the same knowledge and skills (McGill-Franzen & Allington, 2006).

- The stated goal of accountability programs—to improve the quality of classroom teaching and the level of student achievement—cannot be accomplished by programs that rely largely or exclusively on standardized test scores. The conditions under which teaching and learning occur must also be assessed, and professional development initiatives designed to help teachers be more effective must be provided (Camilli, 2003; Cizek, 2003; Linn, 2003).
- If you think of education in terms of inputs (teacher and student characteristics, resources, physical environment), processes (instructional and learning processes), and outputs (student knowledge and skills), the main focus of high-stakes testing programs is the output. Although NCLB requires that failing students receive remedial instruction and, if necessary, be allowed to transfer to different schools, the main thrust of the law is to drive school improvement by the imposition of output standards and accountability. High-stakes systems tend to ignore the contributions of input and process variables, or what might be called opportunity to learn. If, for example, students are not given sufficient time to learn, if the classroom and school environments are chaotic and threatening to the students' well-being, if classroom instruction is dull and unresponsive to individual differences, and if students have low levels of self-efficacy for learning and poor self-regulated learning skills, this diminished opportunity to learn is likely to result in a failing test performance (Sadker & Zittleman, 2004; Starratt, 2003).
- Schools that record consistent gains in achievement (and that would be rated "good" or "excellent" according to state standards) receive no credit for that accomplishment and are classified as "needing improvement" if the gains are too small to meet AYP requirements. This has been cited as a particularly egregious shortcoming when the gains occur among such at-risk groups as students from low-income families, students with limited English proficiency, and students with disabilities (Goldberg, 2005; Hershberg, 2005; Kim & Sunderman, 2005; Nichols & Berliner, 2005).

**Misinterpretation and Misuse of Test Results**    Although high-stakes testing programs do a reasonably good job of assessing mastery of certain learning standards, they do not, because they were not designed to, measure the general quality of a school or an individual teacher's effectiveness. Nevertheless, when faced with district and state report cards that rank schools, many people will draw the intuitively appealing but incorrect inference that high test scores equal good schools and teachers, that low scores equal poor-quality schools and teachers, and that rewarding or punishing schools and teachers on the basis of test scores is appropriate (Camilli, 2003; Cochran-Smith, 2003; Vogler & Kennedy, 2003).

**A One-Size-Fits-All Approach to Motivation**    High-stakes testing programs are based on a limited and simplistic view of motivation. Whether intended or not, the use of rewards and punishments to improve educational outcomes represents a behavioral view of motivation (Clarke et al., 2001). But if you go back to and quickly review Chapter 12 on motivation, you will see that many factors influence an individual's willingness and ability to master learning standards and perform well on standardized assessments. And as we pointed out in other chapters, the values students have about education (which are strongly influenced by parents and peer groups) and the sophistication of their learning skills will also affect their motivation to learn.

For some students, the prospect of gaining rewards and avoiding punishment may be sufficient incentive to work harder. But students who suffer from low self-efficacy, the adoption of avoidance goals, low levels of achievement motivation, maladaptive attributions, inappropriate beliefs about ability, an environment that does not satisfy deficiency needs, a poor academic self-concept, and poorly developed learning skills will likely see learning standards and high-stakes tests as obstacles they cannot overcome regardless of the rewards and punishments.

**A One-Size-Fits-All Approach to Standards** Using a similar line of reasoning as those who have argued that not all students will be motivated by the same rewards and punishments, Nel Noddings (2003) proposes that because students are so different in their interests, abilities, and goals, it is a mistake to hold everyone to the same set of standards. Using the teaching of mathematics as an example, she asks: "To whom shall we teach mathematics? For what ends? Mathematics of what sort? In what relation to students' expressed needs? In what relations to our primary aims?" (p. 87). By raising such questions, Noddings is not necessarily arguing that mathematics should not be taught to some students (although she does believe that the question deserves serious discussion before curriculum and instructional decisions are made). Rather, she suggests that it may be more profitable for more students if they were taught different types of mathematics in different ways and held accountable for the type of mathematics taught. This argument seems particularly cogent when applied to students with disabilities. As we noted in Chapter 6, the main purpose of IDEA is to ensure a free, appropriate education to all children in the least restrictive environment in which they are capable of successfully performing. Obviously, the nature of that education and the environment in which it takes place will be different for children with different disabilities. With respect to taking high-stakes tests, Noddings (2003) says:

> some probably should be encouraged to take them, with only positive stakes attached. It is outrageous, however, to force these tests on all students in special education . . . . If by *equity* we mean providing an appropriate education for every child, it is dead wrong to expect the same performance from each child. Having forgotten our aim, we act as though all children are academically equal and can be held to the same standard. (p. 90)

*A possible negative effect of high-stakes testing programs is that teachers may spend more time preparing students for the test and less time on topics and subjects that are not covered by the test.*

**Undesirable Side Effects** Critics of high-stakes testing argue that the rewards and punishments associated with high-stakes testing programs may produce one or more of the following undesirable side effects.

- Concern with rankings and the rewards and punishments attached to state assessment programs leads many teachers to provide students with intensive test preparation. Although this practice may raise scores, it often comes at the expense of meaningful learning (Center on Educational Policy, 2005; Goldberg, 2004; Nichols & Berliner, 2005). Consequently, there is often little transfer to other tests that purport to measure the same knowledge and skills.

  For example, one study found that scores on a statewide assessment increased almost every year for seven years in reading and math. In the eighth year, a new test of similar reading and math skills was introduced. Scores in both areas fell dramatically, and then rose in subsequent years (Linn, 2000). In another study, 83 percent of students in a Pittsburgh elementary school scored above the national norm on the reading test of the Iowa Test of Basic Skills (a standardized achievement test). But on the reading test of the state assessment, only 26 percent scored within the top two proficiency levels (Yau, 2002). The phenomenon that both studies highlight is sometimes referred to as WYTIWYG: what you test is what you get. In other words, high-stakes assessments lead teachers to focus on preparing students for a particular type of test, and, as a result, there is little carryover to other tests that measure the same or similar skills.

- Many educators fear that the press to meet the demands of NCLB and other state assessment goals will result in more time spent strengthening students' basic math and reading/language arts skills at the expense of time for such subjects as art, music, and foreign languages (Hamilton & Stecher, 2004; Nichols & Berliner, 2005).

- A similar fear has been expressed about the fate of certain forms of instruction. For example, inquiry-based science education has been praised because it emphasizes hands-on science activities as opposed to the traditional reading about science in textbooks and watching the teacher conduct an occasional experiment. But because of the pressure to have students perform well on state-mandated assessments, science educators fear that the amount of time devoted to science instruction will be reduced in favor of test preparation activities and that the instruction that does occur will emphasize drill-and-practice activities because they fit the demands of high-stakes tests (Gallagher, 2005; Nichols & Berliner, 2005).
- To avoid the negative sanctions mandated by NCLB for schools whose students continue to score poorly for several years in a row, states are likely to propose the lowest-level content and performance standards that the federal government will accept (Linn, 2003; Popham, 2005).
- As high-stakes testing programs have proliferated, so have reports of cheating by teachers and administrators (echoing research, summarized earlier in the book, suggesting that most people are susceptible to cheating under the right circumstances). Educators have been accused of such infractions as giving slow students extra time on timed tests, suggesting answers to students, changing students' answers, directly teaching specific portions of a test, and allowing students to have access to dictionaries and thesauruses on writing tests (Nichols & Berliner, 2005; Popham, 2005). In one survey, about 35 percent of teachers said they had either engaged in unethical test-related practices or had seen others engaging in them (Cizek, 2001b). Administrators have been accused of publishing inaccurate graduation and enrollment data to make their school districts look better than they actually are. In one case, a school district claimed that 51 percent of the class of 2002 graduated, but an independent investigation claimed that only 39 percent graduated. The size of another school's freshman class decreased by two-thirds over four years, yet the school reported no dropouts (Goldberg, 2004).
- States that make promotion contingent on achieving a passing score are likely to have higher dropout rates than states that have no such requirement (Goldberg, 2005; Kober et al., 2006; Neill, 2003).

## VIDEO CASE    ◀◀ ▶ ▶▶

HM

### Foundations: Aligning Instruction with Federal Legislation

*Watch the video, study the artifacts in the case, and reflect upon the following questions:*

1. In this Video Case, various school professionals discuss the challenges of complying with NCLB. As a prospective teacher, what aspects of NCLB do you find most daunting?

2. In your opinion, has federal legislation such as NCLB improved the quality of public education? Use the material in this chapter to find information that will support your argument.

## Research on the Effects of High-Stakes Testing

Research on effects of high-stakes testing limited and inconsistent

Given all the argument about the effects of high-stakes testing, actual research on this subject is vital. But because these programs have been in existence for a relatively short time, the research on their effects is limited, the results are inconsistent, and the implications have been hotly debated. In addition, some of the evidence is merely anecdotal. Nevertheless, we will summarize for you what has been reported about the effects these programs appear to have on student achievement, student motivation, teachers' behavior, classroom instruction, and the dropout rate.

**Effect on Achievement**　A major assumption underlying NCLB is that the consequences of failing to meet its accountability standards will drive states and school districts to improve the quality of classroom instruction and the level of student achievement. This hypothesis was tested by a group of researchers (Nichols, Glass, & Berliner, 2006) who classified twenty-five states in terms of how much pressure their testing programs placed on teachers and students and then examined the relationship between these various programs and performance by fourth- and eighth-grade students on the math and reading scores of the National Assessment of Educational Progress (NAEP) tests. They found no relationship between earlier pressure from high-stakes tests and later achievement. Another analysis (Lee, 2006) also concluded that NCLB did not produce increases in NAEP math and reading scores among fourth- and eighth-grade students. On the other hand, the Center on Educational Policy (2005) reported that almost three-fourths of the 314 school districts they surveyed in forty-nine states reported increases in students' scores. The inconsistency between these two findings may be due, as we noted earlier, to the fact that although intensive test preparation boosts scores on state tests, there is often little carryover to other tests, such as those administered by the NAEP (see, for example, Fuller et al., 2006).

**Effect on Motivation**　Some evidence suggests that the presence of high stakes motivates some students to work harder. Among Massachusetts high school students who failed that state's high-stakes test the first time they took it, about two-thirds said they were now working harder and paying more attention in class, and almost 75 percent said that missing too much school was a major reason for failing the test (Cizek, 2003).

In 1996, the Chicago Public Schools instituted a high-stakes testing program that required third, sixth, and eighth graders to pass the reading and mathematics sections of the Iowa Test of Basic Skills in order to be promoted to the next grade. During the school year leading up to the test, students could receive extra help both before school and through an after-school program. Students who failed the test were required to attend a summer program before they could retake the test and be promoted for the fall semester. Those who failed the second test were retained.

An analysis of 102 low-achieving students (Roderick & Engel, 2001) revealed that the program affected different students in different ways. About 53 percent of the students reported greater attention to class work, increased academic expectations and support from their teachers, and greater effort both in and out of class. The students interpreted the higher expectations and support from teachers as evidence that the teachers cared about them and wanted them to succeed. A second and much smaller group (about 9 percent) also worked hard to prepare for the test but received most of their support outside of school from parents and other family members. A third group of students, about 35 percent of the sample, expressed concern about passing the test and was aware of the before- and after-school help that was available but did not take advantage of it. The fourth and smallest group of students (about 4 percent) wasn't worried about passing the test and wasn't considered by teachers to be at risk of failing.

To examine the relationship between effort and test performance, students from the first three groups were reassigned to one of the following categories: Substantial Work Effort Either in or out of School, No Substantial Work Effort, or Substantial Home or Skill Problems. Of the 53 students in the Substantial Work Effort group, 57 percent passed the test in June, 23 percent passed in August, and 20 percent were retained. Of the 28 students in the No Substantial Work Effort group, 11 percent passed in June, 25 percent passed in August, and 64 percent were retained. Of the 17 students in the Substantial Home or Skill Problems group, 12 percent passed in June, 47 percent passed in August, and 41 percent were retained.

These findings clearly show, as have other interventions mentioned in previous chapters, that no single policy or approach will work for all students because classroom learning is an extremely complex phenomenon that is only partly under the teacher's control. Although the threat of retention was sufficient to motivate some students to work harder and take advantage of the additional resources that were provided, it had a much smaller effect on students with serious learning skill deficits and/or problems at home and on students who simply declined to put forth more effort. Retaining students who fall into these latter two groups is likely to cause them to become even more disengaged and eventually drop out of school. Obviously, an alternative to retention is required to motivate these students and raise their achievement levels.

**Effect on Teachers and Teaching**   An examination of Florida's accountability system (Goldhaber & Hannaway, 2004) revealed that high-stakes testing can have both positive and negative effects on teachers, depending on the type of school one teaches in. Like students, Florida schools are given a letter grade that ranges from A to F based on previous years' scores on the Florida Comprehensive Assessment Test (FCAT). Parents and teachers in A schools felt strong pressure to do whatever was necessary to maintain their school's high grade. As a result, the instructional focus at these schools narrowed. One school postponed all field trips and projects until after the FCATs in the spring. One teacher described classrooms as lifeless, boring places in which students sat at their desks doing workbooks keyed to the FCAT. The principal of one A school said, "We are an A school, and we hate it." Teachers and principals in F schools, however, viewed the accountability system more positively. Although they felt that the grade did not reflect their efforts or the strides they had made in recent years, they used their school's low grade as a motivation to make even more of an effort to improve students' test scores. But as we noted earlier, such pressures have led teachers and administrators in all types of schools to engage in cheating (Nichols & Berliner, 2005).

Anecdotal evidence from Vermont and Virginia (Winkler, 2003) also suggests that state assessments can have a beneficial effect. Some teachers said that their states' content and performance standards stimulated them to use more forms of instruction than they had previously. In an attempt to get as many students as possible to score at the proficiency level, teachers were doing more individualized planning and using different materials and methods with different students. This is the concept of differentiated instruction that we mentioned in previous chapters.

High-stakes tests have encouraged teachers to better align state standards with classroom instruction and classroom assessment, a development that some see as beneficial (Hamilton & Stecher, 2004; Jennings & Rentner, 2006) but that others (Gallagher, 2005) see as having detrimental effects. The State of Illinois, for example, encourages its teachers to design their instruction around the Illinois Professional Teaching Standards. At the same time, teachers are also expected to gear their instruction to the Illinois Standards Achievement Test (ISAT), which the state uses to comply with NCLB. One teaching standard, for example, recommends that teachers provide learning opportunities that support students' intellectual, social, and personal development, yet the ISAT does not formally assess social and personal development. It should be clear from the evidence provided so far which set of standards teachers will attend to in deciding what and how to teach.

A national survey of almost 4,200 K–12 teachers found that more teachers in high-stakes states than moderate- or low-stakes states constructed their classroom tests to reflect the format of the state test, spent more time on test preparation, used materials that closely resembled the test (for example, students were not allowed to use computers for writing assignments because the state test was handwritten), and spent more time with students who were close to either passing the test or moving to a higher level (Pedulla et al., 2003), a practice that is sometimes referred to as "educational triage" (Booher-Jennings, 2005).

**Effect on the Curriculum**   According to a survey conducted by the Center on Educational Policy (2005; Jennings & Rentner, 2006), increases in the amount of instruction devoted to reading and math have resulted in decreases in time devoted to other subjects. About 27 percent of districts reported reducing the amount of instruction devoted to social studies, 22 percent spent less time on science, and 20 percent spent less time on art and music. Anecdotal evidence corroborates these survey findings. In one low-scoring Massachusetts school district, reading was dropped for the spring semester to accommodate test preparation activities for English/language arts and mathematics (Vogler & Kennedy, 2003).

**Effect on the Dropout Rate** The question of whether high-stakes exams, particularly high school exit exams, increase the dropout rate (currently about 5 percent of all high school students) is a difficult one to answer definitively. Not only is the research limited, but it is also inconclusive, because states define and count dropouts differently, and it is difficult for researchers to isolate the effect of a high-stakes test from other factors that may also be playing a role. Nevertheless, an expert panel convened by the Center for Education Policy reviewed the existing literature and concluded that the weight of the evidence currently supports the claim that exit exams cause more students to drop out of school than would otherwise be the case (Gayler et al., 2003). A subsequent analysis by the same organization (Kober et al., 2006) supported that finding but also noted that exit exams are just one of several factors that contribute to a student's decision to drop out and does not seem to be one of the most significant factors.

**School Choice and Supplemental Instructional Services** As we mentioned earlier, schools that fail to make AYP for two consecutive years must allow students the option of transferring to another school within the district, and they must provide tutoring (by an outside agency in most circumstances) to students after three consecutive years of not meeting the AYP requirement. As part of a 2004–2005 survey of 314 school districts, the Center on Educational Policy (2005) inquired about the use of these options and reported the following:

1. About 15 percent of school districts were required to let students attend another public school in their district, but only 1 percent of eligible students took advantage of the opportunity. In addition, many schools that took transfer students did so at the cost of larger class sizes.
2. Although letting students transfer from so-called failing schools was supposed to have a positive effect on the students' achievement, only about 3 percent of school districts believed that this was the case. About 28 percent said choice had little or no impact on achievement, and almost 70 percent had no idea what effect changing schools had on student achievement.
3. Only 18 percent of students who were eligible for tutoring services took advantage of them. As with the effect of transferring to another school, most school districts said they did not know whether tutoring was producing its desired effect.

Frederick Hess and Chester Finn (2004) argue that the relatively little use of school choice and tutoring options is attributable to one or more of the following factors:

1. The lack of successful schools for students to transfer to in small districts.
2. Districts that do have successful schools may not have sufficient room to accept all students who wish to transfer.
3. Failing schools may discourage high-scoring students from transferring out for fear that their scores in subsequent years may be even lower, and successful schools may discourage low-scoring students from transferring in for fear that such students will pull their scores down in subsequent years. As presently written, the law provides no incentives to either the sending or receiving school.
4. School administrators see the school-choice and supplemental-services options as disruptive and costly. The choice option necessitates changes in bus schedules and may change the ethnic/racial balance of some schools, and both options require that school districts set aside 20 percent of their Title I budgets to pay for the costs of school choice and tutoring.
5. As noted earlier (Tucker & Toch, 2004), state departments of education often lack the resources to identify failing schools and to ensure that students receive adequate supplemental services in a timely manner.

## Recommendations for Improving High-Stakes Testing

If NCLB and state-mandated assessment programs are to fulfill their goals of improving the quality of instruction and raising achievement levels, they will have to be implemented in such a way that all stakeholders believe they are being treated fairly. On this score, NCLB appears to be off to a rocky start. A handful of school districts around the country have decided to forgo Title I money from the federal government in order to be free of NCLB's requirements (Hoff, 2006), and several states have sued the federal government for not providing sufficient funds to implement all of the law's provisions (Dobbs, 2005).

While political leaders complain about funding, educators argue that the goal of having all students be proficient in math and reading/language arts by 2014 is unrealistic and will bring about the demise of fundamentally sound schools (Nichols & Berliner, 2005; Popham, 2004; Thomas, 2005). Still others (for example, Jones, 2004; Sadker & Zittleman, 2004) argue that most accountability programs have adopted the wrong focus. A more useful accountability system is one that holds policymakers accountable for the effects of their high-stakes accountability systems. In this view, an accountability system that focuses exclusively on the test scores of students, classes, schools, and districts—ignoring wide disparities in educational opportunity because of differences in funding and facilities—is an irresponsible system.

In response to the many criticisms of high-stakes testing programs, five professional organizations (the American Association of School Administrators, the National Association of Elementary School Principals, the National Association of Secondary School Principals, the National Education Association, and the National Middle School Association) created a commission of nationally recognized experts in assessment and instruction to provide recommendations for meeting the annual testing, AYP, and reporting requirements of NCLB in such a way that positive outcomes are more likely than negative ones. They produced the following nine recommendations for state assessment systems:

1. Each state should adopt only those content standards that represent the most important knowledge and skills that students need to learn. This will help states avoid having more standards than teachers can cover, students can master, and test makers can assess. Having a more modest set of standards also allows educators, students, and parents to get feedback about performance for each standard instead of a single score summed over hundreds of standards.
2. A state's content standards should clearly describe exactly what is being assessed so teachers can create lessons that directly address those standards. Phrases such as "express and interpret information and ideas," for example, should be translated into more precise language.
3. Scores on a state assessment should be reported on a standard-by-standard basis for each student, school, and district.
4. States should provide school districts with additional assessment procedures to assess those standards that the required assessment does not cover.
5. States should monitor the curricula of school districts to ensure that instruction addresses all content standards and subjects, not just those assessed by the required state test.
6. State assessments should be designed so that all students have an equal opportunity to demonstrate which of the state's standards they have mastered. This includes providing accommodations and alternative assessments for students with disabilities and those who are limited in their English proficiency.
7. All tests should satisfy the Standards for Educational and Psychological Testing of the American Educational Research Association and similar test-quality guidelines.

**pause & reflect**

Critics of high-stakes testing suggest that teachers try to persuade policymakers to change the worst aspects of such programs. They recommend steps such as these: speak out at school board meetings; organize a letter-writing campaign to the school board and legislators; assemble a delegation to visit legislators; write letters to the local newspaper; set up a workshop on the abuses of high-stakes testing. How many of these activities are you willing to engage in? Why?

8. Teachers and principals should receive professional development training that helps them use test results to optimize children's learning.

9. States should continually seek to improve the quality of their assessments (Commission on Instructionally Supportive Assessment, 2002).

Several years ago, Robert Linn, a prominent expert in educational measurement, wrote the following:

> As someone who has spent his entire career doing research, writing, and thinking about educational testing and assessment issues, I would like to conclude by summarizing a compelling case showing that the major uses of tests for student and school accountability during the past 50 years have improved education and student learning in dramatic ways. Unfortunately, this is not my conclusion. Instead, I am led to conclude in most cases that instruments and technology have not been up to the demands that have been placed on them by high-stakes accountability. . . . The unintended negative effects of the high-stakes accountability uses often outweigh the intended positive effects. (Linn, 2000, p. 14)

If the preceding recommendations are taken seriously by policymakers at the state and national levels, then perhaps Robert Linn and others will express a more favorable opinion of the effects of high-stakes testing several years from now.

## Take a Stand!

### Healing the Patient: Using the Medical Model to Guide Educational Accountability

Almost everybody, including educators, accepts the contention that educators should be held accountable for their efforts. Indeed, every person should be accountable to others in some fashion. What is, and should be, vigorously debated is the way in which accountability is defined and practiced. We believe that the accountability systems of many states are less effective than they could be because their primary focus is on identifying and punishing substandard performance rather than identifying and remediating the causes of those weaknesses.

We agree with measurement expert Gregory Cizek, who argues that if high-stakes programs are to be more widely embraced by educators, students, and parents, they should mimic the assessment approach that physicians use in their practices. Medical tests tend to be diagnostic in nature because of the detailed level at which they report results. A typical analysis of a blood sample, for example, provides information on the levels of more than twenty elements (e.g., blood sugar, sodium, potassium, calcium, protein, HDL cholesterol, LDL cholesterol, and triglyceride). Abnormal results are then followed by specific recommendations for treatment. The patient isn't accused of being inferior and charged twice the doctor's normal fee as a penalty for having "failing" test scores.

Consequently, a reasonable stand for teachers to take regarding high-stakes testing programs is that they should be constructed to provide detailed information about students' strengths and weaknesses; these results should then serve as a basis for additional instruction. In addition, professional development workshops and seminars should be provided, focusing on how teachers can help students learn the knowledge and skills that are assessed.

#### HM TeacherPrepSPACE

Would you agree with using a medical model for high-stakes testing? What can you do in your own school to promote this view of testing? To explore this issue further, see the Take a Stand! section of the textbook's student website.

# STANDARDIZED TESTING AND TECHNOLOGY

Given the prevalence of standardized testing and the large amount of money that schools spend on testing programs, it is not too surprising that technology tools exist for a wide range of assessment formats, including the standard true-false, multiple-choice, and fill-in-the-blank questions, as well as alternative assessments such as essay writing, debate forums, simulations, and electronic exhibitions of student work. As we discuss in this section, technology can be used in all phases of testing, including preparing students for standardized tests, administering tests, and scoring students' responses.

## Using Technology to Prepare Students for Assessments

For students to perform well on standardized tests, they need to have a clear understanding of the standards for which they will be held accountable and the types of items that will be used to assess those standards. Toward that end, many states provide web-based resources to help students become familiar with and prepare for state assessments. On the websites of state departments of education, students, teachers, and parents can read or download copies of their states' content and performance standards, study examples of the types of items that will appear on the test, and, in some cases, take practice tests. The University of Texas, for example, provides online tutorials and practice tests to that state's high school students to help them prepare for the required graduation exam (Carnevale, 2004). During the 2006–2007 school year, 112 Tennessee schools participated in the Tennessee Formative Assessment Pilot Project. Students in grades 3 through 8 took online formative assessments that were aligned with state standards to help teachers monitor which students were and were not on track to pass the end-of-year state assessment (Tennessee Department of Education, 2006).

Some states and school districts also make available the online test preparation services of private, for-profit companies. The Princeton Review, for example, has a 130,000-question test bank that school districts can use to create online practice tests that are aligned with their states' standards for grades 3 through 12. A company called Smarthinking (**www.smarthinking.com**) provides tutoring through online instructors (called "e-structors") and digital whiteboards. Students can correspond with tutors in real time or submit questions and assignments and get a response within twenty-four hours. The digital whiteboard is used by students to demonstrate their understanding of concepts and skills (such as English grammar or mathematical problem solving), and also by the tutor, who adds comments and corrections.

On the website of TestGEAR (**www.testu.com**), students take a diagnostic pretest and are then provided with individualized courses in various aspects of math and language arts. Teachers receive diagnostic reports that analyze students' responses to test questions. A teacher in an Orlando, Florida, school who used the TestGEAR service was convinced that it helped his students improve their scores on that state's high-stakes test, the Florida Comprehensive Assessment Test (Borja, 2003).

## Using Technology to Assess Mastery of Standards

Although only a small percentage of school districts currently have computer-based testing (CBT) programs, you can expect to see more schools at least experiment

---

Standardized Testing and Technology

Websites of state departments of education, private companies provide services that help prepare students for state assessments

*HM TeacherPrepSPACE*

To explore websites mentioned in this chapter, go to the Weblinks section of the textbook's student website.

---

*In coming years, it is likely that increasing numbers of students will take high-stakes and other standardized tests on a computer.*

with this option in the coming years. Consequently, you should be aware of their advantages and disadvantages. On the plus side:

- You can get scores and detailed reports at any time, from immediately after a test is completed to a few days later, and can therefore provide students with timely feedback (Chaney & Gilman, 2005; Olson, 2002; Russo, 2002).
- CBT reduces the chances of cheating by allowing you to create as many random sequences of test items as there are students taking the test (Chaney & Gilman, 2005).
- It is easier to use novel items to assess certain skills. For example, a computer screen could display the periodic table of elements with a question mark in five of the cells and the five elements that belong in those cells above the table. The student would have to drag each element to its correct location and then drop it (release the mouse button) (Zenisky & Sireci, 2002).

On the negative side:

- It is costly to buy and maintain enough computers to test large groups of students. One high school in Indiana, for example, had to close four computer labs for a month to test every student.
- Schools need to have a plan for dealing with interruptions due to a faulty computer or a power loss (Olson, 2003b).
- Claims that paper-and-pencil tests are equivalent to computer versions of the same test are not yet supported by research. Some studies, for example, have found that White males score higher on computer-based versions of a test, whereas Black and Latino students score higher on paper-and-pencil versions. Other studies, however, have found no differences across versions for these groups (Leeson, 2006).

National testing services have shown an interest in using technology to grade essay exam questions as human judgment on national and state tests is fairly subjective and human time is costly. The first of these so-called automated essay scoring programs, called Project Essay Grade (PEG), has demonstrated that it can rate student essays as well as or better than humans. According to its creator, Ellis Page (2003), this tool evaluates such complex and important writing variables as content, organization, style, and creativity, in addition to mechanics and document length. In one experiment, the scores assigned by PEG to more than a thousand essays from the Praxis exam (taken mostly by teacher education students applying for teacher certification) were compared with the scores given by six human judges. PEG's ratings were more similar to the judges' ratings than the judges' ratings were similar to each other's. Computer scoring is not only quicker and more economical, but apparently it is more accurate and consistent than human ratings (Page, 2003).

Although programs such as PEG are used mostly at the college and graduate school levels, they are also being tried out in grades K–12 for scoring essay-type constructed-response questions (Elliot, 2003). Indiana is pilot testing the scoring program used by the Educational Testing Service to assess high school students' essay responses on an English exam (Olson, 2003b). Given the millions of essays rated each year by the Educational Testing Service alone and the addition of essay writing to the SATs and GREs, computer-rated essays may soon become commonplace in standardized testing.

## Computer Adaptive Testing

Computer adaptive testing: computers determine sequence and difficulty level of test items

Technology has also shaped the way tests are put together and administered. Instead of subjecting every student to the same sequence of test items, **computer adaptive testing (CAT)** allows students to take tests that are geared to their own ability levels. When a student begins a test in the CAT format, the computer selects an item that matches his or her estimated ability. If the student responds correctly, the computer selects a slightly more difficult item. An incorrect response results in an easier item. After each correct or incorrect response, the computer estimates the student's ability. The test ends when the computer determines that it has reached the limits of the student's knowledge (Olson, 2005; Wilson, 2005; Yeh, 2006).

The major advantages of CAT are tests that are only as long as they need to be for each examinee, immediate feedback on achievement growth, and information about students' strengths and weaknesses that can help teachers better target their instructional efforts (Olson, 2005). The major disadvantages are increased test anxiety and confusion for those not familiar or comfortable with taking a test on a computer and high test-taking fees because of the high cost involved in developing and implementing such a system (Latu & Chapman, 2002).

In an interesting turn of events, several states that had intended to use CAT to meet the requirements of NCLB had to change course. The reason is that NCLB requires that students be evaluated only according to the expectations for their grade level. Taking a test that contains items that are either easier or harder than what is normal for a grade level, as in the case of computer adaptive tests, is considered "out-of-level" testing and is not allowed (Trotter, 2003). One state, however, believes it has solved this problem. The Idaho Standards Achievement Test is a state assessment that contains the adaptive feature of CAT but also satisfies NCLB requirements. It does this by first presenting students with grade-level test items and then moves into the adaptive portion of the test (Olson, 2005). School districts in other states, such as South Dakota, Kentucky, and California, are using CAT either to satisfy other accountability goals or to promote the use of formative assessment (Stokes, 2005; Trotter, 2003; Wilson, 2005).

In the next section we offer several Suggestions for Teaching that will help you and your students appropriately use standardized tests and interpret the scores from them.

# Suggestions for Teaching in Your Classroom

## Using Standardized Tests

**1** **Before you give a standardized test, emphasize that students should do their best.**

For maximum usefulness, scores on standardized tests should be as accurate a representation of actual ability as possible.

Accordingly, the day before a standardized test is scheduled, tell your students that they should do their best. Emphasize that the scores will be used to help them improve their school performance and will provide useful feedback to you about the quality of your instruction. If you're thinking about ignoring this suggestion because you don't believe that students will score significantly higher on a standardized test in response to a simple pep talk, you might want to reconsider. Research has shown that students who have a positive attitude toward learning and test taking score higher on tests than do students whose attitudes are less positive or are negative (Brown & Walberg, 1993; Gulek, 2003).

**2** **Before your students take a standardized test, give them specific suggestions for taking such tests.**

JOURNAL ENTRY
Explaining Test-Taking Skills

You may be able partly to reduce the anxiety and tension that are almost inevitable under formal testing conditions by giving some test-taking hints in advance. Robert Linn and M. David Miller (2005) note the following tips that might be stressed (depending on the type of test and the grade level of the student):

1. Listen to or read directions carefully.
2. Listen to or read test items carefully.
3. Set a pace that will allow time to complete the test.
4. Bypass difficult items and return to them later.
5. Make informed guesses rather than omit items.
6. Eliminate as many alternatives as possible on multiple-choice items before guessing.
7. Follow directions carefully when marking the answer sheet (for example, be sure to darken the entire space).
8. Check to be sure the item number and answer number match when marking an answer.
9. Check to be sure the appropriate response is marked on the answer sheet.
10. Go back and check the answers if time permits. (p. 466)

**3** **Examine the test booklet and answer sheet in advance so that you are familiar with the test.**

Ideally you might take an earlier released version of the test or a publicly available practice test yourself so that you become thoroughly familiar with what your students will be doing. If there are any aspects of recording answers that are especially tricky or if the test contains unfamiliar terminology, you might mention these when you give your test-taking skills presentation or when you hand out examination booklets and answer sheets. Knowledge of test vocabulary and terminology has been found to have a significant effect on students' performance on high-stakes tests (Gulek, 2003).

**4** **Be cautious when interpreting scores, and always give the student the benefit of the doubt.**

JOURNAL ENTRY
Interpreting Test Scores

The profiles or reports you will receive a few weeks after a test has been administered will contain information that is potentially beneficial to you and your students. If misused or misinterpreted, however, the information is potentially harmful. Misinterpretations of scores can lead to complaints by parents. Therefore, as you examine the scores, concentrate on ways you can make positive use of the results.

For example, if a student's test scores are lower than you expected them to be, examine them to discover areas of weakness but guard against thinking, "Well, I guess he had me fooled. He's not as sharp as I thought he was. Maybe I had better lower his grades a notch on the next report card." There are many reasons a student may not do well on a test (for example, anxiety, fatigue, illness, worry about some home or school interpersonal situation), and scores may not be an accurate reflection of current capability. Thus, whenever there is a discrepancy between test scores and observed classroom performance, always assume that the more favorable impression is the one to use as an indication of general capability. Try to use indications of below-average performance in constructive ways to help students overcome inadequacies.

**5** **Do your best to control the impact of negative expectations.**

As you peruse student test scores, do your best to resist the temptation to label or categorize students, particularly those who have a consistent pattern of low scores.

**Suggestions for Teaching in Your Classroom**

Instead of succumbing to thoughts that such students are incapable of learning, you might make an effort to concentrate on the idea that they need extra encouragement and individualized attention. Use the information on test profiles to help them overcome their learning difficulties, not to justify fatalistically ignoring their problems.

**6**   **Be prepared to offer parents clear and accurate information about their children's test scores.**

*HM TeacherPrepSPACE*

To spur your reflections about standardized tests, see the Thought Questions and Reflective Journal Questions on the textbook's student website.

For a variety of reasons, misconceptions about the nature of standardized tests are common. As a result, many parents do not fully understand what their children's scores mean. Parent-teacher conferences are probably the best time to correct misconceptions and provide some basic information about the meaning of standardized test scores. In an unobtrusive place on your desk, you might keep a brief list of points to cover as you converse with each parent. In one way or another, you should mention that test scores should be treated as *estimates* of whatever was measured (achievement, for example). There are two reasons for representing test scores in this fashion:

- Tests do not (indeed, they cannot) assess everything that students know or that makes up a particular capability. Standardized achievement tests, for example, tend to cover a relatively broad range of knowledge but do not assess any one topic in great depth. Therefore, students may know more than their scores suggest.
- All tests contain some degree of error because of such factors as vaguely worded items, confusing directions, and low motivation on the day the test is administered.

Remember that a student's test score reflects the extent to which the content of that test has been mastered at about the time the test was taken. A student may have strengths and weaknesses not measured by a particular test, and because of changes in such characteristics as interests, motives, and cognitive skills, test scores can change, sometimes dramatically. The younger the student is and the longer the interval is between testings (on the same test), the greater is the likelihood that a test score will change significantly.

What a test score means depends on the nature of the test. If your students took an intelligence or a scholastic aptitude test, point out that such tests measure the current status of those cognitive skills that most closely relate to academic success. Also mention that IQ scores are judged to be below average, average, or above average on the basis of how they compare with the scores of a norm group.

If you are discussing achievement test scores, make sure you understand the differences among diagnostic tests, norm-referenced tests, and criterion-referenced tests:

- Scores from a diagnostic achievement test can be used to discuss a student's strengths and weaknesses in such skills as reading, math, and spelling.
- Scores from a norm-referenced achievement test can be used to discuss general strengths and weaknesses in one or more content areas. For achievement tests that provide multiple sets of norms, start your interpretation at the most local level (school norms, ideally), because they are likely to be the most meaningful to parents, and then move to a more broad-based interpretation (district, state, or national norms).
- Scores from a criterion-referenced achievement test can be used to discuss how well a student has mastered the objectives on which the test is based. If there is a close correspondence between the test's objectives and your own objectives as a teacher, the test score can be used as an indicator of how much the student has learned in class.

The instructional decisions you make in the classroom will be *guided* but not dictated by the test scores. Many parents fear that if their child obtains a low score

**HM** *TeacherPrepSPACE*

*To review this chapter, see the ACE practice tests and PowerPoint slides on the textbook's student website.*

on a test, she will be labeled a slow learner by the teacher and receive less attention than higher-scoring students do. This is a good opportunity to lay such a fear to rest in two ways. First, note that test scores are but *one* source of information about students. You will also take into account how well they perform on classroom tests, homework assignments, and special projects, as well as in classroom discussions. Second, emphasize that you are committed to using test scores not to classify students but to help them learn.

# 15

# Assessment of Classroom Learning

## KEY POINTS

*These key points will help you
learn the important information
in this chapter. To help you study,
they also appear in the margins
of the pages, next to the text
where they are discussed.*

### The Role of Assessment in Teaching

- Measurement: assigning numbers or ratings according to rules to create a ranking
- Evaluation: making judgments about the value of a measure
- Summative evaluation: measure achievement; assign grades
- Formative evaluation: monitor progress; plan remedial instruction
- Tests can positively affect many aspects of students' learning
- Moderate testing produces more learning than no testing or infrequent testing

### Ways to Measure Student Learning

- Written tests measure degree of knowledge about a subject
- Selected-response tests are objectively scored and efficient but usually measure lower levels of learning and do not reveal what students can do
- Short-answer tests easy to write but measure lower levels of learning
- Essay tests measure higher levels of learning but are hard to grade consistently
- Performance tests measure ability to use knowledge and skills to solve realistic problems, create products
- Performance tests may vary in degree of realism
- Rubrics increase objectivity and consistency of scoring, align instruction with assessment, communicate teachers' expectations, help students monitor progress
- Performance tests pose several challenges for teachers
- Reliability and validity of performance tests not yet firmly established

### Ways to Evaluate Student Learning

- Norm-referenced grading: compare one student with others
- Norm-referenced grading based on absence of external criteria
- Norm-referenced grading can be used to evaluate advanced levels of learning
- Criterion-referenced grading: compare individual performance with stated criteria
- Criterion-referenced grades provide information about strengths and weaknesses
- Mastery approach: give students multiple opportunities to master goals at own pace

### Improving Your Grading Methods: Assessment Practices to Avoid

- Be aware of and avoid faulty measurement and grading practices

### Technology for Classroom Assessment

- Digital portfolio: collection of work that is stored and illustrated electronically
- Special rubrics available to assess digital portfolios and presentations

### Suggestions for Teaching in Your Classroom: Effective Assessment Techniques

- Necessary to obtain a representative sample of behavior when testing
- Table of specifications helps ensure an adequate sample of content, behavior
- Elementary grade students tested as much for diagnostic, formative evaluation purposes as for summative purposes
- Rating scales and checklists make evaluations of performance more systematic
- Item analysis tells about difficulty, discriminating power of multiple-choice items

arlier parts of this book discuss three major aspects of the teacher's role: understanding student differences and how to address them properly, understanding the learning process and how to use that knowledge to formulate effective approaches to instruction, and establishing a positive learning environment by influencing motivation to learn and creating an orderly classroom. Now we turn to assessing performance, which is an equally significant aspect of the teacher's role. Virtually everyone connected with public schools, from students to teachers and administrators to state education officials to members of the U.S. Congress, is keenly interested in knowing how much and how well students have learned.

In this and the previous chapter, we describe a twofold process for assessing student learning: using teacher-made measures to assess mastery of the teacher's specific objectives and using professionally prepared standardized tests to measure the extent of a student's general knowledge base and aptitudes. Although the items that make up teacher-made and standardized assessments can be very similar, if not identical, these two types of assessment differ significantly in their construction, in the conditions under which they are administered, and in the purposes for which they are used. In short, standardized tests are designed to highlight where students, classrooms, schools, and districts stand with respect to one another in terms of general levels of performance in various skills and subject areas. Period. Think of this as assessment *of* learning. Teacher-made assessments, by contrast, are designed to highlight students' strengths and weaknesses, to give students timely feedback about the effectiveness of their study habits, and to provide teachers with timely information that can help them make more effective instructional decisions. These assessments may or may not look like traditional "tests." Think of them as assessment *for* learning (Stiggins, 2002). ●

# THE ROLE OF ASSESSMENT IN TEACHING

Assessing student learning is something that every teacher has to do, and usually quite frequently. Written tests, book reports, research papers, homework exercises, oral presentations, question-and-answer sessions, science projects, and artwork of various sorts are just some of the means by which teachers measure student learning, with written tests accounting for about 33 percent of a typical student's course grade (Stiggins, 2001, 2002). One elementary teacher estimated that, on average, students take a written test once every twelve days (Barksdale-Ladd & Thomas, 2000). It is no surprise, then, that the typical teacher can spend about one-third of class time engaged in one or another type of assessment activity (McTighe & Ferrara, 1998).

Assessing student learning is a task that most teachers dislike and few do well. One reason is that many have little or no in-depth knowledge of assessment principles (Guskey, 2003; Mertler, 2000; Stiggins, 2002; Trevisan, 2002), largely because most states do not require prospective teachers to demonstrate competence in assessment in order to obtain a teaching license (Guskey, 2003). Another reason is that the role of assessor is seen as being inconsistent with the role of teacher (or helper). In fact, well-designed classroom assessment schemes contribute to student achievement (Popham, 2006; Stiggins, 2002; Trevisan, 2002). Moreover, teachers with more training in assessment use more appropriate assessment practices than do teachers with less training (McMillan, Myran, & Workman, 2002).

A basic goal of this chapter is to help you understand how to use knowledge about assessment to reinforce, rather than work against, your role as teacher. Toward that end, we will begin by defining what we mean by the term *assessment* and by two key elements of this process: *measurement* and *evaluation*.

## What Is Assessment?

Broadly conceived, classroom assessment involves two major types of activities: collecting information about how much knowledge and skill students have learned (measurement) and making judgments about the adequacy or acceptability of each student's level of learning (evaluation). Both aspects of classroom assessment can be accomplished in a number of ways. The most common ways that teachers determine how much learning has occurred is to have students take exams, respond to oral questions, do homework exercises, write papers, solve problems, create products, and make oral presentations. Teachers can then evaluate the scores from those activities by comparing them either with one another or with an absolute standard (such as an A equals 90 percent correct). In this chapter, we will explain and illustrate the various ways in which you can measure and evaluate student learning with assessments that you create and administer regularly (Airasian, 2005; Nitko & Brookhart, 2006).

Measurement: assigning numbers or ratings according to rules to create a ranking

**Measurement**   For educational purposes, **measurement** is defined as the assignment of either numbers (such as the score from a traditional paper-and-pencil test) or a rating (such as the designation "excellent" or "exceeds standards" from a performance assessment) to certain attributes of people according to a rule-governed system. For example, we can measure someone's level of typing proficiency by counting the number of words the person accurately types per minute. For an oral presentation, we might measure the quality by using a guide called a scoring rubric. In a classroom or other group situation, the rules that are used to assign the numbers or provide the rating ordinarily create a ranking that reflects how much of the attribute different people possess (Airasian, 2005; Nitko & Brookhart, 2006).

| Evaluation: making judgments about the value of a measure

**Evaluation**    **Evaluation** involves using a rule-governed system to make judgments about the value or worth of a set of measures (Airasian, 2005; Nitko & Brookhart, 2006). What does it mean, for example, to say that a student answered eighty out of one hundred earth science questions correctly? Depending on the rules that are used, it could mean that the student has learned that body of knowledge exceedingly well and is ready to progress to the next unit of instruction or, conversely, that the student has significant knowledge gaps and requires additional instruction.

## Why Should We Assess Students' Learning?

This question has several answers. We will use this section to address four of the most common reasons for assessment: to provide summaries of learning, to monitor learning progress, to diagnose specific strengths and weaknesses in an individual's learning, and to motivate further learning.

| Summative evaluation: measure achievement; assign grades

**Summative Evaluation**    The first, and probably most obvious, reason for assessment is to provide to all interested parties a clear, meaningful, and useful summary or accounting of how well a student has met the teacher's objectives. When testing is done for the purpose of assigning a letter or numerical grade, it is often called **summative evaluation** because its primary purpose is to sum up how well a student has performed over time and at a variety of tasks.

| Formative evaluation: monitor progress; plan remedial instruction

**Formative Evaluation**    A second reason for assessing students is to monitor their progress. The main things that teachers want to know from time to time are whether students are keeping up with the pace of instruction and are understanding all of

*Classroom assessments serve several purposes. They provide information about the extent to which students have acquired the knowledge and skills that have recently been taught, they indicate whether students are understanding and keeping up with the pace of instruction, they may identify the particular cause of a student's learning difficulties, and they help students effectively regulate their study efforts.*

the material that has been covered so far. For students whose pace of learning is either slower or faster than average or whose understanding of certain ideas is faulty, you can introduce supplementary instruction (a workbook or a computer-based tutorial program), remedial instruction (which may also be computer based), or within-class ability grouping (recall that we discussed the benefits of this arrangement in Chapter 6, "Accommodating Student Diversity"). Because the purpose of such assessment is to facilitate, or form, learning and not to assign a grade, it is usually called **formative evaluation**.

Formative evaluations are conducted more or less continuously during an instructional unit, using both formal and informal assessment techniques. Periodic quizzes, homework assignments, in-class worksheets, oral reading, responses to teacher questions, and behavioral observations are all examples of formative evaluation if the results are used to generate timely feedback about what students have learned, what the source of any problems might be, and what might be done to prevent small problems from becoming major ones later in the year. Unlike summative evaluation, which is a one-time event conducted only after instruction is finished, formative evaluation has a more dynamic, ongoing, interactive relationship with teaching. The results of formative assessments affect instruction, which affects subsequent performance, and so on.

**Diagnosis**  A third reason for assessing students follows from the second. If you discover a student who is having difficulty keeping up with the rest of the class, you will probably want to know why in order to determine the most appropriate course of action. This purpose may lead you to construct an assessment (or to look for one that has already been made up) that will provide you with specific diagnostic information.

**Effects on Learning**  A fourth reason for assessment of student performance is that it has potentially positive effects on various aspects of learning and instruction. As Terence Crooks (1988) points out, classroom assessment guides students' "judgment of what is important to learn, affects their motivation and self-perceptions of competence, structures their approaches to and timing of personal study (e.g., spaced practice), consolidates learning, and affects the development of enduring learning strategies and skills. It appears to be one of the most potent forces influencing education" (p. 467).

Proof of Crooks's contention that classroom testing helps students consolidate their learning (despite students' arguments to the contrary) was examined by Robert Bangert-Drowns, James Kulik, and Chen-Lin Kulik (1991). They analyzed the results of forty studies conducted in actual classrooms and drew the following conclusions:

- Students who were tested more frequently (six or seven tests over the course of a semester) scored about one-fourth of a standard deviation higher on a final exam than did students who were tested less frequently. (See the chapter on standardized tests for a discussion of standard deviations.) This translated to an advantage of nine percentile ranks for the more frequently tested students.
- The advantage was even larger (twenty percentile ranks) when students who were tested several times were compared with students who were never tested.
- As students took more tests over the course of a semester, they generally scored higher on a final exam, but the increases became successively smaller for each additional test. The benefit of taking multiple tests seemed to peak by the sixth or seventh test.

> Tests can positively affect many aspects of students' learning

> Moderate testing produces more learning than no testing or infrequent testing

## WAYS TO MEASURE STUDENT LEARNING

Just as measurement can play several roles in the classroom, teachers have several ways to measure what students have learned. Which type of measure you choose

## pause & reflect

Over the past ten to twelve years, you have taken probably hundreds of class-room tests. What types of tests best reflected what you learned? Why?

will depend, of course, on the objectives you have stated. For the purposes of this discussion, objectives can be classified in terms of two broad categories: knowing *about* something (for example, that knots are used to secure objects, that dance is a form of social expression, that microscopes are used to study things too small to be seen by the naked eye) and knowing *how to do* something (for example, tie a square knot, dance the waltz, operate a microscope). Measures that attempt to assess the range and accuracy of someone's knowledge are usually called *written tests*. And measures that attempt to assess how well somebody can do something are often referred to as *performance tests*. Keep in mind that both types have a legitimate place in a teacher's assessment arsenal. Which type is used, and to what extent, will depend on the purpose or purposes you have for assessing students. In the next two sections, we will briefly examine the nature of both types.

## Written Tests

Written tests measure degree of knowledge about a subject

As we indicated at the beginning of this chapter, teachers spend a substantial part of each day assessing student learning, and much of this assessment activity involves giving and scoring some type of written test. Most written tests are composed of one or more of the following categories and item types: *selected response* (multiple-choice, true-false, and matching) and *constructed response* (short-answer and essay). In all like-lihood, you have taken hundreds of these types of tests in your school career thus far.

In the next couple of pages, we will briefly describe the main features, advantages, and disadvantages of each test. As you read, bear in mind that what we said about the usefulness of both written and performance tests applies here as well. No one type of written test will be equally useful for all purposes. You are more likely to draw correct inferences about students' capabilities by using a variety of selected- and constructed-response items.

**Selected-Response Tests**    Selected-response tests are so named because the student reads a relatively brief opening statement (called a stem) and selects one of the provided alternatives as the correct answer. Selected-response tests are typically made up of multiple-choice, true-false, or matching items. Quite often all three item types are used in a single test. Although guidelines exist for writing selected-response items (see, for example, the thirty-one guidelines for writing multiple-choice items discussed by Haladyna, Downing, & Rodriguez, 2002), many of these guidelines have not been validated by research. Hence, test-item writing is currently as much an art as a science.

***Characteristics***    Selected-response tests are sometimes called "objective" tests because they have a simple and set scoring system. If alternative b of a multiple-choice item is keyed as the correct response and the student chooses alternative d, the student is marked wrong, and the teacher's desire for a correct response cannot change the result. Selected-response tests are typically used when the primary goal is to assess what might be called *foundational knowledge*. This knowledge comprises the basic factual information and cognitive skills that students need in order to do such high-level tasks as solve problems and create products (Stiggins, 2005).

***Advantages***    A major advantage of selected-response tests is efficiency: a teacher can ask many questions in a short period of time. Another advantage is ease and reliability of scoring. With the aid of a scoring template (such as a multiple-choice answer sheet that has holes punched out where the correct answer is located), many tests can be quickly and uniformly scored. Moreover, there is some evidence that selected-response tests, when well written, can measure higher-level cognitive skills as effectively as constructed-response tests (Martinez, 1999; Nitko & Brookhart, 2006).

Selected-response tests are objectively scored and efficient but usually measure lower levels of learning and do not reveal what students can do

***Disadvantages***   Because items that reflect the lowest level of Bloom's Taxonomy (verbatim knowledge) are the easiest to write, most teacher-made tests (and many standardized tests as well) are composed almost entirely of knowledge-level items (a point we made initially in Chapter 13, "Approaches to Instruction"). As a result, students focus on verbatim memorization rather than on meaningful learning. Another disadvantage is that, although we get some indication of what students know, such tests reveal nothing about what students can do with that knowledge. A third disadvantage is that heavy or exclusive use of selected-response tests leads students to believe that learning is merely the accumulation of universally agreed-upon facts (Martinez, 1999; Nitko & Brookhart, 2006).

**Short-Answer Tests**   As their name implies, short-answer tests require a brief written response from the student.

***Characteristics***   Instead of *selecting* from one or more alternatives, the student is asked to *supply* from memory a brief answer consisting of a name, word, phrase, or symbol. Like selected-response tests, short-answer tests can be scored quickly, accurately, and consistently, thereby giving them an aura of objectivity. They are primarily used for measuring foundational knowledge.

***Advantages***   Short-answer items are relatively easy to write, so a test, or part of one, can be constructed fairly quickly. They allow either broad or in-depth assessment of foundational knowledge because students can respond to many items within a short space of time. Because students have to supply an answer, they have to recall, rather than recognize, information.

Short-answer tests easy to write but measure lower levels of learning

***Disadvantages***   Short-answer tests have the same basic disadvantages as selected-response tests. Because short-answer items ask only for short verbatim answers, students are likely to limit their processing to that level; thus these items provide no information about how well students can use what they have learned. In addition, unexpected but plausible answers may be difficult to score.

**Essay Tests**   Essay items require students to organize a set of ideas and write a somewhat lengthy response to a broad question.

***Characteristics***   The student is given a somewhat general directive to discuss one or more related ideas according to certain criteria. An example of an essay question is, "Compare operant conditioning theory and information-processing theory in terms of basic assumptions, typical research findings, and classroom applications."

***Advantages***   Essay tests reveal how well students can recall, organize, and clearly communicate previously learned information. When well written, essay tests call on such higher-level abilities as analysis, synthesis, and evaluation. Because of these demands, students are more likely to try to meaningfully learn the material on which they are tested (Martinez, 1999; Nitko & Brookhart, 2006).

Essay tests measure higher levels of learning but are hard to grade consistently

***Disadvantages***   Consistency of grading is likely to be a problem. Two students may have essentially similar responses yet receive different letter or numerical grades because of differences in vocabulary, grammar, and style. These test items are also very time-consuming to grade. And because it takes time for students to formulate and write responses, only a few questions at most can be given (Martinez, 1999; Nitko & Brookhart, 2006). But recent developments in essay scoring by computer programs may eliminate or drastically reduce these disadvantages in the near future (Myers, 2003).

**Constructing a Useful Test**   Understanding the characteristics, advantages, and disadvantages of different types of written tests and knowing how to write such test items are necessary but not sufficient conditions for creating an instructionally useful test. James Popham (2006), a noted measurement scholar, maintains that a useful classroom test has the following five attributes:

- *Significance.* The test measures worthwhile skills (such as the last four levels of Bloom's Taxonomy—application, analysis, synthesis, and evaluation) and substantial bodies of important knowledge.
- *Teachability.* Effective instruction can help students acquire the skills and knowledge measured by the test.
- *Describability.* The skills and knowledge measured by the test can be described with sufficient clarity that they make instructional planning easier.
- *Reportability.* The test produces results that allow a teacher to identify areas of instruction that were probably inadequate.
- *Nonintrusiveness.* The test does not take an excessive amount of time away from instruction.

## Performance Tests

In recent years, many teachers, learning theorists, and measurement experts have argued that the typical written test should be used far less often than it is because it reveals little or nothing of the depth of students' knowledge and how students use their knowledge to work through questions, problems, and tasks. These individuals argue that because we are living in a more complex and rapidly changing world than was the case a generation ago, schools can no longer be content to hold students accountable just for how well they can learn, store, and retrieve information in more or less verbatim form. Instead, we need to teach and assess students for such capabilities as how well they can frame problems, formulate and carry out plans, generate hypotheses, find information that is relevant to the solution to a problem, and work cooperatively with others, because those are the types of skills that are necessary to cope successfully with the demands of life after school in the twenty-first century (Cunningham, 2001; Eisner, 1999).

In addition, the learning standards of such professional groups as the National Council of Teachers of Mathematics (**http://standards.nctm.org**), the National Council for the Social Studies (**www.socialstudies.org/standards**), the National Council of Teachers of English (**www.ncte.org/about/over/standards**), and the National Research Council (**www.nap.edu/catalog/10256.html**) call for students to develop a sufficiently deep understanding of subject matter that they can demonstrate their knowledge in socially relevant ways. One way to address these concerns is to use performance tests.

*HM TeacherPrepSPACE*

For direct links to these and other websites, go to the Weblinks section of the textbook's student website.

Performance tests measure ability to use knowledge and skills to solve realistic problems, create products

**What Are Performance Tests?**   **Performance tests** require students to use a wide range of knowledge and skills over an extended period of time to complete a task or solve a problem under more or less realistic conditions. At the low end of the realism spectrum, students may be asked to construct a map, interpret a graph, or write an essay under highly standardized conditions. Everyone in the class completes the same task in the same amount of time and under the same conditions. At the high end of the spectrum, students may be asked to conduct a science experiment, produce a painting, or write an essay under conditions that are similar to those of real life. For example, students may be told to produce a compare-and-contrast essay on a particular topic by a certain date, but the resources students choose to use, the number of revisions they make, and when they work on the essay are left unspecified. When performance testing is conducted under such realistic conditions, it is also called **authentic assessment** (Gronlund, 2006; Janesick, 2001; Nitko & Brookhart, 2006).

Perhaps the clearest way to distinguish between traditional paper-and-pencil tests (such as multiple-choice tests) and performance tests is to say that the former measure

*Performance tests assess how well students complete a task under realistic conditions.*

how much students know, whereas the latter measure what students can do with what they know. In the sections that follow, we will first define four different types of performance tests and then look at their most important characteristics.

**Types of Performance Tests** There are four ways in which the performance capabilities of students are typically assessed: direct writing assessments, portfolios, exhibitions, and demonstrations.

***Direct Writing Assessments*** These tests ask students to write about a specific topic ("Describe the person whom you admire the most, and explain why you admire that person") under a standard set of conditions. Each essay is then scored by two or more people according to a set of defined criteria.

***Portfolios*** A **portfolio** contains one or more pieces of a student's work, some of which demonstrate different stages of completion. For example, a student's writing portfolio may contain business letters; pieces of fiction; poetry; and an outline, rough draft, and final draft of a research paper. Through the inclusion of various stages of a research paper, both the process and the end product can be assessed. Portfolios can also be constructed for math and science, as well as for projects that combine two or more subject areas.

Either the student alone or the student in consultation with the teacher decides what is to be included in the portfolio. The portfolio is sometimes used as a showcase to illustrate exemplary pieces, but it also works well as a collection of pieces that represent a student's typical performances. In its best and truest sense, the portfolio functions not just as a housing for these performances but also as a means of self-expression, self-reflection, and self-analysis for an individual student (Hebert, 2001; LaBoskey, 2000).

***Exhibitions*** Exhibitions involve just what the label suggests: a showing of such products as paintings, drawings, photographs, sculptures, videotapes, and models. As with direct writing assessments and portfolios, the products a student chooses to exhibit are evaluated according to a predetermined set of criteria.

***Demonstrations*** In this type of performance testing, students are required to show how well they can use previously learned knowledge or skills to solve a somewhat

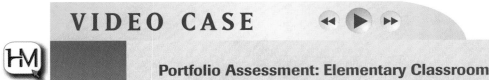

## Portfolio Assessment: Elementary Classroom

*Watch the video, study the artifacts in the case, and reflect upon the following questions:*

1. As previously discussed, portfolios can be time-consuming for teachers to develop and grade. Based on the use of portfolios in this Video Case, do you think that using portfolios would be worth the extra time and effort? Explain your answer.

2. Based on this Video Case, why might some teachers find portfolios to be a more accurate representation of student abilities (as compared with other forms of assessment)?

unique problem (such as conducting a scientific inquiry to answer a question, interpreting a graph, or diagnosing the cause of a malfunctioning engine and describing the best procedure for fixing it) or to perform a task (such as reciting a poem, performing a dance, or playing a piece of music). Figure 15.1 shows a performance item for graph interpretation, the partially correct response of a student, and the corrective feedback offered by two classmates.

**Characteristics of Performance Tests**　Performance tests are different from traditional written tests in that they require the student to make an active response, are more like everyday tasks, contain problems that involve many variables, are closely related to earlier instructional activities, use scoring guides that clearly specify the criteria against which responses will be evaluated, emphasize formative evaluation, and are probably more responsive to cultural diversity.

***Emphasis on Active Responding***　As we pointed out previously, the goal of performance testing is to gain some insight into how competently students can carry out various tasks. Consequently, such tests focus on processes (that is, the underlying skills that go into a performance), products (an observable outcome such as a speech or a painting), or both. For example, an instrumental music teacher may want to know whether students can apply their knowledge of music technique and theory to use the correct fingering and dynamics when playing a woodwind or piano (Clark, 2002).

| Performance tests may vary in degree of realism |

***Degree of Realism***　Although performance tests strive to approximate everyday tasks, not every test needs to be or can be done under the most realistic circumstances. How realistic the conditions should be depends on such factors as time, cost, availability of equipment, and the nature of the skill being measured. Imagine, for example, that you are a third-grade teacher and that one of your objectives is that students will be able to determine how much change they should receive after making a purchase in a store. If this is a relatively minor objective or if you do not have a lot of props available, you might simply demonstrate the situation with actual money and ask the students to judge whether the amount of change received was correct. If, however, you consider this to be a major objective and you have the props available, you might set up a mock store and have each student make a purchase using real money (Gronlund, 2006).

An example of a task that is realistic in content and intellectual demands but not in its setting (it takes place in the classroom) is "Read All About It!" Playing the roles of newspaper staff writers and editorial board members, students put together a special series for their local newspaper that compares and contrasts the five major wars in which the United States was involved during the 1900s (World War I,

**Figure 15.1** Example of a Performance Assessment: Interpreting a Graph

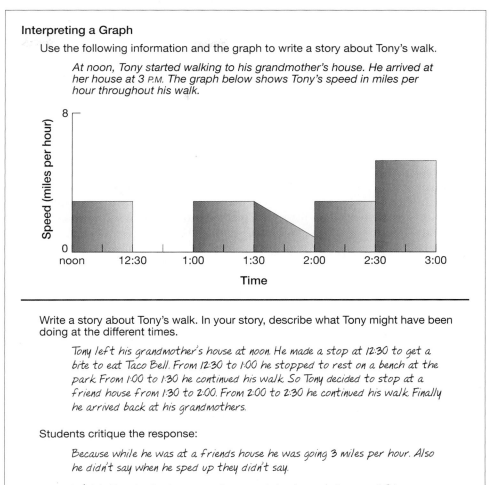

SOURCE: Parke and Lane (1997).

World War II, Korean War, Vietnam War, and Persian Gulf War). Writing assignments include feature articles, opinion columns, and letters to the editor. Editorial responsibilities include story editor, photo editor, mockup editor, layout editor, and copyeditor (Moon, 2002).

***Emphasis on Complex Problems*** To assess how well students can use foundational knowledge and skills in a productive way, the questions and problems they are given should be sufficiently open ended and ill structured (Stiggins, 2005). The problems contained in the Adventures of Jasper Woodbury program that we described in earlier chapters are good examples of complex and somewhat ill-structured tasks. They have several interrelated parts, provide few cues as to how the problem might be solved, and contain some uncertainty about what constitutes an appropriate solution.

***Close Relationship Between Teaching and Testing*** All too often students walk out of an exam in a state of high frustration (if not anger) because the content and format of the test seemed to have little in common with what was covered in class and the way in which it was taught. It's the old story of teaching for one thing and testing for something else. Performance testing strives for a closer match between teaching and testing. Often a performance assessment can be a variation or extension of a task used during instruction. For example, the mock store assessment mentioned earlier could follow an instructional activity in which students practiced making change.

This close relationship between assessment and instruction is not automatic, however; the teacher must deliberately establish it. For example, if in giving an oral book report, a student is expected to speak loudly and clearly enough for everyone to hear, to speak in complete sentences, to stay on the topic, and to use pictures or other materials to make the presentation interesting, the student needs to be informed of these criteria, and classroom instruction should be organized around them. One proponent of performance testing cited the old farm adage "You don't fatten the cattle by weighing them" to make this point. He then went on to note, "If we expect students to improve their performance on these new, more authentic measures, we need to engage in 'performance-based instruction' on a regular basis" (McTighe, 1996/1997, p. 7).

## pause & reflect

Have you ever taken any kind of performance assessment as a student? Did you feel that it accurately reflected what you had learned? To what extent would you use performance measures for such academic subjects as writing, math, science, and social studies? Why?

By the same token, the assessment of students' performances should be limited to just the criteria emphasized during instruction (Nitko & Brookhart, 2006; Taylor, 2003). One reason that proponents of performance testing push for this feature is that it has always been a standard part of successful programs in sports, the arts, and vocational education. Football coaches, for example, have long recognized that if they want their quarterback to know when during a game (the equivalent of a final exam) to attempt a pass and when not to, they must provide him with realistic opportunities to practice making this particular type of decision. Perhaps you recall our mentioning in the chapter on constructivist learning theory that realistic and varied practice are essential if students are to transfer what they learn in an instructional setting to an applied setting.

***Use of Scoring Rubrics***   A **rubric** is a scoring guide that specifies the capabilities students should exhibit (also known as content standards), describes the qualitative levels or categories into which the responses will be sorted (also known as performance standards), and specifies how the responses will be scored (as separate elements or holistically). For writing tasks, which are probably the most common performance measures, some commonly used content criteria are clarity of purpose, organization, voice, word choice, grammatical usage, and spelling (Arter & McTighe, 2001). An example of a scoring rubric for an oral report is provided in Table 15.1.

> Rubrics increase objectivity and consistency of scoring, align instruction with assessment, communicate teachers' expectations, help students monitor progress

Creating and using scoring rubrics and providing them to students at the beginning of a task is highly desirable for at least three reasons:

1. They increase the objectivity, consistency, and efficiency of scoring.
2. They help teachers match their instructional activities to the demands of the performance measure, the goal we discussed in the previous section.
3. By providing students with verbal descriptions and examples of the desired performance or product, teachers clearly communicate to students the types of behaviors that represent the range from unacceptable to exceptional performance and help students better monitor their progress and make productive changes in the quality of their work (Arter & McTighe, 2001; Whittaker, Salend, & Duhaney, 2001). Students with learning disabilities are likely to experience the greatest benefit from being given a scoring rubric and being shown how to use it (Jackson & Larkin, 2002).

Bear in mind, however, that scoring rubrics have their limitations. Although the rubrics used by two teachers to score writing samples may have some of the same

| Table 15.1 | Scoring Rubric for a Group Oral Presentation | | | |
|---|---|---|---|---|
| **Level** | **Content** | **Audiovisual Components** | **Group Members** | **Audience Members** |
| Excellent | Accurate, specific, research based, retold in own words | Are unique, add to presentation quality of materials used, are neat, present a clear message | Each member is equally involved in presentation and is well informed about the topic | Maintain eye contact with presenters, ask many questions |
| Good | Less detailed, lacking depth, limited number of sources used | Support topic but do not enhance presentation; some attempts at originality, clear message | Most members are active; most members are informed about the topic | Some members of the audience not attending; questions are limited or off the topic |
| Minimal | Limited information, general, strays from topic, not presented in own words | Inappropriate, no originality, detract from presentation, message is confusing | One or two members dominate; some members do not seem well prepared or well informed | Audience is not attending; no questions asked or questions are off the topic |

SOURCE: Montgomery (2000).

content standards (such as clarity of purpose, organization, and grammar), they may differ as well (for instance, in the presence or absence of idea development, use of detail, and figurative use of language), because there are different ways to define good writing. Thus any one rubric is not likely to represent the domain of writing fully and may provide few or no opportunities for scorers to reward certain desirable writing skills (Mabry, 1999).

# VIDEO CASE ◀◀ ▶ ▶▶

## Performance Assessment:
## Student Presentations in a High School English Class

*Watch the video, study the artifacts in the case, and reflect upon the following questions:*

**1.** During each presentation in Laura Mosman's class, students assess their peers' performance. How do the peer assessments contribute to the learning of both the presenters and the assessors?

**2.** In this Video Case, Ms. Mosman claims that performance assessment allows students to demonstrate their learning in ways that tests may not. How do such demonstrations affect student learning and motivation?

***Use of Formative Evaluation*** As we pointed out earlier, tests can be used as a source of feedback to help students improve the quality of their learning efforts. Because many real-life performances and products are the result of several feedback and revision cycles, performance testing often includes this feature as well. As anyone who has ever done any substantial amount of writing can tell you (and we are no exception), a satisfactory essay, story, or even personal letter is not produced in one attempt. Usually, there are critical comments from oneself and others and subsequent attempts at another draft. If we believe that the ability to write well, even among people who do it for a living, is partly defined by the ability to use feedback profitably, why should this be any different for students (Stiggins, 2001)? Some specific forms of formative assessment are dress rehearsals, reviews of writing drafts, and peer response groups (Gronlund, 2006).

## Take a Stand!

### Practice Assessment for Learning

The classroom assessments that teachers devise are among the most powerful influences on the quality of students' learning, largely due to their effect on self-efficacy, interest, and the types of learning strategies that students construct. Whether these assessments have positive or negative effects on students depends on how they are constructed and the purpose for which they are primarily intended.

As we have noted in this and other chapters, classroom assessments can be used both to sum up what students have learned (summative evaluation) and to provide information about the effectiveness of instruction and students' specific strengths and weaknesses (formative evaluation). All too often, unfortunately, formative assessment tends to be overshadowed by the summative type. Many teachers are more concerned with giving students grades than with using information gained from assessment to improve their instruction. Although both types of assessment are legitimate, we encourage you to emphasize formative assessment because of its potential to positively shape students' learning.

To ensure that assessments serve as a positive force for learning, we believe teachers should take the following steps:

- Make sure that you are knowledgeable about, understand, and use the basic measurement concepts and practices described in this chapter. Don't fall into the trap that so many teachers have fallen into of treating classroom assessment as a necessary evil.
- Recognize that the most accurate and useful assessments of learning are composed of multiple and varied measures. Use the full range of assessments (written tests, performance tests, checklists, rating scales) available to you.
- Align the content of your assessments with your objectives, and fully inform students about the content and demands of your assessments.
- Finally, use the results to help you work even more productively with your students.

**HM TeacherPrepSPACE**

Have you been in classes in which formative evaluation was downplayed in favor of summative evaluation? What did you think of that? For more on this issue, see the Take a Stand! section of the textbook's student website.

### Responsiveness to Cultural Diversity

Traditional written tests have been criticized over the years for being culturally biased. That is, they are thought to underestimate the capabilities of many ethnic minority students, as well as students of low socioeconomic status, because they rely on a narrow range of item types (mainly selected response) and on content that mostly reflects the experiences of the majority culture (Stobart, 2005). This criticism is based in large part on the constructivist view of learning: that meaningful learning occurs within a cultural context with which one is familiar and comfortable. If this is so, say the critics, then tests should be more consistent with the cultural context in which learning occurs. Performance tests have been promoted as a way to assess more fairly and accurately the knowledge and skills of all students, and particularly minority students, because of their realism (including group problem solving) and closer relationship between instruction and assessment (Hood, 1998; Lee, 1998).

Much research on this issue remains to be done, but there is some evidence to support the arguments of the critics. In one study (Supovitz & Brennan, 1997), White, Black, and Latino first- and second-grade students either took a standardized test of language arts or constructed a language arts portfolio. Although the White students significantly outscored the Black and Latino students on the standardized test, the gap for the portfolio assessment was smaller by about half. In another study (Supovitz, 1998), White, Black, and Latino fourth graders took either an open-ended paper-and-pencil science test or a science performance test. Although the scores of the White students on the paper-and-pencil exam were higher than the scores of the Black and Latino students, there was no difference among the three groups on the performance assessment. Within groups, White students performed better on the paper-and-pencil measures than on the performance measures, and the Black and Latino students scored higher on the performance measures.

**Some Concerns About Performance Assessment** There is no question that alternative assessment methods have excited educators and will be used with increasing frequency. But some of the same features that make these new assessment methods attractive also create problems that may or may not be solvable. For example, a study of performance assessments used by twenty-nine seventh- and eighth-grade teachers in Ontario, Canada (Hargreaves, Earl, & Schmidt, 2002), turned up several problems.

One problem was the amount of time required by these tests. Because the goal of performance assessments is to reveal what students can and cannot do with the knowledge they acquire, they take more time to construct, administer, and score than standard tests. And writing anecdotal comments, conferencing with individual students, and reading through and grading portfolios takes time away from other aspects of instruction. One teacher interviewed by the researchers used the colorful metaphor of "portfolio prison" to denote situations in which one has to give up other activities (such as accompanying students on a field trip) in order to help slower students complete their portfolios. A second problem is that it was harder to explain to parents the relationship between how such tests are often scored (e.g., "meets the standard," "satisfactory performance") and the letter grades on students' report cards.

A third problem involved adopting new responsibilities. With traditional tests, the teacher's primary responsibilities are to provide effective instruction in the subject matter that makes up the curriculum and to determine the extent to which students have acquired that knowledge. The student's primary responsibility is to be prepared to demonstrate that knowledge in whatever way the teacher deems appropriate. Teachers typically spend little time helping students prepare for tests. When using alternative assessments, a teacher becomes more of a collaborator and facilitator than a gatekeeper. The assessment criteria are clear and communicated at the outset of instruction, and the assessment tasks are taken directly from the instructional activities.

| Performance tests pose several challenges for teachers

The last problem concerned the radically different purposes of traditional standardized tests and performance tests. Standardized tests are typically used to satisfy the summative evaluation purpose of testing. They are given at the end of the academic year and are used solely to rank and compare students, schools, and school districts. Performance-based classroom tests, on the other hand, lend themselves to the formative evaluation purpose of testing. They are given periodically to provide teachers, students, and parents with relevant information about the current level of student learning and to generate ideas about how performance might be improved. The challenge for the teachers in this study was not to let the school district's preoccupation with high-stakes tests (those on which poor performance has significant consequences for students, teachers, and administrators) crowd out their use of performance-based tests for formative evaluation purposes.

| Reliability and validity of performance tests not yet firmly established

In addition to the problems identified by Hargreaves and colleagues, there are other questions about the reliability (consistency of performance) and validity (how accurately the test measures its target) of performance measures (Bachman, 2002). In one study (Shavelson & Baxter, 1992), fifth- and sixth-grade students' scores on three science investigations were very inconsistent from task to task, thereby producing a relatively low level of a form of reliability known as *internal consistency*. Thus, to get a clear picture of whether a student understands the use of basic scientific principles, understands how to do scientific projects of a particular type, or can complete only the particular science project that is contained in the assessment, a number of tasks may be needed.

In another study (Herman, Gearhart, & Baker, 1993), samples of students' classroom writing that were included in their portfolios were scored higher than a narrative they wrote in thirty minutes under standardized conditions (an example of a direct writing assessment). The researchers could not determine which writing sample was a better estimate of students' writing ability. A second problem was that overall portfolio scores were substantially higher than the aggregate scores of the individual items that made up the portfolio, truly a case of the whole being greater than the sum of its parts.

Some performance assessments are, however, proving to be valid measures of achievement. The Work Sampling System is a performance assessment that uses checklists, portfolios, and summary reports to measure seven areas of development (personal/social, language/literacy, mathematical thinking, scientific thinking, social studies, the arts, physical development) of kindergarten and primary grade children. In one study (Meisels, Bickel, Nicholson, Xue, & Atkins-Burnett, 2001), it was shown to be a valid measure of achievement by virtue of its moderate to high correlations with a standardized achievement test.

Finally, we have a word about keeping things in perspective. Like most other new ideas, performance assessment has been vigorously debated as *the* solution to the shortcomings and distortions of traditional tests. The truth, of course, is almost always somewhere in between. As we have pointed out in previous chapters and in numerous ways, *nothing works for everyone all the time or under all circumstances.* Writing portfolios, for example, do not engage all students. As one middle school student rather dramatically put it: "I would rather shovel coal in hell than put together another one of these portfolios" (Spalding, 2000, p. 762).

# WAYS TO EVALUATE STUDENT LEARNING

Once you have collected all the measures you intend to collect—for example, test scores, quiz scores, homework assignments, special projects, ratings of products and performances, and laboratory experiments—you will have to give the data some sort of value (the essence of evaluation). As you probably know, this is most often done by using an A-to-F grading scale. There are two general ways to approach this task. One approach is making comparisons among students. Such forms of evaluation are called norm-referenced because students are identified as average (or normal), above average, or below average. An alternative approach is called criterion-referenced because performance is interpreted in terms of defined criteria. Although both approaches can be used, we favor criterion-referenced grading for reasons we will mention shortly.

## Norm-Referenced Grading

A **norm-referenced grading** system assumes that classroom achievement will naturally vary among a group of heterogeneous students because of differences in such characteristics as prior knowledge, learning skills, motivation, and aptitude (to be discussed in the chapter on standardized tests). Under ideal circumstances (hundreds of scores from a diverse group of students), this variation produces a bell-shaped, or "normal," distribution of scores that ranges from low to high, has few tied scores, and has only a very few low scores and only a very few high scores. For this reason, norm-referenced grading procedures are also referred to as "grading on the curve."

Norm-referenced grading: compare one student with others

**The Nature of Norm-Referenced Grading**   Course grades, like standardized test scores, are determined through a comparison of each student's level of performance with the normal, or average, level of other, similar students in order to reflect the assumed differences in amount of learned material. The comparison may be with all other members of the student's class that year, or it may be with the average performance of several classes stretching back over several years. It is probably better for teachers to use a broad base of typical student performance made up of several classes as grounds for comparison than to rely on the current class of students. Doing so avoids two severe distorting effects: (1) when a single class contains many weak students, those with more well-developed abilities will more easily obtain the highest grades; and (2) when the class has many capable students, the relatively weaker students are virtually predestined to receive low or failing grades (Brookhart, 2004; Gronlund, 2006; Kubiszyn & Borich, 2007; Nitko & Brookhart, 2006).

The basic procedure for assigning grades on a norm-referenced basis involves just a few steps:

1. Determine what percentage of students will receive which grades. If, for example, you intend to award the full range of grades, you may decide to give A's to the

top 15 percent, B's to the next 25 percent, C's to the middle 35 percent, D's to the next 15 percent, and F's to the bottom 10 percent.

2. Arrange the scores from highest to lowest.
3. Calculate which scores fall in which category, and assign the grades accordingly.

Many other arrangements are also possible. How large or small you decide to make the percentages for each category will depend on such factors as the nature of the students in your class, the difficulty of your exams and assignments, and your own sense of what constitutes appropriate standards. Furthermore, a norm-referenced approach does not necessarily mean that each class will have a normal distribution of grades or that anyone will automatically fail. For example, it is possible for equal numbers of students to receive A's, B's, and C's if you decide to limit your grading system to just those three categories and award equal numbers of each grade. A norm-referenced approach simply means that the grading symbols being used indicate one student's level of achievement relative to other students.

Proponents of norm-referenced grading typically point to the absence of acceptable external criteria for use as a standard for evaluating and grading student performance. In other words, there is no good way to determine externally how much learning is too little, just enough, or more than enough for some subject. And if there is no amount of knowledge or set of behaviors that all students must master, then grades may be awarded on the basis of relative performance among a group of students (Gronlund, 2006).

**Strengths and Weaknesses of Norm-Referenced Grading**   There are at least two circumstances under which it may be appropriate to use norm-referenced measurement and evaluation procedures:

1. *Evaluating advanced levels of learning.* You might, for example, wish to formulate a two-stage instructional plan in which the first stage involves helping all students master a basic level of knowledge and skill in a particular subject. Performance at this stage would be measured and evaluated against a predetermined standard (such as 80 percent correct on an exam). Once this has been accomplished, you could supply advanced instruction and encourage students to learn as much of the additional material as possible. Because the amount of learning during the second stage is not tied to a predetermined standard and because it will likely vary due to differences in motivation and learning skills, a norm-referenced approach to grading can be used at this stage. This situation also fits certain guidelines for the use of competitive reward structures (discussed in Chapter 13, "Approaches to Instruction") because everyone starts from the same level of basic knowledge.
2. *Selection for limited-enrollment programs.* Norm-referenced measurement and evaluation are also applicable in cases in which students with the best chances for success are selected for a limited-enrollment program from among a large pool of candidates. One example is the selection of students for honors programs who have the highest test scores and grade-point averages (Gronlund, 2006).

The main weakness of the norm-referenced approach to grading is that there are few situations in which the typical public school teacher can appropriately use it. Either the goal is not appropriate (as in mastery of certain material and skills by all students or diagnosis of an individual student's specific strengths and weaknesses), or the basic conditions cannot be met (classes are too small or homogeneous or both). When a norm-referenced approach is used in spite of these weaknesses, communication and motivation problems are often created.

Consider the example of a group of high school sophomores having a great deal of difficulty mastering German vocabulary and grammar. The students may have been underprepared, the teacher

**Norm-referenced grading based on absence of external criteria**

**Norm-referenced grading can be used to evaluate advanced levels of learning**

## pause & reflect

Have you ever taken a class that was graded "on the curve"? Did you feel that your grade accurately reflected how much you had learned? If not, why was the grade too low or too high?

may be doing a poor job of organizing and explaining the material, or both factors may be at work. The top student averages 48 percent correct on all of the exams, quizzes, and oral recitations administered during the term. That student and a few others with averages in the high 40s will receive the A's. Although these fortunate few may realize their knowledge and skills are incomplete, others are likely to conclude falsely that these students learned quite a bit about the German language, as a grade of A is generally taken to mean superior performance.

At the other extreme, we have the example of a social studies class in which most of the students are doing well. Because the students were well prepared by previous teachers, used effective study skills, were exposed to high-quality instruction, and were strongly motivated by the enthusiasm of their teacher, the final test averages ranged from 94 to 98 percent correct. And yet the teacher who uses a norm-referenced scheme would assign at least A's, B's, and C's to this group. Not only does this practice seriously damage the motivation of students who worked hard and performed well, but it also miscommunicates to others the performance of students who received B's and C's (Airasian, 2005).

*Norm-referenced grading systems should rarely, if ever, be used in classrooms because few circumstances warrant their use and because they are likely to depress the motivation of all but the highest-scoring students.*

## Criterion-Referenced Grading

A **criterion-referenced grading** system permits students to benefit from mistakes and improve their level of understanding and performance. Furthermore, it establishes an individual (and sometimes cooperative) reward structure, which fosters motivation to learn to a greater extent than other systems.

**The Nature of Criterion-Referenced Grading**  Under a criterion-referenced system, grades are determined by the extent to which each student has attained a defined standard (or criterion) of achievement or performance. Whether the rest of the students in the class are successful or unsuccessful in meeting that criterion is irrelevant. Thus any distribution of grades is possible. Every student may get an A or an F, or no student may receive these grades. For reasons we will discuss shortly, very low or failing grades may occur less frequently under a criterion-referenced system.

A common version of criterion-referenced grading assigns letter grades on the basis of the percentage of test items answered correctly. For example, you may decide to award an A to anyone who correctly answers at least 85 percent of a set of test questions, a B to anyone who correctly answers 75 to 84 percent, and so on down to the lowest grade. To use this type of grading system fairly, which means specifying realistic criterion levels, you would need to have some prior knowledge of the levels at which students typically perform. You would thus be using normative information to establish absolute, or fixed, standards of performance. However, although both norm-referenced and criterion-referenced grading systems spring from a normative database (that is, from comparisons among students), only the former system uses those comparisons to directly determine grades.

Criterion-referenced grading: compare individual performance with stated criteria

Criterion-referenced grades provide information about strengths and weaknesses·

**Strengths and Weaknesses of Criterion-Referenced Grading**  Criterion-referenced grading systems (and criterion-referenced tests) have become increasingly popular in recent years primarily because of the following advantages:

- Criterion-referenced tests and grading systems provide more specific and useful information about student strengths and weaknesses than do norm-referenced grading systems. Parents and teachers are more interested in knowing that a student received an A on an earth science test because she mastered 92 percent of the objectives for that unit than they are in knowing that she received an A on a test of the same material because she outscored 92 percent of her classmates.

- Criterion-referenced grading systems promote motivation to learn because they hold out the promise that all students who have sufficiently well-developed learning skills and receive good-quality instruction can master most of a teacher's objectives (Gronlund, 2006). The motivating effect of criterion-referenced grading systems is likely to be particularly noticeable among students who adopt mastery goals (which we discussed in Chapter 12 on motivation) because they tend to use grades as feedback for further improvement (Covington, 2000).

One weakness of the criterion-referenced approach to grading is that the performance standards one specifies (such as a grade of A for 90 percent correct) are arbitrary and may be difficult to justify to parents and colleagues. (Why not 87 percent correct for an A? Or 92 percent?) A second weakness is that although a teacher's standards may appear to be stable from one test to another (90 percent correct for an A for all tests), they may in reality fluctuate as a result of unnoticed variation in the difficulty of each test and the quality of instruction (Gronlund, 1998).

## VIDEO CASE  ◄◄ ▶ ▶▶

### Assessment in the Middle Grades: Measurement of Student Learning

*Watch the video, study the artifacts in the case, and reflect upon the following questions:*

1. Evaluate the assessment practices used by Mr. Somers in this Video Case. Which ones did you find particularly effective? Support your answers using information from the textbook about effective assessment practices.

2. In this Video Case, Mr. Somers uses a written test to evaluate student understanding of course material. What are some other forms of assessment that could be used to gauge student understanding of a math unit?

Finally, we would like to alert you to a characteristic of criterion-referenced evaluation that is not a weakness but is an unfortunate fact of educational life that you may have to address. In a variety of subtle and sometimes not so subtle ways, teachers are discouraged from using a criterion-referenced approach to grading because it tends to produce higher test scores and grades than a norm-referenced approach does. The reason for the higher scores is obvious and quite justified. When test items are based solely on the specific instructional objectives that teachers write and when those objectives are clear and provided to students, students know what they need to learn and what they need to do to meet the teacher's objectives. Also, because students' grades depend only on how well they perform, not how well their classmates perform, motivation for learning tends to be higher. The result is that students tend to learn more and score higher on classroom tests. So why should this happy outcome be a cause for concern? Because individuals who are not well versed in classroom measurement and evaluation may believe that the only reason large numbers of students achieve high grades is that the teacher has lower standards than other teachers. Consequently, you may find yourself in a position of having to defend the criteria you use to assign grades. As Tom Kubiszyn and Gary Borich point out, "It is a curious fact of life that everyone presses for excellence in education, but many balk at marking systems that make attainment of excellence within everyone's reach" (2007, p. 226).

**A Mastery Approach**  A particular criterion-referenced approach to grading is often referred to as a mastery approach because it allows students multiple opportunities to

Mastery approach: give students multiple opportunities to master goals at own pace

learn and demonstrate their mastery of instructional objectives. This approach stems in large part from the work of John Carroll (1963) and Benjamin Bloom (1968, 1976) on the concept of *mastery learning*. The basic idea behind mastery learning is that most students can master most objectives if they are given good-quality instruction and sufficient time to learn and are motivated to continue learning (see, for example, Gentile & Lalley, 2003).

In a mastery approach, tests are used for formative as well as summative evaluation purposes. Thus students whose scores indicate deficiencies in learning are given additional instruction and a second chance to show what they have learned. Although pedagogically sound, this approach is often criticized on the grounds that life outside of school often does not give people a second chance. Surgeons and pilots, for example, are expected to do their jobs without error each and every time (Guskey, 2003). In our view, this criticism is flawed because it is shortsighted and involves an apples-and-oranges comparison. First, even surgeons and pilots made mistakes that they were allowed to correct. Surgeons made their mistakes on cadavers and pilots on flight simulators. Second, schooling is about helping students acquire the knowledge and skills they need to move from novices to experts and become self-directed learners. Life outside of school, on the other hand, frequently involves competition among individuals who are, or are expected to be, equally proficient.

If you are interested in using a mastery approach, the following suggestions can be adapted for use at any grade level and any subject area:

**JOURNAL ENTRY**
Trying a Mastery Approach to Grading

1. Go through a unit of study, a chapter of a text, or an outline of a lecture and pick out what you consider to be the most important points—that is, the points you wish to stress because they are most likely to have later value or are basic to later learning.

2. List these points in the form of a goal card (a list of the major concepts and skills that should be acquired by the end of an instructional unit), instructional objectives (as described by Robert Mager, 1997, or Robert Linn and Norman Gronlund, 2000), key points, or the equivalent. If appropriate, arrange the objectives in some sort of organized framework, perhaps with reference to the relevant taxonomy of educational objectives (see Chapter 13, "Approaches to Instruction").

3. Distribute the list of objectives at the beginning of a unit. Tell your students that they should concentrate on learning those points and that they will be tested on them.

4. Consider making up a study guide in which you provide specific questions relating to the objectives and a format that students can use to organize their notes.

5. Use a variety of instructional methods and materials to explain and illustrate objectives-related ideas.

6. Make up exam questions based on the objectives and the study guide questions. Try to write several questions for each objective.

7. Arrange these questions into at least two (preferably three) alternate exams for each unit of study.

8. Make up tentative criteria for grade levels for each exam and for the entire unit or report period (for example, A for not more than one question missed on any exam; B for not more than two questions missed on any exam; C for not more than four questions missed on any exam).

9. Test students either when they come to you and indicate they are ready or when you determine they have all had ample opportunity to learn the material. Announce all exam dates in advance, and remind students that the questions will be based only on the objectives you have mentioned. Indicate the criteria for different grade levels, and emphasize that any student who fails to meet a desired criterion on the first try will have a chance to take an alternate form of the exam.

10. Grade and return the exams as promptly as possible, go over questions briefly in class (particularly those that caused problems for more than a few students),

and offer to go over exams individually with students. Allow for individual interpretations, and give credit for answers you judge to be logical and plausible, even if they differ from the answers you expected.

11. Schedule alternate exams, and make yourself available for consultation and tutoring the day before. (While you are giving alternate exams, you can administer the original exam to students who were absent.)

12. If students improve their score on the second exam but still fall below the desired criterion, consider a safety valve option: invite them to provide you with a completed study guide (or the equivalent) when they take an exam the second time, or give them an open-book exam on the objectives they missed to see whether they can explain them in terms other than those of a written examination. If a student fulfills either of these options satisfactorily, give credit for one extra answer on the second exam.

13. To supplement exams, assign book reports, oral reports, papers, or some other kind of individual work that will provide maximum opportunity for student choice. Establish and explain the criteria you will use to evaluate these assignments, but stress that you want to encourage freedom of choice and expression. (Some students will thrive on free choice; others are likely to feel threatened by open-ended assignments. To allow for such differences, provide specific directions for those who need them and general hints or a simple request that "original" projects be cleared in advance for the more independent thinkers.) Grade all reports Pass or Do Over, and supply constructive criticism on those you consider unsatisfactory. Announce that all Do Over papers can be reworked and resubmitted within a certain period of time. Have the reports count toward the final grade—for example, three reports for an A, two for a B, one for a C. (In addition, students should pass each exam at the designated level.) You might also invite students to prepare extra papers to earn bonus points to be added to exam totals.

This basic technique will permit you to work within a traditional A-to-F framework, but in such a way that you should be able, without lowering standards, to increase the proportion of students who do acceptable work. An example of a mastery-oriented, criterion-referenced approach to grading appears in Figure 15.2.

# IMPROVING YOUR GRADING METHODS: ASSESSMENT PRACTICES TO AVOID

Be aware of and avoid faulty measurement and grading practices

Earlier in this chapter, we noted that the typical teacher has little systematic knowledge of assessment principles and as a result may engage in a variety of inappropriate testing and grading practices. We hope that the information in this chapter will help you become more proficient at these tasks. (In addition, we strongly encourage you to take a course in classroom assessment if you have not already done so.) To reinforce what you have learned here, we will describe some of the more common inappropriate testing and grading practices that teachers commit. The following list is based largely on the observations of Thomas Haladyna (1999), Thomas Guskey (2002), John Hills (1991), and Anthony Nitko (2004).

1. *Worshiping averages.* Some teachers mechanically average all scores and automatically assign the corresponding grade, even when they know an unusually low score was due to an extenuating circumstance. Allowances can be made for physical illness, emotional upset, and the like; a student's lowest grade can be dropped, or he can repeat the test on which he performed most poorly. Although objectivity in grading is a laudatory goal, it should not be practiced to the extent that it prevents you from altering your normal procedures when your professional judgment indicates an exception is warranted.

**Figure 15.2** Page from a Teacher's Grade Book and Instructions to Students: A Mastery Approach

| | 1st Exam 1st Try | 1st Exam 2nd Try | 2nd Exam 1st Try | 2nd Exam 2nd Try | 3rd Exam 1st Try | 3rd Exam 2nd Try | Exam Total Points | Projects 1 | Projects 2 | Projects 3 | Extra Project | Grade |
|---|---|---|---|---|---|---|---|---|---|---|---|---|
| Adams, Ann | 16 | 18 | 17 | 18 | 18 | | | P | P | P | | |
| Baker, Charles | 13 | 14 | 14 | | 10 | 14 | | P | | | | |
| Cohen, Matthew | 14 | 16 | 15 | 16 | 17 | | | P | P | | | |
| Davis, Rebecca | 19 | | 19 | | 20 | | | P | P | P | | |
| Evans, Deborah | 16 | 18 | 17 | 18 | 18 | 18 | | P | P | P | | |
| Ford, Harold | 15 | 16 | 17 | | 15 | | | P | P | | | |
| Grayson, Lee | 10 | 13 | 12 | 14 | 12 | 15 | | P | | | | |
| Hood, Barbara | 16 | | 17 | | 15 | | | P | P | | | |
| Ingalls, Robert | 16 | 18 | 16 | | 15 | | | P | P | | | |
| Jones, Thomas | 11 | 14 | 12 | 16 | 15 | | | P | | | | |
| Kim, David | 18 | | 19 | | 19 | | | P | P | P | | |
| Lapine, Craig | 14 | 16 | 18 | | 16 | | | P | P | P | | |
| Moore, James | 17 | | 17 | | 17 | | | P | P | P | | |
| Nguyen, Tuan | 17 | 18 | 19 | | 16 | 17 | | P | P | P | | |
| Orton, John | 10 | 10 | 11 | | 9 | | | P | | | | |
| Peck, Nancy | 14 | | 15 | | 14 | | | P | | | | |
| Quist, Ann | 16 | 18 | 17 | 18 | 18 | | | P | P | P | | |
| Richards, Mary | 16 | | 17 | | 15 | | | P | P | | | |
| Santos, Maria | 13 | | 15 | | 14 | | | P | P | | | |
| Thomas, Eric | 15 | 16 | 15 | 17 | 15 | | | P | P | | | |
| Wong, Yuen | 14 | | 15 | | 16 | | | P | | | | |
| Vernon, Joan | 11 | 14 | 13 | 14 | 12 | 14 | | P | | | | |
| Zacharias, Saul | 16 | 18 | 17 | | 18 | 19 | | P | P | P | | |

## Instructions for Determining Your Grade in Social Studies

Your grade in social studies this report period will be based on three exams (worth 20 points each) and satisfactory completion of up to three projects.

Here are the standards for different grades:

A—Average of 18 or more on three exams, plus three projects at Pass level
B—Average of 16 or 17 on three exams, plus two projects at Pass level
C—Average of 14 or 15 on three exams, plus one project at Pass level
D—Average of 10 to 13 on three exams
F—Average of 9 or less on three exams

Another way to figure your grade is to add together points as you take exams. This may be the best procedure to follow as we get close to the end of the report period. Use this description of standards as a guide:

A—At least 54 points, plus three projects at Pass level
B—48 to 53 points, plus two projects at Pass level
C—42 to 47 points, plus one project at Pass level
D—30 to 41 points
F—29 points or less

If you are not satisfied with the score you earn on any exam, you may take a different exam on the same material in an effort to improve your score. (Some of the questions on the alternate exam will be the same as those on the original exam; some will be different.) Projects will be graded P (Pass) or DO (Do Over). If you receive a DO on a project, you may work to improve it and hand it in again. You may also submit an extra project, which may earn up to 3 points of bonus credit (and can help if your exam scores fall just below a cutoff point). As you take each exam and receive a Pass for each project, record your progress on this chart.

| First Exam 1st Try | First Exam 2nd Try | Second Exam 1st Try | Second Exam 2nd Try | Third Exam 1st Try | Third Exam 2nd Try | Project 1 | Project 2 | Project 3 | Extra Project | Grade |
|---|---|---|---|---|---|---|---|---|---|---|
| | | | | | | | | | | |

Another shortcoming of this practice is that it ignores measurement error. No one can construct the perfect test, and no person's score is a true indicator of knowledge and skill. Test scores represent estimates of these characteristics. Accordingly, giving a student with an average of 74.67 a grade of D when 75 is the minimum needed for a C pretends that the test is more accurate than it really is. This is why it is so important to conduct an item analysis of your tests. If you discover several items that are unusually difficult, you may want to make allowances for students who are a point or two from the next highest grade (and modify the items if you intend to use them again). We describe a simple procedure for analyzing your test items in the next Suggestions for Teaching section.

2. *Using zeros indiscriminately.* The sole purpose of grades is to communicate to others how much of the curriculum a student has mastered. When teachers also use grades to reflect their appraisal of a student's work habits or character, the validity of the grades is lessened. This occurs most dramatically when students receive zeros for assignments that are late (but are otherwise of good quality), incomplete, or not completed according to directions and for exams on which they are suspected of cheating. This is a flawed practice for two reasons:

- First, and to repeat what we said in point 1, there may be good reasons why projects and homework assignments are late, incomplete, or different from what was expected. You should try to uncover such circumstances and take them into account.
- Second, zeros cause communication problems. If a student who earns grades in the low 90s for most of the grading period is given two zeros for one or more of the reasons just mentioned, that student could easily receive a D or an F. Such a grade is not an accurate reflection of what was learned.

If penalties are to be given for work that is late, incomplete, or not done according to directions and for which there are no extenuating circumstances, they should be clearly spelled out far in advance of the due date, and they should not seriously distort the meaning of the grade. For students suspected of cheating, for example, a different form of the exam can be given.

3. *Providing insufficient instruction before testing.* For a variety of reasons, teachers occasionally spend more time than they had planned on certain topics. In an effort to "cover the curriculum" prior to a scheduled exam, they may significantly increase the pace of instruction or simply tell students to read the remaining material on their own. The low grades that typically result from this practice will unfortunately be read by outsiders (and this includes parents) as a deficiency in students' learning ability when in fact they more accurately indicate a deficiency in instructional quality.

4. *Teaching for one thing but testing for another.* This practice takes several forms. For instance, teachers may provide considerable supplementary material in class through lecture—thereby encouraging students to take notes and study them extensively—but base test questions almost entirely on text material. Or if teachers emphasize the text material during class discussion, they may take a significant number of questions from footnotes and less important parts of the text. A third form of this flawed practice is to provide students with simple problems or practice questions in class that reflect the knowledge level of Bloom's Taxonomy but to give complex problems and higher-level questions on a test. Remember what we said earlier in this book: if you want transfer, then teach for transfer.

5. *Using pop quizzes to motivate students.* If you recall our discussion of reinforcement schedules, you will recognize that surprise tests represent a variable interval schedule and that such schedules produce a consistent pattern of behavior in humans under certain circumstances. Being a student in a classroom is not one of those circumstances. Surprise tests produce an undesirable level of anxiety

## pause & reflect

Because students in American schools feel considerable pressure to obtain high grades, a significant number of them feel driven to cheat. What might you do to reduce your students' tendency to cheat?

in many students and cause others simply to give up. If you sense that students are not sufficiently motivated to read and study more consistently, consult Chapter 12, "Motivation and Perceptions of Self," for better ideas on how to accomplish this goal.

6. *Keeping the nature and content of the test a secret.* Many teachers scrupulously avoid giving students any meaningful information about the type of questions that will be on a test or what the test items will cover. The assumption that underlies this practice is that if students have been paying attention in class, have been diligently doing their homework, and have been studying at regular intervals, they will do just fine on a test. But they usually don't—and the main reason can be seen in our description of a learning strategy (see Chapter 8, "Information-Processing Theory"). A good learning strategist first analyzes all of the available information that bears on attaining a goal. But if certain critical information about the goal is not available, the rest of the strategy (planning, implementing, monitoring, and modifying) will suffer.

7. *Keeping the criteria for assignments a secret.* This practice is closely related to the previous one. Students may be told, for example, to write an essay on what the world would be like if all diseases were eliminated and to give their imagination free rein in order to come up with many original ideas. But when the papers are graded, equal weight is given to spelling, punctuation, and grammatical usage. If these aspects of writing are also important to you and you intend to hold students accountable for them, make sure you clearly communicate that fact.

8. *Shifting criteria.* Teachers are sometimes disappointed in the quality of students' tests and assignments and decide to change the grading criteria as a way to shock students into more appropriate learning behaviors. For example, a teacher may have told students that mechanics will count for one-third of the grade on a writing assignment. But when the teacher discovers that most of the papers contain numerous spelling, punctuation, and grammatical errors, she may decide to let mechanics determine half of the grade. As we indicated before, grades should not be used as a motivational device or as a way to make up for instructional oversights. There are far better ways to accomplish these goals.

9. *Combining apples and oranges.* Students' grades are supposed to indicate how much they have learned in different subject-matter areas. When factors such as effort and ability are combined with test scores, the meaning of a grade becomes unclear. Consequently, measurement experts routinely recommend that teachers base students' grades solely on how well they have performed on written and performance tests. Assessments of effort and ability should be reported separately (Gronlund, 2006). Nevertheless, many teachers do not follow this recommendation. A survey of just over nine hundred third- through fifth-grade teachers revealed that 36 percent factored a student's level of effort into a grade either quite a bit, extensively, or completely and that 47 percent used a student's ability level to help determine a grade either quite a bit, extensively, or completely. Many high school teachers engage in this practice as well (McMillan et al., 2002).

A number of technological formats and products have been developed to make the task of classroom assessment easier, more informative, and less prone to error. The next section describes several of these formats and products.

## TECHNOLOGY FOR CLASSROOM ASSESSMENT

At the beginning of this chapter, we mentioned that assessment activities can account for about one-third of a teacher's time. This large investment in time is partly due to the importance of assessment in both teaching and learning, but it is also related to the fact that many assessment activities involve time-consuming methods of creating, administering, and scoring tests and analyzing and recording scores. Fortunately, computer-based technology supports many of the assessment functions teachers must execute (Cardwell, 2000). As the technological tools for learning and assessment have grown, so have the expectations that aspiring teachers will demonstrate their capacity to use the technology (Yao, 2006).

## Electronic Gradebooks and Grading Programs

Electronic gradebooks can store records of student test performance, compute test averages and cumulative averages, weight scores, note students with particular scores or characteristics, and print grade reports with standard as well as specific student comments. Edward Vockell and Douglas Fiore (1993) found that speed, accuracy, customizability, and organization are the key advantages of these systems (see also Pope, Hare, & Howard, 2002). However, they also admit that there can be distinct disadvantages to electronic gradebooks, such as incorrect data entry, system impersonality, and inflexibility with absent students and special situations. A networked database can compile all teachers' grades and automatically create an electronic report card (McNally & Etchison, 2000).

Computerized grading programs are very popular with teachers because they are designed to be consistent with the point-based grading systems that are used by most middle and high school teachers. These programs can scan and mark students' choices to selected-response test items (true-false, matching, multiple-choice) and allow teachers to track, summarize, and present student performance in a variety of ways. But the efficiency and seeming objectivity of such programs mask a serious potential drawback: they can lead to unfair assignment of grades when used uncritically. The challenge of accurately assigning grades usually involves more than just mathematical precision.

To demonstrate the complex nature of grading and why professional judgment should supplement the use of computerized grading programs, consider the example offered by Thomas Guskey (2002) in Table 15.2.

The table represents a group of seven students, each of whom has been graded using three methods: calculating the simple average of all scores, calculating the median or middle score, and calculating the average with the lowest score deleted. Using the simple arithmetic average produces a grade of C for all students despite the differences in their grade patterns. Student 1, for example, started slowly but gradually improved. Student 2 exhibited the opposite pattern. Student 3's performance was consistently around the average. Student 4 failed the first two unit tests but

| Table 15.2 | Summary Grades Tallied by Three Different Methods | | | | | | | | | | |
|---|---|---|---|---|---|---|---|---|---|---|---|
| **Student** | **Unit 1** | **Unit 2** | **Unit 3** | **Unit 4** | **Unit 5** | **Avg Score** | **Grade** | **Median Score** | **Grade** | **Delete Lowest** | **Grade** |
| 1 | 59 | 69 | 79 | 89 | 99 | 79 | C | 79 | C | 84 | B |
| 2 | 99 | 89 | 79 | 69 | 59 | 79 | C | 79 | C | 84 | B |
| 3 | 77 | 80 | 80 | 78 | 80 | 79 | C | 80 | B | 79.5 | B |
| 4 | 49 | 49 | 98 | 99 | 100 | 79 | C | 98 | A | 86.5 | B |
| 5 | 100 | 99 | 98 | 49 | 49 | 79 | C | 98 | A | 86.5 | B |
| 6 | 0 | 98 | 98 | 99 | 100 | 79 | C | 98 | A | 98.8 | A |
| 7 | 100 | 99 | 98 | 98 | 0 | 79 | C | 98 | A | 98.8 | A |

Grading Scale: 90–100% = A; 80–89% = B; 70–79% = C; 60–69% = D; 59% or lower = F.

SOURCE: Guskey, 2002.

scored near or at the top for the last three. Student 5 exhibited the opposite pattern from student 4. Student 6 had an unexcused absence for the first test and was given a score of zero but scored near or at the top for the last four tests. Student 7 had virtually perfect scores for the first four tests but was caught cheating on the last one and received a score of zero. If giving all seven students the same grade strikes you as inappropriate, note that using the median score or the average with the lowest score deleted produces grades that range from A through C, and that students 4 and 5 could receive either an A, B, or C, depending on which method is used.

Our purpose here is not to tell you which of these methods to use, as that will depend on other information that teachers typically have about student capabilities and teachers' beliefs about the appropriateness of different grading methods, but to remind you that computerized grading books should not be allowed to substitute for a teacher's professional judgment in awarding grades.

## Technology-Based Performance Assessment

As you may recall from our earlier discussion, performance assessments give students the opportunity to demonstrate how well they can use the knowledge and skills that were the focus of an instructional unit to carry out realistic and meaningful tasks. Computer-based technology is an excellent vehicle for this purpose. For example, simulations are likely to be more effective than traditional paper-and-pencil tests for determining how well students understand and can carry out the process of scientific inquiry (for example, planning an investigation, collecting data, organizing and analyzing the data, forming conclusions, and communicating findings). Recent research on the development of performance assessment procedures in complex task domains such as engineering design and medical diagnosis promise even greater effectiveness of technology-based performances in the future (Spector, 2006). A web-based simulation that lends itself to the assessment of scientific inquiry is the GLOBE environmental science education program (www.globe.gov/globe_flash.html). Students who participate in GLOBE collect environmental data at a local site and submit it to a scientific database on the Web. About four thousand schools from countries around the world participate in this program. Teachers could use the GLOBE database to assess how well students analyze and interpret climate data by having them use a set of climate-related criteria (such as temperature at different altitudes, amount of sunshine, and amount of snow) to determine in which of several cities the next Winter Olympics should be held (Means & Haertel, 2002).

Multimedia tools with text, audio, video, and graphics components also offer opportunities for students to demonstrate their ability to solve real-world problems in a number of content areas. Ivan Baugh (1994), for instance, notes that students investigating concepts such as biomes and ecosystems could (1) construct hypermedia stacks such as encyclopedias and pictorial atlases, (2) record narrative voice-overs for such segments, (3) use telecommunications to exchange information with people living near those environments, (4) digitize video taken from the local environment, (5) type environmental reports, newspapers, and brochures, and (6) create brief movies about the different locales that link to other documents.

## Digital Portfolios

**What Is a Digital Portfolio?**    Terry Wiedmer (1998, p. 586) defines a **digital portfolio** as "a purposeful collection of work, captured by electronic means, that serves as an exhibit of individual efforts, progress, and achievements in one or more areas." In their digital portfolios, students can create, store, and manage various products and processes that they want to document and perhaps showcase (Siegle, 2002).

Digital portfolios (also called **electronic portfolios**) are similar in purpose to the more traditional portfolios, but they extend beyond paper versions because they can include sound effects, audio and video testimonials, voice-over explanations of a

Digital portfolio: collection of work that is stored and illustrated electronically

student's thinking process as a project is worked on, and photographs of such products as drawings, paintings, and musical compositions (Siegle, 2002).

**The Components and Contents of Digital Portfolios**   Because the purposes for having students construct a digital portfolio (such as to assign grades, assess students' strengths and weaknesses, evaluate a program or curriculum) are not always the same, the portfolio structure will vary somewhat across teachers and school districts. But some components, such as those in the list that follows, are frequently recommended (for instance, Barrett, 1998; Goldsby & Fazal, 2001; Janesick, 2001; Niguidula, 1997) and should always be seriously considered for inclusion:

- the goals the student was attempting to achieve
- the guidelines that were used to select the included material
- work samples
- teacher feedback
- student self-reflection
- the criteria that were used to evaluate each entry
- examples of good-quality work

Just as the general components of a digital portfolio may vary, so may the particular media that are used. Following are some specific examples of the types of media a student may use and information that would be represented by each medium (Barrett, 2000; Gatlin & Jacob, 2002; Janesick, 2001; O'Lone, 1997; Siegle, 2002):

- *Digitized pictures and scanned images*: photos of the student and/or objects he has created, artwork, models, science experiments over time, fax exchanges with scientists, spelling tests, math work, self-assessment checklists
- *Documents*: electronic copies of student writing, reflection journals, publications, copies of web pages created, and teacher notes and observations
- *Audio recordings*: persuasive speeches, poetry readings, rehearsals of foreign language vocabulary, readings of select passages, self-evaluations, interviews or voice notes regarding the rationale for work included
- *Video clips*: short videos showing the student or teams of students engaged in science experiments and explaining their steps, or showing student performances in physical education or the performing arts
- *Multimedia presentations*: QuickTime movies of interdisciplinary projects

**Advantages and Disadvantages of Digital Portfolios**   The main advantage of a digital portfolio is the ability of students to explain in text and narration why they gave their portfolio its particular content and form. It is very important that each student portfolio submission be linked to self-reflections about why the item was selected, because "without time for reflection, the digital portfolio might be no different from a paper portfolio filed away in a locked cabinet" (Niguidula, 1997, p. 28). Using this opportunity for self-reflection, students can demonstrate what they know, how they came to know it, how their knowledge increased and evolved, and what they have accomplished with that knowledge.

However, many of the same disadvantages that occur when computers are used for other purposes apply to the creation and use of digital portfolios. Because portfolios are personal documents, access to them needs to be restricted. This is typically done with passwords, which, as you probably know, are easily forgotten. Second, portfolios that are stored on a school's server can be altered or destroyed by hackers. Finally, work that is not saved while working on a portfolio can be lost if the computer crashes.

**Rubrics for Digital Portfolios and Presentations**   With all the information a digital portfolio might contain, how can a classroom teacher fairly and efficiently assess student learning? First, electronic writing, just like paper-based compositions, can be assessed holistically in a general impression rating. It can also be analyzed with specific criteria such as whether the work is insightful, well organized, clear, focused, relevant, sequentially flowing, persuasive, inspirational, and original (see Arter & McTighe, 2001). There are also rubrics for analyzing the quality of a portfolio that has been posted to a website. One uses a four-point scale (exceeds requirements, meets requirements, close to meeting standards, clearly does not meet standards) to assess the design and aesthetics of the website, its usability, and the presence and clarity of the portfolio's contents (Goldsby & Fazal, 2001). The website **www.4teachers.org** contains, among other things related to technology, a tool called RubiStar that provides templates for creating rubrics for several types of digital products.

### Performance and Portfolio Assessment Problems

We would be remiss not to point out the problems often associated with technology-based performance and portfolio assessment. High-quality performance assessments require multiple assessments (for both formative and summative purposes), extensive time, electronic equipment, careful planning, and continued modification (McGrath, 2003). Electronic portfolios can become large, complex, and time-consuming to grade fairly and thus can overload teachers with work (Moersch & Fisher, 1995; Pope et al., 2002).

Staff development and teacher training are additional barriers to effective use of performance assessment and digital portfolios. But with proper training, teachers may begin to find ways in which technology-based school and classroom assessment plans are practical, cost-effective, and qualitatively better than traditional assessments.

The following Suggestions for Teaching should help you properly implement the assessment concepts and research findings presented in this chapter.

# Suggestions for Teaching in Your Classroom

## Effective Assessment Techniques

**1** **As early as possible in a report period, decide when and how often to give tests and other assignments that will count toward a grade, and announce tests and assignments well in advance.**

If you follow the suggestions for formulating objectives presented in Chapter 13, "Approaches to Instruction," you should be able to develop a reasonably complete master plan that will permit you to devise a course outline even though you have only limited experience with teaching or with a particular text or unit of study. In doing so, you will have not only a good sense of the objectives you want your students to achieve but also the means by which achievement will be assessed.

Before the term starts is a good time to block out the number of tests you will give in that term. Recall that research cited earlier has shown that students who take six or seven tests per term (two or three per grading period) learn more than students who are tested less frequently or not at all. Don't assume, however, that if giving three tests per grading period is good, then giving five or six tests is better. A point of diminishing returns is quickly reached after the fourth test.

If you announce at the beginning of a report period when you intend to give exams or set due dates for assignments, you not only give students a clear idea of what they will be expected to do, but you also give yourself guidelines for arranging

*For students to effectively plan how they will master your objectives, they need to know as early as possible how many tests they will have to take, when the tests will occur, what types of items each test will contain, and what content they will be tested on.*

lesson plans and devising, administering, and scoring tests. For the most part, it is preferable to announce tests well in advance. (If you will be teaching elementary students, it will be better to announce exams and assignments for a week at a time rather than providing a long-range schedule.) When tests are announced, be sure to let students know exactly what material they will be held responsible for, what kinds of questions will be asked, and how much tests will count toward the final grade. As we noted in the Take a Stand! feature in Chapter 8 on information-processing theory, and as others have pointed out (Guskey, 2003), students need complete information about the content and nature of tests if they are to function strategically. In addition, research indicates that students who are told to expect (and who receive) an essay test or a multiple-choice test score slightly higher on an exam than students who do not know what to expect or who are led to expect one type of test but are given another type (Lundeberg & Fox, 1991).

For term papers or other written work, list your criteria for grading the papers (for example, how much emphasis will be placed on style, spelling and punctuation, research, individuality of expression). In laboratory courses, most students prefer a list of experiments or projects and some description of how they will be evaluated (for example, ten experiments in chemistry, fifteen drawings in drafting, five paintings in art, judged according to posted criteria).

### 2 Prepare a content outline or a table of specifications of the objectives to be covered on each exam, or otherwise take care to obtain a systematic sample of the knowledge and skill acquired by your students.

The more precisely and completely goals are described at the beginning of a unit, the easier and more efficient assessment (and teaching) will be. The use of a clear outline will help ensure an adequate sample of the most significant kinds of behavior.

When the time comes to assess the abilities of your students, you can't possibly observe and evaluate all relevant behavior. You can't listen to more than a few pages of reading by each first grader, for example, or ask high school seniors to answer questions on everything discussed in several chapters of a text. Because of the limitations imposed by large numbers of students and small amounts of time, your evaluation will have to be based on a sample of behavior—a three- or four-minute reading performance and questions covering points made in only a few sections of text material assigned for an exam. It is therefore important to try to obtain a representative, accurate sample.

| Necessary to obtain a representative sample of behavior when testing

**Figure 15.3** Example of a Table of Specifications for Material Covered in This Chapter

| Topic | Objectives | | | | | |
|---|---|---|---|---|---|---|
| | Knows | Comprehends | Applies | Analyzes | Synthesizes | Evaluates |
| *Nature of measurement and evaluation* | | | | | | |
| *Purposes of measurement and evaluation* | | | | | | |
| *Types of written tests* | | | | | | |
| *Nature of performance tests* | | | | | | |

**Suggestions for Teaching in Your Classroom**

Table of specifications helps ensure an adequate sample of content, behavior

Psychologists who have studied measurement and evaluation often recommend that as teachers prepare exams, they use a **table of specifications** to note the types and numbers of test items to be included so as to ensure thorough and systematic coverage. You can draw up a table of specifications by first listing along the left-hand margin of a piece of lined paper the important topics that have been covered. Then insert appropriate headings from the taxonomy of objectives for the cognitive domain (or for the affective or psychomotor domain, if appropriate) across the top of the page. An example of such a table of specifications for some of the information discussed in this chapter is provided in Figure 15.3. A computer spreadsheet program such as Microsoft Excel is an ideal tool for creating a table of specifications.

Test specialists often recommend that you insert in the boxes of a table of specifications the percentage of test items that you intend to write for each topic and each type of objective. This practice forces you to think about both the number and the relative importance of your objectives before you start teaching or writing test items. Thus, if some objectives are more important to you than others, you will have a way of ensuring that these are tested more thoroughly. If, however, a test is going to be brief and emphasize all objectives more or less equally, you may wish to put a check mark in each box as you write questions. If you discover that you are overloading some boxes and that others are empty, you can take steps to remedy the situation. The important point is that by taking steps to ensure that your tests cover what you want your students to know, you will be increasing the tests' validity.

For reasons to be discussed shortly, you may choose not to list all of the categories in the taxonomy for all subjects or at all grade levels. Tables of specifications that you draw up for your own use therefore may contain fewer headings across the top of the page than the table illustrated in Figure 15.3.

**JOURNAL ENTRY**
Using a Table of Specifications

**③ Consider the purpose of each test or measurement exercise in the light of the developmental characteristics of the students in your classes and the nature of the curriculum for your grade level.**

In addition to considering different uses of tests and other forms of measurement when you plan assessment strategies, you should think about the developmental characteristics of the students you plan to teach and the nature of the curriculum at your grade level. As noted in the discussion of Jean Piaget's theory early in this book, there are significant differences among preoperational, concrete operational, and formal thinkers. Furthermore, because primary grade children are asked to master a curriculum that is substantially different from the curriculum upper elementary and secondary school students are expected to learn, different forms of measurement should be used at each level.

Primary grade children are asked to concentrate on learning basic skills, and their progress—or lack of it—will often be apparent even if they are not asked to take tests. A second grader who has difficulty decoding many longer unfamiliar words, for instance, will reveal that inability each time she is asked to read. Upper elementary grade and middle school students are asked to improve and perfect their mastery of skills in reading, writing, and arithmetic and also to study topics in the sciences, social studies, and other subjects. Because their success in dealing with many subjects, learning materials, and tests often depends on reading ability, you may have to create tests to diagnose weaknesses and chart improvement (a formative evaluation function), as well as to establish grades.

At the secondary level, testing is done largely to assign grades and to determine whether students are sufficiently prepared to take more advanced courses (as in Algebra I, Algebra II). Consequently, as you create a table of specifications for a particular instructional unit, you want to make sure that you have identified all of the important concepts and skills for that unit and that your test items cover most, if not all, of the levels of Bloom's Taxonomy.

| Elementary grade students tested as much for diagnostic, formative evaluation purposes as for summative purposes |

### 4 Decide whether a written test or a performance test is more appropriate.

As you think about which types of questions to use in a particular situation, consider the student characteristics and curriculum differences noted earlier. In the primary grades, you may not use any written tests in the strict sense. Instead, you might ask your students to demonstrate skills, complete exercises (some of which may be similar to completion tests), and solve simple problems (often on worksheets). In the upper elementary and middle school grades, you may need to use or make up dozens of measurement instruments, because many subjects must be graded. Accordingly, it may be necessary to make extensive use of completion, short-answer, and short-essay items that can be printed on the board or on paper. If you find it impossible or impractical to make up a table of specifications for each exam, at least refer to instructional objectives or a list of key points as you write questions. At the secondary level, you might do your best to develop some sort of table of specifications for exams not only to ensure measurement of objectives at various levels of the taxonomy but also to remind yourself to use different types of items.

In certain elementary and middle school subjects and in skill or laboratory subjects at the secondary level, performance tests may be more appropriate than written tests. At the primary grade level, for instance, you may be required to assign a grade in oral reading. In a high school home economics class, you may grade students on how well they produce a garment or a soufflé. In a wood shop class, you may base a grade on how well students construct a piece of furniture. In such cases, you can make evaluations more systematic and accurate by using rating scales and checklists and by attempting to equate (or at least take into account) the difficulty level of the performance to be rated.

To evaluate a product such as a garment or a piece of furniture, you might use a checklist that you devised and handed out at the beginning of a course. Such a checklist should state the number of possible points that will be awarded for various aspects of the project—for example, accuracy of measurements and preparation of component parts, neatness of assembly, quality of finishing touches, and final appearance. To evaluate a performance, you might use the same approach, announcing beforehand how heavily you intend to weigh various aspects of execution. In music,

| Rating scales and checklists make evaluations of performance more systematic |

for instance, you might note possible points to be awarded for tone, execution, accuracy, and interpretation. For both project and performance tasks, you might multiply the final score by a difficulty factor. (You have probably seen television coverage of Olympic events in which divers and gymnasts have their performance ratings multiplied by such a difficulty factor.)

## 5  Make up and use a detailed answer key or rubric.

### a.  Evaluate each answer by comparing it with the key or rubric.

**JOURNAL ENTRY**
Preparing a Detailed Key

One of the most valuable characteristics of a test is that it permits comparison of the permanently recorded answers of all students with a fixed set of criteria. A complete key or rubric not only reduces subjectivity but can also save you much time and trouble when you are grading papers or defending your evaluation of questions.

For short-answer, true-false, matching, or multiple-choice questions, you should devise your key as you write and assemble the items. With planning and ingenuity, you can prepare a key that will greatly simplify grading. For essay questions, you should also prepare answers as you write the questions. If you ask students to write answers to a small number of comprehensive essay questions, you are likely to maximize the consistency of your grading process by grading all answers to the first question at one sitting, then grading all answers to the second question, and so on. However, if a test consists of eight or ten short-essay items (which can usually be answered in a half-hour or so), you would have to do too much paper shuffling to follow such a procedure. One way to speed up the grading of short-essay exams (so that you can evaluate up to thirty tests in a single session of forty minutes or so) is to use plus or minus grading. If you use a point scale to grade short-essay answers, you will spend an agonizing amount of time deciding just how much a given answer is worth. But with practice, you should be able to write short-essay questions and answers (on your key) that can be graded plus or minus.

To develop skill in writing such questions, make up a few formative quizzes that will not count toward a grade. Experiment with phrasing questions that require students to reveal that they either know or don't know the answer. Prepare your key as you write the questions. When the time comes to grade papers, simply make a yes or no decision about the correctness of each answer. With a felt-tip pen, make a bold check over each satisfactory answer on an exam, and tally the number of checks when you have read all the answers. (Counting up to eight or ten is obviously a lot quicker and easier than adding together various numbers of points for eight or ten answers.) Once you have developed skill in writing and evaluating short-essay questions that can be graded plus or minus, prepare and use summative exams. If you decide to use this type of exam, guard against the temptation to write items that measure only knowledge. Use a table of specifications, or otherwise take steps to write at least some questions that measure skills at the higher levels of the taxonomy for the cognitive domain.

### b.  Be willing and prepared to defend the evaluations you make.

You will probably get few complaints if you have a detailed key and can explain to the class when exams are returned how each answer was graded. To a direct challenge about a specific answer to an essay or short-essay question, you might respond by showing complainers an answer that received full credit and inviting them to compare it with their own.

*To maintain consistency when scoring exams, teachers should use a scoring key for selected-response and short-answer items and a rubric for essay items.*

Perhaps the best way to provide feedback about responses to multiple-choice questions is to prepare a feedback booklet. As you write each multiple-choice question, also write a brief explanation as to why you feel the answer is correct and why the distracters are incorrect. If you follow this policy (which takes less time than you might expect), you can often improve the questions as you write your defense of the answer. If you go a step further (described in the next point), you can obtain information to use in improving questions after they have been answered. This is a good policy to follow with any exam, multiple choice or otherwise.

**6** **During and after the grading process, analyze questions and answers in order to improve future exams.**

**JOURNAL ENTRY**
Analyzing Test Items

If you prepare sufficient copies of feedback booklets for multiple-choice exams, you can supply them to all students when you hand back scored answer sheets (and copies of the question booklets). After students have checked their papers and identified and examined questions that were marked wrong, invite them to select up to three questions that they wish to challenge. Even after they read your explanation in the feedback booklet, many students are likely to feel that they selected a different answer than you did for logical and defensible reasons. Permit them to write out a description of the reasoning behind their choices. If an explanation seems plausible, give credit for the answer. If several students chose the same questions for comment, you have evidence that the item needs to be revised. (It's also possible that the information reflected in the item was not directly related to your objectives or was poorly taught.)

If you follow the procedure of supplying feedback booklets, it is almost essential to prepare at least two forms of every exam. Having two or more forms also equips you to use a mastery approach. After writing the questions, arrange them into two tests. Make perhaps half of the questions the same and half unique to each exam. (If you have enough questions, you might prepare three forms.) If you teach multiple sections, give the first form to period 1, the next form to period 2, and thereafter use the forms in random order. This procedure will reduce the possibility that some students in later classes will have advance information about most of the questions on the test.

If you find that you do not have time to prepare feedback booklets, you might invite students to select three answers to defend as they record their choices when taking multiple-choice exams. This will supply you with information about ambiguous questions, even though it will not provide feedback to students. It may also provide you with useful information about how well the items were written.

Turning back to multiple-choice questions, you may also want to use simple versions of item-analysis techniques that measurement specialists use to analyze and improve this type of item. These techniques will allow you to estimate the difficulty level and discriminating power of each item. Discriminating power is the ability of a test item to distinguish students who have learned that piece of information from students who have not. To do so, try the following steps:

1. Rank the test papers from highest score to lowest score.
2. If you have 50 or more, select approximately the top 30 percent, and call this the upper group. Select approximately the bottom 30 percent, and call this the lower group. Set the middle group of papers aside. If you have 30–40 students, split the scores in the middle and create upper and lower groups. If you have fewer than 30 students, you have too few to conduct an item analysis (Nitko & Brookhart, 2006).
3. For each item, record the number of students in the upper group and in the lower group who selected the correct answer and each distracter as follows (the correct answer has an asterisk next to it):

| Item 1 Alternatives | A | B* | C | D | E |
|---|---|---|---|---|---|
| Upper group | 0 | 6 | 3 | 1 | 0 |
| Lower group | 3 | 2 | 2 | 3 | 0 |

4. Estimate the item difficulty by calculating the percentage of students who answered the item correctly. The difficulty index for the preceding item is

Item analysis tells about difficulty, discriminating power of multiple-choice items

40 percent (8/20 × 100). Note that the smaller the percentage is, the more difficult the item is.

5. Estimate the item discriminating power by subtracting the number in the lower group who answered the item correctly from the number in the upper group, and divide by one-half of the total number of students included in the item analysis. For the preceding example, the discrimination index is 0.40 (6 − 2 ÷ 10). When the index is positive, as it is here, it indicates that more students in the upper group than in the lower group answered the item correctly. A negative value indicates just the opposite.

As you can see, this type of item analysis is not difficult to do, nor is it likely to be very time-consuming. It is important to remember, however, that the benefits of item analysis can quickly be lost if you ignore certain limitations. One is that you will be working with relatively small numbers of students. Therefore, the results of item analysis are likely to vary as you go from class to class or from test to test with the same class. Because of this variation, you should retain items that a measurement specialist would discard or revise. In general, you should retain multiple-choice items whose difficulty index lies between 50 and 90 percent and whose discrimination index is positive (Gronlund, 2006). Another limitation is that you may have objectives that everyone must master. If you do an effective job of teaching these objectives, the corresponding test items are likely to be answered correctly by nearly every student. These items should be retained rather than revised to meet arbitrary criteria of difficulty and discrimination.

*HM TeacherPrepSPACE*

*To review this chapter, see the ACE practice tests and PowerPoint slides on the textbook's student website. You may also want to try the Glossary Flashcards for glossary terms.*

# 16

# Becoming a Better Teacher by Becoming a Reflective Teacher

As you know from personal experience, some teachers are much more effective than others. Take a moment and think back to as many teachers as you can remember. How many of them were really outstanding in the sense that they established a favorable classroom atmosphere, were sensitive to the needs of students, and used a variety of techniques to help you learn? How many of them did an adequate job but left you bored or indifferent most of the time? How many of them made you dread entering their classrooms because they were either ineffective teachers or insensitive or even cruel in dealing with you and your classmates?

Chances are you remember just a few outstanding teachers and had at least one who was incompetent or tyrannical (and perhaps several of them). You probably know from your experiences as a student that ineffective or vindictive teachers are often dissatisfied with themselves and with their jobs. It seems logical to assume a circular relationship in such cases: unhappy teachers often do a poor job of instruction; teachers who do a poor job of instruction are likely to be unhappy.

If you hope to be an effective teacher who enjoys life in the classroom (most of the time), you must be well prepared and willing to work. You will need a wide variety of skills, sensitivity to the needs of your students, and awareness of many instructional techniques. Each chapter in this book was written to help you acquire these various skills, sensitivities, and techniques. In addition, you will need to develop the reflective attitudes and abilities that help you formulate thoughtful instructional goals and plans, implement those plans, observe their effects, and judge whether your goals were met. This chapter offers some suggestions you might use to enhance such attitudes and abilities.

# IMPROVING YOUR TEACHING AND REFLECTION SKILLS

**HM TeacherPrepSPACE**

The *Psychology Applied to Teaching*'s student website offers many helpful resources. To aid your professional development, go to **login.cengage.com** select the *student website,* and explore the Weblinks section. See especially the links to professional organizations and publications.

Scholars who study instructional processes (e.g., Freiberg, 2002; Howard & McColskey, 2001; Protheroe, 2002) often note that effective teachers know how to coordinate a diverse array of instructional elements (such as planning, lesson design, time management, classroom management, instructional methods, student motivation, and assessment techniques) and adapt them to differences in student needs, materials, and purposes. Their insights highlight the point that to be consistently effective, you will need to observe and analyze what you do in the classroom and use different approaches with different groups of students. In essence, you will be conducting formative evaluations of yourself. Barbara Howard and Wendy McColskey (2001), who helped develop a teacher evaluation system for the state of North Carolina, describe formative teacher evaluation as a structure for individual professional growth that uses self-assessment, goal setting, feedback from peers, and portfolio development. In the sections that follow, we will explore these and other techniques.

## Student Evaluations and Suggestions

In many respects, students are in a better position to evaluate teachers than anyone else. They may not always be able to analyze *why* what a teacher does is effective or ineffective (even an experienced expert observer might have difficulty doing so), but they know, better than anyone else, whether they are responding and learning. Furthermore, students form their impressions after interacting with a teacher for hundreds or thousands of hours. Most principals or other adult observers may watch a teacher in action for only a few minutes at a time. It therefore makes sense to pay attention to and solicit opinions from students.

As a matter of fact, it will be virtually impossible for you to ignore student reactions. Every minute that school is in session, you will receive student feedback in the form of attentiveness (or lack of it), facial expressions, restlessness, yawns, sleeping, disruptive behavior, and the like. If a particular lesson arouses either a neutral or a negative reaction, this should signal to you that you need to seek a better way to present the same material in the future. If you find that you seem to be spending much of your time disciplining students, it will be worth your while to evaluate why and to find other methods.

In addition to informally analyzing the minute-by-minute reactions of your students, you may find it helpful to request more formal feedback. After completing a unit, you might say, "I'd like you to tell me what you liked and disliked about the way this unit was arranged and give me suggestions for improving it if I teach it again next year."

A more comprehensive and systematic approach is to distribute a questionnaire or evaluation form and ask students to record their reactions anonymously. You might use a published form or devise your own. In either case, a common format is to list a series of statements and ask students to rate them on a five-point scale. Some of the published forms use special answer sheets that make it possible to tally the results electronically. Many rating-scale evaluation forms have some disadvantages, however:

- Responses may not be very informative unless you can compare your ratings with those of colleagues. If you get an overall rating of 3.5 on "makes the subject matter interesting," for example, you won't know whether you need to work on that aspect of your teaching until you discover that the average rating of other teachers of the same grade or subject was 4.2.

- Published evaluation forms may not be very helpful unless all other teachers use the same rating scale. Fortunately, this may be possible in school districts that use a standard scale to obtain evidence for use in making decisions about retention, tenure, and promotion.
- Many rating scales are subject to a *leniency problem*. Students tend to give most teachers somewhat above-average ratings on most traits. Although leniency may soothe a teacher's ego, wishy-washy responses do not provide the information needed to improve pedagogical effectiveness.

To get around the leniency problem and to induce students to give more informative reactions, forced-choice ratings are often used. A rating form developed by Don Cosgrove, which provides student perceptions of teacher performance in the areas of knowledge and organization of subject matter, relationships with students, plans and procedures, and enthusiasm, is available on the textbook's student website.

For teachers who adopt a constructivist approach and value students' perceptions of how well constructivist learning principles are implemented in the classroom, the survey instrument in Figure 16.1 may prove useful. Called the Constructivist Learning Environment Survey (CLES) (Aldridge, Laugksch, Seopa & Fraser, 2006; Spinner & Fraser, 2005; Taylor & Fraser, 1998; Taylor, Fraser, & Fisher, 1997), it was designed especially for science teachers. But except for items 3 and 6 through 10, the items are sufficiently general that they can be used for other subject areas.

One way to use the CLES is to administer it at the beginning of the school year to establish a baseline and then again in the middle of the year and at the end.

**HM TeacherPrepSPACE**

To view Cosgrove's rating form, use the Weblinks at the textbook's student website.

**Figure 16.1** The Constructivist Learning Environment Survey

| Learning about the world | Almost Always | Often | Sometimes | Seldom | Almost Never |
|---|---|---|---|---|---|
| In this class . . . | | | | | |
| 1 I learn about the world outside of school. | 5 | 4 | 3 | 2 | 1 |
| 2 My new learning starts with problems about the world outside of school. | 5 | 4 | 3 | 2 | 1 |
| 3 I learn how science can be part of my out-of-school life. | 5 | 4 | 3 | 2 | 1 |
| In this class . . . | | | | | |
| 4 I get a better understanding of the world outside of school. | 5 | 4 | 3 | 2 | 1 |
| 5 I learn interesting things about the world outside of school. | 5 | 4 | 3 | 2 | 1 |
| Learning about science | Almost Always | Often | Sometimes | Seldom | Almost Never |
| In this class . . . | | | | | |
| 6 I learn that science has changed over time. | 5 | 4 | 3 | 2 | 1 |
| 7 I learn that science is influenced by people's values and opinions. | 5 | 4 | 3 | 2 | 1 |
| In this class . . . | | | | | |
| 8 I learn about the different sciences used by people in other cultures. | 5 | 4 | 3 | 2 | 1 |
| 9 I learn that modern science is different from the science of long ago. | 5 | 4 | 3 | 2 | 1 |
| 10 I learn that science involves inventing theories. | 5 | 4 | 3 | 2 | 1 |

*Continued*

**Figure 16.1** The Constructivist Learning Environment Survey—Cont'd

| Learning to speak out | Almost Always | Often | Sometimes | Seldom | Almost Never |
|---|---|---|---|---|---|
| In this class . . . | | | | | |
| 11 It's OK for me to ask the teacher "why do I have to learn this?" | 5 | 4 | 3 | 2 | 1 |
| 12 It's OK for me to question the way I'm being taught. | 5 | 4 | 3 | 2 | 1 |
| 13 It's OK for me to complain about activities that are confusing. | 5 | 4 | 3 | 2 | 1 |
| In this class . . . | | | | | |
| 14 It's OK for me to complain about anything that prevents me from learning. | 5 | 4 | 3 | 2 | 1 |
| 15 It's OK for me to express my opinion. | 5 | 4 | 3 | 2 | 1 |

| Learning to learn | Almost Always | Often | Sometimes | Seldom | Almost Never |
|---|---|---|---|---|---|
| In this class . . . | | | | | |
| 16 I help the teacher to plan what I'm going to learn. | 5 | 4 | 3 | 2 | 1 |
| 17 I help the teacher to decide how well I am learning. | 5 | 4 | 3 | 2 | 1 |
| 18 I help the teacher to decide which activities are best for me. | 5 | 4 | 3 | 2 | 1 |
| In this class . . . | | | | | |
| 19 I help the teacher to decide how much time I spend on activities. | 5 | 4 | 3 | 2 | 1 |
| 20 I help the teacher to decide which activities I do. | 5 | 4 | 3 | 2 | 1 |

| Learning to communicate | Almost Always | Often | Sometimes | Seldom | Almost Never |
|---|---|---|---|---|---|
| In this class . . . | | | | | |
| 21 I get the chance to talk to other students. | 5 | 4 | 3 | 2 | 1 |
| 22 I talk with other students about how to solve problems. | 5 | 4 | 3 | 2 | 1 |
| 23 I explain my ideas to other students. | 5 | 4 | 3 | 2 | 1 |
| In this class . . . | | | | | |
| 24 I ask other students to explain their ideas. | 5 | 4 | 3 | 2 | 1 |
| 25 Other students listen carefully to my ideas. | 5 | 4 | 3 | 2 | 1 |

SOURCE: Taylor & Fraser (1998); Taylor, Fraser, & Fisher (1997). Permission to reproduce the CLES granted personally to the author by Peter Taylor.

Because the students will not have experienced your approach to instruction at the beginning of the year, have them answer on the basis of their experiences in last year's class. A high school teacher who administered the CLES in September and June found that scores on all the scales increased (that is, shifted toward the constructivist end). The largest increases occurred in the Learning About the World, Learning to Speak Out, and Learning to Communicate scales (Johnson, 2000).

## Peer and Self-Assessment Techniques

**Classroom Observation Schedules**   Although your students can supply quite a bit of information that can help you improve your teaching, they cannot always tell

# VIDEO CASE ◄◄ ▶ ►►

## Teaching as a Profession: Collaboration with Colleagues

*Watch the video, study the artifacts in the case, and reflect upon the following questions:*

**1.** The text and this Video Case both show how colleagues play a role in improving the teaching practice of others. Which examples of peer assessment and collaboration do you think would be most helpful to you? Explain your answers.

**2.** In the Video Case, we see several teachers collaborating on an important issue related to their students. Briefly explain what they are trying to achieve and whether or not you think their collaborative process was successful.

you about technical flaws in your instructional technique. This is especially true with younger students. Accordingly, you may wish to submit to a detailed analysis by a colleague of your approach to teaching.

One of the simplest classroom observation instruments to create and use is the checklist. Figure 16.2 contains a set of six relatively brief checklists that reflect many of the topics discussed in this book. You can adopt this instrument as is or modify it to suit your circumstances (such as your grade level and your state's learning standards) to help you evaluate your effectiveness in several important areas.

**Figure 16.2** Examples of Classroom Observation Checklists

**1. Characteristics of a Good Learning Environment**

_____ Samples of exemplary work are displayed.

_____ Criteria charts, rubrics, or expectations are visible.

_____ There is evidence of students making choices.

_____ Furniture arrangements allow for individual, small-group, and whole-class work.

_____ Written expectations for behavior and subject matter are displayed.

_____ There are a variety of materials and activities to address different learning styles.

_____ There are discussions that involve many different students and points of view.

**2. Characteristics of Good Teaching**

_____ Content and standards are being explicitly taught.

_____ A variety of instructional strategies are integrated into all lessons.

_____ Individual progress is monitored.

_____ There are interventions for students not demonstrating mastery.

_____ A variety of assessment techniques are used.

_____ There is evidence of staff development impact.

**3. Patterns of Teacher Behavior**

_____ Gender and racial equity are observed in interactions with students.

_____ There is recognition and positive reinforcement of effort as well as achievement.

_____ Students are treated as individuals.

**4. Characteristics of Student Learning**

_____ Students communicate ideas clearly, orally and in writing.

_____ Students plan and organize their own work.

_____ Students use a variety of resources.

_____ Students create new products and ideas.

_____ Students use prior knowledge to solve problems.

_____ Students collaborate with peers and adults on projects, drafts, and investigations.

*Continued*

**Figure 16.2** Examples of Classroom Observation Checklists—Cont'd

| 5. Questions to Ask Students Who Are On-Task | 6. Observing Individual Students Who Are Not On-Task |
|---|---|
| ____ What are you learning? | ____ What is the student doing while others are learning? |
| ____ Why do you need to know this information? | ____ Where is the student sitting? |
| ____ How is this like other things you've learned? | ____ How often does the teacher make contact with the student? |
| ____ What will this help you do in the future? | ____ What is the nature of the interactions? |
| ____ What do you do if you get stuck? | |
| ____ How do you know if your work is good enough? | *Ask the Student:* |
| ____ If you want to make your work better, do you know how to improve it? | ____ What do you think this lesson is about? |
| ____ Do you talk about your work with your parents or other adults? | ____ What would help you understand this better? |
| | ____ What would make it more interesting? |
| | ____ What do you do if you don't understand something? |
| | ____ How do you get help? |

SOURCE: L. Schmidt (2003).

Another useful observation instrument can be found in an article by Donna Sobel, Sheryl Taylor, and Ruth Anderson in the July/August 2003 issue (Vol. 35, No. 6) of *Teaching Exceptional Children*. Called the Diversity-Responsive Teaching Observation Tool, it was created for a Colorado school district with a broad diversity of students. The instrument contains three sections and focuses on how well teachers address diversity as well as exhibit appropriate classroom instruction and classroom management behaviors. Because the form is too lengthy to reproduce here, we encourage you to consult the article in which it appears if you think you might want to have a colleague use it to evaluate your teaching.

**Audiotaped Lessons**    If it is not possible for you to team up with a colleague, you might consider trying to accomplish the same goal through the use of audiotape. Your first step should be to decide which classes or parts of classes you want to record, for how long, and on what day of the week. The goal should be to create a representative sample of the circumstances under which you teach. Then you should inform your

*Soliciting comments about the effectiveness of one's teaching methods from students and colleagues and reflecting on these comments is an excellent way to become a better teacher.*

students that you intend to tape-record a sample of your lessons over a period of several weeks to study and improve your instructional methods and that you will protect their confidentiality by not allowing anyone else but you to listen to the tapes.

A first-year high school teacher decided after analyzing an audiotape of one of her lessons that she needed to wait longer for students to respond to high-level questions, give students more opportunities to ask questions, give students more feedback, use specific praise, review and integrate previous concepts with new lessons, and stop saying "OK" and "all right." Impressed with these insights, she continued to tape-record and analyze her lessons, and at the end of the year was nominated for an award as the district's best new teacher (Freiberg, 2002).

**Videotaped Lessons**   Allowing yourself to be videotaped as you teach and then analyzing your actions later can be a valuable learning experience because it often reveals (even more clearly than audiotape) discrepancies between the instructional beliefs you espouse and how you put those beliefs into practice. Think of it as putting into practice the old saying, "Actions speak louder than words." The potential of videotaped lessons to reveal these discrepancies and produce major shifts in teaching behavior was illustrated in a study (Wedman, Espinosa, & Laffey, 1999) of eleven individuals whose teaching experience ranged from none to twenty-two years. The participant with twenty-two years of experience, a primary grade teacher who had never had her teaching observed, claimed to have a student-centered philosophy. She believed that teachers should provide students with opportunities to explore and experiment. But her videotaped lessons revealed a strong teacher-directed, teacher-centered approach. She selected all the material and activities for the students and provided few opportunities for student expression, exploration, or questioning. As a result of reviewing and discussing her videotaped lessons, she began to look for ways to be more student centered and to emphasize inquiry rather than information dissemination as her approach to student learning.

Because videotaping is more intrusive than audiotaping, teachers are often concerned that the natural flow of classroom events will be disrupted. Experience has shown, however, that both students and teachers quickly lose their self-consciousness and treat the camera as just part of the background. As with audiotaped lessons, make sure your students are informed of what will occur and why and how you will keep the results confidential (Lonoff, 1997).

**Reflective Lesson Plans**   You may want to try something called reflective lesson plans (Ho, 1995). To do so, follow these four steps:

1. Divide a sheet of paper in half. Label the left-hand side "Lesson Plan." Label the right-hand side "Reflective Notes."
2. On the lesson plan side, note relevant identifying information (fourth period English, January 23, 9:00 A.M.; honors algebra; fourth-grade social studies), the objectives of the lesson, the tasks that are to be carried out in chronological order, the materials and equipment that are to be used, and how much time has been allotted for this lesson.
3. On the reflective notes side, as soon as possible after the lesson, write your thoughts about the worth of the objective that underlies the lesson, the adequacy of the materials, and how well you performed the basic mechanics of teaching.
4. Make changes to the lesson plan based on your analysis of the reflective notes.

**Guided Reflection Protocol**   A technique that is somewhat less structured than the reflective lesson plan is the guided reflection protocol (McEntee et al., 2003). After choosing one or more teaching episodes that you would like to examine, try to answer as honestly as possible the following four questions:

1. *What happened?* The main requirement of this step is simply to describe the incident as fully as possible. Note, for instance, when and where the incident

occurred, who was involved, and what occurred just prior to, during, and immediately after the incident. Avoid analysis and interpretation.

2. *Why did it happen?* If you've provided enough context in answering the first question, you should be able to identify the events that produced the incident.

3. *What might it mean?* Note the conditional wording of this question. Using the word *might* instead of *does* is intended to help you realize that there are usually several possible interpretations of the meaning of an incident. A teacher who reprimands a class for not finishing an assignment on time may, for example, need to examine the clarity of her objectives, the amount of time she budgets for the completion of assignments, the ability of students to use their time productively, or her ability to cope with administrative pressure to cover the curriculum in time for an upcoming high-stakes test.

4. *What are the implications for my practice?* Consider what you might do differently in a similar situation in the light of how you answered the first three questions.

**Developing a Reflective Journal**    Seymour Sarason (1993, 2005; Glazek & Sarason, 2006), who has written extensively about schooling and school reform, points out what may seem obvious but is often missed in practice: every teacher should be an expert in both subject matter and how children learn in classrooms. The goal, and the challenge, is to figure out how to present the subject matter so that students understand it, remember it, and use it. To do that, you must constantly prepare, observe, and reflect on how closely your instructional practices relate to theory and research and produce the desired outcome (Heath, 2002). The Reflective Journal that we mentioned at the beginning of the book is intended to help you begin that process in a systematic way. Now we will give you more detailed suggestions for keeping such a journal.

We recommend that you develop a Reflective Journal for two basic purposes: (1) to serve as a repository of instructional ideas and techniques that you have either created from your own experiences or gleaned from other sources and (2) to give yourself a format for recording your observations and reflections on teaching (Lyons & Kubler LaBoskey, 2002). These two purposes can be separate from each other or, if you choose, related to each other in a cycle of reflectivity that we will describe. As you read this section, refer to Figure 16.3 for an illustration of how a journal page might look.

The form your Reflective Journal takes will probably change over the years to reflect your experiences and changing needs. But to begin, we suggest that you organize your first journal around the marginal notes in each chapter of this book that are labeled "Journal Entry." Use the Journal Entries as just what their name implies: page headings in your Reflective Journal. To allow room for both the expansion of your teaching ideas and the inclusion of your ongoing reflections, you might purchase a three-ring binder so that you can add and drop pages. Alternatively, you might want to create your Reflective Journal as computer files, which would give you unlimited capacity for interaction and expansion.

Under each heading, you can develop a two-part page or multipage entry. As illustrated in the top half of Figure 16.3, the first part should contain your own teaching ideas, custom-tailored from the Suggestions for Teaching sections of the chapters of this book and from personal experience and other sources to fit the grade level and subjects you expect to teach.

To illustrate, let's use a Journal Entry from Chapter 10, "Social Cognitive Theory— Ways to Teach Comprehension Tactics":

- Search your memory for techniques that your past teachers used. Did your fifth-grade teacher, for instance, have a clever way of relating new information to ideas that you had learned earlier in order to make the new information easier to understand? Describe the technique so you will remember to try it yourself. Did a high school teacher have an ingenious way of displaying the similarities and differences among a set of ideas? Exactly how did she or he do it?

**Figure 16.3** Sample Page for Your Reflective Journal

Journal Entry:      *Ways to Teach Comprehension Tactics*
Source:             *"Information-Processing Theory"*

### Ideas for Instruction

Note: All the ideas you list here will pertain to the particular journal entry/instructional goal for this journal page.

- *Customized suggestions for teaching—those points, principles, activities, and examples taken from the text and the Suggestions for Teaching that are most relevant to your own situation.*

- *Ideas generated from past experiences as a student.*

- *Ideas provided by professional colleagues.*

- *Ideas collected from student-teaching experiences.*

- *Ideas gathered from methods textbooks.*

### Reflections: Questions and "Restarter" Suggestions for Instruction

Reflective Question (to focus observation of my teaching and my students' learning):
*Do my students have difficulty understanding the meaning of what they read or of what I present in class?*

*(Record your ongoing reflections, observations, and analytic notes about your instruction and your students' learning of this topic here. If necessary, you may need to "jump-start" or reorient your instruction. One possible idea follows.)*

Suggested Action: *Schedule a series of sessions on how to study. Explain the purpose of various comprehension tactics, and provide opportunities for students to practice these skills on material they have been assigned to read. Give corrective feedback.*

---

- After you exhaust your own recollections, ask roommates or classmates if they can remember any successful ways that their teachers made understanding easier.
- Examine the examples given in the text section in which the Journal Entry "Ways to Teach Comprehension Tactics" appears. Which ones seem most appropriate for the grade level and subject you will be teaching? Jot them down. Do any of the examples suggest variations you can think of on your own? Write them down before you forget them.
- Add ideas that you pick up in methods classes or during your student-teaching experience. If you see a film in a methods class that shows how a teacher helps students understand a particular point, describe it in your journal. If your master teacher uses a successful technique to clarify difficult-to-understand material, record it.

If you follow some or all of these suggestions for using the Journal Entries, you will have a rich source of ideas to turn to when you discover that your students seem confused and anxious because of poor comprehension and you find yourself wondering if there is anything you can do about it.

With this part of the journal under way, you should feel reasonably well prepared when you first take charge of a class. But given the complexity of classroom teaching, lessons or techniques that looked good on paper do not always produce the intended effect. This is the point at which you need to reflect on and analyze what you are doing and how you might bring about improvements. On the bottom half of your journal page, or on a new page, write in question form what the nature of

*Research has shown that keeping a personal journal about one's teaching activities and outcomes helps teachers improve their effectiveness because it forces them to focus on what they do, why they do it, and what kinds of results are typically obtained.*

the problem seems to be. Then try to identify the cause (or causes) of the problem and at least one possible solution. You can use this suggestion to get restarted or headed in a new direction with your teaching. If, for example, some of your students still have difficulty comprehending what they read despite the comprehension-enhancing techniques that you embedded into your lessons, you might reread Chapter 8 on information-processing theory, as well as other articles and books on information processing, and decide that your students really need systematic instruction in how to use various comprehension-directed learning tactics.

**Using a Portfolio with Your Journal**    Middle school teacher Linda Van Wagenen used a personal portfolio along with a Reflective Journal to analyze and improve the quality of her instruction (Van Wagenen & Hibbard, 1998). She compiled a portfolio of her efforts to achieve certain teaching goals and used that to examine her effectiveness. She judged her first two efforts at analysis to be unsatisfactory because they were largely descriptive; they emphasized what she had done and ignored what effects those efforts had on her students (self-assessment), what she thought about the quality of her own instruction (self-evaluation), or what she planned to do next (self-regulation). Her third attempt focused on ways to motivate students to improve their performance in persuasive and expository writing. She identified a set of steps that would help her understand the problem and produce improvements. Evidence of her successes and failures made up the portfolio. In addition, she kept a Reflective Journal because she felt it would help her stay focused on finding a solution to the problem and would stimulate attempts at self-evaluation and self-regulation. The result of this third attempt was judged to be much more useful than either of her first two efforts. In addition to addressing the question, "What did I do?" she also addressed the questions, "What did I learn?" and "Now what will I do?" Essentially, she engaged in "an intentional reflective process" (Lyons & Kubler LaBoskey, 2002, p. 2), which told the story of her teaching and her students' learning. Narrative accounts (i.e., telling the stories of your teaching) have been shown to be an effective form of self-study to improve teaching (Anderson-Patton & Bass, 2002). By asking and answering questions, as Linda Van Wagenen did on her third attempt, you can build a narrative account in your reflective journal.

In thinking about the contents of your own portfolio, you might want to start with the following list of items (Drake & McBride, 2000; Hurst, Wilson, & Cramer, 1998; Lyons, 1999):

1. Title page
2. A table of contents
3. A statement of your educational philosophy, which may include the reasons that you chose teaching as a career
4. A résumé
5. A statement of your teaching goals
6. Example(s) of a lesson plan, keyed to state standards
7. Examples of learning activities (especially those that contain innovative ideas)
8. Samples of students' work
9. Photographs and videotapes
10. Letters of recommendation
11. Teaching evaluations
12. Samples of college work
13. An autobiography
14. Reflections about how teaching (or student teaching) has contributed to your growth as a person and a teacher
15. Official documents (transcripts, teaching certificates, test scores)

# VIDEO CASE  ◀◀ ▶ ▶▶

## Teaching as a Profession:
## What Defines Effective Teaching?

*Watch the video, study the artifacts in the case, and reflect upon the following questions:*

1. In this Video Case, different school professionals share their thoughts on what defines an effective teacher. Of the various teacher attributes that they describe, which ones do you think are most critical (e.g., knowledge of child development, command of subject matter, being organized, knowing your students, etc.)?

2. Based on this Video Case and the content in this text, think about the concept of teacher self-reflection. In your opinion, what are some effective ways for teachers to reflect on their own practice? Which self-reflection techniques make the most sense to you?

## Are Reflective Techniques Effective?

The answer to this question depends very much on the type of evidence one chooses to examine and the characteristics of the teachers who participated in studies on reflection. There are, for example, many positive anecdotes about the benefits of reflection on the quality of one's teaching. Lynn Streib, a primary grade teacher, had this to say about journal writing:

> Keeping a journal has been a realistic way for me to learn about, inquire into, collect data about, and enhance my practice as well as to learn about and plan for the children. Although writing in my journal each day takes time, it is economical and is the genre most compatible with my style of writing, my way of teaching, and my way of thinking.
>
> Since 1980, I have kept some kind of journal. . . . I continue to keep a journal for a variety of reasons. First and most important, it helps me with my teaching. When used in certain ways, the journal allows me to look closely at the curriculum. As I teach, I wonder how my thinking and my students' thinking evolve over time. I wonder what I have valued and what the children are interested in and value. Lesson plans don't tell me this, but the journal does. My journal is a place for planning, for raising questions, for figuring things out, and for thinking. (Streib, 1993, pp. 121–122)

The findings from experiments, on the other hand, have generally found that reflective activities produced little discernible effect on the quality of subsequent teaching behavior (Cornford, 2002). According to Ian Cornford (2002), these negative outcomes are largely due to flawed research designs. Additionally, most studies of teacher effectiveness have failed to differentiate evaluative techniques according to the particular circumstances of teaching, such as subject matter and age of students (Campbell, Kyriakides, Muijs & Robinson, 2004). Cornford believes that for reflection to be effective, teachers need to possess two qualities: broad and in-depth knowledge of the classroom as a teaching-learning environment and strong critical thinking skills. Many of the studies on reflection mentioned by Cornford were conducted with teachers who appeared to lack these qualities, and he was unable to find any studies that first tried to teach critical thinking skills before assessing the effect of reflection. The validity of Cornford's conclusion is supported by the fact that the few positive findings he did locate involved studies done with experienced teachers. For example, teachers with more than three years' experience who learned reflective skills in college were more satisfied with their jobs and had better teacher-student relationships than teachers who had no college training in reflection.

Cornford's analysis also receives support from a study of the effect of self-assessment on the type of instructional talk used by nine experienced elementary school teachers who were teaching reading (Roskos, Boehlen, & Walker, 2000). Much of the instructional talk exhibited by reading teachers involves a social function in that its purpose is to maintain the flow of instruction and provide direction (for example, restating students' comments, providing reinforcement, directing attention, and commenting on students' ideas). Instructional talk that is directed more to the conceptual basis of reading (such as tapping background knowledge, stimulating memory of relevant experiences, suggesting decoding techniques, and defining a concept) occurs much less frequently. For five weeks, the teachers' daily interactions with students in a reading clinic were videotaped and analyzed by both the teachers and researchers with an instrument (The Instructional Talk Analysis Tool) that assessed how frequently the preceding two categories of teacher talk occurred.

One of the major findings of this study is that the Talk Analysis Tool scores generated by the teachers did not match those of the researchers. The teachers saw themselves using social and conceptual talk in about equal proportions, whereas the researchers' analysis showed the split to be about 60/40 in favor of social language. This finding may have been due to the teachers' not having totally mastered the scoring rules of the Talk Analysis Tool, or it may have stemmed from the teachers' seeing and hearing what they wanted to believe.

The other major finding is that the way the teachers described their instructional behavior changed over the five-week period. Early on, most of their comments were evaluations of either their use of social and conceptual talk or their students' reading behaviors. These evaluative comments gradually subsided, whereas comments about the *instructional effects* of their talk increased. Thus, at least for experienced teachers who can engage in some degree of critical thinking, viewing and analyzing one's actions seems to positively affect how one thinks about and interprets them.

The discrepancy in the preceding study between teachers' self-assessment and the assessment made of them by the researchers suggests that teachers may want to supplement self-assessment with forms of assessment that involve colleagues. Elementary and high school teachers in Hong Kong who participated in a study of peer coaching found it to be a beneficial experience (Lam, Yim, & Lam, 2002). Four or five teachers first met to discuss how a certain unit would be taught. The lesson plan was then tried out by one teacher while the others observed. The teachers then met to discuss the strengths and weaknesses of the lesson. The technique has also been used in Japan and is rapidly finding its way into North American schools under the label "lesson study" (Lewis, Perry, & Murata, 2006). In general, teachers who have an opportunity to reflect on their teaching with colleagues improved their teaching and their ability to communicate with one another and said they would participate in the experience again.

## USING TECHNOLOGY FOR REFLECTION

Throughout this book, we have described how you can use various technology tools to help your students become more effective learners. Now it's time to consider how you can use such technologies as the World Wide Web, videotape, and multimedia and hypermedia programs to help you think about and improve your own teaching skills.

### Discussion Forums and Chatrooms

A major source of frustration for teachers is the limited intellectual and social contact they have with one another (Sarason, 1993). Certainly during school hours, there are few opportunities for teachers to engage in meaningful discussions about teaching and learning. And after school, many teachers are either busy grading papers and making lesson plans or are at home with their families. Computer-based technologies can help break down this sense of isolation by providing forums for teachers to discuss instructional ideas and problems from any location and at any time.

You can begin that process now by using the World Wide Web to discuss ideas and field experiences with peers in this country and others. Later, when you have a full-time teaching position, you can use the Web to discuss such issues as teaching philosophy and common classroom problems and their solutions and to explore relevant resources. Numerous websites have been designed for K–12 teachers and contain discussion forums or chatrooms (or both). Here are five you might consider using:

- the Connect page of ALPS, Harvard's Teacher Lab (**learnweb.harvard.edu/alps/bigideas/q5.cfm**)
- the New Teachers Online page of Teachers Network (**www.teachersnetwork.org/ntol**)
- the Interactive Forums page of the International Education and Resource Network (**www.iearn.org/index.html**)
- the Teacher2Teacher page of Teachnet.com (**www.teachnet.com/t2t**)
- the Teachers Helping Teachers Guestbook page of Teachers Helping Teachers (**www.pacificnet.net/~mandel/guestbook.html**)
- the teachers.net "chat center" can direct you to "chatboards" arranged by grade levels, subjects, region, and so forth (**http://teachers.net**)

## Multimedia Case-Based Instruction

In addition to online conferencing, educational researchers and teacher education programs are using multimedia and hypermedia programs that feature case-based learning formats that encourage new models of teaching, learning, and assessment among both preservice and practicing teachers (Abell, Bryan, & Anderson, 1998; Baker, 2000; Hughes, Packard, & Pearson, 2000; Stephens, Leavell, & Fabris, 1999).

These materials—as well the Houghton Mifflin Video Cases that accompany this book—contain video-based stories to provide a context or situation for teacher reflection and introduce a more constructivist teaching orientation. Tools are provided for selecting and displaying problem cases and situations, recording preliminary case solutions, browsing through expert commentary and supplemental case information, exploring library materials for case solutions and alternative cases, and provoking student reflection. And with technology's replay capabilities, a preservice teacher like you could use these multimedia cases to identify key instructional decisions in planning or conducting a lesson. After watching a video sequence a second or third time for critical teaching decisions, you might post some reflection notes or compare that situation with another. Perhaps more important, such tools are not only useful for individual exploration but also promote rich conversations among teachers.

One set of such materials (Baker, 2000) focuses on the reading and writing of an elementary grade student over the course of a school year. Each videotape segment shows the student either reading or writing with classmates or the teacher. The book that the student reads from and the student's written products can be easily read from the videotape. The video segments can be arranged in such a way that one can track the student's performance either over time or across subject-matter areas.

One study (Abell et al., 1998) focused on science education undergraduates who viewed video cases of first graders learning about eggs and seeds. The experience produced significant changes in the future teachers' beliefs about the capabilities of six-year-olds. According to one undergraduate:

> My expectations for a first grade science lesson have really changed after viewing the Seeds and Eggs lesson. The first graders are able to handle hands-on a lot better than I thought they would. I thought the teacher would mainly do all of the talking and experimenting. I saw these students, even though they are young, being able to conduct and observe experiments on their own. I thought they would misbehave if there was not a lot of supervision. This class really surprised me at how well behaved and under control they were. (p. 505)

Technological tools for reflection can be very helpful to teachers at any stage of their professional development. However, as is the case with any tool, understanding a tool's purpose is critical to using it effectively.

**HM** *TeacherPrepSPACE*

For direct links to these and other websites, use the Weblinks at the textbook's student website.

**HM** *TeacherPrepSPACE*

*How will you use reflective teaching in your own career? To prompt your thinking, read the PowerPoint slides and try the ACE practice tests at the textbook's student website.*

# Glossary

## A

**accommodation**   The process of creating or revising a scheme to fit a new experience. (*See* **scheme**)

**achievement batteries**   Sets of tests designed to assess performance in a broad range of subjects.

**active listening**   A way of dealing with a problem-owning student by showing interest and encouraging the talker to continue expressing feelings.

**adaptation**   The process, described by Piaget, of creating a good fit or match between one's conception of reality and one's real-life experiences. (*See* **accommodation; assimilation**)

**adolescent egocentrism**   The introspective, inward turning of a high school student's newly developed powers of thought, with a tendency to project one's self-analysis onto others. (*See* **egocentrism**)

**adventure learning**   A type of learning wherein students might participate in real-life expeditions, virtual field trips, historical reenactments, and local adventures in their community, typically in structured activities with students from other schools.

**affective domain taxonomy**   A classification of instructional outcomes that concentrates on attitudes and values.

**anchored instruction**   Method of embedding important information or skills in authentic problem-solving situations and meaningful contexts for prolonged student exploration. (*See* **inert knowledge; situated learning**)

**aptitude tests**   Tests intended to give educators some idea of the level of knowledge and skill a student could acquire with effective instruction.

**assimilation**   The process of fitting new experience into an existing scheme. (*See* **scheme**)

**assistive technology**   Any item, device, or piece of equipment, from low-tech equipment such as taped stories to more sophisticated technologies such as voice-recognition and speech-synthesis devices, that is used to increase, maintain, or improve the functional abilities of persons with disabilities.

**attention**   The selective focusing on a portion of the information currently stored in the sensory register. (*See* **sensory register**)

**attention-deficit/hyperactivity disorder (ADHD)**   A disorder that begins in childhood; is marked by abnormally high levels of impulsive behavior, distractibility, and motor activity; and leads to low levels of learning.

**attribution theory**   A body of research into the ways that students explain their success or failure, usually in terms of ability, effort, task difficulty, and luck.

**authentic assessment**   (*See* **performance tests**)

**authoritarian parents**   Parents who make demands and wield power without considering their children's point of view.

**authoritative parents**   Parents who provide models of competence to be imitated, based on confidence in their own abilities.

## B

**behavior disorder**   (*See* **emotional disturbance**)

**behavior modification**   The use of operant conditioning techniques to modify behavior, generally by making rewards contingent on certain actions. Also called *contingency management.* (*See* **operant conditioning**)

**between-class ability grouping**   Assigning students of similar learning ability to separate classes based on scores from standardized intelligence or achievement tests.

## C

**cognitive apprenticeship**   A relationship in which help and guidance are provided by a mentor or expert practitioner to a learner, enabling him or her to master a task and gradually participate in a culture or community. (*See* **telementoring**)

**cognitive constructivism**   A form of constructivist learning theory that emphasizes the role of assimilation and accommodation in constructing an understanding of the world in which one lives. (*See* **accommodation; assimilation; constructivism**)

**cognitive domain taxonomy**   A classification scheme of instructional outcomes that stresses knowledge and intellectual skills, including comprehension, application, analysis, synthesis, and evaluation. Also called *Bloom's taxonomy.*

**collaborative learning**   Activities for which groups of learners use and combine their individual talents and areas of expertise to investigate problems, negotiate ideas, generate knowledge, and design products. (*See* **cooperative learning**)

**competency test**   A test to determine a student's ability to handle basic subjects.

**computer adaptive testing (CAT)**   A testing technique in which a computer program adapts the difficulty of questions to the ability level of the examinee based on her responses, thereby resulting in a reduction in test length and greater efficiency.

**computer-assisted instruction (CAI)**   (*See* **computer-based instruction**)

**computer-based instruction (CBI)**   Teaching methods that use interactive software as an aid to learning.

**computer conferencing** An online discussion group, typically organized by topic, that can provide students with access to information, viewpoints, and communities beyond the boundaries of their classrooms.

**concept mapping** A technique for identifying and visually representing on paper the ideas that comprise a section of text and the ways in which they relate to each other.

**conservation** The recognition that certain properties stay the same despite a change in appearance or position.

**constructivism** The view that meaningful learning is the active creation of knowledge structures rather than a mere transferring of objective knowledge from one person to another.

**contingency contracting** A behavior-strengthening technique that specifies desirable behaviors and consequent reinforcement.

**cooperative learning** An approach that uses small heterogeneous groups for purposes of mutual help in the mastery of specific tasks.

**criterion-referenced grading** A system in which grades are determined on the basis of whether each student has attained a defined standard of achievement or performance.

**criterion-referenced tests** Tests in which students are evaluated according to how well they have mastered specific objectives in various well-defined skill areas.

**cultural pluralism** A set of tenets based on three principles: (1) every culture has its own internal coherence, integrity, and logic; (2) no culture is inherently better or worse than another; and (3) all persons are to some extent culture-bound.

**culture** A description of the ways a group of people perceives the world; formulates beliefs; evaluates objects, ideas, and experiences; and behaves.

## D

**decentration** The ability to think of more than one quality of an object or problem at a time. (*See* **perceptual centration**)

**deficiency needs** The first four levels (physiological, safety, belongingness or love, and esteem) in Maslow's hierarchy of needs, so called because these needs cause people to act only when they are unmet to some degree.

**depression** An emotional disorder characterized by self-deprecation, crying spells, and suicidal thoughts, afflicting between 7 and 28 percent of all adolescents.

**diagnostic test** A single-subject achievement test intended to identify the source of a problem in basic subjects and perhaps in study skills. (*See* **single-subject achievement test**)

**digital portfolio** A multimedia collection of student work that documents individual expertise, achievement, accomplishments, and growth in one or more areas over extended periods of time. Also called *electronic portfolio*.

**direct instruction** An approach to instruction that emphasizes the efficient acquisition of basic skills and subject matter through lectures and demonstrations, extensive practice, and corrective feedback.

**discovery learning** A teaching strategy that encourages children to seek solutions to problems either on their own or in group discussion.

**discrimination** A process in which individuals learn to notice the unique aspects of seemingly similar situations and thus learn different ways of responding.

**distributed practice** The practice of breaking up learning tasks into small, easy-to-manage pieces that are learned over several relatively brief sessions.

**drill-and-practice programs** Computer programs that help students practice skills and learn factual information.

**dual coding theory** A theory of elaboration that states that concrete objects and words are remembered better than abstract information because they are coded in memory as both visual images and verbal labels, whereas abstract words are only encoded verbally.

## E

**early-maturing boy** A boy whose early physical maturation typically draws favorable adult responses and promotes confidence and poise, thus contributing to leadership and popularity with peers. (*See* **late-maturing boy**)

**early-maturing girl** A girl whose early physical maturation typically makes her socially out of step with her peers. (*See* **late-maturing girl**)

**educational psychology** The branch of psychology that specializes in understanding how different factors affect the classroom behavior of both teachers and students.

**egocentrism** Difficulty in taking another person's point of view, a characteristic typical of young children.

**elaborative rehearsal** A process that consciously relates new information to knowledge already stored in long-term memory. Also called *elaborative encoding*. (*See* **long-term memory**)

**electronic portfolio** (*See* **digital portfolio**)

**emotional disturbance** An emotional condition in which inappropriate aggressive or withdrawal behaviors are exhibited over a long period of time and to a marked degree, adversely affecting a child's educational performance.

**empirical learning** The use of noticeable characteristics of objects and events to form spontaneous concepts; a form of learning typical of young children.

**epigenetic principle** The notion that a child's personality develops as the ego progresses through a series of interrelated stages, much as the human body takes shape during its fetal development.

**equilibration** The tendency to organize schemes to allow better understanding of experiences. (*See* **scheme**)

**ethnic group** A collection of people who identify with one another on the basis of such characteristics as ancestral origin, race, religion, language, values, political or economic interests, and behavior patterns.

**evaluation** In assessment, the use of a rule-governed system to make judgments about the value or worth of a set of measures.

**exploratory environments** Electronic environments that provide students with materials and resources to discover interesting phenomena and construct new insights; for example, computer simulations. Also called *discovery environments*. (*See* **discovery learning**)

**extinction** The weakening of a target behavior by ignoring it.

**extrinsic motivation** A form of incentive based on a system of rewards not inherent in a particular activity. (*See* **intrinsic motivation**)

## F

**far transfer** The ability to use knowledge and skills learned at an earlier point in time in a particular context to help one learn new information or solve a problem in a very different context at a much later point in time.

**field-dependent style** A learning style in which a person's perception of and thinking about a task or problem are strongly influenced by such contextual factors as additional information and other people's behavior.

**field-independent style** A learning style in which a person's perception of and thinking about a task or problem are influenced more by the person's knowledge base than by the presence of additional information or other people's behavior.

**flow** A mental state of high engagement in an activity that is characterized by such intense concentration, sustained interest, and enjoyment of the activity's challenge, that individuals lose track of the passage of time.

**foreclosure status** An adolescent identity status marked by the unquestioning endorsement of parents' goals and values.

**formative evaluation** A type of assessment that monitors a student's progress in order to facilitate learning rather than to assign a grade.

**full inclusion** The practice of eliminating pullout programs (those outside the classroom) and providing regular teachers with special training so as to keep special needs students in regular classrooms. Also called *inclusion*.

## G

**gender bias** The tendency of teachers to respond differently to male and female students when there is no educationally sound reason for doing so.

**gender roles** Sets of behaviors typically identified with either males or females in a society; young children's awareness of these roles shows up clearly in the different toys and activities that boys and girls prefer.

**generalization** The learned ability to respond in similar ways to similar stimuli.

**general objectives** Objectives that use the three taxonomies (cognitive, affective, and psychomotor) to describe types of behavior that would demonstrate a student's learning. (*See* **affective domain taxonomy; cognitive domain taxonomy; psychomotor domain taxonomy**)

**general transfer** A situation in which prior learning aids subsequent learning due to the use of similar cognitive strategies.

**gifted and talented student** A student who shows unusual ability in any of a variety of ways and who may require services not ordinarily provided by his school.

**grade equivalent score** A measurement that interprets test performance in terms of grade levels.

**growth need** A yearning for personal fulfillment that people constantly strive to satisfy. (*See* **self-actualization**)

**growth spurt** The rapid and uneven physical growth that besets adolescents during the middle school years.

**guided learning** Environments in which teachers, experts, or more knowledgeable peers support student inquiry by helping students set plans and goals, ask questions, discuss issues, solve problems, and reflect on strategies and solutions. Also called *guided discovery learning*. (*See* **cognitive apprenticeship; constructivism**)

## H

**heuristics** General approaches to solving problems, such as studying worked examples and breaking problems into parts, that can be applied to different subject areas.

**high-road transfer** A situation involving the conscious, controlled, somewhat effortful formulation of an "abstraction" (that is, a rule, a schema, a strategy, or an analogy) that allows a connection to be made between two tasks.

**high-stakes testing** The use of standardized test results to make such significant decisions as whether students get promoted to the next grade or graduate from high school, whether teachers and administrators receive financial rewards or demotions, and whether school districts receive additional state funds or lose their accreditation.

**humanistic approach** An approach to instruction that emphasizes the effect of student needs, values, motives, and self-perceptions on learning.

**hypermedia** A technology that combines multimedia and hypertext so that the learner can nonsequentially access and explore interesting and important information resources. (*See* **hypertext; multimedia**)

**hypertext** A system of linking text in a nonlinear way, thereby enabling users to jump from one section of text to another section of the same document or to other documents, often through pressing highlighted or "hot" words.

## I

**IDEA** Acronym for the Individuals with Disabilities Education Act (originally called the Education for All Handicapped Children Act), the principal federal law governing the education of children with disabilities.

**identity** A relatively stable conception of where and how one fits into a society that is strongly influenced by the perception of one's physical appearance, the goals one establishes and achieves, and recognition from significant others in the environment.

**identity achievement status** An adolescent identity status marked by self-chosen commitments with respect to at least some aspects of identity.

**identity diffusion status** An adolescent identity status marked by the avoidance of choices pertaining to jobs, roles, or values and the readiness to change one's position in response to negative or positive feedback.

**identity status** A style or approach that adolescents adopt to deal with such identity-related issues as career goal, gender-role orientation, and religious beliefs. James Marcia identified four identity statuses: identity diffusion, moratorium, foreclosure, and identity achievement.

**ill-structured problems** Vaguely stated problems with unclear solution procedures and vague evaluation standards. (*See* **well-structured problems**)

**I-message** A first-person statement by a teacher that emphasizes the teacher's feelings about a situation rather than her feelings about the students.

**impulsive** A learning style in which students respond relatively quickly to questions or tasks for which there is no obvious correct answer or solution.

**inclusion** An extension of the least restrictive environment provision of IDEA in which students with disabilities are placed in regular classrooms for the entire school day and receive some instruction and support from a special education teacher. (*See also* **full inclusion**)

**individualized education program (IEP)** A written statement describing an educational program designed to meet the unique needs of a child with a particular disability.

**inert knowledge** Information, typically memorized verbatim, that is unconnected, lacking in context, and not readily accessible for application to real-world tasks. (*See* **anchored instruction; drill-and-practice programs; meaningful learning; situated learning**)

**information-processing theory** An area of study that seeks to understand how people acquire, store, and recall information and how their current knowledge guides and determines what and how they will learn.

**instructional objectives** Statements written by teachers that specify the knowledge and skills students should be able to exhibit after a unit of instruction.

**integrated learning systems (ILS)** Computer-based instructional systems that provide sequenced and self-paced learning activities to students in many different content areas as well as appropriate remediation or enrichment activities.

**intelligence** The ability of an individual to use a variety of cognitive and noncognitive capabilities to formulate goals, logically work toward achieving those goals, and adapt to the demands of the environment.

**Internet** *See* **World Wide Web**.

**interpersonal reasoning** The ability to understand the relationship between motives and behavior among a group of people.

**intrinsic motivation** A form of incentive inherent in a particular activity, such as the positive consequence of becoming more competent or knowledgeable. (*See* **extrinsic motivation**)

**irreversibility** The inability of a young child to mentally reverse physical or mental processes, such as pouring water from a tall, thin glass back into a short, squat one.

**issues** Ill-structured problems that arouse strong feelings. (*See* **ill-structured problems**)

**J**

**Joplin Plan** An ability grouping technique that combines students of different grade levels according to their standardized test scores. (*See* **regrouping**)

**L**

**late-maturing boy** A boy whose delayed physical maturation typically causes inferiority feelings and leads to bossy and attention-getting behavior. (*See* **early-maturing boy**)

**late-maturing girl** A girl whose delayed physical maturation typically makes her more poised than others her age and elicits praise from elders, thus conferring leadership tendencies. (*See* **early-maturing girl**)

**learner-centered education** An educational philosophy in which the teacher helps guide students to construct knowledge meaningfully and monitor their own learning by emphasizing student choice, responsibility, challenge, intrinsic motivation, and ownership of the learning process.

**learning disabilities** Problems in otherwise mentally fit students who are unable to respond to certain aspects of the curriculum presented in regular classrooms because of disorders in one or more basic psychological processes.

**learning strategy** A general plan that a learner formulates for achieving a somewhat distant academic goal.

**learning style** A consistent tendency or preference to respond to a variety of intellectual tasks and problems in a particular fashion.

**learning tactic** A specific technique that a learner uses to accomplish an immediate learning objective.

**least restrictive environment** A requirement (under the 1994 Code of Federal Regulations governing the implementation of IDEA) that disabled children be provided with education in the least restrictive setting possible, usually by including them in regular classrooms. (*See* **mainstreaming**)

**long-term memory (LTM)** Storehouse of permanently recorded information in an individual's memory.

**loss of voice** The tendency of adolescent females to suppress their true beliefs about issues and either claim that they have no opinion or state what they think others want to hear because of socialization practices.

**low-road transfer** A situation in which a previously learned skill or idea is almost automatically retrieved from memory and applied to a highly similar current task. (*See* **high-road transfer**)

**M**

**mainstreaming** The policy of placing students with disabilities in regular classes.

**maintenance rehearsal** A rather mechanical process that uses mental and verbal repetition to hold information in short-term memory for some immediate purpose. Also called *rote rehearsal* or *repetition*. (*See* **short-term memory**)

**massed practice**  An approach to learning that emphasizes a few long, infrequently spaced study periods.

**mastery learning**  An approach that assumes most students can master the curriculum if certain conditions are established: (1) sufficient aptitude, (2) sufficient ability to understand instruction, (3) a willingness to persevere, (4) sufficient time, and (5) good-quality instruction.

**meaningful learning**  Learning that occurs when new information or activities are made relevant by relating them to personal interests and prior experiences or knowledge.

**measurement**  The assignment of numbers to certain attributes of objects, events, or people according to a rule-governed system.

**melting pot**  A term referring to the assimilation of diverse ethnic groups into one national mainstream.

**mental retardation**  A condition in which learning proceeds at a significantly slow rate, is limited to concrete experiences, and is accompanied by difficulty functioning in social environments.

**metacognition**  Knowledge about the operations of cognition and how to use them to achieve a learning goal.

**microcomputer-based laboratory (MBL)**  A microcomputer with attached sensors and probes that can quickly represent such data as temperature or speed in multiple ways in order to help students explore concepts, test hypotheses, and repair scientific misconceptions.

**microworld**  A computer scenario intended to foster cognitive development and overcome misconceptions by allowing students the chance to explore relationships among variables or concepts and build personal models of how things work.

**mnemonic device**  A memory-directed tactic that helps a learner transform or organize information to enhance its retrievability.

**morality of constraint**  Piaget's term for the moral thinking of children up to age ten or so, in which they hold sacred rules that permit no exceptions and make no allowance for intentions. Also called *moral realism.*

**morality of cooperation**  Piaget's term for the moral thinking of children age eleven or older, based on flexible rules and considerations of intent. Also called *moral relativism.*

**moratorium status**  An adolescent identity status marked by various kinds of identity crises, often involving experimentation and restless searching.

**multicultural education**  An approach to learning and teaching that seeks to foster an understanding of and mutual respect for the values, beliefs, and practices of different cultural groups.

**multidisciplinary assessment team**  A group of people involved in determining the nature of a child's disability, typically consisting of a school psychologist, guidance counselor, classroom teacher, school social worker, school nurse, learning disability specialist, physician, and psychiatrist.

**multimedia**  The combination of several forms of media such as text, graphics, animation, sound, images, and video that teachers can use to enrich student understanding and address various student learning styles, preferences, and impairments. (*See* **dual coding theory; hypermedia**)

**N**

**near transfer**  The ability to use knowledge and skills learned at an earlier point in time in a particular context to help one learn new information or solve a problem in a very similar context and soon after the original learning.

**negative reinforcement**  A way of strengthening a target behavior by removing an aversive stimulus after a particular behavior is exhibited. (*See* **positive reinforcement**)

**negative transfer**  A situation in which one's prior learning interferes with subsequent learning. (*See* **positive transfer**)

**normal curve**  The bell-shaped distribution of scores that tends to occur when a particular characteristic is measured in thousands of people.

**norm group**  A sample of individuals carefully chosen to reflect the larger population of students for whom a test is intended.

**norm-referenced grading**  A system of grading that assumes classroom achievement will vary among a group of heterogeneous students because of such differences as prior knowledge, learning skills, motivation, and aptitude, and so compares the score of each student to the scores of other students in order to determine grades.

**norm-referenced tests**  Tests in which individual performance is evaluated with reference to the performance of a norm group.

**O**

**observational learning/modeling**  That part of the triadic reciprocal causation model of social cognitive theory that describes the role of observing and imitating the behavior of models in learning new capabilities.

**operant conditioning**  The theory of behavior developed by B. F. Skinner, based on the fact that organisms respond to their environments in particular ways to obtain or avoid particular consequences.

**organization**  The tendency to systematize and combine processes into coherent general systems.

**P**

**peer tutoring**  An approach to learning that involves the teaching of one student by another, based on evidence that a child's cognitive growth benefits from exposure to alternative cognitive schemes.

**percentile rank**  A score that indicates the percentage of students who are at or below a given student's achievement level, providing specific information about relative position.

**perceptual centration**  The tendency to focus attention on only one characteristic of an object or aspect of a problem or event at a time.

**performance tests**  Assessment devices that attempt to gauge how well students can use basic knowledge and skill to perform complex tasks or solve problems under more or less realistic conditions. Also called *performance-based assessment* and *authentic assessment*.

**permissive parents**   Parents who make few demands on their children and fail to discourage immature behavior, thus reflecting their own tendency to be disorganized, inconsistent, and lacking in confidence.

**personal agency**   The idea that people rather than environmental forces are the primary cause of their own behavior.

**personal interest**   Interest in a subject that is characterized by an intrinsic desire to understand the subject that persists for an extended period of time and is based on prior knowledge, personal experience, and emotion.

**portfolio**   A collection of one or more pieces of a person's work, some of which typically demonstrate different stages of completion.

**positive reinforcement**   A way of strengthening a target behavior (increasing and maintaining the probability that a particular behavior will be repeated) by supplying a positive stimulus immediately after a desired response. (*See* **negative reinforcement**)

**positive transfer**   A situation in which prior learning aids subsequent learning, when, for example, a new learning task calls for essentially the same response that was made to a similar earlier-learned task. (*See* **negative transfer**)

**Premack principle**   A shaping technique that allows students to indulge in a favorite activity after completing a set of instructional objectives. Also called *Grandma's rule*. (*See* **shaping**)

**problem-based learning (PBL)**   An instructional method that requires learners to develop solutions to authentic and complex problems through problem analysis, hypothesis generation, collaboration, reflection, and extensive teacher coaching and facilitation.

**problem representation/problem framing**   The process of finding ways to express a problem so as to recall the optimal amount of solution-relevant information from long-term memory. (*See* **long-term memory**)

**problem solving**   The identification and application of knowledge and skills that result in goal attainment.

**project-based learning**   An approach to teaching and learning that attempts to motivate students through collaborative investigations of real-world problems that result in tangible products.

**psychological androgyny**   An acquired sense of gender that combines traditional masculine and feminine traits.

**psychomotor domain taxonomy**   A classification of instructional outcomes that focuses on physical abilities and skills.

**psychosocial moratorium**   A period of identity development marked by a delay of commitment, ideally a time of adventure and exploration having a positive, or at least neutral, impact on the individual and society.

**punishment**   A method of weakening a target behavior by presenting an aversive stimulus after the behavior occurs.

## R

**recognition**   A cognitive process that involves noting key features of a stimulus and relating them to previously stored information in an interactive manner.

**reflective**   A learning style in which students collect and analyze information before offering an answer to a question or a solution to a problem.

**reflective teaching**   A way of teaching that blends artistic and scientific elements through thoughtful analysis of classroom activity.

**regrouping**   A form of ability grouping that brings together students of the same age, ability, and grade but from different classrooms, for instruction in a specific subject, usually reading or mathematics.

**rejecting-neglecting parents**   Parents who make no demands on their children, provide no structure at home, and do not support their children's goals, activities, and emotional needs.

**reliability**   Consistency in test results, related to the assumption that human characteristics are relatively stable over short periods of time.

**response cost**   The withdrawal of previously earned positive reinforcers as a consequence of undesirable behavior, often used with a token economy. (*See* **token economy**)

**ripple effect**   The extent to which an entire class responds to a reprimand directed at only one student.

**role confusion**   Uncertainty as to what behaviors will elicit a favorable reaction from others.

**rubric**   A scoring guide used in performance assessment that helps define and clarify levels of student performance from poor to exemplary.

## S

**scaffolding**   Supporting learning during its early phases through such techniques as demonstrating how tasks should be accomplished, giving hints to the correct solution to a problem or answer to a question, and providing leading questions. As students become more capable of working independently, these supports are withdrawn.

**schemata**   Plural of *schema*, an abstract information structure by which our store of knowledge is organized in long-term memory. *Schemas* is another plural form. (*See* **long-term memory**)

**scheme**   An organized pattern of behavior or thought that children formulate as they interact with their environment, parents, teachers, and agemates.

**scholastic aptitude**   The cognitive skills that most directly relate to and best predict the ability to cope with academic demands. Often used as a synonym for *intelligence*.

**scientific concepts**   A term coined by Russian psychologist Lev Vygotsky to denote such psychological tools as language, formulas, rules, and symbols that are learned mostly with the aid of formal instruction.

**self-actualization**   The movement toward full development of a person's potential talents and capabilities.

**self-concept**   The evaluative judgments people make of themselves in specific areas, such as academic performance, social interactions, athletic performance, and physical appearance.

**self-description**   The way people describe themselves to others, using statements that are largely nonevaluative.

**self-efficacy**   The degree to which people believe they are capable or prepared to handle particular tasks.

**self-esteem**   The overall or general evaluation people make of themselves. Also called *self-worth*.

**self-fulfilling prophecy**   The tendency of students to achieve the levels expected of them by their teachers. Also called the *Pygmalion effect*. (*See* **teacher expectancy effect**)

**self-image**   A mental self-portrait composed of a self-description, self-esteem, and self-concept. (*See* **self-concept; self-description; self-esteem**)

**self-regulated learning**   The conscious and purposeful use of one's cognitive skills, feelings, and actions to maximize the learning of knowledge and skills for a given task and set of conditions.

**self-reinforcement**   A situation in which the individual strives to meet personal standards and does not depend on or care about the reactions of others.

**sensory register (SR)**   The primary memory store that records temporarily (for one to three seconds) an incoming flow of data from the sense receptors.

**serial position effect**   The tendency to learn and remember words at the beginning and end of a list more easily than those in the middle.

**sexually transmitted diseases (STDs)**   Contagious diseases, such as HIV/AIDS, gonorrhea, and herpes, that are spread by sexual contact.

**shaping**   Promoting the learning of complex behaviors by reinforcing successive approximations to the terminal behavior.

**short-term memory (STM)**   The second temporary memory store, which holds about seven bits of information for about twenty seconds. Also called *working memory*.

**simulation programs**   Highly individualized and flexible programs that allow learners to test hypotheses, display knowledge, repair errors in thinking, and solve problems in an artificial environment that imitates the real world.

**single-subject achievement test**   A test designed to assess learning or achievement in a particular basic school subject, such as reading or mathematics.

**situated learning**   The idea that problem-solving skills, cognitive strategies, and knowledge are closely linked to the specific context or environment in which they are acquired; hence, the more authentic, or true to life, the task, the more meaningful the learning. Also called *situated cognition*. (*See* **cognitive apprenticeship; inert knowledge**)

**situational interest**   Interest in a subject that is relatively short-term and is based on situational or context-specific factors, such as the unusualness of the subject and its personal relevance.

**social class**   An individual's or a family's relative standing in society, determined by such factors as income, occupation, education, place of residence, types of associations, manner of dress, and material possessions.

**social cognitive theory**   An explanation of how people learn to become self-regulated learners through the interactive effects of their personal characteristics, behaviors, and social reinforcement. (*See* **triadic reciprocal causation**)

**social constructivism**   A form of constructivist learning theory that emphasizes how people use such cultural tools as language, mathematics, and approaches to problem solving in social settings to construct a common or shared understanding of the world in which they live. (*See* **constructivism**)

**socioeconomic status (SES)**   A quantifiable level of social standing, determined by the federal government on the basis of a person's income, occupation, and education. (*See* **social class**)

**special-purpose achievement test**   A test to determine specific qualifications, such as the College-Level Examination Program or the National Teacher Examination.

**specific objectives**   Objectives that specify the behavior to be learned, the conditions under which it will be exhibited, and the criterion for acceptable performance.

**specific transfer**   A situation in which prior learning aids subsequent learning because of specific similarities between two tasks.

**spontaneous concepts**   A term coined by Russian psychologist Lev Vygotsky to denote the facts, concepts, and rules that young children acquire as a natural consequence of engaging in everyday activities.

**spontaneous recovery**   The reappearance of a seemingly extinguished behavior. (*See* **extinction**)

**standard deviation**   A statistic that indicates the degree to which scores in a group of tests differ from the average or mean.

**standardized tests**   Assessment tools designed by people with specialized knowledge and applied to all students under the same conditions.

**stanine score**   A statistic reflecting a division of a score distribution into nine groups, with each stanine being one-half of a standard deviation unit.

**styles of mental self-government theory**   A theory of learning style formulated by Robert Sternberg that is based on the different functions and forms of civil government. The theory describes thirteen styles that can vary in terms of function, form, level, scope, and learning.

**summative evaluation**   Testing done for the purpose of assigning a letter or numerical grade to sum up a student's performance at a variety of tasks over time.

**T**

**table of specifications**   A table used in exam preparation that notes types and numbers of included test items, ensuring systematic coverage of the subject matter.

**taxonomy** A classification scheme with categories arranged in hierarchical order.

**teacher expectancy effect** The tendency of students to behave in ways they think the teacher expects them to behave. Also called *self-fulfilling prophecy; Pygmalion effect.*

**teaching as an art** A way of teaching that involves intangibles such as emotions, values, and flexibility.

**teaching as a science** A way of teaching based on scientific methods such as sampling, control, objectivity, publication, and replication.

**telementoring** The use of networking technologies by experts, mentors, instructors, and peers to demonstrate ideas, pose questions, offer insights, and provide relevant information that can help learners build new knowledge and effectively participate in a learning community.

**theoretical learning** Learning how to use psychological tools across a range of settings and problem types to acquire new knowledge and skills.

**theory of identical elements** The theory that a similarity between the stimulus and response elements in two different tasks accounts for transfer of learning from one task to the other. (*See* **transfer of learning**)

**theory of mind** The ability, typically developed by children around the age of four, to be aware of the difference between thinking about something and experiencing that same thing and to predict the thoughts of others.

**theory of multiple intelligences** A theory formulated by Howard Gardner that describes intelligence as being composed of eight, mostly independent capabilities.

**time-out** A procedure that weakens a target behavior by temporarily removing the opportunity for the behavior to be rewarded.

**token economy** A behavior-strengthening technique that uses items of no inherent value to "purchase" other items perceived to be valuable.

**transfer of learning** A student's ability to apply knowledge and problem-solving skills learned in school to similar but new situations.

**triadic reciprocal causation** The conceptual foundation of social cognitive theory, which specifies that learned capabilities are the product of interactions among an individual's personal characteristics, behaviors, and social environment. (*See* **social cognitive theory**)

**triarchic theory of intelligence** A theory formulated by Robert Sternberg that describes intelligence as being composed of practical, creative, and analytical components.

**T score** A standardized test score that ranges from 0 to 100 and uses a preselected mean of 50 to avoid negative values. (*See* **z score**)

**tutorial programs** Programs that attempt to teach facts, definitions, concepts, and other new material to students in either a step-by-step or a more individualized, branching approach.

**two-way bilingual (TWB) education** An approach to bilingual education in which instruction is provided to all students in both the minority language and the majority language. Also called *bilingual immersion* or *dual language.*

## V

**validity** The extent to which a test measures what it claims to measure.

**vicarious reinforcement** A situation in which the observer anticipates receiving a reward for behaving in a given way because someone else has been so rewarded.

## W

**well-structured problems** Clearly formulated problems with known solution procedures and known evaluation standards. (*See* **ill-structured problems**)

**within-class ability grouping** A form of ability grouping that involves the division of a single class of students into two or three groups for reading and math instruction.

**withitness** An attribute of teachers who prove to their students that they know what is going on in a classroom and as a result have fewer discipline problems than teachers who lack this characteristic.

**World Wide Web** A global system of interconnected computers that provides access to a wide variety of data in different formats. Also called *the Internet; the Web; WWW.*

## Z

**zero transfer** A situation in which prior learning has no effect on new learning.

**zone of proximal development (ZPD)** Vygotsky's term for the difference between what a child can do on his or her own and what can be accomplished with some assistance.

**z score** A standardized test score that tells how far a given raw score differs from the mean in standard deviation units. (*See* **T score**)

# References

Abedi, J., & Dietel, R. (2004). Challenges in the No Child Left Behind Act for English-language learners. *Phi Delta Kappan, 85*(10), 782–785.

Abell, S. K., Bryan, L. A., & Anderson, M. A. (1998). Investigating preservice elementary science teacher reflective thinking using integrated media case-based instruction in elementary science teacher preparation. *Science Education, 82*(4), 491–510.

Abma, J. C., & Sonenstein, F. L. (2001). *Sexual activity and contraceptive practices among teenagers in the United States, 1988 and 1995.* Hyattsville, MD: National Center for Health Statistics. Retrieved January 2, 2002, from www.cdc.gov/nchs/data/series/sr_23/sr23_21.pdf.

Abrami, P. C., Lou, Y., Chambers, B., Poulsen, C., & Spence, J. C. (2000). Why should we group students within-class for learning? *Educational Research and Evaluation, 6*(2), 158–179.

Adams, G. L., & Engelmann, S. (1996). *Research on direct instruction: 25 years beyond DISTAR.* Seattle, WA: Educational Achievement Systems.

Adams, G. R., Munro, B., Doherty-Poirer, M., Munro, G., Peterson, A. R., & Edwards, J. (2001). Diffuse-avoidance, normative, and informational identity styles: Using identity theory to predict maladjustment. *Identity, 1*(4), 307–320.

Adelson, J. (1972). The political imagination of the young adolescent. In J. Kagan & R. Coles (Eds.), *Twelve to sixteen: Early adolescence.* New York: Norton.

Adelson, J. (1986). *Inventing adolescence: The political psychology of everyday schooling.* New Brunswick, NJ: Transaction Books.

Adey, P. S., Shayer, M., & Yates, C. (2001). *Thinking science* (3rd ed.). London: Nelson Thornes.

Ainley, M., Hidi, S., & Berndorff, D. (2002). Interest, learning, and the psychological processes that mediate their relationship. *Journal of Educational Psychology, 94*(3), 545–561.

Airasian, P. W. (2005). *Classroom assessment: Concepts and applications* (5th ed.). Boston: McGraw-Hill.

Airasian, P. W., & Walsh, M. E. (1997). Constructivist cautions. *Phi Delta Kappan, 78*(6), 444–449.

Akin-Little, K. A., Eckert, T. L., Lovett, B. J., & Little, S. G. (2004). Extrinsic reinforcement in the classroom: Bribery or best practices. *School Psychology Review, 33*(3), 344–362.

Alagic, M., & Palenz, D. (2006). Teachers explore linear and exponential growth: Spreadsheets as cognitive tools. *Journal of Technology and Teacher Education, 14*(3), 633–649.

Alan Guttmacher Institute. (2004, February). *U.S. teenage pregnancy statistics.* Retrieved July 3, 2006, from www.guttmacher.org.

Alasker, F. D., & Olweus, D. (2002). Stability and change in global self-esteem and self-related affect. In T. M. Brinthaupt & R. P. Lipka (Eds.), *Understanding early adolescent self and identity: Applications and interventions* (pp. 193–223). Albany: State University of New York Press.

Alavi, M., & Leidner, D. E. (2001). Technology-mediated learning: A call for greater depth and breadth of research. *Information Systems Research, 12*(1), 1–10.

Alberto, P. A., & Troutman, A. C. (2006). *Applied behavior analysis for teachers* (7th ed.). Upper Saddle River, NJ: Pearson/Merrill Prentice Hall.

Aldridge, J. M., Laugksch, R. C., Seopa, M. A., & Fraser, B. J. (2006). Development and validation of an instrument to monitor the implementation of outcomes-based learning environments in science classrooms in South Africa. *International Journal of Science Education, 28*(1), 45–70.

Alexander, P. A., & Winne, P. H. (Eds.). (2006). *Handbook of educational psychology* (2nd ed.). Mahwah, NJ: Erlbaum.

Alfassi, M. (1998). Reading for meaning: The efficacy of reciprocal teaching in fostering reading comprehension in high school students in remedial reading classes. *American Educational Research Journal, 35*(2), 309–332.

Algozzine, B., & White, R. (2002). Preventing problem behaviors using schoolwide discipline. In B. Algozzine & P. Kay (Eds.), *Preventing problem behaviors: A handbook of successful prevention strategies* (pp. 85–103). Thousand Oaks, CA: Corwin Press.

Allen, N., Christal, M., Perrot, D., Wilson, C., Grote, B., & Earley, M. A. (1999). Native American schools move into the new millennium. *Educational Leadership, 56*(7), 71–74.

Allen, N., Resta, P. E., & Christal, M. (2002). Technology and tradition: The role of technology in Native American schools. *TechTrends, 46*(2), 50–55.

Allison, B. N., & Schultz, J. B. (2001). Interpersonal identity formation during early adolescence. *Adolescence, 36*(143), 509–523.

American Association of University Women. (1999). *Gender gaps: Where schools still fail our children.* New York: Marlowe & Company.

American Association on Mental Retardation. (2002). *The AAMR definition of mental retardation.* Retrieved January 16, 2004, from http://161.58.153.187/Policies/faq_mental_retardation.shtml.

American Educational Research Association. (2000). *AERA position statement concerning high-stakes testing in pre-K–12 education.* Retrieved January 2, 2002, from www.aera.net/about/policy/stakes.html.

American Educational Research Association. (2004, Summer). Teachers matter: Evidence from value-added assessments. *Research Points, 2*(2), 1–4.

American Psychiatric Association. (2000). *Diagnostic and statistical manual of mental disorders* (4th ed., text rev.). Washington, DC: Author.

American Psychological Association. (1997). *Learner-centered psychological principles: A framework for school redesign and reform.* Retrieved July 17, 2006, from www.apa.org/ed/resources.html.

American Psychological Association. (2006, June 1). *Applications of psychological science to teaching and learning task force to present at 2006 AERA conference.* Retrieved June 20, 2006, from www.apa.org/ed/epse/interdivision.html.

Ames, C., & Ames, R. (1984). Systems of student and teacher motivation: Toward a qualitative definition. *Journal of Educational Psychology, 76*(4), 535–556.

Amiram, R., Bar-Tal, D., Alona, R., & Peleg, D. (1990). Perception of epistemic authorities by children and adolescents. *Journal of Youth and Adolescence, 19*(5), 495–510.

Anderman, E. M. (2002). School effects on psychological outcomes during adolescence. *Journal of Educational Psychology, 94*(4), 795–809.

Anderman, E. M., & Maehr, M. L. (1994). Motivation and schooling in the middle grades. *Review of Educational Research, 64*(2), 287–309.

Anderson, J. R., Greeno, J. G., Reder, L. M., & Simon, H. A. (2000). Perspectives on learning, thinking, and activity. *Educational Researcher, 29*(4), 11–13.

Anderson, L. W., Krathwohl, D. R., Airasian, P. W., Cruikshank, K. A., Mayer, R. E., Pintrich, P. R., Raths, J., & Wittrock, M. C. (2001). *A taxonomy for learning, teaching, and assessing: A revision of Bloom's taxonomy of educational objectives.* New York: Addison Wesley Longman.

Anderson-Patton, V., & Bass, E. (2002). Using narrative teaching portfolios for self-study. In N. P. Lyons & V. Kubler LaBoskey (Eds.), *Narrative inquiry in practice: Advancing the knowledge of teaching.* New York: Teachers College Press.

André, M. E. D. A., & Anderson, T. H. (1978/1979). The development and evaluation of a self-questioning study technique. *Reading Research Quarterly, 14*(4), 605–623.

Andrews, K., & Marshall, K. (2000). Making learning connections through telelearning. *Educational Leadership, 58*(2), 53–56.

Angeli, C. (2002). Teachers' practical theories for the design and implementation of problem-based learning. *Science Education International, 13*(3), 9–15.

Angold, A., Worthman, C., & Costello, E. J. (2003). Puberty and depression. In C. Hayward (Ed.), *Gender differences at puberty* (pp. 137–164). Cambridge, England: Cambridge University Press.

Antil, L. R., Jenkins, J. R., Wayne, S. K., & Vadasy, P. F. (1998). Cooperative learning: Prevalence, conceptualizations, and the relation between research and practice. *Review of Educational Research, 35*(3), 419–454.

Applebee, A. N., Langer, J. A., Nystrand, M., & Gamoran, A. (2003). Discussion-based approaches to developing understanding: Classroom instruction and student performance in middle and high school English. *American Educational Research Journal, 40*(3), 685–730.

Appleton, N. (1983). *Cultural pluralism in education.* New York: Longman.

Armstrong, T. (1994). *Multiple intelligences in the classroom.* Alexandria, VA: Association for Supervision and Curriculum Development.

Arnold, M. L. (2000). Stage, sequence, and sequels: Changing conceptions of morality, post-Kohlberg. *Educational Psychology Review, 12*(4), 365–383.

Aronson, E. (2002). Building empathy, compassion, and achievement in the Jigsaw classroom. In J. Aronson (Ed.), *Improving academic achievement: Impact of psychological factors on education* (pp. 209–225). San Diego, CA: Academic Press.

Arter, J., & McTighe, J. (2001). *Scoring rubrics in the classroom.* Thousand Oaks, CA: Corwin Press.

Artiles, A. J., Klingner, J. K., & Tate, W. F. (2006). Representation of minority students in special education: Complicating traditional explanations. *Educational Researcher, 35*(6), 3–5.

Ash, C. (2000). *Voices of a new century: Students' perspectives on the achievement gap.* Chicago: North Central Regional Educational Laboratory. Retrieved July 23, 2003, from www.msanetwork.org/.

Astington, J. W. (1998). Theory of mind goes to school. *Educational Leadership, 56*(3), 46–48.

Atkinson, J. W. (1964). *An introduction to motivation.* Princeton, NJ: Van Nostrand.

Atkinson, R. C. (1975). Mnemotechnics in second language learning. *American Psychologist, 30*(2), 821–828.

Atkinson, R. C., & Raugh, M. R. (1975). An application of the mnemonic keyword method to the acquisition of a Russian vocabulary. *Journal of Experimental Psychology: Human Learning and Memory, 104*(2), 126–133.

Atkinson, R. C., & Shiffrin, R. M. (1968). Human memory: A proposed system and its control processes. In K. W. Spence & J. T. Spence (Eds.), *The psychology of learning and motivation* (Vol. 2). New York: Academic Press.

Atkinson, R. K., Derry, S. J., Renkl, A., & Wortham, D. (2000). Learning from examples: Instructional principles from the worked examples research. *Review of Educational Research, 70*(2), 181–214.

Atkinson, R. K., Renkl, A., & Merrill, M. M. (2003). Transitioning from studying examples to solving problems: Effects of self-explanation prompts and fading worked-out steps. *Journal of Educational Psychology, 95*(4), 774–783.

Ausubel, D. P., Novak, J. D., & Hanesian, H. (1978). *Educational psychology: A cognitive view* (2nd ed.). New York: Holt, Rinehart & Winston.

Azar, B. (2002). The "science of learning" moves mainstream. *Monitor on Psychology, 33*(8), 60–62.

Bachman, L. F. (2002). Alternative interpretations of alternative assessments: Some validity issues in educational performance assessments. *Educational Measurement: Issues and Practice, 21*(5), 5–18.

Bae, Y., Choy, S., Geddes, C., Sable, J., & Snyder, T. (2000). *Trends in educational equity of girls and women.* Washington, DC: National Center for Educational Statistics. Retrieved January 2, 2002, from http://nces.ed.gov/pubs2000/2000030.pdf.

Bailey, S. M. (1996). Shortchanging girls and boys. *Educational Leadership, 53*(8), 5–79.

Baker, E. (2000). Case-based learning theory: Implications for software design. *Journal of Technology and Teacher Education, 8*(2), 85–95.

Baker, J. A. (1999). Teacher-student interaction in urban at-risk classrooms: Differential behavior, relationship quality, and student satisfaction with school. *The Elementary School Journal, 100*(1), 57–70.

Balk, D. E. (1995). *Adolescent development.* Pacific Grove, CA: Brooks/Cole.

Bandura, A. (1986). *Social foundations of thought and action: A social cognitive theory.* Englewood Cliffs, NJ: Prentice-Hall.

Bandura, A. (1997). *Self-efficacy: The exercise of control.* New York: W. H. Freeman.

Bandura, A. (2001). Social cognitive theory: An agentic perspective. In S. T. Fiske, D. L. Schacter, & C. Zahn-Waxler (Eds.), *Annual Review of Psychology, 52*(1), 1–26.

Bandura, A. (2002). Social cognitive theory in cultural context. *Applied Psychology, 51*(2), 269–290.

Bandura, A., Ross, D., & Ross, S. (1961). Transmission of aggression through imitation of aggressive models. *Journal of Abnormal and Social Psychology, 63*(3), 575–582.

Bangert-Drowns, R. L., Kulik, J. A., & Kulik, C-L, C. (1991). Effects of frequent classroom testing. *Journal of Educational Research, 85*(2), 89–99.

Bangert-Drowns, R. L., Kulik, C-L. C., Kulik, J. A., & Morgan, M. (1991). The instructional effect of feedback in test-like events. *Review of Educational Research, 61*(2), 213–238.

Banks, J. A. (1993). The canon debate, knowledge construction, and multicultural education. *Educational Researcher, 22*(5), 4–14.

Banks, J. A. (1994). Transforming the mainstream curriculum. *Educational Leadership, 51*(8), 4–8.

Banks, J. A. (2002). *An introduction to multicultural education* (3rd ed.). Boston: Allyn & Bacon.

Banks, J. A. (2006). *Cultural diversity and education: Foundations, curriculum, and teaching* (5th ed.). Boston: Pearson Education.

Barab, S. A., & Luehmann, A. L. (2003). Building sustainable science curriculum: Acknowledging and accommodating local adaptation. *Science Education, 87*(4), 454–467.

Barak, M. (2005). From order to disorder: The role of computer-based electronics projects on fostering of higher-order cognitive skills. *Computers and Education, 45*(2), 231–243.

Barksdale-Ladd, M. A., & Thomas, K. F. (2000). What's at stake in high-stakes testing: Teachers and parents speak out. *Journal of Teacher Education, 51*(5), 384–397.

Barnett, S. M., & Ceci, S. J. (2002). When and where do we apply what we learn? A taxonomy for far transfer. *Psychological Bulletin, 128*(4), 612–637.

Barrett, H. C. (1998). Strategic questions: What to consider when planning for electronic portfolios. *Learning and Leading with Technology, 26*(2), 6–13.

Barrett, H. C. (2000). Create your own electronic portfolio. *Learning and Leading with Technology, 27*(7), 14–21.

Barron, B. (2000). Problem solving in video-based microworlds: Collaborative and individual outcomes of high-achieving sixth-grade students. *Journal of Educational Psychology, 92*(2), 391–398.

Barron, B., Vye, N., Zech, L., Schwartz, D., Bransford, J., Goldman, S., Pelligrino, J., Morris, J., Garrison, S., & Kantor, R. (1995). Creating contexts for community-based problem solving: The Jasper challenge series. In C. A. Hedley, P. Antonacci, & M. Rabinowitz (Eds.), *Thinking and literacy: The mind at work* (pp. 47–71). Hillsdale, NJ: Erlbaum.

Bartlett, F. C. (1932). *Remembering.* London: Cambridge University Press.

Baugh, I. W. (1994). Hypermedia as a performance-based assessment tool. *The Computing Teacher, 21*(6), 14–17.

Baumrind, D. (1971). Current patterns of parental authority. *Developmental Psychology Monographs, 4*(1, Pt. 2), 1–103.

Baumrind, D. (1991a). Parenting styles and adolescent development. In R. M. Lerner, A. C. Peterson, & J. Brooks-Gunn (Eds.), *Encyclopedia of adolescence.* New York: Garland Publishing.

Baumrind, D. (1991b). The influence of parenting style on adolescent competence and substance abuse. *Journal of Early Adolescence, 11*(1), 56–95.

Baumrind, D., Larzelere, R. E., & Cowan, P. A. (2002). Ordinary physical punishment: Is it harmful? Comment on Gershoff (2002). *Psychological Bulletin, 128*(4), 580–589.

Bay, J. M., Bledsoe, A. M., & Reys, R. E. (1998). State-ing the facts: Exploring the United States. *Mathematics Teaching in the Middle School, 4*(1), 8–14.

Beaumont, C., de Valenzuela, J. S., & Trumbull, E. (2002). Alternative assessment for transitional readers. *Bilingual Research Journal, 26*(2), 241–268.

Beck, A. T. (1972). *Depression: Causes and treatment.* Philadelphia: University of Pennsylvania Press.

Beck, J. (2002). Emerging literacy through assistive technology. *Teaching Exceptional Children, 35*(2), 44–48.

Beiser, M., Erickson, D., Fleming, J. A. E., & Iacono, W. G. (1993). Establishing the onset of psychotic illness. *American Journal of Psychiatry, 150*(9), 1349–1354.

Beishuizen, J. J., & Stoutjesdijk, E. T. (1999). Study strategies in a computer-assisted study environment. *Learning and Instruction, 9*(3), 281–301.

Bell, L. I. (2002/2003). Strategies that close the gap. *Educational Leadership, 60*(4), 32–34.

Bellezza, F. S. (1981). Mnemonic devices: Classification, characteristics, and criteria. *Review of Educational Research, 51*(2), 247–275.

Ben-Hur, M. (1998). Mediation of cognitive competencies for students in need. *Phi Delta Kappan, 79*(9), 661–666.

Benjamin, A. (2003). *Differentiated instruction: A guide for elementary school teachers.* Larchmont, NY: Eye on Education.

Benjamin, A. (2005). *Differentiated instruction using technology: A guide for middle and high school teachers.* Larchmont, NY: Eye on Education.

Bennett, C. I. (2007). *Comprehensive multicultural education: Theory and practice* (6th ed.). Boston: Pearson/Allyn & Bacon.

Bennett, L., & Pye, J. (2000). Using the internet for reflective journals in elementary teacher preparation. *Journal of Social Studies Research, 24*(2), 21–30.

Bennett, N., Desforges, C., Cockburn, A., & Wilkinson, B. (1984). *The quality of pupil learning experiences.* Hillsdale, NJ: Erlbaum.

Benoit, D. A., Edwards, R. P., Olmi, D. J., Wilczynski, S. M., & Mandal, R. M. (2001). Generalization of a positive treatment package for child noncompliance. *Child and Family Behavior Therapy, 23*(2), 19–32.

Bereiter, C. (1997). Situated cognition and how to overcome it. In D. Kirshner & J. A. Whitson (Eds.), *Situated cognition: Social, semiotic, and psychological perspectives* (pp. 281–300). Mahwah, NJ: Erlbaum.

Bergin, D. A. (1999). Influences on classroom interest. *Educational Psychologist, 34*(2), 87–98.

Berk, L. E. (1994). Why children talk to themselves. *Scientific American, 271*(5), 78–83.

Berk, L. E. (2006). *Child development.* Boston: Pearson/Allyn & Bacon.

Berliner, D. C. (2002). Educational research: The hardest science of all. *Educational Researcher, 31*(8), 18–20.

Berliner, D. C. (2006). Educational psychology: Searching for essence throughout a century of influence. In P. A. Alexander & P. H. Winne (Eds.), *Handbook of educational psychology* (2nd ed., pp. 3–27). Mahwah, NJ: Erlbaum.

Berliner, D. C., & Biddle, B. J. (1995). *The manufactured crisis: Myths, fraud, and the attack on America's public schools.* Reading, MA: Addison-Wesley.

Berliner, D. C., & Casanova, U. (1996). *Putting research to work in your school.* Arlington Heights, IL: IRI/Skylight Training and Publishing.

Bernard, R. M., Abrami, P. C., Lou, Y., Borokhovski, E., Wade, A., Wozney, L., Wallet, P. A., Fiset, M., & Huang, B. (2004). How does distance education compare with classroom instruction? A meta-analysis of the empirical literature. *Review of Educational Research, 74*(3), 379–439.

Berry, B., Hoke, M., & Hirsch, E. (2004). The search for highly qualified teachers. *Phi Delta Kappan, 85*(9), 684–689.

Bielefeldt, T. (2005). Computers and student learning: Interpreting the multivariate analysis of PISA 2000. *Journal of Research on Technology in Education, 37*(4), 339–347.

Biemiller, A. (1993). Lake Woebegon revisited: On diversity and education. *Educational Researcher, 22*(9), 7–12.

Billig, S. H. (2000). Research on K–12 school-based service-learning: The evidence builds. *Phi Delta Kappan, 81*(9), 658–664.

Bilsker, D., & Marcia, J. E. (1991). Adaptive regression and ego identity. *Journal of Adolescence, 14*(1), 75–84.

Bjork, R. A. (1979). Information processing analysis of college teaching. *Educational Psychologist, 14*, 15–23.

Bjorklund, D. F. (2005). *Children's thinking: Cognitive development and individual differ-*

ences (4th ed.). Belmont, CA: Thomson/Wadsworth.

Blanchett, W. J. (2006). Disproportionate representation of African American students in special education: Acknowledging the role of White privilege and racism. *Educational Researcher, 35*(6), 24–28.

Block, J. H., Efthim, H. E., & Burns, R. B. (1989). *Building effective mastery learning schools.* New York: Longman.

Blok, H., Oostdam, R., Otter, M. E. & Overmaat, M. (2002). Computer-assisted instruction in support of beginning reading instruction: A review. *Review of Educational Research, 72*(1), 101–130.

Bloom, B. S. (1968). Learning for mastery. *Evaluation Comment, 1*(2), 1–12.

Bloom, B. S. (1976). *Human characteristics and school learning.* New York: McGraw-Hill.

Bloom, B. S. (1984). The two sigma problem: The search for methods of group instruction as effective as one-to-one tutoring. *Educational Researcher, 13*(6), 4–16.

Bloom, B. S., Englehart, M. B., Furst, E. J., Hill, W. H., & Krathwohl, D. R. (Eds.). (1956). *Taxonomy of educational objectives: The classification of educational goals. Handbook I. Cognitive domain.* New York: McKay.

Bloomquist, M. L., & Schnell, S. V. (2002). *Helping children with aggression and conduct problems: Best practices for intervention.* New York: Guilford Press.

Boekarts, M. (1993). Being concerned with well-being and with learning. *Educational Psychologist, 28*(2), 149–167.

Bond, C. L., Miller, M. J., & Kennon, R. W. (1987). Study skills: Who is taking the responsibility for teaching? *Performance & Instruction, 26*(7), 27–29.

Bong, M., & Skaalvik, E. (2003). Academic self-concept and self-efficacy: How different are they really? *Educational Psychology Review, 15*(1), 1–40.

Boniecki, K. A., & Moore, S. (2003). Breaking the silence: Using a token economy to reinforce classroom participation. *Teaching of Psychology, 30*(3), 224–227.

Bonk, C. J., & Cunningham, D. J. (1998). Searching for learner-centered, constructivist, and sociocultural components of collaborative educational learning tools. In C. J. Bonk & K. S. King (Eds.), *Electronic collaborators: Learner-centered technologies for literacy, apprenticeship, and discourse* (pp. 25–50). Mahwah, NJ: Erlbaum.

Bonk, C. J., & Reynolds, T. H. (1992). Early adolescent composing within a generative-evaluative computerized prompting framework. *Computers in Human Behavior, 8*(1), 39–62.

Bonk, C. J., & Sugar, W. A. (1998). Student role play in the World Forum: Analyses of an Arctic learning apprenticeship. *Interactive Learning Environments, 6*(1–2), 1–29.

Booher-Jennings, J. (2005). Below the bubble: "Educational triage" and the Texas accountability system. *American Educational Research Journal, 42*(2), 231–268.

Boonstra, H. (2002). Teen pregnancy: Trends and lessons learned. *The Guttmacher Report on Public Policy, 5*(1), 7–10. Retrieved June 27, 2003, from www.agi-usa.org/pubs/journals/gr050107.html.

Borja, R. R. (2003, May 8). Prepping for the big test. *Education Week, 22*(35), 22–24, 26.

Bornas, X., Servera, M., & Llabrés, J. (1997). Preventing impulsivity in the classroom: How computers can help teachers. *Computers in the Schools, 13*(1–2), 27–40.

Borthick, A. F., Jones, D. R., & Wakai, S. (2003). Designing learning experiences within learners, zones of proximal development: Enabling collaborative learning on-site and on-line. *Journal of Information Systems, 17*(1), 107–134.

Bower, G. H., Clark, M. C., Lesgold, A. M., & Winzenz, D. (1969). Hierarchical retrieval schemes in recall of categorized word lists. *Journal of Verbal Learning and Verbal Behavior, 8*(3), 323–343.

Bowman, D. H. (2002). National survey puts ADHD incidence near 7 percent. *Education Week, 21*(38), 3.

Boyer, E. L. (1983). *High school*. New York: Harper & Row.

Braaksma, M. A. H., Rijlaarsdam, G., & van den Bergh, H. (2002). Observational learning and the effects of model-observer similarity. *Journal of Educational Psychology, 94*(2), 405–415.

Bracey, G. W. (2002). The 12th Bracey report on the condition of public education. *Phi Delta Kappan, 84*(2), 135–150.

Bracey, G. W. (2003). The 13th Bracey report on the condition of public education. *Phi Delta Kappan, 85*(2), 148–164.

Branch, C. W., & Boothe, B. (2002). The identity status of African Americans in middle adolescence: A replication and extension of Forbes and Ashton (1998). *Adolescence, 37*(148), 815–821.

Bransford, J. D., Sherwood, R., Vye, N., & Rieser, J. (1986). Teaching thinking and problem solving: Research foundations. *American Psychologist, 41*(10), 1078–1089.

Bransford, J. D. & Stein, B. S. (1993). *The ideal problem solver* (2nd ed.). New York: W.H. Freeman.

Braun, H. I., & Mislevy, R. (2005). Intuitive test theory. *Phi Delta Kappan, 86*(7), 489–497.

Brewer, D. J., Rees, D. I., & Argys, L. M. (1995). Detracking America's schools: The reform without cost? *Phi Delta Kappan, 77*(3), 210–215.

Britner, S. L., & Pajares, F. (2006). Sources of science self-efficacy beliefs of middle school students. *Journal of Research in Science Teaching, 43*(5), 485–499.

Broekkamp, H., van Hout-Wolters, B. H. A. M., Rijlaarsdam, G., & van den Bergh, H. (2002). Importance in instructional text: Teachers' and students' perceptions of task demands. *Journal of Educational Psychology, 94*(2), 260–271.

Brookfield, S. D., & Preskill, S. (2005). *Discussion as a way of teaching* (2nd ed.). San Francisco: Jossey-Bass.

Brookhart, S. M. (2004). *Grading*. Upper Saddle River, NJ: Merrill Prentice Hall.

Brooks, J. G., & Brooks, M. G. (2001). *In search of understanding: The case for constructivist classrooms*. Upper Saddle River, NJ: Merrill Prentice Hall.

Brophy, J. E. (1979). Teacher behavior and its effects. *Journal of Educational Psychology, 71*(6), 733–750.

Brophy, J. E. (1981). Teacher praise: A functional analysis. *Review of Educational Research, 51*(1), 5–32.

Brophy, J. E. (1983). Research on the self-fulfilling prophecy and teacher expectations. *Journal of Educational Psychology, 75*(5), 631–661.

Brophy, J. E., & Alleman, J. (1991). Activities as instructional tools: A framework for analysis and evaluation. *Educational Researcher, 20*(4), 9–23.

Brophy, J. E., & Evertson, C. M. (1976). *Learning from teaching*. Boston: Allyn & Bacon.

Brouwer, N., & Korthagen, F. (2005). Can teacher education make a difference? *American Educational Research Journal, 42*(1), 153–224.

Brown, A. L., Campione, J. C., & Day, J. D. (1981). Learning to learn: On training students to learn from text. *Educational Researcher, 10*(2), 14–24.

Brown, D. F. (2002). Self-directed learning in an 8th grade classroom. *Phi Delta Kappan, 60*(1), 54–58.

Brown, J. L., Roderick, T., Lantieri, L., & Aber, J. L. (2004). The Resolving Conflict Creatively Program: A school-based social and emotional learning program. In J. E. Zins, R. P. Weissberg, M. C. Wang, & H. J. Walberg (Eds.), *Building academic success on social and emotional learning: What does the research say?* New York: Teachers College Press.

Brown, J. S., Collins, A., & Duguid, P. (1989). Situated cognition and the culture of learning. *Educational Researcher, 18*(1), 32–42.

Brown, R. A. J., & Renshaw, P. D. (2000). Collective argumentation: A sociocultural approach to reframing classroom teaching and learning. In H. Cowie & G. van der Aalsvoort (Eds.), *Social interaction in learning and instruction* (pp. 52–66). Amsterdam: Pergamon.

Brown, S. M., & Walberg, H. J. (1993). Motivational effects on test scores of elementary students. *Journal of Educational Research, 86*(3), 133–136.

Brulle, A. R. (2005). What can you say when research and policy collide? *Phi Delta Kappan, 86*(6), 433–437.

Bruner, J. S. (1983). *In search of mind: Essays in autobiography*. New York: Harper & Row.

Bruning, R. H., Schraw, G. J., Norby, M. M., & Ronning, R. R. (2004). *Cognitive psychology and instruction* (4th ed.). Upper Saddle River, NJ: Merrill Prentice Hall.

Brush, T. A., Armstrong, J., Barbrow, D., & Ulintz, L. (1999). Design and delivery of integrated learning systems: Their impact on student achievement and attitudes. *Journal of Educational Computing Research, 21*(4), 475–486.

Brush, T., & Saye, J. (2001). The use of embedded scaffolds with hypermedia-supported student-centered learning. *Journal of Educational Multimedia and Hypermedia, 10*(4), 333–356.

Bryant, D. P., Vaughn, S., Linan-Thompson, S., Ugel, N., Hamff, A., & Hougen, M. (2000). Reading outcomes for students with and without reading disabilities in general education middle-school content area classes. *Learning Disability Quarterly, 23*(4), 238–252.

Bucher, A. A. (1997). The influence of models in forming moral identity. *International Journal of Educational Research, 27*(7), 619–627.

Bukatko, D., & Daehler, M. W. (2004). *Child development: A thematic approach* (5th ed.). Boston: Houghton Mifflin.

Burch, C. B. (1993). Teachers vs. professors: The university's side. *Educational Leadership, 51*(2), 68–76.

Burchinal, M. R., Peisner-Feinberg, E., Pianta, R., & Howes, C. (2002). The development of academic skills from preschool through second grade: Family and classroom predictors of developmental trajectories. *Journal of School Psychology, 40*(5), 415–436.

Bureau of Labor Statistics. (2003). Most 16- to 18-year-old students work in school year and summer. *Monthly Labor Review: The Editor's Desk*. Retrieved December 12, 2003, from www.bls.gov/news.release/nlsyth.toc.htm.

Burns, M. (2002). From compliance to commitment: Technology as a catalyst for communities of learning. *Phi Delta Kappan, 84*(4), 295–302.

Burris, C. C., & Welner, K. G. (2005). Closing the achievement gap by detracking. *Phi Delta Kappan, 86*(8), 594–598.

Burtch, J. A. (1999). Technology is for everyone. *Educational Leadership, 56*(5), 33–34.

Bushrod, G., Williams, R. L., & McLaughlin, T. F. (1995). An evaluation of a simplified daily report system with two kindergarten pupils. *B.C. Journal of Special Education, 19*(1), 35–43.

Butler, R. (2005). Competence assessment, competence, and motivation between early and middle childhood. In A. J. Elliot & C. S. Dweck (Eds.), *Handbook of competence and motivation* (pp. 202–221). New York: Guilford Press.

Caine, G., Caine, R. N., & McClintic, C. (2002). Guiding the innate constructivist. *Educational Leadership, 60*(1), 70–73.

Calderón, M. E., & Minaya-Rowe, L. (2003). *Designing and implementing two-way bilingual programs*. Thousand Oaks, CA: Corwin Press.

Callahan, C. M., & McIntire, J. A. (1994). *Identifying outstanding talent in American Indian and Alaska native students*. Washington, DC: U. S. Department of Education, Office of Educational Research and Improvement.

Callahan, R. M. (2005). Tracking and high school English learners: Limiting opportunity to learn. *American Educational Research Journal, 42*(2), 305–328.

Cameron, J. (2001). Negative effects of reward on intrinsic motivation—A limited phenomenon: Comment on Deci, Koestner, & Ryan (2001). *Review of Educational Research, 71*(1), 29–42.

Cameron, J., Banko, K. M., & Pierce, W. D. (2001). Pervasive negative effects of rewards on intrinsic motivation: The myth continues. *Behavior Analyst, 24*(1), 1–44.

Camilli, G. (2003). Comment on Cizek's "More unintended consequences of high-stakes testing." *Educational Measurement: Issues and Practice, 22*(1), 36–39.

Campbell, J., Kyriakides, L., Muijs, D., & Robinson, W. (2004). *Assessing teacher effectiveness: Developing a differentiated model*. New York: Routledge/Falmer.

Campbell, L. (1997). How teachers interpret MI theory. *Educational Leadership, 55*(1), 14–19.

Cangelosi, J. S. (2004). *Classroom management strategies: Gaining and maintaining students' cooperation* (5th ed.). New York: Wiley.

Cardon, P. L., & Christensen, K. W. (1998). Technology-based programs for drop-out prevention. *Journal of Technology Studies, 24*(1), 50–54.

Cardwell, K. (2000). Electronic assessment. *Learning and Leading with Technology, 27*(7), 22–26.

Carnevale, D. (2004, May 28). Online study tools help Texas students prepare for graduation exam. *The Chronicle of Higher Education, 50*(38), p. A31.

Carney, R. N., & Levin, J. R. (2002). Pictorial illustrations still improve students' learning from text. *Educational Psychology Review, 14*(1), 5–26.

Carney, R. N., Levin, J. R., & Levin, M. E. (1994). Enhancing the psychology of memory by enhancing memory of psychology. *Teaching of Psychology, 21*(3), 171–174.

Carroll, J. B. (1963). A model of school learning. *Teachers College Record, 64*(8), 723–733.

Carter, C. J. (1997). Why reciprocal teaching? *Educational Leadership, 54*(6), 64–68.

Carter, D. B. (1987). The role of peers in sex role socialization. In D. B. Carter (Ed.), *Current conceptions of sex roles and sex typing*. New York: Praeger.

Case, R. (1975). Gearing the demands of instruction to the developmental capacities of the learner. *Review of Educational Research, 45*(1), 59–88.

Case, R. (1999). Conceptual development in the child and in the field: A personal view of the Piagetian legacy. In E. K. Scholnick, K. Nelson, S. A. Gelman, & P. H. Miller

(Eds.), *Conceptual development: Piaget's legacy*. Mahwah, NJ: Erlbaum.

Center for Applied Linguistics. (2006). *Directory of two-way bilingual immersion programs in the U.S.* Retrieved July 14, 2006, from www.cal.org/twi/directory.

Center on Educational Policy. (2005, March). *From the capital to the classroom: Year 3 of the No Child Left Behind Act*. Washington, DC: Author. Retrieved March 23, 2005, from www.cep-dc.org.

Centers for Disease Control. (2002). Trends in sexual risk behaviors among high school students—United States, 1991–2001. *MMWR, 51*(38), 856–859. Retrieved June 27, 2003, from www.cdc.gov/mmwr/preview/mmwrhtml/mm5138a2.htm.

Chan, C. K. K., & Pang, M. F. (2006). Teacher collaboration in learning communities. *Teaching Education, 17*(1), 1–5.

Chance, P. (1992). The rewards of learning. *Phi Delta Kappan, 74*(3), 200–207.

Chance, P. (1993). Sticking up for rewards. *Phi Delta Kappan, 74*(10), 787–790.

Chaney, E., & Gilman, D. A. (2005). Filling in the blanks: Using computers to test and teach. *Computers in the Schools, 22*(1/2), 157–168.

Chapman, J. W., & Tunmer, W. E. (1995). Development of young children's reading self-concepts: An examination of emerging subcomponents and their relationships with reading achievement. *Journal of Educational Psychology, 87*(1), 154–167.

Chase, K. (2002). The brilliant inventiveness of student misbehavior: Test your classroom management skills. *Phi Delta Kappan, 84*(4), 327–328, 330.

Checkley, K. (1997). The first seven . . . and the eighth: A conversation with Howard Gardner. *Educational Leadership, 55*(1), 8–13.

Chen, M., & Bargh, J. A. (1997). Nonconscious behavioral confirmation processes: The self-fulfilling consequences of automatic stereotype activation. *Journal of Experimental Social Psychology, 33*(5), 541–560.

Choate, J. S. (Ed.). (2003). *Successful inclusive teaching: Proven ways to detect and correct special needs* (4th ed.). Boston: Allyn & Bacon.

Chrenka, L. (2001). Misconstructing constructivism. *Phi Delta Kappan, 82*(9), 694–695.

Cicchetti, D., & Toth, S. L. (1998). The development of depression in children and adolescents. *American Psychologist, 53*(2), 221–241.

Cizek, G. J. (2001a). More unintended consequences of high-stakes testing. *Educational Measurement: Issues and Practices, 20*(4), 19–27.

Cizek, G. J. (2001b). Cheating to the test. *Education Matters, 1*(1), 41–47.

Cizek, G. J. (2003). Rejoinder. *Educational Measurement: Issues and Practice, 22*(1), 40–44.

Clark, J. M., & Paivio, A. (1991). Dual coding theory and education. *Educational Psychology Review, 3*(3), 149–210.

Clark, R. E. (2002). Performance assessment in the arts. *Kappa Delta Pi Record, 39*(1), 29–32.

Clarke, L., & Heaney, P. (2003). Author On-Line: Using asynchronous computer conferencing to support literacy. *British Journal of Educational Psychology, 34*(1), 57–66.

Clarke, M., Abrams, L., & Madaus, G. (2001). The effects and implications of high-stakes achievement tests for adolescents. In T. Urdan & F. Pajares (Eds.), *Adolescence and education. Vol. 1: General issues in the education of adolescents* (pp. 201–229). Greenwich, CT: Information Age Publishing.

Clawson, M. A., & Robila, M. (2001). Relations between parenting style and children's play behavior: Issues in education. *Journal of Early Education and Family Review, 8*(3), 13–19.

Clements, P., & Seidman, E. (2002). The ecology of middle grades schools and possible selves. In T. M. Brinthaupt & R. P. Lipka (Eds.), *Understanding early adolescent self and identity: Applications and interventions* (pp. 133–164). Albany: State University of New York Press.

Cochran-Smith, M. (2003). The unforgiving complexity of teaching: Avoiding simplicity in the age of accountability. *Journal of Teacher Education, 54*(1), 3–5.

Cochran-Smith, M. (2005). The new teacher education: For better or for worse? *Educational Researcher, 34*(7), 3–17.

Cognition and Technology Group at Vanderbilt. (1990). Anchored instruction and its relationship to situated cognition. *Educational Researcher, 19*(6), 2–10.

Cognition and Technology Group at Vanderbilt. (1992a). The Jasper series: A generative approach to improving mathematical thinking. In K. Sheingold, L. G. Roberts, & S. M. Malcolm (Eds.), *This year in school science 1991: Technology for teaching and learning*. Washington, DC: American Association for the Advancement of Science.

Cognition and Technology Group at Vanderbilt. (1992b). The Jasper series as an example of anchored instruction: Theory, program description, and assessment data. *Educational Psychologist, 27*(3), 291–315.

Cognition and Technology Group at Vanderbilt. (1993). Anchored instruction and situated cognition revisited. *Educational Technology, 33*(3), 52–70.

Cognition and Technology Group at Vanderbilt. (1996). Looking at technology in context: A framework for understanding technology and education research. In D. C. Berliner & R. C. Calfee (Eds.), *Handbook of educational psychology* (pp. 807–840). New York: Simon & Schuster.

Colangelo, N., & Davis, G. A. (2003b). Introduction and overview. In N. Colangelo &

G. A. Davis (Eds.), *Handbook of gifted education* (3rd ed., pp. 3–10). Boston: Allyn & Bacon.

Cole, J. M., & Hilliard, V. R. (2006). The effects of web-based reading curriculum on children's reading performance and motivation. *Journal of Educational Computing Research, 34*(4), 353–380.

Coley, R. J. (2003, November). *Growth in school revisited: Achievement gains from the fourth to the eighth grade.* Retrieved July 5, 2006, from Educational Testing Service, Policy Information Center website: www.ets.org/Media/Research/pdf/PICGROWTH.pdf.

Collier, C. (1999). Project-based student technology competencies. *Learning and Leading with Technology, 27*(3), 50–53.

Combs, A. W. (1965). *The professional education of teachers.* Boston: Allyn & Bacon.

Commission on Instructionally Supportive Assessment. (2002, March). *Implementing ESEA's testing provisions.* Retrieved February 9, 2004, from www.nea.org/accountability/images/02eseatesting.pdf.

Conger, J. J., & Galambos, N. L. (1997). *Adolescence and youth* (5th ed.). New York: Longman.

Connor, D. F. (2002). *Aggression and antisocial behavior in children and adolescents: Research and treatment.* New York: Guilford Press.

Cooper, B., & Harries, T. (2005). Making sense of realistic word problems: Portraying working class "failure" on a division with remainder problem. *International Journal of Research and Method in Education, 28*(2), 147–169.

Cooper, H. (2001). Homework for all—in moderation. *Educational Leadership, 58*(7), 34–38.

Cooper, H., & Dorr, N. (1995). Race comparisons on need for achievement: A meta-analytic alternative to Graham's narrative review. *Review of Educational Research, 65*(4), 438–508.

Cooper, H., Robinson, J. C., & Patall, E. A. (2006). Does homework improve academic achievement? A synthesis of research, 1987–2003. *Review of Educational Research, 76*(1), 1–62.

Corbett, D., & Wilson, B. (2002). What urban students say about good teaching. *Educational Leadership, 60*(1), 18–22.

Cornford, I. (2002). Reflective teaching: Empirical research findings and some implications for teacher education. *Journal of Vocational Education and Training, 54*(2), 219–235.

Cothran, J. C. (2006). *A search of African-American life, achievement and culture.* Carrolltown, TX: Stardate Publishing.

Cotterall, S., & Cohen, R. (2003). Scaffolding for second language writers: Producing an academic essay. *ELT Journal, 57*(2), 158–166.

Couzijn, M. (1999). Learning to write by observation of writing and reading processes: Effects on learning and transfer. *Learning and Instruction, 9*(2), 109–142.

Covington, M. V. (1985). Strategic thinking and the fear of failure. In J. W. Segal, S. F. Chipman, & R. Glaser (Eds.), *Thinking and learning skills* (Vol. 1). Hillsdale, NJ: Erlbaum.

Covington, M. V. (2000). Goal theory, motivation, and school achievement: An integrative review. In S. T. Fiske, D. L. Schacter, & C. Zahn-Waxler (Eds.), *Annual review of psychology* (Vol. 51, pp. 171–200). Palo Alto, CA: Annual Reviews.

Covington, M. V. (2002). Rewards and intrinsic motivation: A needs-based developmental perspective. In F. Pajares & T. Urdan (Eds.), *Academic motivation of adolescents* (pp. 169–192). Greenwich, CT: Information Age Publishing.

Cowan, N. (2005). *Working memory capacity.* New York: Psychology Press.

Cox, B. D. (1997). The rediscovery of the active learner in adaptive contexts: A developmental-historical analysis of transfer of training. *Educational Psychologist, 32*(1), 41–55.

Crain, W. (2000). *Theories of development: Concepts and applications* (4th ed.). Upper Saddle River, NJ: Prentice-Hall.

Cramer, P. (2001). Identification and its relation to identity development. *Journal of Personality, 69*(5), 667–688.

Crawford, G. B. (2004). *Managing the adolescent classroom: Lessons from outstanding teachers.* Thousand Oaks, CA: Corwin Press.

Crooks, T. J. (1988). The impact of classroom evaluation practices on students. *Review of Educational Research, 58*(4), 438–481.

Cruickshank, D. R. (1990). *Research that informs teachers and teacher educators.* Bloomington, IN: Phi Delta Kappa Educational Foundation.

Csikszentmihalyi, M. (1975). *Beyond boredom and anxiety.* San Francisco: Jossey-Bass.

Csikszentmihalyi, M. (1996). *Creativity.* New York: Harper/Perennial.

Csikszentmihalyi, M. (2000). *Finding flow: The psychology of engagement with everyday life.* New York; Basic Books.

Csikszentmihalyi, M. (2002). *Flow: The classic work on how to achieve happiness.* London: Rider.

Cuban, L. (1986). *Teachers and machines: The classroom use of technology since 1920.* New York: Teachers College Press.

Cuban, L. (1990). What I learned from what I had forgotten about teaching: Notes from a professor. *Phi Delta Kappan, 71*(6), 479–482.

Cuban, L. (2001). *Oversold and underused: Computers in the classroom.* Cambridge, MA: Harvard University Press.

Cummins, J. (1999). Alternative paradigms in bilingual education research. *Educational Researcher, 28*(7), 26–32, 41.

Cunningham, D. J. (2001, April). *Fear and loathing in the information age.* Paper presented at the annual meeting of the American Educational Research Association, Seattle, WA.

Curtis, D. (2002). The power of projects. *Educational Leadership, 60*(1), 50–53.

Dai, D. Y., Moon, S. M., & Feldhusen, J. F. (1998). Achievement motivation and gifted students: A social cognitive perspective. *Educational Psychologist, 33*(2/3), 45–63.

Daiute, C. (1985). Issues in using computers to socialize the writing process. *Educational Communication and Technology, 33*(1), 41–50.

Dardig, J. C. (2005). The McClurg monthly magazine and 14 more practical ways to involve parents. *Teaching Exceptional Children, 38*(2), 46–51.

Darling-Hammond, L., & Falk, B. (1997). Using standards and assessments to support student learning. *Phi Delta Kappan, 79*(3), 190–199.

Darling-Hammond, L., & Youngs, P. (2002). Defining "highly qualified teachers": What does "scientifically-based research" actually tell us? *Educational Researcher, 31*(9), 13–25.

Dasen, P., & Heron, A. (1981). Cross-cultural tests of Piaget's theory. In H. C. Triandis & A. Heron (Eds.), *Handbook of cross-cultural psychology, developmental psychology* (Vol. 4). Boston: Allyn & Bacon.

Davison, M. L., Seo, Y. S., Davenport, E. C., Jr., Butterbaugh, D., & Davison, L. J. (2004). When do children fall behind? What can be done? *Phi Delta Kappan, 85*(10), 752–761.

DeBell, M., & Chapman, C. (2003). *Computer and Internet use by children and adolescents in 2001.* Washington, DC: National Center for Educational Statistics. Retrieved January 5, 2004, from http://nces.ed.gov/pubsearch/pubsinfo.asp?pubid=2004014.

DeBlois, R. (2005). When to promote students. *Phi Delta Kappan, 87*(4), 306–310.

Deci, E. L., Koestner, R., & Ryan, R. M. (1999). A meta-analytic review of experiments examining the effects of extrinsic rewards on intrinsic motivation. *Psychological Bulletin, 125*(6), 627–668.

Deci, E. L., Koestner, R., & Ryan, R. M. (2001). Extrinsic rewards and intrinsic motivation in education: Reconsidered once again. *Review of Educational Research, 71*(1), 1–27.

De Corte, E. (2003). Transfer as the productive use of acquired knowledge, skills, and motivations. *Current Directions in Psychological Science, 12*(4), 142–146.

de Jong, T., & van Joolingen, W. R. (1998). Scientific discovery learning with computer simulations in conceptual domains. *Review of Educational Research, 68*(2), 179–201.

Delgarno, B. (2001). Interpretations of constructivism and consequences for computer assisted learning. *British Journal of Educational Technology, 32*(2), 183–194.

De Lisi, R. (2006). A developmental perspective on virtual scaffolding for learning in home and school contexts. In A. O'Donnell, C. E. Hmelo-Silver, & G. Erkens (Eds.), *Collaborative learning, reasoning, and technology.* Mahwah, NJ: Erlbaum.

Dempster, F. N. (1988). The spacing effect: A case study in the failure to apply the results of psychological research. *American Psychologist, 43*(8), 627–634.

Denbo, S. J. (2002). Institutional practices that support African American student achievement. In S. J. Denbo & L. M. Beaulieu (Eds.), *Improving schools for African American students* (pp. 55–71). Springfield, IL: Charles C. Thomas.

Derry, S. J. (1996). Cognitive schema theory in the constructivist debate. *Educational Researcher, 31*(3/4), 163–174.

Derry, S. J., Hmelo-Silver, C. E., Nagarajan, A., Chernobilsky, E., Feltovich, J., & Halfpap, B. (2005). Making a mesh of it: A STELLAR approach to teacher professional development. In T. Koschmann, D. D. Suthers, & T.-W. Chan (Eds.), *Proceedings of Computer Support for Collaborative Learning (CSCL) 2005, Taipei, Taiwan.* Mahwah, NJ: Erlbaum.

DeVoe, J. F., Peter, K., Noonan, M., Snyder, T. D., & Baum, K. (2005, November). *Indicators of school crime and safety: 2005* (NCES No. 2006-001/NCJ No. 210697). Washington, DC: U.S. Departments of Education and Justice.. Retrieved August 30, 2006, from www.ojp.usdoj.gov/bjs.

De Vries, B., Van der Meij, Boersma, K., & Pieters, J. M. (2005). Embedding e-mail in primary schools: Developing a tool for collective reflection. *Journal of Educational Computing Research, 32*(2), 167–183.

DeVries, R. (1997). Piaget's social theory. *Educational Researcher, 26*(2), 4–17.

DiGiulio, R. (2000). *Positive classroom management* (2nd ed.). Thousand Oaks, CA: Corwin.

Dill, E. M., & Boykin, A. W. (2000). The comparative influence of individual, peer tutoring, and communal learning contexts of the text recall of African American children. *Journal of Black Psychology, 26*(1), 65–78.

Dillon, A., & Gabbard, R. (1998). Hypermedia as an educational technology: A review of the quantitative research literature on learner comprehension, control, and style. *Review of Educational Research, 68*(3), 322–349.

Dillon, S. (2005, November 26). Students ace state tests, but earn D's from U.S. *The New York Times.* Retrieved November 26, 2005, from www.nytimes.com/2005/11/26/education/26tests.html.

Dobbs, M. (2005, April 21). NEA, states challenge "No Child" program. *Washington Post,* p. A21.

Dochy, F., Segers, M., & Buehl, M. M. (1999). The relation between assessment practices and outcomes of studies: The case of research on prior knowledge. *Review of Educational Research, 69*(2), 145–186.

Doherty, R. W., Hilberg, R. S., Epaloose, G., & Tharp, R. G. (2002). Standards performance continuum: Development and validation of a measure of effective pedagogy. *Journal of Educational Research, 96*(2), 78–89.

Donovan, C. A., & Smolkin, L. B. (2002). Children's genre knowledge: An examination of K–5 students' performance on multiple tasks providing differing levels of scaffolding. *Reading Research Quarterly, 37*(4), 428–465.

Doppelt, Y., & Barak, M. (2002). Pupils identify key aspects and outcomes of a technological learning environment. *Journal of Technology Studies, 28*(1), 22–28.

Dornbusch, S. M., & Kaufman, J. G. (2001). The social structure of the American high school. In T. Urdan & F. Pajares (Eds.), *Adolescence and education* (Vol. 1, pp. 61–91). Greenwich, CT: Information Age Publishing.

Doty, D. E., Popplewell, S. R., & Byers, G. O. (2001). Interactive CD-ROM storybooks and young readers' reading comprehension. *Journal of Research on Computing in Education, 33*(4), 374–384.

Doyle, W. (1983). Academic work. *Review of Educational Research, 53*(2), 159–200.

Drake, F. D., & McBride, L. W. (2000). The summative teaching portfolio and the reflective practitioner of history. *The History Teacher, 34*(1), 41–60.

Drier, H. S. (2001). Conceptualization and design of Probability Explorer. *TechTrends, 45*(2), 2–24.

Drier, H. S., Dawson, K. M., & Garofalo, J. (1999). Not your typical math class. *Educational Leadership, 56*(5), 21–25.

Driscoll, M. P. (2005). *Psychology of learning for instruction* (3rd ed.). Boston: Pearson/Allyn & Bacon.

Duckworth, A. L., & Seligman, E. P. (2006). Self-discipline gives girls the edge: Gender in self-discipline, grades, and achievement test scores. *Journal of Educational Psychology, 98*(1), 198–208.

Duell, O. K. (1986). Metacognitive skills. In G. D. Phye & T. Andre (Eds.), *Cognitive classroom learning.* Orlando, FL: Academic Press.

Duff, C. (2000). Online mentoring. *Educational Leadership, 58*(2), 49–52.

Duffrin, E. (2004a, May). What we know about efforts to end "social promotion." *Catalyst Chicago,* 8–10.

Duffrin, E. (2004b, May). Popular despite the research. *Catalyst Chicago,* 6–7.

Duffy, T. M., & Cunningham, D. J. (1996). Constructivism: Implications for the design and delivery of instruction. In D. Jonassen (Ed.), *Handbook of research for educational communications and technology* (pp. 170–198). New York: Macmillan Library Reference.

Duhaney, L. M., & Duhaney, D. C. (2000). Assistive technology: Meeting the needs of learners with disabilities. *International Journal of Instructional Media, 27*(4), 393–401.

Dweck, C. S. (2002a). The development of ability conceptions. In A. Wigfield & J. S. Eccles (Eds.), *Development of achievement motivation* (pp. 57–88). San Diego, CA: Academic Press.

Dweck, C. S. (2002b). Messages that motivate: How praise molds students' beliefs, motivation, and performance (in surprising ways). In J. Aronson (Ed.), *Improving academic achievement* (pp. 37–59). San Diego, CA: Academic Press.

Eberstadt, M. (2003). The child-fat problem. *Policy Review, 117,* 3–19.

Ebert, E., & Strudler, N. (1996). Improving science learning using low-cost multimedia. *Learning and Leading with Technology, 24*(1), 23–26.

Eby, J. W., Herrell, A., & Hicks, J. L. (2002). *Reflective planning, teaching, and evaluation: K–12.* Upper Saddle River, NJ: Merrill Prentice Hall.

Edelson, D. C., Pea, R. D., & Gomez, L. (1996). Constructivism in the collaboratory. In B. G. Wilson (Ed.), *Constructivist learning environments: Case studies in instructional design* (pp. 151–164). Englewood Cliffs, NJ: Educational Technology Publications.

Education Trust, Inc. (2004). *Education watch: The nation: Key education facts and figures.* Retrieved December 12, 2004, from www2.edtrust.org/edtrust/summaries2004/USA.pdf.

Eisner, E. W. (1999). The uses and limits of performance assessment. *Phi Delta Kappan, 80*(9), 658–660.

Eisner, E. W. (2002). What can education learn from the arts about the practice of education? *Journal of Curriculum and Supervision, 18*(1), 4–16.

Eisenman, G., & Payne, B. D. (1997). Effects of the higher order thinking skills program on at-risk young adolescents' self-concept, reading achievement, and thinking skills. *Research in Middle Level Education Quarterly, 20*(3), 1–25.

Elkind, D. (1968). Cognitive development in adolescence. In J. F. Adams (Ed.), *Understanding adolescence.* Boston: Allyn & Bacon.

Elkind, D. (1989). Developmentally appropriate practice: Philosophical and practical implications. *Phi Delta Kappan, 71*(2), 113–117.

Elkind, D. (2005). Response to objectivism and education. *The Educational Forum 69*(4), 328–334.

Elliot, A. J., & Covington, M. V. (2001). Approach and avoidance motivation. *Educational Psychology Review, 13*(2), 73–92.

Elliot, A. J., & Thrash, T. M. (2001). Achievement goals and the hierarchical model of achievement motivation. *Educational Psychology Review, 13*(2), 139–156.

Elliot, S. (2003). IntelliMetric™: From here to validity. In M. D. Shermis & J. C. Burstein

(Eds.), *Automated essay scoring* (pp. 71–86). Mahwah, NJ: Erlbaum.

Elliott, J. G., & Bempechat, J. (2002). The culture and contexts of achievement motivation. In J. Bempechat & J. G. Elliott (Eds.), *New directions for child and adolescent development, no. 96. Learning in culture and context: Approaching the complexities of achievement motivation in student learning* (pp. 7–26). San Francisco, CA: Jossey-Bass.

Elliott, L., Foster, S., & Stinson, M. (2002). Student study habits using notes from a speech-to-text support service. *Exceptional Children, 69*(1), 25–40.

Ellis, A. K. (2001). *Teaching, learning, and assessment together: The reflective classroom.* Larchmont, NY: Eye on Education.

Ellis, H. C. (1965). *The transfer of learning.* New York: Macmillan.

Ellis, H. C. (1978). *Fundamentals of human learning, memory, and cognition* (2nd ed.). Dubuque, IA: William C. Brown.

Emmer, E. T., Evertson, C. M., Clements, B. S., & Worsham, M. E. (2006). *Classroom management for middle and high school teachers* (7th ed.). Boston: Pearson/Allyn and Bacon.

Emmer, E. T., & Stough, L. M. (2001). Classroom management: A critical part of educational psychology, with implications for teacher education. *Educational Psychologist, 36*(2), 103–112.

Engebretsen, A. (1997). Visualizing least-square lines of best fit. *Mathematics Teacher, 90*(5), 405–408.

Englander, E. K. (2003). *Understanding violence* (2nd ed.). Mahwah, NJ: Erlbaum.

Eom, W., & Reiser, R. A. (2000). The effects of self-regulation and instructional control on performance and motivation in computer-based instruction. *International Journal of Instructional Media, 27*(3), 247–260.

Erdelyi, M. H., & Goldberg, B. (1979). Let's now sweep repression under the rug: Towards a cognitive psychology of repression. In J. Kihlstrom & F. Evans (Eds.), *Functional disorders of memory.* Hillsdale, NJ: Erlbaum.

Ericsson, K. A., Chase, W. G., & Faloon, S. (1980). Acquisition of a memory skill. *Science, 208*(4448), 1181–1182.

Erikson, E. H. (1963). *Childhood and society* (2nd ed.). New York: Norton.

Erikson, E. H. (1968). *Identity: Youth and crisis.* New York: Norton.

Evans, G., & English, K. (2002). The environment of poverty: Multiple exposure, psychophysiological stress, and socioemotional adjustment. *Child Development, 73*(4), 1238–1249.

Evans, R. (2005). Reframing the achievement gap. *Phi Delta Kappan, 86*(8), 582–589.

Evertson, C. M., Emmer, E. T., & Worsham, M. E. (2006). *Classroom management for elementary teachers* (7th ed.). Boston: Pearson/Allyn & Bacon.

Fabes, R. A., Martin, C. L., & Hanish, L. D. (2003). Young children's play qualities in same-, other-, and mixed-sex peer groups. *Child Development, 74*(3), 921–932.

Fadjukoff, P., Pulkkinen, L., & Kokko, K. (2005). Identity processes in adulthood: Diverging domains. *Identity, 5*(1), 1–20.

Falk, B. (2002). Standard-based reforms: Problems and possibilities. *Phi Delta Kappan, 83*(8), 612–620.

Faw, H. W., & Waller, T. G. (1976). Mathemagenic behaviors and efficiency in learning from prose materials. *Review of Educational Research, 46*(4), 691–720.

Fehrenbach, C. R. (1994). Cognitive styles of gifted and average readers. *Roeper Review, 16*(4), 290–292.

Feigenbaum, P. (2002). Private speech: Cornerstone of Vygotsky's theory of the development of higher psychological processes. In D. Robbins & A. Stetsenko (Eds.), *Voices within Vygotsky's non-classical psychology: Past, present, and future* (pp. 161–174). New York: Nova Science.

Feiman-Nemser, S. (2003). What new teachers need to learn. *Educational Leadership, 60*(8), 25–29.

Feist, J., & Feist, G. J. (2001). *Theories of personality* (5th ed). Dubuque, IA: McGraw-Hill.

Feynman, R. P. (1985). *"Surely you're joking, Mr. Feynman."* New York: Norton.

Feyten, C. M., Macy, M. D., Ducher, J., Yoshii, M., Park, E., Calandra, B., & Meros, J. (2002). *Teaching ESL/EFL with the Internet.* Upper Saddle River, NJ: Merrill Prentice Hall.

Finarelli, M. G. (1998). GLOBE: A worldwide environmental science and education partnership. *Journal of Science Education and Technology, 7*(1), 77–84.

Fisher, D. (2006). Keeping adolescents "alive and kickin' it": Addressing suicide in schools. *Phi Delta Kappan, 87*(10), 784–786.

Fitzgerald, J. (1995). English-as-a-second-language learners' cognitive reading processes: A review of the research in the United States. *Review of Educational Research, 65*(2), 145–190.

Flavell, J. H. (1976). Metacognitive aspects of problem solving. In L. B. Resnick (Ed.), *The nature of intelligence.* Hillsdale, NJ: Erlbaum.

Flavell, J. H. (1987). Speculations about the nature and development of metacognition. In F. E. Weinert & R. H. Kluwe (Eds.), *Metacognition, motivation, and understanding.* Hillsdale, NJ: Erlbaum.

Flieller, A. (1999). Comparison of the development of formal thought in adolescent cohorts aged 10 to 15 years (1967–1996 and 1972–1993). *Developmental Psychology, 35*(4), 1048–1058.

Flinders, D. J. (1989). Does the "art of teaching" have a future? *Educational Leadership, 46*(1), 16–20.

Flora, S. R. (2004). *The power of reinforcement.* Albany: State University of New York Press.

Forbes, S., & Ashton, P. (1998). The identity status of African Americans in middle adolescence: A replication and extension of Watson and Protinsky (1991). *Adolescence, 33*(132), 845–849.

Fosnot, C. T. (1996). Constructivism: A psychological theory of learning. In C. T. Fosnot (Ed.), *Constructivism: Theory, perspectives, and practice.* New York: Teachers College Press.

Franzke, M., Kintsch, E., Caccamise, D., Johnson, N., & Dooley, S. (2005). Summary Street®: Computer support for comprehension and writing. *Journal of Educational Computing Research, 33*(1), 53–80.

Freedman, K., & Liu, M. (1996). The importance of computer experience, learning processes, and communication patterns in multicultural networking. *Educational Technology Research and Development, 44*(1), 43–59.

Freiberg, H. J. (2002). Essential skills for new teachers. *Educational Leadership, 59*(6), 56–60.

Frisbie, D. A. (2005). Measurement 101: Some fundamentals revisited. *Educational Measurement: Issues and Practice, 24*(3), 21–28.

Fryer, R. G., Jr., & Torelli, P. (2005, May). *An empirical analysis of "acting white"* (Working Paper No. 11334). Cambridge, MA: National Bureau of Economic Research. Retrieved July 10, 2006, from www.nber.org/papers/w11334.

Fuchs, D., Fuchs, L. S., Mathes, P. G., & Simmons, D. C. (1997). Peer-assisted learning strategies: Making classrooms more responsive to diversity. *American Educational Research Journal, 34*(1), 174–206.

Fuller, B., Gesicki, K., Kang, E., & Wright, J. (2006). *Is the No Child Left Behind Act working?* (Working Paper 06-1). Berkeley: University of California, Policy Analysis for California Education.

Funk, C. (2003). James Otto and the pi man: A constructivist tale. *Phi Delta Kappan, 85*(3), 212–214.

Funkhouser, C. (2002/2003). The effects of computer-augmented geometry instruction on student performance and attitudes. *Journal of Research on Technology in Education, 35*(2), 163–175.

Gabler, I. C., Schroeder, M., & Curtis, D. H. (2003). *Constructivist methods for the secondary classroom.* Boston: Allyn & Bacon.

Gaffney, J. S., & Anderson, R. C. (1991). Two-tiered scaffolding: Congruent processes of teaching and learning. In E. H. Hiebert (Ed.), *Literacy in a diverse society: Perspectives, practices, and policies* (pp. 141–156). New York: Teachers College Press.

Gage, N. L., & Berliner, D. C. (1998). *Educational psychology* (6th ed.). Boston: Houghton Mifflin.

Gagné, E. D., Yekovich, C. W., & Yekovich, F. R. (1993). *The cognitive psychology of school learning* (2nd ed.). New York: HarperCollins.

Gallagher, J. J. (2003). Issues and challenges in the education of gifted students. In

N. Colangelo & G. A. Davis (Eds.), *Handbook of gifted education* (3rd ed., pp. 11–23). Boston: Allyn & Bacon.

Gallagher, W. J. (2005). The contradictory nature of professional teaching standards: Adjusting for common misunderstandings. *Phi Delta Kappan, 87*(2), 112–115.

Gallimore, R., & Tharp, R. (1990). Teaching mind in society: Teaching, schooling, and literate discourse. In L. C. Moll (Ed.), *Vygotsky and education: Instructional implications and applications of sociohistorical psychology.* Cambridge, England: Cambridge University Press.

Gantner, M. W. (1997). Lessons learned from my students in the barrio. *Educational Leadership, 54*(7), 44–45.

García, E. (2002). *Student cultural diversity: Understanding and meeting the challenge* (3rd ed.). Boston: Houghton Mifflin.

Garcia, J. (1993). The changing image of ethnic groups in textbooks. *Phi Delta Kappan, 75*(1), 29–35.

Gardner, H. (1999). *Intelligence reframed: Multiple intelligences for the 21st century.* New York: Basic Books.

Gardner, H., & Hatch, T. (1989). Multiple intelligences go to school. *Educational Researcher, 18*(8), 410.

Gatlin, L., & Jacob, S. (2002). Standards-based digital portfolios: A component of authentic assessment for preservice teachers. *Action in Teacher Education, 23*(4), 35–41.

Gayler, K., Chudowsky, N., Kober, N., & Hamilton, M. (2003, August). *State high school exit exams put to the test.* Retrieved February 18, 2004, from www.cep-dc.org.

Gelman, R. (1994). Constructivism and supporting environments. In D. Tirosh (Ed.), *Implicit and explicit knowledge: An educational approach.* Norwood, NJ: Ablex.

Genesee, F., & Cloud, N. (1998). Multilingualism is basic. *Educational Leadership, 55*(6), 62–65.

Gentile, J. R., & Lalley, J. P. (2003). *Standards and mastery learning.* Thousand Oaks, CA: Corwin Press.

Gentry, M., Gable, R. K., & Rizza, M. G. (2002). Students' perceptions of classroom activities: Are there grade-level and gender differences? *Journal of Educational Psychology, 94*(3), 539–544.

Gershoff, E. T. (2002). Corporal punishment by parents and associated child behaviors and experiences: A meta-analytic and theoretical review. *Psychological Bulletin, 128*(4), 539–579.

Gersten, R. (1999). The changing face of bilingual education. *Educational Leadership, 56*(7), 41–45.

Gersten, R., & Brengelman, S. U. (1996). The quest to translate research into classroom practice: The emerging knowledge base. *Remedial and Special Education, 17*(2), 67–74.

Gersten, R., Fuchs, L. S., Williams, J. P., & Baker, S. (2001). Teaching reading comprehension strategies to students with learning disabilities: A review of research. *Review of Educational Research, 71*(2), 279–320.

Gettinger, M., & Stoiber, K. C. (2006). Functional assessment, collaboration, and evidence-based treatment: Analysis of a team approach for addressing challenging behaviors in young children. *Journal of School Psychology, 44*(3), 231–252.

Gewertz, C. (2005). Ed. dept. allows Chicago to provide NCLB tutoring. *Education Week, 25*(2), 3, 18.

Giaccardi, E. (2005). Metadesign as an emergent design culture. *Leonardo, 38*(4), 342–349.

Gick, M. L. (1986). Problem-solving strategies. *Educational Psychologist, 21*(1,2), 99–120.

Gilberg, C. (2001). Epidemiology of early onset schizophrenia. In H. Remschmidt (Ed.), *Schizophrenia in children and adolescents* (pp. 43–59). New York: Cambridge University Press.

Gillespie, C. W., & Beisser, S. (2001). Developmentally appropriate LOGO computer programming with young children. *Information Technology in Childhood Education Annual,* 229–245.

Gillies, R. M. (2003). Structuring cooperative group work in classrooms. *International Journal of Educational Research, 39*(1–2), 35–49.

Gilligan, C. (1979). Women's place in man's life cycle. *Harvard Educational Review, 49*(4), 431–446.

Gilligan, C. (1987). Adolescent development reconsidered. In C. E. Irwin, Jr. (Ed.), *Adolescent social behavior and health.* San Francisco: Jossey-Bass.

Gilligan, C. (1988). Exit-voice dilemmas in adolescent development. In C. Gilligan, J. Ward, J. Taylor, & B. Bardige (Eds.), *Mapping the moral domain: A contribution of women's thinking to psychological theory and education.* Cambridge, MA: Harvard University Press.

Gilness, J. (2003). How to integrate character education into the curriculum. *Phi Delta Kappan, 85*(3), 243–245.

Ginott, H. (1965). *Between parent and child.* New York: Macmillan.

Ginott, H. (1972). *Teacher and child.* New York: Macmillan.

Ginott, H., G., Ginott, A., & Goddard, H. W. (2003). *Between parent and child* (Revised and updated). New York: Three Rivers Press.

Ginsburg, H. P., & Opper, S. (1988). *Piaget's theory of intellectual development* (3rd ed.). Englewood Cliffs, NJ: Prentice-Hall.

Ginsburg-Block, M. D., Rohrbeck, C. A., & Fantuzzo, J. W. (2006). A meta-analytic review of social, self-concept, and behavioral outcomes of peer-assisted learning. *Journal of Educational Psychology, 98*(4), 732–749.

Glasser, W. (1998). *The quality school: Managing students without coercion* (Rev. ed.). New York: HarperPerennial.

Glasser, W. (2001). *Choice theory in the classroom* (Rev. ed.). New York: Quill.

Glazek, S. D., & Sarason, S. B. (2006). *Productive learning: Science, art, and Einstein's relativity in educational reform.* Thousand Oaks, CA: Corwin Press.

Goldberg, M. (2004). The test mess. *Phi Delta Kappan, 85*(5), 361–366.

Goldberg, M. (2005). Test mess 2: Are we doing better a year later? *Phi Delta Kappan, 86*(5), 389–395.

Goldhaber, D., & Hannaway, J. (2004). Accountability with a kicker: Observations on the Florida A+ accountability plan. *Phi Delta Kappan, 85*(8), 598–605.

Goldsby, D., & Fazal, M. (2001). Now that your students have created web-based digital portfolios, how do you evaluate them? *Journal of Technology and Teacher Education, 9*(4), 607–616.

Gollnick, D. A., & Chinn, P. C. (2002). *Multicultural education in a pluralistic society* (6th ed.). Upper Saddle River, NJ: Merrill.

Gomez, L. M., Fishman, B. J., & Pea, R. D. (1998). *The CoVis project: Building a large scale science education testbed.* Interactive Learning Environments.

Good, T. (1982). *Classroom research: What we know and what we need to know* (R&D Report No. 9018). Austin: University of Texas, Research and Development Center for Teacher Education.

Good, T. L., & Brophy, J. (1995). *Contemporary educational psychology* (5th ed.). New York: Longman.

Good, T. L., & Nicholls, S. L. (2001). Expectancy effects in the classroom: A special focus on improving the reading performance of minority students in first-grade classrooms. *Educational Psychologist, 36*(2), 113–126.

Good, J. M., & Whang, P. A. (2002). Encouraging reflection in preservice teachers through response journals. *Teacher Educator, 37*(4), 254–267.

Goodlad, J. I. (1984). *A place called school.* New York: McGraw-Hill.

Gordon, P. R., Rogers, A. M., Comfort, M., Gavula, N., & McGee, B. P. (2001). A taste of problem-based learning increases achievement of urban minority middle-school students. *Educational Horizons, 79*(4), 171–175.

Gordon, S., & Gilgun, J. F. (1987). Adolescent sexuality. In V. B. van Hasselt & M. Hersen (Eds.), *Handbook of adolescent psychology.* New York: Pergamon Press.

Gordon, T. (1974). *TET: Teacher effectiveness training.* New York: McKay.

Gottfried, A. E., Fleming, J. S., & Gottfried, A. W. (2001). Continuity of academic intrinsic motivation from childhood through late adolescence: A longitudinal study. *Journal of Educational Psychology, 93*(1), 3–13.

Gough, P. B. (1987). The key to improving schools: An interview with William Glasser. *Phi Delta Kappan, 69*(9), 656–662.

Gould, F. (2003). Testing third-graders in New Hampshire. *Phi Delta Kappan, 84*(7), 507–513.

Gould, S. J. (1981). *The mismeasure of man.* New York: Norton.

Grabe, M., & Grabe, C. (2007). *Integrating technology for meaningful learning* (5th ed.). Boston: Houghton Mifflin.

Graham, S., & Hudley, C. (2005). Race and ethnicity in the study of motivation and competence. In A. J. Elliot & C. S. Dweck (Eds.), *Handbook of competence and motivation* (pp. 392–413). New York: Guilford Press.

Graham, S., & Taylor, A. Z. (2002). Ethnicity, gender, and the development of achievement values. In A. Wigfield & J. S. Eccles (Eds.), *Development of achievement motivation* (pp. 121–146). San Diego, CA: Academic Press.

Graue, M. E., & DiPerna, J. (2000). Redshirting and early retention: Who gets the "gift of time" and what are its outcomes? *American Educational Research Journal, 37*(2), 509–534.

Gredler, M., & Shields, C. (2004). Does no one read Vygotsky's words? Commentary on Glassman. *Educational Researcher, 33*(2), 21–25.

Green, C., & Tanner, R. (2005). Multiple intelligences and online teacher education. *ELT Journal, 59*(4), 312–321.

Greenberg, E. R., Canzoneri, C., & Joe, A. (2000). *2000 AMA survey on workplace testing: Basic skills, job skills, psychological measurement.* Retrieved January 2, 2002, from www.amanet.org/research/pdfs/psych.pdf.

Greenfield, R. (2003). Collaborative e-mail exchange for teaching secondary ESL: A case study in Hong Kong. *Language Learning and Technology, 7*(1), 46–70.

Gregory, G. H. (2003). *Differentiated instructional strategies in practice.* Thousand Oaks, CA: Corwin Press.

Gregory, G. H., & Chapman, C. (2002). *Differentiated instructional strategies: One size doesn't fit all.* Thousand Oaks, CA: Corwin Press.

Gregory, G. H., & Kuzmich, L. (2005). *Differentiated literacy strategies for student growth and achievement in grades 7–12.* Thousand Oaks, CA: Corwin Press.

Gresham, F. M., & MacMillan, D. L. (1997). Social competence and affective characteristics of students with mild disabilities. *Review of Educational Research, 67*(4), 377–415.

Griffin, H. C., Williams, S. C., Davis, M. L., & Engleman, M. (2002). Using technology to enhance cues for children with low vision. *Teaching Exceptional Children, 35*(2), 36–42.

Grigorenko, E. L., Jarvin, L., & Sternberg, R. J. (2002). School-based tests of the triarchic theory of intelligence: Three settings, three samples, three syllabi. *Contemporary Educational Psychology, 27*(2), 167–208.

Groeben, N. (1994). Humanistic models of human development. In T. Husen & T. N. Postlewhaite (Eds.), *International encyclopedia of education* (2nd ed., Vol. 5, pp. 2689–2692). New York: Pergamon.

Gronlund, N. E. (1998). *Assessment of student achievement* (6th ed.). Boston: Allyn & Bacon.

Gronlund, N. E. (2004). *Writing instructional objectives for teaching and assessment* (7th ed.). Upper Saddle River, NJ: Merrill Prentice Hall.

Gronlund, N. E. (2006). *Assessment of student achievement* (8th ed.). Boston: Allyn & Bacon.

Grossen, B. J. (2002). The BIG Accommodation model: The direct instruction model for secondary schools. *Journal of Education for Students Placed At Risk, 7*(2), 241–263.

Guay, F., Marsh, H. W., & Boivin, M. (2003). Academic self-concept and academic achievement: Developmental perspectives on their causal ordering. *Journal of Educational Psychology, 95*(1), 124–136.

Guild P. (1994). The culture/learning style connection. *Educational Leadership, 51*(8), 16–21.

Gulek, C. (2003). Preparing for high-stakes testing. *Theory into Practice, 42*(1), 42–50.

Gunn, H., & Hepburn, G. (2003). Seeking information for school purposes on the internet. *Canadian Journal of Learning and Technology, 29*(1), 67–88.

Guskey, T. R. (2002). Computerized gradebooks and the myth of objectivity. *Phi Delta Kappan, 83*(10), 775–780.

Guskey, T. R. (2003). How classroom assessments improve learning. *Educational Leadership, 60*(5), 6–11.

Guskey, T. R., & Bailey, J. M. (2001). *Developing grading and reporting systems for student learning.* Thousand Oaks, CA: Corwin Press.

Gutek, G. L. (1992). *Education and schooling in America* (3rd ed.). Boston: Allyn & Bacon.

Gutiérrez, K. D., & Rogoff, B. (2003). Cultural ways of learning: Individual traits or repertoires of practice. *Educational Researcher, 32*(5), 19–25.

Haag, L., & Stern, E. (2003). In search of the benefits of learning Latin. *Journal of Educational Psychology, 95*(1), 174–178.

Hacker, D. J., & Tenent, A. (2002). Implementing reciprocal teaching in the classroom: Overcoming obstacles and making modifications. *Journal of Educational Psychology, 94*(4), 699–718.

Hadwin, A. F., Winne, P. H., Stockley, D. B., Nesbit, J. C., & Woszczyna, C. (2001). Context moderates students' self-reports about how they study. *Journal of Educational Psychology, 93*(3), 477–487.

Haier, R. J. (2001). PET studies of learning and individual differences. In J. L. McClelland & R. S. Siegler (Eds.), *Mechanisms of cognitive development: Behavioral and neural perspectives* (pp. 123–145). Mahwah, NJ: Erlbaum.

Haladyna, T. (1999). *A complete guide to student grading.* Boston: Allyn & Bacon.

Haladyna, T. M., Downing, S. M., & Rodriguez, M. C. (2002). A review of multiple-choice item-writing guidelines for classroom assessment. *Applied Measurement in Education, 15*(3), 309–334.

Hallfors, D., Vevea, J. L., Iritani, B., Cho, H., Khatapoush, S., & Saxe, L. (2002). Truancy, grade point average, and sexual activity: A meta-analysis of risk indicators for youth substance abuse. *Journal of School Health, 72*(5), 205–211.

Halpern, D. F. (1997). Sex differences in intelligence: Implications for education. *American Psychologist, 52*(10), 1091–1102.

Halpern, D. F. (1998). Teaching critical thinking for transfer across domains. *American Psychologist, 53*(4), 449–455.

Halpern, D. F., & LaMay, M. L. (2000). The smarter sex: A critical review of sex differences in intelligence. *Educational Psychology Review, 12*(2), 229–246.

Halpern, D. F., Wai, J., & Saw, A. (2005). A psychobiosocial model: Why females are sometimes greater than and sometimes less than males in math achievement. In A. M. Gallagher & J. C. Kaufman (Eds.), *Gender differences in mathematics* (pp. 48–72). New York: Cambridge University Press.

Hambrick, D. Z., & Engle, R. W. (2003). The role of working memory in problem solving. In J. E. Davidson & R. J. Sternberg (Eds.), *The psychology of problem solving* (pp. 176–205). Cambridge, England: Cambridge University Press.

Hamilton, L., & Stecher, B. (2004). Responding effectively to test-based accountability. *Phi Delta Kappan, 85*(8), 578–583.

Hamilton, R., & Ghatala, E. (1994). *Learning and instruction.* New York: McGraw-Hill.

Hamman, D., Berthelot, J., Saia, J., & Crowley, E. (2000). Teachers' coaching of learning and its relation to students' strategic learning. *Journal of Educational Psychology, 92*(2), 342–348.

Hamre, B. K., & Pianta, R. C. (2005). Can instructional and emotional support in the first-grade classroom make a difference for children at risk of school failure? *Child Development, 76*(5), 949–967.

Haney, J. J., & McArthur, J. (2002). Four case studies of prospective science teachers' beliefs concerning constructivist teaching practices. *Science Education, 86*(6), 783–802.

Hansgen, R. D. (1991). Can education become a science? *Phi Delta Kappan, 72*(9), 689–694.

Harding, C. G., & Snyder, K. (1991). Tom, Huck, and Oliver Stone as advocates in Kohlberg's just community: Theory-based strategies for moral-based education. *Adolescence, 26*(102), 319–330.

Hardy, C. L., Bukowski, W. M., & Sippola, L. K. (2002). Stability and change in peer relationships during the transition to middle-level school. *Journal of Early Adolescence, 22*(2), 117–142.

Hardy, I., Jonen, A., Möller, K., & Stern, E. (2006). Effects of instructional support within constructivist learning environments for elementary school students' understanding of "floating and sinking." *Journal of Educational Psychology, 98*(2), 307–326.

Hargreaves, A., Earl, L., & Schmidt, M. (2002). Perspectives on alternative assessment reform. *American Educational Research Journal, 39*(1), 69–95.

Harris, K. R., Graham, S., & Mason, L. H. (2006). Improving the writing, knowledge, and motivation of struggling young writers: Effects of self-regulated strategy development with and without peer support. *American Educational Research Journal, 43*(2), 295–340.

Harry, B., & Klingner, J. K. (2006). *Why are so many minority students in special education? Understanding race and disability in schools.* New York: Teachers College Press.

Hart, B., & Risley, T. R. (1995). *Meaningful differences in the everyday experience of young American children.* Baltimore, MD: Paul H. Brookes.

Harter, S. (1990). Self and identity development. In S. S. Feldman & G. R. Elliot (Eds.), *At the threshold: The developing adolescent* (pp. 352–387). Cambridge, MA: Harvard University Press.

Harter, S. (1999). *The construction of the self: A developmental perspective.* New York: Guilford Press.

Harter, S., Waters, P. L., & Whitesell, N. R. (1997). Lack of voice as a manifestation of false self-behavior among adolescents: The school setting as a stage upon which the drama of authenticity is enacted. *Educational Psychologist, 32*(3), 153–174.

Hartshorne, H., & May, M. A. (1929). *Studies in service and self-control.* New York: Macmillan.

Hartshorne, H., & May, M. A. (1930a). *Studies in deceit.* New York: Macmillan.

Hartshorne, H., & May, M. A. (1930b). *Studies in the organization of character.* New York: Macmillan.

Hartup, W. W. (1989). Social relationships and their developmental significance. *American Psychologist, 44*(2), 120–126.

Haskell, R. E. (2001). *Transfer of learning: Cognition, instruction, and reasoning.* San Diego, CA: Academic Press.

Hatch, T. (1997). Getting specific about multiple intelligences. *Educational Leadership, 54*(6), 26–29.

Hattie, J., Biggs, J., & Purdie, N. (1996). Effects of learning skills interventions on student learning: A meta-analysis. *Review of Educational Research, 66*(2), 99–136.

Hay, K. E., & Barab, S. A. (2001). Constructivism in practice: A comparison and contrast of apprenticeship and constructionist learning environments. *The Journal of the Learning Sciences, 10*(3), 281–322.

Healy, L., & Hoyles, C. (2001). Software tools for geometrical problem solving: Potentials and pitfalls. *International Journal of Computers for Mathematical Learning, 6*(3), 235–256.

Heath, M. (2002). Electronic portfolios for reflective self-assessment. *Teacher Librarian, 30*(1), 19–23.

Hebert, E. A. (2001). *The power of portfolios.* San Francisco: Jossey-Bass.

Hecker, L., Burns, L., Elkind, J., Elkind, K., & Katz, L. (2002). Benefits of assistive reading software for students with attention disorders. *Annals of Dyslexia, 52*, 243–272.

Henderson, J. G. (Ed.). (2001). *Reflective teaching: Professional artistry through inquiry.* Upper Saddle River, NJ: Merrill Prentice Hall.

Henry J. Kaiser Family Foundation. (2004, September). *Children, the digital divide, and federal policy.* Retrieved November 9, 2006, from www.kff.org/entmedia/7090.cfm.

Herman, J. L., Gearhart, M., & Baker, E. L. (1993). Assessing writing portfolios: Issues in the validity and meaning of scores. *Educational Assessment, 1*(3), 201–224.

Herr, P. (2000). The changing role of the teacher: How management systems help facilitate teaching. *T.H.E. Journal, 28*(4), 28–34.

Hersh, R. H., Paolitto, D. P., & Reimer, J. (1979). *Promoting moral growth: From Piaget to Kohlberg.* New York: Longman.

Hershberg, T. (2005). Value-added assessment and systemic reform: A response to the challenge of human capital development. *Phi Delta Kappan, 87*(4), 276–283.

Hess, F. M., & Finn, C. E., Jr. (2004). Inflating the life raft of NCLB: Making public school choice and supplemental services work for students in troubled schools. *Phi Delta Kappan, 86*(1), 34–40, 57–58.

Hetherington, E. M., & Parke, R. D. (1993). *Child psychology: A contemporary viewpoint* (4th ed.). New York: McGraw-Hill.

Heward, W. L. (2003). *Exceptional children: An introduction to special education* (7th ed.). Upper Saddle River, NJ: Merrill Prentice Hall.

Hewitt, J. (2002). From a focus on tasks to a focus on understanding: The cultural transformation of a Toronto classroom. In T. Koschmann, R. Hall, & N. Miyake (Eds.), *CSCL2: Carrying forward the conversation* (pp. 11–41). Mahwah, NJ: Erlbaum.

Hickey, D. T., Kindfield, A. C. H., Horwitz, P., & Christie, M. T. (2003). Integrating curriculum, instruction, assessment, and evaluation in a technology-supported genetics learning environment. *American Educational Research Journal, 40*(2), 495–538.

Hickey, D. T., Moore, A. L., & Pellegrino, J. W. (2001). The motivational and academic consequences of elementary mathematics environments: Do constructivist innovations and reforms make a difference? *American Educational Research Journal, 38*(3), 611–652.

Hidi, S. (2001). Interest, reading, and learning: Theoretical and practical considerations. *Educational Psychology Review, 13*(3), 191–209.

Hidi, S., & Ainley, M. (2002). Interest and adolescence. In F. Pajares & T. Urdan (Eds.), *Academic motivation of adolescents* (pp. 247–275). Greenwich, CT: Information Age Publishing.

Hidi, S., & Harackiewicz, J. M. (2000). Motivating the academically unmotivated: A critical issue for the 21st century. *Review of Educational Research, 70*(2), 151–179.

Hiebert, J., Gallimore, R., & Stigler, J. W. (2002). A knowledge base for the teaching profession: What would it look like and how can we get one? *Educational Researcher, 31*(5), 3–15.

Higgins, J. W., Williams, R. L., & McLaughlin, T. F. (2001). The effects of a token economy employing instructional consequences for a third-grade student with learning disabilities: A case study. *Education and Treatment of Children, 24*(1), 99–106.

Hill, J. G., & Johnson, F. (2005). *Revenues and expenditures for public elementary and secondary education: School year 2002–03* (NCES 2005-353R). Washington, DC: U.S. Department of Education, National Center for Educational Statistics. Retrieved October 17, 2006, from http://nces.ed.gov/ccd/pubs/npefs03/findings.asp.

Hill, J. P. (1987). Research on adolescents and their families: Past and prospect. In C. E. Irwin, Jr. (Ed.), *Adolescent social behavior and health.* San Francisco: Jossey-Bass.

Hills, J. R. (1991). Apathy concerning grading and testing. *Phi Delta Kappan, 72*(7), 540–545.

Ho, B. (1995). Using lesson plans as a means of reflection. *ELT Journal, 49*(1), 66–70.

Hoegh, D. G., & Bourgeois, M. J. (2002). Prelude and postlude to the self: Correlates of achieved identity. *Youth & Society, 33*(4), 573–594.

Hoff, D. J. (2006, January 4). Colo. town raises taxes to finance NCLB withdrawal. *Education Week, 25*(16), 3, 9.

Hoffer, T. B. (1992). Middle school ability grouping and student achievement in science and mathematics. *Educational Evaluation and Policy Analysis, 14*(3), 205–227.

Hoffman, J. L., Wu, H.-K., Krajcik, J. S., & Soloway, E. (2003). The nature of middle school learners' science content understandings with the use of on-line resources. *Journal of Reseearch in Science Teaching, 40*(3), 323–346.

Hoffman, M. L. (1980). Moral development in adolescence. In J. Adelson (Ed.), *Handbook of adolescent psychology.* New York: Wiley.

Hoffman, M. L. (2000). *Empathy and moral development: Implications for caring and justice.* Cambridge, England: Cambridge University Press.

Hoge, R. D., & Renzulli, J. S. (1993). Exploring the link between giftedness and self-concept. *Review of Educational Research, 63*(4), 449–465.

Holman, L. J. (1997). Meeting the needs of Hispanic immigrants. *Educational Leadership, 54*(7), 37–38.

Hong, G., & Raudenbush, S. W. (2005). Effects of kindergarten retention policy on children's cognitive growth in reading and mathematics. *Educational Evaluation and Policy Analysis, 27*(3), 205–224.

Hood, S. (1998). Culturally responsive performance-based assessment: Conceptual and psychometric considerations. *Journal of Negro Education, 67*(3), 187–196.

Houston, P. D. (2005). NCLB: Dreams and nightmares. *Phi Delta Kappan, 86*(6), 469–470.

Houston, W. R., & Williamson, J. L. (1992/1993). Perceptions of their preparation by 42 Texas elementary school teachers compared with their responses as student teachers. *Teacher Education and Practice, 8*(2), 27–42.

Howard, B. B., & McColskey, W. H. (2001). Evaluating experienced teachers. *Educational Leadership, 58*(5), 48–51.

Howard, B. C., McGee, S., Shin, N., & Shia, R. (2001). The triarchic theory of intelligence and computer-based inquiry learning. *Educational Technology Research and Development, 49*(4), 49–69.

Howe, C. K. (1994). Improving the achievement of Hispanic students. *Educational Leadership, 51*(8), 42–44.

Howe, N., Rinaldi, C. M., Jennings, M., & Petrakos, H. (2002). "No! the lambs can stay out because they got cozies": Constructive and destructive sibling conflict, pretend play, and social understanding. *Child Development, 73*(5), 1460–1473.

Hrabowski, F. A., III. (2002/2003). Raising minority achievement in science and math. *Educational Leadership, 60*(4), 44–48.

Hughes, F. P., & Noppe, L. D. (1991). *Human development across the life span.* New York: Macmillan.

Hughes, J. E., Packard, B. W.-L., & Pearson, P. D. (2000). The role of hypermedia cases on preservice teachers' views on reading instruction. *Action in Teacher Education, 22*(2A), 24–38.

Hung, D. (2001). Theories of learning and computer-mediated instructional technologies. *Education Media International, 38*(4), 281–287.

Hung, D. (2002). Situated cognition and problem-based learning: Implications for learning and instruction with technology. *Journal of Interactive Learning Research, 13*(4), 393–414.

Hunt, N., & Marshall, K. (2006). *Exceptional children and youth* (4th ed.). Boston: Houghton Mifflin.

Hurst, B., Wilson, C., & Cramer, G. (1998). Professional teaching portfolios: Tools for reflection, growth, and advancement. *Phi Delta Kappan, 79*(8), 578–582.

Huyvaert, S. (1995). *Reports from the classroom: Cases for reflection.* Boston: Allyn & Bacon.

Hyde, J. S. (2005). The gender similarities hypothesis. *American Psychologist, 60*(6), 581–592.

Hyerle, D. (Ed.). (2004). *Student successes with thinking maps.* Thousand Oaks, CA: Corwin Press.

Hyönä, J., Lorch, R. F., Jr., & Kaakinen, J. K. (2002). Individual differences in reading to summarize expository text: Evidence from eye fixations. *Journal of Educational Psychology, 94*(1), 44–55.

Individuals with Disabilities Education Act Amendments of 1997. (1997, June). Retrieved September 15, 2003, from http://frwebgate.access.gpo.gov/cgi-bin/useftp.cgi?IPaddress=162.140.64.21&filename=publ17.105&directory=/diskc/ wais/data/105_cong_public_laws.

International Society for Technology in Education. (2000). *National Educational Technology Standards for Students: Connecting Curriculum and Technology.* Eugene, OR: Author.

Jackson, A. W., & Davis, G. A. (2000). *Turning points 2000: Educating adolescents in the 21st century.* New York: Teachers College Press.

Jackson, C. W., & Larkin, M. J. (2002). Rubric: Teaching students to use grading rubrics. *Teaching Exceptional Children, 35*(1), 40–45.

Jackson, D. B. (2003). Education reform as if student agency mattered: Academic micro-cultures and student identity. *Phi Delta Kappan, 84*(8), 579–585.

Jackson, J. F. (1999). What are the real risk factors for African American children? *Phi Delta Kappan, 81*(4), 308–312.

Jackson, S., & Bosma, H. (1990). Coping and self in adolescence. In H. Bosma & S. Jackson (Eds.), *Coping and self-concept in adolescence.* New York: Springer-Verlag.

Jaffee, S., Hyde, J. S., & Shibley, J. (2000). Gender differences in moral orientation: A meta-analysis. *Psychological Bulletin, 126*(5), 703–726.

James, W. (1899). *Talks to teachers on psychology: And to students on some of life's ideals.* New York: Holt.

Janesick, V. J. (2001). *The assessment debate: A reference handbook.* Santa Barbara, CA: ABC-CLIO.

Jennings, J., & Rentner, D. S. (2006). Ten big effects of the No Child Left Behind Act on public schools. *Phi Delta Kappan, 88*(2), 110–113.

Jensen, L. A., Arnett, J. J., Feldman, S. S., & Cauffman, E. (2002). It's wrong, but everybody does it: Academic dishonesty among high school and college students. *Contemporary Educational Psychology, 27*(2), 209–228.

Jenson, W. R., Olympia, D., Farley, M., & Clark, E. (2004). Positive psychology and externalizing students in a sea of negativity. *Psychology in the Schools, 41*(1), 67–79.

Jimerson, S. R. (2001). Meta-analysis of grade retention research: Implications for practice in the 21st century. *School Psychology Review, 30*(3), 420–437.

Jimerson, S. R., & Kaufman, A. M. (2003). Reading, writing, and retention: A primer on grade retention research. *The Reading Teacher, 56*(7), 622–635.

Jimerson, S. R., Anderson, G. E., & Whipple, A. D. (2002). Winning the battle and losing the war: Examining the relation between grade retention and dropping out of high school. *Psychology in the Schools, 39*(4), 441–457.

Jobe, D. A. (2002/2003). Helping girls succeed. *Educational Leadership, 60*(4), 64–66.

Johnson, J., Farkas, S., & Bers, A. (1997). *What American teenagers really think about their schools: A report from Public Agenda.* New York: Public Agenda.

Johnson, D. W., & Johnson, R. T. (1995). Cooperative learning and nonacademic outcomes of schooling: The other side of the report card. In J. E. Pedersen & A. D. Digby (Eds.), *Secondary schools and cooperative learning* (pp. 81–150). New York: Garland Publishing.

Johnson, D. W., & Johnson, R. T. (1998). Cultural diversity and cooperative learning. In J. W. Putnam (Ed.), *Cooperative learning and strategies for inclusion* (2nd ed.). Baltimore, MD: Brookes Publishing.

Johnson, D. W., Johnson, R. T., & Holubec, E. J. (1994). *The new circles of learning: Cooperation in the classroom and school.* Alexandria, VA: Association for Supervision and Curriculum Development.

Johnson, D. W., Johnson, R. T., & Smith, K. A. (1995). Cooperative learning and individual student achievement in secondary schools. In J. E. Pedersen & A. D. Digby (Eds.), *Secondary schools and cooperative learning* (pp. 3–54). New York: Garland Publishing.

Johnson, K. E. (2000). Constructive evaluations. *Science Teacher, 67*(2), 38–41.

Johnson, R. E. (1975). Meaning in complex learning. *Review of Educational Research, 45*(3), 425–460.

Jonassen, D. H. (2000). *Computers as mindtools for schools: Engaging critical thinking* (2nd ed.). Upper Saddle River, NJ: Merrill Prentice Hall.

Jonassen, D. H., Howland, J., Moore, J., & Marra, R. M. (2003). *Learning to solve problems with technology: A constructivist perspective* (2nd ed.). Upper Saddle River, NJ: Merrill Prentice Hall.

Jones, K. (2004). A balanced school accountability model: An alternative to high-stakes testing. *Phi Delta Kappan, 85*(8), 584–590.

Joo, Y.-J., Bong, M., & Choi, H.-J. (2000). Self-efficacy for self-regulated learning, academic self-efficacy, and internet self-efficacy in web-based instruction. *Educational Technology Research and Development, 48*(2), 5–17.

Jorgenson, O. (2003). Brain scam? Why educators should be careful about embracing "brain research." *The Educational Forum, 67*(4), 364–369.

Jovanovic, J., & King, S. S. (1998). Boys and girls in the performance-based science classroom: Who's doing the performing? *American Educational Research Journal, 35*(3), 477–496.

Juvonen, J. (2000). The social functions of attributional face-saving tactics among early adolescents. *Educational Psychology Review, 12*(1), 15–32.

Joyce, B., & Weil, M. (2004). *Models of teaching* (7th ed.). Boston: Allyn & Bacon.

Jussim, L., Eccles, J., & Madon, S. (1996). Social perception, social stereotypes, and teacher expectations: Accuracy and the quest for the powerful self-fulfilling prophecy. In M. Zanna (Ed.), *Advances in experimental social psychology* (Vol. 28, pp. 281–383). San Diego, CA: Academic Press.

Kagan, J. (1964a). *Developmental studies of reflection and analysis.* Cambridge, MA: Harvard University Press.

Kagan, J. (1964b). Impulsive and reflective children. In J. D. Krumbolz (Ed.), *Learning and the educational process.* Chicago: Rand McNally.

Kail, R. V. (2007). *Children and their development* (4th ed.). Upper Saddle River, NJ: Pearson Prentice Hall.

Kalbaugh, P., & Haviland, J. M. (1991). Formal operational thinking and identity. In R. M. Lerner, A. C. Peterson, & J. Brooks-Gunn (Eds.), *Encyclopedia of adolescence.* New York: Garland Publishing.

Kamii, C. (2000). *Young children reinvent arithmetic: Implications of Piaget's theory* (2nd ed). New York: Teachers College Press.

Karchmer, R. A. (2001). The journey ahead: Thirteen teachers report how the Internet influences literacy and literacy instruction in their K–12 classrooms. *Reading Research Quarterly, 36*(4), 442–466.

Karniol, R., Gabay, R., Ochion, Y., & Harari, Y. (1998). Is gender or gender-role orientation a better predictor of empathy in adolescence? *Sex Roles, 39*(1–2), 45–59.

Karpov, Y. V., & Bransford, J. D. (1995). L. S. Vygotsky and the doctrine of empirical and theoretical learning. *Educational Psychologist, 30*(2), 61–66.

Karpov, Y. V., & Haywood, H. C. (1998). Two ways to elaborate Vygotsky's concept of mediation. *American Psychologist, 53*(1), 27–36.

Katayama, A. D., & Robinson, D. H. (2000). Getting students "partially" involved in notetaking using graphic organizers. *The Journal of Experimental Education, 68*(2), 119–133.

Katz, L. G., & Chard, S. C. (2000). *Engaging children's minds: The project approach* (2nd ed.). Stamford, CT: Ablex Publishing.

Kavale, K. A. (2002). Mainstreaming to full inclusion: From orthogenesis to pathogenesis of an idea. *International Journal of Disability, Development and Education, 49*(2), 201–214.

Keane, G., & Shaughnessy, M. F. (2002). An interview with Robert J. Sternberg: The current "state of the art." *Educational Psychology Review, 14*(3), 313–330.

Keeler, C. M. (1996). Networked instructional computers in the elementary classroom and their effect on the learning environment: A qualitative evaluation. *Journal of Research on Computing in Education, 28*(3), 329–345.

Kehle, T. J., Bray, M. A., Theodore, L. A., Jenson, W. R., & Clark, E. (2000). A multicomponent intervention designed to reduce disruptive classroom behavior. *Psychology in the Schools, 37*(5), 475–481.

Kelley, M. L., & Carper, L. B. (1988). Home-based reinforcement procedures. In J. C. Witt, S. N. Elliott, & F. M. Gresham (Eds.), *Handbook of behavior therapy in education.* New York: Plenum Press.

Kelly, M., & Moag-Stahlberg, A. (2002). Battling the obesity epidemic. *Principal, 81*(5), 26–29.

Kentucky Department of Education (2004). *Commonwealth accountability testing system.* Retrieved from www.education.ky.gov/ KDE/Administrative+Resources/Testing+a nd+Reporting+/CATS/default.htm.

Kernis, M. H. (2002). Self-esteem as a multifaceted construct. In T. M. Brinthaupt & R. P. Lipka (Eds.), *Understanding early adolescent self and identity: Applications and interventions* (pp. 57–87). Albany: State University of New York Press.

Kerr, M. M., & Nelson, C. M. (2006). *Strategies for addressing behavior problems in the classroom* (5th ed.). Upper Saddle River, NJ: Merrill Prentice Hall.

Kim, J. S., & Sunderman, G. L. (2005). Measuring academic proficiency under the No Child Left Behind Act: Implications for educational equity. *Educational Researcher, 34*(8), 3–13.

Kim, Y., Baylor, A. L., & PALS Group. (2006). Pedagogical agents as learning companions: The role of agent competency and type of interaction. *Educational Technology Research and Development, 54*(3), 223–243.

King, A. (1992a). Comparison of self-questioning, summarizing, and notetaking-review as strategies for learning from lectures. *American Educational Research Journal, 29*(2), 303–323.

King, A. (1992b). Facilitating elaborative learning through guided student-generated questioning. *Educational Psychologist, 27*(1), 111–126.

King, A. (1994). Guiding knowledge construction in the classroom: Effects of teaching children how to question and how to explain. *American Educational Research Journal, 31*(2), 338–368.

King, A. (1998). Transactive peer tutoring: Distributing cognition and metacognition. *Educational Psychology Review, 10*(1), 57–74.

King, A. (2002). Structuring peer interaction to promote high-level cognitive processing. *Theory into Practice, 41*(1), 33–39.

Kirk, S. A., Gallagher, J. J., & Anastasiow, N. J. (2006). *Educating exceptional children* (11th ed.). Boston: Houghton Mifflin.

Kirschner, P. A., Sweller, J., & Clark, R. E. (2006). Why minimal guidance during instruction does not work: An analysis of the failure of constructivist, discovery, problem-based, experiential, and inquiry-based teaching. *Educational Psychologist, 41*(2), 75–86.

Klassen, R. (2002). Writing in early adolescence: A review of the role of self-efficacy beliefs. *Educational Psychology Review, 14*(2), 173–203.

Klassen, R. M. (2004). A cross-cultural investigation of the efficacy beliefs of South Asian immigrant and AngloCanadian non-immigrant early adolescents. *Journal of Educational Psychology, 96*(4), 731–742.

Klauer, K. (1984). Intentional and incidental learning with instructional texts: A meta-analysis for 1970–1980. *American Educational Research Journal, 21*(2), 323–339.

Knapp, M. S., & Shields, P. M. (1990). Reconceiving academic instruction for the children of poverty. *Phi Delta Kappan, 71*(10), 753–758.

Knapp, M. S., Shields, P. M., & Turnbull, B. J. (1995). Academic challenge in high-poverty classrooms. *Phi Delta Kappan, 76*(10), 770–776.

Kober, N., Zabala, D., Chudowsky, N., Chudowsky, V., Gayler, K., & McMurrer, J. (2006, August). *State high school exit exams: A challenging year.* Washington, DC: Center on Education Policy. Retrieved September 6, 2006, from www.cep-dc.org.

Kohlberg, L. (1963). The development of children's orientations toward a moral order: 1. Sequence in the development of moral thought. *Vita Humana, 6*(1–2), 11–33.

Kohlberg, L. (1969). Stage and sequence: The cognitive-developmental approach to socialization. In D. A. Goslin (Ed.), *Handbook of socialization theory and research.* Chicago: Rand McNally.

Kohlberg, L. (1976). Moral stages and moralization: The cognitive-developmental approach. In T. Lickona (Ed.), *Moral development and behavior: Theory, research, and social issues.* New York: Holt, Rinehart & Winston.

Kohlberg, L. (1978). Revisions in the theory and practice of moral development. In W. Damon (Ed.), *New directions for child development: Moral development* (No. 2). San Francisco: Jossey Bass.

Kohn, A. (1993). Rewards versus learning: A response to Paul Chance. *Phi Delta Kappan, 74*(10), 783–787.

Kohn, A. (1999). *Punished by rewards: The trouble with gold stars, incentive plans, A's, praise, and other bribes.* Boston: Houghton Mifflin.

Kontos, G., & Mizell, A. P. (1997). Global village classroom: The changing roles of teachers and students through technology. *TechTrends, 42*(5), 17–22.

Kordaki, M., & Potari, D. (2002). The effect of area measurement tools on student strategies: The role of a computer microworld. *International Journal of Computers for Mathematical Learning, 7*(1), 65–100.

Kosunen, T., & Mikkola, A. (2002). Building a science of teaching: How objectives and reality meet in Finnish teacher education. *European Journal of Teacher Education, 25*(2/3), 135–150.

Kounin, J. S. (1970). *Discipline and group management in classrooms.* New York: Holt, Rinehart & Winston.

Kozulin, A., & Presseisen, B. Z. (1995). Mediated learning experience and psychological tools: Vygotsky's and Feuerstein's perspectives in a study of student learning. *Educational Psychologist, 30*(2), 57–75.

Kramarski, B., & Zeichner, O. (2001). Using technology to enhance mathematical reasoning: Effects of feedback and self-regulation learning. *Educational Media International, 38*(2/3), 77–82.

Krashen, S. (1999). What the research really says about structured English immersion: A reply to Keith Baker. *Phi Delta Kappan, 80*(9), 705–706.

Krathwohl, D. R., Bloom, B. S., & Masia, B. B. (1964). *Taxonomy of educational objectives: Handbook II. Affective domain.* New York: McKay.

Krätzig, G. P., & Arbuthnot, K. D. (2006). Perceptual learning style and learning proficiency. *Journal of Educational Psychology, 98*(1), 238–246.

Krulik, S., & Rudnick, J. A. (1993). *Reasoning and problem solving: A handbook for elementary school teachers.* Boston: Allyn & Bacon.

Kubiszyn, T., & Borich, G. (2007). *Educational testing and measurement: Classroom application and practice* (8th ed.). New York: Wiley.

Kuhn, D. (1999). A developmental model of critical thinking. *Educational Researcher, 28*(2), 16–26, 46.

Kuhn, D. (2002). What is scientific thinking and how does it develop? In U. Goswami (Ed.), *Blackwell handbook of childhood cognitive development* (pp. 371–393). Malden, MA: Blackwell.

Kulik, C.-L., Kulik, J. A., & Bangert-Drowns, R. L. (1990). Effectiveness of mastery learning programs. *Review of Educational Research, 60*(2), 265–299.

Kulik, J. A. (2003a, May). *Effects of using instructional technology in elementary and secondary schools: What controlled evaluation studies say.* Arlington, VA: SRI International. Retrieved July 20, 2006, from www.sri.com/csted/reports/sandt/it/.

Kulik, J. A. (2003b). Grouping and tracking. In N. Colangelo & G. A. Davis (Eds.), *Handbook of gifted education* (3rd ed., pp. 268–281). Boston: Allyn & Bacon.

Kulik, J. A., & Kulik, C.-L. (1991). Ability grouping and gifted students. In N. Colangelo & G. A. Davis (Eds.), *Handbook of gifted education.* Boston: Allyn & Bacon.

Kyllonen, P. C. (1996). Is working memory capacity Spearman's g? In I. Dennis & P. Tapsfield (Eds.), *Human abilities: Their nature and measurement.* Mahwah, NJ: Erlbaum.

LaBoskey, V. K. (2000). Portfolios here, portfolios there. . . . Searching for the essence of "educational portfolios." *Phi Delta Kappan, 81*(8), 590–595.

Lach, C., Little, E., & Nazzaro, D. (2003). From all sides now: Weaving technology and multiple intelligences into science and art. *Learning and Leading with Technology, 30*(6), 32–35, 59.

Lacina, J. (2004/2005). Promoting language acquisitions: Technology and English language learners. *Childhood Education, 81* (2), 113–115.

Laczko-Kerr, I., & Berliner, D. C. (2003). In harm's way: How undercertified teachers hurt their students. *Educational Leadership, 60*(8), 34–39.

Ladson-Billings, G. (1994). What we can learn from multicultural education research. *Educational Leadership, 51*(8), 22–26.

Ladson-Billings, G. (2002). But that's just good teaching! The case for culturally relevant pedagogy. In S. J. Denbo & L. M. Beaulieu (Eds.), *Improving schools for African American students* (pp. 95–102). Springfield, IL: Charles C. Thomas.

Lai, S.-L., Chang, T.-S., & Ye, R. (2006). Computer usage and reading in elementary schools: A cross-cultural study. *Journal of Educational Computing Research, 34*(1), 47–66.

Lam, S., Yim, P., & Lam, T. W. (2002). Transforming school culture: Can true collaboration be inititated? *Educational Research, 44*(2), 181–195.

Lampinen, J. M., & Odegard, T. N. (2006). Memory editing mechanisms. *Memory, 14*(6), 649–654.

Lancey, D. F. (2002). Cultural constraints on children's play. In J. L. Roopnarine (Ed.), *Conceptual, social-cognitive, and contextual issues in the fields of play* (pp. 53–60). Westport, CT: Ablex.

Landau, B. M., & Gathercoal, P. (2000). Creating peaceful classrooms: Judicious Discipline and class meetings. *Phi Delta Kappan, 81*(6), 450–452, 454.

Lantieri, L. (1995). Waging peace in our schools: Beginning with the children. *Phi Delta Kappan, 76*(5), 386–388.

Lantieri, L. (1999). Hooked on altruism: Developing social responsibility in at-risk youth. *Reclaiming Children and Youth, 8*(2), 83–87.

Latu, E., & Chapman, E. (2002). Computerised adaptive testing. *British Journal of Educational Technology, 33*(5), 619–622.

Lazear, D. G. (1992). *Teaching for multiple intelligences.* Bloomington, IN: Phi Delta Kappa Educational Foundation.

Leadbeater, B. (1991). Relativistic thinking in adolescence. In R. M. Lerner, A. C. Peterson, & J. Brooks-Gunn (Eds.), *Encyclopedia of adolescence.* New York: Garland Publishing.

Leaver, B. L. (1998). *Teaching the whole class* (5th ed.). Dubuque, IA: Kendall/Hunt.

Lee, C. D. (1998). Culturally responsive pedagogy and performance-based assessment. *Journal of Negro Education, 67*(3), 268–279.

Lee, H. M. J., Lee, F. L., & Lau, T. S. (2006). Folklore-based learning on the web: Pedagogy, case study and evaluation. *Journal of Educational Computing Research, 34*(1), 1–27.

Lee, J. (2002). Racial and ethnic achievement gap trends: Reversing the progress toward equity? *Educational Researcher, 31*(1), 3–12.

Lee, J. (2006, June). *Tracking achievement gaps and assessing the impact of NCLB on the gaps: An in-depth look into national and state reading and math outcome trends.* Cambridge, MA: The Civil Rights Project at Harvard University. Retrieved October 10, 2006, from www.civilrightsproject .harvard.edu/research/esea/esea_gen.php.

Lee, J.-S., & Bowen, N. K. (2006). Parent involvement, cultural capital, and the achievement gap among elementary school children. *American Educational Research Journal, 43*(2), 193–218.

Leeson, H. V. (2006). The mode effect: A literature review of human and technological issues in computerized testing. *International Journal of Testing, 6*(1), 1–24.

Lehrer, R. (1993). Authors of knowledge: Patterns of hypermedia design. In S. Lajoie & S. Derry (Eds.), *Computers as cognitive tools* (pp. 197–227). Hillsdale, NJ: Erlbaum.

LeLoup, J., & Ponterio, R. (2003). Telecollaborative projects: Monsters.com? *Language Learning and Technology, 7*(2), 6–11.

Lepper, M. R., Corpus, J. H., & Iyengar, S. S. (2005). Intrinsic and extrinsic motivational orientations in the classroom: Age differences and academic correlates. *Journal of Educational Psychology, 97*(2), 184–196.

Lerner, J. W. (2003). *Learning disabilities: Theories, diagnosis, and teaching strategies* (9th ed.). Boston: Houghton Mifflin.

Levin, J. R. (1982). Pictures as prose-learning devices. In A. Flammer & W. Kintsch (Eds.), *Advances in psychology: Vol. 8. Discourse processing.* Amsterdam: North-Holland.

Levin, J. R. (1993). Mnemonic strategies and classroom learning: A 20-year report card. *Elementary School Journal, 94*(2), 235–244.

Levine, D. U., & Levine, R. F. (1996). *Society and education* (9th ed.). Boston: Allyn & Bacon.

Levine, S. C., Vasilyeva, M., Lourenco, S. F., Newcombe, N. S., & Huttenlocher, J. (2005). Socioeconomic status modifies the sex difference in spatial skill. *Psychological Science, 16*(11), 841–845.

Lewis, C., Perry, R., & Murata, A. (2006). How should research contribute to instructional improvement? The case of lesson study. *Educational Researcher, 35*(3), 3–14.

Lewis, T. (2005). Creativity: A framework for the design/problem solving discourse in technology education. *Journal of Technology Education, 17*(1). Retrieved September 16, 2006, from http://scholar.lib.vt.edu/ejournals/JTE/v17n1/lewis.html.

Ley, K., & Young, D. B. (2001). Instructional principles for self-regulation. *Educational Technology Research and Development, 49*(2), 93–103.

Leyser, Y., Frankiewicz, L. E., & Vaughn, R. (1992). Problems faced by first-year teachers: A survey of regular and special educators. *Teacher Educator, 28*(1), 36–45.

Li, J. (2002). Learning models in different cultures. In J. Bempechat & J. G. Elliott (Eds.), *Learning in culture and context: Vol. 96. New directions for child and adolescent development* (pp. 45–63). San Francisco: Jossey-Bass.

Liao, Y.-K. C. (2007). Effects of computer-assisted instruction on students' achievement in Taiwan: A meta-analysis. *Computers and Education, 48*(2), 216–233.

Liben, L. S., Bigler, R. S., & Krogh, H. R. (2002). Language at work: Children's gendered interpretations of occupational titles. *Child Development, 73*(3), 810–828.

Lickona, T. (1976). Research on Piaget's theory of moral development. In T. Lickona (Ed.), *Moral development and behavior: Theory, research, and social issues.* New York: Holt, Rinehart & Winston.

Lickona, T. (1998). A more complex analysis is needed. *Phi Delta Kappan, 79*(6), 449–454.

Lickona, T., & Davidson, M. (2005). *Smart and good high schools: Integrating excellence and ethics for success in school, work, and beyond.* Cortland, NY: Center for the 4th and 5th Rs (Respect and Responsibility)/Washington, DC: Character Education Partnership. Retrieved August 25, 2005 from www.cortland.edu/character/highschool/.

Light, P., & Littleton, K. (1999). *Social processes in children's learning.* Cambridge, England: Cambridge University Press.

Ligorio, M. B., Talamo, A., & Pontecorvo, C. (2005). Building intersubjectivity at a distance during the collaborative writing of fairy tales. *Computers and Education, 45*(3), 357–374.

Linderholm, T., & van den Broek, P. (2002). The effects of reading purpose and working memory capacity on the processing of expository text. *Journal of Educational Psychology, 94*(4), 778–784.

Linn, M. C. (1992). Science education reform: Building on the research base. *Journal of Research in Science Teaching, 29*(8), 821–840.

Linn, M. C., Lewis, C., Tsuchida, I., & Songer, N. B. (2000). Beyond fourth-grade science: Why do U.S. and Japanese students diverge? *Educational Researcher, 29*(3), 4–14.

Linn, M. C., & Slotta, J. D. (2000). WISE science. *Educational Leadership, 58*(2), 29–32.

Linn, R. L. (2000). Assessments and accountability. *Educational Researcher, 29*(2), 4–16.

Linn, R. L. (2003). Accountability: Responsibility and reasonable expectations. *Educational Researcher, 32*(7), 3–13.

Linn, R. L., Baker, E. L, & Betebenner, D. W. (2002). Accountability systems: Implications of requirements of the No Child Left Behind Act of 2001. *Educational Researcher, 31*(6), 3–16.

Linn, R. L., & Gronlund, N. E. (2000). *Measurement and assessment in teaching* (8th ed.) Upper Saddle River, NJ: Merrill.

Linn, R. L., & Miller, M. D. (2005). *Measurement and assessment in teaching* (9th ed.). Upper Saddle River, NJ: Pearson Prentice-Hall.

Livson, N., & Peskin, H. (1980). Perspectives on adolescence from longitudinal research. In J. Adelson (Ed.), *Handbook of adolescent psychology.* New York: Wiley.

Llabo, L. D. (2002). Computers, kids, and comprehension: Instructional practices that make a difference. In C. C. Block, L. B. Gambrell, & M. Pressley (Eds.), *Improving comprehension instruction: Rethinking research, theory, and classroom practice* (pp. 275–289). San Francisco: Jossey-Bass.

Lloyd, L. (1999). Multi-age classes and high ability students. *Review of Educational Research, 69*(2), 187–212.

Lockwood, A. (1978). The effects of values clarification and moral development curricula on school age subjects: A critical review of recent research. *Review of Educational Research, 48*(3), 325–364.

Lodewyk, K. R., & Winne, P. H. (2005). Relations among the structure of learning tasks, achievement, and changes in self-efficacy in secondary students. *Journal of Educational Psychology, 97*(1), 3–12.

Lonoff, S. (1997). Using videotape to talk about teaching. *ADE Bulletin, 118,* 10–14.

Lopata, C., Miller, K. A., & Miller, R. H. (2003). Survey of actual and preferred use of cooperative learning among exemplar teachers. *Journal of Educational Research, 96*(4), 232–239.

Lou, Y., Abrami, P. C., & d'Apollonia, S. (2001). Small group learning and individual learning with technology: A meta-analysis. *Review of Educational Research, 71*(3), 499–521.

Lou, Y., Abrami, P. C., & Spence, J. C. (2000). Effects of within-class grouping on student achievement: An exploratory model. *Journal of Educational Research, 94*(2), 101–112.

Loveless, T. (1998). The tracking and ability grouping debate. *Fordham Report, 2*(8). Retrieved January 2, 2002, from www.edexcellence.net/library/track.html.

Loveless, T. (1999). Will tracking reform promote social equity? *Educational Leadership, 56*(7), 28–32.

Lowry, R., Sleet, D., Duncan, C., Powell, K., & Kolbe, L. (1995). Adolescents at risk for violence. *Educational Psychology Review, 7*(1), 7–39.

Lundeberg, M. A., & Fox, P. W. (1991). Do laboratory findings on test expectancy generalize to classroom outcomes? *Review of Educational Research, 61*(1), 94–106.

Lyons, N. (1999). How portfolios can shape emerging practice. *Educational Leadership, 56*(8), 63–65.

Lyons, N. P., & Kubler LaBoskey, V. (2002). Introduction. In N. P. Lyons & V. Kubler LaBoskey (Eds.), *Narrative inquiry in practice: Advancing the knowledge of teaching.* New York: Teachers College Press.

Maag, J. W. (2001). Rewarded by punishment: Reflections on the disuse of positive reinforcement in schools. *Exceptional Children, 67*(2), 173–186.

Mabry, L. (1999). Writing to the rubric: Lingering effects of traditional standardized testing on direct writing assessment. *Phi Delta Kappan, 80*(9), 673–679.

MacArthur, C. (1994). Peers + word processing + strategies = a powerful combination for revising student writing. *Teaching Exceptional Children, 27*(1), 24–29.

Maccini, P., Gagnon, J. C., & Hughes, C. A. (2002). Technology-based practices for secondary students with learning disabilities. *Learning Disability Quarterly, 25*(4), 247–261.

Macedo, D. (2000). The illiteracy of English-only literacy. *Educational Leadership, 57*(4), 62–67.

MacKay, A. P., Fingerhut, L. A., & Duran, C. R. (2000). *Health, United States, 2000. Adolescent health chartbook.* Hyattsville, MD: National Center for Health Statistics. Retrieved January 2, 2002, from www.cdc.gov/nchs/data/hus/hus00cht.pdf.

Mackay, S., McLaughlin, T. F., Weber, K., & Derby, K. M. (2001). The use of precision requests to decrease noncompliance in the home and neighborhood: A case study. *Child and Family Behavior Therapy, 23*(2), 43–52.

MacKinnon, J. L., & Marcia, J. E. (2002). Concurring patterns of women's identity status, attachment styles, and understanding of children's development. *International Journal of Behavioral Development, 26*(1), 70–80.

MacMillan, D. L., Gresham, F. M., & Forness, S. R. (1996). Full inclusion: An empirical perspective. *Behavioral Disorders, 21*(2), 145–159.

Mager, R. F. (1962). *Preparing instructional objectives.* Palo Alto, CA: Fearon.

Mager, R. F. (1997). *Preparing instructional objectives* (3rd ed.). Atlanta, GA: The Center for Effective Performance.

MaKinster, J. G., Beghetto, R. A., & Plucker, J. A. (2002). Why can't I find Newton's third law? Case studies of students' use of the web as a science resource. *Journal of Science Education and Technology, 11*(2), 155–172.

Maloch, B., Fine, J., & Flint, A. S. (2002/2003). Trends in teacher certification and literacy. *Reading Teacher, 56*(4), 348–350.

Marcia, J. E. (1966). Development and validation of ego identity status. *Journal of Personality and Social Psychology, 3*(5), 551–558.

Marcia, J. E. (1967). Ego identity status: Relationship to change in self-esteem, "general adjustment," and authoritarianism. *Journal of Personality, 35*(1), 119–133.

Marcia, J. E. (1980). Identity in adolescence. In J. Adelson (Ed.), *Handbook of adolescent psychology.* New York: Wiley.

Marcia, J. E. (1991). Identity and self-development. In R. M. Lerner, A. C. Peterson, & J. Brooks-Gunn (Eds.), *Encyclopedia of adolescence.* New York: Garland Publishing.

Marcia, J. E. (1999). Representational thought in ego identity, psychotherapy, and psychosocial developmental theory. In I. E. Sigel (Ed.), *Development of mental representation: theories and application* (pp. 391–414). Mahwah, NJ: Erlbaum.

Marcia, J. E. (2001). A commentary on Seth Schwartz's review of identity theory and research. *Identity, 1*(1), 59–65.

Marcia, J. E. (2002). Identity and psychosocial development in adulthood. *Identity, 2*(1), 7–28.

Marquis, J. G., Horner, R. H., Carr, E. G., Turnbull, A. P., Thompson, M., Behrens, G. A., Magito-McLaughlin, D., McAtee, M. L., Smith, C. E., Ryan, K. A., & Doolabh, A. (2000). A meta-analysis of positive behavior support. In R. Gersten, E. P. Schiller & S. R. Vaughn, (Eds.), *Contemporary special education research* (pp. 137–178). Mahwah, NJ: Erlbaum.

Marr, P. M. (2000). Grouping students at the computer to enhance the study of British literature. *English Journal, 90*(2), 120–125.

Marsh, H. W., & Craven, R. G. (2002). The pivotal role of frames of reference in academic self-concept formation: The "big fish–little pond" effect. In F. Pajares & T. Urdan (Eds.), *Academic motivation of adolescents* (pp. 83–123). Greenwich, CT: Information Age Publishing.

Marsh, H. W., & Hattie, J. (1996). Theoretical perspectives on the structure of self-concept. In B. A. Bracken (Ed.), *Handbook of self-concept* (pp. 38–90). New York: Wiley.

Marsh, H. W., & Yeung, A. S. (1998). Longitudinal structural equation models of academic self-concept and achievement: Gender differences in the development of math and English constructs. *American Educational Research Journal, 35*(4), 705–738.

Marsh, R. S., & Raywid, M. A. (1994). How to make detracking work. *Phi Delta Kappan, 76*(4), 314–317.

Martin, J. (2004). Self-regulated learning, social cognitive theory, and agency. *Educational Psychologist, 39*(2), 135–145.

Martinez, M. E. (1998). What is problem solving? *Phi Delta Kappan, 79*(8), 605–609.

Martinez, M. E. (1999). Cognition and the question of test item format. *Educational Psychologist, 34*(1), 207–218.

Marx, R. W., & Winne, P. H. (1987). The best tool teachers have—their students' thinking. In D. C. Berliner & B. V. Rosenshine (Eds.), *Talks to teachers.* New York: Random House.

Marzano, R. J., Pickering, D. J., & Pollock, J. E. (2005). *Classroom instruction that works: Research-based strategies for increasing student achievement.* Upper Saddle River, NJ: Pearson/Prentice Hall.

Maslow, A. H. (1943). A theory of human motivation. *Psychological Review, 50*(4), 370–396.

Maslow, A. H. (1968). *Toward a psychology of being* (2nd ed.). Princeton, NJ: Van Nostrand.

Maslow, A. H. (1987). *Motivation and personality* (3rd ed.). New York: Harper & Row.

Mason, L. H. (2004). Explicit self-regulated strategy development versus reciprocal questioning: Effects on expository reading comprehension among struggling readers. *Journal of Educational Psychology, 96*(2), 283–296.

Mathes, L. (2002). Theme and variation: The Crosshatch portrait. *Arts and Activities, 131*(2), 32–33, 70, 74.

Mathis, W. J. (2005). Bridging the achievement gap: A bridge too far? *Phi Delta Kappan, 86*(8), 590–593.

Matthew, K. I. (1996). The impact of CD-ROM storybooks on children's reading comprehension and reading attitude. *Journal of Educational Multimedia and Hypermedia, 5*(3/4), 379–394.

Matthews, C. E., Binkley, W., Crisp, A., & Gregg, K. (1998). Challenging gender bias in fifth grade. *Educational Leadership, 55*(4), 54–57.

Matthews, M. R. (2002). Constructivism and science education: A further appraisal. *Journal of Science Education and Technology, 11*(2), 121–134.

Mayer, R. E. (1987). Learnable aspects of problem solving: Some examples. In D. E. Berger, K. Pezdek, & W. P. Banks (Eds.), *Applications of cognitive psychology: Problem solving, education, and computing.* Hillsdale, NJ: Erlbaum.

Mayer, R. E. (2001). *Multimedia learning.* Cambridge, England: Cambridge University Press.

Mayer, R. E. (2004). Should there be a three-strike rule against pure discovery learning? The case for guided methods of instruction. *American Psychologist, 59*(1), 14–19.

Mayer, R. E., Mautone, P., & Prothero, W. (2002). Pictorial aids for learning by doing in a multimedia geology simulation game. *Journal of Educational Psychology, 94*(1), 171–185.

Mayer, R. E., & Moreno, R. (2002). Animation as an aid to multimedia learning. *Educational Psychology Review, 14*(1), 87–99.

Mazyck, M. (2002). Integrated learning systems and students of color: Two decades of use in K–12 education. *TechTrends, 46*(2), 33–39.

McCaslin, M., & Good, T. L. (1992). Compliant cognition: The misalliance of management and instructional goals in current school reform. *Educational Researcher, 21*(3), 4–17.

McDevitt, T. M., & Ormrod, J. E. (2004). *Child development: Educating and working with children and adolescents* (2nd ed.). Upper Saddle River, NJ: Pearson/Merrill Prentice Hall.

McEntee, G. H., Appleby, J., Dowd, J., Grant, J., Hole, S., & Silva, P. (2003). *At the heart of teaching: A guide to reflective practice.* New York: Teachers College Press.

McGill-Franzen, A., & Allington, R. (2006). Contamination of current accountability systems. *Phi Delta Kappan, 87*(10), 762–766.

McGrath, D. (2003). Rubrics, portfolios, and tests, oh my! *Learning and Leading with Technology, 30*(8), 42–45.

McInerney, D. M. (2005). Educational psychology–Theory, research, and teaching: A 25-year retrospective. *Educational Psychology, 25*(6), 585–599.

McKenna, M. C., Cowart, E., & Watkins, J. (1997, December). *Effects of talking books on the growth of struggling readers in second grade.* Paper presented at the meeting of the National Reading Conference, Scottsdale, AZ.

McKenzie, W. (2002). *Multiple intelligences and instructional technology: A manual for every mind.* Eugene, OR: International Society for Technology in Education.

McLeskey, J., & Waldron, N. L. (2002). School change and inclusive schools: Lessons learned from practice. *Phi Delta Kappan, 84*(1), 65–72.

McLoyd, V. C. (1998). Socioeconomic disadvantage and child development. *American Psychologist, 53*(2), 185–204.

McMillan, J. H., Myran, S., & Workman, D. (2002). Elementary teachers' classroom assessment and grading practices. *Journal of Educational Research, 95*(4), 203–213.

McNally, L., & Etchison, C. (2000). Streamlining classroom management. *Learning and Leading with Technology, 28*(2), 6–9, 12.

McTighe, J. (1996/1997). What happens between assessments? *Educational Leadership, 54*(4), 6–12.

McTighe, J., & Ferrara, S. (1998). *Assessing learning in the classroom.* Washington, DC: National Education Association.

McVarish, J., & Solloway, S. (2002). Self-evaluation: Creating a classroom without unhealthy competitiveness. *Educational Forum, 66*(3), 253–260.

Means, B., & Haertel, G. (2002). Technology supports for assessing science inquiry. In National Research Council (Ed.), *Technology and assessment: Thinking ahead* (pp. 12–25). Washington, DC: National Academy Press.

Means, B., & Knapp, M. S. (1991). Introduction: Rethinking teaching for disadvantaged students. In B. Means, C. Chelemer, & M. S. Knapp (Eds.), *Teaching advanced skills to at risk students.* San Francisco: Jossey-Bass.

Meier, N. (1999). A fabric of half-truths: A response to Keith Baker on structured English immersion. *Phi Delta Kappan, 80*(9), 704, 706.

Meisels, S. J., Bickel, D. D., Nicholson, J., Xue, Y., & Atkins-Burnett, S. (2001). Trusting teachers' judgments: A validity study of a curriculum-embedded performance assessment in kindergarten to grade 3. *American Educational Research Journal, 38*(1), 73–95.

Meisels, S. J., & Liaw, F.-R. (1993). Failure in grade: Do retained students catch up? *Journal of Educational Research, 87*(2), 69–77.

Melton, R. F. (1978). Resolution of conflicting claims concerning the effect of behavioral objectives on student learning. *Review of Educational Research, 48*(2), 291–302.

Mendoza, J. I. (1994). On being a Mexican American. *Phi Delta Kappan, 76*(4), 293–295.

Mertler, C. A. (2000). Teacher-centered fallacies of classroom assessment validity and reliability. *Mid-Western Educational Researcher, 13*(4), 29–35.

Messick, S. (1989). Meaning and values in test validation: The science and ethics of assessment. *Educational Researcher, 18*(2), 5–11.

Metzger, M. (1996). Maintaining a life. *Phi Delta Kappan, 77*(5), 346–351.

Metzger, M. (1998). Teaching reading: Beyond the plot. *Phi Delta Kappan, 80*(3), 240–246, 256.

Metzger, M. (2002). Learning to discipline. *Phi Delta Kappan, 84*(1), 77–84.

Mevarech, Z., & Susak, Z. (1993). Effects of learning with cooperative-mastery method on elementary students. *Journal of Educational Research, 86*(4), 197–205.

Meyer, M. S. (2000). The ability-achievement discrepancy: Does it contribute to our understanding of learning disabilities? *Educational Psychology Review, 12*(3), 315–337.

Midgley, C. (2001). A goal theory perspective on the current status of middle level schools. In T. Urdan & F. Pajares (Eds.), *Adolescence and education: Vol. 1. General issues in the education of adolescents* (pp. 33–59). Greenwich, CT: Information Age Publishers.

Midgley, C., Middleton, M. J., Gheen, M. H., & Kumar, R. (2002). Stage-environment fit revisited: A goal theory approach to examining school transitions. In C. Midgley (Ed.), *Goals, goal structures, and patterns of adaptive learning* (pp. 109–142). Mahwah, NJ: Erlbaum.

Miller, P. C., & Endo, H. (2004). Understanding and meeting the needs of ESL students. *Phi Delta Kappan, 85*(10), 786–791.

Miller, R. B., & Brickman, S. J. (2004). A model of future-oriented motivation and self-regulation. *Educational Psychology Review, 16*(1), 9–33.

Miltenberger, R. G. (2004). *Behavior modification: Principles and procedures.* Belmont, CA: Wadsworth/Thomson Learning.

Mistler-Jackson, M., & Songer, N. B. (2000). Student motivation and Internet technology: Are students empowered to learn science? *Journal of Research in Science Teaching, 37*(5), 459–479.

Mock, D. R., & Kauffman, J. M. (2002). Preparing teachers for full inclusion: Is it possible? *The Teacher Educator, 37*(3), 202–215.

Moely, B. E., Hart, S. S., Leal, L., Santulli, K. A., Rao, N., Johnson, T., & Hamilton, L. B. (1992). The teacher's role in facilitating memory and study strategy development in the elementary school classroom. *Child Development, 63*(3), 653–672.

Moersch, C., & Fisher, L. M., III (1995). Electronic portfolios—some pivotal questions. *Learning and Leading with Technology, 23*(2), 10–14.

Montgomery, K. (2000). Classroom rubrics: Systematizing what teachers do naturally. *The Clearing House, 73*(6), 324–328.

Moon, T. R. (2002). Using performance assessment in the social studies classroom. *Gifted Child Today, 25*(3), 53–59.

Moore, J. A., & Teagle, H. F. B. (2002). An introduction to cochlear implant technology, activation, and programming. *Language, Speech, and Hearing Services in the Schools, 33*(3), 153–161.

Mora, J. K., Wink, J., & Wink, D. (2001). Dueling models of dual language instruction: A critical review of the literature and program implementation guide. *Bilingual Research Journal, 25*(4), 435–460.

Moreno, R. (2006). Learning in high-tech and multimedia environments. *Current Directions in Psychological Science, 15*(2), 63–67.

Moreno, R., & Mayer, R. E. (2002). Learning science in virtual reality multimedia environments: Role of methods and media. *Journal of Educational Psychology, 94*(3), 598–610.

Moreno, R., & Mayer, R. E. (2005). Role of guidance, reflection, and interactivity in an agent-based multimedia game. *Journal of Educational Psychology, 97*(1), 117–128.

Morgan, H. (1997). *Cognitive styles and classroom learning.* Westport, CT: Praeger.

Morris, P. (1977). Practical strategies for human learning and remembering. In M. J. A. Howe (Ed.), *Adult learning.* New York: Wiley.

Moshavi, D. (2001). "Yes and . . .": Introducing improvisational theatre techniques to the management classroom. *Journal of Management Education, 25*(4), 437–449.

Muhlenbruck, L., Cooper, H., Nye, B., & Lindsay, J. J. (2000). Homework and achievement: Explaining the different strengths at the elementary and secondary levels. *Social Psychology in Education, 3*(4), 295–317.

Mullis, I. V. S., Martin, M. O., Gonzalez, E., O'Connor, K. M., Chrostowski, S. J., Gregory, K. D., Garden, R. A., & Smith, T. A. (2001). *Mathematics benchmarking report TIMSS 1999–eighth grade.* Chestnut Hill, MA: Boston College. Retrieved January 2, 2002, from www.timss.org/timss1999b/publications.html.

Murdoch, K., & Wilson, J. (2004). *How to succeed with cooperative learning.* Carlton, South Australia: Curriculum Corporation.

Murdock, T. B., Miller, A., & Kohlhardt, J. (2004). Effects of classroom context variables on high school students' judgments of the acceptability and likelihood of cheating. *Journal of Educational Psychology, 96*(4), 765–777.

Murphy, B. C., & Eisenberg, N. (2002). An integrative examination of peer conflict: Children's reported goals, emotions, and behavior. *Social Development, 11*(4), 534–557.

Myers, M. (2003). What can computers contribute to a K–12 writing program? In M. D. Shermis & J. C. Burstein (Eds.), *Automated essay scoring* (pp. 3–20). Mahwah, NJ: Erlbaum.

Nagaoka, J., & Roderick, M. (2004, March). *Ending social promotion: The effects of retention.* Chicago: Consortium on Chicago School Research. Retrieved February 15, 2005, from www.consortium-chicago.org/publications/p70.html.

Nagy, P., & Griffiths, A. K. (1982). Limitations of recent research relating Piaget's theory to adolescent thought. *Review of Educational Research, 52*(4), 513–556.

Nakhleh, M. B. (1994). A review of microcomputer-based labs: How have they affected science learning? *Journal of Computers in Mathematics and Science Teaching, 13*(4), 368–381.

Narvaez, D. (2002). Does reading moral stories build character? *Educational Psychology Review, 14*(2), 155–172.

National Board for Professional Teaching Standards. (2003, May 30). *What teachers should know and be able to do: The five core propositions of the National Board.* Retrieved October 23, 2003, from www.nbpts.org/about/coreprops.cfm.

National Center for Health Statistics. (2005). *Health, United States, 2005. With chartbook on trends in the health of Americans.* Hyattsville, MD: Author.

National Coalition to Abolish Corporal Punishment in Schools. (2005, November). *U. S.: Statistics on corporal punishment by state and race.* Retrieved July 18, 2006, from www.stophitting.com/disatschool/statesBanning.php.

National Commission on Excellence in Education. (1983). *A nation at risk: The imperative for educational reform.* Washington, DC: U.S. Department of Education.

National Research Council. (2000). *Inquiry and the National Science Education Standards: A guide for teaching and learning.* Washington, DC: National Academies Press.

National Research Council. (2002). *Minority students in special and gifted education* (Committee on Minority Representation in Special Education, M. S. Donovan & C. T. Cross, Eds., Division of Behavioral and Social Sciences). Washington, DC: National Academy Press.

Naughton, C. C., & McLaughlin, T. F. (1995). The use of a token economy system for students with behaviour disorders. *B.C. Journal of Special Education, 19*(2/3), 29–38.

Neill, M. (2003). High stakes, high risk. *American School Board Journal, 190*(2), 18–21.

Neisser, U. (1976). *Cognition and reality.* San Francisco: Freeman.

Nesbit, J. C., & Adesope, O. O. (2006). Learning with concept and knowledge maps: A meta-analysis. *Review of Educational Research, 76*(3), 413–448.

Newman, B. M., & Newman, P. R. (2003). *Development through life: A psychosocial approach* (8th ed.). Belmont, CA: Wadsworth/Thomson Learning.

Nichols, S. L., & Berliner, D. C. (2005, March). *The inevitable corruption of indicators and educators through high-stakes testing* (EPSL-0503-101-EPRU). Retrieved November 1, 2005, from Arizona State University, Education Policy Studies Laboratory, Education Policy Research Unit Website: www.asu .edu/educ/epsl/EPRU/epru_2005_Research_ Writing.htm.

Nichols, S. L., Glass, G. V., & Berliner, D. C. (2006). High-stakes testing and student achievement: Does accountability pressure increase student learning? *Education Policy Analysis Archives, 14*(1). Retrieved September 12, 2006, from http://epaa .asu.edu/epaa/v14n1/.

Nickerson, R. S. (1994). The teaching of thinking and problem solving. In R. J. Sternberg (Ed.), *Thinking and problem solving.* San Diego, CA: Academic Press.

Nicol, M. P. (1997). How one physics teacher changed his algebraic thinking. *The Mathematics Teacher, 90*(2), 86–89.

Nieto, S. (2002/2003). Profoundly multicultural questions. *Educational Leadership, 60*(4), 6–10.

Nieto, S. (2004). *Affirming diversity: The sociopolitical context of multicultural education* (4th ed.). Boston: Allyn & Bacon.

Niguidula, D. (1997). Picturing performance with digital portfolios. *Educational Leadership, 55*(3), 26–29.

Nitko, A. J., & Brookhart, S. M. (2006). *Educational assessment of students* (5th ed.). Upper Saddle River, NJ: Merrill Prentice Hall.

*No Child Left Behind Act of 2001.* (2001, January). Retrieved September 7, 2006, from www.ed.gov/legislation/ESEA02/ 107-110.pdf.

Noddings, N. (2003). *Happiness and education.* Cambridge, England: Cambridge University Press.

Norman, D. A., & Rumelhart, D. E. (1970). A system for perception and memory. In D. A. Norman (Ed.), *Models of human memory.* New York: Academic Press.

Novak, J. D., & Gowin, D. B. (1984). *Learning how to learn.* Cambridge, England: Cambridge University Press.

Novak, J. D. (1998). *Learning, creating, and using knowledge: Concept maps as facilitative tools in schools and corporations.* Mahwah, NJ: Erlbaum.

Oakes, C. (1996). First grade online. *Learning and Leading with Technology, 24*(1), 37–39.

Oakes, J. (2005). *Keeping track* (2nd ed.). New Haven, CT: Yale University Press.

Oakes, J., & Wells, A. S. (1998). Detracking for high student achievement. *Educational Leadership, 55*(6), 38–41.

Obenchain, K. M., & Taylor, S. S. (2005). Behavior management: Making it work in middle and secondary schools. *The Clearing House, 79*(1), 7–11.

Ochse, R., & Plug, C. (1986). Cross-cultural investigation of the validity of Erikson's theory of personality development. *Journal of Personality and Social Psychology, 50*(6), 1240–1252.

O'Donnell, A. M., Dansereau, D. F., & Hall, R. H. (2002). Knowledge maps as scaffolds for cognitive processing. *Educational Psychology Review, 14*(1), 71–86.

Office of the Federal Register. (1994). *Code of Federal Regulations 34. Parts 300 to 399.* Washington, DC: Author.

Ogbu, J. U. (1992). Understanding cultural diversity and learning. *Educational Researcher, 21*(8), 5–14.

Ogbu, J. U. (2003). *Black American students in an affluent suburb.* Mahwah, NJ: Erlbaum.

Okagaki, L. (2001). Triarchic model of minority children's school achievement. *Educational Psychologist, 36*(1), 9–20.

Okagaki, L. (2006). Ethnicity and learning. In P. A. Alexander & P. H. Winne (Eds.), *Handbook of educational psychology* (2nd ed., pp. 615–634). Mahwah, NJ: Erlbaum.

O'Lone, D. J. (1997). Student information system software: Are you getting what you expected? *NASSP Bulletin, 81*(585), 86–93.

Olson, A. (2002). Technology solutions for testing. *The School Administrator, 59*(4), 20–23.

Olson, A. (2005). Improving schools one student at a time. *Educational Leadership, 62*(5), 37–40.

Olson, L. (2003a, June 18). All states get federal nod on key plans. *Education Week, 22*(41), 1, 20–21.

Olson, L. (2003b, May 8). Legal twists, digital turns. *Education Week, 22*(35), 11–16.

O'Neal, J. (2001). Y = mx+b really is found in real-life situations. *Ohio Journal of School Mathematics, 43*, 18–20.

Ormrod, J. E. (2004). *Human learning* (4th ed.). Upper Saddle River, NJ: Prentice Hall.

Ornstein, A. C., & Levine, D. U. (2006). *Foundations of education* (9th ed.). Boston: Houghton Mifflin.

Osgood, C. E. (1949). The similarity paradox in human learning: A resolution. *Psychological Review, 56*(3), 132–143.

Oshima, J., Scardamalia, M., & Bereiter, C. (1996). Collaborative learning processes associated with high and low conceptual progress. *Instructional Science, 24*(1), 125–155.

Osterman, K. F. (2000). Students' need for belonging in the school community. *Review of Educational Research, 70*(3), 323–367.

Owen, A. M., McMillan, K. M., Laird, A. R., & Bullmore, E. (2005). N-back working memory paradigm: A meta-analysis of normative functional neuroimaging studies. *Human Brain Mapping, 25*(1), 46–59.

Owens, R. F., Hester, J. L., & Teale, W. H. (2002). Where do you want to go today? Inquiry-based learning and technology integration. *Reading Teacher, 55*(7), 616–625.

Owings, W. A., & Kaplan, L. S. (2001). Standards, retention, and social promotion. *NASSP Bulletin, 85*(629), 57–66.

Paavola, S., Lipponen, L., & Hakkarainen, K. (2004). Three metaphors of learning: Models of innovative knowledge communities and three metaphors of learning. *Review of Educational Research, 74*(4), 557–576.

Padilla, A. M., & Gonzalez, R. (2001). Academic performance of immigrant and U.S.-born Mexican heritage students: Effects of schooling in Mexico and bilingual/English language instruction. *American Educational Research Journal, 38*(3), 727–742.

Page, E. B. (2003). Project essay grade: PEG. In M. D. Shermis & J. C. Burstein (Eds.), *Automated essay scoring* (pp. 43–54). Mahwah, NJ: Erlbaum.

Page, M. S. (2002). Technology-enriched classrooms: Effects on students of low socioeconomic status. *Journal of Research on Technology in Education, 34*(4), 389–409.

Palincsar, A., & Brown, A. L. (1984). Reciprocal teaching of comprehension-fostering and comprehension-monitoring activities. *Cognition and Instruction, 1*(2), 117–175.

Palmer, J. (2001). Conflict resolution: Strategies for the elementary classroom. *The Social Studies, 92*(2), 65–68.

Palmer, S. B., & Wehmeyer, M. L. (2003). Promoting self-determination in early elementary school: Teaching self-regulated problem-solving and goal-setting skills. *Remedial and Special Education, 24*(2), 115–126.

Panchaud, C., Singh, S., Feivelson, D., & Darroch, J. E. (2000). Sexually transmitted diseases among adolescents in developed countries. *Family Planning Perspectives, 32*(1), 24–32, 45. Retrieved January 2, 2002, from www.agi-usa.org/pubs/journals/ 3202400.html.

Paris, S. G., & Paris, A. H. (2001). Classroom applications of research on self-regulated learning. *Educational Psychologist, 36*(2), 89–101.

Parke, C. S., & Lane, S. (1997). Learning from performance assessments in math. *Educational Leadership, 54*(6), 26–29.

Parsad, B., & Jones, J. (2005). Internet access in U.S. public schools and classrooms: 1994–2003. *Education Statistics Quarterly, 7*(1 & 2). Retrieved July 23, 2006, from http://nces.ed.gov/programs/quarterly/ vol_7/1_2/4_3.asp.

Parten, M. B. (1932). Social participation among preschool children. *Journal of Abnormal and Social Psychology, 27*(3), 243–269.

Patterson, B. (2002). Creating two-point perspective on the computer. *Arts & Activities, 131*(4), 52.

Patterson, G. R., DeBaryshe, B. D., & Ramsey, E. (1989). A developmental perspective on antisocial behavior. *American Psychologist, 44*(2), 329–335.

Pea, R. D. (1985). Beyond amplification: Using the computer to reorganize mental functioning. *Educational Psychologist, 21*(4), 167–182.

Pea, R. D. (2004). The social and technological dimensions of scaffolding and related theoretical concepts for learning, education, and activity. *Journal of Learning Sciences, 13*(3), 423–451.

Pedersen, S., & Liu, M. (2002). The effects of modeling expert cognitive strategies during problem-based learning. *Journal of Educational Computing Research, 26*(4), 353–380.

Pedersen, S., & Liu, M. (2002/2003). The transfer of problem-solving skills from a problem-based learning environment: The effect of modeling an expert's cognitive processes. *Journal of Research on Technology in Education, 35*(2), 303–320.

Pedulla, J. J., Abrams, L. M., Madaus, G. F., Russell, M. K., Ramos, M. A., & Miao, J. (2003, March). *Perceived effects of state-mandated testing programs on teaching and learning: Findings from a national survey of teachers.* Boston, MA: Boston College, National Board on Educational Testing and Public Policy.

Pellegrini, A. D., & Bjorklund, D. F. (1997). The role of recess in children's cognitive performance. *Educational Psychologist, 32*(1), 35–40.

Pellegrini, A. D., & Bohn, C. M. (2005). The role of recess in children's cognitive performance and school adjustment. *Educational Researcher, 34*(1), 13–19.

Peltier, G. L. (1991). Why do secondary schools continue to track students? *The Clearing House, 64*(4), 246–247.

Pelletier, L. G., Séguin-Lévesque, C., & Legault, L. (2002). Pressure from above and pressure from below as determinants of teachers' motivation and teaching behaviors. *Journal of Educational Psychology 94*(1), 186–196.

Peña, C. M., & Alessi, S. M. (1999). Promoting a qualitative understanding of physics. *Journal of Computers in Mathematics and Science Teaching, 18*(4), 439–457.

Penfield, W. (1969). Consciousness, memory, and man's conditioned reflexes. In K. Pribram (Ed.), *On the biology of learning.* New York: Harcourt Brace Jovanovich.

Pérez, B. (2004). *Becoming biliterate: A study of two-way bilingual immersion education.* Mahwah, NJ: Erlbaum.

Perie, M., Moran, R., & Lutkus, A. D. (2005). NAEP trends in academic progress: Three decades of student performance in reading and mathematics (NCES No. 2005-464). Washington, DC: Government Printing Office. Retrieved 9/20/05 from National Center for Education Statistics website: nces.ed.gov/pubsearch/bubsinfo.aasp?pubid=2005464.

Perkins, D. (1999). The many faces of constructivism. *Educational Leadership, 57*(3), 6–11.

Perkins, D., Tishman, S., Ritchhart, R., Donis, K., & Andrade, A. (2000). Intelligence in the wild: A dispositional view of intellectual traits. *Educational Psychology Review, 12*(3), 269–293.

Perkins, D. F., & Hartless, G. (2002). An ecological risk-factor examination of suicide ideation and behavior of adolescents. *Journal of Adolescent Research, 17*(1), 3–26.

Perry, N. E., VandeKamp, K. O., Mercer, L. K., & Nordby, C. J. (2002). Investigating teacher-student interactions that foster self-regulated learning. *Educational Psychologist, 37*(1), 5–15.

Peters, G. D. (2001). Transformations: Technology and the music industry. *Teaching Music, 9*(3), 20–25.

Peterson, A. C. (1988). Adolescent development. In M. R. Rosenzweig & L. W. Porter (Eds.), *Annual review of psychology* (Vol. 39, pp. 583–607). Palo Alto, CA: Annual Reviews.

Peterson, A. C., Compas, B. E., Brooks-Gunn, J., Stemmler, M., Ey, S., & Grant, K. E. (1993). Depression in adolescence. *American Psychologist, 48*(2), 155–168.

Peverly, S. T., Brobst, K. E., Graham, M., & Shaw, R. (2003). College adults are not good at self-regulation: A study on the relationship of self-regulation, note taking, and test taking. *Journal of Educational Psychology, 95*(2), 335–346.

Pewewardy, C. (2002). Learning styles of American Indian/Alaska Native students: A review of the literature and implications for practice. *Journal of American Indian Education, 41*(3), 22–56.

Piaget, J. (1932). *The moral judgement of the child* (M. Gabain, Trans.). New York: Harcourt Brace.

Piaget, J. (1965). *The moral judgment of the child* (M. Gabain, Trans.). Glencoe, IL: Free Press. (Original work published 1932.)

Piaget, J., & Inhelder, B. (1956). *The child's conception of space.* London: Routledge & Kegan Paul.

Piechowski, M. M. (1997). Emotional giftedness: The measure of intrapersonal intelligence. In N. Colangelo & G. A. Davis (Eds.), *Handbook of gifted education* (2nd ed.). Boston: Allyn & Bacon.

Pintrich, P. R., & De Groot, E. V. (1990). Motivational and self-regulated learning components of classroom academic performance. *Journal of Educational Psychology, 82*(1), 33–40.

Pintrich, P. R., & Schunk, D. H. (2002). *Motivation in education: Theory, research, and applications* (2nd ed.). Upper Saddle River, NJ: Merrill Prentice Hall.

Pleydon, A. P., & Schner, J. G. (2001). Female adolescent friendships and delinquent behavior. *Adolescence, 36*(142), 189–205.

Podoll, S., & Randle, D. (2005). Building a virtual high school . . . click by click. *T.H.E. Journal, 33*(2), 14–19.

Pogrow, S. (1990). A Socratic approach to using computers with at-risk students. *Educational Leadership, 47*(5), 61–66.

Pogrow, S. (1999). Systematically using powerful learning environments to accelerate the learning of disadvantaged students in grades 4–8. In C. M. Reigeluth (Ed.), *Instructional design theories and models: Vol. II. A new paradigm of instructional theory.* Mahwah, NJ: Erlbaum.

Pogrow, S. (2005). HOTS revisited: A thinking development approach to reducing the learning gap after grade 3. *Phi Delta Kappan, 87*(1), 64–75.

Polya, G. (1957). *How to solve it* (2nd ed.). Princeton, NJ: Princeton University Press.

Pomerantz, E. M. (2002). Making the grade but feeling distressed: Gender differences in academic performance and internal distress. *Journal of Educational Psychology, 94*(2), 396–404.

Pope, M., Hare, D., & Howard, E. (2002). Technology integration: Closing the gap between what preservice teachers are taught to do and what they can do. *Journal of Technology and Teacher Education, 10*(2), 191–203.

Popham, W. J. (2003). *What every teacher should know about educational assessment.* Boston: Allyn & Bacon.

Popham, W. J. (2004, May 26). Shaping up the "No Child" act: Is edge-softening really enough? *Education Week, 23*(38), 40.

Popham, W. J. (2005). How to make use of PAP to make AYP under NCLB. *Phi Delta Kappan, 86*(10). 787–791.

Popham, W. J. (2006). *Assessment for educational leaders.* Boston: Allyn & Bacon.

Porter, R. P. (2000). The benefits of English immersion. *Educational Leadership, 57*(4), 52–56.

Portes, P., Dunham, R., & Del Castillo, K. (2000). Identity formation and status across cultures: Exploring the cultural validity of Erikson's theory. In A. L. Comunian & U. Gielen (Eds.), *International perspectives on human development* (pp. 449–459). Lengerich, Germany: Pabst Science Publishers.

Premack, D. (1959). Toward empirical behavior laws: 1. Positive reinforcement. *Psychological Review, 66*(4), 219–233.

Pressley, M., Gaskins, I. W., Solic, K., & Collins, S. (2006). A portrait of benchmark school: How a school produces high achievement in students who previously failed. *Journal of Educational Psychology, 98*(2), 282–306.

Pressley, M., Woloshyn, V., & Associates. (1995). Cognitive strategy instruction that really improves children's strategy instruction (2nd ed.). Cambridge, MA: Brookline Books.

Pretz, J. E., Naples, A. J., & Sternberg, R. J. (2003). Recognizing, defining, and representing problems. In J. E. Davidson & R. J. Sternberg (Eds.), *The psychology of problem solving* (pp. 3–30). Cambridge, England: Cambridge University Press.

Protheroe, N. (2002). Improving instruction through teacher observation. *Principal, 82*(1), 48–51.

Pugh, K. J., & Bergin, D. (2005). The effect of schooling on students' out-of-school experience. *Educational Researcher, 34*(9), 15–23.

Purdie, N., & Hattie, J. (1996). Cultural differences in the use of strategies for self-regulated learning. *American Educational Research Journal, 33*(4), 845–871.

Purdie, N., Hattie, J., & Carroll, A. (2002). A review of the research on interventions for attention deficit hyperactivity disorder: What works best? *Review of Educational Research, 72*(1), 61–99.

Purkey, W. W., & Strahan, D. B. (2002). *Inviting positive classroom discipline.* Westerville, OH: National Middle School Association.

Qin, Z., Johnson, D. W., & Johnson, R. T. (1995). Cooperative versus competitive efforts and problem solving. *Review of Educational Research, 65*(2), 129–143.

Quenneville, J. (2001). Tech tools for students with learning disabilities: Infusion into inclusive classrooms. *Preventing School Failure, 45*(4), 167–170.

Quihuis, G., Bempechat, J., Jiminez, N. V., & Boulay, B. A. (2002). Implicit theories of intelligence across domains: A study of meaning making in adolescents of Mexican descent. In J. Bempechat & J. G. Elliott (Eds.), *New directions for child and adolescent development, no. 96. Learning in culture and context: Approaching the complexities of achievement motivation in student learning* (pp. 87–100). San Francisco: Jossey-Bass.

Rabow, J., Charness, M. A., Kipperman, J., & Radcliffe-Vasile, S. (1994). *William Fawcett Hill's learning through discussion* (3rd ed.). Thousand Oaks, CA: Sage.

Raison, J., Hanson, L. A., Hall, C., & Reynolds, M. C. (1995). Another school's reality. *Phi Delta Kappan, 76*(6), 480–482.

Rakes, G. C., Fields, V. S., & Cox, K. E. (2006). The influence of teachers' technology use on instructional practices. *Journal of Research on Technology in Education, 38*(4), 409–424.

Ramirez, A., & Carpenter, D. (2005). Challenging assumptions about the achievement gap. *Phi Delta Kappan, 86*(8), 599–603.

Ramirez-Valles, J., Zimmerman, M. A., & Juarez, L. (2002). Gender differences of neighborhood and social control processes: A study of the timing of first intercourse among low-achieveing, urban, African American youth. *Youth & Society, 33*(3), 418–441.

Randi, J., & Corno, L. (2000). Teacher innovations in self-regulated learning. In M. Boekaerts, P. R. Pintrich, & M. Zeidner (Eds.), *Handbook of self-regulation* (pp. 651–685). San Diego: Academic Press.

Rathunde, K., & Csikszentmihalyi, M. (2005). Middle school students' motivation and quality of experience: A comparison of Montessori and traditional school environments. *American Journal of Education, 111*(3), 341–371.

Ratner, C. (1991). *Vygotsky's sociohistorical psychology and its contemporary applications.* New York: Plenum Press.

Raudenbush, S. W. (1984). Magnitude of teacher expectancy effects on pupil IQ as a function of the credibility of expectancy induction: A synthesis of findings from 18 experiments. *Journal of Educational Psychology, 76*(1), 85–97.

Raudenbush, S. W., Rowan, B., & Cheong, Y. F. (1993). Higher order instructional goals in secondary schools: Class, teacher, and school influences. *American Educational Research Journal, 30*(3), 523–553.

Raugh, M. R., & Atkinson, R. C. (1975). A mnemonic method for learning a second-language vocabulary. *Journal of Educational Psychology, 67*(1), 1–16.

Ravaglia, R., Alper, T., Rozenfeld, M., & Suppes, P. (1998). Successful pedagogical applications of symbolic computation. In N. Kajler (Ed.), *Computer-human interaction in symbolic computation* (pp. 61–88). New York: Springer-Verlag.

Ravaglia, R., Sommer, R., Sanders, M., Oas, G., & DeLeone, C. (1999). Computer-based mathematics and physics for gifted remote students. *Proceedings of the International Conference on Mathematics/Science Education and Technology* (pp. 405–410). Retrieved January 15, 2004, from www.epgy-stanford.edu/research/index .html?papers.

Rawsthorne, L. J., & Elliot, A. J. (1999). Achievement goals and intrinsic motivation: A meta-analytic review. *Personality and Social Psychology Review, 3*(4), 326–344.

Rea, A. (2001). Telementoring: An A+ initiative. *Education Canada, 40*(4), 28–29.

Redl, F., & Wattenberg, W. W. (1959). *Mental hygiene in teaching* (2nd ed.). New York: Harcourt Brace Jovanovich.

Reed, S. K. (2006). Cognitive architectures for multimedia learning. *Educational Psychologist, 41*(2), 87–98.

Reeve, J., & Jang, H. (2006). What teachers say and do to support students' autonomy during a learning activity. *Journal of Educational Psychology, 98*(1), 209–218.

Reid, C., Romanoff, B., & Algozzine, R. (2000). An evaluation of alternative screening procedures. *Journal for the Education of the Gifted, 23*(4), 378–396.

Reis, S. M., & Renzulli, J. S. (1985). *The secondary triad model.* Mansfield Center, CT: Creative Learning Press.

Reninger, R. D. (2000). Music education in a digital world. *Teaching Music, 8*(1), 24–31.

Renninger, K. A., & Hidi, S. (2002). Student interest and achievement: Developmental issues raised by a case study. In A. Wigfield & J. S. Eccles (Eds.), *Development of achievement motivation* (pp. 173–195). San Diego, CA: Academic Press.

Renzulli, J. S. (2002). Expanding the conception of giftedness to include co-cognitive traits and promote social capital. *Phi Delta Kappan, 84*(1), 33–40, 57–58.

Renzulli, J. S., Gentry, M., & Reis, S. M. (2003). *Enrichment clusters: A practical plan for real-world, student-driven learning.* Mansfield Center, CT: Creative Learning Press.

Renzulli, J. S., & Reis, S. M. (1985). *The schoolwide enrichment model.* Mansfield Center, CT: Creative Learning Press.

Resnick, L. B. (1987). Learning in school and out. *Educational Researcher, 16*(9), 13–20.

Rest, J., Narvaez, D., Bebeau, M. J., & Thoma, S. J. (1999). *Postconventional moral thinking: A neo-Kohlbergian approach.* Mahwah, NJ: Erlbaum.

Reynolds, T. H., & Bonk, C. J. (1996). Creating computerized writing partner and keystroke recording tools with macro-driven prompts. *Educational Technology Research and Development, 44*(3), 83–97.

Ricci, C. M., & Beal, C. R. (2002). The effect of interactive media on children's story memory. *Journal of Educational Psychology, 94*(1), 138–144.

Rice, K. L. (2006). A comprehensive look at distance education in the K-12 context. *Journal of Research on Technology in Education, 38*(4), 425–448.

Richard, A. (2005, December 7). Supplemental help can be hard to find for rural students. *Education Week, 25*(14), 1, 22.

Ridgeway, V. G., Peters, C. L., & Tracy, T. S. (2002). Out of this world: Cyberspace, literacy, and learning. In C. C. Block, L. B. Gambrell, & M. Pressley (Eds.), *Improving comprehension instruction: Rethinking research, theory, and classroom practice.* San Francisco: Jossey-Bass.

Riel, M. (1993). Global education through learning circles. In L. Harasim (Ed.), *Global networks* (pp. 221–236). Cambridge, MA: MIT Press.

Riel, M. (1996). Cross-classroom collaboration: Communication and education. In T. Koschmann (Ed.), *CSCL: Theory and practice* (pp. 187–207). Mahwah, NJ: Erlbaum.

Riel, M., & Fulton, K. (2001). The role of technology in supporting learning communities. *Phi Delta Kappan, 82*(7), 518–523.

Robertson, A. (2001, Sept./Oct.). CASE is when we learn to think. *Primary Science Review, 69*, 20–22.

Robertson, J. S. (2000). Is attribution training a worthwhile classroom intervention for K-12 students with learning difficulties? *Educational Psychology Review, 12*(1), 111–134.

Robledo, M. M., & Cortez, J. D. (2002). Successful bilingual education programs: Development and dissemination of criteria to identify promising and exemplary practices in bilingual education at the national level. *Bilingual Research Journal, 26*(1), 1–21.

Roblyer, M. D. (2006). Virtually successful: Defeating the dropout problem through online school programs. *Phi Delta Kappan, 88*(1), 31–36.

Roderick, M., & Engel, M. (2001). The grasshopper and the ant: Motivational responses of low-achieving students to high-stakes testing. *Educational Evaluation and Policy Analysis, 23*(3), 197–227.

Rodney, L. W., Crafter, B., Rodney, H. E., & Mupier, R. M. (1999). Variables contributing to grade retention among African American adolescent males. *Journal of Educational Research, 92*(3), 185–190.

Roerden, L. (2001). The Resolving Conflict Creatively Program. *Reclaiming Children and Youth, 10*(1), 24–28.

Roeser, R. W., & Lau, S. (2002). On academic identity formation in middle school settings during early adolescence: A motivational contextual perspective. In T. M. Brinthaupt & R. P. Lipka (Eds.), *Understanding early adolescent self and identity: Applications and interventions* (pp. 91–131). Albany: State University of New York Press.

Rogers, C. R. (1967). Learning to be free. In C. R. Rogers & B. Stevens (Eds.), *The problem of being human*. Lafayette, CA: Real People Press.

Rogers, C. R. (1980). *A way of being*. Boston: Houghton Mifflin.

Rogers, C. R. (1983). *Freedom to learn for the 80's*. Columbus, OH: Merrill.

Rogoff, B. (1990). *Apprenticeship in thinking: Cognitive development in social context*. New York: Oxford University Press.

Rogoff, B., & Chavajay, P. (1995). What's become of research on the cultural basis of cognitive development? *American Psychologist, 50*(10), 859–877.

Rohrbeck, C. A., Ginsburg-Block, M. D., Fantuzzo, J. W., & Miller, T. R. (2003). Peer-assisted learning interventions with elementary school students: A meta-analytic review. *Journal of Educational Psychology, 95*(2), 240–257.

Roller, C. M. (2002). Accommodating variability in reading instruction. *Reading & Writing Quarterly, 18*(1), 17–38.

Rolón, C. A. (2002/2003). Educating Latino students. *Educational Leadership, 60*(4), 40–43.

Romance, N. R., & Vitale, M. R. (1999). Concept mapping as a tool for learning: Broadening the framework for student-centered instruction. *College Teaching, 47*(2), 74–79.

Rop, C. (1998). Breaking the gender barrier in the physical sciences. *Educational Leadership, 55*(4), 58–60.

Roschelle, J. (1996). Computer support for knowledge-building communities. In T. Koschmann (Ed.), *CSCL: Theory and practice* (pp. 209–248). Mahwah, NJ: Erlbaum.

Rosenshine, B., & Meister, C. (1994a). Reciprocal teaching: A review of the research. *Review of Educational Research, 64*(4), 479–530.

Rosenshine, B. V., & Meister, C. (1994b). Direct Instruction. In T. Husen & T. N. Postlewhaite (Eds.), *International encyclopedia of education* (2nd ed., Vol. 3, pp. 1524–1530). New York: Pergamon.

Rosenshine, B., Meister, C., & Chapman, S. (1996). Teaching students to generate questions: A review of the intervention studies. *Review of Educational Research, 66*(2), 181–221.

Rosenshine, B. V. (1987). Explicit teaching. In D. C. Berliner & B. V. Rosenshine (Eds.), *Talks to teachers* (pp. 75–92.). New York: Random House.

Rosenthal, R. (1985). From unconscious experimenter bias to teacher expectancy effects. In J. B. Dusek (Ed.), *Teacher expectations*. Hillsdale, NJ: Erlbaum.

Rosenthal, R. (2002). The Pygmalion effect and its mediating mechanisms. In J. Aronson (Ed.), *Improving academic achievement* (pp. 26–36). San Diego: Academic Press.

Rosenthal, R., & Jacobson, L. (1968). *Pygmalion in the classroom*. New York: Holt, Rinehart, & Winston.

Roskos, K., Boehlen, S., & Walker, B. J. (2000). Learning the art of instructional conversations: The influence of self-assessment on teachers' instructional discourse in a reading clinic. *The Elementary School Journal, 100*(3), 229–252.

Ross, D. D., Bondy, E., & Kyle, D. W. (1993). *Reflective teaching for student empowerment*. New York: Macmillan.

Ross, H. S., & Spielmacher, C. E. (2005). Social development. In B. Hopkins, R. G. Barr, G. F. Michel, & P. Rochat (Eds.), *The Cambridge encyclopedia of child development* (pp. 227–233). Cambridge, UK: Cambridge University Press.

Rothstein, R. (1998). Bilingual education: The controversy. *Phi Delta Kappan, 79*(9), 672–678.

Rothstein, R. (2004). A wider lens on the black-white achievement gap. *Phi Delta Kappan, 86*(2), 104–110.

Rothstein-Fisch, C., Greenfield, P. M., & Trumbull, E. (1999). Bridging cultures with classroom strategies. *Educational Leadership, 56*(7), 64–67.

Rowan, B. (1994). Comparing teachers' work with work in other occupations: Notes on the professional status of teaching. *Educational Researcher, 23*(6), 4–17.

Rowe, S. M., & Wertsch, J. V. (2002). Vygotsky's model of cognitive development. In U. Goswami (Ed.), *Blackwell handbook of childhood cognitive development* (pp. 538–554). Oxford, England: Blackwell.

Royer, J. M. (1979). Theories of the transfer of learning. *Educational Psychologist, 14*, 53–72.

Royer, J. M., & Cable, G. W. (1975). Facilitated learning in connected discourse. *Journal of Educational Psychology, 67*(1), 116–123.

Royer, J. M., & Cable, G. W. (1976). Illustrations, analogies, and facilitative transfer in prose learning. *Journal of Educational Psychology, 68*(2), 205–209.

Royer, J. M., Tronsky, L. N., Chan, Y., Jackson, S. J., & Marchant, H., III. (1999). Math-fact retrieval as the cognitive mechanism underlying gender differences in math test performance. *Contemporary Educational Psychology, 24*(3), 181–266.

Rubado, K. (2002). Empowering students through multiple intelligences. *Reclaiming Children and Youth, 10*(4), 233–235.

Rubin, B. C. (2006). Tracking and detracking: Debates, evidence, and best practices for a heterogeneous world. *Theory into Practice, 45*(1), 4–14.

Rubin, K. H., Maioni, T. L., & Hornung, M. (1976). Free play behavior in middle- and lower-class preschoolers: Parten and Piaget revisited. *Child Development, 47*(2), 414–419.

Rubin, L. J. (1985). *Artistry in teaching*. New York: Random House.

Ruder, S. (2000). We teach all. *Educational Leadership, 58*(1), 49–51.

Ruggiero, V. R. (1988). *Teaching thinking across the curriculum*. New York: Harper & Row.

Ruggiero, V. R. (2007). *The art of thinking: A guide to critical and creative thought* (8th ed.). New York: Pearson/Longman.

Ruhland, S. K., & Bremer, C. D. (2002). Professional development needs of novice career and technical educational teachers. *Journal of Career and Technical Education, 19*(1), 18–31.

Rummel, N., Levin, J. R., & Woodward, M. M. (2003). Do pictorial mnemonic text-learning aids give students something worth writing about? *Journal of Educational Psychology, 95*(2), 327–334.

Ruopp, R., Gal, S., Drayton, B., & Pfister, M. (Eds.). (1993). *LabNet: Toward a community of practice*. Hillsdale, NJ: Erlbaum.

Russo, A. (2002). Mixing technology and testing. *The School Administrator, 59*(4), 6–12.

Rutledge, M. (1997). Reading the subtext on gender. *Educational Leadership, 54*(7), 71–73.

Ryan, A. M., & Patrick, H. (2001). The classroom social environment and changes in adolescents' motivation and engagement during middle school. *American Educational Research Journal, 38*(2), 437–460.

Rycek, R. F., Stuhr, S. L., & McDermott, J. (1998). Adolescent egocentrism and cognitive functioning during late adolescence. *Adolescence, 33*(132), 745–749.

Saban, A. (2002). Toward a more intelligent school. *Educational Leadership, 60*(2), 71–73.

Sadker, D., & Zittleman, K. (2004). Test anxiety: Are students failing tests—or are tests failing students? *Phi Delta Kappan, 85*(10), 740–744, 751.

Sadker, M. P., & Sadker, D. M. (1994). *Failing at fairness: How America's schools cheat girls.* New York: Charles Scribner's Sons.

Sadker, M. P., & Sadker, D. M. (2005). *Teachers, schools, and society* (7th ed.). Boston: McGraw-Hill.

Sadoski, M., Goetz, E. T., & Rodriguez, M. (2000). Engaging texts: Effects of concreteness on comprehensibility, interest, and recall in four text types. *Journal of Educational Psychology, 92*(1), 85–95.

Saleh, M., Lazonder, A. W., & De Jong, T. (2004). Effects of within-class ability grouping on social interaction, achievement, and motivation. *Instructional Science, 33*(2), 105–199.

Salmon, M., & Akaran, S. E. (2001). Enrich your kindergarten program with a cross-cultural connection. *Young Children, 56*(4), 30–32.

Salomon, G. (1988). AI in reverse: Computer tools that turn cognitive. *Journal of Educational Computing Research, 4*(2), 123–139.

Salomon, G., Globerson, T., & Guterman, E. (1989). The computer as a zone of proximal development: Internalizing reading-related metacognitions from a reading partner. *Journal of Educational Psychology, 81*(4), 620–627.

Salomon, G., & Perkins, D. N. (1989). Rocky roads to transfer: Rethinking mechanisms of a neglected phenomenon. *Educational Psychologist, 24*(2), 113–142.

Saltzman, J. (2003, July 20). Reinstating two-way bilingual ed is hailed. *The Boston Globe* (Globe West section), p. 1

Sameroff, A., & McDonough, S. C. (1994). Educational implications of developmental transitions: Revisiting the 5- to 7-year shift. *Phi Delta Kappan, 76*(3), 189–193.

Sapon-Shevin, M. (1996). Full inclusion as disclosing tablet: Revealing the flaws in our present system. *Theory into Practice, 35*(1), 35–41.

Sapon-Shevin, M. (2003). Inclusion: A matter of social justice. *Educational Leadership, 61*(2), 25–28.

Saracho, O. N. (2001). Cognitive style and kindergarten pupils' preferences for teachers. *Learning and Instruction, 11*(3), 195–209.

Sarason, S. B. (1993). *The case for change: Rethinking the preparation of educators.* San Francisco: Jossey-Bass.

Sarason, S. B. (2005). *Letters to a serious education president* (2nd ed.). Thousand Oaks, CA: Corwin Press.

Scales, P. (1993). How teachers and education deans rate the quality of teacher preparation for the middle grades. *Journal of Teacher Education, 44*(5), 378–383.

Scardamalia, M., & Bereiter, C. (1991). Higher levels of agency for children in knowledge building: A challenge for the design of new knowledge media. *Journal of the Learning Sciences, 1*(1), 37–68.

Scardamalia, M. & Bereiter, C. (1996). Computer support for knowledge-building communities. In T. Koschmann (Ed.), *CSCL: Theory and practice* (pp. 249–268). Mahwah, NJ: Erlbaum.

Scarr, S., Weinberg, R. A., & Levine, A. (1986). *Understanding development.* San Diego, CA: Harcourt Brace Jovanovich.

Schellenberg, E. G. (2006a). Long-term positive associations between music and IQ. *Journal of Educational Psychology, 98*(2), 457–468.

Schellenberg, E. G. (2006b). Exposure to music: The truth about the consequences. In G. E. McPherson (Ed.), *The child as musician: The handbook of musical development.* Oxford, England: Oxford University Press.

Schery, T., & O'Connor, L. (1997). Language intervention: Computer training for young children with special needs. *British Journal of Educational Technology, 28*(4), 271–279.

Schifter, D. (1996). A constructivist perspective on teaching and learning mathematics. *Phi Delta Kappan, 77*(7), 492–499.

Schlaefli, A., Rest, J. R., & Thoma, S. J. (1985). Does moral education improve moral judgment? A meta-analysis of intervention studies using the Defining Issues Test. *Review of Educational Research, 55*(3), 319–352.

Schlagmüller, M., & Schneider, W. (2002). The development of organizational strategies in children: Evidence from a microgenetic longitudinal study. *Journal of Experimental Child Psychology, 81*(3), 298–319.

Schmidt, L. (2003). Getting smarter about supervising instruction. *Principal, 82*(4), 24–28.

Schmidt, P. (2003, November 28). The label "Hispanic" irks some, but also unites. *Chronicle of Higher Education, 50*(14), A9.

Schneider, W. (2002). Memory development in childhood. In U. Goswami (Ed.), *Blackwell handbook of childhood cognitive development* (pp. 236–256). Malden, MA: Blackwell.

Schneider, W., & Bjorklund, D. F. (1998). Memory. In W. Damon, D. Kuhn, & R. S. Siegler (Eds.), *Handbook of child psychology: Cognition, perception, and language* (Vol. 2, pp. 467–521). New York: Wiley.

Schneider, W., Knopf, M., & Stefanek, J. (2002). The development of verbal memory in childhood and adolescence: Findings from the Munich longitudinal study. *Journal of Educational Psychology, 94*(4), 751–761.

Schraw, G., Flowerday, T., & Lehman, S. (2001). Increasing situational interest in the classroom. *Educational Psychology Review, 13*(3), 211–224.

Schraw, G., & Lehman, S. (2001). Situational interest: A review of the literature and directions for future research. *Educational Psychology Review, 13*(1), 23–52.

Schunk, D. H. (1987). Peer models and children's behavioral change. *Review of Educational Research, 57*(2), 149–174.

Schunk, D. H. (1996). Goal and self-evaluative influences during children's cognitive skill learning. *American Educational Research Journal, 33*(2), 359–382.

Schunk, D. H. (1998). Teaching elementary students to self-regulate practice of mathematical skills with modeling. In D. H. Schunk & B. J. Zimmerman (Eds.), *Self-regulated learning: From teaching to self-reflective practice* (pp. 137–159). New York: Guilford Press.

Schunk, D. H. (2001). Social cognitive theory and self-regulated learning. In B. J. Zimmerman & D. H. Schunk (Eds.), *Self-regulated learning and academic achievement: Theoretical perspectives* (pp. 125–151). Mahwah, NJ: Erlbaum.

Schunk, D. H. (2004). *Learning theories: An educational perspective* (4th ed.). Upper Saddle River, NJ: Merrill Prentice Hall.

Schunk, D. H., & Hanson, A. R. (1985). Peer models: Influence on children's self-efficacy and achievement. *Journal of Educational Psychology, 77*(3), 313–322.

Schunk, D. H., & Hanson, A. R. (1989). Self-modeling and children's cognitive skill learning. *Journal of Educational Psychology, 81*(2), 155–163.

Schunk, D. H., Hanson, A. R., & Cox, P. D. (1987). Peer model attributes and children's achievement behaviors. *Journal of Educational Psychology, 79*(1), 54–61.

Schunk, D. H., & Miller, S. D. (2002). Self-efficacy and adolescents' motivation. In F. Pajares & T. Urdan (Eds.), *Academic motivation of adolescents* (pp. 29–52). Greenwich, CT: Information Age Publishing.

Schunk, D. H., & Pajares, F. (2002). The development of academic self-efficacy. In A. Wigfield & J. Eccles (Eds.), *The development of achievement motivation* (pp. 16–31). San Diego, CA: Academic Press.

Schunk, D. H., & Zimmerman, B. J. (1997). Social origins of self-regulatory competence. *Educational Psychologist, 32*(4), 195–208.

Schuster, E. H. (2004). National and state writing tests: The writing process betrayed. *Phi Delta Kappan, 85*(5), 375–378.

Schvaneveldt, P. L., Miller, B. C., Berry, E. H., & Lee, T. R. (2001). Academic goals, achievement, and age at first sexual intercourse: Longitudinal, bidirectional influences. *Adolescence, 36*(144), 767–787.

Schwartz, D., Gorman, A. H., Nakamoto, J., & Toblin, R. L. (2005). Victimization in the peer group and children's academic functioning. *Journal of Educational Psychology, 97*(3), 425–435.

Schweinhart, L. J., Weikart, D. P., & Hohmann, M. (2002). The High/Scope preschool curriculum: What is it? Why use it? *Journal of At-Risk Issues, 8*(1), 13–16.

Seagoe, M. V. (1970). *The learning process and school practice.* Scranton, PA: Chandler.

Seagoe, M. V. (1975). *Terman and the gifted.* Los Altos, CA: Kaufmann.

Searleman, A., & Herrmann, D. (1994). *Memory from a broader perspective.* New York: McGraw-Hill.

Secules, T., Cottom, C., Bray, M., & Miller, L. (1997). Creating schools for thought. *Educational Leadership, 54*(6), 56–60.

Seddon, F. A., & O'Neill, S. A. (2006). How does formal instrumental music tuition (FIMT) impact on self- and teacher-evaluations of adolescents, computer-based compositions? *Psychology of Music, 34*(1), 27–45.

Seligman, M. E. P. (1975). *Helplessness: On depression, development, and death.* San Francisco: Freeman.

Selman, R. L. (1980). *The growth of interpersonal understanding: Developmental and clinical analyses.* New York: Academic Press.

Selmes, I. (1987). *Improving study skills.* London: Hodder & Stoughton.

Semb, G. B., & Ellis, J. A. (1994). Knowledge taught in school: What is remembered? *Review of Educational Research, 64*(2), 253–286.

Setzer, J. C., & Lewis, L. (2005, March). *Distance education courses for public elementary and secondary school students: 2002-03* (NCES 2005-010). Washington, DC: U.S. Department of Education, National Center for Education Statistics. Retrieved September 12, 2006, from www.nces.ed.gov/pubsearch/pubsinfo.asp?pubid=2005010.

Shachar, H., & Fischer, S. (2004). Cooperative learning and the achievement of motivation and perceptions of students in 11th grade chemistry classrooms. *Learning and Instruction, 14*(1), 69–87.

Shapiro, A. (2002). The latest dope on research (about constructivism): Part I. Different approaches to constructivism—what it's all about. *International Journal of Educational Reform, 11*(4), 347–361.

Shapiro, A. (2003). The latest dope on research (about constructivism): Part II. On instruction and leadership. *International Journal of Educational Reform, 12*(1), 62–77.

Sharan, S. (1995). Group investigation: Theoretical foundations. In J. E. Pedersen & A. D. Digby (Eds.), *Secondary schools and cooperative learning* (pp. 251–277). New York: Garland.

Sharan, Y., & Sharan, S. (1999). Group investigation in the cooperative classroom. In S. Sharan (Ed.), *Handbook of cooperative learning methods* (pp. 97–114). Westport, CT: Greenwood Press.

Shavelson, R. J., & Baxter, G. P. (1992). What we've learned about assessing hands-on science. *Educational Leadership, 49*(8), 20–25.

Shayer, M. (1997). Piaget and Vygotsky: A necessary marriage for effective educational interventions. In L. Smith, J. Dockrell, & P. Tomlinson (Eds.), *Piaget, Vygotsky, and beyond.* London: Routledge.

Shayer, M. (1999). Cognitive acceleration through science education: II. Its effects and scope. *International Journal of Science Education, 21*(8), 883–902.

Shepard, R. N. (1978). Externalization of mental images and the act of creation. In B. S. Randhawa & W. E. Coffman (Eds.), *Visual learning, thinking, and communication.* New York: Academic Press.

Shernoff, D. J., Csikszentmihalyi, M., Schneider, B., & Shernoff, E. S. (2003). Student engagement in high school classrooms from the perspective of flow theory. *School Psychology Quarterly, 18*(2), 158–176.

Sherry, L., & Billig, S. H. (2002). Redefining a "virtual community of learners." *TechTrends, 46*(1), 48–51.

Sherwood, R. D., Petrosino, A. J., Lin, X., & Cognition and Technology Group at Vanderbilt. (1998). Problem-based macro contexts in science instruction: Design issues and applications. In B. J. Fraser & K. G. Tobin (Eds.), *International handbook of science education: Part I* (pp. 349–362). Dordrecht, Netherlands: Kluwer.

Shrader, G., Lento, E., Gomez, L., & Pea, R. (1997). *Inventing interventions: Cases from CoVis–An analysis by SES.* Paper presented at the annual meeting of the American Educational Research Association, Chicago, IL. (ERIC Document Reproduction Service No. ED 412 115).

Shure, M. B. (1999, April). Preventing violence the problem-solving way. *Juvenile Justice Bulletin.* Retrieved January 2, 2002, from http://ojjdp.ncjrs.org/pubs/violvict.html.

Siegel, M. A., & Kirkley, S. E. (1998). Adventure learning as a vision of the digital learning environment. In C. J. Bonk & K. S. King (Eds.), *Electronic collaborators: Learner-centered technologies for literacy, apprenticeship, and discourse* (pp. 341–364). Mahwah, NJ: Erlbaum.

Siegle, D. (2002). Creating a living portfolio: Documenting student growth with electronic portfolios. *Gifted Child Today, 25*(3), 60–63.

Siegler, R. S. (1996). *Emerging minds: The process of change in children's thinking.* New York: Oxford University Press.

Siegler, R. S. (1998). *Children's thinking* (3rd ed.). Upper Saddle River, NJ: Prentice Hall.

Siegler, R. S., & Svetina, M. (2006). What leads children to adopt new strategies? A microgenetic/cross-sectional study of class inclusion. *Child Development, 77*(4), 997–1015.

Sigelman, C. K., & Shaffer, D. R. (1991). *Lifespan human development.* Pacific Grove, CA: Brooks Cole.

Simon, S. (2002). The CASE approach for pupils with learning difficulties. *School Science Review, 83*(305), 73–79.

Simpson, E. J. (1972). *The classification of educational objectives: Psychomotor domain.* Urbana: University of Illinois Press.

Sinatra, G. M., & Pintrich, P. R. (Eds.). (2003). *Intentional conceptual change.* Mahwah, NJ: Erlbaum.

Singer, A. (1994). Reflections on multiculturalism. *Phi Delta Kappan, 76*(4), 284–288.

Singer, D. G., & Revenson, T. A. (1996). *A Piaget primer: How a child thinks* (rev. ed.). New York: Plume.

Singham, M. (2003). The achievement gap: Myths and reality. *Phi Delta Kappan, 84*(8), 586–591.

Singletary, T. J., & Jordan, J. R. (1996). Exploring the globe. *The Science Teacher, 63*(3), 36–39.

Sipe, R. B. (2000). Virtually being there: Creating authentic experiences through interactive exchanges. *English Journal, 90*(2), 104–111.

Sirin, S. R. (2005). Socioeconomic status and academic achievement: A meta-analytic review of research. *Review of Educational Research, 75*(3), 417–453.

Skinner, B. F. (1984). The shame of American education. *American Psychologist, 39*(9), 947–954.

Skrtic, T. M., Sailor, W., & Gee, K. (1996). Voice, collaboration, and inclusion. *Remedial and Special Education, 17*(3), 142–157.

Slavin, R. E. (1989). PET and the pendulum: Faddism in education and how to stop it. *Phi Delta Kappan, 79*(10), 752–758.

Slavin, R. E. (1994). Student teams-achievement divisions. In S. Sharan (Ed.), *Handbook of cooperative learning methods* (pp. 3–19). Westport, CT: Greenwood Press.

Slavin, R. E. (1995). *Cooperative learning: Theory, research, and practice* (2nd ed.). Boston: Allyn & Bacon.

Slavin, R. E., & Cheung, A. (2005). A synthesis of research on language of reading instruction for English language learners. *Review of Educational Research, 75*(2), 247–284.

Sleeter, C. E., & Grant, C. A. (2007). *Making choices for multicultural education* (5th ed.). New York: Wiley.

Smelter, R. W., Rasch, B. W., & Yudewitz, G. J. (1994). Thinking of inclusion for all special needs students? Better think again. *Phi Delta Kappan, 76*(1), 35–38.

Smilansky, S. (1968). *The effects of sociodramatic play on disadvantaged preschool children.* New York: Wiley.

Smith, D. D. (2004). *Introduction to special education* (5th ed.). Boston: Allyn & Bacon.

Smith, L. (2002). Piaget's model. In U. Goswami (Ed.), *Blackwell handbook of childhood cognitive development* (pp. 515–537). Oxford, England: Blackwell.

Smith, P. K. (2005). Play. In B. Hopkins, R. G. Barr, G. F. Michel, & P. Rochat (Eds.), *The Cambridge encyclopedia of child development* (pp. 344–347). Cambridge, England: Cambridge University Press.

Snow, R. E. (1986). Individual differences and the design of educational programs. *American Psychologist, 41*(10), 1029–1039.

Snow, R. E. (1992). Aptitude testing: Yesterday, today, and tomorrow. *Educational Psychologist, 27*(1), 5–32.

Snowman, J. (1986). Learning tactics and strategies. In G. D. Phye & T. Andre (Eds.), *Cognitive classroom learning: Understanding, thinking, and problem solving.* New York: Academic Press.

Snowman, J. (1987, October). *The keys to strategic learning.* Paper presented at the annual meeting of the Mid-Western Educational Research Association, Chicago, IL.

Snyder, H. N., & Sickmund, M. (2006). *Juvenile offenders and victims: 2006 national report.* Washington, DC: U.S. Department of Justice, Office of Justice Programs, Office of Juvenile Justice and Delinquency Prevention. Retrieved November 20, 2006, from http:// ojjdp.ncjrs.org/ojstabb/nr2006/index.html.

Sobel, D. M., Taylor, S. V., & Anderson, R. E. (2003). Shared accountability: Encouraging diversity—responsive teaching in an inclusive classroom. *Teaching Exceptional Children, 35*(6), 46–54.

Soderberg, P., & Price, F. (2003). An examination of problem-based teaching and learning in population genetics and evolution using EVOLVE, a computer simulation. *International Journal of Science Education, 25*(1), 35–55.

Sofronoff, K., Dalgliesh, L., & Kosky, R. (2005). *Out of options: A cognitive model of adolescent suicide and risk-taking.* Cambridge, England: Cambridge University Press.

Soldier, L. L. (1989). Cooperative learning and the Native American student. *Phi Delta Kappan, 71*(2), 161–163.

Soldier, L. L. (1997). Is there an "Indian" in your classroom? Working successfully with urban Native American students. *Phi Delta Kappan, 78*(8), 650–653.

Sorell, G. T., & Montgomery, M. J. (2001). Feminist perspectives on Erikson's theory: Their relevance for contemporary identity development research. *Identity, 1*(2), 97–128.

Spalding, E. (2000). Performance assessment and the new standards project: A story of serendipitous success. *Phi Delta Kappan, 81*(10), 758–764.

Spear, N. E., & Riccio, D. C. (1994). *Memory: Phenomena and principles.* Boston: Allyn & Bacon.

Spear-Swerling, L., & Sternberg, R. J. (1998). Curing our "epidemic" of learning disabilities. *Phi Delta Kappan, 79*(5), 397–401.

Spector, J. M. (2006). A methodology for assessing learning in complex and ill structured task domains. *Innovations in Education and Teaching International, 43*(2), 109–120.

Spelke, E. S. (2005). Sex differences in intrinsic aptitude for mathematics: A critical review. *American Psychologist, 60*(9), 950–958.

Spinner, H., & Fraser, B. J. (2005). Evaluation of an innovative mathematics program in terms of classroom environment, student attitudes, and conceptual development. *International Journal of Science and Mathematics Education, 3*(2), 267–293.

Spitz, H. H. (1999). Beleaguered Pygmalion: A history of the controversy over claims that teacher expectancy raises intelligence. *Intelligence, 27*(3), 199–234.

Sprinthall, N. A., & Sprinthall, R. C. (1987). *Educational psychology: A developmental approach* (4th ed.). New York: Random House.

Sprinthall, N. A., Sprinthall, R. C., & Oja, S. N. (1998). *Educational psychology: A developmental approach* (7th ed.). New York: McGraw-Hill.

Standing, L. (1973). Learning 10,000 pictures. *Quarterly Journal of Experimental Psychology, 25*(2), 207–222.

Standing, L., Conezio, J., & Haber, R. (1970). Perception and memory for pictures: Single trial learning of 2500 visual stimuli. *Psychonomic Science, 19*(2), 73–74.

Stanford, P., & Siders, J. A. (2001). E-pal writing! *Teaching Exceptional Children, 34*(2), 21–25.

Starnes, B. A. (2006). What we don't know *can* hurt them: White teachers, Indian children. *Phi Delta Kappan, 87*(5), 384–392.

Starratt, R. J. (2003). Opportunity to learn and the accountability agenda. *Phi Delta Kappan, 85*(4), 298–303.

Staub, F. C., & Stern, E. (2002). The nature of teachers' pedagogical content beliefs matters for students' achievement gains: Quasi-experimental evidence from elementary mathematics. *Journal of Educational Psychology, 94*(2), 344–355.

Steinberg, L. (1996). *Beyond the classroom: Why school reform has failed and what parents need to do.* New York: Simon & Schuster.

Steinberg, L. (2005). *Adolescence* (7th ed.). New York: McGraw-Hill Higher Education.

Steinberg, L., & Morris, A. S. (2001). Adolescent development. In S. T. Fiske, D. L. Schacter, & C. Zahn-Waxler (Eds.), *Annual review of psychology* (pp. 83–110). Stanford, CA: Annual Reviews.

Stemler, S. E., Elliott, J. G., Grigorenko, E. L., & Sternberg, R. J. (2006). There's more to teaching than instruction: Seven strategies for dealing with the practical side of teaching. *Educational Studies, 32*(1), 101–118.

Stephens, L., Leavell, J. A., & Fabris, M. E. (1999). Producing video-cases that enhance instruction. *Journal of Technology and Teacher Education, 7*(4), 291–301.

Sternberg, R. J. (1985). *Beyond IQ: A triarchic theory of human intelligence.* New York: Cambridge University Press.

Sternberg, R. J. (1994). Allowing for thinking styles. *Educational Leadership, 52*(3), 36–40.

Sternberg, R. J. (1996). Matching abilities, instruction, and assessment: Reawakening the sleeping giant of ATI. In I. Dennis & P. Tapsfield (Eds.), *Human abilities: Their nature and measurement* (pp. 167–181). Mahwah, NJ: Erlbaum.

Sternberg, R. J. (1997a). What does it mean to be smart? *Educational Leadership, 54*(6), 20–24.

Sternberg, R. J. (1997c). Technology changes intelligence: Societal implications and soaring IQ's. *Technos, 6*(2), 12–14.

Sternberg, R. J. (1998). Abilities are forms of developing expertise. *Educational Researcher, 27*(3), 11–20.

Sternberg, R. J. (2002a). Intelligence is not just inside the head: The theory of successful intelligence. In J. Aronson (Ed.), *Improving academic achievement* (pp. 227–244). San Diego, CA: Academic Press.

Sternberg, R. J. (2002b). Raising the achievement of all students: Teaching for successful intelligence. *Educational Psychology Review, 14*(4), 383–393.

Sternberg, R. J. (2003). Construct validity of the theory of successful intelligence. In R. J. Sternberg, J. Lautrey, & T. I. Lubart (Eds.), *Models of intelligence: International perspectives* (pp. 55–77). Washington, DC: American Psychological Association.

Sternberg, R. J. (2005). WICS: A model of positive educational leadership comprising wisdom, intelligence, and creativity synthesized. *Educational Psychology Review 17*(3), 191–262.

Sternberg, R. J., Ferrari, M., Clinkenbeard, P., & Grigorenko, E. L. (1996). Identification, instruction, and assessment of gifted children: A construct validation of a triarchic model. *Gifted Child Quarterly, 40*(3), 129–137.

Sternberg, R. J., & Grigorenko, E. L. (2001). A capsule history of theory and research on styles. In R. J. Sternberg & L. Zhang (Eds.), *Perspectives on thinking, learning, and cognitive styles* (pp. 1–21). Mahwah, NJ: Erlbaum.

Sternberg, R. J., & Grigorenko, E. L. (2004). Successful intelligence in the classroom. *Theory into Practice, 43*(4), 274–280.

Sternberg, R. J., & Zhang. L. (2005). Styles of thinking as a basis of differentiated instruction. *Theory into Practice, 44*(3), 245–253.

Steubing, K. K., Fletcher, J. M., LeDoux, J. M., Lyon, G. R., Shaywitz, S. E., & Shaywitz, B. A. (2002). Validity of IQ-discrepancy classifications of reading disabilities: A meta-analysis. *American Educational Research Journal, 39*(4), 469–518.

Stevens, R. J., & Slavin, R. E. (1995). The cooperative elementary school: Effects on students' achievement, attitudes, and social relations. *American Educational Research Journal, 32*(2), 321–351.

Stier, H., Lewin-Epstein, N., & Braun, B. (2001). Welfare regimes, family-supportive policies, and women's employment along the life-course. *American Journal of Sociology, 106*(6), 1731–1760.

Stiggins, R. J. (2001). The unfulfilled promise of classroom assessment. *Educational Measurement: Issues and Practice, 20*(3), 5–15.

Stiggins, R. J. (2002). Assessment crisis: The absence of assessment FOR learning. *Phi Delta Kappan, 83*(10), 758–765.

Stiggins, R. J. (2005). *Student-involved assessment for learning* (4th ed.). Upper Saddle River, NJ: Merrill Prentice Hall.

Stinson, N., Jr. (2003, August). Working toward our goal: Eliminating racial and ethnic disparities in health. *Closing the Gap,* 1–2. Retrieved January 6, 2004, from www.omhrc.gov/OMH/sidebar/archivedctg.htm.

Stipek, D. (2002). *Motivation to learn: Integrating theory and practice* (4th ed.). Boston: Allyn & Bacon.

Stobart, G. (2005). Fairness in multicultural assessment systems. *Assessment in Education: Principles, Policy & Practice, 12*(3), 275–287.

Stokes, V. (2005). No longer a year behind. *Learning and Leading with Technology, 33*(2), 15–17.

Strassman, B. K., & D'Amore, M. (2002). The write technology. *Teaching Exceptional Children, 34*(6), 28–31.

Streib, L. Y. (1993). Visiting and revisiting the trees. In M. Cochran-Smith & S. L. Lytle (Eds.), *Inside/outside: Teacher research and knowledge*. New York: Teachers College Press.

Sunderman, G. L. (2006, February). *The unraveling of No Child Left Behind: How negotiated changes transform the law.* Cambridge, MA: The Civil Rights Project at Harvard University. Retrieved October 10, 2006, from www.civilrightsproject .harvard.edu/research/esea/esea_gen.php.

Suomala, J., & Alajaaski, J. (2002). Pupils' problem-solving processes in a complex computerized learning environment. *Journal of Educational Computing Research, 26*(2), 155–176.

Supovitz, J. A. (1998). Gender and racial/ethnic differences on alternative science assessments. *Journal of Women and Minorities in Science and Engineering, 4*(2 & 3), 129–140.

Supovitz, J. A., & Brennan, R. T. (1997). Mirror, mirror on the wall, which is the fairest test of all? An examination of the equitability of portfolio assessment relative to standardized tests. *Harvard Educational Review, 67*(3), 472–506.

Susman, E. J. (1991). Stress and the adolescent. In R. M. Lerner, A. C. Peterson, & J. Brooks-Gunn (Eds.), *Encyclopedia of adolescence*. New York: Garland Publishing.

Swanson, C. B. (2004). *Who graduates? Who doesn't? A statistical portrait of public high school graduation, class of 2001.* Washington, DC: The Urban Institute. Retrieved March 10, 2004, from www.urban.org/url.cfm?ID=410934.

Swanson, C. B. (2006). Tracking U.S. trends. *Education Week, 25*(35), 50–53.

Swanson, H. L. (2006). Cross-sectional and incremental changes in working memory and mathematical problem solving. *Journal of Educational Psychology, 98*(2), 265–281.

Swanson, H. L., & Hoskyn, M. (1998). Experimental intervention research on students with learning disabilities: A meta-analysis of treatment outcomes. *Review of Educational Research, 68*(3), 277–321.

Sweeting, H., & West, P. (2001). Being different: Correlates of the experience of teasing and bullying at age 11. *Research Papers in Education: Policy & Practice, 16*(3), 225–246.

Sweller, J., van Merriënboer, J. J. G., & Paas, F. G. W. C. (1998). Cognitive architecture and instructional design. *Educational Psychology Review, 10*(3), 251–296.

Tappan, M. B. (1998). Sociocultural psychology and caring pedagogy: Exploring Vygotsky's "hidden curriculum." *Educational Psychologist, 33*(1), 23–33.

Tappan, M. B. (2006). Moral functioning as mediated action. *Journal of Moral Education, 35*(1), 1–18.

Tauber, R. T., & Mester, C. S. (2007). *Acting lessons for teachers: Using performance skills in the classroom* (2nd ed.). Westport, CT: Praeger.

Taylor, D., & Lorimer, M. (2002/2003). Helping boys succeed. *Educational Leadership, 60*(4), 68–70.

Taylor, G. R. (2003). *Informal classroom assessment strategies for teachers*. Lanham, MD: Scarecrow Press.

Taylor, P. C., & Fraser, B. J. (1998). *The constructivist learning environment survey: Mark 2.* Perth, Australia: Science and Mathematics Education Centre, Curtin University of Technology.

Taylor, P. C., Fraser, B. J., & Fisher, D. L. (1997). Monitoring constructivist classroom learning environments. *International Journal of Educational Research, 27*(4), 293–301.

Tennessee Department of Education. (2006, July 20). *Schools to use technology to enhance achievement.* Retrieved September 15, 2006, from http://tennessee.gov/education/news/nr/2006/07_20_06.shtml.

Tharp, R. G., Estrada, P., Dalton, S. S., & Yamauchi, L. A. (2000). *Teaching transformed: Achieving excellence, fairness, inclusion, and harmony.* Boulder, CO: Westview Press.

Thoma, S. J. (1986). Estimating gender differences in the comprehension and preference of moral issues. *Developmental Review, 6*(2), 165–180.

Thomas, J. (2005). Calling a cab for Oregon students. *Phi Delta Kappan, 86*(5), 385–388.

Thomas, V. G. (2000). Learner-centered alternatives to social promotion and retention: A talent development approach. *Journal of Negro Education, 69*(4), 323–337.

Thomas, W. P., & Collier, V. P. (1997/1998). Two languages are better than one. *Educational Leadership, 55*(4), 23–26.

Thomas, W. P., & Collier, V. P. (1999). Accelerated schooling for English language learners. *Educational Leadership, 56*(7), 46–49.

Thompson, M. S., DiCerbo, K. E., Mahoney, K., & MacSwan, J. (2002, January 25). ¿Exito en California? A validity critique of language program evaluations and analysis of English learner test scores. *Education Policy Analysis Archives, 10*(7). Retrieved January 26, 2004, from http://epaa.asu.edu/epaa/v10n7/.

Thorndike, E. L., & Woodworth, R. S. (1901). The influence of improvement in one mental function upon the efficiency of other functions. *Psychological Review, 8*, 247–261.

Thorndike, R. L., Hagen, E. P., & Sattler, J. M. (1986). *The Stanford-Binet Intelligence Scale—IV.* Chicago: Riverside Publishing.

Tieso, C. L. (2003). Ability grouping is not just tracking anymore. *Roeper Review, 26*(1), 29–39.

Toch, T. (2003). *High schools on a human scale.* Boston: Beacon Press.

Tock, K., & Suppes, P. (2002, June 23). *The high dimensionality of students' individual differences in performance in EPGY's k6 computer-based mathematics curriculum.* Retrieved January 15, 2004, from www.epgy-stanford.edu/research/index .html?trajectories.html.

Tollefson, N. (2000). Classroom applications of cognitive theories of motivation. *Educational Psychology Review, 12*(1), 63–83.

Tomlinson, C. A. (2002). Invitations to learn. *Educational Leadership, 60*(1), 6–10.

Torff, B., & Sessions, D. N. (2005). Principals' perceptions of the causes of teacher ineffectiveness. *Journal of Educational Psychology, 97*(4), 530–537.

Trautwein, U., Ludtke, O., Koller, O., & Baumert, J. (2006). Self-esteem, academic self-concept, and achievement: How the learning environment moderates the dynamics of self-concept. *Journal of Personality and Social Psychology, 90*(2), 334–349.

Trevisan, M. S. (2002). The states' role in ensuring assessment competence. *Phi Delta Kappan, 83*(10), 766–771.

Triandis, H. C. (1986). Toward pluralism in education. In S. Modgil, G. K. Verma, K. Mallick, & C. Modgil (Eds.), *Multicultural education: The interminable debate.* London: Falmer.

Trotter, A. (2003, May 8). A question of direction. *Education Week, 22*(35), 17–18, 20–21.

Trumper, R., & Gelbman, M. (2000). Investigating electromagnetic induction through a microcomputer-based laboratory. *Physics Education, 35*(2), 90–95.

Trumper, R., & Gelbman, M. (2002). Using MBL to verify Newton's second law and the impulse-momentum relationship with an arbitrary changing force. *School Science Review, 83*(305), 135–139.

Tucker, M. S., & Toch, T. (2004). The secret to making NCLB work? More bureaucrats. *Phi Delta Kappan, 86*(1), 28–33.

Tudge, J. R. H., & Rogoff, B. (1989). Peer influences on cognitive development: Piagetian and Vygotskian perspectives. In M. H. Bornstein & J. S. Bruner (Eds.), *Interaction in human development.* Hillsdale, NJ: Erlbaum.

Tudge, J. R. H., & Winterhoff, P. A. (1993). Vygotsky, Piaget, and Bandura: Perspectives on the relations between the social world and cognitive development. *Human Development, 36*(2), 61–81.

Tudge, J., & Scrimsher, S. (2003). Lev S. Vygotsky on education: A cultural-historical, interpersonal, and individual approach to development. In B. J. Zimmerman & D. H. Schunk (Eds.), *Educational psychology: A century of contributions.* Mahwah, NJ: Erlbaum.

Tukey, L. (2002). Differentiation. *Phi Delta Kappan, 84*(1), 63–64, 92.

Tulving, E., & Pearlstone, Z. (1966). Availability vs. accessibility of information in memory for words. *Journal of Verbal Learning and Verbal Behavior, 5*(4), 381–391.

Umar, K. B. (2003, August). Disparities persist in infant mortality: Creative approaches work to close the gap. *Closing the Gap,* 4–5. Retrieved January 6, 2004, from www.omhrc.gov/OMH/sidebar/ archivedctg.htm.

Underwood, J., Cavendish, S., Dowling, S., Fogelman, K., & Lawson, T. (1996). Are integrated learning systems effective learning support tools? In M. R. Kibby & J. R. Hartley (Eds.), *Computer assisted learning: Selected contributions for the CAL 95 symposium.* Oxford, England: Elsevier Science.

Urdan, T., & Mestas, M. (2006). The goals behind performance goals. *Journal of Educational Psychology, 98*(2), 354–365.

Urdan, T., & Midgley, C. (2001). Academic self-handicapping: What we know, what more there is to learn. *Educational Psychology Review, 13*(2), 115–138.

Urdan, T., Midgley, C., & Anderman, E. M. (1998). The role of classroom goal structure in students' use of self-handicapping strategies. *American Educational Research Journal, 35*(1), 101–122.

Urdan, T., Ryan, A. M., Anderman, E. M., & Gheen, M. H. (2002). Goals, goal structures, and avoidance behaviors. In C. Midgley (Ed.), *Goals, goal structures, and patterns of adaptive learning* (pp. 55–83). Mahwah, NJ: Erlbaum.

U.S. Census Bureau (2002, August). *National population projections I. Summary Files: (NP-T4) Projections of the total resident population by 5-year age groups, race, and Hispanic origin with special age categories: Middle series, 1999 to 2100.* Retrieved July 7, 2006, from www.census.gov/www/projections/natsum-T3.html/.

U.S. Census Bureau. (2005a, August). *Table 4. Number in poverty and poverty rates by race and Hispanic origin using 2- and 3-year averages: 2002–2004.* Retrieved July 12, 2006, from www.census.gov/hhes/www/poverty/poverty04/table04.html.

U.S. Census Bureau. (2005b, December). *Table H7. Women 15 to 44 years old who had a child in the last year and children ever born per 1,000 women, by nativity status, region of birth, citizenship status, race, Hispanic origin, and age: Selected years, 1994 to 2004.* Retrieved July 9, 2006, from www.census.gov/population/www/socdemo/fertility.html.

U.S. Census Bureau. (2006, April). *Table 3. People and families in poverty by selected characteristics: 2003 and 2004.* Retrieved July 12, 2006, from www.census.gov/hhes/www/poverty/poverty04/table3.pdf.

U.S. Department of Education, Office of Special Education and Rehabilitative Services, Office of Special Education Programs. (2005). *Twenty-sixth annual (2004) report to Congress on the implementation of the Individuals with Disabilities Education Act.* Washington, DC: Author. Retrieved December 9, 2006, from www.ed.gov/ about/reports/annual/osep/2004/index. html.

U.S. Department of Education. (2004). *Individuals with Disabilities Education Improvement Act of 2004.* Retrieved October 17, 2006, from www.ed.gov/policy/speced/guid/idea/idea2004.html.

U.S. Department of Education. (2006). *The condition of education 2006* (NCES Publication No. 2006-071). Washington, DC: U.S. Government Printing Office. Retrieved October 17, 2006, from http://nces.ed.gov/pubsearch/pubsinfo.asp?pubid=2006071.

U.S. Department of Labor. (2001, October 16). *Occupational classification system manual.* Retrieved June 20, 2006, from www.bls.gov/ncs/ocs/ocsm/comMoga.htm.

U.S. Office of Immigration Statistics. (2006, June). *Yearbook of immigration statistics: 2005. Immigrants. Table 3. Legal permanent resident flow by region and country of birth: Fiscal years 1996 to 2005.* Retrieved July 7, 2006, from www.uscis.gov/graphics/shared/statistics/yearbook/LPR05.htm.

Uyeda, S., Madden, J., Brigham, L. A., Luft, J. A., & Washburne, J. (2002). Solving authentic science problems. *The Science Teacher, 69*(1), 24–29.

Vallecorsa, A. L., deBettencourt, L. U., & Zigmond, N. (2000). *Students with mild disabilities in general education settings.* Upper Saddle River, NJ: Merrill Prentice Hall.

van Drie, J., van Boxtel, C., & van der Linden, J. (2006). Historical reasoning in a computer-supported collaborative learning environment. In A. M. O' Donnell, C. E. Hmelo-Silver, & G. Erkens (Eds.), *Collaborative learning, reasoning, and technology* (pp. 265–296). Mahwah, NJ: Erlbaum.

van Laar, C. (2000). The paradox of low academic achievement but high self-esteem in African American students: An attributional account. *Educational Psychology Review, 12*(1), 33–62.

Van Wagenen, L., & Hibbard, K. M. (1998). Building teacher portfolios. *Educational Leadership, 55*(5), 26–29.

Vartanian, L. R. (2000). Revisiting the imaginary audience and personal fable constructs of adolescent egocentrism: A conceptual review. *Adolescence, 35*(140), 639–661.

Vasquez, J. A. (1990). Teaching to the distinctive traits of minority students. *The Clearing House, 63*(7), 299–304.

Veenman, S., Denessen, E., van den Akker, A., & van der Rijt, J. (2005). Effects of a cooperative learning program on the elaborations of students during help seeking and help giving. *American Educational Research Journal, 42*(1), 115–151.

Veermans, M., & Cesareni, D. (2005). The nature of the discourse in web-based collaborative learning environments: Case studies from four different countries. *Computers and Education, 45*(3), 316–336.

Vekiri, I. (2002). What is the value of graphical displays in learning? *Educational Psychology Review, 14*(3), 261–312.

Vermont Department of Education. (2004). *Vermont's framework of standards and learning opportunities.* Retrieved March 3, 2004 from www.state.vt.us/educ/new/html/pubs/framework.html.

Vitz, P. C. (1990). The use of stories in moral development: New psychological reasons for an old educational method. *American Psychologist, 45*(6), 709–720.

Vockell, E. L., & Fiore, D. J. (1993). Electronic gradebooks: What current programs can do for teachers. *The Clearing House, 66*(3), 141–145.

Vogler, K. E., & Kennedy, R. J., Jr. (2003). A view from the bottom: What happens when your school system ranks last? *Phi Delta Kappan, 84*(6), 446–448.

Volman, M., & van Eck, E. (2001). Gender equity and information technology in education: The second decade. *Review of Educational Research, 71*(4), 613–634.

Vondracek, F. W., Schulenberg, J., Skorikov, V., Gillespie, L. K., & Wahlheim, C. (1995). The relationship of identity status to career indecision during adolescence. *Journal of Adolescence, 18*(1), 17–30.

Vye, N. J., Goldman, S. R., Voss, J. F., Hmelo, C., Williams, S., & Cognition and Technology Group at Vanderbilt. (1997). Complex mathematical problem solving by individuals and dyads. *Cognition and Instruction, 15*(4), 435–484.

Vygotsky, L. S. (1986). *Thought and language* (A. Kozulin, Trans.). Cambridge, MA: MIT Press. (Original work published 1934)

Wadsworth, B. J. (1996). *Piaget's theory of cognitive and affective development* (5th ed.). White Plains, NY: Longman.

Wai, J., Lubinski, D., & Benbow, C. P. (2005). Creativity and occupational accomplishments among intellectually precocious youth: An age 13 to 33 longitudinal study. *Journal of Educational Psychology, 97*(3), 484–492.

Walberg, H. J. (1990). Productive teaching and instruction: Assessing the knowledge base. *Phi Delta Kappan, 71*(6), 470–478.

Walker, J. E., Shea, T. M., & Bauer, A. M. (2007). *Behavior management: A practical approach for educators* (9th ed.). Upper Saddle River, NJ: Pearson/Merrill Prentice Hall.

Wallace-Broscious, A., Serafica, F. C., & Osipow, S. H. (1994). Adolescent career development: Relationships to self-concept and identity status. *Journal of Research on Adolescence, 4*(1), 127–149.

Walsh, W. B., & Betz, N. E. (2001). *Tests and assessment* (4th ed.). Upper Saddle River, NJ: Merrill Prentice Hall.

Wang, M. C., Haertel, G. D., & Walberg, H. J. (1993). Toward a knowledge base for school learning. *Review of Educational Research, 63*(3), 249–294.

Wasserman, S. (1999). Shazam! you're a teacher: Facing the illusory quest for certainty in classroom practice. *Phi Delta Kappan, 80*(6), 464–468.

Waterman, A. S. (1988). Identity status theory and Erikson's theory: Communalities and differences. *Developmental Review, 8*(2), 185–208.

Waterman, A. S., & Archer, S. L. (1990). A life-span perspective on identity formation: Developments in form, function, and process. In P. B. Baltes, D. L. Featherman, & R. M. Lerner (Eds.), *Life-span development and behavior* (Vol. 10, pp. 30–57). Hillsdale, NJ: Erlbaum.

Watson, J. B. (1913). Psychology as the behaviorist views it. *Psychological Review, 20*, 158–177.

Watson, M. F., & Protinsky, H. (1991). Identity status of black adolescents: An empirical investigation. *Adolescence, 26*(104), 963–966.

Watkins, C. (2005). *Classrooms as learning communities: What's in it for schools?* London: Routledge.

Wayne, A. J., & Youngs, P. (2003). Teacher characteristics and student achievement gains: A review. *Review of Educational Research, 73*(1), 89–122.

Weah, W., Simmons, V. C., & Hall, M. (2000). Service-learning and multicultural/multiethnic perspectives: From diversity to equity. *Phi Delta Kappan, 81*(9), 673–675.

Webb, N. M., Nemer, K. M., Chizhik, A. W., & Sugrue, B. (1998). Equity issues in collaborative group assessment: Group composition and performance. *American Educational Research Journal, 35*(4), 607–651.

Webb, N. M., Nemer, K. M, & Zuniga, S. (2002). Short circuits of superconductors? Effects of group composition on high-achieving students' science assessment performance. *American Educational Research Journal, 39*(4), 943–989.

Wechsler, D. (1975). Intelligence defined and undefined: A relativistic appraisal. *American Psychologist, 30*(2), 135–139.

Wechsler, D. (1997). *Wechsler Adult Intelligence Scale—III.* New York: Psychological Corporation.

Wechsler, D. (2003). *Wechsler Intelligence Scale for Children—IV.* New York: Psychological Corporation.

Wedman, J. M., Espinosa, L. M., & Laffey, J. M. (1999). A process for understanding how a field-based course influences teachers' beliefs and practices. *Teacher Educator, 34*(3), 189–214.

Weichold, K., Silbereisen, R. K., & Schmitt-Rodermund, E. (2003). Short-term and long-term consequences of early versus late physical maturation in adolescents. In C. Hayward (Ed.), *Gender differences at puberty* (pp. 241–276). Cambridge, England: Cambridge University Press.

Weiler, G. (2003). Using weblogs in the classroom. *English Journal, 92*(5), 73–75.

Weiner, I. B. (1975). Depression in adolescence. In F. F. Flach & S. C. Draghi (Eds.), *The nature and treatment of depression.* New York: Wiley.

Weinert, F. E., & Hany, E. A. (2003). The stability of individual differences in intellectual development: Empirical evidence, theoretical problems, and new research questions. In R. J. Sternberg, J. Lautrey, & T. I. Lubart (Eds.), *Models of intelligence: International perspectives* (pp. 169–181). Washington, DC: American Psychological Association.

Weiss, R. P. (2000). Howard Gardner talks about technology. *Training & Development, 54*(9), 52–56.

Wentzel, K. R. (2002). Are effective teachers like good parents? Teaching styles and student adjustment in early adolescence. *Child Development, 73*(1), 287–301.

Wertsch, J. V. (1998). *Mind as action.* New York: Oxford University Press.

Wertsch, J. V., & Tulviste, P. (1996). L. S. Vygotsky and contemporary developmental psychology. In H. Daniels (Ed.), *An introduction to Vygotsky.* New York: Routledge.

Westerman, D. A. (1991). Expert and novice teacher decision making. *Journal of Teacher Education, 42*(4), 292–305.

Wheatley, G. H. (1991). Constructivist perspectives on science and mathematics learning. *Science Education, 75*(1), 9–21.

Wheelock, A. (1994). *Alternatives to tracking and ability grouping.* Arlington, VA: American Association of School Administrators.

Whimbey, A., & Lochhead, J. (1999). *Problem solving and comprehension* (6th ed.). Mahwah, NJ: Erlbaum.

White House is easing up on federal requirement for testing in schools. (2004, March 30). *St. Louis Post-Dispatch*, p. A4.

White, R., Algozzine, B., Audette, R., Marr, M. B., & Ellis, E. D., Jr. (2001). Unified Discipline: A school-wide approach for managing problem behavior. *Intervention in School and Clinic, 37*(1), 3–8.

Whittaker, C. R., Salend, S. J., & Duhaney, D. (2001). Creating instructional rubrics for inclusive classrooms. *Teaching Exceptional Children, 34*(2), 8–13.

Wicks-Nelson, R., & Israel, A. C. (2003). *Behavior disorders of childhood* (5th ed.). Upper Saddle River, NJ: Prentice-Hall.

Wiedmer, T. L. (1998). Digital portfolios: Capturing and demonstrating skills and levels of performance. *Phi Delta Kappan, 79*(8), 586–589.

Wigfield, A., Battle, A., Keller, L. B., & Eccles, J. S. (2002). Sex differences in motivation, self-concept, career aspiration, and career choice: Implications for cognitive development. In A. McGillicuddy-De Lisi & R. De Lisi(Eds.), *Biology, society, and behavior: The development of sex differences in cognition* (pp. 93–124). Westport, CT: Ablex.

Wigfield, A., & Eccles, J. S. (2002a). Students' motivation during the middle school years. In J. Aronson (Ed.), *Improving academic achievement* (pp. 159–184). San Diego, CA: Academic Press.

Wigfield, A., & Eccles, J. S. (2002b). The development of competence beliefs, expectancies for success, and achievement values from childhood through adolescence. In A. Wigfield & J. S. Eccles (Eds.), *Development of achievement motivation* (pp. 91–120). San Diego, CA: Academic Press.

Wiles, J., Bondi, J., & Wiles, M. T. (2006). *The essential middle school* (4th ed.). Upper Saddle River, NJ: Pearson/Merrill Prentice Hall.

Williams, J. P., Lauer, K. D., Hall, K. M., Lord, K. M., Gugga, S. S., Bak, S.-J., Jacobs, P. R., & deCani, J. S. (2002). Teaching elementary school students to identify story themes. *Journal of Educational Psychology, 94*(2), 235–248.

Willig, A. C. (1985). A meta-analysis of selected studies on the effectiveness of bilingual education. *Review of Educational Research, 55*(3), 269–318.

Wilson, R. (2005). Targeted growth for every student. *Leadership, 35*(2), 8–12.

Wilson, S. M., Floden, R. E., & Ferrini-Mundy, J. (2002). Teacher preparation research: An insider's view from the outside. *Journal of Teacher Education, 53*(3), 190–204.

Windschitl, M. (2002). Framing constructivism in practice as the negotiation of dilemmas: An analysis of the conceptual, pedagogical, cultural, and political challenges facing teachers. *Review of Educational Research, 72*(2), 131–175.

Windschitl, M., & Sahl, K. (2002). Tracing teachers' use of technology in a laptop computer school: The interplay of teacher beliefs, social dynamics, and institutional culture. *American Educational Research Journal, 39*(1), 165–206.

Winkler, A. M. (2003). The power of the A word. *American School Board Journal, 190*(6), 22–24.

Winne, P. H. (2001). Self-regulated learning viewed from models of information processing. In B. J. Zimmerman & D. H. Schunk (Eds.), *Self-regulated learning and academic achievement: Theoretical perspectives* (2nd ed., pp. 153–189). Mahwah, NJ: Erlbaum.

Winne, P. H., & Jamieson-Noel, D. (2002). Exploring students' calibration of self reports about study tactics and achievement. *Contemporary Educational Psychology, 27*(4), 551–572.

Winne, P. H., & Jamieson-Noel, D. (2003). Self-regulating studying by objectives for learning: Students' reports compared to a model. *Contemporary Educational Psychology, 28*(3), 259–276.

Winne, P. H., & Stockley, D. B. (1998). Computing technologies as sites for developing self-regulated learning. In D. H. Schunk & B. J. Zimmerman (Eds.), *Self-regulated learning: From teaching to reflective practice* (pp. 107–136). New York: Guilford Press.

Winner, E. (1997). Exceptionally high intelligence and schooling. *American Psychologist, 52*(10), 1070–1081.

Witkin, H. A., Moore, C. A., Goodenough, D. R., & Cox, P. W. (1977). Field-dependent and field-independent cognitive styles and their educational implications. *Review of Educational Research, 47*(1), 1–64.

Wlodkowski, R. J. (1978). *Motivation and teaching: A practical guide.* Washington, DC: National Education Association.

Wlodkowski, R. J., & Ginsberg, M. B. (1995). A framework for culturally responsive teaching. *Educational Leadership, 53*(1), 17–21.

Wong, B. Y. L. (1985). Self-questioning instructional research: A review. *Review of Educational Research, 55*(2), 227–268.

Woodhill, B. M., & Samuels, C. A. (2004). Desirable and undesirable androgyny: A prescription for the twenty-first century. *Journal of Gender Studies, 13*(1), 15–42.

Woodul, C. E., III, Vitale, M. R., & Scott, B. J. (2000). Using a cooperative multimedia learning environment to enhance learning and affective self-perceptions of at-risk students in grade 8. *Journal of Educational Technology Systems, 28*(3), 239–252.

Wuthrick, M. A. (1990). Blue jays win! Crows go down in defeat! *Phi Delta Kappan, 71*(7), 553–556.

Wynn, R. L., & Fletcher, C. (1987). Sex role development and early educational experiences. In D. B. Carter (Ed.), *Current conceptions of sex roles and sex typing.* New York: Praeger.

Yager, R. E. (2000). The constructivist learning model. *Science Teacher, 67*(1), 44–45.

Yang, S. C. (2001). Synergy of constructivism and hypermedia from three constructivist perspectives: Social, semiotic, and cognitive. *Journal of Educational Computing Research, 24*(4), 321–361.

Yao, Y. (2006). Technology use as a scoring criterion. In C. Crawford, D. A. Willis, R. Carlsen, I. Gibson, K. McFerrin, J. Price, & R. Weber (Eds.), *Proceedings of the Society for Information Technology and Teacher Education International Conference 2006* (pp. 215–219). Chesapeake, VA: Association for the Advancement of Computing in Education.

Yates, F. A. (1966). *The art of memory.* London: Routledge & Kegan Paul.

Yau, R. (2002). High-achieving elementary schools with large percentages of low-income African American students: A review and critique of the current research. In S. J. Denbo & L. M. Beaulieu (Eds.), *Improving schools for African American students* (pp. 193–217). Springfield, IL: Charles C. Thomas.

Yeh, S. S. (2006). Reforming federal testing policy to support teaching and learning. *Educational Policy, 20*(3), 495–524.

Yelland, N., & Masters, J. (2007). Rethinking scaffolding in the information age. *Computers & Education, 48*(3), 362–382.

Yoerg, K. (2002). Painting patterns with pixels. *Arts & Activities, 131*(4), 50–51.

Yonezawa, S., Wells, A. S., & Serna, I. (2002). Choosing tracks: "Freedom of choice" in detracking schools. *American Educational Research Journal, 39*(1), 37–67.

Young, J. D. (1996). The effect of self-regulated learning strategies on performance in learner controlled computer-based instruction. *Educational Technology Research and Development, 44*(2), 17–27.

Ysseldyke, J. E., Algozzine, B., & Thurlow, M. L. (2000). *Critical issues in special education* (3rd ed.). Boston: Houghton Mifflin.

Ysseldyke, J., Kosciolek, S., Spicuzza, R., & Boys, C. (2003). Effects of a learning information system on mathematics achievement and classroom structure. *Journal of Educational Research, 96*(3), 163–173.

Zeldin, A. L., & Pajares, F. (2000). Against the odds: Self-efficacy beliefs of women in mathematical, scientific, and technological careers. *American Educational Research Journal, 37*(1), 215–246.

Zellermayer, M., Salomon, G., Globerson, T., & Givon, H. (1991). Enhancing writing-related metacognitions through a computerized writing partner. *American Educational Research Journal, 28*(2), 373–391.

Zenisky, A., & Sireci, S. G. (2002). Technological innovations in large-scale assessment. *Applied Measurement in Education, 15*(4), 337–362.

Zhang, L. (2005). Validating the theory of mental self-government in a non-academic setting. *Personality and Individual Differences, 38*(8), 1915–1925.

Zhang, L., & Sternberg, R. J. (2001). Thinking styles across cultures: Their relationships with student learning. In R. J. Sternberg & L.-F. Zhang (Eds.), *Perspectives on thinking, learning, and cognitive styles* (pp. 197–226). Mahwah, NJ: Erlbaum.

Zhang, L., & Sternberg, R. J. (2006). *The nature of intellectual styles.* Mahwah, NJ: Erlbaum.

Zigmond, N., Jenkins, J., Fuchs, L. S., Deno, S., Fuchs, D., Baker, J. N., Jenkins, L., & Couthino, M. (1995). Special education in restructured schools: Findings from three multi-year studies. *Phi Delta Kappan, 76*(7), 531–540.

Zimmerman, B. J. (1990). Self-regulating academic learning and achievement: The emergence of a social cognitive perspective. *Educational Psychology Review, 2*(2), 173–200.

Zimmerman, B. J. (2000). Attaining self-regulation: A social cognitive perspective. In M. Boekaerts, P. R. Pintrich, & M. Zeidner (Eds.), *Handbook of self-regulation* (pp. 13–39). San Diego, CA: Academic Press.

Zimmerman, B. J. (2002). Achieving self-regulation: The trial and triumph of adolescence. In F. Pajares & T. Urdan (Eds.), *Academic motivation of adolescents* (pp. 1–27). Greenwich, CT: Information Age Publishing.

Zimmerman, B. J., & Kitsantas, A. (2002). Acquiring writing revision and self-regulatory skill through observation and emulation. *Journal of Educational Psychology, 94*(4), 660–668.

Zimmerman, B. J., & Kitsantas, A. (2005). The hidden dimension of personal competence: Self-regulated learning and practice. In A. J. Elliot & C. S. Dweck (Eds.), *Handbook of competence and motivation* (pp. 509–526). New York: Guilford Press.

Zimmerman, B. J., & Martinez-Pons, M. (1990). Student differences in self-regulated learning: Relating grade, sex, and giftedness to self-efficacy and strategy use. *Journal of Educational Psychology, 82*(1), 51–59.

Zuo, L., & Cramond, B. (2001). An examination of Terman's gifted children from the theory of identity. *Gifted Child Quarterly, 45*(4), 251–259.

# Credits

## Text Credits

Chapter 1: p. 17, Reprinted with permission from National Education Technology Standards for Students Connecting Curriculum and Technology. Chapter 3: p. 91, T. Lickona, "A More Complex Analysis Is Needed" *Phi Delta Kappan*, 79, pp. 449–454. Reprinted by permission of Thomas Lickona. Chapter 4: p. 117, J. I. Mendoza, "On Being Mexican American" in *Phi Delta Kappan*, 76(40) 1994, pp. 293–295. Chapter 5: p. 131, Figure 5.1, The Three Components of Sternberg's Triarchic Theory. Adapted from Sternberg (1985); Sternberg, Farrari, Clinkenbears & Grigorenko (1996). p. 136, Table 5.2 Table, Adapted from Figure 1—Teaching for Four Abilities, from "What Does It Mean to Be Smart?" by R. J. Sternberg (1997, March). *Educational Leadership*, 54(6), p. 22. Used with permission. The Association for Supervision and Curriculum Development is a worldwide community of educators advocating sound policies and sharing best practices to achieve the success of each learner. To learn more, visit ASCD at www.ascd.org. p. 142, Table 5.3, adapted from R. J. Sternberg, *Educational Leadership*, 52(3), 1994, pp. 36–40. Chapter 8: p. 218, Figure 8.2, G. H. Bower, M. C. Clark, A. M. Lesgold, & D. Winzenz, "Hierarchical retrieval schemes in recall of *categorized* world lists" in *Journal of Verbal Learning and Verbal Behavior*, 8(3), 1969, pp. 323–343. Reprinted with permission of Elsevier. Chapter 9: p. 256–257, A. Whimbey & J. Lochhead, Problem Solving and Comprehension, 6/e pp. 104, 128, 1999. Reprinted with permission of *Lawrence Erlbaum Associates*. Chapter 10: p. 271, "The Triadic Reciprocal Causation Model," from A. Bandura, Self-Efficacy: The Exercise of Control (New York: W. H. Freeman, 1997). Reprinted by permission. p. 276, Figure 10.3, "Phases and Categories of the Self-Regulation Cycle" from Zimmerman, B. J. & Kitsantas, A. (2005). The hidden dimension of personal competence: Self-regulated learning and practice. In A. J. Elliot and C. S. Dweck (eds.), *Handbook of competence and motivation*, pp. 509–526.

Chapter 11: p. 330–331, Adapted excerpts from M. Metzger, "Learning to discipline" from *Phi Delta Kappan*, 84(1), pp. 77–84. Used by permission. Chapter 12: p. 354, Table 12.1, "Guidelines for Effective Praise," from J. E. Brophy, "Teacher Praise: A Functional Analysis" in *Review of Educational Research*, 51(1), 1981, pp. 5–32. Reprinted by permission of American Educational Research. p. 365, Figure 12.3, from "Relationship Between Academic Self-Concept and Achievement" adapted from F. Guay, H. Marsh, and Boivin, "Academic self-concept and academic achievement: Developmental Perspectives on their causal ordering" in *Journal of Educational Psychology*, 95(1), pp. 124–136. Used by permission of American Psychological Association. Chapter 15: p. 451, Figure 15.1, Adapted from Figure 3—Interpreting a Graph, from "Learning from Performance Assessments in Math" (1996/97, December/January). *Educational Leadership* 54(4), p. 28. Used with permission. The Association for Supervision and Curriculum Development is a worldwide community of educators advocating sound policies and sharing best practices to achieve the success of each learner. To learn more, visit ASCD at www.ascd.org. p. 453, Table 15.1, "Scoring Rubric for a Group Oral Presentation" from K. Montgomery, "Classroom Rubrics: Systematizing what teachers do naturally" *The Clearing House*, 73(6), 2000, pp. 324–328. Reprinted by permission of Helen Dwight Reid Educational Foundation. Published by Heldred Publications, 1319 Eighteenth St., NW, Washington, DC 20036-1802. p. 465, Table 15.2, "Summary Grades Tallied by Three Different Methods" from "Computerized Gradebooks and the Myth of Objectivity" by Thomas R. Guskey, *Phi Delta Kappan*, 83(10), 2002, pp. 775–780. Reprinted with permission of the author. Chapter 16: p. 477–478, Figure 16.1, "The Constructivist Learning Environment Survey" from Peter Taylor & B. J. Fraser, "Monitoring constructivist classroom learning environments" in *International Journal of Educational Research*, 27(4), pp. 293–301. Reprinted by permission of Peter Taylor. p. 479–480, Figure 16.2, "Examples of Classroom Observation Checklists" from L. Schmidt, "Getting smarter about supervising instruction" in *Principal*, 82(4), 2003, pp. 24–28. Reprinted with permission. Copyright 2003 National Association of Elementary School Principals. All rights reserved.

**Photo Credits**

Chapter 1: p. 2, David Young-Wolff/PhotoEdit Inc.; p. 5, Flash!Light/Stock Boston; p. 8, Susie Fitzhugh; p. 10, Bill Bachman/PhotoEdit; p. 13, Ken Whitmore/Getty Images. Chapter 2: p. 21, Banana Stock/Alamy; p. 29, Geoffrey Biddle; p. 32, (left) David M. Grossman/Photo Researchers, Inc., (right) Junebug Clark/Photo Researchers Inc.; p. 34, David Young-Wolff/PhotoEdit; p. 39, Angela Hampton/Alamy, p. 40, Elizabeth Crews; p. 44, Adam Smith/Getty Images; p. 47, Richard Hutchings/PhotoEdit. Chapter 3: p. 57, (left) Stewart Cohen/Index Stock Imagery, (right) John Henley/Corbis; p. 63, Paul Conklin/PhotoEdit; p. 67, Flash!Light/Stock Boston; p. 76, (left) Susie Fitzhugh, (right) David Young-Wolff/PhotoEdit; p. 79, Jose Luis Pelaez Inc/Jupiter Images; p. 87, Myrleen Ferguson/PhotoEdit. Chapter 4: p. 99, Bob Daemmrich/PhotoEdit Inc.; p. 102, Catherine Karnow/Corbis; p. 112, John Elk/Stock Boston; p. 113, Li-Hua Lan/Syracuse Newspapers/The Image Works; p. 118, Felicia Martinez/PhotoEdit; p. 123, Bob Daemmrich/Stock Boston. Chapter 5: p. 129, Ray Scott/The Image Works; p. 132, Will Hart/PhotoEdit; p. 135, (right) David Young-Wolff/PhotoEdit (left) Susie Fitzhugh; p. 140, (left) Susie Fitzhugh, (right) Erika Stone; p. 148, Michael Newman/PhotoEdit Inc. Chapter 6: p. 157, Myrleen Ferguson Cate/PhotoEdit Inc.; p. 163, Bob Daemmrich/PhotoEdit Inc.; p. 167, Susie Fitzhugh; p. 173, Laura Dwight; p. 178, Frank Siteman/Stock Boston; p. 183, Bob Daemmrich/The Image Works. Chapter 7: p. 193, Lawrence Migdale/Stock Boston; p. 194, Bob Daemmrich/The Image Works; p. 198, Tim Platt/Iconica/Getty Images; p. 202, Jim Pickerell/Stock Boston; p. 208, Peter Hvizdak/The Image Works. Chapter 8: p. 219, Michael Newman/PhotoEdit; p. 220, Jim Cummins/Getty Images; p. 222, Jeff Greenberg/PhotoEdit; p. 225, VStock Ed/Alamy. Chapter 9: p. 239, (left) Joel Gordon, (right) Will & Deni McIntyre/Photo Researchers, Inc.; p. 249, Bob Daemmrich/PhotoEdit, Inc.; p. 253, Susie Fitzhugh; p. 260, Steve Skjold/Skjold Photographs. Chapter 10: p. 275, Paul Barton/Corbis, p. 280, Michael Newman/PhotoEdit; p. 287, Rick Friedman/Black Star; p. 291, Susie Fitzhugh; p. 300, Michael Newman/PhotoEdit; p. 302, Rhoda Sidney/Stock Boston. Chapter 11: p. 314, Bob Daemmrich/Bob Daemmrich Photography; p. 318, David Young Wolff/PhotoEdit; p. 324, Junebug Clark/Photo Researchers Inc.; p. 328, Ellen B. Senisi/The Image Works; p. 334, Richard Hutchings/PhotoEdit; p. 338, Elizabeth Crews. Chapter 12: p. 344, Tom McCarthy/PhotoEdit, Inc.; p. 349, Elizabeth Crews; p. 359, Richard Hutchings/PhotoEdit; p. 362, John Lei/Stock Boston; p. 365, David Young Wolff/PhotoEdit. Chapter 13: p. 374, (left and right) Robert Finken/Index Stock Imagery; p. 376, Bob Daemmrich/Bob Daemmrich Photography; p. 380, Mary Kate Denny/PhotoEdit, Inc.; p. 384, Jeff Greenberg/PhotoEdit; p. 388, Bob Daemmrich/The Image Works; p. 397, Cindy Charles/PhotoEdit. Chapter 14: p. 412, Don Stevenson/Index Stock Imagery; p. 415, Spencer Grant/PhotoEdit; p. 423, Bob Daemmrich/The Image Works; p. 429, Susie Fitzhugh; p. 436, Michael Newman/PhotoEdit Inc. Chapter 15: p. 444, Mary Kate Denny/PhotoEdit; p. 449, David Young-Wolff/Getty Images; p. 458, Bob Daemmrich/Bob Daemmrich Photography; p. 469, Michael Newman/PhotoEdit; p. 472, Bill Aron/PhotoEdit. Chapter 16: p. 480, Mary Kate Denny/PhotoEdit; p. 484, Michael Newman/PhotoEdit.

# Author/Source Index

# Subject Index